Gourmet
TODAY

HOUGHTON MIFFLIN HARCOURT · BOSTON · NEW YORK · 2009

More than
**1000 ALL-NEW
RECIPES**
for the
**CONTEMPORARY
KITCHEN**

Gourmet
TODAY

EDITED BY
RUTH REICHL

For information about permission to reproduce selections from this book, write to Permissions, Houghton Mifflin Harcourt, 215 Park Avenue South, New York, New York 10003.

www.hmhbooks.com

Library of Congress Cataloging-in-Publication Data

Reichl, Ruth.
  Gourmet today : more than 1000 all-new recipes for the contemporary kitchen / edited by Ruth Reichl.
      p. cm.
  Includes index.
  ISBN 978-0-618-61018-1
  1. Cookery, International. I. Gourmet. II. Title.
  TX725.A1R444 2009
  641.59—dc22   2009019781

For permissions, see page 1008.

Book design by Anne Chalmers
Typefaces: Miller, The Sans, Gotham

Printed in the United States of America.

DOJ 10 9 8 7 6 5 4 3 2 1

ACKNOWLEDGMENTS

You aren't eating the way you used to. None of us are. That realization made us understand that the time had come to create a new cookbook, one dedicated to the way we are eating right now.

But not until we started to work on the project did we understand exactly how enormous this undertaking would be. When executive editor John Willoughby, executive food editor Kemp Minifie, former executive food editor Zanne Stewart, Gourmet Books director Diane Abrams, and I sat down to discuss how the changes in food would be reflected in this book, we embarked on a fascinating conversation about the way America eats. Poring over the recipes we were planning for future issues, we began to understand how different they are from the ones we published as recently as ten years ago. They are lighter than those in the past, relying less on butter and more on powerfully flavorful ingredients that now come from all around the world. The recipes are also much more reflective of the time constraints modern cooks face: although we had not been entirely conscious of the transformation, our recipes have gradually become easier and easier to make. And where we once used luxury ingredients with impunity, these days when we call for an expensive item, it really has to pull its weight.

Before long, Kate Winslow, who wrote all the headnotes, joined the conversation. She is both a young mother and a passionate cook, and her son, Elio, became an ad hoc recipe tester.

As the book progressed, it became clear that modern cooks

need information about all the produce we now find in farmers markets as well as about sustainable fish and meat, and we persuaded the incomparable Jane Daniels Lear to research and write the many sidebars, which I think are worth the price of the book all by themselves. Jane is an indefatigable researcher; she always wants to know why, and she never accepts an easy answer. When she has a question, she goes straight to the expert in the field, and we owe an enormous debt of gratitude to Georgeanne Brennan, Marc Buzzio, Shirley Corriher, Maureen Fant, Darra Goldstein, Ihsan Gurdal, Lynne Rossetto Kasper, David Law, Deborah Madison, Jill Norman, David Rakoff, Jon Rowley, Stephen Schmidt, William Woys Weaver, and Grace Young. When any one of them offers an opinion, you know it is right.

As we progressed to the testing phase, the food editors became an essential part of the process. *Gourmet*'s cooks always test obsessively, but Alexis Touchet, Ruth Cousineau, Paul Grimes, Maggie Ruggiero, Gina Marie Miraglia Eriquez, Melissa Roberts, Ian Knauer, Andrea Albin, Kay Chun, Lillian Chou, and Shelley Wiseman did more than just create the recipes; they redid them over and over again so that any cook, no matter how inexperienced, can make them with ease. Without their intelligence and input and endless inquisitiveness, this book would have been a shadow of itself. With each recipe, they asked: Why this one? Is this as good as it can be? Is this the recipe we want to use to showcase these particular ingredients? The constant questioning was difficult, but it became the heart of this book.

When it came time to test the cocktails in the first chapter, we called in *Gourmet*'s drinks editor, James Rodewald, to supervise and answer our many questions—how much ice, which glass, how many shakes? In his able hands, our libations sang.

Many freelance testers also helped us. Thanks to Jill Anton, Allison Ehri Kreitler, Elizabeth Greene, Penelope Hoblyn, Rebecca Jurkevich, Vivian Lui, Amy Mastrangelo, Molly Rundberg, and David Whiteman. Thanks also to Herta Guhl, Rafael Payano, and Margarita Sanabria, who washed the pots, scrubbed the pans, and kept the ovens clean.

Also working behind the scenes were Margie Dorrian and Stephanie Stehofsky of *Gourmet*'s production department. Marisa Robertson-Textor and Leah Price kept us honest with their fact-checking. Hobby Coudert, who has a stunning eye for detail, edited the recipes on *Gourmet*'s end and made sure that they were consistent.

By the time you have a manuscript in hand, you think you are coming to the end, but in fact you have only just begun. As we moved into the final phase, other professionals moved in. Artist Nina Berkson contributed the hundreds of delightful drawings that dance so delicately across these pages. Designer Anne Chalmers, with the help of Eugenie Delaney, transformed a bunch of typed recipes into a beautiful and accessible book. Teresa Elsey of Houghton Mifflin Harcourt's production team shepherded the book through and made sure everything was perfect, and Jacinta Monniere did a masterful job of deciphering our impossible handwriting and inputting the changes and corrections. Judith Sutton edited the recipes all over again

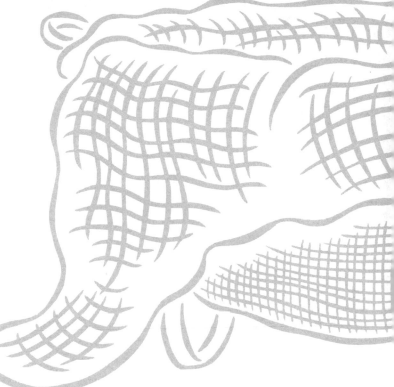

once the manuscript went to the publisher; she is a stickler for detail and a master of precision.

This book would never have seen the light of day without our agent, Doe Coover, who knows more about cookbooks and how they are made than anyone else in the country. Our editor, Rux Martin, is another cookbook genius; she can—and often does—drive you crazy with her incessant desire for one more revision or one more recipe. But, although I am loath to admit this, she is almost always right, and I have yet to regret giving in to any of her demands.

Finally, I'd like to thank Si Newhouse, who made this all possible by giving *Gourmet* the gift of our eight test kitchens, and by understanding that an epicurean magazine, and its books, are only as good as the recipes we produce. Thanks to him, we had the luxury of testing and retesting every one until it was absolutely right.

CONTENTS

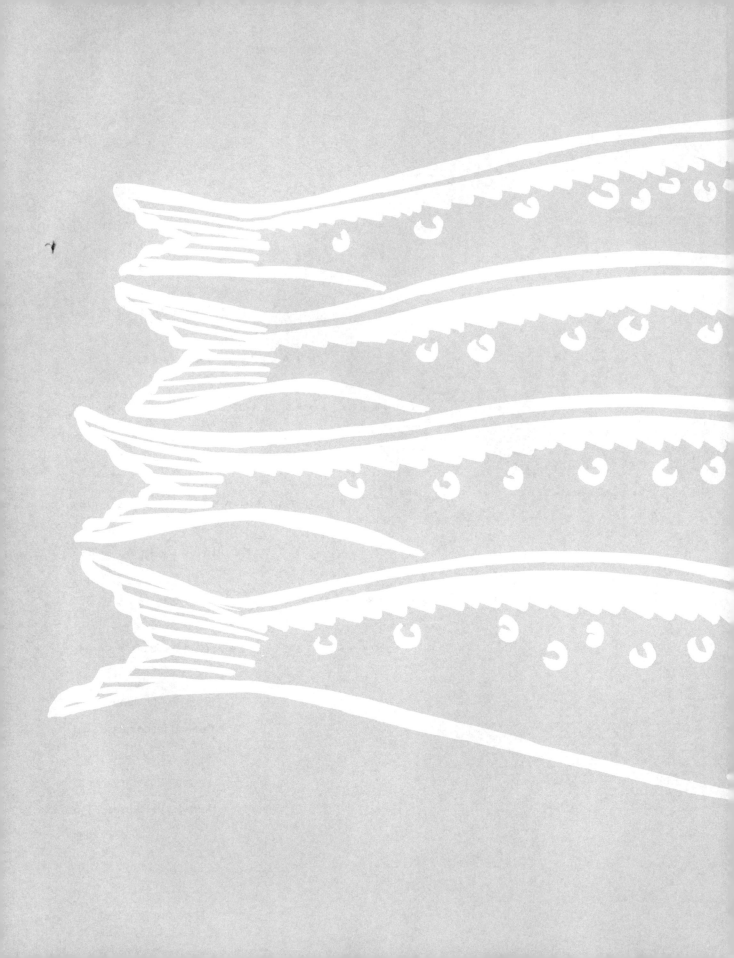

INTRODUCTION

When my son, Nick, was small, he limited his diet to five white foods. Everyone else thought this was hilarious, but I was in despair. I kept hoping that he would change, but the year he was six, he narrowed his menu even more drastically and would only eat the same thing for dinner every single night. "Can a child actually live on nothing but strips of boneless chicken breast?" I asked our doctor. "Stop worrying," she replied. "No sane child ever deliberately starved himself to death."

The one thing that gave me hope was the fact that he liked to cook. All children do, I think, but Nick enjoyed it more than most, and every night he'd come into the kitchen with me to chop vegetables, stir a stew, or roll out piecrust. Some day, I thought wistfully, he might actually eat some of the food he helped me cook.

And that is exactly what happened. Somewhere around the age of nine, Nick began to eat. I don't know what precipitated the change, and I was unwilling to risk jinxing it with questions, but I couldn't help smiling every time I saw him devour a plate of lasagne (one of his favorite foods), or a juicy rare lamb chop (another), or a dish of South Indian shrimp curry. He had been transformed from the world's pickiest eater to an utter omnivore, and I looked on with great joy.

Little did I know that a greater treat lay ahead.

It was one that I never could have anticipated. Nick went off to college, took a bite of dorm food, and instantly decided to cook for himself. And so we entered a new phase in our relationship. For Nick not only cooks, he calls. These days when his number lights up my phone, I know that a cooking question is likely to be coming my way. But I think I have learned as much from Nick as he has learned from me. Through his questions, I have come to realize how dramatically American food has changed. "I'm in the supermarket. What kind of rice should I buy for risotto? Arborio, basmati, jasmine, sushi . . ."

Nick's school is in a small New England town, not a major metropolis. And yet the supermarket carries an array of international products wide enough to please the most sophisticated cook.

Nick still calls almost weekly when he shops, and the surprises keep coming. A few days ago, he phoned to ask if I had a recipe for ramps. Ramps! If he wants to buy organic vegetables, he has options; just about every conventionally raised vegetable in the supermarket has an organic counterpart. He can buy eggs from chickens raised in half a dozen different ways, the variety of fish available has exploded, and the meat department has moved way beyond the display of standard roasts and chops to flavorful cuts like skirt steak and short ribs. These changes, of course, didn't happen overnight, but the transformation has been so gradual that I had to see the supermarket through Nick's eyes in order to open my own. Strolling up and down the aisles with him, I began to understand what it all means. These changes reflect the ongoing revolution in the American kitchen.

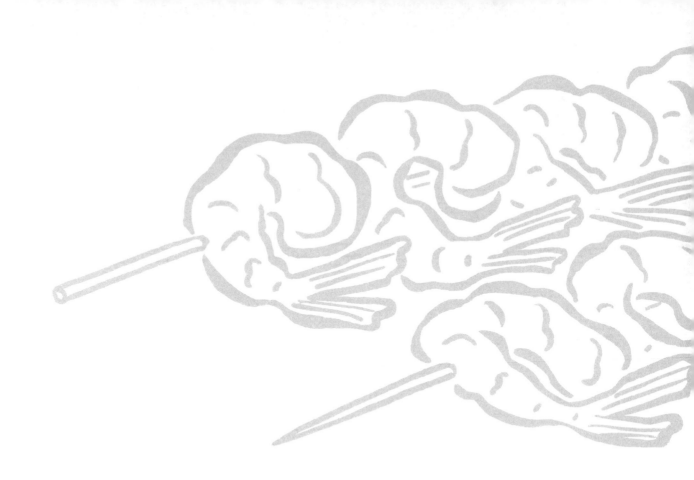

The history of American food has always been about the people who immigrated here; as each wave of newcomers landed on our shores, they brought with them new flavors, new plants, and new recipes that altered the landscape of food. Immigration accelerated over time, and our food began to change faster and faster—as did our appetite for change. Today most of us casually incorporate a global array of spices into recipes without giving it a second thought. Modern children have international appetites, and that is reflected in the supermarket. Salsa is now part of the American repertoire, along with Indian spice pastes, Japanese noodles, and an enormously wide range of vegetables, like chiles, bok choy, chayotes, and edamame.

But immigration is only part of the story. When Nick and his friends think about what they want to cook, they consider issues to which no previous generation gave a second thought.

They are seriously ethical eaters, conscious of the impact that food has on both their bodies and the environment. In deciding what's for dinner, they think about sustainability, ask questions about where the food comes from, and take both food safety and carbon footprint into account. They try to eat seasonally and locally, and many of them are vegetarians.

This new appetite, combined with the new larder, requires a new kind of cookbook. Ten years ago,

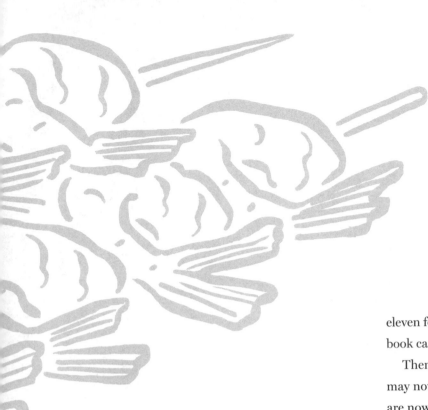

when we were working on *The Gourmet Cookbook*, we were looking back at sixty years of American history, thinking about the past. But as we began working on this book, we looked to the future.

And that future has never seemed more promising. I have been writing about food my entire life, and I can't remember a more exciting time. Americans are the most open-minded eaters in the world, constantly looking for new flavors and new experiences. The way that we eat has changed constantly throughout history, but now, as we welcome a new generation of cooks, we are thinking about food in a particularly interesting way.

For one thing, we've picked up the pace. Time has always been the cook's concern, but never so much as right now. No matter how much you love to cook, there are inevitably nights when you rush in with the need to get dinner on the table fast. Nobody creates better recipes for time-pressed cooks than *Gourmet*'s

eleven food editors, and many of the recipes in this book can be prepared in less than 30 minutes.

Then there is the vegetarian consideration. You may not be a vegetarian, but so many Americans are now eschewing meat that even the most dedicated carnivore is forced to occasionally cook a vegetarian meal. And so we have included a vegetarian main-course chapter, along with dozens of other recipes to make satisfying meatless meals.

We've included basic instructions for A to Z vegetable cookery, if you're just starting out or simply want to know the best ways to cook a particular vegetable. We scoured supermarkets and farmers markets to make sure all the fruits and vegetables that have enriched our repertoire were included. Some of them—radicchio, bok choy, and lacinato kale—are new to our shores. Others, like heirloom tomatoes, ramps, purslane, and a wide array of chiles, are old favorites that had almost been forgotten before they were lovingly restored to our tables.

We gave a great deal of thought to sustainability. As we were testing the fish recipes, I imagined Nick calling from the seafood counter saying, "They don't have any Arctic char. What can I use instead?" As a result, many of our fish recipes suggest substitutes that might be more available (or more sustainable) in your part of the country.

As always, these recipes were tested almost to the point of absurdity. We wanted to make sure that each one was worth both your time and your money, and we always went the extra step, testing it just once more until it was absolutely the best it could be.

As we put the book together, I kept trying to anticipate Nick's questions, wanting every one of them to have an answer here. I imagine a time a few years from now when the book sits on the counter in his kitchen. It is a bit battered, covered with food stains, and rich with scribbles. It is a very different book from the pristine tome it once was. It is, in fact, a much better book. For a brand-new cookbook is merely a starting point, and its future is in your hands. It will become whatever you make of it.

So what are you waiting for? Start cooking it up right now.

— RUTH REICHL

WHAT SALT TO USE WHEN

The ability to use the right amount of salt is one of the things that separate a great cook from an adequate one. Used properly, salt causes all the other flavors in a dish to open up, blend more harmoniously, and become fuller on the tongue. In other words, it makes the dish taste a lot better. But too much can make that same dish inedible.

Once there was only one kind of salt in common use—ordinary iodized table salt. Today, though, there are dozens of salts to choose from, and the kind that a cook chooses has much to do with individual preference and the personality that he or she brings to the stove.

When we call for salt in recipes without specifying what kind, it means that we developed those recipes using regular TABLE SALT. We don't recommend substituting another salt, such as kosher salt or sea salt, because their textures are different, and therefore the amounts when measured by volume will also differ, sometimes by as much as 100 percent. This is especially critical in baking.

KOSHER SALT is preferred by many cooks because it does not contain iodine and other additives, as does table salt. In addition, its larger crystals are easy to grab, which makes for easier sprinkling. Sometimes kosher salt can make all the difference in the success of a recipe: those large crystals are great, for example, if you're putting a rub on a steak, since they draw more liquid out of the meat to mix with the salt and any other spices, deepening the flavor. In instances like that, we specify kosher salt.

SEA SALT, which is available in coarse or fine crystals, adds a briny complexity to food. The coarse kind also brings a particular spiky crunch; we like to sprinkle it on meat and fish dishes as a finishing touch, as well as on salads and sandwiches to brighten them up.

SALT SUBSTITUTION GUIDELINES

- Don't substitute kosher or sea salt for table salt in baking recipes.
- In nonbaking recipes, if you substitute kosher salt for table salt, use 1½ times the amount.
- To substitute table salt for kosher, cut the amount by ¾.
- You can substitute an equal amount of kosher salt for coarse sea salt, but you will not have the same lovely crunch.

Gourmet
TODAY

DRINKS

Reading the books and watching the movies of the thirties and forties, you can't help noticing that *Gourmet* came of age in a time when Americans were a very boozy lot. If an author or a director wanted to indicate a character's extreme sophistication, all he had to do was put a cocktail in his hand. If he wanted to make his characters seem even more urbane, he gave them serious attitudes about alcohol: the result was endless banter about the efficacy of shaking versus stirring or the virtues of one brand of liquor over another.

Gourmet was definitely part of this cocktail conspiracy. To prove its bona fides as the magazine of truly cosmopolitan readers, the editors ran endless stories about various kinds of alcoholic concoctions, written by a veritable who's who of writers; M.F.K. Fisher, for example, wrote a long and wonderful ode to the martini in 1957.

But times changed, and the allure of the cocktail began to fade, owing partly to our increasing interest in wine and partly to a push for increased productivity. (Those three-martini lunches may have been fun, but they didn't do much for the afternoon schedule.)

We're probably too close to the return of the cocktail to understand its sociological significance fully, but there is no doubt that as the twentieth century turned into the twenty-first, sophisticated drinks came roaring back. Long-forgotten manuals were dug out of the shelves as bartenders began to pride themselves on their mastery of the classics. Innovation was prized too, and the mark of a really great party became the cocktails that were served.

Here at *Gourmet*, we welcomed the cocktail's comeback with unalloyed joy. We had hundreds of recipes locked up in our archives, and we imagined long, happy afternoons sipping martinis and French kisses and classic margaritas as we retested them. To our complete surprise, we discovered that the difference between a good drink and a great one can be as small as the shape of the ice, the depth of the pour, or how many times the drink is stirred. It turned out that all that literature about mixing versus stirring and proper proportions was not simply a lot of blather. When it comes to cocktails, tiny variations in the recipe can make an enormous difference to the way it tastes.

So instead of spending delightfully boozy afternoons in the test kitchens, we stood there counting as we stirred the drinks to find out how they changed if they were stirred eight times, twelve times, or twenty times. Even now it sounds absurd, but you really can taste the difference, and if you're going to be a member of the cocktail culture, you want those gimlets and manhattans to be as good as they can be. We're convinced that if you stir up a batch of any of these drinks, you'll be truly happy that cocktails are back.

But it's not all cocktails: if you're after an entirely different kind of drink, you'll find those in this chapter as well. We have included the best lemonade you'll ever taste, along with a wide range of the newer additions to the American repertoire, like Mexican fruit drinks, chai, and refreshing Indian *lassis*.

The truth is that drinks have become, once again, a sign of the good life. But time has wrought one big change: in the past, all you needed to do to prove that you were suave was serve a drink. When you serve a drink these days, it has to be excellent.

DRINKS

Vodka Drinks

Bloody Mary

MAKES 6 DRINKS
ACTIVE TIME: 10 MINUTES ■ START TO FINISH: 10 MINUTES

■ The Bloody Mary—reputedly named for the notorious sixteenth-century Tudor queen Mary I—originated as a simple blend of vodka and tomato juice, created by the bartender Fernand "Pete" Petiot at Harry's American Bar in Paris in 1921. When Petiot moved to the St. Regis Hotel in Manhattan in 1933, customers clamored for a zippier version, and so was born the spiced Bloody Mary that is now the centerpiece of so many Sunday brunches. Everyone claims to make *the* best Bloody Mary, but this one, we think, is especially balanced and tasty. Make sure to use a fresh bottle of Worcestershire sauce—if you're down to the dregs, your drinks will have a fishy taste. ■

    1 (1-quart) bottle tomato juice, chilled
    9 ounces (1 cup plus 2 tablespoons) vodka
    ⅓ cup fresh lemon juice (from about 2 lemons)
    1½ tablespoons drained bottled horseradish
    2 tablespoons Worcestershire sauce
    ½ teaspoon celery salt (optional)
    ¾ teaspoon Tabasco
    ¾ teaspoon freshly ground black pepper
       Ice cubes
GARNISH: lemon slices and/or inner ribs of celery with
    leaves

Stir together all ingredients except ice in a pitcher. Pour into six tall 12-ounce glasses filled with ice.
    Garnish with lemon and/or celery.

Moscow Mule

MAKES 2 DRINKS
ACTIVE TIME: 5 MINUTES ■ START TO FINISH: 5 MINUTES

■ In the 1940s, when businessman John Martin was desperately trying to sell Smirnoff vodka, he teamed up with Los Angeles bar owner Jack Morgan, who was looking for a market for his recently concocted ginger beer. The two tracked down a company that produced copper mugs with a logo of kicking mules stamped on them, and a drink was born. The Moscow mule became one of the most popular cocktails of the 1950s and '60s, and it is well worth reviving—it's easy to make and very refreshing. ■

       Ice cubes
    3 ounces (6 tablespoons) vodka
    2 tablespoons fresh lime juice
    1⅓ cups chilled ginger beer
GARNISH: lime slices

Fill two tall 12-ounce glasses three-quarters full with ice cubes. Add 3 tablespoons vodka, 1 tablespoon lime juice, and ⅔ cup ginger beer to each glass. Garnish with lime slices.

Cosmopolitan

MAKES 2 DRINKS
ACTIVE TIME: 5 MINUTES ■ START TO FINISH: 5 MINUTES

■ Drinks master Dale DeGroff is often credited with starting the cosmo revolution in the mid-1990s at the Rainbow Room in New York City, where he served it with a flamed orange peel, but he points out that other Manhattan and San Francisco establishments were mixing it before he was. Whoever shook the first cosmopolitan started something big—it quickly became a stalwart classic. Over time, fans—including us—have tweaked the classic recipe of lemon-flavored vodka, Cointreau, cranberry juice, and lime juice to suit their own tastes. Our version uses regular vodka and replaces the fresh lime juice with the distinctive

WHICH GLASS FOR WHICH DRINK?

Matching the glass to the drink is just as important as matching the ice to the drink (see page 8). Below are some basic choices that will see you through a variety of social occasions. A good rule of thumb is to always buy more than you think you need, because sooner or later, at least one is going to break.

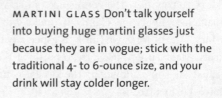

CHAMPAGNE FLUTE Champagne and other sparkling wines don't seem right in anything else. The tall glass (which usually holds 6 ounces) with its narrow opening keeps the effervescence from dissipating too quickly, the reason that this shape is preferred over the iconic Champagne *coupe*, with a wide bowl. (If you inherited a set of coupes from your grandmother, save them for something flirty, like daiquiris.) Word to the wise: when drinking Champagne, hold the glass by its elegant stem—it will stay colder that way.

COLLINS GLASS Tall, slim, and straight-sided, but a little narrower than a highball glass (the two can be used interchangeably), collins glasses hold from 8 to 14 ounces. Perfect for any collins and other long drinks served over ice— Bloody Marys, gin and tonics, or sea breezes, for instance, or simply iced tea or lemonade.

HIGHBALL GLASS Similar to a collins glass, this can be used interchangeably with it; highball glasses hold from 8 to 12 ounces.

MARGARITA GLASS You can serve classic margaritas (the most popular cocktail in the United States) in just about any glass, but the 6- to 10-ounce long-stemmed bowls designed specifically for the drink sure do look like a party. The glasses are also perfect for any slushy blender concoction. Margaritas that are served over ice require a tall glass. The iconic stemmed glass is often simply called a cocktail glass.

MARTINI GLASS Don't talk yourself into buying huge martini glasses just because they are in vogue; stick with the traditional 4- to 6-ounce size, and your drink will stay colder longer.

OLD-FASHIONED GLASS Also known as a rocks glass or tumbler, this sturdy, straight-sided, heavy-bottomed glass is for drinks served over ice; the glasses hold from 8 to 12 ounces.

WINEGLASSES Glasses for red wine traditionally have wider, rounder bowls, which give the wine a chance to breathe. Glasses for white wine usually have straighter sides and are narrower; that reduced surface area helps the wine stay chilled. But does it really matter what you drink your wine from? Many experts (and glass manufacturers) say that we should use a different glass for every type of wine we drink, but despite anecdotal testimonies, scientists haven't found any evidence to back up the claim. It is true, however, that perception enhances an experience, and if you enjoy an array of expensive wineglasses, by all means use them. They range in volume from about 6 to 10 ounces.

sweetness of Rose's lime juice. Beneath the drink's blushing demeanor are tart, sophisticated undertones and an addictive punch. ▪

    Ice cubes
  2 ounces (¼ cup) vodka
  1 ounce (2 tablespoons) Cointreau or Triple Sec
  2 tablespoons cranberry juice cocktail (see Cook's
      Note)
  1 tablespoon Rose's lime juice
GARNISH: two 1½-inch-long lemon twists
SPECIAL EQUIPMENT: a cocktail shaker; a cocktail strainer

Fill cocktail shaker half full with ice. Add remaining ingredients and shake for 15 seconds. Strain into two chilled 6-ounce martini glasses and garnish with lemon twists.

COOK'S NOTE
▪ For the proper sweetness, we recommend using cranberry juice cocktail, which contains high-fructose corn syrup. Do not use cranberry juice labeled 100% fruit (which is actually a combination of cranberry and other fruit juices). And avoid pure unsweetened cranberry juice, which would make the drink overly tangy and brown.

Fizzy Sour Cherry Lemonade

MAKES 8 DRINKS
ACTIVE TIME: 20 MINUTES ▪ START TO FINISH: 20 MINUTES

▪ Sour cherries are more perishable than their sweet cousins, so if you're able to get your hands on a load at the farmers market, snap them up and freeze them. That way, this delightful quaff won't be relegated to the fruit's short summer season. Don't worry about pitting the cherries; they get whizzed in the blender, pits and all, and then strained. Vodka adds a buzz, but virgin cherry lemonade is also delicious. ▪

  2 pounds (1 quart) fresh or thawed frozen sour
      cherries, stemmed
  1 cup fresh lemon juice (from about 4 lemons)
¾–1 cup sugar

 12 ounces (1½ cups) vodka
    Ice cubes
 2–3 cups chilled club soda
OPTIONAL GARNISH: fresh sour cherries with stems

Blend whole cherries in a blender at low speed until skins have broken down enough to brightly color liquid (some pits will be coarsely chopped). Pour through a sieve into a 2-quart pitcher, pressing on solids; discard solids. Add lemon juice and sugar (to taste), stirring until sugar is dissolved.

Pour 1½ ounces (3 tablespoons) vodka into each of eight tall 10-ounce glasses filled with ice. Add ½ cup cherry lemonade to each and top off with club soda to taste. Garnish with cherries, if using.

COOK'S NOTE
▪ The cherry lemonade, without the vodka or club soda, can be made up to 1 day ahead and refrigerated, covered.

Ladybug

MAKES 4 DRINKS
ACTIVE TIME: 10 MINUTES ▪ START TO FINISH: 1¼ HOURS

▪ When life gives you watermelons, make . . . the Ladybug! This recipe came about when we had a surfeit of watermelon in the test kitchen one summer, and the name is a nod to the drink's color, pretty pink dotted with bits of watermelon seeds. Its tart, slushy chill is just the antidote for a hot afternoon. If you are using a seedless watermelon, use a little less sugar—the seeds in a regular watermelon contribute a slight bitterness that tempers the drink's sweetness. ▪

4 cups 1-inch chunks watermelon, including seeds, from a 3-pound wedge
3–4 tablespoons sugar
1–2 limes
4 ounces (½ cup) vodka

Put watermelon in a 1-gallon sealable plastic bag and seal bag. Lay flat in freezer, so pieces are in one layer, and freeze for 1 hour; watermelon will be partially frozen.

Put sugar (to taste) in a small bowl. Zest 1 lime and stir zest into sugar. Squeeze 2 tablespoons juice from lime(s).

Combine watermelon, sugar mixture, lime juice, and vodka in a blender and puree until smooth, 1 to 2 minutes. Pour into four 6- to 8-ounce glasses.

COOK'S NOTES

▪ The watermelon can be frozen for up to 3 days. Thaw partially (15 to 30 minutes) at room temperature before making the drinks.
▪ The sugar and lime zest can be mixed together up to 1 day ahead and refrigerated, covered with plastic wrap. (Wrap the zested lime in plastic so it doesn't dry out.) Squeeze the lime juice just before making the drinks.

Ruby Red Sea Breeze

MAKES 2 DRINKS
ACTIVE TIME: 5 MINUTES ▪ START TO FINISH: 5 MINUTES

▪ A variation on the Cape Codder (vodka with cranberry juice), the sea breeze adds grapefruit juice to the mix. We like to use juice from Ruby Red grapefruit, which has a more luscious color and flavor than regular grapefruit. ▪

Ice cubes
2 ounces (¼ cup) vodka
½ cup chilled Ruby Red grapefruit juice
½ cup chilled cranberry juice cocktail
GARNISH: 2 small grapefruit twists

Fill two 10-ounce long-stemmed glasses with ice cubes. Add 2 tablespoons vodka, ¼ cup grapefruit juice, and ¼ cup cranberry juice to each glass and stir well. Garnish with grapefruit twists.

ICE: THE SECRET INGREDIENT

Ice cubes aren't what they used to be. The big cubes that came out of those old-fashioned metal trays stayed frozen a good long time in a drink, keeping it cold without diluting it. Today's ice-cube trays are designed for faster freezing and increased surface area, but the ice they make melts so quickly that your drink is diluted and warm before you know it. The ideal Scotch or bourbon on the rocks or in a highball calls for large cubes or, ideally, just one very large, dense rock. Avoid half cubes, quarter cubes, and those odious ice disks, which melt almost immediately.

Cracked ice works best in sweet drinks, juice drinks, and specialty drinks such as daiquiris, mint juleps, and caipirinhas. It should also be used for blender concoctions, because it results in the right amount of slushiness without turning to water or ruining your blender.

One last thing: any good bartender will stress the importance of pristine ice. Keep your freezer as cold as possible and use bottled water for the cubes if you don't have good-tasting water. You wouldn't dream of cooking with rancid oil, after all, so why would you ever use anything but clean, fresh ice?

Raspberry Lime Rickey

MAKES 6 TO 8 DRINKS
ACTIVE TIME: 15 MINUTES ■ START TO FINISH: 1¼ HOURS

■ This spin on the traditional rickey, made with vodka instead of gin, is sweet but not too sweet, with a little Pernod adding an interesting accent. One sip will remind you of a melting Popsicle—just what you want on a hot summer's day. (See page 29 for a virgin Cherry Lime Rickey.) ■

   1 (10-ounce) package frozen raspberries in light syrup, thawed
1¼ cups fresh lime juice (from about 10 limes)
   1 cup water
   4 ounces (½ cup) vodka
   2 ounces (¼ cup) Pernod
   ¾ cup superfine sugar
   1 (10-ounce) bottle club soda or seltzer, chilled
     Ice cubes
GARNISH: fresh raspberries and lime slices

Drain raspberries in a fine-mesh sieve set over a bowl; press gently on berries with back of a spoon if necessary to yield ½ cup liquid. Reserve raspberries for another use. Stir together raspberry liquid, lime juice, water, vodka, Pernod, and sugar in a pitcher until sugar is dissolved. Refrigerate until cold.

Just before serving, add club soda to pitcher, along with raspberries and lime slices for garnish.

Serve rickeys in tall glasses filled with ice, garnished with more raspberries and lime slices.

COOK'S NOTE

■ The raspberry-lime mixture, without the club soda, can be refrigerated, covered, for up to 3 hours.

Gin Drinks

Gin Rickey

MAKES 1 DRINK
ACTIVE TIME: 5 MINUTES ■ START TO FINISH: 5 MINUTES

■ A gin and tonic with fizzy club soda stepping in for the tonic water, a gin rickey is light, refreshing, and effervescent. ■

     Ice cubes
1½ ounces (3 tablespoons) gin
   1 tablespoon fresh lime juice
6–8 tablespoons chilled club soda or seltzer
GARNISH: lime wedge
SPECIAL EQUIPMENT: a cocktail shaker; a cocktail strainer

Fill cocktail shaker half full with ice cubes. Add gin and lime juice. Shake for 5 seconds, then strain into a tall 8- to 10-ounce glass filled with ice cubes. Top off with club soda. Squeeze juice from lime wedge into drink, drop wedge into glass, and stir to combine.

Gimlet

MAKES 2 DRINKS
ACTIVE TIME: 5 MINUTES ■ START TO FINISH: 5 MINUTES

■ "A real gimlet is half gin and half Rose's lime juice and nothing else. It beats martinis hollow." Or so says Terry Lennox in Raymond Chandler's *The Long Goodbye*. Maybe Lennox and his pal Philip Marlowe had a sweeter tooth than we do, but we like the more modern proportions of 4 parts gin to 1 part Rose's. Now *that's* a drink that will give a martini a run for its money. ■

     Ice cubes
   4 ounces (½ cup) gin
   2 tablespoons Rose's lime juice, or to taste
GARNISH: 2 lime wedges
SPECIAL EQUIPMENT: a cocktail shaker; a cocktail strainer

Fill cocktail shaker three-quarters full with ice cubes. Add gin and lime juice and stir for 10 seconds. Strain into two 8- to 10-ounce old-fashioned glasses filled with ice or two chilled 6-ounce martini glasses without ice. Garnish with lime wedges.

Classic Martini

MAKES 2 DRINKS
ACTIVE TIME: 5 MINUTES ■ START TO FINISH: 5 MINUTES

■ Like many cocktails, the martini, which has been around for 100 years, was originally much sweeter than its contemporary counterpart. What started off as a half-gin, half-vermouth concoction morphed into a bone-dry cocktail with only the faintest whisper of vermouth. But we think what makes a martini is the vermouth—otherwise, it's just a glass of cold gin. Although this version is quite dry, it has just enough of the aromatized wine to lend presence. ■

Ice cubes
6 ounces (¾ cup) gin or vodka
¾ ounce (1½ tablespoons) dry vermouth
GARNISH: pimiento-stuffed green olives or lemon twists
SPECIAL EQUIPMENT: a cocktail shaker; a cocktail strainer

Fill cocktail shaker three-quarters full with ice cubes. Add gin and vermouth and stir well.

Strain into two chilled 4-ounce martini glasses and garnish with olives or lemon twists.

COOK'S NOTE

■ If you add a little olive juice to your martini, it's a "dirty martini." If you substitute a cocktail onion for the olive or twist, it becomes a Gibson.

Negroni

MAKES 2 DRINKS
ACTIVE TIME: 5 MINUTES ■ START TO FINISH: 5 MINUTES

■ As Italian as a Vespa but with more bracing zip, the Negroni is not for the faint of heart. A healthy jigger of Campari adds a complex bitterness, which is the essence of the drink. If you find it a little too intense, you can cut back on the sweet vermouth and add a dash of fresh orange juice (see Cook's Note); it's not traditional, but it is smoother. ■

Ice cubes
2 ounces (¼ cup) gin
2 ounces (¼ cup) Campari
2 ounces (¼ cup) sweet vermouth
SPECIAL EQUIPMENT: a cocktail shaker; a cocktail strainer

Fill cocktail shaker half full with ice. Add remaining ingredients and shake for 15 seconds. Strain into two 10- to 12-ounce old-fashioned glasses filled with ice.

COOK'S NOTE

■ For a smoother-tasting drink, reduce the amount of vermouth to 1 ounce (2 tablespoons) and add ½ cup fresh orange juice.

Tom Collins

MAKES 2 DRINKS
ACTIVE TIME: 5 MINUTES ■ START TO FINISH: 5 MINUTES

■ A London barkeep named John Collins is credited with inventing this refreshing gin drink in the late 1800s. It originally called for sweet Old Tom brand gin, but over the years, dry gin was substituted. Generations who have grown up with bottled sour mixes don't know what they're missing—using fresh lemon juice makes all the difference. A true Tom Collins couldn't be easier to make, and nothing beats it. A John Collins usually replaces the gin with bourbon. ■

Ice cubes

3 tablespoons fresh lemon juice

1 tablespoon superfine sugar

4 ounces (½ cup) gin

Chilled club soda

GARNISH: 2 lemon slices

SPECIAL EQUIPMENT: a cocktail shaker; a cocktail strainer

Fill cocktail shaker three-quarters full with ice cubes. Add lemon juice, sugar, and gin and shake for 15 seconds. Strain into two tall 12-ounce glasses filled with ice cubes. Add club soda to taste. Garnish with lemon slices.

WHEN TO STIR, WHEN TO SHAKE

Martinis and manhattans are classically stirred together in a cocktail shaker or pitcher of ice, which blends them and makes them icy cold but prevents them from clouding up and becoming frothy, the way they would if they were shaken. You want them to be silken on the palate, not effervescent. Try stirring a martini with freshly shattered big dense ice cubes, and see how satiny it is. Stir for at least 10 seconds to properly dilute it and chill it down.

Because some ingredients—cream, sugar, and fruit juice, for instance—are heavier than alcohol, however, you need to use more vigorous action to blend them. And some drinks, such as daiquiris and margaritas, should be light and frothy. When you shake, always add the ice first and then shake the ingredients vigorously, using a diagonal motion, for at least 10 seconds; the bigger the ice cubes, the harder and longer you need to shake. (Never shake a tomato juice–based drink, though, or it will become unpleasantly foamy.) Store your shaker in the freezer if possible.

Rhubarb Collins

MAKES 8 DRINKS

ACTIVE TIME: 20 MINUTES ■ START TO FINISH: 2 HOURS

■ A collins—just about any spirit combined with lemon juice, sugar, and club soda—is traditionally served in a tall narrow glass of the same name. Likewise, any drink served in a collins glass is often called a collins by default. This tangy pink drink, for instance: it calls for lime, Cointreau, and rhubarb, which complements the taste of gin surprisingly well (without the alcohol, it's a delicious fruit cooler). ■

2 pounds rhubarb, trimmed and cut into ½-inch pieces (6 cups)

1 cup sugar

3 cups water

⅓ cup fresh lime juice (from about 3 limes), or to taste

12 ounces (1½ cups) gin

1½ ounces (3 tablespoons) Cointreau or Triple Sec

Ice cubes

Chilled seltzer or club soda

8 small lime wedges

Combine rhubarb, sugar, and water in a 3-quart heavy saucepan and bring to a boil, stirring until sugar is dissolved. Reduce heat and simmer, partially covered, until rhubarb falls apart, about 15 minutes. Remove from heat and cool, uncovered, for 15 minutes.

Pour rhubarb mixture into a large fine-mesh sieve set over a large bowl and let drain for 15 minutes. Press gently on solids, then discard solids. Skim off any foam, pour syrup into a pitcher, and refrigerate, uncovered, until cold, about 1 hour (see Cook's Note).

Stir lime juice, gin, and Cointreau into chilled syrup. Pour into eight tall 10-ounce glasses filled with ice, stopping about 1 inch from rim. Top off drinks with seltzer. Run a wedge of lime around rim of each glass, then squeeze into drink.

COOK'S NOTES

■ The rhubarb syrup can be quick-chilled in a metal bowl

set in a larger bowl of ice; stir occasionally until cold, about 15 minutes.

- The syrup can be refrigerated, covered, for up to 1 day or frozen for up to 1 week.
- The collins mixture (without the seltzer) can be refrigerated, covered, for up to 4 hours.

Sloe Gin Fizz

MAKES 2 DRINKS
ACTIVE TIME: 10 MINUTES ■ START TO FINISH: 10 MINUTES

■ Sloe gin isn't a gin at all, but a liqueur made of neutral spirits flavored with sloes, tart plums native to Eurasia. It has a lovely candy-apple-red color and a fruity sweetness with undercurrents of almond. We love this drink, which combines sloe gin with regular gin, simple syrup, fresh lemon juice, and a top-off of fizzy club soda, for its good looks and unique sweet-tart flavor. ■

⅓ cup Simple Syrup (recipe follows)
2 ounces (¼ cup) sloe gin
2 ounces (¼ cup) gin
¼ cup fresh lemon juice
   Ice cubes
   Chilled club soda
GARNISH: 2 maraschino cherries

Stir together simple syrup, sloe gin, gin, and lemon juice in a small pitcher. Pour into two tall 10-ounce glasses half filled with ice. Top off with club soda and stir. Garnish each drink with a cherry.

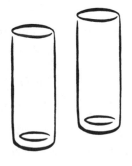

Simple Syrup

MAKES ABOUT 1 CUP
ACTIVE TIME: 5 MINUTES ■ START TO FINISH: 35 MINUTES

■ Simple syrup, sometimes called sugar syrup, is a great way to add sweetness to a drink without clouding it, as straight sugar can. Simple syrup couldn't be easier to make, and it keeps well. ■

1 cup sugar
1 cup water

Bring sugar and water to a boil in a 1-quart saucepan, stirring until sugar is dissolved. Boil, stirring, for 1 minute. Transfer to a heatproof bowl and refrigerate, uncovered, until cold, about 30 minutes.

COOK'S NOTE
- Simple syrup keeps, refrigerated in an airtight container, for up to 6 months.

Rum Drinks

Planter's Punch

MAKES 4 DRINKS
ACTIVE TIME: 10 MINUTES ■ START TO FINISH: 10 MINUTES

■ Caribbean sugar plantations were the homes of the first versions of planter's punch, which were simply made by mixing the estate's own rum and sugar with local citrus juice. Since then, recipes for this tropical drink have become more involved, with bitters, orange-flavored liqueur, and various rums added to the mix. Our easy-to-make version is festive and fun. ■

   Ice cubes
4 ounces (½ cup) dark rum
½ cup fresh orange juice (from about 1½ oranges)
⅓ cup pineapple juice
2 tablespoons fresh lime juice
1 ounce (2 tablespoons) Cointreau or Triple Sec

1 tablespoon grenadine
½ teaspoon Angostura bitters
GARNISH: 4 orange wedges; 4 lime wedges; 4 maraschino
   cherries
SPECIAL EQUIPMENT: a cocktail shaker; a cocktail
   strainer

Fill a cocktail shaker three-quarters full with ice. Add remaining ingredients and shake for 15 seconds. Strain into four tall 8-ounce glasses filled with ice. Garnish each drink with an orange wedge, a lime wedge, and a maraschino cherry.

COOK'S NOTE
■ You can find bitters and grenadine in your supermarket in the soda aisle, with the mixers.

Classic Daiquiri

MAKES 4 DRINKS
ACTIVE TIME: 10 MINUTES ■ START TO FINISH: 10 MINUTES

■ Named for the little village on the southeastern coast of Cuba where it originated more than 100 years ago, the daiquiri takes three of the country's most famous exports—rum, limes, and sugar—and combines them into frosty, frothy perfection. Made well, a daiquiri has just enough sugar to balance the rich rum and tart lime juice. Ernest Hemingway and J.F.K.—two daiquiri connoisseurs—would approve of this terrific version. ■

Ice cubes
6 ounces (¾ cup) gold rum
6 tablespoons fresh lime juice (from about
   3 limes)
6 tablespoons superfine sugar
GARNISH: 4 lime slices
SPECIAL EQUIPMENT: a cocktail shaker; a cocktail
   strainer

Fill cocktail shaker three-quarters full with ice. Add remaining ingredients and shake vigorously for 15 seconds. Strain into four 5-ounce martini glasses. Garnish with lime slices.

Mango Frozen Daiquiri

MAKES 4 DRINKS
ACTIVE TIME: 15 MINUTES ■ START TO FINISH: 2¼ HOURS
(INCLUDES FREEZING)

■ Fresh mango adds musky sweetness and alluring color to the traditional frozen daiquiri. For the best flavor, seek out very ripe, sweet-smelling mangoes. ■

3 cups 1-inch mango chunks (from two 1-pound
   mangoes)
¾ cup cracked ice
4 ounces (½ cup) gold rum
⅓ cup water
¼ cup fresh lime juice (from about 2 limes)
¼ cup superfine sugar

Line a baking sheet with parchment paper. Spread mango chunks on baking sheet and freeze until hard, about 2 hours.

Combine mango with remaining ingredients in a blender and blend until smooth, about 1 minute. Pour into four 8-ounce stemmed glasses.

COOK'S NOTE

■ The frozen mango chunks can be transferred to an airtight container and kept frozen for up to 1 week.

Strawberry Frozen Daiquiri

MAKES 4 DRINKS
ACTIVE TIME: 15 MINUTES ■ START TO FINISH: 2¼ HOURS
(INCLUDES FREEZING)

■Fresher, more sprightly, and less sugary than many fruity daiquiris (which are often made from packaged mixes), this smooth, frozen version goes down easily. ■

1 pound strawberries, hulled and quartered (3 cups)
¾ cup cracked ice
4 ounces (½ cup) gold rum
⅓ cup water
¼ cup fresh lime juice (from about 2 limes)
¼ cup superfine sugar

Line a baking sheet with parchment paper. Spread strawberries on baking sheet and freeze until hard, about 2 hours.

Combine strawberries with remaining ingredients in a blender and blend until smooth, about 1 minute. Pour into four 8-ounce stemmed glasses.

COOK'S NOTE

■ The frozen strawberries can be transferred to an airtight container and kept frozen for up to 1 week.

TOOLS OF THE TRADE

If you enjoy entertaining, it makes sense to have a well-stocked bar.

BAR NAPKINS/COASTERS You'll find a festive high-quality assortment of both in any cookware shop.

BAR SPOON This spoon, with a long, twisted handle that makes it easier to navigate around ice cubes, and a flattened bowl, comes in handy for all sorts of things. If you want to make a layered drink with liquids of different densities, for instance, pour the heaviest one (usually syrup) into the glass first. Then hold the bar spoon in the glass, with the bowl just touching the liquid, and pour the lighter liquid around either side of the handle.

BAR TOWELS You'll want a large thin cotton towel designated for drying glasses and other dish towels for mopping up spills.

BLENDER For blender drinks, you need one with a heavy-duty motor that will grind ice.

BOTTLE/CAN OPENER In this day of pop-tops and screw caps, your children may never have seen an old-fashioned beer can opener, but if you buy a large can of juice or imported bottles of beer, you'll need one.

CITRUS JUICER Options here include the simple handheld wooden reamer and the classic juicer set in its own shallow bowl. For squeezing lots of limes, though, it's hard to beat a Mexican lime press, which turns a lime inside out to extract as much juice as possible; this gadget is available at cookware shops. If you serve lots of fruity drinks, an electric juicer makes sense.

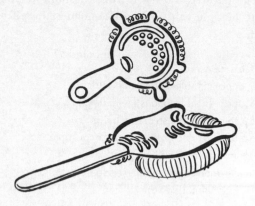

GLASS PITCHER For stirred cocktails, it should be large so that it can hold enough ice to properly chill the drinks.

ICE CRACKER An old-fashioned metal one fits the bill nicely, although a muddler (see below) works well too (hold an ice cube in the palm of your hand and bash it). You can also wrap the ice cubes in a clean kitchen towel and whack them with a rolling pin, although the ice tends to stick to the towel.

COCKTAIL SHAKER/STRAINER Look for a large shaker that's stainless steel and heavy for its size, to get drinks as cold as possible. Some have built-in strainers so you don't need to buy a separate one. Most professional bartenders use what's known as a Boston shaker: the bottom half is stainless steel and the top half is glass (the top is also used for mixing stirred drinks). If you buy a coil-rimmed cocktail strainer, choose one that's sturdy.

ICE BUCKET WITH TONGS OR SCOOP The bucket should be large and insulated.

CORKSCREW A common waiter's corkscrew, with a folding knife to cut the foil of a wine bottle, is inexpensive and reliable, although it can be a little tricky to use. A wing-type corkscrew, with a curly screw that looks like a drill bit, is pretty foolproof. The rabbit-ear type of lever is excellent, but the cheaper versions won't last as long as the (really) expensive ones, which can set you back $80 or so.

JIGGER Correct proportions are important to well-made cocktails. A double jigger with a different measure on each end Is useful. In fact, It's a smart idea to have two jiggers—one with ¾-ounce and 1½-ounce measures, the other ½-ounce and 1-ounce.

MUDDLER This is a wooden rod used for crushing fruit or herbs such as mint.

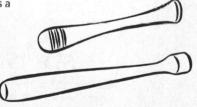

VEGETABLE PEELER This makes it easy to remove only the aromatic peel from citrus fruits, not the bitter white pith beneath it.

Mojito

MAKES 1 DRINK
ACTIVE TIME: 5 MINUTES ■ START TO FINISH: 5 MINUTES

■ This summery drink of rum, lime, and mint muddled with sugar became popular with American glitterati during Prohibition, when frequent "rum flights" and overnight boats carried parched revelers from Miami to Havana. Happily for us, the mojito eventually came back with them. This recipe came to us from Sloppy Joe's Bar in Havana. ■

2 tablespoons fresh lime juice
3 fresh mint sprigs
1 tablespoon sugar
1 ounce (2 tablespoons) light rum
Ice cubes
⅓ cup chilled club soda

SPECIAL EQUIPMENT: a cocktail shaker; a cocktail strainer

Combine lime juice, mint sprigs, and sugar in cocktail shaker. Crush mint with a muddler or back of a wooden spoon until sugar is dissolved. Add rum and fill shaker three-quarters full with ice cubes. Shake vigorously for 15 seconds. Strain into a tall 12-ounce glass filled with ice, top off with club soda, and stir well.

Mai Tai

MAKES 1 DRINK
ACTIVE TIME: 5 MINUTES ■ START TO FINISH: 5 MINUTES

■ Legend has it that Trader Vic Bergeron mixed this drink for the first time in 1944 at his bar outside San Francisco. He served it to a friend visiting from Tahiti, who took one sip and remarked, *Mai tai—roa aé!*" Or, "Out of this world—the best!" Since those glory days, the drink has become a kitschy catchall for concoctions of bad rum and sugary fruit juices. A proper mai tai should be sweet but frisky, with depth provided by the dark and amber rums, as in this recipe. Sweet almond-flavored orgeat syrup offers a subtle foil to the citrus, but you can substitute almond extract if you must. ■

Ice cubes
1 ounce (2 tablespoons) dark rum
1 ounce (2 tablespoons) gold rum
2 tablespoons fresh orange juice
½ ounce (1 tablespoon) Cointreau or Triple Sec
1 tablespoon fresh lime juice
1 teaspoon orgeat syrup (see Sources) or 1 drop pure almond extract
1 teaspoon superfine sugar
Dash of grenadine

GARNISH: a fresh mint sprig
SPECIAL EQUIPMENT: a cocktail shaker; a cocktail strainer

Fill cocktail shaker three-quarters full with ice. Add remaining ingredients and shake for 15 seconds. Strain into an 8-ounce old-fashioned glass filled with ice cubes. Garnish with mint sprig.

Piña Colada

MAKES 6 DRINKS
ACTIVE TIME: 5 MINUTES ■ START TO FINISH: 5 MINUTES

■ A great piña colada should show some restraint, striking the perfect balance between pineapple, cream of coconut, and good rum. This delicious version fits the bill. Paper umbrellas optional. ■

3 cups cracked ice
1½ cups canned unsweetened pineapple juice
8 ounces (1 cup) gold rum
½ cup well-stirred cream of coconut, such as Coco Lopez

GARNISH: pineapple wedges and maraschino cherries

Combine all ingredients in a blender and blend until very smooth, about 30 seconds. Immediately pour into six 8-ounce stemmed glasses, and stir if drink begins to separate. Garnish rims of glasses with pineapple wedges and maraschino cherries.

No-Cook Eggnog

MAKES 8 DRINKS
ACTIVE TIME: 5 MINUTES ■ START TO FINISH: 5 MINUTES

■ This super-easy eggnog recipe, based on vanilla ice cream, is perfect for people who are nervous about the raw eggs traditionally used in the drink. (For a more traditional take on eggnog, see page 21.) The result doesn't have as much of that distinctly eggy flavor, but it's still delicious, rich, and creamy. ■

3 pints super-premium vanilla ice cream
4 ounces (½ cup) dark rum
½ teaspoon freshly grated nutmeg

Soften ice cream (see Cook's Note); it should remain cold. Transfer to a blender, add rum and nutmeg, and blend until smooth. Serve, or refrigerate, covered, until ready to serve.

COOK'S NOTES
■ You can soften the ice cream, 1 pint at a time, in a microwave at high power for about 1 minute.
■ The eggnog can be refrigerated for up to 1 day.

Tequila Drinks

Classic Margarita

MAKES 2 DRINKS
ACTIVE TIME: 5 MINUTES ■ START TO FINISH: 5 MINUTES

■ We adore this margarita for its balance and simplicity: just mix together equal parts tequila, Cointreau, and fresh lime juice, shake, and serve it up. For a more mellow version, replace half the lime juice with fresh orange juice. ■

2 small lime wedges (optional)
  Kosher salt (optional)
  Ice cubes
¼ cup fresh lime juice (from about 2 limes)

2 ounces (¼ cup) good-quality tequila, preferably *reposado*
2 ounces (¼ cup) Cointreau or Triple Sec

SPECIAL EQUIPMENT: a cocktail shaker; a cocktail strainer

If desired, rim glasses with salt: Run 1 lime wedge each around rims of two 6-ounce margarita glasses to moisten. Put salt on a small plate and roll outside rims of glasses in salt to coat lightly, then tap glasses gently to knock off excess salt. Garnish rims with lime wedges.

Fill cocktail shaker half full with ice. Add lime juice, tequila, and Cointreau and shake vigorously for 15 seconds, then strain into glasses.

COOK'S NOTE
■ To serve on the rocks, fill two 8-ounce old-fashioned glasses with ice cubes and strain the margaritas into the glasses.

TEQUILA: THE SPIRIT OF MEXICO

Tequila is made from blue agave, a succulent, not a cactus, as many presume. Until fairly recently, Mexican government regulations described just three tequila styles. *Blanco* ("white" or "silver"), which is how all tequila starts, can be aged in wood barrels for up to 60 days, but in practice it is aged for only a short time or not at all, and so it retains the most agave flavor. *Reposado* ("rested") must be aged in wood barrels for at least 60 days. *Añejo* ("aged") must spend at least 1 year in wood. Wood-aging smooths some of the rough edges, but it can also mute the agave flavor. A new category, *extra-añejo*, sees a minimum of 3 years in wood. Tequilas in this group sell for around $250 a bottle, and although they are impeccably made, they tend to taste more like oak than tequila.

It's the blue agave that makes tequila special. Hundreds of varieties of agave are grown in Mexico, and the liquor made from these other species, known as mescal, is produced in many regions of Mexico. Tequila is made only from the blue agave plant, and it can be produced in only a handful of approved areas.

HOW TO RIM A GLASS WITH SALT

The goal is a delicate frost on the lip of a glass, not a thick crust. Be sure the inside of the lip is dry; otherwise, the crystals will stick to it and get into the drink, ruining it. Pour kosher (not iodized table) salt onto a small plate. Moisten just the outside rim of the glass with a lemon or lime wedge (1). Holding the glass with the stem parallel to the plate, slowly roll the rim in the salt until the circumference is completely covered (2). Tap the glass gently to knock off excess salt.

Raspberry Orange Margarita

MAKES 4 DRINKS
ACTIVE TIME: 15 MINUTES ■ START TO FINISH: 15 MINUTES

■ Pleasant tartness and a smooth, light texture make this limeless margarita easy to drink. ■

- 1½ cups (8 ounces) raspberries
- ¾ cup fresh orange juice (from about 2½ oranges)
- 6 ounces (¾ cup) white tequila (also called silver or *blanco*)
- 1–2 tablespoons sugar
  Ice cubes

Combine raspberries, orange juice, tequila, and sugar (to taste) in a blender and puree until smooth. Force through a fine-mesh sieve into a pitcher, pressing on solids; discard solids. Pour into four tall 10-ounce glasses filled with ice.

Frozen Margarita

MAKES 4 DRINKS
ACTIVE TIME: 10 MINUTES ■ START TO FINISH: 10 MINUTES

■ A traditional margarita is shaken with ice, but many people love the slushy frozen version.■

- 4 small lime wedges (optional)
  Kosher salt (optional)
- 3 cups small ice cubes or cracked large ice cubes
- ½ cup fresh lime juice (from about 4 limes)
- 4 ounces (½ cup) white tequila (also called silver or *blanco*)
- 4 ounces (½ cup) Cointreau or Triple Sec

If desired, rim glasses with salt: Run 1 lime wedge each around rims of four 8- to 10-ounce margarita glasses to moisten. Put salt on a small plate and roll outside rims of glasses in salt to coat lightly; tap glasses gently to knock off excess salt. Garnish each rim with a lime wedge.

Put ice in a blender. Add remaining ingredients and blend until smooth, 1 to 2 minutes. Pour into glasses.

Blackberry Frozen Margarita

MAKES 4 DRINKS
ACTIVE TIME: 15 MINUTES ■ START TO FINISH: 15 MINUTES

■ An unusual alternative to the traditional margarita, this version gets an earthy sweetness from blackberries. ■

- 2 cups (8 ounces) blackberries
- ½ cup fresh lime juice (from about 4 limes)
- 6 ounces (¾ cup) white tequila (also called silver or *blanco*)
- ⅓ cup sugar, or to taste
- 3 cups small ice cubes or cracked large ice cubes

Combine blackberries with lime juice, tequila, and sugar in a blender and puree. Force puree through a fine-mesh sieve into a pitcher, pressing on solids; discard solids. Add ice to blender, then add puree and blend until smooth, 1 to 2 minutes. Divide among four 6-ounce margarita glasses.

Bourbon and Other Whiskey Drinks

Tequila Sunrise

MAKES 2 DRINKS
ACTIVE TIME: 5 MINUTES ■ START TO FINISH: 5 MINUTES

■ Some say that the tequila sunrise was invented at a Tijuana racetrack called the Agua Caliente, a playground for the rich and famous during Prohibition. The original drink was made with tequila, crème de cassis, grenadine, and lime juice, which settled into beautiful striations of color, but it eventually evolved into the orange-juice-tequila-grenadine mix most people know today. We find that a little fresh lime juice gives the drink just the right poise. The grenadine floated on top makes the sunrise; the key is to pour slowly, so the layers stay separate. ■

        Ice cubes
¾ cup fresh orange juice (from about 2½ oranges)
 3 ounces (6 tablespoons) tequila, preferably white
        (also called silver or *blanco*)
 1 tablespoon fresh lime juice
 1 tablespoon grenadine, or to taste
GARNISH: 2 orange slices
SPECIAL EQUIPMENT: a cocktail shaker; a cocktail
        strainer

Fill a cocktail shaker half full with ice. Add orange juice, tequila, and lime juice and shake vigorously for 15 seconds, then strain into two tall 12- to 14-ounce glasses filled with ice. Slowly pour 1½ teaspoons grenadine on top of each drink; do not stir. Garnish with orange slices.

Mint Julep

MAKES 8 DRINKS
ACTIVE TIME: 15 MINUTES ■ START TO FINISH: 15 MINUTES

■ Juleps—medicinal tonics made of herbs mixed with sugar and water—date back to the fifteenth century. In America, they evolved to include spirits, originally brandy or Cognac, and later rye or bourbon. This, the most famous julep incarnation, is sweet and strong, with a nice herbal kick from the mint. The official drink of the Kentucky Derby, mint juleps are meant to be served icy cold. Though they are traditionally made one at a time by muddling fresh mint with the sugar in individual silver julep cups, we've adapted the recipe to make a large batch. ■

12 ounces (1½ cups) bourbon
 2 tablespoons plus 2 teaspoons superfine sugar,
        or to taste
 1 cup loosely packed fresh mint leaves
        About 12 cups crushed ice
GARNISH: 8 fresh mint sprigs

Stir together bourbon and 4 teaspoons sugar in a small bowl until sugar is dissolved.

Lightly crush mint leaves with remaining 4 teaspoons sugar in a medium metal bowl with a muddler or back of a wooden spoon until sugar is dissolved, about 5 minutes. Add 4 cups crushed ice. Add ¾ cup bourbon mixture and stir well.

Using a ladle, divide mint mixture among eight 12-ounce glasses. Add enough of remaining crushed ice to almost fill glasses. Divide remaining bourbon mixture among drinks and stir well. Garnish with mint sprigs.

Bourbon is an American whiskey that is made by cooking a variety of grains, which must include at least 51 percent corn, in water (this is the mash), then adding yeast to make the mixture ferment, distilling the result, and aging it in new charred-oak barrels for a minimum of 2 years. Most bourbons are aged for longer to give them a mellow, rich complexity. Bourbon must not be over 160 proof (80 percent alcohol), and only water is used to lower the alcohol level. The sour-mash method entails adding fermented mash from a previous batch—much like a starter for sourdough bread or a mother for vinegar—to the fresh mash, but few bourbon distillers put the term "sour mash" on the label. Bourbon gets its name from Bourbon County, Kentucky, where most of the whiskey was produced during the late 1700s and 1800s. Today, although bourbon can legally be made anywhere in the United States, virtually all of it is still made in Kentucky. (Tennessee whiskey, such as Jack Daniel's, is very much like bourbon, but it's been filtered through sugar-maple charcoal, which gives it a sweeter flavor.)

Rye whiskey, which has a spicier, more assertive flavor than bourbon and is more closely identified with Maryland and Pennsylvania, must be made with a minimum of 51 percent rye. Like bourbon and Tennessee whiskey, it must be aged for a minimum of 2 years.

Manhattan

MAKES 2 DRINKS
ACTIVE TIME: 5 MINUTES ■ START TO FINISH: 5 MINUTES

■ The story goes that the manhattan was created in 1874 by a bartender at the Manhattan Club in New York City for a party thrown to celebrate the state's new governor, Samuel Tilden. Originally made with rye whiskey, bolstered with sweet vermouth and a dash of Angostura bitters, the drink quickly became one of the great classic cocktails. In later years, bourbon or blended whiskey replaced the rye. We mixed manhat-

tans using a wide variety of whiskeys and found that blended whiskey produces the smoothest drink. ■

Ice cubes
4 ounces (½ cup) blended whiskey, such as Seagram's 7
2 ounces (¼ cup) sweet vermouth
2 dashes Angostura bitters
GARNISH: 2 maraschino cherries
SPECIAL EQUIPMENT: a cocktail shaker; a cocktail strainer

Fill a cocktail shaker half full with ice. Add remaining ingredients and stir well. Strain into two chilled martini glasses. Garnish each drink with a cherry.

Old-Fashioned

MAKES 1 DRINK
ACTIVE TIME: 5 MINUTES ■ START TO FINISH: 5 MINUTES

■ This irresistible drink tempers the distinctively strong flavor of rye with a hint of sweetness and the mysterious complexity of Angostura bitters. We adapted our old-fashioned (short for "Old-Fashioned Whiskey Cocktail") from the version served at the Pegu Club in Manhattan, where the bartenders use 100-proof Rittenhouse, a Kentucky rye that has enjoyed a resurgence in popularity owing to its deep, bold flavor. Indeed, a fine-quality rye makes all the difference (a generous hand with the bitters also adds immeasurably to the drink's suaveness). The Pegu Club offers a sweeter, fruitier version too (see Cook's Note). Stirring the drink twenty-eight times may sound finicky, but it's an important step in achieving the proper dilution and chill. ■

½ cup cracked ice, plus 6 large ice cubes
1 tablespoon Simple Syrup (page 12)
3 generous dashes Angostura bitters
2 ounces (¼ cup) rye
1 lemon twist
SPECIAL EQUIPMENT: a cocktail shaker; a cocktail stirrer; a cocktail strainer

Put cracked ice and 3 ice cubes into cocktail shaker. Add simple syrup, bitters, and rye and give mixture 28 stirs with cocktail stirrer.

Put remaining 3 ice cubes into a 12-ounce old-fashioned glass and rim edge of glass with lemon twist. Add twist to glass, then strain rye mixture into glass.

COOK'S NOTE

■ For an old-fashioned with fruit, muddle 2 slices of orange and a maraschino cherry with the simple syrup in the cocktail shaker. Then add the ice, bitters, and rye and stir 28 times. Strain into the ice-filled glass and garnish with 2 thin orange slices and another cherry.

Eggnog

MAKES 6 TO 8 DRINKS
ACTIVE TIME: 25 MINUTES ■ START TO FINISH: 3½ HOURS
(INCLUDES CHILLING)

■ Christmas-tree trimming isn't complete without a cup of homemade eggnog. Forget the heavy, thick grocery store versions—this one has a fresh, custardy flavor and a light, velvety mouthfeel. (And you can imbibe without worry, because the eggs are completely cooked.) Bourbon and brandy add boozy zing, but the drink is just as delicious without them. ■

    3 cups whole milk
    7 large eggs
    1 cup sugar
    2 cups heavy cream
    ⅓ cup bourbon
    ⅓ cup Cognac or other brandy
    1 teaspoon vanilla extract
    ½ teaspoon freshly grated nutmeg
GARNISH: freshly grated nutmeg
SPECIAL EQUIPMENT: an instant-read thermometer

Bring milk just to a boil in a 2-quart heavy saucepan. Meanwhile, whisk together eggs and sugar in a large bowl. Add hot milk in a slow stream, whisking constantly. Pour back into saucepan and cook over moderately low heat, stirring constantly with a wooden spoon, until mixture is slightly thickened and registers 165°F on thermometer, 6 to 7 minutes.

Pour custard through a fine-mesh sieve into a (clean) large bowl. Stir in cream, bourbon, brandy, vanilla, and nutmeg. Cool completely, uncovered, then refrigerate, covered, until very cold, at least 3 hours.

Transfer eggnog to a pitcher. Serve in punch cups or other small cups, sprinkled with nutmeg.

COOK'S NOTE

■ The eggnog can be enjoyed after 3 hours of chilling, but it will improve in flavor if refrigerated longer, for up to 1 day.

Wine and Champagne Drinks

Classic Sangria

MAKES 8 DRINKS
ACTIVE TIME: 10 MINUTES ■ START TO FINISH: 1¼ HOURS

■ Long enjoyed in Spain, sangria gained more far-reaching popularity when it was served at the Spanish Pavilion at the 1964 World's Fair in Queens, New York. Its name derives from *sangre*, the Spanish word for "blood," because of the ruby color of the drink. Keeping the sliced fruit to a minimum makes the sangria easier to sip. ■

    1 (750-ml) bottle dry red wine
    ½ cup fresh orange juice (from about 1½ oranges)
    ½ lemon, sliced
    ½ large navel orange, sliced
    ½ cup sugar
    ½ cup water
    4 ounces (½ cup) brandy
    4 ounces (½ cup) Cointreau or Triple Sec
      Ice cubes

Put wine, juice, and fruit slices in a heatproof pitcher. Combine sugar, water, brandy, and Cointreau in a small saucepan and bring just to a simmer, stirring until sugar is dissolved. Add to wine mixture. Refrigerate, covered, for at least 1 hour.

Pour sangria into eight white wine glasses or old-fashioned glasses filled with ice.

COOK'S NOTE

■ The sangria can be refrigerated for up to 1 day.

Peach–White Wine Sangria

MAKES 8 TO 10 DRINKS
ACTIVE TIME: 15 MINUTES ■ START TO FINISH: 1½ HOURS

■ This is one of our very favorite summer drinks: chilled white wine and sweet peach nectar combined with the herbal balm of fresh basil. ■

    1 cup loosely packed fresh basil leaves, plus
        8–10 fresh basil sprigs
    ¾ cup sugar
    ¼ cup fresh lemon juice
    2 (11.5-ounce) cans peach nectar
    1 (750-ml) bottle dry white wine, chilled
    1 large peach, peeled if desired (see Tips, page 913),
        pitted, and diced
        Ice cubes

Put basil leaves, sugar, and lemon juice in a small saucepan and bruise leaves by gently mashing with a wooden spoon. Add 1 can nectar and bring just to a simmer, stirring until sugar is dissolved. Remove from heat and let stand for 5 minutes.

Pour nectar mixture through a medium-mesh sieve into a heatproof pitcher; discard basil leaves. Stir in wine, diced peach, remaining nectar, and basil sprigs. Refrigerate, covered, for at least 1 hour.

Pour sangria into white wine or old-fashioned glasses filled with ice.

COOK'S NOTE

■ The sangria can be refrigerated for up to 1 day.

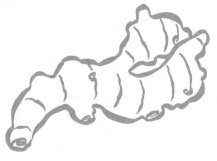

Cucumber, Ginger, and Sake Sangria

MAKES 8 TO 10 DRINKS
ACTIVE TIME: 10 MINUTES ■ START TO FINISH: 10 MINUTES

■ An Eastern spin on the classic Spanish cocktail, this sake sangria gets warmth from ginger. Fresh cucumber lends it a cool celadon hue. ■

    1 large (1-pound) seedless cucumber (usually plastic-
        wrapped)
    2 cups water
    ⅔ cup sugar
    1 tablespoon finely grated peeled fresh ginger
    2 tablespoons fresh lemon juice, or to taste
    1 (720-ml) bottle dry sake, chilled
    2 tablespoons finely chopped crystallized ginger
        (optional)
        Ice cubes

Cut cucumber into 3 equal pieces. Peel and chop 2 pieces and put into a blender. Peel 4 lengthwise strips from remaining piece, leaving stripes of green. Halve piece lengthwise and scoop out seedy center with a spoon. Thinly slice.

Add water, sugar, fresh ginger, and lemon juice to cucumber in blender and puree until smooth. Pour through a medium-mesh sieve into a pitcher. Stir in sake, crystallized ginger (if using), and cucumber slices.

Pour sangria into white wine or old-fashioned glasses filled with ice.

COOK'S NOTE

■ The sangria can be refrigerated, covered, for up to 2 hours.

Mimosa

MAKES 6 DRINKS
ACTIVE TIME: 10 MINUTES ■ START TO FINISH: 10 MINUTES

■ For many people, a mimosa is the only way to ease into a Sunday morning brunch, and it couldn't be easier to make a batch for a crowd. When the mood strikes, experiment with other citrus juices, such as tangerine, grapefruit, or even blood orange. Should you find yourself craving a mimosa in England, ask for a Buck's fizz. ■

3 cups chilled strained fresh orange juice (from about 9 oranges)
1 (750-ml) bottle Champagne or other sparkling white wine, chilled

Pour juice and Champagne into a large pitcher and stir gently. Serve immediately in Champagne flutes or wineglasses.

Bellini

MAKES 6 DRINKS
ACTIVE TIME: 15 MINUTES ■ START TO FINISH: 1¼ HOURS
(INCLUDES MAKING PUREE)

■ The original Bellini, invented in 1948 at Harry's Bar in Venice by owner Giuseppe Cipriani, enjoyed a very short season—only as long as sweet white peaches were available. With the advent of fine-quality frozen white peach puree, we can toast with Bellinis all year long. Don't consider making these with yellow peaches—both the color and the taste will be off. ■

1½ cups white peach puree (recipe follows, or see Sources), thawed if frozen
1 (750-ml) bottle Prosecco, chilled

Pour peach puree into a 2-quart pitcher. Tilt pitcher and very slowly add about 1 cup Prosecco. Gently stir, allowing foam to subside, then add remaining Prosecco in same manner. Stir again and pour into six Champagne flutes. Serve immediately.

COOK'S NOTE

■ To make individual servings, pour ¼ cup peach puree into each of six Champagne flutes. Very slowly pour about ½ cup Prosecco at a time into each glass, allowing foam to subside before adding more. Gently stir drinks and serve immediately.

White Peach Puree

MAKES ABOUT 1½ CUPS
ACTIVE TIME: 10 MINUTES ■ START TO FINISH: 1¼ HOURS

■ Though it may seem odd, the vitamin C tablet is a vital ingredient; it helps prevent the puree from discoloring. ■

1 pound white peaches (about 3 medium), left unpeeled, quartered, and pitted
1 (500-mg) vitamin C tablet, crushed
2 tablespoons sugar
2 tablespoons fresh lemon juice

Combine all ingredients in a food processor and puree until smooth (there will be flecks of peach skin). Pour through a fine-mesh sieve into a bowl; discard solids. Refrigerate puree, its surface covered with wax paper to prevent darkening and bowl covered with foil, until cold, about 1 hour.

Stir puree before using.

COOK'S NOTE

■ The puree can be refrigerated in an airtight container for up to 3 days or frozen for up to 3 months.

Kir

MAKES 1 DRINK
ACTIVE TIME: 5 MINUTES ■ START TO FINISH: 5 MINUTES

■ An apéritif, that lovely liquid prelude to a meal, should be daintier than a cocktail and stimulating to the appetite. A kir fits the bill on both counts. The components are white Burgundy (or any good crisp white wine) and crème de cassis, a sweet black currant liqueur from Dijon, France. In fact, the drink was named for a famous war hero and mayor of Dijon, Canon Félix Kir. We also like the less traditional Beaujolais kir: cassis mixed with well-chilled fruity Beaujolais in place of white wine. ■

  4 ounces (½ cup) chilled white wine, preferably
     white Burgundy
  ½ ounce (1 tablespoon) crème de cassis
  1 lemon twist

Pour wine into a 6-ounce wineglass. Add crème de cassis and lemon twist and stir.

Kir Royale

MAKES 1 DRINK
ACTIVE TIME: 5 MINUTES ■ START TO FINISH: 5 MINUTES

■ A kir royale makes any occasion feel like a celebration. If you're a Champagne purist and find it hard to add anything to a good bubbly, choose a fine-quality sparkling wine instead. ■

  5 ounces (½ cup plus 2 tablespoons) chilled
     Champagne or sparkling white wine
  ½ ounce (1 tablespoon) crème de cassis

Pour Champagne into a 6-ounce Champagne flute and wait for foam to subside. Add crème de cassis and stir gently if necessary to mix.

French Kiss

MAKES 6 DRINKS
ACTIVE TIME: 15 MINUTES ■ START TO FINISH: 3¼ HOURS
(INCLUDES FREEZING ICE CUBES)

■ This classic apéritif is wonderfully complex, with a taste reminiscent of a sophisticated iced tea. It gets its depth from sweet vermouth, its kick from dry

vermouth, and its singular verve from lemonade ice cubes. And the drink only gets more delicious the longer you sip it, as the ice cubes melt and release their tart sweetness. ■

FOR LEMONADE ICE CUBES
  ½ cup fresh lemon juice (from about 2 lemons)
  2 tablespoons sugar
  1½ cups water
FOR DRINKS
  12 ounces (1½ cups) dry vermouth
  12 ounces (1½ cups) sweet vermouth
  6 strips lemon zest, removed with a vegetable peeler

MAKE THE ICE CUBES: Stir together juice and sugar in a pitcher or large glass measuring cup until sugar is dissolved. Stir in water. Pour into an ice cube tray and freeze until solid, about 3 hours.

MAKE THE DRINKS: Stir together vermouth and lemonade ice cubes in a pitcher until vermouth is cold. Run a strip of zest around rim of each of six 6-ounce glasses and drop into glass. Add vermouth mixture, with ice, to glasses.

COOK'S NOTE
■ The lemon ice cubes keep for up to 1 week.

Other Alcoholic Drinks

Caipirinha

MAKES 8 DRINKS
ACTIVE TIME: 20 MINUTES ■ START TO FINISH: 20 MINUTES

■ Considered Brazil's national drink, the caipirinha ("kai-pee-*reen*-ya") is made from cachaça ("kah-*shah*-sah"), a liquor that is distilled from fermented sugarcane juice (rum, its close cousin, is made from the molasses left from processing sugarcane). Although the ingredients seem similar to those of a daiquiri, the effect is brasher and more tart, thanks to the sharpness of the cachaça and the oil from the lime peel. ∎

    4 limes
    ½ cup sugar
      Ice cubes
   12 ounces (1½ cups) cachaça

Quarter limes lengthwise, then cut each quarter crosswise in half. Divide pieces among eight 6-ounce glasses.

Add 1 tablespoon sugar to each glass. Muddle lime pieces, pounding and pressing with a muddler or wooden spoon, until sugar is dissolved. Fill glasses with ice, then add 1½ ounces (3 tablespoons) cachaça to each drink, stirring well.

Pimm's Cup

MAKES 1 DRINK
ACTIVE TIME: 5 MINUTES ∎ START TO FINISH: 5 MINUTES

∎ Pimm's Cup is the quintessential British cocktail and the signature drink of Wimbledon. The London oyster bar owner James Pimm first brewed a batch of Pimm's No. 1 Cup in the 1840s, using gin, quinine, and a secret batch of herbs. The aromatic concoction is usually mixed with English lemonade—a sort of fizzy lemonade similar to limonata—and the result is refreshing, with the Pimm's herbal, not-too-sweet flavor acting as a true tonic. A garnish of cucumber spears, borage leaves, and mixed fruit slices is also traditional, but we prefer to keep things simple and uncrowded. Before World War II, the Pimm's line expanded to No. 2 (based on whiskey), No. 3 (brandy), and No. 4 (rum); in the 1960s, No. 5 (rye) and No. 6 (vodka) were added. Numbers 1, 3, and 6 are still available today. ∎

    1 cucumber spear
    1 lemon slice
    ½ orange slice
      Ice cubes
1–1½ ounces (2–3 tablespoons) Pimm's No. 1 Cup
    ¼ cup San Pellegrino limonata (sparkling bitter
       lemon soda)

Put cucumber spear and citrus slices in a tall 8-ounce glass. Fill glass three-quarters full with ice cubes. Add Pimm's to taste and top off drink with limonata.

COOK'S NOTE
∎ To make a pitcher (or punch bowl) of Pimm's Cup (6 to 8 drinks), fill a 2-quart pitcher three-quarters full with ice cubes. Add 5 thin slices each of cucumber, lemon, and orange. Add 8 ounces (1 cup) Pimm's and top off with 1½ cups limonata.

Pisco Sour

MAKES 1 DRINK
ACTIVE TIME: 5 MINUTES ∎ START TO FINISH: 5 MINUTES

∎ This South American cocktail is made with pisco, a potent brandy distilled from Muscat grapes. Tasted on its own, pisco has an almost grappalike intensity. A spoonful of sugar, as well as bitters and tart lemon and lime juices, tames the pisco's fiery strength and helps it go down—delightfully. The drink gets its distinctive foamy head from egg white, a classic ingredient in a number of old-fashioned cocktails. ∎

      Ice cubes
   1½ ounces (3 tablespoons) pisco
    1 tablespoon fresh lemon juice
    1 tablespoon fresh lime juice
    1 tablespoon superfine sugar
    1 large egg white (see Cook's Note)
      A few drops of Angostura bitters
SPECIAL EQUIPMENT: a cocktail shaker; a cocktail strainer

Fill cocktail shaker half full with ice. Add remaining ingredients except bitters and shake vigorously for 15 seconds. Strain into an old-fashioned or martini glass and sprinkle bitters onto froth.

COOK'S NOTE
∎ The egg white in this recipe is not cooked. If that is a concern, see page 915. Alternatively, you can substitute ½ teaspoon powdered egg white, such as Just Whites, or 2 tablespoons liquid pasteurized egg whites.

Rob Roy

MAKES 2 DRINKS
ACTIVE TIME: 5 MINUTES ■ START TO FINISH: 5 MINUTES

■ Following a tradition at the end of the nineteenth century of naming cocktails for new plays and musicals, the Rob Roy was created to commemorate the opening of an 1894 Broadway show about a Scottish Robin Hood. Essentially a variation on a manhattan, the drink replaces the rye with Scotch. A dry Rob Roy substitutes dry vermouth for sweet and a twist of lemon for the maraschino cherry garnish, while a "perfect" Rob Roy calls for equal amounts of dry and sweet vermouth. ■

Ice cubes
3 ounces (6 tablespoons) blended Scotch
3 ounces (6 tablespoons) sweet vermouth
2 dashes of Angostura bitters
GARNISH: 2 maraschino cherries
SPECIAL EQUIPMENT: a cocktail shaker; a cocktail strainer

Fill cocktail shaker half full with ice. Add remaining ingredients and stir with a bar spoon for about 15 seconds. Strain into two chilled 6-ounce martini glasses and garnish each drink with a cherry.

Limoncello and Mint Sparkler

MAKES 6 DRINKS
ACTIVE TIME: 15 MINUTES ■ START TO FINISH: 1¼ HOURS

■ Limoncello, a liqueur made by steeping lemon peels in a neutral spirit, has long been a staple in the lemon-producing region along Italy's Amalfi Coast, where it is usually served well chilled in the summer months. It offers even more of a lift when infused with mint and mixed with club soda and fresh lemon juice. ■

1 cup loosely packed fresh mint leaves
8 ounces (1 cup) chilled limoncello
½ cup fresh lemon juice (from about 2 lemons)
3 cups chilled club soda
Ice cubes
GARNISH: fresh mint sprigs and lemon slices

Combine mint and limoncello in a bowl and bruise mint by gently mashing with a wooden spoon. Refrigerate, covered, for 1 hour.

Pour limoncello through a fine-mesh sieve into a pitcher, pressing firmly on mint; discard mint. Stir lemon juice and club soda into limoncello, then add enough ice to fill pitcher. Pour drink and ice into six 8-ounce glasses. Garnish with mint sprigs and lemon slices.

COOK'S NOTE

■ The strained limoncello-mint infusion can be refrigerated, covered, for up to 2 hours.

Long Island "Iced Tea"

MAKES 2 DRINKS
ACTIVE TIME: 5 MINUTES ■ START TO FINISH: 5 MINUTES

■ Stories differ as to how this potent drink came to be, but the most commonly accepted one is that Robert "Rosebud" Butt shook it up first in the 1970s at the Oak Beach Inn, a popular bar located at the end of a pier in Hampton Bays on, yes, Long Island. Its strength is infamous, but holding the five alcohols to a restrained ½ ounce each for 2 cocktails keeps things civilized. However, the brew does taste just enough like ordinary iced tea to merit a warning: one is probably enough. ■

Ice cubes
½ ounce (1 tablespoon) gin
½ ounce (1 tablespoon) vodka
½ ounce (1 tablespoon) light rum
½ ounce (1 tablespoon) tequila
½ ounce (1 tablespoon) Cointreau or Triple Sec
1½ tablespoons fresh lemon juice
1 teaspoon superfine sugar, or to taste
½ cup cola

GARNISH: 2 lemon wedges

SPECIAL EQUIPMENT: a cocktail shaker; a cocktail
	strainer

Put 1 cup ice in cocktail shaker, add gin, vodka, rum, tequila, Cointreau, lemon juice, and sugar, and shake vigorously for 15 seconds. Strain into two tall 8-ounce glasses filled with ice. Add ¼ cup cola to each drink and stir. Garnish with lemon wedges.

Mulled Red Wine

MAKES 8 TO 10 DRINKS
ACTIVE TIME: 10 MINUTES ■ START TO FINISH: 20 MINUTES

■ A perfect warm-up after an afternoon of sledding, this mulled wine gets a fruity kick from kirsch and strips of lemon and orange zest. Simmering it only briefly keeps its fresh flavor vibrant. ■

    8 whole cloves
    4 black peppercorns
    4 (3-by-½-inch) strips lemon zest, removed
        with a vegetable peeler
    4 (4-by-½-inch) strips orange zest, removed
        with a vegetable peeler
   32 ounces (4 cups) dry red wine (from two
        750-ml bottles)
    4 ounces (½ cup) kirsch or other cherry-flavored
        brandy
   1½ cups water
   ¾ cup sugar
    1 (3-inch) cinnamon stick
    1 vanilla bean, halved lengthwise
GARNISH: cinnamon sticks
SPECIAL EQUIPMENT: a 4-inch square of cheesecloth;
	kitchen string

Put cloves, peppercorns, and zests in center of cheesecloth, then pull up edges and tie to form a bag. Combine cheesecloth bag and remaining ingredients in a 4-quart saucepan, bring to a simmer, and simmer, stirring occasionally, for 10 minutes.

Ladle wine into heatproof small glasses or cups and garnish with cinnamon sticks.

Bridge Punch

MAKES 50 CUPS
ACTIVE TIME: 15 MINUTES ■ START TO FINISH: 2¼ HOURS
(INCLUDES CHILLING)

■ Every great host needs a great punch, and this one, from contributor Don Summers in 1942, turns any gathering into a party. It's a bit like Planter's Punch (page 12) but much less sweet. The iced tea gives it backbone, bracing up the fruit juices, maraschino, and crushed pineapple (don't be tempted to use fresh pineapple; it doesn't have the requisite sweetness, and besides, you're going retro here). Before the guests arrive, kick back and sample "thoughtfully." As Summers wrote, "This is the Punch Master's privilege and gives [you] a head start on the mob." ■

    1 bunch fresh mint
    4 cups sugar
    4 cups strong black tea, cooled
    1 (750-ml) bottle brandy
   ½ cup dark rum
   ¾ cup fresh orange juice (from 2 oranges)
   ¾ cup fresh grapefruit juice
   ¾ cup fresh lemon juice or lime juice (from 3 lemons or
        6 limes)
    1 (20-ounce) can crushed pineapple in juice
    1 (10-ounce) jar maraschino cherries, drained and
        minced
       A block of ice
    1 (1-liter) bottle club soda, chilled

Cut off tender sprigs of mint and put them in a large bowl or pitcher. Add sugar and muddle lightly with a muddler or a potato masher until mint is bruised. Add tea, brandy, rum, juices, pineapple, and cherries, and stir to combine. Refrigerate for at least 2 hours.

Put ice in a punch bowl, pour punch over ice, and add club soda. Ladle punch into small cups.

COOK'S NOTES

■ The punch (without the ice and club soda) can be
   refrigerated for up to 8 hours.
■ You can make your own block of ice by freezing water
   in a loaf pan or similar container.

Brandy Alexander

MAKES 1 DRINK
ACTIVE TIME: 5 MINUTES ■ START TO FINISH: 5 MINUTES

■ The Alexander was developed during Prohibition as a way to make homemade hooch more palatable—cream and sugar (now crème de cacao) certainly did the trick. Gin was originally the most popular liquor, but today brandy is the norm. The ultimate nightcap—or a bewitching alternative to dessert—a brandy Alexander is cool, creamy, and smooth. If you opt to use nutmeg, use it sparingly (too much may overwhelm). ■

Ice cubes
1 ounce (2 tablespoons) brandy
1 ounce (2 tablespoons) crème de cacao
2 tablespoons heavy cream
OPTIONAL GARNISH: freshly grated nutmeg
SPECIAL EQUIPMENT: a cocktail shaker; a cocktail
      strainer

Fill cocktail shaker half full with ice. Add brandy, crème de cacao, and cream and shake vigorously for 5 seconds. Strain into a 4- to 5-ounce martini glass. Sprinkle lightly with nutmeg if desired.

Hot Buttered Rum

MAKES 4 DRINKS
ACTIVE TIME: 10 MINUTES ■ START TO FINISH: 15 MINUTES

■ Warm and sweet, with a pleasant spice and rummy bite, hot buttered rum is a true toddy, forcing you to slow down, sip, relax, and unwind. Most versions involve making a compound butter with spices and stirring a pat into each drink until it melts. Our method—boiling the butter with the spices and water—results in a more rounded drink. ■

2 cups water
½ stick (4 tablespoons) unsalted butter

⅓ cup packed dark brown sugar
1 teaspoon ground cinnamon
½ teaspoon freshly grated nutmeg
¼ teaspoon ground cloves
⅛ teaspoon salt
5⅓ ounces (⅔ cup) dark rum

Combine water, butter, brown sugar, cinnamon, nutmeg, cloves, and salt in a 1- to 2-quart saucepan and bring to a simmer. Simmer, whisking occasionally, for 10 minutes to blend flavors. Remove from heat and stir in rum. Pour into four 6-ounce mugs.

Irish Coffee

MAKES 4 DRINKS
ACTIVE TIME: 10 MINUTES ■ START TO FINISH: 10 MINUTES

■ A delicious excuse to pull those stemmed mugs out of the china closet (though regular mugs work fine), Irish coffee is warming and invigorating. Don't add too much sugar to the whipped cream, though, or the drink will be cloying. ■

6 ounces (¾ cup) Irish whiskey
2 tablespoons sugar, or to taste
3 cups freshly brewed strong hot coffee
   Lightly sweetened whipped cream

Combine 3 tablespoons whiskey and 1½ teaspoons sugar each in four 8-ounce mugs. Divide coffee among mugs and stir until sugar is dissolved; stir in more sugar if desired. Top each drink with a dollop of whipped cream.

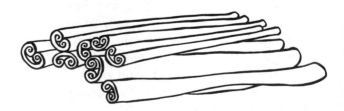

Nonalcoholic Drinks

Classic Lemonade

MAKES 8 DRINKS
ACTIVE TIME: 15 MINUTES ■ START TO FINISH: 15 MINUTES

■ Now here's a lemonade stand–worthy quaff: sweet and clean tasting, with just the right amount of mouth-puckering tartness. ■

        2 cups fresh lemon juice (from about 8 lemons)
1¼ 1⅓ cups superfine sugar
        6 cups water
           Ice cubes

Stir together lemon juice and sugar (to taste) in a 3-quart pitcher until sugar is dissolved. Add water and stir until combined. Pour into eight tall 10-ounce glasses filled with ice.

COOK'S NOTE
■ The lemonade can be refrigerated, covered, for up to 1 day. Stir before serving over ice.

Cherry Lime Rickey

MAKES 6 DRINKS
ACTIVE TIME: 15 MINUTES ■ START TO FINISH: 50 MINUTES

■ Refreshing and not too sweet, these colorful virgin drinks will please kids and adults alike. Their play of flavors comes from tart lime juice, simple syrup, and a splash of maraschino cherry juice. Topping off the drinks with club soda adds a fizzy sparkle. ■

        1 cup sugar
        ⅓ cup water
           Pinch of salt
½–⅔ cup strained fresh lime juice (from about 5 limes)

        3 tablespoons maraschino cherry liquid (from a
           10-ounce jar of maraschino cherries)
           Ice cubes
        2 (10-ounce) bottles club soda or seltzer, chilled
GARNISH: 6 maraschino cherries with stems and 6 lime
           wedges

Bring sugar, water, and salt to a simmer in a small saucepan over medium heat, stirring until sugar is dissolved. Simmer until slightly syrupy, about 5 minutes, then transfer to a bowl and stir in ½ cup lime juice. Refrigerate until cool, about 30 minutes.

Add maraschino cherry liquid to lime mixture and stir to combine. Taste and stir in additional lime juice if desired. Fill six tall 8- to 10-ounce glasses half full with ice and divide cherry lime syrup among glasses. Top off drinks with club soda and garnish with cherries and lime wedges.

COOK'S NOTE
■ The cherry lime syrup can be refrigerated for up to 2 days.

Fresh Tomato Juice

MAKES 5 DRINKS
ACTIVE TIME: 20 MINUTES ■ START TO FINISH: 3 HOURS

■ This juice is pale in color, but it is surprisingly flavorful—the essence of tomato. It proves a lovely tonic for a hot summer day, or add a little chilled aquavit for a Norwegian Mary. ■

        3 pounds ripe beefsteak tomatoes (about 4 large),
           cored and coarsely chopped
        2 celery ribs, coarsely chopped
        2 teaspoons fine sea salt
SPECIAL EQUIPMENT: four 20-inch squares of cheesecloth

Pulse tomatoes and celery in batches in a food processor until finely chopped (tomatoes will be almost pureed). Transfer to a large bowl and stir in salt. Let stand, loosely covered, at room temperature for 1½ hours.

Line a large sieve with layered cheesecloth squares, allowing excess cloth to drape over sides. Set sieve over a large bowl. Pour tomato mixture into center of cheesecloth, gather up edges to form a large sack, and squeeze solids to extract as much liquid as possible. Discard solids.

Refrigerate juice until cold, about 1 hour. Stir before serving.

COOK'S NOTE

■ The tomato juice can be refrigerated, covered, for up to 1 day.

Mango Lassi

MAKES 4 DRINKS
ACTIVE TIME: 5 MINUTES ■ START TO FINISH: 35 MINUTES

■ As much a refreshing pick-me-up as a drink, the yogurt coolers known as *lassis* are popular throughout India—and, increasingly, throughout the world. For this classic version, we found that the most intense mango flavor comes from sweetened mango puree rather than fresh mangoes (which require a lot more work). When buying cans of puree, check the expiration date—you want the mango to taste fresh and sweet, not tinny. ■

1⅓ cups sweetened mango puree (see Sources)
¼ cup sugar
1½ cups whole-milk yogurt
2 cups crushed ice
2 teaspoons fresh lime juice, or to taste
Pinch of salt
Ice cubes
GARNISH: lime wedges

Combine all ingredients except ice cubes in a blender and blend until smooth. Refrigerate for at least 30 minutes to allow flavors to blend.

Stir *lassi* and pour into four 10-ounce glasses half-filled with ice cubes. Garnish with lime wedges.

COOK'S NOTE

■ The *lassi* can be refrigerated, covered, for up to 4 hours.

Mint Lassi

MAKES 4 DRINKS
ACTIVE TIME: 5 MINUTES ■ START TO FINISH: 35 MINUTES

■ Perfect for a sweltering day, this lightly salted *lassi* with toasted cumin and fresh mint is a wonderful restorative. Like sports drinks that have a bit of a salty taste, it can replenish the electrolytes you've lost after strenuous exercise or a long day in the sun. It's a more delicious alternative, and healthier as well. ■

½ teaspoon cumin seeds, toasted (see Tips, page 911)
½ cup loosely packed fresh mint leaves
1 teaspoon salt, or to taste
2 cups whole-milk yogurt
2 cups crushed ice
Ice cubes
GARNISH: lemon wedges and fresh mint sprigs

Pulse cumin seeds and mint with salt in a blender until finely chopped. Add yogurt and crushed ice and blend until smooth. Refrigerate, covered, for at least 30 minutes to allow flavors to blend.

Stir *lassi* and pour into four 8-ounce glasses half-filled with ice cubes. Garnish with lemon wedges and mint sprigs.

COOK'S NOTE

■ The *lassi* can be refrigerated for up to 4 hours.

Mexican Fruit Cooler
Agua Fresca de Fruta

MAKES 4 DRINKS
ACTIVE TIME: 10 MINUTES ■ START TO FINISH: 1¾ HOURS

■ *Aguas frescas*, literally "fresh waters," are refreshing Mexican drinks made from a wide variety of fruits and herbs, sold at street stands from clear glass barrels. Our basic recipe is good with any of the fruits suggested below. If you're feeling ambitious, make several different kinds and set them out in glass pitchers for a summer cookout—their colors are great and your guests will be mightily impressed. ∎

> 2 cups cold water
> 1 cup ice cubes, plus additional for serving
> 2 cups fruit (see Cook's Note for options), cut into 1-inch pieces unless otherwise specified
> ¼ cup sugar, or to taste
> 1 tablespoon fresh lime juice, or to taste

Combine water, ice cubes, fruit, sugar, and lime juice in a blender and blend on high speed until completely smooth. Pour through a fine-mesh sieve into a pitcher, pressing hard on solids; discard solids. Refrigerate, covered, for at least 1½ hours.

Stir cooler again and pour into four 8-ounce glasses half-filled with ice cubes.

COOK'S NOTES
- Use one of the following fruits, or a combination: honeydew or cantaloupe; mango (about 1); pineapple with a few fresh basil leaves; watermelon; strawberries (halved) with a few fresh mint leaves; papaya (very ripe); or seedless red grapes (whole).
- The cooler can be refrigerated for up to 1 day.

Hibiscus Flower Cooler
Agua de Jamaica

MAKES 6 DRINKS
ACTIVE TIME: 10 MINUTES ∎ START TO FINISH: 2 HOURS

∎ This traditional cooler, popular in Latin America, gets its glorious red color from the dried calyxes of the *Jamaica* ("hah-*my*-cah") or hibiscus flower. Hibiscus has a tart, almost cranberry-like flavor that is tempered by adding sugar to the drink. The name is sometimes mistranslated as "rose hip petals," so when shopping, specify *flor de Jamaica*. ∎

> 4 cups water
> 1 cup (about 1½ ounces) dried hibiscus flowers (also called *flor de Jamaica*; see Sources)

> ⅓ cup sugar, or to taste
> 2 cups ice cubes, plus additional for serving

Bring water to a boil in a 1½-quart saucepan. Add flowers, reduce heat, and simmer, uncovered, for 5 minutes. Remove from heat and let mixture steep for 30 minutes.

Pour infusion through a fine-mesh sieve into a pitcher, pressing on flowers; discard flowers. Add sugar and ice cubes, stirring until sugar is dissolved. Refrigerate, covered, for at least 1½ hours.

Stir cooler again and pour into six 8-ounce glasses filled with ice cubes.

COOK'S NOTE
- The infusion, with the sugar but not the ice cubes, can be made up to 2 days ahead. Cool, uncovered, then refrigerate, covered. Stir in the ice 30 minutes before serving, and keep refrigerated.

Cantaloupe Cooler
Agua de Melón

MAKES 4 DRINKS
ACTIVE TIME: 10 MINUTES ∎ START TO FINISH: 10 MINUTES

∎ Cantaloupe seeds are the unlikely basis of this delicious cooler. When they are blended with sugar and water and then strained, the result is a sweet, musky drink with an alluring nuttiness. We adapted this recipe from one by reader Maria A. Garza Jeffery of Ottawa, Canada. ∎

> 1 medium cantaloupe (2½–3 pounds)
> ⅓ cup sugar, or to taste
> 3 cups very cold water
>   Ice cubes (optional)

Cut cantaloupe in half. Scoop seeds, with juice, into a blender; reserve fruit for another use. Add sugar and 2 cups water and blend on high speed for 1 minute; seeds will still be visible. Pour through a fine-mesh sieve into a pitcher, pressing on solids; discard solids. Stir in remaining 1 cup water.

Serve chilled or over ice.

COOK'S NOTE

- The cooler can be made up to 4 hours ahead and refrigerated, covered.

Chocolate Egg Cream

MAKES 1 DRINK
ACTIVE TIME: 5 MINUTES ■ START TO FINISH: 5 MINUTES

■ This fountain treat is a New York classic. It became popular there in the early twentieth century at the city's many corner candy stores. Enthusiasts insist that egg creams—which contain neither eggs nor cream— should be made with fresh seltzer (from a glass bottle with a siphon) for the best fizz and Fox's U-Bet Original Chocolate Flavor Syrup, a Brooklyn institution for almost 100 years, for the best flavor. No matter what brand you use, the drink will be delicious. ■

½ cup very cold whole milk
  Chilled seltzer
¼ cup chocolate syrup
SPECIAL EQUIPMENT: a long-handled spoon; a seltzer
  siphon (optional)

Pour milk into a 16-ounce glass and put long-handled spoon in glass. Pour seltzer (or squirt it if using siphon) into glass to ½ inch below rim; a white foam will develop. Pour syrup into center of foam, stir it in, and remove spoon through center of foam.

Mexican Hot Chocolate

MAKES 8 DRINKS
ACTIVE TIME: 15 MINUTES ■ START TO FINISH: 15 MINUTES

■ Mexican chocolate, with its signature hint of cinnamon, is the backbone of this deeply flavored cocoa from the restaurant Noche on St. Thomas in the Virgin Islands. The tiny amounts of almond extract and cayenne add complexity, while the half-and-half, milk, and a bit of cream contribute richness. If you own a *molino*, the traditional wooden tool for mixing and foaming Mexican chocolate, by all means use it, but a regular whisk gets equally good results. ■

½ cup very cold heavy cream
2 teaspoons confectioners' sugar
2 drops pure almond extract
2 cups whole milk
2 cups half-and-half
1½ tablets (4¾ ounces) Mexican chocolate, such as
  Ibarra or Abuelita (see Sources), chopped
  Pinch of cayenne, or to taste
4 macadamia nuts, chopped

Using an electric mixer, beat cream with confectioners' sugar and almond extract in a small bowl until it holds soft peaks. Refrigerate, covered.

Bring milk and half-and-half just to a boil in a 2-quart heavy saucepan. Add chocolate and cayenne, whisking vigorously until chocolate is melted and mixture is smooth and foamy on top. Pour hot chocolate into eight demitasse or other small cups. Top each serving with a dollop of whipped cream and sprinkle with nuts.

Spiced Milk Tea
Masala Chai

MAKES 4 DRINKS
ACTIVE TIME: 10 MINUTES ■ START TO FINISH: 15 MINUTES

■ *Masala chai*, a spiced, sweetened black tea mixed with milk enjoyed by millions in India, is now popular around the world. It is sold all over India by *chai wallahs*, or tea vendors, who pour the tea from big kettles into small cups. Americans have incorrectly shortened the name to *chai* (which means simply "milk tea"); *masala* refers to the combination of spices, which often includes cardamom, cinnamon, ginger, cloves, pepper, fennel, and star anise. Although there are many chai blends now available in supermarkets, making your own is quick and satisfying and the results are much better. ■

10 green cardamom pods, cracked, seeds removed, and pods discarded (see Sources), or ½ teaspoon cardamom seeds or ground cardamom

1 (1½-inch) piece cinnamon stick

4 peppercorns, preferably white

¼ teaspoon fennel seeds

2 cups whole milk

3½ tablespoons packed light brown sugar, or to taste

⅛ teaspoon salt, or to taste

½ teaspoon ground ginger

2 cups water

5 teaspoons loose orange pekoe tea or other black tea

SPECIAL EQUIPMENT: a mortar and pestle or an electric coffee/spice grinder

Grind together cardamom, cinnamon stick, peppercorns, and fennel seeds with mortar and pestle or coffee/spice grinder.

Bring milk just to a simmer in a 2-quart heavy saucepan. Stir or whisk in brown sugar, salt, ground spice mixture, and ginger. Reduce heat to low and simmer gently, stirring occasionally, for 3 minutes to infuse flavors.

Meanwhile, bring water to a boil in a 1-quart saucepan, add tea, and boil for 1 minute.

Pour tea through a fine-mesh sieve into hot milk mixture (discard tea leaves) and cook, still over low heat, for 1 minute. Stir before serving.

COOK'S NOTE

■ The spices can be ground up to 2 hours ahead and kept in an airtight container at room temperature.

Spiced Milk Tea with Saffron and Pistachios

Kashmiri Masala Chai

MAKES 4 DRINKS
ACTIVE TIME: 10 MINUTES ■ START TO FINISH: 15 MINUTES

■ A variation on traditional *masala chai*, this milk tea incorporates saffron, almonds, and pistachios for a rich and hearty concoction. The ground nuts make the drink wholly unusual and absolutely wonderful. ■

1½ tablespoons blanched whole almonds

1½ tablespoons peeled shelled pistachios (raw or roasted salted)

10 green cardamom pods, cracked, seeds removed, and pods discarded (see Sources), or ½ teaspoon cardamom seeds or ground cardamom

1 (1-inch) piece cinnamon stick

Pinch of saffron threads (15–20)

2 cups whole milk

3½ tablespoons packed light brown sugar, or to taste

⅛ teaspoon salt, or to taste

¼ teaspoon freshly grated nutmeg

2 cups water

5 teaspoons loose orange pekoe tea or other black tea

SPECIAL EQUIPMENT: a mortar and pestle or an electric coffee/spice grinder

Grind together almonds, pistachios, cardamom, cinnamon stick, and saffron with mortar and pestle or coffee/spice grinder.

Bring milk just to a simmer in a 2-quart heavy saucepan. Stir or whisk in brown sugar, salt, ground nut mixture, and nutmeg. Reduce heat to low and simmer gently, stirring occasionally, for 3 minutes to infuse flavors.

Meanwhile, bring water to a boil in a 1-quart saucepan, add tea, and boil for 1 minute.

Pour tea through a fine-mesh sieve into hot milk mixture (discard tea leaves) and cook, still over low heat, for 1 minute. Stir before serving.

COOK'S NOTE

■ The spices and nuts can be ground up to 2 hours ahead and kept in an airtight container at room temperature.

HORS D'OEUVRES AND FIRST COURSES

If you want to throw a really great party—the kind that people talk about for years—all you really need are a few fabulous hors d'oeuvres and an incredible dessert. The stuff in the middle will pretty much take care of itself. That's always been my theory of entertaining, and it is one of the reasons we put so much energy into this chapter.

Chefs understand this. Anyone who spends a lot of time in restaurants knows that the first course is always the most exciting part of a menu. I've never thought it makes much sense for home cooks to try to act like restaurant chefs—none of us have the staff and few of us have the equipment—but if you're going to take your cues from a restaurant, this is the time to do it.

I remember the very first moment I tasted Wolfgang Puck's curried oysters with cucumber sauce and salmon roe. I fell in love with the way each little oyster looked—like a beautiful piece of jewelry—and then I took a bite and was wowed by the sensuous flavor combination. It seemed like a perfect party dish, so I asked for the recipe. That was twenty years ago, and I've been serving it ever since. I had the same experience when I tasted the smoked salmon croque monsieur at Le Bernardin. It is such an incredibly clever notion—an everyday sandwich transformed into something small, elegant, and irresistibly tasty. It has everything a good appetizer needs: it looks good, it tastes great, and it's a fantastic conversation starter.

The truth is that appetizers have a heavier responsibility than any other course. Their job is to set the tone for the evening and to make sure the conversational ball gets rolling. If you want your guests to have something to talk about from the moment they sit down, you could not have better insurance than an exciting appetizer.

That doesn't mean that it has to be complicated. You could simply start your party with something thrillingly unfamiliar from another corner of the world. That is why we've included *bhel poori*, the delightfully crisp, crunchy, and slightly spicy mixture that is a staple in Indian households. It's nothing fancy—it's just exotic street food—but it is deliciously aromatic, and the first time you taste it is always an adventure. If your friends are not familiar with *arepas*, the irresistible cornmeal cakes of Central America, they will be intrigued by the savory layers of flavor they discover when they put these delectable little black-bean-and-cheese-filled pockets into their mouths. What you are giving them is not just a fleeting taste, but something to talk about, a story to take home.

Hors d'oeuvres also present the perfect opportunity to offer something unabashedly rich without worrying about the calorie count. You may be reluctant to fill out your menu with a surfeit of butter and cream, but who can resist a little bite of bacon and cheddar toast? Miniature Camembert walnut pastries are as gorgeously opulent as they sound, but they are also so small that no reasonable person could possibly object to eating one or two.

But, in the end, the best thing about these first bites is that they allow me to indulge my taste for foreign flavors without committing to an entire ethnic meal. One of my favorite ways to spend an afternoon is wandering through Chinatown soaking in the smells. Yet serving an entire Chinese menu has always struck me as an arduous way to entertain—almost everything needs to be made at the last minute. So instead I share pork belly buns with my guests, or the crackling excitement of Vietnamese fried spring rolls, before going on to something less involved for the main course.

If you're entertaining a large group of people, it's easiest to follow up with a dish you can make ahead, or one that's very basic. Roast chicken. Poached salmon. Leg of lamb or a simply seared steak. Looking back, people will remember the care that you took with the opening course, the surprisingly exotic flavor you offered them as the evening started.

HORS D'OEUVRES AND FIRST COURSES

Hors d'Oeuvres

Spicy Cashews

MAKES 2 CUPS
ACTIVE TIME: 10 MINUTES ■ START TO FINISH: 15 MINUTES

■ These fried cashews, adapted from a recipe by the Indian cooking authority Madhur Jaffrey, have a wonderful texture, simultaneously crisp and tender. Don't worry if the toasted spices adhere to some nuts better than others—there is a cumulative effect of gentle heat. When shopping for the cashews, make sure to buy whole raw nuts (not pieces) from a natural foods store with a brisk turnover, or order them by mail (see Sources). ■

- ¾ teaspoon cumin seeds, toasted (see Tips, page 911)
- ¼ teaspoon salt
- ¼ teaspoon cayenne
- ⅛ teaspoon freshly ground black pepper
  About 4 cups vegetable oil for deep-frying
- 2 cups (11 ounces) raw cashews (see headnote)

SPECIAL EQUIPMENT: a mortar and pestle or an electric coffee/spice grinder; a deep-fat thermometer

Finely grind cumin seeds in mortar with pestle or in coffee/spice grinder. Stir together ground cumin, salt, cayenne, and black pepper in a small bowl. Set a sieve over a large metal bowl and set near stove. Line another bowl with paper towels.

Heat 1 inch oil in a 10-inch 2- to 3-inch-deep skillet over moderately high heat until it registers 350°F on thermometer. Fry cashews, stirring carefully but constantly, until golden brown, about 1 minute.

With a slotted spoon, transfer cashews to sieve and carefully shake off excess oil. Transfer cashews to lined bowl to drain, then remove and discard paper towels and toss cashews well with cumin mixture.

Serve cashews warm or at room temperature.

COOK'S NOTE
■ The spiced cashews can be kept for up to 3 days in an airtight container at room temperature.

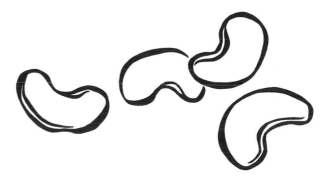

Smoky Peanuts

MAKES ABOUT 1 CUP
ACTIVE TIME: 5 MINUTES ■ START TO FINISH: 40 MINUTES

■ The subtle smokiness of these nuts comes from Lapsang souchong, a smoky black tea from China's Fujian Province. Although tea might sound like an exotic embellishment, many chefs use it as a natural flavoring agent for everything from red meats to fish to beans. ■

- 1 tablespoon lightly beaten egg white
- 1 teaspoon sugar
- ¾ teaspoon Lapsang souchong tea leaves (see Sources), crushed with side of a large heavy knife if coarse
- ¼ teaspoon salt
- 1 cup salted cocktail peanuts

SPECIAL EQUIPMENT: parchment paper

Put a rack in middle of oven and preheat oven to 350°F. Line a baking sheet with parchment paper.

Whisk together egg white, sugar, tea, and salt in a small bowl. Stir in peanuts and spread in one layer on baking sheet.

Bake, stirring occasionally, until nuts are dry, about 7 minutes. Cool on baking sheet on a rack. (Nuts will crisp as they cool.)

COOK'S NOTE
■ The smoky peanuts can be kept for up to 5 days in an airtight container at room temperature.

OLIVES

The olive—the fruit of a long-lived tree (*Olea europaea*) with distinctive silvery green leaves—evokes the rough, scrubby swath of the Mediterranean, which arcs from Spain to Greece and down through the Middle East and northern Africa. Whether you are setting out a bowl of glistening Gaetas at cocktail time or fishing pimiento-stuffed green Manzanillas out of a jar for your mother's cut-glass relish tray, you are looking at a food that's been revered since prehistoric times. Biblical, classical, artistic, and literary allusions, rich and inviting, are everywhere. Novelist Lawrence Durrell recorded his fascination with olives in *Prospero's Cell*: "The whole Mediterranean . . . the wine, the ideas, the ships, the moonlight, the winged gorgons, the bronze men, the philosophers—all of it seems to rise in the sour, pungent taste of these black olives between the teeth. A taste older than meat, older than wine. A taste as old as cold water."

There are about 700 cultivated varieties of *Olea europaea*, and each one produces a different kind of fruit—think of the difference between a large full-flavored almond-shaped Kalamata and a tiny, briny Niçoise. Some are grown for eating and others for pressing into oil. Their color—green, purple, or black—depends on stage of ripeness when harvested, not on the variety. You can't eat any just-picked olives out of hand, by the way, no matter how ripe they are, because they contain a compound that makes them extremely bitter—they must be cured.

Artisanal methods of curing olives differ and all have their place. The Greek black olive called Thasos is simply dried in the sun until its flesh is crinkly and its flavor deep and concentrated. WATER-CURING involves repeated soaks and rinses over months; BRINE-CURING soaks the olives in a brine solution for one to six months; and DRY-CURING works its magic by way of salt. OIL-CURING means either that the olives are soaked in oil for some months or that dry-cured olives are rubbed with oil. Herbs and other seasonings—garlic, for instance, or fresh or preserved lemons—are often added afterward, for flavor. LYE-CURING is primarily used for the "black ripe" olives sold in cans. They are quickly cured with a strong alkaline solution and get a color boost from an iron compound. But lye-curing can also be used in combination with brine-curing to produce mild green olives such as Cerignola or Lucques.

GREEN OLIVES are picked unripe. Their firm flesh is often cracked slightly to give the seasonings a better chance to penetrate during the curing process. PURPLE OLIVES are further along the road to ripeness. Their flesh is oilier and meatier than that of green olives. BLACK

OLIVES are completely ripe, with very oily flesh that is soft but not mushy.

If you don't know which to choose, buy a tub of mixed olives from a specialty foods shop or high-end supermarket and find out what you like. Then have fun making your own mixes.

Olives taste best at room temperature or slightly warm, so take them out of the refrigerator at least 30 minutes ahead or warm them in a low oven for 10 minutes before serving. If you've bought olives that are more salty or vinegary than you'd like, put them in a sieve and rinse them under cool running water.

Because saltiness enhances the perception of sweetness, briny olives can bring out the fruit in a wine. Olives cured with a generous amount of citrus zest, however, might be too acidic to pair well with a glass of wine; a very dry sherry or even a gin and tonic would work better.

FROM ITALY
CERIGNOLA ("che-ree-*nyo*-la") These very large, crisp-fleshed olives from Puglia can be green or black. They taste mild and almost grassy.

GAETA ("*gaye*-ta") Small olives from central Italy, Gaetas may be dry-cured, which makes them black and wrinkled, or brine-cured, in which case they're dark purple and smooth-skinned. They are salty but mellow.

FROM FRANCE
LUCQUES Meaty green olives from the Hérault region in the South of France, Lucques have a mild, nutty flavor.

NIÇOISE These dark little nuggets of brine-cured intensity from Provence are indispensable in regional specialties such as *salade niçoise*, *pissaladière*, and *pan bagnat*.

NYONS Matte-black wrinkled olives from southern France, these are dry-cured, then aged in brine. They have a deep, rich flavor.

PICHOLINE Brine-cured green olives from the South of France, Picholines are firm-fleshed and mild. They are great cooked in chicken or fish dishes.

"CRACKED PROVENÇAL OLIVES" The green olives often labeled this way are cracked so the cure can penetrate their firm unripe flesh. Although they are given Provençal seasonings, they are not a true French variety but in fact are usually Spanish Manzanillas or one of any number of Sicilian olives.

FROM SPAIN
ARBEQUINA Very small, round olives from Catalonia in northeastern Spain, Arbequinas are brown and nutty-tasting.

MANZANILLA These green olives come from Spain or California. Commonly stuffed with pimientos, hot peppers, or garlic, they are the classic martini olives.

FROM GREECE
AMPHISSA Picked when they're very ripe, these purple-black olives are very soft and briny sweet.

KALAMATA These brine-cured, purplish black, smooth-skinned olives from the valley of Messina are meaty and tangy.

NAFPLION Cracked green olives with a nutty flavor, these come from the valley of Argos.

THASOS Shriveled yet meaty, these intense olives come from the island of Thasos.

FROM MOROCCO
The Moroccan olives most commonly found in the United States are dry-cured black olives that are marinated in a blend of North African spices; their texture is almost prunelike.

Marinated Green Olives

MAKES 2 CUPS
ACTIVE TIME: 20 MINUTES ■ START TO FINISH: 1 DAY
(INCLUDES MARINATING)

■ These days, almost every supermarket in America carries a selection of marinated fresh olives. So why bother making these? Because they taste spectacular, with a freshness and vitality that supermarket mixes can't touch. ■

½ cup plus 2 tablespoons olive oil
2 large garlic cloves, thinly sliced lengthwise
½ cup white wine vinegar
1 large shallot, thinly sliced lengthwise
1 tablespoon packed dark brown sugar
¼ teaspoon whole allspice, lightly crushed
    with the side of a large heavy knife
1 teaspoon pink peppercorns, lightly crushed
    (optional)
1 (3-inch) cinnamon stick
2 Turkish bay leaves or 1 California bay leaf
2 (3-by-1-inch) strips lemon zest, removed
    with a vegetable peeler
2 (4-by-1-inch) strips orange zest, removed
    with a vegetable peeler
2 cups (12 ounces) brine-cured small green
    olives, drained

Heat 2 tablespoons oil in a small heavy skillet over moderate heat until hot but not smoking. Add garlic and cook, stirring, until pale golden, about 30 seconds. With a slotted spoon, transfer garlic to a small bowl; reserve oil separately (to prevent garlic from continuing to brown in hot oil).

Combine ¼ cup vinegar, shallot, and brown sugar in a 1-quart heavy saucepan, bring to a simmer, and simmer, stirring occasionally, until liquid is reduced to about 1 tablespoon, about 4 minutes.

Add garlic, garlic oil, remaining ½ cup olive oil, remaining ¼ cup vinegar, spices, bay leaves, zests, and olives and bring to a simmer. Transfer mixture to a medium bowl and cool to warm, then cover and marinate olives, refrigerated, for at least 24 hours.

If desired, reheat olives in marinade in a saucepan over low heat, stirring, until warm. With a slotted spoon, transfer olives to a serving dish.

COOK'S NOTE
■ The olives can marinate for up to 5 days.

Crostini

MAKES 24 TOASTS; SERVES 6 TO 8
ACTIVE TIME: 5 MINUTES ■ START TO FINISH: 20 MINUTES

■ Crostini—lightly toasted thin slices of bread brushed with olive oil—make a great base for all sorts of toppings. In addition to the recipes that follow, consider raiding the fridge for other topping ideas. Try a smear of goat cheese and a dab of fig jam (or a fresh fig half), or a slice of sharp cheddar cheese with a dollop of mango chutney. The quality of your crostini has everything to do with the quality of your bread—start with a fresh baguette from a reputable bakery (supermarket loaves are often bland and cottony). ■

24 (⅓-inch-thick) baguette slices (from a baguette at
    least 14 inches long and 2 inches wide)
3 tablespoons olive oil
½ teaspoon kosher salt
¼ teaspoon freshly ground black pepper

Put a rack in middle of oven and preheat oven to 350°F.

Arrange baguette slices in one layer on a large baking sheet and lightly brush both sides of bread with oil. Sprinkle tops with salt and pepper.

Bake until very lightly toasted, 8 to 10 minutes. Cool completely.

COOK'S NOTE
■ The crostini can be kept for up to 1 day in an airtight container at room temperature.

Garlic and Cheese Crostini

MAKES 24 HORS D'OEUVRES
ACTIVE TIME: 20 MINUTES ■ START TO FINISH: 30 MINUTES

■ Unlike classic crostini, these toasts are topped with a light sprinkling of minced garlic, fresh parsley, and sharp pecorino Romano before being baked. Garlicky and salty, they are a great accompaniment to cocktails. ∎

    24 (⅓-inch-thick) baguette slices (from a baguette
         at least 14 inches long)
    ¼ cup olive oil
    ¾ cup finely grated pecorino Romano, preferably
         imported
    5 large garlic cloves, minced
         Kosher salt
    ¼ teaspoon freshly ground black pepper
    2 tablespoons finely chopped fresh flat-leaf parsley

Put a rack in middle of oven and preheat oven to 350°F.

Arrange bread slices in one layer on a large baking sheet and brush tops with 3 tablespoons oil.

Stir together remaining 1 tablespoon oil, cheese, garlic, ¼ teaspoon salt, and pepper in a small bowl. Sprinkle each slice with about 1 teaspoon cheese mixture, mounding it slightly.

Bake until topping just starts to melt, 6 to 8 minutes. Sprinkle with parsley and salt to taste. Serve warm.

COOK'S NOTE

∎ The cheese mixture can be made up to 1 day ahead and refrigerated, covered.

Tomato and Basil Topping

MAKES ABOUT 1½ CUPS (ENOUGH FOR 24 CROSTINI)
ACTIVE TIME: 30 MINUTES ∎ START TO FINISH: 1 HOUR

∎ Wonderful by itself, this topping also takes nicely to easy additions. Try stirring in ⅓ cup chopped pitted Kalamata olives or ⅓ cup crumbled feta or ricotta salata cheese. ∎

    1 pound ripe tomatoes, cut into ¼-inch pieces
    1 large garlic clove, minced
    2 teaspoons balsamic vinegar
    ¼ teaspoon kosher salt
    ¼ teaspoon freshly ground black pepper
    3 tablespoons chopped fresh basil
    3 tablespoons extra-virgin olive oil
ACCOMPANIMENT: Crostini (page 40)

Stir together tomatoes, garlic, vinegar, salt, pepper, basil, and olive oil in a bowl. Let stand, covered, at room temperature for 30 minutes to develop flavors.

Mound about 1 tablespoon tomato mixture on each crostini and serve immediately.

Chickpea, Garlic, and Mint Topping

MAKES ABOUT 1½ CUPS (ENOUGH FOR 24 CROSTINI)
ACTIVE TIME: 30 MINUTES ∎ START TO FINISH: 1½ HOURS

∎ Tender chickpeas brightened with the Mediterranean flavors of mint, red onion, and lemon juice make a lively topping for crostini. ∎

    1 small garlic clove
    ¾ teaspoon kosher salt
    ¼ teaspoon freshly ground black pepper
    1 tablespoon fresh lemon juice
    2 tablespoons water
    ¼ cup olive oil
    1 (14- to 15-ounce) can chickpeas, rinsed and drained
    2 tablespoons finely chopped red onion
    3 tablespoons finely chopped fresh mint
ACCOMPANIMENT: Crostini (page 40)

Using a mortar and pestle, mash garlic to a paste with salt and pepper; or mince and mash with a large heavy knife. Transfer to a small bowl, add lemon juice, water, and oil, and whisk until well blended.

Combine chickpeas and garlic mixture in a medium bowl and coarsely mash with a fork until mixture just holds together. Stir in onion and mint. Add more water, 1 teaspoon at a time, if mixture seems dry.

Let stand, covered, at room temperature for 1 hour to develop flavors.

Mound about 1 tablespoon chickpea mixture on each crostini and serve immediately.

COOK'S NOTE

∎ The chickpea topping, without the onion and mint, can be made up to 1 day ahead and refrigerated, covered. Bring to room temperature, then stir in onion and mint before serving.

Chicken Liver, Sage, and Onion Topping

MAKES ABOUT ½ CUP (ENOUGH FOR 24 CROSTINI)
ACTIVE TIME: 45 MINUTES ■ START TO FINISH: 45 MINUTES

■ A coarsely pureed chicken liver spread seasoned with allspice and fresh sage pairs well with sweet sautéed onions. ■

FOR ONION MIXTURE
- 1 tablespoon vegetable oil
- 1 small onion, halved lengthwise and thinly sliced crosswise
- 1 garlic clove, chopped
- ⅛ teaspoon kosher salt
- ¼ teaspoon freshly ground black pepper

FOR LIVER MIXTURE
- 6 ounces chicken livers, trimmed and halved
- 1 tablespoon vegetable oil
- 1 garlic clove, chopped
- 2 tablespoons chopped fresh sage
- ⅛ teaspoon ground allspice
- ¼ teaspoon kosher salt
- ¼ teaspoon freshly ground black pepper

GARNISH: finely chopped fresh sage
ACCOMPANIMENT: Crostini (page 40)

MAKE THE ONION MIXTURE: Heat oil in a 10-inch skillet, preferably nonstick, over moderate heat until hot but not smoking. Add onion and garlic and cook, stirring occasionally, until pale golden, 8 to 10 minutes. Stir in salt and pepper. Transfer to a bowl and cover to keep warm. (Set pan aside.)

MAKE THE LIVER MIXTURE: Pat chicken livers dry. Heat oil in same skillet over moderately high heat. Add garlic and cook, stirring, until golden, about 30 seconds. Add chicken livers and cook, turning once, until golden and just springy to the touch, 2 to 3 minutes. Transfer to a food processor, add sage, allspice, salt, and pepper, and pulse to a coarse puree.

Mound about 1 teaspoon liver mixture on each crostini and top with about ¼ teaspoon onion mixture. Sprinkle with chopped sage and serve immediately.

COOK'S NOTE

■ The onion mixture can be made up to 2 days ahead and, once cooled, refrigerated, covered. Reheat before serving.

Catalan Tomato Bread
Pa Amb Tomàquet

MAKES ABOUT 10 LARGE TOASTS
ACTIVE TIME: 15 MINUTES ■ START TO FINISH: 30 MINUTES

■ A rustic dish of grilled bread rubbed with garlic and tomatoes, *pa amb tomàquet* exemplifies Catalan cuisine, the assertive, earthy food from the northeastern corner of Spain. Serve this when friends come over for a cookout and are hanging around the grill. It almost goes without saying that you should make this simple recipe only with the very best ingredients—good-quality sourdough bread, juicy ripe tomatoes, and excellent extra-virgin olive oil. ■

- 1 (8-inch) round sourdough loaf or 20-inch-long sourdough baguette
- 2 large garlic cloves, halved crosswise
- 3–4 small ripe tomatoes, halved crosswise
- 3–4 tablespoons extra-virgin olive oil
  Coarse salt

If using a charcoal grill, prepare it for direct-heat cooking over medium-hot coals; if using a gas grill, prepare it for direct-heat cooking over medium-high heat (see Grilling Basics, page 512).

Cut bread into ¾-inch-thick slices if using a round loaf, or cut baguette on a long diagonal to get 6-inch-long slices.

Oil grill rack. Working in batches of 3 or 4 slices, grill bread (covered if using a gas grill), turning once, until grill marks appear, 1 to 2 minutes per batch. Remove bread from grill and immediately rub one side of each slice with cut side of a garlic half. Then rub with cut side of a tomato half, using 1 tomato half for 1 to 2 slices of bread and allowing most of pulp to be absorbed by bread (discard remainder of garlic and tomatoes after last batch). Brush bread with oil, sprinkle with coarse salt, and serve immediately.

COOK'S NOTES
■ The bread can also be grilled in a hot, lightly oiled, well-seasoned ridged grill pan over moderately high heat.
■ If your salt is very coarse, crush it using the side of a large heavy knife.

Dried Apricots with Goat Cheese and Pistachios

MAKES 30 HORS D'OEUVRES
ACTIVE TIME: 20 MINUTES ■ START TO FINISH: 30 MINUTES

■ Soaked in orange juice, dried apricots become soft, plump foundations for a spread of creamy goat cheese and chopped pistachios. ■

30 (4 ounces) dried California apricot halves or 15 (3½ ounces) dried whole Turkish apricots, halved
⅓ cup fresh orange juice
3 ounces soft mild goat cheese
2½ tablespoons salted roasted shelled pistachios, finely chopped

Toss apricots with orange juice in a bowl. Let stand, tossing occasionally, for 20 minutes. Drain cut side down on paper towels.

Stir together goat cheese and 2 tablespoons pistachios. Turn apricot halves cut side up and top each with ½ teaspoon goat cheese mixture. Sprinkle with remaining 1½ teaspoons pistachios.

COOK'S NOTE
■ The hors d'oeuvres can be assembled up to 1 hour ahead and kept, loosely covered, at room temperature.

Beet Chips with Curried Sour Cream

MAKES ABOUT 24 HORS D'OEUVRES
ACTIVE TIME: 20 MINUTES ■ START TO FINISH: 2 HOURS

■ Soaking the beets in sugar water enhances their natural sweetness, and the sugar, like salt, draws out moisture and helps crisp the chips. This recipe works as a casual chips-and-dip appetizer or, with each chip crowned by a dollop of curried sour cream and a dusting of chopped fresh chives, as an elegant hors d'oeuvre. If you opt for the latter, assemble them at the last minute to keep the chips from getting soggy. ■

FOR CHIPS
2 medium beets, stems trimmed to 1 inch
1 cup water
1 cup sugar
Salt and freshly ground black pepper
FOR CURRIED SOUR CREAM
2 tablespoons finely chopped shallot
1 tablespoon olive oil
¾ teaspoon curry powder, preferably Madras
¾ cup sour cream
1½ tablespoons finely chopped fresh chives
¼ teaspoon salt
¼ teaspoon freshly ground black pepper
GARNISH: chopped fresh chives
SPECIAL EQUIPMENT: a mandoline or other adjustable-blade vegetable slicer; a nonstick baking sheet liner, such as a Silpat

MAKE THE CHIPS: Peel beets, then slice paper-thin with slicer, using stems as "handles."

Bring water and sugar to a boil in a 3-quart heavy saucepan, stirring until sugar is dissolved. Add beets, remove pan from heat, and let stand for 15 minutes.

Drain beets in a colander, then let drain in colander for 15 minutes more.

Put a rack in middle of oven and preheat oven to 225°F.

Line a large baking sheet with nonstick liner. Arrange beet slices in one snug layer (discard any partial or torn slices) on pan and season with salt and pepper. Bake beets until dry, about 1 hour. Immediately transfer chips to a rack to cool (chips will crisp as they cool).

MEANWHILE, MAKE THE CURRIED SOUR CREAM: Cook shallot in oil in a small skillet over moderate heat, stirring frequently, until golden, 3 to 4 minutes. Stir in curry powder and cook, stirring, for 1 minute. Remove from heat and let cool.

Combine sour cream, chives, salt, and pepper in a bowl, and stir in shallot until well blended. Refrigerate, covered, until ready to serve.

Serve beet chips topped with sour cream and chives.

COOK'S NOTES
- The beet chips can be kept for up to 5 days in a sealed plastic bag at room temperature.
- The curried sour cream can be made up to 1 day ahead and refrigerated, covered.

Zucchini Chips

SERVES 8 TO 10
ACTIVE TIME: 30 MINUTES ■ START TO FINISH: 30 MINUTES

■ These chips are incredibly light and delicate. Their snap is the result of slicing the zucchini almost paper-thin (quick work on an adjustable-blade slicer), then shaking off all the excess flour before frying. ■

3–4 cups vegetable oil for deep-frying
1 cup all-purpose flour
1 large or 2 medium zucchini
Salt

SPECIAL EQUIPMENT: a deep-fat thermometer; a mandoline or other adjustable-blade vegetable slicer; 2 sieves

Fill a 10- to 12-inch deep heavy skillet, preferably cast-iron, halfway with oil and heat over moderate heat until oil registers 360°F on thermometer.

Meanwhile, put flour in a shallow bowl. Fill another bowl halfway with cold water. Cut zucchini into almost paper-thin rounds with mandoline and separate slices.

Put 12 zucchini slices in one sieve and dip into water, shaking off excess, then transfer dampened slices to flour and dredge. Gently shake in second sieve to remove excess flour. Fry coated slices in oil, turning and separating them with a wire-mesh skimmer or slotted spoon, until golden brown, 1 to 2 minutes. Transfer chips to paper towels to drain, then season lightly with salt. Coat and fry remaining slices in same manner. Serve warm.

COOK'S NOTE
- The chips can be made up to 2 hours ahead and kept at room temperature. Reheat in a 350°F oven for 8 to 10 minutes.

Baba Ghanouj

MAKES ABOUT 2½ CUPS
ACTIVE TIME: 1 HOUR ■ START TO FINISH: 1¼ HOURS

■ This classic Middle Eastern dip never goes out of style. Though the eggplant is often broiled or baked, we love it best when the vegetable's silky flesh is perfumed with smoke from an outdoor grill. Draining the liquid exuded in the grilling process helps remove any bitterness. Because tahini can spoil quickly, stir it well and taste it before using. ■

2 medium eggplants
3 small garlic cloves, finely chopped
¼ cup well-stirred tahini (Middle Eastern sesame paste)
2–3 tablespoons fresh lemon juice
1 teaspoon salt
¼ teaspoon freshly ground black pepper
3 tablespoons extra-virgin olive oil, plus additional for drizzling
1 tablespoon chopped fresh flat-leaf parsley

ACCOMPANIMENTS: grilled or toasted pita bread; chopped tomato, chopped red onion, and chopped Kalamata olives

If using a charcoal grill, prepare it for direct-heat cooking over hot coals; if using a gas grill, prepare it for direct-heat cooking over medium-high heat (see Grilling Basics, page 512).

Generously oil grill rack. Prick eggplants in several places with a fork and grill, turning every 5 minutes, until charred all over and very soft, 20 to 25 minutes. Cool for about 15 minutes, then peel off and discard skin.

Transfer eggplant pulp to a colander set over a bowl and drain for 20 minutes. (Discard any liquid in bowl.)

Combine eggplant, garlic, tahini, lemon juice (to taste), salt, pepper, and oil in a food processor and blend until smooth and creamy. Transfer to a shallow bowl, drizzle with oil, and sprinkle with parsley. Serve with accompaniments.

COOK'S NOTES
- If you can't grill outdoors, cook the eggplants in a hot, well-seasoned grill pan or cast-iron skillet, turning every 5 minutes, until charred all over and very soft, 45 to 55 minutes.
- The dip can be made up to 1 day ahead and refrigerated, covered. Bring to room temperature before serving, then drizzle with the oil and sprinkle with the parsley.

Sun-Dried Tomato Dip

MAKES ABOUT 1 CUP
ACTIVE TIME: 15 MINUTES ■ START TO FINISH: 20 MINUTES

■ During the eighties, leathery disks of sun-dried tomatoes showed up in salads and pastas and everything in between. Well, they've changed. Good-quality oil-packed sun-dried tomatoes (rather than those packaged dry, in pouches) are plump, pliable, and intensely tomatoey. This rosy dip is delicious with crudités or crackers. If you have any left over, try it on a cold roast pork sandwich. ■

¼ cup drained oil-packed sun-dried tomatoes
2 tablespoons chopped drained bottled roasted red peppers
½ cup walnuts, toasted (see Tips, page 911)
1 teaspoon finely chopped shallot
1½ tablespoons red wine vinegar

2 tablespoons water
¼ cup olive oil
Salt

Combine all ingredients except oil and salt in a food processor and puree until smooth. With motor running, add oil in a slow stream, blending until incorporated. Season with salt to taste.

COOK'S NOTE
- The dip can be made up to 1 day ahead and refrigerated, covered.

Chive and Pine Nut Dip with Sourdough Toasts

MAKES ABOUT 1 CUP DIP
ACTIVE TIME: 15 MINUTES ■ START TO FINISH: 1¼ HOURS

■ Think of this as onion dip for the twenty-first century, with verdant chive oil taking the place of the instant soup mix, and mascarpone and cream cheese stepping in for the sour cream. It's great on the toasts, but we also love it with crudités, crackers, or potato chips. ■

¾ cup coarsely chopped fresh chives, plus
   2 tablespoons finely chopped fresh chives
   (2–3 bunches)
¼ cup vegetable oil
   Salt
1 (12-inch-long) sourdough baguette, cut diagonally into ⅛-inch-thick slices
¼ cup pine nuts
⅔ cup mascarpone, at room temperature
2 tablespoons cream cheese, softened

Combine coarsely chopped chives, oil, and ⅛ teaspoon salt in a blender and blend until smooth. Refrigerate for 1 hour.

Meanwhile, put racks in upper and lower thirds of oven and preheat oven to 375°F.

Divide bread slices between two baking sheets and toast in oven, switching position of sheets halfway through, until golden, 8 to 10 minutes. Set aside. (Leave oven on.)

Spread pine nuts in a shallow baking pan and toast in lower third of oven, shaking pan occasionally, until pale golden, 4 to 5 minutes. Cool completely, then coarsely chop.

Pour chive oil through a fine-mesh sieve into a small bowl, pressing on solids; discard solids. Stir in pine nuts and finely chopped chives.

Whisk together mascarpone, cream cheese, and ¼ teaspoon salt in a bowl until smooth. Fold in chive oil mixture until cream is streaked (do not mix in thoroughly). Transfer dip to a shallow bowl and serve with toasts.

COOK'S NOTE

■ The dip can be made up to 6 hours ahead and refrigerated, covered. Bring to room temperature before serving.

Taramasalata

MAKES ABOUT 3 CUPS
ACTIVE TIME: 20 MINUTES ■ START TO FINISH: 20 MINUTES

■ In this traditional Greek dip, humble ingredients—salty salmon-colored carp roe, or *tarama*, bread, lemon juice, and olive oil—are transformed into a sublimely creamy and savory dip that tastes wonderful with crisp toasts or soft triangles of pita. This version—the best we've ever tasted—comes from the Athens restaurant Estiatorio Milos, which has outposts in Montreal and New York City. Milos prepares whole fish, pristine and gorgeous, and prices it by the pound, and a meal there is as memorable as it is expensive. Happily, taramasalata is affordable and easy to make at home. When shopping for *tarama*, look for roe that is neither too pink (which may be an indication of food coloring) nor too brown (which may mean it's been sitting around too long). The only ingredients listed on the jar should be carp roe, salt, and extra-virgin olive oil. ■

    6 cups 1-inch torn pieces crustless bread (from a
       30-inch-long Italian loaf)
    ¼ cup chopped red onion
    ¼ cup (2 ounces) *tarama* (carp roe; see Sources)
    ½ teaspoon salt
    ½ teaspoon freshly ground white pepper
    ¼ cup fresh lemon juice
    ½ cup olive oil
ACCOMPANIMENT: lightly toasted bread slices

Soak bread in water to cover by 1 inch in a large bowl until very soft, about 5 minutes.

Meanwhile, mince onion in a food processor. Add roe, salt, white pepper, 2 tablespoons lemon juice, and ¼ cup oil and blend until smooth.

Squeeze as much water as possible from bread, then add bread to roe mixture and blend until smooth. With motor running, add remaining 2 tablespoons lemon juice and ¼ cup oil and blend until well combined.

Serve dip with toasts.

COOK'S NOTE

■ The taramasalata can be made up to 6 hours ahead and refrigerated, covered.

Smoked Trout Spread

MAKES ABOUT 4 CUPS
ACTIVE TIME: 25 MINUTES ■ START TO FINISH: 8½ HOURS
(INCLUDES CHILLING)

■ Adding water while processing the smoked trout, butter, and seasonings creates a mousselike texture that sets this fish spread worlds apart from most others. Because it must be made ahead to allow the flavors to develop, it is excellent for company. ■

    1 pound smoked trout fillets, skin discarded, any
       remaining silvery skin scraped off
    2 sticks (½ pound) unsalted butter,
       softened
    ⅓ cup finely chopped shallots
    ¼ cup finely chopped fresh dill
    1 tablespoon fresh lemon juice
    ½ teaspoon hot sauce, such as Tabasco
    ¼ teaspoon freshly ground black pepper
    1 cup cold water
ACCOMPANIMENT: whole-grain crackers

Flake trout. Transfer 2 cups to a food processor (reserve remaining trout), add butter, shallots, dill, lemon juice, hot sauce, and pepper, and blend until smooth.

With motor running, add water to trout mixture in a slow stream, then process until water is completely absorbed, about 1 minute. Transfer to a bowl and fold in reserved trout. Pack mixture into a 4-cup glass or ceramic mold or bowl. Cover surface with wax paper, cover tightly with plastic wrap, and refrigerate for at least 6 hours to blend flavors.

Bring spread to room temperature before serving. Serve with crackers.

COOK'S NOTE
■ The spread can be refrigerated for up to 5 days.

Caviar Tart

SERVES 8 TO 10
ACTIVE TIME: 30 MINUTES ■ START TO FINISH: 3½ HOURS
(INCLUDES DRAINING SOUR CREAM)

■ Finely chopped hard-boiled eggs, sour cream, and onion are traditional accompaniments to caviar. Here they are transformed into a thin sumptuous tart, spread with caviar, and cut into neat wedges meant for eating with toasts. We used supermarket lumpfish caviar, but if you're feeling flush, use the good stuff. ■

¾ cup sour cream
8 hard-boiled large eggs (see Cook's Note), finely chopped
½ cup finely chopped onion
¾ stick (6 tablespoons) unsalted butter, melted and cooled
2 tablespoons finely chopped fresh dill
2 teaspoons finely grated lemon zest
¼ teaspoon salt
¼ teaspoon freshly ground black pepper
1 tablespoon finely chopped fresh chives
2 (3½-ounce) jars black lumpfish caviar, drained (see Cook's Note)
OPTIONAL GARNISH: 2 tablespoons finely chopped fresh chives

ACCOMPANIMENTS: lemon wedges; thin slices whole wheat bread, toasted, buttered, and halved or quartered diagonally
SPECIAL EQUIPMENT: a 9-inch nonstick springform pan

Put ½ cup sour cream in a paper-towel-lined sieve set over a bowl. Refrigerate, covered with plastic wrap, and let drain for 3 hours.

Stir together remaining ¼ cup sour cream, eggs, onion, butter, dill, zest, salt, pepper, and chives in a bowl until well combined.

Invert bottom of springform pan (to make it easier to slide tart off bottom) and lock on sides. Spread egg mixture evenly in pan with an offset spatula or back of a spoon, smoothing top. Cover surface with plastic wrap, pressing gently, and refrigerate until firm, at least 3 hours.

Remove plastic wrap from egg mixture and spread drained sour cream evenly over it with offset spatula or spoon.

Gently spread half of caviar on several layers of paper towels to absorb excess ink, then carefully lift caviar from paper towels with offset spatula or a spoon and spread evenly on top of egg mixture (be careful not to smash caviar). Repeat with remaining caviar.

To serve, remove side of pan and cut tart into wedges. Sprinkle with chives if desired, and serve with small bowls of lemon wedges and toasts.

COOK'S NOTES
■ To hard-boil eggs, put them in a heavy saucepan, cover them with cold water by 1½ inches, partially cover pan, and bring to a rolling boil. Reduce the heat to low, cover completely, and cook the eggs for 30 seconds. Remove from the heat and let stand, covered, for 15 minutes. Transfer the eggs to a bowl of ice and cold water and let stand for 30 minutes; drain and peel.
■ Draining the caviar removes the excess ink, which would stain the cream (this is not necessary for higher-quality caviar). For a caviar alternative, try Cavi-Art, a caviar substitute made of seaweed (see Sources).

Improv Hors d'Oeuvres

Sometimes spur-of-the-moment gatherings turn out to be the most fun, especially when you have all sorts of delicious things handy in the refrigerator, freezer, and pantry. Never be embarrassed to offer simple food to your guests.

- Toast GREEN (HULLED) PUMPKIN SEEDS (PEPITAS) in a dry skillet over moderate heat, then drizzle with a little of your best olive oil and sprinkle with sea salt. This is fast and will make your house smell wonderful as well. Use any leftover roasted pumpkin seeds to garnish soups.

- An ASSORTMENT OF OLIVES (for suggestions, see page 38) will keep in the refrigerator for a couple of weeks. To enjoy them at their most flavorful, warm them in a low oven for about 10 minutes before serving.

- The SUMMER'S FIRST RADISHES—crisp, juicy, mildly peppery—are worth showcasing the way the French do, with sea salt and European-style sweet butter. If you find long narrow pink-and-white French Breakfast radishes, pounce. Trim the radishes of their roots and all but the smallest leaves. Arrange on a pretty plate, along with a generous slab of butter and a small bowl of sea salt for sprinkling, and let guests butter and salt their radishes to taste.

- Make a VERSATILE DIP of equal parts mayonnaise and sour cream, and flavor it with all kinds of things, including curry powder (to take the raw taste out of it, toast it first in a dry skillet over low heat until it's fragrant), chutney, minced fresh herbs (chives, tarragon, basil, or cilantro), flaked smoked fish, canned chipotles in adobo (whiz them up in a blender and add to taste), or wasabi paste. For an EASY SPREAD, work chopped olives or smoked salmon into cream cheese. Both dips and spreads are best made ahead of time and chilled, to give the flavors a chance to develop. Bring them to room temperature before serving.

- PITA POCKETS split into their thin halves, then cut into wedges and toasted, make an excellent vehicle for dips. After you split them, lightly brush the rough sides with olive oil and sprinkle with coarse salt and/or a combination of seeds such as nigella (shiny black seeds often incorrectly labeled "onion seeds"), cumin, and sesame. Or, instead of spices, use minced fresh herbs such as rosemary and/or thyme. Cut each round into 8 wedges and bake on a baking sheet in a preheated 375°F oven until golden and crisp.

- Toss unblanched whole ALMONDS with tamari (a type of Japanese soy sauce), spread them out on a parchment-lined baking sheet, and bake in a low oven until dry and crisp, 10 to 20 minutes. Or toast almonds in a dry skillet over moderate heat, then add a knob of butter to them and toss to coat. Finish with a sprinkle of sea salt.

- PICKLED VEGETABLES, found in the canned-vegetable aisle in the supermarket, are treasures. Look for jars of pickled okra, pickled carrots, and "dilly beans," as well as the Italian assortment of pickled vegetables called *giardiniera* (literally, "gardener's-style").

- DRIED FRENCH SAUSAGES (*saucissons secs*) are delicious sliced thin and served on a board with a ramekin of mustard. You can do the same thing with Spanish chorizo or Italian soppressata, but hold the mustard. A combination of any of the sausages with any of the pickled vegetables mentioned above is perfection.

- Even POTATO CHIPS can be improved upon. Spread them on a baking sheet and warm them in the middle of a preheated 350°F oven for about 5 minutes. They are delicious as is or topped with something delicate—a dab of crème fraîche, for instance, and a sliver of smoked salmon, or even a dollop of *tobiko,* flying-fish roe (see page 97).

- Mash some COOKED WHITE BEANS (or rinsed canned white beans) with some top-quality CANNED TUNA packed in olive oil (use the oil too), and serve on toasted rounds of French bread.

- Thinly sliced PROSCIUTTO keeps beautifully, well wrapped, in the freezer. Use it to wrap the thin Italian breadsticks called *grissini* and serve with fresh cantaloupe or figs. It's also delicious wrapped around slender stalks of asparagus that have been steamed until they are crisp-tender, or strips of thin white sandwich bread that's been buttered and toasted until golden.

- If you are lucky enough to have a perfectly ripe AVOCADO, coarsely mash it with a little lime juice, and maybe a little minced green chile if you've got one sitting around (hot sauce is an able substitution). Spread it lavishly on pieces of toasted country-style white bread, drizzle with olive oil, and season with salt and pepper. Top with cilantro leaves—or some toasted cumin for more punch if desired.

- FRESH RICOTTA CHEESE (from a cheese shop or Italian market, not the supermarket) has an appealingly moist texture. Mash it in a bowl with some snipped fresh chives and a little milk, to give it a creamy consistency. Sprinkle it with cracked black pepper and serve it with cool, crisp leaves of endive. Experiment with other fresh white cheeses such as feta or *queso fresco.*

- When serving a CHEESE PLATE, it's not necessary to buy a huge assortment. Keep it focused. You might buy three or four Spanish cheeses and pair them with bowls of olives, almonds, and the quince paste called *membrillo* (found in specialty shops and such supermarkets as Whole Foods). Add a bowl of oranges or clementines and you've got an after-dinner cheese course and dessert rolled into one. Or serve a selection of goat cheeses, in a beautiful array of sizes, shapes, wrappings, and flavors.

- Sometimes all you really need is some PARMIGIANO-REGGIANO. Pry into chunks and serve it drizzled with aged balsamic vinegar.

Vegetables with Thai Pork-Chile Dipping Sauce

SERVES 4 TO 6

ACTIVE TIME: 1½ HOURS ■ START TO FINISH: 1½ HOURS

■ This traditional northern Thai dip—a chunky relish of diced pork, fiery chiles, tomatoes, shallots, and garlic called *nam prik ong*—becomes increasingly addictive with each bite. The small amounts of Thai shrimp paste and fish sauce are essential to underscoring the layers of flavor for which this dip is famous. Indeed, *nam prik* is a wonderful example of the hot-sour-salty-sweet balance that defines Thai cooking. The cool, crisp long beans, carrots, and cabbage are traditionally dipped into the relish and then eaten, but you might find it easier to use a plate. Because this dish is quite spicy even with just a few chiles, we suggest using the lesser amount the first time you make the recipe. ■

10–18 (2- to 3-inch-long) dried Thai red chiles (see Sources)
     Salt
  6 ounces Chinese long beans (see Sources) or green beans, trimmed and cut into 3-inch pieces
  ½ cup chopped shallots
  4 garlic cloves, chopped
  ¼ teaspoon Thai shrimp paste (see Sources)
  ⅛ teaspoon sugar
  ½ pound cherry tomatoes, quartered
  ½ pound boneless pork shoulder, cut into ¼-inch pieces
  2 tablespoons vegetable oil
  1 tablespoon Asian fish sauce
  4 carrots, cut diagonally into ¼-inch-thick slices
  ½ head (1½ pounds) cabbage, cut into 8 wedges (including core)

SPECIAL EQUIPMENT: a large (at least 2-cup) mortar and pestle, preferably granite (see Cook's Note)

Cut chiles in half with kitchen shears, discard seeds, and cut into ¼-inch pieces. Soak in warm water until softened, about 20 minutes. Drain.

Meanwhile, blanch beans in a large saucepan of boiling salted water (1 tablespoons salt per every 4 quarts water) for 1 minute. Transfer to a bowl of ice and cold water to stop the cooking. Drain well.

Combine chiles, shallots, garlic, ½ teaspoon salt, shrimp paste, and sugar in mortar and pound to a coarse paste with pestle, about 8 minutes. Transfer half of paste to a small bowl. Add half of tomatoes to mortar and pound until tomatoes begin to break up and form a chunky sauce. Transfer tomato mixture to another bowl, return reserved chile paste to mortar, and pound with remaining tomatoes in same manner.

Pat pork dry. Heat oil in wok (see Cook's Note) over moderate heat until hot but not smoking. Add pork and cook, stirring, until no longer pink, 3 to 4 minutes. Add tomato mixture and cook, stirring occasionally, until reduced and slightly thickened, 3 to 5 minutes. Add fish sauce and cook, stirring occasionally, for 1 minute.

Serve relish warm or at room temperature, with vegetables for dipping.

COOK'S NOTES

■ The chile paste can also be made in a mini food processor. Combine all the ingredients except the tomatoes in the processor and blend to a coarse paste, scraping down the sides occasionally. Add the tomatoes in batches, pulsing until a chunky sauce forms.

■ You can substitute a 12-inch heavy skillet, preferably cast-iron, for the wok.

■ The relish, without the fish sauce, can be made up to 1 day ahead and refrigerated, covered. Reheat over moderate heat, stirring, until hot before adding the fish sauce.

Pork Rillettes

SERVES 12 TO 14
ACTIVE TIME: 30 MINUTES ■ START TO FINISH: 2½ DAYS
(INCLUDES MARINATING AND CHILLING)

■ A classic component of French charcuterie, pork *rillettes* ("rih-*yet*") are made by braising marinated pork in fat and a little water at low temperature until it is very tender. The meat is then shredded, packed into a terrine, and sealed with a thin layer of fat for further curing. Like pâté, *rillettes* go well with cornichons, caper berries, or pickled onions. Don't be put off by the long start-to-finish time—this recipe is actually simple. Because the spread keeps well, you can divide the *rillettes* between two 2-cup terrines and save one for another time—or use it for gift-giving. ■

- 2 garlic cloves
- 1 tablespoon kosher salt
- 3 fresh thyme sprigs, plus ¼ teaspoon chopped fresh thyme
- ⅓ teaspoon ground allspice
- ¼ teaspoon freshly grated nutmeg
- ¼ teaspoon freshly ground black pepper
- 1 (2-pound) piece boneless pork shoulder, cut into 1½-inch pieces
- 3 fresh flat-leaf parsley sprigs
- 1 Turkish bay leaf or ½ California bay leaf
- ¾ pound skinned pork fatback (from a 1-pound piece with skin; see Cook's Note), cut into ½-inch pieces
- 2 cups water

GARNISH: fresh thyme sprigs
ACCOMPANIMENT: toasted baguette slices or crackers
SPECIAL EQUIPMENT: cheesecloth; kitchen string; a 3½- to 4-cup terrine mold or crock

MARINATE THE PORK: Mince garlic and mash to a paste with salt, chopped thyme, allspice, nutmeg, and pepper, using side of a large heavy knife. Put pork into a bowl and rub pieces with spice mix. Refrigerate, covered, for 12 to 24 hours.

COOK THE PORK: Put a rack in lower third of oven and preheat oven to 300°F.

Wrap parsley sprigs, thyme sprigs, and bay leaf in cheesecloth and tie with string to make a bouquet garni. Put pork in a 3- to 4-quart heavy ovenproof saucepan, add bouquet garni, fatback, and water, and bring to a simmer over moderate heat. Cover with tight-fitting lid and transfer to oven. Braise, stirring once or twice, until meat is very tender, about 4 hours.

Drain pork mixture in a fine-mesh sieve set over a bowl; reserve cooking liquid and discard bouquet garni. Transfer meat and fatback, 1 cup at a time, to a plate and finely shred pork with two forks; transfer to a large bowl. Lightly mash fatback with fork to break into tiny pieces and add to bowl with pork.

Skim fat from cooking liquid; reserve fat. Stir ¼ cup cooking liquid (if you have less, that's okay; do not add water) into shredded pork. Transfer mixture to terrine, pressing down lightly and smoothing top. Garnish top with thyme sprigs and pour reserved fat over top. Let *rillettes* cool, then refrigerate, covered, for at least 8 hours.

Bring *rillettes* to room temperature before serving. Just before serving, remove top layer of fat only from portion to be served (the protective layer of fat will keep the *rillettes* moist). Serve with baguette toasts or crackers.

COOK'S NOTES

- Fatback is unsmoked, unsalted fresh fat that comes from the back of the pig. (Do not confuse it with salt pork.) It's available in supermarkets and it will keep, refrigerated, for up to 1 week.
- The *rillettes* can be refrigerated for up to 6 weeks.

Roasted Grape Relish with Cheddar Crisps

MAKES 24 HORS D'OEUVRES
ACTIVE TIME: 45 MINUTES ■ START TO FINISH: 1¼ HOURS

■ Roasted grapes on savory cheddar crisps make an unlikely yet delicious combination. We roast the grapes just long enough for them to become soft and tender, then add celery, red onion, jalapeño, pine nuts, and green olives to make a relish that is also good on fowl or fish. Though we call for red grapes, green grapes or a mixture of the two can be substituted. ■

FOR CHEDDAR CRISPS

1 cup coarsely grated extra-sharp cheddar, preferably white (4 ounces)

½ cup all-purpose flour

⅛ teaspoon cayenne

2 tablespoons unsalted butter, softened

FOR GRAPE RELISH

1 pound seedless red grapes (see headnote), stemmed and halved lengthwise (3 cups)

¼ teaspoon salt

⅛ teaspoon freshly ground black pepper

2 tablespoons plus 1 teaspoon olive oil

½ cup finely chopped pitted green olives

¼ cup finely chopped celery

¼ cup finely chopped red onion

½ teaspoon finely chopped jalapeño, including seeds

½ teaspoon minced garlic

½ teaspoon finely grated orange zest

1 tablespoon red wine vinegar

⅓ cup pine nuts, toasted (see Tips, page 911)

SPECIAL EQUIPMENT: 2 nonstick mini muffin pans with twelve 2-tablespoon cups each

MAKE THE CHEDDAR CRISPS: Put a rack in middle of oven and preheat oven to 400°F.

Pulse cheddar, flour, and cayenne in a food processor until well combined. Add butter and process until dough starts to clump, 30 seconds to 1 minute. Turn out onto a work surface and gently knead until well combined. Using palms of your hands, roll dough into a 12-inch-long log.

Cut log into twenty-four ½-inch-thick slices. Press 1 piece onto bottom and halfway up sides of each mini muffin cup.

Bake until crisps are golden and puffed slightly in centers, about 10 minutes. Cool in pan on a rack for 10 minutes, then invert onto rack to cool completely. (Leave oven on.)

MEANWHILE, MAKE THE GRAPE RELISH: Line a baking sheet with foil and turn up edges of foil. Toss grapes with salt, pepper, and 1 teaspoon oil in a bowl, then spread on baking sheet. Roast until shriveled, about 25 minutes.

Slide foil onto a rack and cool grapes completely.

Transfer grapes to a bowl and toss together with remaining ingredients, including remaining 2 tablespoons oil. Let stand for 15 minutes to develop flavors.

Just before serving, spoon relish onto cheddar crisps.

COOK'S NOTES

- The cheddar crisps can be made up to 3 days ahead and kept in an airtight container at room temperature. Recrisp in a 375°F oven for 3 minutes before serving.

- The grape relish can be made up to 8 hours ahead and refrigerated, covered.

Stilton Cheese Puffs

MAKES ABOUT 40 HORS D'OEUVRES
ACTIVE TIME: 30 MINUTES ■ START TO FINISH: 1 HOUR

■ In this variation on gougères, the famous English blue cheese steps in for the traditional Gruyère, and ale adds extra depth of flavor. The light-as-air puffs are perfect as a cocktail snack or as an accompaniment to a post-dinner salad, scuttling the need for a cheese course. When preparing any *pâte à choux* dough, make sure it has cooled sufficiently before you add the eggs; if the dough is too hot, the eggs will partially cook and the puffs will not rise properly. ■

½ cup pale ale, such as Bass (pour beer slowly into measuring cup—do not measure foam)

3 tablespoons unsalted butter

Rounded ⅛ teaspoon salt

½ cup all-purpose flour

2 large eggs

½ cup crumbled Stilton cheese (from a 4-ounce piece, rind discarded)

SPECIAL EQUIPMENT: a pastry bag fitted with a plain ½-inch tip; parchment paper

Put a rack in middle of oven and preheat oven to 400°F.

Combine ale, butter, and salt in a 1½- to 2-quart heavy saucepan and bring to a full boil over high heat, stirring until butter is melted. Reduce heat to moderate, add flour all at once, and stir vigorously with a wooden spoon until mixture pulls away from sides of pan, about 30 seconds. Continue to cook, stirring and flattening dough against bottom of pan, until excess moisture evaporates and a film forms on bottom of pan. Remove from heat and cool for 5 minutes.

Add eggs one at a time, beating well with wooden spoon after each addition. (Dough will appear to separate initially but will become smooth as it is beaten.) Add cheese and stir until well combined.

Spoon dough into pastry bag. Line a large baking sheet with parchment paper and secure parchment by piping a dab of batter under each corner. Pipe approximately 3-inch lengths of dough 1 inch apart on baking sheet, making about 40 total.

Bake until puffed, golden, and crisp, 20 to 25 minutes. Cool slightly before serving.

COOK'S NOTE

- The cheese puffs are best when freshly baked, but they can be made up to 4 hours ahead and reheated in a 350°F oven for 10 minutes.

Miniature Camembert Walnut Pastries

MAKES 42 HORS D'OEUVRES
ACTIVE TIME: 30 MINUTES ■ START TO FINISH: 50 MINUTES

■ These tiny pastries are light in texture, though rich in flavor. A bit of freshly ground pepper on top gives them just the right edge. ■

FOR PASTRY
¼ cup walnuts, finely chopped
2 teaspoons unsalted butter, melted
⅛ teaspoon fine sea salt
1 sheet frozen puff pastry (from a 17.3-ounce package), thawed
1 large egg, lightly beaten with 1 tablespoon water for egg wash

FOR CHEESE FILLING
6 ounces Camembert (not runny), rind discarded
⅓ cup walnuts, finely chopped and toasted (see Tips, page 911)

Freshly ground black pepper
SPECIAL EQUIPMENT: parchment paper; a 1½-inch round cookie cutter

MAKE THE PASTRY: Put a rack in middle of oven and preheat oven to 400°F. Line a large baking sheet with parchment paper.

Stir together walnuts, butter, and salt in a small bowl.

With a lightly floured rolling pin, roll out pastry on a lightly floured surface into a 14-by-12-inch rectangle. Cut out 42 rounds with lightly floured cookie cutter; discard trimmings.

Brush tops of rounds with egg wash, then sprinkle each with about ¼ teaspoon walnut mixture. Transfer to lined baking sheet. Bake until golden and puffed, 10 to 15 minutes. Slide pastries, on parchment, onto a rack to cool slightly. (Leave oven on.)

MEANWHILE, MAKE THE FILLING: Mash together cheese and toasted walnuts with a fork.

FILL THE PASTRIES: While pastries are still warm, gently pull each one apart, keeping tops and bottoms together. Lightly press down any puffed inner layers.

Spoon a ½-teaspoon mound of cheese filling into each pastry bottom, cover with pastry top, and arrange on same parchment-lined baking sheet. Bake until cheese begins to melt, 2 to 3 minutes.

Sprinkle tops of pastries with pepper and serve immediately.

COOK'S NOTES

- The puff pastry rounds can be baked and separated into tops and bottoms up to 1 day ahead. Cool completely, then store in an airtight container at room temperature.
- The pastries can be filled (but not baked) up to 1 hour ahead and kept, loosely covered, at room temperature.

Anchovy Puffs

MAKES 108 PUFFS
ACTIVE TIME: 20 MINUTES ■ START TO FINISH: 1¼ HOURS

■ Store-bought puff pastry is great entertaining insurance. Even better is having a bag of these unfussy savory snacks in the freezer, waiting to be baked at a doorbell's notice. It's important to prick the unbaked pastry all over with a fork, or the puffs will splay apart. ■

1 (2-ounce) can anchovy fillets in oil, rinsed, drained, and chopped

3 tablespoons mayonnaise

1 (17.3-ounce) package frozen puff pastry (2 sheets), thawed

1 large egg, lightly beaten with 1 tablespoon water for egg wash

Mash together anchovy fillets and mayonnaise in a bowl with a fork until well blended (small bits of anchovy will remain).

Roll out 1 sheet of dough on a lightly floured surface into a 12-by-9-inch rectangle. Carefully transfer to a baking sheet and spread evenly with anchovy mayonnaise. Roll out remaining pastry sheet in same manner and cover anchovy layer with it. Lightly roll rolling pin over top pastry sheet to help layers adhere. Brush top with egg wash and freeze pastry for 1 minute to set glaze (reserve remaining egg wash).

Remove pastry from freezer and brush with egg wash again. Prick pastry all over with a fork and freeze until firm, about 20 minutes.

Put a rack in middle of oven and preheat oven to 400°F.

Transfer pastry to a cutting board, placing it with a short side nearest you. Cut lengthwise into nine 1-inch-wide strips, then cut crosswise into twelve 1-inch-wide strips (to form 108 squares).

Using a spatula, carefully transfer squares to a large baking sheet, arranging them ¼ inch apart. Bake until puffed and golden brown, 12 to 15 minutes. Serve warm.

COOK'S NOTES

- The puffs can be baked up to 3 hours ahead. Cool completely, then store, separated by wax paper, in an airtight container at room temperature. Just before serving, reheat in a 350°F oven for 3 to 5 minutes.
- The unbaked squares can be frozen for up to 1 week. Freeze on a baking sheet until firm, then transfer to a sealed plastic bag and freeze. (Frozen puffs will not rise as high as those baked immediately after being cut.)

Hazelnut and Olive Rugelach

MAKES 32 HORS D'OEUVRES
ACTIVE TIME: 45 MINUTES ■ START TO FINISH: 7½ HOURS
(INCLUDES CHILLING DOUGH)

■ Who says rugelach have to be sweet? The Hanukkah tradition gets a makeover with a filling of pungent green olives and toasted hazelnuts rolled up in tender cream cheese dough. Although it is easy to work with, the dough can soften very quickly; if it becomes too soft, simply refrigerate briefly, until firm, and then continue with the recipe. ■

1 cup all-purpose flour, plus additional for dusting

¾ teaspoon dried thyme, crumbled

¼ teaspoon salt

½ teaspoon coarsely ground black pepper

1 stick (8 tablespoons) unsalted butter, softened

¼ pound cream cheese, softened

⅓ cup hazelnuts, toasted (see Tips, page 911), loose skins rubbed off in a kitchen towel, and very finely chopped

⅓ cup brine-cured green olives, drained, patted dry, pitted, and very finely chopped

SPECIAL EQUIPMENT: parchment paper

Whisk together flour, thyme, salt, and pepper in a bowl.

Beat together butter and cream cheese in a large bowl with an electric mixer until well combined. Add flour mixture and mix at low speed until a soft dough forms. Gather dough into a ball, then halve dough and wrap each half in plastic wrap. Flatten each half, in plastic wrap, forming it into a 4-inch disk. Refrigerate for 6 hours (to allow gluten to relax).

Put a rack in middle of oven and preheat oven to 350°F. Cut four 17-by-12-inch sheets of parchment paper.

Bring dough to cool room temperature (this will take 15 to 20 minutes).

Remove and discard plastic wrap from 1 disk of dough, keeping other disk wrapped. Flour one sheet of parchment paper and put dough in center of paper. Dust dough with flour, cover with another sheet of parchment, and roll out into a 9-inch round. Carefully peel off top sheet of parchment and set aside. (If dough is too sticky to remove parchment cleanly, refrigerate on a baking sheet until firm, 10 to 20 minutes.) Repeat procedure with remaining dough.

Sprinkle hazelnuts and olives evenly over rounds of dough. Reposition top sheets of parchment on dough and press gently to help nuts and olives adhere. Remove and discard top sheets of parchment. Cut each round into 16 wedges. Beginning at base of 1 wedge, roll up dough as tightly as possible toward point and transfer, point side down, to an unlined large baking sheet. Repeat with remaining wedges of dough, arranging rugelach 1½ inches apart. (If dough becomes too soft to roll up, refrigerate to firm.)

Bake until golden brown, 20 to 25 minutes. Cool on baking sheet on a rack. Serve warm or at room temperature.

COOK'S NOTES

- The dough can be refrigerated for up to 1 day or frozen for up to 1 month.
- The rugelach are best eaten the day they are made, but they can be made up to 1 day ahead and, once cooled, kept in an airtight container at room temperature. Reheat in a 325°F oven for 10 to 12 minutes.

Caramelized Onion Tartlets

MAKES 24 HORS D'OEUVRES
ACTIVE TIME: 30 MINUTES ■ START TO FINISH: 1 HOUR

■ These miniature versions of a traditional Alsatian onion tart fall squarely into the "simple yet spectacular" category. The recipe makes great use of pantry items, including refrigerated pie dough (be sure to buy the rolled dough in a box, not the sort already fitted into a tin). Once the components are ready, the tartlets take just minutes to assemble. ■

    3 tablespoons unsalted butter
    4 cups very thinly sliced halved onions (1¼ pounds)
    ¾ teaspoon salt
    ¼ teaspoon freshly ground black pepper

    ¼ cup water
    2 (9-inch) refrigerated rolled-up piecrusts (1 [15-ounce] package)
    6 tablespoons crème fraîche, at room temperature
    1 tablespoon finely chopped fresh chives
SPECIAL EQUIPMENT: a 2¼-inch round cookie cutter; 2 mini muffin pans with twelve 2-tablespoon cups each

Put a rack in middle of oven and preheat oven to 375°F.

Melt butter in a 10-inch heavy skillet over moderately low heat. Stir in onions, salt, pepper, and 2 tablespoons water, cover, and cook, stirring once or twice, for 10 minutes. Remove lid and cook, stirring frequently and adding remaining 2 tablespoons water to deglaze pan as needed, until onions are deep golden brown and very tender, 30 to 35 minutes. Transfer onions to a small bowl and cool slightly.

While onions cook, unroll dough circles and cut out 12 rounds from each with cookie cutter. Lightly press rounds into mini-muffin cups. Bake until pale golden, 10 to 12 minutes. Remove tartlet shells from muffin pans and cool completely on a rack.

Stir together crème fraîche and chives in a small bowl. Divide among tartlet shells, top with caramelized onions, and serve.

COOK'S NOTES

- The caramelized onions can be made up to 2 days ahead and refrigerated, covered. Rewarm in a skillet before serving.
- The tartlet shells can be baked up to 2 days ahead and kept in an airtight container at room temperature.
- The tartlets can be assembled up to 1 hour ahead and kept, loosely covered, at room temperature.

Hunan Scallion Pancakes

MAKES 48 HORS D'OEUVRES
ACTIVE TIME: 20 MINUTES ■ START TO FINISH: 20 MINUTES

■ Traditionally this favorite Chinese appetizer of flaky fried dough studded with chopped scallions requires a time-consuming method of rolling homemade dough to distribute the scallions evenly. Our pancakes are much simpler. We use store-bought flour tortillas, which we sandwich with the scallions and fry. The resulting pancakes are crisp, chewy, and surprisingly authentic-tasting. ∎

12 (8- to 9-inch) flour tortillas
2½ tablespoons Asian sesame oil
1 large egg, lightly beaten
½ teaspoon salt
¾ cup minced scallions (about 1 bunch)
About 4 cups vegetable oil for deep-frying
SPECIAL EQUIPMENT: a deep-fat thermometer

Arrange 6 tortillas on a work surface. Lightly brush top of each with sesame oil, then brush with beaten egg and sprinkle with salt. Sprinkle 3 of the tortillas with 2 tablespoons scallions each. Invert remaining 3 brushed tortillas on top and press firmly to sandwich scallions in between. Stack pancakes on a plate with sheets of plastic wrap between them and gently weight with an empty skillet or saucepan. Repeat with remaining 6 tortillas.

Heat 1 inch of oil in a heavy 10-inch skillet over moderate heat until it registers 400°F on thermometer. Set a large rack on a baking sheet. Add 1 pancake to pan and fry, turning several times, until golden and puffed, about 1 minute. Transfer with tongs to rack, tilting pancake to let excess oil drip back into skillet, and let drain while you fry remaining pancakes. (Return oil to 400°F for each pancake.)

Cut each pancake into 8 wedges and serve.

COOK'S NOTES
- The pancakes can be assembled up to 2 hours ahead. Cover the stacked pancakes, weight them as above, and refrigerate.
- The fried pancakes can be kept in one layer on the rack at room temperature for up to 2 hours. Reheat on the rack on the baking sheet in a 350°F oven for 7 to 8 minutes.

Smoked Salmon Croque Monsieur

MAKES 24 HORS D'OEUVRES
ACTIVE TIME: 20 MINUTES ∎ START TO FINISH: 20 MINUTES

∎ Eric Ripert, the chef of Le Bernardin, the four-star New York City restaurant, based these hors d'oeuvres on *croque monsieurs*, the toasted ham and cheese sandwiches his grandmother made for him as a child. Smoked salmon stands in for the ham, with the Gruyère adding its richness. But the real genius lies in the preserved lemon, which amplifies all the flavors and makes these something truly special. (Note that the preserved lemons must be made 5 days ahead, though you can substitute lemon zest if you wish.) Be sure to seek out good-quality sandwich bread. ∎

12 slices firm white sandwich bread, crusts discarded
½ pound thinly sliced smoked salmon
1 tablespoon finely chopped fresh chives
1 tablespoon finely chopped rind from Preserved Lemons (recipe follows) or finely grated lemon zest
6 ounces Gruyère, sliced very thin
1 stick (8 tablespoons) unsalted butter, well softened

Lay out 6 bread slices on a work surface and top with salmon. Sprinkle with chives and lemon rind. Cover with cheese and remaining bread slices. Spread tops with half of butter.

Heat a 12-inch nonstick skillet or griddle over moderate heat until hot. Add 3 sandwiches, buttered side down, and cook until undersides are golden and cheese is beginning to melt, 3 to 4 minutes. Spread tops with half of remaining butter, turn over, and cook until undersides are pale golden, about 1 minute more. Transfer to a cutting board and cover loosely to keep warm. Cook remaining 3 sandwiches in same manner.

Quarter sandwiches diagonally and serve.

COOK'S NOTE
- The sandwiches can be assembled and the tops buttered up to 1 hour ahead and kept, loosely covered, at room temperature.

Preserved Lemons

MAKES 48 PIECES
ACTIVE TIME: 15 MINUTES ■ START TO FINISH: 5 DAYS

11–12 lemons
⅔ cup kosher salt
¼ cup olive oil

SPECIAL EQUIPMENT: a 6-cup canning jar with lid and
screw band

Blanch 6 lemons in boiling water for 5 minutes; drain and cool.

Cut each blanched lemon into 8 wedges. Toss with kosher salt in a bowl, then pack into jar.

Juice enough of remaining lemons to measure 1¼ cups juice. Add enough juice to cover lemons, and seal jar. Let stand at room temperature, shaking gently once a day, for 5 days.

Add oil to lemons and refrigerate.

COOK'S NOTE

■ The preserved lemons keep, refrigerated, for up to 6 months.

Wasabi Shrimp Crackers

MAKES 30 HORS D'OEUVRES
ACTIVE TIME: 20 MINUTES ■ START TO FINISH: 20 MINUTES

■ Think of this as a postmodern sushi roll, with crunchy rice crackers instead of rice and a topping of briny shrimp and wasabi-spiked cream cheese. It's a delicious, beautiful, and easy hors d'oeuvre that your guests will go wild for. ■

Salt
1 pound medium shrimp (31–35 per pound),
peeled and deveined
1 (8-ounce) package cream cheese, softened
3–4 teaspoons wasabi paste
30 (2-inch) thin rice crackers
Greens from 1 scallion, thinly sliced

Fill a 2-quart saucepan three-quarters full with water, add 1 tablespoon salt, and bring to a boil. Add shrimp and boil until just cooked through, about 2 minutes. Drain, transfer to a bowl of ice and cold water, and cool in water for 3 minutes. Drain and pat dry. Halve shrimp lengthwise.

Combine cream cheese and wasabi (to taste) in a food processor and blend until smooth.

Mound 1 teaspoon cream cheese mixture on each cracker and top with 2 shrimp halves. Sprinkle with scallion. Serve immediately.

COOK'S NOTE

■ The cream cheese mixture can be made up to 1 day ahead and refrigerated, its surface covered with plastic wrap.

Lobster Salad Cucumber Canapés

MAKES 36 HORS D'OEUVRES
ACTIVE TIME: 45 MINUTES ■ START TO FINISH: 1½ HOURS

■ Cucumber rounds topped with colorful lobster salad are festive-looking, but the real fireworks happen when you take a bite. The sweet lobster sparkles with ripe mango, crunchy celery, jalapeño, and fresh cilantro, and the tang of lime juice ups the "wow" factor. The long, skinny seedless cucumbers, often called English cucumbers, make a sturdier, crisper base than regular cukes, which are too watery. ■

Salt
1 (1½-pound) live lobster
1–2 seedless cucumbers (usually plastic-wrapped; at
least 1¾ inches in diameter)
2 tablespoons mayonnaise
2–3 teaspoons fresh lime juice
1½ teaspoons minced jalapeño chile, including seeds
Pinch of freshly ground black pepper
⅓ cup diced (⅛-inch) firm but ripe mango
¼ cup finely chopped celery
2 tablespoons finely chopped red onion
2 tablespoons finely chopped fresh cilantro
GARNISH: thinly sliced fresh cilantro leaves

Bring 6 quarts water with 1½ tablespoons salt to a boil in an 8-quart pot over high heat. Plunge lobster headfirst into water and cook, covered, for 7 minutes. Using tongs, transfer to sink to drain and cool.

While lobster is cooling, cut cucumber(s) into thirty-six ¼-inch-thick slices (see Cook's Note); then, using a 1½-inch scalloped round cookie cutter, trim each cucumber slice; discard trimmings.

Whisk together mayonnaise, lime juice (to taste), jalapeño, ¼ teaspoon salt, and pepper in a medium bowl.

When lobster is cool enough to handle, crack shell and remove meat from claws, joints, and tail (see page 385), discarding tomalley, any roe, and shells. Cut meat into ¼-inch pieces.

Add lobster, mango, celery, onion, and cilantro to mayonnaise mixture and toss well.

Top each cucumber round with 1 rounded teaspoon lobster salad and garnish with sliced cilantro. Serve immediately.

COOK'S NOTES

- In place of the lobster, you can use 6 ounces large shrimp, peeled and, if desired, deveined. Bring 4 cups water with ¾ teaspoon salt to a boil in a 2-quart saucepan. Add the shrimp, reduce the heat, and poach at a bare simmer until just cooked through, about 2 minutes. With a slotted spoon, transfer the shrimp to a bowl of ice and cold water to stop the cooking. Let the shrimp cool for 2 minutes, then drain and pat dry. Cut into ¼-inch pieces and proceed with the recipe.
- The lobster can be cooked and the meat removed from the shell up to 1 day ahead; refrigerate, covered. Cut the meat just before assembling the salad.
- Instead of trimming the cucumber slices with a scalloped cutter, you can simply peel the cucumber(s) before slicing them.
- The salad can be made up to 6 hours ahead and refrigerated, covered.

■ A refinement of a grilled cheese and bacon sandwich, these treats are worthy of becoming a family tradition. They're that easy and that good. Toasted, the trimmed crusts make decadent croutons or a "cook's treat" for nibbling. ■

- ½ pound extra-sharp white cheddar, coarsely grated (2 cups)
- ½ pound cold lean bacon (chilled bacon is easier to chop), finely chopped
- 1 small onion, finely chopped
- 1½ tablespoons drained bottled horseradish
- ½ teaspoon salt
- ¼ teaspoon freshly ground black pepper
- 14 very thin slices firm white sandwich bread

Stir together cheese, bacon, onion, horseradish, salt, and pepper in a bowl with a rubber spatula until well blended.

With a small offset spatula or butter knife, spread about 1½ tablespoons cheese mixture evenly to edges of each slice of bread. Arrange slices in one layer on a large baking sheet, cover with wax paper, and freeze until firm, about 15 minutes.

Put a rack in middle of oven and preheat oven to 375°F.

Trim crusts off bread and reserve if desired (see Cook's Note). Cut each slice into 4 squares.

Arrange toasts on baking sheet and bake until edges begin to brown, about 20 minutes. Serve warm.

COOK'S NOTES

- The unbaked toasts can be prepared up to 2 weeks ahead and frozen, layered between sheets of wax paper in an airtight container. Thaw before baking.
- The reserved crusts (with some of the filling still on them) can be baked in a 375°F oven until lightly browned, about 10 minutes. Cool, then break up the crusts and sprinkle over salads (or just nibble on them).

Bangers and Mash

MAKES ABOUT 34 HORS D'OEUVRES
ACTIVE TIME: 1 HOUR ■ START TO FINISH: 1 HOUR

■ *Bangers* is British slang for sausages made of pork or beef and bread crumbs, which are traditionally paired with mashed potatoes. Here we miniaturize and spiff up the pub staple by topping rounds of browned sausages with potato puree and roasted cherry tomato halves. ■

FOR TOMATOES

- 20 cherry or grape tomatoes, halved
- 1 tablespoon olive oil
- ¼ teaspoon sugar
- ¼ teaspoon salt
- ¼ teaspoon freshly ground black pepper
- 1 teaspoon balsamic vinegar

FOR MASHED POTATOES

- 1 (8-ounce) russet (baking) potato, peeled and cut into ½-inch pieces
- 2½ tablespoons truffle butter (see Sources) or unsalted butter
- 1 tablespoon heavy cream
- ⅛ teaspoon salt

FOR BANGERS

- 5 (4-ounce) English-style sausages (1–1¼ inches thick; see Cook's Note)
- 1 tablespoon olive oil

ROAST THE TOMATOES: Put a rack in middle of oven and preheat oven to 400°F.

Toss tomatoes with oil, sugar, salt, and pepper. Transfer to a shallow baking pan and roast until collapsed, about 20 minutes. Remove from oven and drizzle with vinegar.

MEANWHILE, MAKE THE MASHED POTATOES: Put potato in a small saucepan, cover with cold well-salted water by 1 inch, and bring to a simmer. Simmer until potato is very tender, about 10 minutes.

Drain potato and return to saucepan. Add butter, cream, and salt and mash until smooth. Cover pan loosely to keep potatoes warm.

COOK THE SAUSAGES: Combine sausages and ½ cup water in a 12-inch heavy skillet and bring just to a simmer. Cover and simmer sausages, turning once, until cooked through, 10 to 12 minutes. Remove from heat and cool to warm, about 6 minutes.

Cut sausages into ½-inch-thick slices; discard end pieces.

Heat oil in cleaned skillet over moderately high heat until hot but not smoking. Add sausage slices and brown, turning once, 4 to 5 minutes.

ASSEMBLE THE HORS D'OEUVRES: Mound 1 teaspoon potato mixture on top of each sausage slice and top each with a tomato half.

COOK'S NOTES

■ When shopping for bangers, seek out good-quality sausages with only a modest amount of bread filler. (Whole Foods is one source.) If you can't find bangers, substitute bratwurst or weisswurst. If the sausages are already cooked, just slice them and brown in the olive oil.

■ The mashed potatoes, roasted tomatoes, and browned sausage slices can be prepared up to 1 day ahead and refrigerated separately, covered. Just before serving, assemble the hors d'oeuvres and heat, covered with foil, in a 350°F oven for about 15 minutes.

Armenian Lamb Pizzas
Lahmajoon

MAKES 128 HORS D'OEUVRES
ACTIVE TIME: 1 HOUR ■ START TO FINISH: 2½ HOURS

■ *Lahmajoon*—thin rounds of dough topped with a savory mixture of ground lamb, green pepper, parsley, onion, and garlic and baked—are a beloved Armenian snack food, often rolled up to be eaten on the go. They make a great hors d'oeuvre when cut into wedges. They're easy to grab, they're good at room temperature, and they make an unusual addition to cocktail party fare. *Lahmajoon*'s enticing spiciness comes from Aleppo chile pepper, a Syrian chile that lends depth and a fruity, mild heat. Cayenne can be substituted, though the flavor will not be as complex. ■

FOR DOUGH

- 1 (¼-ounce) package active dry yeast
- ¼ teaspoon sugar
- 1½ cups warm water (105°–115°F)
- 4 cups unbleached all-purpose flour, plus additional for kneading
- 2 teaspoons salt
- ¼ cup olive oil

FOR TOPPING

- 2 tablespoons olive oil
- 1 medium onion, chopped
- 2 garlic cloves, chopped
- 1 green bell pepper, chopped
- 1 cup chopped fresh curly parsley (see Cook's Note)
- 1¾ pounds ground lamb
- 3 tablespoons tomato paste
- 1 tablespoon chopped fresh thyme
- 2–2½ teaspoons Aleppo pepper (see headnote and Sources) or ½ teaspoon cayenne
- 1 teaspoon salt
- ¾ teaspoon ground allspice
- ½ teaspoon freshly ground black pepper

SPECIAL EQUIPMENT: parchment paper

MAKE THE DOUGH: Whisk together yeast, sugar, and 1 cup warm water in a large bowl until yeast is dissolved. Let stand until foamy, about 5 minutes. (If mixture doesn't foam, discard and start over with new yeast.)

Whisk together flour and salt in another bowl. Stir oil and remaining ½ cup warm water into yeast mixture. Add flour mixture and stir until a dough forms. Turn dough out onto a floured surface and knead, adding more flour as necessary, until dough is smooth and elastic but still slightly sticky, 5 to 10 minutes.

Transfer dough to a generously oiled large bowl and turn to coat with oil. Cover bowl with a clean kitchen towel (not terry cloth) and let rise in a warm, draft-free place until doubled in bulk, 1½ to 2 hours.

MEANWHILE, MAKE THE TOPPING: Heat oil in a 10- to 12-inch heavy skillet over moderately high heat until hot but not smoking. Add onion and cook, stirring occasionally, until softened and golden brown, about 5 minutes. Add garlic and cook, stirring, for 1 minute. Transfer to a food processor.

Add bell pepper and parsley to onion and pulse until vegetables are finely chopped. Add lamb, tomato paste, thyme, Aleppo pepper (to taste), salt, allspice, and black pepper and pulse until well combined. Transfer to a bowl and refrigerate, covered, for at least 30 minutes.

ASSEMBLE AND BAKE THE PIZZAS: Put a rack in lower third of oven and preheat oven to 500°F. Cut eight pieces of parchment large enough to line a 17-by-13-inch baking sheet.

Turn dough out onto a work surface and knead several times to remove air bubbles. Divide dough into 16 equal pieces and cover with kitchen towel or oiled plastic wrap. Lightly dust 1 piece of dough with flour and form into a disk. Transfer dough to one side of a piece of lightly floured parchment and roll out with a lightly floured rolling pin into a 7-inch circle. Roll out a second piece of dough on other half of parchment in same manner.

Slide dough rounds, on parchment, onto baking sheet and bake for 2 minutes. Remove baking sheet from oven and turn dough rounds over with tongs. With a small offset spatula or back of a spoon, spread ⅓ cup of topping evenly over each dough round, leaving a ¼-inch border around edges. Return to oven and bake until topping and dough are cooked through, 4 to 5 minutes. Slide pizzas, on parchment, onto a rack to cool.

Form and bake 14 more pizzas with remaining dough and topping, 2 at a time, using a fresh piece of parchment for each batch.

Cut each pizza into 8 wedges and serve warm or at room temperature.

COOK'S NOTES

- Curly parsley is traditionally used for the topping, but you can substitute flat-leaf.
- Once cooled, the pizzas can be frozen, stacked between squares of parchment paper in sealed plastic bags, for up to 1 month. Reheat in batches in a 350°F oven (do not thaw before reheating) on an unlined baking sheet for 6 to 8 minutes. Or, for a crisper crust, reheat directly on the oven rack.

Spanakopita

Spinach and Feta Phyllo Triangles

MAKES 30 HORS D'OEUVRES
ACTIVE TIME: 45 MINUTES ■ START TO FINISH: 1½ HOURS

■ Spanakopita was the ubiquitous appetizer of the 1970s and '80s, monopolizing catering trays all over the country. Sadly, too many indifferent versions made us forget what all the fuss was about. Our take—crisp phyllo enfolding a fresh-tasting filling of spinach, creamy feta, and aromatic nutmeg—brings flavor to the fore and restores spanakopita to its glory. ■

    1 stick (8 tablespoons) plus 1 tablespoon unsalted
       butter
    1 pound baby spinach
    ½ pound feta, crumbled (scant 2 cups)
    ½ teaspoon freshly grated nutmeg
    ½ teaspoon salt
    ½ teaspoon freshly ground black pepper
   10 (17-by-12-inch) phyllo sheets, thawed if frozen

Melt 1 tablespoon butter in a 12-inch heavy skillet over moderate heat. Add spinach and cook, stirring, until wilted and tender, about 4 minutes. Remove from heat and cool.

Squeeze spinach by handfuls to remove as much liquid as possible, then coarsely chop. Transfer to a bowl and stir in feta, nutmeg, salt, and pepper.

Put a rack in middle of oven and preheat oven to 375°F.

Melt remaining 1 stick butter in a small saucepan; cool.

Put phyllo stack on a work surface and cover with two overlapping sheets of plastic wrap.

Transfer 1 phyllo sheet to a work surface, with a long side nearest you (keep remaining sheets covered), and brush with some melted butter. Top with another phyllo sheet and brush with more butter. Cut phyllo stack crosswise into 6 (roughly 12-by-2¾-inch) strips.

Put a heaping teaspoon of filling near one bottom corner of each strip, then fold corner of phyllo over to enclose filling and form a triangle (1). Continue folding strip (like a flag), maintaining triangle shape (2, 3, 4). Put triangle seam side down on a large bak-

ing sheet and brush top with butter. Make more triangles in same manner, using remaining phyllo and filling.

Bake triangles until golden brown, about 20 minutes. Transfer to a rack to cool slightly before serving.

COOK'S NOTE

■ The unbaked pastry triangles can be frozen for up to 1 month. Arrange in one layer on a baking sheet and freeze until firm, then transfer to sealable plastic bags and freeze. Do not thaw pastries before baking; the baking time may be slightly longer.

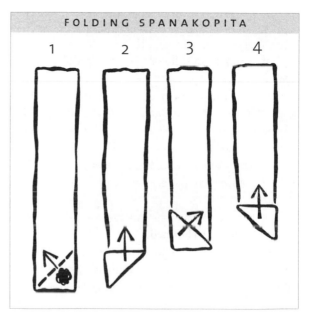

FOLDING SPANAKOPITA

Mushroom Strudels

MAKES 32 HORS D'OEUVRES
ACTIVE TIME: 1 HOUR ■ START TO FINISH: 1¼ HOURS

■ Mushrooms cooked gently in butter and wine, then rolled up in phyllo and baked until the pastry is golden and crisp, make a luxe finger food. If you have some black truffle oil lurking in your pantry, this is the place for it—dotting the tiniest amount on the strudels when they come out of the oven makes them even more fabulous. ■

½ cup boiling water

¼ ounce (½ cup) dried porcini (cèpes)

½ pound white mushrooms, trimmed and halved lengthwise

2 tablespoons unsalted butter

¼ cup finely chopped shallots

¼ cup dry white wine

¼ teaspoon salt

⅛ teaspoon freshly ground black pepper

2½ tablespoons finely chopped fresh flat-leaf parsley

4 (17-by-12-inch) phyllo sheets, thawed if frozen

2 tablespoons duck or goose fat (see Sources), unsalted butter, melted, or olive oil

Black truffle oil for brushing (optional; see Sources)

Put a rack in middle of oven and preheat oven to 450°F.

Pour boiling water over porcini in a small bowl and let soak until softened, 10 to 12 minutes. Lift out porcini and squeeze excess liquid back into bowl; reserve liquid. Rinse porcini well to remove any grit and pat dry. Pour soaking liquid through a sieve lined with a dampened paper towel into another bowl; reserve.

Pulse porcini and white mushrooms in a food processor until finely chopped.

Melt butter in a 9- to 10-inch heavy skillet over moderate heat. Add shallots and cook, stirring, until beginning to soften, about 1 minute. Add mushrooms, reserved soaking liquid, wine, salt, and pepper and cook, stirring occasionally, until liquid has evaporated, about 8 minutes. Stir in parsley, then spread filling on a plate and refrigerate, uncovered, until cold, about 10 minutes.

Meanwhile, put stack of phyllo sheets on a work surface and cut crosswise in half. Stack halves and cover with plastic wrap.

Remove 1 phyllo sheet from stack (keep remaining sheets covered) and arrange with a long side nearest you, then brush generously with some fat (or butter). Top with another phyllo sheet and brush generously with fat. Spread about 2 tablespoons mushroom filling in a narrow strip along edge nearest you, then roll up phyllo tightly around filling, like a jelly roll. Transfer roll seam side down to a baking sheet. Make 3 more rolls in same manner.

Bake until golden brown, 12 to 14 minutes. Cool slightly on baking sheet on a rack, then, using a cotton swab, brush length of each roll with a very thin line of truffle oil, if using. Carefully cut each roll into 8 pieces with a serrated knife, preferably a wide-toothed one. Serve warm or at room temperature.

COOK'S NOTES

- The mushroom filling can be made up to 2 days ahead and cooled completely, then refrigerated; cover once completely cooled.

- The unbaked strudels can be refrigerated for up to 1 day, covered, or frozen for up to 2 weeks, wrapped well in plastic wrap. Bake (do not thaw first if frozen) in a 350°F oven for 12 to 14 minutes if refrigerated, about 20 minutes if frozen.

Arepas with Black Beans and Feta

MAKES ABOUT 60 HORS D'OEUVRES
ACTIVE TIME: 2½ HOURS ■ START TO FINISH: 12½ HOURS
(INCLUDES PICKLING ONION)

■ The Colombian fried cornmeal cakes known as *arepas* are fantastic as bite-sized hors d'oeuvres and can be served as a casual meal. Here they are topped neatly with mashed black beans, creamy feta cheese, and pickled red onion. Everything can be prepped well in advance and assembled at the last minute. ■

FOR PICKLED ONION

1 medium red onion, cut into ¾-inch-thick wedges and very thinly sliced crosswise

1–2 habanero or Scotch bonnet chiles (to taste), seeded and very finely chopped

½ cup distilled white vinegar

½ teaspoon dried oregano, preferably Mexican, crumbled

½ teaspoon salt, or to taste

FOR AREPAS

3 cups whole milk

½ stick (4 tablespoons) unsalted butter, cut into pieces

1½ cups white *arepa* flour (see Sources)

1 tablespoon sugar

1 teaspoon salt

1 cup coarsely grated mozzarella (about 4 ounces)

About 3 tablespoons vegetable oil

FOR TOPPING

5 tablespoons vegetable oil

1 cup finely chopped white onion

3 large garlic cloves, minced

1 green serrano chile, finely chopped, including seeds

2 (19-ounce) cans black beans, rinsed and drained, or 4 cups cooked black beans (see Cook's Note)

1 cup finely chopped tomatoes

½ cup finely chopped fresh cilantro

½ cup water or reserved bean cooking liquid

1 teaspoon salt

½ pound mild feta, crumbled (about 2 cups)

PICKLE THE ONION: Stir together all ingredients in a bowl. Refrigerate, covered, for at least 12 hours.

MAKE THE AREPAS: Bring milk to a simmer in a small saucepan; remove from heat. Pour ½ cup milk into a small bowl and reserve. Add butter to hot milk remaining in pan and stir until melted.

Toss together arepa flour, sugar, salt, and mozzarella in a large bowl. Add hot milk and stir until combined. Let mixture stand until dry ingredients absorb enough milk to form a soft dough, 1 to 2 minutes (dough will continue to stiffen as it stands).

With palms of your hands, form 1 tablespoon dough into a ball. Flatten ball on a sheet of wax paper to a 1½- to 1¾-inch disk. Transfer to a wax-paper-lined tray and cover with plastic wrap. Form disks with remaining dough in same manner, stirring in some of reserved milk if dough becomes too stiff or if edges of disks crack when flattened.

Heat 1½ teaspoons oil in a 12-inch nonstick skillet over moderately low heat until hot but not smoking. Cook arepas in batches of 10 to 12, turning once, until cooked through and golden in patches on both sides, 8 to 12 minutes per batch; add more oil to skillet between batches as needed. Transfer arepas to baking sheets.

MAKE THE BEAN TOPPING: Heat oil in a 12-inch heavy skillet over moderately high heat until hot but not smoking. Add onion and cook, stirring frequently, until well browned, 8 to 10 minutes. Add garlic and chile and cook, stirring, until softened, about 1 minute. Add beans, tomatoes, cilantro, water, and salt

and cook, stirring and mashing with a bean masher or wire potato masher, until beans are slightly drier and coarsely mashed, about 5 minutes.

ASSEMBLE AND HEAT THE AREPAS: Put a rack in middle of oven and preheat oven to 350°F.

Reheat arepas in batches (as needed for serving) on baking sheets, covered with foil, until heated through, 10 to 15 minutes.

Top each warm arepa with about 1½ teaspoons bean topping, then sprinkle with cheese and pickled onion. Serve warm.

COOK'S NOTES

- If you would like to use dried black beans, 1 pound beans yields about 5½ cups cooked. Rinse the beans, then soak in 10 cups water in a 4- to 5-quart heavy pot at room temperature (refrigerate if kitchen is very warm) for 6 to 12 hours (or see page 129 for quick-soaking procedures). Bring to a boil (in the same water, to preserve the color) and simmer, uncovered, until the beans are tender, 1 to 1½ hours. Drain, reserving ½ cup of the cooking liquid.

- The pickled onion can be refrigerated for up to 1 week.

- The arepas can be cooked up to 1 day ahead. Cool completely, then wrap in foil packages in 1 layer (10 per package) and refrigerate. Reheat, still in foil, in a 350°F oven for 10 to 15 minutes. The arepas can also be frozen, wrapped in foil in sealed plastic bags, for up to 2 weeks. Thaw for 30 minutes at room temperature before reheating.

- The bean topping can be made up to 1 day ahead and refrigerated, covered. Reheat, covered, in a heatproof bowl set over a saucepan of simmering water, stirring occasionally and adding a little water if it seems very dry, until heated through, 10 to 15 minutes.

Samosas

MAKES 32 HORS D'OEUVRES
ACTIVE TIME: 1½ HOURS ■ START TO FINISH: 2¾ HOURS
(NOT INCLUDING MAKING FILLING)

■ Who could resist these popular Indian snacks, dumplings filled with any number of savory fillings, fried until bubbling, and served with sweet and spicy chutney? We offer two different fillings, a traditional vegetarian version made with potatoes and peas and a slightly racier lamb and tomato one. Though the samosas taste best when freshly fried, the fillings can be made ahead. Let the samosas stand, uncovered, for 30 to 60 minutes before frying—they will dry slightly and fry up better. ■

FOR DOUGH
2¾ cups unbleached all-purpose flour
1 teaspoon salt
6½ tablespoons vegetable oil
½ cup plus 2 tablespoons water

Potato and Pea Filling or Spiced Lamb Filling
(recipes follow)
6 cups vegetable oil for deep-frying
ACCOMPANIMENT: bottled mango chutney
SPECIAL EQUIPMENT: a deep-fat thermometer

MAKE THE DOUGH: Stir together flour and salt in a bowl until well combined. Drizzle oil over mixture, then blend together by rubbing with your fingertips until mixture holds together when squeezed. Add water and stir until a dough forms and pulls away from sides of bowl; add more water, 1 tablespoon at a time, if necessary.

Turn out dough onto a lightly floured surface and knead until smooth, about 5 minutes. Transfer to a lightly oiled bowl, turn to coat with oil, and let stand, covered, at room temperature for 30 minutes.

FORM AND FRY THE SAMOSAS: Halve dough and leave one half in bowl, covered. Roll out other half of dough with a rolling pin on an unfloured surface to a 13-inch square. Let stand, covered with plastic wrap, for 15 minutes.

Set plastic wrap aside, trim dough to a 12-inch square with a large sharp knife, and then cut into six-

teen 3-inch squares. Cover again with plastic wrap.

Place 1 square of dough on an unfloured surface, keeping remaining squares covered. Lightly moisten 2 adjacent edges of square with a finger dipped in water, then spread 1 level tablespoon of filling across center of square from one moistened corner to opposite moistened corner, leaving a ½-inch border at edges. Fold unmoistened corner of dough over filling to form a triangle, then press edges together to seal (you can trim edges slightly if they become too elongated as you shape the samosa). Transfer to a baking sheet; do not cover. Repeat with remaining squares of dough, then roll out remaining dough, let it stand, and make more samosas in same manner.

Let samosas stand, uncovered, at room temperature for 30 minutes to 1 hour, turning over several times for even drying.

Heat oil in a 4-quart heavy pot over high heat until thermometer registers 350°F. Working in batches of 8, fry samosas, stirring frequently to ensure even browning, until golden, 3 to 5 minutes. Transfer with a slotted spoon to paper towels to drain. (Return oil to 350°F between batches.)

Serve samosas warm or at room temperature, with chutney.

COOK'S NOTE
■ The samosas can be kept warm on a baking sheet in a 200°F oven for up to 1 hour.

Potato and Pea Filling

MAKES ABOUT 2 CUPS
ACTIVE TIME: 1 HOUR ■ START TO FINISH: 1 HOUR

■ Potatoes and peas are a classic Indian combination, and here they make an almost creamy filling for the crisp samosas. ■

½ pound yellow-fleshed potatoes, such as Yukon Gold
(about 2 medium or 3 small)
4 teaspoons vegetable oil
1 small onion, finely chopped
⅔ cup frozen baby peas, thawed
1 teaspoon minced peeled fresh ginger
½ (2½-inch-long) fresh hot green chile, such as serrano
or Thai, minced, including seeds
2 tablespoons water

½ teaspoon salt

Rounded ¼ teaspoon garam masala
(see page 536 and Sources)

Rounded ¼ teaspoon ground cumin

Rounded ¼ teaspoon ground coriander

1½ tablespoons finely chopped fresh cilantro

2 teaspoons fresh lemon juice

Combine potatoes and well-salted water to cover by 2 inches in a 3-quart saucepan and bring to a boil. Reduce heat and simmer, uncovered, until potatoes are tender, 15 to 25 minutes. Drain and cool, then peel potatoes and cut into ¼-inch dice.

Heat oil in a 10- to 12-inch heavy skillet over moderate heat until hot but not smoking. Add onion and cook, stirring occasionally, until edges are golden, 3 to 5 minutes. Add peas, ginger, chile, and water and bring to a boil. Reduce heat and simmer, covered, until peas are just tender, 2 to 3 minutes. Add potatoes, salt, garam masala, cumin, and coriander and cook, uncovered, over moderately low heat, stirring occasionally, for 3 minutes to blend flavors. Transfer to a bowl and let cool, then stir in cilantro and lemon juice.

COOK'S NOTE

- The filling, without the cilantro and lemon juice, can be made up to 1 day ahead and refrigerated, covered. Bring to room temperature and stir in the cilantro and lemon juice before using.

Spiced Lamb Filling

MAKES ABOUT 2 CUPS
ACTIVE TIME: 30 MINUTES ■ START TO FINISH: 30 MINUTES

■ In this standout filling, ground lamb is seasoned with a balanced mix of intriguing spices, plus tomato, ginger, garlic, and chile. ■

¾ pound ground lamb (not lean)

2 tablespoons vegetable oil

1 small onion, finely chopped

1 tablespoon minced peeled fresh ginger

2 medium garlic cloves, minced

1 (2½-inch-long) fresh hot green chile, such as serrano or Thai, minced, including seeds

2¼ teaspoons ground cumin

1½ teaspoons ground coriander

¼ teaspoon turmeric

Pinch of ground cloves

Pinch of ground cinnamon

½ teaspoon salt

1 medium tomato, chopped

Cook lamb in 1 tablespoon oil in a 10- to 12-inch heavy skillet over moderately low heat, stirring constantly and breaking up lumps, until no longer pink, 4 to 6 minutes; do not brown. Transfer to a bowl.

Add remaining tablespoon oil to skillet, then add onion and cook, stirring, until softened, 4 to 5 minutes. Add ginger, garlic, and chile and cook, stirring, for 1 minute. Add cumin, coriander, turmeric, cloves, cinnamon, and salt and cook, stirring, for 1 minute. Add tomato and cook, stirring occasionally, until tomato falls apart and forms a thick sauce, 3 to 5 minutes.

Stir in lamb, with any juices accumulated in bowl, and simmer, stirring occasionally, until most of liquid has evaporated and filling is dry, 3 to 5 minutes. Remove from heat and let cool.

COOK'S NOTE

- The filling can be made up to 1 day ahead and refrigerated, covered.

Korean Pancakes
Bindaedok

MAKES 32 HORS D'OEUVRES
ACTIVE TIME: 45 MINUTES ■ START TO FINISH: 2¾ HOURS
(INCLUDES SOAKING BEANS)

■ Savory pancakes are much loved in Korea, where they are sold by street vendors who mix chopped vegetables and bits of fish or meat into a batter. Cut into wedges and dipped into a light, salty sauce flavored with red pepper flakes and sesame seeds, *bindaedok* make a memorable hors d'oeuvre. This colorful vegetarian version, dotted with carrots, scallions, and red chile, gets its airy texture from a batter of dried mung beans, flour, eggs, and water. ■

    1 cup dried yellow (hulled) mung beans
        (see Sources)
    2 medium carrots
    1 bunch scallions, white and pale green
        parts only
    1 (5-inch-long) fresh red chile, thinly sliced,
        including seeds
    1 tablespoon minced garlic
    1 cup water
    2 large eggs
    2 tablespoons all-purpose flour
    1 teaspoon salt
    ¼ cup vegetable oil

FOR DIPPING SAUCE

    3 tablespoons soy sauce
    2 teaspoons rice vinegar (not seasoned)
    1 tablespoon sesame seeds, toasted (see Tips,
        page 911)
    ¼ teaspoon red pepper flakes
    ¼ teaspoon Asian sesame oil

SOAK THE BEANS: Rinse mung beans in a sieve under cold water until water runs clear. Soak beans in cold water to cover by 2 inches, refrigerated, for at least 2 hours.

MEANWHILE, MAKE THE DIPPING SAUCE: Stir together all the ingredients in a small bowl.

MAKE THE PANCAKES: Cut carrots into 1/16-inch-thick matchsticks, preferably using a mandoline or other adjustable-blade vegetable slicer. Halve scallions lengthwise and cut into 2-inch pieces. Combine carrots, scallions, chile, and garlic in a large bowl.

Drain mung beans and transfer to a food processor. Add water and puree until smooth, about 1 minute. Add eggs, flour, and salt and blend until smooth, about 30 seconds. Pour mixture over vegetables in bowl and stir with a flexible spatula. (Batter will be thick.)

Heat 1 tablespoon oil in a large heavy nonstick skillet (at least 8 inches across bottom) over moderate heat until hot but not smoking, then swirl to coat pan. Stir batter and ladle 1 cup into skillet, pressing down lightly with a large spatula to flatten and evenly distribute vegetables, making an 8-inch pancake (less than ½ inch thick). Cook until edges begin to bubble and turn golden, 1 to 2 minutes, then turn with spatula and cook until other side is golden, 1 to

2 minutes more. Transfer pancake to paper towels to drain. Make 3 more pancakes in same manner, stacking them, after draining briefly, if desired.

Transfer pancakes, one at a time, to a cutting board and cut into 8 wedges. Serve warm or at room temperature, with dipping sauce.

COOK'S NOTE

■ The mung beans can be soaked for up to 12 hours.

Shrimp Cocktail with Sauce Verte

SERVES 8 TO 10
ACTIVE TIME: 1 HOUR ■ START TO FINISH: 1 HOUR

■ When you want a change from standard cocktail sauce, dunk your shrimp into this extraordinary dipping sauce loaded with fresh watercress, parsley, tarragon, and chives. We prefer medium shrimp for shrimp cocktail—they're big enough to look impressive on the plate, but small enough to dip easily. ■

FOR SAUCE

    3 bunches watercress, torn into 2- to 3-inch-long
        sprigs (6 cups packed)
    1 cup mayonnaise
    ¼ cup packed fresh flat-leaf parsley leaves
    2 tablespoons chopped fresh chives
    1 tablespoon chopped fresh tarragon
    1 tablespoon Dijon mustard
    ½ teaspoon hot sauce, such as Tabasco
    2 teaspoons bottled mango chutney
    1 teaspoon fresh lemon juice

FOR SHRIMP

    2 tablespoons salt
    2 pounds medium shrimp in shells (31–35 per pound),
        peeled, leaving tail and last segment of shell
        intact, and deveined

MAKE THE SAUCE: Blanch watercress in a 2- to 3-quart saucepan of boiling well-salted water for 30 seconds. Drain in a colander and transfer to a bowl of ice and cold water to stop the cooking, then drain briefly in colander (do not squeeze dry).

Put mayonnaise in a blender and add herbs, mustard, hot sauce, chutney, and lemon juice, and then watercress. Blend until smooth and very bright green, about 2 minutes. Transfer to a serving bowl.

COOK THE SHRIMP: Fill a 4-quart saucepan halfway with water, add 2 tablespoons salt, and bring to a boil. Add shrimp and boil until just cooked through, about 2 minutes. Drain in a colander and rinse briefly under cold running water to stop the cooking, then drain well.

Serve shrimp with sauce for dipping.

COOK'S NOTE
■ The sauce can be made up to 1 day ahead and refrigerated, covered tightly with plastic wrap.

Mini Shrimp Cornets

MAKES 48 HORS D'OEUVRES
ACTIVE TIME: 45 MINUTES ■ START TO FINISH: 1¼ HOURS

■ *Cornet* ("cor-*nay*") means "cone" in French, and these festive puff pastry wraps are a wonderful vehicle for shrimp. They look fancy, but they aren't difficult to assemble, and even if your folding technique isn't perfect, the cornets will be delicious. ■

    1 tablespoon unsalted butter
    ¼ cup finely chopped onion
    1 pound large shrimp in shells (21–25 per pound),
        peeled, deveined, and coarsely chopped
    2 tablespoons medium-dry sherry
    1 tablespoon chopped fresh tarragon
    ½ teaspoon salt
    ¼ teaspoon freshly ground black pepper
    1 (17.3-ounce) package frozen puff pastry sheets,
        thawed
      All-purpose flour for dusting
    1 large egg
    1 tablespoon milk

SPECIAL EQUIPMENT: parchment paper

Put racks in upper and lower thirds of oven and preheat oven to 400°F. Line two large baking sheets with parchment paper.

Heat butter in an 8-inch heavy skillet over moderately low heat until foam subsides, then add onion

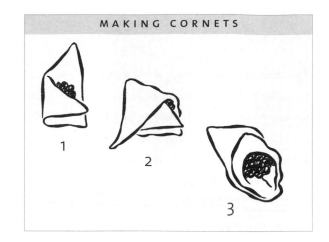

MAKING CORNETS

and cook, stirring occasionally, until softened, about 2 minutes. Transfer to a medium bowl to cool.

Add shrimp, sherry, tarragon, salt, and pepper to onion and stir until well combined.

Roll out 1 sheet of pastry on a lightly floured surface into a 12-inch square. Cut into thirds in one direction, then into quarters in the other direction, to make 12 rectangles. Cut each rectangle diagonally in half to form 2 triangles. Place 1 triangle on a work surface with shortest side nearest you and longest side to the left, and put 1 teaspoon shrimp filling in center of triangle. Bring left corner of short side over filling (**1**), drape top of triangle over it (**2**), and then wrap tip around and pinch to seal (**3**). Transfer to a lined baking sheet. Form more cornets with remaining triangles in same manner, arranging them ½ inch apart on baking sheet. Refrigerate first baking sheet of cornets, loosely covered, while you make second sheet of cornets with remaining dough and filling.

Whisk together egg and milk and lightly brush some of egg wash over top of each cornet.

Bake, switching position of sheets halfway through baking, until golden, 18 to 20 minutes. Cool cornets on sheets on racks for 5 minutes, then gently loosen from parchment with a spatula. Serve warm.

COOK'S NOTE
■ The cornets can be formed—but not brushed with the egg wash—up to 3 days ahead. Freeze on baking sheets until firm, then transfer to a sealable plastic bag and freeze. Do not thaw before brushing with egg wash and baking.

PARTY PLANNING

If you have endless resources, giving a party is a snap: hire a wonderful caterer and go curl up in an armchair with a good book until the guests come. For those of us who must be (or want to be) a little more hands-on, the key thing to remember is to get as much done beforehand as possible so that you can enjoy being a host. And if you are worried about wine stains on that white rug, for example, roll it up and tuck it away. Then everyone, including you, can relax.

MAKE LISTS Several of them. (This is enormously satisfying, because then you get to check things off. If only life were always so orderly.) In terms of food and drinks, write down everything you need to buy and where to buy it. List other things too, such as cocktail napkins (you can never have enough), lemons/limes, and forks, if you are not serving only finger food. Don't forget to buy ice. Lots of it. Go over each thing you are serving and make a list of what implements/platters/bowls you will need. Decide what food goes on what platters. (Post-it notes come in handy.) Trays are a smart investment, and they don't have to be fancy: Asian markets, for instance, often have beautiful ones that are not expensive at all, as well as stackable small bowls that are good for nuts, dips, and olive pits.

DO A WALK-THROUGH Pretend you're a guest and walk through your door. Coats—where do they go? What if it's raining or snowing? Is there room for boots or umbrellas? Figure out where to put the dog during the party. If you have a cat, figure out where to stash the litter box. And hire a babysitter and order a pizza for the children.

TRAFFIC FLOW Put something stationary—the bar or a table with a big bowl of shrimp cocktail on it, for instance—in a corner of the room, and guests will follow. And bear in mind that no matter what you do, people will gravitate toward the kitchen, so make them welcome. Move the chairs out of the kitchen so there's room.

SET THE MOOD A party needs music, so stack the CD changer or put the iPod on shuffle. Do the flowers the day before. Avoid lilies and other flowers with a heavy fragrance; the same holds true for candles. Everyone looks great by candlelight, so don't skimp on the votives—you can find clear ones for next to nothing at a discount store. (Add a little water to each votive before you pop in the candle, and that will make the melted remains easy to remove. Substitute cranberry juice for the water, and the result will be a rosy pink glow.)

BAR TALK It's not necessary to stock an entire bar. Instead, have a pitcher of one cocktail—manhattans, say—along with red and white wine and something nonalcoholic. If you are expecting sixteen or more guests, hire a bartender (who will clean up at the end of the evening; for a bigger party, hire someone to pass trays of hors d'oeuvres as well). Tip generously and in cash.

You can't have enough glassware, so rent it. Rent triple the number of glasses you think you will need, because you don't want to have to wash them during a party and you don't want to run out. (If you need to round out a minimum order for glasses, order a couple of trays too.) The beauty of renting glasses is that you don't have to wash them; simply empty them and put them back in the boxes. A trash can next to the bar is a smart idea.

QUICK TIP FOR CHILLING A CASE OF WHITE WINE Put the bottles in the bathtub, pour ice and cold water over them, and they will be chilled in 25 minutes (the greater the ratio of ice to water, the faster they will chill). One of our food editors with years of catering experience has been known to use his top-loading washing machine, filled with ice, as a wine cooler. If you need to chill a few bottles of beer or wine on the spur of the moment, put them in a large ice bucket or bowl and pour ice and cold water over them, adding about a tablespoon of salt for each quart of water; because salt lowers the freezing point of water, it helps the water stay colder longer.

FOOD AND ITS PRESENTATION Keeping things simple is always better than going overboard. Many a great party has been provisioned with nothing more complicated than cheeses, cured meats, nuts and/or dried fruit, olives, and bread or crackers. If you are buying a very large piece of **cheese** (five or six pounds, for instance) for a party, don't put it all out at once; instead, cut it in half, and when the cheese platter is looking ravaged, you can take it back into the kitchen, replenish, and hear people exclaim, "Wow, look at all that cheese!" one more time. The idea is to keep things looking bountiful. Also, choose things that can be served at room temperature—humble **meat loaf** (you might not think your mom's recipe is special, but it is), sliced thin and served with cornichons, for example, or a large baking sheet of **quiche** cut into bite-sized squares. Cook a **beef tenderloin** the day beforehand and slice it after chilling it (you get paper-thin slices that way). Bring it to room temperature an hour before the party and serve it with toasts and mustard.

Serve uncomplicated food with a high drama quotient, and serve larger quantities of fewer things. An enormous **bowl of shrimp** is a surefire draw, and here's how to do it easily: This may sound heretical, but buy frozen peeled cooked shrimp. Thaw them, toss with lemon slices, a little Old Bay seasoning, and salt, and pile into your largest, most beautiful bowl. Fill another bowl with a lavish assortment of **cherry tomatoes** from the farmers market and put a small bowl of vinaigrette or seasoned salt next to it. Add bowls of blanched sugar snap peas, pita or bagel crisps, and dip (half sour cream, half mayonnaise, a little curry powder, cumin, and chives—you get the idea), and you are *done*.

You will give food on trays or platters more of a presence by placing something between it and the surface. Line a tray with sprigs of fresh herbs or a layer of raw dried beans, lentils, chickpeas, or rice. Keep in mind that a contrasting color will make an hors d'oeuvre pop: a bed of black beans shows off sliced radishes with a dab of herbed cream cheese or butter on top; a layer of white rice makes baby lettuce leaves filled with shrimp salad even prettier. The sleek soupspoons found at Asian markets are not expensive. Fill them with **smoked salmon** or **sablefish salad** from the deli. Then arrange the spoons on a tray, nestled in a bed of dried wasabi peas so they don't slide around or topple over while being passed, with a plate nearby where guests can deposit the empties.

Grilled Shrimp Saté with Spiced Pistachio Chutney

MAKES ABOUT 22 HORS D'OEUVRES
ACTIVE TIME: 45 MINUTES ■ START TO FINISH: 2 HOURS

■ Skewered shrimp are as easy to broil and serve as they are for guests to nibble on while chatting and drinking. Plus, they look—and taste—wonderful with the verdant chutney. Keep this nutty, spicy condiment in mind—it is also delicious with almost any grilled seafood or chicken. ■

FOR CHUTNEY
- 1 (8-ounce) container plain yogurt
- ½ cup unsalted shelled pistachios, toasted (see Tips, page 911)
- 1 teaspoon ground coriander
- ½ teaspoon ground cumin
- 1½ teaspoons olive oil
- 4 jalapeño chiles, coarsely chopped, including seeds
- 1 cup loosely packed fresh cilantro sprigs
- 1 tablespoon fresh lime juice
- Salt

FOR SHRIMP
- 1 pound large shrimp in shells (21–25 per pound), peeled and deveined
- 1½ teaspoons minced garlic
- 1½ tablespoons olive oil
- 1 tablespoon fresh lime juice
- ½ teaspoon salt

SPECIAL EQUIPMENT: an electric coffee/spice grinder; about twenty-five 6- to 8-inch bamboo skewers, soaked in water for 30 minutes

DRAIN THE YOGURT: Put yogurt into a fine-mesh sieve set over a bowl and drain, refrigerated, for 1 hour.

MEANWHILE, MARINATE THE SHRIMP: Butterfly shrimp by cutting them almost in half, but not quite all the way, down the backs. Toss in a bowl with garlic, oil, lime juice, and salt. Marinate, refrigerated, for 30 minutes to 1 hour.

MAKE THE CHUTNEY: Finely grind pistachios in coffee/spice grinder.

Cook coriander and cumin in oil in a small heavy skillet over moderate heat, stirring occasionally, until fragrant, 1 to 2 minutes; cool.

Combine chiles, drained yogurt, coriander mixture, and cilantro in a blender and puree until smooth. Transfer to a bowl and stir in lime juice, pistachios, and salt to taste.

GRILL THE SATÉS: If using a charcoal grill, prepare it as for indirect-heat cooking over hot coals; if using a gas grill, prepare it as for indirect-heat cooking over high heat (see Grilling Basics, page 512).

Meanwhile, gently press 1 shrimp open and thread lengthwise onto a skewer, so shrimp is near pointed end of skewer. Repeat with remaining shrimp and skewers.

Lightly oil grill rack. Arrange shrimp over hot coals or burner(s), with exposed part of skewers over cooler parts of grill. Grill (covered if using a gas grill), turning once, until just cooked through, 1½ to 2 minutes.

Serve saté with chutney for dipping.

COOK'S NOTES

■ The chutney can be made up to 1 day ahead and refrigerated, covered.

■ Alternatively, you can broil the saté. Arrange the skewers in a row along one long side of a broiler pan so that the blunt ends of the skewers point toward the middle of the pan. Cover the ends of the skewers with a sheet of foil (don't cover the shrimp). Arrange another row of skewers over the foil, and cover the ends of the skewers with foil. Continue adding rows of saté and layers of foil until the pan is full, making sure to cover the exposed ends of the last row of skewers. Broil the shrimp 4 to 6 inches from heat, without turning, until just cooked through, 3 to 4 minutes.

Salt and Pepper Shrimp

MAKES ABOUT 24 HORS D'OEUVRES
ACTIVE TIME: 45 MINUTES ■ START TO FINISH: 45 MINUTES

■ In this dish, a perennial on Sichuan menus, the shrimp are fried in their shells and magically assume a texture similar to that of soft-shell crab, the crisp exterior protecting the tender flesh. Should your guests balk at eating the shells, which become almost papery in the hot oil, suggest that they at least lick off the seasonings before peeling and eating the shrimp. The simple secret here is five-spice powder, the Chinese seasoning blend of cinnamon, cloves, fennel seed, star anise, and Sichuan peppercorns (depending on the manufacturer, there may also be small amounts of ginger and cardamom). ■

    1 pound large shrimp in shells (21–25 per pound)
    6 cups vegetable oil for deep-frying
    ¾ teaspoon fine sea salt
    ½ teaspoon freshly ground black pepper
    ½ teaspoon Chinese five-spice powder (see Sources)

SPECIAL EQUIPMENT: a deep-fat thermometer

Cut each shrimp shell open down the back with scissors, leaving tail and last segment intact, and devein shrimp, leaving shell in place. Cut off feathery legs and sharp pointed section of shell above soft tail fins. Rinse shrimp and dry thoroughly.

Heat oil in a well-seasoned 14-inch flat-bottomed wok or 4- to 5-quart deep heavy pot over high heat until it registers 400°F on thermometer. Deep-fry shrimp in 4 batches until shells bubble and shrimp are bright pink, 45 to 60 seconds (they will be slightly undercooked), then transfer with a wire-mesh skimmer or slotted spoon to paper towels to drain. (Return oil to 400°F between batches.)

Carefully pour oil into a heatproof bowl (to cool before discarding). Wipe wok clean with paper towels, or use a large heavy skillet. Stir together salt, pepper, and five-spice powder. Heat wok or skillet over moderate heat until hot but not smoking. Add shrimp and spice mixture and stir-fry for 10 seconds. Serve immediately.

HOW TO SHELL AND DEVEIN SHRIMP

If the shrimp have heads, twist them off. Peel back the rest of the shell, which is composed of overlapping layers. Then, unless you need the tail and last section of the shell—the one adjoining the tail—for a little handle (if the shrimp are to be dipped in a sauce), pinch the end of the tail to crack the shell; that will make it easier to remove. Shrimp heads don't freeze well, but toss the rest of the shells into a sealable plastic bag and freeze for stock.

The dark vein down the back (dorsal) curve of a shrimp is actually the intestinal tract. To devein or not to devein is often a matter of personal preference. People who grow up in shrimp-eating areas tend not to fuss with the procedure, but that dark line can be gritty, especially in medium or large shrimp. To devein, simply slide a small knife down the back, making a shallow slit to expose the vein (1). Pull out the vein with the edge of the knife or with your fingers (2).

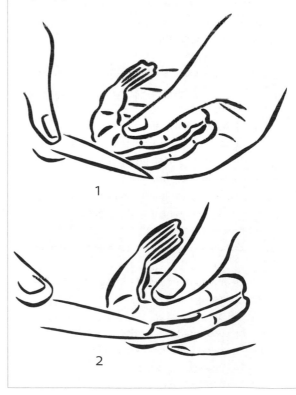

1

2

Vietnamese Fried Spring Rolls
Cha Gio

MAKES 50 HORS D'OEUVRES
ACTIVE TIME: 1¾ HOURS ■ START TO FINISH: 2 HOURS

■ Every Tet, or Lunar New Year, contributor Bich Minh Nguyen's grandmother Noi made hundreds of these wonderful spring rolls—lightly crunchy on the outside, each ingredient in the filling inside distinct and fresh-tasting. The golden pyramid of *cha gio* would disappear quickly as family and friends wrapped the rolls in lettuce leaves, tucking cilantro and mint leaves inside, and dunked them one after another in the savory dipping sauce called *nuoc cham*. After Nguyen's family had to flee Saigon in 1975, they settled in Grand Rapids, Michigan, where they did their weekly shopping at a local Vietnamese market. Vietnamese rice-flour wrappers (*banh trang*) weren't widely available, so Noi used wheat-flour wrappers from China and Singapore; though it's easier to get *banh trang* these days, Nguyen still uses wheat wrappers. Many supermarket wrappers are too thick, so it's worth seeking out the delicate ones labeled "spring roll pastry" at Asian markets. ■

FOR DIPPING SAUCE (*NUOC CHAM*)
- 5½ tablespoons sugar
- ¾ cup warm water
- 5 tablespoons Asian fish sauce
- 2 tablespoons rice vinegar (not seasoned)
- 2 teaspoons fresh lime juice (optional)
- 2 garlic cloves, minced
- 2 (2- to 3-inch-long) fresh Thai chiles, preferably red, thinly sliced, including seeds

FOR SPRING ROLLS
- 7½ ounces bean thread (cellophane) noodles (see Sources)
- 2 ounces dried wood ear mushrooms (see Sources)
- 1 medium shallot
- 2 garlic cloves
- 2 cups shredded carrots (4–5)
- 1 pound ground pork shoulder
- ¼ cup Asian fish sauce
- ¼ cup plus 1 teaspoon sugar
- 2 teaspoons salt
- 2½ teaspoons freshly ground black pepper
- 1 pound shrimp in shells, peeled and deveined
- 25 (8-inch) square frozen wheat-flour spring roll wrappers (see headnote), thawed
- 1 large egg yolk, lightly beaten

About 6 cups vegetable oil for deep-frying
ACCOMPANIMENTS: lettuce leaves; fresh mint leaves and small cilantro sprigs
SPECIAL EQUIPMENT: a deep-fat thermometer

MAKE THE DIPPING SAUCE: Stir together sugar and water in a bowl until sugar is dissolved. Stir in remaining ingredients. Refrigerate, covered, for at least 2 hours to develop flavors.

MEANWHILE, PREPARE THE FILLING: Put noodles in a large bowl and cover with hot water by several inches. Soak, stirring occasionally and pulling noodles apart, for 10 minutes. Drain noodles and cut with kitchen shears into 2- to 3-inch lengths (you should have about 3 cups). Transfer to another large bowl.

Meanwhile, put mushrooms in a medium bowl, cover with hot water by several inches, and soak for 15 minutes. Drain mushrooms and rinse thoroughly, then drain again. Trim off and discard any hard parts. Finely chop mushrooms. (You should have about 2 cups.) Add to noodles.

Pulse shallot and garlic in a food processor until finely chopped. Add to noodles, along with carrots, pork, fish sauce, sugar, salt, and pepper. Pulse shrimp in processor until coarsely ground; do not overprocess, or it will become pasty. Add to noodle mixture and mix with your hands until well combined. Refrigerate filling, covered, until cold.

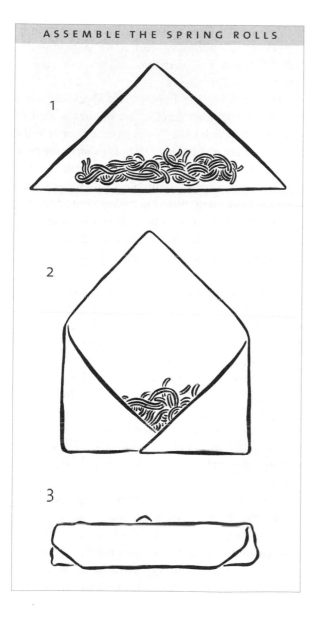

ASSEMBLE THE SPRING ROLLS

1

2

3

making sure ends stay tucked inside (3). Place on a tray, seam side down. Repeat with remaining triangle, then make more rolls in same manner with remaining wrappers and filling (transfer first tray to refrigerator once it is filled). Refrigerate spring rolls, loosely covered, until ready to fry.

Heat 1½ inches of oil in a 5- to 6-quart heavy pot over moderately high heat until it registers 365°F on thermometer. Line a colander with paper towels. Fry rolls in batches of 5 or 6, using a slotted spoon to keep rolls apart during first minute of frying so they won't stick together, until golden brown and cooked through, 4 to 5 minutes. Transfer to colander, standing rolls on end, and drain for 2 to 3 minutes. (Return oil to 365°F between batches.)

Serve rolls hot or warm, with dipping sauce. To eat, wrap rolls in lettuce leaves, tucking in mint and cilantro leaves, then dip in sauce.

COOK'S NOTES

■ The sauce and filling can be made up to 4 hours ahead and refrigerated separately, covered.

■ The rolls can be assembled up to 1 month ahead and frozen, wrapped well in foil. Thaw in the refrigerator before frying.

Shrimp and Pork Pot Stickers

MAKES 24 DUMPLINGS
ACTIVE TIME: 1½ HOURS ■ START TO FINISH: 1½ HOURS

■ Making the panfried Chinese dumplings called pot stickers at home is a deliciously worthwhile endeavor. Hand-rolling and pleating the dough results in a pleasing wrapper that is both delicate and engagingly chewy—and far better than store-bought wrappers. The juicy filling of well-seasoned pork, shrimp, and crunchy water chestnuts is classic, as is the cooking technique used. The dumplings are fried and then steamed in one pan, then cooked until their bottoms become golden and crisp. Invert the dumplings onto a serving plate so their beautifully burnished sides are facing up. Sealing the dumplings may take some practice, so the last one you form will probably be prettier than your first, but they will all taste wonderful. ■

ASSEMBLE THE SPRING ROLLS: Line two trays with wax paper. Transfer one quarter of filling to a small bowl; keep remainder refrigerated, covered.

Place 1 wrapper on a work surface; keep remaining wrappers covered with a clean kitchen towel to prevent them from drying out. Cut wrapper diagonally in half, to form 2 triangles. Arrange 1 triangle so longest side is nearest you, put 2 tablespoons filling along middle of long edge, and shape filling into a thin 5-inch-long log (1). Fold left and right corners of wrapper over filling (2), overlapping filling slightly and aligning bottom edges. (Wrapper will resemble an open envelope.) Dab top corner with yolk, then roll up wrapper away from you into a long thin roll,

FOR DUMPLINGS

1½–1¾ cups all-purpose flour, plus additional
    for dusting
½ cup lukewarm water
3 fresh or 4 canned water chestnuts (see Cook's Note)
½ pound shrimp in shells, peeled, deveined, and
    coarsely chopped
¼ pound ground fatty pork (from shoulder)
¾ cup chopped scallions (about 1 bunch)
2 teaspoons minced peeled fresh ginger
1½ tablespoons soy sauce
1 teaspoon Asian sesame oil
1 tablespoon peanut or vegetable oil

FOR SAUCE

⅓ cup soy sauce
2 tablespoons Chinese black vinegar, preferably
    Chinkiang (see Sources)
2 tablespoons water
1 teaspoon Asian chile oil, or to taste

SPECIAL EQUIPMENT: a 3½-inch round cookie cutter

MAKE THE DUMPLINGS: Stir together 1½ cups flour and lukewarm water in a bowl until a shaggy dough forms. Turn out onto a lightly floured surface and knead, adding more flour as needed if dough is sticky, until smooth, 1 to 2 minutes. Dust dough lightly with flour, cover with an inverted bowl, and let stand at room temperature for 10 minutes to 1 hour (to let gluten relax).

If using fresh water chestnuts, scrub very well, peel with a sharp paring knife, and rinse (see Cook's Note). Cover with 1½ cups water in a 1-quart saucepan, bring to a boil, and boil until chestnuts are crisp-tender and slightly translucent, about 5 minutes. Drain in a colander and rinse under cold water to cool. If using canned water chestnuts, rinse well.

Cut water chestnuts into ¼-inch dice and put in a medium bowl. Add shrimp, pork, scallions, ginger, soy sauce, and sesame oil and knead until just combined. Refrigerate, covered, while you roll out and cut dough.

Line a large baking sheet with paper towels and dust lightly with flour. Lightly dust work surface with flour. Halve dough and cover one half with inverted bowl. Pat remaining half into a flat square, then roll out with a lightly floured rolling pin into a 13-inch square (less than ⅛ inch thick), dusting work surface

with additional flour as needed. Cut out 12 rounds, very close together, using cutter (if dough sticks to cutter, lightly dip cutter in flour and shake off excess). Reroll scraps if necessary.

Transfer rounds to lined baking sheet and cover loosely with another layer of paper towels. Lightly dust paper towels with flour. Roll out remaining dough and cut out 12 more rounds in same manner. Transfer rounds to top layer of paper towels.

Line another large baking sheet with paper towels and dust lightly with flour. Put 1 dough round on your fingers, near your palm, put 1 tablespoon pork mixture in center of round, and fold dough over filling to form an open half-moon shape. With a wet finger, moisten lower inner edge of round. Use your forefingers and thumb to make the first pleat along the edge closest to you, starting at one corner (1). Press down on the pleat so that it stays in place (2). Keeping your thumb on the first pleat, begin making the second (3). As you form the pleats, that edge will become shorter, curving the dumpling into a crescent moon. After finishing the pleats, pinch the top together to seal (4) and stand dumpling on baking sheet. Form remaining dumplings in same manner (you may have some filling left over), arranging them about ½ inch apart on baking sheet. Cover loosely with paper towels.

MAKE THE SAUCE: Stir together all ingredients in a small bowl. (Stir again just before serving.)

COOK THE DUMPLINGS: Heat peanut oil in a 10-inch nonstick skillet over moderately high heat until hot but not smoking. Arrange 7 dumplings, seam sides up, in a tight spiral pattern in center of skillet. Arrange remaining dumplings around outer edges (they should touch one another). Fry dumplings until bottoms are pale golden, 2 to 3 minutes. Add ½ cup water, tilting skillet to distribute, then cover tightly and cook until liquid is evaporated and bottoms of dumplings are crisp and golden, 7 to 10 minutes. (Use a spatula to loosen and lift edges to check bottoms after 7 minutes; replace lid and continue cooking if necessary, checking every 1 to 2 minutes.)

Remove lid and invert a large rimmed plate over skillet. Using pot holders, and holding plate and skillet tightly together, invert dumplings onto plate. Serve with dipping sauce.

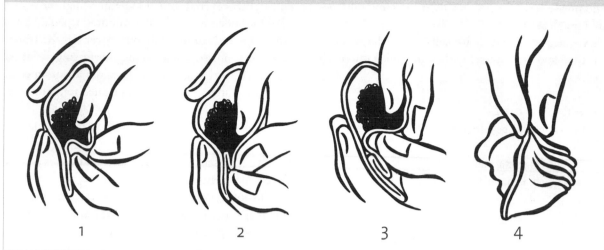

1   2   3   4

COOK'S NOTES

- You can find fresh water chestnuts at Asian markets. Look for clean, firm chestnuts, then buy twice as many as you think you'll use, since you will need to cut into each one to determine if it is usable. Cut off the top and bottom of each chestnut with a sharp paring knife, then cut off the remaining peel; the water chestnut should be firm and off-white in color. Rinse and cut as directed. You can eat any extra chestnuts raw.

- The dumplings can be formed (but not cooked) up to 1 day ahead. Refrigerate in an airtight container, in one layer on lightly floured paper towels, not touching, and loosely covered with more paper towels.

- The sauce can be made up to 8 hours ahead and kept at room temperature.

Mussels on the Half-Shell with Ravigote Sauce

MAKES ABOUT 48 HORS D'OEUVRES
ACTIVE TIME: 30 MINUTES ■ START TO FINISH: 1½ HOURS

■ When we revisited this recipe from 1964, we found it bracing, sophisticated, and definitely worth resurrecting. The mussels are marinated in a piquant sauce of onion, Dijon mustard, fresh herbs, and sieved hard-boiled egg. ■

1½ pounds mussels (about 48), preferably cultivated, scrubbed and beards removed
¼ cup dry white wine
1 hard-boiled large egg
½ cup olive oil
3 tablespoons white wine vinegar
1 medium onion, finely chopped
2 teaspoons bottled capers, drained and rinsed, chopped if large
1 teaspoon Dijon mustard
1 teaspoon finely chopped fresh flat-leaf parsley
1 teaspoon finely chopped fresh chervil
1 teaspoon finely chopped fresh chives
¼ teaspoon salt
⅛ teaspoon freshly ground black pepper

Cook mussels in wine in a 5- to 6-quart heavy pot, tightly covered, over moderately high heat just until they open wide, checking frequently after 4 minutes and transferring opened mussels to a baking sheet using a slotted spoon. Discard any mussels that remain unopened after 8 minutes; reserve liquid remaining in pot.

When mussels are cool enough to handle, detach from shells and discard 1 half-shell from each one. Reserve mussels (with any juice) and remaining shells separately.

Peel and halve egg. Using back of a spoon, force egg through a medium-mesh sieve into a small bowl. Whisk in oil, vinegar, onion, capers, mustard, parsley, chervil, chives, salt, and pepper until well combined. Add mussels, stirring to coat, then cover and refrigerate for at least 1 hour.

Arrange reserved half-shells on a large platter, then spoon a mussel with some sauce into each shell.

COOK'S NOTES
- The mussels can be refrigerated in the sauce for up to 6 hours.
- The mussels on the half-shell can be assembled on the platter up to 1 hour before serving and refrigerated.

Mussels with Serrano Ham

MAKES ABOUT 60 HORS D'OEUVRES
ACTIVE TIME: 1 HOUR ■ START TO FINISH: 1¼ HOURS

■ These tapas-style hors d'oeuvres couldn't be simpler to make. Toss steamed mussels with a quick vinaigrette, chopped piquillo peppers, toasted almonds, and matchsticks of serrano ham, then nestle them back in their shells. Each bite will have a little savor, a little crunch, a little sharpness. Piquillo peppers—red peppers from northern Spain that are traditionally roasted over an open fire, peeled, and packed in their own juices in jars or tins—contribute a sweet and smoky piquancy to the mix. ■

2 pounds mussels (about 60), preferably cultivated, scrubbed and beards removed
⅓ cup extra-virgin olive oil
2½ tablespoons sherry vinegar
1 teaspoon Dijon mustard
½ teaspoon finely chopped garlic
⅛ teaspoon salt
⅛ teaspoon freshly ground black pepper
2 (⅛-inch-thick) slices serrano ham (about 1½ ounces), cut into 1-inch-long matchsticks
⅓ cup sliced almonds, toasted (see Tips, page 911)
¼ cup drained bottled piquillo peppers (see Sources), finely chopped
2 tablespoons chopped fresh flat-leaf parsley

Cook mussels in a dry 3- to 4-quart deep heavy pot, tightly covered, over moderately high heat just until they open wide, about 4 minutes; open lid after 3 minutes and stir once, then re-cover tightly. Transfer opened mussels to a baking sheet using a slotted spoon. Discard any mussels that remain unopened after 8 minutes; reserve mussel juice remaining in pot.

When mussels are cool enough to handle, detach from shells and discard 1 half-shell from each one. Reserve mussels (with any juice) and remaining shells separately.

Whisk together oil, vinegar, mustard, garlic, salt, and pepper in a large bowl. Add ham, almonds, piquillo peppers, parsley, mussels, and 3 to 4 tablespoons of reserved juices and toss until mussels are coated.

Arrange reserved half-shells on a large plate. Spoon 1 mussel with some of dressing into each reserved shell and serve.

COOK'S NOTE
- The mussels can be tossed with the dressing up to 1 hour ahead. Add the ham, almonds, piquillo peppers, and parsley before spooning them into the shells.

Clams with Ponzu and Panko

MAKES 24 HORS D'OEUVRES
ACTIVE TIME: 45 MINUTES ■ START TO FINISH: 1 HOUR

■ *Ponzu*, a Japanese sauce made of citrus juice, soy sauce, and *dashi*, the sea stock that provides the backbone for so many Japanese dishes, is a natural with broiled fresh clams. A sprinkling of the Japanese bread crumbs known as panko mixed with citrus zest and garlic plays up the flavor and fragrance while adding a nice crispness to the clams. Making *dashi* is simple enough, but because this recipe only calls for a small amount, we prefer to use instant powder. Stabilizing the clams on a bed of raw rice is a nifty catering trick that translates easily to home entertaining and looks impressive. Try black or purple Philippine rice for a very dramatic presentation; inexpensive white rice, tapioca pearls, or kosher salt also looks great. ■

FOR PANKO TOPPING
  1 small garlic clove
    Salt
  ¼ teaspoon finely grated orange zest
  ¼ teaspoon finely grated lemon zest
  ¼ teaspoon finely grated lime zest
  2 teaspoons finely chopped scallion greens
  ⅓ cup panko (Japanese bread crumbs)
FOR PONZU SAUCE
  ¼ cup *dashi* (Japanese sea stock), made from instant
     dashi (see Sources)
  3 tablespoons mirin (Japanese sweet rice wine) or
     cream sherry
  2 tablespoons fresh orange juice
  1 tablespoon fresh lemon juice
  1 tablespoon fresh lime juice
  1 tablespoon rice vinegar (not seasoned)
  1 tablespoon soy sauce
FOR CLAMS
  3½ cups uncooked rice (for stabilizing clamshells)
  24 small hard-shelled clams (about 2 inches wide),
     scrubbed

SPECIAL EQUIPMENT: a clam knife

MAKE THE PANKO TOPPING: Mince garlic and mash to a paste with a pinch of salt, using side of a large heavy knife. Transfer to a small bowl and stir in remaining topping ingredients.

MAKE THE PONZU SAUCE: Combine all sauce ingredients in a small saucepan, bring to a simmer, and simmer until reduced to about ¼ cup, about 15 minutes. Remove from heat and set aside.

SHUCK AND BROIL THE CLAMS: Spread 2 cups rice on a baking sheet.

Grip 1 clam in a kitchen towel, with its hinge side toward you. Slide clam knife between the two shells at a point opposite hinge and rotate clam, sliding knife between shells, until knife reaches hinge. Cut through hinge, being careful to avoid center of clam. Open shells, sliding knife along underside of top shell to detach clam. Pull off top shell and discard. Slide knife under clam to detach it from bottom shell and transfer clam to a bowl; reserve bottom shell. Repeat with remaining clams.

Scrub reserved shells inside and out, then dry. Return clams to shells, nestling shells in rice on baking sheet to keep them stable.

Preheat broiler. Add ¼ teaspoon *ponzu* sauce to each clam and sprinkle with 1 teaspoon topping. Broil clams 4 to 6 inches from heat until topping is browned and clams are just cooked through, 2 to 3 minutes.

Meanwhile, spread remaining 1½ cups rice on a platter.

Nestle clams in rice on platter and serve warm.

COOK'S NOTES
■ The panko topping can be made up to 3 hours ahead and refrigerated, covered.
■ The *ponzu* sauce can be made up to 3 days ahead and refrigerated, covered.
■ The clams will be much easier to shuck if you put them in the freezer for 20 minutes first.

Oysters with Champagne-Vinegar Mignonette

MAKES 24 HORS D'OEUVRES
ACTIVE TIME: 15 MINUTES ■ START TO FINISH: 45 MINUTES

■ In this elegant hors d'oeuvre, tiny pearl-like Champagne grapes and a Champagne-vinegar mignonette raise the glamour quotient of the ultimate aphrodisiac. It's a wonderful treat in which the brine of the sea meets with the sweet pop of the earth, all balanced by the sharpness of the vinegar in the mignonette. ■

FOR MIGNONETTE
  2 tablespoons Champagne vinegar
  4 teaspoons finely chopped shallot
  ¼ teaspoon coarsely ground black pepper
  ¼ teaspoon sugar
  1 tablespoon finely chopped fresh flat-leaf parsley
FOR OYSTERS
  6 cups kosher salt (for stabilizing oyster shells)
  2 tablespoons unsalted butter
  24 small oysters, such as Kumamoto or Prince Edward
     Island, scrubbed well and shucked, liquor and
     bottom shells reserved
     Several clusters of Champagne grapes, left whole,
     or 5 seedless red grapes, quartered and thinly
     sliced

MAKE THE MIGNONETTE: Stir together vinegar, shallot, pepper, and sugar in a small bowl. Let stand for 30 minutes.

PREPARE THE OYSTERS: Preheat broiler. Spread 2½ to 3 cups salt in a flameproof shallow baking pan (about 15 by 10 inches). Cut butter into 24 small pieces. Arrange oyster shells in salt, leveling shells. Place 1 oyster in each shell, with some of oyster liquor, and top each with a piece of butter.

Broil oysters 4 to 6 inches from heat until butter is melted and sizzling and edges of oysters are beginning to curl, 1 to 2 minutes.

Meanwhile, stir parsley into mignonette. Spread remaining salt on a platter.

Carefully transfer oysters to platter, keeping them level. Spoon ¼ teaspoon mignonette over each oyster and sprinkle each one with 3 or 4 Champagne grapes (or a few grape slices). Serve warm.

COOK'S NOTES

- The mignonette, without the parsley, can be made up to 1 day ahead and refrigerated, covered.
- The oysters can be arranged in the baking pan, with the liquor and butter, up to 1 hour ahead and refrigerated, loosely covered.

Curried Oysters with Cucumber Sauce and Salmon Roe

MAKES 24 HORS D'OEUVRES
ACTIVE TIME: 30 MINUTES ■ START TO FINISH: 45 MINUTES

■ This fanciful combination is as stunningly delicious as it is beautiful. Fried oysters, gilded with curry powder, nestle in the pools of cucumber sauce, topped with orange pearls of salmon roe. Editor in chief Ruth Reichl adapted this recipe from one that Wolfgang Puck serves at his Santa Monica restaurant Chinois. Good-quality salmon roe is imperative here. ■

FOR CUCUMBER SAUCE
½ seedless cucumber (usually plastic-wrapped), left unpeeled, chopped (1⅓ cups)

¼ cup rice vinegar (not seasoned)
¾ teaspoon salt
¼ teaspoon freshly ground black pepper
2½ tablespoons Asian sesame oil
2½ tablespoons peanut oil

FOR CURRIED OYSTERS
24 small oysters, such as Kumamoto or Prince Edward Island, shucked (see page 379), bottom shells reserved
2 tablespoons curry powder, preferably Madras
2 tablespoons all-purpose flour
¼ teaspoon salt
⅓ cup vegetable oil
¼ cup (2 ounces) salmon roe

ACCOMPANIMENT: lemon wedges

MAKE THE CUCUMBER SAUCE: Combine cucumber with vinegar, salt, and pepper in a blender and puree until very smooth, about 1 minute. With motor running, add both oils in a slow stream, blending until well blended.

MAKE THE CURRIED OYSTERS: Scrub reserved bottom oyster shells. Boil in a 6- to 8-quart pot of boiling water for 3 minutes to remove any grit or traces of raw oyster. Drain shells in a colander, rinse, and dry thoroughly.

Whisk together curry powder, flour, and salt in a shallow bowl. Pat oysters dry. Dredge one at a time in curry mixture, shaking off excess flour, and transfer to a plate.

Heat oil in a 10-inch heavy skillet over moderate heat until hot but not smoking. Panfry oysters in 2 batches, turning once, until plump and golden, 1 to 2 minutes per batch. Transfer fried oysters to paper towels to drain.

Arrange reserved oyster shells on a large platter. Spoon a scant tablespoon of cucumber sauce into each shell and top with a fried oyster (you will have some sauce left over). Top each oyster with ½ teaspoon salmon roe and serve with lemon wedges.

COOK'S NOTE

- The cucumber sauce can be made up to 1 day ahead and refrigerated, covered.

Stone Crab Claws
with Parsley Sauce

MAKES 24 OR 36 HORS D'OEUVRES
ACTIVE TIME: 35 MINUTES ■ START TO FINISH: 35 MINUTES

■ The stone crab is native to South Atlantic and Gulf Coast waters. Its body has little meat, but its chubby black-tipped claws are loaded with sweet flesh. (Happily, no crabs are sacrificed—fishermen simply break off one claw and return the crab to the ocean, where it generates another, smaller claw.) Most of the stone crabs eaten in the United States come from Florida, where the season runs from mid-October to mid-May. All stone crab claws are cooked immediately after harvesting and sold fresh or frozen. Because the meat becomes tough if reheated, the claws taste best chilled, served with a flavorful dipping sauce—traditionally a mustard-mayo dip. We think this mix of fresh parsley, horseradish, and mayonnaise is even more appealing. To help your guests get to the succulent meat, crack the claws and set out oyster forks. ■

1 cup packed fresh flat-leaf parsley leaves
¼ cup drained bottled horseradish
3 tablespoons water
1 cup mayonnaise
1 tablespoon distilled white vinegar
¼ teaspoon salt
¼ teaspoon freshly ground white pepper
24 large or 36 medium cooked stone crab
    claws (5 pounds; see Sources), rinsed if
    necessary
Crushed ice for serving

Combine parsley, horseradish, and water in a blender and blend until smooth. Transfer to a bowl and stir in mayonnaise, vinegar, salt, and white pepper until combined.

Crack crab claws with a mallet and arrange on a platter lined with crushed ice. Serve with sauce for dipping.

COOK'S NOTE

■ The sauce can be made up to 1 day ahead and refrigerated, covered.

Grilled Chicken Wings
with Two Asian Sauces

MAKES 24 TO 28 HORS D'OEUVRES
ACTIVE TIME: 1¼ HOURS ■ START TO FINISH: 1¾ HOURS
(INCLUDES MARINATING)

■ Chicken wings are casual fare—easy to make, messy to eat, loved by all. Because of their high proportion of crispy skin and bone to meat, wings don't need much to perk them up. We do, however, like to serve them with these two Asian-inspired dipping sauces. One, a traditional *nuoc cham*, is light but flavor-packed; the other, a chunky peanut sauce, shimmers with Thai red curry paste. ■

¼ cup vegetable oil
3 tablespoons fresh lemon juice
1 teaspoon salt
3 pounds chicken wings, tips discarded and wings
    halved at joint
ACCOMPANIMENTS: Red Curry Peanut Dipping Sauce and
    Nuoc Cham (recipes follow)

Whisk together oil, lemon juice, and salt in a large bowl. Add wings and stir to coat. Cover and marinate, refrigerated, for at least 1 hour.

If using a charcoal grill, prepare it for direct-heat cooking over medium-hot coals; if using a gas grill, prepare it for direct-heat cooking over medium-high heat (see Grilling Basics, page 512).

Drain wings and pat dry. Lightly oil grill rack. Grill wings, uncovered, turning occasionally, until cooked through and golden brown, 12 to 15 minutes.

Serve wings warm or at room temperature, with dipping sauces.

COOK'S NOTES

■ The wings can be marinated for up to 8 hours.
■ The wings can also be broiled on a lightly oiled broiler pan 4 to 6 inches from the heat, turning occasionally, until cooked through and golden brown, about 16 minutes.

Red Curry Peanut Dipping Sauce

MAKES ABOUT ⅔ CUP
ACTIVE TIME: 20 MINUTES ■ START TO FINISH: 40 MINUTES

¼ cup salted peanuts
1 tablespoon palm sugar (see Sources) or dark brown sugar
1½–3 teaspoons Thai red curry paste (see Cook's Note)
½ cup water, or as needed
2 tablespoons peanut or vegetable oil
3 large garlic cloves, finely chopped
1 shallot, finely chopped
2 (2- to 3-inch-long) fresh Thai chiles, preferably red, thinly sliced, including seeds

SPECIAL EQUIPMENT: an electric coffee/spice grinder

Pulse 3 tablespoons peanuts with sugar in grinder until finely ground. Finely chop remaining tablespoon of peanuts by hand.

Stir together curry paste and water in a small bowl until paste is dissolved.

Heat oil in a 10-inch heavy skillet over moderately high heat until hot but not smoking. Add garlic, shallot, and chiles and cook, stirring constantly, until garlic and shallot are golden, 1½ to 2 minutes. Stir in ground peanut mixture and cook, stirring, until a shade darker, about 1 minute. Stir in curry mixture and bring just to a boil, stirring constantly and adding more water 1 teaspoon at a time if sauce is too thick. Remove from heat and stir in chopped peanuts, then cool to room temperature.

COOK'S NOTES
■ The sauce can be made up to 4 hours ahead and refrigerated, covered. Bring to room temperature before serving, and add water, 1 teaspoon at a time, if necessary to reach the desired consistency.
■ If you use supermarket red curry paste, use 3 teaspoons (1 tablespoon) paste; if you use curry paste made in Thailand, use only 1½ teaspoons, since it is spicier.

Nuoc Cham
Vietnamese Dipping Sauce

MAKES ABOUT ¾ CUP
ACTIVE TIME: 10 MINUTES ■ START TO FINISH: 10 MINUTES

¼ cup Asian fish sauce
3 tablespoons fresh lime juice
3 tablespoons water
3 tablespoons sugar, palm sugar (see Sources), or dark brown sugar
2 small (1- to 1½-inch-long) fresh Thai chiles, seeded if desired and minced
1 garlic clove, minced

Stir together all ingredients in a small bowl until sugar is dissolved.

COOK'S NOTE
■ The sauce can be made up to 1 day ahead and refrigerated, covered.

Broiled Chicken Wings with Asian Plum Sauce

MAKES ABOUT 24 HORS D'OEUVRES
ACTIVE TIME: 30 MINUTES ■ START TO FINISH: 10 HOURS
(INCLUDES MARINATING)

■ Deeply flavored and well balanced, this plum sauce is a far cry from the pale imitation served at so many Chinese takeout restaurants, and it's absolutely delicious with the broiled wings. A bit of sugar tempers the plums' natural tartness, while anise seeds, fresh ginger, and dried tangerine peel add complexity. ■

1 teaspoon anise seeds
1 pound prune plums or red or black plums, halved lengthwise, pitted, and cut into ½-inch pieces
½ cup water
½ cup rice vinegar (not seasoned)
¼ cup sugar
2 garlic cloves, smashed and peeled

1 (1-inch) cube peeled fresh ginger, smashed
1 (1½-inch) piece dried tangerine peel (see Sources)
    or a 3-inch-long strip orange zest, removed with a
    vegetable peeler
¼ teaspoon red pepper flakes
2 tablespoons mild honey
    Salt
2 tablespoons soy sauce
3 pounds chicken wings, tips discarded

SPECIAL EQUIPMENT: a 4-inch square of cheesecloth

MAKE THE PLUM SAUCE: Put anise seeds in middle of cheesecloth, wrap up in cloth, and tie into a knot. Combine anise seeds, plums, water, vinegar, sugar, garlic, ginger, tangerine peel, red pepper flakes, 1 tablespoon honey, and ½ teaspoon salt in a 3- to 4-quart heavy saucepan, cover, and bring to a simmer over moderate heat. Continue to simmer, stirring occasionally, until plums fall apart, 15 to 20 minutes. Remove from heat and let stand, covered, for 30 minutes to develop flavors.

Discard anise seeds, and puree plum mixture in a blender (use caution when blending hot liquids) until very smooth. Cool sauce, and transfer ½ cup to a large bowl for marinade. Refrigerate remaining sauce, covered.

MARINATE THE WINGS: Add soy sauce and remaining 1 tablespoon honey to sauce in bowl, stirring to combine, then add wings, turning to coat. Transfer to a heavy-duty sealable plastic bag. Marinate, refrigerated, turning bag occasionally, for at least 8 hours.

COOK THE WINGS: Put a rack in middle of oven and preheat oven to 375°F. Line a large baking sheet with foil. Bring plum sauce to room temperature.

Arrange wings in one layer on lined baking sheet. Sprinkle with ½ teaspoon salt. Bake for 20 minutes. Turn wings over and bake until tender, about 15 minutes more.

Preheat broiler. Broil wings 4 to 6 inches from heat until browned, 2 to 3 minutes. Turn wings and broil until browned on other side, 2 to 3 minutes more. Serve hot, with reserved plum sauce.

COOK'S NOTES

- The plum sauce can be made up to 3 days ahead and refrigerated, covered.
- The wings can be marinated for up to 24 hours.

Sweet-and-Spicy Beef Skewers

MAKES 24 HORS D'OEUVRES
ACTIVE TIME: 30 MINUTES ■ START TO FINISH: 1¾ HOURS

■ These delicious skewers get their sizzle from red pepper flakes and guajillo ("gwa-*hee*-oh"), a dried chile common in Mexico and increasingly available in the United States. Guajillos, 4 to 6 inches long and leathery, have a mild to medium heat tempered by a hint of sweetness and smoke that pairs beautifully with beefy skirt steak. ■

1½ ounces dried guajillo chiles (about 7; see headnote
    and Sources)
½ cup chopped fresh cilantro
¼ cup mild honey
2 tablespoons fresh lime juice
3 garlic cloves
1¼ teaspoons salt
½ teaspoon dried oregano, preferably Mexican
½ teaspoon red pepper flakes
3 tablespoons olive oil
1 pound skirt steak, trimmed

SPECIAL EQUIPMENT: twenty-four 10-inch bamboo skewers,
    soaked in water for 30 minutes

Soak chiles in boiling water to cover, turning occasionally, until softened, about 45 minutes.

Drain chiles and transfer to a cutting board. When chiles are cool enough to handle, stem, halve, and seed them. Scrape pulp from skin with a sharp knife; discard skin. Transfer pulp to a blender and add cilantro, honey, lime juice, garlic, salt, oregano, red pepper flakes, and 2 tablespoons oil. Puree until very smooth, about 30 seconds.

Cut steak diagonally across the grain into slices 3 inches long and ¼ inch thick. Toss with half of chile puree in a bowl. Marinate steak, covered, for 30 minutes to 1 hour at room temperature.

Meanwhile, heat remaining tablespoon oil in a small heavy skillet or saucepan over moderately low heat until hot but not smoking. Add remaining chile puree and cook, stirring frequently, until reduced to about ⅓ cup, 3 to 4 minutes. Pour into a bowl to serve as a dipping sauce.

If using a charcoal grill, prepare it for indirect-heat cooking over medium-hot coals; if using a gas grill, prepare it for indirect-heat cooking over high heat (see Grilling Basics, page 512).

Thread 1 or 2 pieces of steak onto each skewer. Lightly oil grill rack. Arrange skewers on grill rack with meat over coals or hot burner(s) and exposed part of skewers over cooler parts of grill. Grill, turning once, until grill marks appear and meat is medium-rare, 1½ to 2 minutes. Serve with dipping sauce.

COOK'S NOTES

- The beef can be marinated for up to 2 hours. Refrigerate after 1 hour.
- The beef skewers can also be cooked in a well-seasoned ridged grill pan over moderately high heat for 2 to 3 minutes.

Rice-Studded Chinese Meatballs

MAKES ABOUT 30 HORS D'OEUVRES
ACTIVE TIME: 20 MINUTES ■ START TO FINISH: 2¾ HOURS
(INCLUDES SOAKING RICE)

■ *Shen shu*, literally "pearls" in Chinese, are a staple in many homes in New York City's Chinatown, where they are often served as part of a large family-style meal. The gently seasoned meatballs are a delicious study in contrasts—in one bite, you get tender meat with scallions and crunchy water chestnuts, all coated with satisfyingly chewy sticky rice. There's no reason to save these for a special Chinese meal—they are a delicious addition to any cocktail party. ■

    1 cup Chinese or Japanese short-grain sticky ("sweet")
        rice (see Cook's Note)
  2–4 outer iceberg or romaine lettuce leaves
    1 pound mix of ground pork (not lean) and veal or
        meat loaf mix (equal parts ground beef, pork, and
        veal)
    1 small bunch scallions (white and pale green parts
        only), minced (⅓ cup)
    ½ cup diced (¼-inch) rinsed and drained canned water
        chestnuts

    1 tablespoon cornstarch
    1 tablespoon Chinese rice wine, preferably Shaoxing,
        or medium-dry sherry
    1 tablespoon lightly beaten egg white
    1 teaspoon sugar
    ½ teaspoon Asian sesame oil
    1 teaspoon salt
    ¼ teaspoon freshly ground white pepper

SPECIAL EQUIPMENT: a large collapsible metal steamer rack

Cover rice with cold water by 1 inch in a bowl and soak for at least 2 hours.

Meanwhile, put a metal steamer rack in a deep 12-inch skillet or a wide 6-quart pot and add enough water to come to ½ inch below bottom of rack, then remove rack from skillet and line rack with lettuce.

Stir together remaining ingredients (except rice) in a bowl until well combined.

Drain rice in a sieve and rinse well under cold water. Drain again and transfer to a shallow dish.

Roll about 1 tablespoon meat mixture into a ball, roll in rice to coat, and transfer to steamer rack. Make more coated balls in same manner, using all of meat mixture (there will be leftover rice), and arrange in one layer on steamer rack.

Set steamer rack in skillet and bring water to a boil. Cover tightly and steam over high heat until meatballs are cooked through, about 25 minutes. Check water occasionally, adding more as necessary. Serve on a platter with toothpicks.

COOK'S NOTE

- Long-grain white rice can be substituted for the sticky rice; rinse it briefly in a sieve under cold running water.

Pork Belly Buns

MAKES 16 BUNS
ACTIVE TIME: 1¼ HOURS ■ START TO FINISH: 1 DAY
(INCLUDES BRINING)

■ This classic Chinese pork bun is the signature dish of David Chang, the chef and owner of several Momofuku restaurants in New York City. Make these at home, and the first bite—soft, savory, sweet, and crunchy—will prove they are worth the effort. If you live near a Chinatown, you may be able to find the steamed dough wrappers there and save yourself the trouble of making them. Look for plain unstuffed "flour rolls" or *bao*. If you can't find flattish ones that are simply folded over (which Chang prefers), split round ones and stuff accordingly. ■

FOR PORK
  ½ cup kosher salt
  ½ cup sugar
  4½ cups water
  2½ pounds boneless, skinless pork belly, cut into
      quarters (see Sources)
  ⅓ cup Chicken Stock (page 153) or store-bought
      reduced-sodium broth
FOR BUNS
  1 cup warm water (105°–115°F)
  1 teaspoon active dry yeast
  3 tablespoons sugar, plus a pinch
  2 tablespoons nonfat dried milk
  3½ cups cake flour (not self-rising), plus additional for
      kneading
  1½ teaspoons baking powder
  Canola oil for brushing
ACCOMPANIMENTS: hoisin sauce; thinly sliced cucumber;
      chopped scallions
SPECIAL EQUIPMENT: parchment paper; a deep 12-inch
      skillet with a domed lid or a well-seasoned 14-inch
      flat-bottomed wok with a lid

BRINE THE PORK: Stir together salt, sugar, and 4 cups water in a bowl until sugar and salt are dissolved. Put pork belly in a large sealable bag and pour in brine. Carefully press out air and seal bag. Lay in a shallow dish and brine, refrigerated, for at least 12 hours.

MAKE THE DOUGH: Stir together ¼ cup warm water with yeast and pinch of sugar in a small bowl. Let stand until foamy, 5 to 10 minutes. (If mixture doesn't foam, start over with new yeast.) Whisk in dried milk and remaining ¾ cup warm water.

Stir together flour and remaining 3 tablespoons sugar (do not add baking powder) in a large bowl, then stir in yeast mixture with a fork until a dough forms. Knead dough in bowl until all flour is incorporated. Turn out dough onto a floured surface and knead, dusting surface and your hands with just enough flour to keep dough from sticking, until dough is smooth and elastic but still soft, about 5 minutes.

Form dough into a ball, put into an oiled large bowl, and turn to coat. Cover with plastic wrap and let rise in a warm, draft-free place until doubled in bulk, about 2 hours.

WHILE THE DOUGH RISES, ROAST THE PORK: Put a rack in middle of oven and preheat oven to 300°F.

Discard brine and put pork fat side up in an 8- to 9-inch square baking pan. Pour in chicken stock and remaining ½ cup water. Cover tightly with foil and roast until pork is very tender, about 2½ hours.

Remove foil, increase oven temperature to 450°F, and roast until fat is golden, about 20 minutes more. Cool for 30 minutes, then refrigerate, uncovered, until cold, about 1 hour.

Cut chilled pork across the grain into ¼-inch-thick slices. Refrigerate slices in pan juices, covered, while you make buns.

MAKE THE BUNS: Punch down dough, transfer to a lightly floured surface, and flatten slightly into a disk. Sprinkle baking powder over center of dough, then gather edges of dough and pinch to seal in baking powder. Knead dough with just enough flour to keep dough from sticking until baking powder is incorporated, about 5 minutes. Return dough to bowl, cover with plastic wrap, and let stand for 30 minutes.

Cut out sixteen 3-by-2-inch pieces of parchment paper.

Form dough into a 16-inch-long log. Cut into 16 equal pieces. Lightly dust with flour and cover loosely with plastic wrap. Roll out 1 piece of dough into a 6-by-3-inch oval, lightly dusting surface, your hands,

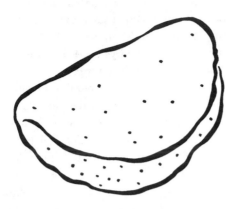

- The pork can be roasted and sliced up to 2 days ahead and refrigerated (in liquid), covered.
- The buns can be steamed up to 1 day ahead. Cool completely, then refrigerate, wrapped tightly in a double layer of plastic wrap. They can also be frozen for up to 1 week; when ready to serve, thaw the wrapped frozen buns in the refrigerator. Remove the plastic, wrap the buns in a dampened kitchen towel (not terry cloth) and then tightly in foil, and reheat in a 350°F oven until soft and heated through, about 15 minutes.

and a rolling pin with flour as necessary. Pat oval between your palms to remove excess flour, then brush half of oval lightly with oil and fold crosswise in half (do not pinch to seal). Place bun on a piece of parchment on a large baking sheet and cover loosely with plastic wrap. Make more buns with remaining dough. Let stand, loosely covered, until slightly risen, about 30 minutes.

Set a large steamer rack inside skillet (or wok), add enough water to come to ½ inch below bottom of rack, and bring to a boil over high heat. Carefully place 5 or 6 buns (still on parchment) in steamer rack; do not let buns touch. Cover tightly and steam until buns are puffed and cooked through, about 7 minutes. Transfer buns to a plate with tongs, discard parchment paper, and wrap buns in kitchen towels (not terry cloth) to keep warm. Steam remaining buns in 2 batches, adding boiling water to pan as needed.

Return buns (still wrapped in towels) to steamer rack in pan, off heat, and cover to keep warm.

ASSEMBLE THE BUNS: Preheat oven to 350°F.

Heat sliced pork (in liquid in baking dish), covered, until hot, 15 to 20 minutes.

Open each bun at seam with your fingers, brush bottom half of bun with hoisin sauce, and sandwich with 2 or 3 pork slices and some cucumber and scallions. Serve warm.

COOK'S NOTES
- The pork belly can be brined for up to 24 hours.

First Courses

Roasted Asparagus with Feta

SERVES 6
ACTIVE TIME: 10 MINUTES ■ START TO FINISH: 25 MINUTES

■ This is one of those simple dishes that never fail to impress. Roasting the asparagus spears caramelizes and concentrates their flavor, and then their residual heat warms the feta, releasing its tangy pungency. ■

   2½ pounds medium asparagus, trimmed
    2 tablespoons extra-virgin olive oil
    ½ teaspoon salt
    ¼ teaspoon freshly ground black pepper
    2 ounces feta, preferably French, crumbled

Put a rack in lower third of oven and preheat oven to 500°F.

Toss asparagus with oil, salt, and pepper on a baking sheet and spread out in one layer. Roast, shaking pan once about halfway through roasting, until asparagus is just tender when pierced with a fork, 8 to 12 minutes. Serve asparagus sprinkled with cheese.

COOK'S NOTE
- We prefer French feta because it is less astringent and salty than most supermarket choices.

Asparagus Flan with Cheese Sauce

SERVES 8
ACTIVE TIME: 25 MINUTES ■ START TO FINISH: 2 HOURS

■ Asparagus, joyfully celebrated every spring in the Piedmont region of Italy, becomes silky when pureed, which makes it an ideal component of a rich savory flan. Its fresh distinctive flavor pairs beautifully with another Piedmontese specialty, *fonduta*, a satiny sauce starring luscious Fontina d'Aosta cheese. Do not substitute the red-wax-wrapped Fontina from Scandinavia; only the gently nutty semifirm Italian cheese will do. This elegant recipe comes from the Andrea Hotel Ristorante in Santena, a small town outside Turin. ■

FOR FLAN
  2 pounds asparagus, trimmed
  4 large eggs
  1⅓ cups whole milk
  2 tablespoons finely grated Parmigiano-Reggiano
  1½ teaspoons salt
  ½ teaspoon freshly ground black pepper
  ¼ teaspoon freshly grated nutmeg, or to taste
FOR SAUCE
  ¼ pound Italian Fontina, rind discarded and coarsely grated (or cut into ¼-inch dice if too soft to grate; 1¼ cups)
  ½ cup whole milk
  2 large egg yolks
  1 tablespoon unsalted butter
SPECIAL EQUIPMENT: an 8-by-2-inch round cake pan; an instant-read thermometer

MAKE THE FLAN: Put a rack in middle of oven and preheat oven to 325°F. Butter cake pan and line bottom with a round of wax paper, then butter paper.

Steam asparagus in a steamer rack set over boiling water in 2 batches (or on two levels if using a multi-tiered steamer), covered, until very tender, 7 to 10 minutes. Puree asparagus in a food processor until smooth, 1 to 2 minutes. (You will have about 2 cups puree.)

Whisk together eggs, milk, cheese, salt, pepper, and nutmeg in a bowl. Whisk in asparagus puree. Pour mixture into cake pan.

Put cake pan in a larger baking pan and pour enough boiling water into baking pan to reach halfway up sides of cake pan. Bake until flan is set and a wooden pick or skewer inserted in center comes out clean, 50 minutes to 1 hour. Remove cake pan from water and transfer to a rack to cool slightly, 10 to 15 minutes.

MAKE THE SAUCE WHILE THE FLAN COOLS: Put all sauce ingredients in a metal bowl, set bowl over a saucepan of barely simmering water, and heat, whisking, until cheese and butter are melted. Stir with a wooden spoon until sauce is slightly thickened and registers 160°F on thermometer, 5 to 8 minutes. Pour sauce through a medium-mesh sieve into a sauceboat.

To serve, run a thin knife around edges of flan to loosen it, then invert a serving plate over pan and invert flan onto plate. Remove pan and discard paper. Cut flan into wedges and serve with sauce.

COOK'S NOTE
■ The flan can be made up to 1 day ahead and cooled completely in the pan, then refrigerated, covered. Reheat in a hot water bath (as above), loosely covered with foil, in a 350°F oven until a knife inserted in the center comes out very warm, about 30 minutes.

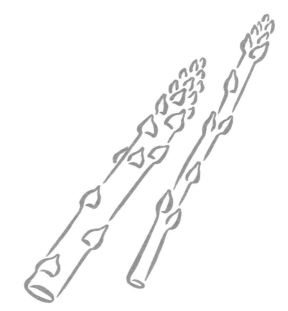

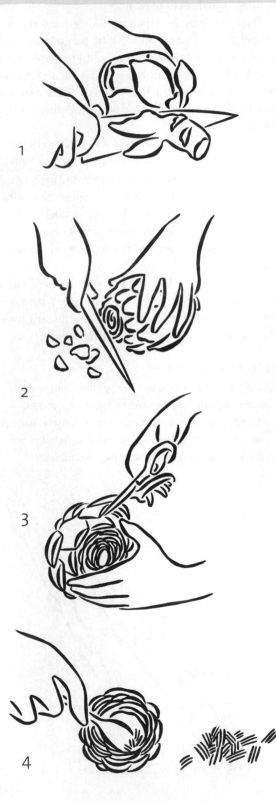

1

2

3

4

Stuffed Artichokes

SERVES 4
ACTIVE TIME: 1½ HOURS ■ START TO FINISH: 2 HOURS

■ A filling of sweet sausage, cheese, and toasted bread crumbs stuffed between the leaves gives these artichokes a heartiness worthy of a special course. Eat them as you normally would, scraping the leaves with your teeth—but in this case you'll get a flavor-packed filling too. Using a pressure cooker not only speeds up the cooking time, it results in incredibly tender leaves and hearts. Just one bite justifies making room in your kitchen for this time-saving appliance. ■

FOR STUFFING
  2 cups fine fresh bread crumbs from an Italian loaf
  ½ cup finely grated Parmigiano-Reggiano
  1½ tablespoons finely chopped garlic
  ¼ cup finely chopped fresh flat-leaf parsley
  ¼ cup minced sweet soppressata (dried Italian sausage; see Cook's Note)
  1 teaspoon finely grated lemon zest (optional)
  1 teaspoon salt
  ¼ teaspoon freshly ground black pepper
  ¼ cup olive oil
FOR ARTICHOKES
  4 medium artichokes (8–9 ounces each)
  1 lemon, halved
  4 thin slices provolone
FOR COOKING ARTICHOKES
  1½ cups water
  ½ cup dry white wine
  ¼ cup olive oil
  ½ cup finely chopped onion
  1½ teaspoons finely chopped garlic
  ½ teaspoon salt
  ¼ teaspoon freshly ground black pepper
SPECIAL EQUIPMENT: a melon ball cutter or a grapefruit spoon

MAKE THE STUFFING: Put a rack in middle of oven and preheat oven to 350°F.

Spread bread crumbs on a baking sheet and toast in oven until pale golden, about 10 minutes. Cool completely.

Toss crumbs in a bowl with Parmesan, garlic,

parsley, soppressata, zest (if using), salt, and pepper. Drizzle oil over crumbs and toss to moisten evenly.

TRIM AND STUFF THE ARTICHOKES: Cut off artichoke stems so artichokes will stand upright (1). Cut off top ½ inch of 1 artichoke with a serrated knife (2). Cut about ½ inch off all remaining leaf tips with kitchen shears (3). Rub cut leaves with a lemon half. Gently pull open center of artichoke and scoop out sharp leaves and choke from center with melon ball cutter or grapefruit spoon (4). Squeeze some lemon juice into cavity. Trim remaining artichokes in same manner.

Spoon about 2 tablespoons stuffing into cavity of each artichoke, then, starting with outer leaves, spreading leaves open as much as possible without breaking, spoon a rounded ½ teaspoon stuffing inside each large leaf. Top each artichoke with a slice of provolone.

COOK THE ARTICHOKES: Combine water, wine, oil, onion, garlic, salt, and pepper in a pressure cooker (without insert) or a large wide pot with a tight-fitting lid and stand artichokes in liquid.

Lock lid on pressure cooker and cook at high pressure, according to manufacturer's instructions, for 10 minutes. Put pressure cooker in sink (do not remove lid) and run cold water over lid until pressure reduces completely. Or, if using pot, cover, bring to a simmer, and simmer gently until leaves are tender, about 50 minutes.

With tongs, transfer artichokes to four soup plates. Spoon some cooking liquid around each one.

COOK'S NOTES

■ Genoa salami can be substituted for the soppressata.
■ The stuffing can be made up to 1 day ahead and refrigerated, covered.

Beet Carpaccio with Onion Marmalade

SERVES 6
ACTIVE TIME: 40 MINUTES ■ START TO FINISH: 2½ HOURS

■ In this interpretation of carpaccio, paper-thin slices of tender roasted beet stand in for the traditional raw beef and are lapped over a slow-cooked onion marmalade. Shavings of Parmigiano-Reggiano complete the trompe l'oeil and provide just the right counterpoint to

the sweet beets. Break out your best olive oil here—it will make a real difference. ■

6 large or 12 medium beets (3 pounds with greens), stems trimmed to 1 inch
3 medium onions, halved lengthwise and thinly sliced crosswise
3 tablespoons unsalted butter
Salt
½ teaspoon sugar
2 teaspoons balsamic vinegar
⅓ cup dry white wine
Freshly ground black pepper
¼ cup extra-virgin olive oil
1 (8-ounce) piece Parmigiano-Reggiano for shaving

SPECIAL EQUIPMENT: a mandoline or other adjustable-blade vegetable slicer

Put a rack in middle of oven and preheat oven to 400°F.

Tightly wrap beets in double layers of foil, making 3 packages (2 large beets or 4 medium per package). Put on a baking sheet and roast until tender, 1¼ to 1½ hours. Cool to warm in foil packages (the steam makes beets easier to peel), about 30 minutes.

Meanwhile, cook onions in butter in a 12-inch heavy skillet, covered, over moderately low heat, stirring occasionally, until soft, about 20 minutes.

Add ½ teaspoon salt, sugar, and vinegar to onions and cook, uncovered, stirring occasionally, until onions are very tender and caramelized to a deep brown, about 20 minutes more.

Add wine to onions, bring to a boil, and boil, stirring occasionally, until liquid is reduced to about 2 tablespoons, 3 to 5 minutes. Transfer mixture to a food processor and pulse to a coarse puree. Return to skillet and season with salt and pepper.

Just before serving, reheat onion marmalade, covered, over low heat.

Meanwhile, peel beets, discarding stems. Cut into ⅛-inch-thick slices with slicer (discard end pieces).

Divide marmalade among six large plates and spread evenly in a thin layer to cover plate, using an offset spatula or back of a spoon. Arrange beet slices in one layer over marmalade, overlapping them only enough to cover marmalade. Drizzle 2 teaspoons oil over each serving and season with pepper. With a vegetable peeler, shave 4 to 6 curls of Parmigiano-Reggiano over beets.

- The beets can be roasted and peeled up to 1 day ahead; cool completely, then refrigerate in a sealable plastic bag. To reheat, slice the beets, stack the slices in two piles, wrap in foil, and heat in a 400°F oven for about 10 minutes.
- The onion marmalade can be made up to 1 day ahead and refrigerated, covered. Reheat before serving.

Bhel Poori

SERVES 8
ACTIVE TIME: 50 MINUTES ■ START TO FINISH: 50 MINUTES
(INCLUDES MAKING CHUTNEYS)

■ The popular Indian snack known as *bhel poori* gets its flavors—at once savory, sweet, and spicy—from a combination of fresh vegetables and chutneys, while puffed rice and the fried chickpea noodles called *sev* contribute crunch. The ingredients are folded together and eaten immediately, before the mixture has a chance to gets soggy. *Bhel poori* is traditionally served with crackers, but we like to eat it with a fork. This colorful version comes from Gwen Oliveira, the mother of *Gourmet* art director Erika Oliveira. ■

½ pound white boiling potatoes
¾ cup finely chopped onion
1½ pounds firm but ripe tomatoes, cut into ¼-inch dice and drained in a sieve for 20 minutes
1 (1-pound) underripe mango, peeled, pitted, and cut into ¼-inch dice
½ cup coarsely chopped fresh cilantro
2½ cups (2 ounces) Indian puffed rice (see Sources)
2 cups (4½ ounces) unseasoned *sev* (thin crispy chickpea noodle pieces; see Sources)
Sweet Tamarind Chutney (recipe follows)
Spicy Cilantro and Mint Chutney (recipe follows)

Peel potatoes. Cover with well-salted water by 1 inch in a 2- to 3-quart saucepan, bring to a boil, and boil, uncovered, until just tender. Drain in a colander. When potatoes are cool enough to handle, cut into ¼-inch dice.

Just before serving, stir together potatoes and remaining ingredients except chutneys in a large bowl. Stir in ½ cup tamarind chutney and 2 tablespoons cilantro and mint chutney. Serve immediately, with remainder of chutneys on the side.

Sweet Tamarind Chutney

MAKES ABOUT ¾ CUP
ACTIVE TIME: 15 MINUTES ■ START TO FINISH: 15 MINUTES

■ If possible, use a block of Asian (Thai) tamarind rather than the Indian kind. It's usually thicker, softer, and easier to work with. Jaggery, an unrefined sugar made from sugarcane or date palm juice, has a distinctive winey sweetness that makes it indispensable to Indian cooks; if you can't find it, substitute dark brown sugar. ■

1 (4-ounce) piece tamarind from a pliable block (see headnote and Sources)
¾ cup hot water
¼ cup packed jaggery sugar (chop to measure if necessary; see Sources) or dark brown sugar
1 teaspoon coriander seeds
1 teaspoon cumin seeds
1 teaspoon anise seeds
½ teaspoon hot chile power, preferably Indian (see Sources)
½ teaspoon salt
SPECIAL EQUIPMENT: an electric coffee/spice grinder

Gently mash tamarind with water in a small bowl until pulp is softened. Force pulp through a sieve into a 2- to 3-quart saucepan, pressing on seeds and thick fibers; discard solids. Add sugar and cook over low heat, stirring, just until sugar is dissolved. Return mixture to cleaned bowl.

Toast coriander, cumin, and anise seeds in a dry small skillet over moderate heat, stirring, until fragrant and a shade darker, about 2 minutes. Cool completely, then finely grind in grinder.

Stir ground spices into tamarind mixture, along with chile powder and salt.

COOK'S NOTE

- The chutney can be made up to 2 days ahead and refrigerated, covered.

Spicy Cilantro and Mint Chutney

MAKES ABOUT ⅓ CUP
ACTIVE TIME: 15 MINUTES ■ START TO FINISH: 15 MINUTES

■ This herb chutney is delicious served with samosas (page 64), dosas, chicken, or fish. ■

  ½ teaspoon cumin seeds
  1 cup firmly packed fresh cilantro leaves (from 1 large bunch)
  1 cup firmly packed fresh mint leaves (from 1 large bunch)
  5–7 (1½- to 2-inch-long) fresh green Thai chiles (to taste), stemmed
  2 teaspoons *amchoor* (ground dried mango; see Sources)
  ¼ teaspoon salt
  3 tablespoons fresh lemon juice

Toast cumin seeds in a dry small skillet over moderate heat, stirring, until fragrant and a shade darker, about 2 minutes. Transfer to a food processor. Add cilantro, mint, chiles, *amchoor*, and salt and blend until herbs are very finely chopped. Transfer to a small bowl and stir in lemon juice.

COOK'S NOTE

■ The chutney can be up to made 4 hours ahead and refrigerated, covered (it will discolor if made further ahead).

Salt Cod in Tomato Garlic Confit

SERVES 6
ACTIVE TIME: 40 MINUTES ■ START TO FINISH: 1¾ HOURS,
PLUS 1 TO 3 DAYS FOR SOAKING COD

■ A rich reduction of tomatoes and golden garlic makes a wonderful accent to tender, snowy white salt cod in this Spanish-inspired first course. Lightly glazing the fish with mayonnaise and crème fraîche gives it a golden crown. ■

  1 pound center-cut skinless, boneless salt cod (*bacalao*), rinsed well and cut into 1½-inch pieces (see Cook's Note)

  8 large garlic cloves
  ⅓ cup extra-virgin olive oil
  4 (14- to 15-ounce) cans diced tomatoes in juice, drained
  ¼ teaspoon sugar
    Salt and freshly ground black pepper
  6 tablespoons mayonnaise
  ¼ cup crème fraîche

Cover cod with 2 inches of cold water in a large bowl and soak, refrigerated, changing water 3 times a day, for up to 3 days (see Cook's Note).

Drain cod and transfer to a 3-quart saucepan. Add 6 cups water, bring just to a simmer, and remove from heat. (Cod will be just beginning to flake; do not boil, or it will become tough.) With a slotted spatula, gently transfer cod to a paper towel lined plate to drain. Cover with a dampened paper towel and refrigerate.

Cook garlic in oil in a 12-inch heavy skillet over moderately low heat, turning occasionally, until golden, 10 to 15 minutes. Add tomatoes and sugar and cook, stirring frequently, until tomatoes break down into a very thick sauce and oil separates out, 45 minutes to 1 hour.

Mash garlic cloves into sauce and add salt and pepper to taste. Spread sauce in a 3-quart gratin dish or other flameproof shallow baking dish and arrange fish over sauce.

Preheat broiler. Whisk together mayonnaise, crème fraîche, and 1 tablespoon water and spread over fish. Broil fish 5 to 6 inches from heat just until mayonnaise mixture is lightly browned, about 2 minutes.

COOK'S NOTES

■ When shopping for the salt cod, look for a center cut, or *lomo*, which is preferable to the chewier end pieces.

■ Salt cod differs in degree of saltiness depending on the producer. A less salty variety may need only 1 day of soaking, while another could require up to 3. To test it, simply taste a small piece after 1 day of soaking; you want it to be pleasantly salty, not overwhelmingly so. When your cod is ready, remove it from the water, and, if not using immediately, cover and refrigerate (once desalted, it is as perishable as fresh fish).

■ The tomato confit can be made up to 2 days ahead and, once cooled, refrigerated, covered. Reheat before serving.

PRESERVING FISH

Long before the days of refrigeration and modern transport, cooks in maritime cultures around the world discovered how to preserve fish using techniques such as drying, brining, salt-curing, fermenting, smoking, and pickling, or some combination thereof. By happy coincidence, these treatments change and intensify the flavors of seafood, giving us delicious products that include smoked salmon, salt cod, and pickled herring.

DRYING Drying fish outdoors in the sun and wind is perhaps the most ancient method of preserving, and it's still used today. It works best with lean fish and shellfish, since fatty fish can turn rancid in the process. (Fatty fish are usually brined, salt-cured, or smoked instead.) In Southeast Asia and China, the world's largest producers and consumers of dried seafood, cooks use whole or ground dried shrimp as a seasoning; they also add reconstituted dried seafood, such as scallops, shark fins, and abalone, to soups.

BRINING The process of soaking fish in a concentrated saltwater solution inhibits bacterial growth yet allows complex flavors to develop through fermentation. As the fish sits in the brine, the salt penetrates the tissues and draws moisture out of them all at the same time. (Sugar acts in a similar fashion, and it sometimes replaces part of the salt in a brine.) Fatty fish such as herring are often brined (or pickled; see opposite page) in barrels.

SALT-CURING Coating fish in salt preserves it by drawing moisture out of the fish; at the same time, some of the salt is absorbed. One of the most common salt-cured fish is salt cod. The Swedish specialty called gravlax (see page 92) is another example of salt-curing, as are salt-cured anchovies, an indispensable ingredient as far as we're concerned. Canned anchovies or anchovy paste acts as a secret weapon in many of our recipes; used judiciously, the complex, concentrated-yet-not-fishy flavor gives a deep resonance to everything from spaghetti sauces to salad dressings.

FERMENTING Drawing hard-and-fast lines between drying, brining, salt-curing, and fermenting isn't easy, because bacteria play a part in all methods, and most fermentation begins with an initial salting, to control the bacterial action. The fermentation technique originated thousands of years ago in China and Southeast Asia, and it was used in ancient Europe as well (the Roman version of fermented fish, called *garum*, was used as both an ingredient and a condiment). Today you'll see a wealth of fermented fish sauces and pastes in any Asian or Indian market. Like anchovies, they are used to give a meaty, savory back note of flavor to dishes.

PICKLING Because a pickle can be any food preserved by submerging it in a brine or an acid such as vinegar, this category often overlaps brining and fermenting. (Brines generally encourage fermentation, and fermentation, in turn, encourages the development of preservative acids.) One pickling treatment popular in the Mediterranean is *escabeche*, a dish made by sautéing or frying seafood and then marinating it in a vinegar mixture (see page 339).

SMOKING Smoking fish both preserves and flavors it. Fruitwoods and other hardwoods all give different nuances to smoked fish (old oak whiskey barrels are used for producing the finest Scottish smoked salmon); hickory and mesquite can be overwhelming. There are two different kinds of smoking. **Hot-smoking** flavors the seafood and cooks it to an internal temperature of 150° to 170°F, giving it a flaky texture and an opaque appearance. Hot-smoked, or kippered, salmon and other fish is usually served in thick, generous pieces to prevent it from falling apart. **Cold-smoking** is a gentler method; it takes place, not surprisingly, at a cooler temperature, below 90°F, and the fish keeps its silky texture. It looks almost translucent and is usually served in thin slices. (Both hot- and cold-smoked fish are usually brined first.) Scottish smoked salmon, Nova, and pretty much everything else labeled "smoked salmon" is of the cold-smoked type. Though the term *lox* is often used to refer to cold-smoked salmon, true lox is not smoked at all; it's salmon that has been salt-cured.

Arctic Char Gravlax with Cucumber Jelly

SERVES 6
ACTIVE TIME: 30 MINUTES ■ START TO FINISH: 1½ DAYS
(INCLUDES CURING)

■ Gravlax—fish cured with salt and sugar—is usually made with salmon, but we like the milder, buttery flavor of Arctic char for this sophisticated first course. The shimmering, refreshing cucumber jelly has just enough gelatin to give it shape, and the jelly's delicate subtle cucumber flavor is sparked with fresh dill. If you choose not to make the jelly, the gravlax served on its own, with crispbread or buttered thin slices of rye bread, makes a great hors d'oeuvre. Note that the fish needs to be turned every 12 hours or so for 36 hours as it cures. ■

FOR GRAVLAX
   1 (1¼-pound) center-cut piece Arctic char fillet with skin, any pin bones removed
   ½ cup sugar
   ¼ cup kosher salt
   1 tablespoon coarsely ground black pepper
   3 cups coarsely chopped fresh dill (from 2 large bunches)
FOR CUCUMBER JELLY
   3 seedless cucumbers (usually plastic-wrapped)
   ¾ teaspoon salt
   2 teaspoons unflavored gelatin
   1 tablespoon distilled white vinegar
   1 tablespoon tiny fresh dill fronds
ACCOMPANIMENT: thin Scandinavian crispbread, such as Kavli

MAKE THE GRAVLAX: Pat fish dry and place skin side up on a large sheet of plastic wrap. Stir together sugar, salt, and pepper and rub 3 tablespoons of mixture onto skin side of fish. Turn fish over and thickly coat with remaining sugar mixture. Pack dill onto top of fish.

Wrap fish tightly in plastic wrap, then wrap in one or two more sheets of plastic (to prevent leakage; salt mixture will liquefy as fish cures). Transfer to a baking sheet and put another baking sheet or a cutting board on top of fish. Set a 3-pound weight (such as three or four soup cans) on top. Let fish cure, refrigerated, turning wrapped fillet over about every 12 hours and replacing weight, for 36 hours.

MEANWHILE, MAKE THE JELLY: Peel cucumbers, making sure to remove all skin, for a clearer jelly. Halve lengthwise, seed, and coarsely chop. Transfer cucumbers to a food processor and puree until smooth. Drain puree in a large fine-mesh sieve set over a bowl, pressing hard on solids to extract 2 cups liquid. Discard solids.

Stir together salt and ½ cup cucumber liquid in a small saucepan, sprinkle with gelatin, and let stand for 1 minute to soften. Heat over moderate heat, stirring, just until gelatin is dissolved, about 2 minutes. Cool mixture to room temperature.

Stir gelatin mixture into remaining 1½ cups cucumber liquid, along with vinegar. Pour mixture into an 8-inch square glass baking dish. Sprinkle dill fronds over liquid, pressing gently to submerge them. Refrigerate, covered, until set, at least 8 hours.

To serve, unwrap gravlax, discard liquid, and gently scrape off dill. Transfer gravlax skin side down to a cutting board. Holding a very sharp, long, thin-bladed knife at a 30-degree angle, cut gravlax across the grain into very thin slices, being careful not to cut through skin. Discard skin.

GRAVLAX

This lightly salted cured salmon, a Swedish specialty, has a compact, luscious texture and a clean yet rich flavor. Fresh dill is a classic seasoning. Along with salt and sugar, it's sprinkled evenly over the surface of a side of salmon or large salmon fillets, then the fish is weighted and refrigerated for a few days. The weighting allows the salt and sugar to penetrate and simultaneously draw out excess moisture from the fish, creating the brine and giving gravlax its characteristic tenderness. Gravlax (literally, "buried salmon") was first made in the Middle Ages by Scandinavian fishermen.

Gravlax is traditionally served sliced into paper-thin slices with a mustard- or dill-based sauce, but it's also delicious served like smoked salmon, on canapés or small pieces of buttered thin dark bread.

Cut jelly into 6 pieces and transfer to six plates, using a wide spatula. Arrange several slices each of gravlax next to jelly and serve with crispbread.

COOK'S NOTES
■ The cured gravlax can be drained and scraped, then wrapped in new plastic wrap and refrigerated for up to 5 days.
■ The jelly can be refrigerated for up to 4 days.

Mexican Shrimp Cocktail

SERVES 4 TO 6
ACTIVE TIME: 25 MINUTES ■ START TO FINISH: 25 MINUTES

■ Traditionally served in tall parfait glasses in Mexico, this colorful shrimp cocktail is almost like a cold tomato soup, bobbing with the sweet crustaceans, creamy avocado, and chopped onion. It's very refreshing and just spicy enough. A combination of Clamato juice, fresh lime juice, and hot sauce is the basis for the cocktail's signature flavor. ■

¾ pound medium shrimp (31–35 per pound), peeled and deveined
1½ cups chilled Clamato juice or 1 cup chilled tomato juice plus ½ cup chilled bottled clam juice
¼ cup ketchup
¼ cup fresh lime juice
1 teaspoon hot sauce, such as Tabasco
1 teaspoon salt, or to taste
½ cup finely chopped white onion
¼ cup chopped fresh cilantro
1 firm but ripe California avocado, halved, pitted, peeled, and cut into small chunks
OPTIONAL ACCOMPANIMENT: oyster crackers or saltines

Cook shrimp in 6 cups boiling well-salted water in a 2-quart saucepan until just cooked through, about 2 minutes. Drain, transfer to a bowl of ice and cold water, and cool in water for 3 minutes. Drain and pat dry.

Stir together Clamato juice, ketchup, lime juice, hot sauce, salt, onion, and cilantro in a large bowl.

Gently stir in avocado and shrimp. Spoon into 6- to 8-ounce glasses, parfait or margarita glasses, or cups. Serve with crackers if desired.

COOK'S NOTE
■ The shrimp cocktail can be made up to 1 hour ahead and refrigerated, covered.

Shrimp Gribiche

SERVES 4
ACTIVE TIME: 20 MINUTES ■ START TO FINISH· 1¾ HOURS
(INCLUDES CHILLING)

■ *Gribiche,* a classic French sauce made with hard-boiled eggs, cornichons, capers, and fresh herbs, deserves a return to vogue. We use white balsamic vinegar for this because it won't darken the sauce the way regular balsamic would. ■

- 1 pound medium shrimp in shells (31–35 per pound), peeled and deveined
- 3 tablespoons balsamic vinegar, preferably white
- ½ teaspoon Dijon mustard
- ½ teaspoon salt
- ¼ teaspoon freshly ground black pepper
- ⅓ cup olive oil
- 3 tablespoons chopped fresh basil
- 1 tablespoon chopped fresh flat-leaf parsley
- ¼ cup finely chopped drained cornichons (tiny French gherkins)
- 2 tablespoons drained capers, finely chopped
- 3 hard-boiled large eggs, finely chopped

ACCOMPANIMENT: soft-leaf lettuce leaves

Cook shrimp in 6 cups boiling well-salted water in a 2-quart saucepan until just cooked through, about 2 minutes. Drain and transfer to a bowl of ice and cold water. Cool in water for 3 minutes, then drain shrimp and pat dry.

Put vinegar, mustard, salt, and pepper in a blender and pulse until combined. With motor running, add oil in a slow stream, blending until well combined. Add herbs and pulse until finely chopped.

Transfer dressing to a bowl and stir in cornichons, capers, eggs, and shrimp. Refrigerate, covered, until cold, or for up to 1 hour.

Arrange lettuce on four plates and top with shrimp.

Hot Pepper and Garlic Shrimp

SERVES 8
ACTIVE TIME: 35 MINUTES ■ START TO FINISH: 35 MINUTES

■ *Gambas al ajillo,* served all over Spain in both rustic tapas joints and elegant restaurants, is the picture of simplicity, with the sweetness of the shrimp playing against the twang and spice of the hot red pepper and garlic. If you have a set of small earthenware *cazuelas,* this would be the time to use them. ■

- 10 large garlic cloves, thinly sliced
- ¼ teaspoon red pepper flakes
- ½ teaspoon fine sea salt
- ⅓ cup extra-virgin olive oil
- 2 pounds large shrimp in shells (21–25 per pound), peeled, deveined, and patted dry
- 1 tablespoon fresh lemon juice

ACCOMPANIMENT: lemon wedges

Cook garlic, red pepper flakes, and sea salt in oil in a 12-inch heavy skillet over moderately low heat, stirring occasionally, until garlic is pale golden, 4 to 5 minutes. Increase heat to moderately high, add shrimp, and cook, turning occasionally, until just cooked through, 3 to 4 minutes. Remove from heat and stir in lemon juice.

Transfer to a serving bowl and serve warm or at room temperature, with lemon wedges.

COOK'S NOTE
■ The shrimp can be cooked up to 1 hour ahead and kept, covered, at room temperature.

Vietnamese Summer Rolls

SERVES 4
ACTIVE TIME: 45 MINUTES ■ START TO FINISH: 45 MINUTES
(INCLUDES MAKING SAUCE)

■ Summer rolls with pungent herbs, crisp carrot, and bean sprouts are light and refreshing, a mainstay of Vietnamese cuisine. Our version of *nuoc cham*, the dipping sauce found at every Vietnamese meal, is a careful balance of fish sauce, lime juice, sugar, garlic, and chiles, and it's similar to those served in southern Vietnam. Organize yourself before assembling the rolls: clear off your work surface and line up your bowls of fillings in the order you want to layer them in (the order doesn't matter so much as rolling the bundles up snugly). ■

1½ ounces rice stick noodles (rice vermicelli; see Sources)
    Salt
8 medium shrimp in shells (31–35 per pound)
2 medium carrots
1 teaspoon sugar
1 cup bean sprouts
½ cup loosely packed fresh mint leaves
½ cup loosely packed fresh cilantro leaves
4 Boston lettuce leaves, halved lengthwise, center ribs discarded
8 (8½-inch) rice paper rounds (*bahn trang*; see Sources), plus a few extra in case some tear
    Nuoc Cham (Vietnamese Dipping Sauce, page 80)

SPECIAL EQUIPMENT: a mandoline or other adjustable-blade vegetable slicer, preferably with a fine julienne blade

Cover noodles with hot water in a large bowl and soak for 15 minutes.

Meanwhile, bring 6 cups water with 1 teaspoon salt to a boil in a 3-quart saucepan over high heat. Add shrimp, reduce heat, and poach at a bare simmer, uncovered, until just cooked through, 1 to 2 minutes. With a slotted spoon, transfer shrimp to a sieve (reserve cooking water in pan) and rinse briefly under cold running water, then drain.

When shrimp are cool enough to handle, peel, then halve lengthwise, devein, and transfer to a small bowl.

Drain soaked vermicelli in a colander. Return reserved cooking water to a boil over high heat and cook vermicelli until just tender, 2 to 3 minutes. Drain in colander, rinse briefly under cold running water, and drain well. Transfer to a small bowl.

Cut carrots into 2- to 3-inch sections. Cut lengthwise into fine julienne strips (about 1⁄16 inch) using slicer. Alternatively, thinly slice carrot sections lengthwise on slicer, then cut lengthwise into fine julienne with a sharp knife. Toss carrots with sugar in a small bowl and let stand for 5 minutes.

Lay a clean dry kitchen towel on a work surface. Put bean sprouts, herbs, and lettuce leaves in separate bowls and arrange near towel, along with bowls of shrimp, vermicelli, and carrots. Fill a 12-inch skillet halfway with water and heat to warm over low heat, then turn off heat. Check 1 rice paper round to make sure it doesn't have any holes, soak in warm water until pliable, about 15 seconds, and then carefully transfer to towel with your fingers. Arrange 2 shrimp halves in a row, cut sides up, on bottom third of soaked rice paper. Roll up a lettuce leaf half from a long side and put on top of shrimp, then layer one eighth of each remaining ingredient (except sauce) on top of lettuce, leaving about a 2-inch border on either side. Fold bottom of rice paper over filling and roll up tightly, folding in sides as soon as filling is enclosed. Transfer roll seam side down to a platter. Make 7 more rolls in same manner, reheating water in skillet as necessary.

Serve rolls whole (2 per person), or cut rolls crosswise into quarters and stand up 8 pieces on each of four plates. Serve nuoc cham on the side.

COOK'S NOTE

■ The summer rolls can be assembled (but not cut) up to 4 hours ahead and refrigerated, wrapped in plastic wrap. Cut into quarters just before serving if desired.

Mussel Cassoulette

SERVES 8 TO 10
ACTIVE TIME: 40 MINUTES ■ START TO FINISH:
40 MINUTES

■ In this recipe, steamed mussels are bathed in a deeply flavored sauce of tomatoes, the reserved mussel cooking liquid, Dijon mustard, and crème fraîche, which adds a slightly tangy, creamy character to the mix. The dish is very rich, so a small bowl with a side of golden toasts is all you need to make you very happy. ■

20 (¼-inch-thick) baguette slices
2 tablespoons extra virgin olive oil
2 pounds mussels, preferably cultivated, scrubbed
    and beards removed
1 (12-ounce) can lager
3 tablespoons unsalted butter
1 medium onion, finely chopped
2 medium celery ribs, finely chopped
3 garlic cloves, finely chopped
1 (14- to 15-ounce) can diced tomatoes in juice,
    drained
1 California bay leaf or 2 Turkish bay leaves
1 teaspoon finely chopped fresh thyme
    Salt and freshly ground black pepper
1 (7 ounce) container (¾ cup plus 2 tablespoons)
    crème fraîche
1 tablespoon Dijon mustard
¼ cup chopped fresh flat-leaf parsley

Preheat broiler. Arrange bread slices in one layer on a baking sheet and lightly brush tops with oil. Broil 4 to 6 inches from heat until golden, about 30 seconds. Turn toasts over and brush with remaining oil, then broil until golden, about 30 seconds more.

Cook mussels in lager in a 5- to 6-quart wide heavy pot, tightly covered, over moderately high heat just until they open wide, checking frequently after 4 minutes and transferring opened mussels to a baking sheet with a slotted spoon. Discard any mussels that remain unopened after 8 minutes. Remove pot from heat and reserve cooking liquid.

When mussels are cool enough to handle, shuck and transfer to a small bowl (discard shells). Cover with plastic wrap. Pour reserved liquid through a fine-mesh sieve into another small bowl.

Heat butter in a 2-quart heavy saucepan over moderately high heat until foam subsides. Add onion, celery, garlic, tomatoes, bay leaf, thyme, ½ teaspoon salt, and ¼ teaspoon pepper and cook, stirring occasionally, until vegetables are softened, about 6 minutes. Whisk in mussel broth, crème fraîche, and mustard, reduce heat to moderate, and cook, whisking occasionally, until sauce is slightly thickened, 12 to 15 minutes. Remove bay leaf.

Add mussels and parsley and simmer just until mussels are heated through. Season with salt and pepper. Transfer mussels and sauce to small bowls and serve with toasts.

COOK'S NOTES
■ The toasts can be made up to 2 hours ahead and kept, covered, at room temperature.
■ The sauce (without the mussels and parsley added) can be made and the mussels cooked up to 1 day ahead. Cool the sauce, uncovered, then refrigerate, covered. Cover and refrigerate the shucked mussels. Just before serving, reheat the sauce gently, then stir in the mussels and parsley and simmer gently until heated through.

Goan Curried Clams or Mussels

SERVES 4
ACTIVE TIME: 20 MINUTES ■ START TO FINISH: 25 MINUTES

■ Goa, on the western coast of India, was a Portuguese colony for hundreds of years, and this mild seafood curry, from writer Laxmi Hiremath, is a delicious example of how the two cuisines mixed over the centuries. It's well spiced—with ginger, paprika, coriander, and cumin—but not spicy, and it's finished with fresh cilantro, grated coconut, and lime juice. Be sure to serve soft Portuguese rolls on the side to soak up the sauce. ■

1½ tablespoons vegetable oil

1 medium onion, finely chopped

1 tablespoon finely grated peeled fresh ginger

2 teaspoons sweet paprika

1 teaspoon ground coriander

½ teaspoon ground cumin

¼ teaspoon cayenne

½ cup well-stirred canned unsweetened coconut milk

2 pounds small hard-shelled clams (less than 2 inches wide) or cockles, scrubbed, or mussels, preferably cultivated, scrubbed and beards removed

1 tablespoon fresh lime or lemon juice

2 tablespoons chopped fresh cilantro

½ cup unsweetened dried coconut

Heat oil in a 5- to 6-quart heavy pot over moderate heat until hot but not smoking. Add onion and ginger and cook, stirring occasionally, until lightly browned, 5 to 6 minutes. Add spices and cook, stirring, until fragrant, about 1 minute. Add coconut milk and bring to a gentle boil. Add clams (or mussels), cover, and boil gently, stirring occasionally, until opened wide, 6 to 8 minutes; check frequently after 6 minutes and transfer opened clams to a bowl. Discard any clams that haven't opened after 10 minutes.

Divide clams and cooking liquid among four bowls and sprinkle with lime juice, cilantro, and coconut.

Deviled Crab

SERVES 8

ACTIVE TIME: 30 MINUTES ■ START TO FINISH: 50 MINUTES

■ We adapted this classic Charleston recipe from the Southern food expert John Martin Taylor, who insists that it must be seasoned with the traditional sherry pepper sauce. This robust Bermuda condiment, made from sherry, peppers, and spices, offers layers of both heat and sweetness (you can substitute cayenne if necessary). Taylor likes to bake and serve the deviled crabmeat in crab backs (shells). If you buy crabmeat already picked from the shell, bake the deviled crab in store-bought scallop shells or ramekins. ■

1 stick (8 tablespoons) unsalted butter

½ cup finely chopped sweet onion, such as Vidalia

½ cup finely chopped celery

1 pound jumbo lump crabmeat, picked over for shells and cartilage

1½ tablespoons fresh lemon juice

8 saltines

¼ cup medium-dry sherry, such as Amontillado, or to taste

Sherry pepper sauce (see Sources) or cayenne

¼ teaspoon salt, or to taste

SPECIAL EQUIPMENT: eight 5-inch scallop shells (see Sources) or 3-ounce shallow ramekins

Put a rack in middle of oven and preheat oven to 350°F.

Heat butter in a 10-inch heavy skillet over moderate heat until foam subsides. Add onion and celery and cook, stirring, until softened, about 2 minutes. Remove from heat and cool.

Gently toss crab with lemon juice. Coarsely crush saltines with your hands in a large bowl. Stir in onion mixture, sherry, sherry pepper sauce to taste, and salt. Fold in crab.

Divide crab among scallop shells (or ramekins). Put on a large baking sheet and bake until lightly browned on top, about 20 minutes.

Scrambled Eggs en Coque with Caviar

SERVES 6

ACTIVE TIME: 45 MINUTES ■ START TO FINISH: 45 MINUTES

■ Eggshells—the *"coque"* part of the recipe title—filled with creamy scrambled eggs and topped with glistening caviar are a pure French indulgence that will make any meal instantly memorable. Whisking eggs constantly in a double boiler produces a voluptuous, custardlike result—a delightful contrast to the briny snap of the caviar.

Fans of soft-boiled eggs are old hands at carefully removing the tops of shells by tapping them with the edge of a knife; for the rest of us, there are egg toppers. These nifty little tools, which cleanly lop off the tops of eggs, range from inexpensive plastic cutters to fancy spring-loaded plungers and can be found at many kitchenware shops. ■

 6 large eggs (still in shells)
 2 tablespoons heavy cream
 5 tablespoons unsalted butter
 ¼ teaspoon salt
 ¼ teaspoon freshly ground black pepper
 3 (½-inch-thick) slices firm white bread, crusts discarded
 1 (50-gram) jar caviar

SPECIAL EQUIPMENT: 6 eggcups; 6 demitasse spoons

Holding 1 egg narrow end up, remove top ½ inch of shell with an egg topper or a sharp paring knife and discard. Pour egg into a bowl and reserve shell. Repeat with remaining eggs, combining eggs in bowl.

Rinse eggshells gently in water. Submerge in a 2-quart saucepan of water and bring to a boil, covered. Remove from heat, leaving shells in water to keep warm.

Add cream to eggs and whisk until well combined. Melt 4 tablespoons butter in a double boiler or in a metal bowl set over a saucepan of barely simmering water. Add egg mixture and cook, whisking gently but constantly, until eggs are the consistency of pudding (thick enough to mound), 15 to 20 minutes. Remove from heat and whisk in salt, pepper, and remaining tablespoon butter. Transfer to a 2-cup glass measuring cup and cover to keep warm.

Toast bread and cut into long ½-inch-wide strips.

While bread toasts, drain eggshells upside down on paper towels.

Put shells in eggcups, then pour egg mixture into shells, guiding flow with a small spoon. (Alternatively, put shells in an empty egg carton to stabilize while filling, then wipe shells clean before transferring to eggcups.) Spoon caviar on top of eggs and serve with toast fingers and demitasse spoons.

SUSTAINABLE CAVIAR

The most prized caviar comes from sturgeon in the Caspian Sea, but those fish are threatened by pollution, habitat loss, and overfishing. Perhaps the future of caviar is on the farm: several domestic caviars from farmed fish have the wonderful, burst-in-the-mouth texture of the real thing. We like Sterling Classic white sturgeon caviar from Stolt Sea Farm, in California, and the domestic osetra from Russ & Daughters, a specialty foods shop in New York City: both have a clean taste and a terrific texture. The rainbow trout caviar produced by Sunburst Trout Company, in Canton, North Carolina, has a lovely flavor that is concentrated yet mild at the same time.

As for wild-fish choices, crisp-textured orange-red Japanese *tobiko* (flying-fish roe), commonly used as a topping for sushi, also comes in handy as a garnish (see page 49). Salmon roe, which usually comes from wild Alaskan fish, is another sustainable choice. For most preparations, we don't recommend the lumpfish caviar available in supermarkets; although it looks somewhat like sturgeon caviar, that's where the similarity ends.

Creamy Shad Roe
with Lime Salt

SERVES 6
ACTIVE TIME: 20 MINUTES ■ START TO FINISH: 25 MINUTES

■ As much as asparagus, ramps, and the first tender lettuces at the farmers market, shad roe is a herald of spring. That's when the fish move from the sea to the refuge of coastal rivers to spawn. Though shad roe is often served with lemon butter as a main course, we love chef Thomas Keller's approach. He treats the roe as the eggs they are, gently "scrambling" them in butter until just cooked and then sprinkling them with lime salt and dried bonito flakes, which amplify the roe's briny flavor. The result is very rich; a spoonful or two is all you need to make a big impression at the beginning of a meal. When shopping for shad roe, look for lobes that are creamy and fresh-looking. ■

1 pair shad roe (about 8 ounces)
½ teaspoon flaky sea salt, such as Maldon
2 tablespoons cold unsalted butter, cut
   into ½-inch cubes
   Lime Salt (recipe follows)
   Dried bonito flakes (*katsuobushi;* see
   Sources)

Rinse roe briefly and pat dry, handling it gently to prevent membranes from tearing. Put roe on a plate and carefully slit egg sac lengthwise from end to end with a sharp knife. Open egg sac and gently scrape roe from membranes with a rubber spatula into a medium-mesh sieve set over a bowl. Force roe through sieve with spatula to remove any membranes. Gently stir sea salt into roe, transfer roe to a small saucepan, and add butter. Cook over low heat, stirring gently but constantly, until thickened, 2 to 3 minutes.

Divide roe among six small plates or shot glasses. Top each serving with a pinch of lime salt and bonito flakes.

COOK'S NOTE

■ The roe can be removed from the egg sac up to 3 hours before cooking and refrigerated, covered.

Lime Salt

MAKES 1 TEASPOON
ACTIVE TIME: 2 MINUTES ■ START TO FINISH: 2 MINUTES

½ teaspoon flaky sea salt, such as Maldon
½ teaspoon finely grated lime zest

Mix together salt and zest with your fingers until blended.

Spring Vegetable
Terrine en Gelée

SERVES 8
ACTIVE TIME: 1 HOUR ■ START TO FINISH: 6 HOURS
(INCLUDES CHILLING)

■ This gorgeous terrine is a sophisticated change of pace from a green salad to start the meal. Don't be tempted to substitute large red beets for the baby yellow and pink ones called for here; they would muddy the terrine's delicate color and flavor. Since the vegetables are cooked until very tender, the terrine slices beautifully. ■

1¾ pounds mixed baby (1- to 1½-inch) golden and
   Chioggia (candy-stripe) beets (12–18 beets),
   stems trimmed to 1 inch
   Salt
1½ cups dry white wine
2 large leeks (about 1½ pounds total), root ends
   trimmed, discolored leaves discarded, coarsely
   chopped and washed well
2 carrots, sliced
2 shallots, sliced
1 small celery rib, sliced
10 black peppercorns
3¼ cups water
1 large bunch fresh chives
1 large bunch fresh chervil or flat-leaf parsley,
   small sprigs removed (about ½ cup), stems
   reserved
1 large bunch fresh tarragon, leaves removed
   (about ⅓ cup), stems reserved
   Freshly ground black pepper

4 teaspoons unflavored gelatin (from two ¼-ounce
   envelopes)
1½ pounds thin asparagus
¼ cup extra-virgin olive oil
   Fleur de sel

SPECIAL EQUIPMENT: a 6-cup terrine mold or loaf pan
(about 8½ by 4½ by 2¾ inches deep)

ROAST THE BEETS: Put a rack in middle of oven and
preheat oven to 450°F.

Divide beets into 2 mounds and wrap each mound
in heavy-duty foil or a double layer of regular foil. Put
packets on a small baking sheet and roast until beets
are very tender, 1¼ to 1½ hours.

Let beets stand, still wrapped in foil, for 15 minutes (the steam makes peeling easier), then carefully
unwrap, peel, discarding stems, and quarter lengthwise. Season lightly with salt.

MEANWHILE, MAKE THE GELÉE: Combine wine,
leeks, carrots, shallots, celery, 1 teaspoon salt, peppercorns, and 3 cups water in a 4-quart saucepan and
bring to a boil. Simmer, uncovered, for 45 minutes.

Cut off bottom third of chives (reserve remainder)
and add to leek stock, along with stems and about
one third each of chervil and tarragon leaves. Continue to simmer until liquid is reduced to about 2½
cups, about 10 minutes.

Pour stock through a fine-mesh sieve into a 1-quart
measuring cup or a bowl; discard solids. (If you have
more than 2½ cups liquid, boil until reduced.) Season with salt and pepper.

Sprinkle gelatin over remaining ¼ cup cold water
in a small bowl and let stand for about 1 minute to
soften. Add to hot stock and stir until dissolved.

STEAM THE ASPARAGUS: Trim asparagus to 6- or
7-inch lengths and peel with a vegetable peeler. Steam
in a steamer basket set over simmering water, covered, until very tender, 8 to 10 minutes. Transfer to a
bowl of ice and cold water to stop the cooking, then
drain and pat dry with paper towels. Season with salt
and pepper.

ASSEMBLE THE TERRINE: Very lightly oil terrine
mold. Line bottom and long sides with a sheet of
plastic wrap (cut to fit mold if necessary), smoothing out any wrinkles and allowing enough overhang
on both sides to fold over and cover top. Pour about
½ cup gelée into terrine and refrigerate until set,

about 45 minutes. (Or quick-chill in freezer, about
10 minutes.)

Meanwhile, coarsely chop enough of remaining
chervil, tarragon, and chives to measure ¼ cup. Refrigerate remaining herbs for garnish, covered.

Arrange one third of asparagus lengthwise in
terrine, trimming as necessary. Sprinkle with half
of chopped herbs, then top with half of beets, leaving spaces between vegetables for gelée. Arrange
another third of asparagus on top of beets. Sprinkle with remaining herbs and top with a layer of
remaining beets and then remaining asparagus.
Stir remaining gelée and reserve ½ cup. Carefully
pour remaining gelée over terrine, pushing down
vegetables if necessary, to just cover. Cover terrine
and extra gelée and refrigerate until terrine is just
set, about 2 hours.

Reheat reserved gelée over low heat, stirring, just
until liquified but not hot. Pour evenly over terrine.
Fold overhanging plastic wrap over top of terrine and
refrigerate until set, at least 2 hours.

To serve, pull back plastic from top of terrine. Invert a platter or cutting board over terrine and invert
terrine onto platter. Holding down plastic overhang,
lift off terrine mold, then discard plastic.

Cut terrine into 8 slices and put in center of eight
plates. Drizzle olive oil around plates and sprinkle
plates and terrine with fleur de sel and pepper. Scatter remaining herbs decoratively over plates.

COOK'S NOTE
■ The terrine can be refrigerated for up to 2 days.

Salmon
and Scallop Terrine
with Frisée Salad

SERVES 8
ACTIVE TIME: 1 HOUR ■ START TO FINISH: 2 HOURS

■ This leek-wrapped seafood terrine has a cloudlike
texture. Surprisingly, its lusciousness comes not from
cream but from a combination of olive oil and broth. It
can be served warm, or you can make the terrine a day
ahead and serve it at room temperature. ■

A terrine can be fancy, or it can be rustic. What it is *not* is a Frenchified exercise in nostalgia, nor do you need a degree from a cooking school to make one. Even though you do need to allot a fair amount of time, the techniques are within the skill set of every home cook. Most terrines must be made at least a day ahead of time to be at their peak, so, generally speaking, there is no last-minute fuss or frenzy in the kitchen, and they are enormously versatile. But the most important reason to make terrines is that they let you combine rich, deep flavors in interesting ways—plus almost all of them have the added benefit of deeply satisfying textures, at once reassuringly solid and gracefully yielding.

The terms *pâté* and *terrine* are used interchangeably these days, but strictly defined, a pâté has a pastry crust and sometimes a little layer of aspic that fills the space created when the baked meat has shrunk away from the crust. A terrine is essentially a crustless pâté named (like a casserole) for the container or mold in which it is baked. While the term *terrine* is most often applied to meat-based combinations, it can also refer to seafood, or even to an ethereally light assortment of tender spring vegetables suspended in gelée (see page 98).

Fat is crucial to any meat or fish terrine. The suspension of tiny particles of fat in the protein enriches and binds the terrine. Fat also acts as a preservative, keeping the terrine moist and delicious for weeks or even longer. In order to make that suspension happen, you need just the right proportion of fat to protein, and you need to keep everything *very cold,* from the moment you begin until you tuck the terrine into its water bath and slide it into the oven; otherwise, the fat may soften or melt before baking. The more fat absorbed by the forcemeat (the ground or pureed meat or fish, from the French word

farcir, "to stuff"), the moister the finished terrine will be. Keeping things cold is just one of the many reasons to plan ahead: read the recipe, assemble all the equipment and ingredients, and chill them.

The range of seasonings in many terrines may seem excessive and their amounts may seem persnickety. But careful seasoning is especially important when you are serving something at room temperature or chilled. If the right seasonings aren't there, or if they're in the wrong amounts, a finished terrine will taste flat and all of your time and effort will have been for naught.

As for what type of mold to use, it almost doesn't matter, aside from the volume. All sorts of suitable rectangular containers are available in many different price categories and materials, including earthenware and metal. Even a Pyrex loaf pan works, although a heavier pan will cook the terrine more uniformly.

A meat terrine needs to be weighted and chilled in the pan for a day after baking so that it will hold together and not crumble when sliced. To unmold it, let the mold sit in a pan of hot water for a couple of minutes to loosen the bottom. Pour off the liquid that has accumulated in the mold after the terrine has been weighted and invert the terrine onto a cutting board. Gently blot the outside (the bacon strips, in the case of the country terrine on page 102) with a paper towel and let the terrine stand for half an hour before serving. Then set it out on a buffet table with little toasts, cornichons, pickled onions, and Dijon mustard, and watch it disappear.

2 long medium-thick leeks

1½ cups water

½ cup dry white wine

¼ cup chopped onion

2 tablespoons finely chopped carrot

4 large fresh cilantro sprigs, plus 2 tablespoons chopped fresh cilantro

2 tablespoons minced peeled fresh ginger

1 teaspoon coriander seeds, toasted (see Tips, page 911) and crushed with side of a large heavy knife

Salt and freshly ground white pepper

⅓ pound salmon fillet, skin and any pin bones and dark flesh discarded

⅔ pound medium sea scallops, tough ligament removed from side of each if necessary

1 large egg white, lightly beaten

6 tablespoons mild olive oil

FOR SALAD

2 tablespoons white wine vinegar

¼ teaspoon salt

⅛ teaspoon freshly ground white pepper

¼ cup extra-virgin olive oil

¼ pound frisée (French curly endive), torn into bite-sized pieces (4 cups)

2 Belgian endives, halved lengthwise, cored, and sliced crosswise

1 cup thinly sliced radicchio leaves (from 1 head)

1 teaspoon fleur de sel or kosher salt

½ teaspoon coriander seeds, toasted (see Tips, page 911) and crushed

2 tablespoons finely chopped fresh cilantro

SPECIAL EQUIPMENT: a 4-cup loaf pan (about 8 by 4 by 2¼ inches deep)

PREPARE THE LEEKS AND BROTH: Discard any discolored leaves from leeks, then cut off root end and discard. Thinly slice enough of dark green parts to measure ¼ cup. Wash well and reserve for broth. Set aside remainder of leeks for lining terrine.

Combine water, wine, sliced leek greens, onion, carrot, cilantro sprigs, 1 tablespoon ginger, ½ teaspoon crushed coriander seeds, ⅛ teaspoon salt, and ⅛ teaspoon white pepper in a 2-quart saucepan and bring to a boil. Partially cover and simmer for 20 minutes. Pour broth through a fine-mesh sieve into a bowl, pressing hard on solids; discard solids. (You

will have 1 to 1½ cups broth.) Set bowl in a larger bowl of ice and cold water and refrigerate until cold, 5 to 10 minutes.

Meanwhile, slit 1 side of each leek open lengthwise, cutting only to center, and peel off layers. Rinse layers in warm water to remove any grit. Cook in a 6- to 8-quart pot of boiling well-salted water until tender, about 10 minutes. Transfer with tongs to a bowl of ice and cold water to stop the cooking. Drain, spread leek layers flat on paper towels, and pat dry.

MAKE THE TERRINE: Put a rack in middle of oven and preheat oven to 325°F.

Lightly oil loaf pan. Line bottom and long sides of pan by draping some of leeks crosswise over bottom and up sides of pan, allowing at least 1 inch overhang on each side.

Cut salmon into 1-inch cubes. Add enough scallops (about 3) to total ½ pound and set aside.

Combine remaining scallops, 1 tablespoon egg white, ⅛ teaspoon salt, and ⅛ teaspoon white pepper in a food processor and puree until smooth. Add ½ cup cooled broth and blend well. With motor running, add 3 tablespoons oil in a slow stream, blending until incorporated.

Transfer scallop puree to terrine, using a rubber spatula, and smooth top (do not clean processor). Stir together chopped cilantro, ⅛ teaspoon salt, and remaining tablespoon ginger and ½ teaspoon crushed coriander seeds in a small bowl, then sprinkle evenly over scallop puree.

Add salmon and scallop mixture to processor, along with remaining tablespoon egg white, ⅛ teaspoon salt, and ⅛ teaspoon white pepper, and puree until smooth. Add ½ cup cooled broth and blend well. With motor running, add remaining 3 tablespoons oil in a slow stream until incorporated.

Spoon salmon puree evenly over herb mixture in terrine and smooth top. Fold ends of leeks over puree to cover, filling in any bare spots with pieces of remaining leeks. Cover surface of terrine with an oiled piece of parchment or wax paper (oiled side down).

Put loaf pan in a larger baking pan and add enough boiling water to reach halfway up sides of terrine. Bake until terrine is just cooked through (terrine will be firm to the touch and will come away from sides of pan), about 30 minutes.

Let terrine stand in loaf pan on a rack for at least 15 minutes before unmolding.

MEANWHILE, MAKE THE SALAD: Whisk together vinegar, salt, and white pepper in a small bowl. Add oil in a slow stream, whisking until well combined.

Toss frisée, endive, and radicchio in a large bowl with just enough vinaigrette to coat.

To serve, divide salad among eight plates. Put a cutting board over terrine and carefully invert terrine onto board. Cut into 8 slices. Divide among plates, then drizzle with remaining vinaigrette and sprinkle with fleur de sel, crushed coriander seeds, and cilantro.

COOK'S NOTES

- The broth can be refrigerated, covered, for up to 1 day or frozen for up to 1 month.
- The leeks for lining the terrine can be cooked up to 1 day ahead and refrigerated, rolled up in paper towels, in a sealed plastic bag.
- The terrine can be assembled up to 3 hours ahead and refrigerated, covered.
- The terrine can be cooked up to 1 day ahead and served at room temperature. Cool in the pan, uncovered, then unmold and refrigerate, covered with plastic wrap. Bring to room temperature before serving (this will take about 1 hour).
- The vinaigrette can be made up to 6 hours ahead and refrigerated, covered.

Terrine de Campagne

SERVES 12 TO 14
ACTIVE TIME: 1 HOUR ■ START TO FINISH: 3 DAYS
(INCLUDES MARINATING AND CHILLING)

■ This classic French country pâté, made of pork, veal, and chicken livers seasoned with Cognac, thyme, and allspice, can be served as an hors d'oeuvre or first course with the traditional accompaniments (see below), or as part of a picnic lunch with a hearty salad and a crusty loaf. Or put it on the table as an easy make-ahead supper with *céleri rémoulade* (see page 591) and steamed haricots verts on the side. ■

1 cup finely chopped onion
2 tablespoons unsalted butter
2 garlic cloves, finely chopped
1 tablespoon chopped fresh thyme or 1 teaspoon dried thyme, crumbled
2 teaspoons salt
1 teaspoon black peppercorns
½ teaspoon whole allspice or ¼ teaspoon ground allspice
¼ teaspoon freshly grated nutmeg
1 Turkish bay leaf or ½ California bay leaf
½ pound chicken livers, trimmed
1 pound ground pork shoulder or ½ pound ground lean pork plus ½ pound ground pork fatback
½ pound fatty ground veal, preferably veal breast
3 tablespoons Cognac or other brandy
2 large eggs
½ cup heavy cream
½ pound baked ham, cut into ½-inch dice
6–11 slices (about 8 ounces) bacon

ACCOMPANIMENTS: cornichons (tiny French gherkins); grainy mustard; crusty bread or crackers

SPECIAL EQUIPMENT: an electric coffee/spice grinder; a 6-cup terrine mold or loaf pan (about 8½ by 4½ by 2¾ inches deep); an instant-read thermometer

PREPARE AND MARINATE THE PÂTÉ: Cook onion in butter in a 10-inch heavy skillet over moderately low heat, covered, stirring frequently, until soft, about 10 minutes. Add garlic and thyme and cook, stirring, for 1 minute. Remove from heat and cool.

Combine salt, peppercorns, allspice, nutmeg, and bay leaf in grinder and pulse until finely ground.

Pulse livers in a food processor to a coarse puree. Transfer to a large metal bowl set in a larger bowl of ice. Add pork, veal, brandy, onion mixture, and spice mixture and mix with your hands or a wooden spoon. Whisk together eggs and cream until well combined, then stir into meats, along with ham.

Line terrine mold, covering bottom and long sides, with 6 to 8 crosswise strips of bacon, arranging slices close together but not overlapping and leaving a ½- to 2-inch overhang on either side. Fill terrine evenly with pâté mixture. Rap terrine on counter to compact it (it will mound slightly above edges). If overhang of bacon slices is not long enough to cover top of terrine, cover top of pâté with 2 or 3 lengthwise strips of bacon. Fold overhang of bacon strips over top of terrine. Cover with plastic wrap and refrigerate for at least 12 hours to allow flavors to blend.

BAKE THE PÂTÉ: Put a rack in middle of oven and preheat oven to 325°F.

Discard plastic wrap and cover terrine tightly with a double layer of foil. Put terrine in a small roasting pan and add enough boiling water to reach halfway up sides of terrine. Bake until thermometer inserted diagonally through foil at least 2 inches into center of pâté registers 160° to 165°F, 1½ to 1¾ hours.

Remove foil and transfer terrine to a rack. Let stand for 30 minutes (temperature will rise about 5 degrees). Pour out water and dry roasting pan.

WEIGHT THE PÂTÉ: Return terrine to roasting pan and put a sheet of parchment or wax paper over top of terrine. Place another terrine mold or loaf pan of the same size over paper (or use a foil-wrapped piece of wood or thick cardboard cut to fit inside top of terrine) and put a 2-pound weight (such as two or three soup cans) in pan (or on wood or cardboard) to weight pâté.

Refrigerate weighted pâté until completely cold, at least 4 hours. Then refrigerate, with or without weights, for at least 24 hours to allow flavors to develop.

TO SERVE: Remove paper and any congealed fat from top of pâté. Run a knife around edges of pâté, then put terrine mold in a pan of hot water for 1 minute to loosen bottom. Invert onto a cutting board and blot outside of pâté with a paper towel to clean. Let stand, loosely covered, at room temperature for 30 minutes.

Transfer pâté to a plate and cut into ½-inch-thick slices with a sharp knife. Serve with accompaniments.

COOK'S NOTES

- The pâté can be refrigerated before baking for up to 24 hours.
- The cooked pâté keeps, wrapped in plastic wrap and refrigerated, for up to 2 weeks.

Chicken Empanada with Chorizo, Raisins, and Olives

SERVES 16 AS A FIRST COURSE, 8 AS A MAIN COURSE
ACTIVE TIME: 1 HOUR ■ START TO FINISH: 3 HOURS

■ The word *empanada* comes from the Spanish *empanar*, or "to cover in bread." This wonderfully savory version may be Galician-inspired, but the salty sweetness of the added olives and raisins is Moorish through and through. We simplify the process in two ways: by making one large pie rather than the more traditional small ones and by using frozen pizza dough. Cut into squares, it is equally impressive as a first course or as part of a tapas party or cocktail buffet. Or pair with a salad and serve as a main course. ■

3 whole chicken legs, including thighs (2–2¼ pounds total)
Salt and freshly ground black pepper
About 4½ tablespoons extra-virgin olive oil
2 large onions, halved lengthwise and cut lengthwise into ¼-inch-wide strips
2 large garlic cloves, minced
2 Turkish bay leaves or 1 California bay leaf
⅓ cup finely diced (casings discarded if desired) Spanish chorizo (cured spicy pork sausage; see Sources)
½ teaspoon sweet *pimentón* (Spanish smoked paprika; see Sources)
¼ cup chopped green olives
¼ cup golden raisins
½ cup dry white wine
½ cup Chicken Stock (page 153) or store-bought reduced-sodium broth
1 pound frozen pizza dough, thawed
All-purpose flour for rolling

MAKE THE FILLING: Pat chicken dry and sprinkle with 1 teaspoon salt and ¼ teaspoon pepper. Heat 2 tablespoons oil in a 12-inch heavy skillet over moderately high heat until hot but not smoking. Add chicken and brown, turning once, about 6 minutes. Transfer to a plate.

Add onions, garlic, and bay leaves to fat remaining in skillet and cook, stirring frequently, until onions are softened, 4 to 5 minutes. Add chorizo and *pimentón* and cook, stirring, for 1 minute. Add olives, raisins, wine, and stock and bring to a boil, stirring and scraping up any brown bits. Return chicken to skillet, along with any juices accumulated on plate, reduce heat to moderately low, cover, and simmer, turning chicken once, until tender, 25 to 30 minutes.

Transfer chicken to a clean plate. Sauce in skillet should be the consistency of heavy cream; if it's not, briskly simmer until slightly thickened, about 5 minutes; remove from heat.

When chicken is cool enough to handle, discard skin and bones and coarsely chop meat. Stir chicken into sauce and discard bay leaves. Season with salt and pepper. Let filling cool, uncovered, while dough rests.

Form dough into a ball, wrap in oiled plastic wrap, and let stand at room temperature for 30 minutes.

FORM AND BAKE THE EMPANADA: Put a rack in middle of oven and preheat oven to 400°F. Grease a 15-by-10-inch baking sheet (jelly-roll pan) with 1 tablespoon oil.

Divide dough in half. On a floured surface, roll out one half (keep remaining dough covered with plastic wrap) with a floured rolling pin into a 15-by-10-inch rectangle. Transfer to baking sheet. Spread filling evenly over dough, leaving a 1-inch border all around.

Roll out remaining dough in same manner. Moisten exposed border of bottom dough rectangle with water. Place top crust over filling, pressing edges together to seal. Roll edges in and press to form a decorative rim. Cut a 1-inch hole to serve as a steam vent in center of empanada.

Bake empanada for 15 minutes. Brush dough with scant tablespoon oil and bake until crust is golden brown, 20 to 25 minutes more. Brush empanada with scant tablespoon oil and cool for 10 minutes in pan on a rack.

Slide empanada onto rack, using a wide metal spatula, and cool to warm, about 30 minutes.

Cut empanada into squares and serve warm or at room temperature.

COOK'S NOTE

■ The filling can be made up to 2 days ahead and, once cooled, refrigerated, covered. Bring to room temperature before using.

Sicilian Fried Stuffed Rice Balls
Arancini

SERVES 8
ACTIVE TIME: 1½ HOURS ■ START TO FINISH: 2 HOURS

■ These *arancini*, from reader Bridget Miraglia, are the best we've ever tasted. The crisp bread crumb coating gives way to tender, cheesy rice, revealing an inner pocket of savory meat ragù. Miraglia's family traditionally serves these fried rice balls at New Year's, but we think the morsels are worth the effort any time of year. ■

    4½ cups water
        Salt
     2 cups Arborio rice
     3 tablespoons unsalted butter
     2 tablespoons olive oil
     1 medium onion, chopped
     2 large garlic cloves, finely chopped
     ¼ pound white or cremini mushrooms, halved if large, thinly sliced
     ¼ pound sweet Italian sausage, casings removed
     ¼ pound ground beef chuck
     1 (8-ounce) can tomato sauce
     2 teaspoons finely chopped fresh oregano
     ½ cup frozen baby peas, thawed
        Freshly ground black pepper
     3 large eggs, lightly beaten
    1¼ cups finely grated Parmigiano-Reggiano (about 3½ ounces)
     3 cups fine dry bread crumbs
     8 cups vegetable oil for deep-frying

SPECIAL EQUIPMENT: a deep-fat thermometer

Bring water and 1½ teaspoons salt to a boil in a 3- to 4-quart heavy saucepan. Add rice, cover, and simmer undisturbed until water is absorbed and rice is tender, about 20 minutes. Remove pan from heat and add butter, stirring until melted. Spread rice out on a baking sheet to cool completely.

Meanwhile, heat olive oil in a 12-inch heavy skillet over moderate heat until hot but not smoking. Add onion and garlic and cook, stirring, until slightly softened, about 4 minutes. Add mushrooms and cook, stirring occasionally, until liquid they give off has evaporated and mushrooms are lightly browned, about 5 minutes.

Add sausage and beef and cook, stirring and breaking up lumps, until meat is no longer pink, about 3 minutes. Stir in tomato sauce and oregano and boil until sauce is slightly thickened, about 3 minutes. Stir in peas, ½ teaspoon salt, and ¼ teaspoon pepper. Transfer to a bowl.

Transfer cooled rice to a large bowl. Add eggs, cheese, and ¼ teaspoon pepper, stirring until well combined.

Stir together bread crumbs and ¼ teaspoon salt in a shallow bowl. Put some bread crumbs in cupped palm of one hand (crumbs help keep rice from sticking) and top with a level ¼ cup rice. Make a large cavity in center of rice mound with your finger. Spoon 1 tablespoon filling into cavity, then cover with another tablespoon of rice and form mixture into a ball. Roll ball in bread crumbs to coat, knocking off excess, and transfer to a wax-paper-lined baking sheet. Form more rice balls in same manner.

Heat vegetable oil in a 5- to 6-quart heavy pot over moderately high heat until thermometer registers 375°F. Fry rice balls in batches of 3, turning frequently, until golden brown, 1½ to 2 minutes. With a slotted spoon, transfer to paper towels to drain. (Return oil to 375°F between batches.) Serve warm or at room temperature.

COOK'S NOTE
- The rice balls can be fried up to 1 day ahead. Cool, uncovered, then refrigerate, loosely covered. Reheat in a shallow baking pan in a 350°F oven for about 15 minutes.

SOUPS

Soup is the ultimate comfort food. It is the endlessly simmering pot that sits on the stove all afternoon, whispering promises. It is the stuff of fairy tales. It is at the same time a dish so satisfying that it can make an entire meal and one so delicate that a few spoonfuls can whet the appetite for everything that follows. A good soup is the ultimate sign of a fabulous cook. And despite all that, soup is the most forgiving thing you'll ever make, the easiest kind of cooking.

Looking back, you find that once upon a time in America almost every meal began with soup. But as our dinners became less elaborate (and soup increasingly came from cans), we went through a period when serious cooks all but forgot how wonderful soup can be. That, however, is over. Many cultures consider soup an important part of any meal, and as we became acquainted with Vietnamese *pho,* tortilla soup with Mexican chiles, and spicy African chicken and peanut soup, we realized how much we were missing.

Soup was once the most familiar food on any menu, but it has turned into the most intriguing moment of the meal. All the interesting soups of the world have been appearing on American tables, from hearty Italian *zuppa di pesce,* filled with an intriguing array of fish and shellfish, to an outrageous Vietnamese chicken and pineapple soup whose bright flavors are enhanced by large handfuls of fresh herbs. There are cool soups for summer (chilled carrot honey soup with the flavors of Morocco) and thick soups that make a hearty winter meal (Italian wedding soup, gingered pork wonton soup with bok choy, and the great New Orleans classic, gumbo z'herbes).

If you still think that every fancy meal deserves a good soup to get it started, don't despair. This chapter has those too. Some offer an extraordinarily elegant way to kick off a gala event. What could be more delicate than clear, colorless chilled tomato consommé? Garnished with feathery slivered fennel and tiny bits of colorful tomatoes, it looks like a beautiful glass paperweight. Or more surprising than watermelon lemongrass soup with crabmeat? And for sheer impact, there is almost nothing like mushroom consommé with pastry hats. It was inspired by the famous truffle soup cooked up by master chef Paul Bocuse at his restaurant in Lyon, and it will leave your dinner party speechless.

Although these showstoppers take some time to produce, many of the other soups in this chapter come together very quickly. I believe that the best gift you can give yourself is a freezer stocked with homemade chicken stock, but should yours be bare, we have a solution: you can whip up a pressure-cooker stock in only 30 minutes, which means that the whole wide and wonderful world of soups is available on the spur of almost any moment.

You owe it to yourself. More than anything you'll ever cook, soup offers incredible dividends. Nothing else can send so much rich aroma into the air, and nothing else so effectively makes every house into a home.

SOUPS

Classic White Gazpacho

SERVES 4 AS A FIRST COURSE (MAKES ABOUT 4 CUPS)
ACTIVE TIME: 30 MINUTES ■ START TO FINISH:
3½ HOURS (INCLUDES CHILLING)

■ When we hear the term *gazpacho* today, we most often think of a chilled raw-tomato soup, but the earliest Andalusian gazpachos were true peasant food, made of stale bread, olive oil, vinegar, garlic, and water. Over the years, different areas of southern Spain developed their own gazpachos, including tomato versions, as the fruit began to be exported from the New World. This white gazpacho, adapted from the restaurant Parador de Gibralfaro in the port city of Málaga, gets its snowy color and creamy consistency from blanched almonds. Sweet green grapes are the essential counterpoint to the tang of garlic and vinegar. We love the restaurant's addition of shrimp. ■

  1 (3-inch-long) piece baguette, crust discarded
  ½ cup water
  1 garlic clove
    Salt
  ¼ pound blanched whole almonds
  1 tablespoon sherry vinegar, preferably "reserva" (see Cook's Note and Sources), plus additional to taste
  ½ cup mild extra-virgin olive oil
  2 cups ice water
  24 seedless green grapes, peeled
  12 peeled cooked small shrimp (about ⅓ pound)

Soak bread in ½ cup water for 1 minute, then drain and squeeze dry.

Mince garlic and mash to a paste with ½ teaspoon salt, using side of a large heavy knife.

Blend garlic paste and almonds in a food processor until nuts are as finely ground as possible. Add bread and vinegar. With motor running, add oil in a slow stream, then add ice water and blend well.

Force puree through a fine-mesh sieve into a bowl; discard solids. Refrigerate, covered, until cold, about 3 hours.

Before serving, season gazpacho with salt and vinegar if necessary. Serve topped with grapes and shrimp.

COOK'S NOTES

■ Regular sherry vinegar can be found in most supermarkets. "Reserva" is a finer-quality vinegar, which can be found in specialty food stores.
■ The gazpacho can be refrigerated for up to 2 days.

Peach and Tomato Gazpacho

SERVES 4 AS A FIRST COURSE (MAKES ABOUT 5 CUPS)
ACTIVE TIME: 20 MINUTES ■ START TO FINISH: 20 MINUTES

■ Drippingly ripe peaches and tomatoes hit the farmers market at the same time, so it seems natural to combine them in two ways in this refreshing gazpacho: first in the smooth soup itself, and then in the chunky salsa served on top. As your spoon swirls the salsa into the gazpacho, the interplay of textures and flavors—musky sweetness, gentle tartness, and the anisey note of tarragon—is a delight. The ice in the recipe gives the soup just the right chill, so you don't have to refrigerate it. If you don't have crushed ice, crush about ¼ cup ice in a blender. ■

  1½ pounds tomatoes, chopped
  1 pound peaches, pitted and chopped
  ¼ cup crushed ice
  2 tablespoons chopped shallot
  2 tablespoons olive oil
  1½ tablespoons white wine vinegar
  1 tablespoon chopped fresh tarragon
    Salt and freshly ground black pepper
  ¼–½ cup cold water

Combine two thirds of tomatoes, half of peaches, ice, shallot, 1 tablespoon oil, 1 tablespoon vinegar, 2 teaspoons tarragon, ¾ teaspoon salt, and ¼ teaspoon pepper in a blender and puree until very smooth, about 1 minute. Force through a medium-mesh sieve into a large glass measure; discard solids. Stir in enough water to reach desired consistency.

MAKE THE SALSA: Combine remaining tomatoes and peaches in a bowl and toss together with remaining tablespoon oil, remaining 1½ teaspoons vinegar, remaining teaspoon tarragon, and ½ teaspoon each salt and pepper.

Serve soup topped with salsa.

COOK'S NOTE
■ The gazpacho can be made up to 2 hours ahead and refrigerated, covered.

Chilled Tomato Consommé

SERVES 6 AS A FIRST COURSE (MAKES ABOUT 4 CUPS)
ACTIVE TIME: 1¼ HOURS ■ START TO FINISH: 3½ HOURS
(INCLUDES CHILLING)

■ It's not simple, but this delicate chilled consommé, best made with ripe plum tomatoes, is a showstopper. To clarify the broth, we whisk an egg white into the hot liquid; the floating egg-white "raft" attracts particles from the simmering broth, resulting in a crystal-clear consommé. The crucial thing is not to disturb or break up the raft. Mixing herbs into the egg whites gently flavors the broth, while a quick salad of pear tomatoes and fennel added to the soup just before serving contributes punch. ■

1½   pounds fennel bulbs with stalks and fronds (2 small bulbs or 1 large)
2   tablespoons olive oil
2   medium onions, coarsely chopped
2   garlic cloves, coarsely chopped
5   pounds tomatoes, preferably plum, quartered and pureed in a food processor
     Fine sea salt and freshly ground black pepper
8   large egg whites, chilled
¼   cup coarsely chopped fresh flat-leaf parsley
2   tablespoons coarsely chopped fresh basil
1   tablespoon coarsely chopped fresh tarragon
½   cup ice cubes, lightly crushed if cubes are large
10   ounces mixed yellow and red pear or cherry tomatoes, halved lengthwise
1½   teaspoons sherry vinegar

Cut fronds from fennel stalks and reserve. Halve fennel (with stalks) lengthwise and core. Separate layers and reserve 3 or 4 tender inner pieces. Coarsely chop remaining fennel, including stalks.

Heat oil in a 5- to 6-quart heavy pot over moderate heat until hot but not smoking. Add onions, garlic, and chopped fennel and cook, stirring frequently, until softened, 10 to 12 minutes. Stir in pureed tomatoes, 1 teaspoon sea salt, and ½ teaspoon pepper and simmer, uncovered, stirring occasionally, for 20 minutes.

Pour tomato mixture through a fine-mesh sieve into a 4-quart saucepan, pressing hard on solids; discard solids. Bring tomato broth to a full boil.

Whisk together egg whites, herbs, ice, ½ teaspoon sea salt, and ½ teaspoon pepper in a bowl until frothy, then quickly add to boiling broth, whisking vigorously 2 or 3 times; egg mixture will rise to surface and form a "raft." When broth returns to a simmer, find a place where bubbles are breaking through raft and gently enlarge hole to the size of a ladle. Cook broth, uncovered, at a bare simmer, without stirring (but keep raft opening clear by gently spooning out any froth), until broth is clear, 15 to 20 minutes.

Meanwhile, line cleaned fine-mesh sieve with a double layer of dampened paper towels and set over a bowl or large glass measure. Remove saucepan from heat and, disturbing raft as little as possible, carefully ladle out consommé through opening in raft, tilting pan as necessary, and transfer to lined sieve; discard raft. Refrigerate consommé, uncovered, until cold, about 1½ hours.

Just before serving, slice reserved tender fennel into thin slivers and toss with fennel fronds, pear tomatoes, and vinegar. Season consommé with salt and divide consommé and tomato salad among bowls.

COOK'S NOTE
■ The consommé can be refrigerated for up to 3 days; cover once it is cold.

Sweet and Spicy Chilled Carrot Soup

SERVES 6 AS A FIRST COURSE (MAKES ABOUT 6 CUPS)
ACTIVE TIME: 20 MINUTES ■ START TO FINISH: 1½ HOURS
(INCLUDES CHILLING)

■ Seasoned with cumin, coriander, and lemon juice, this soup grew out of our fondness for Moroccan carrot salad, one of the small plates traditionally set out at the start of a Moroccan meal. Its lushness belies its lack of dairy. ■

    1 pound carrots, cut into ½-inch pieces
    3 cups water
 1¾ cups Chicken Stock (page 153) or store-bought
       reduced-sodium broth
    1 medium onion, chopped
    1 teaspoon salt, or to taste
  ¼ teaspoon ground coriander
  ¼ teaspoon ground cumin
  ¼ teaspoon paprika
  ⅛ teaspoon cayenne
    2 tablespoons mild honey
 2½ tablespoons fresh lemon juice
GARNISH: 6 thin lemon slices; mild honey for drizzling

Combine all ingredients except ½ tablespoon lemon juice in a 3-quart heavy saucepan and bring to a boil over moderate heat, stirring occasionally. Reduce heat and simmer, covered, until carrots are tender, 30 to 40 minutes.

Puree soup in 2 batches in a blender (use caution when blending hot liquids) until very smooth; transfer to a metal bowl. Place bowl in a larger bowl of ice and cold water and stir occasionally until soup is cold, about 30 minutes. (Alternatively, cool soup, uncovered, then refrigerate, covered, until cold, about 4 hours.)

Stir in remaining ½ tablespoon lemon juice and salt to taste. Divide soup among six bowls. Float a lemon slice on top of each serving, drizzle with honey, and serve.

COOK'S NOTE

■ The soup can be made up to 3 days ahead and refrigerated, covered once it is cold.

Cold Curried Squash Soup with Chutney

SERVES 4 AS A FIRST COURSE (MAKES ABOUT 6 CUPS)
ACTIVE TIME: 20 MINUTES ■ START TO FINISH: 6½ HOURS
(INCLUDES CHILLING)

■ This chilled soup is much more delicious than its modest list of ingredients may suggest. The gentle nature of yellow squash is elevated by the zip of curry powder and turmeric, which also yield a sunny color. Dollops of sour cream round out the spice, and the chutney adds a sweet-hot note. ■

    1 tablespoon extra-virgin olive oil
    1 medium leek (white and pale green parts
       only), halved lengthwise, thinly sliced,
       and washed well
    1 teaspoon curry powder
  ¼ teaspoon turmeric
 1½ pounds yellow squash (about 3 large), halved
       lengthwise and thinly sliced
    4 cups water
    Salt and freshly ground black pepper
ACCOMPANIMENTS: sour cream and mango chutney,
       preferably Major Grey's

Heat oil in a 3- to 4-quart heavy saucepan over moderately low heat until hot but not smoking. Add ½ cup leeks (reserve remainder for another use) and cook, stirring occasionally, until softened, about 4 minutes. Add curry powder and turmeric and cook, stirring, until fragrant, about 30 seconds. Add squash, water, 1 teaspoon salt, and ¼ teaspoon pepper, bring to a simmer, and simmer, uncovered, stirring occasionally, until squash is very tender, 15 to 20 minutes. Remove from heat and cool mixture slightly.

Puree squash mixture in batches in a blender (use caution when blending hot liquids) until smooth and transfer to a bowl. Season soup with salt and pepper. Refrigerate, covered, until cold, at least 6 hours.

Serve soup with dollops of sour cream topped with chutney.

COOK'S NOTE

■ The soup can be refrigerated for up to 3 days.

Zucchini and Saffron Vichyssoise with Scallops

SERVES 6 AS A FIRST COURSE (MAKES ABOUT 8½ CUPS)
ACTIVE TIME: 1 HOUR ■ START TO FINISH: 5½ HOURS
(INCLUDES CHILLING)

■ This saffron-tinged vichyssoise is lighter than most, thanks to zucchini—its flesh is pureed with the potatoes and the julienned green outer portions make a pretty bed for the seared scallop garnish. Serve the soup in shallow bowls for a fancy opener to a dinner party. ■

2 pounds small (5-inch-long) zucchini
1 medium onion, chopped
3 tablespoons unsalted butter
1 pound boiling potatoes, peeled and cut
   into ½-inch pieces
1 teaspoon chopped garlic
¼ teaspoon finely crumbled saffron threads
5 cups Chicken Stock (page 153) or store-bought
   reduced-sodium broth
1 Turkish bay leaf or ½ California bay leaf
½ teaspoon fresh thyme leaves
½ cup very cold heavy cream
2 teaspoons fresh lemon juice
   Salt and freshly ground black pepper
4 large sea scallops (about 4 ounces total),
   tough ligament removed from side of
   each if necessary
1 tablespoon vegetable oil
SPECIAL EQUIPMENT: a mandoline or other adjustable-
   blade vegetable slicer with a julienne blade

With slicer, julienne each zucchini lengthwise into ¼-inch-thick ribbons, stopping when you reach seedy center. Turn zucchini and continue in same manner, turning zucchini as necessary. Cut zucchini centers into ½-inch pieces.

Cook onion in butter in a 5-quart heavy pot over moderate heat, stirring occasionally, until softened, about 10 minutes. Add potatoes, garlic, and saffron and cook, stirring, for 1 minute. Add stock, bay leaf, and thyme, bring to a simmer, and simmer, uncov-ered, until potatoes are tender, about 20 minutes.

Add chopped zucchini and simmer, uncovered, until zucchini is very tender, about 8 minutes. Discard bay leaf.

Puree soup in batches in a blender (use caution when blending hot liquids) until very smooth, then pour through a fine-mesh sieve into a bowl; discard solids. Stir in cream, lemon juice, 1¼ teaspoons salt, and ¼ teaspoon pepper. Cool, uncovered, then refrigerate, covered, until cold, at least 4 hours.

Meanwhile, blanch julienned zucchini in a 4- to 5-quart pot of boiling salted water (1 tablespoon salt) until crisp-tender, about 30 seconds. Drain and transfer to a bowl of ice and cold water to stop the cooking. Drain and pat dry with paper towels. Season with salt and pepper and refrigerate, covered.

Just before serving, cut each scallop horizontally into 3 rounds; pat dry. Heat oil in a large nonstick skillet over high heat until hot but not smoking. Add scallops and sear just until golden brown, 20 to 30 seconds on each side. Season with salt.

Serve soup with zucchini mounded in center and topped with scallops.

COOK'S NOTES

■ The soup can be refrigerated for up to 2 days.
■ The julienned zucchini can be blanched up to 2 days ahead.

Watermelon Lemongrass Soup with Crabmeat

SERVES 4 AS A FIRST COURSE (MAKES ABOUT 4 CUPS)
ACTIVE TIME: 1 HOUR ■ START TO FINISH: 1 HOUR
(3 HOURS IF SERVING CHILLED)

■ The rich red-orange color of this soup may fool your guests into thinking it's tomato, and they might take a sip or two before they realize they're actually tasting watermelon. Despite its robust color, this is quite a delicate soup, with warm hints of lemongrass, ginger, and chile. Paired with sweet lump crab, it makes an elegant first course served hot or chilled. ■

FOR SOUP

5 cups coarsely chopped seeded watermelon (from a 4-pound piece, rind discarded)
1 stalk lemongrass, root end trimmed and tough outer leaves discarded
1½ tablespoons mild olive oil
3 tablespoons finely chopped shallots
1½ tablespoons finely chopped peeled fresh ginger
1 tablespoon finely chopped garlic
1 small fresh hot green chile, such as Thai or serrano, finely chopped, including seeds, or to taste
2 tablespoons fresh lime juice, or to taste
Salt

FOR CRAB

10 ounces (2 cups) jumbo lump crabmeat, picked over for shells and cartilage
¼ cup finely chopped fresh cilantro
1½ tablespoons mild olive oil
¼ teaspoon salt, or to taste

ACCOMPANIMENT: lime wedges

MAKE THE SOUP: Puree watermelon in a blender until smooth and transfer to a bowl. (Set blender container aside.)

Thinly slice lower 5 to 6 inches of lemongrass stalk, then mince; discard remainder.

Heat oil in a 2-quart heavy saucepan over moderately low heat until hot but not smoking. Add lemongrass, shallots, ginger, and garlic and cook, stirring, until pale golden, about 5 minutes. Add about one third of watermelon puree, increase heat to moderate, and simmer, stirring, for 5 minutes.

Transfer watermelon mixture to blender and add chile, lime juice, and ¾ teaspoon salt. Blend until smooth (use caution when blending hot liquids). Add remaining watermelon puree and blend briefly. Season with more chile, lime juice, and/or salt if desired, blending if necessary.

Pour soup through a sieve into a bowl, pressing on solids; discard solids. Refrigerate soup, uncovered, for about 2 hours if serving cold, or reheat gently in cleaned saucepan to serve hot.

PREPARE THE CRAB: Toss crabmeat with cilantro, oil, and salt.

Divide crab among four soup plates, piling it in center; pour soup around it. Serve with lime wedges.

COOK'S NOTES

■ The soup can be made up to 1 day ahead and refrigerated; cover once chilled. Serve chilled or reheat gently to serve hot.

■ The crabmeat can be picked over up to 1 day ahead. The crab mixture can be prepared up to 1 hour ahead and refrigerated, covered.

Moroccan Minted Melon Soup

SERVES 4 AS A FIRST COURSE (MAKES ABOUT 4 CUPS)
ACTIVE TIME: 20 MINUTES ■ START TO FINISH: 1¼ HOURS
(INCLUDES CHILLING)

■ Melon soups are often served for dessert, but there's no question that this one belongs at the beginning of a meal. Its flavors are more modern Marrakech than country club. Lime, yogurt, and a hint of toasted cumin temper honeydew's sweetness, and the scattering of toasted sesame seeds seals the deal—they provide an unexpected nuttiness. ■

½ large honeydew melon, rind discarded and cut into 1-inch pieces (4 cups)
½ cup plain yogurt, preferably Greek
¼ cup packed fresh mint leaves
½ teaspoon ground cumin
¼ teaspoon salt
¼ teaspoon freshly ground black pepper
1 teaspoon fresh lime juice, or to taste
2 teaspoons sesame seeds, toasted (see Tips, page 911)

Combine all ingredients except sesame seeds in a blender and blend until smooth, about 30 seconds. Transfer to a bowl and refrigerate, covered, until cold, about 1 hour.

Serve soup with additional salt and pepper, if necessary, and sprinkled with sesame seeds.

COOK'S NOTE
■ The soup can be refrigerated for up to 8 hours.

Easy Carrot Soup with Toasted Pecans

SERVES 4 AS A FIRST COURSE OR LIGHT MAIN COURSE
ACTIVE TIME: 15 MINUTES ■ START TO FINISH: 45 MINUTES

■ The sweet essence of carrots, enlivened with a bit of cumin, is the star of the show here. A topping of buttery pecans adds a nice textural counterpoint to the smooth, cheery soup. ■

FOR SOUP
- 1 large onion, chopped
- ½ stick (4 tablespoons) unsalted butter
- 1¼ pounds large carrots, thinly sliced
- 1 teaspoon ground cumin
- 1 teaspoon salt
- 4 cups water

FOR PECANS
- ½ cup pecans, coarsely chopped
- 1 tablespoon unsalted butter, softened
- Salt

Put a rack in middle of oven and preheat oven to 350°F.

MAKE THE SOUP: Cook onion in butter in a 4-quart heavy saucepan over moderate heat, stirring, until softened, about 5 minutes. Add carrots, cumin, and salt and cook, stirring, until fragrant, about 1 minute. Add water, bring to a simmer, and simmer, covered, until carrots are very tender, 25 to 30 minutes.

MEANWHILE, PREPARE THE PECANS: Toast pecans on a baking sheet in oven until fragrant and a shade darker, about 8 minutes. Toss them with butter and salt to taste.

Puree carrot mixture in a blender in 2 batches (use caution when blending hot liquids) until smooth.

Serve soup sprinkled with pecans.

COOK'S NOTE
■ The soup can be made up to 2 days ahead. Cool, uncovered, then refrigerate, covered.

Cauliflower Soup with Stilton

SERVES 4 AS A FIRST COURSE (MAKES ABOUT 4½ CUPS)
ACTIVE TIME: 25 MINUTES ■ START TO FINISH: 1 HOUR

■ Even people who claim to dislike cauliflower fall over themselves to praise it when they taste this soup. The cruciferous vegetable and blue cheese seem to gentle each other's flavors and the result is suave and creamy. ■

- 1 medium onion, finely chopped
- 2 celery ribs, strings removed with a vegetable peeler, ribs finely chopped
- 2¼ cups 1-inch florets cauliflower (from about 8 ounces)
- 3 tablespoons unsalted butter
- 2 cups Chicken Stock (page 153) or store-bought reduced-sodium broth
- 1 cup whole milk
- ⅓ cup crumbled Stilton
- ½ cup half-and-half
- ¼ teaspoon salt
- ¼ teaspon freshly ground white pepper

GARNISH: croutons and crumbled Stilton

Cook onion, celery, and cauliflower in butter in a 3½- to 4-quart heavy saucepan over moderate heat, stirring occasionally, until onion and celery are softened, 8 to 10 minutes. Add stock and milk, bring to a simmer, and simmer, covered, until cauliflower is very tender, about 25 minutes.

Puree cauliflower mixture in 2 batches in a blender (use caution when blending hot liquids) until very smooth, then return to cleaned saucepan. Bring to a simmer, then add remaining ingredients and cook over low heat, whisking, until Stilton is melted and soup is smooth, 1 to 2 minutes.

Served topped with croutons and crumbled Stilton.

COOK'S NOTE
■ The soup can be made up to 1 day ahead. Cool, uncovered, then refrigerate, covered. Reheat, stirring, over moderate heat.

Creamy Chinese Celery Soup

SERVES 6 AS A FIRST COURSE (MAKES ABOUT 5 CUPS)
ACTIVE TIME: 30 MINUTES ■ START TO FINISH: 1½ HOURS

■ Chinese celery has long, skinny stems, a flurry of parsleylike leaves, and an aromatic pungence. Its pronounced flavor mellows and sweetens when it is cooked, while maintaining an elusive mystery that makes this soup special. Look for Chinese celery year-round at Asian markets; it is not as crisp as ordinary "supermarket" celery, but it shouldn't be limp. It will keep for a few days in a plastic bag in the refrigerator. ■

FOR SOUP
- ½ cup chopped shallots
- 2 tablespoons unsalted butter
- 1 tablespoon olive oil
- 1 medium leek (white and pale green parts only), chopped and washed well
- 2 bunches (1 pound) Chinese celery, top leaves discarded, stalks cut into 2-inch pieces
- 1 medium russet (baking) potato (8 ounces), peeled and chopped
- ½ cup dry white wine
- 4 cups Chicken Stock (page 153) or store-bought reduced-sodium broth
- ½ cup heavy cream
- ½ teaspoon salt
- ¼ teaspoon freshly ground black pepper

FOR CROÛTES
- 6 (¼-inch-thick) baguette slices (cut on the diagonal)
- ¼ cup extra-virgin olive oil
- Kosher salt and freshly ground black pepper

GARNISH: fresh cilantro or flat-leaf parsley leaves

MAKE THE SOUP: Cook shallots in butter and oil in a 3-quart heavy saucepan over moderate heat, stirring, until softened, about 2 minutes. Add leek and cook, stirring, until softened, about 5 minutes. Add celery and potato and cook, stirring, for 2 minutes. Add wine, bring to a boil, and boil for 1 minute. Add chicken stock, bring to a simmer, covered, and simmer until celery is very tender, about 1 hour.

MEANWHILE, MAKE THE CROÛTES: Put a rack in middle of oven and preheat oven to 350°F.

Brush baguette slices with oil and season generously with salt and pepper. Arrange in one layer on a baking sheet and bake until golden brown and crisp, 12 to 15 minutes. Set aside.

Puree soup in batches in a blender (use caution when blending hot liquids) until very smooth, then pour through a large medium-mesh sieve into a bowl. Press hard on solids; discard solids.

Transfer soup to cleaned saucepan, stir in cream, salt, and pepper, and heat over low heat until hot. Thin with water if desired.

Serve soup topped with croûtes.

COOK'S NOTES
- The soup can be made up to 3 days ahead. Cool, uncovered, then refrigerate, covered.
- The croûtes can be made up to 2 days ahead. Once cooled completely, store in an airtight container at room temperature.

Smooth Chayote Soup

SERVES 4 AS A FIRST COURSE (MAKES ABOUT 4 CUPS)
ACTIVE TIME: 30 MINUTES ■ START TO FINISH: 45 MINUTES

■ Chayote, also known as vegetable pear or mirliton, is a pear-shaped member of the gourd family that is native to North America but now grows around the world. Its smooth pale green skin can be tough, so it is often peeled. The vegetable's subtle squashlike flavor takes well to cream and butter. Indeed, this soup of palest celadon tastes as though it's rich, when in fact there's only a jot of butter. ■

½ tablespoon unsalted butter
2 scallions, minced
1 small garlic clove, minced
¼ teaspoon minced small fresh hot green chile, such as serrano or Thai, or to taste
1½ pounds chayote (2–3; see Sources), peeled, quartered lengthwise, pitted if desired (see Cook's Note), and cut into ½-inch pieces
Salt
2 tablespoons finely chopped fresh cilantro
1¾ cups water
GARNISH: fresh cilantro sprigs

Melt butter in a 3-quart heavy saucepan over moderately low heat. Add scallions, garlic, and chile and cook, stirring, until softened, about 3 minutes. Add chayote, ½ teaspoon salt, and 1 tablespoon cilantro and cook, stirring, for 2 minutes. Add water, bring to a simmer, and simmer, covered, until chayote is very tender, 15 to 20 minutes.

Stir in remaining tablespoon cilantro. Puree mixture in 2 batches in a blender (use caution when blending hot liquids) until smooth. Season soup with salt and garnish with cilantro sprigs.

COOK'S NOTES

■ Chayote pits are soft enough to puree in a blender; they have a faintly almondy flavor.

■ The soup can be made up to 1 day ahead. Cool, uncovered, then refrigerate, covered.

Harvest Corn Chowder with Bacon

SERVES 8 AS A FIRST COURSE (MAKES ABOUT 11 CUPS)
ACTIVE TIME: 40 MINUTES ■ START TO FINISH: 1¼ HOURS

■ Brimming with fresh corn, sweet potato, red bell pepper, and carrots, this vibrant chowder has flavor to spare. We adapted the colorful recipe from one served at Suzanne Fine Regional Cuisine, a restaurant in Lodi, New York, that overlooks Seneca Lake. ■

½ cup diced (¼-inch) slab bacon (2 ounces; rind discarded if necessary)
2 cups diced (¼-inch) sweet onion, such as Vidalia or Walla Walla
2 large carrots, cut into ¼-inch dice
1 celery rib, cut into ¼-inch dice
1 red bell pepper, cored, seeded, and cut into ¼-inch dice
½ pound yellow-fleshed potatoes, such as Yukon Gold (2 small), peeled and cut into ¼-inch dice
1 medium sweet potato (8 ounces), peeled and cut into ¼-inch dice
5 cups Chicken Stock (page 153) or store-bought reduced-sodium broth
2 fresh thyme sprigs
3 cups corn (from about 6 ears)
1½ cups heavy cream
1 teaspoon salt
1 teaspoon freshly ground black pepper
GARNISH: 2 plum tomatoes, seeded and diced; finely chopped fresh chives

Cook bacon in a 6- to 8-quart wide heavy pot over moderate heat, stirring frequently, until crisp, about 5 minutes. Transfer with a slotted spoon to paper towels to drain.

Add onion, carrots, celery, and bell pepper to bacon fat remaining in pot and cook, stirring, until onion is softened, 8 to 10 minutes. Add both potatoes, stock, and thyme, bring to a simmer, and simmer, covered, until potatoes are just tender, about 15 minutes.

Add corn and cream and simmer, uncovered, for 10 minutes. Add salt and pepper and stir in bacon. Serve sprinkled with tomatoes and chives.

COOK'S NOTE

■ The chowder can be made up to 3 days ahead. Cool, uncovered, then refrigerate, covered.

Tunisian Soup with Egg Noodles and Chard

SERVES 8 TO 10 AS A FIRST COURSE
(MAKES ABOUT 10 CUPS)
ACTIVE TIME: 35 MINUTES ■ START TO FINISH: 1¼ HOURS

■ Punctuated by strands of egg noodles and leafy chard, this rustic soup makes a wonderful start to a meal. Harissa, the traditional Tunisian hot sauce, lends a brick-red color and deep, spicy warmth. Toast the cumin deeply, so that the flavor comes alive. ■

- 1 teaspoon cumin seeds
- 1 pound Swiss chard, stems and center ribs removed and chopped, leaves coarsely chopped and reserved separately
- 1 medium red onion, chopped
- 2 large garlic cloves, minced
  Salt
- ¼ teaspoon freshly ground black pepper
- 3 tablespoons extra-virgin olive oil
- 2 tablespoons tomato paste
- 8 cups Rich Chicken Stock (page 153) or 5 cups store-bought reduced-sodium broth plus 3 cups water
- 1–2 tablespoons harissa (see Sources)
- 1 tablespoon fresh lemon juice
- 3½ ounces (about 1½ cups) fine egg noodles

ACCOMPANIMENT: lemon wedges
SPECIAL EQUIPMENT: an electric coffee/spice grinder

Toast cumin in a dry small heavy skillet, preferably cast-iron, over moderate heat, stirring, until deeply fragrant and dark brown, 2 to 3 minutes; be careful not to burn it. Cool, then grind to a powder in grinder.

Cook chard stems and ribs, onion, and garlic with ½ teaspoon cumin, ½ teaspoon salt, and pepper in oil in a large heavy pot over moderate heat, stirring occasionally, until beginning to brown, about 12 minutes. Add tomato paste and cook, stirring, for 2 minutes. Add stock, harissa, and lemon juice, bring to a simmer, and simmer, covered, for 30 minutes.

Add chard leaves, noodles, and ½ teaspoon salt and simmer, covered, until chard and noodles are tender, about 7 minutes.

Sprinkle with remaining cumin and serve with lemon wedges.

COOK'S NOTE

- The soup, without the noodles, can be made up to 3 days ahead. Cool, uncovered, then refrigerate, covered. Bring to a simmer and cook the noodles in the soup before serving.

Silky Lettuce Soup

SERVES 4 AS A FIRST COURSE OR LIGHT LUNCH
(MAKES ABOUT 4 CUPS)
ACTIVE TIME: 25 MINUTES ■ START TO FINISH: 35 MINUTES

■ Lettuces take on all sorts of interesting characteristics when cooked. Indeed, the tough outer leaves and ribs that often land in the compost heap make a delicate but surprisingly flavorful and nuanced soup. In this version, buttery sautéed onions bolster the sweetness factor, while a bit of ground coriander adds a citrusy undertone. You can use any salad greens, including arugula, spinach, and watercress, and any kind of potato. ■

- 3 tablespoons unsalted butter
- 1 cup chopped onion, scallions, and/or shallots
- 1 garlic clove, chopped
- ¾ teaspoon ground coriander
  Salt and freshly ground black pepper
- ¾ cup diced (⅓-inch) peeled potato
- 8 cups coarsely chopped lettuce leaves, including ribs (12 ounces)
- 3 cups water

Melt 2 tablespoons butter in a 4- to 5-quart heavy pot over moderately low heat. Add onion and garlic and cook, stirring, until softened, 3 to 5 minutes. Add coriander, ¾ teaspoon salt, and ¼ teaspoon pepper and cook, stirring, for 1 minute. Stir in potato, lettuce, and water and bring to a boil, then reduce heat and simmer, covered, until potato is very tender, about 10 minutes.

Puree soup in batches in a blender (use caution when blending hot liquids), and transfer to a 2- to 3-quart saucepan. Bring soup to a simmer, then whisk in remaining tablespoon butter and salt and pepper to taste.

COOK'S NOTE
- The soup can be made up to 1 day ahead. Cool, uncovered, then refrigerate, covered.

Gumbo Z'Herbes

SERVES 8 AS A MAIN COURSE (MAKES ABOUT 12 CUPS)
ACTIVE TIME: 40 MINUTES ■ START TO FINISH: 2 HOURS

■ Deeply nourishing and delicious, this gumbo is like a tonic. In Louisiana, the Creole gumbo z'herbes (from the French *gumbo aux herbes*) is traditionally served during Lent, especially on Holy Thursday or Good Friday, when Catholics are supposed to abstain from eating meat. Original versions contained only greens, but as time went on, Louisiana palates began to override religious customs, and seasoning meats and seafood were included in the mix. Ideally, you should use a mix of bitter and milder greens; each contributes its own sweet or pungent voice, resulting in a loud chorus of flavor.

If you can't find mustard or turnip greens, which are bitter, increase the greens you can find proportionately to equal the total amount called for in the recipe. ■

    4 quarts water
    2 pounds meaty smoked ham hocks (2 medium)
    8 large cabbage leaves
    ¾ pound turnip greens, coarse ribs and stems discarded
    1 pound mustard greens, coarse ribs and stems discarded (see headnote)
    ½ pound beet greens, including stems (from 1 bunch beets)
    3 tablespoons unsalted butter
    2 medium onions, finely chopped
    2 tablespoons all-purpose flour
    2 garlic cloves, minced
    1 tablespoon fresh thyme leaves or 1 teaspoon dried thyme, crumbled
  1–2 small (2- to 3-inch-long) fresh hot red chiles (to taste), minced, including seeds

    10 ounces baby spinach
    ¼ cup finely chopped fresh flat-leaf parsley
    1 teaspoon salt, or to taste
  ACCOMPANIMENTS: white rice; hot sauce, such as Tabasco; cider vinegar (optional)

Bring water and ham hocks to a boil in a 6- to 8-quart heavy pot. Reduce heat and simmer, partially covered, until meat is very tender, 1½ to 2 hours.

With tongs, transfer ham hocks to a cutting board to cool; reserve cooking liquid. When cool enough to handle, discard skin, bones, and fat and finely chop ham.

Add cabbage to reserved cooking liquid, bring to a simmer, and simmer, covered, until tender, about 10 minutes. With tongs, transfer cabbage to a colander set over a large bowl. Add half of turnip, mustard, and beet greens to cooking liquid in pot and simmer, uncovered, stirring occasionally, for 5 minutes. With a slotted spoon, transfer greens to colander with cabbage. Cook remaining greens in same manner and transfer to colander; set pot aside. When greens are cool enough to handle, finely chop; reserve cooking liquid in bowl.

Pour cooking liquid in pot into bowl of cooking liquid. Add water if necessary to bring total to 8 cups.

Melt butter in cleaned pot over moderate heat. Add onions and cook, stirring frequently, until golden, 5 to 7 minutes. Add flour and cook, stirring, for 3 minutes, until beginning to brown. Add garlic and cook, stirring, for 1 minute, until pale golden. Add cooking liquid in a slow stream, stirring constantly, and bring to a boil, stirring constantly. Add chopped greens, ham, thyme, and chiles and simmer, uncovered, stirring occasionally, until greens are tender, about 8 minutes.

Gradually add spinach and cook, stirring, until wilted. Stir in parsley and salt.

Serve gumbo over rice with hot sauce and, if desired, cider vinegar.

COOK'S NOTE
- The gumbo, without the spinach, parsley, and salt, can be made up to 2 days ahead. Cool completely, uncovered, then refrigerate, covered. Reheat before adding the remaining ingredients.

GUMBO GREENS

Gumbo z'herbes comes together out of greens as a restorative after a chilly, damp winter. Though it's traditionally served on Holy Thursday, we happen to like it even better in the late spring and early days of summer, when there are lots of fresh young greens to be had at the farmers market. It is also a cheerful reminder that the word *herb*—which has lost much of its original digestive or medicinal connotations in the United States—became something larger and much more encompassing when it morphed into the French *herbes* or Creole *zhèbes*, an almost infinite number of shades and flavors of green.

Leah Chase, the guiding light of New Orleans' Dooky Chase Restaurant, is renowned for her gumbo z'herbes, and she notes that the key to the soup is variety, and thus complexity of flavor. "Kale, collards, and chard will always work, and spinach mellows things out," she said. "Sometimes I put green cabbage in there. You could also use some arugula and watercress, or old-time pepper cress, if you can find it. But shy away from dandelion greens; they will give the gumbo a whole different flavor." In general, when shopping for greens, look for fairly thin-stemmed leaves that are vibrant, not yellow and dry. Store them in the refrigerator, wrapped loosely in dampened paper towels in a plastic bag.

BEET GREENS At the farmers market and increasingly at supermarkets, beets come with their greens attached, so you are, in essence, getting two vegetables for the price of one. The thick, lush greens (they are closely related to Swiss chard, a good substitute) have a mild, minerally taste that plays off sharper, more pungent varieties such as turnip and mustard greens. Beet greens become silky-soft when cooked and give depth and body to gumbo.

TURNIP GREENS These add an earthy succulence, brightness, and bite to gumbo. They are popular all over the American South, where they are typically sold, sans turnips, at the supermarket. In other parts of the country, you'll find them at Asian markets as well as farmers markets.

MUSTARD GREENS Botanically speaking, mustard greens are a single species of *Brassica juncea* that most likely originated in Central Asia and spread to China, India, Africa, and points west. But experts have identified at least seventeen subspecies that are wildly different in flavor (ranging from delicate to pungent), texture (from smooth to fuzzy to fibrous), and color (parrot green to reddish purple). The most common type is called southern, American, or curled mustard. The leaves are large, frilly, and thinner than either beet or turnip greens; the flavor is peppery and herbaceous. Look for them too at Asian markets, farmers markets, and, in the South, at supermarkets. Keep mustard greens moist and cold. They can develop an unpleasant smell if they're stored airtight, so store them in a perforated plastic bag or one that isn't tightly sealed.

Mushroom Consommé Topped with Puff Pastry

SERVES 6 AS A FIRST COURSE (MAKES ABOUT 5½ CUPS)
ACTIVE TIME: 40 MINUTES ■ START TO FINISH: 4½ HOURS

■ Inspired by chef Paul Bocuse's legendary truffle soup, which is served topped with a billowy dome of puff pastry, we created an equally elegant version featuring mushroom consommé laced with morels and snips of chives. The key to the dramatic pastry "hat" is leaving enough headroom between the soup and the puff pastry so that steam can build up and lift the pastry. (If you add too much broth to the bowls, the pastry may be drawn down into the soup and become partially submerged.) The woodsy intensity that the dried morels add to the consommé is delicious, but other dried exotic mushrooms, such as porcini, can be substituted. ■

FOR MUSHROOM CONSOMMÉ
- 2 pounds white mushrooms, finely chopped, preferably in a food processor
- 2 medium onions, chopped
- 8 cups cold water
- Salt
- ¼ teaspoon freshly ground black pepper
- 2 tablespoons 1-inch pieces fresh chives

FOR MORELS
- 1½ cups boiling water
- ¾ ounce (about ¾ cup) dried morels (see Sources)
- ¾ cup Sercial (dry) Madeira

FOR PASTRY
- All-purpose flour for rolling
- 1 (17.3-ounce) package frozen puff pastry (2 sheets), thawed
- 1 large egg, lightly beaten
- 1 large egg yolk

SPECIAL EQUIPMENT: 6 deep 16- to 18-ounce ovenproof bowls (4 to 4½ inches across the top), such as "lion's head" bowls (see Sources)

MAKE THE MUSHROOM CONSOMMÉ: Combine mushrooms, onions, water, and 1 teaspoon salt in a 6-quart stockpot, bring to a simmer, and simmer, uncovered, for 1½ hours.

MEANWHILE, PREPARE THE MORELS: Pour boiling water over morels in a small bowl and soak until softened, about 20 minutes.

With a slotted spoon, transfer morels to a medium-mesh sieve set over a bowl. Press on them with back of spoon to remove excess liquid, then add liquid from morels to soaking liquid and reserve.

Rinse morels to remove any grit, transfer to a small saucepan, and add Madeira. Bring to a simmer and simmer, covered, for 5 minutes.

FINISH THE CONSOMMÉ: Strain mushroom consommé through a large sieve lined with a damp paper towel into a large saucepan, pressing gently on solids to extract as much liquid as possible; discard solids. There should be about 4 cups consommé (if there is less, add water; if there is too much, boil until reduced to 4 cups). Season consommé with salt and pepper.

Add morels and Madeira to consommé. Let reserved soaking liquid settle, then slowly pour into consommé, leaving last tablespoon (containing sediment) in bowl.

Add chives to consommé and simmer, covered, for 3 minutes. Refrigerate, uncovered, until cold, about 1 hour.

MEANWHILE, PREPARE THE PASTRY: On a lightly floured surface, roll out each sheet of pastry into a 13-inch square with a lightly floured rolling pin. Refrigerate on baking sheets until firm, about 1 hour.

Using a lid or plate 1½ inches large than diameter of tops of bowls, cut out 3 rounds from each sheet of puff pastry. Brush any excess flour from both sides of pastry rounds, then brush tops with some of beaten egg. Refrigerate pastry rounds on baking sheets until firm, about 1 hour.

FINISH THE SOUP: Put a rack in middle of oven and preheat oven to 425°F.

Divide cold soup among bowls. Lightly beat yolk. Brush egg wash around rim and down sides of each bowl to make a ½-inch-wide strip. Working quickly, place each pastry round over a bowl, pull slightly so pastry is taut, and press edges down against sides of bowl to seal tightly.

Arrange bowls on a large baking sheet and bake until pastry is puffed and golden brown, 15 to 20 minutes. Serve immediately.

Onion and Fennel Bisque

SERVES 10 TO 12 AS A FIRST COURSE
(MAKES ABOUT 6 CUPS)
ACTIVE TIME: 30 MINUTES ■ START TO FINISH: 1 HOUR

■ Sublimely elegant, this vegetarian bisque is so lush that demitasse cups make an ideal serving size. Stirring in a bit of Pernod just before serving amplifies the fennel's anise notes and the onions' mellow sweetness. We adapted the recipe from one served at Blue Heron Inn in Sechelt, British Columbia. ■

- 3 medium red onions, chopped
- 2 leeks (white and pale green parts only), chopped and washed well
- 1 medium fennel bulb (8 ounces), stalks discarded, bulb cored and chopped
- 1 large garlic clove, minced
- 2 tablespoons unsalted butter
- ¼ cup dry white wine
- 2 cups Vegetable Stock (page 155) or store-bought reduced-sodium broth
- 1¼ cups water
- 1 teaspoon salt
- ¼ teaspoon freshly ground black pepper
- ⅛ teaspoon freshly grated nutmeg
- 1 cup heavy cream
- 2 teaspoons Pernod

GARNISH: chopped fresh chives

Cook onions, leeks, fennel, and garlic in butter in a 5- to 6-quart heavy pot over moderate heat, covered, stirring occasionally, until softened, about 15 minutes. Add wine and boil, uncovered, until evaporated, about 1 minute. Add stock, water, salt, pepper, and nutmeg, bring to a simmer, and simmer, uncovered, until vegetables are tender, about 10 minutes.

Stir in cream, bring to a simmer, and simmer, stir-ring occasionally, until liquid is slightly thickened and reduced to about 6 cups, about 15 minutes.

Puree soup in batches in a blender (use caution when blending hot liquids) until smooth, then transfer to a soup tureen. Stir in Pernod and serve sprinkled with chives.

COOK'S NOTE

■ The soup can be made up to 2 days ahead. Cool, uncovered, then refrigerate, covered. Add more water if necessary to thin to the desired consistency when reheating.

Ramp and Sweet Onion Soup

SERVES 4 AS A FIRST COURSE (MAKES ABOUT 4 CUPS)
ACTIVE TIME: 45 MINUTES ■ START TO FINISH: 1¼ HOURS

■ This creamy soup, adapted from one served at chef Bruce Sherman's Chicago restaurant, North Pond, captures the essence of ramps, which flourish so briefly during the spring. Cooking the oniony bulbs brings out their sweetness, and the briefly blanched green stems lend a cheerful color. Sherman likes to drizzle the finished soup with a bit of almond oil, a chef's touch that adds a smoothing roundness to the soup, but extra-virgin olive oil will also work. ■

- 1 pound ramps
- ½ sweet onion, such as Vidalia or Walla Walla, thinly sliced
- ¼ teaspoon freshly ground white pepper
  Salt
- 2 tablespoons vegetable oil
- ⅓ cup dry white wine
- 3½ cups Chicken Stock (page 153) or store-bought reduced-sodium broth
- ¼ cup finely grated Parmigiano-Reggiano
- 2 tablespoons unsalted butter

GARNISH: almond oil (see Sources) or extra-virgin olive oil

Trim roots from ramps and slip outer skin from bulbs if loose. Cut off green tops and coarsely chop enough greens to measure 3 cups (reserve remainder for another use). Thinly slice ramp bulbs, including pink stems.

Cook ramp bulbs, onion, white pepper, and ½ teaspoon salt in vegetable oil in a large heavy saucepan over moderate heat, stirring occasionally, until ramps and onion are softened, about 10 minutes. Add wine and boil over high heat, stirring occasionally, until completely evaporated. Add stock, partially cover, reduce heat, and simmer, stirring occasionally, until ramps and onion are very soft, about 20 minutes. Stir in ramp greens and boil for 1 minute.

Puree mixture in batches in a blender (use caution when blending hot liquids) until very smooth, about 1 minute per batch, and pour through a fine-mesh sieve into a large bowl. Press hard on solids; discard solids. Return soup to cleaned pot and bring just to a boil. Whisk in cheese and butter until smooth. Season with salt.

Serve drizzled with almond oil or olive oil.

COOK'S NOTE

- The soup can be made up to 1 day ahead. Cool, uncovered, then refrigerate, covered. To reheat, bring just to a boil.

Tuscan Yellow Pepper Soup

SERVES 8 AS A FIRST COURSE (MAKES ABOUT 8 CUPS)
ACTIVE TIME: 15 MINUTES ■ START TO FINISH: 1¼ HOURS

■ A remarkably simple soup, this has long been a specialty at the famous trattoria Cibrèo in Florence, owned by Fabio Picchi. Its backbone comes from beef stock, and potatoes offer creamy body, but what you'll remember is the bright yellow color and intense flavor of the peppers. The soup can also be served chilled. ■

¼ cup plus 1½ teaspoons olive oil
1 medium carrot, finely chopped
1 medium onion, finely chopped
1 celery rib, finely chopped
4 yellow bell peppers, cored, seeded, and cut into 1-inch pieces

1 pound boiling potatoes, peeled and cut into ¼-inch pieces
1 cup Beef Stock (page 153) or store-bought reduced-sodium broth
4 cups water
1½ teaspoons salt
¼ teaspoon freshly ground black pepper

Heat ¼ cup oil in a 6-quart heavy pot over moderately high heat until hot but not smoking. Add carrot, onion, and celery and cook, stirring, until softened and pale golden, about 10 minutes. Add bell peppers, potatoes, stock, and water and bring to a boil, then reduce heat and simmer until vegetables are very soft, about 40 minutes.

Puree pepper mixture in batches in a blender (use caution when blending hot liquids) until smooth, and pour through a sieve into a large bowl. Stir in remaining 1½ teaspoons oil, salt, and pepper.

COOK'S NOTE

- The soup can be made up to 2 days ahead. Cool, uncovered, then refrigerate, covered. Serve chilled or reheat to serve hot.

Curried Potato and Leek Soup with Spinach

SERVES 4 AS A MAIN COURSE (MAKES ABOUT 8 CUPS)
ACTIVE TIME: 25 MINUTES ■ START TO FINISH: 1 HOUR

■ Chopped spinach and a generous pinch of curry powder smarten up classic potato-leek soup. Instead of blending the soup to a smooth puree, we leave it slightly chunky. Since the leeks are chopped but not pureed, make sure yours are tender. ■

3 tablespoons unsalted butter
4 cups chopped leeks (white and pale green parts only; from 4–6 medium leeks), washed well
1 pound boiling potatoes, preferably Yukon Gold, peeled and cut into ¼-inch pieces
1 teaspoon curry powder, preferably Madras
1 teaspoon salt

¼ teaspoon freshly ground black pepper

2⅔ cups water

1¾ cups Chicken Stock (page 153) or store-bought reduced-sodium broth

1 cup whole milk

5 ounces baby spinach, coarsely chopped

Heat butter in a 3- to 3½-quart heavy saucepan over moderate heat until foam subsides. Add leeks, potatoes, curry powder, salt, and pepper and cook, stirring occasionally, until leeks are softened, about 5 minutes. Stir in water and stock, bring to a simmer, and simmer, uncovered, until potatoes are very tender, about 20 minutes.

Transfer 1 cup of soup to a blender (use caution when blending hot liquids) and puree until smooth. Return puree to pan, stir in milk, and bring to a simmer. Stir in spinach and simmer until spinach is wilted, about 1 minute more.

COOK'S NOTE

- The soup, without the spinach, can be made up to 2 days ahead. Cool, uncovered, then refrigerate, covered. To serve, bring to a simmer, stir in spinach, and simmer until wilted, about 1 minute.

Chunky Butternut Squash, White Bean, and Tomato Soup

SERVES 4 AS A MAIN COURSE (MAKES ABOUT 6 CUPS)
ACTIVE TIME: 15 MINUTES ■ START TO FINISH: 35 MINUTES

■ It's nice to have several dishes in your repertoire that are nourishing and don't require any special trips to the store. This is one of our favorites. It comes together in a flash. ■

1 large garlic clove, minced

1–2 tablespoons extra-virgin olive oil

½ small butternut squash, peeled, seeded, and cut into ½-inch pieces (2 cups)

2 cups water

1¾ cups Chicken Stock (page 153) or store-bought reduced-sodium broth

1 (16- to 19-ounce) can white beans, preferably cannellini, rinsed and drained

2 canned tomatoes, coarsely chopped

1 teaspoon finely chopped fresh sage

¼ cup green (hulled) pumpkin seeds (*pepitas*; optional)

Salt

½ cup finely grated Parmigiano-Reggiano, plus additional for serving

Freshly ground black pepper

Cook garlic in 1 tablespoon oil in a 3-quart heavy saucepan over moderate heat, stirring frequently, until golden, about 1 minute. Add squash, water, stock, beans, tomatoes, and sage, bring to a simmer, cover, and simmer, stirring occasionally, until squash is tender, about 20 minutes.

Meanwhile, cook pumpkin seeds, if using, in remaining 1 tablespoon oil in a small skillet over moderately low heat, stirring, until seeds are puffed and lightly toasted, 2 to 4 minutes. Transfer to a bowl and season with salt.

Mash some of squash against sides of saucepan to thicken soup. Remove from heat and stir in cheese and salt and pepper to taste. Serve sprinkled with pumpkin seeds, if using, and cheese.

COOK'S NOTE

- The soup can be made up to 3 days ahead. Cool, uncovered, then refrigerate, covered.

Pumpkin Soup with Red Pepper Mousse

SERVES 12 AS A FIRST COURSE, 6 TO 8 AS A MAIN COURSE
(MAKES ABOUT 14 CUPS)
ACTIVE TIME: 1 HOUR ■ START TO FINISH: 3 HOURS
(INCLUDES CHILLING MOUSSE)

■ This gorgeous soup reminds us of a bolt of paisley silk, shot through with rusty reds and shimmering oranges. Its flavor is intoxicating, with the smoked paprika adding a gypsy heat to the red pepper mousse. Although we originally created the soup as part of a Thanksgiving menu, it will turn any cold winter night into a celebration. ■

FOR MOUSSE

- 1 (12-ounce) jar roasted red peppers, drained, rinsed, and patted dry
- 1 tablespoon extra-virgin olive oil
- 1 teaspoon sherry vinegar
- ¼ teaspoon hot *pimentón* (Spanish smoked paprika; see Sources)
- ¼ teaspoon salt
- ½ teaspoon unflavored gelatin
- 2 tablespoons water
- ⅓ cup heavy cream

FOR SOUP

- 3 tablespoons extra-virgin olive oil
- 5 medium carrots, chopped
- 1 large onion, chopped
- 2 garlic cloves, minced
- 1 Turkish bay leaf or ½ California bay leaf
- 1 (4- to 4½-pound) pumpkin or butternut squash, halved, seeded, peeled, and cut into 1-inch pieces (9 cups)
- ¾ teaspoon ground cumin
- 1 teaspoon salt
- ¼ teaspoon freshly ground black pepper
- 5 cups Chicken Stock (page 153) or store-bought reduced-sodium broth
- 3½ cups water

MAKE THE MOUSSE: Combine peppers, oil, vinegar, *pimentón*, and salt in a blender or food processor and puree until very smooth.

Sprinkle gelatin over water in a 1-quart heavy saucepan and let stand for 1 minute to soften. Heat over low heat, stirring, just until gelatin is dissolved. Remove from heat and whisk in pepper puree 1 tablespoon at a time.

Beat cream in a small deep bowl with an electric mixer at medium speed until it just holds soft peaks. Gently but thoroughly fold in pepper mixture. Cover surface of mousse with plastic wrap and refrigerate until set, at least 2 hours.

MEANWHILE, MAKE THE SOUP: Heat oil in a 6- to 8-quart heavy pot over moderate heat until hot but not smoking. Add carrots, onion, garlic, and bay leaf and cook, stirring occasionally, until vegetables are softened, 5 to 6 minutes. Add pumpkin, cumin, salt, and pepper and cook, stirring occasionally, until pumpkin begins to soften around edges, about 15 minutes.

Stir in stock and water and bring to a boil, then reduce heat and simmer, covered, until vegetables are very tender, 35 to 45 minutes. Discard bay leaf.

Blend soup in batches in blender (use caution when blending hot liquids) until smooth, and transfer to a bowl.

Just before serving, return soup to cleaned pot and reheat over low heat. Ladle soup into bowls and top each serving with 1½ tablespoons mousse.

COOK'S NOTES

- The mousse can be refrigerated for up to 2 days.
- The soup can be made up to 3 days ahead. Cool, uncovered, then refrigerate, covered.

Baby Spinach Soup with Croutons

SERVES 4 TO 6 AS A LIGHT MAIN COURSE
(MAKES ABOUT 6 CUPS)
ACTIVE TIME: 30 MINUTES ■ START TO FINISH: 30 MINUTES

■ Baby spinach has a more delicate flavor and is easier to clean than mature spinach. Cooking the spinach quickly and then immediately blending it helps preserve the vegetable's bright color. Add some cream and a handful of savory croutons, and you end up with a seductive, surprisingly substantial soup. ■

FOR CROUTONS

- 2 cups ½-inch cubes baguette (including crust) or other white bread
- 2 tablespoons olive oil
- ⅛ teaspoon salt
- ⅛ teaspoon freshly ground black pepper

FOR SOUP

- ½ stick (4 tablespoons) unsalted butter
- 1 cup chopped onion
- 2 tablespoons all-purpose flour
- 2 cups Chicken Stock (page 153) or store-bought reduced-sodium broth
- 1 cup water
- Salt and freshly ground black pepper
- About 1 pound baby spinach (12 cups packed)

1 cup heavy cream
½ teaspoon freshly grated nutmeg, or to taste

MAKE THE CROUTONS: Put a rack in upper third of oven and preheat oven to 400°F.

Toss bread cubes with oil, salt, and pepper on a baking sheet. Bake, stirring once, until golden, about 5 minutes. Set aside.

MAKE THE SOUP: Heat 3 tablespoons butter in a 5- to 6-quart heavy pot over moderately low heat, add onion, and cook, stirring occasionally, until soft, 6 to 8 minutes. Add flour and cook, stirring, for 2 minutes. Stir in stock, water, ¾ teaspoon salt, and ¼ teaspoon pepper and bring to a boil, stirring occasionally. Add spinach by handfuls, stirring to wilt it slightly as you add it, then cover and cook, stirring occasionally, until it is completely wilted, about 3 minutes total.

Puree soup in 2 batches in a blender (use caution when blending hot liquids) until smooth, then return to cleaned pot. Add cream, nutmeg, and salt and pepper to taste and bring to a simmer. Add remaining tablespoon butter, swirling pot until incorporated. Serve soup with croutons.

COOK'S NOTES

- The croutons are best made no more than 1 hour before serving.
- The soup can be made up to 1 day ahead. Cool, uncovered, then refrigerate, covered. Reheat gently before serving.

Spinach Stracciatella Soup

SERVES 6 AS A FIRST COURSE, 4 AS A MAIN COURSE
(MAKES ABOUT 6 CUPS)
ACTIVE TIME: 20 MINUTES ■ START TO FINISH: 20 MINUTES

■ *Stracciatella* means "little rags" in Italian, which captures the way the eggs take shape when stirred into the hot soup. We've added spinach to this classic recipe to create a dish that's both filling and delicious. Best of all, it's on the table in just 20 minutes. ■

3 cups Chicken Stock (page 153) or store-bought reduced-sodium broth

2 cups water
½ teaspoon salt
Freshly ground black pepper
1 (10-ounce) package frozen chopped spinach (not thawed)
½ cup finely grated Parmigiano-Reggiano, plus additional for serving
2 large eggs, lightly beaten

Combine stock, water, salt, and ¼ teaspoon pepper in a 2- to 2½-quart saucepan and heat over moderate heat until hot. Stir in spinach and cheese, cover, and simmer, stirring occasionally to break up spinach and distribute cheese, until spinach is just tender, about 8 minutes.

Add eggs to soup in a slow stream, stirring constantly to form ribbons.

Ladle soup into bowls. Grind pepper and sprinkle some cheese over each serving.

Greek Egg and Lemon Soup
Soupa Avgolemono

SERVES 8 AS A FIRST COURSE (MAKES ABOUT 7 CUPS)
ACTIVE TIME: 45 MINUTES ■ START TO FINISH: 4½ HOURS
(INCLUDES MAKING STOCK)

■ As with the famous Greek sauce of the same name (pronounced "ahv-go-*leh*-mo-no"), lemon is the star of the show here: a strong, tart flavor is key to the soup's success. Well-beaten eggs give the soup an ethereal creaminess, while a little rice provides a nice textural contrast. ■

6 cups Chicken Stock (page 153)
Salt and freshly ground white pepper
½ cup long-grain white rice
2 large eggs, left at room temperature for 30 minutes
6 tablespoons fresh lemon juice
1½ tablespoons chopped fresh dill

Bring stock, 1¼ teaspoons salt, and ¼ teaspoon white pepper to a boil in a 3- to 4-quart heavy saucepan. Stir in rice, reduce heat to low, and cook, covered, until it is tender, 15 to 17 minutes. Remove from heat.

Beat eggs in a bowl with an electric mixer at high speed until thick and pale, 3 to 5 minutes. Add lemon juice in a slow stream, beating (mixture will thicken, then thin out). Add 1 cup hot stock mixture in a slow stream (to temper eggs), beating, then beat egg mixture into remaining stock mixture. Stir in dill and season with salt and white pepper if necessary.

COOK'S NOTE

■ The soup can be made up to 3 days ahead. Cool, uncovered, then refrigerate, covered. Reheat over low heat, stirring constantly, just until hot (do not boil, or eggs will curdle).

Roasted Tomato Soup with Parmesan Wafers

SERVES 6 TO 8 AS A FIRST COURSE (MAKES ABOUT 8 CUPS)
ACTIVE TIME: 20 MINUTES ■ START TO FINISH: 1¾ HOURS

■ Roasting tomatoes concentrates their flavor, transforming them into something intensely rich and deep—like a tomato to the tenth power. This silky soup, touched with cream and sweetened with roasted garlic, gets even better when the lacy Parmesan wafer floating on top starts to soften and mingle with it. ■

4 pounds tomatoes, halved lengthwise
6 garlic cloves, left unpeeled
3 tablespoons olive oil
  Salt and freshly ground black pepper
2 tablespoons unsalted butter
1 medium onion, finely chopped
½ teaspoon dried oregano, crumbled
2 teaspoons sugar
3 cups Chicken Stock (page 153) or store-bought reduced-sodium broth
½ cup heavy cream
GARNISH: fresh oregano sprigs
ACCOMPANIMENT: Parmesan Wafers (recipe follows)

Put a rack in middle of oven and preheat oven to 350°F.

Arrange tomatoes cut side up in one layer on a large baking sheet. Scatter garlic around tomatoes. Drizzle tomatoes with oil and sprinkle with ½ teaspoon salt and ¼ teaspoon pepper.

Roast until tomatoes are browned around edges but still juicy, about 1 hour. Cool in pan on a rack, then peel garlic.

Melt butter in a 6- to 8-quart heavy pot over moderately low heat. Add onion, oregano, and sugar and cook, stirring frequently, until onion is softened, about 5 minutes. Add tomatoes, garlic, and stock, bring to a simmer, and simmer, covered, for 20 minutes to allow flavors to blend.

Puree soup in batches in a blender (use caution when blending hot liquids), then pour through a fine-mesh sieve into cleaned pot, pressing on solids; discard solids. Stir in cream and salt and pepper to taste and simmer for 2 minutes.

Divide soup among bowls and float a Parmesan wafer, topped with an oregano sprig, in center of each.

COOK'S NOTE

■ The soup can be made up to 1 day ahead. Cool, uncovered, then refrigerate, covered.

Parmesan Wafers

MAKES 8 WAFERS
ACTIVE TIME: 10 MINUTES ■ START TO FINISH: 35 MINUTES

■ These delicate savory crisps are just the right embellishment for Roasted Tomato Soup, but they also make a wonderful snack or appetizer in their own right. ■

1½ cups coarsely grated Parmigiano-Reggiano (4–5 ounces; use a box grater, not a food processor)
1 tablespoon all-purpose flour
SPECIAL EQUIPMENT: a nonstick baking sheet liner, such as a Silpat (see Sources)

Put a rack in middle of oven and preheat oven to 350°F. Line a large baking sheet with nonstick liner.

Stir together cheese and flour in a bowl. Make 4 mounds of cheese mixture (about 3 tablespoons each) about 5 inches apart on baking sheet and spread each mound into a 4- to 5-inch round.

Bake until melted and golden, about 10 minutes. Cool for 2 minutes on baking sheet on a rack. Carefully transfer each wafer (they are very delicate) with a wide metal spatula to rack to cool completely.

Stir cheese in bowl (to redistribute flour) and make 4 more wafers in same manner.

COOK'S NOTE
■ The wafers can be made up to 2 days ahead and kept, layered between sheets of wax paper, in an airtight container at room temperature.

French Tomato Soup with Rice

SERVES 4 AS A MAIN COURSE (MAKES ABOUT 8 CUPS)
ACTIVE TIME: 25 MINUTES ■ START TO FINISH: 1 HOUR

■ A far cry from the canned tomato soup so many of us grew up with, this French country-style soup delivers the warming taste of sun-ripened tomatoes, luxurious saffron, and fragrant orange zest. ■

    2 pounds tomatoes
    2 medium onions, halved lengthwise and thinly
        sliced crosswise
    1 medium carrot, coarsely grated
    1 celery rib, finely chopped
    4 large garlic cloves, finely chopped
    3 (3-by-1-inch) strips fresh orange zest, removed
        with a vegetable peeler, finely chopped
    1 teaspoon finely chopped fresh thyme
       Scant ¼ teaspoon red pepper flakes
    ¼ teaspoon fennel seeds
    1 Turkish bay leaf or ½ California bay leaf
    3 tablespoons extra-virgin olive oil
    2 tablespoons tomato paste
    3 cups water
    1¾ cups Chicken Stock (page 153) or store-bought
        reduced-sodium broth
       Salt
    ¼ teaspoon freshly ground black pepper
       Pinch of crumbled saffron threads
    1 teaspoon sugar, or to taste
    ¼ cup long-grain white rice
    2 tablespoons chopped fresh flat-leaf parsley
    ¼ cup chopped fresh basil

Cut a shallow X in bottom of each tomato with a paring knife. Blanch tomatoes in batches of 2 or 3 in a 5- to 6-quart pot of boiling water for 10 seconds, then transfer with a slotted spoon to a bowl of ice and cold water to stop the cooking.

Peel tomatoes and halve crosswise. Squeeze halves gently, cut side down, over a sieve set over a bowl to extract seeds and juices. Press on seeds and discard them; reserve juice and tomatoes.

Cook onions, carrot, celery, garlic, zest, thyme, red pepper flakes, fennel seeds, and bay leaf in oil in a 2½- to 3-quart heavy saucepan over moderate heat, stirring occasionally, until vegetables are softened, about 5 minutes. Add tomatoes, reserved juice, tomato paste, water, stock, ¾ teaspoon salt, pepper, saffron, and 1 teaspoon sugar, bring to a simmer, and simmer, uncovered, stirring and breaking up tomatoes with spoon occasionally, for 20 minutes.

Stir in rice and simmer, uncovered, until rice is tender, about 15 minutes. Discard bay leaf and stir in parsley, basil, and additional sugar and salt to taste if necessary.

COOK'S NOTE
■ The soup can be made up to 1 day ahead. Cool, uncovered, then refrigerate, covered. Add water if necessary to thin to the desired consistency when reheating.

Christmas Chestnut Soup with Sourdough Sage Croutons

SERVES 8 TO 10 AS A FIRST COURSE
(MAKES ABOUT 10 CUPS)
ACTIVE TIME: 1¼ HOURS ■ START TO FINISH: 1¼ HOURS

■ This first course makes the most of chestnuts, in both starring and supporting roles. Pureed to a silky essence, they become the body of the soup, which is then garnished generously with chopped toasted chestnuts and crisp sage-flecked croutons. Light yet flavorful, this soup holds its own in the lineup of a large holiday meal. ■

FOR SOUP

- 2 (7½-ounce) jars peeled cooked whole chestnuts, rinsed and drained
- 1 tablespoon olive oil
- 1 tablespoon unsalted butter
- 2 large leeks (white and pale green parts only), coarsely chopped and washed well
- 1 large onion, coarsely chopped
- 2 celery ribs, coarsely chopped
- 2 medium carrots, coarsely chopped
- 1½ Turkish bay leaves or 1 California bay leaf
- 1 tablespoon tamari or soy sauce
- 10 cups water
   Salt
- ⅓ cup chopped fresh flat-leaf parsley
- 1 teaspoon chopped fresh sage
- 2 tablespoons medium-dry sherry or Madeira
- ½ teaspoon freshly ground black pepper

FOR TOPPING

- 2 tablespoons olive oil
- 2 tablespoons unsalted butter
- ½ sourdough loaf, crust discarded and cut into ¼-inch cubes (4 cups)
- 1 teaspoon chopped fresh sage
- 2 (7½-ounce) jars peeled cooked whole chestnuts, rinsed, drained, and chopped
- 1 teaspoon flaky sea salt, preferably Maldon

MAKE THE SOUP: Put a rack in upper third of oven and preheat oven to 375°F.

Spread chestnuts in one layer on a large baking sheet. Roast until dry and slightly darkened, about 20 minutes. Set aside.

Heat oil and butter in a 5- to 6-quart heavy pot over moderately high heat until foam subsides. Add leeks, onion, celery, carrots, and bay leaves and cook, stirring occasionally, until vegetables are pale golden, 8 to 10 minutes. Add chestnuts and tamari and cook, stirring, until most of liquid has evaporated, 1 to 2 minutes. Add water and 2 teaspoons salt and bring to a boil, then reduce heat and simmer, uncovered, stirring occasionally, until vegetables are tender, about 30 minutes. Remove from heat and stir in parsley and sage; discard bay leaves.

Puree soup in 3 batches in a blender (use caution when blending hot liquids) until smooth, then transfer to a bowl. Pour through a medium-mesh sieve into cleaned pot, pressing hard on solids; discard solids. Bring soup to a simmer and stir in sherry, pepper, and salt to taste.

MEANWHILE, MAKE THE TOPPING: Heat oil and butter in a 12-inch heavy skillet over moderately high heat until foam subsides. Add bread cubes and sage and cook, turning occasionally, until croutons are golden, 6 to 10 minutes. Add chestnuts and cook, stirring, for 2 minutes. Transfer to a large bowl and toss with sea salt.

Ladle soup into bowls and sprinkle each serving with about ⅓ cup topping.

COOK'S NOTES

- The soup, without the sherry, can be made up to 3 days ahead. Cool, uncovered, then refrigerate, covered. Bring to a simmer and stir in the sherry before serving.
- The topping can be made up to 3 days ahead and, once cooled completely, kept in an airtight container at room temperature. Reheat in one layer on a baking sheet in a 350°F oven until the bread is crisp, 10 to 20 minutes.

BOTTLED CHESTNUTS

Nothing beats freshly roasted chestnuts for eating, but odds are you'll cook with them more frequently if you use bottled vacuum-packed whole chestnuts that are already cooked and peeled. They're also extremely convenient at Thanksgiving (see Sources).

White Bean and Tuscan Kale Soup with Chestnuts

SERVES 6 AS A FIRST COURSE (MAKES ABOUT 7 CUPS)
ACTIVE TIME: 30 MINUTES ■ START TO FINISH: 1½ HOURS
PLUS SOAKING TIME FOR BEANS

■ Tuscan kale, also known as *cavolo nero*, lacinato, and dinosaur kale, has long ruffled dark green leaves, a rich sweet flavor, and a more delicate texture than regular kale. It pairs beautifully with chestnuts and white beans. Both the kale and bottled chestnuts are found in some supermarkets and natural food stores. Although this hearty soup is traditionally served as a first course in Italian homes, we love it as a casual entrée. ■

½ pound (about 1¼ cups) dried white beans, such as cannellini, great northern, or navy, picked over and rinsed
3 tablespoons extra-virgin olive oil
¼ pound thinly sliced pancetta, chopped
1 large onion, chopped
3 garlic cloves, finely chopped
1 (14- to 15-ounce) can whole tomatoes in juice, drained, juice reserved, and chopped
3½ cups Chicken Stock (page 153) or store-bought reduced-sodium broth
2 cups water
1 (3-by-2-inch) piece Parmigiano-Reggiano rind (about ½ inch thick)
1½ teaspoons salt
¼ teaspoon freshly ground black pepper
1 (7½-ounce) jar peeled cooked whole chestnuts, rinsed, drained, and halved (see Sources)
½ pound Tuscan kale (see headnote) or regular kale, stems and center ribs discarded, leaves torn into bite-sized pieces
2 teaspoons chopped fresh thyme
Finely grated Parmigiano-Reggiano
GARNISH: Parmigiano-Reggiano shavings; extra-virgin olive oil for drizzling; freshly ground black pepper; fresh thyme sprigs; peeled cooked whole chestnuts, coarsely chopped

QUICK-SOAKING BEANS

We would all love to be the sort of cook who remembers to soak beans overnight in preparation for cooking them the next day. More often than not, though, inspiration strikes at the last minute, and so we rely on the quick-soaking method; it still takes an hour, but that gives us enough time to get the rest of the meal under way.

Put the beans in a saucepan and cover with cold water by 2 inches. Bring to a boil and boil for 2 minutes, remove from the heat, and let the beans soak, covered, for 1 hour. Drain.

Soak beans in cold water to cover by 2 inches at room temperature (refrigerate if kitchen is warm), for 8 to 12 hours (or see above for quick-soaking procedure); drain.

Heat oil in a 6- to 8-quart wide heavy pot over moderate heat until hot but not smoking. Add pancetta, onion, and garlic and cook, stirring occasionally, until browned, about 8 minutes. Add tomatoes with juice, beans, stock, water, cheese rind, salt, and pepper and bring to a boil, then reduce heat and simmer, uncovered, until beans are tender, 45 minutes to 1 hour.

Discard cheese rind and stir in chestnuts. Transfer 2 cups soup to a blender and puree (use caution when blending hot liquids) until smooth. Return to pot. Stir in kale and simmer, uncovered, stirring occasionally, until leaves are tender, 10 to 15 minutes. Stir in thyme.

Sprinkle soup with Parmesan to taste and serve with remaining garnishes.

COOK'S NOTE

■ The soup can be made up to 3 days ahead. Cool, uncovered, then refrigerate, covered. Add water if necessary to thin to the desired consistency when reheating.

Venetian-Style Bean and Pasta Soup

SERVES 8 AS A MAIN COURSE (MAKES ABOUT 12 CUPS)
ACTIVE TIME: 45 MINUTES ■ START TO FINISH: 3¾ HOURS
PLUS SOAKING TIME FOR BEANS

■ Many versions of *pasta fagioli* ("fah-*zhool*") are simply minestrone with some pasta added. Not so this sublime Venetian rendition. The focus is on the beans, which are simmered gently with a piece of Parmesan rind, pureed, and then topped with a small amount of tubetti pasta and a drizzle of olive oil. That's it, but, oh, the result: a voluptuous, elegant, and satisfying soup that will make you want to lick your bowl clean before asking for seconds. Borlotti beans are the traditional choice for Venetian *pasta fagioli*. They have thin tan skins speckled with red and take on a creamy consistency when cooked. ■

- 1 pound (2¾ cups) dried borlotti beans (see Cook's Note and Sources), picked over and rinsed
- ½ cup plus 2 tablespoons extra-virgin olive oil, plus additional for serving
- 2½ cups chopped onions
  Salt
- 2 medium carrots, chopped
- 2 celery ribs, chopped
- 5 large garlic cloves, finely chopped
- ¼ cup chopped fresh flat-leaf parsley
- 1 teaspoon dried rosemary, crumbled
  Freshly ground black pepper
- 1 (3-by-2-inch) piece Parmigiano-Reggiano rind (about ½ inch thick)
- ¾ pound ditalini or other small tubular pasta

Soak beans in cold water to cover by 2 inches at room temperature (refrigerate if kitchen is very warm) for 8 to 12 hours (or see page 129 for quick-soaking procedure). Drain in a colander set over a large bowl; reserve soaking liquid. Add enough water to soaking liquid to make 12 cups.

Heat ¼ cup oil in a 6- to 8-quart heavy pot over moderately high heat until hot but not smoking. Add onions with ½ teaspoon salt and cook, stirring occasionally, until beginning to brown, 8 to 9 min-utes. Add carrots, celery, garlic, parsley, rosemary, and ¼ teaspoon pepper and cook, stirring, for 5 minutes.

Add beans, cheese rind, and bean-soaking liquid, bring to a simmer, and simmer, uncovered, stirring occasionally, until beans are very tender, 2 to 3 hours, depending on age of beans; add more water if necessary to keep them covered and stir more frequently toward end of cooking. Stir in ¼ cup oil and 1¼ teaspoons salt, remove from heat, and cool for 20 minutes.

Discard cheese rind. Coarsely puree soup in batches in a blender (use caution when blending hot liquids), and transfer to a large bowl.

Return soup to pot and reheat over moderately low heat, stirring frequently and thinning soup with additional water if desired (soup is traditionally quite thick). Season with salt and pepper.

Meanwhile, cook pasta in a 6- to 8-quart pot of boiling salted water (3 tablespoons salt) until al dente. Drain in a colander, transfer to a large bowl, and toss with remaining 2 tablespoons oil and pepper to taste.

To serve, ladle soup into bowls, top with pasta, and drizzle with olive oil.

COOK'S NOTES

- Dried cranberry beans can be substituted for the borlotti beans, but the soup won't have quite the same depth of flavor. To compensate, add 1 tablespoon balsamic vinegar after the soup is pureed.
- The soup can be made in about one third the time in a 6- to 8-quart pressure cooker. Follow the recipe, but sauté the vegetables in the pressure cooker, uncovered, then add the beans, cheese rind, and only 8 cups liquid. Lock on the lid and bring to high pressure, then cook at high pressure (according to the manufacturer's instructions), for 45 minutes. Put the pressure cooker in the sink and run cold water over the lid until the pressure goes down completely.
- The soup, without the pasta, can be made up to 1 week ahead. Cool, uncovered, then refrigerate, covered (it will thicken considerably). Reheat over moderately low heat, thinning with water as necessary. The soup can also be frozen in an airtight container for up to 3 months.

Parmigiano-Reggiano is a cheese of many uses. It commonly appears as a condiment, of course, grated or shaved into and over pastas, risottos, salads, and soups. Or pass a large wedge of it around the table after dinner and let people help themselves to the golden, crumbly shards. "There's something about the cheese," says Italian cooking authority Lynne Rossetto Kasper, "that brightens other flavors without overpowering them."

Even the rind, carefully saved for the soup pot, has mystique. "Parmigiano has always been expensive, and Italians can't bear to throw any of it away," explains Kasper. "They use the last ounce of its soul."

What do you do with the gooey remnant once you've fished it out of the soup? "The rind is just hardened cheese," Kasper says. "Smear it on a piece of toasted bread and enjoy it."

When buying Parmigiano, make sure you are getting the genuine article. Production is closely regulated, so look for the words "Parmigiano-Reggiano" stamped on the rind. (If they're not there, you are probably looking at an Italian Grana Padano or an American *grana*, which should be much cheaper.)

For storage tips, we turned to Ihsan Gurdal of Formaggio Kitchen, in Cambridge, Massachusetts. "Buy only what you need, because freshly cut cheese tastes better," he says. "Wrap it in cheese paper, wax paper, or parchment paper; plastic wrap will suffocate the cheese and give it an off flavor." (If you buy Parmigiano-Reggiano from a shop that sells it in plastic-wrapped wedges, remove it from the plastic once you get home and rewrap it.) Store it in the crisper drawer of your refrigerator to keep it moist.

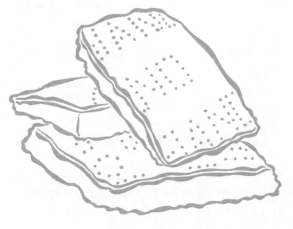

Mexican Black Bean Soup with Ancho Chiles

SERVES 6 TO 8 AS A MAIN COURSE
(MAKES ABOUT 12 CUPS)
ACTIVE TIME: 1 HOUR ■ START TO FINISH: 2½ HOURS

■ This vegetarian black bean soup is from the Cocinar Mexicano Cooking School in the small town of Tepoztlán, Mexico, just fifty miles south of Mexico City. The recipe calls for traditional ingredients and techniques to produce a soup that is both refined and a bit wild. The pureed beans are velvety—not too thin, not too thick—while anchos, both in the soup itself and as a garnish, add their own layer of smoky flavor and a touch of heat. Brash-tasting epazote has long been a common addition to black bean recipes in Mexico; the herb mellows as it cooks, adding an ineffable depth to the soup. Finally, frying the pureed tomatoes with the garlic and onion before adding them to the soup helps reduce the juices and concentrate their flavor. ■

1 pound (about 2⅓ cups) dried black beans, picked over and rinsed
3 quarts water
1 (3-inch) sprig fresh epazote (see headnote) or cilantro
  Salt
1 pound tomatoes, chopped
1 garlic clove
1 large white onion, chopped
3 tablespoons olive oil
4 dried ancho chiles (see Sources), wiped clean
3–4 cups vegetable oil for deep-frying
6 (5- to 6-inch) corn tortillas, cut into ½-inch-wide strips

ACCOMPANIMENTS: *crema* (see Sources) or sour cream

Combine beans, water, epazote, and 1 teaspoon salt in a 6- to 8-quart heavy pot and bring to a boil, then reduce heat and simmer, covered, until beans are tender, 1½ to 2 hours. Remove from heat.

Puree tomatoes with garlic and ½ cup chopped onion in a blender.

Heat 1 tablespoon olive oil in a 10-inch heavy skillet over moderate heat until it shimmers. Add tomato puree (it will spatter) and cook, stirring occasionally, for 5 minutes. Remove sauce from heat.

Slit chiles lengthwise and stem, seed, and remove ribs. Heat a dry large heavy skillet, preferably cast-iron, over moderate heat until hot. Open chiles out flat and toast, turning and pressing with tongs, until more pliable and slightly darker, 30 seconds to 1 minute. Transfer to a plate.

Heat remaining 2 tablespoons olive oil in same skillet over moderately high heat until it shimmers. Add half of chiles and remaining onion and sauté, stirring occasionally, until onion is just tender, about 8 minutes.

Drain beans, reserving cooking liquid, and add beans to skillet. Cook over moderate heat, stirring frequently, for 5 minutes.

Puree bean mixture with reserved cooking liquid in batches in blender (use caution when blending hot liquids), then return to pot. Bring to a simmer, stir in tomato sauce and ¾ teaspoon salt, and simmer, stirring occasionally, for 15 minutes.

Meanwhile, heat 1 inch vegetable oil in a 12-inch skillet until it shimmers. Add tortilla strips, in batches, in a single layer, and fry, stirring occasionally, until crisp and golden, 2 to 3 minutes per batch. Transfer to paper towels to drain.

Cut remaining toasted chiles into thin julienne with kitchen shears.

Thin soup with water if desired and season with salt. Serve drizzled with *crema* and topped with tortilla and chile strips.

COOK'S NOTE

■ The soup can be made up to 3 days ahead. Cool, uncovered, then refrigerate, covered.

Best Red Bean Soup

SERVES 8 TO 10 AS A MAIN COURSE
(MAKES ABOUT 14 CUPS)
ACTIVE TIME: 40 MINUTES ■ START TO FINISH: 2 HOURS
PLUS SOAKING TIME FOR BEANS

■ Based on the hearty bean versions found throughout the Caribbean, this red bean soup is so full-flavored that you might never guess that it is vegetarian. It gets its phenomenal depth from a *sofrito*, a sautéed mix of onion, garlic, sun-dried tomatoes, and peppers, notably *ají dulce* chiles. Commonly used in Puerto Rican cooking, these little lantern-shaped peppers, which range in color from green to red, are not at all hot but rather have a fruity sweetness (Cubanelles will give a slightly different result, but will work.) The last-minute sprinkling of gremolata is not traditional, but it adds a final blast of freshness that we find irresistible. ■

FOR SOUP
  1 pound (about 2½ cups) dried red kidney beans, picked over and rinsed
  1 large onion, chopped
  4 large garlic cloves, chopped
  4 *ají dulce* chiles (see Cook's Note and Sources), stemmed and seeded
  2 Cubanelle or Italian frying peppers, seeded and finely chopped
  ½ cup packed chopped cilantro leaves
  ¼ cup chopped sun-dried tomatoes, preferably oil-packed
  ¼ cup extra-virgin olive oil, plus additional for drizzling
  1 Turkish bay leaf or ½ California bay leaf
  ½ teaspoon sweet *pimentón* (Spanish smoked paprika; see Sources)
  10 cups water
    Salt and freshly ground black pepper
  1 tablespoon fresh lemon juice
FOR GREMOLATA
  1 teaspoon finely grated lemon zest
  1 garlic clove, minced
  ¼ cup finely chopped fresh flat-leaf parsley

SOAK THE BEANS AND MAKE THE SOUP: Soak beans in cold water to cover by 2 inches at room temperature (refrigerate if kitchen is very warm) for 8 to 12 hours (or see page 129 for quick-soaking procedure); drain.

Cook onion, garlic, chiles, peppers, cilantro, and sun-dried tomatoes in olive oil in a large heavy pot over moderate heat, stirring occasionally, until browned, about 12 minutes. Add bay leaf and *pimentón* and cook, stirring, for 2 minutes.

Add drained beans and water, bring to a simmer, and simmer, covered, until beans are very tender, about 1½ hours. Discard bay leaf.

Puree soup in batches in a blender (use caution when blending hot liquids). Reheat in cleaned pot over moderately low heat. Season with salt and pepper and stir in lemon juice.

MAKE THE GREMOLATA: Stir together gremolata ingredients in a small bowl.

Serve soup sprinkled with gremolata and drizzled with oil.

COOK'S NOTES

■ If *ají dulce* chiles are not available, substitute an additional Cubanelle pepper.

■ The soup, without the gremolata, can be made up to 3 days ahead. Cool, uncovered, then refrigerate, covered. Add water if necessary to thin to the desired consistency when reheating.

Gascon White Bean Soup

SERVES 4 TO 6 AS A MAIN COURSE (MAKES ABOUT 12 CUPS)
ACTIVE TIME: 30 MINUTES ■ START TO FINISH: 3 HOURS
PLUS SOAKING TIME FOR BEANS

■ Hearty country soups known as *garbures* have long been a staple in southwestern France. Made with a combination of beans, preserved meats, and vegetables (cabbage is traditional), they are meant to be substantial enough that a spoon can stand upright in them. Though not quite that thick, our version is redolent of smoked ham, loaded with cabbage and potato, and seasoned with thyme, parsley, and garlic. ■

1 cup (7 ounces) dried white beans, such as great northern, navy, or cannellini, picked over and rinsed
2 large meaty smoked ham hocks (2½ pounds total)
3 quarts water
1 whole clove
1 medium onion, peeled
6 fresh parsley sprigs
1 fresh thyme sprig
1 Turkish bay leaf or ¼ California bay leaf
2 garlic cloves, finely chopped
1 pound yellow-fleshed potatoes, such as Yukon Gold (3–4 medium)
1 pound cabbage, cored and cut into ½-inch pieces (6 cups)
  Salt and freshly ground black pepper
½ stick (4 tablespoons) unsalted butter, softened
12 (½-inch-thick) baguette slices

Soak beans in cold water to cover by 2 inches at room temperature (refrigerate if kitchen is very warm), for 8 to 12 hours (or see page 129 for quick-soaking procedure); drain.

Bring ham hocks and water to a boil in a 6- to 7-quart wide heavy pot, skimming off any froth. Reduce heat and simmer, covered, for 1 hour.

Stick clove into onion. Add onion, beans, parsley, thyme, bay leaf, and garlic to pot and simmer, uncovered, stirring occasionally, until beans are almost tender, 40 to 50 minutes.

When beans are almost done, peel potatoes and

cut into 1-inch pieces. Add potatoes and cabbage to beans and simmer, uncovered, until vegetables are very tender, 20 to 25 minutes. Remove from heat, remove ham hocks, and let cool slightly.

When ham hocks are cool enough to handle, discard skin and bones and cut meat into bite-sized pieces. Stir into soup and season with salt and pepper to taste. Discard onion and bay leaf.

Spread butter on both sides of bread slices and toast in a 12-inch heavy skillet over moderate heat, turning once, until golden, about 2 minutes.

Serve soup with toasts.

COOK'S NOTE

- The soup improves in flavor if made at least 1 day ahead, and it can be made up to 3 days ahead. Cool, uncovered, then refrigerate, covered. Remove any solidified fat, then reheat, adding water if necessary to thin soup to the desired consistency.

Lentil, Sausage, and Escarole Soup

SERVES 6 AS A MAIN COURSE (MAKES ABOUT 7 CUPS)
ACTIVE TIME: 20 MINUTES ■ START TO FINISH: 45 MINUTES

■ Hearty and homey, this soup dresses up brown lentils with sweet Italian sausage and escarole. Put out some crusty bread and a leafy green salad, and your meal is complete. ■

- 1⅓ cups (11 ounces) brown lentils, picked over and rinsed
- 5 cups water
- 3½ cups Chicken Stock (page 153) or store-bought reduced-sodium broth
- 1 Turkish bay leaf or ½ California bay leaf
- 4 garlic cloves, finely chopped
- 2 tablespoons extra-virgin olive oil
- 1 pound sweet Italian sausage links, cut into 1-inch pieces
- 1 medium onion, finely chopped
- 2 medium carrots, finely chopped
- 2 celery ribs, finely chopped
  Salt and freshly ground black pepper
- 2 tablespoons tomato paste

- ½ pound escarole, chopped (4 cups packed)
- 1–2 tablespoons red wine vinegar
  ACCOMPANIMENT: croutons

Combine lentils, water, stock, bay leaf, and half of garlic in a 4-quart pot and bring to a simmer.

Meanwhile, heat oil in a 5- to 6-quart wide heavy pot over moderately high heat. Add sausage and brown, turning occasionally, about 7 minutes. Transfer with a slotted spoon to a bowl. Reduce heat to moderate and add onion, carrots, celery, remaining garlic, 1 teaspoon salt, and ½ teaspoon pepper. Cook, stirring occasionally, until vegetables are softened, about 5 minutes. Stir in tomato paste and cook, stirring, for 2 minutes. Add sausage and lentils, with cooking liquid, and simmer, uncovered, just until lentils are tender, 5 to 10 minutes.

Stir in escarole and cook until tender, about 3 minutes. Discard bay leaf. Stir in vinegar (to taste) and season with salt and pepper.

Serve soup topped with croutons.

COOK'S NOTE

- The soup can be made up to 2 days ahead. Cool, uncovered, then refrigerate, covered.

Split Pea Soup with Pumpernickel Croutons

SERVES 6 TO 8 AS A MAIN COURSE (MAKES ABOUT 12 CUPS)
ACTIVE TIME: 35 MINUTES ■ START TO FINISH: 4 HOURS

■ If you've always thought of pea soup as drab, this one will change your mind. It's light, even colorful, due to an extra handful of sliced carrots and frozen peas added toward the end of cooking. To get every ounce of flavor from the ham hocks, we first make a light broth with them and then simmer the bones in the soup, reserving the meat to stir in later. Pumpernickel croutons add crunch and contrast. ■

- 2 meaty smoked ham hocks (1¾–2 pounds total)
- 4 quarts water
- 5 tablespoons olive oil
- 4 large carrots, 2 chopped, 2 halved lengthwise and cut into ¼-inch-thick slices

1 large onion, chopped

2 celery ribs, chopped

1 pound (2¼ cups) dried green split peas, picked over and rinsed

Kosher salt

¼ teaspoon freshly ground black pepper

5 cups ½-inch cubes pumpernickel bread (from a 1¼-pound loaf)

1 cup frozen peas (not thawed)

Combine ham hocks and water in a deep 6-quart pot, bring to a simmer, and simmer, uncovered, until meat is tender, 1½ to 2 hours.

Transfer ham hocks to a cutting board. Measure broth: If you have more than 12 cups, boil it until reduced; if less, add enough water to make 12 cups. Set aside.

When hocks are cool enough to handle, discard skin and cut meat into ¼-inch pieces; reserve bones.

Heat 2 tablespoons oil in a 6- to 8-quart heavy pot over moderate heat until hot but not smoking. Add chopped carrots, onion, and celery and cook, stirring, until softened, 6 to 8 minutes. Add split peas, 1 teaspoon salt, pepper, ham hock broth, and reserved bones, bring to a simmer, and simmer, uncovered, stirring occasionally, until peas are falling apart and soup is slightly thickened, about 1½ hours.

Meanwhile, put a rack in middle of oven and preheat oven to 400°F.

Toss bread with remaining 3 tablespoons oil and 1 teaspoon salt in a large bowl. Spread in one layer on a large baking sheet and bake until crisp, about 10 minutes. Cool on pan on a rack.

Remove bones from soup with tongs or a slotted spoon and discard. Add sliced carrots and ham to soup and simmer, uncovered, until carrots are tender, 10 to 15 minutes.

Add frozen peas and simmer, uncovered, stirring, just until hot, about 3 minutes. Season with salt.

Serve soup topped with croutons.

COOK'S NOTES

■ The soup is best when made, without the frozen peas, up to 1 day ahead, to allow the flavors time to develop. Cool, uncovered, then refrigerate, covered. When reheating, add water if necessary to thin to the desired consistency, stir in the peas, and simmer just until hot.

■ The croutons can be made up to 3 days ahead and, once cooled completely, kept in an airtight container at room temperature.

Buttered Barley and Onion Soup

SERVES 8 AS A MAIN COURSE (MAKES ABOUT 10 CUPS)
ACTIVE TIME: 30 MINUTES ■ START TO FINISH: 1½ HOURS
(DOES NOT INCLUDE MAKING STOCK)

■ Taking the time to toast barley before cooking it amplifies and deepens the grain's nuttiness. That step, along with making a rich chicken stock, elevates this simple soup into an instant classic. Butter, stirred in at the end, imparts velvetiness, while a small amount of chopped carrots, celery, and parsley adds sweetness and color. Be aware that the barley will continue to absorb liquid if you make the soup ahead—you'll need to add extra stock or water when you reheat it. ■

1 cup (7 ounces) pearl barley

2 tablespoons olive oil

4 medium onions, finely chopped

2 celery ribs, finely chopped

2 carrots, finely chopped

3 garlic cloves, finely chopped

Salt and freshly ground black pepper

5 cups water

4 cups Chicken Stock (page 153) or Pressure-Cooker Chicken Stock (page 152)

½ stick (4 tablespoons) unsalted butter, cut into 8 pieces

⅓ cup finely chopped fresh flat-leaf parsley

Put a rack in middle of oven and preheat oven to 375°F.

Spread barley in a shallow baking pan and toast in oven, shaking pan occasionally, until aromatic, 5 to 7 minutes. Cool in pan on a rack.

Heat oil in a 5- to 6-quart heavy pot over moderately high heat. Add onions, celery, carrots, garlic, 2 teaspoons salt, and ½ teaspoon pepper and cook, stirring occasionally, until onions are golden brown, about 10 minutes. Add barley, water, and stock and bring to a boil, then reduce heat and simmer, partially covered, until barley is tender, 1 to 1¼ hours.

Add butter, stirring until melted, then stir in parsley. Season with salt and pepper.

COOK'S NOTE

- The soup can be made up to 4 days ahead. Cool, uncovered, then refrigerate, covered. When reheating, add up to 2 cups water or stock if necessary to thin to the desired consistency, stirring occasionally.

Salmon and Potato Chowder

SERVES 4 AS A MAIN COURSE (MAKES ABOUT 8 CUPS)
ACTIVE TIME: 25 MINUTES ■ START TO FINISH: 45 MINUTES

■ Chowders are usually plain-looking, but this one, with its cream-white canvas dotted with pink salmon, pale green celery, and verdant dill, is pretty. ■

- 4 bacon slices, cut crosswise into 1-inch pieces
- 1 medium onion, cut into ½-inch cubes
- 2 celery ribs, cut into ½-inch cubes
- 1 pound boiling potatoes, peeled and cut into 1-inch cubes
- 1 teaspoon salt
- ¼ teaspoon freshly ground black pepper
- 1 cup water
- 2 cups whole milk
- 1 pound skinless salmon fillet, trimmed of any dark flesh and cut into 1-inch pieces
- 2 tablespoons chopped fresh dill
- 1 tablespoon unsalted butter

Cook bacon in a 3-quart heavy saucepan over moderate heat, stirring frequently, until crisp. With a slotted spoon, transfer to paper towels to drain.

Pour off all but 2 tablespoons fat from saucepan. Add onion, celery, potatoes, salt, and pepper and cook, stirring occasionally, until onion is softened, 5 to 7 minutes. Stir in water and bring to a boil, then reduce heat and simmer, covered, until potatoes are almost tender, about 10 minutes.

Add milk, bring to a simmer, and simmer, uncovered, until potatoes are tender, 4 to 5 minutes. Stir

in salmon, dill, and butter and simmer gently until salmon is just cooked through, 3 to 4 minutes.

Serve chowder sprinkled with bacon.

Creamless Clam Chowder

SERVES 6 AS A FIRST COURSE OR LIGHT MAIN COURSE
(MAKES ABOUT 7 CUPS)
ACTIVE TIME: 45 MINUTES ■ START TO FINISH: 1 HOUR

■ A simple clam chowder for purists, this contains neither cream nor tomatoes, highlighting the clams themselves. To ensure that there's not a speck of grit, we cook the clams separately and strain their cooking liquid before adding it to the soup. ■

- ½ cup water
- 24 small hard-shelled clams (less than 2 inches wide), such as littlenecks, scrubbed well
- ½ stick (4 tablespoons) unsalted butter
- 1 large onion, chopped
- 1 large garlic clove, finely chopped
- 1 pound russet (baking) potatoes (2 medium), peeled and cut into ⅓-inch cubes
- 2 celery ribs, chopped
- 2 medium carrots, chopped
- 1 Turkish bay leaf or ½ California bay leaf
  Salt and freshly ground black pepper
- ½ cup dry white wine
- 3 (8-ounce) bottles clam juice
- 2 tablespoons chopped fresh flat-leaf parsley

Bring water to a simmer in a 2- to 3-quart heavy saucepan. Add clams and simmer, covered, until they open wide, 6 to 8 minutes; check frequently after 6 minutes and transfer opened clams to a bowl. Discard any that have not opened after 8 minutes. Remove pan from heat; reserve cooking liquid.

When clams are cool enough to handle, remove from shells and chop. Pour cooking liquid through a sieve lined with a dampened paper towel into a bowl.

Heat butter in a 3- to 4-quart heavy saucepan over moderate heat until foam subsides. Add onion and garlic and cook, stirring occasionally, until softened but not browned, about 6 minutes.

Add potatoes, celery, carrots, bay leaf, ½ teaspoon

salt, and ½ teaspoon pepper and cook, stirring occasionally, until vegetables begin to soften, about 4 minutes. Add wine and simmer until liquid is reduced by half, about 5 minutes. Add bottled clam juice, bring to a simmer, and simmer, covered, until vegetables are tender, 8 to 10 minutes. Remove bay leaf.

Transfer 1 cup soup (with vegetables) to a blender (use caution when blending hot liquids) and puree. Stir puree back into soup. Stir in parsley, chopped clams, reserved clam cooking liquid, and salt and pepper to taste and reheat gently (do not simmer).

COOK'S NOTE

- The soup can be made up to 1 day ahead. Cool, uncovered, then refrigerate, covered. Reheat gently before serving.

Shellfish Chowder with Bacon and Herbs

SERVES 6 AS A FIRST COURSE, 4 AS A MAIN COURSE
(MAKES ABOUT 7 CUPS)
ACTIVE TIME: 20 MINUTES ■ START TO FINISH: 40 MINUTES

■ Utterly luxurious-tasting but easy enough to pull together for a weeknight dinner party, this chowder is filled with shrimp, scallops, lobster, and salty nuggets of bacon. Using whole milk instead of cream is the key to satisfaction without heaviness. ■

- 5 bacon slices, finely chopped
- 2 boiling potatoes (12 ounces), cut into ¼-inch dice
- ½ cup finely chopped shallots
- ¾ cup bottled clam juice
- 2½ cups whole milk
- ⅛ teaspoon cayenne
- ¼ pound shrimp in shells, peeled, deveined, and cut into ½-inch pieces
- ½ pound sea scallops, tough ligament removed from side of each if necessary, scallops quartered
- 1 teaspoon salt
- ½ pound cooked lobster meat, cut into ½-inch pieces, or ½ pound lump crabmeat, picked over for shells and cartilage
- 2 tablespoons chopped fresh cilantro
- 2 tablespoons chopped fresh chives

Cook bacon in a 5-quart heavy pot over moderate heat, stirring occasionally, until crisp, about 5 minutes. With a slotted spoon, transfer bacon to paper towels to drain.

Pour off all but 1 tablespoon fat from pot and stir in potatoes, shallots, and clam juice. Bring to a boil, then reduce heat and simmer, covered, until potatoes are tender and most of liquid has evaporated, about 8 minutes.

Stir in milk and cayenne and return just to a simmer. Add shrimp, scallops, and salt and simmer, stirring occasionally, until shellfish is just cooked through, 3 to 5 minutes. Stir in lobster and half of herbs and simmer for 1 minute.

Serve chowder sprinkled with bacon and remaining herbs.

Oyster Soup with Frizzled Leeks

SERVES 8 AS A FIRST COURSE (MAKES ABOUT 11 CUPS)
ACTIVE TIME: 1 HOUR ■ START TO FINISH: 1¼ HOURS

■ A topping of frizzled leeks adds distinctive crunch to this creamy soup studded with oysters. It's important to use small oysters, such as Kumamoto or Prince Edward Island; when we tested the recipe with larger ones, the flavor was too briny. ■

FOR FRIED LEEKS
- 2 large leeks (white and pale green parts only)
- 4 cups vegetable oil for deep-frying

FOR SOUP
- 1½ cups shucked small oysters, such as Kumamoto or Prince Edward Island (about 6 dozen), with 1½ cups of their liquor (if necessary, add enough bottled clam juice to make 1½ cups)
- 2 medium leeks (white and pale green parts only), chopped and washed well
- 2 large russet (baking) potatoes (1 pound total), peeled and cut into ½-inch cubes
- Salt
- 3 tablespoons unsalted butter
- 3½ cups water
- 1 cup half-and-half
- Pinch of cayenne

SPECIAL EQUIPMENT: a deep-fat thermometer

FRY THE LEEKS: Trim leeks and cut into 2-inch lengths, then cut lengthwise into thin strips; you need 2 cups. Wash leek strips well and pat dry.

Heat oil in a 4-quart deep heavy saucepan until it registers 360°F on thermometer. Fry leeks in 8 batches, stirring, until golden, about 10 seconds per batch; transfer with a slotted spoon to paper towels to drain (leeks will crisp as they cool).

MAKE THE SOUP: Pick over oysters, discarding any bits of shell, and rinse well.

Cook chopped leeks and potatoes with 1 teaspoon salt in butter in a 4-quart heavy saucepan, covered, over low heat, stirring occasionally, until leeks are golden and potatoes are beginning to soften, about 15 minutes. Add water and bring to a boil. Reduce heat and simmer, covered, over moderate heat until potatoes are very tender, about 10 minutes.

Puree soup in batches in a blender (use caution when blending hot liquids) until very smooth; transfer to a bowl. Return soup to cleaned saucepan. Add oyster liquor and half-and-half and bring to a simmer over moderate heat, stirring occasionally; do not boil. Add oysters and cayenne and cook, stirring occasionally, just until oysters become plump and edges curl, about 3 minutes. Season with salt.

Serve soup topped with fried leeks.

COOK'S NOTES

- The fried leeks can be made up to 3 days ahead and kept in a sealed plastic bag at room temperature.
- The soup base (without the oyster liquor, half-and-half, oysters, and cayenne) can be made and pureed up to 2 days ahead. Cool, uncovered, then refrigerate, covered. Reheat over moderate heat before proceeding.

Italian Seafood Soup
Zuppa di Pesce

SERVES 6 TO 8 AS A MAIN COURSE (MAKES ABOUT 14 CUPS)
ACTIVE TIME: 1 HOUR ■ START TO FINISH: 1 HOUR

■ This is the *zuppa di pesce* of your dreams, a luxuriously fragrant taste of the sea, with squid, shrimp, mussels, clams, and fish. The distinctive taste of each ingredient shines through. The base is homemade fish stock (or bottled clam juice if you want to save time), enriched with chopped tomatoes, white wine, and fresh herbs. With garlic toasts and a leafy green salad, this soup makes a meal. ■

FOR SOUP
- 1 pound cleaned squid, bodies and tentacles separated
- ½ pound large shrimp in shells (21–25 per pound), peeled and deveined
- Salt
- ⅛ teaspoon freshly ground black pepper
- ¼ cup olive oil
- 3 garlic cloves, finely chopped
- ½ teaspoon red pepper flakes
- ¼ teaspoon dried oregano, crumbled
- 1 cup dry white wine
- 4½ cups water
- 12 small hard-shelled clams (less than 2 inches wide), scrubbed
- 12 mussels, preferably cultivated, scrubbed and beards removed
- 4 cups Fish Stock (page 154) or bottled clam juice
- 2 (14- to 15-ounce) cans diced tomatoes in juice
- 1 teaspoon sugar
- 1 pound skinless halibut fillet or other thick meaty white fish fillets, cut into 1-inch pieces
- ¼ cup chopped fresh basil
- ¼ cup chopped fresh flat-leaf parsley

FOR GARLIC TOASTS
- 1 (12-inch-long) Italian loaf, cut into ½-inch-thick slices
- 2 tablespoons olive oil
- Salt
- 1 garlic clove, halved crosswise
- 2 tablespoons finely chopped fresh flat-leaf parsley

ACCOMPANIMENT: extra-virgin olive oil

MAKE THE SOUP: Rinse squid and pat dry. If they are large, halve rings of tentacles. Cut longer tentacles into 2-inch pieces. Pull off flaps from bodies and cut into ¼-inch-thick slices. Cut bodies crosswise into ¼-inch-wide rings.

Pat shrimp dry and sprinkle with ¼ teaspoon salt and pepper. Heat oil in a 6- to 8-quart wide heavy pot over moderately high heat until hot but not smoking. Add shrimp in 2 batches and sear, turning once, until golden but not cooked through, about 2 minutes per batch. Transfer with a slotted spoon to a bowl.

Add garlic, red pepper flakes, and oregano to pot and cook, stirring, until garlic is golden, about 30 seconds. Add wine and ½ cup water and bring to a boil. Add clams and simmer, covered, until they open wide; check frequently after 6 minutes and transfer opened clams to bowl with shrimp. (Discard any clams that have not opened after 8 minutes.) Stir mussels into pot and cook, covered, until shells just open wide; check frequently after 3 minutes and transfer opened mussels to bowl with shrimp. (Discard any mussels that have not opened after 6 minutes.)

Add stock to pot, along with tomatoes with juice, sugar, remaining 4 cups water, and ½ teaspoon salt, bring to a simmer, and simmer, uncovered, for 15 minutes.

MEANWHILE, MAKE THE TOASTS: Put a rack in middle of oven and preheat oven to 425°F.

Arrange bread slices in one layer on a baking sheet, drizzle with oil, and sprinkle with salt. Bake, turning once, until golden, about 10 minutes.

Transfer toasts to a rack to cool slightly, then rub lightly with cut sides of garlic and sprinkle with parsley.

FINISH THE SOUP: Add halibut to stock mixture and cook at a bare simmer, covered, until just cooked through, about 2 minutes. Stir in squid and shellfish, then remove from heat and let stand, covered, for 1 minute. Stir in basil and parsley.

Ladle into bowls, drizzle with olive oil, and serve with toasts alongside for dipping.

COOK'S NOTE
- The garlic toasts can be made up to 1 day ahead and kept in an airtight container at room temperature.

Quick and Easy Cioppino

SERVES 4 AS A MAIN COURSE (MAKES ABOUT 10 CUPS)
ACTIVE TIME: 10 MINUTES ■ START TO FINISH: 40 MINUTES

■ The legacy of San Francisco's Italian and Portuguese immigrants—many of them fishermen—lives on in this fast and fuss-free take on the North Beach favorite, with fresh fennel adding a subtle touch of anise to the tomato-based seafood stew. ■

1 medium fennel bulb, stalks discarded, bulb cut into 6 wedges
1 medium onion, quartered
3 garlic cloves, smashed and peeled
3 tablespoons extra-virgin olive oil
2 Turkish bay leaves or 1 California bay leaf
1½ teaspoons dried thyme, crumbled
⅛ teaspoon red pepper flakes
1½ teaspoons salt
½ teaspoon freshly ground black pepper
1 (28-ounce) can crushed tomatoes in juice
1½ cups water
1 cup full-bodied red wine, such as Zinfandel or Syrah
1 (8-ounce) bottle clam juice
1 pound skinless thick white-fleshed fish fillets, such as halibut, hake, or pollack, cut into 2-inch chunks
1 pound mussels, preferably cultivated, scrubbed and beards removed

Pulse fennel, onion, and garlic in a food processor until coarsely chopped.

Heat oil in a 5- to 6-quart heavy pot over moderately high heat until it shimmers. Stir in chopped vegetables, bay leaves, thyme, red pepper flakes, salt, and pepper, cover, and cook over moderate heat, stirring once or twice, until vegetables begin to soften, about 4 minutes.

Add tomatoes with juice, water, wine, and clam juice, bring to a boil, and boil, covered, for 20 minutes to allow flavors to blend.

Stir in seafood and cook, uncovered, until fish is just cooked through and mussels have opened wide, 4 to 6 minutes; discard any mussels that remain unopened after 6 minutes. Discard bay leaves.

Provençal Fish Soup with Croûtes and Saffron Rouille

SERVES 10 TO 12 AS A FIRST COURSE, 6 AS A MAIN COURSE
(MAKES ABOUT 12 CUPS)
ACTIVE TIME: 1¼ HOURS ■ START TO FINISH: 1¾ HOURS

■ The summer sun of the South of France shines through this robust fish soup, with its heady aromas of tomatoes, orange zest, and fennel. We cook the soup until the ingredients have combined into a fragrant mash and then press it all through a food mill. It's a job that requires a bit of elbow grease, but the rewards are worth it. We like whiting, either fresh or frozen, for this soup because its delicate structure passes relatively easily through the mill. Perch, cod, and smelts also work well. ■

⅓ cup extra-virgin olive oil
4 medium leeks (white and pale green parts only), halved lengthwise, chopped, and washed well
1 large fennel bulb, small fronds reserved for garnish, stalks discarded, bulb cored and cut into ¼-inch pieces
3 medium carrots, chopped
2 celery ribs, chopped
4 large garlic cloves, finely chopped
1 tablespoon herbes de Provence
4 Turkish bay leaves or 2 California bay leaves
1 tablespoon salt
½ teaspoon freshly ground black pepper
¼ teaspoon cayenne
⅛ teaspoon crumbled saffron threads
5 tomatoes, chopped
2 cups dry white wine
4 (1-by-3-inch) strips orange zest, removed with a vegetable peeler
5 pounds whole whiting (with heads), cleaned, rinsed well to remove all traces of blood and gills, and cut crosswise into 2- to 3-inch-wide pieces (see headnote)
6 cups water
3 tablespoons tomato paste
6–12 (¾-inch-thick) slices baguette (1 slice per serving)

ACCOMPANIMENT: Saffron Rouille (recipe follows)
SPECIAL EQUIPMENT: a food mill fitted with a fine disk

Heat oil in an 8-quart heavy pot over moderate heat until hot but not smoking. Add leeks, fennel, carrots, celery, garlic, herbes de Provence, bay leaves, salt, black pepper, cayenne, and saffron and cook, stirring occasionally, until vegetables are softened, about 10 minutes.

Add tomatoes, wine, and zest, bring to a boil, and boil for 30 seconds (to reduce acidity). Add fish, water, and tomato paste, bring to a simmer, and simmer, uncovered, stirring occasionally, until fish completely falls apart, about 30 minutes.

MEANWHILE, MAKE THE CROÛTES: Put a rack in middle of oven and preheat oven to 350°F.

Arrange baguette slices in one layer on a baking sheet and bake until golden brown and dried, about 20 minutes. Set aside.

Force soup through food mill into a large heavy pot; discard solids. Reheat soup, stirring occasionally.

Mound rouille on croûtes and put 1 in bottom of each of 6 to 12 soup bowls. Pour soup over croûtes and garnish with fennel fronds.

COOK'S NOTES

■ The soup can be made up to 2 days ahead. Cool, uncovered, then refrigerate, covered. Reheat gently before serving.
■ The croûtes can be made up to 2 days ahead and, once cooled completely, kept in an airtight container at room temperature.

Saffron Rouille

MAKES ABOUT 1½ CUPS
ACTIVE TIME: 10 MINUTES ■ START TO FINISH: 10 MINUTES

■ A traditional garnish to bouillabaisse and other fish stews and soups, rouille ("roo-*ee*") is usually made by pounding garlic, bread crumbs, roasted red peppers, chiles, and olive oil with a mortar and pestle. This delicious, saffron-tinted version, which uses bottled red peppers and mayonnaise, is faster. ■

⅛ teaspoon crumbled saffron threads
¼ teaspoon hot water
1 cup mayonnaise
¼ cup bottled roasted red peppers, drained
¼ cup extra-virgin olive oil
½ teaspoon fresh lemon juice

2 teaspoons finely chopped garlic

½ teaspoon cayenne

¼ teaspoon salt

Sprinkle saffron over hot water and let stand for 1 minute. Blend saffron mixture with remaining ingredients in a blender until smooth.

COOK'S NOTE

■ The rouille can be made up to 2 days ahead and refrigerated, covered.

Classic Matzo Ball Soup

SERVES 8 AS A FIRST COURSE OR LIGHT MAIN COURSE
(MAKES ABOUT 10 CUPS)
ACTIVE TIME: 20 MINUTES ■ START TO FINISH: 1¾ HOURS
(DOES NOT INCLUDE MAKING STOCK)

■ These matzo balls are everything they should be: big, delicious, light, and fluffy. To achieve the airy texture, use a quick, deft touch when shaping them; if you overmix them, they will be tough and heavy. And work quickly so the dough doesn't get too warm, or bits may float off when you drop the matzo balls into the simmering water. For depth of flavor, these are made the traditional way, with schmaltz, or rendered chicken fat, which is available in the refrigerated kosher section of the supermarket. ■

FOR MATZO BALLS

¼ cup minced onion

¼ cup rendered chicken fat

4 large eggs, lightly beaten

1¼ cups matzo meal

¼ cup water

1 tablespoon chopped fresh flat-leaf parsley

1¼ teaspoons salt

¼ teaspoon freshly ground black pepper

FOR SOUP

Salt

10 cups Chicken Stock (page 153)

Freshly ground black pepper

1 cup finely chopped parsnip (about 1 medium)

1 cup finely chopped carrots (about 2 medium)

2 tablespoons chopped fresh dill

RENDERING CHICKEN FAT (SCHMALTZ)

Chicken fat must be rendered, or melted, before it can be used. Save raw chicken fat and fatty pieces of skin in the freezer until you have enough to render. (Six ounces of fat and three ounces of skin will render about 1 cup schmaltz.) Put the fat and pieces of skin, along with about ¼ cup water (to prevent scorching), into a heavy skillet and cook over moderately low heat until the fat melts and the skin turns golden brown and crunchy. Strain the fat through cheesecloth into a container and cool. It will keep for up to 1 month in the refrigerator or up to 3 months in the freezer. The bits of skin (gribenes) can be eaten while hot or added to mashed potatoes.

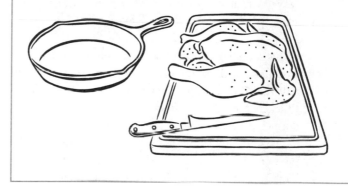

MAKE THE MATZO BALLS: Cook onion in chicken fat in a 10-inch skillet over moderate heat, stirring occasionally, until just golden, about 5 minutes. Transfer mixture to a large bowl. Stir in eggs, matzo meal, water, parsley, salt, and pepper until combined. Refrigerate, covered, for at least 1 hour.

Bring an 8-quart pot of salted water (2 tablespoons salt) to a boil. Meanwhile, with dampened hands, roll matzo mixture into 8 balls, each about 1¾ inches in diameter (balls will expand as they cook).

Add matzo balls to boiling water and simmer, covered, until cooked through, 35 minutes.

MEANWHILE, MAKE THE SOUP: About 15 minutes before matzo balls are cooked, bring stock to a simmer in a 4- to 6-quart pot and season with salt and pepper to taste. Add parsnip and carrots and cook, uncovered, until just tender, about 6 minutes.

With a slotted spoon, transfer matzo balls to broth

and simmer, uncovered, for 5 minutes. Sprinkle with chopped fresh dill.

COOK'S NOTES

- The uncooked matzo mixture can be refrigerated, covered, for up to 1 day.
- The soup (with the matzo balls) can be made up to 3 days ahead. Cool, uncovered, then refrigerate, covered. Reheat gently, covered, until the matzo balls are heated through, then add the dill.

Chicken Soupy Noodles

SERVES 4 TO 6 AS A MAIN COURSE (MAKES ABOUT 10 CUPS)
ACTIVE TIME: 25 MINUTES ■ START TO FINISH: 1¼ HOURS
(INCLUDES MAKING PRESSURE-COOKER STOCK)

■ This soup begs for the body and depth of homemade stock, and with a pressure cooker, you can make it in half the time. (If you don't own one, make our Rich Chicken Stock.) The stock is so rich that the soup doesn't need any extra chicken, which leaves room for lots of noodles. Lasagne noodles are more satisfying than the usual thin ones, and breaking them up by hand gives the soup a pleasantly homey look. Be sure to get dried noodles made with eggs, which will further enrich the broth. ■

  3 tablespoons olive oil
1¾ pounds leeks (white and pale green parts only), coarsely chopped and washed well
    Salt
  3 celery ribs, coarsely chopped
  ½ pound carrots, coarsely chopped
  1 teaspoon finely chopped fresh rosemary
  7 cups Rich Pressure-Cooker Chicken Stock (page 153) or Rich Chicken Stock (page 153)
 12 oven-ready (no-boil) egg lasagne noodles
    ACCOMPANIMENT: finely grated Parmigiano-Reggiano

Heat oil in a large heavy pot over medium heat, add leeks and ½ teaspoon salt, and cook, covered, stirring occasionally, until softened, about 3 minutes. Add celery, carrots, and rosemary and cook, covered, stirring occasionally, for 3 minutes.

Add stock and 1 teaspoon salt, bring to a simmer, and simmer, partially covered, until vegetables are tender, about 10 minutes.

Break lasagne noodles into 1- to 1½-inch pieces into simmering soup, stirring them in as you add them. Simmer briskly, uncovered, stirring occasionally, until noodles are tender, about 6 minutes. Serve with cheese.

COOK'S NOTE

- The soup, without the egg noodles, can be made up to 3 days ahead. Cool, uncovered, then refrigerate, covered. To serve, bring to a brisk simmer, add the noodles, and cook as directed above.

Thai-Style Chicken and Rice Soup

SERVES 8 AS A MAIN COURSE
ACTIVE TIME: 50 MINUTES ■ START TO FINISH: 1½ HOURS

■ This fragrant Thai-inspired version of chicken and rice soup offers both succor and intrigue. Simmering chicken stock with curry paste, garlic, ginger, and cilantro is a quick way to achieve the authentic flavor. ■

  8 cups Chicken Stock (page 153) or store-bought reduced-sodium broth
  4 cups water
  1 tablespoon Thai green curry paste (see Sources)
  4 garlic cloves, coarsely chopped
  1 (2-inch) piece fresh ginger, peeled and coarsely chopped
  1 teaspoon coriander seeds, crushed
  2 cups loosely packed fresh cilantro leaves, plus ½ cup chopped fresh cilantro (from 2 large bunches)
  1 cup jasmine rice
  ¾ pound boneless, skinless chicken breast, thinly sliced crosswise and slices cut lengthwise into thin strips, or ¾ pound medium shrimp in shells (31–35 per pound), peeled and deveined
  1 (13- to 14-ounce) can unsweetened coconut milk, well stirred
  ¼ pound snow peas, trimmed and cut diagonally into ¼-inch-wide strips

2 tablespoons Asian fish sauce

2 tablespoons fresh lime juice

1½ teaspoons salt, or to taste

ACCOMPANIMENT: lime wedges

Combine stock, water, curry paste, garlic, ginger, coriander seeds, and whole cilantro leaves in a 3- to 4-quart saucepan and bring to a boil. Reduce heat and simmer, uncovered, until ginger is softened, about 15 minutes.

Pour broth through a paper-towel-lined sieve into a 5- to 6-quart heavy pot; discard solids. Stir in rice and bring to a boil, then reduce heat and simmer, uncovered, stirring occasionally, until rice is tender, about 15 minutes.

Add chicken (or shrimp) and poach at a bare simmer, uncovered, until just cooked through, about 3 minutes. Stir in coconut milk, snow peas, and fish sauce and simmer, uncovered, just until snow peas are crisp-tender, about 2 minutes. Remove from heat and stir in lime juice, salt, and chopped cilantro.

Serve with lime wedges.

COOK'S NOTE

■ The soup can be made up to 1 day ahead. Cool, uncovered, then refrigerate, covered.

Smoky Tortilla Soup with Duck

SERVES 6 TO 8 AS A FIRST COURSE, 4 AS A MAIN COURSE
(MAKES ABOUT 8 CUPS)
ACTIVE TIME: 2 HOURS ■ START TO FINISH: 3 HOURS

■ The broth for this tortilla soup, thicker and heartier than most versions, is made with dried pasilla and smoked pasilla de Oaxaca chiles, which enhance the flavor of the duck. Pasilla de Oaxaca chiles are worth seeking out for their subtle mix of sweetness and smokiness (regular pasilla chiles—long, black, and faintly licorice-flavored—are not smoked). If you want a thicker soup, add more fried tortilla strips to the broth. The cool creaminess of the avocados balances the soup's richness. We adapted this recipe from one by reader Erin Franzman of New York City. ■

1 dried pasilla or mulato chile (see Sources)

1 dried pasilla de Oaxaca chile or other dried smoked chile, such as chipotle or chipotle mora, or 1 canned chipotle chile in adobo (see Sources)

5 cups water

1½ pounds duck legs (2–4, depending on size; see Sources)

Salt

4 cups Chicken Stock (page 153) or store-bought reduced-sodium broth

¼–½ cup corn or other vegetable oil

1 (8-ounce) package 5- to 6-inch corn tortillas (10–12), cut in half, then cut crosswise into ⅛-inch-wide strips

1 (14- to 15-ounce) can diced tomatoes in juice

1 medium white onion, chopped

½ cup packed fresh cilantro sprigs, plus fresh cilantro leaves for serving

2 large garlic cloves

1 whole clove or a pinch of ground cloves

5 whole allspice or ¼ teaspoon ground allspice

2 California avocados, quartered, pitted, peeled, and cut crosswise into thick slices

2 limes, halved crosswise, each half quartered

Heat a 12-inch heavy skillet over moderate heat until hot. Cut dried chiles open lengthwise and open out flat (if chiles are too brittle to cut open, toast whole chiles for a few seconds on each side, pressing down with tongs, to soften slightly, and then cut open); discard seeds and stems. Toast chiles in hot skillet, pressing down with tongs, turning once, until color changes slightly and chiles are more fragrant, 10 to 15 seconds. (If using a canned chipotle, simply discard seeds; do not toast.) Transfer dried chiles to blender, add 1 cup water, and let soak for at least 20 minutes (without blending); add canned chipotle if using. Set skillet aside.

Meanwhile, remove skin and fat from duck legs. Coarsely chop skin and fat and transfer to same skillet. Cook over moderate heat, stirring occasionally, until some of fat is rendered, about 3 minutes. Pat duck legs dry and season with ½ teaspoon salt. Brown duck legs in fat, turning once and continuing to stir skin and fat, until all fat is rendered and cracklings are golden brown and crisp, 5 to 7 minutes. Remove from heat and, using a slotted spoon, transfer cracklings to paper towels to drain. Transfer duck legs to a 3- to 4-quart heavy saucepan; reserve fat in skillet.

Add stock and remaining 4 cups water to duck legs and bring to a simmer, partially covered. Remove from heat.

Add enough oil to duck fat in skillet to measure ¼ inch and heat over moderately high heat until hot but not smoking. Fry tortilla strips in 4 batches, stirring, until golden brown, 1½ to 2 minutes per batch; transfer to paper towels to drain. Pour out fat from skillet and reserve ¼ cup. Wipe skillet clean.

Add tomatoes with juice, onion, cilantro sprigs, garlic, 1¾ teaspoons salt, clove, and allspice to chiles in blender and blend until smooth (you will have about 3⅓ cups sauce).

Return reserved ¼ cup fat to skillet and heat over moderately high heat until hot but not smoking. Pour sauce into skillet (use caution: fat will spatter) and cook, stirring occasionally, until thickened and reduced to about 2¼ cups, about 10 minutes.

Add chile sauce to duck legs and crumble in a handful of fried tortilla strips (or 2 handfuls for a thicker soup). Bring to a simmer and simmer, partially covered, over low heat until duck is tender, about 2 hours. Remove from heat and remove duck legs from soup.

When duck legs are cool enough to handle, coarsely shred meat. Skim fat from soup and return duck meat to soup. Season with salt and bring to a simmer.

Put remaining tortilla strips, avocados, cilantro leaves, cracklings, and lime wedges in separate small bowls and serve with soup.

COOK'S NOTE

■ The soup (without the toppings) can be made up to 1 day ahead. Cool, uncovered, then refrigerate, covered. Refrigerate the cracklings, covered; before serving, reheat in a small skillet over moderate heat until crisp, 2 to 3 minutes. Store the fried tortilla strips in an airtight container at room temperature.

Vietnamese Chicken and Pineapple Soup

SERVES 6 TO 8 AS A FIRST COURSE (MAKES ABOUT 14 CUPS)
ACTIVE TIME: 1 HOUR ■ START TO FINISH: 1 HOUR

■ Traditional Vietnamese pineapple soup can be made with beef, chicken, shrimp, or fish, and it usually includes tomatoes, mushrooms, and a shower of herbs. This version, a complex, colorful concoction of salty, sweet, sour, and spicy from reader Kia Ly Dickinson of Miami, calls for chicken, a whole pineapple, and a healthy dose of fish sauce (although the fish sauce seems extremely pungent when it is first added, it will have a mild flavor in the finished soup). If you can get your hands on fresh herbs in the winter, do make this soup then—it's a wonderful pick-me-up. ■

    1 pineapple, preferably labeled "extra sweet" (about
        3½ pounds)
      About 8 cups water
    2 skinless, boneless chicken breast halves (12 ounces
        total)
    ¼ cup vegetable oil
    4 (1-inch-long) fresh red Thai chiles, minced, including
        seeds
    3 tablespoons minced garlic
    6 tablespoons Asian fish sauce
    ½ pound shiitake mushrooms, stems discarded, caps
        thinly sliced
    2 large tomatoes, chopped
    1 cup (2 ounces) bean sprouts, rinsed
      Freshly ground black pepper
    ⅓ cup coarsely chopped fresh basil
    ⅓ cup coarsely chopped fresh mint
    ⅓ cup coarsely chopped fresh lemon verbena (see
        Cook's Note)
    1 tablespoon chopped fresh oregano
    ½ teaspoon salt

Cut peel from pineapple, removing just a thin layer, and discard. Trim pineapple, cutting only deep enough to remove eyes, and transfer trimmings to a blender. Quarter pineapple lengthwise and cut out core. Coarsely chop core and transfer to blender. Puree trimmings and core with 2 cups water until smooth. Pour through a fine-mesh sieve into a 2-quart glass measure, pressing hard on solids; discard solids. Add enough water to measure 8 cups.

Cut remaining pineapple into ½-inch pieces and put in a bowl.

Place chicken between two sheets of plastic wrap and gently pound to ¼ inch thick with flat side of a meat pounder or a rolling pin. Cut chicken across the grain into ¼-inch-wide strips. Cut strips into 2-inch pieces and transfer to another bowl. Refrigerate, covered.

Heat 2 tablespoons oil in a 5- to 6-quart heavy pot over moderately high heat until hot but not smoking. Add chiles and 2 tablespoons garlic and cook, stirring, until fragrant, about 30 seconds. Add ¼ cup fish sauce and boil until reduced by half, about 2 minutes.

Add pineapple broth and bring to a boil. Stir in pineapple, mushrooms, tomatoes, sprouts, and ¼ teaspoon pepper and bring to a boil, then reduce heat and simmer, uncovered, stirring occasionally, for 10 minutes.

Meanwhile, heat remaining 2 tablespoons oil in a 12-inch heavy skillet over moderately high heat until hot but not smoking. Add remaining tablespoon garlic and cook, stirring, until fragrant, about 30 seconds. Add remaining 2 tablespoons fish sauce and simmer until reduced by half, about 2 minutes.

Sprinkle chicken with pepper. Add to garlic mixture and cook, stirring, until just cooked through, about 4 minutes.

Stir chicken into soup, along with herbs and salt, and simmer for 1 minute.

COOK'S NOTES

- Substitute 1 stalk lemongrass if lemon verbena is not available. Trim the root end and discard the tough outer leaves, then thinly slice the lower 6 inches of the stalk. Finely chop and sauté with the chiles and garlic.
- The soup can be made up to 3 days ahead. Cool, uncovered, then refrigerate, covered. (The herbs may discolor if the soup is made ahead.)

LEMON VERBENA

Lemon verbena (*Aloysia triphylla*), native to South America, is an intoxicatingly fragrant herb that has the clean, clear sweetness of lemon without the acidity. It's most famously used in tisanes, or herbal infusions (pour boiling water over a handful of leaves and let steep to taste). But it's also employed to great effect in chicken or fish dishes (chop and add to a sauce or marinade, or simply put a few sprigs in the cavity of a whole chicken or fish before roasting). It can also be used in lemonade, iced tea, or sorbet, or in a syrup for poaching fruit. It has a great affinity as well for flavorings such as basil and mint. The fresh leaves can be hard to find—look for them at farmers markets during the summer months—but, happily, the bushy perennial, available at plant shops and nurseries, is easy to grow.

Spicy African Chicken and Peanut Soup

SERVES 6 TO 8 AS A MAIN COURSE (MAKES ABOUT 14 CUPS)
ACTIVE TIME: 35 MINUTES ■ START TO FINISH: 1¼ HOURS

■ In the huge and varied culinary lexicon of Africa, there is no single definitive recipe for peanut soup—some versions use fish, others chicken or beef; some are loaded with vegetables, others are a study in minimalism. This spicy variation is similar to the soups made in the countries of West Africa. It's full of chicken, sweet potatoes, and eggplant and is thickened with okra. Like many modern African cooks, we use peanut butter rather than grinding the nuts ourselves. ■

⅔ cup smooth peanut butter

5 cups water

¼ cup peanut oil

4 chicken drumsticks

 Salt

4 chicken thighs

1 large onion, halved lengthwise and thinly sliced
   lengthwise

2 tablespoons tomato paste

1 (14- to 15-ounce) can diced tomatoes in juice,
   drained

1¾ cups Chicken Stock (page 153) or store-bought
   reduced-sodium broth

2 (3-inch-long) fresh hot red chiles, such as cayenne or
   Thai, minced, including seeds

1 medium eggplant (1 pound)

1 large sweet potato (1 pound)

1 cup fresh or frozen sliced okra

Stir together peanut butter and 1 cup water in a medium bowl until smooth.

Heat oil in a 7- to 8-quart heavy pot over moderately high heat until hot but not smoking. Pat drumsticks dry with paper towels and sprinkle with ¼ teaspoon salt. Brown drumsticks in oil, turning occasionally, until golden, about 6 minutes. Transfer to a bowl. Pat thighs dry and sprinkle with ¼ teaspoon salt, then brown in same manner and transfer to bowl.

Pour off all but 2 tablespoons fat from pot. Add onion and cook over moderate heat, stirring occasionally, until golden around edges, about 2 minutes. Add tomato paste and cook, stirring, for 1 minute. Add peanut butter mixture, remaining 4 cups water, diced tomatoes, stock, chicken with any juices accumulated in bowl, chiles, and 1 teaspoon salt and bring to a boil. Reduce heat and simmer, partially covered, stirring occasionally, until chicken is tender, 30 minutes (see Cook's Note).

Meanwhile, trim eggplant and cut into ½-inch pieces. Add eggplant to soup and simmer, partially covered, for 5 minutes. While eggplant simmers, peel sweet potato and cut into ½-inch pieces. Add sweet potato and okra, partially cover, and simmer, stirring occasionally, until potato is tender, 15 to 18 minutes. Season with salt if necessary.

COOK'S NOTES

- If desired, remove and discard the skin and bones from the chicken after cooking it in the soup. Tear the meat into bite-sized pieces and return to the soup to heat through.
- The soup, without the eggplant, sweet potato, and okra, can be made up to 1 day ahead. Cool, uncovered, then refrigerate, covered. Bring the soup to a simmer before adding the vegetables and proceeding; thin with water if necessary.

Chunky Beef and Vegetable Soup

SERVES 8 TO 10 AS A MAIN COURSE
(MAKES ABOUT 16 CUPS)
ACTIVE TIME: 45 MINUTES ■ START TO FINISH: 4 HOURS
PLUS SOAKING TIME FOR BEANS

■ Pure Americana, this homage to farmhouse cooking gets its body from slowly cooked beef shanks. Lima beans and an entire gardenful of vegetables round out the soup. For best flavor, make it ahead. ■

½ pound (about 1 cup) dried large lima beans, picked
   over and rinsed

8 cups water, plus additional for soaking beans

3 pounds meaty crosscut beef shanks (also
   called beef shins; 2 inches thick), trimmed of
   excess fat

 Salt

¼ teaspoon freshly ground black pepper

2 tablespoons olive oil

1 large onion, chopped

2 garlic cloves, chopped

3 carrots, halved lengthwise and cut diagonally into
   1½-inch pieces

3½ cups Beef Stock (page 153) or store-bought reduced-
   sodium broth

1 pound yellow-fleshed potatoes, such as Yukon Gold

1 (14- to 15-ounce) can diced tomatoes in juice

¼ pound cabbage, preferably savoy, tough stems
   discarded, leaves coarsely chopped

¼ pound green beans, trimmed and cut into 1-inch
   pieces

Soak lima beans in cold water to cover by 2 inches at room temperature (refrigerate if kitchen is very warm) for 8 to 12 hours (or see page 129 for quick-soaking procedure); drain.

Simmer lima beans in 4 cups water in a 4-quart saucepan, covered, until just tender, 20 to 30 minutes. Drain in colander set over a large bowl; reserve cooking liquid.

Pat shanks dry and sprinkle with 1 teaspoon salt and pepper. Heat oil in a 6- to 8-quart wide heavy pot over moderately high heat until hot but not smoking. Brown shanks (in batches if necessary), turning once, about 6 minutes per batch; transfer with tongs to a bowl.

Cook onion in fat remaining in pot over moderate heat, stirring, until golden, about 5 minutes. Add garlic and cook, stirring, for 1 minute. Add browned meat, along with any juices accumulated in bowl, carrots, reserved bean cooking liquid, remaining 4 cups water, stock, and ½ teaspoon salt, bring to a simmer, and simmer, covered, until meat is very tender, about 1½ hours. Remove from heat.

Remove shanks with tongs and transfer to a cutting board. When cool enough to handle, cut meat into 1-inch pieces; discard bones. Return meat to soup.

Peel potatoes and cut into ¾-inch cubes, then add to soup, along with lima beans and tomatoes with juice, and simmer, covered, until potatoes are tender, about 15 minutes. Add cabbage and green beans and simmer, uncovered, until tender, 5 to 8 minutes.

COOK'S NOTE

■ The soup is best when made at least 1 day, or up to 3 days, ahead (to give the flavors time to develop). Cool, uncovered, then refrigerate, covered. Remove any solidified fat and reheat, thinning with water, if necessary.

Italian Wedding Soup

SERVES 8 TO 10 AS A MAIN COURSE
(MAKES ABOUT 20 CUPS)
ACTIVE TIME: 1½ HOURS ■ START TO FINISH: 3 HOURS

■ Welcome at almost any family gathering, this rich chicken soup, full of tiny, tender meatballs and esca-

role, comes from the grandmother of one of our food editors, Gina Marie Miraglia Eriquez. We've used her trick of adding a piece of pecorino Romano rind to the soup; it adds both body and flavor. If you can't find pecorino with the rind on it, substitute ⅓ cup finely grated cheese. ■

FOR STOCK
1 (3½-pound) chicken, rinsed, patted dry, and cut into 8 pieces
2 celery ribs, cut into 2-inch lengths
2 carrots, quartered
1 large onion, left unpeeled, trimmed and halved
2 garlic cloves
6 fresh parsley stems (without leaves)
1 Turkish bay leaf or ½ California bay leaf
½ teaspoon black peppercorns
4 quarts cold water
1½ teaspoons salt

FOR MEATBALLS
1 cup ¼-inch pieces Italian bread
1 cup whole milk
1 pound meat loaf mix (equal parts ground beef, pork, and veal)
2 garlic cloves, minced
2 large eggs, lightly beaten
¾ cup finely grated pecorino Romano
¼ cup finely chopped fresh flat-leaf parsley
¾ teaspoon salt
½ teaspoon freshly ground black pepper
About 2 cups vegetable oil

FOR SOUP
5 cups water
1 large onion, cut into ¼-inch pieces
3 medium carrots, halved lengthwise and thinly sliced
2 celery ribs, halved lengthwise and thinly sliced
1 (3-by-2-inch) piece pecorino Romano rind (about ⅓ inch thick; see headnote)
1 medium head escarole, tough stems discarded, leaves chopped (about 5 cups)
Salt and freshly ground black pepper

ACCOMPANIMENT: finely grated pecorino Romano

MAKE THE STOCK: Combine all ingredients in an 8- to 10-quart pot and bring to a boil; skim froth. Reduce heat and simmer gently, uncovered, skimming froth occasionally, for 2 hours. Remove from heat.

MEANWHILE, FORM AND FRY THE MEATBALLS: Stir together bread and milk in a large bowl and let stand for 10 minutes. Add meat, garlic, eggs, cheese, parsley, salt, and pepper and blend with your hands just until well combined (do not overmix). Form scant tablespoons into meatballs; you will have about 60 (meatballs will be very moist).

Heat 1 inch oil in a 12-inch heavy skillet over moderately high heat until hot but not smoking. Cook meatballs in 3 batches (do not overcrowd), turning occasionally, until well browned and cooked through, about 6 minutes per batch. Transfer to paper towels to drain.

MAKE THE SOUP: Remove chicken from pot and pour stock through a fine-mesh sieve into a large bowl; discard solids. If using stock immediately, skim off and discard fat. If not, cool stock completely, uncovered, then refrigerate, covered, until cold; remove congealed fat from chilled stock. You should have about 3 quarts stock; if you have less, add enough water to make 3 quarts.

When chicken is cool enough to handle, discard skin and bones and coarsely shred enough chicken into bite-sized pieces to measure about 3 cups (reserve remaining chicken for another use).

Return stock to cleaned pot and add 5 cups water. Add onion, carrots, celery, and cheese rind and bring to a boil, then reduce heat and simmer, covered, until vegetables are crisp-tender, about 15 minutes. Stir in escarole, cover, and bring to a boil. Add meatballs and simmer, uncovered, until escarole is very tender and meatballs are heated through, about 10 minutes. Discard cheese rind, stir in shredded chicken, and season with salt and pepper.

Serve with grated cheese.

COOK'S NOTES

- The cooled stock can be refrigerated, covered, for up to 3 days or frozen for up to 1 month.
- The soup can be made up to 4 days ahead. Cool, uncovered, then refrigerate, covered. The soup can also be frozen for up to 1 month (the meatballs will swell slightly).

Hanoi Beef Noodle Soup
Pho Bo

SERVES 6 AS A MAIN COURSE
ACTIVE TIME: 1½ HOURS ■ START TO FINISH: 4½ HOURS

■ Traditionally eaten for breakfast, Vietnam's favorite convenience food is usually purchased at street stands, where the quality of the broth can make or break a cook's reputation. Almost all versions include the elusive fragrance of star anise, meaty beef shanks, and charred ginger and onions. Blanching the shanks briefly and then pouring off the water before getting on with the recipe ensures a clear, uncloudy broth. ■

- 2 large onions, halved lengthwise
- 1 (3-inch) piece fresh ginger, left unpeeled
- 4 pounds meaty crosscut beef shanks (also called beef shins; 1½ inches thick), trimmed of excess fat
- 7 quarts cold water
- 2 teaspoons star anise pieces
- 1 (3-inch) cinnamon stick
- 3 whole cloves
- 1 tablespoon black peppercorns
- 1 (8-ounce) piece boneless beef sirloin steak or tenderloin (see Cook's Note)
- 1 pound dried flat thin or medium rice noodles (*banh pho* or pad Thai; see Sources)
- ⅓ –½ cup Asian fish sauce
- ½ teaspoon salt, or to taste

ACCOMPANIMENTS: bean sprouts, rinsed; very thinly sliced onion, rinsed and drained; fresh leaves of cilantro, mint, and basil, preferably Thai; thinly sliced scallions; lime wedges; thinly sliced fresh Thai or serrano chiles; Asian fish sauce

SPECIAL EQUIPMENT: cheesecloth; kitchen string

MAKE THE BROTH: Roast onions and ginger directly on grate of a gas burner over high heat, turning with tongs, until blistered and blackened, 10 to 15 minutes. (Alternatively, broil onions and ginger on a foil-lined broiler pan about 5 inches from heat, turning occasionally, until charred, 20 to 25 minutes for onions, 25 to 30 minutes for ginger.) Transfer to a bowl to cool.

Meanwhile, cover shanks with 8 cups cold water in a 6- to 8-quart pot and bring to a boil. Drain in a large colander and rinse well with cold water. Clean pot.

When onions are cool enough to handle, rinse and rub under cold running water to remove any blackened pieces (some areas will still be browned).

Wrap star anise, cinnamon stick, cloves, and peppercorns in a square of cheesecloth and tie into a bundle with kitchen string to make a spice bag. Add to cleaned pot, along with 4 quarts water, shanks, onions, and ginger. Bring to a boil, reduce heat, and simmer, uncovered, skimming froth occasionally, for 2 hours.

Add remaining 4 cups water and bring to a boil, reduce heat, and simmer, skimming froth occasionally, until shanks are very tender, about 1 hour more.

MEANWHILE, PREPARE THE SIRLOIN AND NOODLES: Freeze steak until firm but not frozen solid, 30 to 45 minutes. With a sharp thin knife, slice across the grain into slices less than ⅛ inch thick.

Soak rice noodles in cold water to cover until softened, about 30 minutes; drain. Cook noodles in a 6-quart pot of boiling (unsalted) water, uncovered, stirring, for 1 minute, then drain.

FINISH THE SOUP: Transfer shanks with tongs to a cutting board.

When shanks are cool enough to handle, remove meat from bones and cut into small pieces; discard bones, fat, and sinew. Set aside 2 cups beef (reserve remainder for another use).

Pour broth through a fine-mesh sieve into a large heatproof bowl; discard solids. Measure broth: If you have more than 3 quarts, boil in cleaned pot until reduced; if you have less, add enough water to make 3 quarts. Let broth stand until fat rises to top, 1 to 2 minutes, then skim off fat if desired.

Combine broth and shank meat in cleaned 6- to 8-quart pot and bring to a boil.

Meanwhile, divide noodles among six large deep bowls. Top noodles with sliced uncooked steak.

Add ⅓ cup fish sauce and salt to broth and return to a boil. Taste, add more fish sauce if desired, and ladle hot broth (with pieces of beef shanks) over steak and noodles (hot broth will cook steak).

Put accompaniments in separate small bowls and serve with soup.

COOK'S NOTES
■ In place of the sirloin steak or tenderloin, you can use thinly sliced rare roast beef (from the deli counter), torn into pieces.
■ The broth can be made (and strained) up to 3 days ahead. Cool, uncovered, then refrigerate, with the 2 cups beef, covered. Bring to a boil before serving.

Chinese Hot-and-Sour Soup

SERVES 6 TO 8 AS A FIRST COURSE (MAKES ABOUT 6 CUPS)
ACTIVE TIME: 1 HOUR ■ START TO FINISH: 1¼ HOURS

■ Not just a meal but an ancient curative, this pungent soup from the Chinese cooking authority Bruce Cost is designed to get your *chi* flowing. Dried tree ear mushrooms and dried lily buds are prized for their circulation-stimulating qualities, while vinegar adds pep and a generous amount of white pepper provides heat. For help finding the Asian ingredients, see Sources. ■

5 ounces boneless pork loin, cut into ¼-inch-thick strips
2 teaspoons dark soy sauce
4 small dried Chinese black mushrooms
12 small dried tree ear mushrooms
12 dried lily buds (also called golden needles)
½ cup rinsed canned sliced bamboo shoots, cut lengthwise into ⅛-inch-wide strips
1½ tablespoons cornstarch
2 tablespoons red wine vinegar
2 tablespoons rice vinegar (not seasoned)
1 tablespoon light soy sauce
1½ teaspoons sugar
1 teaspoon kosher salt
2 tablespoons peanut oil
4 cups Chicken Stock (page 153) or store-bought reduced-sodium broth
3–4 ounces firm tofu (about ¼ block), rinsed, drained, and cut into ¼-inch-wide strips
2 large eggs
2 teaspoons Asian sesame oil
1½ teaspoons freshly ground white pepper
2 tablespoons thinly sliced scallion greens
2 tablespoons fresh cilantro leaves

Toss pork with dark soy sauce in a bowl until well coated. Marinate at room temperature while mushrooms soak.

Soak black and tree ear mushrooms in 3 cups boiling water to cover in a small bowl, turning black mushrooms occasionally, until softened, about 30 minutes. (Tree ears will expand significantly.)

Meanwhile, soak lily buds in about 1 cup warm water until softened, about 20 minutes; drain.

Cover bamboo shoots with cold water by 2 inches in a small saucepan and bring just to a boil (to remove bitterness); drain.

Lift black mushrooms from bowl, cut out and discard stems, and squeeze excess liquid from caps into bowl, then thinly slice caps. Lift tree ears from bowl and trim off any hard nubs. Cut tree ears, if large, into bite-sized pieces. Stir together ¼ cup mushroom soaking liquid (discard remainder) and cornstarch in a small bowl; set aside.

Trim tough tips of lily buds. Cut buds crosswise in half and tear each half lengthwise into 2 or 3 shreds.

Stir together vinegars, light soy sauce, sugar, and salt in a small bowl until sugar and salt are dissolved.

Heat a well-seasoned 14-inch flat-bottomed wok (see Cook's Note) over high heat until a drop of water vaporizes upon contact. Pour peanut oil down side of wok, then swirl oil, tilting wok to coat sides, and heat until oil is just smoking. Add pork and stir-fry until meat just changes color, about 1 minute. Add black mushrooms, tree ears, lily buds, and bamboo shoots and stir-fry for 1 minute.

Transfer pork mixture to a 3- to 4-quart heavy saucepan, add stock, and bring to a boil. Stir in vinegar mixture. Stir cornstarch mixture, add to soup, and return to a boil, stirring (liquid will thicken). Reduce heat to moderate and simmer for 1 minute. Add tofu and return to a simmer.

Lightly beat eggs with a fork and add a few drops of sesame oil. Add eggs to soup in a thin stream, stirring soup slowly in one direction with a spoon. Stir in white pepper, then drizzle in remaining sesame oil.

Divide soup among six to eight bowls and sprinkle with scallion greens and cilantro.

COOK'S NOTES

- You can substitute a 12-inch skillet for the wok.
- The dried mushrooms and lily buds can be soaked up to 1 day ahead and refrigerated, covered.
- The pork and vegetables can be stir-fried up to 6 hours ahead. Add to the stock and refrigerate, covered. Bring to a boil before proceeding.

Gingered Pork Wonton Soup with Bok Choy

SERVES 6 AS A MAIN COURSE (MAKES ABOUT 13 CUPS)
ACTIVE TIME: 1 HOUR ■ START TO FINISH: 8 HOURS
(INCLUDES CHILLING)

■ Wontons look complicated, but they are actually easy to make and you'll soon get the hang of forming them. The broth, which is made with both pork ribs and chicken, has a deep meatiness. ■

FOR STOCK
- 2 pounds country-style (meaty) pork ribs
- 2 pounds chicken thighs, legs, and/or wings
- 4 scallions, coarsely chopped
- 1 (2-inch) piece fresh ginger, peeled and chopped
- 3 quarts water

FOR WONTONS
- ½ pound ground pork (not lean)
- 1 large egg yolk
- 2 scallions, finely chopped
- 1 (1½-inch) piece fresh ginger, peeled and finely chopped
- 1 tablespoon soy sauce
- 1 teaspoon rice vinegar (not seasoned)
- ½ teaspoon Asian sesame oil
- ½ teaspoon salt
- ¼ teaspoon freshly ground white pepper
  All-purpose flour for sprinkling
  About 30 wonton wrappers, thawed if frozen

FOR SOUP
- 1½ pounds bok choy, leaves and stalks halved lengthwise and thinly sliced crosswise
- 1½ teaspoons salt
- ¼ teaspoon freshly ground white pepper

MAKE THE STOCK: Combine all ingredients in a tall narrow 6- to 8-quart stockpot, bring to a simmer, and simmer, uncovered, until meat is falling-apart tender, 4½ to 5 hours.

Pour stock through a sieve into a large bowl; discard solids. Cool stock, uncovered, then refrigerate, covered, until cold, at least 1½ hours.

MEANWHILE, MAKE THE WONTONS: Mix pork, yolk, scallions, ginger, soy sauce, vinegar, sesame oil, salt, and white pepper in a bowl, stirring in one direction with your hand (see Cook's Note) until just combined (do not overwork, or filling will be tough).

Sprinkle a baking sheet lightly with flour. Put 1 wonton wrapper on a work surface (keep remaining wrappers covered with plastic wrap). Spoon a rounded teaspoon of filling into center of wrapper (1), and brush edges with water. Lift 2 opposite corners together to form a triangle, press edges together firmly around mound of filling to eliminate air pockets, and seal (2). Moisten opposite corners of long side, curl moistened corners toward each other, overlapping them, and carefully press them together to seal (3). Transfer wonton to floured baking sheet and make more wontons in same manner.

FINISH THE SOUP: Skim any fat from stock and bring to a simmer in a 5- to 6-quart pot. Stir in bok choy, salt, and white pepper and simmer, uncovered, until bok choy is crisp-tender, 3 to 4 minutes. Add wontons and simmer uncovered, stirring gently to keep them from sticking, until filling is just cooked through, about 3 minutes (cut one open to check).

COOK'S NOTES

- The stock can be refrigerated for up to 3 days or frozen for up to 1 month.
- Stirring the wonton filling in one direction compacts it properly.
- The wontons can be made up to 1 month ahead. Freeze in one layer on a plastic-wrap-lined baking sheet until firm, about 30 minutes, then transfer to a sealable plastic bag and freeze (do not thaw before adding to broth).

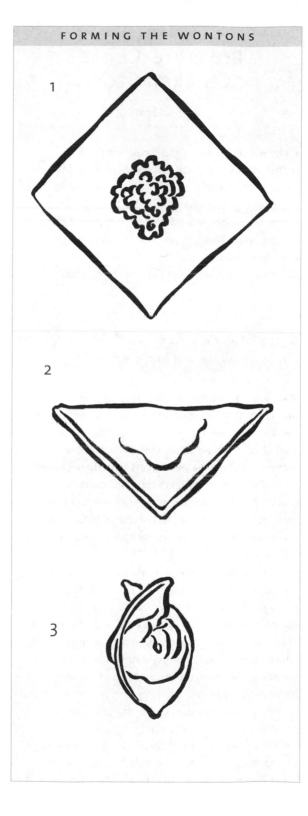

FORMING THE WONTONS

1

2

3

Pressure-Cooker Chicken Stock

MAKES ABOUT 7 CUPS
ACTIVE TIME: 15 MINUTES ■ START TO FINISH: 45 MINUTES

■ The ability to make great chicken stock in a flash is reason enough to own a pressure cooker. This can be made with a whole chicken or the equivalent weight in wings or pieces. So we can use the meat for another dish, we cook the stock for only 15 minutes. For a richer stock, cook it longer and discard the chicken; see the variation. ■

1 (3½-pound) chicken, neck and giblets (except liver) reserved
2 celery ribs, cut into 2-inch lengths
2 carrots, quartered
2 medium onions, left unpeeled, trimmed and halved
1 garlic clove
6 fresh parsley stems (without leaves)
1 Turkish bay leaf or ½ California bay leaf
2 fresh thyme sprigs
4 black peppercorns
7 cups cold water
1½ teaspoons salt

SPECIAL EQUIPMENT: a 6- to 8-quart pressure cooker

A NEW GENERATION OF PRESSURE COOKERS

If you were born before the Kennedy administration, you may flinch at the mention of pressure cookers, recalling the time when your mother's cooker, with that sinister, hissing valve, blew its top—literally. But the pressure cookers of today are a world apart from the old jiggle-top models. Even if you forget to turn the heat down once the cooker reaches high pressure, at least one vent (sometimes more) will release as a matter of course. In fact, most of the cookers manufactured today have three backup shut-off features.

Once you've locked the lid, with its airtight gasket, and put the pressure cooker over high heat, the liquid inside produces steam as it comes to a boil. Tightly sealed inside the cooker, the steam causes the internal pressure to increase to up to 15 pounds per square inch, which makes it harder for the water molecules to escape the liquid; therefore, the boiling point of the water is increased. (In other words, water boils in modern pressure cookers at 230°F to 266°F, so chemical reactions occur much faster.)

Our favorite type of modern cooker has a spring-valve pressure regulator on the lid. The design varies depending on the brand, but there is often some sort of visual cue—such as a rod that pops up—to tell you when the cooker has reached high pressure. Then you adjust the heat so that you can maintain a steady pressure. A cooker with a heavy three-ply bottom prevents foods from sticking or burning; not a worry if you are just making stock, but important if you are browning meat in it.

Pressure cookers are terrific for stews and braises and for cooking dried beans (but avoid quick-cooking varieties like lentils and split peas). There is a knack to cooking your tried-and-true recipes under pressure, because the amount of liquid needed is probably going to be different (you don't lose as much to evaporation). For a wealth of recipes developed for the cooker, see *Cooking Under Pressure* and *Pressure Perfect*, both by Lorna Sass. Good pressure cookers aren't inexpensive: they start around $75.

Bring all ingredients to a boil in pressure cooker. Lock on lid and bring to high pressure over moderately high heat, then reduce heat to maintain high pressure (following manufacturer's instructions) and cook for 15 minutes. Transfer pressure cooker to sink and run cold water over lid until pressure is completely reduced.

Open lid, remove chicken, and reserve for another use. Pour stock through a fine-mesh sieve into a bowl; discard solids. If using stock immediately, skim off and discard fat. If not, cool stock completely, uncovered, then refrigerate, covered, until cold; scrape congealed fat from chilled stock.

COOK'S NOTE
- The stock can be refrigerated for up to 3 days or frozen for up to 1 month.

VARIATION
- RICH PRESSURE-COOKER CHICKEN STOCK: Use 3½ pounds chicken parts (preferably backs, necks, wings, and feet, if you can find them). Increase the water to 8 cups and cook at high pressure for 30 minutes. Strain as directed and discard the solids, including the chicken. If necessary, boil the stock to reduce it to 7 cups.

Chicken Stock

MAKES ABOUT 10 CUPS
ACTIVE TIME: 30 MINUTES ■ START TO FINISH: 4½ HOURS

■ There isn't a lot of work involved in making good chicken stock. What you do need is the patience to let the chicken, vegetables, herbs, and water transform into a savory golden broth. If you want to make this fabulous stock even richer, see the variation. ■

    1 (3- to 3½-pound) chicken, cut into 8 pieces, neck and
        giblets (except liver) reserved
    4 quarts cold water
    2 onions, left unpeeled, halved

    2 whole cloves
    4 garlic cloves, left unpeeled
    1 celery rib, halved
    2 carrots, halved
    1 teaspoon salt
    6 long fresh parsley sprigs
    8 black peppercorns
    ½ teaspoon dried thyme, crumbled
    1 Turkish bay leaf or ½ California bay leaf

Put chicken pieces (including neck and giblets) in an 8-quart stockpot, add cold water, and bring to a boil, skimming froth. Add remaining ingredients and simmer, uncovered, skimming froth occasionally, for 3 hours.

Pour stock through a fine-mesh sieve into a bowl; discard solids. If using stock right away, skim off and discard fat. If not, cool stock completely, uncovered, then refrigerate, covered, until cold; scrape congealed fat from chilled stock.

COOK'S NOTE
- The stock can be refrigerated for up to 1 week or frozen for up to 3 months.

VARIATION
- RICH CHICKEN STOCK: Use 5½ pounds chicken parts, including 3 pounds wings.

Beef Stock

MAKES ABOUT 8 CUPS
ACTIVE TIME: 30 MINUTES ■ START TO FINISH: 6½ HOURS

■ The difference between a good beef stock and a truly memorable one is taking the time to brown the bones (or, here, beef and veal shanks) really well. Use a large roasting pan so they have plenty of room to caramelize, and when you deglaze the pan, scrape up every browned bit that you can. Once that's done, you just have to wait for the ingredients to cook down to a rich, fragrant stock, ready to be used in all sorts of dishes. ■

2 pounds meaty beef shanks, sawed crosswise into
   1-inch slices by the butcher
2 pounds meaty veal shanks, sawed crosswise into
   1-inch slices by the butcher
2 onions, left unpeeled, quartered
1 carrot, quartered
4 fresh parsley sprigs
1 fresh thyme sprig
1 Turkish bay leaf or ½ California bay leaf
4 quarts cold water
2 celery ribs, quartered
1½ teaspoons salt
SPECIAL EQUIPMENT: cheesecloth; kitchen string

Put a rack in middle of oven and preheat oven to 450°F.

Spread beef shanks, veal shanks, onions, and carrot in a large roasting pan. Roast, turning occasionally, until well browned, about 1 hour.

Meanwhile, wrap parsley, thyme, and bay leaf in a square of cheesecloth and tie into a bundle with string to make a bouquet garni.

With a slotted spoon, transfer meat and vegetables to a 6- to 8-quart stockpot. Set roasting pan across two burners, add 2 cups water to pan, and deglaze by boiling over high heat, stirring and scraping up brown bits, for about 2 minutes. Add liquid to stockpot, along with remaining 3½ quarts water, celery, salt, and bouquet garni, bring to a boil, and skim froth. Reduce heat and simmer gently, uncovered, skimming froth occasionally, until stock is reduced to about 8 cups, 3 to 5 hours.

Pour stock through a fine-mesh sieve into a bowl, pressing hard on solids; discard solids. If using right away, skim off and discard fat. If not, cool stock completely, uncovered, then refrigerate, covered, until cold; scrape congealed fat from chilled stock.

COOK'S NOTE

■ The stock can be refrigerated for up to 1 week or frozen for up to 3 months.

Fish Stock

MAKES ABOUT 3 CUPS
ACTIVE TIME: 15 MINUTES ■ START TO FINISH: 45 MINUTES

■ Quick and easy to make, this delicate fish stock is great for fish soups or seafood risottos. Or use some to make a fast pan sauce for fish. Because parsley leaves can discolor the stock, we use only the stems. ■

1 tablespoon unsalted butter, softened
1 pound mixed bones and heads of white-fleshed fish,
   such as Pacific cod, porgy, striped bass, or turbot,
   or any combination, gills removed, rinsed well, and
   roughly chopped
1 small onion, sliced
12 fresh parsley stems (without leaves)
2 tablespoons fresh lemon juice
½ teaspoon salt
3½ cups cold water
½ cup dry white wine

Spread butter over bottom of a 4-quart heavy saucepan (to prevent bones from sticking). Add fish bones and heads, onion, parsley stems, lemon juice, and salt and cook, covered, over moderately high heat until bones are opaque, about 5 minutes. Add water and wine, bring to a boil, and skim froth. Reduce heat and simmer, uncovered, for 25 minutes.

Pour stock through a fine-mesh sieve into a bowl, pressing hard on solids; discard solids. If not using stock right away, cool completely, uncovered, then refrigerate, covered.

COOK'S NOTE

■ The stock be can refrigerated for up to 2 days or frozen for up to 1 month.

Vegetable Stock

MAKES ABOUT 6 CUPS
ACTIVE TIME: 30 MINUTES ■ START TO FINISH: 1 HOUR

■ Adapted from chef Jean-Georges Vongerichten's *Simple Cuisine*, this stock freezes beautifully. ■

  8 cups water
  ¾ cup chopped onion
  ½ cup chopped carrot
  ½ cup chopped celery
  ½ cup chopped zucchini
  ½ cup chopped cabbage
  ½ cup chopped turnips
  ½ cup chopped mushrooms
  1 bunch fresh flat-leaf parsley
  ½ cup mixed chopped fresh herbs, such as basil, tarragon, and chives

Put all ingredients in a 4-quart heavy saucepan and bring to a boil over moderately high heat. Boil, uncovered, for 20 minutes.

Pour stock through a large fine-mesh sieve into a large bowl, pressing hard on solids; discard solids. If not using right away, cool completely, uncovered, then refrigerate, covered.

COOK'S NOTE

■ The stock can be refrigerated for up to 1 week or frozen for up to 3 months.

Roasted Vegetable Stock

MAKES ABOUT 3½ CUPS
ACTIVE TIME: 30 MINUTES ■ START TO FINISH: 2 HOURS

■ Roasting the vegetables before simmering them in water and wine results in a more deeply flavored stock that makes a great base for vegetarian soups or gravies. ■

  ¾ pound cremini mushrooms, trimmed and halved
  ½ pound shallots (6 small or 4 medium), left unpeeled, quartered
  ½ pound carrots (3 medium), cut into 1-inch pieces
  1 red bell pepper, cored, seeded, and cut into 1-inch pieces
  2 garlic cloves, coarsely chopped
  4 fresh flat-leaf parsley sprigs (including long stems)
  3 fresh thyme sprigs
  1 tablespoon olive oil
  ½ cup dry white wine
  1 Turkish bay leaf or ½ California bay leaf
  ½ cup canned crushed tomatoes
  4 cups water
  ¾ teaspoon salt

Put a rack in middle of oven and preheat oven to 425°F.

Toss mushrooms, shallots, carrots, bell pepper, garlic, and parsley and thyme sprigs with oil in a flameproof roasting pan. Roast, stirring occasionally, until vegetables are golden, 35 to 40 minutes.

Transfer vegetables with a slotted spoon to a 4-quart saucepan. Straddle roasting pan across two burners, add wine, and deglaze by boiling over moderate heat, scraping up brown bits, 1 to 2 minutes. Transfer liquid to saucepan, add remaining ingredients, and bring to a boil. Reduce heat and simmer, covered, stirring occasionally, for 45 minutes.

Pour stock through a fine-mesh sieve into a bowl, pressing hard on solids; discard solids. If not using right away, cool completely, uncovered, then refrigerate, covered.

COOK'S NOTE

■ The stock can be refrigerated for up to 1 week or frozen for up to 1 month.

SALADS

What is a salad?

It used to be a reliable but unremarkable dish that you could always count on. Everybody knew where a salad belonged: at the side of the plate or toward the end of the meal. And everybody knew what a salad was: essentially an easy way to eat your greens. It even had its own special implement, the salad fork, which made every table look more attractive. A salad might contain the occasional odd ingredient—grapes, seeds, a nut or two—but when someone offered you a salad, you pretty much knew what you were going to get.

That, however, was before we turned into a society of salad eaters. Today's salad is a versatile dish that can show up anytime, anywhere. It might be the perfectly arranged and elegantly adorned first course sitting on the table when guests sit down to dinner: arugula with pancetta-wrapped peaches, melon carpaccio, or roasted red peppers with walnuts and raisins. It might be the simply dressed greens that arrive at the end of the meal—red leaf lettuce with citrus dressing or spinach with strawberry vinaigrette—a light little interlude before dessert. Or it might be the meal itself: chicken salad with grapes and walnuts or steak salad with pickled vegetables, a one-dish dinner so satisfying that nobody needs a single other bite to eat.

But when we eat our salads is not the only change time has wrought. Who is eating salads has changed too. Not so long ago, salads were reserved strictly for women. Offered a salad, my father would push the plate away, refusing to eat "rabbit food." And if truth be told, most women weren't all that enthusiastic about leafy greens either: as far as I could tell, they ate them only because they were convinced that salads contained no calories. Today, however, real men do eat salads—and real women eat them with gusto.

Why did things change? One major cause was certainly the green-market movement. As we began to have access to really fine, really fresh produce, we began looking at new ways to serve it. Strolling through our markets, we began to wonder what to do with purslane, bitter greens, Tuscan kale, and jicama. As fascinating new vegetables began to appear, we seized the opportunity to make jicama slaw or to mix kohlrabi and pea shoots with sesame dressing. Intrigued, we discovered that seaweed is also a wonderful salad vegetable. Grains became more available too, and we were suddenly looking at the possibilities of quinoa, wheat berries, barley, wild rice, and farro.

Access to just-picked produce also meant that we began looking at more familiar vegetables in new ways. Exploring the possibilities of eating them raw, we discovered that Brussels sprouts, which we were accustomed to boiling, were extraordinarily sweet and delicious when simply shaved and tossed with walnuts and pecorino. And if you can get fresh-from-the-garden zucchini, why bother to cook it? It is beautiful sliced into thin ribbons and served as a salad.

Still, it is the salad as meal that has changed the most. In the past we tended to think of chicken or seafood salad as something invariably involving mayonnaise. But as we learned more about the cooking of the Mediterranean and Asia, we discovered a whole new range of flavor palettes. On the one hand, we have the olive-oil-and-vinegar medley in dishes like grilled tuna salade Niçoise and chicken salad with tomatoes, olives, and green beans. On the other, the deliciously pungent fish-sauce-dressed salads of Southeast Asia, such as the great Thai grilled beef salad, *yam neua*.

What's next in the ever-evolving definition of a salad? My guess is that it won't be long before we're eating it for breakfast. Come to think of it, that sounds like a pretty perfect way to start the day.

SALADS

Minted Green Salad

SERVES 6
ACTIVE TIME: 20 MINUTES ■ START TO FINISH: 20 MINUTES

■ Carrots, cucumber, lettuce . . . sounds like a regular salad, right? But add a generous amount of tender mint leaves and watch that salad explode with an invigorating freshness. This is a wonderful side to serve with a hearty lasagne or other baked casserole, and it easily can be doubled for a crowd. ■

- 1 carrot
- 1½ Kirby cucumbers, halved lengthwise and thinly sliced
- 1 large head Boston lettuce, torn into bite-sized pieces
- ½ heart of romaine, torn into bite-sized pieces
- ¾ cup packed small fresh mint leaves
- 2 tablespoons extra-virgin olive oil
- ¼ teaspoon fine sea salt or kosher salt
- 1 tablespoon red wine vinegar

Halve carrot crosswise, then shave into wide ribbons using a vegetable peeler.

Toss carrot with cucumbers, lettuces, mint, and oil in a large bowl. Sprinkle with sea salt and toss, then sprinkle with vinegar and toss again.

WASHING AND STORING GREENS

Most salad greens require a little TLC to keep them at their best. After you get home, look for any bruised, wilted, or torn leaves and discard them—they're a breeding ground for slimy decay. Truth be told, greens will stay fresher longer if you don't wash them ahead of time, but, frankly, most of us at the magazine do anyway. Time is usually in short supply when getting dinner on the table—especially during the week—and if the greens aren't already clean, it's all too easy to put that salad off until another night. So we tend to wash our greens (even if they're organic or labeled "prewashed") all at once in a very large bowl or clean sink of cold water. Gently swish the greens to dislodge any grit, sand, or stray insects, and then give the debris a chance to settle at the bottom of the bowl or sink. (Particularly sandy greens, such as watercress and spinach, often benefit from a second bath.)

Dry the greens in a salad spinner (how did we live without one?) before transferring them to bags. Some people swear by muslin storage bags; others roll the greens loosely in paper towels or tea towels and then put the roll in a sealable plastic bag. The goal is to get rid of the excess water on the greens (to prevent decay) while still retaining their natural moisture, as well as to give them circulating air within a closed space. Greens will keep from 2 to 4 days this way, depending on the type; heartier varieties will keep longer, obviously, than tender arugula and delicate lettuces. Watercress keeps best with its stems in a bowl of water, covered loosely with a plastic bag.

Red Leaf Lettuce with Citrus Dressing and Toasted Pine Nuts

SERVES 4
ACTIVE TIME: 10 MINUTES ■ START TO FINISH: 20 MINUTES

■ Sometimes it doesn't take much to make a recipe memorable. Here two little additions—citrus zest in the dressing and nicely toasted pine nuts—transform this easy weeknight salad into something fabulous. Fresh and vibrant, it tastes like a jolt of sunshine. ■

¼ cup extra-virgin olive oil
¼ teaspoon finely grated lemon zest
¼ teaspoon finely grated orange zest
1 tablespoon fresh lemon juice
1 tablespoon fresh orange juice
  Rounded ¼ teaspoon salt
  Rounded ¼ teaspoon freshly ground
    black pepper
1 large head red leaf lettuce, torn into
    bite-sized pieces
6 radishes, cut lengthwise into wedges
¼ cup pine nuts, toasted (see Tips, page 911)

Whisk together oil, zests, juices, salt, and pepper in a large bowl until salt is dissolved. Add lettuce and radishes and toss until well coated, then sprinkle with toasted pine nuts.

Spinach Salad with Strawberry Vinaigrette

SERVES 6
ACTIVE TIME: 30 MINUTES ■ START TO FINISH: 1¼ HOURS
(INCLUDES MAKING VINEGAR)

■ Surprisingly, this gorgeous salad is not so much sweet as aromatic. The spinach plays well with fresh berries and toasted pecans. Raspberries work here too. ■

2½ tablespoons Strawberry Vinegar (recipe follows)
  Rounded 1 teaspoon salt
⅛ teaspoon freshly ground black pepper
3 tablespoons olive oil
5 ounces baby spinach (about 8 cups)
½ pound strawberries, hulled and cut lengthwise into
    thick slices (1½ cups)
½ cup pecan halves, toasted (see Tips, page 911)

Whisk together vinegar, salt, and pepper in a small bowl until salt is dissolved. Add oil in a slow stream, whisking well.

Put spinach, strawberries, and pecans in a large bowl and toss with just enough vinaigrette to coat lightly.

Strawberry Vinegar

MAKES ABOUT 2 CUPS
ACTIVE TIME: 15 MINUTES ■ START TO FINISH: 1¼ HOURS

■ Making your own fruit vinegar with uncooked strawberries results in a subtle, fresh-from-the-berry-patch flavor. ■

1 pound strawberries, hulled (3 cups)
2 tablespoons sugar (optional—if berries are not
    sweet)
2 cups white balsamic vinegar

Pulse berries with sugar (if using) in a food processor until finely chopped and very juicy. Transfer to a bowl and add vinegar. Let stand for 1 hour.

Pour vinegar through a fine-mesh sieve into a bowl; discard solids.

COOK'S NOTE
■ The vinegar keeps, covered and refrigerated, for up to 2 weeks.

Spinach and Endive Salad with Pecans and Blue Cheese

SERVES 6
ACTIVE TIME: 10 MINUTES ■ START TO FINISH: 20 MINUTES

■ This elegant winter salad packs a dramatic punch: pale wisps of endive stand out against the dark spinach, the leaves glistening with maple syrup vinaigrette and dotted with ruby-red cranberries, toasted pecans, and crumbles of blue cheese. Each bite will be deliciously different, depending on what your fork picks up. ■

¼ cup extra-virgin olive oil
2 tablespoons finely chopped shallot
2 tablespoons white wine vinegar
1 tablespoon pure maple syrup
½ teaspoon salt
¼ teaspoon freshly ground black pepper
2 Belgian endives, thinly sliced on a long diagonal
10 ounces baby spinach
1 cup (about 3½ ounces) pecans, chopped and toasted (see Tips, page 911)
½ cup dried cranberries
⅓ cup crumbled blue cheese, preferably Danish

Whisk together oil, shallot, vinegar, syrup, salt, and pepper in a large bowl until salt is dissolved. Add endives and spinach and toss to combine.

Sprinkle salad with pecans, cranberries, and blue cheese.

Watercress and Mango Salad

SERVES 4
ACTIVE TIME: 20 MINUTES ■ START TO FINISH: 20 MINUTES

■ A new twist on slaw, this colorful mix is sweet, peppery, and refreshing. With its plethora of fresh herbs and Vietnamese-style dressing, it definitely skews in a Southeast Asian direction, but the salad tastes great with anything grilled. ■

FOR DRESSING
2 tablespoons vegetable oil
1½ tablespoons Asian sesame oil
¼ cup fresh lime juice
1 tablespoon Asian fish sauce
2 tablespoons sugar
2 dashes hot sauce, such as Tabasco
    Salt and freshly ground white pepper to taste
FOR SALAD
¾ pound watercress, coarse stems discarded (about 6 cups loosely packed)
1¾ cups thinly sliced Napa cabbage
1 (1- to 1½-pound) firm but ripe mango, peeled, pitted, and cut into ½-inch dice
½ cup coarsely grated carrot
¼ cup torn fresh cilantro leaves
¼ cup torn fresh basil leaves
¼ cup torn fresh mint leaves

MAKE THE DRESSING: Whisk together all ingredients in a small bowl until sugar and salt are dissolved.

MAKE THE SALAD: Gently toss all ingredients together in a large bowl. Toss with just enough dressing to coat.

Green Leaf Lettuce, Pomegranate, and Almond Salad

SERVES 8
ACTIVE TIME: 30 MINUTES ■ START TO FINISH: 30 MINUTES

■ With their rosy glitter and tart, juicy crunch, pomegranate seeds make an impression in autumn salads. This crisp salad of watercress and leaf lettuce tossed with toasty almonds and pomegranate seeds sets the stage nicely for a holiday meal. ■

2 tablespoons fresh lime juice
1½ teaspoons sugar
¾ teaspoon salt
¼ teaspoon freshly ground black pepper
5 tablespoons extra-virgin olive oil
2 heads green leaf lettuce, torn into 2-inch pieces (20 cups)
2 bunches watercress, coarse stems discarded, sprigs cut into 1-inch pieces (6 cups)
 Seeds from 1 large pomegranate (1¼ cups)
¾ cup sliced almonds, toasted (see Tips, page 911)

Whisk together lime juice, sugar, salt, and pepper in a small bowl until sugar and salt are dissolved. Add oil in a slow stream, whisking until combined.

Combine lettuce, watercress, and half of pomegranate seeds in a large bowl. Toss with just enough dressing to coat. Sprinkle with almonds and remaining pomegranate seeds.

COOK'S NOTES

- The pomegranate can be seeded up to 1 day ahead. Refrigerate the seeds in an airtight container.
- The almonds can be toasted up to 1 day ahead and, once cooled, kept in an airtight container at room temperature.

Frisée and Celery Salad with Toasted Fennel Seed Dressing

SERVES 8
ACTIVE TIME: 30 MINUTES ■ START TO FINISH: 30 MINUTES

■ Infusing olive oil with toasted fennel seeds and then making a lemony vinaigrette with it adds an intriguing hint of licorice to this salad of bitter greens and crunchy celery. ■

2 teaspoons fennel seeds, toasted (see Tips, page 911)
¼ cup olive oil
3 tablespoons fresh lemon juice
3 tablespoons finely chopped shallots
1 teaspoon salt

½ teaspoon sugar
½ pound frisée (French curly endive), torn into bite-sized pieces (10 cups)
3 Belgian endives, cut crosswise into ½-inch-wide slices
3 celery ribs, thinly sliced (2 cups)

SPECIAL EQUIPMENT: an electric coffee/spice grinder

Grind fennel seeds in grinder until ground but not powdery. Transfer to a small bowl or cup and stir in oil until combined. Let stand for 15 minutes to infuse flavors.

Whisk together lemon juice, shallots, salt, and sugar in another small bowl or cup until salt and sugar are dissolved. Stir fennel oil, then add to shallot mixture in a slow stream, whisking until combined.

Toss frisée, endive, and celery in a large bowl with just enough dressing to coat.

COOK'S NOTE

- The fennel oil can be made up to 1 day ahead and refrigerated, covered. Bring to room temperature before using.

Watercress and Frisée Salad with Green Apple and Celery Root

SERVES 6
ACTIVE TIME: 25 MINUTES ■ START TO FINISH: 25 MINUTES

■ Clean and fresh—just what you want after a rich main course. Watercress and frisée are two of our favorite salad greens, and the slivers of tart green apple and crisp celery root prove to be the right foils to their lively bitterness. If you've only had celery root cooked, tasting it raw will be a revelation—its earthy sweetness and crunchy texture are a delight. ■

6 ounces watercress, coarse stems discarded (6 cups)
¼ pound frisée (French curly endive), torn into 2-inch pieces (5 cups)
2 tablespoons extra-virgin olive oil
2 tablespoons red wine vinegar
2 teaspoons finely chopped shallot

Salt and freshly ground black pepper
1 Granny Smith apple
½ medium celery root (celeriac; 8 ounces), peeled
SPECIAL EQUIPMENT: a mandoline or other adjustable-
blade vegetable slicer with an ⅛-inch julienne
blade

Put watercress and frisée in a large bowl.

Whisk together oil, vinegar, shallot, ¼ teaspoon salt, and ⅛ teaspoon pepper in a small bowl until salt is dissolved.

Using slicer, julienne apple lengthwise until you reach core, then turn apple and continue; repeat process all around apple. Add apple to greens. Julienne celery root and add to greens.

Toss salad with vinaigrette and add salt and pepper to taste if necessary.

Spicy Napa Cabbage Slaw with Cilantro Dressing

SERVES 4
ACTIVE TIME: 15 MINUTES ■ START TO FINISH: 25 MINUTES

■ A nice switch from the usual mayo-heavy slaw, this version gets its zing from ginger and rice vinegar. A bit of serrano chile sparks just the right amount of heat. ■

¼ cup rice vinegar (not seasoned)
2 teaspoons sugar
1 teaspoon grated peeled fresh ginger
1 serrano chile, finely chopped, including seeds
2 tablespoons vegetable oil
½ teaspoon salt
1 pound Napa cabbage, cored and cut crosswise into
½-inch-wide slices (8 cups)
1 bunch scallions, sliced
½ cup coarsely chopped fresh cilantro

Whisk together vinegar, sugar, ginger, chile, oil, and salt in a large bowl until salt is dissolved. Add remaining ingredients and toss well. Let stand, tossing occasionally, until vegetables are slightly wilted, for about 10 minutes before serving.

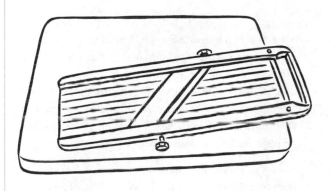

Napa Cabbage Salad with Buttermilk Dressing

SERVES 6 TO 8
ACTIVE TIME: 20 MINUTES ■ START TO FINISH: 20 MINUTES

■ Buttermilk adds a light, creamy tang to this salad chock-full of ruffly cabbage, bits of red radish, and sliced crisp celery. Take this to your next barbecue potluck and wait for the raves. ■

SOME FAVORITE SEA VEGETABLES

The marine plants most Americans call seaweeds are known, more appropriately, as sea vegetables in Japan, where they've been cultivated and eaten for centuries. They're also popular in Britain and an important indigenous food in two places that don't have many native vegetables, Hawaii and Iceland. Generally speaking, sea vegetables are packed with minerals and amino acids, which give them a briny savor. Their aroma reminds one of the seacoast, says food scientist Harold McGee, because they, in fact, help perfume it. For practical purposes, edible sea vegetables can be classified into three groups: green, red, and brown. The sea vegetables that you'll find in the United States are mostly dried and need to be soaked briefly before using.

KOMBU

ARAME This brown sea vegetable, which grows in deep waters, is somewhat similar to hijiki in flavor and texture but is sweeter, milder, and softer. It's also known as sea oak, because its thick, large, irregular fronds look like oak leaves. *Arame* ("ah-*rah*-may") is sold in thin brown strips that turn black when cooked. It helps give the miso stew on page 332 texture and nuance.

DULSE You will find these dramatic reddish purple, ribbonlike fronds growing in rocky crannies along the northern coasts of the Atlantic and Pacific Oceans. Considered a red sea vegetable, dulse is popular in Ireland, Iceland, and Atlantic Canada. (One Nova Scotia miniature variety is marketed as Sea Parsley.) Crisp, almost leathery, dulse can be eaten raw or cooked; we use dried dulse flakes to season the miso stew on page 332.

HIJIKI This calcium-and-iron-rich brown sea vegetable (when dried, it's almost jet black), with its wrinkled spaghetti-thin fronds, grows along the coasts of Japan, China, and Korea. It's used in vegetable dishes, soups, and a tealike infusion in Japan and China. We combine it with carrots in a homey preparation on page 586.

KOMBU This salty-sweet brown sea vegetable (aka kelp), harvested mainly around the northern Japanese island of Hokkaido, is several yards long; dried kombu is sold packaged in different lengths that are easily cut with scissors. Kombu is renowned as a flavor enhancer, which is why it's long been used as a base for the sea stock called *dashi;* it's known for the savory, almost meaty taste called *umami,* perhaps best translated as "richness" or "deliciousness." (*Umami* is also present in various fermented foods, including soy sauce, wine, and cheese.)

NORI This green sea vegetable is commonly used as a sushi wrap. In Britain it is called *laver* (*sloke* in Scotland), and it is used in bread and cakes. In Wales, the gathering of it, primarily in the south along the Pembrokeshire and Gower coasts, begins in the spring. There, unlike in Japan, where it's dried in sheets, laver is sold either wet and fresh from the sea or washed well and pureed.

WAKAME Despite its deep green color when soaked and softened, mineral-rich dried wakame ("wah-*kah*-may") is considered a brown sea vegetable. The tangled fronds add a mild sweetness and delicate succulence to seaweed salad and are also delicious in miso soup.

½ cup well-shaken buttermilk

3 tablespoons mayonnaise

2 tablespoons cider vinegar

2 tablespoons minced shallot

1 tablespoon sugar

½ teaspoon salt

¼ teaspoon freshly ground black pepper

3 tablespoons finely chopped fresh chives

1 pound Napa cabbage, cored and thinly sliced
crosswise (8 cups)

6 radishes, diced

2 celery ribs, thinly sliced diagonally

Whisk together buttermilk, mayonnaise, vinegar, shallot, sugar, salt, and pepper in a large bowl until sugar and salt are dissolved, then whisk in chives. Add cabbage, radishes, and celery and toss with dressing.

Seaweed Salad

■ Granny Smith apple adds a note of crisp familiarity to this unusual seaweed salad. Wakame, a sea alga that is rich in minerals, often looks almost black, but when it is soaked and softened, its deep green color reemerges. At her restaurant, Rialto, in Cambridge, Massachusetts, chef Jody Adams serves the salad with grilled clams, but it makes a sprightly side dish for any kind of seafood. ■

¾ ounce dried wakame seaweed (whole or cut; see
Sources)

3 tablespoons rice vinegar (not seasoned)

3 tablespoons soy sauce

2 tablespoons Asian sesame oil

1 teaspoon sugar

1 teaspoon finely grated peeled fresh ginger

½ teaspoon minced garlic

1 small tart apple, such as Granny Smith

2 scallions, thinly sliced

2 tablespoons chopped fresh cilantro

1 tablespoon sesame seeds, toasted (see Tips,
page 911)

Soak wakame in warm water to cover for 5 minutes. Drain and squeeze out excess water. If wakame is uncut, cut into ½-inch-wide strips.

Whisk together vinegar, soy sauce, sesame oil, sugar, ginger, and garlic in a medium bowl until sugar is dissolved. Cut apple into ¼-inch dice and add to dressing, along with seaweed, scallions, and cilantro, tossing to combine well. Sprinkle salad with sesame seeds.

Grilled Caesar Salad

■ It's hard to improve on classic Caesar salad, but this recipe does it. Grilling the romaine and croutons is a neat trick, adding a sultry, smoky edge (the romaine's leaves char slightly but stay crisp). Contrasting cool and warm, crunchy and soft, this Caesar is revolutionary yet familiar. ■

2 anchovy fillets, drained and chopped

1 small garlic clove, chopped

½ cup extra-virgin olive oil
Salt

¼ teaspoon freshly ground black pepper

12 (½-inch-thick) slices baguette

1 large egg

2 tablespoons fresh lemon juice, or to taste

3 hearts of romaine, halved lengthwise

½ cup finely grated Parmigiano-Reggiano

If using a charcoal grill, prepare it for direct-heat cooking over medium-hot coals; if using a gas grill, prepare it for direct-heat cooking over medium heat (see Grilling Basics, page 512).

Meanwhile, combine anchovies, garlic, oil, ¼ teaspoon salt, and pepper in a blender and puree until smooth. Brush both sides of baguette slices with some of anchovy mixture and transfer to a platter.

Add egg and lemon juice to dressing in blender and blend until smooth, 1 to 2 minutes; season with salt to taste. Transfer to a small bowl and refrigerate until ready to use.

Grill anchovy bread, turning occasionally, until

toasted, 1 to 2 minutes. Grill romaine, cut side down (covered only if using a gas grill), just until grill marks appear, about 2 minutes.

Cut romaine crosswise into 2-inch-wide strips and transfer to a bowl. Halve or quarter toasts and add to romaine, along with Parmigiano-Reggiano. Toss salad with just enough dressing to coat and serve immediately.

COOK'S NOTES

- The egg in this recipe is not cooked. If that is a concern, see page 915.
- The bread can be brushed with the anchovy mixture up to 4 hours ahead and refrigerated, covered.
- The dressing can be made up to 4 hours ahead and refrigerated, covered.

Boston Lettuce Salad with Dubliner Cheese and Chive Dressing

SERVES 4 AS A FIRST COURSE, 2 AS A MAIN COURSE
ACTIVE TIME: 30 MINUTES ■ START TO FINISH: 30 MINUTES

■ A bed of thinly sliced Boston lettuce holds crisp cucumbers in a rich dressing of crème fraîche and chives, with a healthy sprinkling of Dubliner cheese (a firm sharp cheese similar to Irish cheddar) and a sweet topping of hazelnuts and dates. The flavor is phenomenal and the salad is substantial enough to serve as an entrée. If you can't find Dubliner, any sharp cheddar will do. We adapted this recipe from one served at the Huntington House Inn in Rochester, Vermont. ■

FOR HAZELNUT-DATE TOPPING
  ½ tablespoon unsalted butter
  ¼ cup hazelnuts
  ¼ teaspoon sugar
  ¼ teaspoon salt
  1 pitted date, preferably Medjool
FOR DRESSING
  1 cup (8 ounces) crème fraîche
  2 tablespoons extra-virgin olive oil

  2 teaspoons fresh lemon juice
  ¾ teaspoon salt
  ¾ teaspoon freshly ground black pepper
  2 tablespoons coarsely grated Dubliner cheese or sharp cheddar
  2 tablespoons finely chopped fresh chives
FOR CUCUMBERS
  1 seedless cucumber (usually plastic-wrapped), peeled and cut into slices less than ⅛ inch thick
  1 tablespoon finely chopped shallot
  1 tablespoon chopped fresh dill
  1 tablespoon cider vinegar
  ¼ teaspoon salt
FOR SALAD
  2 heads Boston lettuce
  ½ cup coarsely grated Dubliner cheese or sharp cheddar
OPTIONAL ACCOMPANIMENTS: fresh lemon juice and extra-virgin olive oil

MAKE THE HAZELNUT-DATE TOPPING: Heat butter in a small heavy skillet over moderate heat until foam subsides. Add hazelnuts and swirl skillet until nuts are coated. Add sugar and salt and cook, shaking skillet occasionally, until sugar melts into a golden caramel and coats nuts, 2 to 4 minutes. Transfer nuts to a plate to cool.

When nuts are completely cool, reserve 1 tablespoon, then pulse remaining nuts in a food processor until coarsely chopped. Transfer to a bowl. Grind reserved nuts in food processor until very finely ground, being careful not to process to a paste. Add date and pulse until date is finely chopped. Toss date mixture with coarsely chopped nuts.

MAKE THE DRESSING: Whisk together all ingredients in a bowl until combined.

MAKE THE CUCUMBERS: Toss together all ingredients until combined.

ASSEMBLE THE SALAD: Remove 8 outer leaves of lettuce and reserve. Slice remaining lettuce into ¼-inch-wide strips. Arrange reserved leaves on four plates and place a tall mound of shredded lettuce in center of each. Drizzle each serving with 3 to 4 tablespoons dressing. Top salads with cucumbers and sprinkle evenly with cheese and hazelnut-date topping. Drizzle with lemon juice and olive oil if desired.

- The hazelnut-date topping can be made up to 1 week ahead and kept in an airtight container at room temperature.
- The dressing can be made up to 1 day ahead and refrigerated, covered. Whisk well before using.

Romaine, Radish, and Cucumber Salad with Tahini Dressing

SERVES 4
ACTIVE TIME: 25 MINUTES ■ START TO FINISH: 25 MINUTES

■ A welcome change of pace from oil and vinegar, this tahini dressing is creamy and nutty, with a lemony kick. It goes beautifully with the crisp vegetables. For a delicious summery sandwich, stuff the salad into a pita with some leftover grilled lamb or chicken. ■

FOR TAHINI DRESSING
- ¼ cup well-stirred tahini (Middle Eastern sesame paste)
- ¼ cup water
- 2½ tablespoons fresh lemon juice
- 2 tablespoons soy sauce
- 1 tablespoon mild honey
- 1 small garlic clove, minced
- ½ teaspoon salt
- ⅛ teaspoon cayenne

FOR SALAD
- ½ pound romaine, torn into bite-sized pieces (6 cups)
- 1 bunch radishes, trimmed, halved, and thinly sliced
- ½ seedless cucumber (usually plastic-wrapped), halved lengthwise and thinly sliced
- 4 scallions, thinly sliced

MAKE THE DRESSING: Combine all ingredients in a blender and blend until smooth. (If desired, blend in more water, 1 teaspoon at a time, to thin dressing.)

MAKE THE SALAD: Toss together all ingredients in a large bowl with just enough dressing to coat.

- The dressing can be made up to 3 days ahead and refrigerated, covered. Stir before using, thinning with additional water if necessary.

Clementine, Olive, and Endive Salad

SERVES 6 TO 8
ACTIVE TIME: 1 HOUR ■ START TO FINISH: 1 HOUR

■ Clementines, a cross between the Mediterranean mandarin and a sour orange, are a favorite for snacking out of hand during the few fleeting winter months they're available. Here they combine with black olives, pickled cocktail onions, and gently bitter endive. It's a great kickoff to a hearty meal of short ribs, duck, or braised lamb shanks. ■

- 2 tablespoons red wine vinegar
- 1 teaspoon sugar, or to taste
- ½ teaspoon salt, or to taste
- ¼ cup extra-virgin olive oil
- Freshly ground black pepper
- 1¾ pounds clementines (7–11)
- 2 pounds Belgian endives (6–8)
- 4 pale inner celery ribs with leaves
- ½ cup Kalamata or other brine-cured black olives, pitted and cut lengthwise into slivers
- 1 cup (5 ounces) drained cocktail (pickled) onions, quartered
- ¾ cup loosely packed fresh flat-leaf parsley leaves

Whisk together vinegar, sugar, and salt in a small bowl until sugar and salt are dissolved. Add oil in a slow stream, whisking until well blended. Season with pepper.

Cut off tops and bottoms of clementines to expose fruit. Stand fruit on a cutting board and remove peel, including all white pith, by cutting it off in vertical strips with a sharp paring knife. Cut segments free from membranes.

Halve endives lengthwise. Cut out and discard cores, cut endives diagonally into ½-inch-wide strips, and put in a large salad bowl. Separate celery leaves from ribs and cut ribs diagonally into very thin slices. Add leaves and ribs to endive, along with olives, onions, parsley, and clementine segments. Whisk dressing and gently toss salad with just enough dressing to coat.

COOK'S NOTES

- The salad ingredients can be cut up to 4 hours ahead and refrigerated separately in sealable plastic bags.
- The dressing can be made up to 4 hours ahead and refrigerated, covered.

Bitter Green Salad with Roasted Pears

SERVES 10 TO 12
ACTIVE TIME: 35 MINUTES ∎ START TO FINISH: 1 HOUR

∎ Even pears that aren't quite ripe taste extraordinary when roasted until caramelized. Here they are the counterpoint to a colorful combination of bitter greens dressed with a honey-sweetened vinaigrette. This big, beautiful salad makes a statement at the end of a holiday meal. Happily, most of the work can be done well ahead of time. ∎

FOR SALAD
  8 firm but ripe Bosc pears, peeled, cored, and cut into 8 wedges each
1½ tablespoons extra-virgin olive oil
    Salt and freshly ground black pepper
  1 small head chicory
  1 small head escarole
  1 small head radicchio
  1 bunch watercress, coarse stems discarded
  1 bunch mizuna, coarse stems discarded (see Cook's Note)
  1 small head romaine
FOR DRESSING
  1 tablespoon finely chopped shallot
2½ tablespoons cider vinegar
  ½ teaspoon honey
  ¼ teaspoon salt
  ⅛ teaspoon freshly ground black pepper
  5 tablespoons extra-virgin olive oil

ROAST THE PEARS: Put a rack in middle of oven and preheat oven to 425°F.

Toss pears with oil and spread in one layer on a large baking sheet. Season with salt and pepper. Roast pears, stirring and turning twice, until tender and beginning to brown, 20 to 30 minutes. Cool for about 15 minutes.

MEANWHILE, PREPARE THE GREENS: Tear enough tender chicory and escarole leaves (discard ribs) into bite-sized pieces to measure 6 cups total. Tear enough radicchio, watercress, mizuna, and romaine into bite-sized pieces to measure 10 cups total. Toss torn greens together in a large bowl (reserve any remaining greens for another use).

MAKE THE DRESSING: Whisk together shallot, vinegar, honey, salt, and pepper in a small bowl until salt is dissolved. Add oil in a slow stream, whisking until well combined.

Just before serving, add roasted pears and dressing to greens and toss to combine well.

COOK'S NOTES

- The pears can be roasted up to 4 hours head and kept at room temperature.
- If you can't find some of the greens, such as mizuna, you can substitute more of another kind, to measure 16 cups total.

Ribboned Zucchini Salad

SERVES 6
ACTIVE TIME: 30 MINUTES ∎ START TO FINISH: 30 MINUTES

∎ Floppy ribbons of zucchini weave through a jumble of herbs and frisée, all punctuated by briny black olives. Preparing the zucchini for this dish won't heat up your kitchen—simply salting the thin slices is enough to tenderize them. ∎

  2 pounds small zucchini, trimmed
  1 teaspoon salt
  2 tablespoons extra-virgin olive oil
  2 teaspoons finely grated lemon zest
  2 teaspoons fresh lemon juice
  2 teaspoons Dijon mustard

- 1 teaspoon anchovy paste
- ¼ teaspoon freshly ground black pepper
- 3 ounces frisée (French curly endive), trimmed and torn into small pieces (4 cups loosely packed)
- ½ cup loosely packed fresh flat-leaf parsley leaves
- ½ cup loosely packed fresh mint leaves, torn lengthwise in half if large
- ½ cup loosely packed fresh basil leaves, torn into small pieces
- 12 Kalamata or other brine-cured black olives, pitted and thinly sliced lengthwise
- 1 small red onion, halved lengthwise and thinly sliced crosswise (½ cup)

SPECIAL EQUIPMENT: a mandoline or other adjustable-blade vegetable slicer

Cut zucchini lengthwise into ⅛-inch-thick slices with slicer and transfer to a colander set over a bowl. Sprinkle with salt and toss well. Let stand for 5 minutes.

Rinse zucchini under cold running water. Transfer to a clean kitchen towel and spread out in one layer, then gently roll up in towel and let stand for 5 minutes to absorb excess moisture.

Whisk together oil, zest, juice, mustard, anchovy paste, and pepper in a large bowl until combined.

Add zucchini and remaining ingredients and toss well. Serve immediately.

Grilled Zucchini Salad with Purslane and Tomatoes

SERVES 4 TO 6
ACTIVE TIME: 30 MINUTES ■ START TO FINISH: 30 MINUTES

■ Tossed in a fresh, lemony dressing, the smoky slices of grilled zucchini contrast nicely with juicy, slightly acidic tomatoes and succulent purslane. ■

- 1 teaspoon finely grated lemon zest
- 3 tablespoons fresh lemon juice
- 1 tablespoon finely chopped shallot

- ¼ teaspoon Dijon mustard
- ½ teaspoon salt
- ⅓ cup extra-virgin olive oil, plus more for brushing zucchini
- ¼ teaspoon freshly ground black pepper
- 3 tablespoons chopped fresh flat-leaf parsley
- 4 zucchini (1¾–2 pounds total), halved lengthwise
- ¾ pound purslane, thick stems discarded (4 cups)
- 10 ounces pear or cherry tomatoes, halved lengthwise

If using a charcoal grill, prepare it for direct-heat cooking over medium-hot coals; if using a gas grill, prepare it for direct-heat cooking over medium-high heat (see Grilling Basics, page 512).

MAKE THE DRESSING: Whisk together zest, lemon juice, shallot, mustard, and salt in a small bowl until salt is dissolved. Add oil in a slow stream, whisking until well blended. Whisk in pepper and parsley.

GRILL THE ZUCCHINI: Lightly brush zucchini all over with oil. Grill zucchini (covered only if using a gas grill), starting cut side down and turning once, until just tender, 8 to 12 minutes. Transfer to a cutting board and let cool slightly, then cut diagonally into ½-inch-thick slices.

Toss zucchini with purslane, tomatoes, and dressing in a large bowl. Serve immediately.

TOMATOES

Each year, more and more tomatoes in a wide variety of shapes and colors appear in supermarkets and farmers markets across the country, displayed like voluptuous starlets. One of the most popular and versatile varieties—meaty, with relatively few seeds—is what's commonly called a beefsteak. According to the master gardener and author William Woys Weaver, the original beefsteak was a purple-brown tomato that looked like raw beef inside. Named in 1869 by Thomas Campbell and used in ketchup and canning, that variety is now extinct. Because it was oblate (flat at the top and bottom), its steaklike shape became associated with the name, which was subsequently given to all tomatoes of similar form.

For consumers, the most important development on the tomato front in recent years has been the rise of heirloom varieties. Unlike hybrids—which are controlled crosses that, in subsequent generations, revert to types from both parental lines—heirlooms breed "true" to their forebears year after year. They are also open-pollinated, meaning that there's no artificial crossing or genetic engineering. Much of the popularity of heirlooms stems from their depth of flavor and differences in acidity, fruitiness, and their tomatoey taste. The thin-skinned Pink Brandywine is one of the most famous heirloom varieties, and it's one of the most versatile; it's meaty and juicy and it holds its shape well when cooked. It's not of Amish origin, as is often claimed; it's a commercial cultivar, introduced by a Philadelphia seed company in 1889.

Heirlooms come in a far greater range of colors than commercial hybrids do because the latter are designed to meet standards for certain industries, such as canning. Some heirlooms, such as Cherokee Purple and Black Russian, are deep red, almost brown in color. Others, including Aunt Ruby's German Green, Evergreen, and Green Zebra (a new heirloom dating from the 1980s), have skins tinged with yellow when ripe, but their flesh remains green. In general, these ripe green tomatoes are sweeter and less acidic than red ones. Richly hued cherry tomatoes are just the ticket for salads or snacks. They are also delicious simply pan-seared and piled on top of a steak.

Tomatoes are generally treated like a vegetable rather than a tropical fruit (their ancestral home is South America). That's probably because ripe tomatoes have large amounts of glutamic acid and sulfur compounds, both more common in meats than in fruits, and enough acid to balance that steak.

Because tomatoes are tropical, it takes a stretch of hot, sunny weather to bring them to their peak. They are so sensitive to the cold, in fact, that you should never keep them in the refrigerator; their flesh will lose its firmness and become mealy, and much of the flavor will be irrevocably lost as well. They keep best stem end up (to prevent bruised shoulders) at room temperature and in indirect light. Under those conditions, ripe tomatoes will keep for at least a day or so; underripe ones can take up to a week to reach their peak. And as you savor each variety, keep one thing in mind: there are thousands more out there.

Cucumber, Mustard, and Dill Salad

SERVES 4
ACTIVE TIME: 10 MINUTES ■ START TO FINISH: 10 MINUTES

■ Fast, crisp, and flavorful, this salad is great with fish, especially salmon. ■

- 2 teaspoons white wine vinegar
- 2 teaspoons Dijon mustard
- 1½ teaspoons sugar
- ½ teaspoon salt, or to taste
- 1 tablespoon mild olive oil
- 1 large seedless cucumber (usually plastic-wrapped; 1 pound), peeled, halved lengthwise, seedy center scooped out, and cut into ⅛-inch-thick slices
- 2 tablespoons chopped fresh dill

Whisk together vinegar, mustard, sugar, and salt in a bowl until sugar and salt are dissolved. Add oil in a slow stream, whisking. Add cucumber, along with dill, tossing to coat.

Summer Tomato Salad

SERVES 6
ACTIVE TIME: 10 MINUTES ■ START TO FINISH: 10 MINUTES

■ Adding just a tiny amount of dressing to perfectly ripe summer tomatoes boosts their flavor into the stratosphere. Whether you use heirloom, beefsteak, or cherry, be sure to use the ripest tomatoes you can find. ■

- 3 tablespoons extra-virgin olive oil
- 2 tablespoons malt vinegar
- ¾ teaspoon packed light brown sugar
- ½ teaspoon salt
- ½ teaspoon coarsely ground black pepper
- 2 pounds ripe tomatoes, cut into ½-inch-thick slices
- 1 scallion, thinly sliced on the diagonal

Whisk together oil, vinegar, brown sugar, salt, and pepper in a small bowl until sugar and salt are dissolved.

Arrange one third of tomatoes in one layer on a large plate. Drizzle with about one third of dressing and sprinkle with one third of scallion. Make 2 more layers of tomatoes, drizzling each with dressing and sprinkling with scallion.

Tomato Salad with Red Onion and Herbs

SERVES 6 TO 8
ACTIVE TIME: 20 MINUTES ■ START TO FINISH: 1½ HOURS

■ An easy vinaigrette with sherry vinegar and Dijon mustard marries the juicy sweetness of ripe tomatoes with the bite of red onion and shallots. Although a mix of fresh basil, parsley, tarragon, and mint scattered over the salad plays up its multidimensional flavors, it will be wonderful even if you use only one or two herbs. ■

- 1 garlic clove
- ¾ teaspoon salt
- 1½ tablespoons fresh lemon juice
- 1½ tablespoons sherry vinegar
- 1½ teaspoons Dijon mustard
- ¾ teaspoon sugar
- ¼ teaspoon freshly ground black pepper
- 6 tablespoons extra-virgin olive oil
- 2½ pounds tomatoes (about 6 medium), cored and cut into ½-inch-thick slices
- ½ cup thin red onion rounds, separated into rings
- 2 shallots, thinly sliced
- ⅓ cup coarsely chopped mixed fresh herbs, such as basil, flat-leaf parsley, tarragon, and/or mint

Mince garlic and mash to a paste with salt, using side of a large heavy knife. Transfer to a bowl, add lemon juice, vinegar, mustard, sugar, and pepper, and whisk until combined. Add oil in a stream, whisking until well blended.

Arrange tomato slices on a deep platter and scatter onion rings and shallots over them. Pour dressing over salad and let stand at room temperature, basting tomatoes with juices occasionally, for 1 hour to allow flavors to blend.

Just before serving, sprinkle with herbs.

Tomato and Pita Bread Salad

Fattoush

SERVES 4
ACTIVE TIME: 1¼ HOURS ■ START TO FINISH: 1½ HOURS

■ It's best to dress most salads just before serving, so the greens and vegetables stay light and crisp. Not so with Lebanese fattoush—you want to prepare it well in advance so the lettuce, onion, cucumber, and herbs can drink up the vinaigrette. The result is an intensely tasty salad, punctuated by crunchy triangles of toasted pita. Fattoush's most distinct flavor comes from sumac, a brick-red powder of ground dried sumac berries that contributes a tart, lemony taste. If you can find purslane at your farmers market (or growing wild in your yard), by all means use it—it adds a succulence. ■

1 medium red onion, halved lengthwise and cut crosswise into very thin slices (1½ cups)

6 large romaine leaves, cut lengthwise into 1-inch-wide strips, then crosswise into 1-inch pieces (3½ cups)

1 seedless cucumber (usually plastic-wrapped), peeled, halved lengthwise, seedy center scooped out, and cut into ¼-inch pieces (2 cups)

½ cup coarsely chopped fresh flat-leaf parsley

½ cup coarsely chopped purslane, thick stems discarded (optional)

¼ cup coarsely chopped fresh mint

2 teaspoons ground sumac (see Sources)
Freshly ground black pepper

2 garlic cloves
Salt

¼ cup fresh lemon juice

⅓ cup extra-virgin olive oil

3 (6-inch) pita breads (with pockets)

½ stick (4 tablespoons) unsalted butter

¼ cup olive oil

4 medium tomatoes (1½ pounds), cut into ½-inch pieces

Cover onion with very cold water and soak for 10 minutes (to make onion flavor milder). Drain in a colander and pat dry with paper towels.

Toss together onion, romaine, cucumber, parsley, purslane (if using), mint, sumac, and ¼ teaspoon pepper in a large serving bowl.

Mince garlic and mash to a paste with 1 teaspoon salt, using side of a large heavy knife. Whisk together garlic paste, lemon juice, and extra-virgin olive oil in a small bowl until combined, then pour over salad and toss well. Refrigerate salad, covered, for at least 30 minutes to allow flavors to develop.

Meanwhile, split pitas horizontally to make 6 rounds. Cut each round into 8 wedges. Heat 1 tablespoon butter and 1 tablespoon olive oil in a 12-inch heavy skillet over moderate heat until foam subsides. Fry 12 pita wedges, turning occasionally, until golden and crisp, about 2 minutes. With a slotted spatula, transfer to paper towels to drain. Fry remaining pita wedges in remaining butter and oil in batches in same manner.

About 10 minutes before serving, add pita wedges, tomatoes, and salt and pepper to taste to salad and toss to combine.

COOK'S NOTE

■ The dressed salad, without the pitas and tomatoes, can be refrigerated for up to 2 hours.

Tomato, Cucumber, and Pineapple Salad with Asian Dressing

SERVES 6
ACTIVE TIME: 30 MINUTES ■ START TO FINISH: 30 MINUTES

■ This fabulous salad is the epitome of flavor synergy. Combining sweet pineapple and fiery serrano with cooling cucumber and mint catapults you out of your backyard and into a very sophisticated café somewhere in Vietnam. ■

1 large garlic clove
Salt

2 tablespoons fresh lime juice

1 tablespoon sugar

2 tablespoons vegetable oil

1 (2-inch-long) serrano or jalapeño chile, minced, including seeds

¼–½ teaspoon Asian fish sauce

½ seedless cucumber (usually plastic-wrapped), halved lengthwise and thinly sliced

½ pineapple, peeled, quartered lengthwise, cored, and sliced crosswise ¼ inch thick (2 cups)

½ cup coarsely chopped fresh cilantro

¼ cup coarsely chopped fresh mint

1 pound tomatoes (about 3 medium), cut into ½-inch-thick wedges

Mince garlic and mash to a paste with ¼ teaspoon salt, using side of a large heavy knife.

Whisk together lime juice and sugar in a large bowl until sugar is dissolved. Whisk in oil, garlic paste, chile, and fish sauce (to taste). Add remaining ingredients, tossing to coat, then add salt to taste.

Melon Carpaccio

SERVES 6
ACTIVE TIME: 20 MINUTES ■ START TO FINISH: 20 MINUTES

■ A simple, stylish starter, this salad is a knockout every time. Though you might instinctively reach for a drippingly ripe cantaloupe, it could be too juicy here, dissolving into mush under the peeler's blade. Instead, look for one that is just ripe but fragrant. The fresh lime juice, sea salt, and tarragon amplify the melon's musky sweetness. ■

1 (3-pound) cantaloupe, halved lengthwise and seeded

1½ teaspoons fresh lime juice

1 tablespoon extra-virgin olive oil

1 bunch fresh tarragon with small leaves

Coarse sea salt (lightly crushed if grains are very large) and freshly ground black pepper

ACCOMPANIMENT: 6 thin lime wedges

SPECIAL EQUIPMENT: a Y-shaped vegetable peeler

Cut each cantaloupe half into 3 wedges. Shave thin slices from one wedge, starting from seeded side,

with peeler (first slice may be irregular), stopping when you get close to rind. Arrange slices, overlapping slightly, on one plate. Repeat with remaining cantaloupe, putting slices from each wedge on a separate plate.

Drizzle each serving with ¼ teaspoon lime juice and ½ teaspoon oil, then scatter about 10 tarragon leaves on top. Season with sea salt and pepper and serve with lime wedges.

COOK'S NOTE

■ The carpaccio can be arranged on the plates, without the tarragon and seasoning, up to 1 hour ahead. Sprinkle with the tarragon, salt, and pepper just before serving.

Arugula with Pancetta-Wrapped Peaches

SERVES 8
ACTIVE TIME: 40 MINUTES ■ START TO FINISH: 40 MINUTES

■ Salty ham wrapped around juicy melon or ripe figs is a favorite Italian antipasto. This first-course salad reprises that idea by enrobing peach slices in pancetta and cooking them until the meat becomes crisp. Add baby arugula and a sprinkling of snow-white ricotta salata, and you've got a dish that is as impressive as it is delicious. ■

1 tablespoon balsamic vinegar

2 teaspoons fresh lemon juice

¼ teaspoon salt

3 tablespoons extra-virgin olive oil

4 ripe peaches

24 thin slices pancetta (Italian unsmoked bacon; 1¼ pounds)

2 tablespoons olive oil

6 ounces baby arugula (6 cups)

½ cup finely crumbled ricotta salata

Coarsely ground black pepper

Whisk together vinegar, lemon juice, and salt in a small bowl until salt is dissolved. Add extra-virgin olive oil in a stream, whisking until well blended.

Cut an X in bottom of each peach. Immerse peaches in a pot of boiling water for 15 seconds, then transfer to a bowl of ice and cold water. Peel peaches and cut each into 6 wedges. Wrap 1 slice of pancetta around each wedge, overlapping ends of pancetta.

Heat olive oil in a 12-inch nonstick skillet over moderate heat until hot but not smoking. Add half of peaches and cook, turning occasionally with tongs, until pancetta is browned on all sides, about 5 minutes per batch. Transfer to a plate and cover loosely with foil to keep warm while you cook remaining peaches in same manner.

Divide arugula and peaches among eight salad plates. Drizzle with dressing, sprinkle with ricotta salata and pepper, and serve immediately.

COOK'S NOTES
- The dressing can be made up to 2 hours ahead and kept, covered, at room temperature.
- The peaches can be peeled, tossed with an additional teaspoon of lemon juice, and wrapped with the pancetta up to 1 hour ahead. Refrigerate, covered with plastic wrap.

Winter Salad

SERVES 4
ACTIVE TIME: 35 MINUTES ■ START TO FINISH: 35 MINUTES

■ This very special salad, which balances sweet, bitter, peppery, and tangy notes, comes from the Peerless Restaurant in Ashland, Oregon. White truffle oil, misused by overzealous chefs, is essential here. A restrained teaspoon adds just a whiff of the woods, playing beautifully against the snowy celery root and Granny Smith apple. The recipe makes more dressing than you'll need, but it's so good you'll want to have extra. ■

- 2 teaspoons finely chopped shallot
- 1 teaspoon honey
- 2 tablespoons fresh orange juice
- 2 tablespoons sherry vinegar
  Salt and freshly ground white pepper
- ¾ cup extra-virgin olive oil

- 3 Belgian endives, halved lengthwise, cored, and cut lengthwise into ½-inch-wide strips
- 1 small red onion, halved lengthwise and thinly sliced crosswise (½ cup)
- ½ fennel bulb, stalks discarded, bulb cored and thinly sliced lengthwise (½ cup)
- ¼ celery root (celeriac), peeled and cut into ⅛-inch-thick matchsticks (½ cup)
- ½ Granny Smith apple, cored and cut into ⅛-inch-thick matchsticks (½ cup)
- 2 cups mizuna or mustard greens (if using mustard greens, stems and tough center ribs discarded, leaves torn into 2-inch pieces)
- 2 ounces firm aged goat cheese, shaved with a vegetable peeler
- 1 teaspoon white truffle oil (see Sources)

Whisk together shallot, honey, orange juice, vinegar, ½ teaspoon salt, and ¼ teaspoon white pepper in a bowl until salt is dissolved. Add olive oil in a stream, whisking until well blended.

Toss endives, onion, fennel, celery root, apple, and mizuna with ½ cup dressing in a large bowl. Season with salt and white pepper.

Serve salad topped with cheese and drizzled with truffle oil.

COOK'S NOTE
- Leftover dressing keeps, covered and refrigerated, for up to 2 days. Bring to room temperature before using.

Sweet-Hot Mustard Green and Avocado Salad

SERVES 4
ACTIVE TIME: 20 MINUTES ■ START TO FINISH: 25 MINUTES

■ How do raw mustard greens, avocado, and a boiling-hot dressing of rice vinegar, honey, and raisins go together? Fabulously, it turns out. This barely wilted salad from the vegetable expert and cookbook author Elizabeth Schneider retains a fluffy freshness, while the butteriness of the avocado and the dressing's sweet tang help temper the mustardy bite. It's a wholly fresh take on a "mess o' greens." ∎

⅓ cup rice vinegar (not seasoned)
⅓ cup golden raisins
1 tablespoon finely chopped shallot
1 tablespoon minced peeled fresh ginger
1 tablespoon mild honey
¾ pound tender mustard greens, stems discarded
1 large California avocado
⅛ teaspoon salt, or to taste
3 tablespoons vegetable oil

Combine vinegar, raisins, shallot, ginger, and honey in a small saucepan and bring to a boil, stirring. Remove from heat and let stand for 10 minutes.

Meanwhile, cut mustard greens crosswise into thin slices and put in a heatproof serving bowl. Halve, pit, and peel avocado and cut into ½-inch dice.

Add salt and oil to vinegar mixture and bring to a boil, stirring. Drizzle dressing over mustard greens, tossing well to coat. Add avocado and toss gently.

Shaved Brussels Sprout Slaw with Walnuts and Pecorino

SERVES 6
ACTIVE TIME: 25 MINUTES ∎ START TO FINISH: 35 MINUTES

∎ Brussels sprouts, sliced very thin, make for a delicate slaw. If you have a sharp knife and good skills, you can slice the Brussels sprouts by hand, but it's much easier to use an adjustable-blade slicer. In the fall, when walnuts are fresh and in season, chef Jonathan Waxman uses just-shelled ones in this salad, which he serves at his Manhattan restaurant, Barbuto. Pecorino Romano varies in saltiness; after tasting, you may want to add a little more cheese than we call for here. ∎

1½ pounds Brussels sprouts, preferably on the stalk, any discolored leaves discarded, any stems left intact
1 cup (about 3½ ounces) walnuts, lightly toasted (see Tips, page 911)

2 tablespoons finely grated pecorino Romano, or more to taste
¼ cup olive oil
3 tablespoons fresh lemon juice
Freshly ground black pepper

Holding each Brussels sprout by stem end, cut into very thin slices using a mandoline or other adjustable-blade slicer; discard stems. Or, using a sharp knife, halve sprouts lengthwise and cut crosswise into very thin slices. Transfer to a large bowl. Toss to separate leaves.

Lightly crush walnuts with your hands. Add to Brussels sprouts, along with cheese, oil, and lemon juice, and toss to combine. Season with pepper.

COOK'S NOTES
∎ The Brussels sprouts can be sliced up to 3 hours ahead and refrigerated, covered.
∎ The walnuts can be toasted up to 1 day ahead and kept in an airtight container at room temperature.

Jicama Slaw

SERVES 8
ACTIVE TIME: 30 MINUTES ∎ START TO FINISH: 30 MINUTES

∎ Jicama is all about crunch, and this slaw makes the most of it. It's also very pretty, with the pink of the chopped red onion and the cilantro-flecked dressing against the ivory matchsticks of jicama. ∎

1 medium red onion, finely chopped
Salt
2½ tablespoons fresh lime juice (from about 2 limes)
⅓ cup extra-virgin olive oil
1 teaspoon sugar
¼ teaspoon freshly ground black pepper
2½ pounds jicama, peeled and cut into matchsticks (9–10 cups)
⅓ cup finely chopped fresh cilantro

Soak onion in 1 cup cold water with ½ teaspoon salt for 15 minutes (to make onion flavor milder). Drain in a sieve, rinse under cold water, and pat dry.

Whisk together lime juice, oil, sugar, ¾ teaspoon salt, and pepper in a large bowl until sugar and salt are dissolved. Add onion, jicama, and cilantro, season with salt to taste, and toss well.

sing will be thick; thin slightly with additional water if desired.)

Drizzle salad with some of dressing and serve remainder on the side.

COOK'S NOTE
- The jicama can be cut into matchsticks up to 6 hours ahead and refrigerated, covered.

COOK'S NOTE
- The salad and dressing can be made up to 1 day ahead and refrigerated separately, covered. If the dressing is too thick to drizzle, thin with a teaspoon of water.

Kohlrabi Slivers and Pea Shoots with Sesame Dressing

SERVES 6
ACTIVE TIME: 20 MINUTES ■ START TO FINISH: 20 MINUTES

■ Combining bright green pea shoots and crunchy white matchsticks of raw kohlrabi makes for a very Japanese presentation. Indeed, such a dish could come from no other cuisine, but it's also perfectly at home served with non-Japanese dishes—plain grilled salmon or meaty steak. The nutty dressing is a nice match for kohlrabi's distinctive turnipy sweetness. ■

    Salt
  2 ounces pea shoots, cut in half (2 cups)
 12 ounces trimmed kohlrabi, peeled and cut into fine
    matchsticks
 ⅓ cup sesame seeds, toasted (see Tips, page 911)
  3 tablespoons plus 1 teaspoon reduced-sodium soy
    sauce
  2 teaspoons sugar
  2 teaspoons mirin (Japanese sweet rice wine)
  1 tablespoon water

SPECIAL EQUIPMENT: an electric coffee/spice grinder

Bring a 3-quart pot of salted water (1 tablespoon salt) to a boil. Blanch pea shoots just until color brightens, about 10 seconds. Drain immediately and transfer to a bowl of ice and cold water to stop the cooking. Drain and pat dry. Toss kohlrabi together with shoots in a serving dish.

Finely grind sesame seeds in spice grinder. Transfer to a bowl and stir in remaining ingredients. (Dres-

Roasted Cauliflower, Romaine, and Radicchio Salad

SERVES 8 TO 12
ACTIVE TIME: 45 MINUTES ■ START TO FINISH: 1¼ HOURS

■ This vibrant salad is a great winter first course. For a more casual meal, pair it with a lentil soup for a vegetarian dinner, or with fillet of beef as part of a buffet. If you're cooking for a smaller group, the recipe can be easily halved. ■

  1 large head cauliflower (3–3½ pounds), cut into
    1-inch-wide florets (9 cups)
 ½ cup plus 1 tablespoon extra-virgin olive oil
    Salt and freshly ground black pepper
 ¼ cup white wine vinegar
 1½ tablespoons finely chopped shallot
  2 heads romaine (2 pounds total), cut crosswise into
    ¼-inch-wide strips
  1 large head radicchio (12 ounces), cut crosswise into
    ¼-inch-wide strips
  1 cup loosely packed fresh flat-leaf parsley leaves
 ½ cup hazelnuts, toasted (see Tips, page 911), any loose
    skins rubbed off in a kitchen towel, and coarsely
    chopped

Put a rack in middle of oven and preheat oven to 450°F.

Toss cauliflower with ¼ cup oil, ½ teaspoon salt, and ⅛ teaspoon pepper in a large bowl. Spread in one layer on a baking sheet and roast, turning with tongs halfway through roasting, until tender and golden brown, 25 to 30 minutes. Cool on pan on a rack.

Whisk together vinegar, shallot, ¼ teaspoon salt,

and ⅛ teaspoon pepper in a small bowl until salt is dissolved, then add remaining 5 tablespoons oil in a slow stream, whisking until well blended.

Transfer cauliflower to a large bowl. Add half of dressing and toss to coat. Add romaine, radicchio, parsley, half of nuts, and remaining dressing and toss to coat. Season with salt and pepper and sprinkle with remaining nuts.

COOK'S NOTES

- The cauliflower can be cut into florets up to 1 day ahead and refrigerated in sealable plastic bags lined with paper towels.
- The cauliflower can be roasted up to 4 hours ahead and kept, covered, at room temperature.
- The hazelnuts can be toasted and chopped up to 1 day ahead and kept in an airtight container at room temperature.

Grilled Mushroom Salad with Arugula

SERVES 8
ACTIVE TIME: 40 MINUTES ■ START TO FINISH: 1 HOUR

■ This combination of pungent arugula and robust mushrooms interlaced with thin ribbons of Parmigiano-Reggiano is as much side dish as it is salad (try pairing it with roast capon or chicken). It may look like a lot of mushrooms when you're putting it together, but it allows everyone to have a generous helping. You can grill the mushrooms outside or indoors on a grill pan. ■

½ cup Champagne vinegar
½ cup finely chopped shallots
2 teaspoons sugar
  Salt and freshly ground black pepper
1 cup extra-virgin olive oil
½ pound portobello mushrooms, stems discarded
½ pound shiitake mushrooms, stems discarded
½ pound cremini mushrooms, trimmed
¾ pound chanterelle mushrooms, trimmed (see Cook's Note)
½ pound baby arugula, or regular arugula, torn into bite-sized pieces (16 cups)

⅔ cup Parmigiano-Reggiano shavings (made with a vegetable peeler from a 2-ounce piece)
SPECIAL EQUIPMENT: a perforated grill sheet (see page 511 and Cook's Note)

Whisk together vinegar, shallots, sugar, 1½ teaspoons salt, and 1 teaspoon pepper in a large bowl until sugar and salt are dissolved. Add oil in a slow stream, whisking until combined.

Pour half of vinaigrette into a cup and add mushrooms to remaining vinaigrette. Toss to coat and marinate for 5 minutes. Drain mushrooms, discarding marinade.

If using a charcoal grill, prepare it for direct-heat cooking over medium-hot coals; if using a gas grill, prepare it for direct-heat cooking over medium heat (see Grilling Basics, page 512).

Put perforated grill sheet on grill rack and oil sheet. Grill shiitakes, cremini, and chanterelles on perforated sheet and portobellos directly on grill rack (covered only if using a gas grill), turning occasionally, until golden brown and tender, 5 to 7 minutes. Transfer to a platter and cool to room temperature.

Cut portobellos into ½-inch-wide wedges. Halve shiitakes and cremini. If they are large, cut chanterelles lengthwise into ½-inch pieces. Toss mushrooms, arugula, and cheese in a large bowl with enough reserved vinaigrette to coat. Season with salt and pepper and toss again.

COOK'S NOTES

- The vinaigrette can be made up to 1 day ahead and refrigerated, covered.
- If desired, you can substitute more or less of a particular kind of mushroom to equal a total of 2¼ pounds.
- The mushrooms can be grilled and sliced up to 4 hours ahead. Once cool, keep, loosely covered, at room temperature. Pour off any juices before tossing with the vinaigrette.
- Alternatively, the mushrooms can be grilled indoors on a well-seasoned large (2-burner) ridged grill pan, preferably cast-iron. Heat the lightly oiled grill pan over moderately high heat until hot but not smoking. Grill the mushrooms in 3 batches, turning frequently, until golden brown, about 5 minutes per batch.
- The cheese can be shaved up to 1 day ahead and refrigerated in a sealable plastic bag.

Tuscan Kale and Ricotta Salata Salad

SERVES 6
ACTIVE TIME: 25 MINUTES ■ START TO FINISH: 25 MINUTES

■ Tuscan kale's substantial leaves are usually cooked, but this robust salad proves how delicious they are raw. Inspired by a popular antipasto at New York City's Lupa, the kale is sliced very thin and tossed with a shalloty dressing and grated ricotta salata. ■

    2 tablespoons finely chopped shallot
    1½ tablespoons fresh lemon juice
        Salt and freshly ground black pepper
    4½ tablespoons extra-virgin olive oil
    ¾–1 pound Tuscan kale (also called lacinato kale, *cavolo nero*, or dinosaur kale) or regular kale, stems and ribs discarded, leaves cut crosswise into thin slices
    2 ounces ricotta salata, coarsely grated

Whisk together shallot, lemon juice, ¼ teaspoon salt, and ¼ teaspoon pepper in a small bowl until salt is dissolved. Add oil in a slow stream, whisking until well combined.

Toss kale and ricotta salata in a large bowl with enough dressing to coat well. Season with salt and pepper.

Roasted Red Peppers with Walnuts and Raisins

SERVES 8 TO 10
ACTIVE TIME: 45 MINUTES ■ START TO FINISH: 1¼ HOURS

■ Roasting, peeling, and chopping eight large red bell peppers takes a bit of time, but this suave salad is well worth the effort. The peppers are scattered with raisins and crisp walnuts, and a light sherry vinaigrette highlights the Spanish undertones of the dish. Utterly delicious all by itself, the salad can take its place as part of a platter of cheese, dried sausages, olives, and crusty bread. ■

    8 large red bell peppers (4 pounds), halved lengthwise, cored, and seeded
    ⅓ cup plus 2 tablespoons extra-virgin olive oil
    2 tablespoons sherry vinegar
    1 tablespoon walnut oil
    ½ teaspoon finely chopped garlic
    ¼ teaspoon ground cumin
    ½ teaspoon salt
    ¼ teaspoon freshly ground black pepper
    ¾ cup walnuts, toasted (see Tips, page 911) and coarsely chopped
    ¾ cup raisins

Preheat broiler. Line two large baking sheets with foil. Rub or brush skin sides of bell peppers with 2 tablespoons olive oil and put 8 pepper halves, skin side up, on each baking sheet. Broil (in 2 batches) about 2 inches from heat until skins are blistered and charred, about 15 minutes per batch. With tongs, transfer peppers to a bowl, cover tightly with plastic wrap, and let steam until cool enough to handle.

Meanwhile, whisk together remaining ⅓ cup olive oil, vinegar, walnut oil, garlic, cumin, salt, and pepper in a large bowl until salt is dissolved.

Peel peppers. Tear lengthwise into 1-inch-wide strips or cut into 1-inch pieces.

Add peppers, walnuts, and raisins to vinaigrette and toss until well coated. Cover and marinate at room temperature for at least 30 minutes.

COOK'S NOTE

■ The marinated peppers can be refrigerated, covered, for up to 2 days. Bring to room temperature before serving.

Roasted Vegetable Panzanella

SERVES 6 TO 8 AS A FIRST COURSE, 4 AS A MAIN COURSE
ACTIVE TIME: 35 MINUTES ■ START TO FINISH: 1 HOUR

■ Classic Italian panzanella—a tomato and bread salad that was developed as a way to use up day-old loaves—gets an inspired makeover. The combination of roasted green beans and cherry tomatoes, cannellini beans, and fresh mozzarella makes this a satisfying main course, and the cubes of crusty-chewy toasted bread soak up the lusty balsamic vinaigrette. ∎

1 large garlic clove
    Salt
½ cup plus 3 tablespoons extra-virgin olive oil
3 (12-inch) lengths crusty baguette, cut into 1-inch cubes (12 cups)
¾ pound cherry tomatoes, halved
    Freshly ground black pepper
1 pound green beans, trimmed and halved crosswise
3 tablespoons balsamic vinegar, preferably white
3 tablespoons capers, rinsed, drained, and chopped
½ teaspoon sugar
1 (19-ounce) can cannellini beans or chickpeas, rinsed and drained
1 pound lightly salted fresh mozzarella, cut into ⅓-inch dice
¾ cup chopped fresh basil

Arrange racks in upper and lower thirds of oven and preheat oven to 425°F.

Mince garlic and mash to a paste with a pinch of salt, using side of a large heavy knife. Transfer to a small bowl and add ½ cup olive oil in a slow stream, whisking until well combined. Put bread cubes in a large bowl and drizzle with 3 tablespoons garlic oil, tossing to combine. Divide bread between two large baking sheets, spreading cubes out in one layer. Toast in oven, stirring once or twice, until golden, 10 to 12 minutes. Remove from oven; leave oven on.

Gently toss tomatoes with 1 tablespoon olive oil, ¼ teaspoon salt, and ⅛ teaspoon pepper in a bowl. Arrange in one layer on a large baking sheet. Toss green beans in same bowl with remaining 2 tablespoons oil, ¼ teaspoon salt, and ⅛ teaspoon pepper. Arrange in one layer on another large baking sheet. Roast vegetables, switching position of pans halfway through roasting and shaking pans once or twice, until tomatoes are very tender but not falling apart and beans are just tender and browned in spots, 12 to 16 minutes. Cool vegetables on pans until ready to assemble salad.

Meanwhile, add vinegar to remaining garlic oil, along with capers, sugar, ½ teaspoon salt, and ¼

teaspoon pepper, and whisk until sugar and salt are dissolved.

Put green beans, tomatoes and any pan juices, toasted bread, cannellini beans, mozzarella, and basil in a large bowl. Drizzle with dressing and stir to combine well. Let stand for 10 to 15 minutes to allow flavors to develop, and stir again just before serving.

COOK'S NOTES

∎ The vinaigrette can be made up to 1 day ahead and refrigerated, covered.

∎ The bread can be toasted up to 1 day ahead and kept in an airtight container at room temperature.

Celery, Sesame, and Tofu Salad

SERVES 4
ACTIVE TIME: 15 MINUTES ∎ START TO FINISH: 15 MINUTES

∎ With its contrast of crisp celery and soft tofu, which absorbs the rich sesame oil and tangy rice vinegar, this is a salad for all seasons. It's excellent during the winter when you're ready to take a break from hearty greens and root vegetables, but its cool, refreshing flavors and easy preparation also make it just the thing for a sultry summer day. ∎

1 (14-ounce) block firm tofu
2 tablespoons vegetable oil
¾ teaspoon Asian sesame oil
2 teaspoons rice vinegar (not seasoned)
1 teaspoon soy sauce
½ teaspoon freshly ground black pepper
4 large celery ribs
2 teaspoons sesame seeds, toasted (see Tips, page 911)
    Salt

Rinse tofu and pat dry. Cut crosswise into ¼-inch-thick slices. Arrange slices in one layer on a triple thickness of paper towels and cover with another triple thickness of paper towels. Put a small baking sheet on top of tofu, weight with three 1-pound cans, and let stand for 10 minutes to remove excess moisture.

Meanwhile, whisk together oils, vinegar, soy sauce, and pepper in a large bowl. Trim celery, then remove tough strings with a vegetable peeler and slice very thin diagonally.

Cut tofu crosswise into ¼-inch-wide sticks and transfer to a bowl. Gently toss tofu with dressing, celery, sesame seeds, and salt to taste.

Combine jalapeños with cilantro, shallots, garlic, oil, and remaining 3 tablespoons vinegar in a food processor and pulse until finely chopped.

Toss potatoes with salsa.

COOK'S NOTE

■ The salsa can be made up to 1 day ahead and refrigerated, covered.

Potato Salad with Green Chile–Cilantro Salsa

SERVES 8
ACTIVE TIME: 15 MINUTES ■ START TO FINISH: 45 MINUTES

■ If you're seeking a fresh alternative to Mom's old standby potato salad, this is it: slender fingerlings flecked with a vibrant green salsa. The cilantro and jalapeños will get your taste buds humming. It's important to cool the potatoes before tossing them with the salsa to keep the cilantro from discoloring. ■

    4 pounds fingerling potatoes or other small boiling
        potatoes
      Salt
    ¼ cup cider vinegar
      Freshly ground black pepper
    3 jalapeño chiles, seeds and ribs removed from 2,
        all 3 chiles coarsely chopped
    2 cups fresh cilantro sprigs, coarsely chopped
  1½ shallots, coarsely chopped
    1 garlic clove, coarsely chopped
    ¼ cup extra-virgin olive oil

Cover potatoes with cold salted water (2½ table-spoons salt) by 1 inch in a 5- to 6-quart pot, bring to a boil, and simmer until just tender, 10 to 15 minutes. (Hot potatoes will continue to cook after draining; do not overcook, or they will break apart.) Drain potatoes in a colander and rinse under cold water until slightly cooled; drain well.

Halve potatoes lengthwise. While still warm, gently toss with 1 tablespoon vinegar. Cool potatoes to room temperature, then season with salt and pepper.

Herbed Potato Salad

SERVES 6
ACTIVE TIME: 15 MINUTES ■ START TO FINISH: 2 HOURS

■ Unobscured by mayo, this salad brings potatoes' earthy goodness to the fore, and it comes together in a trice. It's especially good with Yukon Golds. Because some varieties of thyme are stronger than others, we've given a range. ■

    2 pounds fingerling, boiling, or all-purpose
        potatoes
      Salt
    ¼ cup packed fresh flat-leaf parsley leaves,
        chopped
  2–3 teaspoons fresh thyme leaves, chopped
    3 tablespoons extra-virgin olive oil
    1 tablespoon minced shallot
      Freshly ground black pepper

Cover potatoes with cold salted water (2½ table-spoons salt) by 1 inch in a 5-quart pot, bring to a boil, and simmer until just tender, about 10 minutes for small fingerling potatoes, or up to 25 minutes for larger boiling or all-purpose potatoes. Drain potatoes and let cool to room temperature.

Cut cooled potatoes into 1½-inch pieces and transfer to a bowl. Gently toss with herbs, oil, shallot, and salt and pepper to taste. Serve at room temperature.

Roasted Potato, Okra, and Fava Bean Salad

SERVES 6 AS A FIRST COURSE, 4 AS A MAIN COURSE
ACTIVE TIME: 40 MINUTES ■ START TO FINISH: 1 HOUR

■ This potato salad is a beautiful thing. Small roasted potatoes—their crisp, burnished skin giving way to soft and creamy flesh—are mixed with tender roasted okra, sweet corn, and bright fava beans, dressed with a lemony, rosemary-scented vinaigrette. The substantial salad makes a great side to grilled burgers or pork chops; it also works as a vegetarian main course. ■

2 pounds small fingerling, red, or yellow-fleshed potatoes
1 large bunch scallions, white parts halved lengthwise (greens reserved for another use)
2 large fresh rosemary sprigs, plus ½ teaspoon chopped fresh rosemary
¼ cup olive oil
Salt and freshly ground black pepper
¾ pound (2- to 3-inch-long) okra, trimmed
2 cups shelled fava beans (2½ pounds in pods) or fresh or frozen edamame (soybeans; 1½ pounds in pods if fresh)
1 cup corn kernels (from 1–2 ears)
1½ tablespoons fresh lemon juice
1 tablespoon finely chopped shallot

FRESH FAVA BEANS AND GREEN SOYBEANS

The fava bean has been a staple food of the Old World for a long time—its ancestral lineage, in fact, is lost to the ages—but here in the United States, it's only recently become the legume du jour of restaurant chefs and home cooks who don't mind the labor-intensive preparation. Favas are the only variety that usually must be both shucked and peeled, which is why the shiny, spring-green beans are often used sparingly in other dishes rather than served on their own.

When shopping for favas, look for large, fat pods. Feel each pod to make sure it contains beans; some are only half full. To shuck favas, simply run your thumb down the seam of each pod and pop the beans out of the pod. (If you have young children in your life, this will keep them entertained and let them feel useful as well.) Blanch the beans in boiling salted water for 3 minutes, then drain and rinse them under cold water to loosen their skins. Make a slit in the thick green skin with your thumbnail and either peel it off or pinch out the bean.

One caveat: favas should be avoided by some people of Mediterranean, African, and Pacific Rim descent (those who have an inherited deficiency of glucose-6-phosphate dehydrogensase) or anyone taking MAO-inhibitor-type antidepressants.

FAVA

GREEN SOYBEAN

Another fresh bean in the pod that is relatively new to the American table is the green soybean, more commonly known by its Japanese name, edamame ("ed-ah-*mah*-may"). Edamame have been bred especially for eating at an immature stage; they're a different variety from the field soybeans used to make tofu, miso, fermented black beans, soy sauce, and soy milk. Boiled, salted, and served in the pod, fresh edamame are a fixture on the menus of Japanese restaurants, where the firm yet tender little nuggets are popped out of their jackets and into the mouth. Frozen edamame (either in the pod or already shucked) are available in the frozen foods section of many supermarkets. In the summer and early fall, they're sold on the stem at Asian produce markets and some farmers markets.

ROAST THE POTATOES AND OKRA: Put a rack in middle of oven and preheat oven to 450°F.

Halve potatoes lengthwise and toss with scallions, rosemary sprigs, 2 tablespoons olive oil, ¾ teaspoon salt, and ½ teaspoon pepper. Spread in a large roasting pan and roast, stirring once, for 20 minutes.

Stir potatoes and add okra to pan, tossing to coat. Continue to roast until okra and potatoes are tender, about 30 minutes more.

MEANWHILE, COOK THE BEANS AND CORN: Cook beans in 4 cups (unsalted) boiling water in a 3- to 4-quart saucepan for 3 minutes. Immediately transfer with a slotted spoon to a bowl of ice and cold water to stop the cooking, then transfer with slotted spoon to another bowl. If using favas, gently peel off skins.

Return water to a boil and add 1 teaspoon salt. Add corn and cook until tender, about 4 minutes. Drain and immediately transfer to bowl of ice and cold water to stop the cooking. Drain again.

MAKE THE DRESSING AND ASSEMBLE THE SALAD: Whisk together lemon juice, shallot, chopped rosemary, remaining 2 tablespoons oil, ½ teaspoon salt, and ½ teaspoon pepper in a large bowl until salt is dissolved. Remove rosemary sprigs from potato mixture and discard, then add hot potatoes and okra to dressing, along with beans, corn, and salt to taste, tossing to combine. Cool to warm before serving.

COOK'S NOTES

- Be aware that fava beans can cause a potentially fatal reaction in some people (see page 181).
- The salad can be made up to 1 day ahead and refrigerated, covered. Bring to room temperature before serving.

Orzo with Feta and Cherry Tomatoes

SERVES 8
ACTIVE TIME: 30 MINUTES ■ START TO FINISH: 30 MINUTES

■ Fresh lemon zest adds a little sunburst to this summery orzo salad. Made with supermarket ingredients, it is a perfect addition to a weeknight dinner or casual barbecue. ■

2 garlic cloves
  Salt
3 tablespoons olive oil
2 tablespoons red wine vinegar
1 teaspoon finely grated lemon zest
½ teaspoon freshly ground black pepper
1 pound (about 2½ cups) orzo
½ cup pine nuts
1 pound cherry tomatoes, quartered
½ cup chopped fresh flat-leaf parsley
½ pound feta, preferably Greek, crumbled (about 2 cups)

Mince garlic and mash to a paste with a pinch of salt, using side of a large heavy knife. Transfer to a large bowl and whisk in 2 tablespoons oil, vinegar, zest, ¾ teaspoon salt, and pepper.

Cook orzo in a 5- to 6-quart pot of boiling salted water (1 tablespoon salt) until al dente.

Meanwhile, toast pine nuts in remaining 1 tablespoon oil in a small heavy skillet over moderate heat, stirring frequently, until golden, 3 to 5 minutes. Transfer to paper towels to cool.

Drain orzo well, transfer to a bowl, and add vinaigrette, tossing to coat. Stir in nuts, tomatoes, parsley, and feta. Serve warm or at room temperature.

Israeli Couscous Salad with Grilled Shrimp and Vegetables

SERVES 6 TO 8
ACTIVE TIME: 1 HOUR ■ START TO FINISH: 1 HOUR

■ Toasting the small orbs of Israeli couscous before cooking them adds an extra layer of nutty flavor, which harmonizes with the smoky grilled shrimp, onions, and zucchini. ■

3 tablespoons red wine vinegar
3 tablespoons chopped fresh oregano
2 tablespoons chopped fresh thyme
1 large garlic clove, finely chopped
  Salt and freshly ground black pepper
⅓ cup plus ¼ cup olive oil

2¼ cups Israeli couscous

1¾ cups Chicken Stock (page 153) or store-bought
    reduced-sodium broth

1 cup water

¼ teaspoon crumbled saffron threads

2 pounds large shrimp in shells (21–25 per pound),
    peeled and, if desired, deveined

2 medium red onions

2 pounds large zucchini (about 4), cut diagonally into
    ½-inch-thick slices

6 ounces feta, crumbled (about 1½ cups)

SPECIAL EQUIPMENT: about twelve 8-inch wooden skewers
    and 20 round wooden toothpicks, soaked in water
    for 30 minutes

Whisk together vinegar, oregano, thyme, garlic, ½ teaspoon salt, and ¼ teaspoon pepper in a small bowl until salt is dissolved. Add ⅓ cup oil in a slow stream, whisking until combined.

Heat 1 tablespoon oil in a 3-quart wide heavy saucepan over moderate heat until hot but not smoking. Toast couscous, stirring occasionally, until fragrant and pale golden, 3 to 5 minutes.

Meanwhile, stir together stock, water, and saffron in a large glass measure. Add saffron mixture to couscous, along with ½ teaspoon salt, and bring to a simmer. Simmer, covered, until liquid is absorbed and couscous is al dente, 10 to 12 minutes. Remove from heat and let stand, covered, for 10 minutes.

Stir vinaigrette to combine, then stir 2 tablespoons into couscous. Let stand, uncovered, at room temperature.

If using a charcoal grill, prepare it for direct-heat cooking over medium-hot coals; if using a gas grill, prepare it for direct-heat cooking over medium heat (see Grilling Basics, page 512).

Meanwhile, toss shrimp with 1 tablespoon oil, ¼ teaspoon salt, and ¼ teaspoon pepper in a bowl. Thread 4 or 5 shrimp onto each skewer (don't crowd, or shrimp won't cook evenly).

Halve onions lengthwise, leaving root ends intact, and cut lengthwise into ½-inch-wide wedges. Insert a toothpick through each wedge to hold layers together while grilling, and put onions in a large bowl. Add zucchini and toss with remaining 2 tablespoons oil, ½ teaspoon salt, and ¼ teaspoon pepper.

Oil grill rack. Grill shrimp (covered if using a gas grill), turning once with tongs, until just cooked

through, 3 to 4 minutes. Transfer shrimp to a clean bowl, discarding skewers, and toss with 2 tablespoons vinaigrette.

Grill vegetables on lightly oiled grill rack (covered if using a gas grill), turning once, until just tender, about 5 minutes; transfer to bowl with shrimp. Remove and discard toothpicks from onions. Drizzle vegetables with remaining vinaigrette and toss to combine.

Spoon couscous onto a large platter or into a shallow serving bowl. Arrange shrimp and vegetables on top of couscous and sprinkle with feta. Serve warm or at room temperature.

COOK'S NOTES

- The vinaigrette can be made up to 3 hours ahead and kept, covered, at room temperature.
- The shrimp skewers can be assembled up to 2 hours ahead and refrigerated, covered.
- The vegetables can be cut and the onions skewered up to 2 hours ahead. Refrigerate, covered.

Antipasto Pasta Salad

SERVES 8 TO 10 AS A FIRST COURSE, 6 AS A MAIN COURSE
ACTIVE TIME: 15 MINUTES ■ START TO FINISH: 30 MINUTES

■ Everything you love about an antipasto platter—plus pasta. This zesty combination of rotini, vegetables, mozzarella, soppressata, and olives will quickly become a family favorite. ■

1 pound rotini (corkscrew pasta)
  Salt

2 tablespoons red wine vinegar

¼ cup extra-virgin olive oil

1 (12-ounce) jar marinated artichokes, drained and
    chopped

1 (12-ounce) jar roasted red peppers, drained and cut
    into ¼-inch-wide strips

½ pound mozzarella, cut into ½-inch cubes

½ pound thinly sliced sweet soppressata or salami, cut
    into 1-inch pieces

¼ pound Kalamata or other brine-cured black olives,
    pitted and chopped (½ cup)

1½ cups loosely packed fresh flat-leaf parsley leaves
    Freshly ground black pepper

Cook pasta in an 8-quart pot of boiling salted water (3 tablespoons salt) until al dente. Drain in a colander, rinse under cold water, and drain thoroughly.

Whisk together vinegar and olive oil in a large bowl. Add pasta and remaining ingredients except pepper and toss to combine. Season with salt and pepper to taste. Serve at room temperature.

COOK'S NOTE
■ The salad can be made up to 4 hours ahead and refrigerated, covered. Bring to room temperature before serving.

Lemony Rice Salad with Peas and Mint

SERVES 6
ACTIVE TIME: 20 MINUTES ■ START TO FINISH: 20 MINUTES

■ Arborio rice isn't just for risotto. When boiled like pasta and tossed with peas, lemon zest, and fresh mint, it makes a great salad, light yet satisfying. Keep this in mind for a summer buffet—it's delicious served alongside cold roast chicken or grilled leg of lamb. ■

> 2 cups Arborio rice
> Kosher salt
> 1 (10-ounce) package frozen baby peas, thawed
> ¼ cup extra-virgin olive oil
> 1 teaspoon finely grated lemon zest
> 2 tablespoons fresh lemon juice
> ½ teaspoon freshly ground black pepper
> ⅓ cup torn fresh mint leaves

Cook rice in a 6- to 8-quart pot of boiling salted water (3 tablespoons salt) for 10 minutes. Add peas and cook until rice is tender, 4 to 5 minutes. Drain in a colander, rinse under cold water, and drain well. Transfer to a large bowl.

Whisk together oil, lemon zest, juice, 1 teaspoon salt, and pepper in a small bowl until salt is dissolved. Add to rice and peas and toss to coat.

Just before serving, sprinkle salad with mint and toss again.

COOK'S NOTE
■ The salad, without the mint, can be made up to 1 day ahead and refrigerated, covered. Stir in the mint just before serving.

Wild Rice Salad with Smoked Fish and Snap Peas

SERVES 6 TO 8 AS A MAIN COURSE
ACTIVE TIME: 40 MINUTES ■ START TO FINISH: 1¼ HOURS

■ This salad brings together nutty wild rice and a snappy dill-flecked vinaigrette. We call for hot-smoked salmon because it breaks apart into big, supple flakes rather than sheets, as does the cold-smoked kind. Sugar snap peas and cool wedges of hard-boiled eggs make the salad a meal. ■

> Salt
> 2 cups wild rice
> 1 pound sugar snap peas, trimmed
> 3 tablespoons cider vinegar
> 3 tablespoons whole-grain mustard
> 2½ teaspoons sugar
> ⅓ cup vegetable oil
> ⅓ cup chopped fresh dill
> ½ pound hot-smoked salmon or smoked trout, skin discarded and fish flaked into ½-inch-wide pieces
> 4 scallions, thinly sliced
> 6 hard-boiled large eggs, quartered lengthwise

Bring 4 quarts salted water (2 teaspoons salt) to a boil in a 5-quart pot. Add wild rice and simmer, partially covered, until grains are tender and have split open, 1 to 1¼ hours. Drain well.

Meanwhile, cook snap peas in a 4-quart saucepan of salted boiling water (1 tablespoon salt) until crisp-tender, about 2 minutes Drain and transfer to a bowl of ice and cold water to stop the cooking. Drain peas and pat dry between paper towels, then cut diagonally in half.

Whisk together vinegar, mustard, sugar, and ¾ teaspoon salt in a bowl until sugar and salt are dissolved. Add oil in a slow stream, whisking until well combined. Whisk in dill.

Combine peas, salmon, scallions, and eggs with warm rice in a large bowl. Drizzle with dressing and toss gently. Serve warm or at room temperature.

COOK'S NOTE

■ The salad can be made up to 1 day ahead and refrigerated, covered. Bring to room temperature before serving.

Winter Tabbouleh

SERVES 4 TO 6 AS A SIDE DISH, 2 TO 3 AS A MAIN COURSE
ACTIVE TIME: 45 MINUTES ■ START TO FINISH: 45 MINUTES

■ Before we came across this recipe, which hails from chefs Samuel and Samantha Clark of Moro in London, few of us had ever heard of a tabbouleh that wasn't based on parsley, cucumber, and tomato. This winter version of the Middle Eastern classic is a colorful mixture of endive, fennel, cauliflower, walnuts, jewel-like pomegranate seeds, and chewy bulgur. It embodies the sort of Spanish-Moorish cuisine that the Clarks have perfected. Pomegranate molasses is essential; it contributes a unique sweet sourness, not unlike a good aged balsamic vinegar. ■

FOR TABBOULEH

1¼ cups (7 ounces) coarse bulgur
1 large Belgian endive, halved lengthwise, cored, and coarsely chopped
1 medium fennel bulb, stalks discarded, bulb quartered lengthwise, cored, and coarsely chopped
1½ cups tiny cauliflower florets (no larger than ½ inch in diameter)
6 tablespoons coarsely chopped fresh flat-leaf parsley
3 tablespoons coarsely chopped fresh mint
3 tablespoons walnuts, coarsely chopped
Seeds from 1 large pomegranate (about 1⅓ cups)
½ teaspoon fine sea salt
¼ teaspoon freshly ground black pepper

FOR DRESSING

1 garlic clove, minced
¼ teaspoon ground cinnamon
3 tablespoons pomegranate molasses (see Sources)

POMEGRANATE MOLASSES

The pomegranate most likely originated in northern Persia, and it spread throughout the ancient world. (The earliest sherbet was pomegranate juice mixed with snow.) Dark, thick pomegranate molasses—essentially, cooked-down pomegranate juice—gives a complex, fruity, tart boost to many Middle Eastern and Indian dishes, but don't stop there: it will add an alluring, mysterious backnote of flavor to braised lamb, a pan sauce or glaze for poultry or pork, or even a salad dressing.

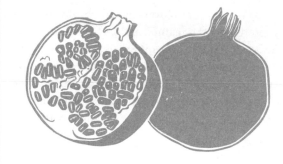

1 tablespoon water
¼ teaspoon fine sea salt
Pinch of freshly ground black pepper
6 tablespoons extra-virgin olive oil
½ teaspoon sugar (optional)

MAKE THE TABBOULEH: Cover bulgur with warm water by 2 inches in a bowl and soak for 10 minutes.

Drain bulgur well in a sieve and transfer to a large bowl. Stir in endive, fennel, cauliflower, parsley, mint, walnuts, and pomegranate seeds until combined.

MAKE THE DRESSING: Stir together garlic, cinnamon, molasses, water, sea salt, and pepper in a small bowl. Add oil in a slow stream, whisking until emulsified. Dressing will be very tart; add sugar to sweeten if desired.

FINISH THE SALAD: Just before serving, toss tabbouleh with dressing, sea salt, and pepper.

COOK'S NOTES

■ The tabbouleh, without the herbs and dressing, can be prepared up to 4 hours ahead and kept at room temperature. Just before serving, toss with the herbs, dressing, sea salt, and pepper.

- The dressing can be made up to 4 hours ahead and kept, covered, at room temperature.

Farro Tricolore

SERVES 4 TO 6
ACTIVE TIME: 30 MINUTES ■ START TO FINISH: 30 MINUTES

■ Green arugula, white endive, and red radicchio wilt slightly under a warm dressing enlivened with pancetta, gently cooked tomatoes, and garlic. Farro, or emmer wheat, is a staple in Tuscany and is growing in popularity in the United States. Chewier and more substantial than rice, it makes this simple salad arrayed in the colors of the Italian flag into a meal. Farro can sometimes be found in the pasta section of the supermarket. ■

Salt
1 cup (about 7 ounces) farro (see Sources)
1 large bunch arugula, stems discarded, leaves torn into bite-sized pieces (about 6 cups)
1 head radicchio, cut into ½-inch pieces
1 large Belgian endive, cored and cut into ½-inch pieces
3 tablespoons extra-virgin olive oil
¼ pound sliced pancetta (Italian unsmoked bacon), cut into ½-inch pieces
¾ pound grape or cherry tomatoes
2 garlic cloves, minced
¼ teaspoon freshly ground black pepper
2–3 tablespoons balsamic vinegar

Bring a 2- to 3-quart pot of salted water (1½ teaspoons salt) to a boil. Add farro and cook until just tender, about 20 minutes. Drain in a sieve.

Meanwhile, toss arugula, radicchio, and endive in a large bowl.

Heat 2 tablespoons olive oil in a 12-inch heavy skillet over moderate heat. Add pancetta and cook, stirring occasionally, until most of fat is rendered and pancetta is just golden, about 6 minutes. With a slotted spoon, transfer pancetta to paper towels to drain, leaving fat in skillet.

Add remaining tablespoon oil to skillet, along with tomatoes, garlic, ¾ teaspoon salt, and pepper, and cook, stirring occasionally, until tomatoes begin to wilt but still hold their shape, 5 to 7 minutes. Add 2 tablespoons vinegar, scraping up any brown bits from bottom of skillet.

Add farro and pancetta to bowl with greens. Pour hot dressing over salad and toss well to coat. Add another tablespoon of vinegar if desired.

COOK'S NOTE
- The salad can be made up to 3 hours ahead and kept, covered, at room temperature.

Wheat Berry Waldorf Salad

SERVES 8 TO 10 AS A SIDE DISH, 4 TO 6 AS A MAIN COURSE
ACTIVE TIME: 1 HOUR ■ START TO FINISH: 2½ HOURS

■ We've always suspected that if it got out from under its heavy mantle of mayonnaise, Waldorf salad could be a delightful thing. And it is, especially with the addition of chewy wheat berries. A handful of dried cherries and a tart dressing dotted with fresh orange zest brighten the dish. ■

FOR WHEAT BERRIES
1 cup wheat berries (whole-grain wheat)
½ teaspoon salt
FOR VINAIGRETTE
1 teaspoon finely grated orange zest
3 tablespoons fresh orange juice
3 tablespoons fresh lemon juice
3 tablespoons cider vinegar
1 teaspoon sugar
½ teaspoon salt
¼ teaspoon freshly ground black pepper
⅓ cup extra-virgin olive oil
FOR SALAD
3 celery ribs, halved lengthwise and thinly sliced
3 scallions, halved lengthwise and thinly sliced
2 Gala or Golden Delicious apples, cored and cut into ⅓-inch pieces

¾ cup coarsely chopped dried sour cherries
  Salt and freshly ground black pepper
1 head Boston lettuce, torn into bite-sized pieces
  (6 cups)
1 cup torn fresh mint leaves
¾ cup walnuts, toasted (see Tips, page 911)
  and coarsely chopped

COOK THE WHEAT BERRIES: Bring 4 cups water and wheat berries to a boil in a 2- to 3-quart saucepan. Reduce heat and simmer wheat berries, partially covered, until tender but still chewy, 1¼ to 1½ hours.

Drain wheat berries, then return to pan and stir in salt. Cool to room temperature.

MAKE THE VINAIGRETTE: Whisk together all ingredients in a bowl until sugar and salt are dissolved.

ASSEMBLE THE SALAD: Combine celery, scallions, apples, dried cherries, and cooled wheat berries in a bowl. Stir in ½ cup vinaigrette, and let stand at room temperature for 15 minutes to allow flavors to blend. Season with salt and pepper.

Toss together lettuce and mint on a platter and top with wheat berry mixture. Sprinkle with walnuts and drizzle with remaining vinaigrette.

COOK'S NOTE
■ The vinaigrette can be made up to 1 day ahead and refrigerated, covered. Bring to room temperature before using.

Southwestern Quinoa Salad

SERVES 4 AS A SIDE DISH, 2 AS A MAIN COURSE
ACTIVE TIME: 50 MINUTES ■ START TO FINISH: 50 MINUTES

■ Quinoa ("*keen*-wa") is considered a "supergrain" because it contains all eight essential amino acids. The grains are coated in a bitter substance called saponin and must be thoroughly rinsed before cooking. Steamed with a towel over the pot to absorb excess moisture, the grain becomes a light and fluffy base for this salad, brimming with roasted poblanos, sweet corn, nutty pumpkin seeds, salty cheese, and a tart citrus dressing. ■

1 cup quinoa
  Salt
2 ears corn, shucked
1 white onion, chopped
¼ cup green (hulled) pumpkin seeds (*pepitas*;
  see Cook's Note)
1 teaspoon cumin seeds
3 large poblano chiles (8 ounces total), roasted (see
  Tips, page 914), peeled, seeded, and cut into
  ½-inch pieces
1 tomato, chopped
3 tablespoons chopped fresh cilantro
¼ pound *queso fresco* (Mexican fresh white cheese;
  see Sources) or feta, crumbled
1½ tablespoons extra-virgin olive oil
½ cup fresh orange juice
2–3 tablespoons fresh lime juice
¼ teaspoon freshly ground black pepper

Rinse quinoa in 3 changes of cold water in a bowl, rubbing grains and letting them settle each time before draining in a fine-mesh sieve after each rinse.

Cook quinoa in a 3- to 4-quart saucepan of boiling salted water (1 teaspoon salt), uncovered, for 10 minutes. Drain in sieve and rinse under cold water.

Bring about 1½ inches water to a boil in same saucepan. Set sieve with quinoa over saucepan (quinoa should not touch water). Cover with a kitchen towel and a lid; fold edges of towel up over lid so towel won't burn. Steam quinoa until fluffy and dry, 10 to 15 minutes; check water level occasionally and add boiling water if necessary. Transfer quinoa to a large bowl.

Bring a large pot of water to a boil and add corn. When water returns to a boil, cover pot, remove from heat, and let stand for 10 minutes. With tongs, transfer corn to a cutting board. When cool enough to handle, cut off kernels with a sharp knife.

Heat a dry 10-inch cast-iron skillet over moderate heat until hot. Add corn and onion and cook, stirring frequently, until golden brown, about 10 minutes. Add to quinoa.

Add pumpkin and cumin seeds to same skillet and cook, stirring frequently, until pumpkin seeds puff, about 2 minutes. Add to quinoa mixture. Stir in chiles, tomato, cilantro, cheese, and oil and gently toss with two forks.

Whisk together orange juice and lime juice (to taste), 1 teaspoon salt, and pepper in a bowl until salt is dissolved. Drizzle over salad and toss until combined.

COOK'S NOTES

- The quinoa can be boiled and steamed up to 2 days ahead. Cool, uncovered, then refrigerate, covered.
- If you are unable to find raw pumpkin seeds, salted toasted ones can be substituted; do not toast them with the cumin seeds.

Quinoa and Bulgur Salad with Feta

SERVES 4 AS A SIDE DISH, 2 AS A MAIN COURSE
ACTIVE TIME: 20 MINUTES ▪ START TO FINISH: 40 MINUTES

▪ With crisp radishes, Bibb lettuce, salty olives, and feta dressed with minted olive oil and lemon, this colorful grain salad sings. ▪

⅓ cup quinoa
Salt
⅓ cup bulgur
2 tablespoons olive oil
2 tablespoons fresh lemon juice
¾ teaspoon dried mint, crumbled
¼ teaspoon freshly ground black pepper
4 brine-cured black olives, such as Kalamata, pitted and cut into slivers
2 radishes, quartered and thinly sliced
2 ounces feta, coarsely crumbled
1 head Bibb lettuce, cut into ¼-inch-wide strips (4 cups)

Wash quinoa in 3 changes of cold water in a bowl, draining in a sieve between changes of water.

Stir together quinoa, 4 cups water, and ¾ teaspoon salt in a 2- to 3-quart saucepan. Bring to a boil, reduce heat, and simmer, uncovered, until quinoa is just tender and germs are starting to separate from grains, about 20 minutes. Drain well in sieve and transfer to a medium bowl.

Meanwhile, cover bulgur with warm water by 2 inches in a bowl and soak until tender and chewy, 10 to 20 minutes. Drain well in sieve.

Stir bulgur into drained quinoa. Cool completely.

Meanwhile, stir together oil, lemon juice, mint, ¾ teaspoon salt, and pepper in a small bowl and let stand for 15 minutes.

Stir dressing into grains, along with olives, radishes, feta, and lettuce. Serve immediately, so lettuce stays crisp.

COOK'S NOTE

- The grains can be cooked and combined up to 1 day ahead. Once cool, refrigerate in an airtight container. Bring to room temperature while the dressing stands.

Barley, Corn, and Grape Tomato Salad

SERVES 8
ACTIVE TIME: 40 MINUTES ▪ START TO FINISH: 2 HOURS
(INCLUDES CHILLING)

▪ A trinity of tomatoes, corn, and basil is the focus of this late-summer treat. (Don't even think about using frozen or canned corn.) Vegetarians can enjoy the salad as a colorful, nutritionally rich main course or pair it with any kind of grilled food. We prefer to use pearl barley here; this polished form of the grain gives the salad a bright look. Though you can use hulled barley (which still has the bran attached) in a pinch, it will impart a grayish cast. ▪

Salt
2 cups (14 ounces) pearl barley
8 ears corn, shucked
⅔ cup extra-virgin olive oil
1½ cups packed fresh basil leaves
⅓ cup white wine vinegar
½ teaspoon freshly ground black pepper
1 large garlic clove
1 bunch scallions, chopped (1 cup)
2 cups halved grape tomatoes
½ pound feta, crumbled (about 2 cups)

Bring 8 cups salted water (1 tablespoon salt) to a boil in a 3½- to 4-quart pot. Stir in barley and simmer, covered, until tender, 30 to 40 minutes.

Meanwhile, cook corn in an 8-quart pot of boiling (unsalted) water until tender, about 5 minutes. Transfer with tongs to a colander to cool. Working with 1 ear at a time, lay each cob on its side on a cutting board and cut off kernels with a large knife.

Combine oil, basil, vinegar, 1 teaspoon salt, pepper, and garlic in a blender and blend until smooth.

Drain barley in a colander and rinse under cold water, then drain again and transfer to a large bowl. Add dressing, corn, and scallions and toss until well combined. Refrigerate salad, covered, for 1 hour so barley absorbs dressing.

Add tomatoes and feta and toss salad to distribute.

COOK'S NOTE
- The salad, without the tomatoes and feta, can be prepared up to 8 hours ahead and refrigerated, covered. Just before serving, add the tomatoes and cheese and toss.

Lentil Salad with Tomato and Dill

SERVES 4 TO 6 AS A SIDE DISH, 2 AS A MAIN COURSE
ACTIVE TIME: 25 MINUTES ■ START TO FINISH: 35 MINUTES

■ Chopped ripe tomatoes, dill, and basil impart a welcome freshness and vitality to lentils. This salad works equally well as a colorful vegetarian centerpiece or a side dish. It's important to seek out small French green or black lentils for this; they hold their shape well. Regular brown ones, the kind often used for soup, are too starchy. ■

- 1 cup small French green or black beluga lentils, picked over and rinsed
- 1 large garlic clove, chopped
  Salt
- ¾ pound tomatoes, seeded and diced (2 cups)
- ½ cup thinly sliced scallions
- ¼ cup chopped fresh dill

- ¼ cup thinly sliced fresh basil
- 2 tablespoons red wine vinegar, or to taste
- ¼ cup extra-virgin olive oil
- ¼ teaspoon freshly ground black pepper

Combine lentils, garlic, ½ teaspoon salt, and 4 cups water in a 2-quart heavy saucepan and bring to a boil. Reduce heat and simmer, uncovered, until lentils are tender but not falling apart, 15 to 25 minutes. Drain in a sieve and transfer to a large bowl.

Toss hot lentils with tomatoes, scallions, dill, basil, vinegar, oil, ½ teaspoon salt, or to taste, and pepper. Serve warm or at room temperature.

COOK'S NOTE
- The salad can be made up to 2 days ahead and refrigerated, covered. Bring to room temperature before serving.

Herbed Chickpea Salad

SERVES 8 TO 10
ACTIVE TIME: 1 HOUR ■ START TO FINISH: 2½ HOURS
(INCLUDES SOAKING CHICKPEAS)

■ Speckled with fresh parsley and oregano and tossed with a lemon dressing, this salad is great at a picnic, as a side dish, or as a first course. Cooking your own dried chickpeas results in beans with a nice, firm texture that hold together well in salads (canned chickpeas can be substituted, but the texture will be softer). Removing the thin, chewy skins from the cooked chickpeas may sound finicky, but it adds refinement to both the taste and the look of the salad. ■

- 1 pound (about 2¼ cups) dried chickpeas, picked over (see Cook's Note)
  Salt
- ¼ cup fresh lemon juice
- ½ cup extra-virgin olive oil
- ½ cup finely chopped sweet onion, such as Vidalia or Walla Walla
- 2 garlic cloves, finely chopped
- ½ teaspoon freshly ground black pepper
- ⅔ cup chopped fresh flat-leaf parsley
- 2 tablespoons chopped fresh oregano

Cook chickpeas in a 4- to 5-quart pot of boiling (unsalted) water, covered, for 2 minutes. Remove from heat and let stand, covered, for 1 hour.

Drain chickpeas and return to pot. Cover with water again and bring to a boil. Reduce heat and simmer, uncovered, until chickpeas are tender, 35 to 40 minutes; add 2 teaspoons salt during last 10 minutes of cooking.

Meanwhile, whisk together lemon juice, oil, onion, garlic, and pepper in a large bowl until well combined. Let stand for about 15 minutes.

Drain chickpeas and transfer to a bowl of cold water. Slip skins from chickpeas by rubbing them with your fingers. Drain well.

Add chickpeas to onion mixture. Stir in parsley, oregano, and ½ teaspoon salt and let stand, uncovered, for about 30 minutes to allow flavors to blend.

COOK'S NOTES

- Three 19-ounce cans of chickpeas can be substituted for the dried chickpeas. Rinse and drain them, and for best results, remove the skins as described above.
- The salad can be made, without the parsley and oregano, up to 1 day ahead and refrigerated, covered. Just before serving, stir in the herbs and salt.

HOW TO STORE FRESH HERBS

Fresh herbs are a huge return on a small investment. The vegetarian cooking authority Deborah Madison compares them to border collies, because they urge fruits and vegetables in one direction or another. You can cook the same vegetable every night of the week with a different herb and never have it taste the same.

Storing herbs properly helps them keep their lively flavors and textures. In a perfect world, everyone would have a refrigerator (spacious and organized to the *n*th degree) filled with garden-fresh bouquets of basil, parsley, and cilantro stored in Mason jars of water, their leaves loosely covered by a plastic or muslin hood. We don't have room for that, and we bet you don't either. Here's what we recommend: when you get home from the market (or from a stroll in your backyard), examine the herbs carefully and discard any bruised, wilted, or torn leaves—they're a breeding ground for decay. You'll be more apt to use them if they are washed and ready to go. If they are held together by a wire or rubber band, discard that and trim the bruised stems. (Many herbs are sold in plastic clamshell boxes; get rid of those too.) Rinse the herbs (except for basil and tarragon, which are especially delicate; wash them just before using) and spin them dry in a salad spinner. Spread them out on paper towels to dry thoroughly. Gently and loosely roll the herbs up in the towels before tucking them into plastic bags. This rids them of excess water (and prevents decay) while helping them keep their natural moisture.

Use a sharp knife when chopping herbs. A dull one smashes the leaves when it cuts them, and all those aromatic oils end up on your cutting board, not in your food.

White Bean, Red Onion, and Celery Salad

SERVES 8 TO 10 AS A FIRST COURSE, 4 TO 5 AS A MAIN COURSE
ACTIVE TIME: 25 MINUTES ■ START TO FINISH: 11 HOURS
(INCLUDES SOAKING BEANS)

■ The orange zest in this salad—both cooked with the beans and added to the dressing—works in concert with the black olives and capers to produce a dish that belongs on the French Riviera. Don't quick-soak the beans for this recipe; it makes them mushy. A traditional longer soak in cold water produces tender yet sturdy beans. ■

FOR BEANS

- 1 pound (2½ cups) dried white beans, such as great northern or navy, picked over and rinsed (see Cook's Note)
- 1 large carrot, quartered
- 1 celery rib, quartered
- 1 onion, quartered
- 3 large fresh thyme sprigs
- 2 Turkish bay leaves or 1 California bay leaf
- 1 (1-by-3-inch) strip orange zest, removed with a vegetable peeler
- 1 large garlic clove, crushed and peeled
- 1 whole clove
- 2 teaspoons salt

FOR SALAD

- ½–1 teaspoon finely grated orange zest
- ½ teaspoon finely chopped garlic
- 1 teaspoon salt
- ½ teaspoon freshly ground black pepper
- ¼ cup fresh lemon juice
- 1 teaspoon finely chopped fresh oregano
- ¼ cup finely chopped brine-cured black olives, preferably Gaeta
- 2 tablespoons drained capers, finely chopped
- 2 tablespoons finely chopped fresh flat-leaf parsley
- ½ cup extra-virgin olive oil
- 1½ cups thinly sliced celery
- 1 cup thinly sliced red onion, rinsed (see Cook's Note)

SOAK AND COOK THE BEANS: Soak beans in cold water to cover by 2 inches at room temperature (re-frigerated if kitchen is very warm) for 8 to 12 hours. Drain.

Transfer beans to a 6- to 8-quart pot and add carrot, celery, onion, thyme sprigs, bay leaves, orange zest, garlic, and clove. Stir in 10 cups water, bring to a simmer, and simmer until beans are tender, 35 to 45 minutes.

Remove from heat, stir in salt, and cool beans to room temperature.

Drain beans in a colander and discard carrot, celery, onion, thyme, bay leaves, zest, garlic, and clove.

MAKE THE SALAD: Whisk together zest (to taste), garlic, salt, pepper, lemon juice, oregano, olives, capers, parsley, and oil in a large bowl until just combined. Add beans, celery, and red onion and toss until well coated.

Refrigerate, covered, for at least 1 hour to allow flavors to blend. Bring to room temperature before serving.

COOK'S NOTES

- Three 19-ounce or four 15-ounce cans of white beans, rinsed and drained, can be substituted for the dried beans.
- Rinsing the sliced onion makes its flavor milder.
- The salad can be refrigerated for up to 12 hours.

Three-Bean Salad with Cilantro-Chile Dressing

SERVES 8 TO 10
ACTIVE TIME: 25 MINUTES ■ START TO FINISH: 1½ HOURS

■ Green beans, chickpeas, and edamame all contribute different textures and shapes to this contemporary spin on traditional three-bean salad, but it's the dressing that makes the dish such a standout. It combines the fresh flavors of cilantro and lemon juice with serrano chile, cumin, and a touch of cayenne to make a vibrant counterpoint to the vegetables and beans. This colorful salad goes beautifully with any type of fish. ■

1 pound green beans, trimmed and cut into
   1-inch pieces
Salt
1 (14-ounce) bag frozen shelled edamame (soybeans)
1 (19-ounce) can chickpeas, rinsed and drained
1 large garlic clove
1 cup loosely packed fresh cilantro leaves
½ teaspoon finely chopped serrano chile, including
   seeds, or to taste
3 tablespoons fresh lemon juice
6 tablespoons extra-virgin olive oil
½ teaspoon cumin seeds, toasted (see Tips,
   page 911)
Rounded ⅛ teaspoon cayenne
ACCOMPANIMENT: 2 lemons, cut into wedges

Cook green beans in a 6- to 8-quart pot of boiling salted water (2 tablespoons salt), uncovered, until crisp-tender, 6 to 8 minutes. With a wire skimmer or a slotted spoon, immediately transfer beans to a large bowl of ice and cold water to stop the cooking. When beans are cool, transfer with spoon or skimmer to paper towels to drain.

Return water to a boil and cook edamame until crisp-tender, 5 to 6 minutes. Drain and transfer to bowl of ice water to stop the cooking. When edamame are cool, drain and transfer to dry paper towels to drain.

Pat green beans dry and transfer to a large bowl. Pat edamame dry and add to green beans. Stir in chickpeas.

Mince garlic and mash to a paste with ½ teaspoon salt, using side of a large heavy knife. Transfer garlic paste to a blender. Add remaining ingredients and blend, scraping down sides occasionally, until smooth.

Add dressing to beans and season with salt. Let stand at room temperature for 1 hour to allow flavors to blend.

Serve salad with lemon wedges.

COOK'S NOTES
- The beans, without the dressing, can be cooked and combined up to 1 day ahead and refrigerated, covered.
- The salad can be made up to 6 hours ahead and refrigerated, covered. Bring to room temperature before serving.

Tuna Pasta Salad

SERVES 6 AS A MAIN COURSE
ACTIVE TIME: 15 MINUTES ■ START TO FINISH: 30 MINUTES

■ Fresh flavors and utter ease of preparation are two reasons to make this main-dish salad a summertime staple. ■

1 pound penne rigate or other short pasta
Salt
¾ cup mayonnaise
2 tablespoons fresh lemon juice (grate zest first)
1 tablespoon finely grated lemon zest
1 (6-ounce) can tuna packed in olive oil, drained
1 (15-ounce) can navy or cannellini beans, rinsed and
   drained
½ cup thinly sliced fresh basil
¾ pound cherry tomatoes, halved
Freshly ground black pepper

Cook pasta in an 8-quart pot of boiling salted water (3 tablespoons salt) until al dente. Drain in a colander and rinse under cold running water, then drain again.

Whisk together mayonnaise and lemon juice in a large bowl. Add pasta, zest, tuna, white beans, basil, and tomatoes and toss to combine. Season with salt and pepper.

COOK'S NOTE
■ The salad, without the tomatoes and basil, can be made up to 1 day ahead and refrigerated, covered. Toss with the tomatoes and basil just before serving.

Grilled Tuna Salade Niçoise

SERVES 6 AS A MAIN COURSE
ACTIVE TIME: 1 HOUR ■ START TO FINISH: 1½ HOURS

■ Salade Niçoise includes ingredients classically associated with the French Riviera—tomatoes, anchovies, capers, and olives (small Niçoise ones). It's traditionally made with fine-quality canned tuna packed in olive oil, but it's even better with grilled fresh tuna. Potatoes and green beans round out this one-dish meal. ■

FOR DRESSING
- 1 large garlic clove
  Salt
- ¼ cup red wine vinegar
- 2½ tablespoons minced shallots
- 2 teaspoons Dijon mustard
  Rounded ½ teaspoon anchovy paste
- 1 cup extra-virgin olive oil
- 1½ teaspoons minced fresh thyme
- 1½ tablespoons finely chopped fresh basil
  Freshly ground black pepper

FOR SALAD
- ¾ pound green beans, preferably haricots verts, trimmed
  Salt
- 1½ pounds small (1- to 2-inch) boiling potatoes, preferably Yukon Gold
- 1½ pounds (1-inch-thick) tuna steaks
  Vegetable oil for brushing
  Freshly ground black pepper
- ¼ cup drained capers
- 2 heads Boston lettuce (12 ounces total), torn into bite-sized pieces
- 1 pint cherry or grape tomatoes
- ⅔ cup Niçoise or other small brine-cured black olives
- 4 hard-boiled large eggs, quartered
- 3 tablespoons finely chopped fresh flat-leaf parsley and/or basil

MAKE THE DRESSING: Mince garlic and mash to a paste with ½ teaspoon salt, using side of a large heavy knife. Whisk together vinegar, shallots, mustard, garlic paste, and anchovy paste in a small bowl until well combined. Add oil in a slow stream, whisking until well blended. Whisk in thyme, basil, and salt and pepper to taste.

MAKE THE SALAD: Cook beans in a 4- to 6-quart pot of boiling salted water (2 tablespoons salt), uncovered, until crisp-tender, 4 to 6 minutes. Immediately transfer with a wire skimmer or a slotted spoon to a bowl of ice and cold water to stop the cooking.

Add potatoes to boiling water and simmer, uncovered, until tender, 15 to 20 minutes; drain in a colander. Halve potatoes while still warm, peel if desired, and toss with 2 tablespoons dressing in a bowl. Let cool.

If using a charcoal grill, prepare it for direct-heat cooking over medium-hot coals; if using a gas grill, prepare it for direct-heat cooking over medium-high heat (see Grilling Basics, page 512).

Brush tuna with oil and season with salt and pepper. Oil grill rack and grill tuna uncovered, turning once, until browned but still pink in center, 6 to 8 minutes. Let tuna stand for 3 minutes, then break into 3-inch pieces. Transfer to one part of large platter and drizzle with 2 to 3 tablespoons dressing. Sprinkle top with capers.

Transfer potatoes to another part of platter (set bowl aside). Drain beans and pat dry. Toss beans with 1 tablespoon dressing and salt and pepper to taste in same bowl and transfer to platter. Toss lettuce with 2 tablespoons dressing and salt and pepper to taste and transfer to platter. Toss tomatoes with 1 tablespoon dressing and salt and pepper to taste and transfer to platter.

Arrange olives and eggs on platter and sprinkle salad with parsley and/or basil. Serve with remaining dressing on the side.

COOK'S NOTE
■ The beans and potatoes can be cooked up to 1 hour ahead and kept at room temperature. Toss the potatoes with the dressing while still warm, but do not dress the beans until just before serving.

Grilled Spice-Crusted Tuna with Jicama and Avocado Salad

SERVES 4
ACTIVE TIME: 1 HOUR ■ START TO FINISH: 1¼ HOURS

■ With chunks of grilled tuna nestled in a verdant mix of greens and avocado accented by matchsticks of jicama, this salad is both crunchy and creamy and just a little bit spicy from the chipotle in the vinaigrette. ■

6 tablespoons olive oil

3 tablespoons fresh lime juice (from about 2 limes)

1½ tablespoons distilled white vinegar

1½ tablespoons finely chopped red onion

1½ teaspoons minced canned chipotles in adobo
   Salt

½ teaspoon ground coriander

½ teaspoon ground cumin

1 teaspoon chili powder

¼ teaspoon freshly ground black pepper

1¼ pounds sushi-grade tuna steaks

3 cups ⅛-inch-thick matchsticks peeled jicama
   (from 1 pound jicama)

1 cup coarsely chopped fresh cilantro

3 cups loosely packed baby arugula

2 firm but ripe avocados

ACCOMPANIMENT: lime wedges

Whisk together 5 tablespoons oil, lime juice, vinegar, onion, chipotles, and ½ teaspoon salt in a bowl until salt is dissolved.

Toast coriander, cumin, chili powder, ¼ teaspoon salt, and pepper in a dry 6- to 7-inch heavy skillet over moderately low heat, stirring, until very fragrant, about 2 minutes. Transfer to a shallow bowl to cool slightly.

If using a charcoal grill, prepare it for direct-heat cooking over medium-hot coals; if using a gas grill, prepare it for direct-heat cooking over medium-high heat (see Grilling Basics, page 512).

Brush tuna all over with remaining 1 tablespoon oil and sprinkle all over with spice mixture. Oil grill rack and grill tuna (covered if using a gas grill), turning once, until browned but still rare in center, 6 to 8 minutes for 1-inch-thick steaks. Let tuna stand for 5 minutes.

Meanwhile, toss jicama, cilantro, and arugula with lime vinaigrette in a large bowl. Halve, pit, and peel avocados, and cut into 1-inch pieces.

Cut tuna into ½-inch-thick slices. Transfer salad to a large platter and top with sliced tuna and avocado. Serve with lime wedges.

Squid Salad with Olives and Tomatoes

SERVES 8

ACTIVE TIME: 30 MINUTES ■ START TO FINISH: 45 MINUTES

■ To become tender, squid must be cooked either slowly or in a flash. Here we quickly blanch it and toss it with olives, tomatoes, celery, and a lemony vinaigrette. Although it is delicious when eaten right away, the salad's flavor improves if you have time to refrigerate it for 8 hours (bring it to room temperature before tucking in). ■

1½ pounds cleaned squid, rinsed inside and out and
   patted dry
   Salt

2 tablespoons fresh lemon juice

1 tablespoon red wine vinegar

⅓ cup extra-virgin olive oil

1 large garlic clove, minced
   Freshly ground black pepper

1 small red onion, halved lengthwise and thinly sliced
   crosswise (1 cup)

⅓ cup pitted Kalamata or other brine-cured black
   olives, halved lengthwise

¾ pound cherry or grape tomatoes, halved, or
   quartered if large

2 celery ribs, cut into ¼-inch-thick slices

1 cup loosely packed fresh flat-leaf parsley leaves

Halve rings of squid tentacles lengthwise and cut longer tentacles into 2-inch lengths. Cut bodies (including flaps, if attached) into ⅓-inch-wide rings.

Cook squid in a 5- to 6-quart pot of boiling salted water (1 tablespoon salt), uncovered, until just opaque, 40 to 60 seconds. Drain and immediately transfer to a bowl of ice and cold water to stop the cooking. When squid is cool, drain and pat dry.

Whisk together lemon juice, vinegar, oil, garlic, ½ teaspoon salt, and ¼ teaspoon pepper in a small bowl. Stir in onion and let stand for 5 minutes to soften onion slightly.

Combine squid, olives, tomatoes, celery, and parsley in a large bowl. Toss with dressing and season with salt and pepper. Let stand for at least 15 minutes to allow flavors to develop.

- The salad, without the parsley, can be tossed with the dressing up to 8 hours ahead and refrigerated, covered. Add the parsley just before serving.

Southeast Asian Grilled Squid Salad

SERVES 4
ACTIVE TIME: 1 HOUR ■ START TO FINISH: 1 HOUR

■ With just a short visit to the grill, squid becomes tender. Carrots, cucumber, and peanuts give a nice crunch to this salad, and a generous shower of cilantro and mint ups the freshness factor. ■

- ¼ cup fresh lime juice (from about 2 limes)
- 2½ tablespoons Asian fish sauce
- 1½–2 tablespoons sugar
- ½ teaspoon salt
- 1–2 (1½- to 2-inch-long) fresh hot chiles, such as Thai or serrano, finely chopped, including seeds
- ¼ cup vegetable oil
- 1¼ pounds cleaned medium squid, rinsed inside and out and patted dry
- 2 carrots, halved crosswise, then cut lengthwise into wide ribbons using a vegetable peeler
- 1 seedless cucumber (usually plastic-wrapped), halved crosswise, then cut lengthwise into wide ribbons using peeler
- 1 head Boston lettuce, torn into bite-sized pieces
- 1 cup loosely packed fresh cilantro leaves
- 1 cup loosely packed fresh mint leaves
- 4 scallions, thinly sliced diagonally
- ½ cup coarsely chopped salted dry-roasted peanuts

ACCOMPANIMENT: lime wedges

If using a charcoal grill, prepare it for direct-heat cooking over hot coals; if using a gas grill, prepare it for direct-heat cooking over high heat (see Grilling Basics, page 512).

Whisk together lime juice, fish sauce, sugar (to taste), salt, chiles, and 3 tablespoons oil in a large bowl until sugar and salt are dissolved.

Toss squid bodies (including flaps, if attached) and tentacles with remaining 1 tablespoon oil. Oil grill rack. Grill squid bodies (covered if using gas grill), turning once, until grill marks appear and squid is just cooked through (it will curl up as it cooks), about 4 minutes. Transfer to a cutting board and cover loosely with foil to keep warm. Grill tentacles in same manner.

Cut squid bodies crosswise into ¾-inch-wide rings. If rings of tentacle are large, halve lengthwise. Cut longer tentacles into 2-inch lengths.

Toss together carrot and cucumber ribbons, lettuce, cilantro, mint, and scallions in a large bowl. Add squid and dressing and toss to coat. Sprinkle peanuts over salad and serve immediately, with lime wedges.

Thai-Style Crab Salad in Papaya

SERVES 4 AS A LIGHT MAIN COURSE
ACTIVE TIME: 20 MINUTES ■ START TO FINISH: 20 MINUTES

■ Sometimes the vessel is as important as its contents. Every bite of cool crab salad, its flavors so evocative of Southeast Asian cuisine, melds with the sweet, soft papaya flesh as it gets scooped up. Gold or strawberry papayas are especially sweet and fragrant, and they are the right size for this salad. Looks for papayas with skins that are mostly yellow and that yield slightly to the touch. ■

- ¼ cup rice vinegar (not seasoned)
- 3 tablespoons sugar
- 2 tablespoons water
- 4 teaspoons Asian fish sauce
- ½ teaspoon salt
- ½ cup chopped green bell pepper
- ½ cup chopped red bell pepper
- 1½ teaspoons minced serrano chile, including seeds
- 2 tablespoons chopped fresh cilantro
- ½ pound jumbo lump crabmeat, picked over for shells and cartilage
- 2 ripe small papayas, halved lengthwise and seeded

ACCOMPANIMENT: lime wedges

Whisk together vinegar, sugar, water, fish sauce, and salt in a bowl until sugar and salt are dissolved. Add bell peppers, chile, cilantro, and crab and toss gently to combine.

Serve crab salad mounded in papaya halves, with lime wedges.

Lobster, Avocado, and Grapefruit Salad

SERVES 4 AS A FIRST COURSE, 2 AS A MAIN COURSE
ACTIVE TIME: 45 MINUTES ■ START TO FINISH: 2¾ HOURS
(INCLUDES CHILLING)

■ A collage of pinks and greens with both sweetness and tang, this salad is sure to impress. What makes it so doable is that all of the components can be prepped ahead of time and then put together at the last minute (you can save time by buying 1⅓ pounds cooked lobster meat instead of cooking your own). ■

   Salt
2 (1¼- to 1½-pound) live lobsters
1 tablespoon finely chopped shallot
2 tablespoons fresh lemon juice
¼ cup extra-virgin olive oil
2 pink or Ruby Red grapefruits
1 firm but ripe California avocado
4 ounces baby arugula, or regular arugula torn into bite-sized pieces (4 cups)
   Coarse sea salt (optional; lightly crushed if grains are very large)

Bring 6 quarts salted water (1½ tablespoons salt) to a boil in an 8-quart pot over high heat. Plunge lobsters headfirst into water and cook, covered, for 6 minutes for 1¼-pound lobsters, 7 minutes for 1½-pound lobsters, from the time they enter water. Transfer with tongs to sink to drain.

When lobsters are cool enough to handle, crack shells and remove meat from tails and claws, keeping meat intact. Discard tomalley, any roe, and shells. Refrigerate lobster, covered, until cold, at least 1 hour.

Meanwhile, stir together shallot, lemon juice, and ½ teaspoon salt in a small bowl and let stand at room temperature for 30 minutes to allow flavors to blend.

Add oil to lemon juice mixture in a stream, whisking until well combined.

Cut off tops and bottoms of grapefruits to expose fruit. Stand fruit on a cutting board and remove peel, including all white pith, by cutting it off in vertical strips with a sharp paring knife. Cut segments free from membranes.

Halve and pit avocado. Cut each avocado half lengthwise in half and peel, then cut crosswise into ⅓-inch-thick slices.

Cut lobster tail meat crosswise into ½-inch-thick slices. Divide avocado and lobster meat among four plates and arrange grapefruit around them. Top with arugula and drizzle with dressing. Sprinkle lightly with sea salt, if using, and serve immediately.

COOK'S NOTES

■ The lobsters can be cooked and the meat removed from the shells up to 1 day ahead; refrigerate, covered. Slice the tail meat just before assembling the salad.

■ The dressing can be made up to 1 day ahead and refrigerated, covered. Whisk well just before using.

■ The grapefruit segments can be cut up to 2 hours ahead and refrigerated in one layer on a paper-towel-lined plate, covered with plastic wrap.

■ The avocado can be cut up to 1 hour ahead and refrigerated on a plate, its surface covered with plastic wrap.

Chicken Salad with Grapes and Walnuts

SERVES 4 AS A MAIN COURSE
ACTIVE TIME: 15 MINUTES ■ START TO FINISH: 30 MINUTES

■ Throw some salty capers into chicken salad, and the classic pairing of walnuts and juicy grapes tastes instantly new. Chicken tenders and a dressing of yogurt, mayonnaise, and Dijon mustard make the salad come together very quickly. ■

1½ pounds chicken tenders
   Salt
1¾ cups Chicken Stock (page 153) or store-bought reduced-sodium broth

⅓ cup plain yogurt

⅓ cup mayonnaise

1 tablespoon Dijon mustard

1 cup seedless grapes, halved crosswise

1 cup (about 3½ ounces) coarsely chopped walnuts

3 tablespoons drained capers, chopped

Freshly ground black pepper

Toss chicken with 2 teaspoons salt.

Bring stock and 5 cups water to a boil in a large saucepan. Add chicken and cook, uncovered, at a bare simmer, stirring occasionally, until just cooked through, about 5 minutes. Drain and cool, then tear into 1-inch chunks.

Stir together yogurt, mayonnaise, and mustard in a large bowl.

Stir chicken, grapes, walnuts, and capers into dressing, then season with salt and pepper to taste.

COOK'S NOTES

- The chicken can be cooked up to 1 day ahead and refrigerated, covered.

- The dressing can be made up to 1 day ahead and refrigerated, covered.

Chicken Salad with Tomatoes, Olives, and Green Beans

SERVES 4 AS A MAIN COURSE
ACTIVE TIME: 40 MINUTES ■ START TO FINISH:
40 MINUTES

■ Crisp-tender green beans and a spunky tomato-olive relish transform poached chicken from wallflower to wonderful. Our fail-safe poaching method, which has its roots in Chinese cooking, always produces moist, flavorful meat. This striking dish is best served at room temperature, rather than chilled, to show off its fresh, bold flavors. ■

4 skinless, boneless chicken breast halves (1¾ pounds)

Kosher salt

1¾ cups Chicken Stock (page 153) or store-bought reduced-sodium broth

1 fresh thyme sprig

¾ pound haricots verts or other thin green beans, trimmed

5 tablespoons extra-virgin olive oil

Freshly ground black pepper

1 pound tomatoes, cut into ¼-inch dice (3 cups)

½ cup mixed brine-cured green and black olives, such Picholine and Kalamata, pitted and chopped

1 tablespoon torn fresh oregano leaves

Sprinkle chicken all over with 1 tablespoon salt. Set aside.

Bring 5 cups water, stock, and thyme to a boil in a 4- to 6-quart heavy pot. Add beans and cook, uncovered, until crisp-tender, 3 to 6 minutes. With a slotted spoon, transfer beans to a bowl. Toss with 1 tablespoon oil and season with salt and pepper.

Add chicken to stock mixture and cook at a bare simmer, uncovered, for 6 minutes. Remove pot from heat and let stand, covered, until chicken is cooked through, about 15 minutes. With tongs, transfer chicken to a cutting board and let cool.

Meanwhile, stir together tomatoes, olives, oregano, ¼ teaspoon salt, ⅛ teaspoon pepper, and remaining ¼ cup oil in a bowl.

Cut chicken diagonally across the grain into 1-inch-thick slices.

Divide green beans among four plates. Arrange sliced chicken over beans and top with tomato-olive mixture.

COOK'S NOTE

- The beans, chicken, and tomato-olive mixture can be made up to 2 hours ahead and refrigerated separately, covered. Bring to room temperature before serving.

Beef Salad with Potatoes and Cornichons

SERVES 4 AS A MAIN COURSE
ACTIVE TIME: 30 MINUTES ■ START TO FINISH: 1½ HOURS

■ Shredded beef and warm potatoes pair up with a lively mustard vinaigrette to create a satisfying meal. ■

When we need a sharp, bright flavor to balance out a dish like this hearty beef salad, we turn to cornichons. The tiny sour pickles are so important in France, according to the French cooking authority Georgeanne Brennan, that French seed companies have hybridized special cucumbers that are ready to pick at the small cornichon size. The brine, she notes, usually has tarragon in it, which gives it a distinctive flavor. Cornichons and their juices are also used in sauces such as rémoulade and *gribiche*, and the pickles are a traditional accompaniment to pâtés and charcuterie platters; in casual restaurants in France, a whole crock or jar of them is sometimes brought to the table with the charcuterie.

- 2 large boiling potatoes (1 pound total)
- 3 cups shredded leftover pot roast
- 3 tablespoons red wine vinegar
- 1½ tablespoons Dijon mustard
- ¼ cup finely chopped shallots
- ¾ teaspoon sugar
- 1 teaspoon salt
- ¼ teaspoon freshly ground black pepper
- 5 tablespoons mild olive or vegetable oil
- ⅓ pound haricots verts or small regular green beans, trimmed and halved diagonally
- 1 large head Bibb lettuce, separated into leaves
- 6 cornichons (tiny French gherkins), cut into ⅛-inch-thick matchsticks
- ¼ cup chopped fresh flat-leaf parsley

Put a rack in middle of oven and preheat oven to 400°F.

Place potatoes on a 12-inch square of foil, prick each with a fork, and wrap in foil. Bake until tender, about 1 hour. (Potatoes are done when a small knife pierces centers easily.) Carefully unwrap potatoes and cool slightly.

Heat beef in a small baking dish, covered, in hot oven or in microwave until warm.

While beef is heating, whisk together vinegar, mustard, shallots, sugar, salt, and pepper in a small bowl until sugar and salt are dissolved. Add oil in a slow stream, whisking until well blended.

Steam beans in a steamer over boiling water, covered, until just tender, about 5 minutes.

Meanwhile, peel potatoes and cut crosswise into ¼-inch-thick slices; transfer to a large bowl. Add hot beans to warm potatoes, along with 2 tablespoons vinaigrette, gently tossing to coat.

Line a platter or four plates with lettuce leaves and arrange potato mixture on top. Toss meat, cornichons, and parsley with remaining vinaigrette and mound on top of potato mixture.

Steak Salad with Pickled Vegetables

SERVES 2 GENEROUSLY AS A MAIN COURSE
ACTIVE TIME: 20 MINUTES ■ START TO FINISH: 20 MINUTES

■ You can use leftover beef in this salad, but the mixture of flavors and textures is so delicious that it's worth cooking a steak just for it. Adding tart, crunchy, colorful *giardiniera* (pickled vegetables—usually carrots, cauliflower, and celery—available at the grocery store) means there's no need to make a separate dressing. ■

- 1 (12-ounce) jar *giardiniera* (assorted pickled vegetables), drained
- About 1 pound leftover cooked boneless steak, thinly sliced
- 1 celery rib, thinly sliced diagonally
- ¼ cup chopped drained bottled roasted red peppers
- ¼ cup chopped fresh flat-leaf parsley
- 2 tablespoons olive oil
- 1 teaspoon Worcestershire sauce, or to taste
  Salt and freshly ground black pepper
  Green lettuce leaves for lining plates

Cut any large pieces of *giardiniera* in half and transfer *giardiniera* to a large bowl. Add steak, celery, roasted peppers, parsley, oil, Worcestershire sauce, and salt and pepper to taste and toss to combine well.

Line two plates with lettuce and mound steak salad on top.

Ground Beef Salad with Shallots, Lemongrass, Cilantro, and Mint

SERVES 4
ACTIVE TIME: 1 HOUR ∎ START TO FINISH: 1 HOUR

∎ In northern Thailand and Laos, where this salad originated, the ground beef is often served raw, but in the American adaptation here, it is fully cooked. Crisp cucumbers, romaine, and carrots, along with fresh cilantro and mint, offer cool relief to the meat's complex heat, which comes from a well-balanced combination of dried red chiles, lemongrass, garlic, shallots, and galangal. ∎

2 tablespoons jasmine rice
4–6 (2- to 3-inch long) dried hot red chiles
2 fresh lemongrass stalks, root ends trimmed and tough outer leaves discarded
¾ cup chopped shallots
6 garlic cloves, chopped
2 tablespoons chopped peeled fresh or thawed frozen galangal (see Cook's Note and Sources)
3 tablespoons water
1¼ teaspoons salt
3 tablespoons fresh lime juice
1 tablespoon Asian fish sauce
1 teaspoon packed light brown sugar
2 tablespoons vegetable oil
1 pound lean ground beef chuck
½ cup loosely packed fresh cilantro leaves
½ cup loosely packed fresh mint leaves

ACCOMPANIMENTS: romaine leaves, sliced cucumbers, and thinly sliced carrots
SPECIAL EQUIPMENT: an electric coffee/spice grinder; a mini food processor

Toast rice in a dry small heavy skillet over moderate heat, shaking skillet, until golden, 5 to 7 minutes (skillet will smoke). Cool, then grind to a powder in grinder.

Toast chiles in a dry heavy 12-inch skillet over moderate heat, turning occasionally, until fragrant and lightly browned, 1 to 2 minutes. Transfer to a bowl to cool.

Thinly slice lower 6 inches of lemongrass stalks, then finely chop. Discard any stems from chiles and crumble chiles, with seeds, into mini processor. Add lemongrass, shallots, garlic, galangal, water, and salt, in 2 batches if necessary, and puree until finely ground.

Stir together lime juice, fish sauce, and brown sugar in a small bowl until sugar is dissolved.

Heat oil in 12-inch heavy skillet over moderate heat until warm, about 30 seconds. Add chile puree and cook, stirring constantly, until very fragrant and a shade darker, 3 to 4 minutes. Add beef, increase heat to moderately high, and cook, stirring and breaking up lumps, until meat is no longer pink, 4 to 5 minutes. Transfer to a bowl and stir in lime juice mixture and rice powder until well combined.

Mound beef on a platter and top with cilantro and mint. Arrange romaine, cucumbers, and carrots around meat.

COOK'S NOTE

∎ If you are unable to find galangal, you can substitute fresh ginger.

Thai Grilled Beef Salad
Yam Neua

SERVES 4 AS A MAIN COURSE
ACTIVE TIME: 1 HOUR ∎ START TO FINISH: 4 HOURS
(INCLUDES MAKING RICE)

∎ There are probably as many versions of *yam neua* as there are cooks in Thailand (ours comes from the cookbook authors Jeffrey Alford and Naomi Duguid), and although no ingredient is hard to find, the salad's cumulative flavor is out of this world. Each bite of tenderloin, tossed with fresh herbs, chile, lime, and fish sauce, will taste just a little bit different from the one before. A dish with such intensity is not meant to be eaten on its own, but is served as an accompaniment to sticky rice, the country's national staple. ∎

1 (1-pound) piece center-cut beef tenderloin
1 teaspoon freshly ground black pepper
¼ cup fresh lime juice (from about 2 limes), or
   to taste
2 tablespoons Asian fish sauce
½ teaspoon sugar
2–3 (1¼- to 1½-inch-long) fresh hot chiles, such as Thai or
   serrano (to taste), seeded and minced
⅓ cup thinly sliced shallots
3 scallions, thinly sliced
½ cup packed fresh cilantro leaves
3 tablespoons finely chopped fresh mint
1 seedless cucumber (usually plastic-wrapped)

GARNISH: fresh cilantro sprigs
ACCOMPANIMENT: Thai Sticky Rice (page 258)

If using a charcoal grill, prepare it for direct-heat cooking over hot coals; if using a gas grill, prepare it for direct-heat cooking over medium-high heat (see Grilling Basics, page 512).

Cut tenderloin horizontally in half to form 2 pieces about 1 inch thick (see Cook's Note). Pat meat dry, then rub all over with pepper, pressing it into meat.

Oil grill rack, then grill beef (covered if using a gas grill), turning occasionally, for 7 to 8 minutes for medium-rare. Transfer beef to a cutting board and let stand, uncovered, for 30 minutes (see Cook's Note).

Cut beef across the grain into very thin slices.

Stir together lime juice, fish sauce, sugar, and chiles in a large bowl until sugar is dissolved. Add beef, shallots, scallions, cilantro, and mint and toss until well combined.

Score cucumber lengthwise with tines of a fork and cut into thin slices. Arrange cucumber slices around edges of a platter. Mound beef salad in center and garnish with cilantro sprigs. Serve with rice.

COOK'S NOTE

■ To facilitate cutting the raw tenderloin, freeze it for 15 minutes. To facilitate slicing the grilled beef thin, cool completely, uncovered, then refrigerate, covered, for up to 1 day. Slice while still cold and bring to room temperature before assembling the salad.

Grilled Steak Salad with Mustard Vinaigrette

SERVES 4 AS A MAIN COURSE
ACTIVE TIME: 35 MINUTES ■ START TO FINISH: 45 MINUTES

■ Watercress boldly dressed with white wine vinegar, mustard, diced dill pickle, and capers makes a piquant bed for boneless top loin steak, cucumber, and red bell pepper. ■

6 tablespoons white wine vinegar
¼ cup Dijon mustard
6 tablespoons olive oil
2 teaspoons sugar
½ cup finely diced red bell pepper
½ cup finely diced peeled and seeded cucumber
¼ cup finely diced dill pickle
¼ cup finely chopped shallots
¼ cup small capers, drained and patted dry
   (chopped if large)
   Salt and freshly ground black pepper
2 (1¼-inch-thick) boneless beef top loin steaks (also
   known as strip steaks; about 2 pounds total)
2 bunches watercress (1 pound total), coarse stems
   discarded

SPECIAL EQUIPMENT: an instant-read thermometer

If using a charcoal grill, prepare it for direct-heat cooking over medium-hot coals; if using a gas grill, prepare it for direct-heat cooking over medium-high heat (see Grilling Basics, page 512).

Meanwhile, whisk together vinegar, mustard, oil, and sugar in a large bowl until sugar is dissolved. Stir in bell pepper, cucumber, pickle, shallots, capers, and salt and pepper to taste.

Pat steaks dry and sprinkle all over with ½ teaspoon salt and ½ teaspoon pepper (total). If using a gas grill, turn off one burner (the middle one if there are three burners). Oil grill rack and grill steaks (covered if using a gas grill), turning once, and moving to cooler area of grill if flare-ups occur, until thermometer inserted horizontally 2 inches into meat registers 120°F, 10 to 12 minutes. Transfer steak to a cutting board and let stand, loosely covered with foil, for 10 minutes (steak will continue to cook, reaching medium-rare).

Holding knife at a 45-degree angle, cut steak into ¼-inch-thick slices.

Add watercress to vinaigrette and toss until coated. Divide among four plates and arrange steak slices on salad.

Vietnamese Caramelized Grilled Pork and Rice Noodle Salad

SERVES 4 AS A MAIN COURSE
ACTIVE TIME: 35 MINUTES ■ START TO FINISH: 35 MINUTES

■ Popular in Vietnam, rice noodle salads offer an array of flavors—salty, sweet, sour, and sometimes spicy—and a mix of temperatures, the cool, refreshing salad contrasting with the caramelized pork cutlets. ■

FOR RICE NOODLES
  ¼ pound thin rice vermicelli (rice stick noodles)
  ¼ cup rice vinegar (not seasoned)
  1 tablespoon Asian fish sauce
  1 tablespoon sugar
  ¼ teaspoon salt
  1 carrot, coarsely shredded
  2 scallions, thinly sliced
  ¼ cup chopped unsalted dry-roasted peanuts
  ¼ cup loosely packed mixed fresh cilantro, mint, and/or basil leaves, torn if large
FOR PORK
  6 (¼-inch-thick) boneless pork loin chops
  ⅓ cup sugar
  ¼ cup finely chopped shallots
  1 tablespoon fresh lime juice
  1 tablespoon Asian fish sauce
  ½ teaspoon salt
ACCOMPANIMENT: Daikon and Carrot Pickle (recipe follows) or lime slices

MAKE THE NOODLES: Soak noodles in hot water for 10 minutes, then drain in a large sieve.

Meanwhile bring a 4-quart pot of unsalted water to a boil.

Boil noodles until tender, about 1 minute. Drain in sieve and rinse under cold water until cold. Drain well and pat dry.

Whisk together vinegar, fish sauce, sugar, and salt in a large bowl until sugar and salt are dissolved. Add noodles, carrot, scallions, and peanuts, tossing to combine.

GRILL THE PORK: Pound chops between two large sheets of plastic wrap with flat side of a meat pounder or rolling pin to less than ⅛ inch thick. Make several small ¼-inch-deep slits around edges of each chop to prevent curling. Cut chops lengthwise in half and transfer to a bowl.

Cook sugar in a 1-quart dry heavy saucepan over moderate heat, undisturbed, until it begins to melt. Continue to cook, stirring occasionally with a wooden spoon, until sugar is melted into a golden caramel. Add remaining ingredients (caramel will harden) and cook, stirring constantly, until caramel is dissolved and shallots are softened, about 2 minutes. Pour sauce over pork and toss until well coated.

Heat a lightly oiled ridged grill pan over moderately high heat until hot but not smoking. Grill pork in batches, turning once, until just cooked through, about 1 minute per side. (Discard any remaining caramel sauce.)

Add herbs to salad and toss to combine. Divide salad among bowls and top with pork. Serve with pickle or lime slices.

Daikon and Carrot Pickle

MAKES ABOUT 2 CUPS
ACTIVE TIME: 30 MINUTES ■ START TO FINISH: 45 MINUTES

■ Try this extraordinarily easy pickle to serve with Asian-style ribs, grilled chicken, or even burgers. ■

  2 medium carrots
  ½ pound daikon radish, peeled
  ½ cup rice vinegar (not seasoned)
  ¼ cup sugar
  1 teaspoon salt
SPECIAL EQUIPMENT: a mandoline or other adjustable-blade vegetable slicer with a julienne blade

Cut carrots and daikon into 2-inch-long, ⅛-inch-thick matchsticks with slicer.

Whisk together vinegar, sugar, and salt in a bowl until sugar and salt are dissolved. Add vegetables and toss to combine. Let stand, tossing occasionally, until wilted, about 15 minutes.

PASTA, NOODLES, AND DUMPLINGS

A confession: If I could have only one food for the rest of my life, it would be pasta. So when I tell you that I have eaten my way from one end of this chapter to the other, you can believe me.

I have, in fact, cooked almost every one of these recipes for my family, and it is tempting to offer you an account of what happened on each occasion. I could, for instance, tell you about the first time I made the lasagne Bolognese: as my son and I stood in the kitchen, rolling out the pasta, we discovered that it was as ethereal as butterfly wings. I could tell you how we reveled in the wonderful aroma that wafted up from the sauce as it cooked and the sheer pleasure we got from watching the delight of our guests as they ate. And if I were going to tell you that, I'd add that since that night, it has been the single most requested dish in my household.

I might talk about discovering spaghetti *cacio e pepe* (simple spaghetti with pecorino Romano and black pepper) in a working-men's trattoria in the spring of 2002, when a group of us went off to research an issue on Rome, and how it has been a weeknight staple in my house from that time on. Or about the joyful summer simplicity of fettuccine with arugula puree and cherry tomato sauce, a dish so lovely you can hardly believe that it is so easy to make.

Or perhaps I'd want to tell you about the first time I tried orzo risotto, which tastes so much richer than it actually is. It's easier than a classic risotto, and it's become one of the side dishes I serve on harried nights when I've rushed home from the office. Or I might recall the time I walked into our test kitchens, my nose twitching, to discover an almost forgotten but entirely familiar scent: the cooks were gathered around a dish of egg noodles with cabbage and onions, and when I stuck my fork into that seductively buttery tangle, I was back in my grandmother's kitchen, eating her favorite dish (and, in fact, the only one she knew how to cook).

The truth is that no matter where you are in the world, noodles of some kind are probably on the menu, and they are such classic comfort food that they almost always bring back welcome memories. Whether they are *bahmi goreng,* the exotic fried noodles of Indonesia, or classic American tuna noodle casserole, one bite is enough to evoke the taste of good times. It might be the clear, clean flavor of Japanese mint and scallion soba noodles, the rich delicate lightness of Italy's gnocchi alla romana, or the strong rustic heartiness of *aushak,* the garlicky scallion dumplings of Afghanistan, but each is able to offer someone a taste of home.

Even if you are cooking these dishes for the first time, I promise that you're going to love them. And so will your family and friends. The world of pasta is large, generous, and delicious, and there is something here to please every taste.

PASTA, NOODLES, AND DUMPLINGS

Capellini
with Fresh Tomato Sauce

SERVES 6 AS A FIRST COURSE, 4 AS A MAIN COURSE
ACTIVE TIME: 20 MINUTES ■ START TO FINISH: 25 MINUTES

■ This summery dish focuses on the goodness of ripe tomatoes, letting them be just what they're meant to be. Mixing together the chopped and grated raw tomatoes creates a fresh sauce with enough body to coat each strand of capellini with bright flavor. ■

1 small garlic clove
  Salt
3 pounds ripe tomatoes
2 tablespoons fresh lemon juice
1 teaspoon sugar (optional)
½ teaspoon freshly ground black pepper
1 pound dried capellini (angel hair pasta)
½ cup chopped fresh basil
ACCOMPANIMENTS: finely grated Parmigiano-Reggiano; extra-virgin olive oil (optional)

Mince garlic and mash to a paste with a pinch of salt, using side of a large heavy knife.

Core and coarsely chop two thirds of tomatoes. Halve remaining tomatoes crosswise. Rub cut sides against large holes of a box grater set in a large bowl; reserve pulp and discard skin. Toss pulp with chopped tomatoes, garlic paste, lemon juice, 1 teaspoon salt, sugar (if using), and pepper. Let stand for at least 10 minutes, or until ready to use.

Cook pasta in an 8-quart pot of boiling salted water (3 tablespoons salt) until al dente, about 2 minutes. Drain and immediately add to tomato mixture, tossing to combine. Sprinkle with basil. Serve with grated cheese and, if desired, olive oil for drizzling.

COOK'S NOTE
■ The tomato mixture can stand at room temperature for up to 2 hours.

PASTA COOKING WATER

You'll notice that in our pasta recipes we say to salt the cooking water, and we tell you how much salt to use: 3 tablespoons for 8 quarts water. In our experience, most home cooks are too timid about salting pasta cooking water, and it's a detail that makes a huge difference. The pasta won't taste salty (most of the salt will be drained away in the cooking water), but it will be really flavorful. In the grand Italian tradition, after all, pasta dishes are about the pasta, not about the sauce. And the salt also hinders the separation of starch molecules and thus minimizes stickiness. We've even upped the amount of salt from that given in the first *Gourmet Cookbook* (about 1 tablespoon for every 4 quarts of water), since we realized that most of us salt the water more liberally at home than we do in the test kitchens.

One last tip: Always reserve a ladleful of the cooking water before turning the pasta out into a colander. It comes in handy if you need to moisten the pasta or if you want to extend the sauce. (The secret to great pesto when serving it over pasta is to add a little cooking water: it helps the cheese to melt and the sauce to coat the pasta more easily.) And if you are cooking a big batch of pasta or an artisanal pasta (see page 213), which throws off more starch, the water will have a greater starch content and can be used to help thicken a sauce.

Spaghetti with Pecorino Romano and Black Pepper

SERVES 4 AS A FIRST COURSE, 2 AS A MAIN COURSE
ACTIVE TIME: 20 MINUTES ■ START TO FINISH: 20 MINUTES

■ The southern half of Italy is so rugged that it's difficult for cows to graze, so most of the cheese there is made from sheep's milk. Indeed, every region in southern Italy produces some kind of pecorino (from *pecora*, Italian for "sheep"), but sharp, salty pecorino Romano, produced in the Roman countryside, is the most famous. It's the key ingredient in *cacio e pepe*, a classic Roman dish that is so sublimely simple that initially we wondered if you would even need a recipe to make it. As it turns out, perfecting it was challenging, but ultimately we found the ideal combination of spaghetti, melting pecorino Romano, and crushed black pepper. ■

- 2 teaspoons black peppercorns
- ½ pound spaghetti
  Salt
- ¾ cup plus 2 tablespoons very finely grated pecorino Romano or Parmigiano-Reggiano (use the ragged-edged holes of a box grater), plus additional for serving

Toast peppercorns in a dry small heavy skillet over moderately high heat, swirling skillet, until fragrant and beginning to jump, 2 to 3 minutes. Coarsely crush peppercorns in a mortar with a pestle or wrap in a kitchen towel and press on peppercorns with bottom of a heavy skillet to crush them.

Cook spaghetti in an 8-quart pot of boiling salted water (3 tablespoons salt) until al dente.

Fill a large glass or ceramic bowl with some hot water to warm bowl; just before spaghetti is cooked, drain bowl, but do not dry.

Reserve ½ cup pasta cooking water and drain pasta quickly (do not shake off excess water), then add to warm pasta bowl. Sprinkle ¾ cup cheese and 3 tablespoons cooking water evenly over spaghetti and toss quickly. If pasta seems dry, toss with more cooking water.

Divide pasta among plates and sprinkle with pepper and remaining 2 tablespoons cheese. Serve with additional cheese on the side.

Spaghetti with Olive and Pine Nut Salsa

SERVES 8 AS A FIRST COURSE, 4 AS A MAIN COURSE
ACTIVE TIME: 30 MINUTES ■ START TO FINISH: 30 MINUTES

■ Adapted from Latteria San Marco di Arturo e Maria, an intimate little restaurant that is a favorite of Milanese cognoscenti, this pretty dish is sure to become a weekday standby. Not only is it easy to prepare, but you've probably got all the ingredients in your fridge. The trick is to hand-chop everything very fine, so that the salsa speckles the spaghetti evenly and you get just the right amount of fiery crunch in each bite. ■

- ¾ cup Gaeta olives, pitted
- ¼ cup drained capers
- ¼ cup pine nuts
- ¼ cup chopped fresh flat-leaf parsley
- 1 teaspoon red pepper flakes
- ½ cup extra-virgin olive oil
- 1 pound spaghetti
  Salt

Very finely chop together olives, capers, and pine nuts with a large heavy knife. Transfer to a large serving bowl, add parsley and red pepper flakes, and stir in oil until combined.

Cook spaghetti in an 8-quart pot of boiling salted water (3 tablespoons salt) until al dente. Reserve 1 cup pasta cooking water and drain spaghetti.

Add spaghetti to olive mixture and toss until well combined. If pasta seems dry, moisten with some reserved cooking water.

Spaghetti with Ramps

SERVES 8 AS A FIRST COURSE, 4 AS A MAIN COURSE
ACTIVE TIME: 25 MINUTES ■ START TO FINISH: 25 MINUTES

■ We look to the arrival of ramps in the farmers market as our first marker of spring. The robust flavor of these wild leeks is like that of a very garlicky onion, and it is a wonderful tonic after a winter of sweet root vegetables and hearty stews. We enjoy ramps all sorts of ways—sautéed, roasted, pickled—but this quick, pungent pesto is an especially fine introduction to the vegetable. Don't skip the toasted bread crumb topping; it adds a nice crunch. ■

½ pound ramps
  Salt
1 teaspoon finely grated lemon zest
¼ cup extra-virgin olive oil
1 pound spaghetti
2 tablespoons finely grated Parmigiano-Reggiano

ACCOMPANIMENT: Toasted Bread Crumb Topping (recipe follows; see Cook's Note)

Trim roots from ramps and slip off outer skin from bulbs if loose. Blanch ramps in an 8-quart pot of boiling salted water (3 tablespoons salt) for 2 to 3 seconds, then transfer to a cutting board with tongs. Coarsely chop ramps, transfer to a blender, and add zest and oil.

Add spaghetti to boiling water and cook for a few minutes, then ladle out ½ cup pasta water and add to blender. Puree ramps until smooth and season with salt.

Meanwhile, continue to cook spaghetti until al dente. Reserve 1 cup pasta water and drain spaghetti. Return pasta to pot, add ramp puree and cheese, and toss over moderate heat for 1 to 2 minutes, thinning sauce with a little pasta water as needed to coat pasta. Serve pasta with bread crumbs for sprinkling.

COOK'S NOTE
■ Make the bread crumbs before you cook the pasta.

Toasted Bread Crumb Topping for Pasta

MAKES ABOUT 1½ CUPS
ACTIVE TIME: 5 MINUTES ■ START TO FINISH: 20 MINUTES

3 (½-inch-thick) slices whole-grain bread, cut into cubes
2 tablespoons extra-virgin olive oil
  Sea salt

Put a rack in middle of oven and preheat oven to 350°F.

Grind bread cubes to coarse crumbs, in batches, in

THE BEAUTY OF BREAD CRUMBS

We have executive food editor Kemp Minifie to thank for the Toasted Bread Crumb Topping recipe. She makes a substantial investment in artisanal whole-grain bread every week at the Union Square Greenmarket, and she refuses to waste a literal crumb of it. (The better the bread, the better the crumbs.) On Saturdays, she gathers up the uneaten end pieces from that week, coarsely grinds them, and then freezes them. (She cubes the bread first and grinds it in small batches in the blender; the results are superior to what you get using a food processor, because you get a more even texture.) When she's accumulated a quart-size sealable bag of crumbs in the freezer, she spreads them out on a baking sheet and toasts them in a 350°F oven until they are deep golden. She dumps them into a bowl and drizzles them with extra-virgin olive oil, about ¼ cup for every 2 cups of crumbs, then seasons them with salt. Many recipes suggest tossing the crumbs with oil before toasting them, but adding the oil afterward instead allows its fresh, clean, green taste to come through. It's important to distribute the oil evenly (Minifie uses a fork) and season confidently with salt.

What do you do with seasoned toasted crumbs? We love the crisp textural contrast they add to pasta. Bring a bowl of them to the table and, in true Sicilian tradition, scatter them on top in place of Parmigiano-Reggiano, or be extravagant and use them in addition to the cheese. By the time you get to the bottom of your bowl, the crumbs have plumped up in whatever flavorful sauce remains. We find the crumbs delicious on vegetables as well, or on a salad in place of croutons.

The toasted crumbs keep beautifully in the freezer. To take the chill off them before serving, heat them for 20 to 30 seconds in the microwave, until just warmed through. They'll be as good as freshly made.

a blender or food processor. Spread on a baking sheet and bake, stirring occasionally, until golden, 10 to 15 minutes. Pour crumbs into a bowl and stir in oil and salt to taste.

COOK'S NOTE

- The toasted crumbs keep in an airtight container in the freezer for up to 3 months. Heat them in the microwave until they are just warmed through, 20 to 30 seconds, before serving.

Linguine with Zucchini and Mint

SERVES 8 AS A FIRST COURSE, 4 AS A MAIN COURSE
ACTIVE TIME: 40 MINUTES ■ START TO FINISH: 40 MINUTES

■ Supermarkets carry zucchini all year round, but it's worth waiting until the end of summer, when squash and mint are running riot, to make this dish. Slicing and lightly frying the zucchini is the only step that takes a bit of time. The pale golden wafer-thin disks practically melt into the pasta, and their sweetness is accentuated by the garlic, mint, and lemon. ■

  2 pounds zucchini (about 3 large)
  1 cup olive oil
  4 garlic cloves, finely chopped
  1 pound dried linguine
    Salt
  ¾ cup chopped fresh mint
  1 tablespoon finely grated lemon zest
  ¼ teaspoon freshly ground black pepper

Slice zucchini very thin with a mandoline or other adjustable-blade vegetable slicer or a sharp knife.

Heat oil in a 12-inch heavy skillet over moderately high heat until hot but not smoking. Fry zucchini in 3 batches, stirring occasionally, until softened and very pale golden, 3 to 4 minutes per batch. Transfer with a slotted spoon to a baking sheet lined with paper towels to drain and cover with foil to keep warm.

Add garlic to oil remaining in skillet and cook,

stirring, until very pale golden, about 30 seconds. Remove skillet from heat.

Cook pasta in an 8-quart pot of boiling salted water (3 tablespoons salt) until al dente. Reserve 1 cup pasta cooking water, drain pasta, and transfer to a large shallow bowl.

Toss pasta with garlic oil, zucchini, mint, zest, 1 teaspoon salt, and pepper. Add some of reserved cooking water to moisten if necessary.

Fettuccine with Arugula Puree and Cherry Tomato Sauce

SERVES 8 AS A FIRST COURSE, 4 AS A MAIN COURSE
ACTIVE TIME: 20 MINUTES ■ START TO FINISH: 30 MINUTES

■ Arugula is transformed from peppery leaf to powerhouse pesto in this dish, adapted from one devised by the chef, cookbook author, and radio host Evan Kleiman. Topping the pesto-dressed pasta with an easy chunky tomato sauce bumps up the flavors and textures. For this recipe, we prefer to use dried fettuccine that is not made with eggs; it has a firmness and bite that contrasts nicely with the softened tomatoes. ■

FOR ARUGULA PUREE
  2 tablespoons pine nuts, lightly toasted (see Tips, page 911)
  5 ounces baby arugula, coarsely chopped (7 cups)
  ½ cup extra-virgin olive oil
  ¼ cup finely grated pecorino Romano
  1 teaspoon salt
FOR CHERRY TOMATO SAUCE
  3 tablespoons extra-virgin olive oil
  2 garlic cloves, crushed with side of a large heavy knife
  1½ pounds cherry tomatoes
    Salt
FOR PASTA
  1 pound dried fettuccine, preferably not made with eggs (see headnote)
ACCOMPANIMENT: finely grated pecorino Romano

MAKE THE PUREE: Pulse pine nuts in a food processor until finely ground; be careful not to grind to a paste. Add arugula, oil, cheese, and salt and pulse until almost smooth.

MAKE THE TOMATO SAUCE: Heat oil in a 12-inch heavy skillet over moderate heat until hot but not smoking. Add garlic and cook, stirring, until golden, about 2 minutes. Discard garlic. Add tomatoes and ¾ teaspoon salt and cook, stirring occasionally, until tomatoes are collapsed but not falling apart, 15 to 20 minutes.

MEANWHILE, COOK THE PASTA: Cook fettuccine in an 8-quart pot of boiling salted water (3 tablespoons salt) until al dente. Drain and return to pot.

Add arugula puree to pasta and toss until well coated. Transfer to a platter and top with tomato sauce. Serve with grated cheese.

COOK'S NOTE
■ The arugula puree can be made up to 1 day ahead and refrigerated, covered. Bring to room temperature before using.

Penne with Tomatoes and Goat Cheese

SERVES 8 AS A FIRST COURSE, 4 TO 6 AS A MAIN COURSE
ACTIVE TIME: 20 MINUTES ■ START TO FINISH: 25 MINUTES

■ With its hits of fresh basil and salty olives, this is one of the fastest, most flavorful combinations we know (and the only thing you need to cook is the pasta). Tossed with the hot penne, the mild goat cheese melts and becomes a creamy sauce, while the tomatoes add a note of sweetness. For an especially vibrant presentation, use cherry tomatoes in a variety of shapes and colors. ■

  1 pound penne or gemelli
2¾ pounds cherry tomatoes, halved
     Salt
5–6 ounces soft mild goat cheese, crumbled
  ⅔ cup coarsely chopped Kalamata or other brine-cured black olives
  ¾ cup torn fresh basil leaves
     Freshly ground black pepper

Cook pasta in an 8-quart pot of boiling salted water (3 tablespoons salt) until al dente; drain.

Meanwhile, toss tomatoes with salt to taste in a bowl. Let stand to release juices.

Toss hot pasta with goat cheese in a large bowl until cheese melts and coats pasta. Add tomatoes with juices, olives, basil, and salt and pepper to taste and toss to combine.

COOK'S NOTE
■ To prevent the basil leaves from discoloring, don't tear them until just before the pasta is done.

Pasta with Lentils and Kale

SERVES 6 TO 8 AS A MAIN COURSE
ACTIVE TIME: 45 MINUTES ■ START TO FINISH: 1¼ HOURS

■ Onions cooked "low and slow" so they become sweet nuggets of flavor are the backbone of this dish. The step cannot be rushed, so we like to cook the onions earlier in the day and reheat them later. This recipe is particularly good in the fall, since Tuscan kale tastes best when picked after the first frost. ■

  ½ cup small French green lentils
  2 cups water
     Salt
  6 tablespoons extra-virgin olive oil
  1 pound onions, chopped
1¼ pounds Tuscan kale (also called lacinato kale, *cavolo nero*, or dinosaur kale)
     Freshly ground black pepper
  1 pound rotini (corkscrew pasta) or small tubular pasta

Combine lentils, water, and ¼ teaspoon salt in a 1- to 1½-quart saucepan, bring to a simmer, and simmer, uncovered, until tender but not falling apart, 20 to 25 minutes; add more water if necessary to keep lentils barely covered. Remove from heat and season with additional salt if desired.

Meanwhile, heat ¼ cup oil in a 12-inch heavy skillet over moderately high heat until hot but not smoking. Add onions and ½ teaspoon salt and cook, stirring, for 1 minute. Reduce heat to low, cover, and cook, stirring occasionally (more frequently toward end of cooking), until onions are soft and golden, about 30 minutes. Remove lid and cook, stirring frequently, until onions are golden brown, 5 to 10 minutes more.

While onions cook, cut out and discard stems and center ribs from kale. Bring 6 quarts water to a boil in a 7- to 8-quart pot and stir in 3 tablespoons salt. Stir in kale and boil, uncovered, stirring occasionally, until just tender, 5 to 7 minutes. With tongs, transfer kale to a colander to drain, pressing lightly on kale. (Keep water at a boil.)

Coarsely chop kale. Add to onions, along with lentils (including cooking liquid), and simmer, stirring, for 1 minute. Season with salt and pepper.

Meanwhile, add pasta to pot of boiling water and cook until al dente. Reserve about 1 cup pasta cooking liquid and drain pasta.

Add pasta to lentil mixture and cook over high heat, tossing, for 1 minute, adding ⅓ cup of pasta cooking liquid, or enough to keep pasta moist. Season with pepper and drizzle with remaining 2 tablespoons oil.

COOK'S NOTE
- Both the lentils and the onions can be cooked up to 5 days ahead. Cool, uncovered, then refrigerate—separately or together—in an airtight container.

3 ounces pancetta (Italian unsmoked bacon), chopped (scant 1 cup)
1 tablespoon extra-virgin olive oil
1 small onion, finely chopped
4 garlic cloves, minced
2 tablespoons finely chopped fresh sage
½ pound bottled peeled cooked whole chestnuts, coarsely crumbled (1½ cups; see Sources)
½ pound dried egg tagliatelle or fettuccine
   Salt
1 cup finely grated Parmigiano-Reggiano (about 3 ounces)
2 tablespoons unsalted butter
   Freshly ground black pepper
1 tablespoon finely chopped fresh flat-leaf parsley

Cook pancetta in oil in a 12-inch heavy skillet over moderate heat, stirring frequently, until beginning to brown, 3 to 4 minutes. Add onion and cook, stirring frequently, until beginning to brown, 2 to 3 minutes. Add garlic and 1 tablespoon sage and cook, stirring, for 1 minute. Stir in chestnuts and remove from heat.

Cook pasta in an 8-quart pot of boiling salted water (3 tablespoons salt) until al dente. Reserve 1½ cups cooking water and drain pasta.

Add pasta to pancetta mixture in skillet, then add 1 cup reserved cooking water, cheese, and butter and cook, tossing constantly, over high heat until pasta is well coated (add more reserved water if necessary), about 1 minute. Season with salt and pepper to taste and sprinkle with parsley and remaining tablespoon sage. Serve immediately.

Tagliatelle with Chestnuts, Pancetta, and Sage

SERVES 6 AS A SIDE DISH, 4 AS A MAIN COURSE
ACTIVE TIME: 30 MINUTES ■ START TO FINISH: 30 MINUTES

■ Perfect for a cool evening, this pasta features a classic trio of Italian ingredients. The small amount of pancetta has an enormous impact, giving a salty sheen to the sweet crumbles of chestnuts and chopped sage. Bottled cooked chestnuts—one of our favorite pantry items—make the preparation surprisingly quick. ■

Crab and Herb Fettuccine

SERVES 8 AS A FIRST COURSE, 6 AS A MAIN COURSE
ACTIVE TIME: 30 MINUTES ■ START TO FINISH: 30 MINUTES

■ Fine-quality lump crabmeat is expensive, so we like to save it for recipes that showcase its sweet essence. Here delicate crabmeat and a light, herb-flecked *beurre blanc* provide a luxurious complement to fettuccine. This makes an elegant centerpiece to a summery menu. ■

¼ cup dry white wine

¼ cup tarragon vinegar or white wine vinegar

⅓ cup finely chopped shallots

1¼ sticks (10 tablespoons) cold unsalted butter, cut into tablespoons

1 pound jumbo lump crabmeat, picked over for shells and cartilage

3 tablespoons chopped fresh tarragon

3 tablespoons chopped fresh chives

⅓ cup chopped fresh flat-leaf parsley

1½ teaspoons finely grated lemon zest

3 tablespoons fresh lemon juice

Salt

½ pound dried egg fettuccine

Freshly ground black pepper

Combine wine, vinegar, and shallots in a 2½- to 3-quart heavy saucepan, bring to a boil over moderate heat, and boil until liquid is reduced to about 1 tablespoon, about 3 minutes. Add a few tablespoons butter, whisking constantly. Add remaining butter one piece at a time, whisking constantly, adding each new piece before previous one has completely melted and lifting pan from heat occasionally to cool sauce. Reduce heat to low, add crabmeat, and cook, stirring occasionally, until just heated through, about 2 minutes. Remove pan from heat and stir in herbs, zest, lemon juice, and ½ teaspoon salt.

Meanwhile, cook pasta in an 8-quart pot of boiling salted water (3 tablespoons salt) until al dente. Reserve 3 tablespoons pasta cooking water and drain pasta.

Toss pasta with crab sauce and reserved cooking water in a serving bowl. Season with salt and pepper to taste.

Campanelle with Squid, Tomatoes, and Capers

SERVES 4 AS A FIRST COURSE, 2 AS A MAIN COURSE
ACTIVE TIME: 45 MINUTES ■ START TO FINISH: 1 HOUR

■ Pairing squid with capers, raisins, and tomatoes might strike you as unusual, but the elements har-

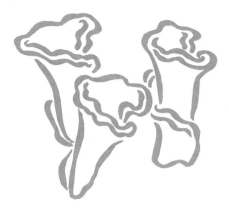

monize perfectly on the palate. This recipe, from Wendy Artin, an artist who lives in Rome, is light, vibrant, and very fresh. We call for a Thai or serrano chile because these are easier to find than the small, thin Italian hot chiles that Artin buys at her local market. ■

1 pound cleaned squid, bodies and tentacles separated

6 tablespoons extra-virgin olive oil

4 large garlic cloves, finely chopped

1 (1½-inch long) fresh hot chiles, such as Thai or serrano, halved crosswise

½ pound grape or cherry tomatoes, halved

⅓ cup dry white wine

½ cup raisins

¼ cup capers, rinsed, drained, patted dry, and coarsely chopped

½ pound campanelle (small bell-shaped pasta) or fusilli

Salt

½ cup loosely packed torn fresh basil leaves

¼ cup pine nuts, lightly toasted (see Tips, page 911)

1 (1-by-½-inch) strip lemon zest, removed with a vegetable peeler, finely chopped

Freshly ground black pepper

If squid are large, halve each ring of tentacles. Cut longer tentacles into 2-inch pieces. Pull off flaps from squid bodies and cut flaps into ¼-inch-thick slices. Cut bodies crosswise into ¼-inch-wide rings. Pat squid dry.

Heat 3 tablespoons oil in a 12-inch heavy skillet

over moderately high heat until hot but not smoking. Add garlic and chile and cook, stirring, until fragrant, about 30 seconds. Add squid and cook, stirring, for 1 minute. Add tomatoes and wine and simmer, stirring, for 2 minutes. Add raisins and capers and simmer, stirring, for 30 seconds. Remove from heat.

Cook pasta in an 8-quart pot of boiling salted water (3 tablespoons salt) until al dente. Reserve ½ cup pasta cooking water and drain pasta.

Add pasta and ¼ cup reserved cooking water to tomato mixture and cook over moderately high heat, stirring constantly, for 1 minute. Remove from heat and stir in basil, pine nuts, zest, and salt and pepper to taste; discard chile. If pasta looks dry, moisten with more cooking water.

Divide pasta among plates and drizzle with remaining 3 tablespoons oil.

Fideos with Mussels

SERVES 6 AS A MAIN COURSE
ACTIVE TIME: 1½ HOURS ■ START TO FINISH: 2 HOURS
(INCLUDES MAKING STOCK)

■ *Fideos*, nests of thin pasta, are popular on the eastern coast of Spain. They are often first toasted in oil, then added to a sauce so that they absorb it as they continue to cook. In this recipe, the flavorful cooking liquid in which the mussels are steamed is enhanced with a *sofrito*, a concentrated sauté of onions, garlic, and tomato, and chopped Spanish chorizo. ■

 6 tablespoons extra-virgin olive oil
10 ounces *fideos* (see Cook's Note and Sources)
1⅓ cups chopped onions
 2 teaspoons minced garlic
 2 (14- to 15-ounce) cans diced tomatoes in juice
   Salt
   Pinch of sugar
½ cup finely chopped Spanish chorizo (cured spicy pork sausage)
 1 Turkish bay leaf or ½ California bay leaf
 1 cup dry white wine
 5 cups Fish Stock (page 154)
 3 pounds mussels, preferably cultivated, scrubbed and beards removed
 2 tablespoons chopped fresh flat-leaf parsley

Heat ¼ cup oil in a 6-quart wide heavy pot over moderately low heat until hot but not smoking. Add *fideos* and cook, stirring and turning frequently, until golden brown (nests will break up), 10 to 15 minutes. Transfer pasta with a slotted spoon to a bowl.

Add ⅔ cup onion and 1 teaspoon garlic to oil remaining in pot and cook, stirring occasionally, until softened, 4 to 5 minutes. Stir in tomatoes with juice, ½ teaspoon salt, and sugar, increase heat to moderately high, and bring to a simmer. Simmer, stirring frequently, until tomatoes have broken down into a very thick paste, about 25 minutes.

While *sofrito* simmers, cook chorizo and remaining ⅔ cup onion and 1 teaspoon garlic with bay leaf in remaining 2 tablespoons oil in an 8-quart heavy pot over moderate heat, stirring occasionally, until onion is softened, 4 to 5 minutes. Add wine, bring to a boil, and boil for 5 minutes. Add stock and ½ teaspoon salt and return to a boil. Add mussels and cook, tightly covered, over moderate heat, until mussels open wide, 3 to 6 minutes. (Discard any mussels that remain unopened after 6 minutes.) Transfer mussels with a slotted spoon to a bowl. Discard bay leaf.

Add mussel cooking liquid and browned *fideos* to *sofrito* and boil, uncovered, stirring frequently, until pasta is tender and has absorbed most of liquid, 12 to 15 minutes. Add mussels and 1 tablespoon parsley and cook, tossing, until mussels are heated through, 1 to 2 minutes. Serve sprinkled with remaining tablespoon parsley.

COOK'S NOTES
- You can substitute 10 ounces spaghetti, broken into 2-inch lengths, for the *fideos*.
- The pasta can be browned up to 1 day ahead and, once cooled, kept, loosely covered, at room temperature. Then use 2 additional tablespoons olive oil to cook the onion and garlic and continue with recipe.
- The *sofrito* can be cooked up to 1 day ahead. Cool, uncovered, then refrigerate, covered.

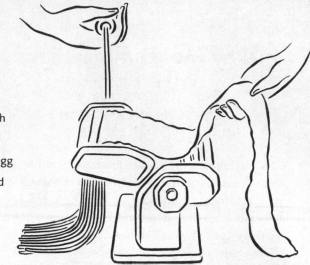

PASTA: FRESH VERSUS DRIED

One of the most enduring culinary myths is that homemade fresh pasta is superior to manufactured dried pasta. You might as well say apples are better than oranges! With the exception of dried egg noodles, which are a relatively small part of the market, dried and fresh pastas are made with different ingredients, using different methods, and are best suited to different sauces.

FRESH PASTA Made from all-purpose flour and eggs and rolled out before being cut, fresh pasta has a tender texture and a clean flavor. It's more porous than dried pasta, so it works best with creamy or buttery sauces that are meant to be absorbed. It's perishable, and it should be cooked as soon as it's rolled out or wrapped and refrigerated. Fresh pasta expands more when cooked than dried, and it's richer, because of the eggs; a half pound will feed four people. Making fresh pasta at home might seem daunting, but it doesn't take much time at all (see the directions on page 224)—and it's worlds better than any of the so-called fresh pastas found in the refrigerator case at the supermarket. Those are pasteurized and they've been packaged in a way that extends their shelf life for weeks. We've found that the next best thing to homemade fresh pasta is thin, light Cipriani-brand dried egg pasta (see Sources).

DRIED PASTA This is made from hard durum wheat (semolina) flour and water in factories, where it's extruded through dies into all sorts of shapes, including long noodles such as spaghetti and linguine, short tubes such as penne and rigatoni, and more

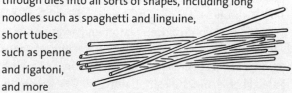

complex shapes such as fusilli and campanelle, which are designed to trap sauces in their nooks and crannies.

Although dried pasta is such a simple, straightforward product—or perhaps *because* of that—all brands are not created equal. Good-quality dried pasta has a nutty, wheaty flavor that tastes great with nothing more than the tiniest bit of olive oil and freshly grated Parmigiano-Reggiano. When cooked with care to the al dente stage—when the center of the noodle is just slightly underdone—it has a wonderful firmness and chewiness, and it goes best with tomato- or oil-based sauces. If using a dried pasta that contains egg, you might notice that the packages contain a smaller amount than those of regular no-egg pastas and that the recommended serving portions are smaller. That's because the egg causes the pasta to expand, so it's more filling.

Pastas made in Italy are not necessarily better than those made elsewhere, but Italian law does require that they be made of 100 percent durum wheat (much of which is, in fact, imported from the United States). Durum's high protein content is what gives the pasta its characteristic bite when cooked. The way the pasta is extruded and dried also makes a big difference. Pasta pressed through Teflon-coated stainless steel dies is uniformly smooth and glossy, so it won't grab a sauce, whereas pasta pressed through classic bronze dies has an appealingly rough texture that a sauce just wants to cling to. That coarser texture also causes the pasta to release more starch into the cooking water, which makes it a terrific thickening agent if you're adding a little of it to a sauce. Modern quick-drying techniques produce firmer cooked pasta, but traditionalists will tell you that long, slow drying results in better flavor.

More and more artisanal brands—pastas that are made in small batches using bronze dies—are becoming available in supermarkets as well as specialty foods shops. Most of the time, we're happy with a good supermarket brand such as De Cecco, but as far as Italian luxuries go, artisanal pasta is a lot more affordable than a white truffle, a Super Tuscan wine, or a Ferrari.

Turkey Meatballs in Sauce with Pasta

SERVES 4 TO 6 AS A MAIN COURSE
ACTIVE TIME: 1 HOUR ■ START TO FINISH: 3¼ HOURS
(INCLUDES MAKING SAUCE)

■ Sunday supper at *nonna*'s house is a tradition in many Italian-American families. We can't imagine a more gourmet grandmother than the chef, cookbook author, and cooking show host Lidia Bastianich, who regularly gathers her children, grandchildren, and other relatives together for a big family-style meal on Sunday afternoons. She often serves a wholly American combination—a big bowl of pasta with meatballs. But her meatballs are enlivened with pine nuts and raisins, ingredients that reflect her childhood in Istria (now part of Croatia). She always makes these meatballs with ground turkey thighs, because the meat is much moister and more flavorful than breast meat. ■

¼ cup finely chopped onion
  Salt
3 tablespoons extra-virgin olive oil
2 slices (2 ounces) stale white bread from an Italian loaf or sandwich loaf, torn into pieces
1 cup whole milk
¼ cup golden raisins
1 large egg
1 pound ground turkey (not breast meat)
¼ cup pine nuts, toasted (see Tips, page 911)
1 tablespoon chopped fresh flat-leaf parsley
1½ teaspoons porcini mushroom powder (see Sources), or 3 grams dried porcini ground in an electric coffee/spice grinder
⅛ teaspoon freshly ground black pepper
  About ⅔ cup all-purpose flour for dredging
  About 1 cup vegetable oil for shallow-frying
  Lidia's Pasta Sauce (recipe follows)
1 pound fusilli, rigatoni, or cavatappi (ridged corkscrew pasta)
½ cup finely grated Parmigiano-Reggiano, plus additional for serving

Cook onion with a pinch of salt in 1 tablespoon olive oil in a small heavy skillet over moderate heat, stirring occasionally, until softened and beginning to brown, 4 to 5 minutes. Transfer to a small bowl to cool.

Soak bread in milk in a bowl until completely softened, 4 to 5 minutes. Firmly squeeze milk from bread; discard milk.

Meanwhile, soak raisins in warm water to cover in a small bowl until plumped; drain.

Lightly beat egg with a pinch of salt.

Lightly crumble turkey into a large bowl. Add egg and cooled onion, scatter pine nuts, raisins, parsley, porcini powder, ¼ teaspoon salt, and pepper on top, and crumble moistened bread over mixture. Gently mix with your hands until ingredients are evenly distributed. Shape into 1½-inch balls; you will have 16 to 18 meatballs. Dredge meatballs in flour to coat, tossing them gently from hand to hand to remove excess flour.

Heat ¼ inch vegetable oil in a 12-inch heavy skillet until hot but not smoking. Fry meatballs, turning frequently, until golden brown on all sides, about 6 minutes. Remove from heat.

Bring sauce to a simmer in a 4- to 5-quart heavy pot.

With a slotted spoon, transfer meatballs and any stray pine nuts to simmering sauce, spreading meatballs out in one layer (discard oil). Simmer, stirring occasionally, for 30 minutes.

Meanwhile, cook pasta in an 8-quart pot of boiling salted water (3 tablespoons salt) until barely al dente, about 7 minutes; drain.

Ladle 3 cups sauce into cleaned 12-inch heavy skillet and bring to a boil over high heat. Add pasta and remaining 2 tablespoons olive oil and cook, tossing constantly, until pasta has absorbed most of sauce, about 4 minutes.

Spoon pasta onto a deep platter and arrange meatballs around it. Nap meatballs with some of sauce left in pot and sprinkle pasta with cheese. Serve with grated cheese and, if desired, remaining sauce on the side.

COOK'S NOTE

■ The meatballs can be cooked up to 1 day ahead and refrigerated, covered. Reheat them in the sauce before proceeding.

Lidia's Pasta Sauce

MAKES ABOUT 8 CUPS
ACTIVE TIME: 30 MINUTES ■ START TO FINISH: 1½ HOURS

■ Lidia Bastianich's addition of a cinnamon stick to the *sugo*, or sauce, harks back to her native Istria's proximity to Venice, long in control of the spice route. The cinnamon lends an ineffable perfume and sweetness to the sauce. ■

    1 large onion, coarsely chopped
    2 medium carrots, coarsely chopped
    ¼ cup extra-virgin olive oil
    2 tablespoons finely chopped shallot
    2 celery ribs, coarsely chopped
    1 tablespoon minced garlic
    ¼ teaspoon salt
    4 Turkish bay leaves or 2 California bay leaves
    2 tablespoons tomato paste
    1½ cups canned whole plum tomatoes in juice (from a
       28-ounce can), passed, with juice, through a food
       mill into a bowl
    ½ cup water
    1 (2- to 3-inch) cinnamon stick
    6 cups Chicken Stock (page 153) or Turkey Stock
       (page 420)

Pulse onion in a food processor until finely chopped and transfer to a bowl. Pulse carrots until finely chopped; set aside.

Heat oil in a 4- to 5-quart heavy pot over moderate heat, add onion and shallot, and cook, stirring occasionally, until softened, 4 to 5 minutes. Stir in carrots and cook, stirring, for 2 minutes. Add celery, garlic, salt, and bay leaves and cook, stirring frequently, until vegetables are softened and beginning to brown and any liquid has evaporated, about 8 minutes.

Push vegetables to one side of pot. Add tomato paste to other side and cook, stirring paste constantly, until it caramelizes, about 1 minute. Stir together vegetables and paste. Stir in tomatoes with juice. Rinse tomato bowl with ½ cup water, then add water and cinnamon stick to pot. Bring to a boil, then reduce heat and simmer, stirring occasionally, until sauce begins to thicken, about 5 minutes.

Meanwhile, bring stock to a boil.

Stir stock into thickened sauce and simmer, uncovered, stirring occasionally, for 1 hour. Sauce will be thin but full of flavor. Discard cinnamon stick and bay leaves.

COOK'S NOTE

■ The sauce can be made up to 3 days ahead. Cool, uncovered, then refrigerate, covered.

Orecchiette with Rabbit Ragù

SERVES 4 AS A MAIN COURSE
ACTIVE TIME: 1¼ HOURS ■ START TO FINISH: 1¾ HOURS

■ Orecchiette is the signature pasta of Puglia, in the heel of Italy's boot. The name means "little ears," and orecchiette are formed by pressing a thumb into a small disk of dough. In Puglia, the pasta is often served with a ragù made from rabbit or its wild cousin, hare. Maria Teresa Guarini serves this version at the farmhouse resort Masseria Marzalossa, owned by her family. The rich, deeply flavored ragù is like the most delicious cacciatore you've ever tasted, and the dimpled orecchiette are the ideal vehicles for catching the lustrous sauce and shreds of meat. ■

    1 (3-pound) rabbit (see Sources), cut into 6 pieces
       Salt and freshly ground black pepper
    ¼ cup plus 3 tablespoons extra-virgin olive oil
    1 large onion, finely chopped
    1 carrot, finely chopped
    1 celery rib, finely chopped
    2 garlic cloves, finely chopped
    2 Turkish bay leaves or 1 California bay leaf
    ¾ teaspoon finely chopped fresh rosemary
    1 cup dry white wine
    1 (28-ounce) can whole tomatoes in juice, preferably
       San Marzano, drained and chopped
    ½ cup Chicken Stock (page 153) or store-bought
       reduced-sodium broth
       Fresh Semolina Orecchiette (recipe follows) or
       1 pound dried orecchiette
    ACCOMPANIMENT: finely grated Grana Padano

Pat rabbit dry and sprinkle with ½ teaspoon salt and ¼ teaspoon pepper. Heat ¼ cup oil in a deep 12-inch heavy skillet over moderately high heat until hot but not smoking. Brown rabbit in 2 batches, turning once, about 7 minutes per batch. Transfer to a platter, reserving fat in skillet.

Add remaining 3 tablespoons oil to fat in skillet and heat until hot but not smoking. Add onion, carrot, celery, garlic, bay leaves, rosemary, and ¼ teaspoon salt and cook, stirring occasionally, until vegetables are golden brown, 8 to 10 minutes.

Add wine, bring to a boil, stirring and scraping up any brown bits, and boil until most of liquid has evaporated, about 3 minutes. Stir in tomatoes, stock, and ½ teaspoon salt and bring to a boil. Return rabbit, along with juices accumulated on platter, to skillet and nestle into sauce. Cover and simmer, stirring and turning rabbit occasionally, until both saddle pieces are tender, about 15 minutes.

Transfer saddle pieces to a plate, then continue to simmer leg pieces until tender, about 10 minutes more. Transfer remaining rabbit pieces to plate; set skillet aside.

When rabbit is cool enough to handle, remove meat from bones, discarding bone and gristle, and shred. Return meat, along with any juices, to sauce in skillet. Add ¼ teaspoon salt and ¼ teaspoon pepper and bring to a boil. Discard bay leaves.

Meanwhile, cook pasta in an 8-quart pot of boiling salted water (3 tablespoons salt) until al dente. Drain.

Transfer pasta to a large serving dish and top with sauce, stirring to combine. Serve with cheese.

COOK'S NOTE
■ The sauce can be made up to 3 days ahead. Cool, uncovered, then refrigerate, covered.

Fresh Semolina Orecchiette

MAKES ABOUT 1½ POUNDS
ACTIVE TIME: 1½ HOURS ■ START TO FINISH: 2½ HOURS

■ Made of semolina, flour, and water, this pasta dough may seem a bit stiff to work with, but it is perfect for crafting into sturdy shapes. You'll soon sink into the meditative rhythm of forming the "little ears." ■

2 cups semolina (sometimes called semolina flour; see Sources)
2 cups unbleached all-purpose flour
  Pinch of salt
1 cup lukewarm water

Stir together semolina, flour, and salt in a large bowl and make a well in center. Add lukewarm water to well and, using a fork, gradually stir in flour, pulling in flour closest to water, until a dough forms (some of flour will not be incorporated). Transfer dough to a work surface. Sift remaining flour mixture in bowl through a medium-mesh sieve into another bowl; discard any hard clumps.

Knead dough, incorporating some of sifted flour mixture as dough becomes sticky, until smooth and elastic, about 8 minutes. Divide dough into 8 pieces. Wrap each piece in plastic wrap and let stand at room temperature for 1 hour. Reserve remaining flour mixture.

Line two large trays with clean kitchen towels (not terry cloth) and dust your hands with some of remaining flour mixture. Unwrap 1 piece of dough and roll under your palms on work surface into a ½-inch-thick rope, 2 to 3 feet long. Cut into ⅓-inch pieces with a sharp knife, separating cut pieces so they do not touch. Lightly toss cut pieces with some of flour mixture.

Put 1 piece of dough cut side down on work surface (keep remaining pieces covered with a clean kitchen towel); if necessary, re-form round shape. Dust your thumb with flour mixture and press down on dough, pushing away from you and twisting thumb slightly to form an indented curled shape (like an ear). Transfer to a lined tray. Shape more orecchiette with remaining cut pieces in same manner, transferring to lined tray, then repeat rolling, cutting, and forming with remaining 7 pieces of dough.

COOK'S NOTE
■ The orecchiette can be made up to 2 days ahead and refrigerated on the towel-lined trays, wrapped in plastic wrap.

Gemelli and Mushrooms with Parmesan Crumb Topping

SERVES 4 AS A MAIN COURSE
ACTIVE TIME: 40 MINUTES ■ START TO FINISH: 1¼ HOURS

■ This dish has all the deep, woodsy flavor of stuffed mushrooms, with the delightful addition of gemelli, their twisted edges capturing every drop of savory goodness. A cascade of garlicky, cheesy bread crumbs seals the deal. ■

¼ ounce (about ¼ cup) dried porcini mushrooms
½ cup boiling water
2¾ cups coarse fresh bread crumbs (from an Italian or French loaf)
4 garlic cloves, finely chopped
⅓ cup finely chopped fresh flat-leaf parsley
3 tablespoons olive oil
Freshly ground black pepper
1 cup finely grated Parmigiano-Reggiano (about 3 ounces)
2 tablespoons unsalted butter
2 tablespoons extra-virgin olive oil
1 medium onion, finely chopped
1¼ pounds cremini mushrooms, trimmed and quartered
1 teaspoon dried oregano, crumbled
Salt
1 cup Chicken Stock (page 153) or store-bought reduced-sodium chicken or vegetable broth
½ pound gemelli, campanelle (small bell-shaped pasta), or short spiral pasta

Put a rack in middle of oven and preheat oven to 425°F. Butter a 13-by-9-inch or other 3-quart glass or ceramic baking dish.

Soak porcini in boiling water in a bowl until softened, about 20 minutes.

Meanwhile, spread out crumbs on a baking sheet and bake, stirring occasionally, until golden, about 6 minutes. Cool completely on pan on a rack. (Leave oven on.)

Toss toasted crumbs with half of garlic, parsley, olive oil, ¼ teaspoon pepper, and ½ cup cheese.

Lift porcini out of soaking liquid, squeezing excess liquid back into bowl, and rinse to remove any grit. Pour soaking liquid through a sieve lined with a dampened paper towel into another bowl and reserve. Finely chop porcini.

Heat butter and extra-virgin olive oil in a 12-inch heavy skillet over moderately high heat until foam subsides. Add onion and remaining garlic and cook, stirring, until onion is golden, about 8 minutes. Add cremini mushrooms, oregano, ½ teaspoon salt, and ¼ teaspoon pepper and cook, stirring occasionally, until liquid mushrooms give off has evaporated and mushrooms are browned, about 10 minutes. Stir in chopped porcini, reserved soaking liquid, and stock, bring to a simmer, and simmer for 1 minute.

Meanwhile, cook pasta in an 8-quart pot of boiling salted water (3 tablespoons salt) until al dente. Drain and transfer to baking dish. Stir in mushroom mixture and remaining ½ cup cheese.

Sprinkle bread crumb topping evenly over pasta and bake, uncovered, until crumbs are golden, 15 to 20 minutes.

COOK'S NOTE

■ The casserole can be made up to 1 day ahead. Cool, uncovered, and refrigerate, covered. Bring to room temperature and reheat, covered, in a 350°F oven.

CREMINI

PORCINI

Macaroni
with Four Cheeses

SERVES 8 TO 10 AS A FIRST COURSE, 6 AS A MAIN COURSE
ACTIVE TIME: 30 MINUTES ■ START TO FINISH: 30 MINUTES

■ This pasta dish, adapted from the historic hotel Villa d'Este on the west shore of Italy's Lake Como, is seriously cheesy, and judicious amounts of bacon, herbs, and tomato sauce add refinement. Buttery Bel Paese lends just the right creaminess, while the Fontina and Gruyère reinforce each other's nuttiness. The Parmesan is the great amplifier, helping the other three sing a little louder. If you have everything chopped and prepped, this comes together in a trice. But it won't wait—have people seated and ready to eat before you toss the pasta. ■

  6 bacon slices, diced
1½ pounds elbow macaroni
     Salt
  6 ounces Italian Fontina, cut into ⅓-inch dice (1 cup)
  6 ounces Bel Paese, cut into ⅓-inch dice (1 cup)
  6 ounces Gruyère, cut into ⅓-inch dice (1 cup)
  3 tablespoons canned tomato sauce
  ¼ cup heavy cream, plus additional if necessary
  ½ teaspoon minced fresh rosemary
  ½ teaspoon minced fresh sage
  ½ teaspoon minced fresh oregano
  1 large egg yolk
  1 cup finely grated Parmigiano-Reggiano (about 3 ounces)
     Freshly ground black pepper

Cook bacon in a 10-inch heavy skillet over moderate heat, stirring frequently, until browned and crisp, about 5 minutes. Transfer with a slotted spoon to paper towels to drain.

Cook macaroni in an 8-quart pot of boiling salted water (3 tablespoons salt) until al dente; drain.

Meanwhile, heat Fontina, Bel Paese, and Gruyère with tomato sauce, cream, and herbs in a 5- to 6-quart heavy pot over moderately low heat, stirring, until melted and smooth. Put egg yolk in a cup and stir in ½ cup sauce to temper, then whisk into sauce remaining in pot.

Remove sauce from heat and add macaroni, ba-con, and Parmesan, tossing to combine well. Season with salt and pepper to taste, and stir in more cream to thin sauce if necessary.

COOK'S NOTE

■ The egg yolk in this recipe will not be fully cooked. If that is a concern, see page 915.

Mexican Macaroni
and Cheese

SERVES 6 AS A FIRST COURSE, 4 AS A MAIN COURSE
ACTIVE TIME: 40 MINUTES ■ START TO FINISH:
40 MINUTES

■ One of Mexico's most famous dishes, *rajas con cre-ma*—strips of roasted poblano chiles with cream—is a natural tossed with pasta. On first taste, the pasta is seductively creamy, but after a few bites, you begin to get a pleasant zing from the poblano and serrano chiles. The tang of the crumbled *queso fresco* adds cool contrast. ■

  ½ large white onion, cut lengthwise into ¼-inch-wide slices
     Salt
  2 tablespoons unsalted butter
  ¾ pound poblano chiles (about 4), roasted (see Tips, page 914), peeled, seeded, and cut into ¼-inch-wide strips
  ½ serrano chile, minced, including seeds
  2 large garlic cloves, minced
  ½ teaspoon dried oregano, preferably Mexican, crumbled
  6 ounces dried cavatappi (ridged corkscrew pasta) or penne
  ⅔ cup *crema* (see Sources) or crème fraîche
  ¼ pound *queso fresco* (Mexican fresh white cheese; see Sources) or ricotta salata, crumbled (1 cup)

Cook onion with ½ teaspoon salt in butter in a 12-inch heavy skillet over moderately low heat, stirring occasionally, until golden, 10 to 12 minutes. Add poblanos, serrano, garlic, and oregano and cook, stirring, until fragrant, about 1 minute. Remove from heat.

Meanwhile, cook pasta in an 8-quart pot of boil-

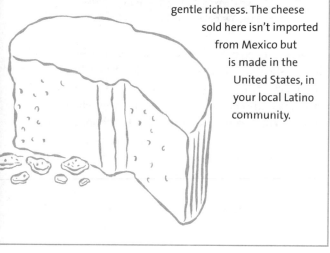
ing salted water (3 tablespoons salt) until tender. Reserve ¼ cup pasta cooking water and drain pasta.

Add pasta to chile mixture, along with *crema* and reserved cooking water. Increase heat to high and cook, tossing, until pasta is well coated, about 1 minute. Stir in cheese.

Tuna Noodle Casserole

SERVES 4 TO 6 AS A MAIN COURSE
ACTIVE TIME: 1 HOUR ■ START TO FINISH: 1½ HOURS

■ Tuna noodle—the king of casseroles—has a well-deserved place in nostalgic American hearts. With just two cans and a box of egg noodles, harried cooks could get dinner on the table in no time. But when we revisited this family favorite, we opted to trade some convenience for flavor and freshness. We lost the canned cream of mushroom soup, which is full of salt and additives, and prepared a simple white sauce, embellishing it with extra mushrooms and a little sherry—outrageously delicious and well worth the effort. ■

1 medium onion, finely chopped
Salt
4½ tablespoons unsalted butter
10 ounces white mushrooms, trimmed and sliced ¼ inch thick (4 cups)
2 teaspoons soy sauce
¼ cup sherry (any kind)
¼ cup all-purpose flour
2 cups Chicken Stock (page 153) or store-bought reduced-sodium broth
1 cup whole milk
2 teaspoons fresh lemon juice
1 (6-ounce) can tuna in olive oil, drained
Freshly ground black pepper
6 ounces (about 3¼ cups) dried curly egg noodles, preferably Pennsylvania Dutch–style
1½ cups coarse fresh bread crumbs (from 3 slices firm white sandwich bread)
¼ pound cheddar, coarsely grated (about 1 cup)
1 tablespoon vegetable oil

Put a rack in middle of oven and preheat oven to 375°F. Butter a shallow 2-quart baking dish.

Cook onion with a pinch of salt in 1½ tablespoons butter in a 12-inch heavy skillet over moderately low heat, covered, stirring occasionally, until softened, about 5 minutes. Increase heat to moderately high, add mushrooms, and cook, stirring occasionally, until they begin to give off liquid, about 2 minutes. Add soy sauce and continue to cook, stirring, until liquid mushrooms give off has evaporated. Add sherry and boil, stirring occasionally, until evaporated. Remove from heat.

Melt remaining 3 tablespoons butter in a 2- to 3-quart heavy saucepan over moderately low heat. Add flour and cook, whisking, for 3 minutes to make a roux. Add stock in a steady stream, whisking constantly, and bring to a boil, whisking. Whisk in milk, reduce heat, and simmer, whisking frequently, for 5 minutes.

Stir mushroom mixture, lemon juice, and ¼ teaspoon salt into sauce. Flake tuna into sauce and stir gently. Season with salt and pepper to taste. Remove from heat.

Cook noodles in a 6-quart pot of boiling salted water (3 tablespoons salt) until al dente. Drain noodles and return to pot. Add sauce and stir gently to combine. Transfer mixture to baking dish, spreading it evenly.

Toss together bread crumbs and cheese in a bowl. Drizzle with oil and toss again, then sprinkle evenly over casserole. Bake until topping is crisp and sauce is bubbling, 20 to 30 minutes.

COOK'S NOTE

- The casserole can be assembled, without the topping, up to 1 day ahead and refrigerated, covered. Make the topping and add it to the casserole just before baking.

Penne and Chicken Gratin

SERVES 10 TO 12 AS A MAIN COURSE
ACTIVE TIME: 2 HOURS ■ START TO FINISH: 4 HOURS
(INCLUDES MAKING STOCK)

■ Think chicken tetrazzini—but ten times better. This sophisticated gratin combines nutty Gruyère, sharp Parmesan, and juicy poached chicken, topping it off with a crisp, cheesy crust. If you're short on time, feel free to use cooked rotisserie chickens (see Cook's Note) and canned chicken broth. We love to serve this for a casual holiday meal, but you can easily halve the recipe to make just one gratin. ■

FOR CHICKEN AND STOCK

- 2 (3½- to 4-pound) chickens, giblets reserved
- 10 cups cold water
- 1 celery rib, quartered
- 1 carrot, quartered
- 1 medium onion, quartered
- 1 large garlic clove, smashed
- 2 fresh thyme sprigs
- 1 teaspoon salt
- ¼ teaspoon black peppercorns

FOR CHEESE SAUCE AND GRATIN

- 1 stick (8 tablespoons) unsalted butter
- 1 garlic clove, minced
- ½ cup all-purpose flour
- 3 cups whole milk
- 1 cup (8 ounces) crème fraîche
- Salt
- ½ teaspoon freshly ground black pepper
- ¼ teaspoon cayenne
- 1 pound Gruyère, coarsely grated (about 5 cups)
- 1¼ cups finely grated Parmigiano-Reggiano (1 ounce; use a rasp grater)
- 1 pound penne rigate or other short tubular pasta
- 6 cups fine fresh bread crumbs (from 18 slices firm white sandwich bread)

SPECIAL EQUIPMENT: two 2½- to 3-quart gratin dishes or other shallow baking dishes

MAKE THE STOCK: Using a large sharp knife or poultry shears, cut down each side of backbone of each chicken to remove it; reserve backbones. Cut wing tips and second joints of wings from chickens. Cut each chicken into quarters. Put backbones, wing tips, second joints, and giblets, except livers, in a 6- to 8-quart pot, add water, celery, carrot, onion, garlic, thyme, salt, and peppercorns. Bring to a boil. Add chicken quarters and return to a boil, skimming off any foam, then reduce heat and simmer, uncovered, for 10 minutes. Remove from heat and let stand, covered, for 40 minutes.

With tongs, transfer chicken quarters to a shallow baking pan. When chicken is cool enough to handle, remove meat from skin and bones. Transfer meat to a cutting board and return skin and bones to pot. Cut chicken into 1-inch pieces and reserve in a large bowl.

Bring stock to a boil and boil for 40 minutes. Pour stock through a fine-mesh sieve into a large bowl; discard solids. Let stand for 5 minutes, then skim off fat. Set aside 4 cups stock for sauce. (Reserve remaining stock for another use.)

MAKE THE SAUCE AND COOK THE PASTA: Put a rack in middle of oven and preheat oven to 425°F. Butter gratin dishes.

Melt butter in a 4-quart heavy pot over moderate heat. Add garlic and cook, whisking, for 1 minute. Reduce heat to moderately low, add flour, and cook, whisking, for 3 minutes to make a roux. Add milk and reserved 4 cups stock in a steady stream, whisking constantly, and bring to a boil, whisking. Reduce heat and simmer, whisking frequently, until sauce is slightly thickened, about 10 minutes. Remove from heat and stir in crème fraîche, 1 teaspoon salt, pepper, cayenne, 2 cups Gruyère, and ½ cup Parmigiano-Reggiano.

Meanwhile, cook pasta in an 8-quart pot of boiling salted water (3 tablespoons salt) until not quite al dente (pasta should still be firm).

ASSEMBLE THE GRATIN: Drain pasta and return it to pot. Add chicken and sauce, tossing to coat. Divide pasta mixture between gratin dishes.

Toss bread crumbs with remaining Gruyère and ¾ cup Parmigiano-Reggiano and sprinkle evenly over pasta mixture. Bake gratins until crumbs are golden brown and sauce is bubbling, 20 to 30 minutes. Let stand for 10 minutes before serving.

COOK'S NOTES

- If using rotisserie chickens, pull the meat from the bones and reserve. Make the stock by cooking the skin and bones with the celery, carrot, onion, garlic, thyme, salt, peppercorns, and 8 cups water for 40 minutes (total).

- The casserole, without the topping, can be assembled up to 1 day ahead and refrigerated, covered. Add the topping to the casserole just before baking.

Timballo

SERVES 6 TO 8 AS A MAIN COURSE
ACTIVE TIME: 1¾ HOURS ■ START TO FINISH: 3 HOURS

■ Think of this colorful baked pasta dish as a drum-shaped lasagne, with ziti taking the place of flat lasagne noodles. As the timballo bakes gently in a water bath, the meaty tomato sauce and rich, chard-flecked béchamel work their way into the tubes of pasta and mingle with the creamy mozzarella and sharp Parmesan. The result is magnificent and well worth the effort (both sauces can be made ahead). For added flair, arrange the ziti in a decorative pattern as you assemble the first layer of the timballo. ■

FOR MEAT SAUCE
  1½ tablespoons extra-virgin olive oil
  ½ pound sweet Italian sausage, casings removed if in links
  1 medium onion, finely chopped
  1 Turkish bay leaf or ½ California bay leaf
  1 carrot, finely chopped
  1 celery rib, finely chopped

  ¼ teaspoon salt
  1 tablespoon tomato paste
  ½ cup dry red wine
  1 (14- to 15-ounce) can whole tomatoes in juice, passed, with juices, through a food mill into a bowl
  Pinch of sugar

FOR PASTA
  ¾ pound ziti
  Salt

FOR CHARD IN BÉCHAMEL SAUCE
  1 pound green Swiss chard, stems and center ribs discarded, leaves coarsely chopped
  1½ tablespoons unsalted butter
  2 garlic cloves, minced
  1 tablespoon all-purpose flour
  1 cup whole milk
  ¼ teaspoon salt
  ⅛ teaspoon freshly ground white pepper
  ⅛ teaspoon freshly grated nutmeg
  2 tablespoons finely grated Parmigiano-Reggiano

FOR ASSEMBLY
  ¼ pound mozzarella, preferably fresh (not unsalted), cut into ½-inch cubes (scant 1 cup)
  6 tablespoons finely grated Parmigiano-Reggiano

SPECIAL EQUIPMENT: a 2-quart soufflé dish; parchment paper

MAKE THE MEAT SAUCE: Heat oil in a 12-inch heavy skillet over moderately high heat until hot but not smoking. Add sausage and cook, stirring and breaking up lumps with a fork, until no longer pink, about 5 minutes. Add onion and bay leaf and cook, stirring frequently, until onion begins to brown, 5 to 7 minutes. Add carrot, celery, and salt and cook, stirring occasionally, until vegetables begin to soften, about 4 minutes. Add tomato paste and cook, stirring constantly, for 1 minute. Add wine and deglaze by boiling, scraping up any brown bits, until most of liquid has evaporated, 1 to 2 minutes. Add tomato puree and sugar, bring to a boil, and boil, stirring frequently, until thickened, 8 to 10 minutes. Remove from heat and cool; discard bay leaf.

COOK THE PASTA: Cook pasta in a 6- to 8-quart pot of boiling salted water (3 tablespoons salt) until al dente. Using a wire skimmer, transfer pasta to a colander to drain (do not rinse); keep water at a boil.

Spread pasta in an oiled baking pan to cool while you prepare chard.

MAKE THE CHARD: Add chard to boiling water, reduce heat, and simmer, uncovered, until tender, 3 to 5 minutes. Drain and transfer to a bowl of ice and cold water to stop the cooking. Drain chard and squeeze by handfuls to eliminate excess water, then finely chop.

Heat butter in a 1½- to 2-quart heavy saucepan over moderate heat until foam subsides. Add garlic and cook, whisking, for 1 minute. Add flour and cook, whisking, for 1 minute, to make a roux. Add milk in a slow stream, whisking, and bring to a boil, whisking. Reduce heat and simmer, whisking occasionally, until sauce is slightly thickened, about 5 minutes. Stir in chard, salt, white pepper, nutmeg, and Parmesan and remove from heat.

ASSEMBLE AND BAKE THE TIMBALLO: Put a rack in lower third of oven and preheat oven to 375°F.

Oil soufflé dish, line bottom with a round of parchment paper, and oil parchment. Cover bottom of dish with a single layer of pasta, arranging pasta in a decorative pattern if you wish. Sprinkle ½ cup mozzarella and 3 tablespoons Parmesan over pasta, then spoon half of meat sauce in an even layer over cheese. Arrange one third of remaining pasta over meat sauce and top with all of chard and another layer of pasta (about half of remainder). Sprinkle with remainder of cheeses, then spoon remaining meat sauce over cheese. Top with remaining pasta (fill dish only to top; you may have extra pasta). Cover pasta with an oiled round of parchment (oiled side down) and cover dish with foil.

Put soufflé dish in a wide 6- to 8-quart pot and add enough boiling water to pot to come halfway up sides of dish. Bake until sauce is bubbling and a metal skewer or thin knife inserted in center of timballo comes out hot to the touch, about 1 hour. Remove soufflé dish from water bath and let stand, covered, for 15 minutes.

Remove foil and parchment and run a knife around edge of timballo to loosen, then invert a platter over soufflé dish and invert timballo onto platter. Remove remaining parchment.

COOK'S NOTE

■ The meat sauce and the chard in the béchamel sauce can be made up to 1 day ahead. Cool, uncovered, then refrigerate separately, covered. Bring to room temperature before proceeding.

Vegetable Lasagne

SERVES 8 AS A MAIN COURSE
ACTIVE TIME: 1½ HOURS ■ START TO FINISH: 2½ HOURS

■ This lasagne is all about the vegetables—layers of roasted eggplant, zucchini, and creamed spinach, along with homemade tomato sauce and two cheeses. No-boil noodles are easy to use and the result is light and delicate. Be sure to squeeze the spinach well so that it is very dry, or water will collect in the bottom of the pan. ■

FOR SAUCE
   3 tablespoons olive oil
   1 medium onion, finely chopped
   4 garlic cloves, minced

2 tablespoons tomato paste

2 (28-ounce) cans whole tomatoes in juice, preferably Italian, drained, juice reserved, and finely chopped

1 teaspoon sugar

1 teaspoon salt

½ teaspoon freshly ground black pepper

3 tablespoons chopped fresh basil or flat-leaf parsley

FOR RICOTTA FILLING

1½ pounds (3 cups) whole-milk ricotta

1 large egg, lightly beaten

½ cup finely grated Parmigiano-Reggiano

¼ cup finely chopped fresh flat-leaf parsley

½ teaspoon salt

¼ teaspoon freshly ground black pepper

Pinch of freshly grated nutmeg

FOR VEGETABLES

1 pound eggplant, cut lengthwise into ¼-inch-thick slices

1 pound zucchini, cut lengthwise into ¼-inch-thick slices

3 tablespoons olive oil

1 teaspoon salt

½ teaspoon freshly ground black pepper

FOR CREAMED SPINACH

1½ cups whole milk

3 tablespoons olive oil

3 garlic cloves, minced

3 tablespoons all-purpose flour

3 tablespoons finely grated Parmigiano-Reggiano

2 (10-ounce) packages frozen chopped spinach, thawed and squeezed dry

Salt and freshly ground black pepper

FOR ASSEMBLY

16 oven-ready (no-boil) lasagne noodles (from two 9-ounce packages)

1 pound mozzarella, preferably fresh, coarsely grated (about 4 cups)

MAKE THE SAUCE: Heat oil in a 4- to 5-quart heavy pot over moderately high heat until hot but not smoking. Add onion and cook, stirring, until golden, about 6 minutes. Add garlic and cook, stirring, for 1 minute. Add tomato paste, tomatoes with juice, sugar, salt, and pepper and bring to a boil. Simmer, stirring occasionally, until sauce is thickened, about 45 minutes. Stir in basil and remove from heat.

MEANWHILE, MAKE THE RICOTTA FILLING: Stir together all ingredients in a bowl until combined. Cover and refrigerate until ready to use.

COOK THE VEGETABLES: Put racks in upper and lower thirds of oven and preheat oven to 400°F. Oil two large baking sheets.

Arrange eggplant slices on one baking sheet and zucchini slices on the other. Brush tops of slices with oil and sprinkle with salt and pepper. Bake until tender, turning once, 15 to 20 minutes. Transfer baking sheets to racks to cool completely. Reduce oven temperature to 375°F and move rack to middle of oven.

MAKE THE SPINACH LAYER: Heat milk in a small saucepan over moderate heat, stirring, until warm.

Meanwhile, heat oil in a 3-quart heavy saucepan over moderately low heat until hot. Add garlic and cook, stirring occasionally, until softened, about 4 minutes. Add flour and cook, whisking, for 2 minutes to make a roux. Add warm milk in a steady stream, whisking constantly, then simmer sauce, whisking frequently, until thickened, 3 to 4 minutes. Stir in cheese, spinach, and salt and pepper to taste and cook, stirring, until heated through. Remove from heat.

ASSEMBLE THE LASAGNE: Oil a 13-by-9-inch glass or ceramic baking dish. Spread 2 cups tomato sauce in baking dish and cover with 4 lasagne noodles, slightly overlapping them. Spread with ricotta mixture, then cover with eggplant, overlapping to fit. Top with 4 more noodles and spread with 1½ cups tomato sauce. Spread spinach mixture over sauce and cover with 4 more noodles. Top with zucchini, overlapping to fit, and cover with remaining 4 noodles. Spread with remaining sauce and sprinkle top evenly with mozzarella.

Cover lasagne with well-buttered foil and bake for 45 minutes. Remove foil and bake until top is bubbling and lightly browned, 10 to 15 minutes more. Let stand for 15 minutes before serving.

COOK'S NOTES

- The tomato sauce and creamed spinach can be made up to 2 days ahead. Cool, uncovered, then refrigerate separately, covered.
- The lasagne can be assembled up to 1 day ahead and refrigerated, covered. Bring to room temperature before baking.

THE SIMPLE JOYS OF MAKING PASTA

Why make pasta at home when you can pluck a package of "fresh" pasta from the refrigerated aisle in supermarkets almost everywhere? Because there's no comparison in taste and texture: the light yet rich and satisfying taste and texture of homemade pasta is far better than anything you can buy (and most packaged fresh pasta contains additives to give it prolonged shelf life). And even if you are not an especially ambitious cook, you'll find that knowing how to make fresh pasta is a significant key to broadening your kitchen repertoire. You do have to take your time, but the process is easy and something you can master in an hour or so. The first time you roll out a long, satiny, almost transparent sheet of pasta dough, not only will you be amazed at what you've just accomplished, but there will be no doubt in your mind that dinner will be extraordinary.

Making pasta dough in the food processor is a breeze, but if you don't have one, don't let that stop you: the traditional well method has worked beautifully for centuries, and it couldn't be simpler. The trick, if there is one, is realizing that the eggs (or sometimes just yolks) are in charge. Although recipes will give you a set amount of flour, the eggs will absorb just so much of it and no more. Depending on the temperature of your hands, the room, and your work surface, the dough will be a little different every time, but the more often you make pasta, the more the method will become intuitive. The specific ingredients in the dough depend on the recipe, but the general technique is the same.

Mound the flour on a work surface, preferably wood (marble or stone is too cold). Form a well in the center, but don't make it too big—you want to keep a strong wall around it (1).

Add the eggs (or yolks) and any other ingredients to the well and gently beat with a fork until the mixture turns into a little lake (2).

Gradually draw in flour from the inside of the wall, working your way around evenly so that the wall doesn't collapse. Help keep the wall intact by cupping one hand around it (3).

Continue to stir with the fork (4). When the mixture becomes too sloppy and cumbersome to work with a fork, use your hands to work in the flour, still a little at a time, until the dough forms a ball. Then knead the dough until it's smooth and elastic, 5 to 10 minutes (5).

For rolling out the dough, you'll need a pasta machine (available at kitchenware stores for $40 to about $70; the pasta attachment for the KitchenAid stand mixer is another, though pricier, alternative). Don't buy a pasta machine with nonstick rollers; these make the pasta too slick, and the sauce won't cling the way it's supposed to. If your pasta machine is new, you'll need to sacrifice a piece of dough by running it through the rollers to remove the oil from the machine. It's a good idea to put the pasta machine on a large surface, since the strips of dough will get longer each time you put them through the rollers. If your machine has a clamp, find an area on your counter that will give you the most space for handling the dough as it comes out of the machine. Or use your kitchen table.

Pat the dough into a flat rectangle and dust with flour. Set the rollers of the pasta machine on the widest setting and center the rectangle so that it goes through evenly, short end first. Fold the rectangle into thirds, like a letter, dust it with flour, and feed it, short end first, through the rollers again. Repeat 7 more times, folding it into thirds and dusting with flour so it won't (literally) gum up the works. Turn the dial to the next (narrower) setting and feed the dough through the rollers without folding it, short end first, flouring it as needed and cranking continuously, catching it on the other side with your free hand, until it's through the rollers. Before you put the strip through again, run your hand along it to check for any sticky spots. Dust those with a little flour, brushing off any excess. Hang the rolled-out dough sheets on the back of a chair or a pasta rack, if you have one, while you roll the remaining sheets.

If you are making the dough sheets into spaghetti or fettuccine, don't dry the dough for too long, or it will be too brittle to put through the cutters.

Lasagne Bolognese

SERVES 8 AS A MAIN COURSE
ACTIVE TIME: 2 HOURS ■ START TO FINISH: 3 HOURS
(INCLUDES MAKING PASTA)

■ This is the most miraculous lasagne we've ever tasted—delicate, refined, and ethereal. Adapted from a recipe from the New York City chef Mario Batali and modeled on a classic from Emilia-Romagna, it features whisper-thin sheets of freshly made pasta flecked with spinach and a rich yet understated ragù of tomatoes, veal, pork, and pancetta that is cooked down to its essence. A *besciamella* gently marries it all together. Though we ordinarily include a food-processor option for making pasta dough, the success of this recipe really rests on the otherworldly lightness of hand-kneaded dough. You may have more pasta than you'll need, and because it is a bit of an endeavor to make, you'll want to save it (see Cook's Note). ■

FOR RAGÙ
- 5 tablespoons extra-virgin olive oil
- 3 tablespoons unsalted butter
- 1 carrot, finely chopped
- 1 medium onion, finely chopped
- 1 celery rib, finely chopped
- 1 garlic clove, thinly sliced
- ¼ pound sliced pancetta (Italian unsmoked bacon), slices cut into quarters
- 1 pound ground veal
- 1 pound ground pork (not lean)
- ¼ cup tomato paste
- 1 cup whole milk
- 1 cup dry white wine
- 1 teaspoon salt
- ½ teaspoon freshly ground black pepper

FOR PASTA DOUGH (see Cook's Note)
- Salt
- 1 cup firmly packed spinach (coarse stems removed)
- 4 extra-large eggs
- ½ teaspoon extra-virgin olive oil
- About 4 cups unbleached all-purpose flour

FOR BESCIAMELLA
- 5 tablespoons unsalted butter
- ¼ cup unbleached all-purpose flour
- 3 cups whole milk
- 1½ teaspoons salt
- ½ teaspoon freshly grated nutmeg

FOR ASSEMBLING LASAGNE
- Salt
- 2 tablespoons extra-virgin olive oil
- 9 tablespoons finely grated Parmigiano-Reggiano

SPECIAL EQUIPMENT: a pasta machine

MAKE THE RAGÙ: Heat oil and butter in a 6- to 8-quart wide heavy pot over moderate heat until butter is melted. Add carrot, onion, celery, and garlic and cook, stirring occasionally, until tender but not browned, 10 to 15 minutes.

Meanwhile, pulse pancetta in a food processor until finely chopped.

When vegetables are tender, increase heat to high and stir in veal, pork, and pancetta. Cook, stirring occasionally and breaking up any lumps, until meat is starting to brown, 10 to 15 minutes. Stir in tomato paste, milk, and wine, bring to a simmer, and gently simmer, uncovered, over low heat, stirring occasionally, until almost all liquid has evaporated but ragù is still moist, 1 to 1½ hours. Stir in salt and pepper and remove from heat.

MEANWHILE, MAKE THE DOUGH: Bring 3 quarts water to a boil in a 4- to 5-quart pot and add 1 tablespoon salt. Blanch spinach in boiling water for 45 seconds, then drain in a sieve and immediately transfer to a bowl of ice and cold water to stop the cooking. Drain spinach and squeeze dry in a kitchen towel, removing as much liquid as possible. Chop very fine.

Stir together spinach, eggs, and oil in a small bowl until well combined.

Mound 3½ cups flour on a work surface, preferably wooden, and make a well in center with your fingertips (page 224). Add egg mixture and gently beat with a fork, keeping egg mixture enclosed in well, until combined. Gradually stir in enough flour to form a paste, pulling in flour closest to egg mixture while supporting outside of wall with your other hand and keeping wall intact. When you have a thick paste that you can't stir any more, and about half of the flour is incorporated, start kneading dough with both hands, using your palms (not fingers) and kneading in some remaining flour from work surface. Once you have a cohesive mass (you will have ½ to 1 cup unincorporated flour), remove dough from work surface and scrape clean with a pastry scraper or a knife, discarding any left-over bits of dough and flour. Lightly dust work surface with clean flour and continue kneading until dough is firm and elastic, about 8 minutes. (Dough will be firm.)

Wrap dough in plastic wrap and let stand at room temperature for 30 to 45 minutes. (Dough will soften as it rests.)

MEANWHILE, MAKE THE BESCIAMELLA: Melt butter in a 2- to 3-quart heavy saucepan over moderate heat. Add flour, whisking to make a roux, then cook roux, whisking frequently, until pale golden brown, 4 to 6 minutes.

Meanwhile, heat milk in a 1- to 1½-quart saucepan until just about to boil. Add milk 1 cup at a time to roux, whisking constantly until very smooth. Bring sauce to a boil, whisking, and cook, whisking, for 30 seconds. Remove from heat and whisk in salt and nutmeg. Cover with a buttered round of wax paper (buttered side down) and cool to room temperature, stirring occasionally.

MEANWHILE, ROLL OUT THE PASTA: Cut pasta dough into 8 equal pieces. Cover 7 pieces with plastic wrap. Pat out remaining piece of dough into a flat rectangle and lightly dust with flour.

Set rollers of pasta machine on widest setting. Feed rectangle, a short end first, through rollers. Fold rectangle crosswise in half and feed it, folded end first, through rollers 7 more times in same manner, folding dough in half and dusting with flour if necessary to prevent sticking. Turn dial to next (narrower) setting and feed dough through rollers without folding, a short end first. Continue to feed dough through rollers without folding, once on each setting, until you reach narrowest setting. Lay pasta sheet on a lightly floured surface to dry until slightly leathery but still flexible, about 10 minutes. Meanwhile, roll out remaining pieces of dough in same manner.

Trim ends and cut pasta sheets into 5-inch lengths. Cover with a barely dampened kitchen towel.

ASSEMBLE AND BAKE THE LASAGNE: Put a rack in middle of oven and preheat oven to 375°F.

Bring an 8-quart pot of water to a boil and add 2 tablespoons salt. Set a bowl of ice and cold water next to the stovetop and add oil to ice bath. Drop 6 pieces of pasta into boiling water and cook until just tender, about 1 minute. Transfer with a slotted spoon to ice bath to chill, then transfer to clean kitchen towels, laying pasta flat, and pat dry. Keep water at a boil.

Spread 1 cup ragù over bottom of lasagne pan (ragù will barely cover bottom) and sprinkle with 1½ tablespoons Parmigiano-Reggiano. Cover with cooked pasta (pieces can overlap slightly), and spread ½ cup besciamella over pasta (layer will be thin).

Cook, chill, and dry remaining pasta 6 pieces at a time (you may have some leftover uncooked pasta; see Cook's Note) and layer with remaining ingredients in same sequence 4 more times (ragù, cheese, pasta, and besciamella), ending with 1 cup besciamella. Sprinkle top of lasagne with remaining 1½ tablespoons cheese.

Bake lasagne, uncovered, until top is pale golden in spots and sauces are bubbling, about 45 minutes. Let stand for 10 minutes before serving.

COOK'S NOTES

- For more information on making pasta, see page 224.
- The ragù and besciamella can be made up to 2 days ahead. Cool completely, uncovered, then refrigerate separately, covered. Warm the ragù over low heat just until stirrable before using.
- The lasagne can be assembled up to 4 hours ahead and refrigerated, covered.
- Any leftover uncooked pasta can be lightly dusted with flour and frozen in a sealable plastic bag; do not thaw before cooking.

Arugula and Goat Cheese Ravioli

SERVES 8 AS A FIRST COURSE, 4 AS A MAIN COURSE
ACTIVE TIME: 2 HOURS ■ START TO FINISH: 2½ HOURS

■ Stuffed with a combination of goat cheese, ricotta, peppery arugula, and lemon zest, these ravioli offer loads of flavor with each bite. A brown-butter pine-nut sauce is light enough that the taste of the homemade pasta comes shining through. ■

FOR PASTA DOUGH (see Cook's Note)

- 2 cups cake flour (not self-rising)
- ½ cup all-purpose flour, plus additional for kneading
- 4 large egg yolks
- 3 tablespoons extra-virgin olive oil
- 1 teaspoon salt
- ½ cup water

FOR FILLING

- 2 tablespoons unsalted butter
- 1½ teaspoons finely chopped garlic
- ¾ teaspoon salt
- ¾ teaspoon freshly ground black pepper
- 1 pound arugula, tough stems discarded
- 1 teaspoon finely grated lemon zest
- ½ cup soft mild goat cheese
- ½ cup whole-milk ricotta, preferably fresh (for homemade, see page 231)

FOR SAUCE

- ½ stick (4 tablespoons) unsalted butter
- ⅓ cup pine nuts
- 1 tablespoon finely chopped garlic
- ¼ teaspoon salt
- ½ teaspoon freshly ground black pepper
- 2 teaspoons fresh lemon juice
- ¼ cup extra-virgin olive oil
- ½ cup chopped arugula

SPECIAL EQUIPMENT: a pasta machine

TO MAKE THE DOUGH IN A FOOD PROCESSOR: Blend together all ingredients in processor until mixture just begins to form a ball. Transfer to a lightly floured surface and knead, incorporating only as much additional flour as necessary to keep dough from sticking, until smooth and elastic, 6 to 8 minutes. Cover dough with an inverted bowl and let stand at room temperature for 1 hour (to make rolling easier).

TO MAKE THE DOUGH BY HAND: Whisk together flours in a bowl, then mound on a work surface, preferably wooden, and make a well in center with your fingertips (see page 224). Add yolks, oil, salt, and water to well and gently beat with a fork, keeping egg mixture enclosed in well, until combined. Gradually stir in enough flour to form a paste, pulling in flour closest to egg mixture while supporting outside of wall with your other hand and keeping wall intact. Knead remaining flour into mixture to form a dough

HOW TO FORM RAVIOLI

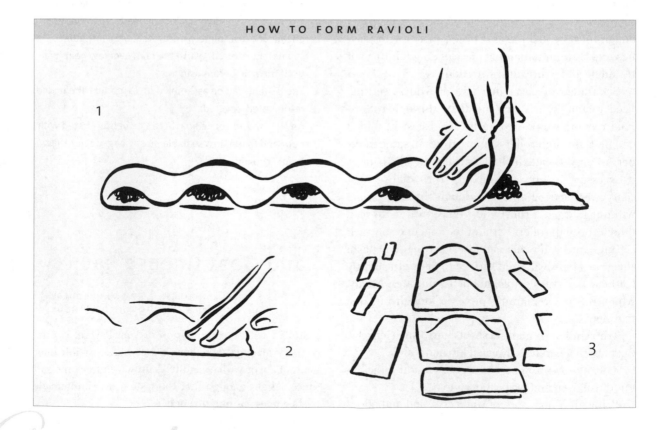

(it will be soft and sticky). Knead dough until smooth and elastic, 8 to 10 minutes. Cover with an inverted bowl and let stand for 1 hour (to make rolling easier).

MEANWHILE, MAKE THE FILLING: Heat butter in a 12-inch heavy skillet over moderate heat until foam subsides. Add garlic, salt, and pepper and cook, stirring occasionally, until garlic begins to turn golden, 1 to 2 minutes. Add arugula and zest and cook, turning with tongs, until arugula is wilted, 2 to 4 minutes. Transfer arugula mixture to a fine-mesh sieve set over a bowl and press with back of a wooden spoon to extract excess liquid.

Finely chop arugula mixture. Stir together arugula mixture and cheeses in a bowl.

MAKE THE RAVIOLI: Cut dough into 8 equal pieces. Cover 7 pieces with a clean kitchen towel (not terry cloth). Pat out remaining piece into a flat rectangle and generously dust with flour.

Set rollers of pasta machine on widest setting. Feed rectangle, a short end first, through rollers. Fold rectangle in thirds, like a letter, and feed it, a short end first, through rollers. Repeat 7 more times in same manner, folding dough in thirds and dusting with flour as necessary to prevent sticking. Turn dial to next (narrower) setting and feed dough through rollers without folding, a short end first. Continue to feed dough through without folding, once on each setting, until you reach the second-to-narrowest setting. (Do not roll too thin, or pasta will tear when filled.)

Put sheet of dough on a lightly floured surface with a long side nearest you. Starting ¾ inch from end of sheet, drop 5 or 6 rounded teaspoon-sized mounds of filling 1½ inches apart in a row down center of right half of sheet. Lift left half of sheet and drape over mounds (1). Press down firmly but gently around each mound, forcing out air (2). Air pockets increase the chance that ravioli will break during cooking. With a fluted pastry wheel or sharp knife, cut pasta (between mounds) into ravioli and trim edges as necessary to make roughly 2-inch squares (3). Line a large baking sheet with a clean kitchen towel (not terry cloth) and arrange ravioli in one layer in it. Make more ravioli with remaining dough and filling in same manner, transferring to baking sheet.

MAKE THE SAUCE: Heat butter in a 12-inch heavy skillet over moderate heat until foam subsides. Add

pine nuts and toast, stirring frequently, until pale golden, about 4 minutes. Add garlic, salt, and pepper and cook, stirring frequently, until garlic begins to turn golden, about 2 minutes. Add lemon juice and oil, swirling skillet to combine, and remove from heat.

COOK THE RAVIOLI: Bring an 8-quart pot of salted water (3 tablespoons salt) to a boil, then reduce heat to a gentle boil. Meanwhile, reheat sauce over low heat if necessary.

Add half of ravioli to gently boiling water, carefully stirring to separate, and cook, adjusting heat to keep at a gentle boil, until pasta is just tender, 2 to 3 minutes. Lift out ravioli with a slotted spoon, draining well over pot, transfer to skillet with sauce, and gently swirl skillet to coat. Transfer ravioli, with half of sauce, to a platter and sprinkle evenly with half of chopped arugula. Repeat with remaining pasta, sauce, and arugula.

COOK'S NOTES

- For more information on making pasta, see page 224.
- The dough can be made up to 6 hours ahead and refrigerated, tightly wrapped in plastic wrap.
- The filling can be made up to 2 days ahead and refrigerated, covered.
- The ravioli can be made up to 4 hours ahead and refrigerated on the towel-lined baking sheet, covered with plastic wrap.

Pork and Pancetta Ravioli with Vegetable "Bolognese" Sauce

SERVES 6 TO 8 AS A MAIN COURSE
ACTIVE TIME: 1½ HOURS ■ START TO FINISH: 3 HOURS

■ These luxurious little packets are worth every ounce of effort. Silky fresh pasta is rolled very thin, then stuffed with a meaty filling of ground pork, finely chopped pancetta, and shallot. The tomato sauce shares many of the ingredients of a classic Bolognese—carrots, celery, wine—but omits the milk and meat. The result is homey but very special. ■

FOR PASTA DOUGH (see Cook's Note)
- 3 cups unbleached all-purpose flour
- 4 large eggs
- 2–3 tablespoons water
- Salt

FOR SAUCE
- 1 (28-ounce) can whole tomatoes in juice, preferably Italian
- 3 tablespoons olive oil
- 1 medium onion, finely chopped
- 1 carrot, finely chopped
- 2 celery ribs, finely chopped
- 3 garlic cloves, minced
- ½ cup dry red wine
- 1 cup water
- ½ teaspoon salt

FOR FILLING
- 2 tablespoons olive oil
- ¼ pound thinly sliced pancetta (Italian unsmoked bacon), minced
- 1 large shallot, finely chopped
- 10 ounces ground pork (not lean)
- 1 large egg
- 1 large egg yolk
- ⅔ cup finely grated pecorino Romano or Parmigiano-Reggiano
- 2 tablespoons minced fresh flat-leaf parsley
- ½ teaspoon salt
- ¼ teaspoon freshly ground black pepper

ACCOMPANIMENT: finely grated pecorino Romano or Parmigiano-Reggiano

SPECIAL EQUIPMENT: a pasta machine

TO MAKE THE DOUGH IN A FOOD PROCESSOR: Blend flour, eggs, 2 tablespoons water, and 1 teaspoon salt in a food processor until mixture just begins to form a ball, adding more water drop by drop if dough is too dry (dough should be firm and not sticky). Process dough for 15 seconds more to knead it. Transfer to a floured surface, cover with an inverted bowl, and let stand for 1 hour (to make rolling easier).

TO MAKE THE DOUGH BY HAND: Mound flour on a work surface, preferably wooden, and make a well in center with your fingertips (page 224). Add eggs, 2 tablespoons water, and salt to well and gently beat with a fork, keeping egg mixture enclosed in well, until combined. Gradually stir in enough flour to form a paste, pulling in flour closest to egg mixture while supporting outside of wall with your other hand and keeping wall intact. Knead remaining flour into mixture to form a dough, adding more water drop by drop if dough is too dry (dough should be firm and not sticky). Knead dough until smooth and elastic, 8 to 10 minutes. Cover with an inverted bowl and let stand for 1 hour (to make rolling easier).

MAKE THE SAUCE: Puree tomatoes with their juice in a blender until almost smooth; set aside.

Heat oil in a 5- to 6-quart heavy pot over moderately high heat until hot but not smoking. Add onion, carrot, celery, and garlic and cook, stirring, until golden, 10 to 12 minutes. Add wine, bring to a boil, and cook until all liquid is evaporated. Add tomatoes, water, and salt, bring to a simmer, and simmer, uncovered, stirring occasionally, until sauce is thickened, about 30 minutes. Remove from heat.

MAKE THE FILLING: Heat oil in a 12-inch heavy skillet over moderately high heat until hot but not smoking. Add pancetta and cook, stirring, until golden, about 4 minutes. Transfer with a slotted spoon to a bowl. Add shallot to skillet and cook, stirring, until golden, about 5 minutes. Add to pancetta and let cool slightly, about 5 minutes.

Add pork, egg, yolk, cheese, parsley, salt, and pepper and stir just until combined; do not overmix. Refrigerate, covered, until ready to use.

MAKE THE RAVIOLI: Cut dough into 6 equal pieces. Pat out each piece into a flat rectangle and cover with a clean kitchen towel (not terry cloth).

Set rollers of pasta machine on widest setting. Lightly dust 1 rectangle with flour and feed, a short end first, through rollers. Fold rectangle in thirds, like a letter, and feed it, a short end first, through rollers. Repeat 7 times in same manner, folding dough in thirds and dusting with flour as necessary to prevent sticking. Turn dial to next (narrower) setting and feed dough through rollers without folding, a short end first. Continue to feed dough through rollers without folding, once on each setting, until you reach the narrowest setting. Put sheet on a lightly floured surface and cover with a clean kitchen towel (not terry cloth). Roll out and cut remaining pieces of dough in same manner.

Put 1 sheet of dough on a lightly floured surface with a long side nearest you. Starting ¾ inch from end of sheet, drop 5 or 6 rounded teaspoon-sized mounds of filling 1½ inches apart in a row down center of right half of sheet. Lift left half of sheet and drape over mounds (see page 228). Press down firmly but gently around each mound, forcing out air. Air pockets increase the chance that the ravioli will break during cooking. With a fluted pastry wheel or a sharp knife, cut pasta (between mounds) into ravioli and trim edges as necessary to make roughly 2-inch squares. Transfer to a floured baking sheet. Repeat with remaining dough sheets and filling. Let ravioli dry on baking sheet, covered with a clean kitchen towel (not terry cloth), for at least 30 minutes, and up to 3 hours.

COOK THE RAVIOLI: Bring an 8-quart pot of boiling salted water (3 tablespoons salt) to a boil, then reduce heat to a gentle boil. Meanwhile, reheat sauce over low heat.

Cook ravioli in 2 batches, gently stirring to separate it, until pasta is tender and filling is cooked through, 4 to 6 minutes. Transfer ravioli to a large serving bowl with a slotted spoon and spoon sauce over. Serve with grated cheese.

COOK'S NOTES

■ For more information on making pasta, see page 224.
■ The sauce can be made up to 4 days ahead. Cool, uncovered, then refrigerate, covered.
■ The ravioli can be made up to 4 hours ahead and refrigerated on the floured baking sheet, covered with a kitchen towel.

Ricotta Gnudi with Roasted Tomatoes

SERVES 4 AS A MAIN COURSE
ACTIVE TIME: 35 MINUTES ■ START TO FINISH: 1¼ HOURS

■ These delicate cheese dumplings are like ravioli fillings that have lost their wrappers (*gnudi* translates as "naked"), but you won't miss the pasta. If you can get fresh ricotta, by all means use it—it produces light, very tender dumplings—or make your own. Roasting concentrates the sweetness of the tomatoes and will pep up even lesser specimens, though it's well worth starting off with the best plum tomatoes you can find. ■

GOT FIVE MINUTES? MAKE RICOTTA

Fresh homemade ricotta is more delicate in flavor than any store-bought version, has a dry curd, and takes just a few minutes of active time. This recipe, from *Gourmet*'s creative director, Richard Ferretti, yields about 2 cups and can easily be doubled. Drizzled with honey and spread on toast, it's good for breakfast. Or top it with honey and cinnamon and serve for dessert.

Line a large sieve with a layer of heavy-duty (fine-mesh) cheesecloth or dampened paper towel and place it over a large bowl. Slowly bring 2 quarts whole milk, 1 cup heavy cream, and ½ teaspoon salt to a rolling boil in a 6-quart heavy pot over moderate heat, stirring occasionally to prevent scorching. Add 3 tablespoons fresh lemon juice, reduce the heat to low, and simmer, stirring constantly, until the mixture curdles, about 2 minutes. Pour the mixture into the lined sieve and let it drain for 1 hour. After discarding the liquid, chill the ricotta, covered; it will keep in the refrigerator for up to 2 days.

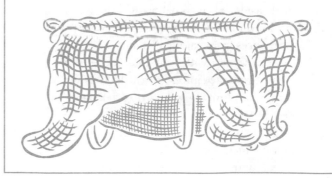

2 pounds plum tomatoes, cored and halved lengthwise
½ stick (4 tablespoons) unsalted butter
Salt and freshly ground black pepper
3 large eggs
1¾ cups (15 ounces) whole-milk ricotta, preferably fresh (see above for homemade)
1 cup all-purpose flour
¼ cup water
¼ cup thinly sliced fresh basil leaves
ACCOMPANIMENT: finely grated Parmigiano-Reggiano

ROAST THE TOMATOES: Put a rack in middle of oven and preheat oven to 400°F.

Put tomatoes cut side up in one layer in a 13-by-9-inch baking dish. Dot with 2 tablespoons butter and sprinkle with 1 teaspoon salt and ½ teaspoon pepper. Roast until skins are wrinkled and beginning to brown, about 45 minutes. Cool in baking dish.

MEANWHILE, MAKE THE *GNUDI*: Bring an 8-quart pot of salted water (3 tablespoons salt) to a boil.

Beat together eggs and ricotta in a large bowl with a handheld electric mixer until blended. Stir in flour, 1 teaspoon salt, and ½ teaspoon pepper until combined (batter will be soft).

Use 2 teaspoons (flatware, not measuring spoons) to form *gnudi:* scoop up a rounded spoonful of batter, then use second spoon to push mixture off spoon and into boiling water. Make 9 more *gnudi* in same matter. Simmer briskly until *gnudi* are cooked through and just firm in center, about 5 minutes. Transfer with a slotted spoon to a platter and cover with a dampened paper towel. Continue making gnudi in batches of 10.

MAKE THE SAUCE: When tomatoes are cool enough to handle, peel and seed them over baking dish; set dish aside. Slice tomatoes lengthwise ¼ inch thick and put in a medium saucepan. Scrape skins, seeds, and juices from baking dish into a fine-mesh sieve set over saucepan with tomatoes and press on solids in sieve to extract juices; discard skins and seeds. Stir water into tomatoes and bring to a bare simmer over low heat.

Meanwhile, melt remaining 2 tablespoons butter in a 12-inch nonstick skillet over moderate heat. Add *gnudi* and cook, turning gently, until heated through, 4 to 5 minutes.

Add basil and salt and pepper to taste to tomatoes. Transfer *gnudi* to a platter and drizzle tomatoes over *gnudi.* Serve immediately, with grated cheese.

COOK'S NOTE

- The tomatoes can be roasted up to 1 day ahead. Cool, uncovered, then refrigerate, covered.

Gnocchi alla Romana

SERVES 6 AS A FIRST COURSE
ACTIVE TIME: 30 MINUTES ■ START TO FINISH: 2 HOURS

■ Two distinct styles of gnocchi battle for attention in Rome: the familiar potato-based dumplings and ones like this recipe, made of semolina. The cooled semolina is cut into rounds, then arranged in a baking dish, dotted with butter and dusted with cheese, and baked until golden. It couldn't be easier and, paired with a green salad, makes a luscious supper. ■

    3 cups whole milk
    ¾ cup semolina (also called semolina flour; see
         Sources)
    1 teaspoon salt
    6 tablespoons (¾ stick) unsalted butter, melted
    1½ cups finely grated Parmigiano-Reggiano (about
         4½ ounces)
    1 large egg

SPECIAL EQUIPMENT: a 2-inch round cookie cutter

Whisk together milk, semolina, and salt in a 2-quart heavy saucepan and bring to a boil over moderate heat, whisking. Simmer, stirring constantly with a wooden spoon, until very stiff, 5 to 8 minutes. Remove from heat and stir in 2 tablespoons melted butter and ¾ cup cheese. Beat in egg.

Spread semolina mixture ½ inch thick on an oiled baking sheet. Refrigerate, uncovered, until very firm, about 1 hour.

Put a rack in middle of oven and preheat oven to 425°F. Generously butter a 13-by-9-inch baking dish.

Cut out rounds from semolina mixture with 2-inch cutter (push scraps into remaining mixture as you go) and arrange in one layer, slightly overlapping, in baking dish. Make a small second layer in center of dish with any extra rounds. Brush gnocchi with remaining ¼ cup melted butter and sprinkle with remaining ¾ cup cheese.

Bake until gnocchi are beginning to brown, 15 to 20 minutes. Let stand for 5 minutes before serving.

■ The semolina mixture can be refrigerated for up to 1 day; cover with plastic wrap after 1 hour in the refrigerator.

Fresh Manicotti

SERVES 12 AS A FIRST COURSE, 6 AS A MAIN COURSE
ACTIVE TIME: 1¼ HOURS ■ START TO FINISH: 2 HOURS

■ Food editor Gina Marie Miraglia Eriquez's mother, Marie, regularly makes manicotti for their immediate family of forty, but we've scaled her recipe down to feed a smaller group. What sets these manicotti apart is the tenderness of the crêpe wrappers. They are sturdy enough to stand up to the ricotta and mozzarella filling, but not at all heavy. The dish is a breeze to assemble if you make the crêpes ahead and freeze them (see Cook's Note). Gina's tomato sauce is a great basic recipe that is wonderful on plain spaghetti or with meatballs. ■

FOR SAUCE
3 tablespoons olive oil
1 medium onion, chopped
3 garlic cloves, minced
2 (28- to 32-ounce) cans whole tomatoes in juice, preferably Italian, drained, juice reserved, and finely chopped
½ cup water
1 teaspoon sugar
1 teaspoon salt
¼ cup chopped fresh basil
FOR CRESPELLE
3 large eggs
1½ cups water
1¼ cups all-purpose flour
½ teaspoon salt
1 tablespoon unsalted butter, melted
FOR FILLING
2 pounds (4 cups) whole-milk ricotta, preferably fresh (for homemade, see page 231)
2 large eggs
½ cup finely grated Parmigiano-Reggiano
⅓ cup chopped fresh flat-leaf parsley

½ teaspoon salt
½ teaspoon freshly ground black pepper
FOR ASSEMBLY
½ pound fresh mozzarella

MAKE THE SAUCE: Heat oil in a 5- to 6-quart heavy pot over moderately high heat until hot but not smoking. Add onion and cook, stirring occasionally, until golden, about 6 minutes. Add garlic and cook, stirring, until golden, about 1 minute. Add tomatoes, with juice, water, sugar, and salt, bring to a simmer, and simmer, uncovered, stirring occasionally, until thickened, about 30 minutes. Stir in basil and remove from heat.

MEANWHILE, MAKE THE *CRESPELLE:* Break up eggs with a wooden spoon in a medium bowl. Stir in water (don't beat) until combined. Sift in flour and salt and stir until just combined. Force through a medium-mesh sieve into another bowl.

Lightly brush an 8-inch nonstick skillet with melted butter and heat over moderate heat until hot but not smoking. Ladle about ¼ cup batter into skillet, tilting and rotating skillet to coat bottom, then

CRESPELLE

Think of the Italian crêpes called *crespelle* as an easier way to make fresh pasta. Made from a batter, not a dough, the *crespelle* are quick-cooking (use a nonstick pan and stay close) and infinitely versatile. Chop herbs such as parsley, chives, or tarragon and add them to the batter, then cut the *crespelle* into strips and sauce them like pasta. Or turn them into something sweet for dessert or even breakfast, topped with cinnamon sugar (or Nutella) and berries.

pour excess batter back into bowl. (If batter sets before skillet is coated, reduce heat slightly for next *crespella*.) Cook until just set and underside is lightly browned, about 30 seconds. Invert *crespella* onto a clean kitchen towel (not terry cloth) to cool completely. Make at least 11 more *crespelle* in same manner, brushing skillet with butter as needed and stacking *crespelle* in 3 piles.

MAKE THE FILLING: Stir together all ingredients in a bowl.

ASSEMBLE THE MANICOTTI: Put a rack in middle of oven and preheat oven to 425°F.

Cut mozzarella lengthwise into ¼-inch-thick sticks.

Spread 2 cups sauce in a 13-by-9-inch glass or ceramic baking dish. Spread 1 cup in an 8-inch square glass or ceramic baking dish. Place 1 *crespella* browned side up on a work surface. Spread about ¼ cup filling in a line across center and top with a mozzarella strip. Fold over top and bottom to enclose filling, leaving ends open, and place crosswise in large baking dish, seam side down. Fill 11 more *crespelle* in same manner, arranging snugly in one layer in baking dishes (8 in large dish, 4 in smaller). Spread 1 cup sauce over manicotti in large dish and ½ cup over manicotti in smaller dish.

Cover dishes tightly with foil and bake until sauce is bubbling and filling is hot, 15 to 20 minutes. Let stand for about 10 minutes.

Reheat remaining sauce and serve on the side.

COOK'S NOTES

- The *crespelle* can be made up to 3 days ahead. Stack the cooled *crespelle,* separated by wax paper, wrap the stacks tightly in plastic wrap, and refrigerate. They can also be frozen for up to 1 month. Stack the cooled *crespelle* in piles of 6, separated by wax paper, wrap the stacks in plastic wrap, and freeze them in a sealable plastic bag. Thaw them in the refrigerator. Bring the *crespelle* to room temperature before assembling the manicotti.
- The manicotti can be assembled up to 1 day ahead and refrigerated, covered with foil. Refrigerate the extra sauce, covered. Let the manicotti stand at room temperature for 15 minutes before baking (covered with foil). Reheat the sauce, thinning it slightly as necessary with water, before serving.

Salmon Cannelloni with Lemon Cream Sauce

SERVES 6 AS A MAIN COURSE
ACTIVE TIME: 45 MINUTES ■ START TO FINISH: 1 HOUR

■ Most seafood cannelloni is stuffed with chopped fish or shellfish, a time-consuming operation that can be fussy. This version, which uses salmon fillets, is both easier and more elegant. Wrapping the fillets in *crespelle* (Italian crêpes; see page 233) flecked with fresh tarragon keeps the fillets moist. The lemon sauce is the perfect finishing touch. ■

FOR *CRESPELLE*
- 2 large eggs
- ⅔ cup water
- ½ cup all-purpose flour
- ¼ teaspoon salt
- 1 tablespoon finely chopped fresh tarragon
- 3 tablespoons unsalted butter, melted

FOR SAUCE
- 2 tablespoons unsalted butter, cut into pieces
- 2 tablespoons all-purpose flour
- 1 (8-ounce) bottle clam juice
- ⅓ cup water
- ¼ cup heavy cream
- 2 teaspoons finely grated lemon zest
- ¼ teaspoon freshly ground black pepper

FOR ASSEMBLY
- 6 (5-ounce) center-cut pieces salmon fillet (1 inch thick), preferably wild, skinned, any pin bones removed with tweezers
- 2 tablespoons unsalted butter, softened
- 1 shallot, finely chopped
- 1 teaspoon salt
- ½ teaspoon freshly ground black pepper

MAKE THE *CRESPELLE*: Blend eggs, water, flour, and salt in a blender until smooth. Transfer to a bowl and stir in tarragon.

Lightly brush a 10-inch nonstick skillet with melted butter and heat over moderate heat until hot but not smoking. Ladle about ¼ cup batter into skillet, tilting and rotating skillet to coat bottom, then pour excess batter back into bowl. (If batter sets before skillet is coated, reduce heat slightly for next *crespella*.) Cook until just set and underside is lightly browned, about 30 seconds. Invert *crespella* onto a clean kitchen towel (not terry cloth) to cool completely. Make 5 more *crespelle* with remaining batter in same manner, brushing skillet with melted butter as needed and arranging *crespelle* in one layer on towel.

MAKE THE SAUCE: Heat butter in a 1- to 2-quart heavy saucepan over moderately low heat until foam subsides. Add flour and cook, whisking, for 2 minutes to make a roux. Add clam juice and water in a slow stream, whisking, then bring to a boil, whisking. Reduce heat and simmer, whisking occasionally, for 5 minutes. Stir in cream, zest, and pepper and remove from heat.

ASSEMBLE THE CANNELLONI: Put a rack in middle of oven and preheat oven to 425°F. Butter a 13-by-9-inch or other 3-quart glass or ceramic baking dish.

Pat salmon dry. Stir together butter, shallot, salt, and pepper in a small bowl. Spread 1 teaspoon butter mixture on top of each fillet.

Spread half of sauce in baking dish. Put 1 *crespella*, browned side up, on a work surface. Place 1 salmon fillet, buttered side down, in center of *crespella*, and fold top and bottom of *crespella* over salmon, leaving ends open. Transfer to baking dish, seam side down. Make 5 more cannelloni with remaining salmon and *crespelle* in same manner, arranging them in baking dish. Spoon remaining sauce over cannelloni.

Bake until salmon is just cooked through and sauce is bubbling, 15 to 20 minutes.

COOK'S NOTES

■ The *crespelle* can be made up to 3 days ahead. Stack the cooled *crespelle,* separated by wax paper, wrap tightly in plastic wrap, and refrigerate. They can also be frozen for up to 1 month. Stack the cooled *crespelle* in piles of 6, separated by wax paper, wrap the stacks in plastic wrap, and freeze them in a sealable plastic bag. Bring *crespelle* to room temperature before assembling the cannelloni.

■ The sauce can be made up to 1 day ahead. Cool, uncovered, then refrigerate, covered. Reheat before using, thinning with water if necessary.

■ The cannelloni can be assembled (covered with sauce) up to 1 day ahead. Refrigerate, tightly wrapped in plastic wrap. Bring to room temperature before baking.

Sausage and Broccoli Rabe Torta

SERVES 4 TO 6 AS A MAIN COURSE
ACTIVE TIME: 2 HOURS ■ START TO FINISH: 3 HOURS

■ Perfect for entertaining, this gorgeous savory pie—sheets of delicate *crespelle* (Italian crêpes; see page 233) layered with rich *besciamella* (white sauce), broccoli rabe, and sweet Italian sausage, baked in a springform pan—will wow your guests. ■

FOR *CRESPELLE*
    2 large eggs
    ⅔ cup whole milk
    ½ cup all-purpose flour
    ¼ teaspoon salt
    3 tablespoons unsalted butter, melted
FOR FILLING
    ¾ pound broccoli rabe
    3 tablespoons olive oil
    4 garlic cloves, finely chopped
    ½ teaspoon red pepper flakes
    ¾ pound sweet Italian sausage, casings removed
FOR *BESCIAMELLA* SAUCE
    ½ stick (4 tablespoons) unsalted butter
    ¼ cup all-purpose flour
    1¾ cups whole milk
    ¼ teaspoon salt
    ¼ teaspoon freshly ground black pepper
    ½ cup finely grated Parmigiano-Reggiano
FOR ASSEMBLY
    1 tablespoon unsalted butter, melted
    ¼ cup dry bread crumbs
    ¼ pound Italian Fontina, chilled and coarsely grated
        (about 1 cup)
    ½ cup finely grated Parmigiano-Reggiano
SPECIAL EQUIPMENT: an 8-inch springform pan

MAKE THE *CRESPELLE:* Blend eggs, milk, flour, and salt in a blender until smooth. Transfer to a bowl.

Lightly brush a 10-inch nonstick skillet with melted butter and heat over moderate heat until hot but not smoking. Ladle about ¼ cup batter into skillet, tilting and rotating skillet to coat bottom, then pour excess batter back into bowl. (If batter sets before skillet is coated, reduce heat slightly for next *crespella*.) Cook until just set and underside is lightly browned, about 30 seconds. Invert *crespella* onto a clean kitchen towel (not terry cloth) to cool completely. Make 5 more *crespelle* with remaining batter in same manner, brushing skillet with melted butter as needed and arranging *crespelle* in one layer on towel.

MAKE THE FILLING: Cut off and discard bottom inch from stems of broccoli rabe. Coarsely chop remainder.

Cook broccoli rabe in a 6- to 8-quart pot of boiling salted water (2 tablespoons salt), uncovered, until just tender, about 5 minutes. Transfer with a slotted spoon to a large bowl of ice and cold water to stop the cooking. Drain well and pat dry.

Heat oil in a 12-inch nonstick skillet over moderate heat. Add garlic and red pepper flakes and cook, stirring occasionally, until golden, about 8 minutes. Add sausage and cook, breaking it up with back of a wooden spoon, until no longer pink inside, about 5 minutes. Stir in broccoli rabe and cook, stirring, until heated, about 3 minutes. Remove from heat.

MAKE THE SAUCE: Heat butter in a 2- to 3-quart heavy saucepan over moderately low heat until foam subsides. Add flour and cook, whisking, for 3 minutes to make a roux. Add milk in a slow stream, whisking, and bring to a boil, whisking. Reduce heat and simmer, whisking occasionally, for 5 minutes. Stir in salt, pepper, and cheese and remove from heat.

ASSEMBLE THE TORTA: Put a rack in middle of oven and preheat oven to 425°F. Invert bottom of springform pan (to make it easier to slide torta off bottom), then lock on side. Wrap outside of pan in a double layer of foil. Generously brush bottom and sides of pan with butter, then sprinkle bread crumbs over bottom.

Stir together Fontina and Parmesan in a bowl. Put 1 *crespella* in springform pan, sprinkle with one sixth of filling, and drizzle with ⅓ cup sauce. Make 5 more layers of *crespella*, filling, and sauce, ending with sauce. Sprinkle cheese mixture evenly over top.

Bake, uncovered, until top is bubbling and golden, about 25 minutes. Cool in pan on a rack for 15 minutes.

Remove side of pan and carefully slide torta off pan bottom onto a plate. Cut into wedges.

Couscous with Dates

SERVES 4 AS A SIDE DISH
ACTIVE TIME: 15 MINUTES ■ START TO FINISH: 20 MINUTES

■ Toasting couscous, a granular form of pasta, with spices in hot oil imparts a nice warm color and creates layers of depth and flavor. A smattering of finely chopped dates adds little jolts of sweetness, while grated orange zest offers a fragrant grace note. This is a natural with lamb, but we also love it with roast chicken. ■

½ teaspoon ground allspice
¼ teaspoon ground cinnamon
¼ teaspoon cayenne
2 tablespoons olive oil
1¾ cups (about 10 ounces) couscous
¼ cup finely chopped dried dates
   Salt
½ teaspoon finely grated orange zest
2 cups boiling water
¼ cup finely chopped scallions

Toast allspice, cinnamon, and cayenne in oil in a 3-quart heavy saucepan over moderate heat, stirring frequently, until fragrant, 1 to 2 minutes. Add couscous and toast, stirring occasionally, until fragrant and just a shade darker, about 2 minutes. Stir in dates, ¾ teaspoon salt, and zest, then add boiling water (mixture will bubble vigorously). Remove pan from heat and let couscous stand, covered, for 5 minutes.

Fluff couscous with a fork, stir in scallions, and season with salt.

Israeli Couscous with Mixed Mushrooms

SERVES 6 AS A SIDE DISH
ACTIVE TIME: 25 MINUTES ■ START TO FINISH: 35 MINUTES

■ Pea-sized Israeli, or pearl, couscous is a pasta made from a hard wheat dough that is rolled or extruded into tiny balls, then toasted to give it more flavor and color. Its pleasantly chewy texture pairs well with meaty mushrooms. ■

- 3 tablespoons unsalted butter
- 1 tablespoon olive oil
- 2 large shallots, finely chopped
- 1 pound mixed mushrooms, such as porcini, morels, cremini, and stemmed shiitakes, trimmed if necessary and cut into ¼-inch-thick slices
- 2 teaspoons soy sauce
- 1 teaspoon sugar
  Salt
- ½ teaspoon freshly ground black pepper
- 2¼ cups (12 ounces) Israeli couscous
- ½ cup loosely packed fresh flat-leaf parsley leaves, chopped

Heat 2 tablespoons butter and oil in a 12-inch heavy skillet over moderately high heat until foam subsides. Add shallots and cook, stirring, for 2 minutes. Add mushrooms, soy sauce, and sugar and cook, stirring, until liquid mushrooms give off has evaporated and mushrooms begin to brown, 10 to 12 minutes. Sprinkle with ¼ teaspoon salt and pepper.

Meanwhile, cook couscous in a 5-quart pot of boiling salted water (1 tablespoon salt) until just tender, 8 to 10 minutes. Drain.

Add couscous to mushroom mixture, along with parsley and remaining 1 tablespoon butter, tossing

to combine. Season with salt. Serve warm or at room temperature.

Orzo Risotto

SERVES 6 TO 8 AS A SIDE DISH
ACTIVE TIME: 40 MINUTES ■ START TO FINISH: 40 MINUTES

■ Orzo, the rice-shaped pasta, makes a dish just as creamy and rich as traditional risotto, but a bit easier and with a more delicate texture. ■

- 3 cups water
- 2 cups Chicken Stock (page 153) or store-bought reduced-sodium broth
- 1½ cups finely chopped onions
- 2 tablespoons olive oil
- ¾ teaspoon finely chopped fresh thyme
- 1½ cups (about 10 ounces) orzo
- ½ cup dry white wine
- ½ cup finely grated Parmigiano-Reggiano
- 2 tablespoons unsalted butter
- 1 teaspoon finely grated lemon zest
  Salt
- ½ teaspoon freshly ground black pepper

Combine water and stock in a small saucepan and bring to a simmer, then keep at a bare simmer.

Meanwhile, cook onions in oil in a 2½- to 3-quart heavy saucepan over moderate heat, stirring occasionally, until softened, 8 to 10 minutes. Stir in thyme and cook until just fragrant, about 1 minute. Add orzo and cook, stirring frequently, until it smells toasted and is just a shade darker, about 3 minutes. Add wine and cook at a strong simmer until almost evaporated. Add 1 cup stock mixture and cook, stirring constantly, until absorbed. Continue adding stock ¼ cup at a time, stirring frequently and letting each addition be absorbed before adding the next, until orzo is al dente and creamy looking, 12 to 15 minutes. (There may be some stock left over.)

Remove orzo from heat and stir in cheese, butter, zest, ½ teaspoon salt, and pepper. Season with additional salt if necessary and serve immediately.

Egg Noodles with Brown Butter and Feta

SERVES 8 TO 10 AS A SIDE DISH
ACTIVE TIME: 10 MINUTES ■ START TO FINISH: 30 MINUTES

■ Looking at this recipe and its short ingredients list, you might think, Why? But the alchemy created by tossing hot noodles with nutty brown butter and tangy hunks of feta is remarkable. Like many of the Greek cooking authority and author Diane Kochilas's recipes, this dish is big on flavor and equally big on simplicity. It's wonderful no matter what egg pasta you use, and Greek feta can be found at most supermarkets. Serve with roast chicken or lamb. ■

1 pound dried egg noodles or egg pasta
Salt
1 stick (8 tablespoons) unsalted butter
6 ounces Greek feta, preferably Mt. Vikos or Dodoni brand, crumbled (about 1½ cups)
Freshly ground black pepper

Cook noodles in an 8-quart pot of boiling salted water (3 tablespoons salt) until just tender. Drain well.

Meanwhile, melt butter in a small heavy skillet over low heat and cook until it begins to turn golden brown, about 6 minutes. Remove from heat.

Spread one third of noodles on a large platter and sprinkle with one third of cheese. Repeat layering with remaining noodles and cheese in 2 batches, then pour brown butter over noodles and toss with two forks to combine. Spread noodles out on platter and season with pepper to taste.

Egg Noodles with Cabbage and Onions

SERVES 4 AS A SIDE DISH OR 2 AS A MAIN COURSE
ACTIVE TIME: 30 MINUTES ■ START TO FINISH: 1¾ HOURS

■ This simple dish may sound like peasant food, but one bite will make you very envious of those peasants. Rich with browned onions, it's a truly heartwarming side dish (the optional poppy seeds add a nice crunch). We adapted the recipe from the cookbook author Faye Levy, and though we love to serve it with pot roast or roast chicken, it also makes a homey vegetarian meal in itself. ■

1½ pounds green cabbage, quartered, cored, and cut crosswise into ½-inch-wide strips
Salt
1 large onion, finely chopped
5 tablespoons unsalted butter
1 teaspoon sugar
Freshly ground black pepper
¼ pound (about 2½ cups) wide egg noodles
1 teaspoon poppy seeds (optional)

Toss cabbage with 2 teaspoons salt in a large bowl. Let stand, tossing occasionally, for 45 minutes. Squeeze cabbage by handfuls to remove as much liquid as possible.

Cook onion in 4 tablespoons butter in a 12-inch heavy skillet over moderate heat, stirring occasionally, until softened, about 5 minutes. Stir in cabbage, sugar, and ¼ teaspoon pepper, cover, reduce heat to low, and cook, stirring occasionally, until cabbage is very tender, about 30 minutes.

Remove lid, increase heat to moderately high, and cook, stirring frequently, until onion and cabbage are golden, 6 to 8 minutes.

Meanwhile, cook noodles in a 4- to 6-quart pot of boiling salted water (3 tablespoons salt) until al dente. Drain well and add to browned cabbage, along with remaining tablespoon butter. Cook over low heat, stirring occasionally, until butter is melted. Add salt and pepper to taste and sprinkle with poppy seeds, if using.

Browned Onion Kugels

SERVES 12 AS A SIDE DISH, 6 AS A MAIN COURSE
ACTIVE TIME: 30 MINUTES ■ START TO FINISH: 1¼ HOURS

■ Noodle pudding may be delicious, but it's not pretty. However, using a muffin tin rather than a single large pan produces a much more sophisticated result (as well as an abundance of tasty browned edges). It's a great way to dress up your brisket or baked chicken; the individual kugels can even be a brunch centerpiece. ■

- 6 ounces (1¾ cups) medium egg noodles
- Salt
- 1 stick (8 tablespoons) unsalted butter
- 3 cups chopped onions
- 1¼ cups sour cream
- 1¼ cups (10 ounces) small-curd cottage cheese
- 1 tablespoon poppy seeds
- 4 large eggs
- ¼ teaspoon freshly ground black pepper

SPECIAL EQUIPMENT: a muffin tin with twelve ½-cup cups

Put a rack in middle of oven and preheat oven to 425°F.

Cook noodles in an 8-quart pot of boiling salted water (3 tablespoons salt) until al dente. Drain in a colander, rinse under cold water, and drain well.

Melt butter in a 12-inch heavy skillet over moderate heat. Brush muffin cups with some of butter. Add onions to skillet and cook, stirring occasionally, until well browned, about 20 minutes.

Transfer onions to a large bowl and stir in noodles, sour cream, cottage cheese, and poppy seeds. Lightly beat eggs with 1 teaspoon salt and pepper, then stir into noodle mixture until well combined.

Divide mixture among muffin cups. Bake until puffed and golden, 20 to 25 minutes. Loosen edges of kugels with a thin knife and cool kugels in pan for 5 minutes before serving.

COOK'S NOTE

■ The kugels can be assembled up to 3 hours ahead and refrigerated, covered. Bake, uncovered, as directed.

Mint and Scallion Soba Noodles

SERVES 6 AS A SIDE DISH
ACTIVE TIME: 10 MINUTES ■ START TO FINISH: 15 MINUTES

■ Chewy buckwheat noodles are a great healthful staple. Perk them up with a rice vinegar and soy sauce dressing, plus lots of fresh mint and scallions, and you have a nutty-tasting side for grilled flank or skirt steak or a light accompaniment for fish. ■

- ¾ pound soba noodles (Japanese buckwheat noodles)
- ⅓ cup rice vinegar (not seasoned)
- 1 tablespoon vegetable oil
- 1 tablespoon soy sauce
- 1¼ teaspoons sugar
- ¾ teaspoon salt
- ½ cup chopped fresh mint
- 1½ cups thinly sliced scallions (1½ bunches)

Cook noodles in a large pot of boiling (unsalted) water until just tender, about 5 minutes. Drain in a colander, rinse under cold water to stop the cooking, and drain well.

Meanwhile, stir together vinegar, oil, soy sauce, sugar, and salt in a small bowl until sugar and salt are dissolved.

Toss noodles with dressing, mint, and scallions.

Spicy Soba Noodles with Lacquered Eggplant

SERVES 4 AS A MAIN COURSE
ACTIVE TIME: 50 MINUTES ■ START TO FINISH: 50 MINUTES

■ Brush a slice of eggplant with soy sauce and mirin, and it will caramelize beautifully under the high heat of the broiler. Combine that with protein-rich soba noodles and a spicy sauce with ginger and chile paste, and you have a meal that is equally delicious served warm, cold, or at room temperature. We prefer to use the long, narrow Chinese or Japanese eggplants for this dish because of their sweetness and their ability to hold their shape. ■

ASIAN NOODLES

Intriguingly slurpy and slippery, Asian noodles have become a culinary obsession in the United States, but the enormous variety that is now available in Asian markets and, increasingly, in well-stocked supermarkets can be more intimidating than inspirational. What kind is that? How do I cook it? Do I need to soak it first?

Asian noodles differ from what we call pasta primarily in the wider range of flours and starches used, as well as in their length. Often considered a symbol of long life and happiness, they're usually produced in longer strands than western pastas are. (By the way, the claim that Marco Polo introduced Italy to noodles upon his return from China in 1295 is one of the great undying myths of the culinary world. Boiling pasta is documented in a tenth-century Persian recipe, and the earliest European reference—to "macaroni," dated 1279—comes from the Genoa city archives.)

Here are some of our favorite Asian noodles.

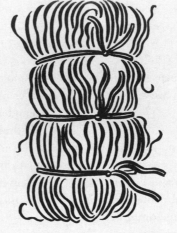

BEAN THREAD NOODLES ("CELLOPHANE" OR "GLASS" NOODLES) These silvery dried strands are made from mung bean starch, and sometimes tapioca starch, blended with water. They commonly come in thin, round strands but also can be flat and fettuccine-like. They become almost clear after being heated. Practically flavorless, bean threads have a pleasingly gelatinous texture and they soak up broths easily. Bean threads are generally softened in water before being used.

FRESH FLAT CHINESE STIR-FRY EGG NOODLES These resemble fresh linguine and are usually cooked in stir-fries. They are usually cooked twice: once in boiling water and then finished another way. Do not buy precooked noodles for our recipes.

DRIED FLAT RICE NOODLES About the width of fettuccine but much longer, these translucent noodles, made from rice flour and sometimes tapioca flour, are used in such Thai dishes as pad Thai and other Southeast Asian dishes. Their texture is different from that of bean threads, because they're not as gelatinous. They should be softened in water before cooking.

FRESH THIN CHINESE EGG NOODLES ("HONG KONG NOODLES")

These noodles are nicely chewy (they are firmer than flat stir-fry egg noodles; see opposite page) and range in color from golden to bright yellow. Some brands don't contain eggs but get their hue from yellow food coloring, so always check the ingredients list. Like flat stir-fry egg noodles, they are first cooked in boiling water, then finished another way—fried into a cake, for instance, or added to a stir-fry or a braising sauce. Take care not to overcook them when boiling; they should have an al dente firmness. Look for them in the refrigerated section at Asian markets; do not buy precooked noodles for our recipes.

SOBA NOODLES

Made with buckwheat flour or a combination of buckwheat and wheat or yam flour, these straight, taupe colored dried Japanese noodles are usually square in cross section. They're nutty in flavor and are eaten in soups or cold, on their own, with a dipping sauce. It's not necessary to soak them before cooking.

FRESH WIDE RICE NOODLES (*HE FUN, HO FUN,* OR *HO FAN*)

These are sold either precut or, more commonly, in loosely folded oiled sheets that can be cut into wide noodles for panfried *chow fun*. Although they absorb sauces and flavors well, they are really all about texture—simultaneously supple and chewy. The Vietnamese call these noodles *banh uot* or *pho*; the Thais call them *gueyteow*.

SWEET POTATO VERMICELLI (*DANG MYUN*)

These thin dried Korean noodles, made of sweet potato flour, are pearly gray in color. (Korean sweet potatoes have flesh that is ivory rather than orange.) They cook to a wonderful slippery chewiness and have a mild yet earthy flavor. They don't need to be soaked before cooking.

2½ pounds Asian eggplants, halved crosswise and cut
     lengthwise into ¼-inch-thick slices
½ cup plus 2 tablespoons mirin (Japanese sweet
     rice wine)
½ cup soy sauce
3 tablespoons vegetable oil
¾ cup water
1½ teaspoons cornstarch
1–1½ teaspoons Asian chile paste with garlic
     (see Sources)
2 teaspoons finely grated peeled fresh ginger
5 scallions, thinly sliced
¾ pound soba noodles (Japanese buckwheat noodles)
3 tablespoons chopped fresh cilantro
     Salt and freshly ground black pepper

Preheat broiler. Line two large baking sheets with
foil and lightly oil foil.

Arrange eggplant slices on baking sheets (slices
will be crowded). Stir together ¼ cup mirin, 2 tablespoons soy sauce, and 2 tablespoons oil in a small
bowl, then brush onto tops of eggplant slices. Broil
one pan of eggplant, rotating pan as needed, until
eggplant is browned, about 5 minutes. (Watch eggplant carefully; it can burn easily.) Turn eggplant
over, brush with some of remaining mirin mixture,
and broil until browned and tender, 3 to 5 minutes.
Set aside. Broil second pan of eggplant in same
manner.

Stir together water, cornstarch, chile paste, and
remaining 6 tablespoons each mirin and soy sauce
in a bowl. Heat remaining tablespoon oil in a 1- to
2-quart heavy saucepan over moderate heat until hot
but not smoking. Add ginger and half of scallions and
cook, stirring, until fragrant, about 30 seconds. Add
cornstarch mixture and simmer, stirring occasionally,
until slightly thickened, about 2 minutes. Remove
from heat and cover to keep warm.

Meanwhile, cook noodles in a 6- to 8-quart pot of
boiling (unsalted) water until just al dente, about 6
minutes. Drain noodles in a colander and rinse well
under cold water; leave in colander to drain well.

Cut eggplant crosswise into ½-inch-wide pieces.
Rinse noodles with very hot water to reheat if serving
warm.

Toss noodles with eggplant, sauce, cilantro, and
remaining scallions. Season with salt and pepper.

COOK'S NOTE

■ If you are serving the noodles chilled, they can be
tossed with the eggplant and sauce, but not the cilantro and remaining scallions, and refrigerated, covered,
for up to 3 days.

Spicy Singapore-Style Rice Noodles

SERVES 4 AS A MAIN COURSE
ACTIVE TIME: 45 MINUTES ■ START TO FINISH: 45 MINUTES

■ These slightly sweet, salty rice noodles, with lots of
garlic and a jab of heat, are popular street food in Singapore, Malaysia, and Thailand. The fresh rice noodles
have a wonderful chewiness and soak up flavor. Look
for them in the refrigerated section of Asian markets.
For the other Asian ingredients, see Sources. ■

1 pound skinless, boneless chicken breasts
½ teaspoon Asian sesame oil
     Salt
½ cup Chicken Stock (page 153) or store-bought
     reduced-sodium broth
¼ cup oyster sauce
2 tablespoons *ketjap manis* (Indonesian sweet soy
     sauce) or mixture of 1 tablespoon each soy sauce
     and molasses (not robust)
2 tablespoons soy sauce
1 tablespoon *sambal oelek* or Sriracha (Asian chile
     sauces), or to taste
1 large carrot
½ pound *choy sum* (also called Chinese flowering
     cabbage; see Sources) or baby bok choy
3 tablespoons peanut or vegetable oil
2 links Chinese sweet sausage (*lop cheong*), halved
     lengthwise and cut diagonally into ¼-inch-thick
     slices
2 large shallots, halved lengthwise and cut crosswise
     into ¼-inch-thick slices
2 tablespoons finely chopped garlic
1 teaspoon sliced fresh mild red chile, including
     seeds
½ pound (3 cups) fresh soybean or mung bean
     sprouts

1 bunch scallions, cut into 2-inch lengths

1 pound fresh wide rice noodles (also called *he fun*, *ho fun*, or *ho fan*; see headnote)

¾ cup loosely packed fresh cilantro sprigs

SPECIAL EQUIPMENT: a mandoline or other adjustable-blade vegetable slicer with a julienne blade

Halve chicken breasts lengthwise, cut across the grain into ¼-inch-thick slices, and put in a bowl. Add sesame oil and a pinch of salt and stir to coat.

Stir together stock, oyster sauce, *ketjap manis*, soy sauce, and *sambal oelek* in a small bowl.

Holding carrot at a 45-degree angle to slicer, cut into thin (⅛-inch) matchsticks.

Cut *choy sum* crosswise into 2½- to 3-inch pieces. Halve any thick stem pieces lengthwise.

Heat a well seasoned 14-inch flat-bottomed wok (see Cook's Note) over high heat until a drop of water evaporates instantly on contact. Add 1 tablespoon peanut oil and swirl to coat bottom and sides of wok. When oil begins to smoke, add sausage and stir-fry until browned, about 1 minute. Add chicken and stir-fry until just opaque, about 3 minutes (chicken will not be cooked through). Transfer to a clean bowl. Add remaining 2 tablespoons peanut oil to wok, swirling to coat, then add carrot, shallots, garlic, and chile and stir-fry for 3 minutes. Add *choy sum*, bean sprouts, and scallions and stir-fry until *choy sum* is crisp-tender, about 3 minutes.

Stir in stock mixture and bring to a boil. Add noodles and stir-fry gently until heated through and tender. Return sausage and chicken to wok and stir until chicken is just cooked through, about 1 minute. Serve sprinkled with cilantro.

COOK'S NOTE

■ You can substitute a 12-inch heavy skillet, preferably cast-iron, for the wok.

CHINESE SWEET SAUSAGES

Indonesian Fried Noodles

SERVES 4 TO 6 AS A MAIN COURSE
ACTIVE TIME: 1¼ HOURS ■ START TO FINISH: 1¼ HOURS

■ It's hard to refuse seconds of this stir-fried noodle dish, called *bahmi goreng*. Tender Chinese egg noodles, snow peas, and Chinese long beans mingle with rich, garlicky sauce, cubes of tofu, and shredded omelet. For help finding the Asian ingredients, see Sources. ■

3 large shallots

½ cup peanut or vegetable oil

1 pound fresh flat Chinese stir-fry egg noodles (do not use those labeled "precooked"; see page 240 and Cook's Note)

½ cup Chicken Stock (page 153), store-bought reduced-sodium broth, or water

3 tablespoons *ketjap manis* (Indonesian sweet soy sauce) or mixture of 1½ tablespoons each soy sauce and molasses (not robust)

1½ tablespoons Asian fish sauce

1 tablespoon *sambal oelek* or Sriracha (Asian chile sauces), or to taste

Salt

½ teaspoon freshly ground black pepper

1 (14- to 16-ounce) package firm tofu

4 large eggs

2 large onions, halved lengthwise and cut crosswise into ½-inch slices

2 teaspoons finely chopped garlic

¼ teaspoon minced fresh red or green chile, such as Thai or serrano, including seeds

6 ounces snow peas, trimmed and cut diagonally into 1-inch pieces

6 ounces Chinese long beans (see Sources) or green beans, trimmed and cut into 2-inch pieces

2 scallions, cut diagonally into very thin slices

GARNISH: sliced cucumber; sliced tomatoes; lime wedges; *sambal oelek* or Sriracha (Asian chile sauces)

SPECIAL EQUIPMENT: a well-seasoned 14-inch flat-bottomed wok

Cut shallots crosswise into very thin slices (less than ⅛ inch thick) with an adjustable-blade vegetable slicer or a sharp knife.

Heat oil in wok over moderate heat until hot but not smoking. Add shallots, reduce heat to moderately low, and fry, stirring frequently, until golden brown, 8 to 12 minutes. Carefully pour shallot mixture into a fine-mesh sieve set over a heatproof bowl. Transfer shallots to paper towels to drain; reserve shallot oil. (Shallots will crisp as they cool.) Wipe wok clean with paper towels.

Cook noodles in a 6- to 8-quart pot of boiling (unsalted) water, stirring to separate, until just tender, 15 seconds to 1 minute. Drain in a colander and rinse under cold water to stop the cooking. Shake colander briskly to drain excess water, then drizzle noodles with 2 teaspoons reserved shallot oil and toss to coat.

Stir together stock, *ketjap manis*, fish sauce, *sambal oelek*, ½ teaspoon salt, and pepper in a small bowl. Set aside.

Cut tofu into 1-inch cubes and pat dry.

Beat together eggs with a pinch of salt. Heat 1 tablespoon reserved shallot oil in wok over moderately high heat until hot but not smoking. Add eggs, swirling in wok, and cook until barely set in center, about 2 minutes. Gently slide omelet out onto a cutting board. Roll into a loose cylinder and cut crosswise into ½-inch-wide strips (do not unroll). Keep warm, loosely covered with foil.

Heat 3 tablespoons reserved shallot oil (reserve remainder for another use) in wok over high heat until hot but not smoking. Add onions with ¼ teaspoon salt and stir-fry until deep golden, 8 to 10 minutes. Add garlic and chile and stir-fry for 1 minute. Add tofu and stir-fry for 3 minutes. Add snow peas and long beans and stir-fry until crisp-tender, about 5 minutes. Add sauce and bring to a boil, then add noodles and stir-fry (use two spatulas to stir if necessary) until noodles are hot.

Transfer noodles to a large platter and scatter egg over noodles. Sprinkle with scallions and half of shallots. Serve remaining shallots on the side. Serve sliced cucumber, tomatoes, and lime wedges on a separate plate, and serve chile sauce in a shallow bowl.

COOK'S NOTES

- The shallots can be fried up to 1 day ahead and, once cooled completely, kept in an airtight container at room temperature.
- Fresh (not cooked) lo mein noodles can be substituted

for the stir-fry noodles. Boil until just tender, 2 to 3 minutes (or follow the package directions), then drain and rinse.

Rice Noodles with Duck and Spicy Orange Sauce

SERVES 4 AS A MAIN COURSE
ACTIVE TIME: 20 MINUTES ■ START TO FINISH: 45 MINUTES

■ Two common pantry items—orange marmalade and Asian chile sauce—make a wonderful sweet-hot sauce for meaty duck breasts and chewy rice noodles in this quick weeknight supper. ■

- 2 cups water
- ½ pound dried flat rice noodles (see page 240 and Sources)
- ½ cup sweet orange marmalade
- 2–3 teaspoons Sriracha or *sambal oelek* (Asian chile sauces; see Sources), or to taste
- ½ cup chopped scallions
  Salt
- 2 (1-pound) Muscovy or Moulard duck breast halves with skin or 4 (7- to 8-ounce) Long Island (Pekin) duck breast halves with skin (see Sources)
- ½ teaspoon freshly ground black pepper

ACCOMPANIMENT: lime wedges
SPECIAL EQUIPMENT: an instant-read thermometer

Remove rack from oven broiler pan, add 2 cups water to broiler pan, and replace rack. Put pan under broiler, with top of pan 5 to 6 inches from heat, and preheat.

Meanwhile, soak noodles in hot water to cover for 10 minutes; drain.

Combine marmalade, Sriracha, ¼ cup scallions, and ½ teaspoon salt in a 1-quart heavy saucepan and cook over moderately low heat, stirring, until marmalade is melted, about 2 minutes. Remove from heat.

Pat duck breasts dry. Score skin at 1-inch intervals with a sharp knife (do not cut into meat). Sprinkle all over with 1 teaspoon salt and pepper. Broil duck breasts, skin sides down, for 4 minutes if using Long Island duck, 8 minutes if using Muscovy or Moulard. Turn and broil until thermometer inserted horizontally into center of a breast registers 130°F for medium-rare (see Cook's Note), 8 to 10 minutes more. Transfer to a cutting board and let rest for 10 minutes. Carefully pour pan juices into a heatproof measure.

While duck stands, cook rice noodles in a 4- to 6-quart pot of boiling (unsalted) water, stirring occasionally, until tender, about 3 minutes. Drain, transfer to a bowl, and add remaining ¼ cup scallions. Skim 2 tablespoons duck fat from top of pan juices, add to noodles, and toss to coat.

Skim off and discard remaining fat from pan juices. Add pan juices and any juices accumulated on cutting board to orange sauce, bring to a simmer, and simmer, stirring occasionally, for 1 minute.

Holding a sharp knife at a 45-degree angle, cut duck into thin slices.

Divide noodles among four plates and top with duck and sauce. Serve with lime wedges.

COOK'S NOTE

- The USDA recommends cooking duck breasts to an internal temperature of 170°F, but since we prefer the meat medium-rare, we cook it only to 130°F. More than that, and the duck gets tough and liverlike.

Beef Chow Mein

SERVES 4 AS A MAIN COURSE
ACTIVE TIME: 45 MINUTES ■ START TO FINISH: 45 MINUTES

■ This authentic Cantonese version of chow mein features fresh egg noodles, which are fried into a crisp cake that softens slightly when topped with the meat and vegetable sauce. It is perfectly delicious with baby bok choy, but if you go to an Asian market for Chinese egg noodles, you would do well to seek out *choy sum*. Related to bok choy, it has slender stems, kelly green leaves, and tiny yellow flowers. One taste of this mild, tender vegetable will make you understand why it's such a ubiquitous green in Chinese cooking.

Be careful not to mistake wonton noodles for Chinese egg noodles; although they look similar, wonton noodles don't have the same rich texture. ■

- ½ pound fresh thin Chinese egg noodles (also called Hong Kong noodles; see page 241 and Sources)
- ½ pound flank steak
- ¼ teaspoon sugar
- ¼ teaspoon Asian sesame oil
- 3 tablespoons soy sauce
- 3 tablespoons Chinese rice wine, preferably Shaoxing, or medium-dry sherry
- 3 tablespoons oyster sauce
- 1 tablespoon cornstarch
- ½ teaspoon freshly ground white pepper
- 1 cup Chicken Stock (page 153) or store-bought reduced-sodium broth
- ½ cup plus 2 tablespoons peanut or vegetable oil
- 1 teaspoon finely chopped peeled fresh ginger
- 1 teaspoon finely chopped garlic
- 3 scallions, cut into 2½-inch pieces
- 6 ounces shiitake mushrooms, stems discarded, caps quartered
- ½ pound *choy sum* (also called Chinese flowering cabbage; see Sources), cut into 2½ inch pieces, or baby bok choy

SPECIAL EQUIPMENT: a well-seasoned 14-inch flat-bottomed wok

Bring 8 cups unsalted water to a boil in a 4-quart pot. Add noodles, stirring to separate, and cook for 15 seconds. Drain in a colander and rinse under cold water until cool, then shake colander briskly to drain excess water.

Cut steak with the grain into 1½- to 2-inch-wide strips, then cut each strip across grain into ¼-inch-thick slices and put in a medium bowl. Using your hands, toss beef with sugar, sesame oil, 1 tablespoon soy sauce, 1 tablespoon rice wine, 1 tablespoon oyster sauce, and 1 teaspoon cornstarch. Let beef marinate at room temperature while you prepare remaining ingredients.

Stir together remaining 2 tablespoons soy sauce, 2 tablespoons rice wine, 2 tablespoons oyster sauce, and 2 teaspoons cornstarch with white pepper in a small bowl until smooth, then stir in stock.

Heat wok over high heat until a drop of water

evaporates within 1 to 2 seconds. Add ½ cup peanut oil and heat until just smoking. Carefully add noodles all at once, flattening them to form a 9-inch cake. Cook, rotating cake with a metal spatula so it browns evenly and lifting edges occasionally to check color, until underside is golden, 4 to 5 minutes. Carefully flip noodle cake over with spatula and tongs and cook, again rotating cake, until other side is golden, 2 to 3 minutes more. Transfer noodle cake to a large paper-towel-lined plate to drain, then transfer to a platter and loosely cover with foil to keep warm. Discard any oil remaining in wok and wipe out wok with paper towels.

Heat wok over high heat until a drop of water evaporates on contact. Pour 1 tablespoon peanut oil down side of wok, then swirl oil, tilting wok to coat sides. Add beef, spreading pieces in one layer over bottom and sides as quickly as possible. Cook, undisturbed, until beef begins to brown, about 1 minute, then stir-fry until meat is just browned on all sides but still pink in center, about 1 minute. Transfer meat and any juices to a plate.

Add remaining tablespoon oil to wok. When oil just begins to smoke, add ginger, garlic, and scallions and stir-fry for 30 seconds. Add mushrooms and stir-fry until softened, about 3 minutes. Add *choy sum* and stir-fry until leaves are bright green and just wilted, 2 to 3 minutes (if using baby bok choy, cook until almost crisp-tender). Stir stock mixture, pour into wok, and stir-fry until sauce is slightly thickened, about 2 minutes. Add beef and stir to coat. Bring mixture just to a boil and pour over noodle cake.

Korean-Style Noodles with Meat and Vegetables

Jap Chae

SERVES 6 AS A MAIN COURSE
ACTIVE TIME: 45 MINUTES ■ START TO FINISH: 1¼ HOURS

■ *Jap chae* is a beloved Korean party dish. One bite might comprise a bit of jade-green spinach and a cloud of omelet, the next juxtapose savory rib eye and sweet red bell pepper, and the third play meaty mushrooms against matchsticks of carrot. Every mouthful will contain threads of *dang myun*, the wonderful Korean sweet potato vermicelli. These dried noodles are pearly gray and cook to a slippery chewiness. Each component is cooked separately, tossed in a garlicky sauce, and then arranged neatly in the serving bowl. Because *jap chae* is so pretty, we like to take the bowl to the table and toss everything together just before serving. ■

    6 dried Korean *pyogo*, Chinese *xianggu*, or Japanese
       shiitake mushrooms (see Sources)
    4 garlic cloves, minced
    ½ cup soy sauce
   2½ tablespoons Asian sesame oil
    1 tablespoon sesame seeds, toasted (see Tips,
       page 911)
    2 tablespoons sugar
    ¼ teaspoon salt
    ¼ teaspoon freshly ground black pepper
   10 ounces boneless rib-eye steak (¾ inch thick), cut
       crosswise into ⅛-inch-thick strips
    2 bunches spinach (about 1½ pounds total), stems
       discarded
   12 ounces Korean sweet potato vermicelli (see page 241
       and Cook's Note)
    2 large eggs
    ¼ cup vegetable oil
    1 medium onion, halved lengthwise and thinly sliced
       crosswise
    ½ red bell pepper, cut lengthwise into thin strips
    3 scallions, halved lengthwise and cut into 2-inch
       lengths
    2 carrots, cut into matchsticks

Soak mushrooms in 2 cups boiling water in a bowl, turning them occasionally, until softened, about 1 hour.

Meanwhile, combine garlic, soy sauce, sesame oil, sesame seeds, sugar, salt, and pepper in a small bowl, stirring until sugar and salt are dissolved.

Toss beef with 3 tablespoons garlic soy sauce in another bowl.

Blanch spinach in an 8-quart pot of boiling (unsalted) water just until bright green, about 30 seconds. With a slotted spoon, transfer to a bowl of ice and cold water to stop the cooking. Keep water at a boil. Drain spinach and squeeze out excess water. Coarsely chop spinach, toss with 2 tablespoons garlic soy sauce, and transfer to a large serving dish.

Cook noodles in the boiling water until just tender but still slightly chewy, 4 to 5 minutes. Drain in a colander and rinse under cold water. Cut noodles into 5- to 6-inch pieces with kitchen shears. Toss with 1 tablespoon garlic soy sauce and place next to spinach in serving dish.

Lift mushrooms from soaking liquid, squeezing excess liquid back into bowl (discard liquid). Cut away and discard stems, then thinly slice caps.

Lightly beat eggs. Heat 1 tablespoon vegetable oil in a 12-inch heavy skillet over moderately high heat until hot but not smoking. Add eggs, swirling skillet to distribute evenly. Cook until just set but not dry, about 1 minute, then turn over and cook for 30 seconds more. Gently slide omelet out onto a cutting board. Fold loosely in half and cut crosswise into thin strips. Add to serving dish.

Add 2 tablespoons vegetable oil to skillet, add mushrooms, and cook over moderate heat, stirring frequently, for 2 minutes. Add onion and cook, stirring, for 3 minutes. Add bell pepper, scallions, and carrots and cook, stirring, until vegetables are just crisp-tender, 4 to 5 minutes. Transfer to a bowl, toss with 3 tablespoons garlic soy sauce until well coated, and transfer to serving dish.

Add remaining 1 tablespoon vegetable oil to skillet, add beef, and cook over moderately high heat, stirring, until just barely cooked through, 1 to 2 minutes. Transfer to serving dish.

Just before serving, toss all ingredients together with remaining garlic soy sauce.

COOK'S NOTE

- Although we prefer the Korean sweet potato vermicelli in this recipe, ½ pound cellophane noodles can be substituted. Soak them in cold water for 15 minutes, then cook in boiling water until just tender, 2 to 3 minutes, drain, and rinse.

DRIED ASIAN MUSHROOMS

Dried Asian mushrooms add a deep, foresty aroma and dense texture to hearty braises and noodle dishes. Their labeling, however, can be confusing. Korean *pyogo*, Chinese *xianggu*, and Japanese shiitake are all actually the same mushroom, *Lentinula edodes*, so use whichever one is most easily available to you (see Sources). The best specimens have thick, lightly spotted caps with deep cracks in them; they've been harvested at the end of the season, during the late fall and early winter, when the reduced moisture in the air tends to create fissures on the surface of the caps. Late-season mushrooms grow more slowly, which is why the caps are thicker, and the end result is a more concentrated flavor.

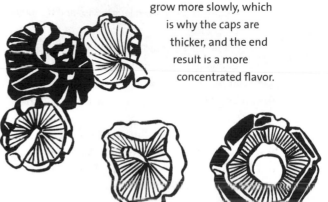

Pierogi

SERVES 6 AS A MAIN COURSE
ACTIVE TIME: 2 HOURS ■ START TO FINISH: 2¾ HOURS

■ Pierogi, classic Polish dumplings, are made with any number of fillings, from sauerkraut to plums. Most Americans, unfortunately, are familiar only with commercially made pierogi, the uniform half-moons of potato-filled dough found in supermarket freezers. There is simply no comparison to homemade. In this traditional version, a dough so tender that it holds the impression of the cook's hands is folded over a smooth, cheesy potato filling. Tossing the cooked pierogi with buttery browned onions takes the dish over the top. These dumplings make a vegetarian main course with just a leafy salad. ■

FOR DOUGH
- 3 cups all-purpose flour, plus additional for kneading
- 1 cup water
- 1 large egg
- 2 teaspoons vegetable oil
- Salt

FOR POTATO FILLING
- 1½ pounds russet (baking) potatoes
- 6 ounces extra-sharp white cheddar, coarsely grated (about 1½ cups)
- ¼ teaspoon salt
- ¼ teaspoon freshly ground black pepper
- ⅛ teaspoon freshly grated nutmeg

FOR ONION COATING
- 1 medium onion, halved lengthwise and thinly sliced crosswise
- 1 stick (8 tablespoons) unsalted butter
- Salt and freshly ground black pepper

ACCOMPANIMENT: sour cream

SPECIAL EQUIPMENT: a 2½-inch round cookie cutter

MAKE THE DOUGH: Put flour in a large shallow bowl and make a well in center. Add water, egg, oil, and 1 teaspoon salt to well and carefully beat together with a fork (without incorporating flour). Then stir with a wooden spoon, gradually incorporating flour, until a soft dough forms.

Transfer dough to a lightly floured surface and knead, dusting with flour as needed to keep it from sticking, until smooth and elastic, about 8 minutes (dough will be very soft). Invert a bowl over dough and let stand for 1 hour.

MEANWHILE, MAKE THE FILLING: Peel potatoes and cut into 1-inch pieces. Bring a large saucepan of salted water (1 tablespoon salt) to a boil. Add potatoes and cook until tender, about 8 minutes. Drain and transfer to a bowl. Add cheese, salt, pepper, and nutmeg to hot potatoes and mash with a potato masher, or beat with a handheld electric mixer at low speed, until smooth.

When potatoes are cool enough to handle, spoon out a rounded teaspoon and lightly roll into a ball between your palms. Transfer to a plate and cover with plastic wrap. Continue making balls in same manner; you want a total of 48 potato balls (there may be a little filling left over).

MAKE THE ONION COATING: Cook onion in butter in a 4- to 5-quart heavy pot over moderately low heat, stirring occasionally (more frequently toward end of cooking) until golden brown, about 30 minutes. Remove from heat and season with salt and pepper to taste.

FORM AND COOK THE PIEROGI: Halve dough, and keep 1 half under inverted bowl. Roll out remaining dough on a lightly floured surface (do not overflour surface, or dough will slide instead of stretch) with a lightly floured rolling pin into a 15-inch round. Cut out 24 rounds with lightly floured cookie cutter. Invert 1 round into palm of your hand, put a potato ball in center of round, and close your hand to fold round in half, enclosing filling. Firmly pinch edges together to seal. If edges don't adhere, brush them lightly with water, then seal; do not leave any gaps, or pierogi may open during cooking. Transfer pierogi to a lightly floured kitchen towel (not terry cloth) and cover with another towel. Form more pierogi in same manner with remaining dough rounds, then roll out and cut remaining dough to make more pierogi.

Bring an 8-quart pot of salted water (3 tablespoons salt) to a boil. Add half of pierogi, stirring once or twice to keep them from sticking together, and cook for 5 minutes from time pierogi float to surface. Transfer with a wire skimmer or slotted spoon to onion coating and toss gently to coat. Cook remaining pierogi in same manner and add to onions.

Reheat pierogi in onion coating over low heat, gently tossing to coat. Serve with sour cream.

COOK'S NOTES

- The potato filling can be made up to 2 days ahead and refrigerated, covered.
- The onion coating can be made up to 2 days ahead. Cool, uncovered, then refrigerate, covered.
- The pierogi can be formed ahead and frozen for up to 1 month. Freeze in one layer on a tray until firm, about 2 hours, then transfer to sealable plastic bags. Do not thaw before cooking.
- Leftover cooked pierogi can be refrigerated for up to 3 days. Refrigerate in one layer on a tray until firm, then refrigerate in an airtight container. Reheat in butter in a skillet over moderately low heat, gently stirring occasionally, until well browned and crisp in spots, about 5 minutes.

Afghani Spicy Scallion Dumplings with Yogurt and Meat Sauces

Aushak

SERVES 4 AS A MAIN COURSE
ACTIVE TIME: 50 MINUTES ■ START TO FINISH: 50 MINUTES

■ These Afghani dumplings taste both exotic and comforting, and their ingredients are reassuringly familiar. The colors and flavors of the two sauces swirl into each other: the yogurt sauce is cool and creamy, sharp and garlicky, a nice complement to the spiced ground beef sauce. Ruth Reichl first shared the dish in her book *Garlic and Sapphires*. ■

FOR MEAT SAUCE
- 3 tablespoons vegetable oil
- 1 medium onion, finely chopped
- ½ pound ground beef
- 1 garlic clove, minced
- 1 teaspoon ground coriander
- ½ teaspoon grated peeled fresh ginger
- ¼ cup water
- 2 tablespoons tomato paste
- ½ teaspoon salt
- ¼ teaspoon freshly ground black pepper

FOR YOGURT SAUCE
- 2 large garlic cloves
- ½ teaspoon salt
- 1 cup whole-milk yogurt

FOR DUMPLINGS
- 1¼ cups finely chopped scallion greens (from 2 bunches)
- Salt
- ½ teaspoon freshly ground black pepper
- 1 teaspoon red pepper flakes
- 1 teaspoon minced garlic
- 1½ teaspoons olive oil
- 25–30 wonton or gyoza wrappers, preferably round
- GARNISH: finely chopped fresh mint

MAKE THE MEAT SAUCE: Heat oil in a 10-inch heavy skillet over moderate heat until hot but not smoking. Add onion and cook, stirring occasionally until beginning to brown, 5 to 7 minutes. Add beef, garlic, coriander, and ginger and cook, breaking up meat with a fork, just until meat is no longer pink, 3 to 4 minutes.

Stir together water and tomato paste and add to beef. Bring to a simmer and simmer until liquid is reduced by half, about 4 minutes. Remove from heat and season with salt and pepper. Skim off and discard fat and cover to keep warm.

MAKE THE YOGURT SAUCE: Mince garlic and mash to a paste with salt, using side of a large heavy knife. Stir into yogurt.

MAKE THE DUMPLINGS: Stir together scallions, ½ teaspoon salt, pepper, red pepper, garlic, and olive oil in a bowl. Put a wonton wrapper on a work surface and brush edges with water. Spoon 1 teaspoon scallion mixture into center and fold wrapper in half to enclose filling, pressing edges to seal. Make more dumplings with remaining wrappers and filling in same manner.

Cook dumplings in a 6- to 8-quart pot of boiling salted water (3 tablespoons salt) for 5 minutes; drain.

Spread ¼ cup yogurt sauce on a platter and put dumplings on top, then spread with remaining yogurt sauce. Spoon meat sauce around dumplings. Sprinkle with mint and serve immediately.

COOK'S NOTES
- The meat sauce can be made up to 1 day ahead. Cool, uncovered, then refrigerate, covered. Add 3 tablespoons water while reheating.
- The yogurt sauce can be made up to 1 day ahead and refrigerated, covered. Bring to room temperature before using.
- The dumpling filling can be made up to 1 day ahead and refrigerated, covered.

GRAINS AND BEANS

I suspect that my mother, who had an extraordinary fondness for good old Uncle Ben, would be shocked to open my cupboard and discover how many different kinds of rice are sitting on my shelves. At the moment I've got Arborio, Carnaroli, jasmine, basmati, black, bomba, sticky, and brown rice.

And I am certainly not alone. Of all the changes in our diets over the last decade or so, our increased consumption of rice is most telling, most dramatic.

How did it begin? Perhaps it was when Chinese restaurants began asking which kind of rice you would like with your order, or when Thai restaurants began serving sticky rice in little baskets. Or maybe it began with the Latinization of the American diet; while salsa was becoming more common than ketchup, rice and beans were beginning to stand in for potatoes more and more often.

I first began to pay attention to the great rice revolution when I realized that risotto was showing up on the menus of restaurants across the country. All at once it seemed that risotto was so ubiquitous that chefs were using it as a means of personal expression. Risotto has become such a familiar part of the American diet that we've included seven different recipes in this chapter, from a traditional Italian mushroom version to a gorgeous radicchio and red wine risotto that looks like a sunset on the plate. And we could not omit the butternut squash risotto that is fast becoming a new American favorite. Each one makes a lovely meal, and risotto will also snuggle up to a chop or a chicken leg, taking the place on the plate once reserved for the baked potato.

Risotto is only the beginning. There are around eight thousand edible varieties of rice in the world, and each has its own unique qualities. The Italian short-grain versions—Arborio, Carnaroli, Vialone Nano—all have spines of steel, which give them the ability to retain their inner integrity while becoming tender on the outside. Asian sticky rice is entirely different, with a fabulous elasticity that makes it melt into dishes like sticky rice with Chinese sausage.

Indian basmati behaves in another fashion, growing longer rather than plumper as it cooks. This means that when you lift the lid off ginger basmati rice pilaf, you get not only the elegantly subtle aroma of basmati, but also a dish where each little kernel is distinct unto itself. Cook up some jasmine rice pilaf with mustard seeds, and the result is every bit as fragrant, but the perfume is gentler and sweeter, the texture fluffier.

Rice is not the only grain that is now capturing our kitchens and captivating our tables. One of the happiest recent developments has been the return of real stone-ground grits; they cook up into something so deliciously creamy that you'll be reminded of the true flavor of the past.

We've also been reconnecting with other familiar grains, like barley, bulgur, and buckwheat, but preparing them in new and exciting ways. In the past few years, many more exotic grains have appeared on our plates as well. Quinoa, the ancient and nutritious grain that has been a staple in Peru for thousands of years, is endlessly versatile. My favorite way to eat it is with mango and curried yogurt, a dish as lovely as it is delicious. Farro is starting to show up on tables all across the country as well; this wheat makes a fascinating stand-in for rice, as in farro risotto with cauliflower. The smoked green wheat of the Middle East is another find; here we turn it into a pilaf with currants and pine nuts.

Sometimes I imagine my mother opening the cupboard and staring at my canisters of grains and jars of dried beans. And then I imagine taking them down and cooking up a pot of black rice with scallions and sweet potatoes or black beans with garlic, cumin, and cilantro and watching her face as she eats. At moments like that, it occurs to me how lucky we are to be living in this particular moment.

GRAINS AND BEANS

Rice

Spinach and Rice with Lemon

SERVES 4 TO 6 AS A SIDE DISH
ACTIVE TIME: 45 MINUTES ■ START TO FINISH: 45 MINUTES

■ Combining a nutritious vegetable with rice in one tasty side dish is a great trick for weeknight meals. Don't be startled by the large quantity of spinach called for—it cooks down to a manageable amount. ■

- 2 tablespoons unsalted butter
- ¼ cup finely chopped shallots
- 1 cup long-grain white rice
- 1⅔ cups Chicken Stock (page 153) or store-bought reduced-sodium broth
- 2 tablespoons extra-virgin olive oil
- 1 tablespoon chopped garlic
- 3 (10-ounce) bags spinach, tough stems discarded
- Salt and freshly ground black pepper
- 2–3 teaspoons fresh lemon juice

Heat butter in a 1- to 2-quart heavy saucepan over moderately low heat until foam subsides. Add shallots and cook, stirring occasionally, until beginning to turn golden, about 2 minutes. Add rice and cook, stirring constantly, until grains turn opaque, about 2 minutes. Stir in stock and bring to a boil, then reduce heat to low and cook, covered, until liquid is absorbed and rice is just tender, about 15 minutes. Remove from heat and let stand, covered, for 5 minutes.

Meanwhile, heat oil in a 6- to 8-quart heavy pot over moderate heat until hot but not smoking. Add garlic and cook, stirring, until it begins to turn golden, about 1 minute. Add spinach, 1 teaspoon salt, and ¼ teaspoon pepper and cook, turning and stirring with tongs, until spinach is wilted and tender, about 3 minutes.

Stir 2 teaspoons lemon juice into spinach, then add rice and stir until just combined. Season with salt and pepper and add remaining teaspoon lemon juice if desired.

Coconut Rice

SERVES 8 AS A SIDE DISH
ACTIVE TIME: 10 MINUTES ■ START TO FINISH: 35 MINUTES

■ Though coconut rice is commonly served in Thailand, it is also a staple in the Caribbean, the provenance of this version. Radiating subtle warmth, it is just the thing when you want to serve something special alongside plain roast chicken or chops but don't have a lot of time. ■

- 2 cups long-grain white rice
- 1 tablespoon unsalted butter
- 1 (13- to 14-ounce) can unsweetened coconut milk
- 1 cup water
- 1 (3-inch) cinnamon stick
- ¼ teaspoon salt

Wash rice in several changes of water in a bowl until water runs clear, then drain well in a large sieve.

Melt butter in a 2- to 3-quart heavy saucepan over moderately high heat. Add rice and cook, stirring constantly, until it becomes opaque, about 3 minutes. Stir in remaining ingredients and bring to a boil. Reduce heat to low and simmer, covered, until rice is just tender, about 20 minutes. Remove from heat and let stand, covered, for 5 minutes.

Discard cinnamon stick and fluff rice with a fork.

Green Rice
Arroz Verde

SERVES 6 AS A SIDE DISH
ACTIVE TIME: 35 MINUTES ■ START TO FINISH: 1¼ HOURS

■ In Mexico, rice—red, white, or green—is often served as a *sopa seca,* or "dry soup," between soup and the main course, though it may also be a side dish. Unlike everyday red rice, which is flavored with tomatoes, *arroz verde* rarely appears on restaurant menus—it is usually made at home and reserved for special occasions. Soaking rice briefly in boiling water softens it, which in turn helps it to cook more quickly and to absorb the flavors of the other ingredients (in this case, roasted poblanos, onion, garlic, parsley, and cilantro). The result is a pretty pale green dish with a gentle bite that goes well with traditional Mexican dishes. It is also a fine side to fish or even something as unorthodox as Indian-spiced lamb kebabs. ∎

- 2 cups long-grain white rice
- 1 large or 2 small poblano chiles (6 ounces total), roasted (see Tips, page 914), peeled, seeded, deveined, and coarsely chopped
- ¼ cup packed fresh cilantro sprigs
- ¼ cup packed fresh flat-leaf parsley sprigs
- 3¼ cups Chicken Stock (page 153) or store-bought reduced-sodium broth
- ¼ cup vegetable oil
- ½ cup finely chopped white onion
- 3 garlic cloves, finely chopped
- 1 teaspoon salt

Rinse rice in a large sieve and transfer to a heatproof bowl. Add boiling water to cover and soak for 15 minutes.

Drain rice well in sieve and let stand in sieve over bowl for 10 to 15 minutes to dry.

Meanwhile, puree chiles with cilantro, parsley, and 1 cup stock in a blender until smooth. Pour through a medium-mesh sieve into a small bowl, pressing on solids; discard solids.

Heat oil in a 4-quart wide heavy pot over moderately high heat until hot but not smoking. Add onion and garlic and cook, stirring, until pale golden, 3 to 4 minutes. Add rice and cook, stirring, until it is

opaque and pale golden, 3 to 4 minutes. Stir in chile puree, salt, and remaining 2¼ cups stock and bring to a simmer. Cover rice, reduce heat to low, and cook until just tender, about 15 minutes. Remove from heat and let stand, covered, for 5 minutes.

Fluff rice with a fork before serving.

Yellow Rice
Arroz Amarillo

SERVES 4 AS A SIDE DISH
ACTIVE TIME: 20 MINUTES ∎ START TO FINISH: 50 MINUTES

∎ *Sofrito*, a sautéed vegetable mixture that typically contains garlic, onion, and bell pepper, is used as a seasoning in much of Latin America and the Caribbean. Here it flavors yellow rice. The color of *arroz amarillo* comes from saffron or, more commonly and less expensively, annatto seeds, which have an astringent, slightly peppery flavor. ∎

- 1 tablespoon annatto (achiote) seeds (see Sources)
- ¼ cup mild olive or vegetable oil
- ½ cup finely chopped onion
- ¼ cup finely chopped green bell pepper
- 2 large garlic cloves, finely chopped
- ¼ cup chopped fresh cilantro
- 1¾ cups long-grain white rice
- 3 cups water
- 1 teaspoon salt

Heat annatto seeds and oil in a very small saucepan over low heat, swirling pan frequently, until oil turns bright red-orange and begins to simmer, 1 to 2 minutes. Remove from heat and let stand for 10 minutes. Pour oil through a fine-mesh sieve into a small bowl; discard seeds.

Cook onion, bell pepper, garlic, and cilantro in 1½ tablespoons annatto oil (reserve leftover oil for another use) in a 2- to 3-quart heavy saucepan over moderate heat, stirring, until vegetables are softened, 3 to 5 minutes. Add rice and cook, stirring, until most of grains are opaque, 1 to 2 minutes. Stir in water and salt and bring to a boil. Stir rice again, reduce heat to low, and cook, covered, until it is just tender, about 15 minutes. Remove from heat and let stand, covered, for 5 minutes.

Fluff rice with a fork before serving.

COOK'S NOTES

■ You can substitute ¼ teaspoon saffron for the annatto. Use only 1½ tablespoons oil and crumble the saffron into the oil just before adding it to the vegetables.

■ The leftover annatto oil can be refrigerated in an airtight container for up to 1 month. You can use it to flavor rice.

Fried Rice
with Eggs and Scallions

SERVES 4 AS A SIDE DISH OR LIGHT MAIN COURSE
ACTIVE TIME: 10 MINUTES ■ START TO FINISH: 10 MINUTES

■ When you order Chinese takeout, ask for an extra container of rice—it's a great thing to keep on hand so you can make this quick fried rice from Fuchsia Dunlop, an authority on Chinese cooking. Tossed with stir-fried eggs, scallions, and sesame oil, it couldn't be simpler.

If you cook your own rice, chill it before you add it to the wok, or it will clump together. ■

1 tablespoon peanut oil
4 large eggs, lightly beaten
4 cups cold unsalted steamed white rice (left over, or see page 256)
¾ teaspoon salt
½ cup thinly sliced scallion greens
1–2 teaspoons Asian sesame oil, or to taste
SPECIAL EQUIPMENT: a well-seasoned flat-bottomed 14-inch wok

Heat wok over high heat until a drop of water evaporates on contact. Add peanut oil, swirling to coat wok evenly, and heat until just smoking. Add eggs, tilting wok and swirling eggs to form a thin even layer, and cook for 30 seconds. Add rice and salt and stir-fry, breaking up eggs and waiting several seconds between stirs, until rice is hot, 2 to 3 minutes. Add

scallion greens and sesame oil and stir-fry until well combined.

Savory Rice Cakes

SERVES 4 AS A SIDE DISH
ACTIVE TIME: 40 MINUTES ■ START TO FINISH: 40 MINUTES

■ Formed into patties and fried until golden, leftover rice gets a whole new life. The rice cakes' edges become addictively crisp, and the chopped carrot, celery, and scallion add punctuations of flavor. ■

5 tablespoons olive oil
3 scallions, finely chopped
1 carrot, finely chopped
1 celery rib, finely chopped
2 garlic cloves, finely chopped
1 teaspoon finely chopped fresh thyme
¾ teaspoon salt
¼ teaspoon freshly ground black pepper
2 cups unsalted steamed white rice (left over, or see page 256), at room temperature
2 large eggs, lightly beaten
1 cup fresh bread crumbs (from 2 slices firm white sandwich bread)

Heat 2 tablespoons oil in a 12-inch heavy nonstick skillet over moderate heat until hot but not smoking. Add scallions, carrot, celery, garlic, thyme, salt, and pepper and cook, stirring, until carrot is softened, about 8 minutes.

Transfer vegetables to a bowl. Add rice, eggs, and bread crumbs and stir together. Form into eight 2½-by-½-inch patties, pressing mixture so cakes hold together (mixture will be loose); transfer to wax paper.

Heat 2 tablespoons oil in cleaned skillet over moderately high heat until hot but not smoking. Cook 4 rice cakes, carefully turning once, until browned, about 7 minutes. Transfer to a plate and cover loosely with foil to keep warm. Add remaining tablespoon oil to oil remaining in pan, heat until hot, and cook remaining 4 cakes in same manner.

Steamed White Rice

SERVES 6
ACTIVE TIME: 5 MINUTES ■ START TO FINISH: 30 MINUTES

■ No salt is used in this traditional Asian recipe. Folding the rice from the top to the bottom of the pan after cooking helps distribute the moisture evenly. ■

    2 cups long-grain white rice
 2⅔ cups water

Rinse rice well in a sieve under cold running water; drain. Transfer to a 2- to 3-quart heavy saucepan, add water, and bring to a boil, then reduce heat to low, cover with a tight-fitting lid, and cook for 20 minutes. Remove from heat and let stand, covered, for 5 minutes.

Stir rice gently with a heatproof rubber spatula, folding from top to bottom of pan.

Herbed Jasmine Rice

SERVES 4 AS A SIDE DISH
ACTIVE TIME: 20 MINUTES ■ START TO FINISH: 20 MINUTES

■ People who think they don't know how to cook rice will love this recipe: it's as simple as boiling pasta and produces very tender grains. The method can be applied to any long-grain variety. Choose gentle herbs; assertive flavors like sage will overpower the rice. ■

 1½ cups jasmine rice
     Salt
   2 tablespoons unsalted butter
   ½ cup chopped mixed delicate, tender-leaved fresh
        herbs, such as flat-leaf parsley, chives, tarragon,
        cilantro, dill, and/or basil
   ¼ teaspoon freshly ground black pepper

Cook rice in a 4-quart saucepan of boiling salted water (2 to 3 teaspoons salt), uncovered, stirring occasionally, until tender, about 12 minutes. Drain well

in a large sieve, then toss with butter, herbs, and pepper in a bowl.

Jasmine Rice Pilaf with Mustard Seeds

SERVES 4 AS A SIDE DISH
ACTIVE TIME: 10 MINUTES ■ START TO FINISH: 25 MINUTES

■ Mustard seeds add a delicate crunch and gentle bite to this pilaf, which goes well with most poultry or meats. ■

   1 tablespoon vegetable oil
   ¼ cup thinly sliced shallots
   1 tablespoon mustard seeds
   1 cup jasmine or long-grain white rice
 1¾ cups water
   ¾ teaspoon salt
   ¼ cup thinly sliced scallion greens

Heat oil in a 1½- to 2-quart heavy saucepan over moderately low heat until hot but not smoking. Add shallots and cook, stirring occasionally, until pale golden, about 6 minutes. Add mustard seeds and cook, stirring occasionally, for 1 minute. Stir in rice and cook, stirring occasionally, for 1 minute. Add water and salt and bring to a boil. Stir rice once, reduce heat to low, and cook, covered, for 15 minutes. Remove from heat and let stand, covered, for 5 minutes.

Fluff rice gently with a fork and stir in scallions.

Spiced Basmati Rice

SERVES 6 TO 8 AS A SIDE DISH
ACTIVE TIME: 10 MINUTES ■ START TO FINISH: 30 MINUTES

■ Frying the cinnamon stick and bay leaves in oil before adding the rice and water, a common practice in Indian cooking, permeates this dish with subtle flavor. ■

   2 cups basmati rice
 1–2 (3-inch) cinnamon sticks
   4 Turkish bay leaves or 2 California bay leaves

1 tablespoon vegetable oil

3 cups water

1 teaspoon salt

Wash rice in several changes of cold water in a bowl until water runs clear. Drain well in a large sieve.

Cook spices in oil in a 3- to 4-quart heavy saucepan over moderate heat, stirring, until fragrant, about 1 minute. Stir in rice and cook, stirring, for 1 minute. Stir in water and salt and bring to a boil. Reduce heat to low and cook, covered, until rice is tender and liquid is absorbed, about 15 minutes. Remove from heat and let stand, covered, for 5 minutes.

Discard cinnamon and bay leaves and fluff rice gently with a fork.

Brown Rice with Toasted Almonds and Parsley

SERVES 4 AS A SIDE DISH
ACTIVE TIME: 20 MINUTES ■ START TO FINISH: 1½ HOURS

■ Cooking the aromatic vegetables separately from the rice keeps the flavors distinct and the finished dish from becoming mushy. The clean bite of parsley plays off the toasted almonds (pecans also work well). ■

1 cup long-grain brown rice

1¾ cups Chicken Stock (page 153) or store-bought reduced-sodium broth

3 tablespoons unsalted butter

1 large onion, finely chopped

2 celery ribs, cut into ¼-inch pieces

2 garlic cloves, finely chopped

½ teaspoon salt

¼ teaspoon freshly ground black pepper

½ cup coarsely chopped fresh flat-leaf parsley

GARNISH: ⅓ cup sliced almonds, lightly toasted (see Tips, page 911)

Bring rice and stock to a boil in a 2- to 3-quart heavy saucepan over moderately high heat. Reduce heat to low and simmer, covered, until stock is absorbed and rice is tender, about 40 minutes. Remove

rice from heat and let stand, covered, for 10 minutes.

While rice stands, melt butter in a 12-inch heavy skillet over moderately high heat. Add onion, celery, garlic, salt, and pepper and cook, stirring, until vegetables are golden brown, 10 to 12 minutes.

Fluff rice with a fork and stir into vegetables, along with parsley, until well combined. Serve sprinkled with almonds.

Ginger Basmati Rice Pilaf with Cumin and Scallions

SERVES 6 AS A SIDE DISH
ACTIVE TIME: 15 MINUTES ■ START TO FINISH: 35 MINUTES

■ As it cooks, basmati rice expands lengthwise rather than plumping up as other types of rice do. The cooked grains have a wonderfully nutty fragrance. Though both white and brown basmati rices are available, we prefer white because of its more delicate taste and texture—plus, it cooks in a flash. Fresh ginger, scallions, and a smattering of toasted whole cumin seeds play up the rice's flavor. ■

1½ cups white basmati rice

1 tablespoon vegetable oil

½ cup thinly sliced scallions

1 tablespoon finely chopped peeled fresh ginger

¾ teaspoon cumin seeds, toasted (see Tips, page 911)

2¼ cups water

¾ teaspoon salt

Wash rice in several changes of cold water in a bowl until water runs clear. Drain well in a sieve.

Heat oil in a 2- to 3-quart heavy saucepan over moderate heat until hot but not smoking. Add scallions and ginger and cook, stirring, until scallions are softened, about 2 minutes. Add rice and cumin seeds and cook, stirring, until fragrant, about 1 minute. Stir in water and salt and bring to a boil. Reduce heat to low and cook, covered, until rice is tender and liquid is absorbed, 10 to 12 minutes. Remove from heat and let stand, covered, for 5 minutes.

Fluff rice gently with a fork.

Ginger is a rhizome, or underground stem, of a lush, bushy plant. Fresh ginger should be firm, unwrinkled, and heavy for its size, with a tan skin and crisp, not fibrous, flesh. To keep it at its peak, wrap it in a paper towel and store it in the vegetable crisper; it will last a good 10 days that way. Inspect it every once in a while and cut off any moldy or dry, woody bits. In cool, dry weather, some of our food editors keep it out on their kitchen counter, next to the salt and pepper.

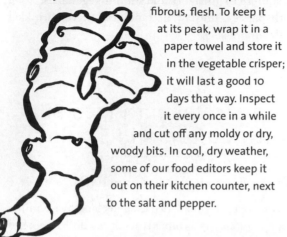

Wash rice in several changes of water in a bowl until water runs clear, then drain well in a large sieve.

Bring rice and water to a boil in a 3-quart heavy saucepan. Reduce heat and cook, covered, over very low heat until water is absorbed and rice is tender, 20 to 25 minutes. Remove from heat and let stand, covered, for 10 minutes, then fluff rice gently with a fork.

Heat oil in a deep 12-inch heavy skillet over moderately high heat until hot but not smoking. Add mustard seeds and cook, stirring, until beginning to pop. Add ginger and ¼ cup peanuts and cook, stirring, for 2 minutes. Add turmeric, rice, and salt to taste, stirring to coat rice thoroughly. Remove skillet from heat and stir in lemon juice. Sprinkle with remaining peanuts and zest.

Lemon Rice with Peanuts

SERVES 6 TO 8 AS A SIDE DISH
ACTIVE TIME: 20 MINUTES ■ START TO FINISH: 45 MINUTES

■ Turmeric and black mustard seeds enliven this South Indian dish, and lemon—both zest and juice—adds brightness. This rice is a great foil for chicken, lamb, or shrimp. ■

  2 cups basmati rice
  3 cups water
  1 tablespoon vegetable oil
  2 teaspoons mustard seeds, preferably black (see Sources)
  1 tablespoon minced peeled fresh ginger
  ⅓ cup finely chopped salted roasted peanuts
  ½ teaspoon turmeric
    Salt
  3 tablespoons fresh lemon juice
  1 tablespoon thin strips lemon zest (use a zester, or remove wide strips of zest with a vegetable peeler and thinly slice)

Foolproof Thai Sticky Rice

SERVES 4
ACTIVE TIME: 10 MINUTES ■ START TO FINISH: 3½ HOURS
(INCLUDES SOAKING RICE)

■ No Thai meal is complete without sticky rice. In fact, sticky rice, sometimes called sweet rice or glutinous rice, is the main event around which all the other dishes revolve. Diners put small bites of each dish on their plates, then form walnut-sized amounts of rice into balls with their fingers and use them to pick up a slice of meat or vegetable. ■

  2 cups Thai (long-grain) sticky rice (see Cook's Note)
SPECIAL EQUIPMENT: cheesecloth

Wash rice in several changes of cold water in a bowl until water runs clear. Soak rice in fresh water to cover for at least 3 hours.

Drain rice and put in a cheesecloth-lined sieve or colander. Set over 1 inch of boiling water in a large pot; do not let rice touch boiling water. Cover pot and steam rice, checking water level occasionally and adding more boiling water if necessary, until shiny and tender, about 20 minutes. Remove from heat and let stand, covered, for 5 minutes before serving.

- When shopping for the sticky rice, which is available at Asian markets and by mail (see Sources), make sure you buy long-grain rice from Thailand, not short-grain sticky rice from China.
- The rice can be soaked, covered and refrigerated, for up to 8 hours.

Wild Rice with Roasted Peppers and Toasted Almonds

SERVES 8 AS A SIDE DISH
ACTIVE TIME: 30 MINUTES ■ START TO FINISH: 1¼ HOURS

■ Cooking shallots and garlic in olive oil until golden brown before stirring in the wild rice deepens the flavor of this pilaf. Roasted red bell peppers add sweetness and color. This dish is a natural with roast turkey, but it is equally delicious with beef tenderloin. ■

¼ pound shallots (about 4 medium), thinly sliced
4 garlic cloves, thinly sliced
2 tablespoons olive oil
2 cups wild rice, rinsed and drained
3½ cups Chicken Stock (page 153) or store-bought reduced-sodium broth
3½ cups water
2 red bell peppers, halved lengthwise, cored, and seeded
1 tablespoon unsalted butter
1 cup (about 3½ ounces) sliced unblanched almonds
1 teaspoon salt
¼ teaspoon freshly ground black pepper
1 tablespoon sherry vinegar

Cook shallots and garlic in oil in a 4- to 5-quart heavy pot over moderately low heat, stirring occasionally, until golden brown, about 10 minutes. Add rice and cook, stirring, until it releases a nutty aroma, about 3 minutes. Add stock and water and bring to a boil, stirring occasionally, then reduce heat and sim-

mer, covered, until rice is tender and grains are split open, about 1¼ hours.

Meanwhile, preheat broiler. Oil a shallow baking pan. Put bell peppers cut side down in 1 layer in baking pan and broil 2 inches from heat until charred and softened, 15 to 18 minutes. Transfer to a bowl, cover with plastic, and let steam for 15 minutes.

Peel peppers and cut into ½-inch pieces.

Melt butter in a 12-inch heavy skillet over moderate heat. Add almonds and cook, stirring, until golden, 5 to 8 minutes. Set aside.

Drain rice well and return to pot. Stir in salt, pepper, red peppers, almonds, and vinegar.

- The rice can be cooked (don't drain it) and the peppers roasted and diced up to 1 day ahead. Cool the rice, uncovered, then refrigerate the rice and peppers separately, covered. Reheat the rice in a heavy pot, covered, over low heat, for 10 to 15 minutes; drain before adding the seasonings, peppers, almonds, and vinegar.

Wild Rice and Bulgur with Braised Vegetables

SERVES 8 AS A SIDE DISH
ACTIVE TIME: 45 MINUTES ■ START TO FINISH: 2 HOURS

■ We've never been particular fans of wild rice mixed with white rice (especially in its packaged incarnations), but we do love how fluffy bulgur adds a lightness to wild rice's chewiness. This goes well with poultry. ■

8 cups water
Salt
1 cup bulgur
1 cup wild rice
3 tablespoons unsalted butter
2 medium leeks (8 ounces total; white and pale green parts only), finely chopped and washed well
1 cup finely chopped onion
1 cup finely chopped carrots
1 cup finely chopped celery
Freshly ground black pepper

Bring water and 2 teaspoons salt to a boil in a 3-quart saucepan. Put bulgur in a large heatproof bowl, pour half of boiling water over it, and soak, uncovered, until tender, about 1 hour. Drain in a large colander.

Meanwhile, add wild rice to water remaining in pan, bring to a simmer, and simmer, covered, until rice is tender and grains are split open, 1 to 1¼ hours. Drain in colander with bulgur.

Melt butter in a 3- to 4-quart wide heavy saucepan over moderately low heat. Add leeks, onion, carrots, celery, and ½ teaspoon salt and cook, stirring occasionally, until vegetables are tender, about 10 minutes. Stir in rice and bulgur and cook, covered, stirring occasionally, until heated through, 5 to 10 minutes. Season with salt and pepper to taste.

COOK'S NOTE
- The bulgur can be soaked and the rice cooked up to 1 day ahead. Drain and cool, uncovered, then refrigerate, covered.

Wild Rice Stuffing with Sausage and Fennel

SERVES 12 TO 16 AS A SIDE DISH
ACTIVE TIME: 55 MINUTES ■ START TO FINISH: 2¼ HOURS

■ We can't get enough of this homey, nubbly stuffing. It's terrific with an oven-bronzed Thanksgiving turkey, a majestic crown roast of pork, or, for a more casual affair, roast chicken or pork loin. ■

1½   cups wild rice, rinsed well and drained
2   teaspoons fennel seeds
3½   cups Chicken Stock (page 153) or store-bought reduced-sodium broth
3½   cups water
1   pound sweet Italian sausage, casings discarded if in links
½   stick (4 tablespoons) unsalted butter
2   cups finely chopped onions
3   cups finely chopped fennel (two 1-pound bulbs)
½   teaspoon salt, or to taste
½   teaspoon freshly ground black pepper, or to taste

Combine rice, fennel seeds, stock, and water in a 3- to 4-quart heavy saucepan and bring to a boil, then reduce heat to low and simmer, covered, until rice is tender and grains are split open, 1 to 1¼ hours.

Meanwhile, cook sausage in a 10-inch heavy skillet over moderate heat, stirring and breaking up lumps, until no longer pink, about 5 minutes. Transfer to a large bowl.

Melt butter in same skillet over moderately low heat, then add onions and cook, stirring, until pale golden, 10 to 15 minutes. Add chopped fennel and cook, stirring, until fennel and onions are golden brown, 15 to 20 minutes. Remove from heat.

Put a rack in middle of oven and preheat oven to 400°F.

Drain rice in a large sieve and add to sausage, along with onion mixture, salt, and pepper, tossing until well combined. Transfer to a 3-quart baking dish and cover with foil.

Bake stuffing for 15 minutes. Remove foil and bake until heated through, 10 to 15 minutes more.

COOK'S NOTES
- The stuffing can be made up to 1 day ahead. Cool, uncovered, then refrigerate, covered.
- You can stuff any bird with the cooled stuffing just before cooking, and bake any remaining stuffing in a baking dish as described above.

Black Rice with Scallions and Sweet Potatoes

SERVES 4 AS A SIDE DISH
ACTIVE TIME: 15 MINUTES ■ START TO FINISH: 40 MINUTES

■ The stunning color of this rice comes from the layers of black bran surrounding the white kernel. Sometimes labeled "forbidden rice," it makes a dramatic—and nutritious—presentation when paired with sautéed sweet potatoes. The dish goes especially well with grilled or roasted meats. ■

¾   cup Chinese black rice (see Sources)
1½   cups water
     Salt

2 tablespoons vegetable oil
1 bunch scallions, chopped
1 tablespoon minced peeled fresh ginger
1 large sweet potato (12–14 ounces), peeled and cut into ½-inch pieces
Freshly ground black pepper
GARNISH: chopped scallion greens

Wash rice in several changes of water in a bowl until water runs clear, then drain in a sieve.

Bring rice, water, and ½ teaspoon salt to a boil in a 1½- to 2-quart heavy saucepan, then reduce heat to low and cook, covered, until rice is tender and most of water is absorbed, about 30 minutes. Remove from heat and let stand, covered for 10 minutes.

Meanwhile, heat oil in a 12-inch heavy nonstick skillet over moderately high heat until hot but not smoking. Add scallions, ginger, and sweet potato and cook, stirring, until well coated, about 2 minutes. Reduce heat to moderate, add ¼ teaspoon salt and pepper to taste, and cook, covered, stirring occasionally, until potato is just tender, about 12 minutes.

Add rice and toss gently to combine. Sprinkle with scallion greens.

Mushroom Risotto

SERVES 8 AS A FIRST COURSE, 6 AS A MAIN COURSE
ACTIVE TIME: 45 MINUTES ■ START TO FINISH: 1 HOUR

■ Soy sauce may not be a traditional ingredient in risotto, but just a small amount intensifies the flavor of the mushrooms, a mix of dried porcini and fresh cremini. The result needs only a leafy green salad to complete the meal. You may want to set aside some of the risotto to make Mushroom Risotto Cakes (see Cook's Note). ■

1 ounce (1 cup) dried porcini mushrooms
3¾ cups hot water
5¼ cups Chicken Stock (page 153) or store-bought reduced-sodium broth
1 tablespoon soy sauce

1 tablespoon olive oil
¾ stick (6 tablespoons) unsalted butter
1 small onion, finely chopped
2 garlic cloves, finely chopped
¾ pound cremini mushrooms, trimmed and thinly sliced
2⅓ cups Carnaroli or Arborio rice
⅔ cup dry white wine
½ cup finely grated Parmigiano-Reggiano
1 teaspoon salt
½ teaspoon freshly ground black pepper
¼ cup chopped fresh flat-leaf parsley
GARNISH: Parmigiano-Reggiano shavings

Soak porcini in 1½ cups hot water in a bowl until softened, about 20 minutes. Lift porcini out of soaking liquid and squeeze excess liquid back into bowl. Rinse porcini well to remove any grit, and coarsely chop.

Pour porcini soaking liquid through a fine-mesh sieve lined with a dampened paper towel into a 3- to 4-quart saucepan. Add stock, soy sauce, and remaining 2¼ cups hot water to pan and bring to a simmer. Reduce heat and keep at a bare simmer.

Meanwhile, heat oil with 1 tablespoon butter in a 4- to 5-quart heavy pot over moderately high heat until foam subsides. Add onion and cook, stirring, until just softened, about 5 minutes. Add garlic and cremini and cook, stirring, until mushrooms are browned and any liquid they give off has evaporated, about 8 minutes. Stir in porcini and cook, stirring, for 1 minute. Add rice and cook, stirring, for 1 minute. Add wine and cook, stirring, until absorbed, about 1 minute.

Add 1 cup simmering stock and cook, stirring and keeping it at a strong simmer, until absorbed. Continue cooking and adding stock about 1 cup at a time, stirring frequently and letting each addition be absorbed before adding the next, until rice is tender and creamy-looking but still al dente, 18 to 20 minutes (there will be about 1 cup stock left over).

Remove pot from heat and stir in cheese, salt, pepper, and remaining 5 tablespoons butter until butter is melted. (If planning to make Mushroom Risotto Cakes, set aside 3 cups now.) If desired, thin risotto with some of remaining stock. Stir in parsley and serve immediately, topped with Parmigiano-Reggiano shavings.

■ To make the Mushroom Risotto Cakes (recipe follows), transfer the 3 cups risotto, without the parsley, to a bowl and cool to room temperature. Then refrigerate, covered with plastic wrap, until well chilled. (Or, to quick-chill the 3 cups risotto, spread it on a parchment-paper-lined baking sheet, cover with another sheet of parchment, and cool to room temperature; then refrigerate until cold, about 30 minutes.) The risotto keeps, covered and refrigerated, for up to 4 days.

Mushroom Risotto Cakes

SERVES 4 AS A SIDE DISH
ACTIVE TIME: 25 MINUTES ■ START TO FINISH: 2 HOURS
(INCLUDES MAKING AND CHILLING RISOTTO)

■ The charm of these tender little cakes lies in their many textures: the creaminess of the risotto, the meatiness of the mushrooms, and the crisp bread crumb coating. Serve alongside chops or roasted chicken. ■

- 3 cups Mushroom Risotto (page 261), chilled
- 1 cup all-purpose flour
- 2 large eggs, lightly beaten
- 2 cups coarse fresh bread crumbs (from about 4 slices firm white sandwich bread)
- 6 tablespoons olive oil

Put a rack in middle of oven and preheat oven to 350°F.

With wet hands, form chilled risotto into eight ¾-inch-thick patties. Put flour, eggs, and bread crumbs in three separate shallow bowls. Coat 1 cake with flour, tapping off excess, then with egg (letting excess drip off), then with bread crumbs. Transfer to a sheet of wax paper. Repeat with remaining cakes.

Heat 3 tablespoons oil in a 12-inch heavy nonstick skillet over moderately high heat until hot but not smoking. Add 4 cakes and cook, turning once, until browned, 5 to 6 minutes. Transfer with a slotted spatula to a paper-towel-lined baking pan and keep warm in oven. Heat remaining 3 tablespoons oil and cook remaining 4 cakes in same manner.

Risotto with Asparagus, Peas, and Mushrooms

SERVES 6 TO 8 AS A FIRST COURSE, 4 AS A MAIN COURSE
ACTIVE TIME: 1 HOUR ■ START TO FINISH: 1 HOUR

■ This risotto has a lively, fresh taste because the vegetables are cooked separately from the rice and then spooned over it as a tasty ragout. A touch of lemon zest and a dusting of fresh chives bring alive the flavors of the morels, asparagus, and baby peas. ■

- ¾ ounce (1 cup) dried morels or ¼ pound fresh morels, trimmed
- 6½ cups Chicken Stock (page 153) or store-bought reduced-sodium broth
- 2 cups water
- 1 pound medium asparagus, trimmed and cut diagonally into 1-inch pieces
- 2 tablespoons olive oil
- ½ small onion, finely chopped
- 2 cups Carnaroli or Arborio rice
- ½ cup dry white wine
- ⅔ cup finely grated Parmigiano-Reggiano, plus additional for serving
  Salt and freshly ground black pepper
- ½ stick (4 tablespoons) unsalted butter, cut into tablespoons
- 1 teaspoon finely chopped garlic
- ½ cup frozen baby peas
- 1 teaspoon finely grated lemon zest
- 2 teaspoons chopped fresh chives

If using dried morels, soak in warm water to cover for 30 minutes. Agitate dried morels in soaking water (or fresh morels in cold water) to dislodge grit, then lift from water, squeezing out excess; discard soaking water. Pat mushrooms dry with paper towels.

Cut morels crosswise into ¼-inch-thick slices.

Bring stock and water to a boil in a 4-quart saucepan. Add asparagus and cook, uncovered, stirring occasionally, until crisp-tender, 3 to 4 minutes. With a slotted spoon, transfer asparagus to a large bowl of ice and cold water to stop the cooking, then drain and pat dry. Remove and reserve 1 cup stock mixture for ragout; keep remaining stock at a bare simmer.

Heat oil in a 5- to 6-quart heavy pot over moderate heat. Add onion and cook, stirring, until softened, about 3 minutes. Add rice and cook, stirring constantly, for 1 minute. Add wine and simmer briskly, stirring constantly, until absorbed, about 1 minute. Add ½ cup hot stock mixture and simmer briskly, stirring constantly, until broth is absorbed. Continue simmering and adding hot broth mixture about ½ cup at a time, stirring constantly and letting each addition be absorbed before adding the next, until rice is just tender and creamy-looking, 18 to 22 minutes. (There will be leftover stock; reserve for thinning risotto.) Stir cheese, ¼ teaspoon salt, and ¼ teaspoon pepper into risotto, then remove from heat and let stand, covered, while you make ragout.

Heat 2 tablespoons butter in a 10-inch heavy skillet over moderately high heat until foam subsides. Add morels and garlic and cook, stirring occasionally, until garlic is pale golden, about 4 minutes. Pour in reserved 1 cup stock and bring to a boil. Stir in peas, asparagus, zest, ¼ teaspoon salt, and ¼ teaspoon pepper and simmer, stirring occasionally, until vegetables are heated through, about 2 minutes. Remove from heat, add remaining 2 tablespoons butter, swirling skillet until butter is incorporated, and season with salt and pepper.

Thin risotto to desired consistency with leftover stock and season with salt and pepper. Divide risotto among shallow bowls. Spoon asparagus and morel ragout, with liquid, on top and sprinkle with chives.

COOK'S NOTE

- The dried morels can be soaked up to 1 day ahead. Drain, pat dry, and refrigerate, covered.

Beet Risotto

SERVES 4 TO 6 AS A MAIN COURSE
ACTIVE TIME: 45 MINUTES ■ START TO FINISH: 2¼ HOURS

■ So bright it shimmers, this vivid magenta dish incorporates the nutritious greens and stems of the beets. A generous dusting of Parmesan tempers the earthy sweetness. You can prep the beets ahead (see Cook's Note, page 265). ■

2¼ pounds beets with greens (9 medium beets), trimmed, leaving about 1 inch of stems attached to beets, greens and stems reserved separately
5½ cups water
5 tablespoons unsalted butter
1 medium onion, chopped
4 large garlic cloves, finely chopped
 Salt
1½ cups Carnaroli or Arborio rice
½ cup dry white wine
½ cup finely grated Parmigiano-Reggiano, plus additional for serving
½ teaspoon freshly ground black pepper

Put a rack in middle of oven and preheat oven to 450°F.

Wrap beets (together) tightly in foil. Roast until tender, about 1½ hours. Carefully unwrap beets and let stand until cool enough to handle. Peel beets (discard attached stems).

Meanwhile, wash reserved beet stems and cut into ¼-inch pieces. Wash and drain leaves and coarsely chop. Set stems and leaves aside separately.

Cut enough beets into ½-inch pieces to make 2 cups. Puree remaining beets with 1 cup water in a blender until smooth, then transfer to a 3- to 4-quart saucepan. Stir in remaining 4½ cups water and bring to a simmer. Reduce heat and keep at a bare simmer.

Heat butter in a 5- to 6-quart heavy pot over moderate heat until foam subsides. Add onion, garlic, chopped beet stems, and 1 teaspoon salt and cook, stirring, until vegetables are softened, about 8 minutes. Stir in rice and cook, stirring, for 1 minute. Add wine and cook, stirring, until absorbed.

Add ½ cup beet broth and cook, stirring constantly and keeping it at a strong simmer, until absorbed. Continue simmering and adding beet broth about ½ cup at a time, stirring constantly and letting each addition be absorbed before adding the next, until you've added about half of broth. Stir in chopped beets and beet greens and continue to cook, adding broth in same manner, until rice is tender and creamy-looking but still al dente, about 18 minutes (there may be broth left over).

Stir in cheese, salt to taste, and pepper. Serve immediately, sprinkled with Parmesan.

Risotto

Risotto is simultaneously simple and luxurious. It takes rice out of the side dish category and makes it a course of its own. You'll spend 20 minutes standing over the stove, it's true, but stirring a pot of risotto isn't exactly onerous, and you can drink a glass of wine and visit with the friends you've invited over for dinner. (They'll have gravitated to the kitchen anyway.) There are any number of variations—see the recipes on pages 261–266, or let the contents of your refrigerator be your guide—that will leave the people sitting around your table feeling blissful. Because risotto is all about layering flavors, you should use top-drawer ingredients. Good butter. Good wine. Real Parmigiano-Reggiano. Fresh, firm garlic cloves. Homemade chicken stock, if you can swing it. (Canned broth works fine, but it doesn't have the body that stock, rich with gelatin, has.) The rice, obviously, is crucial, but there's no great mystery to it: an Italian medium-grain variety such as Carnaroli, Arborio, or Vialone Nano (available at Italian markets, specialty foods shops, and many supermarkets) will retain its shape and chewy kernel as it becomes almost suspended in creaminess. In effect, the rice makes its own sauce, as Harold McGee says—and goes on to explain how—in *On Food and Cooking:* medium- and short-grain rices have a large amount of the starch molecules called amylopectins, which give them their stickiness; stirring the rice releases the amylopectins, thus thickening the cooking liquid. For perfect risotto, after you've cooked the onion (and sometimes garlic) in olive oil and a little butter until they're translucent (don't let them brown), add the rice and stir until it's glossy with oil and looks a bit like milk glass. Add some wine—you'd miss that clean, acidic note

if it wasn't there—and let it bubble away. Then begin adding the hot stock or broth a little at a time, stirring until it's absorbed by the rice. (At this point, it's helpful to set a kitchen timer for, say, 18 minutes, so that you can keep track of how long you cook the rice.) To test for when to add more liquid, drag a wooden spoon (a flat-edged spatula-like one covers a large surface area) through the middle of the rice: if there's only a small amount of liquid, the rice is ready for more. Risotto is done when the rice is tender but still al dente. We like to thin it with a little of the remaining hot stock to make it, as the Italians say, *all'onda* ("wavy"). Chilled leftovers, if there are any, can be shaped into cakes (see the recipe on page 262) and panfried, then served with a salad for lunch, with an egg for breakfast, or as a side dish.

- The beets can be roasted and peeled up to 1 day ahead. Cool completely, unwrapped, then refrigerate, wrapped in foil. The beet stems and leaves can be chopped up to 1 day ahead and refrigerated separately, in dampened paper towels in sealable plastic bags.

Radicchio and Red Wine Risotto

SERVES 6 AS A FIRST COURSE, 4 AS A MAIN COURSE
ACTIVE TIME: 45 MINUTES ■ START TO FINISH: 45 MINUTES

■ The bitterness of radicchio melts away when it's cooked. Its color mellows too, from a vibrant burgundy to a warm mahogany, making this classic Venetian risotto a good choice for autumn or winter. ■

- 3½ cups Chicken Stock (page 153) or store-bought reduced-sodium broth
- 3½ cups water
- 3 tablespoons unsalted butter
- 1 cup finely chopped onion
- 1 Turkish bay leaf or ¼ California bay leaf
  Salt
- ½ pound radicchio, quartered lengthwise, cored, and cut crosswise into ½-inch-wide slices
- 1½ cups Carnaroli or Arborio rice
- 1½ cups dry red wine
- ¾ cup finely grated Parmigiano-Reggiano
  Freshly ground black pepper

Combine stock and water in a 2½- to 3-quart heavy saucepan and bring to a simmer. Reduce heat and keep stock at a bare simmer.

Melt butter in a 4-quart wide heavy pot over moderate heat. Add onion, bay leaf, and ½ teaspoon salt and cook, stirring, until onion is pale golden, about 10 minutes.

Meanwhile, cook radicchio in a 4- to 6-quart pot of boiling salted water (1 tablespoon salt) until just tender, about 3 minutes. Drain and transfer to a bowl of ice and cold water to stop the cooking. Drain and squeeze dry.

Add rice to onion and cook, stirring, for 2 min-

utes. Add wine, bring to a boil, and boil, stirring, until wine is absorbed, about 5 minutes. Add ½ cup simmering stock and cook, stirring constantly and keeping it at a strong simmer, until stock is absorbed. Continue cooking and adding stock about ½ cup at a time, stirring frequently and letting each addition be absorbed before adding the next, until rice is tender and creamy-looking but still al dente, about 18 minutes total (there will be stock left over).

Discard bay leaf, add radicchio and cheese, and cook, stirring, until heated through, about 1 minute. Add salt and pepper to taste. If desired, thin risotto with some of remaining stock. Serve immediately.

Gorgonzola Risotto

SERVES 8 TO 10 AS A SIDE DISH
ACTIVE TIME: 25 MINUTES ■ START TO FINISH: 35 MINUTES

■ In 1926, Beatrice Ruggeri, known to friends and family as Bice, opened a quaint trattoria in Milan. From that one restaurant grew the Bice empire, which helped move northern Italian dishes, like this lush, creamy risotto, from the back to the front burner. Another advantage of Bice's creation is its relative speediness, since the chicken stock is added all at once rather than gradually, as in most risottos. Originally a first course, it may be too rich for that role today, but it's a great side for beef, grilled chicken, veal, or lamb. ■

- 5 cups Chicken Stock (page 153) or store-bought reduced-sodium broth
- ¾ stick (6 tablespoons) unsalted butter, cut into tablespoons
- 2 tablespoons olive oil
- 2½ cups Carnaroli or Arborio rice
- 1⅓ cups heavy cream
- 6 ounces Gorgonzola dolce (see Sources), cut into ¼-inch pieces
- ½ teaspoon salt
- ½ teaspoon freshly ground black pepper
- ½ cup finely grated Parmigiano-Reggiano
- 2 tablespoons chopped fresh flat-leaf parsley

Bring stock to a simmer in a 3-quart heavy saucepan; turn off heat.

Meanwhile, heat 2 tablespoons butter and oil in a 4- to 5-quart heavy pot over moderately high heat until foam subsides. Stir in rice and cook, stirring, for 3 minutes.

Add all of stock to rice and cook, stirring frequently to prevent rice from sticking, for 12 minutes.

Meanwhile, heat cream and Gorgonzola in same 3-quart saucepan over moderately low heat, stirring, until cheese is completely melted. Stir in salt and pepper and remove from heat.

When rice has cooked for 12 minutes, add cream sauce and simmer, stirring, until sauce is absorbed, rice is very tender, and risotto is thickened, 8 to 10 minutes.

Remove from heat and stir rice with a fork, then stir in remaining 4 tablespoons butter and Parmesan until incorporated. Sprinkle with parsley and serve immediately.

Butternut Squash Risotto

SERVES 4 AS A FIRST COURSE, 6 AS A SIDE DISH
ACTIVE TIME: 30 MINUTES ■ START TO FINISH: 1¼ HOURS

■ Roasted diced butternut squash infuses this risotto with a subtle squashy sweetness, while garlic and snips of fresh chives help temper its richness. Don't skimp on top-quality rice and Parmesan—they make all the difference in this simple dish. ■

1 (2-pound) butternut squash, peeled, halved, seeded, and cut into ¼-inch pieces
2½ tablespoons olive oil
¾ teaspoon salt
¼ teaspoon freshly ground black pepper
5½ cups Chicken Stock (page 153) or 4 cups store-bought reduced-sodium broth plus 1½ cups water
½ stick (4 tablespoons) unsalted butter
1 small onion, chopped
1 tablespoon finely chopped garlic
1½ cups Carnaroli or Arborio rice
½ cup dry white wine

½ cup finely grated Parmigiano-Reggiano, plus additional for serving
3 tablespoons finely chopped fresh chives

Put a rack in middle of oven and preheat oven to 450°F.

Toss squash with oil, salt, and pepper on a baking sheet and spread out in one layer. Roast, stirring occasionally, until squash is tender and golden brown, 35 to 45 minutes. Remove from oven.

About 10 minutes before squash is done, bring stock (or broth and water) to a simmer in a 2- to 3-quart heavy saucepan. Reduce heat and keep at a bare simmer.

Melt 2 tablespoons butter in a 4-quart wide heavy saucepan over moderate heat. Add onion and cook, stirring occasionally, until softened, 3 to 4 minutes. Add garlic and cook, stirring, for 1 minute. Add rice and cook, stirring, for 1 minute. Add wine and simmer, stirring, until absorbed, 1 to 2 minutes.

Add 1 cup simmering stock and cook, stirring constantly and keeping it at a strong simmer, until absorbed. Continue cooking and adding stock about ½ cup at a time, stirring frequently and letting each addition be absorbed before adding the next, until rice is tender and creamy-looking but still al dente, 18 to 23 minutes (there will be stock left over).

Stir in roasted squash, cheese, chives, and remaining 2 tablespoons butter. If desired, thin risotto with some of remaining broth. Serve immediately, with additional grated cheese.

Hoppin' John Risotto

SERVES 6 AS A MAIN COURSE, 10 AS A SIDE DISH
ACTIVE TIME: 1 HOUR ■ START TO FINISH: 1¼ HOURS

■ New Sammy's Cowboy Bistro, in Talent, Oregon, northwest of Ashland, is a singular shack of a restaurant that turns out exceptional food, much of it made with the organic produce and herbs grown right on the property. Run by Charlene and Vernon Rollins, it has just six tables. Charlene's hoppin' John risotto is a riff on the traditional Southern dish of black-eyed peas and salt pork served with rice. Under her deft touch, it becomes a risotto dotted with black-eyed peas and flavored with bacon, pancetta, caramelized onion, and the zing of lemon. This is an unconventional method for making risotto—rather than slowly adding hot stock to the rice, Rollins adds it, unheated, in just two batches. ∎

- 4 bacon slices, chopped
- ¾ stick (6 tablespoons) unsalted butter, cut into tablespoons
- 2 pounds yellow onions (5 medium), halved lengthwise and thinly sliced crosswise
  Salt
- 1 (10-ounce) package frozen black-eyed peas, thawed, or 1 (15-ounce) can black-eyed peas, rinsed and drained
- 1 cup finely chopped red onion
- ¼ cup finely chopped celery
- 1 tablespoon finely chopped garlic
- 2½ cups Carnaroli or Arborio rice
- ½ cup dry white wine
- 2 ounces sliced pancetta (Italian unsmoked bacon), cut into ¼-inch pieces
- 1 tablespoon chopped fresh lemon thyme or other thyme
- ½ teaspoon red pepper flakes
- 8 cups Chicken Stock (page 153) or store-bought reduced-sodium broth
- 2 tablespoons fresh lemon juice, or to taste
- ¾ teaspoon coarsely ground black pepper
- 3 tablespoons finely chopped fresh flat-leaf parsley

Cook bacon in a 12-inch heavy skillet over moderate heat, stirring occasionally, until crisp, about 6 minutes. Transfer with a slotted spoon to paper towels to drain. Add 2 tablespoons butter to fat remaining in skillet and heat over moderate heat until foam subsides. Add yellow onions with ½ teaspoon salt and cook, stirring occasionally, until golden, 30 to 35 minutes.

Meanwhile, if using frozen black-eyed peas, simmer them in 2 cups water in a 2-quart saucepan, uncovered, over moderate heat until just tender, about 15 minutes; drain.

Transfer ½ cup caramelized onions to a bowl (for topping) and set remaining onions aside in skillet.

Heat 2 tablespoons butter in a 5- to 6-quart wide heavy pot over moderate heat until hot but not smoking. Add red onion and celery and cook, stirring occasionally, until softened, 5 to 7 minutes. Add garlic and cook, stirring, until fragrant, about 1 minute. Add rice and cook, stirring, for 1 minute. Stir in wine, increase heat to moderately high, and boil until liquid is reduced by half, about 2 minutes.

Add caramelized onions from skillet, black-eyed peas (cooked or canned), pancetta, thyme, red pepper flakes, ¾ teaspoon salt, and 4 cups stock, bring to a strong simmer, and simmer briskly, uncovered, over moderate heat, stirring occasionally, until most of liquid is absorbed, 15 to 20 minutes. Add remaining 4 cups stock and simmer briskly, stirring occasionally, until most of liquid is absorbed and rice is just tender and creamy-looking, 15 to 20 minutes.

Add remaining 2 tablespoons butter and lemon juice, stirring until butter is incorporated. Divide risotto among bowls or plates and sprinkle with bacon and black pepper. Top with reserved caramelized onions, sprinkle with parsley, and serve immediately.

Grilled Paella with Rabbit and Artichokes

SERVES 6
ACTIVE TIME: 2 HOURS ∎ START TO FINISH: 2 HOURS

∎ With its deeply smoky flavor, this is the most delicious version of paella we've ever tasted. The combination is a classic in the Valencia region of Spain, where cookbook author Jeff Koehler learned to make it from his Spanish mother-in-law. Brick-red smoked paprika, artichokes, and golden saffron contribute beautiful color, while the browned rabbit infuses the rice with a meaty richness. Cooking it on the grill adds enormous depth. Short-grain bomba rice, grown in Spain's Calasparra region, in the southeast part of the country, is absorbent enough to absorb the chicken stock without becoming mushy. ∎

1 lemon, halved

6 medium artichokes

1 (2- to 2½-pound) rabbit, cut into 12 pieces (2 fore-
legs; 2 hind legs, each cut into 2 pieces; saddle
split lengthwise, each half cut crosswise into
3 pieces)

Salt

½ teaspoon freshly ground black pepper

6 tablespoons extra-virgin olive oil

1 red bell pepper, cored, seeded, and cut into
1-inch pieces

2 pounds tomatoes (4 large), peeled (see Tips,
page 913), seeded, and finely chopped

4 garlic cloves, finely chopped

1 teaspoon sweet *pimentón* (Spanish smoked paprika;
see Sources)

8 cups Chicken Stock (page 153) or store-bought
reduced-sodium broth

⅛ teaspoon crumbled saffron threads

3 cups short- or medium-grain rice, preferably
Spanish bomba (see Cook's Note)

SPECIAL EQUIPMENT: a 22½-inch-wide charcoal grill and a
6-pound bag of hardwood charcoal, or a 26-by-
20-inch gas grill; a 16- to 18-inch polished-carbon-
steel paella pan (see Cook's Note and Sources)

PREPARE THE ARTICHOKES AND RABBIT: Squeeze
juice from 1 lemon half into a bowl of cold water; reserve remaining half. Cut off top 2 inches of 1 artichoke (1). Bend back outer leaves until they snap off
close to base; remove and discard several more layers
of leaves in same manner until you reach leaves that
are pale green at top and yellow at base (2). Leaving
stem attached, trim dark green fibrous parts from
base and sides with a sharp paring knife (3). Rub cut
surfaces with reserved lemon half. Trim ¼ inch from
bottom of stem and trim sides of stem down to pale
inner core—don't worry if remaining stem is very
thin. Cut artichoke into 8 wedges and cut out fuzzy
choke (4). Rub cut surfaces with reserved lemon half
and drop artichoke into acidulated water. Trim and
cut remaining artichokes in same manner.

If using a charcoal grill, prepare it for direct-heat
cooking over medium-hot coals; if using a gas grill,
prepare it for direct-heat cooking over medium-high
heat (see Grilling Basics, page 512).

Drain artichokes and pat dry between paper towels. Pat rabbit dry and sprinkle with 1 teaspoon salt
and pepper.

TO COOK THE RABBIT AND VEGETABLES: Heat oil
in paella pan on grill rack, covered with grill lid, until
oil is hot but not smoking. Using pot holders, swirl
oil in pan to distribute it evenly. Add rabbit and cook,
uncovered, turning, until well browned on all sides,
about 8 minutes. Move browned rabbit pieces to
outer edges of pan (to slow down cooking while artichokes and bell pepper cook).

Add artichokes and bell pepper to center of pan and
cook, stirring and turning artichokes frequently, and
turning rabbit pieces occasionally to prevent burning,
until artichokes are golden brown, about 4 minutes.

Add tomatoes, garlic, and 1 teaspoon salt and cook,
stirring, until mixture is thickened, about 6 minutes.
Sprinkle with *pimentón* and cook, undisturbed, for
1 minute, then stir rabbit into tomato mixture. Stir
in stock and saffron. Increase heat to high by stok-
ing the charcoal or by turning burners to high, cover
grill with lid, and bring stock to a boil. Sprinkle rice
evenly into pan, avoiding pieces of rabbit. With a
wooden spoon, stir gently to make sure rice is evenly
distributed and all rice grains are submerged (do not
stir again).

TO FINISH THE PAELLA USING A CHARCOAL GRILL:
Cook, uncovered, rotating pan a quarter turn every 5
minutes, until liquid is absorbed and grains of rice are
distinct and just tender (similar to al dente), 20 to 25
minutes. (If all liquid evaporates and rice is still not
tender, sprinkle tepid water, a tablespoon at a time,
over rice where needed and cook for 1 to 2 minutes
more.) Carefully remove pan from grill, cover with a
clean kitchen towel, and let stand for 5 minutes before serving.

TO FINISH THE PAELLA USING A GAS GRILL: Cook,
following instructions for charcoal grill, until rice has
cooked for 10 minutes. Reduce heat to medium and
cook, continuing to turn pan a quarter turn every 5
minutes, until liquid is absorbed and grains of rice
are distinct and just tender (similar to al dente), 10
to 15 minutes more. (If all liquid evaporates and rice
is still not tender, sprinkle tepid water, a tablespoon
at a time, over rice where needed and cook for 1 to 2
minutes more.) Carefully remove pan from grill, cover
with a clean kitchen towel, and let stand for 5 minutes
before serving.

- Spanish bomba or American CalRose rice gives the best results, but Italian Carnaroli and Japanese sushi rice will also work. Do not use long-grain or parboiled varieties (such as Uncle Ben's Converted Rice), which do not absorb as much liquid as short- or medium-grain rice.

- If your paella pan does not have heatproof handles, wrap a double thickness of foil around the handles before placing the pan on the grill.

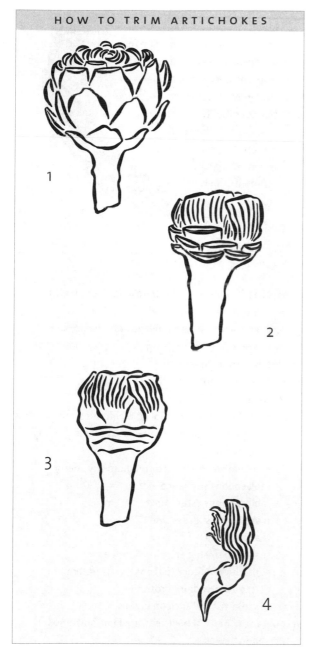

HOW TO TRIM ARTICHOKES

1

2

3

4

Smoked Sausage and Okra Dirty Rice

SERVES 8 AS A SIDE DISH
ACTIVE TIME: 45 MINUTES ■ START TO FINISH: 1 HOUR

■ Dirty rice gets its name from chicken giblets, which give it a distinctive dark ("dirty") color. This Louisiana mainstay forgoes the giblets but includes okra and hot smoked sausage (andouille or kielbasa also works well). It can anchor a Cajun buffet or make a simple dinner, paired with a plain green salad. ■

4¼ cups water
2½ cups long-grain white rice
    Salt
2 tablespoons vegetable oil
1 pound smoked hot pork sausage links, quartered lengthwise and cut crosswise into ½-inch pieces
½ pound okra, stem and blossom ends discarded, thinly sliced
2 medium onions, chopped
1 medium green bell pepper, cored, seeded, and chopped
1 medium red bell pepper, cored, seeded, and chopped
2 large garlic cloves, finely chopped
1¾ cups Chicken Stock (page 153) or store-bought reduced-sodium broth
½ teaspoon freshly ground black pepper
6 scallions, thinly sliced

Bring 4 cups water to a boil in a 4-quart heavy saucepan. Add rice and ½ teaspoon salt and cook, covered, over low heat until water is absorbed and rice is tender, about 20 minutes. Remove from heat and let stand, covered, for 10 minutes, then fluff rice with a fork and keep covered.

Meanwhile, heat 1 tablespoon oil in a 10- to 12-inch heavy skillet, preferably cast-iron, over moderately high heat until hot but not smoking. Add sausage, in 2 batches, and cook, stirring occasionally, until browned, 2 to 3 minutes per batch; transfer with a slotted spoon to a bowl. Add okra to skillet and cook, stirring occasionally, until browned, 2 to 3 minutes. Transfer to another bowl.

Heat remaining tablespoon oil in skillet over moderately high heat until hot but not smoking. Add onions and bell peppers and cook, stirring occasionally, until softened and browned, about 5 minutes. Add garlic and cook, stirring, for 1 minute. Add okra, stock, remaining ¼ cup water, 1 teaspoon salt, and pepper, bring to a simmer, and simmer, uncovered, stirring occasionally, until liquid is slightly thickened and reduced to just below surface of solids, 10 to 15 minutes.

Stir in sausage and toss with rice, scallions, and salt and pepper to taste.

COOK'S NOTE

■ The sausage mixture and the rice can be made up to 1 day ahead. Cool, uncovered, then refrigerate separately, covered. To serve, reheat the rice; heat the sausage mixture in a large saucepan over moderate heat, covered, stirring occasionally, until hot, then toss with the rice and scallions.

Sticky Rice with Chinese Sausage

SERVES 8 TO 10 AS A SIDE DISH
ACTIVE TIME: 25 MINUTES ■ START TO FINISH: 3 HOURS
(INCLUDES SOAKING)

■ Adults and kids alike love this dish, with its sweet Chinese sausages, intensely flavored dried mushrooms, and firm chestnuts, all balanced by the tender sticky rice. The crust that develops on the bottom of the pot is prized. After scooping out most of the rice, you can cook the crust a bit longer, then chip off the tasty morsels to scatter on top of the rice or to enjoy as a cook's treat. This is a delicious alternative to the traditional Thanksgiving dressing. It's also good with a simple roast chicken or stir-fried vegetables, and there's nothing better than leftovers served with a fried egg on top. ■

3 cups Chinese or Japanese short-grain sticky ("sweet") rice (see Sources)

CHINESE SAUSAGE

The rich, sweet, intense flavor of Chinese sausage—*lop cheong* in Cantonese and "pork candy" to legions of aficionados—is similar to that of chorizo and andouille, but it's milder than its Spanish and French counterparts and has a dense, chewy texture. It's often steamed first, until its nuggets of fat are translucent, before being added to a stir-fry or served on its own as a side dish. The *lop cheong* available in the United States is sold in pairs tied together with jute twine or in vacuum-sealed packages. It keeps for several weeks in the refrigerator or for months in the freezer.

1 cup (1½ ounces) dried shiitake (Chinese black) mushrooms
5 links Chinese sweet sausage (*lop cheong*; see Sources)
1 tablespoon peanut oil
1 tablespoon minced peeled fresh ginger
½ cup thinly sliced scallions
1½ cups bottled peeled cooked whole chestnuts (from a 14- to 15-ounce jar), drained and coarsely chopped (see Sources)
⅓ cup Chinese rice wine or medium-dry sherry
3 tablespoons soy sauce
2 tablespoons oyster sauce
2 teaspoons Asian sesame oil
1 teaspoon salt
½ teaspoon freshly ground white pepper
2 cups Chicken Stock (page 153) or store-bought reduced-sodium broth
GARNISH: thinly sliced scallion greens
SPECIAL EQUIPMENT: a well-seasoned flat-bottomed 14-inch wok

Cover rice with cold water by 1 inch in a large bowl and soak for 2 hours. Drain in a large sieve and rinse well under cold water.

Meanwhile, soak mushrooms in warm water for 30 minutes. Drain, squeezing excess liquid back into bowl, and discard liquid. Rinse mushrooms to remove any grit. Discard stems and coarsely chop caps.

Quarter sausages lengthwise and cut crosswise into ½-inch pieces.

Heat wok over high heat until a drop of water evaporates on contact. Add peanut oil, swirling to coat wok evenly, and heat until just smoking. Add ginger and scallions and stir-fry for 30 seconds. Add sausage and stir-fry for 1 minute, then add mushrooms and stir-fry for 1 minute. Add chestnuts and stir-fry for 1 minute. Stir in rice wine, soy sauce, oyster sauce, sesame oil, salt, and white pepper and remove from heat.

Add rice to sausage mixture and stir to coat. Transfer to a 4- to 6-quart heavy pot and add stock (stock will not completely cover rice). Bring to a simmer, then stir once, reduce heat to low, cover, and cook until rice is tender, about 25 minutes.

Remove rice from heat and stir from bottom up to distribute ingredients. Let stand, covered, for 10 minutes before serving. Stir in some scallion greens and sprinkle remainder on top.

COOK'S NOTE

- The rice can be made up to 2 days ahead. Cool, uncovered, then refrigerate, covered. Reheat in a microwave or in a sieve set over a pot of simmering water, covered.

Other Grains

Creamy
Stone-Ground Grits

SERVES 6 AS A SIDE DISH
ACTIVE TIME: 20 MINUTES ■ START TO FINISH: 1¼ HOURS

■ Save this recipe until you can get your hands on hand-milled—stone-ground—grits, which have a complexity that their supermarket counterpart can't touch. Grits' cracked-corn taste shines through best when they are freshly cooked, but they can be made ahead and gently reheated. We suggest storing raw grits in the freezer until you're ready to use them. ■

    4 cups water
    ¾ teaspoon salt
    2 tablespoons unsalted butter
    1 cup coarse stone-ground white grits (see Sources)
    1 cup whole milk
    ¼ teaspoon freshly ground black pepper

Combine water, salt, and 1 tablespoon butter in a 3- to 4-quart heavy saucepan and bring to a boil. Gradually add grits, stirring constantly with a wooden spoon, then reduce heat and cook at a bare simmer, covered, stirring frequently, until water is absorbed and grits are thickened, about 15 minutes.

Stir in ½ cup milk and simmer, partially covered, stirring occasionally to keep grits from sticking to bottom of pan, for 10 minutes. Stir in remaining ½ cup milk and simmer, partially covered, stirring occasionally, until liquid is absorbed and grits are thickened and tender, about 35 minutes more. (Grits will have a soft mashed-potato-like consistency.)

Stir in pepper and remaining 1 tablespoon butter.

COOK'S NOTE

- The grits can be made up to 1 day ahead. Cool, uncovered, then refrigerate, covered with lightly buttered wax paper pressed against the surface (buttered side down). Reheat in a saucepan with 1 to 1¼ cups water, uncovered, stirring occasionally.

Spoon Bread

SERVES 4 TO 6 AS A SIDE DISH
ACTIVE TIME: 15 MINUTES ■ START TO FINISH: 1 HOUR

■ Recipes for this soufflélike side dish first appeared in Mary Randolph's *The Virginia House-Wife* in 1824, and it continues to be associated with Southern cooking in general and Virginia cooking in particular. Light and fluffy enough to be eaten with a spoon, this ethereal version from reader Walter V. Hall of Alexandria, Virginia, rises high and then settles softly. ■

⅓ cup fine dry bread crumbs

3 cups whole milk

1 cup stone-ground white or yellow cornmeal

1 tablespoon unsalted butter

1 teaspoon salt

1 teaspoon sugar

3 large eggs, separated

Put a rack in middle of oven and preheat oven to 375°F. Butter a 2-quart soufflé dish or glass baking dish and coat with bread crumbs, knocking out excess. Refrigerate dish until ready to use.

Heat milk in a large metal bowl set over a saucepan of simmering water until very hot. Gradually add cornmeal, whisking constantly, and cook, whisking frequently, until thick and smooth, about 3 minutes. Remove bowl from pan and stir in butter.

Cool for 5 minutes, then stir in salt, sugar, and yolks until well combined.

Beat whites in a bowl with an electric mixer at medium speed until they just hold stiff peaks. Gently fold one third of whites into cornmeal mixture to lighten it, then fold in remaining whites gently but thoroughly.

Pour batter into soufflé dish and bake until puffed and golden, 40 to 45 minutes. Serve immediately (like a soufflé, spoon bread collapses quickly).

Fresh Corn Spoon Bread

SERVES 6 AS A SIDE DISH
ACTIVE TIME: 15 MINUTES ■ START TO FINISH: 35 MINUTES

■ Sweet corn adds its sunny flavor as well as a bit more substance to traditional spoon bread. ■

2 cups whole milk

⅓ cup stone-ground white or yellow cornmeal

1½ cups fresh corn kernels (from 2–3 ears)

1 tablespoon unsalted butter

Salt

4 large eggs, separated

Put a rack in middle of oven and preheat oven to 425°F. Butter a 9½-inch deep-dish glass pie plate or 1½-quart shallow casserole.

Combine milk, cornmeal, corn kernels, butter, and 1 teaspoon salt in a 3-quart heavy saucepan and bring to a boil over moderately high heat, stirring frequently. Reduce heat and simmer, stirring constantly, until thick, 3 to 4 minutes. Remove saucepan from heat and cool for 5 minutes, stirring occasionally.

Whisk egg yolks into corn mixture.

Beat egg whites and a pinch of salt in a bowl with an electric mixer at medium speed until whites just hold soft peaks. Whisk one quarter of whites into cornmeal mixture to lighten it, then fold in remaining whites gently but thoroughly.

Spread mixture evenly in buttered pie plate and bake until puffed and golden, 15 to 20 minutes. Serve immediately (like a soufflé, spoon bread falls quickly).

Buttered Polenta

SERVES 4
ACTIVE TIME: 45 MINUTES ■ START TO FINISH: 1 HOUR

■ Montreal's Quincaillerie Dante, owned by Elena Faita-Venditelli and her brother Rudy, is part cookware shop, part gun and ammo shop, and it has become a lively meeting place for Montreal chefs and home cooks, who book Elena's cooking classes months in advance. She learned much of what she teaches, like this traditional slow-cooked polenta, from her Italian-born mother. When polenta is cooked properly, each grain of cornmeal slowly absorbs the liquid until it swells, becoming perfectly tender and seeming to disappear within the whole. This makes a natural bed for sausages or any type of stew. ■

7 cups water

1½ tablespoons extra-virgin olive oil

2 teaspoons coarse sea salt

1½ cups polenta (not quick-cooking)

2 tablespoons unsalted butter

Bring water, oil, and sea salt to a boil in a 4-quart heavy saucepan. Add polenta in a slow stream, whisking constantly. Reduce heat to moderate and cook, whisking, for 2 minutes. Reduce heat to low and cook at a bare simmer, stirring frequently with a long-handled wooden spoon, for 45 minutes, or until water is absorbed.

Remove from heat, add butter, and stir until incorporated. Serve immediately.

Barley with Toasted Cumin and Mint

SERVES 4 AS A SIDE DISH
ACTIVE TIME: 15 MINUTES ■ START TO FINISH: 30 MINUTES

■ Quick-cooking barley is a great convenience food. Because it has been presteamed, it only takes about 10 minutes to cook, as opposed to almost an hour for pearl barley. Fresh-tasting and light, this dish is a surprise for people who expect barley to be heavy. A pinch of turmeric adds a sunny hue. ■

POLENTA

Polenta has been a staple in Italy since the early days of Rome. It was originally made mostly from millet, but that was supplanted by corn when the latter arrived from the New World. The word *polenta* means both the cornmeal and the porridge made from it. As for the differences between cooked polenta, grits, and cornmeal mush, they are one and the same, although cornmeal for mush is generally a finer grind. (Regular corn grits, incidentally, are called hominy grits in the Low Country of South Carolina and Georgia; they're different from the fat kernels of dried corn, also called hominy, which are treated with lime to remove the hard-to-digest hulls and used to make tamale dough and pozole.) The best polenta, like the best grits, comes from old-fashioned grist mills, where dried whole corn kernels are ground slowly between cool millstones so that the nutritious germ and sweet, deep corn flavor are preserved. If you can't find polenta in your local supermarket or specialty foods shop, you can use yellow grits, such as Bob's Red Mill brand (see Sources). Like any stone-ground whole-grain product, polenta should be stored in the freezer to keep it fresh.

The most important thing to remember about polenta is that you can't rush it. It cooks in its own good time, and making it the old-fashioned way requires a fair amount of stirring. Once you get the hang of it, though, cooking polenta takes on a comforting, almost ritualistic quality. To cook it, slowly trickle the polenta into a pot of boiling water with one hand while whisking with the other. Whisk for a couple of minutes to get everything working, then lower the heat to a bare simmer. As the polenta absorbs the water during its long, slow time on the stove (about 45 minutes), you'll want to stir the soupy mass often. (A long-handled wooden spoon keeps spatters at bay.) Polenta is done when it feels tender and smooth to the tongue; it shouldn't be gritty or chewy. When stirred, it will pull away from the side of the pot.

You may want to make extra polenta. It sets up as it cools, and it will keep, covered, for several days in the refrigerator. After slicing the firm polenta, fry it until golden and crunchy on the outside, or sprinkle with grated Parmesan and pop it under the broiler. It's great as is or with your favorite tomato sauce.

2 cups water
1 cup quick-cooking barley
Salt
⅛ teaspoon turmeric
¼ cup finely chopped fresh mint
2–3 tablespoons finely chopped red onion
1½ tablespoons fresh lemon juice
¾ teaspoon cumin seeds, toasted (see Tips, page 911)
1 teaspoon extra-virgin olive oil
Freshly ground black pepper

Combine water, barley, ½ teaspoon salt, and turmeric in a 2-quart heavy saucepan and bring to a boil, then reduce heat and simmer, covered, until barley is tender, about 10 minutes. Remove pan from heat and let stand, covered, for 5 minutes.

Drain barley and transfer to a bowl. Stir in mint, onion (to taste), lemon juice, cumin, and oil and season with salt and pepper.

Mushroom Barley Pilaf

SERVES 4 TO 6 AS A SIDE DISH
ACTIVE TIME: 40 MINUTES ■ START TO FINISH: 1 HOUR

■ Dried shiitakes add a deep woodsy note to this homey pilaf, complementing the hearty barley. Cooking the barley and the vegetable mixture separately preserves the nutty texture of the barley and the vegetables' distinct flavors. ■

FOR BARLEY
1 cup pearl barley (not quick-cooking)
1¾ cups Chicken Stock (page 153) or store-bought reduced-sodium broth
¼ cup water
FOR DRIED MUSHROOMS
¾ cup boiling water
½ cup (½ ounce) dried shiitake (Chinese black) mushrooms
FOR VEGETABLES
2 tablespoons unsalted butter
2 tablespoons olive oil
1 large onion, finely chopped
2 carrots, cut into ¼-inch pieces
2 celery ribs, cut into ¼-inch pieces

2 garlic cloves, finely chopped
½ pound cremini mushrooms, trimmed and quartered
½ teaspoon salt
¼ teaspoon freshly ground black pepper
3 tablespoons finely chopped fresh flat-leaf parsley

COOK THE BARLEY: Bring barley, stock, and water to a boil in a 3-quart heavy saucepan over high heat, then reduce heat to low, and simmer, partially covered, until liquid is absorbed, about 40 minutes.

MEANWHILE, PREPARE THE MUSHROOMS: Pour boiling water over shiitakes in a small bowl and let stand, turning occasionally, until softened, about 20 minutes. Lift shiitakes out of soaking liquid and squeeze excess liquid back into bowl (reserve liquid). Rinse shiitakes to remove any grit. Cut off and discard stems and coarsely chop. Pour soaking liquid through a sieve lined with a dampened paper towel into another bowl; set aside.

COOK THE VEGETABLES WHILE THE MUSHROOMS SOAK: Heat butter and oil in a 12-inch heavy skillet over moderately high heat until hot but not smoking. Add onion, carrots, celery, and garlic and cook, stirring, until golden, 12 to 15 minutes. Reduce heat to moderate, stir in cremini mushrooms, salt, and pepper, and cook, stirring, until vegetables are tender and golden brown, about 10 minutes. Remove vegetables from heat and set skillet aside.

FINISH THE PILAF: Remove cooked barley from heat and let stand, covered, for 10 minutes, then fluff with a fork.

Reheat vegetables in skillet over moderate heat, stirring. Add shiitakes and reserved mushroom soaking liquid and cook, stirring, until all of liquid is absorbed, about 3 minutes. Stir in barley and parsley.

Bulgur Pilaf

SERVES 4 AS A SIDE DISH
ACTIVE TIME: 15 MINUTES ■ START TO FINISH: 40 MINUTES

■ Coarsely crushed coriander seeds bring a floral note to this Middle Eastern pilaf. Consider serving this with fish or poultry, especially Cornish game hens or poussins. ■

- 2 tablespoons extra-virgin olive oil
- ½ cup finely chopped onion
- 1½ teaspoons coriander seeds
- 1 scant cup bulgur
- 1 cup boiling water
- ⅓ cup slivered almonds, toasted (see Tips, page 911)
- ½ teaspoon salt
- ¼ teaspoon freshly ground black pepper

Heat oil in a 2-quart heavy saucepan over moderate heat until hot but not smoking. Add onion and cook, stirring occasionally, until golden brown, 5 to 7 minutes.

Meanwhile, wrap coriander seeds in a clean kitchen towel and coarsely crush by pressing with side of a large heavy knife.

Add coriander and bulgur to onion and cook, stirring, for 2 minutes. Stir in boiling water, remove from heat, and let stand, covered, until bulgur is softened, 25 to 30 minutes.

Fluff bulgur with a fork, then stir in almonds, salt, and pepper. Serve warm or at room temperature.

Quinoa with Mango and Curried Yogurt

SERVES 6 AS A SIDE DISH
ACTIVE TIME: 20 MINUTES ■ START TO FINISH: 45 MINUTES

■ Picture fluffy steamed quinoa lightened with creamy spiced yogurt and tossed with roasted peanuts, mango, chile, and mint, and you'll get an idea of what this beautiful side is all about. Because its flavors are so lively, the dish dresses up any plain grilled chicken or fish. ■

- ⅓ cup plain yogurt
- 1 tablespoon fresh lime juice
- 2 teaspoons curry powder
- 1 teaspoon finely grated peeled fresh ginger
  Salt
- ¼ teaspoon freshly ground black pepper
- 2 tablespoons vegetable or peanut oil
- 1⅓ cups quinoa

- 1 (1-pound) firm but ripe mango, peeled, pitted, and cut into ½-inch chunks
- 1 red bell pepper, cored, seeded, and cut into ¼-inch dice
- 1 jalapeño chile, seeded if desired (for less heat) and minced
- ⅓ cup chopped fresh mint
- ½ cup salted roasted peanuts, chopped

Whisk together yogurt, lime juice, curry powder, ginger, ¾ teaspoon salt, and pepper in a large bowl. Add oil in a slow stream, whisking until combined.

Rinse quinoa in 3 changes of cold water in a bowl, draining in a sieve between changes of water. Cook quinoa in a 4- to 5-quart pot of boiling salted water (2 teaspoons salt), uncovered, for 10 minutes. Drain in a large sieve and rinse and rub under cold water.

Set sieve with quinoa over a saucepan containing 1½ inches boiling water (sieve should not touch water), cover with a kitchen towel and the lid, and steam quinoa until fluffy and dry, 10 to 12 minutes.

Toss quinoa with curried yogurt and remaining ingredients in a large bowl. Serve warm or at room temperature.

COOK'S NOTE

■ The dish can be made up to 1 day ahead. Cool, uncovered, then refrigerate, covered. Bring to room temperature before serving.

Farro Risotto with Cauliflower

SERVES 6 TO 8 AS A FIRST COURSE, 4 AS A MAIN COURSE
ACTIVE TIME: 35 MINUTES ■ START TO FINISH: 35 MINUTES

■ Almost any grain can be cooked like risotto, including nutritious farro. While it doesn't develop the same creaminess as traditional risotto, "farrotto" absorbs all the flavors of the chicken stock scented with lemon and bay, and its hearty chewiness plays beautifully against the silky cauliflower. Paired with a simple leafy salad, this makes a great casual meal. ■

5½ cups Chicken Stock (page 153) or store-bought reduced-sodium broth
1 Turkish bay leaf or ½ California bay leaf
1 (3-by-1-inch) strip lemon zest, removed with a vegetable peeler
2 teaspoons fresh lemon juice
½ stick (4 tablespoons) unsalted butter
½ cup finely chopped onion
1½ cups farro (see Sources)
½ cup dry white wine
2 cups finely chopped cauliflower
½ cup finely grated Parmigiano-Reggiano
1 tablespoon finely chopped fresh flat-leaf parsley
½ teaspoon salt
¼ teaspoon freshly ground black pepper

Combine stock, bay leaf, lemon zest, and lemon juice in a 3-quart saucepan and bring to a simmer. Reduce heat and keep at a bare simmer.

Melt 2 tablespoons butter in a 3- to 4-quart heavy saucepan over moderate heat. Add onion and cook, stirring often, until softened, 3 to 4 minutes. Add farro and cook, stirring, for 1 minute. Add wine, bring to a simmer, and simmer, stirring, until it is absorbed.

Add 1 cup simmering stock and cauliflower and cook, stirring and keeping stock at a strong simmer, until it is absorbed. Continue cooking and adding stock about 1 cup at a time, stirring frequently and letting each addition be absorbed before adding the next, until farro is tender and creamy-looking but still slightly al dente and cauliflower is tender, about 25 minutes (there will be stock left over).

Stir in cheese, parsley, remaining 2 tablespoons butter, salt, and pepper. If desired, thin with some of remaining stock (discard bay leaf and zest). Serve immediately.

Spiced Green Wheat with Currants and Pine Nuts

SERVES 4 AS A SIDE DISH
ACTIVE TIME: 45 MINUTES ■ START TO FINISH: 2 HOURS

■ The distinctively smoky, almost meaty kernels of green wheat are complemented by spices, sweet cur-

rants, and toasted pine nuts. We love this with poussin or quail, as a stuffing or on the side (see Cook's Note). Because green wheat can turn rancid easily, it's best stored in your freezer. ■

1¼ cups green wheat (also called *farīk*; see Sources)
 Salt
2 tablespoons olive oil
1 large onion, finely chopped
½ teaspoon ground coriander
½ teaspoon ground ginger
½ teaspoon ground cinnamon
¼ teaspoon freshly ground black pepper
⅓ cup dried currants
¼ cup pine nuts, toasted (see Tips, page 911)

Soak wheat in cold water to cover by 2 inches at room temperature, skimming off any debris that floats to the surface and changing water twice, for 20 minutes. Drain well in a sieve.

Put a rack in middle of oven and preheat oven to 375°F.

Cook wheat, uncovered, in a 3- to 4-quart pot of boiling salted water (1 teaspoon salt), stirring and skimming froth occasionally, until just tender, 12 to 15 minutes. Drain well in sieve.

Meanwhile, heat oil in a 10-inch heavy skillet over moderate heat until hot but not smoking. Add onion and cook, stirring frequently, until softened, about 7 minutes. Add spices and ½ teaspoon salt and cook, stirring, for 1 minute.

Transfer onion to an 8-inch square baking dish and stir in drained cooked wheat, along with currants and pine nuts. Bake, covered with foil, for 20 minutes, or until heated through.

COOK'S NOTE
■ The wheat mixture can be cooled and used to stuff 4 poussins or Cornish hens or one 3½- to 4-pound chicken. Any extra stuffing can be baked separately.

Some of Our Favorite Grains

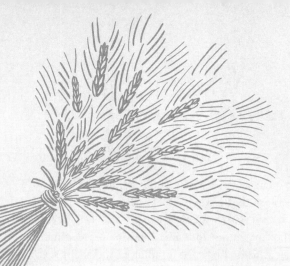

BARLEY was probably the first cereal grain to be domesticated. Because of its relatively short growing season and hardiness, it's cultivated from the Arctic Circle to northern India. In the West, most of the production is used for animal feed and to make malt for beer and some liquors. That's our loss: barley is mild, versatile, and fairly fast-cooking—it takes about 40 minutes and doesn't need to be soaked first. The type most commonly used in the kitchen is called pearl barley, which has had the hull and part of the bran removed during milling. (Quick-cooking pearl barley has been presteamed so that it takes only 10 minutes or so to cook.) Because the amount of pearling varies from brand to brand, look for barley that is fairly dark—that's a sign of how much bran (rich with protein, fiber, and B vitamins) remains.

BULGUR, wheat berries that have been parboiled, dried, and cracked into rough different-sized particles ranging from coarse to fine, is a staple in the Middle East and North Africa. The parboiling turns a slow-cooking grain into one that is ready in about 15 minutes. In the United States, bulgur is known primarily as the main ingredient in tabbouleh (see page 185), for which the grain is merely soaked in boiling water. It also works beautifully in all sorts of side dishes.

FARRO is often said to be the Italian name for spelt (the two wheat varieties are similar in appearance), but it is actually a different variety, called *emmer*. It was probably the second wheat to be cultivated, after einkorn wheat, and it was grown from the Near East to Europe until it was supplanted by durum and "bread wheats" during Roman times. (Interestingly, the words *accompany* and *companion* both come from the Latin word meaning "to share bread.") Farro has a rustic flavor and a pleasantly chewy, dense texture that works well in soups and other hearty dishes. Because it's been pearled so that little of the bran layer is left, it cooks in 20 to 30 minutes; depending on the preparation, sometimes it's soaked or toasted first.

GREEN WHEAT is used throughout the Middle East, but it is particularly popular in Egypt, where it's known as *farīk*. It is harvested when immature, and its grains are still soft and creamy. They are dried and roasted over a fire, which gives the wheat a distinctive but subtle smoky flavor. Then it's dried further and threshed to remove the hulls. We soak the wheat, then boil it for no more than 15 minutes for the spicy dish on page 276.

KASHA is the name for buckwheat groats, which have usually been toasted to deepen their distinctive earthy, "love it or hate it" flavor. Although kasha resembles a whole grain and is used like one, it's not a member of the cereal grain family at all, but is botanically related to sorrel and rhubarb. Depending on the preparation, kasha is sometimes toasted again before cooking; traditionally, it's coated with egg beforehand to prevent the individual grains from falling apart.

QUINOA ("*keen*-wah") is, botanically speaking, the seed of an herb, but it is used as a grain. It's nutty in flavor and is slightly sweet, light in texture, disk-shaped, and protein-rich, loaded with all the essential amino acids as well as lots of minerals and vitamins. It cooks in about 20 minutes. More than 100 varieties are grown in the Andes, and they come in various colors: ivory/tan, black, and red. (Most of the quinoa found in natural foods stores is imported from Ecuador and Bolivia.) Quinoa is coated with a hard natural substance called saponin that repels insects and other pests. It has a bitter, soapy taste, and so quinoa is generally washed or abraded before it is packaged, but it's still a good idea to give it a thorough rinse before cooking.

WHEAT BERRIES are not berries at all but the hulled whole kernels of wheat from which flour is milled. They have a gratifying chewiness. Wheat berries come in two types: hard-wheat (high-protein) berries, which are reddish brown and cook in about an hour, and soft-wheat (low-protein) berries, which are blonder and cook in about 50 minutes. Both types work in the recipes in this book.

Wheat Berries and Wild Rice with Porcini

SERVES 6 AS A SIDE DISH
ACTIVE TIME: 45 MINUTES ■ START TO FINISH: 2 HOURS

■ Though wheat berries are nutritious, it's their nutty sweetness that is their chief selling point. Here they are paired with wild rice, which is cooked separately so the two grains' individual flavors stay distinct. Because it needn't be served piping hot, this dill-scented dish makes a great choice for a buffet, alongside roast chicken or beef. ■

10 cups water
1 cup wild rice
  Salt
1 cup wheat berries (whole-grain wheat)
1½ ounces (1½ cups) dried porcini mushrooms, rinsed
2 tablespoons unsalted butter
3 large garlic cloves, minced
½ cup dry white wine
1 (14- to 15-ounce) can diced tomatoes in juice
¼ teaspoon freshly ground black pepper, or to taste
⅓ cup chopped fresh dill
GARNISH: chopped fresh dill

COOK THE RICE: Bring 4 cups water to a boil in a 2-quart heavy saucepan. Add rice and ½ teaspoon salt, reduce heat to low, and simmer, covered, until rice is tender and grains are split open, 1 to 1¼ hours. Drain in a colander.

MEANWHILE, COOK THE WHEAT BERRIES: Bring remaining 6 cups water to a boil in a 3-quart heavy saucepan. Stir in wheat berries and porcini, reduce heat to low, and simmer, covered, until wheat berries are tender, 1 to 1½ hours. Remove from heat, stir in ½ teaspoon salt, and let stand for 5 minutes.

Drain wheat berry mixture in a large sieve set over a saucepan, then transfer wheat berries and porcini to a bowl. (Cut up any porcini that are large.) Boil cooking liquid in saucepan until reduced to about 1 cup and add to wheat berry mixture.

Melt butter in a 12-inch heavy skillet over moderately low heat. Add garlic and cook, stirring, for 1 minute. Add wine, bring to a boil over high heat, and boil, stirring occasionally, until reduced by half, about 3 minutes. Add tomatoes with juice, ¼ teaspoon salt, and pepper and cook, stirring, for 3 minutes.

Add wild rice and wheat berry mixture (including liquid) and bring to a boil, stirring occasionally. Stir in dill and season with salt and pepper. Serve sprinkled with chopped dill.

COOK'S NOTES

■ The wild rice can be cooked and drained up to 1 day ahead. Cool, uncovered, then refrigerate, covered.

■ The wheat berry mixture can be cooked up to 1 day ahead. Cool in the reduced cooking liquid, uncovered, then refrigerate, covered.

Kasha with Bow-Tie Pasta
Kasha Varnishkes

SERVES 6 AS A SIDE DISH
ACTIVE TIME: 30 MINUTES ■ START TO FINISH: 1 HOUR

■ In this classic Jewish dish, the toastiness of kasha, or roasted buckwheat groats, is emphasized by combining the cooked grain with onions and mushrooms that have been well browned in chicken or duck fat. Because the preparation ties up a few burners, you'll want to make this when you have something like a brisket or roast chicken going in the oven. ■

2 cups Chicken Stock (page 153) or store-bought reduced-sodium broth
¼ teaspoon salt
¼ teaspoon freshly ground black pepper
1 cup coarse kasha (roasted buckwheat groats; see Sources)
1 large egg, lightly beaten
¼ cup rendered chicken or duck fat (see Cook's Note or Sources)
1 large onion, chopped
10 ounces white mushrooms, trimmed and coarsely chopped
2 cups farfalle (bow-tie pasta)
2 tablespoons chopped fresh flat-leaf parsley
1 tablespoon chopped fresh dill

Bring stock, salt, and pepper to a simmer in a 1-quart saucepan.

Toast kasha in a dry 4-quart heavy pot over moderate heat, stirring constantly, until dry, about 2 minutes. Vigorously stir in egg and cook, stirring constantly, until kasha is well coated and egg is browned, 2 to 3 minutes. Stir in hot stock, reduce heat to low, and cook, covered, until kasha is barely tender, 13 to 15 minutes. Remove from heat and let stand, covered, for 10 minutes.

Meanwhile, melt chicken fat in a 12-inch heavy skillet over moderate heat. Add onion and cook, stirring frequently, until well browned, 12 to 15 minutes. Add mushrooms and cook, stirring occasionally, until well browned, about 15 minutes.

Cook pasta in a large pot of boiling salted water (3 tablespoons salt) until al dente; drain.

Add pasta to onion mixture and cook over moderately high heat, tossing to combine, for 2 minutes. Remove from heat and add kasha and herbs, tossing with a fork to combine.

COOK'S NOTES

- You can substitute vegetable oil for the chicken or duck fat, but the dish will not be as flavorful.
- The onions and mushrooms can be cooked up to 1 hour ahead and kept at room temperature. Reheat before adding the pasta.
- The pasta can be cooked up to 1 hour ahead. Drain, rinse with cold water, and keep at room temperature.

Kasha with Browned Onions and Walnuts

SERVES 4 AS A SIDE DISH
ACTIVE TIME: 20 MINUTES ■ START TO FINISH: 35 MINUTES

■ In Russia and eastern Europe, kasha is most often made into a thick gruel, but coating the grain with egg and toasting it before simmering allows it to retain its nubbly texture. Butter-browned walnuts, caramelized onions, and fresh thyme play up the aroma. ■

1 large egg
1 cup coarse kasha (roasted buckwheat groats; see Sources)
2 cups boiling water
Salt and freshly ground black pepper
¾ cup walnuts, coarsely chopped
1½ tablespoons unsalted butter
2 tablespoons olive oil
1 medium onion, coarsely chopped
2 teaspoons fresh thyme leaves
3 tablespoons chopped fresh flat-leaf parsley

Lightly beat egg in a small bowl, add kasha, and stir until well coated. Add mixture to a dry heavy 3½- to 4-quart saucepan and cook over moderate heat, stirring constantly, until grains smell toasty and begin to separate, about 2 minutes. Add boiling water, ½ teaspoon salt, and ¼ teaspoon pepper and simmer, covered, over low heat until kasha is barely tender and most of water is absorbed, about 12 minutes. Remove from heat and let stand, covered, for 10 minutes.

Meanwhile, toast walnuts in 1 tablespoon butter in a 12-inch heavy skillet over moderate heat, stirring frequently, until fragrant and a shade darker, about 5 minutes. Transfer nuts to a plate. Add oil and remaining ½ tablespoon butter to skillet and heat until foam subsides. Add onion and thyme and cook, stirring occasionally, until onion is softened and browned, about 15 minutes.

Stir kasha into onion, along with walnuts, parsley, ¼ teaspoon salt, and ¼ teaspoon pepper.

COOK'S NOTE

- The dish, without the walnuts and parsley, can be made up to 1 day ahead. Cool, uncovered, then refrigerate, covered. Reheat before adding the nuts and parsley.

Beans

White Beans with Roasted Tomatoes

SERVES 8 AS A SIDE DISH
ACTIVE TIME: 1 HOUR ■ START TO FINISH: 1¼ HOURS
PLUS SOAKING TIME FOR BEANS

■ The flavor and sweetness of this combination of white beans, tomatoes, and cipollini onions come from cooking the tomatoes until they become caramelized and start to fall apart. Arranged on a large, rustic platter, this is an enticing dish. ■

FOR BEANS
- 1 pound dried cannellini beans, picked over and rinsed
- 1 pound cipollini (see Sources) or small (about 1½ inches in diameter) boiling onions, left unpeeled
- 1½ teaspoons salt, or to taste

FOR TOMATOES
- 2 pounds large tomatoes, cored and halved crosswise (see Cook's Note)
- 1 pound (4 cups) cherry tomatoes, preferably mixed colors
- 1 teaspoon salt, preferably sea salt
- 1 teaspoon sugar
- ½ cup extra-virgin olive oil
- ¼ cup torn fresh basil leaves

COOK THE BEANS: Soak beans in cold water to cover by 2 inches at room temperature (refrigerate if kitchen is very warm) for 8 to 12 hours (or see page 129 for quick-soaking procedure). Drain.

To make peeling easier, blanch onions in a 2- to 3-quart pot of boiling salted water (1 teaspoon salt) for 1 minute. Drain and peel.

Cover beans with cold water by about 1 inch in a 5- to 6-quart pot and bring to a boil. Add onions, reduce heat, and simmer, partially covered, skimming froth as necessary, until beans and onions are tender, 40 minutes to 1 hour. Stir in salt, remove from heat, and let beans stand in cooking liquid, uncovered.

MEANWHILE, ROAST THE TOMATOES: Put a rack in upper third of oven and preheat oven to 500°F.

Toss tomato halves and cherry tomatoes with salt, sugar, and oil in a shallow 3-quart baking dish. Turn tomato halves cut side up. Roast, uncovered, until large tomatoes are very tender with brown patches and cherry tomatoes are falling apart, 35 to 50 minutes.

FINISH THE DISH: With a slotted spoon, transfer warm beans and onions to a large deep platter. Arrange tomatoes decoratively on top of beans and pour tomato pan juices on top. Sprinkle with basil.

COOK'S NOTES

■ The beans can be cooked up to 1 day ahead. Cool in the liquid, uncovered, then refrigerate, covered. Reheat in the liquid over low heat, covered, stirring occasionally, before serving.

■ You can use whatever kind(s) of tomatoes you want; cherry tomatoes are attractive because they keep their shape when roasted.

■ The tomatoes can be roasted up to 2 hours ahead and kept, uncovered, at room temperature. Reheat, covered with foil, in a 350°F oven for 15 to 20 minutes.

Herbed Bean Ragout

SERVES 6 AS A SIDE DISH OR 3 AS A LIGHT MAIN COURSE
ACTIVE TIME: 40 MINUTES ■ START TO FINISH: 1 HOUR

■ This delicate version of a ragout includes three types of beans (haricots verts, edamame, and white beans). For an easy summer dinner party, serve it as a bed for broiled or grilled fish. ■

- 6 ounces haricots verts, trimmed and cut into thirds
  Salt
- 1 (1-pound) bag frozen edamame (soybeans) in pods or 1 (14-ounce) bag frozen shelled edamame, not thawed
- 1 tablespoon olive oil
- ⅔ cup finely chopped onion
- 2 garlic cloves, minced

1 Turkish bay leaf or ½ California bay leaf
1 teaspoon finely chopped fresh rosemary
¼ teaspoon freshly ground black pepper
1 medium carrot, cut into ⅛-inch pieces
1 medium celery rib, cut into ⅛-inch pieces
1 (15- to 16-ounce) can small white beans, rinsed
   and drained
1½ cups Chicken Stock (page 153) or store-bought
   reduced-sodium broth
2 tablespoons unsalted butter
2 tablespoons finely chopped fresh flat-leaf
   parsley
1 tablespoon finely chopped fresh chervil
   (optional)
OPTIONAL GARNISH: chervil sprigs

Cook haricots verts in a large pot of boiling salted water (1 tablespoon salt), uncovered, until just tender, 4 to 8 minutes. Transfer with a slotted spoon to a bowl of ice and cold water to stop the cooking. Drain in a colander and transfer to a bowl.

Add edamame to boiling water and cook, uncovered, for 4 minutes. Drain in colander, then rinse under cold water to stop the cooking. If using edamame in pods, shell them; discard pods.

Heat oil in a 3- to 4-quart heavy saucepan over moderately low heat until hot but not smoking. Add onion, garlic, bay leaf, rosemary, ½ teaspoon salt, and pepper and cook, stirring, until onion is softened, about 3 minutes. Add carrot and celery and cook, stirring, until softened, about 3 minutes. Add white beans and stock, bring to a simmer, and simmer, covered, stirring occasionally, for 10 minutes.

Add haricots verts and edamame and simmer, uncovered, until heated through, 2 to 3 minutes. Add butter, parsley, and chervil, if using, and stir gently. Discard bay leaf and add salt to taste.

Serve ragout garnished with chervil sprigs, if using.

COOK'S NOTE
■ The ragout, without the haricots, butter, and herbs, can be made up to 1 day ahead. Cool, uncovered, then refrigerate, covered. Just before serving, blanch and drain the beans. Add to the ragout, bring to a boil, and stir in the butter and herbs. Discard the bay leaf and season with salt.

Black Beans
with Garlic, Cumin, and Cilantro

SERVES 4 AS A SIDE DISH
ACTIVE TIME: 10 MINUTES ■ START TO FINISH: 15 MINUTES

■ An easy fix for canned beans, this tasty alternative to refried black beans is much faster and lighter than the traditional versions found in Mexico and Central America. ■

¼ cup olive oil
4 garlic cloves, chopped
2 teaspoons ground cumin
2 (16- to 19-ounce) cans black beans,
   rinsed and drained
⅔ cup tomato juice
½ teaspoon salt
¼ cup chopped fresh cilantro

Heat oil in a 12-inch nonstick skillet over moderate heat until hot but not smoking. Add garlic and cumin and cook, stirring, until fragrant, about 1 minute. Add black beans, tomato juice, and salt and cook, stirring, until beans are heated through, about 5 minutes. Stir in cilantro.

Black Beans
and Rice
with Sweet Potatoes

SERVES 4 AS A MAIN COURSE
ACTIVE TIME: 45 MINUTES ■ START TO FINISH: 2¼ HOURS
(1 HOUR IF USING PRESSURE COOKER;
INCLUDES MAKING BLACK BEANS)

■ *Gourmet*'s executive food editor Kemp Minifie jazzes up this rice and bean dish with toppings including toasted pumpkin seeds, avocado, onion, and salsa, transforming it into a festive meal for casual get-togethers. The recipe doubles easily. ■

FOR ROASTED SWEET POTATO CUBES

- 1 pound sweet potatoes, peeled and cut into ½-inch cubes
- 2 tablespoons olive oil
- ½ teaspoon salt

FOR RICE

- 2¼ cups water
- 1½ cups long-grain white rice
- ¾ teaspoon salt

FOR TOASTED PUMPKIN SEEDS

- 1 cup green (hulled) pumpkin seeds (*pepitas*; see Cook's Note)
- 2 teaspoons olive oil
- Salt

- ½ recipe (4–4½ cups) Kemp's Black Beans (recipe follows)

ACCOMPANIMENTS: cubes of avocado tossed with lime juice; store-bought tomatillo salsa; lime wedges; chopped white onion; fresh cilantro sprigs

ROAST THE SWEET POTATO CUBES: Put a rack in middle of oven and preheat oven to 450°F.

Toss sweet potatoes with oil and salt, then spread in one layer on a baking sheet. Roast, stirring and turning once or twice, until tender and browned, 35 to 40 minutes.

MEANWHILE, COOK THE RICE: Bring water, rice, and salt to a boil in a 2- to 3-quart heavy saucepan, then reduce heat and cook, covered, until rice is tender and water is absorbed, about 15 minutes. Remove from heat and let stand for 5 minutes, then fluff rice with a fork.

TOAST THE PUMPKIN SEEDS: Toast the seeds in a dry 10- to 12-inch heavy skillet, preferably cast-iron, over moderate heat, stirring, until seeds are puffed and pale golden, 3 to 4 minutes. Transfer to a bowl and stir in oil and salt to taste.

TO SERVE: Reheat black beans, thinning with water if necessary. Serve with rice, sweet potatoes, pumpkin seeds, and accompaniments in separate bowls.

COOK'S NOTE

■ If you are unable to find raw pumpkin seeds, salted toasted ones can be substituted (don't toast them again).

Kemp's Black Beans

MAKES 8 TO 9 CUPS
ACTIVE TIME: 15 MINUTES ■ START TO FINISH: 2¼ HOURS
(50 MINUTES IF USING PRESSURE COOKER)

■ Don't be misled by the short ingredient list; Kemp Minifie's black beans are surprisingly complex, thanks to the trinity of sherry, balsamic vinegar, and soy sauce. Leftovers are wonderful to have in the freezer—use them as you would canned beans in soups or stews. Minifie skips soaking her beans in order to preserve their ebony color. ■

- 1 pound dried black beans, picked over and rinsed
- 1 medium onion, finely chopped
- 3 tablespoons olive oil
- 8 cups water
- Salt
- ¼ cup cream sherry or medium-dry sherry
- 1–2 tablespoons soy sauce
- 1–2 tablespoons balsamic vinegar

Combine black beans, onion, oil, water, and ½ teaspoon salt in a 6- to 8-quart heavy pot and bring to a boil, then reduce heat and simmer, covered, until beans are tender, 1½ to 2 hours (depending on age of beans). Thin to desired consistency with additional water if necessary.

Stir in sherry and 1 teaspoon salt, then stir in soy sauce and vinegar (to taste) and simmer, uncovered, stirring occasionally, for 5 minutes to blend flavors.

COOK'S NOTES

■ The beans can be cooked in about one third the time in a 6- to 8-quart pressure cooker. Combine the beans, onion, oil, water, and salt in the pressure cooker. Seal the pressure cooker with the lid and cook at high pressure, according to the manufacturer's instructions, until the beans are tender, 30 to 45 minutes. Put the pressure cooker in the sink (do not remove the lid) and run cold water over the lid until the pressure goes down completely.

■ The beans improve in flavor if cooked at least 8 hours ahead. Refrigerate, uncovered, until cooled, then cover and refrigerate for up to 1 week, or freeze for up to 3 months. The beans thicken considerably as they stand; thin with water as necessary when reheating over moderately low heat.

Spinach and Chickpeas with Bacon

SERVES 4 AS A SIDE DISH
ACTIVE TIME: 25 MINUTES ■ START TO FINISH: 25 MINUTES

■ A line of hungry locals and tourists winds its way out the door of Cal Pep, a tiny, fast-paced tapas restaurant in Barcelona. Though there are a few tables in the back room, most diners wait for a coveted counter seat, where they can watch dishes of sardines, langoustines, and fried squid travel the short distance from stove to plate and listen to the good-natured joking of the waiters. This recipe—inspired by one of our favorite dishes at Cal Pep—is terrific with pork chops or roast chicken. ■

 3 slices thick-cut bacon
 3 tablespoons extra-virgin olive oil
 1 (15-ounce) can chickpeas, rinsed and drained
 ¼ teaspoon red pepper flakes
 6 ounces baby spinach (8 cups)
 1 garlic clove, minced
   Salt and freshly ground black pepper

Bring a 3-quart pot of water to a boil. Add bacon and boil for 2 minutes to remove excess salt and smokiness. Drain bacon in a sieve and rinse under cold water. Drain on paper towels and pat dry. Cut crosswise into ¼-inch pieces.

Cook bacon in a 12-inch heavy skillet over moderate heat, stirring, until browned. Leaving bacon in skillet, spoon off all but 1 tablespoon fat. Add 2 tablespoons oil, chickpeas, and red pepper flakes and cook over high heat, stirring occasionally, until chickpeas begin to brown, 3 to 4 minutes. Stir in spinach and garlic and cook, stirring, until spinach is wilted. Season with salt and pepper and drizzle with remaining tablespoon oil.

Black-Eyed Peas with Dill

SERVES 4 AS A SIDE DISH
ACTIVE TIME: 10 MINUTES ■ START TO FINISH: 1¼ HOURS

■ In the South, black-eyed peas are often cooked with ham or bacon, and most preparations are quite starchy. This Greek-inspired dish is a whole different thing— it's light and refreshing, especially when spritzed with lemon just before eating. Using frozen black-eyed peas makes it a snap to pull together, and it tastes equally good warm and at room temperature. ■

 1½ cups water
  2 fresh dill sprigs, plus 2 tablespoons chopped fresh dill
  2 large scallions, white and pale green parts cut into 1-inch pieces, dark green parts chopped (keep separate)
    Salt
 ¼ cup extra-virgin olive oil
  1 (10-ounce) package frozen black-eyed peas
ACCOMPANIMENT: lemon wedges

Combine water, dill sprigs, white and pale green parts of scallions, ½ teaspoon salt, and 2 tablespoons oil in a 2-quart heavy saucepan and bring to a boil, covered. Reduce heat to moderately low, add peas, and simmer, covered, stirring occasionally, until peas are tender, 30 to 35 minutes.

Transfer black-eyed peas to a shallow bowl and cool, uncovered, to warm or room temperature.

Discard dill sprigs. Stir in chopped dill, scallion greens, and remaining 2 tablespoons oil. Season with salt and serve with lemon wedges.

COOK'S NOTE
■ The black-eyed peas can be cooked, cooled, and dressed up to 1 day ahead and refrigerated, covered. Bring to room temperature before serving.

LENTILS AND OTHER LEGUMES

LENTILS

Lentils cook much faster than dried beans, and they are nutrition-rich (their protein content is higher than that of any other vegetable except the soybean). They're one of the easiest legumes to work into your culinary repertoire because they don't usually require soaking and they cook in 20 to 30 minutes. Today India produces about a third of the world's lentils, and most of them are consumed there as well. Saskatchewan, Canada, is the biggest producer of lentils for export, and North Dakota and eastern Washington are the most significant producers in the United States. In fact, a lentil festival is held in Pullman, Washington, each year.

BLACK BELUGA When these small, plump, mild lentils are cooked, their dark, rich sheen is reminiscent of beluga caviar—hence the name. It wasn't until recently, however, that scientists discovered that the color of black belugas is due to a previously unidentified anthocyanin—a natural pigment occurring in the reds, blues, and purples of many vegetables, fruits, and flowers that is rich in antioxidants and has health benefits.

BROWN These "regular" lentils don't look very fancy but they have a lovely hearty flavor. They are larger and coarser in texture than black beluga or French green lentils. If you are preparing them for a salad, take care not to overcook them; they fall apart more easily than beluga or French green lentils.

FRENCH GREEN (also called *lentilles du Puy*) We're especially fond of these tiny lentils. They have a nutty flavor and they hold their shape and color beautifully, even if you cook them for a long time.

RED Hulled and split, these lentils are perhaps best known in India (where they're called *masoor dal*), but they're favorites all over the Middle East, North Africa, and South Asia. Their beautiful salmon color turns to yellow during cooking. They contain less fiber than green lentils but are a little grainier in texture.

OTHER LEGUMES

MUNG BEANS Dull, olive-green, and about the size of BBs, these are known as *sabat moong* in India, where they're considered the most digestible of legumes and used in a great variety of ways: soaked and simmered to velvety tenderness, for instance, or pureed into batters or pastes. When they're dried, hulled, and split to reveal their yellow interiors, mung beans are called *moong dal*.

SPLIT PEAS These field peas, cultivated especially for drying, come in yellow and green varieties. When they're dried, their indigestible skins are removed and the peas are split along the natural seam. Because they're split, they don't hold their shape after cooking, so they make great soups and purees. Unsoaked split peas take about an hour to cook.

Spiced Lentils

SERVES 4 TO 6 AS A SIDE DISH
ACTIVE TIME: 30 MINUTES ■ START TO FINISH: 1¼ HOURS

■ April Bloomfield, the chef of the Spotted Pig, a wildly popular pub in Manhattan's West Village, likes to serve these spicy lentils with roasted rack of lamb. Be sure that your spices haven't been sitting in your cupboard for too long—freshness makes all the difference. ■

    2 tablespoons coriander seeds
    1 teaspoon cumin seeds
    1½ teaspoons fennel seeds
    ¼ teaspoon turmeric
    ¼ teaspoon ground ginger
    ¼ teaspoon ground cinnamon
    ¼ teaspoon ground allspice
    ¼ teaspoon chili powder
    1½ tablespoons extra-virgin olive oil
    1½ tablespoons finely chopped garlic
    ½ cup drained canned tomatoes (not in puree),
       chopped
    1 tablespoon finely grated peeled fresh ginger
    1⅓ cups small French green lentils
    5 cups water
    ½ teaspoon coarse sea salt

SPECIAL EQUIPMENT: an electric coffee/spice grinder or a
    mortar and pestle

Toast coriander, cumin, and fennel seeds in a dry heavy skillet over moderate heat, stirring, until fragrant and a shade or two darker, 1½ to 2 minutes. Finely grind toasted spices in grinder (or with mortar and pestle). Stir together with remaining spices in a bowl until blended.

Heat oil in a 3-quart heavy saucepan over moderately high heat until hot but not smoking. Add garlic and cook, stirring constantly, until golden, 20 to 30 seconds. Add spices and cook, stirring constantly, until fragrant, about 1 minute. Add tomatoes and half of fresh ginger and cook over moderate heat, stirring constantly, until almost all liquid is evaporated, about 2 minutes.

Add lentils and water, bring to a simmer, and simmer, partially covered, over low heat until lentils are tender but not falling apart, 25 to 30 minutes. Stir in sea salt and remaining fresh ginger. Turn off heat and let stand for 15 minutes to allow flavors to infuse lentils.

Serve lentils with a slotted spoon, leaving most of liquid behind.

COOK'S NOTE

■ The dish can be prepared up to 1 day ahead. Cool, uncovered, then refrigerate, covered. Reheat over low heat, adding water if necessary.

Lentils with Curried Butternut Squash and Walnuts

SERVES 4 AS A SIDE DISH
ACTIVE TIME: 15 MINUTES ■ START TO FINISH: 45 MINUTES

■ Curry and lime juice provide the flavor highlights in this dish, which plays lentils off sweet roast squash and crunchy walnuts. ■

    1 small butternut squash (about 2 pounds), halved,
       peeled, seeded, and cut into ½-inch pieces
    ¼ cup finely chopped shallots
    ¼ cup olive oil
    2 teaspoons curry powder, preferably Madras
       Salt and freshly ground black pepper
    1 cup (about 3½ ounces) walnuts, chopped
    4 cups water
    1 cup small French green lentils, picked over and
       rinsed
    ¼ cup chopped fresh cilantro
    2 teaspoons fresh lime juice, or to taste

Put a rack in middle of oven and preheat oven to 425°F.

Toss squash with shallots, oil, curry powder, ½ teaspoon salt, and ¼ teaspoon pepper on a baking sheet until coated, then spread squash out. Bake for 15 minutes. Sprinkle walnuts over squash and bake until walnuts are lightly toasted and squash is tender, about 10 minutes more.

Meanwhile, bring water to a boil in a 2- to 2½-quart saucepan. Add lentils and ½ teaspoon salt, reduce heat, and simmer, partially covered, until lentils are tender but not falling apart, 20 to 25 minutes. Drain in a sieve and transfer to a bowl.

Add squash mixture, cilantro, lime juice, and salt and pepper to taste to lentils and toss until well combined.

COOK'S NOTE

■ The dish can be made up to 1 day ahead. Cool, uncovered, then refrigerate, covered. Reheat, covered, in a 350°F oven.

Italian Lentil Stew

SERVES 4 AS A MAIN COURSE
ACTIVE TIME: 45 MINUTES ■ START TO FINISH: 2 HOURS

■ This hearty stew comes from the tiny medieval village of Santo Stefano di Sessanio, in Abruzzo, Italy, which is celebrated for its lentils. Tomatoes and fresh herbs brighten the legumes; golden potatoes and fried toasts make it a filling meal-in-one. Santo Stefano's prized lentils are not available in the United States, but any small Italian lentils can be used; if you can't find Italian lentils, small French lentils make a good substitute. ■

8 cups water
1 Turkish bay leaf or ½ California bay leaf
  Generous 1 cup small Italian lentils or small French
    green lentils, picked over and rinsed
2 ounces fresh pork fat, chopped, or 3 bacon slices,
    chopped (½ cup)
3 tablespoons olive oil
4 (½-inch-thick) slices Italian bread (about 3 inches
    in diameter)
  Salt
½ pound boiling potatoes (2 medium), peeled and cut
    into ¼-inch dice
1 large onion, finely chopped
2 large garlic cloves, finely chopped
1 (14- to 15-ounce) can whole tomatoes in juice,
    drained, juice reserved, and finely chopped
1 teaspoon sugar
  Freshly ground black pepper

3 tablespoons chopped fresh basil
1 tablespoon finely chopped fresh oregano

Bring 3 cups water and bay leaf to a boil in a 2- to 3-quart saucepan. Add lentils and simmer, uncovered, for 2 minutes. Remove pan from heat and let lentils soak for 1 hour; drain.

Cook pork fat in a 6-quart heavy pot over moderate heat, stirring occasionally, until it is deep golden and has rendered some fat, 6 to 8 minutes; remove solids with a slotted spoon and discard (if using bacon, transfer with a slotted spoon to paper towels to drain and reserve for garnish).

Add oil to fat in pot and heat over moderately high heat until hot but not smoking. Add bread and fry, turning once, until golden, about 1 minute. Transfer toasts to paper towels to drain and season lightly with salt.

Add potatoes to fat in pot and cook, stirring, until golden, 7 to 8 minutes. Transfer with a slotted spoon to paper towels to drain.

Add onion and garlic to pot and cook, stirring, until golden, 6 to 8 minutes. Stir in lentils, tomatoes with juice, sugar, 1 teaspoon salt, ½ teaspoon pepper, and remaining 5 cups water, bring to a simmer, and simmer, uncovered, stirring occasionally, until lentils are just tender and stew is thickened, 40 to 45 minutes.

Discard bay leaf and stir in potatoes, basil, oregano, and salt and pepper to taste. Thin stew with water if desired, and serve over toasts or with toasts on the side, sprinkled with bacon if using.

COOK'S NOTES

■ Pork fat is available at butcher shops, and most supermarkets can supply it on request.

■ The stew can be made up to 1 day ahead. Cool, uncovered, then refrigerate, covered.

Indian Lentil Stew

SERVES 4 TO 6 AS A MAIN COURSE
ACTIVE TIME: 40 MINUTES ■ START TO FINISH: 2¼ HOURS
(INCLUDES SOAKING TIME AND MAKING SPICE BLEND)

■ From the Cape Malay Kitchen, a restaurant in Cape Town, South Africa, this recipe showcases the legacy of the region's Indian immigrants. The dal is layered with flavors and spice, but it's a comfortable heat. Zucchini slices are laid on top of the lentils at the very end and briefly cooked, so they retain their color and texture. ■

1½ cups brown lentils, picked over and rinsed
2 (3-inch) cinnamon sticks
2 green or white cardamom pods (see Sources)
¼ cup vegetable oil
2 large onions, chopped
3 medium ripe tomatoes (about 1 pound total), chopped, or 2 cups chopped drained canned tomatoes (from a 28-ounce can)
1 serrano chile, seeded if desired (for less heat) and finely chopped
2 teaspoons minced garlic
1 tablespoon Indian Spice Blend (recipe follows)
1 teaspoon ground cumin
1 teaspoon ground coriander
½ teaspoon turmeric
4 cups water
1½ teaspoons salt, or to taste
3 medium zucchini (about 1 pound total), cut into ⅛-inch-thick slices
GARNISH: ¼ cup chopped fresh cilantro
ACCOMPANIMENT: basmati rice
SPECIAL EQUIPMENT: cheesecloth; kitchen string

Soak lentils in water to cover for 1 hour.

Wrap cinnamon sticks and cardamom pods in a small square of cheesecloth and tie into a bundle with string.

Heat oil in a 4-quart heavy pot over moderate heat until hot but not smoking. Add onions and cheesecloth bundle and cook, stirring occasionally, until onions are softened, 6 to 8 minutes. Stir in tomatoes, chile, garlic, spice blend, cumin, coriander, and turmeric, bring to a simmer, and simmer, stirring occasionally, until tomatoes have broken down, about 10 minutes.

Drain lentils in a sieve and add to onion mixture. Stir in water, bring to a simmer, and simmer, uncovered, adding more water if necessary to keep ingredients just covered with liquid, until lentils are very soft, about 40 minutes.

Discard cheesecloth bundle and stir in salt. Ar-

range zucchini in an even layer on top of stew. Cook, covered, until zucchini is tender, about 10 minutes.

Sprinkle stew with cilantro and serve over rice.

COOK'S NOTE
■ The stew, without the zucchini and cilantro, can be made up to 1 day ahead. Remove the cheesecloth bundle and cool, uncovered, then refrigerate, covered. Reheat over moderate heat before adding the zucchini.

Indian Spice Blend

MAKES ABOUT 1 CUP
ACTIVE TIME: 10 MINUTES ■ START TO FINISH: 20 MINUTES

■ This spice blend adds a fragrant kick to any curry, and it is also great as a rub for grilled meats and fish. ■

1 cup coriander seeds
¾ cup cumin seeds
¼ cup red pepper flakes
1½ teaspoons turmeric
1½ teaspoons ground ginger
1½ teaspoons black peppercorns
3 green or white cardamom pods (see Sources)
½ teaspoon whole cloves
1 (1-inch) piece cinnamon stick
SPECIAL EQUIPMENT: an electric coffee/spice grinder

Put a rack in middle of oven and preheat oven to 350°F.

Toast coriander and cumin seeds in a shallow baking pan in oven until fragrant, about 5 minutes. Cool for 10 minutes.

Combine seeds with remaining ingredients in a bowl and grind, in batches, to a powder in grinder.

COOK'S NOTE
■ The spice blend can be kept in an airtight container in a cool, dark place for up to 6 months or frozen for up to 1 year.

Curried Lentil Stew
with Vegetables

SERVES 6 AS A MAIN COURSE
ACTIVE TIME: 30 MINUTES ■ START TO FINISH: 1¾ HOURS

■ In India, lentil-based dals are often served as a side dish, but adding a host of vibrant vegetables turns this one into a main course. Suffused with turmeric, garlic, ginger, and spices, the red lentils are cooked down into a creamy puree. Best of all, the stew improves with time, so you can make it ahead for a night when you need a quick supper. We serve it with roasted cauliflower on the side—the two dishes have an affinity for each other. ■

- 6 tablespoons vegetable oil
- 1 medium onion, finely chopped
- Salt
- 1 (2-by-1-inch) piece fresh ginger, peeled and quartered
- 5 large garlic cloves, coarsely chopped
- About 6 cups water
- 1½ teaspoons curry powder
- ½ teaspoon ground cumin
- ½ teaspoon turmeric
- 1 cup red lentils, picked over and rinsed
- 3 medium carrots, quartered lengthwise and cut crosswise into ½-inch pieces
- 3 cups (about 3 ounces) loosely packed baby spinach leaves
- 1 cup frozen peas (not thawed)
- ½ cup chopped fresh cilantro
- Freshly ground black pepper
- ¼ teaspoon cumin seeds
- ¼ teaspoon red pepper flakes

GARNISH: chopped fresh cilantro

ACCOMPANIMENTS: basmati rice and roasted cauliflower (page 587)

Heat ¼ cup oil in a 4-quart heavy pot over moderately high heat until hot but not smoking. Add onion with ¼ teaspoon salt and cook, stirring occasionally, for 2 minutes. Reduce heat to moderate and cook, stirring occasionally, until onion is golden, about 8 minutes more.

Meanwhile, when onion is almost done, puree ginger and garlic with ⅓ cup water in a blender. Add puree to onion and cook, stirring, until water has evaporated and oil separates from onion mixture, about 5 minutes. Add curry powder, ground cumin, and turmeric, reduce heat to low, and cook, stirring, for 1 minute.

Stir in lentils and 5 cups water, bring to a simmer, and simmer, uncovered, stirring occasionally, for 30 minutes.

Add carrots and ¾ teaspoon salt to lentils and simmer until carrots are tender and lentils have broken down to a coarse puree, 40 to 50 minutes more; add more water if necessary to keep lentils covered and stir more frequently toward end of cooking.

Stir in spinach and peas and simmer, stirring, until peas are tender, about 3 minutes. Stir in cilantro and season with salt and pepper to taste. If necessary, add enough water to thin stew so that it can be ladled easily over rice.

Meanwhile, just before serving, heat remaining 2 tablespoons oil in a small skillet over moderately high heat until hot but not smoking. Add cumin seeds and red pepper flakes and cook, stirring, until spices are a shade or two darker and fragrant, about 30 seconds (be careful not to burn spices). Pour hot oil and spices in a swirl over stew.

Serve stew over rice, sprinkled with cilantro, with roasted cauliflower on the side.

COOK'S NOTE

■ The stew, without the spinach, peas, cilantro, and spice oil, can be made up to 5 days ahead. Cool completely, uncovered, then refrigerate, covered. Or freeze in an airtight container for up to 3 months. Reheat over moderately low heat, thinning with water to a pourable consistency (the stew thickens as it stands) and stirring frequently, before adding the remaining ingredients.

Yellow Split Pea Stew with Coconut Chips

Cholar Dal

SERVES 4 AS A MAIN DISH
ACTIVE TIME: 30 MINUTES ■ START TO FINISH: 1½ HOURS
PLUS SOAKING TIME FOR PEAS

■ This colorful dal, adapted from one by the Bengali writer Chitrita Banerji, is one of the best we've ever tasted. Spicy, slightly sweet, and studded with fresh coconut chips fried in ghee, it is delicious served with rice and green beans on the side, or as a bed for seared mild white fish fillets. ■

1¼ cups yellow split peas, picked over and rinsed
1 small coconut (see Cook's Note)
5 cups water
1 teaspoon finely grated peeled fresh ginger
1 teaspoon turmeric
6 (2- to 3-inch-long) fresh hot chiles, preferably green, slit lengthwise down one side
1 tablespoon garam masala (see page 536 or Sources)
2–4 teaspoons sugar
Salt
½ cup plus 1 tablespoon ghee (see page 490)
2 dried hot chiles (about 3 inches long), stems removed
1 teaspoon cumin seeds
3 Turkish bay leaves or 1½ California bay leaves
1 (1-inch) piece cinnamon stick, broken in half
2 green or white cardamom pods (see Sources)
2 whole cloves

ACCOMPANIMENT: basmati rice
SPECIAL EQUIPMENT: a well-seasoned 14-inch flat-bottomed wok

Soak split peas in cold water to cover by 1 inch at room temperature (refrigerate if kitchen is very warm) for 8 to 12 hours. (Alternatively, cover with boiling water and let stand for 30 minutes.) Drain.

Put a rack in middle of oven and preheat oven to 400°F.

Pierce 2 softest eyes of coconut with a metal skewer or a small screwdriver and drain and discard liquid. Bake coconut for 15 minutes.

Crack open coconut shell with a hammer or back of a heavy cleaver and remove flesh, levering it out carefully with screwdriver or point of a strong knife. With an adjustable-blade slicer or a vegetable peeler, cut one quarter of coconut into thin slices, 1 to 2 inches long and about ¹⁄₁₆ inch thick (reserve remaining coconut for another use).

Bring water to a boil in a 3-quart heavy saucepan. Add split peas, ginger, and turmeric, reduce heat, and simmer, covered, stirring occasionally, until peas are just tender, about 20 minutes.

Add fresh chiles, garam masala, 2 teaspoons sugar, and ½ teaspoon salt to peas and simmer, uncovered, stirring occasionally, until dal is thickened and resembles a thick soup, 30 to 35 minutes.

Meanwhile, heat ½ cup ghee in wok over moderately high heat until hot but not smoking. Add coconut slices, in 2 or 3 batches, and cook, stirring occasionally, until golden brown, 2 to 4 minutes per batch. Transfer with a slotted spoon to paper towels to drain. Discard ghee, then wipe out wok and set aside.

When dal is cooked, heat remaining tablespoon ghee in wok over moderate heat until hot but not smoking. Add dried chiles, cumin seeds, bay leaves, cinnamon, cardamom, and cloves and cook, stirring, until fragrant and chiles have turned just a shade darker, about 1 minute.

Stir spice mixture into dal, along with ¼ teaspoon salt, up to 2 teaspoons more sugar if desired, and coconut chips. Discard bay leaves, as well as dried chiles, cinnamon stick, cardamom pods, and cloves if desired. Serve with rice.

COOK'S NOTES

■ Coconuts are sometimes rancid; you may want to buy an extra one.
■ Any leftover coconut can be frozen in a sealable plastic bag for up to 1 month.
■ The dal, without the final spice oil and coconut chips, can be made up to 1 day ahead. Cool, uncovered, then refrigerate, covered. Reheat the dal, thinning it with water as necessary, before finishing the dish with the spice oil, salt, sugar, and coconut chips.

VEGETARIAN MAIN COURSES

Unless you count potatoes, my father never met a vegetable he liked. He could tolerate the occasional spear of asparagus, provided it was white, and he was known to eat a few forkfuls of red cabbage every once in a while. But to my knowledge, nothing green ever got into his mouth without a fight.

You can imagine, therefore, his horror when, sometime in the early seventies, he was invited to lunch at a health food emporium. He staggered out looking pale; the waitress had talked him into trying vegetarian beef Stroganoff. "It was made out of soybeans," he groaned. And then he announced that he would have to take the rest of the day off to recover.

I sympathized, but a year later, when I moved out to the West Coast, I changed my tune. Like many people of my generation, I read *Diet for a Small Planet* and learned how much more food there would be for the world if we all ate vegetables instead of feeding the plants to the animals and eating their meat. I went through a brief vegetarian phase. But, as with many people of my generation, that period didn't last very long.

Yet time has marched on, and it is becoming increasingly clear that we do need to reconsider our eating habits. We live in a society that consumes more meat than any other group in history. There are currently three billion domesticated cattle, sheep, and goats in the world—and that number does not include the millions of pigs or the nine billion chickens we consume every year in this country alone. Global livestock grazing and feed production now use 30 percent of the surface of the planet, and that takes a toll on the environment. Most health professionals agree that eating so much meat takes a toll on us as well.

All that aside, it seems to me that it is time to put the joy back into the act of eating vegetables. Isn't it time we began to think of all the grains and greens that grow in the earth as a gift? And isn't it time we realized that vegetarian dishes are neither penance nor virtue, but simply another mealtime option?

In this chapter, you'll find everything you'll need to keep you happy, from easy weeknight meals like seductively aromatic Welsh rabbit and zucchini curry to festive party fare like vegetable enchiladas with creamy poblano sauce, and flavors from all around the world. Should you be looking for a showstopper, the fennel, Taleggio, and cardamom tart is just the thing for a holiday meal—and the classic masala dosas of India will wow everyone who is lucky enough to taste them. As for the wild rice crêpes with mushroom filling, they are guaranteed to make any dinner party perfect.

You won't make these dishes because they're good for the earth, and you won't make them because they're good for you. You won't even make them because they're so inexpensive. You will make them because they are very, very delicious.

VEGETARIAN MAIN COURSES

OTHER VEGETARIAN MAIN DISHES IN THIS BOOK

Asparagus Flan with Cheese Sauce (page 85)

Tunisian Soup with Egg Noodles and Chard (page 117; if made with vegetable broth)

Curried Potato and Leek Soup with Spinach (page 122; if made with vegetable broth or water)

Chunky Butternut Squash, White Bean, and Tomato Soup (page 123; if made with vegetable broth or water)

Pumpkin Soup with Red Pepper Mousse (page 123; if made with vegetable broth or water)

Spinach Stracciatella Soup (page 125; if made with vegetable broth or water)

French Tomato Soup with Rice (page 127; if made with vegetable broth or water)

Venetian-Style Bean and Pasta Soup (page 130)

Mexican Black Bean Soup with Ancho Chiles (page 131)

Best Red Bean Soup (page 132)

Buttered Barley and Onion Soup (page 135; if made with vegetable broth)

Boston Lettuce Salad with Dubliner Cheese and Chive Dressing (page 166)

Roasted Vegetable Panzanella (page 178)

Roasted Potato, Okra, and Fava Bean Salad (page 181)

Winter Tabbouleh (page 185)

Southwestern Quinoa Salad (page 187)

Quinoa and Bulgur Salad with Feta (page 188)

Barley, Corn, and Grape Tomato Salad (page 188)

Lentil Salad with Tomato and Dill (page 189)

White Bean, Red Onion, and Celery Salad (page 191)

Three-Bean Salad with Cilantro-Chile Dressing (page 191)

Capellini with Fresh Tomato Sauce (page 205)

Spaghetti with Pecorino Romano and Black Pepper (page 206)

Spaghetti with Olive and Pine Nut Salsa (page 206)

Spaghetti with Ramps (page 206)

Linguine with Zucchini and Mint (page 208)

Fettuccine with Arugula Puree and Cherry Tomato Sauce (page 208)

Penne with Tomatoes and Goat Cheese (page 209)

Pasta with Lentils and Kale (page 209)

Gemelli and Mushrooms with Parmesan Crumb Topping (page 217; if made with vegetable broth)

Mexican Macaroni and Cheese (page 218)

Vegetable Lasagne (page 222)

Arugula and Goat Cheese Ravioli (page 227)

Ricotta Gnudi with Roasted Tomatoes (page 231)

Gnocchi alla Romana (page 232)

Fresh Manicotti (page 233)

Egg Noodles with Cabbage and Onions (page 238)

Browned Onion Kugels (page 239)

Spicy Soba Noodles with Lacquered Eggplant (page 239)

Pierogi (page 247)

Fried Rice with Eggs and Scallions (page 255)

Mushroom Risotto (page 261; if made with vegetable broth)

Risotto with Asparagus, Peas, and Mushrooms (page 262; if made with vegetable broth)

Beet Risotto (page 263)

Radicchio and Red Wine Risotto (page 265; if made with vegetable broth)

Gorgonzola Risotto (page 265; if made with vegetable broth)

Butternut Squash Risotto (page 266; if made with vegetable broth)

Farro Risotto with Cauliflower (page 275; if made with vegetable broth)

Herbed Bean Ragout (page 280)

Black Beans and Rice with Sweet Potatoes (page 281)

Lentils with Curried Butternut Squash and Walnuts (page 285)

Indian Lentil Stew (page 286)

Curried Lentil Stew with Vegetables (page 288)

Yellow Split Pea Stew with Coconut Chips (page 289)

Grilled Eggplant with Spicy Peanut Sauce (page 554)

Grilled Zucchini and Tomatoes with Feta Sauce (page 559)

Rolled Omelet with Arugula–Goat Cheese Filling (page 648)

Parsley-Crouton Omelets with Gruyère (page 649)

Fluffy Egg White Omelets with Basil and Tomatoes (page 650)

Baked Eggs with Roasted Vegetable Hash (page 653)

Poached Eggs with Tomato Cilantro Sauce (page 653)

Grilled Cheddar and Fennel Sandwiches with Curry Mayo

SERVES 4
ACTIVE TIME: 25 MINUTES ■ START TO FINISH: 25 MINUTES

■ Everyone loves grilled cheese sandwiches, but some easy additions—crisp fennel, zesty curry mayo—transform this old standard into something very tasty and sophisticated. Cooking the shallots with the curry powder before mixing them into the mayonnaise makes the flavor bloom. ■

- 1 teaspoon vegetable oil
- 2 tablespoons finely chopped shallot
- 2 teaspoons curry powder, preferably Madras
- ½ cup mayonnaise
- 1 tablespoon fresh lemon juice
- 1 baguette
- 1½ tablespoons unsalted butter, softened
- ½ pound extra-sharp cheddar
- ¼ cup very thinly sliced fennel (quarter bulb lengthwise and core before slicing)

Put a rack in middle of oven and preheat oven to 250°F.

Heat oil in a 12-inch heavy nonstick skillet over moderate heat until hot but not smoking. Add shallot and curry powder and cook, stirring, for 2 minutes. Transfer to a small bowl and stir in mayonnaise and lemon juice. Wipe skillet clean and set aside.

Cut sixteen ¼-inch-thick diagonal slices (about 6 inches long) from baguette and arrange on a sheet of wax paper. Spread one side of each slice with butter, turn over, and spread other side with curry mayonnaise. Cut cheese into thin slices no wider than bread slices. Divide cheese among 8 slices of bread and top with fennel and remaining slices of bread, buttered sides up.

Heat skillet over moderate heat until hot. Add half of sandwiches and cook, turning once and pressing down on bread occasionally, until bread is browned and cheese is melted, about 7 minutes per batch. Transfer to a baking sheet and keep warm, uncovered,

in the oven while you cook remaining sandwiches in same manner.

Cut sandwiches in half to serve.

Grilled Provolone and Broccoli Rabe Panini

SERVES 4
ACTIVE TIME: 20 MINUTES ■ START TO FINISH: 30 MINUTES

■ The messy hoagies loaded with sharp provolone and broccoli rabe at Tony Luke's in Philadelphia were the inspiration for these neater panini. The greens are cooked with garlic until they're meltingly tender, then layered with thinly sliced provolone between slices of Italian bread and grilled in a sandwich press (a ridged grill pan will also do the job). Although we love broccoli rabe's bite, escarole and arugula also work well here. ■

- 1 pound broccoli rabe, 2 inches of lower stems trimmed
- 2 garlic cloves, minced
- 5 tablespoons extra-virgin olive oil
  Salt and freshly ground black pepper
- 8 (½-inch-thick) slices bread cut from an 8- to 9-inch round Italian loaf
- ⅔ pound sliced provolone

SPECIAL EQUIPMENT: a panini or sandwich press or a well-seasoned ridged grill pan (see Cook's Note)

Cook broccoli rabe in a 4-quart pot of boiling salted water (1 tablespoon salt), uncovered, until tender, about 6 minutes. Drain well in a colander and cool slightly. Squeeze out excess water and chop.

Cook garlic in 2½ tablespoons oil in a 10-inch heavy skillet over moderate heat, stirring, until it just begins to turn golden, about 1 minute. Add broccoli rabe and cook, stirring, for 1 minute. Season with salt and pepper and remove from heat.

Heat panini or sandwich press according to manufacturer's instructions until hot or heat grill pan over moderate heat. Meanwhile, brush slices of bread on one side with remaining 2½ tablespoons oil. Turn 4 slices over and divide half of cheese among them. Top with broccoli rabe, remaining cheese, and remaining 4 bread slices, oiled side up.

Put 2 sandwiches on press, close press, and cook sandwiches until browned and crisp, 4 to 8 minutes. Or, if using grill pan, put a heavy pan on top of sandwiches and cook, turning sandwiches once. Cook remaining 2 sandwiches in same manner.

Cut sandwiches in half to serve.

COOK'S NOTES

- For additional flavor, nonvegetarians can add anchovies to the broccoli rabe: Add 4 anchovies, rinsed, patted dry, and chopped, along with the garlic and cook in the oil as directed.
- If you have a large two-burner griddle, you can grill all 4 sandwiches at the same time. Weight the sandwiches with a baking sheet and two 28- to 30-ounce cans.

Hummus and Vegetable Lavash Wraps

SERVES 4
ACTIVE TIME: 30 MINUTES ■ START TO FINISH: 30 MINUTES
(INCLUDES MAKING HUMMUS)

■ Lavash, a type of Middle Eastern flatbread, comes in two styles. The first kind is flat, crisp, and almost crackerlike, and the second, the kind we call for here, has a soft, pliable texture similar to that of a flour tortilla. Lavash is found in many supermarkets. Filled with hummus and a medley of raw vegetables, the wraps are like a Middle Eastern *meze* platter, all rolled up. ■

Hummus (page 298)
1 (16- to 18-inch) very thin, pliable round lavash (sometimes called mountain shepherd bread; see Sources)
½ seedless cucumber (usually plastic-wrapped), cut into ⅛-inch-thick slices
1 large carrot, cut into ribbons with a vegetable peeler
1 small sweet onion, cut into ⅛-inch-thick slices
6 radishes, shredded on large holes of a box grater
½ cup alfalfa sprouts
1 tablespoon sesame seeds, toasted (see Tips, page 911)

BROCCOLI RABE

Broccoli rabe (pronounced "rahb") is actually more closely related to turnips than to regular broccoli. The succulent, slender stalks topped with clusters of small buds and dark green leaves pack an assertive wallop of flavor (as well as vitamins and minerals) and have a great affinity for garlic and olive oil. Introduced to the United States by the immigrant D'Arrigo brothers in 1927 (they were also the first marketers of regular broccoli), the vegetable has outgrown its "ethnic green" pigeonhole and is available in supermarkets across the country, where its aliases include "broccoli raab," "rapini," "cime di rapa," and "Italian broccoli." When buying broccoli rabe, look for bunches with crisp deep green leaves, resilient stalks, and tight buds with a minimum of yellow flowers. It's generally available year-round, but it's at its best in the colder months.

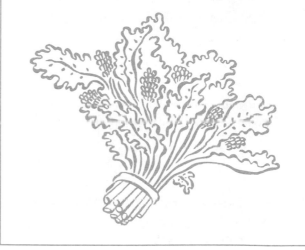

GARNISH: alfalfa sprouts; sesame seeds, toasted (see Tips, page 911) if desired

Spread hummus evenly over lavash. Top with remaining ingredients. Roll lavash up tightly, jelly-roll fashion, and trim ends. Cut into 8 slices with a serrated knife. Garnish sandwiches with sprouts and sesame seeds.

COOK'S NOTE

- The sandwiches can be made up to 1 hour ahead and kept, covered, at room temperature.

QUICK VEGETARIAN MEALS

The key to a satisfying vegetarian meal isn't quantity or heft, but flavor and texture. That's where a well-stocked pantry and refrigerator are worth their weight in gold. Condiments and sauces that have been fermented, like aged balsamic vinegar, naturally brewed soy sauce, and dry sherry, have umami flavors reminiscent of the savory complexity of meat. Other big-ticket flavor items include sun-dried tomatoes, tomato paste, Parmigiano-Reggiano, capers, olives, lemons, dried chiles, Sriracha (Asian chile sauce), fresh herbs, and spices like cumin and *pimentón* (smoked Spanish paprika). The crunch of toasted nuts, *pepitas* (toasted pumpkin seeds), sunflower seeds, and homemade dried bread crumbs makes vegetables, beans, and grains just a little more satisfying.

As with any cooking, creating vegetarian meals becomes easier and more instinctive once you have built a repertoire of a dozen tried-and-true dishes. After mastering the basics of your favorites, you'll be able to effortlessly vary them each season. Here are some quick ideas.

■ **TOSS SEASONAL VEGETABLES** with oil, garlic, and sturdy herbs such as rosemary or thyme and roast in a hot (450°F) oven. Halfway through cooking, drizzle them with a little balsamic vinegar or soy sauce or add a few tablespoons of butter for richness.

■ **DRIED BEANS COOKED FROM SCRATCH** can't be beat. Soak and cook large quantities of dried beans on the weekends—let them simmer away on the back of the stove while you're doing something else—then refrigerate or freeze in small containers to use on weeknights. One of the easiest and most satisfying ways to serve them is a "bean bar," a make-your-own vegetarian buffet. Set a large bowl of soupy beans in the center of the table and surround with mix-ins: rice, cubed roasted sweet potatoes, corn, avocado, jicama, toasted *pepitas,* cilantro, lime

wedges, and just about anything else. Puree the leftover beans with stock to make soup and serve with corn bread and salad.

■ **A BEAN GRATIN** is delicious. Puree half a batch of cooked beans and fold in the remaining whole beans, along with sautéed onions and garlic and fresh thyme or rosemary. Top with fresh bread crumbs tossed with Parmesan and olive oil and bake. For a Mexican twist, use crumbled or ground cumin seeds in place of the herbs and top with crushed tortilla chips.

■ **FOR A MEATLESS CASSOULET,** sauté leeks, carrots, and garlic in oil, add cooked cannellini beans, water, thyme, parsley, and a bay leaf, and simmer until everything is tender. Mash some of the beans to thicken the stew. Meanwhile, toss fresh bread crumbs with oil and finely chopped garlic and bake on a baking sheet until crisp and golden. Top the cassoulet with the crumbs.

■ COOK A POT OF MINESTRONE over the weekend and add heft to leftovers by serving with hot cheese toasts — rub a raw garlic clove over slices of toast, drizzle with olive oil, sprinkle with salt and good cheese, and broil until the cheese melts.

■ FOR SWISS CHARD STEW, cook chopped chard stems and leaves with garlic, olives, and raisins in stock and sprinkle with feta cheese just before serving.

■ KALE RISOTTO is ideal in winter. Cook the stems, then the leaves, in the broth for the risotto until tender, then finely chop. Cook the risotto, stir in the greens, along with some grated Parmesan at the end, and garnish with a handful of toasted pine nuts.

■ ENRICH CANNED BLACK BEAN SOUP with a dash of balsamic vinegar or dry sherry when you're really in a hurry. Cumin, smoked paprika, and fresh cilantro are other options. Or doctor canned lentil soup with chopped kale and fresh thyme.

■ TO MAKE A MEAL OF FRIED EGGS, serve them over any steamed grain spiced up with a bit of salsa or hot sauce.

■ GRAINS can be cooked in advance and refrigerated. They need only to be reheated in the microwave or in a sieve set over a pan of simmering water, covered with a folded kitchen towel and a lid.

■ FOLD SAUTÉED ONIONS, SQUASH, AND EGGPLANT INTO HOT COOKED GRAINS, such as barley, and serve over baby greens and basil dressed with a vinaigrette.

■ A BLOCK OF GOOD TOFU needs nothing more than grated fresh ginger, sliced scallions, and a drizzle of soy sauce or hot chile sauce — no cooking needed. Firm tofu takes especially well to curries, absorbing the rich, spiced sauces while tempering their heat. It also fries well, turning golden and crisp. Cut a block of firm tofu into slices, pat dry, and sear on both sides in hot oil. Sauté garlic, ginger, and sliced red bell pepper in the same skillet, then stir in coconut milk and soy sauce. Pour the sauce over the tofu and top with toasted cashews.

Hummus

MAKES ABOUT 2 CUPS
ACTIVE TIME: 15 MINUTES ■ START TO FINISH: 15 MINUTES

■ This Middle Eastern chickpea dip is a great thing to have in the fridge for an impromptu healthy snack. We like to set it out with fresh vegetables, toasted pita, and olives. ■

    2 large garlic cloves
      Salt
    1 (16- to 19-ounce) can chickpeas, rinsed
      and drained
    ⅓ cup well-stirred tahini (Middle Eastern
      sesame paste)
    2 tablespoons fresh lemon juice
    2 tablespoons olive oil
    1¼ teaspoons ground cumin
    3 tablespoons water
    3 tablespoons minced fresh flat-leaf parsley
      Freshly ground black pepper

Mince garlic and mash to a paste with ½ teaspoon salt, using side of a large heavy knife. Transfer garlic paste to a food processor, add chickpeas, tahini, lemon juice, oil, and cumin, and blend, scraping down sides as necessary, until smooth. Add water, parsley, and salt and pepper to taste and pulse until just combined.

COOK'S NOTE

■ The hummus can be made up to 2 days ahead and refrigerated, covered.

Creamy Tofu Salad Sandwiches

SERVES 4
ACTIVE TIME: 15 MINUTES ■ START TO FINISH: 20 MINUTES

■ We guarantee everyone will want seconds of this egg salad doppelgänger. ■

    1 (14-ounce) package firm tofu, rinsed and drained
    ½ cup mayonnaise
    1 teaspoon fresh lemon juice
    1 teaspoon turmeric
    ½ teaspoon dry mustard
    2 celery ribs, finely chopped
    ¼ cup chopped fresh chives
    ½ teaspoon salt, or to taste
    ¼ teaspoon freshly ground black pepper, or to
      taste
    8 slices whole wheat sandwich bread
    8 Boston lettuce leaves
    8 tomato slices

Finely mash tofu with a fork in a bowl. Transfer to a sieve set over another bowl and let drain for 15 minutes (discard liquid).

Whisk together mayonnaise, lemon juice, turmeric, and mustard in a bowl. Stir in tofu, celery, chives, salt, and pepper.

Make sandwiches with bread, tofu salad, lettuce, and tomatoes.

COOK'S NOTE

■ The salad can be made up to 4 hours ahead and refrigerated, covered.

Tempeh Burgers

SERVES 8
ACTIVE TIME: 1 HOUR ■ START TO FINISH: 3 HOURS
(INCLUDES CHILLING)

■ These vegetarian burgers—the best we've ever tasted—are a nice introduction to tempeh, the dense, protein-rich cake of fermented soybeans that originated in Indonesia. Tempeh is chewy, nutty, and faintly bitter but soaks up any flavor you pair it with. Here, we crumble it and cook it in a paste of onion, garlic, spices, and cilantro as well as sun-dried tomatoes and chipotles. Bulgur and green pumpkin seeds provide the needed texture. You won't mistake these rich, savory patties for hamburger, but they're delicious in their own right. Tempeh is available refrigerated or frozen in most natural foods stores and many supermarkets (look for it near the tofu). ■

⅓ cup packed sun-dried tomatoes (not packed in oil)

½ cup green (hulled) pumpkin seeds (*pepitas;* see Cook's Note)

1 medium onion, quartered

2 garlic cloves

½ cup fresh cilantro stems

½ cup olive oil

1 pound tempeh, crumbled

1 teaspoon ground cumin

1 teaspoon chili powder

1½ cups water

½ cup bulgur

2 tablespoons soy sauce

1 tablespoon chopped canned chipotle chiles in adobo

1 tablespoon Dijon mustard

½ teaspoon salt

¼ teaspoon freshly ground black pepper

ACCOMPANIMENT: grilled or toasted hamburger buns

Cover sun-dried tomatoes with boiling water and soak for 10 minutes; drain and set aside.

Meanwhile, heat a dry 12-inch heavy skillet over moderate heat until hot. Add pumpkin seeds and toast, stirring constantly, until puffed and beginning to pop, about 5 minutes. Transfer to a cutting board and cool slightly, then coarsely chop.

Puree onion, garlic, and cilantro stems in a food processor. Heat 2 tablespoons oil in same skillet over moderate heat until hot but not smoking. Add onion mixture and cook, stirring occasionally, until beginning to brown, about 8 minutes. Add 2 tablespoons oil and tempeh and cook, stirring occasionally, until tempeh is pale golden, about 4 minutes. Add cumin and chili powder and cook, stirring, for 1 minute. Add water, bulgur, and soy sauce, bring to a bare simmer, cover, and simmer, stirring once or twice, until liquid is absorbed, about 10 minutes.

Remove lid and cook until tempeh is the consistency of ground meat, 4 to 5 minutes. Transfer half of tempeh mixture to food processor, add sun-dried tomatoes, chipotles, mustard, salt, pepper, and half of pumpkin seeds, and puree until smooth. Transfer to a large bowl and stir in remaining tempeh mixture and pumpkin seeds. Refrigerate, uncovered, until cool, about 1 hour.

Form mixture into 8 patties and place on a wax-paper-lined baking sheet. Cover with plastic wrap and refrigerate for at least 1 hour.

Put a rack in middle of oven, put a baking sheet on rack, and preheat oven to 200°F.

Heat remaining ¼ cup oil in cleaned skillet over moderate heat until hot but not smoking. Add 4 burgers and cook, turning once, until browned and heated through, about 8 minutes. Transfer burgers to warm baking sheet and keep warm, covered with foil, in oven. Cook remaining 4 burgers in oil remaining in pan in same manner.

Serve burgers on hamburger buns.

COOK'S NOTES

- If you are unable to find raw pumpkin seeds, salted toasted pumpkin seeds can be substituted (don't toast them).
- The patties can be refrigerated for up to 8 hours.

Black Bean Quesadillas

SERVES 4

ACTIVE TIME: 20 MINUTES ■ START TO FINISH: 20 MINUTES

■ Quesadillas should be swift and satisfying, and this version fits the bill. A filling of canned black beans, pepper Jack cheese, and a fillip of salsa offers plenty of flavor. Assembling the quesadillas in the skillet while the bottom of the tortilla cooks is both neat and easy. The key here is not to overload the tortilla with too much filling— you want the quesadillas pleasantly crisp, not soggy. ■

1⅓ cups coarsely grated pepper Jack cheese (about 5 ounces)

½ cup rinsed canned black beans

2 tablespoons finely chopped fresh cilantro

½ teaspoon ground cumin

1–2 tablespoons vegetable oil

8 (6-inch) flour tortillas

½ cup chunky salsa

Put a rack in middle of oven, put a large heatproof plate on rack, and preheat oven to 200°F.

Stir together cheese, beans, cilantro, and cumin in a bowl.

Heat ½ teaspoon oil in an 8-inch nonstick skillet over moderate heat until hot but not smoking. Add 1 tortilla and top half nearest you with 2 to 3 tablespoons cheese mixture, spreading it evenly. Spread cheese mixture with 1 tablespoon salsa. Using a spatula, fold uncovered half of tortilla over and cook until underside is golden, about 1 minute. Carefully turn over tortilla using spatula, and cook until underside is golden, 1 to 2 minutes more. Transfer to plate in oven and cover loosely with foil. Make 7 more quesadillas in same manner, stacking them on plate in oven.

Bean Burritos

SERVES 6

ACTIVE TIME: 45 MINUTES ■ START TO FINISH: 45 MINUTES

■ Full of beans, pepper Jack, and one of our very favorite condiments—quick Mexican pickled onions—these burritos are outrageously good. Panfrying melts the cheese and crisps the outside of the tortillas. We especially like the creaminess of pinto beans here. ■

FOR PICKLED ONIONS
- 2 cups water
- 3 tablespoons red wine vinegar
- 2 tablespoons sugar
- 1 teaspoon salt
- 1 medium red onion, halved lengthwise and thinly sliced crosswise

FOR BEAN FILLING
- 3 tablespoons vegetable oil
- 5 garlic cloves, finely chopped
- 1 teaspoon ground cumin
- ½ teaspoon salt
- ¼ teaspoon freshly ground black pepper
- 2 (14- to 15-ounce) cans pinto or black beans, rinsed and drained
- ⅓ cup water
- 3 scallions, finely chopped

FOR ASSEMBLING AND COOKING BURRITOS
- 6 (8- to 10-inch) flour tortillas
- 2 cups coarsely grated pepper Jack cheese (about 8 ounces)

- ⅓ cup finely chopped fresh cilantro
- 1½ tablespoons vegetable oil

ACCOMPANIMENTS: salsa and sour cream

PREPARE THE ONIONS: Bring water, vinegar, sugar, and salt to a boil in a 1-quart heavy saucepan. Add onion and simmer, uncovered, until crisp-tender, about 3 minutes. Drain and cool to room temperature.

MAKE THE BEAN FILLING: Heat oil in a 12-inch skillet over moderate heat until hot but not smoking. Add garlic, cumin, salt, and pepper and cook, stirring, until garlic is golden, about 1 minute. Stir in beans, coarsely mashing them with a potato masher or a large fork until combined. Add water and scallions and cook, stirring, until most of water is absorbed, about 5 minutes. Remove from heat.

ASSEMBLE THE BURRITOS: Spread one sixth of bean filling across middle of 1 tortilla, leaving a 1-inch border at either end. Sprinkle with ⅓ cup cheese, 1 heaping tablespoon pickled onions, and scant 1 tablespoon cilantro. Fold ends of tortilla over filling, then roll up tightly, enclosing filling. Transfer seam side down to a plate and assemble 5 more burritos in same manner.

COOK THE BURRITOS: Heat 1½ teaspoons oil in a 10- to 11-inch cast-iron or other heavy skillet over moderately high heat until hot but not smoking. Add 2 burritos, seam side down, and fry until lightly browned on underside, 1 to 2 minutes. Using tongs or a spatula, turn over and fry until golden, 1 to 2 minutes more. Transfer to paper towels to drain briefly, then transfer to a platter and cover loosely with foil to keep warm. Fry remaining 4 burritos in 2 batches in remaining oil in same manner.

Serve with salsa and sour cream.

Welsh Rabbit

SERVE 4
ACTIVE TIME: 20 MINUTES ■ START TO FINISH: 20 MINUTES

■ Also known as Welsh rarebit, cheesy sauce ladled over toasted bread dates back hundreds of years in the annals of British cooking. An aged yellow cheddar offers the best visual appeal and the most complex flavor. We tested this with several types of beer and found that pilsner-style beers (think Budweiser) taste best. You can serve it with a salad as a light meal, but John Thorne, author of the newsletter *Simple Cooking,* prefers Welsh rabbit as a savory postmeal alternative to dessert that keeps the conversation (and the wine) flowing late into the night. ■

16 (⅓-inch-thick) baguette slices, cut on a
      diagonal
½ stick (4 tablespoons) unsalted butter,
      softened
 1 large egg yolk
 2 tablespoons all-purpose flour
½ cup pilsner beer
¼ cup whole milk
 1 teaspoon dry mustard
⅛ teaspoon freshly ground black pepper
 6 ounces extra-sharp cheddar, coarsely grated
      (about 1½ cups)

Preheat broiler. Spread one side of bread slices with 2 tablespoons butter. Arrange slices buttered side up on a baking sheet. Broil 4 to 6 inches from heat until golden brown, 1 to 4 minutes (do not turn slices over). Set aside.

Lightly beat yolk in a medium heatproof bowl.

Melt remaining 2 tablespoons butter in a 1- to 2-quart heavy saucepan over moderately low heat. Add flour and cook, whisking, for 1 minute to make a roux. Add beer and milk in a steady stream, whisking constantly, then whisk in mustard and pepper. Bring to a simmer, whisking, and cook, whisking frequently, until thickened, 1 to 2 minutes. Gradually add cheese and cook, whisking, until smooth, about 2 minutes. Remove from heat and whisk into beaten yolk until combined.

Serve cheese sauce on toasts.

Cheddar Tomato Fondue

SERVES 4
ACTIVE TIME: 15 MINUTES ■ START TO FINISH: 20 MINUTES

■ Unlike the usual versions, which require two or more cheeses and a vigilant eye, this fondue offers almost instant gratification. The addition of tomatoes keeps things interesting down to the last gooey bite. ■

 2 tablespoons unsalted butter
⅔ cup finely chopped drained canned tomatoes
 2 garlic cloves, lightly crushed
 3 tablespoons dry white wine
 1 tablespoon cornstarch
¾ pound cheddar, coarsely grated (about 3 cups)
ACCOMPANIMENT· 1-inch cubes of French bread (from 1
      baguette)
SPECIAL EQUIPMENT: a fondue pot set

Melt butter in a 4-quart heavy saucepan over moderately low heat. Add tomatoes and garlic and cook, stirring occasionally, until most of liquid is evaporated, about 5 minutes. Stir together wine and cornstarch in a small bowl, then stir into tomatoes and simmer gently, stirring, for 1 minute. Discard garlic. Add cheddar by handfuls, stirring until completely melted.

Serve in a fondue pot set over a flame, with bread cubes and fondue forks.

Pizza with Stracchino Cheese and Fresh Arugula

MAKES ONE 14-INCH PIZZA
ACTIVE TIME: 45 MINUTES ■ START TO FINISH: 2 HOURS
(INCLUDES MAKING DOUGH)

■ It doesn't get much prettier: a crisp, chewy crust topped with oozy cheese is showered with handfuls of baby arugula at the moment the pizza is plucked from the hot oven. We like to use Stracchino, sometimes labeled "Crescenza," a tart, fruity soft cheese from the Lombardy region of Italy. If you can't find it, fresh mozzarella will also work. ■

2 tablespoons extra-virgin olive oil
6 large garlic cloves, thinly sliced
  Basic Pizza Dough (recipe follows), shaped into a
    ball and allowed to rise
  About 1 tablespoon cornmeal
10 ounces Stracchino cheese or fresh mozzarella
  Salt and freshly ground black pepper
2 cups loosely packed baby arugula
SPECIAL EQUIPMENT: a pizza stone and a baker's peel (see
  Cook's Note), both at least 14 inches in diameter
  (see Sources)

Put pizza stone on oven floor if using a gas oven, or on lowest oven rack if using electric. Remove other racks and preheat oven to highest setting (500° to 550°F). Allow about 1 hour to preheat stone.

Heat oil in a small skillet over moderately low heat until hot but not smoking. Add garlic and cook, stirring constantly, until golden, 1 to 2 minutes. With a slotted spoon, transfer garlic to a small bowl; reserve oil and garlic separately.

Shape dough into a 14-inch round according to instructions for Basic Pizza Dough (recipe follows).

Rub baker's peel with flour and sprinkle with 1 tablespoon cornmeal. Carefully slide dough onto peel, then jerk peel once or twice; if dough sticks, lift it and sprinkle a little more cornmeal underneath. Lightly brush dough with reserved garlic oil, then pull off small pieces of cheese and scatter evenly over pizza, leaving a 1-inch border. Season pizza with salt and pepper.

Line up far edge of peel with far edge of stone and tilt peel, jerking it gently to start pizza moving. When edge of pizza touches stone, quickly pull back peel to transfer pizza to stone (do not pull pizza back). Bake until crust is golden brown, 10 to 12 minutes. Slide peel under pizza to remove from oven, then scatter garlic and arugula over it.

COOK'S NOTE

■ If you don't own a baker's peel, build your pizza on a sheet of parchment laid on a flat baking sheet (sprinkle it with flour and cornmeal as you would a peel). Use the baking sheet as a peel for sliding the pizza and parchment onto the hot stone. When the pizza has finished baking, grab a corner of parchment to slide the pizza back onto the baking sheet.

Basic Pizza Dough

MAKES ENOUGH DOUGH FOR ONE 14-INCH PIZZA
ACTIVE TIME: 30 MINUTES ■ START TO FINISH: 1¾ HOURS

■ The Phoenix chef Chris Bianco makes the best pizza we know, and the secret is his dough. He likes to leave as much air in the risen dough as possible, so he handles it gently when forming the pizza round. It emerges from the oven with a thin, blistered crust that is crisp all across the bottom and chewy on the edges. ■

1 (¼-ounce) package (2¼ teaspoons) active dry yeast
  About 1¾ cups unbleached all-purpose flour, plus
    additional for kneading and dredging
¾ cup warm water (105°–115°F)
1½ teaspoons salt
1½ teaspoons olive oil

MAKE THE DOUGH AND LET IT RISE: Stir together yeast, 1 tablespoon flour, and ¼ cup warm water in a measuring cup and let stand until surface appears creamy, about 5 minutes. (If mixture doesn't appear creamy, discard and start over with new yeast.)

Stir together 1¼ cups flour and salt in a large bowl. Add yeast mixture, oil, and remaining ½ cup warm water and stir until smooth. Stir in enough of remaining flour (about ½ cup) so dough comes away from side of bowl. (The dough will be wetter than other pizzas doughs you may have made.)

Knead dough on a dry surface with lightly floured hands (reflour hands when dough becomes too sticky) until smooth, soft, and elastic, about 8 minutes. Form into a ball, put on a lightly floured surface, and generously dust with flour. Cover loosely with plastic wrap and let rise in a warm, draft-free place until doubled in bulk, about 1¼ hours.

SHAPE THE DOUGH INTO A ROUND: Do not punch down dough. Carefully dredge dough in a bowl of flour to coat and transfer to dry work surface. Holding one edge of dough in the air with both hands and letting bottom just touch work surface, quickly and carefully move your hands around edge of dough as though you were turning a steering wheel, allowing weight of dough to stretch round to roughly 10 inches.

Lay dough on a lightly floured surface and con-

tinue to work edges with your fingers, stretching it into a 14-inch round.

Top and bake pizza according to selected recipe.

COOK'S NOTES

- The dough can be allowed to rise, covered and refrigerated in a bowl, for up to 1 day. Bring to room temperature before shaping.
- The dough (after rising) can be frozen in a sealable plastic bag for up to 1 month. Thaw and bring to room temperature before shaping.

Mushroom and Caramelized Onion Pizza

MAKES ONE 14-INCH PIZZA
ACTIVE TIME: 1¼ HOURS ■ START TO FINISH: 2¼ HOURS
(INCLUDES MAKING DOUGH)

■ Earthy, tangy, and nutty, this pizza is a brilliant change of pace from traditional Italian pies: sweet caramelized onions tangle with sautéed mushrooms and melted shreds of Emmental cheese. It makes a great hors d'oeuvre when cut into small pieces. We also like it with a combination of Emmental and Gruyère or with Italian Fontina. ■

5 tablespoons extra-virgin olive oil
1 pound yellow onions, halved lengthwise and thinly sliced lengthwise
Salt and freshly ground black pepper
1 pound white mushrooms or mixed wild mushrooms, such as shiitake (stemmed), cremini, and oyster, trimmed if necessary and sliced
1 teaspoon red wine vinegar
Basic Pizza Dough (opposite page), shaped into a ball and allowed to rise
About 1 tablespoon cornmeal
2¾ cups coarsely grated Swiss Emmental cheese (about 8 ounces)
½ cup finely grated Parmigiano-Reggiano
1 tablespoon fresh thyme leaves

SPECIAL EQUIPMENT: parchment paper; a pizza stone and a baker's peel (see Cook's Note), both at least 14 inches in diameter (see Sources)

Put pizza stone on oven floor if using a gas oven, or on lowest oven rack if using electric. Remove other racks and preheat oven to highest setting (500° to 550°F). Allow about 1 hour to preheat stone.

Meanwhile, heat 3 tablespoons oil in a 12-inch heavy skillet over moderate heat until hot but not smoking. Add onions, ¼ teaspoon salt, and ⅛ teaspoon pepper, cover directly with a round of parchment paper, and cook, stirring occasionally, until onions are softened and golden brown, 18 to 20 minutes. Transfer to a bowl.

Add remaining 2 tablespoons oil to skillet and heat until hot but not smoking. Add mushrooms, ½ teaspoon salt, ¼ teaspoon pepper, and vinegar and cook, stirring occasionally, until liquid mushrooms give off has evaporated and mushrooms are browned, 8 to 10 minutes. Remove from heat.

Shape dough into a 14-inch round according to instructions for Basic Pizza Dough (see opposite page).

Rub baker's peel with flour and sprinkle with 1 tablespoon cornmeal. Carefully slide dough onto peel, then jerk peel once or twice: if dough sticks, lift it and sprinkle a little more cornmeal underneath. Sprinkle Emmental evenly over dough, leaving a 1-inch border. Scatter mushrooms and onions over cheese, then sprinkle with Parmesan.

Line up far edge of peel with far edge of stone and tilt peel, jerking it gently to start pizza moving. When edge of pizza touches stone, quickly pull back peel to transfer pizza to stone (do not pull pizza back). Bake until crust is golden, about 10 minutes, then open oven door and carefully scatter thyme over pizza. Close door and continue baking until crust is golden brown, about 2 minutes more. Slide peel under pizza to remove from oven.

COOK'S NOTES

- If you don't own a baker's peel, build your pizza on a sheet of parchment laid on an upside down baking sheet (sprinkle it with flour and cornmeal as you would a peel). Use the baking sheet as a peel for sliding the pizza and parchment onto the hot stone. When the pizza has finished baking, grab a corner of parchment to slide the pizza back onto the baking sheet.

- The caramelized onions can be made up to 2 days ahead. Cool, uncovered, then refrigerate, covered. Bring to room temperature before topping the pizza.

Asparagus Quiche

SERVES 4
ACTIVE TIME: 1 HOUR ■ START TO FINISH: 2¾ HOURS
(INCLUDES CHILLING DOUGH)

■ This delicate leek- and tarragon-accented quiche makes a wonderful light dinner, preceded by a soup. ■

FOR PASTRY
  1 cup all-purpose flour
  ½ teaspoon salt
  ¾ stick (6 tablespoons) unsalted butter, cut into
      ½-inch cubes and chilled
  1 large egg, lightly beaten
FOR FILLING
  1 pound medium asparagus, trimmed
  1 tablespoon unsalted butter
  1 medium leek (white and pale green parts only),
      quartered lengthwise, cut crosswise into ⅓-inch-
      thick slices, and washed well
    Salt and freshly ground black pepper
  1⅓ cups heavy cream
  2 large eggs
  2 teaspoons finely chopped fresh tarragon

  1 large egg, lightly beaten with 2 teaspoons water for
    egg wash
SPECIAL EQUIPMENT: a 9- to 9½-inch fluted tart pan with a
  removable bottom

MAKE THE PASTRY: Blend together flour, salt, and butter in a bowl with your fingertips or a pastry blender (or pulse in a food processor) until most of mixture resembles coarse meal with some small (roughly pea-sized) butter lumps. Drizzle evenly with egg and gently stir with a fork (or pulse in processor) just until a dough forms.

Turn dough out onto a lightly floured surface and divide into 4 portions. With heel of your hand, smear each portion once or twice in a forward motion to help distribute butter. Gather dough into a ball, then flatten into a 5-inch disk. Wrap in plastic wrap and refrigerate until firm, at least 30 minutes.

MEANWHILE, MAKE THE FILLING: Cook asparagus in a 4- to 5-quart wide pot of boiling salted water (2 tablespoons salt), uncovered, until just tender, about 5 minutes. Transfer asparagus with tongs to a bowl of ice and cold water to stop the cooking, then drain and pat dry. Cut off and reserve tips (leave some stalk if asparagus is thin) and thinly slice stalks.

Heat butter in a 10- to 12-inch heavy skillet over moderately low heat until foam subsides. Add leek with ¼ teaspoon salt and cook, stirring, until softened, 6 to 8 minutes. Stir in sliced asparagus and ¼ teaspoon pepper and remove from heat.

Put a rack in middle of oven, put a baking sheet on rack, and preheat oven to 375°F.

Whisk together cream, eggs, tarragon, ¼ teaspoon salt, and ¼ teaspoon pepper.

ASSEMBLE AND BAKE THE TART: Roll out dough on a lightly floured surface with a floured rolling pin into an 11-inch round. Fit dough into tart pan, pressing against sides of pan. Run rolling pin over top edge of pan to trim pastry flush with rim. Brush tart shell all over with egg wash. Spoon asparagus mixture into shell, spreading it evenly, then pour cream mixture over asparagus.

Put tart pan on hot baking sheet and bake until filling is just beginning to set but is still loose on top, 20 to 25 minutes. Scatter asparagus tips over top, pressing lightly on them if necessary to help them settle into filling, and continue to bake until quiche is golden and just set but still slightly wobbly in center, about 30 minutes more (filling will continue to set as it cools).

Cool quiche on baking sheet on a rack until warm, about 30 minutes. Remove rim of pan and serve quiche warm or at room temperature.

COOK'S NOTES

- The pastry dough can be refrigerated for up to 1 day. Let stand at room temperature until slightly softened before rolling out.

- The tart can be baked up to 2 hours ahead. Cool completely, then keep, loosely covered with plastic wrap, at room temperature. If desired, reheat in a 350°F oven until warm, 15 to 20 minutes.

Tomato, Goat Cheese, and Onion Tart

SERVES 4
ACTIVE TIME: 20 MINUTES ■ START TO FINISH: 1½ HOURS
(INCLUDES MAKING PASTRY)

■ Everyday ingredients become something truly special in this savory summer classic. The key is using perfectly ripe tomatoes, which are a fine foil for the sweet caramelized onions and mousselike goat cheese. The tart is remarkable when made with homemade pastry, but if you're in a hurry, store-bought pie dough speeds things up. ■

Basic Pastry Dough for a tart shell (page 781) or 1 (9-inch) round prepared pie dough (not pie shell), thawed if frozen
3 tablespoons olive oil
1 large onion, very thinly sliced
  Salt and freshly ground black pepper
6 ounces soft mild goat cheese, crumbled (about 1⅓ cups)
¾ pound tomatoes (3 medium), thinly sliced
GARNISH: sliced fresh basil leaves
SPECIAL EQUIPMENT: a 9- to 9½-inch fluted tart pan with a removable bottom

Put a rack in middle of oven and preheat oven to 375°F.

Roll out dough on a lightly floured surface with a floured rolling pin into an 11-inch round. Fit dough into tart pan. Trim excess dough, leaving a ½-inch overhang, then fold overhang inward and press against sides of pan to reinforce edges of tart shell. Lightly prick bottom and sides of shell all over with a fork.

Line tart shell with foil and fill with pie weights or dried beans. Bake until edges are pale golden, about 20 minutes. Carefully remove foil and weights and bake shell until golden, 8 to 10 minutes more. Cool on a rack. Increase oven temperature to 400°F.

Meanwhile, heat 2 tablespoons oil in a 12-inch heavy skillet over moderate heat until hot but not smoking. Add onion with salt and pepper to taste and cook, stirring frequently, until golden brown, 15 to 20 minutes.

Spread onion over bottom of tart shell. Top with all but ⅓ cup goat cheese. Arrange tomatoes, slightly overlapping, in concentric circles over cheese. Sprinkle with remaining ⅓ cup cheese and salt and pepper to taste. Drizzle with remaining tablespoon oil.

Bake until cheese begins to brown slightly, 10 to 15 minutes. Cool tart on a rack for 5 minutes, then remove rim of pan and garnish tart with basil.

Three Mushroom Tart

SERVES 4 AS A MAIN COURSE, 6 AS A FIRST COURSE
ACTIVE TIME: 1 HOUR ■ START TO FINISH: 1½ HOURS

■ With just a splash of cream and egg, this chic tart is all about the mushrooms, their boskiness heightened by a dram of sherry. Slender enoki mushrooms, which are native to Japan, lend a graceful note. Resembling a long hat pin, with narrow white stems topped by tiny caps, they are increasingly available in supermarkets, but you can omit them if you can't find them. The tart is so rich that all it needs is a leafy green salad as an accompaniment; it also makes an appealing first course. ■

10 ounces white mushrooms, trimmed
5 ounces shiitake mushrooms, stems discarded
3 tablespoons unsalted butter
½ cup minced shallots
2 teaspoons Worcestershire sauce
Salt and freshly ground black pepper
¼ cup cream sherry
1½ teaspoons balsamic vinegar
¼ cup heavy cream
1 large egg, lightly beaten
1 frozen puff pastry sheet (from a 17.3-ounce package), thawed
3 ounces enoki mushrooms (optional; see headnote)

SPECIAL EQUIPMENT: a 9- to 9½-inch fluted tart pan with a removable bottom

Reserve 3 white and 4 shiitake mushrooms for topping tart. Quarter remaining mushrooms and pulse in a food processor just until finely chopped.

Melt 2 tablespoons butter in a 10- to 12-inch heavy skillet over moderately high heat. Add shallots and cook, stirring, until softened, 3 to 4 minutes. Add finely chopped mushrooms, Worcestershire sauce, ¾ teaspoon salt, and ¼ teaspoon pepper and cook, stirring occasionally, until any liquid mushrooms give off has evaporated and mushrooms are browned, 8 to 10 minutes. Add sherry and vinegar and cook, stirring occasionally, until all liquid has evaporated, 3 to 5 minutes. Transfer mixture to a bowl and cool.

Whisk cream, egg, ¼ teaspoon salt, and ¼ teaspoon pepper into mushroom mixture; set aside.

Roll out pastry on a floured surface with a floured rolling pin into a 12-inch square and brush off excess flour. Fit it, without stretching, into tart pan. Run a rolling pin over top of pan to trim pastry flush with rim. Prick bottom of shell all over with a fork and freeze shell for 10 minutes.

Put a rack in lower third of oven, put a baking sheet on rack, and preheat oven to 425°F.

Thinly slice reserved white mushrooms. Holding knife at a 45-degree angle, thinly slice reserved shiitakes. Trim enoki mushrooms, if using, to 2-inch lengths. Melt remaining tablespoon butter in cleaned skillet over moderate heat. Remove from heat and add all uncooked mushrooms, ¼ teaspoon salt, and ¼ teaspoon pepper, tossing to coat.

Spread filling evenly in tart shell, smoothing top.

Mound remaining mushrooms evenly over filling.

Bake tart on hot baking sheet until filling is set and pastry is golden, 20 to 25 minutes. Cool tart in pan on a rack to warm (at least 10 minutes) or to room temperature. Remove rim of pan before serving.

COOK'S NOTES

■ The filling can be made up to 1 day ahead and refrigerated, covered. Refrigerate the whole mushrooms for the topping wrapped in a paper towel in a plastic bag.

■ For a striking presentation, we like to use a 13¾-by-4-inch fluted rectangular tart pan with a removable bottom. Roll out the pastry into a 16-by-10-inch rectangle, and follow directions for preparing the shell.

Roasted Butternut Squash and Caramelized Onion Tart

SERVES 4
ACTIVE TIME: 40 MINUTES ■ START TO FINISH: 2½ HOURS
(INCLUDES MAKING PASTRY)

■ Roasted butternut squash combines with deeply caramelized onions to take the taste of this indulgent tart toward sweetness, but the Fontina and Parmesan pull it back. A reader requested this recipe after dining at chef Tom Douglas's Dahlia Lounge in Seattle. ■

Basic Pastry Dough for a single-crust tart (page 781) or 1 (9-inch) round prepared pie dough (not pie shell), thawed if frozen
1 small butternut squash (about 1 pound)
1½ teaspoons olive oil, plus about 2 teaspoons for brushing squash
1½ tablespoons unsalted butter
1 small onion, halved lengthwise and thinly sliced lengthwise
1 large egg
½ large egg yolk (1½ teaspoons; lightly beat egg yolk to measure)
⅓ cup heavy cream
¾ cup coarsely grated Italian Fontina
½ cup finely grated Parmigiano-Reggiano

¼ cup crumbled mild soft goat cheese

1½ teaspoons minced fresh herbs, such as rosemary, thyme, and/or marjoram

½ teaspoon salt

Freshly ground black pepper

⅓ cup fine fresh bread crumbs (from 1 slice firm white sandwich bread)

SPECIAL EQUIPMENT: a 9- to 9½-inch fluted tart pan with a removable bottom

Roll out dough on a lightly floured surface with a floured rolling pin into an 11-inch round. Fit dough into tart pan, then fold overhang inward and press against sides of pan to reinforce sides of tart shell. Lightly prick bottom all over with a fork. Freeze shell for 15 minutes.

Put a rack in middle of oven and preheat oven to 375°F.

Line chilled shell with foil and fill with pie weights or dried beans. Bake until edges are pale golden, about 20 minutes. Carefully remove foil and weights and bake shell until golden, 8 to 10 minutes more. Cool shell on a rack. (Leave oven on.)

While shell cools, halve squash and scoop out and discard seeds. Lightly brush cut sides with about 2 teaspoons oil and put, cut side down, in a small baking pan. Bake until soft, 40 to 50 minutes. Remove from oven and cool slightly. (Leave oven on.)

Meanwhile, heat ½ tablespoon butter and remaining 1½ teaspoons oil in an 8-inch heavy skillet over low heat until foam subsides. Add onion and cook, stirring occasionally, until soft and golden brown, about 20 minutes. Remove from heat.

When squash is cool enough to handle, scoop flesh into a food processor and puree. Add egg, yolk, and cream and blend well. Transfer mixture to a large bowl and stir in cheeses, herbs, onion, salt, and pepper to taste. Pour filling into shell, smoothing top.

Melt remaining tablespoon butter in a small skillet over low heat. Remove from heat and stir in bread crumbs until evenly moistened. Sprinkle crumb mixture evenly over filling.

Cover edges of tart with a pie shield or strips of foil and bake until filling is set and slightly puffed, 35 to 40 minutes. Cool tart in pan on a rack for 10 minutes, then carefully remove rim.

COOK'S NOTES

■ The tart shell can be baked up to 1 day ahead and kept, loosely covered, at room temperature.

■ The filling (without the crumb topping) can be made up to 1 day ahead. Cool, uncovered, then refrigerate, covered. Bring to room temperature before filling the shell.

Fennel, Taleggio, and Cardamom Tart

SERVES 6
ACTIVE TIME: 40 MINUTES ■ START TO FINISH: 3 HOURS
(INCLUDES CHILLING DOUGH)

■ The cardamom underscores the fennel's gentle anise flavor in this dreamy tart, while crème fraîche and Taleggio, a rich cow's-milk cheese from northern Italy, offer tangy creaminess, further enriched by the cream and eggs. This recipe is adapted from Tamasin Day-Lewis's book *The Art of the Tart*. ■

FOR DOUGH

1½ cups unbleached all-purpose flour

¾ stick (6 tablespoons) unsalted butter, cut into ½-inch cubes and chilled

¼ teaspoon fine sea salt

4 5 tablespoons ice water

FOR FILLING

3 medium fennel bulbs (2½ pounds total)

8 green cardamom pods (see Sources)

¼ cup dry white wine

¼ cup water

¼ cup olive oil

2 tablespoons unsalted butter

Fine sea salt and freshly ground black pepper

2 large eggs

1 large egg yolk

½ cup whole milk

½ cup heavy cream

¼ cup crème fraîche

3 ounces Taleggio cheese, chilled, rind discarded, cheese cut into ⅓-inch cubes

SPECIAL EQUIPMENT: an 11- to 11½-inch fluted tart pan with a removable bottom

Green cardamom (*Elettaria cardamomum*) is the fruit of a large-leaved perennial bush native to the rain forests of southern India, and it has been used in that country for more than 2,000 years. It's now also cultivated in Sri Lanka, Vietnam, Tanzania, and Guatemala. The warm, penetrating aroma and flavor enhance both sweet and savory dishes, and thanks to the caravan trade routes, the spice is as much at home in Swedish coffee cakes as it is in a fiery Ethiopian *berbere*, thick Bedouin coffee, or a fragrant Indian pilaf. You will find "decorticated" cardamom (i.e., just the seeds) and ground cardamom at the supermarket, but for optimum freshness, buy plump whole pods. To remove the small dark seeds, simply crack the pods by using the side of a large heavy knife, or open them with your fingernails. (You will sometimes see recipes that call for a cracked whole pod, which imparts a milder flavor to a dish.) The stickier the seeds are, the fresher the cardamom. White cardamom pods are green ones that have been bleached. Black cardamom (*Amomum* and *Aframomum* genera) is indigenous to the Himalayas; it has a smoky, more camphor-like flavor. Do not substitute it for green cardamom.

MAKE THE DOUGH: Blend together flour, butter, and salt in a bowl with your fingertips or a pastry blender (or pulse in a food processor) just until most of mixture resembles coarse meal with some small (roughly pea-sized) butter lumps. Drizzle evenly with ¼ cup ice water and gently stir with a fork (or pulse) until incorporated. Squeeze a small handful of dough: if it doesn't hold together, add more ice water, ½ tablespoon at a time, stirring (or pulsing) until incorporated, then test again. (Do not overwork, or pastry will be tough.)

Turn dough out onto a work surface and divide into 4 portions. With heel of your hand, smear each portion once or twice in a forward motion to help distribute butter. Gather dough together and form into a disk. Wrap in plastic wrap and refrigerate until firm, about 1 hour.

MEANWHILE, MAKE THE FILLING: Cut off and discard fennel stalks and fronds. Quarter bulbs lengthwise. Cut out core and cut each quarter crosswise into ¼-inch-thick slices.

Crush cardamom pods with side of a large heavy knife. Remove black seeds and discard pods. Crush seeds as much as possible with side of knife, then finely chop.

Combine wine, water, oil, butter, cardamom, ½ teaspoon salt, and ¼ teaspoon pepper in a 12-inch heavy skillet and bring to a simmer. Add fennel and cook, covered, over moderately low heat, stirring occasionally, until tender, 20 to 25 minutes. Let cool.

ASSEMBLE AND BAKE THE TART: Roll out dough on a lightly floured surface with a floured rolling pin into a 15-inch round. Fit into tart pan, then run rolling pin over edge of pan to trim pastry flush with rim. Lightly prick bottom and sides of shell all over with a fork. Refrigerate for 30 minutes.

Put a rack in middle of oven and preheat oven to 375°F.

Line tart shell with foil and fill with pie weights or dried beans. Put on a baking sheet and bake until sides are set and edges are pale golden, 15 to 20 minutes. Carefully remove weights and foil and bake shell until golden, 10 to 15 minutes more. Transfer to a rack.

Whisk together eggs and yolk in a large bowl until foamy. Whisk in milk, cream, crème fraîche, ½ teaspoon salt, and ¼ teaspoon pepper.

Transfer fennel mixture to shell with a slotted spoon, spreading it evenly. Dot with cheese. Pour custard into shell.

Bake tart until set, 20 to 25 minutes. Cool on a rack for 15 minutes and remove rim before serving.

COOK'S NOTES

- The tart shell can be baked up to 1 day ahead and kept, loosely covered, at room temperature.
- The tart can be made up to 1 day ahead. Cool, uncovered, then refrigerate, loosely covered. Reheat in a 350°F oven for 10 to 15 minutes.

Creamy Ricotta and Farro Quiche

SERVES 4 TO 6
ACTIVE TIME: 15 MINUTES ■ START TO FINISH: 1¼ HOURS

■ Farro adds a nutty, chewy element to the ricotta filling of this tart. There's no need for a crust: buttering the pan and then sprinkling it with bread crumbs makes unmolding neat and easy. Pair wedges of the quiche with a leafy salad for a healthy, casual supper. ■

- 1 cup farro (see Sources)
- Salt
- 2 tablespoons fine dry bread crumbs
- 2 tablespoons unsalted butter
- 2 garlic cloves, chopped
- 2 (15-ounce) containers (3½ cups) whole-milk ricotta
- 1 large egg
- 2 large egg yolks
- ⅔ cup finely grated Parmigiano-Reggiano
- ¼ cup coarsely chopped fresh flat-leaf parsley
- ½ teaspoon freshly ground black pepper
- ½ teaspoon freshly grated nutmeg

Cook farro in a 2- to 3-quart pot of boiling salted water (1 tablespoon salt) until just tender, about 10 minutes. Drain in a sieve and cool to room temperature.

Put a rack in middle of oven and preheat oven to 375°F. Butter a 9-inch glass pie plate or other shallow ovenproof dish and lightly coat with bread crumbs, knocking out excess.

Melt butter in a small heavy skillet over low heat. Add garlic and cook, stirring, for 1 minute. Transfer garlic and butter to a medium bowl. Stir in farro, ricotta, egg, yolks, Parmigiano-Reggiano, parsley, ¾ teaspoon salt, pepper, and grated nutmeg until well combined.

Spoon mixture into dish and bake until quiche is just set and top is pale golden, 35 to 45 minutes. Transfer to a rack to cool slightly.

Serve warm, cut into wedges.

Herb and Cheese Phyllo Pie
Tiropita

SERVES 4 TO 6
ACTIVE TIME: 40 MINUTES ■ START TO FINISH: 2½ HOURS

■ Most people know *tiropita* as little triangular hors d'oeuvres, rather like spanakopita minus the spinach. It is much easier to make one large pie than bite-sized ones. Greek cooks use lots of wild fennel; we approximate that pungent anise flavor with regular fennel and fresh dill. Greeks like to cut the saltiness of feta with myzithra, a cheese similar to ricotta. Cottage cheese works well too—it keeps the pie light. ■

- 1 medium fennel bulb (1 pound) with stalks and fronds
- 1 stick (8 tablespoons) unsalted butter
- 1 bunch scallions, chopped
- Salt
- 1 pound (3 cups) 4% cottage cheese
- ½ pound feta, crumbled (about 2 cups)
- 4 large eggs, lightly beaten
- 2 tablespoons semolina (sometimes labeled "semolina flour"; see Sources)
- ¼ cup chopped fresh dill
- ¼ teaspoon freshly ground black pepper
- 2 tablespoons fine dry bread crumbs
- 8 (17-by-12-inch) phyllo sheets, thawed if frozen

SPECIAL EQUIPMENT: a 9-inch springform pan

Put a rack in lower third of oven and preheat oven to 400°F.

Cut off stalks from fennel bulb. Chop enough fronds to measure ¼ cup; discard stalks. Cut bulb into ¼-inch dice.

Melt 2 tablespoons butter in a 10-inch heavy skillet over moderate heat. Add diced fennel, scallions, and ¼ teaspoon salt and cook, covered, stirring occasionally, until fennel is tender, about 10 minutes. Remove lid and cook until any liquid has evaporated, 1 to 2 minutes.

Transfer fennel to a large bowl and stir in cheeses, eggs, semolina, fennel fronds, dill, ¼ teaspoon salt, and pepper until combined.

Melt remaining 6 tablespoons butter. Brush springform pan with some of butter and sprinkle bottom with 1 tablespoon bread crumbs. Unroll phyllo and cover stack with plastic wrap and a dampened kitchen towel. Keeping remaining phyllo covered, brush 1 phyllo sheet with butter and gently fit it into springform pan, allowing ends to hang over. Rotate pan slightly, butter another phyllo sheet, and place on top (sheets should not align). Sprinkle with remaining tablespoon bread crumbs. Butter and fit 4 more phyllo sheets into pan, rotating pan for each sheet; overhang should cover entire rim.

Spread cheese mixture in phyllo shell. Butter another phyllo sheet, fold it crosswise in half, and butter again. Fold in half again (to quarter), brush with butter, and lay over center of filling. Repeat with remaining phyllo sheet, laying it over folded sheet in opposite direction (see illustration). Fold overhanging phyllo over to enclose filling and folded phyllo, and brush top with butter.

Bake pie until puffed and deep golden brown, 40 to 50 minutes; once it is golden brown, loosely cover pan with a sheet of foil to prevent overbrowning. Cool in pan on a rack for 5 minutes. Remove side of pan and cool pie on rack to warm or room temperature.

Cut into wedges to serve.

COOK'S NOTE

■ The pie can be baked up to 6 hours ahead and kept, uncovered, at room temperature.

Chickpea, Eggplant, and Tomato Phyllo Tarts

SERVES 4
ACTIVE TIME: 45 MINUTES ■ START TO FINISH: 1¼ HOURS

■ This robust Mediterranean stew enclosed in crisp phyllo is so outstanding that you can serve it for Thanksgiving, as a main dish for vegetarians and a side for everyone else. But don't save it for the holidays—it's too good for that. Serve these individual tarts plain or embellish them with Roasted Vegetable Gravy (page 330). ■

1 (1-pound) eggplant
   Salt
½ cup extra-virgin olive oil
1 medium onion, halved lengthwise and cut crosswise into ½-inch-thick slices
1 Turkish bay leaf or ½ California bay leaf
3 garlic cloves, minced
1 (14- to 15-ounce) can stewed tomatoes, drained, juice reserved, and coarsely chopped
½ teaspoon sweet paprika
⅛ teaspoon ground cumin
1 (15- to 19-ounce) can chickpeas, rinsed and drained
1 teaspoon sugar
   Freshly ground black pepper
¼ cup coarsely chopped fresh flat-leaf parsley
6 (17-by-12-inch) phyllo sheets, thawed if frozen
GARNISH: fresh flat-leaf parsley leaves, torn into pieces

MAKE THE FILLING: Peel eggplant and cut into ½-inch cubes. Toss with 1 teaspoon salt in a large bowl and let stand for 15 minutes. Transfer eggplant to a colander, rinse under cold water, and squeeze out excess water.

Heat 2 tablespoons oil in a 12-inch heavy skillet over moderately high heat until hot but not smoking. Add onion with bay leaf and cook, stirring occasionally, until golden, about 5 minutes. Add 1 tablespoon oil, then add eggplant and garlic and cook, stirring, until eggplant is tender, 8 to 10 minutes.

Add tomatoes (reserve juice), paprika, and cumin and cook, stirring, for 3 minutes. Add reserved tomato juice, chickpeas, sugar, ¾ teaspoon salt, and ½ teaspoon pepper, and simmer, stirring occasionally, until filling is thickened and most of liquid has evaporated, about 5 minutes. Remove from heat and stir in parsley; discard bay leaf.

MAKE THE TARTS: Put a rack in middle of oven and preheat oven to 425°F. Line a large baking sheet with foil.

Unroll phyllo and cover stack with plastic wrap and a dampened kitchen towel. Keeping remaining phyllo covered, lightly brush 1 phyllo sheet with some of remaining oil. Top with 2 more sheets, brushing each with oil. Sprinkle with ½ teaspoon pepper, then cut stack crosswise in half with a sharp knife. Spoon 1 cup filling into center of each stack. Crumple edges of phyllo up and around filling, leaving filling exposed. Transfer to lined baking sheet using a spatula. Make 2 more tarts in same manner, arranging about ½ inch apart on baking sheet.

Bake, rotating baking sheet after 10 minutes, until edges of tarts are golden, 15 to 20 minutes. Sprinkle with parsley and serve immediately.

COOK'S NOTES

- The filling, without the parsley, can be made up to 1 day ahead and refrigerated, covered. Stir in the parsley before using.
- The tarts can be baked up to 6 hours ahead and kept, uncovered, at room temperature. Reheat in a 350°F oven for 15 to 20 minutes.

Scallion–Wild Rice Crêpes with Mushroom Filling

SERVES 6
ACTIVE TIME: 1¾ HOURS ■ START TO FINISH: 3½ HOURS
(INCLUDES STANDING TIME)

■ It's easy to be a vegetarian in the summer, when farmers markets and supermarkets are filled with fresh, local vegetables. In the colder months, the pickings are slimmer. This dish makes great use of what's available. Wild rice contributes texture to the crêpes, resulting in wrappers that can stand up to the hearty mushroom filling. The rosy roasted red pepper sauce adds a smoky tang. When you make the crêpes, be sure

the rice is evenly distributed throughout the batter; this will make folding the finished crêpes easier. All the components can be prepared in advance. ■

FOR CRÊPES
  4 cups water
  1 cup wild rice
    Salt
  1¾ cups whole milk
  4 large eggs
  1 stick (8 tablespoons) unsalted butter, melted and cooled slightly
  1 cup all-purpose flour
  ¼ teaspoon freshly ground black pepper
  ¾ cup thinly sliced scallions
FOR SAUCE
  3 red bell peppers, roasted (see Tips, page 914), peeled, and seeded
  ½ cup water
  2 tablespoons olive oil
  1½ teaspoons balsamic vinegar
  ¾ teaspoon salt
    Freshly ground black pepper
FOR FILLING
  1½ ounces (1½ cups) dried porcini mushrooms
  ¾ cup boiling water
  2 tablespoons olive oil
  2 tablespoons unsalted butter
  1½ pounds cremini mushrooms, trimmed and thinly sliced
  3 large garlic cloves, minced
  ¾ teaspoon minced fresh rosemary
  ¾ teaspoon minced fresh thyme
    Salt and freshly ground black pepper
GARNISH: thinly sliced scallions
SPECIAL EQUIPMENT: a well-seasoned 6- to 7-inch crêpe pan or nonstick skillet

COOK THE WILD RICE: Bring water to a boil in a 2-quart heavy saucepan. Add rice and ½ teaspoon salt, reduce heat to low, and cook, covered, until rice is tender and grains are split open, 1 to 1¼ hours. Drain well and cool to warm.

MEANWHILE, MAKE THE SAUCE: Coarsely chop bell peppers. Puree with water, oil, vinegar, and salt in a blender until smooth. Season with pepper to taste and pour into a small heavy saucepan.

MAKE THE CRÊPE BATTER: Combine milk, eggs, 3

tablespoons butter, flour, 1 teaspoon salt, pepper, and 1 cup cooked wild rice in cleaned blender and puree until smooth, about 1 minute. Transfer to a large bowl and stir in scallions and 1½ cups cooked wild rice (reserve remainder for another use). Let batter stand, covered, at room temperature for 1 hour.

MEANWHILE, MAKE THE FILLING: Soak porcini in boiling water in a small bowl until softened, about 20 minutes. Lift porcini out, squeezing liquid back into bowl, then rinse porcini (to remove any grit) and finely chop. Pour soaking liquid through a sieve lined with a dampened paper towel into another small bowl.

Heat oil and 1 tablespoon butter in a 12- to 13-inch nonstick skillet over moderately high heat until foam subsides. Add porcini and cremini and cook, tossing with two wooden spatulas or spoons, until wilted and any liquid mushrooms give off has evaporated, 3 to 5 minutes. Add garlic, rosemary, thyme, ¾ teaspoon salt, and remaining tablespoon butter and cook, stirring, for 1 minute. Add porcini soaking liquid and boil until most of liquid has evaporated and mushrooms are tender, 3 to 5 minutes. Season with salt and pepper. Remove from heat.

COOK THE CRÊPES: Line a plate with wax paper. Heat crêpe pan over moderate heat until hot. Brush lightly with some of remaining melted butter and spoon about 3 tablespoons batter into pan, tilting and rotating to coat bottom. (If batter sets before skillet is coated, reduce heat slightly for next crêpe.) Cook until underside is lightly browned, about 1 minute, then loosen crêpe with a heatproof plastic spatula and flip over with your fingers. Cook until other side is lightly browned, about 1 minute, then transfer to wax-paper-lined plate. Top crêpe with a piece of wax paper. Make more crêpes with remaining batter in same manner, brushing pan lightly with butter as needed. (You probably will have a few extra crêpes.)

ASSEMBLE AND BAKE THE CRÊPES: Put a rack in upper third of oven and preheat oven to 400°F.

Brush some melted butter over bottom of a large baking sheet. Spread ¼ cup filling over half of 1 crêpe, then fold other half over filling to form a half-moon. Fold half-moon in thirds, overlapping outer sections, and transfer seam side up to baking sheet. Repeat with 11 more crêpes.

Brush crêpes generously with remaining melted butter. Bake until outsides are crisp and filling is

heated through, about 15 minutes.

Meanwhile, heat sauce over low heat until hot, about 5 minutes.

Put 2 crêpes on each of six plates and serve with sauce.

COOK'S NOTES

■ The wild rice can be cooked up to 2 days ahead. Cool, uncovered, then refrigerate, covered.

■ The red pepper sauce can be made up to 2 days ahead and refrigerated, covered.

■ The filling can be made up to 1 day ahead. Cool, uncovered, then refrigerate, covered.

■ The crêpes can be filled up to 1 day ahead. Refrigerate, wrapped in foil. Brush with melted butter just before baking.

Dosas with Two Fillings

SERVES 4 (MAKES 10 TO 12 DOSAS)
ACTIVE TIME: 2¼ HOURS ■ START TO FINISH: 1½ DAYS
(INCLUDES SOAKING AND FERMENTING TIMES)

■ Unique to southern India, dosas are large, thin, crisp crêpelike wrappers that are usually folded around savory vegetarian fillings and served with an array of chutneys. The crêpes are made from a batter of ground rice and *urad dal* that have been soaked and fermented for about 24 hours. Commonly called black lentils but more closely related to mung beans, *urad dal* are split to reveal their creamy white or pale yellow interior (look for them in Indian markets and natural foods stores, or see Sources). At restaurants, dosas may arrive simply folded in half, dwarfing the plate; rolled up to form a neat cone; or in any other number of shapes. These dosas are much smaller, which makes them easier. You have to cook them one at a time, so prepare the fillings in advance and simply reheat them when you are ready to fill them.

Note that each filling recipe makes enough for the full yield of dosas, so if you want to make both, you will have extra—leftovers make a delicious lunch served with warm naans or other flatbreads. ■

1½ cups long-grain white rice
¾ cup *urad dal* (see headnote)

2⅓ cups water

Salt

About ½ cup vegetable oil for cooking dosas

Potato Cumin Filling and/or Zucchini Tomato Filling
(recipes follow)

ACCOMPANIMENT: bottled mango chutney and/or coconut
chutney

In separate bowls, soak rice and *urad dal* in water to cover by 2 inches for 4 hours.

Drain *urad dal* in a sieve. Puree with ¾ cup water in a food processor until light and fluffy, 3 to 5 minutes. Transfer puree to a large bowl. Drain rice in a sieve and puree in processor with ⅓ cup water until a gritty paste forms, about 1 minute. Stir rice paste and ¾ teaspoon salt into *urad dal* paste.

Let mixture ferment, covered with plastic wrap, in a warm place (about 80°F) until doubled in bulk (mixture will be light and foamy), about 24 hours.

Stir remaining 1¼ cups water and ¼ teaspoon salt into rice mixture. Let batter stand, covered, in a warm place for 1½ to 2½ hours.

Put a rack in middle of oven and preheat oven to 250°F.

Pour 1 teaspoon oil on a well-seasoned 10-inch round cast-iron griddle or in a 10-inch nonstick skillet, spread it with a paper towel, and heat over moderate heat until hot but not smoking. Fill a ⅓-cup measure with batter, gently scooping it, and pour onto center of griddle (use a rubber spatula to scrape out batter remaining in measuring cup). With back of a small spoon, quickly spread batter in a circular motion to thinly cover griddle (dosa may be lacy around edges). Drizzle edges and top of dosa with 1 teaspoon oil and cook until underside is golden and crisp, about 2 minutes. Turn dosa over with a metal spatula and cook, pressing occasionally with spatula, until second side is pale golden, about 1 minute more. (Adjust heat if necessary to prevent overbrowning.) Transfer dosa to a large baking sheet and keep warm, loosely covered with foil, in oven. Make more dosas in same manner, oiling griddle each time; transfer to baking sheet and separate layers with foil.

Just before serving, spread ⅓ cup hot filling down middle of each dosa and loosely fold sides over filling (like folding a letter). Serve, seam side down, with chutney.

COOK'S NOTES

■ The batter can be refrigerated (after fermenting), covered, for up to 24 hours. Let it stand at room temperature for 30 minutes before proceeding and stir just before cooking.

■ The dosas can be made up to 1 hour ahead and kept, covered with foil, at room temperature. Reheat in a 350°F oven until warm, about 10 minutes, before filling.

Potato Cumin Filling

MAKES ABOUT 3½ CUPS (ENOUGH FOR 10 TO 12 DOSAS)
ACTIVE TIME: 30 MINUTES ■ START TO FINISH: 1¼ HOURS

■ Spiced with nutty brown mustard seeds and cumin, this traditional filling has a vivid golden hue. ■

1½ pounds Yukon Gold potatoes of uniform size

Salt

¼ cup vegetable oil

1 teaspoon brown mustard seeds (see Sources)

8 fresh or thawed frozen curry leaves (optional;
see Sources)

½ teaspoon cumin seeds

1 medium onion, chopped

1 (2½-inch-long) fresh hot green chile, such as Thai or
serrano, minced, including seeds

½ teaspoon turmeric

1 cup water

Cover potatoes with 2 inches salted cold water (1½ teaspoons salt) in a 2½- to 3-quart saucepan and bring to a boil. Reduce heat and simmer, uncovered, until potatoes are just tender, 15 to 25 minutes; drain. When potatoes are just cool enough to handle, peel and cut into ½-inch cubes.

Heat oil in a 10- to 12-inch heavy skillet over moderately high heat until hot but not smoking. Add mustard seeds, partially cover, and fry until they just begin to pop, about 10 seconds. Add curry leaves (if using) and cumin and fry, stirring, until cumin turns a shade darker, 10 to 15 seconds. Reduce heat to moderately low, add onion, and cook, stirring occasionally, until softened but not browned, 8 to 10 minutes.

Add chile and turmeric and cook, stirring, for 1 minute. Add potatoes, water, and ¾ teaspoon salt and bring to a boil. Reduce heat to moderately low and simmer, covered, stirring occasionally and mashing potatoes slightly, until filling is thickened, 8 to 10 minutes. Discard curry leaves (if you used them).

COOK'S NOTE

■ The filling can be made up to 1 day ahead. Cool, uncovered, then refrigerate, covered. Reheat before cooking the dosas.

Zucchini Tomato Filling

MAKES ABOUT 3¾ CUPS (ENOUGH FOR 10 TO 12 DOSAS)
ACTIVE TIME: 40 MINUTES ■ START TO FINISH: 1¼ HOURS

■ Zucchini cooked with tomatoes, thickened with coconut, and warmed with ginger and garam masala isn't the usual dosa filling. We think it should be. ■

⅓ cup finely shredded unsweetened dried coconut
1 (2½-inch-long) fresh hot green chile, such as Thai or serrano, seeded and minced
1 small onion, chopped
1 teaspoon finely chopped peeled fresh ginger
1 garlic clove, minced
½ cup packed fresh cilantro sprigs
1 teaspoon salt
¼ teaspoon turmeric
1⅓ cups water
2 tablespoons vegetable oil
1½ pounds zucchini (4 medium), cut into ½-inch pieces
¾ pound tomatoes (3 medium), peeled (see Tips, page 913), seeded, and coarsely chopped
1 teaspoon garam masala (see page 536 and Sources)

Cover coconut with warm water in a small bowl and soak for 30 minutes; drain in a sieve.

Combine coconut, chile, onion, ginger, garlic, cilantro, salt, turmeric, and ⅓ cup water in a blender or mini food processor and blend to a coarse puree.

Heat oil in a deep 12-inch skillet over moderately high heat until hot but not smoking. Add coconut mixture and cook, stirring, until liquid is evaporated, about 4 minutes. Add zucchini, tomatoes, garam masala, and remaining 1 cup water and bring to a boil. Reduce heat to moderately low and simmer, partially covered, stirring occasionally, until zucchini is tender, 25 to 30 minutes.

Remove lid and boil, stirring frequently, until most of liquid has evaporated, about 5 minutes.

COOK'S NOTE

■ The filling can be made up to 1 day ahead. Cool, uncovered, then refrigerate, covered. Reheat before cooking the dosas.

Vegetable Enchiladas with Creamy Poblano Sauce

SERVES 4 TO 6
ACTIVE TIME: 1½ HOURS ■ START TO FINISH: 2 HOURS

■ Typical Mexican ingredients—fresh corn, zucchini, tomatoes, and chiles—are transformed into outrageously good enchiladas. Tangy *crema* tempers and adds lushness to the piquant poblano sauce. The time these enchiladas take to assemble is definitely worth it—your guests will rave. ■

FOR SAUCE
3 poblano chiles, roasted (see Tips, page 914) and peeled
½ cup chopped white onion
1 large garlic clove
1 teaspoon salt, or to taste
1¼ cups water
2 tablespoons vegetable oil, preferably corn oil
1 cup Mexican *crema* (see Sources) or crème fraîche

FOR FILLING
3 tablespoons vegetable oil, preferably corn oil
1 cup chopped white onion
2 large garlic cloves, chopped
1 teaspoon salt
2 cups corn kernels (from 2–3 ears) or 1 (10-ounce) package frozen corn
1 pound zucchini (3 medium), cut into ⅓-inch dice
1 (14- to 15-ounce) can whole tomatoes in juice, drained, juice reserved, and chopped
¼ cup chopped fresh cilantro
2 teaspoons chopped jalapeño chile, including seeds, or to taste

FOR ENCHILADAS
3 tablespoons vegetable oil, preferably corn oil
12 (6- to 7-inch) corn tortillas

¼ pound Monterey Jack cheese, coarsely grated
  (about 1 cup)
2 tablespoons Mexican *crema* or crème fraîche
2 tablespoons water

MAKE THE SAUCE: Open chiles and spread flat; discard seeds and stems and cut out ribs. Coarsely chop chiles. Combine chiles, onion, garlic, salt, and water in a blender and puree until smooth.

Heat oil in a 10-inch heavy skillet over moderately high heat until hot but not smoking. Carefully add sauce (it will spatter) and cook, stirring frequently, until slightly thickened, about 8 minutes. Stir in *crema* and remove from heat.

MAKE THE FILLING: Heat oil in a 12-inch heavy skillet over moderate heat until hot but not smoking. Add onion, garlic, and salt and cook, stirring, until onion is softened, about 5 minutes. Stir in corn and zucchini and cook, covered, stirring occasionally, until vegetables are tender, about 8 minutes. Add tomatoes with juice, cilantro, and jalapeño and cook, uncovered, over moderately high heat, stirring occasionally, until most of liquid has evaporated, about 10 minutes. Transfer filling to a large bowl to cool.

MAKE THE ENCHILADAS: Put a rack in upper third of oven and preheat oven to 450°F. Lightly oil a 13-by-9-inch baking pan or flameproof baking dish. Line a baking sheet with paper towels.

Reheat sauce over moderately high heat until warm, if necessary, and transfer to a shallow bowl or pie plate. Add oil to cleaned 10-inch skillet and heat over moderate heat until hot but not smoking. Add 1 tortilla and cook, turning once with tongs, until softened, 4 to 6 seconds. Transfer to paper-towel-lined baking sheet and blot each side. Repeat procedure with remaining tortillas, stacking them once blotted.

Dip 1 tortilla in warm sauce, turning it with your fingers to coat both sides, and transfer to baking dish. Spoon about ⅓ cup filling down middle of tortilla and roll up to enclose filling. Push enchilada to one long side of baking dish; you will be forming 2 rows of 6 enchiladas each. Make more enchiladas in same manner, arranging them tightly side by side in dish.

Pour remaining sauce over enchiladas and sprin-

kle with cheese. Stir together *crema* and water with a fork in a cup and drizzle over top.

Bake enchiladas, uncovered, until hot and bubbling, about 15 minutes. If desired, brown under broiler 2 to 3 inches from heat, about 3 minutes. Transfer to a rack to cool for 10 minutes before serving.

COOK'S NOTE
■ The filling and sauce can be made 1 day ahead. Cool, uncovered, then refrigerate separately, covered. Bring the filling to room temperature and reheat the sauce to warm before proceeding.

POBLANO CHILES

Poblanos, which Mexican cooking authority Diana Kennedy considers "one of the most delicious foods in the world," are medium- to thick-fleshed forest-green chiles that are ideal for stuffing (page 322). About 4½ inches long with broad shoulders that taper to a point, they resemble large triangles with undulating indentations. While all poblanos share a complex, fruity flavor, they can range from mild to ferocious. Kennedy recommends giving them a sniff when you're preparing, peeling, and seeding them: you'll be able to smell the hotter ones distinctly—be sure to cut out their ribs completely. We also like her trick of marking the hottest chiles with a toothpick before frying them so that guests will know which ones are fiery.

Dried poblanos are often labeled incorrectly in American supermarkets as "pasillas" (and fresh ones are sometimes erroneously referred to as "fresh pasillas"). When poblanos are ripened on the plant, then dried until wrinkled, they're called ancho chiles.

Mixed Mushroom Tamales

SERVES 6

ACTIVE TIME: 1 HOUR ■ START TO FINISH: 2½ HOURS

■ Making tamales can be a meditative activity when you're all alone and not racing the clock, but it's more fun when friends and family get involved. *Tamaladas*, family get-togethers in which everyone lends a hand in making huge quantities of tamales, are a popular tradition in Mexico, especially around Christmastime (the tamales can be made ahead and frozen). Our tamales are very tender, with a rich, almost meaty flavor. ■

- 36 large dried corn husks (3 ounces; see Sources), separated, any damaged husks discarded
- ½ ounce (½ cup) dried porcini mushrooms
- 1 cup boiling water
- 2 sticks (½ pound) unsalted butter, softened
- ½ small onion, finely chopped
- 1 tablespoon minced garlic
- 1 pound mixed mushrooms, such as (stemmed) shiitakes, white button, and cremini, coarsely chopped
- 1 teaspoon dried epazote (optional; see Sources), crumbled
- 2 teaspoons salt
- ½ teaspoon freshly ground black pepper
- 2 cups fine-ground masa harina
- ½ teaspoon baking powder
- 1 teaspoon sugar
- 1½ cups very hot water

SPECIAL EQUIPMENT: a large pasta pot with a perforated insert or a deep pot and a large collapsible vegetable steamer

Cover husks with hot water by 2 inches in a large bowl and use an inverted plate to keep them submerged. Soak, turning husks occasionally, until soft, about 30 minutes.

Meanwhile, cover porcini with boiling water in a small bowl and soak for 30 minutes. Lift out porcini, squeezing liquid back into bowl, and rinse mushrooms to remove any grit. Coarsely chop porcini. Pour soaking liquid through a paper-towel-lined sieve into a glass measure and reserve.

Rinse corn husks one at a time under cold water. Pile 24 of largest husks on a plate and cover with a dampened kitchen towel. Tear twenty-four ½-inch-wide strips lengthwise from remaining husks to use as ties (keep damp as well).

Heat ½ stick butter (4 tablespoons) in a 12-inch heavy nonstick skillet over high heat until foam subsides. Add onion and garlic and cook, stirring, for 1 minute. Add mushrooms, including porcini, and

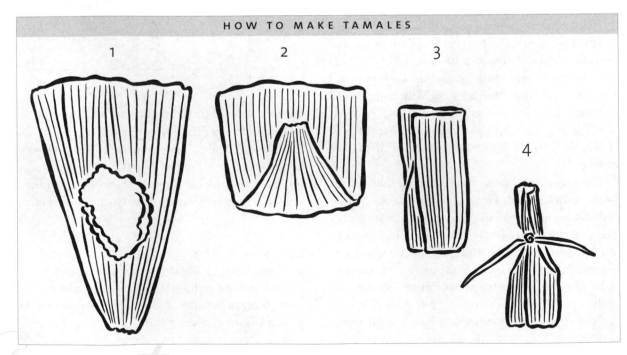

HOW TO MAKE TAMALES

1   2   3   4

Masa is a foundation of Mexican cuisine. Although the word simply means "dough" in Spanish, in the context of cooking it means "corn dough," and masa is transformed into everything from tortillas to tamales to empanadas.

Fresh masa is made by an ancient process of treating dried field corn kernels with a solution of slaked lime (calcium oxide) to help dissolve the indigestible outer hull and increase the nutritional value. After the kernels are thoroughly rinsed, they're stone-ground into a malleable dough with a distinctive fresh flavor. The first grinding results in a coarse dough, which is used only for tamales. The second grinding, when the masa is smoothed out by rollers, produces a fine-grained dough that's used for tortillas and everything else. When purchasing the dough at Latino markets or by mail-order (see Sources), you'll want to specify "tamale masa" or "tortilla masa." (Avoid "masa preparada," which has lard and other flavorings.) Fresh masa is highly perishable, so plan to use it right away or put it in the freezer for no more than a few days.

Commercially prepared dehydrated powdered masa harina is a great, and more readily available, alternative to fresh masa. Available at Latino markets and many supermarkets (or see Sources), it's sometimes labeled "masarica," or "instant corn masa mix." It has a year-long shelf life and needs only water to become tortilla dough. It's not quite as earthy and sweet as fresh masa, but it delivers reliable results with little effort. When used for tamales (opposite page), the dough develops a wonderfully light texture.

Although masa harina looks like cornmeal, you cannot substitute one for the other. (Cornmeal and corn flour are ground dried corn kernels that were not treated with slaked lime.) *Masarepa*, the flour used primarily for making *arepas*, the round corn cakes of Venezuela and Colombia, cannot be used in place of masa harina either. It's made from corn that's been dried, cracked, precooked with steam, pressed into flakes, and ground. It hasn't been treated with slaked lime, so it has a more neutral, less earthy flavor.

epazote, if using, and cook, stirring occasionally, until liquid is released from mushrooms, about 3 minutes. Add porcini soaking liquid, bring to a simmer, and simmer, stirring occasionally, until most of liquid has evaporated and mushrooms are slightly browned, 3 to 5 minutes. Sprinkle with ½ teaspoon salt and pepper and transfer to a bowl to cool.

Beat remaining 1½ sticks butter in a large bowl with an electric mixer at medium-high speed until light and fluffy, about 30 seconds.

Sift masa harina, baking powder, sugar, and remaining 1½ teaspoons salt into another bowl. Stir in 1½ cups very hot water until a thick paste forms. Beat masa mixture into butter in 3 batches, beating until smooth after each addition. Reduce speed to low and mix in mushroom mixture until just combined.

Put 1 husk on a work surface, pointed end closest to you. Spreading husk flat, mound 3 tablespoons filling in center and flatten slightly into a rough oval (about ½ inch thick) with back of a spoon, leaving a 1-inch border on both sides (1). Bring pointed end of husk up over mound of filling to cover (2). Fold sides of husk over filling to enclose (3). Gather together open end of husk at top of filling, creating a flat pouch, and tie with a corn husk strip (4). Assemble 23 more tamales in same manner.

Arrange tamales upright in one layer in steamer insert (or collapsible steamer) so they resemble falling dominoes in rows. Set steamer over boiling water in pot and cover with a folded kitchen towel (towel will absorb condensation so tamales won't get soggy). Steam tamales, tightly covered with a lid, adding more water as necessary, until filling is tender, about 30 minutes. To check for doneness, open 1 tamale; if any part of filling is still gummy, steam for 5 to 10 minutes more.

■ The cooked tamales can be frozen for up to 1 month. Cool completely, then wrap well in foil. To reheat, discard the foil (do not thaw the tamales) and steam over boiling water until heated through, 5 to 10 minutes; or microwave until hot.

Poblano Tortilla Gratin

SERVES 4
ACTIVE TIME: 45 MINUTES ■ START TO FINISH: 1¼ HOURS

■ Similar to an enchilada casserole, this Tex-Mex dish is easy to pull together. Triangles of toasted corn tortillas are layered with a rich, classic cheese sauce and a zesty tomato sauce studded with *rajas*, or strips of roasted poblano chiles. It's a great dish for a Super Bowl party. ■

FOR FILLING
- 9 (6- to 7-inch) corn tortillas
- ¾ pound poblano chiles (3 large), roasted (see Tips, page 914) and peeled
- 2 tablespoons vegetable oil
- 2 cups chopped white onions
- 1 tablespoon minced garlic
- 1 teaspoon salt
- 1 (14- to 15-ounce) can stewed tomatoes, diced

FOR SAUCE AND TOPPING
- 2 tablespoons unsalted butter
- 2 tablespoons all-purpose flour
- 1½ cups whole milk
- 3 cups coarsely grated cheddar or Monterey Jack (about 12 ounces)
- ½ teaspoon salt
- ¼ teaspoon freshly ground black pepper

TOAST THE TORTILLA WEDGES: Put racks in upper and lower thirds of oven and preheat oven to 400°F.

Stack tortillas and cut into 8 wedges. Spread tortilla triangles in one layer on two large baking sheets and bake, stirring occasionally and switching position of pans halfway through baking, until crisp and pale golden, 15 to 20 minutes. Cool tortillas. (Leave oven on.)

PREPARE THE CHILES: Open chiles and spread flat; discard seeds and stems and cut out ribs. Cut chiles lengthwise into ¼-inch-wide strips. Reserve about ¼ cup for garnish.

MAKE THE FILLING: Heat oil in a 10-inch heavy skillet over moderately low heat until hot but not smoking. Add onions and garlic and cook, stirring occasionally, until softened, about 5 minutes. Stir in salt, tomatoes with juice, and remaining poblano strips and simmer for 2 minutes. Remove from heat.

MAKE THE SAUCE: Melt butter in a 2-quart heavy saucepan over moderately low heat. Add flour, and cook, whisking, for 2 minutes to make a roux. Add milk in a steady stream, whisking, and cook, whisking, for 2 minutes. Remove from heat and gradually add 2 cups cheese, stirring until cheese is melted, then add salt and pepper.

ASSEMBLE AND BAKE THE GRATIN: Arrange half of tortillas in a buttered 2-quart gratin or other shallow baking dish. Spoon filling evenly over top. Cover with remaining tortillas. Pour sauce over tortillas (tips of tortillas will stick up) and sprinkle with remaining 1 cup cheese and reserved poblano strips.

Bake, uncovered, in upper third of oven until gratin is bubbling and top is golden, about 30 minutes.

Vegetable Casserole with Tofu Topping

SERVES 4 TO 6
ACTIVE TIME: 1 HOUR ■ START TO FINISH: 1½ HOURS

■ Loaded with kale, cabbage, and carrots, this casserole is substantial and satisfying, and the sweetness of the vegetables shines through. A topping of tofu and bread crumbs adds a wonderful textural accent. (Dried bread crumbs create a crisp crust; fresh crumbs produce a more tender result—your choice.) Cynthia Knauer, the mother of *Gourmet*'s food editor Ian Knauer, shared the recipe. ■

FOR VEGETABLES
- 2 tablespoons olive oil
- 2 medium onions, halved lengthwise and thinly sliced lengthwise

1 pound cabbage, quartered lengthwise, cored, and
    cut crosswise into ⅓-inch-thick slices
1 pound kale, stems and center ribs removed, leaves
    coarsely chopped
½ pound carrots, cut into ¼-inch-thick matchsticks
½ cup water
2 tablespoons soy sauce
½ teaspoon salt

FOR TOPPING

1½ cups fine fresh bread crumbs (from 5 slices firm
    sandwich bread) or dried bread crumbs, preferably
    whole wheat
7–8 ounces firm tofu, rinsed and drained
½ cup finely grated Parmigiano-Reggiano
⅓ cup olive oil
2 teaspoons dried basil, crumbled
1½ teaspoons dried oregano, crumbled
1 teaspoon paprika
1 garlic clove, finely chopped
¼ teaspoon salt

Put a rack in middle of oven and preheat oven to
350°F.

PREPARE THE VEGETABLES: Heat oil in a deep 12-
to 14-inch heavy skillet over moderately high heat
until hot but not smoking. Add onions and cook,
stirring occasionally, until softened and beginning
to brown, about 5 minutes. Reduce heat to moderate, add cabbage, kale, carrots, water, soy sauce,
and salt (skillet will be full, but volume will reduce
as vegetables steam). Cook, covered, stirring occasionally, until vegetables are just tender, 10 to 15
minutes. Transfer to a 13-by-9-inch glass or ceramic
baking dish.

MAKE THE TOPPING AND BAKE THE CASSEROLE:
Combine all ingredients in a food processor and
pulse until well combined. Sprinkle topping over
vegetables in baking dish and bake, uncovered, until
topping is golden brown and vegetables are hot, 15
to 20 minutes.

COOK'S NOTE

■ The casserole can be made up to 1 day ahead. Cool,
  uncovered, then refrigerate, covered. Reheat in a 350°F
  oven until hot.

Eggplant Parmesan

SERVES 8
ACTIVE TIME: 1 HOUR ■ START TO FINISH: 2½ HOURS

■ Each element here is distinct—crisp bread crumbs
enveloping velvety eggplant, lightly cooked tomato
sauce with an herbal hit of basil, just enough gooey
mozzarella—but they come together into a glorious
whole. ■

2½ pounds medium eggplants (about 3), cut into
    ⅓-inch-thick rounds
    Salt
2 (28- to 32-ounce) cans whole Italian tomatoes
    in juice, drained, juice reserved, and coarsely
    chopped
1½ cups plus 3 tablespoons olive oil
2 large garlic cloves, finely chopped
20 fresh basil leaves, torn in half
    Freshly ground black pepper
¼ teaspoon red pepper flakes
1 cup all-purpose flour
5 large eggs
3½ cups packaged fine bread crumbs
1 cup finely grated Parmigiano-Reggiano (about
    3 ounces)
1 pound fresh mozzarella, chilled (for easier slicing)
    and thinly sliced

Toss eggplant with 2 teaspoons salt in a colander
set over a bowl. Let drain for 30 minutes.

Meanwhile, coarsely puree tomatoes with juice, in
batches, in a blender.

Heat 3 tablespoons oil in a 5-quart heavy pot over
moderately high heat until hot but not smoking. Add
garlic and cook, stirring, until golden, about 30 seconds. Add tomato puree, basil, ½ teaspoon salt, ½
teaspoon black pepper, and red pepper flakes. Bring
to a simmer and simmer, uncovered, stirring occasionally, until slightly thickened, 25 to 30 minutes.
Remove from heat.

Put a rack in middle of oven and preheat oven to
375°F.

Stir together flour, ¼ teaspoon salt, and ¼ teaspoon pepper in a shallow bowl. Lightly beat eggs in

a second shallow bowl. Stir together bread crumbs and ½ cup Parmesan in a third shallow bowl.

Working with 1 slice at a time, dredge eggplant in flour, shaking off excess, dip in egg to coat, letting excess drip off, and dredge in bread crumbs until evenly coated. Transfer to wax paper, arranging slices in one layer.

Heat remaining 1½ cups oil in a deep 12-inch skillet, preferably nonstick, over moderately high heat until hot but not smoking. Fry eggplant, 4 slices at a time, turning once, until golden brown, 5 to 6 minutes per batch. Transfer to paper towels to drain.

Spread 1 cup tomato sauce in bottom of a 13-by-11-inch or other 3½-quart baking dish. Arrange one third of eggplant slices in one layer over sauce, overlapping slightly if necessary. Cover eggplant with one third of remaining sauce (about 1¼ cups) and one third of mozzarella. Continue layering with remaining eggplant, sauce, and mozzarella in same manner. Sprinkle top with remaining ½ cup Parmesan.

Bake, uncovered, until cheese is melted and golden and sauce is bubbling, 35 to 40 minutes.

COOK'S NOTE

■ The tomato sauce can be made up to 1 day ahead. Cool, uncovered, then refrigerate, covered.

Vegetable Potpie with Cheddar Biscuit Topping

SERVES 8
ACTIVE TIME: 1 HOUR ■ START TO FINISH: 1½ HOURS

■ This homey potpie is crowned with fluffy cheddar scallion biscuits, ideal for sopping up the rich vegetarian gravy. Because the filling improves when made a day ahead, we like to prep it on a leisurely Sunday, knowing that Monday's dinner will be hassle-free. ■

FOR FILLING

1 (1-pound) package frozen pearl onions (not thawed)
2½ cups water
5 tablespoons unsalted butter
1 fresh thyme sprig, plus ½ teaspoon chopped fresh thyme
Salt and freshly ground black pepper
1 medium onion, coarsely chopped
3 carrots, coarsely chopped
2 celery ribs, coarsely chopped
1 large parsnip, peeled and coarsely chopped
1 medium boiling potato, peeled and coarsely chopped
10 ounces white mushrooms, trimmed and quartered
1 garlic clove, minced
2 tablespoons all-purpose flour
1 cup whole milk
1 (10-ounce) package frozen peas, thawed

FOR BISCUIT TOPPING

2¼ cups all-purpose flour
2 teaspoons baking powder
1 teaspoon baking soda
¾ teaspoon salt
¼ teaspoon freshly ground black pepper
¾ stick (6 tablespoons) unsalted butter, cut into ½-inch cubes and chilled
1 cup coarsely grated extra-sharp cheddar (about 4 ounces)
3 tablespoons finely grated Parmigiano-Reggiano
2 scallions, finely chopped
1½ cups well-shaken buttermilk

MAKE THE FILLING: Combine pearl onions, water, 1 tablespoon butter, thyme sprig, ½ teaspoon salt, and ¼ teaspoon pepper in a 2-quart heavy saucepan and bring to a boil. Reduce heat and simmer, covered, until onions are tender, about 8 minutes. Drain in a sieve set over a bowl; reserve liquid and discard thyme sprig.

Meanwhile, heat remaining ½ stick butter in a 12-inch deep heavy skillet over moderately high heat until foam subsides. Add chopped vegetables, mushrooms, garlic, chopped thyme, and ½ teaspoon salt and cook, stirring occasionally, until vegetables begin to brown (bottom of skillet will become crusty), about 15 minutes.

Sprinkle vegetables with flour and cook, stirring, for 1 minute. Add reserved onion cooking liquid and milk and bring to a boil, stirring and scraping up brown bits. Reduce heat to moderate and simmer, covered, until vegetables are barely tender, about 10 minutes.

Remove from heat and stir in peas, pearl onions, and salt and pepper to taste. Pour into a 13-by-9-inch or other 3-quart baking dish.

MAKE THE TOPPING AND BAKE THE POTPIE: Put a rack in middle of oven and preheat oven to 450°F.

Whisk together flour, baking powder, baking soda, salt, and pepper in a large bowl. Blend in butter with your fingertips or a pastry blender until mixture resembles coarse meal. Stir in cheeses and scallions, add buttermilk, and stir just until combined.

Drop biscuits onto filling in 12 equal mounds, leaving spaces in between. Bake until topping is golden and filling is bubbling, 25 to 30 minutes. Let stand for 5 minutes before serving.

COOK'S NOTES

- The filling can be made up to 1 day ahead. Cool, uncovered, then refrigerate, covered. Reheat before topping with the biscuits.
- The biscuit mixture, without the buttermilk, can be made up to 1 day ahead and refrigerated, covered. Stir in the buttermilk to make the topping.

Bulgur-Stuffed Tomatoes, Zucchini, and Bell Peppers

SERVES 4
ACTIVE TIME: 1 HOUR ■ START TO FINISH: 2½ HOURS

■ The moist filling of bulgur, smoky eggplant, currants, and tomatoes makes each of these vegetables taste delicious. And because the little jewels can be fully prepared up to a day ahead, just set out the platter and join the party. ■

1 large eggplant (1½ pounds)
8 small tomatoes (about 2½ inches in diameter; 2½ pounds total)
Salt
4 small zucchini (1½ pounds total), trimmed and halved lengthwise
6 tablespoons extra-virgin olive oil, plus additional for brushing vegetables
2 cups chopped onions
⅔ cup bulgur

½ teaspoon sugar
½ teaspoon ground allspice
Freshly ground black pepper
⅓ cup dried currants
4 small yellow or orange bell peppers with stems, halved lengthwise through stem, ribs and seeds discarded
¼ cup chopped fresh flat-leaf parsley

Heat a well-seasoned 12-inch cast-iron or other heavy skillet over moderate heat until hot. Add eggplant and cook, turning occasionally with tongs, until blackened on all sides and tender, 35 to 45 minutes. Transfer to a cutting board.

Meanwhile, core tomatoes and cut off top ½ inch from each. Cut tops into ¼-inch dice and set aside. With a melon ball cutter or a spoon, scoop out insides of tomatoes into a medium-mesh sieve set over a bowl, leaving shells intact. Force pulp and juice through sieve; discard seeds. Add enough water to juice to total 2 cups; set aside. Sprinkle tomato shells with ¼ teaspoon salt, invert onto a rack set in a baking pan, and drain for 20 minutes.

Using melon ball cutter or spoon, scoop flesh from zucchini halves into a bowl, leaving ¼-inch thick shells. Coarsely chop flesh; set aside.

When eggplant is cool enough to handle, peel and cut flesh into ½-inch pieces.

Heat ¼ cup oil in a 12-inch heavy skillet over moderate heat. Add chopped zucchini and onions and cook, stirring occasionally, until softened and beginning to brown, 5 to 7 minutes. Add bulgur, sugar, allspice, 1 teaspoon salt, and ¼ teaspoon pepper and cook, stirring, until bulgur is coated, about 1 minute. Add tomato juice mixture, diced tomatoes, and currants and bring to a boil. Remove from heat, cover, and let stand until liquid is absorbed and bulgur is tender, about 10 minutes.

Meanwhile, put racks in upper and lower thirds of oven and preheat oven to 400°F. Oil a large baking sheet and a 13-by-9-inch baking pan.

Arrange tomato and zucchini shells cut side up on oiled baking sheet. Brush insides of shells with oil and sprinkle with ¼ teaspoon pepper (total). Sprinkle zucchini with ¼ teaspoon salt. Put bell pepper halves in oiled baking pan, brush insides with oil, and sprinkle with ¼ teaspoon salt and ¼ teaspoon pepper.

Stir eggplant, 2 tablespoons parsley, and salt and pepper to taste into bulgur mixture. Spoon stuffing into vegetable shells. Drizzle stuffing with remaining 2 tablespoons oil and cover pans loosely with foil.

Bake, switching position of pans halfway through baking, until vegetable shells are just tender but not falling apart, 20 to 30 minutes for tomatoes and zucchini, 30 to 40 minutes for bell peppers. Cool vegetables to room temperature, about 30 minutes.

Sprinkle vegetables with remaining 2 tablespoons parsley just before serving.

COOK'S NOTES

- The eggplant can also be broiled, 4 to 6 inches from heat, in a preheated broiler, turning occasionally, until it collapses, 15 to 20 minutes.
- The stuffed vegetables can be baked up to 1 day ahead. Cool completely, uncovered, then refrigerate, covered. Bring to room temperature before serving (this will take about 1 hour).

Chile Rellenos with Tomato Sauce

SERVES 4
ACTIVE TIME: 1½ HOURS ■ START TO FINISH: 1½ HOURS

■ Voluptuous chile rellenos are complemented by a slightly tangy tomato sauce. A light touch with the frothy egg batter is key. ■

FOR TOMATO SAUCE

- 1 (14- to 15-ounce) can whole tomatoes in juice
- 1 cup water
- ¼ cup chopped white onion
- 2 large garlic cloves
- 1 tablespoon distilled white vinegar
- 2 teaspoons sugar
- 1 teaspoon dried oregano, preferably Mexican, crumbled
- ¾ teaspoon salt
- 2 tablespoons corn or other vegetable oil

FOR CHILES

- 4 large poblano chiles with stems (1 pound total; see Cook's Note), roasted and allowed to steam (see Tips, page 914)
- ½ pound Monterey Jack cheese, coarsely grated (2½ cups packed)

FOR COATING AND FRYING

- About 2 cups corn or other vegetable oil
- 3 large eggs, separated
- ¼ teaspoon salt
- ¼ cup all-purpose flour

ACCOMPANIMENT: white rice

MAKE THE TOMATO SAUCE: Combine all ingredients except oil in a blender and blend until smooth.

Heat oil in a deep heavy 12-inch skillet or shallow flameproof casserole over moderately high heat until hot but not smoking. Carefully pour in sauce (it may spatter) and simmer, stirring occasionally, for 10 minutes (sauce will still be thin). Remove from heat.

PEEL AND STUFF THE CHILES: Peel off charred skin from chiles, leaving stems attached. Cut a lengthwise slit in each chile and carefully cut out seed pod, including attached ribs, with kitchen shears; be careful not to tear chile. Wipe chiles clean with a paper towel if necessary.

Stuff each chile with one quarter of cheese, enclosing it by overlapping slit slightly if possible. Transfer them to a large plate.

COAT AND FRY THE CHILES: Heat ½ inch oil in a 12-inch heavy skillet over moderately low heat until hot but not smoking. Meanwhile, beat egg whites with ⅛ teaspoon salt with an electric mixer just until they hold stiff peaks. Whisk together yolks and remaining ⅛ teaspoon salt in a medium bowl. Gently fold whites into yolks.

Put flour in a fine-mesh sieve and dust chiles with flour, turning to lightly coat all sides.

Reheat sauce over low heat.

Coat and fry chiles in 2 batches. Holding 1 chile by the stem, dip in egg coating, using a rubber spatula to help coat chile completely, then transfer, still holding by stem, to oil. Increase heat to moderately high, then coat and add another chile in same manner. Fry, turning once with a slotted spoon and basting sides with hot oil to brown evenly, until golden, 4 to 5 minutes. Transfer with slotted spoon to paper towels to drain, then transfer chiles to sauce. Coat and fry second batch of chiles in same manner, adjusting heat as necessary; transfer to sauce.

Serve immediately, with rice.

COOK'S NOTES

- If you cannot find 4 large chiles with stems, substitute 6 medium chiles or 8 small chiles (with stems). Coat and fry them in 2 batches.
- The sauce can be made up to 1 day ahead. Cool, uncovered, then refrigerate, covered.
- The chiles can be stuffed (but not coated) up to 1 day ahead. Refrigerate, covered. Bring to room temperature before coating and frying.

Eggplant Soufflé

SERVES 4 TO 6 AS A LIGHT MAIN COURSE
ACTIVE TIME: 10 MINUTES ■ START TO FINISH: 1½ HOURS

■ When we revisited this simple Persian-inspired soufflé from 1966, we were amazed by how light, airy, and deep-flavored it was. Pair it with a salad, plus some feta, olives, and grilled bread. ■

Olive oil
1 (1½- to 1¾-pound) eggplant, halved lengthwise
6 large eggs, separated
½ cup finely grated Parmigiano-Reggiano (use a rasp grater)
1 garlic clove, minced
2½ tablespoons fresh lemon juice
Salt
¼ teaspoon freshly ground black pepper
2 tablespoons unsalted butter, melted

GARNISH: chopped fresh mint
ACCOMPANIMENT: whole-milk yogurt

Put a rack in middle of oven and preheat oven to 350°F. Oil a small baking sheet with olive oil.

Put eggplant cut side down on baking sheet and bake until very tender, about 30 minutes. Remove from oven and cool slightly.

When eggplant is cool enough to handle, scrape flesh into a food processor; discard skin. Puree until smooth. Add egg yolks, Parmesan, garlic, lemon juice, ¾ teaspoon salt, and pepper and pulse until blended. Transfer to a bowl.

Pour melted butter into a 1½-quart gratin dish or a 9½-inch deep-dish pie plate and tilt to coat bottom. Beat egg whites with ¼ teaspoon salt in a large bowl

FRYING SAUCES IN MEXICAN CUISINE

It's not just the bold spices and gutsy combinations of onions, garlic, chiles, and tomatoes that give Mexican cuisine its signature flavors; cooking techniques play a large role as well. Take, for instance, the cooked sauces that coat chile rellenos (opposite) and enchiladas (page 314).

What gives these sauces their nuance and savor is an initial frying of the pureed ingredients: the puree is added to shimmering hot oil (or, more traditionally, lard) and cooked over moderately high heat until it thickens into a paste. This technique concentrates and melds together the natural sweetness, piquancy, spiciness, and aroma of the ingredients. Unlike sauces that are slowly simmered over low heat, these take on a slightly charred depth.

with an electric mixer at medium speed until they just hold stiff peaks. Fold one third of whites into eggplant mixture to lighten it, then fold in remaining whites gently but thoroughly. Spoon mixture into gratin dish.

Bake until golden and puffed, 25 to 30 minutes.

Sprinkle gratin with mint, then scoop into servings and dollop with yogurt.

Chinese Vegetable Stir-Fry

SERVES 4
ACTIVE TIME: 1 HOUR ■ START TO FINISH: 1 HOUR

■ Pea shoots (or watercress), Napa cabbage, crunchy water chestnuts, green beans, and dried shiitake mushrooms combine in this stir fry. The soaking liquid from the mushrooms helps deepen the traditional Chinese sauce of ginger, garlic, soy sauce, and rice wine. Since everything cooks so quickly, it's important to have all the ingredients chopped and lined up next to the wok when you start—once you turn on the burner, there's no time to prep anything more. When making stir-fries with lots of leafy greens, using two wooden spatulas to lift and toss the vegetables gives the best control. ■

3 cups boiling water
2 cups (about 2 ounces) small dried shiitake (Chinese black) mushrooms
¼ cup soy sauce
¼ cup Chinese rice wine or medium-dry sherry
4 teaspoons sugar
2 teaspoons cornstarch
2 tablespoons peanut or vegetable oil
1 tablespoon finely chopped peeled fresh ginger
1 tablespoon finely chopped garlic
6 ounces Chinese long beans (about 15; see Sources) or ¾ pound green beans, cut into 2-inch pieces
1 bunch scallions, halved lengthwise and cut into 2-inch pieces
10 fresh water chestnuts, peeled and cut into ¼-inch-thick slices, or 1 (8-ounce) can sliced water chestnuts, rinsed and drained
1 (2-pound) Napa cabbage, halved lengthwise, cored, and cut crosswise into 2-inch-wide pieces
1 pound pea shoots, coarsely chopped, or 3 bunches watercress, tough stems discarded, coarsely chopped
2 teaspoons Asian sesame oil
½ teaspoon salt
¼ teaspoon freshly ground black pepper

ACCOMPANIMENT: white rice
SPECIAL EQUIPMENT: a well-seasoned 14-inch flat-bottomed wok

Pour boiling water over mushrooms in a medium bowl and soak, turning occasionally, until softened, about 30 minutes.

Lift out mushrooms, squeezing out excess liquid; reserve 1 cup liquid (add water if necessary to bring to 1 cup). Cut out and discard stems and halve caps. Transfer caps to a 1½- to 2-quart saucepan and add 2 tablespoons soy sauce, 2 tablespoons rice wine, 2 teaspoons sugar, and reserved soaking liquid. Bring to a boil, then reduce heat and simmer, covered, stirring occasionally, for 10 minutes. Remove from heat and keep covered.

Stir together remaining 2 tablespoons soy sauce, 2 tablespoons rice wine, 2 teaspoons sugar, and cornstarch in a small bowl until smooth.

Heat wok over high heat until a drop of water evaporates on contact. Pour oil down side of wok, then swirl wok to coat sides. Stir in ginger, garlic, beans, scallions, and water chestnuts and stir-fry for 2 minutes. Add cabbage and, using two wooden spatulas (wok will be very full), toss until cabbage is wilted, 4 to 6 minutes. Add pea shoots and stir-fry until wilted, 2 to 4 minutes. Add mushrooms, with liquid, and bring to a boil. Stir cornstarch mixture, then stir into vegetables and bring to a boil. Boil, stirring constantly, until sauce begins to thicken slightly. Stir in sesame oil, salt, and pepper.

Serve immediately over rice.

COOK'S NOTE

■ The recipe can be halved and served as a side dish for 4.

THE ART OF THE STIR-FRY

If you do lots of stir-frying, you owe it to yourself to buy a flat-bottomed wok. Because the bottom gets very hot and the sides heat up more slowly, you can sear the food, then push it partly up the sides with a shovel-like Chinese spatula, letting it fall back onto the bottom; using this continuous tumbling motion allows you to cook everything quickly and evenly. You can use a large skillet, but you won't have as much control, since it is so wide and the sides aren't a cooking surface. Your spatula will lift only a small amount of food at a time, and you can only move it to the edges rather than up the cooler sides. You'll also need more oil, since the bottom of a large skillet is much larger than that of a wok. And keep in mind that a skillet, particularly a heavy one, takes longer to heat than a wok does.

A wok will also add authenticity to stir-fries, and not just because of its appearance. It will help you achieve *wok hay*, which the Chinese-cooking authority Grace Young describes as "the elusive seared quality—part taste, part smell—prized by Chinese cooks." Young uses a well-seasoned 14-inch carbon-steel wok, modified for Western kitchens with a long wooden handle and a small "helper" handle. It's about 4 inches deep, with a small flat bottom. Flatness is crucial—a round-bottomed wok is too unstable on a Western stove and a wok ring lifts the wok too far from the heat source. (For where to buy a wok and spatula, see Sources.)

Intense heat is the key to a great stir-fry. Because our stoves aren't as powerful as those in China or in Chinese restaurants in the United States, Young recommends allowing as little time as possible to pass between taking the food from the wok and serving it, because *wok hay* lasts for only a few minutes.

When stir-frying beef, cut the meat into short, thin slices, preferably on the bias, so there is more surface area to sear. Young advises against buying presliced steak. "You don't know what cut you're getting," she says. "And often it's sliced all wrong, which can make even tender meat become tough." Once all of the ingredients are sliced and diced, crank up the heat. After a minute, hold your hand about an inch above the bottom of the wok—it should feel like a hot radiator. A few drops of water sprinkled in should evaporate immediately. When you add the meat, unless you have a professional-style stove, don't begin moving it around right away. Give it time to sear first, or it will turn gray and stick. When it comes time to stir-fry the vegetables, make sure they are absolutely bone-dry and cook them just until they crackle invitingly and their aroma blooms. Use your spatula to keep the food you're cooking in contact with the sides of the blistering-hot wok at all times.

Young also has some tips on cleaning a wok. Instead of using one of those stiff bamboo brushes, which are meant for restaurants ("they'll take the seasoning right off your wok"), run some hot water into the wok and let it sit for 10 minutes. Drain, wipe it out with a sponge recommended for cleaning a nonstick pan, removing any sticky bits with the rough side of the sponge, and then put the wok over low heat until thoroughly dry. Properly cared for, your wok will be just as much an heirloom as your grandmother's cast-iron skillet.

TOFU

The very innocuousness of snowy blocks of tofu, or soybean curd, is an opportunity for the cook, since they soak up the flavor of marinades or sauces like a sponge. Choose the texture according to what you're cooking: extra-firm and firm tofu are sturdy, so they hold their shape well, soft tofu is more delicate, and silken tofu is generally reserved for soups, added at the end of cooking to preserve its custardy texture.

Tofu keeps, submerged in a covered container of water, for 3 or 4 days in the refrigerator. (Change the water every day.)

Vegetable Tofu Stir-Fry on Crispy Noodles

SERVES 4
ACTIVE TIME: 45 MINUTES ■ START TO FINISH: 1½ HOURS

■ A good stir-fry proves that a single fresh, colorful dish can deliver a complete meal. This version revs up supermarket ingredients—tofu, broccoli, red bell pepper, canned baby corn—with Asian chile paste. Some of the bright-white fried rice stick noodles are softened by the sauce, while others stay crisp. ■

- 1 (14- to 16-ounce) block firm tofu, rinsed and drained
- ¼ cup plus 2 teaspoons soy sauce
- 1 teaspoon medium-dry sherry
- 1½ teaspoons Asian sesame oil
- 1 tablespoon plus ½ teaspoon cornstarch
- 1 cup water
- 1 tablespoon sugar
- 1½ pounds broccoli (about 1½ medium bunches)
- 2 cups vegetable oil
- ¼ pound thin rice stick noodles (rice vermicelli), separated slightly
- 1 medium red bell pepper, halved crosswise, cored, seeded, and cut into ¼-inch-wide strips
- 2 tablespoons minced scallions
- 1 tablespoon minced peeled fresh ginger
- 1 garlic clove, minced
- 1½ teaspoons Asian chile paste
- 1 (15-ounce) can baby corn, rinsed, drained, and cut into 1-inch pieces if large

SPECIAL EQUIPMENT: a well-seasoned 14-inch flat-bottomed wok

Wrap tofu in several layers of paper towels, set on a plate, and weight with a heavy skillet for 30 minutes to remove excess liquid.

Cut tofu into ½-inch cubes. Stir together 2 teaspoons soy sauce, sherry, ½ teaspoon sesame oil, and ½ teaspoon cornstarch in a medium bowl until smooth. Add tofu and stir gently until marinade is absorbed. Let stand for 30 minutes.

Stir 2 tablespoons water and remaining tablespoon cornstarch together in a small bowl until smooth. Add remaining ¾ cup plus 2 tablespoons water, remaining ¼ cup soy sauce, sugar, and remaining teaspoon sesame oil, stirring until sugar is dissolved.

Cut stalks from broccoli and peel with a paring knife, trimming away any fibrous parts. Cut into ¼-inch-thick slices. Cut remaining broccoli into 1-inch-wide florets.

Cook broccoli stems in a 4-quart pot of boiling salted water (1 tablespoon salt) for 1 minute. Add florets and cook until crisp-tender, about 1 minute more. Drain and plunge into a large bowl of ice and cold water to stop the cooking; drain well.

Heat oil in wok over high heat until hot but not smoking. Add one quarter of noodles and fry (noodles will puff up), turning constantly, until pale golden, 10 to 15 seconds. Transfer with a slotted spoon to paper towels to drain. Fry remaining noodles in 3 batches in same manner.

Pour oil from wok into a heatproof bowl and wipe out wok with paper towels. Pour 2 tablespoons oil back into wok (reserve remainder for another use or discard) and heat over high heat until hot but not smoking. Add bell pepper and stir-fry for 1 minute. Add scallions, ginger, garlic, and chile paste and stir-fry for 15 seconds. Stir soy sauce mixture, add to wok, and bring to a boil, stirring. Cook, stirring, until sauce is thickened, about 1 minute. Add tofu, broccoli, and corn and stir-fry until heated through, about 2 minutes.

Serve immediately over noodles.

Broiled Tofu with Cilantro Pesto

SERVES 4 AS A LIGHT MAIN COURSE
ACTIVE TIME: 15 MINUTES ■ START TO FINISH: 25 MINUTES

■ In this easy Pan-Asian dish, tofu pairs with a sassy cilantro–pine nut sauce accented by soy sauce, sesame oil, and lime juice. If you're not a vegetarian, using fish sauce instead of soy adds even deeper flavor. Broiling tofu is simple and gives it a nice crisp crust. ■

  2 (14- to 16-ounce) blocks firm tofu, rinsed and drained
  ¼ cup mild olive or vegetable oil, plus additional for brushing broiler pan rack and tofu
  2 cups packed fresh cilantro leaves
  2 tablespoons pine nuts
  1 tablespoon fresh lime juice
  2 teaspoons soy sauce
  1 teaspoon Asian sesame oil
  1 teaspoon sugar
  ½ teaspoon salt
  ⅛ teaspoon freshly ground black pepper
GARNISH: pine nuts; fresh cilantro leaves
ACCOMPANIMENTS: lime wedges; white rice

Preheat broiler and generously oil broiler pan rack with some olive oil. Cut each block of tofu crosswise into 6 slices and pat dry between several layers of paper towels. Arrange in one layer on broiler pan rack and lightly brush tops of slices with some oil. Broil 4 to 6 inches from heat, without turning, until golden brown, about 15 minutes.

Meanwhile, combine cilantro, pine nuts, lime juice, soy sauce, sesame oil, sugar, ¼ cup olive oil, salt, and pepper in a food processor and blend until bright green and smooth, about 1 minute.

Spread cilantro pesto on a platter. Using a slotted spatula, arrange tofu on pesto. Scatter pine nuts and cilantro leaves over tofu. Serve with lime wedges and rice.

Grilled Tofu with Sautéed Asian Greens

SERVES 4 TO 6
ACTIVE TIME: 30 MINUTES ■ START TO FINISH: 30 MINUTES

■ Marinated tofu on a bed of wilted greens makes a quick and tasty one-dish dinner. Adding a dash of salt in addition to the soy sauce may seem unnecessary, but it helps the flavor pop. ■

  2 (14- to 16-ounce) blocks firm tofu, rinsed and drained
  ½ cup low-sodium soy sauce
  2 teaspoons Asian sesame oil
  1 tablespoon packed dark brown sugar
  1 tablespoon finely grated peeled fresh ginger
  1 large garlic clove, minced
  ½ teaspoon Tabasco or red pepper flakes
  ¼ teaspoon salt
  2 tablespoons plus 1 teaspoon vegetable oil
  1¼ pounds Asian greens or baby spinach

Cut each block of tofu crosswise into 6 slices. Arrange in one layer on a triple layer of paper towels and top with another triple layer of towels. Weight with a shallow baking pan or a baking sheet and let stand for 2 minutes. Repeat weighting, using dry paper towels, 2 more times to remove excess liquid.

Stir together soy sauce, sesame oil, brown sugar, ginger, garlic, Tabasco, salt, and 2 tablespoons vegetable oil in a glass pie plate or small baking dish. Add tofu slices in one layer and marinate, turning every couple of minutes, for 8 minutes.

Heat a lightly oiled well-seasoned ridged grill pan over moderately high heat until hot but not smoking. Lift tofu from marinade with a slotted spatula (reserve marinade) and grill, carefully turning once with spatula, until grill marks appear and tofu is heated through, 4 to 6 minutes.

Meanwhile, heat remaining teaspoon vegetable oil in a 12-inch heavy skillet over moderately high heat until hot but not smoking. Add greens and cook, tossing with tongs, until beginning to wilt, 1 to 2 minutes. Add reserved marinade and cook, tossing, until greens are just wilted, about 1 minute. Lift greens from skillet with tongs, letting excess marinade drain off, and divide among four to six plates.

Serve greens topped with tofu slices.

Garlic Potato Puree with Shiitake Ragout and Potato Crisps

SERVES 4
ACTIVE TIME: 40 MINUTES ■ START TO FINISH: 1½ HOURS

■ Vegetarians rejoice: shiitake mushrooms make a lush, glossy sauce for a rich potato puree with a whole head of garlic. Adding potato crisps may seem like gilding the lily—and that's just the point. ■

FOR CRISPS
    2 tablespoons vegetable oil
    1 large russet (baking) potato
        Salt
FOR PUREE
    2 pounds russet (baking) potatoes (about 4 medium), peeled and cut into 1-inch pieces
    1 large garlic head, cloves separated and peeled
    ¾ cup whole milk
    ¾ stick (6 tablespoons) unsalted butter, cut into pieces
    ½ teaspoon salt
    ¼ teaspoon freshly ground black pepper
FOR RAGOUT
    2 tablespoons extra-virgin olive oil
    1 pound shiitake mushrooms, stems discarded, caps quartered, or mixed wild mushrooms, trimmed and cut into equal-sized pieces
    3 garlic cloves, minced
        Salt and freshly ground black pepper

    1 cup medium-dry sherry
    1 cup plus 1 tablespoon water
    3 tablespoons soy sauce
    2 teaspoons cornstarch
    3 tablespoons minced fresh flat-leaf parsley
SPECIAL EQUIPMENT: a mandoline or other adjustable-blade vegetable slicer; a ricer or a food mill fitted with a medium disk

MAKE THE CRISPS: Put a rack in middle of oven and preheat oven to 400°F. Generously brush a baking sheet with some of oil.

With slicer, cut potato on the diagonal into very thin (1/16-inch-thick) slices. Immediately arrange slices in one layer on baking sheet. Brush with remaining oil and season with salt. Bake until golden brown, 15 to 20 minutes.

Transfer crisps to a rack with a metal spatula to cool.

MAKE THE PUREE: Steam potatoes and garlic cloves in a steamer set over boiling water, covered, until potatoes are very tender, 12 to 15 minutes.

Bring milk just to a boil in a small saucepan; remove from heat. Force garlic and potatoes through ricer or food mill into a large bowl. Stir in butter, milk, salt, and pepper. Cover to keep warm.

MAKE THE RAGOUT: Heat oil in a large heavy skillet over moderately high heat until hot but not smoking. Add mushrooms, garlic, and salt and pepper to taste and cook, stirring occasionally, until liquid mushrooms give off has evaporated, about 5 minutes. Add sherry, bring to a boil, and boil until most of liquid has evaporated, about 3 minutes.

Add 1 cup water and soy sauce and bring to a boil. Stir together cornstarch and remaining tablespoon water until smooth and stir into ragout. Simmer, stirring occasionally, for 2 minutes. Stir in parsley.

To serve, mound puree on plates and stand 3 crisps in each mound. Spoon ragout over and around puree.

COOK'S NOTES
■ The ragout can be made up to 1 day ahead. Cool, uncovered, then refrigerate, covered.
■ The extra crisps will keep in a sealable plastic bag at room temperature for up to 2 days.

Fall Vegetables with Broiled Polenta Sticks, Frizzled Onions, and Gravy

SERVES 6
ACTIVE TIME: 2¼ HOURS ■ START TO FINISH: 4½ HOURS
(INCLUDES MAKING ACCOMPANIMENTS
AND STOCK FOR GRAVY)

■ Long and uniformly narrow, delicata squash is a breeze to work with—its thin, pale golden skin with green striations needs no peeling. It's fantastic roasted, tossed with meaty mushrooms, and piled high over creamy polenta sticks. Throw in some fried onions, broccolini, and a roasted vegetable gravy, and you have a meal to remember. ■

- ½ cup plus 2 tablespoons olive oil
- 1 tablespoon chopped fresh thyme
  Salt and freshly ground black pepper
- 2 pounds delicata squash (3 medium), halved lengthwise, seeded, and cut crosswise into ½-inch-thick slices
- 2 pounds mixed mushrooms, such as cremini, shiitake, and oyster, trimmed (stems discarded if using shiitakes) and halved (or quartered if large)
- 1¼ pounds broccolini (3 bunches), stem ends trimmed
- 2 large garlic cloves, finely chopped

ACCOMPANIMENTS: Broiled Polenta Sticks, Roasted Vegetable Gravy , and Frizzled Onions (recipes follow)

Put racks in upper and lower thirds of oven and preheat oven to 425°F.

Stir together 6 tablespoons oil, thyme, ¾ teaspoon salt, and ½ teaspoon pepper in a small bowl. Toss squash with 2 tablespoons thyme oil on a baking sheet, then arrange in one layer. Toss mushrooms with remaining ¼ cup thyme oil on another baking sheet and arrange in one layer.

Roast squash and mushrooms, stirring occasionally and switching position of pans halfway through roasting, until vegetables are tender and liquid mushrooms give off has evaporated, 25 to 30 minutes.

Meanwhile, cook broccolini in a 6- to 8-quart pot of boiling salted water (2 tablespoons salt), uncovered, until stems are crisp-tender, about 5 minutes; drain.

Heat 2 tablespoons oil in a 12-inch heavy skillet over moderately high heat until hot but not smoking. Add half of garlic and cook, stirring, until pale golden, about 30 seconds. Add half of broccolini, ¼ teaspoon salt, and ⅛ teaspoon pepper and cook, stirring, until heated through, about 2 minutes. Transfer to a bowl and cook remaining garlic and broccolini in remaining 2 tablespoons oil with ¼ teaspoon salt and ⅛ teaspoon pepper in same manner.

Arrange polenta sticks on six plates, pile broccolini and roasted vegetables on top of polenta, and top with gravy and frizzled onions. Serve immediately.

Broiled Polenta Sticks

SERVES 6
ACTIVE TIME: 30 MINUTES ■ START TO FINISH: 1 HOUR

■ Try serving these "fries" with a fried egg and a leafy salad for a vegetarian lunch, or pair them with something saucy like chicken fricassee. ■

- 6½ cups cold water
- 1½ teaspoons salt
- 2 cups yellow cornmeal (not stone-ground)
- 2 teaspoons olive oil
- ⅓ cup finely grated Parmigiano-Reggiano

Brush a 13-by-9-inch baking pan with some water.

Combine 6½ cups cold water with salt and cornmeal in a 5-quart heavy pot and bring to a boil over moderate heat, whisking. Reduce heat to moderately low and cook, stirring constantly with a long-handled wooden spoon, until polenta begins to pull away from sides of pot, 20 to 25 minutes.

Pour polenta into baking pan, spreading it evenly with a dampened heatproof rubber spatula. Cool in pan on a rack until lukewarm and set, about 20 minutes.

Preheat broiler. Oil a baking sheet with olive oil and invert polenta onto sheet. Brush polenta with oil and sprinkle with cheese. Broil about 4 inches from heat until pale golden, 5 to 7 minutes.

Cool for 5 minutes. Cut into 3-by-1½-inch sticks.

COOK'S NOTE
■ The polenta can be cooked and unmolded up to 1 day ahead. Refrigerate on the oiled baking sheet, the

surface covered with lightly oiled parchment (oiled side down), then tightly covered with plastic wrap. Bring to room temperature before brushing with the oil, sprinkling with the cheese, and broiling.

Roasted Vegetable Gravy

MAKES ABOUT 3½ CUPS
ACTIVE TIME: 45 MINUTES ■ START TO FINISH: 2¾ HOURS
(INCLUDES MAKING STOCK)

■ This is delicious ladled over mashed or roasted potatoes, rice, barley . . . You get the picture. ■

2 tablespoons plus 1 teaspoon unsalted butter
3 tablespoons plus 1 teaspoon all-purpose flour
Roasted Vegetable Stock (page 155), heated
¼ teaspoon salt
¼ teaspoon freshly ground black pepper

Melt butter in a 1½- to 2-quart heavy saucepan over moderate heat. Whisk in flour to make a roux and cook, whisking, until pale golden, 2 to 3 minutes. Add stock in a steady stream, whisking constantly, and bring to a boil, whisking. Reduce heat and simmer, whisking occasionally, until slightly thickened, about 8 minutes. Stir in salt and pepper.

COOK'S NOTE
■ The gravy can be made up to 1 day ahead. Cool completely, uncovered, then refrigerate, covered. Reheat over moderately low heat.

Frizzled Onions

MAKES ABOUT 3 CUPS
ACTIVE TIME: 30 MINUTES ■ START TO FINISH: 30 MINUTES

■ These fried onions make everything taste better. Scatter them over pasta, beans, or salads or tuck them into sandwiches. ■

1 large onion, halved lengthwise
About 3 cups vegetable oil for deep-frying
Salt
SPECIAL EQUIPMENT: a deep-fat thermometer

Very thinly slice onion lengthwise with a mandoline or other adjustable-blade vegetable slicer or a sharp knife.

Heat 2 inches oil in a 2-quart heavy saucepan over moderate heat until thermometer registers 340°F. Add one sixth of onions and fry, stirring occasionally, until golden brown, 1 to 1½ minutes (watch closely, as onions burn easily). Quickly transfer with a slotted spoon to paper towels to drain and season lightly with salt (onions will crisp as they cool). Fry remaining onions in 5 batches, draining on fresh paper towels and seasoning with salt. (Return oil to 340°F between batches.)

COOK'S NOTE
■ The onions can be fried up to 6 hours ahead and kept, uncovered, at room temperature.

Asparagus with Roasted Potatoes and Fried Eggs

SERVES 6
ACTIVE TIME: 30 MINUTES ■ START TO FINISH: 55 MINUTES

■ Food editor Paul Grimes has a great method for cooking a dozen eggs at a time: crack all of them into a bowl and slide them into the hot oil at the same time—they'll do a little snap, crackle, and pop. Cover the skillet with a baking sheet (most nonstick pans don't come with lids) until the whites are cooked through but the yolks are still a bit runny. Although you won't have the picturesque rounds you would get if you cooked the eggs two at a time, you do get the pleasure of having everyone sit down at the same time. ■

1½ pounds Yukon Gold potatoes (about 4 medium), peeled and cut into 1-inch pieces
½ cup extra-virgin olive oil
Salt and freshly ground black pepper
¼ cup finely grated Parmigiano-Reggiano
1 tablespoon fresh lemon juice
1 pound arugula, coarse stems discarded
1 pound asparagus, very thinly sliced on a long diagonal
12 large eggs
SPECIAL EQUIPMENT: a 12-inch heavy nonstick skillet

Put a rack in lower third of oven and preheat oven to 425°F.

Toss potatoes with 2 tablespoons oil, ¼ teaspoon

salt, and ⅛ teaspoon pepper in a large shallow baking pan. Spread out in pan and roast, stirring and turning once halfway through roasting, for 20 minutes.

Sprinkle 3 tablespoons cheese evenly over potatoes and continue roasting until potatoes and cheese are golden, about 10 minutes more. Cool to warm.

Meanwhile, whisk together lemon juice, ¼ teaspoon salt, and ⅛ teaspoon pepper in a large bowl. Add 3 tablespoons oil in a slow stream, whisking until combined. Add arugula and asparagus to dressing and toss to coat. Divide among six plates.

Break eggs into a large bowl. Heat remaining 3 tablespoons olive oil in skillet over high heat until just beginning to smoke. Gently pour eggs into hot oil and sprinkle with ¼ teaspoon salt and ⅛ teaspoon pepper. Cover pan completely with a large baking sheet and cook until whites are set and puffy around edges but still loose in center of skillet and yolks are still runny, about 3 minutes. Remove skillet from heat and cut eggs into pairs with a spatula.

Top asparagus salad with potatoes and eggs and sprinkle with remaining tablespoon cheese.

COOK'S NOTE

■ The egg yolks in this recipe are not fully cooked. If that is a concern, see page 915.

CURRY POWDER

No self-respecting Indian cook would use packaged curry powder—a commercial blend of spices that was, in fact, a British invention—but because it is such a convenient way to add great color and flavor, it has a proud place in our pantry. The blends vary widely in strength and quality (sometimes they are harsh and flat-tasting). We prefer what is called Madras curry powder (Sun brand), which includes coriander, turmeric, chiles, salt, cumin, fennel, black pepper, garlic, ginger, fenugreek seeds, cinnamon, cloves, anise, and mustard. Neither too hot nor too mild, it's mellow and well balanced.

Zucchini Curry

SERVES 6
ACTIVE TIME: 20 MINUTES ■ START TO FINISH: 35 MINUTES

■ Zucchini benefits from strong seasoning, and that's what it gets in this finely tuned curry. Mustard seeds, cumin, ginger, chile, and garlic do the trick, while coconut milk adds lushness. Don't skimp on the cashews and cilantro—they make a nice counterpoint to the tender squash. If you can find fresh Cocozelle zucchini at your farmers market, snap it up. This striped, ridged variety has a sweeter and more pronounced flavor than regular zucchini. ■

½ teaspoon yellow or brown mustard seeds (see Sources)
½ teaspoon cumin seeds
1 garlic clove, chopped
1–2 teaspoons chopped jalapeño chile, including seeds
2 teaspoons finely grated peeled fresh ginger
Salt
1 tablespoon curry powder, preferably Madras
¼ teaspoon ground coriander
3 tablespoons vegetable oil
1 large onion, thinly sliced
6 medium Cocozelle or regular zucchini (3 pounds), cut into ½-inch-thick slices
1 (13- to 14-ounce) can unsweetened coconut milk, well stirred
¼ cup chopped fresh cilantro
½ cup roasted cashews, chopped
ACCOMPANIMENT: basmati rice

Toast mustard and cumin seeds in a dry small heavy skillet over moderate heat, stirring, until cumin seeds are fragrant and a shade darker and mustard seeds pop, about 2 minutes. Cool.

Using a mortar and pestle, pound garlic, jalapeño (to taste), ginger, and 1 teaspoon salt to a paste (or mince and mash with a large heavy knife). Stir in curry powder, coriander, and toasted mustard and cumin seeds.

Heat oil in a 6-quart wide heavy pot over moderately high heat until hot but not smoking. Add onion and cook, stirring, until golden, about 8 minutes. Add curry paste and cook over moderately low heat, stirring, for 2 minutes. Add zucchini and cook, stirring, until it begins to look moist, 3 to 5 minutes. Add coconut milk and 1 teaspoon salt and bring to a boil, then reduce heat and simmer, covered, stirring occasionally, until zucchini is just tender, 10 to 12 minutes.

Sprinkle with cilantro and cashews and serve with rice.

Italian Vegetable Stew
Ciambotta

SERVES 6 TO 8
ACTIVE TIME: 45 MINUTES ■ START TO FINISH: 45 MINUTES

■ As a child, our food editor Gina Miraglia Eriquez regularly enjoyed the hearty vegetarian stew that her grandmother, Mary Pacella, made throughout the fall and winter. Mary learned how to prepare this southern Italian classic from *her* mother, as a way to use up vegetables that had passed their prime, but now Gina's entire family makes it as often as they can, using garden vegetables at their peak. A loaf of crusty bread is all you need to complete the meal. ■

⅓ cup olive oil
2 medium onions, chopped
2 celery ribs, halved lengthwise and cut into ¼-inch-thick slices
3 carrots, halved lengthwise and cut into ¼-inch-thick slices
4 garlic cloves, finely chopped
1¼ pounds eggplant, cut into 1-inch pieces
½ cup water
1 (28-ounce) can whole Italian tomatoes in juice, drained, juice reserved, and chopped
2 red bell peppers, cored, seeded, and cut into ¾-inch pieces
Salt
¾ pound green beans, trimmed and cut into 2-inch pieces
1¼ pounds zucchini, halved lengthwise and cut into ¼-inch-thick slices
¾ pound boiling potatoes (about 2 medium), peeled and cut into 1-inch pieces
½ teaspoon freshly ground black pepper

Heat oil in a 7- to 8-quart heavy pot over moderately high heat until hot but not smoking. Add onions, celery, carrots, and garlic and cook, stirring occasionally, until pale golden, about 10 minutes. Add eggplant and water and cook, covered, until eggplant is slightly soft, stirring occasionally, about 10 minutes.

Stir in tomatoes with juice and bell peppers, reduce heat to low, and cook, uncovered, stirring occasionally, for 15 minutes.

Meanwhile, bring a 3- to 4-quart saucepan of well-salted water (1 tablespoon salt) to a boil. Add green beans and cook until crisp-tender, about 5 minutes. Transfer with a wire skimmer or slotted spoon to a large bowl. Add zucchini to boiling water and cook until crisp-tender, about 5 minutes. Transfer with wire skimmer to bowl with green beans. Add potatoes to boiling water and cook until just tender, about 10 minutes. Drain and add to beans and zucchini.

Add boiled vegetables to tomato mixture and simmer, stirring, until all vegetables are very soft, about 15 minutes. Stir in 1½ teaspoons salt and pepper.

COOK'S NOTE
■ The stew can be made up to 1 week ahead. Cool, uncovered, then refrigerate, covered.

Miso Stew

SERVES 4
ACTIVE TIME: 45 MINUTES ■ START TO FINISH: 45 MINUTES

■ The sea vegetables *arame* and kombu are loaded with beneficial minerals, while quinoa and tofu are rich in protein. White miso contains healthful microorganisms; to preserve them, the Manhattan-based vegan chef Alexandra Jamieson adds the miso after the stew has finished cooking. For help in finding the Asian ingredients, see Sources. ■

¼ cup *arame* (see page 164)
⅔ cup quinoa
1 (1-inch) piece kombu (dried kelp; see page 164)
1 tablespoon extra-virgin olive oil
1 medium onion, cut into ¾-inch pieces
4 garlic cloves, thinly sliced

1 (14- to 16-ounce) block firm tofu, rinsed, drained, cut crosswise into ¼-inch-thick slices, and each slice quartered

1 carrot, halved lengthwise and cut into ¼-inch-thick slices

5 ounces shiitake mushrooms, stems discarded, caps thinly sliced

5–6 tablespoons white miso (also called *shiro miso*), preferably made with white rice

2 cups very thinly sliced bok choy or Napa cabbage

2 teaspoons tamari, or to taste

2 scallions, thinly sliced

1 teaspoon dulse flakes

Cover *arame* with 2 cups water in a small bowl and set aside to soak.

Wash quinoa in 3 changes of cold water in a bowl, draining quinoa in a sieve each time. Combine quinoa, kombu, and 2 cups water in a 2- to 3-quart saucepan. Bring to a simmer, and simmer, uncovered, until quinoa is just tender, about 20 minutes. Drain in a sieve.

About 10 minutes before quinoa is done, heat oil in a 4- to 5-quart heavy pot over moderate heat until hot but not smoking. Add onion and cook, stirring frequently, until beginning to brown, about 5 minutes. Add garlic and cook, stirring, for 30 seconds. Add tofu, carrot, shiitakes, and 5 cups water, bring to a simmer, and simmer, covered, until carrot is just tender, about 5 minutes.

Remove kombu from quinoa and discard. Stir quinoa into stew and remove from heat.

Put miso in a small bowl and add ½ cup stew liquid, whisking until miso is incorporated. Stir mixture into stew. Drain and rinse *arame* and add to stew, along with bok choy and tamari, stirring to combine.

Divide stew among bowls and sprinkle with scallions and dulse flakes.

MISO

Miso is a protein-rich fermented paste of soybeans, grains (rice, barley, wheat, or occasionally millet), salt, and a beneficial mold. Fermentation gives miso its complex flavor, and it imparts body and aroma to everything from soups to sauces. Miso is loosely classified as either light or dark, although there are a whole range of colors as well as flavors and degrees of saltiness in between. In Japan, where miso has a strong regional identity, there are hundreds of types. (Elizabeth Andoh, an expert on Japanese cuisine, likens it to the regional affiliations that Europeans have toward cheese and wines.) White miso (also called *shiro miso*) is pale beige in color. *Shiro miso* made with rice is less sweet than other kinds of *shiro*. Pungent *aka miso* has been fermented longer than *shiro*; it ranges in color from russet to fudge-colored and is almost meaty in flavor.

Miso is available at Asian markets and natural foods stores. It keeps in the refrigerator for several months.

FISH AND SHELLFISH

It would probably be safe to say that at this very moment there is not a single town in America where someone is not sitting down to a fine kettle of fish.

It was not always that way. My mother, like most American women of her generation, was extremely fond of fish, but she did not like to cook it. It frightened her. For one thing, there was the smell: it was, well, fishy. Then there were all those bones to contend with. Mom might deign to bake up a few frozen fish sticks now and then, but when it came to anything more complicated, she was happy to leave it to the professionals. To her, and many American housewives, fish was what you ate when you went out.

But things have changed. In the past twenty years, American fish consumption has gone up by one third, and it continues to rise each year. The many reasons driving this increased interest in fish include the modern obsession with healthy eating, improvements in refrigerated transportation, the almost ubiquitous home grill (salmon, anyone?), and the seductions of sushi. Most important, however, the new abundance of seafood is due to the frighteningly efficient technology of the modern fishing fleet, as well as the advent of fish farming.

Today we face a completely different dilemma from that of our mothers. Our fish is so fresh that odor is not a problem (if your store smells fishy, find a new one). Those who are worried by bones need only purchase fillets. And we now know foolproof methods to ensure that your fish is cooked perfectly every time (see page 341). As a result, we have become so fond of fish that our voracious appetite is endangering the supply. Those of us who love to eat fish are now obliged to pay attention to the sustainability of what we purchase; if we fail to do so, it is entirely possible that there will be no wild fish left for future generations to enjoy.

The good news is that it is increasingly easy to find information on which fish to eat at any given moment (see Sustainable Seafood, page 343). The bad news is that those answers change frequently — with the weather, with the seasons, with where you happen to be — and vigilance is required. These days the honorable fish eater has to ask a lot of questions. "Where was this caught?" is a good place to start. "How was it caught?" is another. Ask what is freshest today — we have given many possible substitutes throughout — and your fishmonger may suggest that one variety is most appealing at the moment. Creating a dialogue with your supplier is important; while you may learn a lot from your fishmonger, he might also learn a lot from you. The more you question your suppliers, the more they will question the fishermen. This is one instance in which the consumer can have a powerful impact on the marketplace.

If you wonder whether that is true, just look at the increasing variety of fish now being sold. Many of the fish in this chapter, like Arctic char, branzino, and tilapia, could not have appeared in earlier cookbooks, because they are new to the market. Others, such as fresh sardines and bluefish, were available but underused.

There is good news on the seafood front as well. Squid, which once hid behind its Italian name, calamari, has come out of the frying pan and into its own. (You won't want to miss the squid in vinegar sauce.) Mussels, which are inexpensive, nutritious, and flavorful, are becoming a new American favorite. And our oyster supply, which had been depleted at the beginning of the twentieth century, is now extremely robust, thanks to responsible aquaculture. Good-quality cultivated clams, too, are now plentiful.

One more thing: bivalves are filter feeders, which means that they are actually beneficial to the waters in which they are raised. So with each one you eat, you strike another blow for clean water. It's just one more reason to make seafood an important part of your diet.

FISH AND SHELLFISH

Broiled Arctic Char with Basil Oil and Tomato

SERVES 4
ACTIVE TIME: 25 MINUTES ■ START TO FINISH: 30 MINUTES

■ Quick, beautiful, and delicious—what more could you ask for? Because the fish is cooked skin side down on the foil-lined broiler pan, you don't have to worry about skinning the fillets—when they're done, just lift them up and leave the skin behind. Any leftover basil oil is good drizzled over pasta or incorporated into a salad dressing. ■

2 cups firmly packed fresh basil leaves
1 large garlic clove
  Salt
¾ cup plus 1 tablespoon extra-virgin olive oil
4 (6-ounce) pieces Arctic char fillet with skin (see Cook's Note)
¼ teaspoon freshly ground black pepper
¾ pound tomatoes (2–3 medium), thinly sliced
1 teaspoon packed light brown sugar
1½ tablespoons red wine vinegar

ACCOMPANIMENT: lemon wedges

Blanch basil in a 3-quart saucepan of boiling water for 15 seconds. Drain in a sieve and immerse, in sieve, in a large bowl of ice and cold water to stop the cooking. Drain and squeeze excess liquid from basil.

Puree basil with garlic, ¼ teaspoon salt, and ¾ cup oil in a blender until smooth. Pour puree into sieve lined with a dampened paper towel set over a bowl. Let drain until only solids remain in sieve, about 5 minutes; discard solids.

Preheat broiler. Line rack of a broiler pan with foil (don't oil foil).

Put fish skin side down on foil-lined pan. Sprinkle with ¼ teaspoon salt and pepper and drizzle with remaining 1 tablespoon oil. Broil fish about 3 inches from heat, without turning, until just cooked through, 6 to 8 minutes for 1-inch-thick fillets.

Meanwhile, arrange tomato slices in centers of four plates and sprinkle with ¼ teaspoon salt (total). Stir together brown sugar and vinegar in a small bowl until sugar is dissolved, then drizzle over tomatoes.

Lift fillets off skin (which will stick to foil) with a large metal spatula and put on top of tomatoes. Spoon some basil oil over fish. Serve with lemon wedges.

COOK'S NOTES
■ You can also use wild salmon.
■ Any leftover basil oil will keep, refrigerated and tightly covered, for up to 5 days.

Arctic Char with Hazelnut Pesto

SERVES 4
ACTIVE TIME: 20 MINUTES ■ START TO FINISH: 40 MINUTES

■ Cilantro and hazelnuts make a delightfully fresh-tasting pesto—the perfect complement to mild Arctic char fillets. And you'll love how quickly it all comes together. ■

1 large garlic clove
1 cup fresh cilantro sprigs
½ cup hazelnuts, toasted (see Tips, page 911)
¼ teaspoon cayenne
  Salt
⅓ cup olive oil
4 (6-ounce) pieces Arctic char fillet with skin (see Cook's Note)

ACCOMPANIMENT: lime wedges

Put a rack in middle of oven and preheat oven to 375°F. Lightly oil a baking dish large enough to hold fish in one layer.

With motor running, drop garlic into a food processor to finely chop. Add cilantro, nuts, cayenne, and ¼ teaspoon salt and blend until cilantro and nuts are coarsely chopped. With motor running, add oil, blending until incorporated. (Sauce should be coarse.)

Arrange fillets skin side down in oiled baking dish. Sprinkle with ¼ teaspoon salt and spoon pesto over fish. Bake until fish is opaque and just cooked through, 12 to 17 minutes, depending on thickness of fillets. Serve with lime wedges.

COOK'S NOTE
■ You can also use wild salmon.

THE SAVVY SHOPPER

Because freshness is critical, patronize a fish market or supermarket seafood department that does a brisk business. It should smell oceanic rather than fishy; a fishy odor means the fish are past their prime or surfaces aren't clean. Whole fish should be well iced and steaks and fillets refrigerated. Don't be shy about asking questions—what the freshest catch is, where it's from, how it was caught, if it is sustainable (see page 343)—and giving feedback.

HOW TO CHOOSE A FISH FILLET OR STEAK It should have the bright, translucent appearance known as "bloom" in the trade; it will say "Choose me, choose me, choose me" to the eye. Dull-looking fish isn't fresh. If you are buying plastic-wrapped fillets or steaks, avoid those with liquid in the bottom of the package. After you've purchased them, take a moment to poke a hole through the wrapper, and if it smells dubious, return it.

HOW TO CHOOSE A WHOLE FISH Whole fish are sold either head on or head off, and the tail may have also been cut off. Look for bright, clear eyes, red gills, shiny, close-fitting scales, and firm yet resilient flesh. Keep in mind, though, that not every indicator holds true for every type of fish. Large fish eyes are more likely to cloud with age, for example, so the eyes of a small-eyed fish, like a salmon, may change very little. A very fresh fish, especially one that is still in rigor mortis (the stiffening that occurs a few hours after death), will have a luminous slime that resembles an aspic that hasn't set, and that is actually the best of all the freshness and quality indicators.

Arctic Char Escabeche

SERVES 8
ACTIVE TIME: 50 MINUTES ■ START TO FINISH: 1 DAY
(INCLUDES MARINATING)

■ Dating from the Middle Ages, *escabeche* is a technique for preserving fish by frying it and then marinating it, traditionally in a sweet-and-sour sauce. Marinating after frying may sound like the wrong order, but the long, slow soak is an excellent a way to layer flavors and textures. This version is adapted from Vecchia Lanterna restaurant in Turin, Italy. Because the fish must marinate for 18 hours and is served at room temperature, it's a great choice for entertaining, especially when paired with sautéed greens and coriander-scented Bulgur Pilaf (page 274). ■

    8 (6-ounce) pieces Arctic char or wild salmon fillet
       with skin
       Salt
    ⅔ cup all-purpose flour
    ¾ cup olive oil
    1 cup chopped onion
    2 garlic cloves, minced
    2 small sprigs fresh sage or ¼ teaspoon dried sage,
       crumbled
    1 Turkish bay leaf or ½ California bay leaf
    ½ cup raisins
    ¼ cup pine nuts, lightly toasted (see Tips, page 911)
    ¾ cup sweet Muscat wine, such as Beaumes-de-Venise
    ¾ cup Chicken Stock (page 153) or store-bought
       reduced-sodium broth
    ⅔ cup distilled white vinegar
    2 tablespoons well-shaken bottled clam juice
    1½ teaspoons sugar
    ¼ teaspoon freshly ground black pepper

Pat fish dry and sprinkle all over with 1 teaspoon salt. Put flour in a shallow dish. Dredge fish in flour, shaking off excess, and transfer to a large baking sheet, arranging in one layer.

Heat oil in a 12-inch heavy skillet over moderately high heat until hot but not smoking. Add 3 pieces fish, skin side up, and fry, turning once, until just cooked through, about 4 minutes for 1-inch-thick fillets. (Reduce heat to moderate if fish begins to brown too quickly.) With a slotted spatula, remove fish from pan, letting excess oil drip back into skillet, and transfer, skin side up, to a shallow glass baking dish large enough to hold all fillets in one layer (or use two dishes). Fry remaining fish in 2 batches in oil remaining in skillet in same manner, and transfer to baking dish.

Pour off all but 3 tablespoons oil from skillet. Add onion, garlic, sage, and bay leaf and cook over moderately low heat, stirring occasionally, until onion is softened, 4 to 5 minutes. Add raisins, pine nuts, wine, stock, vinegar, clam juice, sugar, ½ teaspoon salt, and pepper and bring to a boil over high heat. Reduce heat to moderately low and simmer, stirring occasionally, until mixture is reduced to about 2⅔ cups, 8 to 10 minutes.

Spoon hot vinegar mixture evenly over fish. Cool completely, uncovered.

Cover fish and marinate, refrigerated, turning several times, for 18 to 24 hours.

Discard bay leaf and transfer fish, skin side down, to a serving dish. Spoon marinade evenly over fish and let stand at cool room temperature for 1 hour before serving.

Salmon with Soy Glaze

SERVES 6
ACTIVE TIME: 10 MINUTES ■ START TO FINISH: 30 MINUTES

■ When treated judiciously, a mere three ingredients can equal big taste. Boiling soy sauce and maple syrup until reduced to a rich, sticky glaze and brushing the salmon with the glaze at different stages of cooking permeates the fish with flavor. The dish is a great choice for entertaining. ■

    ¼ cup soy sauce
    ¼ cup pure maple syrup
    1 (2-pound) piece center-cut wild salmon fillet with
       skin

Put a rack in middle of oven and preheat oven to 450°F. Line bottom of a broiler pan with foil, then oil broiler rack.

Bring soy sauce and maple syrup to a boil in a small saucepan over moderate heat, uncovered, and boil until reduced to ⅓ cup, about 5 minutes. Remove from heat.

Place salmon skin side down on broiler rack and pat dry. Reserve 1½ tablespoons glaze in a small bowl. Brush salmon generously with some of remaining glaze. Let stand for 5 minutes, then brush with more glaze.

Roast salmon for 10 minutes. Turn on broiler. Brush salmon with glaze again and broil 4 to 5 inches from heat until just cooked through, 3 to 5 minutes for a 1½-inch-thick fillet.

With two wide metal spatulas, transfer salmon to a platter. Brush with reserved glaze, using a clean brush. Cut into serving pieces.

Pat salmon dry and sprinkle with ½ teaspoon salt. Heat oil in a 12-inch nonstick skillet over moderately high heat until hot but not smoking. Add salmon, skin side up, and cook, turning once, until golden and just cooked through, 5 to 6 minutes for 1¼- to 1½-inch-thick fillets. Transfer to a plate and cover to keep warm.

Add mushrooms to oil in skillet and cook, stirring, until wilted and golden, about 3 minutes. Add garlic, then add bok choy, with water still clinging to leaves, and cook, tossing with tongs, until just tender, about 3 minutes. Remove from heat and add spinach, ginger, sesame oil, soy sauce, and ¼ teaspoon salt, or to taste, tossing to combine.

Serve vegetables topped with salmon and sprinkled with sesame seeds.

Seared Salmon with Sesame Bok Choy and Spinach

SERVES 4
ACTIVE TIME: 45 MINUTES ■ START TO FINISH: 45 MINUTES

■ Wilted spinach, crisp baby bok choy, and meaty shiitake mushrooms make a savory bed for salmon fillets. We love this colorful dish with jasmine rice. ■

    4 (6-ounce) center-cut pieces wild salmon fillet with
        skin
      Salt
    ¼ cup vegetable oil
    ½ pound shiitake mushrooms, stems discarded, caps
        sliced ½ inch thick
    2 garlic cloves, chopped
    1 pound baby bok choy, trimmed, quartered
        lengthwise, rinsed, and drained
    1 (5-ounce) bag baby spinach
    1½ tablespoons finely grated peeled fresh ginger
    1 teaspoon Asian sesame oil
    1 tablespoon soy sauce
    1 tablespoon sesame seeds, toasted (see Tips,
        page 911)

Slow-Roasted Glazed King Salmon

SERVES 8 TO 10
ACTIVE TIME: 30 MINUTES ■ START TO FINISH: 2¼ HOURS

■ Slow-roasting at a very low temperature results in extremely tender salmon. Here the richness of the fish is accented by a salty-sweet red wine sauce, which thickens into a syrupy glaze during cooking. Repeated basting produces a lustrous look. We prefer this made with wild king salmon, which has a complex flavor and unctuous texture. ■

    1 (4-inch) piece fresh ginger, peeled
    1 cup soy sauce
    2 cups dry red wine
    1⅓ cups mirin (Japanese sweet rice wine)
    ¼ cup packed dark brown sugar
    2 teaspoons fresh lime juice
    1 tablespoon olive oil
    1 (4½-pound) wild king salmon fillet with skin (about
        1½ inches at thickest point)
ACCOMPANIMENT: lime wedges

Put a rack in middle of oven and preheat oven to 225°F.

Finely grate ginger into a fine-mesh sieve. Set sieve

over a bowl and press on ginger to extract 2 teaspoons juice. Transfer ginger juice to a 3- to 3½-quart heavy saucepan, add soy sauce, wine, mirin, and brown sugar, and bring to a simmer. Reduce heat and simmer briskly, stirring occasionally, until glaze is syrupy and reduced to about 1 cup, 45 to 55 minutes.

Transfer glaze to a metal bowl and quick-chill, by setting bowl in a larger bowl of ice water and stirring occasionally for 5 minutes. Stir in lime juice. Transfer ½ cup glaze to a small bowl and reserve for brushing after roasting.

Line a 17-by-12-inch heavy baking sheet with foil and coat foil with oil.

Place salmon, skin side down, diagonally in pan. Spoon about 2 tablespoons remaining glaze over salmon, spreading it evenly with back of spoon. Let stand for 5 minutes, then spread another 2 tablespoons glaze over salmon.

Roast for 15 minutes. Remove from oven and glaze again (use a clean spoon each time to avoid cross-contamination), then roast for 10 minutes more. Repeat glazing and continue to roast until fish is just cooked through (opaque), 10 to 20 minutes more (35 to 45 minutes total, depending on thickness of fish; check frequently after 35 minutes).

With two wide metal spatulas, transfer salmon to a platter and coat with a final layer of reserved glaze (about 2 tablespoons), using a clean spoon. Serve with lime wedges and with remaining glaze on the side if desired.

COOK'S NOTE

■ The glaze can be made up to 2 days ahead and refrigerated, covered. Bring to room temperature before using.

Salmon Steaks with Red Wine Butter

SERVES 4
ACTIVE TIME: 35 MINUTES ■ START TO FINISH: 35 MINUTES

■ Salmon steaks are not only less expensive than fillets but more succulent, and these are made even more so by a rich, brightly flavored wine butter. The bone that

CHECKING FOR DONENESS

Judging the degree of doneness in fish is, like most everything in life, helped along by experience. Although the general rule for cooking fish is to measure the thickness and calculate 10 minutes per inch, we think that is too long. We start checking after 7 minutes, because there are so many factors to take into account—the temperature and density of the raw fish, for instance, and the type of pan used. Always check the thickest part of a piece of fish (which, of course, takes the longest to cook). Simply cut into a fillet or steak and peek inside: the flesh should have turned from translucent to opaque. But if you're serving a whole fish—such as the roasted striped bass on page 357—you don't want to mar its appearance by digging around in the midsection. We suggest inserting a knife or metal spatula horizontally into the top of the back and checking for

opaqueness that way. You want to take the fish out of the pan just when it's becoming opaque, because its residual heat will continue to cook the flesh until it is perfect—not undercooked and almost slithery, as is fashionable in many restaurants these days, and not overcooked and dry. If it flakes easily to the touch, you've gone too far, and odds are it's going to taste cottony—or it would if you didn't have the fish's lovely pan juices to save the day.

Gourmet food editor and stylist Paul Grimes likes to bone salmon steaks and skewer the halves together, as cooks do in France. Use a boning knife to cut along both sides of the large bone in the center of each steak, working your way down the rather odd-looking "flaps" (1). You will end up with what are essentially 2 narrow pieces of fillet. Flip one half over so that they look like yin and yang (2). Then dovetail the 2 pieces and secure them with a skewer (3). "This way," Grimes says, "they are easy to turn with tongs, hold together well, cook evenly, and look beautiful."

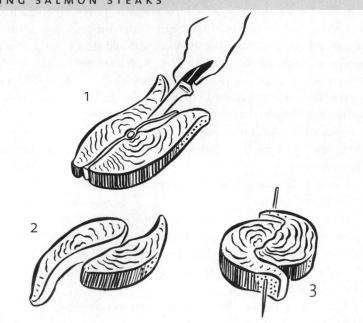

runs through the center can be a drawback for diners. However, if you remove it and then skewer the halves of the steaks together, you end up with a dish that's both eye-catching and easy to eat. Whether you choose to bone them or not, these steaks will create a stir at the table. If you have any leftover red wine butter, use it on beef, lamb chops, chicken, or mushrooms. ∎

- 1 cup full-bodied dry red wine, such as
Côtes du Rhône
- ½ cup fresh orange juice (from about 1½ oranges; grate zest first)
- ¼ cup balsamic vinegar
- ⅓ cup finely chopped shallots
- 1 teaspoon tomato paste
- 1 Turkish bay leaf or ½ California bay leaf
- 1 teaspoon finely grated orange zest
- 1 stick (8 tablespoons) unsalted butter, softened
Salt and freshly ground black pepper
- 4 (8-ounce) wild salmon steaks, boned and skewered if desired (see above)
- 2 tablespoons olive oil

Combine wine, juice, vinegar, shallots, tomato paste, and bay leaf in a 1- to 2-quart heavy sauce-pan, bring to a boil over moderately high heat, and boil until mixture is thick and jamlike and reduced to about ⅓ cup, about 20 minutes.

Discard bay leaf and transfer wine mixture to a small bowl set in a bowl of ice and cold water. Stir until cold to the touch, about 5 minutes. Remove from ice water and stir in zest, butter, ¼ teaspoon salt, and ⅛ teaspoon pepper with a rubber spatula until incorporated.

Preheat broiler. Line rack of a broiler pan with foil.

Pat fish dry, brush all over with oil, and sprinkle with ¾ teaspoon salt and ⅛ teaspoon pepper. Broil fish about 5 inches from heat, turning once, until just cooked through, 8 to 10 minutes for 1-inch-thick steaks.

Top each steak with 1 to 2 tablespoons red wine butter.

COOK'S NOTES

- You can bone the salmon steaks up to 6 hours ahead and refrigerate them, covered.
- Leftover red wine butter can be refrigerated, covered, for up to 3 days or frozen for up to 2 weeks.

SUSTAINABLE SEAFOOD
What Most Other Cookbooks Don't Tell You

You're sitting at a sushi bar savoring a piece of beautifully marbled *chu-toro,* bluefin-tuna belly. Or you page through a fancy menu, avoiding the veal for ethical reasons and choosing instead swordfish or Atlantic halibut. Or perhaps you're in the doctor's office, thumbing through an article on the benefits of fish's omega-3 fatty acids. But you may not realize that many of the fish we love are at risk of vanishing.

Laser-accurate fish-finding technology, indiscriminate harvest methods by factory trawlers, and failed federal management of fisheries in some regions are just a few of the factors that have resulted in overfishing and the collapse of once-abundant fish stocks. Pollution, loss of spawning habitats, and climate change compound the problem. Bluefin tuna, swordfish, Chilean sea bass, Atlantic halibut, Atlantic cod, Atlantic flounder, Gulf red snapper, grouper, and several species of Pacific rockfish are some of the species in serious trouble or even in danger of extinction. And fish farming—especially of carnivorous species such as salmon—has generated a set of environmental problems all its own. (A farmed salmon eats several times its weight in commercial feed made from oceangoing smaller fish.) Fish manure and dead fish have created pollution, and smaller wild fish such as herring and anchoveta have been overharvested for fishmeal. The antibiotics and other drugs used to treat farmed fish end up in both their meat and that of wild fish caught nearby. Escaped penned fish not only compete with wild fish for food sources and spawning grounds but crossbreed with them, passing along traits such as small fins and chubby bodies that don't benefit fish in the wild.

What can a conscientious consumer do? Aside from swearing off fish altogether, you can become informed so that you can make wise decisions and use your food dollars to make a difference. For starters, whether at a restaurant or fish market, ask questions about the fish you usually take for granted. Is it from a sustainable fishery? (That is, from a wild population that is abundant and soundly managed?) Was it caught by a method that does minimal damage to other sea life and habitat? If it's farmed, was it farmed responsibly?

The **Monterey Bay Aquarium Seafood Watch** program (www.mbayaq.org/cr/seafoodwatch.asp) has taken the lead in encouraging the consumption of sustainable seafood. Both wild and farmed fish and shellfish are grouped into green (sustainable; recommended), yellow (species with problems; eat infrequently), and red (species in trouble; avoid) categories. The aquarium publishes handy color-coded wallet-sized guides (which can be downloaded) for each region of the country. The **Blue Ocean Institute** (www.blueocean.org) has guides as well. Many restaurant chefs and fish markets are members of the **Seafood Choices Alliance** (www.seafoodchoices.com), which issues a "Sourcing Seafood" directory of sustainable seafood suppliers.

Pan-Seared Tilapia with Chile Lime Butter

SERVES 6
ACTIVE TIME: 25 MINUTES ■ START TO FINISH: 25 MINUTES

■ We like tilapia for a midweek dinner because it's sustainable, affordable, and easy to find, but it's bland. A dab of citrusy, spicy butter wakes it up. ■

FOR CHILE LIME BUTTER
- ½ stick (4 tablespoons) unsalted butter, softened
- 1 tablespoon finely chopped shallot
- 1 teaspoon finely grated lime zest
- 2 teaspoons fresh lime juice
- 1 teaspoon minced fresh hot chile, such as Thai or serrano, preferably red, including seeds
- ½ teapoon salt

FOR FISH
- 6 (5- to 6-ounce) pieces skinless tilapia fillet or striped bass fillet with skin (see Cook's Note)
- ½ teaspoon salt
- 2 tablespoons vegetable oil

MAKE THE CHILE LIME BUTTER: Stir together all ingredients in a bowl.

PREPARE THE FISH: If using striped bass, score skin in 3 or 4 places with a thin sharp knife to prevent fish from curling (do not cut through flesh). Pat fish dry and sprinkle with salt. Heat 1 tablespoon oil in a 12-inch nonstick skillet over moderately high heat until just smoking. Add 3 pieces fish, skin side up, and cook, turning once with a spatula, until golden and just cooked through, 4 to 5 minutes. Transfer to a plate and cover loosely to keep warm. Cook remaining fish in remaining tablespoon oil in same manner.

Top each piece of fish with a dollop of chile lime butter.

COOK'S NOTES
- You can also use catfish or any other white fish fillet.
- The chile lime butter can be made up to 1 day ahead and refrigerated, covered. Bring to room temperature before using.

Tilapia with Prosciutto and Sage

SERVES 4
ACTIVE TIME: 20 MINUTES ■ START TO FINISH: 20 MINUTES

■ Wrapping thin slices of prosciutto around tilapia not only keeps the fish moist, it punches up the mild flavor. Prosciutto is a natural with fresh sage, which gets tucked in among the slices. Separating the two sides of the fillets helps to keep the thinner part from overcooking. ■

- 4 (8-ounce) pieces skinless tilapia fillet
  Freshly ground black pepper
- 8 thin slices (not paper-thin) prosciutto (6 ounces total)
- 12 fresh sage leaves, stems discarded
- 4 teaspoons olive oil

Cut fillets lengthwise to separate smaller and larger sides. Pat dry and season with pepper to taste. Wrap each piece of fillet crosswise in a slice of prosciutto, tucking 1 or 2 sage leaves in between prosciutto and fillet (use 1 leaf for smaller pieces, 2 for larger pieces) and leaving ends of fillet exposed if necessary.

Heat 2 teaspoons oil in a 12-inch heavy nonstick skillet over moderately high heat until hot but not smoking. Cook larger pieces of fish for 4 minutes. Turn and cook until just cooked through, about 3 minutes more. Transfer to a platter and cover loosely with foil to keep warm. Wipe skillet clean and heat remaining 2 teaspoons oil, then cook smaller pieces of fish, turning once, until just cooked through, about 4 minutes.

Catfish with Green Olives

SERVES 4
ACTIVE TIME: 15 MINUTES ■ START TO FINISH: 25 MINUTES

■ Pimiento-stuffed green olives make a sprightly relish for catfish. We turn to this dish often on weeknights because it can be made in less than 30 minutes. Covering the fish with a round of parchment as it cooks is a simple way to seal in the moisture. ▪

1 cup pimiento-stuffed green olives, rinsed, drained, and chopped
2 tablespoons extra-virgin olive oil
1 teaspoon finely grated lemon zest
3 tablespoons chopped fresh flat-leaf parsley
4 (6-ounce) catfish fillets (see Cook's Note)
  Salt and freshly ground black pepper

ACCOMPANIMENT: lemon wedges

Stir together olives, oil, zest, and 2 tablespoons parsley in a bowl.

Oil a 12-inch nonstick skillet with a tight-fitting lid. Season catfish with salt and pepper and arrange skinned (smooth) side down in skillet, tucking thinner ends of each fillet under.

Mound olive mixture on top of fillets. Put a round of parchment or wax paper on top of mixture and cover skillet. Cook catfish over moderate heat until just cooked through, 8 to 10 minutes. Sprinkle with remaining tablespoon parsley and serve with lemon wedges.

COOK'S NOTE

▪ You can also use tilapia, striped bass, Pacific cod, or haddock.

Spicy Catfish Tenders with Cajun Tartar Sauce

SERVES 2 AS A MAIN COURSE, 4 AS A FIRST COURSE
ACTIVE TIME: 20 MINUTES ▪ START TO FINISH: 30 MINUTES

▪ A mix of yellow cornmeal and flour ensures a light, crunchy coating for fried catfish strips, which are wonderful dipped in homemade tartar sauce enlivened with a dash of Cajun seasoning. We adapted these tenders from ones served at Buddy Guy's Legends, a blues club in Chicago that prepares its own Cajun spice blend. Packaged Cajun seasoning, available in supermarkets, usually contains cayenne or chile powder, black pepper, and onion and garlic powders, plus a myriad of dried herbs. ▪

FOR FISH
1 large egg
2 tablespoons hot sauce
1¼ pounds catfish fillets, cut diagonally into
  ½-inch-wide strips (see Cook's Note)
  About 8 cups vegetable oil for deep-frying
½ cup all-purpose flour
½ cup yellow cornmeal (not coarse)
1 teaspoon salt
1 tablespoon Cajun seasoning

FOR TARTAR SAUCE
1 cup mayonnaise
½ cup sweet pickle relish
2 tablespoons capers, rinsed, drained, and chopped
1 tablespoon fresh lemon juice
1 tablespoon prepared horseradish
2 teaspoons hot sauce
2 teaspoons Cajun seasoning

ACCOMPANIMENT: lemon wedges
SPECIAL EQUIPMENT: a deep-fat thermometer

PREPARE THE FISH: Whisk together egg and hot sauce in a wide shallow dish. Stir in fish strips and let stand at room temperature for at least 10 minutes, or up to 30 minutes.

MEANWHILE, MAKE THE TARTAR SAUCE: Stir together all ingredients in a bowl. Refrigerate, covered, until ready to serve.

FRY THE FISH: Heat 2 inches oil in a 4- to 5-quart heavy pot over moderate heat until thermometer registers 350°F. Meanwhile, stir together flour, cornmeal, salt, and Cajun seasoning in a wide shallow dish.

Drain fish well in a colander. Working quickly, dredge one quarter of fish in flour mixture, shaking off excess, and transfer to hot oil. Fry, stirring occasionally with a slotted spoon, until golden and just cooked through, 1½ to 2 minutes. Transfer with slotted spoon to paper towels to drain. Repeat procedure with remaining fish strips in 3 batches. (Return oil to 350°F between batches.)

Serve fish tenders hot, with tartar sauce and lemon wedges.

COOK'S NOTES

▪ You can also use tilapia or lake whitefish.
▪ The tartar sauce can be made up to 2 days ahead.

Steamed Bass with Ginger and Scallions

SERVES 6
ACTIVE TIME: 15 MINUTES ■ START TO FINISH: 35 MINUTES

■ One of our favorite ways of cooking fish, this Chinese preparation contrasts the mildness of the steamed bass with the sharpness of soy and frizzled ginger. It's delicate yet satisfying. Make sure to choose a serving dish that can also hold the cooking juices—they are delicious spooned over rice. ■

6 (6-ounce) pieces striped bass or black sea bass fillet, preferably with skin (see Cook's Note)
1 large bunch scallions, cut into very thin matchsticks
3 tablespoons soy sauce
¼ teaspoon sugar
2 tablespoons peanut or vegetable oil
1 (1-inch) piece fresh ginger, peeled and cut into very thin matchsticks

GARNISH: fresh cilantro leaves
ACCOMPANIMENT: white rice
SPECIAL EQUIPMENT: a well-seasoned 14-inch flat-bottomed wok with a lid (see Cook's Note); a collapsible steamer rack or a 10-inch round metal rack; a 10-inch deep-dish glass pie plate

Fill wok about one third full of water and place steamer rack in wok (water should be just below bottom of steamer rack). Bring to a boil, covered.

Meanwhile, pat fish dry and arrange skin side down in pie plate. Sprinkle with half of scallions. Stir together soy sauce and sugar until sugar is dissolved, then drizzle evenly over fillets. Carefully transfer plate with fish to rack in wok, cover tightly, and steam over moderately high heat until fish is just cooked through, 10 to 15 minutes, depending on thickness.

Carefully remove plate from wok and sprinkle fish with remaining scallions. Drain water from wok and dry wok, then heat over high heat until a drop of water evaporates on contact. Drizzle oil around sides of wok, tilting wok to coat sides, and heat until smoking. Add ginger and stir-fry until just pale golden, about 15 seconds, then pour ginger mixture over fish.

Sprinkle fish with cilantro and spoon sauce in bottom of pie plate over fish. Serve immediately, with rice.

COOK'S NOTES

■ You can also use barramundi.
■ Fish fillets vary in size and thickness. You may need to fold thinner fillets in half, skin sides in, to fit into the pie plate; these will cook more quickly than thicker fillets.
■ You can substitute a large pot with a steamer rack or a pasta insert for the wok and steamer rack.

Striped Bass in Agrodolce

SERVES 8
ACTIVE TIME: 40 MINUTES ■ START TO FINISH: 2 HOURS

■ Agrodolce ("agro-*dol*-chay"), an Italian sweet-and-sour sauce, combines wine, vinegar, and sugar. Although it may seem odd to call for red wine and white balsamic vinegar in the same dish, the pale vinegar dilutes the wine, preventing the sauce from turning an unappetizing dark color. Folding the fillets before cooking is a convenient way to fit them in the pan. ■

½ cup olive oil
1½ pounds shallots (about 10 large or 15 medium), trimmed, leaving root end intact, and quartered lengthwise (halved if small)
1½ cups dry red wine
1 cup white balsamic vinegar
⅔ cup water
⅓ cup sugar
¼ cup golden raisins
   Salt and freshly ground black pepper
2 Turkish bay leaves or 1 California bay leaf
8 (6- to 7-ounce) skinless pieces striped bass fillet (see Cook's Note)

GARNISH: chopped fresh flat-leaf parsley

Heat ¼ cup oil in a 12- to 13-inch heavy skillet over moderately high heat until hot but not smoking. Add shallots and cook, stirring occasionally, until browned and just tender, about 8 minutes.

Remove pan from heat and add wine, vinegar, water, sugar, raisins, 1¼ teaspoons salt, ¼ teaspoon pepper, and bay leaves. Return to heat, bring to a simmer, and simmer briskly, stirring occasionally, until shallots are very tender and sauce is thick and syrupy, 40 to 45 minutes. (If liquid reduces before shallots are tender, add ½ cup water and continue to simmer.)

About 10 minutes before sauce is ready, pat fish dry and sprinkle with ½ teaspoon salt and ¼ teaspoon pepper. Fold fillets in half, skinned side out.

Heat 2 tablespoons oil in 12-inch skillet over moderately high heat until hot but not smoking. Add 4 folded fillets and cook, turning once, until deep golden, 4 to 6 minutes. Transfer fish (still folded) to sauce (in skillet). Carefully wipe out 12-inch skillet and cook remaining 4 fillets in remaining 2 tablespoons oil in same manner; transfer to sauce.

Cook fish in sauce, partially covered, over moderate heat until fish is just cooked through, 2 to 3 minutes. Transfer to plates and sprinkle with parsley.

COOK'S NOTES
- You can also use catfish or tilapia.
- The sauce can be made up to 1 day ahead. Cool, uncovered, then refrigerate, covered. Reheat over moderate heat before cooking the fish.

Sea Bass with Porcini Mushroom Sauce

SERVES 4
ACTIVE TIME: 45 MINUTES ■ START TO FINISH: 1¼ HOURS

■ In this recipe, we've borrowed one of New York City chef Daniel Boulud's methods for giving body to a light sauce, stirring translucent pearls of tapioca into the mushroom broth. A tiny amount of curry powder adds a Midas touch to the sea bass's flour coating and makes the mushrooms' flavor shine. Once the broth is made (which can be done 2 days in advance), the dish is quick to prepare. ■

FOR BROTH
- 1 tablespoon olive oil
- 1¼ cups chopped leeks (white and pale green parts only), washed well and patted dry
- 1 cup chopped onion
- ¾ cup chopped carrots
- 1 large garlic clove, smashed and peeled
- ⅓ cup dry white wine
- 3½ cups water
- 2 teaspoons soy sauce
- 2 fresh flat-leaf parsley sprigs
- 2 fresh thyme sprigs
- 1 Turkish bay leaf or ½ California bay leaf
- 1½ tablespoons crumbled (or torn into small pieces) dried porcini mushrooms
- 1½ tablespoons quick-cooking tapioca
- Salt and freshly ground black pepper

FOR MUSHROOMS
- 1 tablespoon unsalted butter
- 1 tablespoon olive oil
- ¾ pound mixed mushrooms, such as oyster and chanterelle, trimmed and halved lengthwise (quartered if large)
- ½ teaspoon salt
- ¼ teaspoon freshly ground black pepper
- 2 celery ribs, thinly sliced diagonally

FOR FISH
- 3 tablespoons all-purpose flour
- ½ teaspoon curry powder, preferably Madras
- 4 (5- to 6-ounce) pieces sea bass fillet with skin (see Cook's Note)
- 1 teaspoon salt
- ¼ teaspoon freshly ground black pepper
- 3 tablespoons unsalted butter

MAKE THE BROTH: Heat oil in a 3- to 4-quart heavy saucepan over moderately high heat until hot but not smoking. Add leeks, onion, carrots, and garlic and cook, stirring frequently, until vegetables are soft and well browned, about 10 minutes.

Stir in wine and deglaze by boiling, scraping up any brown bits, for 1 minute. Add water, soy sauce, parsley and thyme sprigs, bay leaf, and porcini, bring to a simmer, and simmer, uncovered, for 20 minutes.

Pour broth through a fine-mesh sieve into a glass measure, lightly pressing on solids; discard solids.

Broth should be reduced to about 1½ cups. If you have slightly more, boil in a small saucepan for a few minutes to reduce; if you have less, add water to make 1½ cups and transfer to saucepan.

FINISH THE SAUCE: Bring broth to a simmer. Remove from heat and stir in tapioca. Let stand, covered, stirring occasionally, for 15 minutes.

MEANWHILE, COOK THE MUSHROOMS: Heat butter and oil in a 10-inch heavy skillet until hot but not smoking. Add mushrooms, salt, and pepper and cook, stirring, until mushrooms are just tender and golden brown, about 4 minutes. Add celery and cook, stirring, until bright green and crisp-tender, about 2 minutes. Remove from heat and cover with foil to keep warm.

COOK THE FISH: Stir together flour and curry powder in a wide shallow bowl. Pat fish dry and sprinkle with salt and pepper, then dredge in flour mixture, shaking off excess, and transfer to a plate.

Heat 1½ tablespoons butter in a 12-inch heavy skillet over moderately high heat until foam subsides. Add 2 fillets, skin side down, and cook, turning once, until golden brown and just cooked through, 5 to 7 minutes, depending on thickness of fish. Transfer to a plate and cover to keep warm. Wipe out skillet and cook remaining 2 fillets in remaining 1½ tablespoons butter in same manner.

Reheat sauce and season with salt and pepper. Serve fish with mushrooms and sauce.

COOK'S NOTES

- You can also use haddock or Pacific halibut.
- The broth can be made up to 2 days ahead. Cool, uncovered, then refrigerate, covered.

Black Sea Bass with Ginger

SERVES 4
ACTIVE TIME: 15 MINUTES ■ START TO FINISH: 30 MINUTES

■ Darina Allen, head of the renowned Ballymaloe Cooking School in County Cork, Ireland, is famous for her elegant yet approachable recipes. This lush dish is a case in point. There is just enough ginger to flavor the sauce without overwhelming the sea bass, and the traditionally Asian ingredient works well with the French triumvirate of cream, butter, and shallots. This pairs nicely with steamed asparagus. ■

1 (¾-inch-long) piece fresh ginger, peeled
1 tablespoon minced shallot
4 (6- to 7-ounce) pieces skinless black sea bass fillet (½ inch thick; see Cook's Note)
½ teaspoon salt
¼ teaspoon freshly ground white pepper
1 cup Fish Stock (page 154)
⅓ cup heavy cream
2 tablespoons cold unsalted butter, cut into ½-inch pieces
1 teaspoon fresh lemon juice, or to taste

Put a rack in middle of oven and preheat oven to 400°F. Butter a baking dish large enough to hold fish in one layer.

Cut ginger lengthwise into 1/16-inch-thick slices, then cut slices lengthwise into julienne strips.

Sprinkle shallot and ginger into baking dish, arrange fish in dish, and sprinkle with salt and white pepper. Pour stock over fish and put a sheet of buttered wax paper (buttered side down) on top of fish.

Bake fish until opaque and just cooked through, 5 to 10 minutes, depending on thickness. Transfer fish with a slotted spatula to a platter and cover to keep warm.

Pour cooking liquid into a 2- to 3-quart heavy saucepan, bring to a boil, and boil until reduced by half, 5 to 8 minutes. Add cream and boil until thick enough to coat back of a spoon, 1 to 2 minutes. Reduce heat to low and whisk in butter 1 piece at a time, adding each new piece before the previous one has completely melted and occasionally lifting pan from heat to cool mixture. (Do not allow sauce to get too hot, or it will separate.) Remove pan from heat and whisk in lemon juice.

Blot up any liquid that has accumulated on platter with paper towels and pour sauce over fish.

COOK'S NOTE

- You can also use tilapia, barramundi, or Pacific halibut.

Sea Bass with Curried Cucumber-Tomato Water and Tomato Herb Salad

SERVES 6
ACTIVE TIME: 35 MINUTES ■ START TO FINISH: 1¼ HOURS

■ This dish tops mild sea bass with a colorful salad of tomatoes, herbs, and lemon. Tomato water—a distillation of tomatoes and cucumber with a smidgen of curry powder—is the breakout star. The pale, unassuming liquid surprises with its pure tomato flavor. A mix of heirloom tomatoes in all different colors makes an especially striking salad. ■

FOR CUCUMBER-TOMATO WATER

1½ cups chopped peeled cucumber
¾ cup chopped tomato
¼ teaspoon curry powder, preferably Madras
¼ teaspoon salt

FOR TOMATO HERB SALAD

1 lemon
1 pound assorted small tomatoes (see headnote), halved (quartered if large)
¼ cup loosely packed fresh flat-leaf parsley leaves
2 tablespoons thinly sliced fresh basil leaves
1 tablespoon extra-virgin olive oil
2 teaspoons finely chopped fresh chives
1 teaspoon finely chopped fresh lemon balm (optional)
¼ teaspoon freshly ground black pepper
¼–½ teaspoon sugar (to taste)
¼ teaspoon salt

FOR FISH

6 (5- to 7-ounce) pieces skinless mild white-fleshed fish fillet, such as sea bass, Pacific halibut, or haddock
1 tablespoon extra-virgin olive oil
Salt and freshly ground black pepper

MAKE THE CUCUMBER-TOMATO WATER: Puree cucumber and tomato with curry powder and salt in a blender until smooth, about 30 seconds.

Line a fine-mesh sieve with a dampened paper towel and set over a large glass measure. Transfer cucumber mixture to sieve and let drain until liquid measures ⅔ cup, about 20 minutes.

If liquid measures less than ⅔ cup after draining, gently squeeze paper towel over sieve until liquid totals ⅔ cup. Discard solids and transfer liquid to a 2- to 3-quart saucepan. Bring to a boil and boil until reduced to about ⅓ cup. Cool to room temperature.

MAKE THE TOMATO HERB SALAD: Cut off top and bottom of lemon to expose fruit. Stand lemon on a cutting board and remove peel, including all white pith, by cutting it off in vertical strips with a sharp paring knife. Working over a bowl, cut segments free from membranes, letting segments fall into bowl. Chop segments; reserve juice in bowl.

Gently toss lemon segments and reserved juice with remaining salad ingredients in a large bowl. Stir in cooled cucumber-tomato water.

BAKE THE FISH: Put a rack in middle of oven and preheat oven to 500°F. Lightly oil a baking sheet large enough to hold fillets in one layer.

Rinse fish and pat dry. Brush fillets all over with oil and season with salt and pepper. Arrange on oiled baking sheet and bake until just cooked through, 4 to 8 minutes, depending on thickness of fish.

Serve tomato herb salad on top of fish.

COOK'S NOTE

■ The cucumber-tomato water can be made up to 1 day ahead and refrigerated, covered.

Sautéed Cod with Lentils

SERVES 4
ACTIVE TIME: 45 MINUTES ■ START TO FINISH: 45 MINUTES

■ This virtual one-dish meal is satisfying without being at all rich or fatty—slow-cooked golden onions are the savory secret. We recommend using French lentils for this recipe because they become tender without falling apart. ■

FOR LENTILS

- 1 cup small French green lentils, picked over and rinsed
- 2 tablespoons unsalted butter
- 1 cup finely chopped onion
- 2 large garlic cloves, chopped
- ¾ teaspoon salt
- 3 tablespoons chopped fresh flat-leaf parsley
- 1 tablespoon fresh lemon juice
- ¼ teaspoon freshly ground black pepper
- 1 tablespoon extra-virgin olive oil

FOR FISH

- 4 (6-ounce) pieces Pacific cod, Pacific halibut, or haddock fillet
- ½ teaspoon salt
- ⅛ teaspoon freshly ground black pepper
- 1 tablespoon unsalted butter
- 1 tablespoon olive oil

GARNISH: extra-virgin olive oil (optional); chopped fresh flat-leaf parsley; lemon wedges

COOK THE LENTILS: Cover lentils with cold water by 1½ inches in a 2-quart saucepan and bring to a boil. Reduce heat and simmer, uncovered, until lentils are just tender but not falling apart, 12 to 25 minutes. Drain in a sieve set over a bowl and reserve ½ cup cooking liquid.

Meanwhile, melt butter in a 2- to 3-quart heavy saucepan over moderately low heat. Stir in onion, garlic, and salt and cook, covered, stirring occasionally, until onion is pale golden, about 10 minutes. Remove lid and cook, uncovered, stirring occasionally, until onion is golden, 5 to 10 minutes more.

MEANWHILE, COOK THE FISH: Pat fish dry and sprinkle with salt and pepper. Heat butter and oil in a 10- to 12-inch nonstick skillet over moderately high heat until foam subsides. Add fish and cook, turning once, until browned and just cooked through, 6 to 8 minutes for ¾- to 1-inch-thick fillets.

MEANWHILE, FINISH THE LENTILS: Stir lentils into onion, along with enough reserved cooking liquid to moisten, and heat through. Just before serving, stir in parsley, lemon juice, pepper, and oil.

Serve fish, drizzled with olive oil if desired and sprinkled with parsley, with lentils and lemon wedges.

Pan-Seared Cod with Creamy Fennel Ragout

SERVES 4
ACTIVE TIME: 30 MINUTES ■ START TO FINISH: 45 MINUTES

■ Think of this dish as a deconstructed fish chowder, with golden pieces of seared cod sitting atop a creamy ragout seasoned with bacon and fennel. For all its sophisticated taste, the dish is made with supermarket ingredients. ■

- 4 bacon slices, cut crosswise into ¼-inch-wide strips
- 3 tablespoons olive oil
- 2 large fennel bulbs (2 pounds total), stalks discarded (reserve fronds for garnish), bulbs cut into 1-inch wedges
- Salt and freshly ground black pepper
- 1¾ cups Chicken Stock (page 153) or store-bought reduced-sodium broth
- ⅔ cup heavy cream
- ¼ cup chopped drained sun-dried tomatoes (packed in oil)
- 2 garlic cloves, finely chopped
- 4 (6- to 7-ounce) pieces Pacific cod, haddock, or Pacific halibut fillet
- 1 tablespoon Dijon mustard

GARNISH: chopped fennel fronds

Cook bacon in a 10- to 12-inch heavy skillet over moderate heat, stirring occasionally, until slightly crisp, 6 to 8 minutes. Transfer with a slotted spoon to a bowl, then pour off and discard all but 2 tablespoons fat from pan.

Add 1 tablespoon oil to skillet, then add fennel, a scant ¼ teaspoon salt, and ⅛ teaspoon pepper. Cook over moderate heat, turning occasionally, until fennel is lightly browned, 6 to 8 minutes. Add stock, cream, sun-dried tomatoes, and garlic, reduce heat to moderately low, and cook, partially covered, stirring occasionally, until fennel is tender and cream is slightly thickened, about 20 minutes.

About 10 minutes before fennel is done, pat fish dry and sprinkle with ¼ teaspoon salt and ⅛ teaspoon pepper. Heat remaining 2 tablespoons oil in a 12-inch nonstick skillet over moderately high heat until hot but not smoking. Add fish and cook, turning once, until just cooked through, about 6 minutes for 1-inch-thick fillets.

Stir mustard and bacon into fennel ragout and season with salt and pepper. Serve fish over fennel ragout, sprinkled with chopped fennel fronds.

COOK'S NOTE

■ The fennel ragout can be made up to 1 day ahead. Cool, uncovered, then refrigerate, covered. Reheat over low heat, thinning with water if necessary.

ATLANTIC AND PACIFIC COD

Although Atlantic cod (*Gadus morhua*) and Pacific cod (*Gadus macrocephalus*) are two separate species, even fish people would be hard-pressed to tell them apart. It's fair to say that there are no dramatic differences in flavor and texture, but Atlantic cod does have a slightly firmer flake, while Pacific cod has more moisture. However, in terms of sustainability—another issue that many cooks and eaters are concerned about—there are some appreciable differences. First, the good news: Pacific cod stocks are in pretty decent shape. The Monterey Bay Aquarium's Seafood Watch Program (www.mbayaq.org/cr/seafoodwatch.asp) rates hook-and-line-caught Pacific cod a "Best Choice" and trawl-caught Pacific cod a "Good Choice." Incidentally, most Pacific cod are taken in Alaskan waters, and because of the distance to market, most of that catch is frozen at sea, ensuring good quality.

Atlantic cod fisheries have collapsed and are currently on Monterey Bay's "Avoid" list. Atlantic cod from Iceland's waters are in better shape; they're considered a "Good Choice" if hook-and-line caught. For more information about seafood sustainability in general, see page 343.

Fresh Cod Cakes

SERVES 4
ACTIVE TIME: 30 MINUTES ■ START TO FINISH: 40 MINUTES

■ Traditional cod cakes are made with dried salt cod and potatoes, but we wanted something lighter and faster. This delicate version uses fresh cod and replaces the potatoes with a mix of celery, scallions, and parsley. ■

5 slices firm white sandwich bread
1 large celery rib, cut into 2-inch pieces
2 scallions, cut into 2-inch pieces
¼ cup loosely packed fresh flat-leaf parsley
1 pound Pacific cod or haddock fillet, coarsely chopped
1 large egg, lightly beaten
  Salt and freshly ground black pepper
3 tablespoons vegetable oil

ACCOMPANIMENT: lemon wedges and/or tartar sauce

Tear bread into pieces and pulse to fine crumbs in a food processor. Transfer a scant cup of crumbs to a large bowl for fish cakes and reserve remaining 1½ cups in a shallow bowl for coating.

Pulse celery and scallions in processor until coarsely chopped. Add parsley and pulse until finely chopped. Combine celery mixture with crumbs in large bowl for fish cakes.

Pulse fish in processor until finely chopped (be careful not to process to a paste). Add fish to celery-crumb mixture, along with egg, ¼ teaspoon salt, and ⅛ teaspoon pepper, stirring until well combined.

Stir ¼ teaspoon salt and ⅛ teaspoon pepper into reserved bread crumbs for coating. Gently shape fish mixture into four 4-inch patties (mixture will be soft). Coat well with bread crumbs. Transfer to a wax-paper-lined large plate and refrigerate, uncovered, for 10 minutes.

Heat oil in a 12-inch nonstick skillet over moderate heat until hot but not smoking. Add fish cakes and cook, turning once, until golden brown and just cooked through, 8 to 10 minutes. Transfer with a slotted spatula to paper towels to drain. Serve with lemon wedges and/or tartar sauce.

COOK'S NOTE

■ The cod cakes can be prepared and breaded up to 4 hours ahead and refrigerated, covered.

Peanut-Crusted Trout with Pineapple Cilantro Relish

SERVES 4
ACTIVE TIME: 25 MINUTES ■ START TO FINISH: 25 MINUTES

■ A coating of finely chopped peanuts combined with cilantro, ginger, garlic, and lime juice adds big flavor to the trout and insulates the delicate fish, protecting it from overcooking. A lively pineapple cilantro relish, made while the fish broils, rounds out the Southeast Asian tones. ■

    1   large bunch fresh cilantro, including stems
    ⅓   cup unsalted dry-roasted peanuts
    1   teaspoon finely chopped peeled fresh ginger
    1   garlic clove
        Salt
    ½   teaspoon freshly ground black pepper
    3   tablespoons vegetable oil
    2   tablespoons fresh lime juice
    1   teaspoon finely chopped serrano chile, including
        seeds
    4   (4- to 5-ounce) trout fillets with skin
    3   cups chopped peeled pineapple (preferably labeled
        "extra-sweet")
    2   teaspoons Asian fish sauce

Preheat broiler. Oil broiler pan rack.

Chop enough cilantro stems to measure ½ cup (set leaves aside). Transfer to a food processor. Add peanuts, ginger, garlic, 1 teaspoon salt, pepper, 2 tablespoons oil, 1 tablespoon lime juice, and ½ teaspoon chile and process until finely chopped, about 30 seconds. Transfer to a bowl; do not clean processor.

Pat fillets dry and arrange skin side down, close together, on broiler pan rack (fillets should just touch). Spread peanut mixture evenly over tops of fillets. Broil fish 3 to 4 inches from heat until lightly browned and just cooked through, about 4 minutes.

Meanwhile, chop enough cilantro leaves to measure 1 cup. Transfer to processor, add pineapple, fish sauce, remaining tablespoon each oil and lime juice,

¼ teaspoon salt, and remaining ½ teaspoon chile, and pulse until combined but still chunky.

Serve fish topped with pineapple relish.

COOK'S NOTE

■ The relish can be made up to 1 day ahead and refrigerated, covered.

Seared Mahimahi with Hot-and-Sour Mango Relish

SERVES 4
ACTIVE TIME: 40 MINUTES ■ START TO FINISH:
40 MINUTES

■ Mahimahi has sturdy and substantial flesh that can hold its own against bright, assertive pairings. Here Asian fish sauce tempers the mango's sweetness and acidity and keeps the fruit from running away with the dish. Try it with Coconut Rice (page 253). ■

    3   tablespoons peanut or vegetable oil
    ⅓   cup finely chopped shallots
    1   (1½- to 2-inch-long) fresh hot chile, such as Thai
        or serrano, minced, including seeds
    2   (1-pound) firm but ripe mangoes, peeled, pitted,
        and cut into ¾-inch pieces
    1½ tablespoons Asian fish sauce
    1   tablespoon sugar
        Salt
    2   tablespoons fresh lime juice, or to taste
    4   (6-ounce) pieces mahimahi fillet with skin
        Freshly ground black pepper
ACCOMPANIMENT: lime wedges

Heat 2 tablespoons oil in a 12-inch nonstick skillet over moderate heat until hot but not smoking. Add shallots and cook, stirring occasionally, until golden, 3 to 5 minutes. Add chile and cook, stirring, until softened, about 1 minute. Add mangoes, fish sauce, sugar, and ¼ teaspoon salt and cook, stirring occasionally, until mango is softened and mixture is slightly thickened, 3 to 7 minutes.

Remove from heat and stir in lime juice. Transfer relish to a bowl.

Pat fish dry and season with salt and pepper. Heat remaining tablespoon oil in cleaned skillet over moderately high heat until it just begins to smoke. Add mahimahi, skin side down, and cook, turning once, until skin is golden and crisp and fish is just cooked through, 12 to 16 minutes for 1 to 1½-inch-thick fillets.

Serve topped with relish, with lime wedges on the side.

Catfish with Red Curry Sauce

SERVES 4 TO 6
ACTIVE TIME: 40 MINUTES ■ START TO FINISH:
40 MINUTES

■ Dredging the fish in rice flour results in a delicate coating when it is fried (cornstarch may be substituted, but the results will not be as crisp). A red curry sauce clings to the fish, with dried shrimp—a classic addition to Thai curries—contributing a briny depth. Chinese long beans, sometimes called yard-long beans for their impressive length, taste similar to green beans but are more pliable. The beans turn bright green as they fry and add a colorful accent to this curry, adapted from one served at Celadon restaurant at the Sukhothai Hotel in Bangkok. Because the sauce is quite rich, it's good to serve the dish with lots of rice (plan on about ⅛ cup raw rice per person). For the Asian ingredients, see Sources. ■

2 tablespoons dried shrimp
About 5 cups vegetable oil for deep-frying, plus 1 tablespoon
2 tablespoons Thai red curry paste
1 (13- to 14-ounce) can unsweetened coconut milk, well stirred
1½ teaspoons Asian fish sauce
2 teaspoons sugar
1½ pounds catfish fillets, cut into 2-inch pieces
⅛ teaspoon salt
¼ cup Asian rice flour or cornstarch
10 Chinese long beans (see Sources) or ¼ pound green beans, cut into 2-inch pieces

ACCOMPANIMENT: jasmine rice; lime wedges
SPECIAL EQUIPMENT: an electric coffee/spice grinder; a deep-fat thermometer

Grind dried shrimp in grinder until fluffy, about 30 seconds.

Heat 1 tablespoon oil in a 12-inch heavy skillet over moderate heat until hot but not smoking. Add curry paste and cook, stirring constantly, until fragrant, about 30 seconds. Gradually add coconut milk, whisking until smooth, then add fish sauce and sugar and cook, stirring, until sugar is dissolved. Stir in ground shrimp, remove from heat, and cover to keep warm.

Heat 1 inch oil in a 4-quart wide pot over high heat until it registers 375°F on thermometer. Meanwhile, pat fish dry and sprinkle with salt. Dredge in rice flour, shaking off excess, and arrange in one layer on a plate.

Pat beans dry and fry in oil until blistered, about 30 seconds (oil will bubble up); transfer with a slotted spoon to paper towels to drain. Return oil to 375°F and fry fish in 2 batches, gently stirring, until golden brown, 2 to 3 minutes per batch for ¾-inch-thick fillets. Transfer fish to paper towels to drain. (Return oil to 375°F between batches.)

Bring curry sauce to a simmer. Add fish and cook, turning fish gently to coat with sauce, about 1 minute.

Transfer fish curry to a large shallow bowl and scatter beans on top. Serve with rice and lime wedges.

Fried Perch with Garlic Chile Sauce

SERVES 4
ACTIVE TIME: 45 MINUTES ■ START TO FINISH: 1 HOUR

■ In this appealing Chinese dish, strips of perch are fried until they curl prettily and then topped with a sauce spiced with garlic, scallions, *sambal oelek,* and brown sugar. (Soak up extra sauce with fluffy steamed white rice.) The dish is equally tasty made with catfish or even shrimp. Carp, which represents good fortune in Chinese lore, would be more authentic, but it's too bony for our tastes. ■

½ cup Chicken Stock (page 153) or store-bought
  reduced-sodium broth
3 tablespoons Asian fish sauce
3 tablespoons packed light brown sugar
2 tablespoons *sambal oelek* (Asian chile sauce; see
  Sources)
2 tablespoons distilled white vinegar
  About ½ cup Asian rice flour (see Cook's Note and
  Sources) or cornstarch
1½ pounds lake perch or Pacific ocean perch fillets,
  preferably with skin (see Cook's Note)
½ teaspoon salt
  About 3 cups peanut or vegetable oil for deep-frying
2 cups finely chopped scallions (2–3 bunches)
3 tablespoons chopped garlic
3 (2-inch-long) dried red chiles

GARNISH: fresh cilantro sprigs
ACCOMPANIMENT: white rice
SPECIAL EQUIPMENT: a deep-fat thermometer

Preheat oven to 200°F. Line a baking dish with a double thickness of paper towels.

Whisk together stock, fish sauce, brown sugar, *sambal oelek*, vinegar, and 2 teaspoons rice flour in a small bowl until rice flour and sugar are dissolved.

Pat fish dry and cut crosswise into 1-inch-wide pieces. Toss with salt in a bowl, then coat with remaining 7 tablespoons rice flour. Transfer fish to a large-mesh sieve set over a bowl and shake off excess rice flour.

Heat 1 inch oil in a well-seasoned 14-inch flat-bottomed wok (see Cook's Note) over moderately high heat to 400°F. Fry fish in 3 batches, turning gently with a slotted spoon, until cooked through and pale golden, 2 to 3 minutes per batch. Transfer with a slotted spoon to paper-towel-lined dish and keep warm in oven. (Skim off and discard any solids from oil and return oil to 400°F between batches.)

Carefully pour hot oil into a heatproof bowl and wipe wok clean. Return 2 tablespoons oil to wok and heat over high heat until it just begins to smoke. Stir in scallions, garlic, and chiles and stir-fry until scallions are softened, about 2 minutes. Stir fish sauce mixture, stir into scallion mixture, and bring to a boil. Remove chiles. Boil sauce until slightly thickened, about 2 minutes.

Transfer fish to a platter and pour sauce over fish. Top with cilantro and serve immediately, with rice.

COOK'S NOTES

- Asian rice flour is similar in texture to cornstarch. Either can be used to coat the fish, but rice flour makes a crisper coating.
- You can also use catfish, Alaskan pollack, and shrimp.
- You can substitute a 12-inch heavy skillet, preferably cast-iron, for the wok.

Pan-Glazed Mackerel with Citrus and Soy

SERVES 4
ACTIVE TIME: 20 MINUTES ■ START TO FINISH: 35 MINUTES

■ The meaty flavor of an oily fish such as mackerel stands up nicely to this easy Japanese-style marinade, which we adapted from a recipe by the cookbook author Elizabeth Andoh. ■

4 (4-ounce) pieces Spanish mackerel fillet (see Cook's
  Note)
1 tablespoon fresh grapefruit juice
1 tablespoon fresh lime juice
2 tablespoons sake
3 tablespoons mirin (Japanese sweet rice wine)
3 tablespoons Japanese light soy sauce
1 tablespoon water
2 teaspoons sugar
2 teaspoons vegetable oil

ACCOMPANIMENT: lime slices

Place fish in a glass or ceramic baking dish just large enough to hold fillets in one layer. Stir together citrus juices in a small bowl. Combine 1 tablespoon mixed juices with sake in another small bowl and pour over fillets. Marinate fish, covered, at room temperature, for 10 minutes.

Stir together mirin and 2 tablespoons soy sauce, pour over fillets, and marinate, covered, at room temperature, for 5 minutes more.

Stir together water, sugar, and remaining tablespoon each mixed citrus juices and soy sauce in a small bowl.

Remove fish from marinade and pat dry; discard marinade. Heat oil in a 12-inch heavy skillet over moderately high heat until hot but not smoking. Add fillets skin side down and cook until just crisp and golden brown, 1 to 2 minutes. Turn fillets and cook until browned on second side, about 1 minute more. Add soy mixture to skillet and cook, swirling skillet occasionally, until sauce is reduced to a glaze and fillets are just cooked through, about 3 minutes. If sauce reduces before fish is cooked through, swirl in 1 additional tablespoon water; repeat as necessary until fish is done.

Serve fish with lime slices.

COOK'S NOTES
- If you prefer milder-flavored fish, try Pacific cod or bass.
- Light soy sauce refers to the first pressing. It is lighter in color and has a more delicate flavor than dark soy. "Lite" soy refers to a low-sodium alternative.
- The fish can marinate, with the mirin and soy sauce added, for up to 1 hour, refrigerated, covered.

Sesame Tuna Burgers

SERVES 4
ACTIVE TIME: 30 MINUTES ■ START TO FINISH: 30 MINUTES

■ A coating of sesame seeds gives these burgers such an impressive crunch that you don't need a bun. Serve them with a green salad tossed with a lemony vinaigrette. ■

¾ cup sesame seeds, toasted (see Tips,
    page 911)
1 pound sushi-grade tuna steaks, preferably albacore
    (see Cook's Note), well chilled
1 tablespoon soy sauce
5 tablespoons vegetable oil
    Salt and freshly ground black pepper
ACCOMPANIMENT: pickled ginger and/or Wasabi
    Mayonnaise (recipe follows)

Put toasted sesame seeds in a wide shallow bowl. Finely chop tuna (about ⅛-inch pieces) with a large wet knife. Stir together soy sauce, 2 tablespoons oil, ¼ teaspoon salt, and ¼ teaspoon pepper in a bowl, then stir in tuna. Divide tuna mixture into 4 portions. Pack 1 portion into a ½-cup measure, then invert onto seeds in bowl. Gently press tuna to form a patty 3½ inches in diameter, coat completely with seeds, and transfer to a wax-paper-lined plate. Form, coat, and transfer 3 more burgers in same manner. Refrigerate, covered with plastic wrap, until ready to cook. (Discard any remaining sesame seeds.)

Heat remaining 3 tablespoons oil in a 12-inch heavy skillet over moderately high heat until hot but not smoking. Add burgers and cook, turning once, for about 2 minutes for medium-rare (seeds should be golden brown).

Serve burgers with slices of pickled ginger and/or wasabi mayonnaise.

COOK'S NOTES
- You can also use bigeye or yellowfin (ahi) tuna.
- The raw burgers can be refrigerated for up to 4 hours.

Wasabi Mayonnaise

MAKES ABOUT ½ CUP
ACTIVE TIME: 5 MINUTES ■ START TO FINISH: 5 MINUTES

■ Pantry ingredients plus a jot of wasabi paste equals a condiment with flavor to spare. ■

½ cup mayonnaise
2 teaspoons soy sauce
¾ teaspoon sugar
1 teaspoon fresh lemon juice
1 teaspoon wasabi paste, or to taste

Stir together all ingredients in a small bowl until sugar is dissolved.

COOK'S NOTE
- The mayonnaise can be refrigerated, covered, for up to 2 days.

Sicilian Tuna

SERVES 4

ACTIVE TIME: 30 MINUTES ■ START TO FINISH: 1 HOUR

■ Even those who prefer their tuna raw or quickly seared will be won over by this preparation. Marinated in a savory anchovy-lemon dressing, the tuna steaks are pan-grilled until their centers are pale pink but still very juicy. The bold flavors continue in the colorful sauce of briefly cooked tomatoes, black olives, capers, celery, and basil. ■

FOR TUNA

- 2 tablespoons olive oil
- 2 tablespoons fresh lemon juice
- 3 anchovy fillets, finely chopped
- 1 garlic clove, finely chopped
- 2 teaspoons finely chopped fresh oregano
- 4 (6-ounce) tuna steaks, preferably albacore (1 inch thick; see Cook's Note)

FOR SAUCE

- 2 tablespoons extra-virgin olive oil
- 2 celery ribs, cut into ¼-inch dice, plus 3 tablespoons celery leaves, coarsely chopped
- 2 ripe tomatoes, cut into ¼-inch dice
- ¼ cup Kalamata or other brine-cured black olives, pitted and coarsely chopped
- 2 tablespoons drained small capers, chopped
- 3 tablespoons finely chopped fresh basil
- 1 tablespoon fresh lemon juice
- ¼ teaspoon salt
- ¼ teaspoon freshly ground black pepper

SPECIAL EQUIPMENT: a well-seasoned large (2-burner) ridged grill pan

MARINATE THE TUNA: Combine oil, lemon juice, anchovies, garlic, oregano, and tuna in a large sealable plastic bag and seal bag, pressing out excess air. Let stand at room temperature, turning occasionally, for 30 minutes.

GRILL THE TUNA: Remove tuna from marinade and shake off any excess. Lightly oil grill pan and heat over moderately high heat until pan smokes. Add tuna to pan and grill, turning once, until pale pink in center, 5 to 7 minutes. Transfer to a platter and cover with foil to keep warm.

MEANWHILE, MAKE THE SAUCE: Heat oil in a 12-inch heavy skillet over moderately high heat until hot but not smoking. Add diced celery and cook, stirring, until tender, about 5 minutes. Stir in tomatoes, olives, and capers and cook until sauce is slightly thickened, about 5 minutes.

Stir in basil, lemon juice, salt, and pepper and remove from heat. Spoon sauce over tuna and sprinkle with celery leaves.

COOK'S NOTE

■ You can also use bigeye or yellowfin (ahi) tuna.

Tuna with Green Olive–Lemon Relish

SERVES 4

ACTIVE TIME: 30 MINUTES ■ START TO FINISH: 35 MINUTES

■ The citrusy fragrance of coriander seeds and the clean, anise flavor of fennel seeds are naturals with fish. Chef Judy Rodgers of San Francisco's Zuni Café puts them together to season meaty tuna steaks and give them a bit of golden crunch. Her Mediterranean-style relish of almonds, olives, and capers is also delicious with chicken, pork, or grilled vegetables. Rodgers likes to use Lucques olives for this recipe. You can substitute Picholines, but in that case, she recommends rinsing them and blanching them in simmering water for 2 minutes before pitting them, a process that softens the olives and allows their fruitiness to shine through. ■

FOR RELISH

- 12 blanched whole almonds, lightly toasted (see Tips, page 911) and coarsely chopped
- 1 cup pitted green olives, such as Lucques (see headnote), rinsed, patted dry, and coarsely chopped
- 2 tablespoons capers, rinsed, patted dry, and coarsely chopped
- 1 teaspoon finely grated lemon zest
- 1 tablespoon fresh lemon juice
- ½ cup extra-virgin olive oil
  Freshly ground black pepper to taste

FOR FISH

- 1 teaspoon fennel seeds
- 1 teaspoon coriander seeds
- ¼ teaspoon salt
- 4 (6-ounce) tuna steaks, preferably albacore (see Cook's Note)
- 3 tablespoons olive oil

SPECIAL EQUIPMENT: a mortar and pestle or an electric coffee/spice grinder

MAKE THE RELISH: Stir together all ingredients in a bowl.

PREPARE THE FISH: Grind together fennel seeds, coriander seeds, and salt in mortar with pestle (or coarsely grind in grinder).

Pat tuna steaks dry and sprinkle both sides evenly with spice mixture, pressing to help it adhere.

Heat oil in a 12-inch nonstick skillet over moderate heat until hot but not smoking. Add fish and cook, turning once, until golden and just cooked through, about 8 minutes for 1-inch-thick steaks. Serve topped with relish.

COOK'S NOTE

- You can also use bigeye or yellowfin (ahi) tuna.

Panfried Trout with Pecan Butter Sauce

SERVES 2 TO 4
ACTIVE TIME: 40 MINUTES ■ START TO FINISH:
40 MINUTES

■ A thin coating of flour helps the trout's skin crisp up beautifully, and the pecan butter sauce, lightened with a splash of lemon juice, makes a savory counterpoint to the sweet, tender fish. ■

- 1 stick (8 tablespoons) unsalted butter
- 2 (8- to 12-ounce) whole trout, cleaned, heads and tails left intact, rinsed, and patted dry
  Salt
- ¾ cup all-purpose flour
- 3 tablespoons vegetable oil

- ¼ cup pecans, coarsely chopped
- 2 tablespoons chopped fresh flat-leaf parsley
- ¼ teaspoon freshly ground black pepper
- 1 tablespoon fresh lemon juice

ACCOMPANIMENT: lemon wedges

Preheat oven to 200°F.

Melt 2 tablespoons butter in a 12-inch heavy skillet, preferably oval, over low heat. Remove from heat.

Brush trout with melted butter inside and out and season all over with ¾ teaspoon salt. Mound flour on a sheet of wax paper and dredge each fish in flour to coat completely, shaking off excess.

Add oil and another 2 tablespoons butter to skillet and heat over moderately high heat until foam subsides. Add both trout and cook, gently turning once using two spatulas, until golden brown and almost cooked through, about 8 minutes (fish will continue to cook as it stands). Transfer trout to plates and keep warm in oven.

Pour off fat from skillet and wipe skillet clean. Melt remaining ½ stick butter over moderately low heat. Add pecans and cook, stirring, until fragrant and a shake darker, 1 to 2 minutes. Add parsley, ¼ teaspoon salt, and pepper, swirling skillet to combine, and remove from heat. Add lemon juice, swirling skillet to incorporate.

Spoon butter over trout. Serve immediately, with lemon wedges.

Roasted Striped Bass with Pistachio Sauce

SERVES 4
ACTIVE TIME: 35 MINUTES ■ START TO FINISH: 45 MINUTES
(INCLUDES MAKING PISTACHIO SAUCE)

■ This recipe, from chefs Sam and Samantha Clark of the London restaurant Moro, is one of our favorite ways to prepare whole fish. Stuffing the striped bass with parsley stems and sliced lemon, fresh fennel, and red onion takes mere minutes and permeates the fish's delicate flesh with flavor. Don't skip the gutsy pistachio sauce—it makes the dish even more memorable. ■

1 (3-pound) whole striped bass (see Cook's Note),
  cleaned, head and tail left intact, rinsed, and
  patted dry
Flaky sea salt, such as Maldon
Coarsely ground black pepper
4 fresh flat-leaf parsley stems
4 thin lemon slices
½ fennel bulb, stalks discarded, bulb thinly sliced
1½ teaspoons fennel seeds
½ red onion, thinly sliced
2 Turkish bay leaves or 1 California bay leaf, preferably
  fresh, halved lengthwise
½ cup dry white wine
6 tablespoons extra-virgin olive oil

ACCOMPANIMENT: Pistachio Sauce (recipe follows)

Put a rack in middle of oven and preheat oven to 425°F.

Put fish in a large roasting pan or on a baking sheet. Sprinkle inside and out with 1 teaspoon sea salt and ¼ teaspoon pepper. Place parsley stems, lemon, fennel bulb and seeds, onion, and bay leaves in cavity of fish. (Aromatics may spill into pan.) Drizzle some of wine and olive oil over fish, then add remainder of both to pan. Sprinkle fish with 1 teaspoon sea salt and ¼ teaspoon pepper.

Roast until fish is just cooked through, 25 to 30 minutes. Discard bay leaves. Transfer fish to a platter using two spatulas, and pour any juices in pan around fish. Serve with pistachio sauce.

COOK'S NOTE
■ You can also use California white sea bass.

Pistachio Sauce

MAKES ABOUT 1½ CUPS
ACTIVE TIME: 20 MINUTES ■ START TO FINISH: 20 MINUTES

■ The Clarks refer to this as a sauce, but it's more of a chunky relish—so intense that a little bit goes a long way. The combination of coarsely chopped pistachios, fresh parsley and mint, and orange-flower water (a fragrant distillate of orange blossoms) also pairs nicely with quail, grilled lamb, or chicken. Persian pistachios have a fuchsia hue and make the dish quite colorful. It's worth spending a bit more to get good-quality orange-flower water, because cheaper versions, made from orange-blossom extract, can have an overwhelmingly perfumey flavor. ■

1¼ cups (about 5½ ounces) unsalted shelled pistachios,
  preferably Persian (see Sources)
1 small garlic clove
  Sea salt
¼ teaspoon finely grated lemon zest
5 tablespoons extra-virgin olive oil
2 tablespoons fresh lemon juice
1 tablespoon water
1–3 teaspoons orange-flower water (also called orange-
  blossom water), preferably French or Lebanese
  (see Sources)
½ cup coarsely chopped fresh flat-leaf parsley
1 tablespoon coarsely chopped fresh mint
⅛ teaspoon freshly ground black pepper

Pulse pistachios in a food processor until coarsely chopped. Transfer to a bowl.

Mince garlic and mash to a paste with a pinch of sea salt, using side of a large heavy knife. Stir garlic paste into pistachios, along with remaining ingredients, until well combined.

COOK'S NOTE
■ The sauce is best if made no more than 2 hours ahead; do not refrigerate.

Branzino Roasted with Fennel, Parsley, and Wine

SERVES 2
ACTIVE TIME: 15 MINUTES ■ START TO FINISH: 45 MINUTES

■ Branzino is a European sea bass that is prized in the Mediterranean (and, increasingly, on our shores) for its delicacy. Because it is so easy to bone, it's an ideal choice to cook whole; the fish in the market usually weigh about a pound. Cooking the bass on an aromatic bed of roasted fennel with dry white wine perfumes it ever so gently and keeps it very moist. Since everything is cooked in one dish, preparation and cleanup are a snap. This recipe can be easily doubled—just use two baking dishes. ■

2 medium fennel bulbs (1½ pounds total)
1 cup chopped fresh flat-leaf parsley
6 tablespoons extra-virgin olive oil
2 garlic cloves, finely chopped
2 teaspoons fennel seeds, crushed
   Salt and freshly ground black pepper
2 (1-pound) whole branzino (European sea bass) or
   other small sea bass (see Cook's Note), cleaned,
   heads and tails left intact, rinsed, and patted dry
⅔ cup dry white wine

Put a rack in middle of oven and preheat oven to 450°F.

Cut off and discard fennel stalks. Cut each bulb lengthwise in half and cut out cores. Cut fennel lengthwise into thin slices.

Stir together fennel slices, parsley, oil, garlic, fennel seeds, ¼ teaspoon salt, and ⅛ teaspoon pepper in a 13-by-9-inch glass or ceramic baking dish. Roast fennel mixture, uncovered, stirring occasionally, until fennel is almost tender, about 20 minutes.

Sprinkle fish inside and out with ½ teaspoon salt and ⅛ teaspoon pepper (total). Place fish on top of fennel, then tilt baking dish and spoon oil over fish. Pour wine around fish and roast until fish is just cooked through, 10 to 15 minutes.

With a large spatula, transfer each fish to a plate. Spoon fennel and sauce over fish.

COOK'S NOTE

■ You can also use black sea bass, Pacific ocean perch, or lake whitefish.

Roasted Bluefish with Coriander in Vinegar Sauce

SERVES 6
ACTIVE TIME: 20 MINUTES ■ START TO FINISH: 1¼ HOURS

■ When the ceramic artist and renowned cook Siglinda Scarpa leads cooking classes in the Piedmont area of North Carolina, where she now lives, she draws on old family recipes and memories of growing up in another Piedmont—Italy's. This marvelous dish, with its al-luring scents of coriander and bay, tastes like a virtual tour of the ancient spice trade route. Although bluefish is categorized as oily, it won't taste that way provided it's fresh, and its luxurious meatiness lends itself well to assertive Mediterranean flavorings like these.

Scarpa starts the fish in a cold oven, so it cooks gently as the oven heats up. ■

FOR FISH
¾ stick (6 tablespoons) unsalted butter,
   2 tablespoons softened
20 Turkish bay leaves or 10 California
   bay leaves
2 tablespoons coriander seeds
2 tablespoons coarse sea salt
1 (4-pound) whole bluefish, cleaned, head and tail left
   intact, rinsed, and patted dry
1½ cups (8 ounces) whole almonds, toasted (see Tips,
   page 911) and coarsely chopped
1 lemon, thinly sliced
FOR SAUCE
1 cup white wine vinegar
2 Turkish bay leaves or 1 California bay leaf
6 black peppercorns, slightly crushed
¼ teaspoon coarse sea salt

COOK THE FISH: Rub softened butter over bottom of a 17-by-14-inch roasting pan and sprinkle with 12 bay leaves (6 California bay leaves), 1 tablespoon coriander seeds, and 1 tablespoon sea salt.

Place fish diagonally in roasting pan. (If tail curls up side of pan, wrap tail in foil to prevent burning.)

Stir together almonds, ½ teaspoon coriander seeds, and 1 teaspoon sea salt. Stuff fish with lemon slices, almond mixture, and 2 tablespoons butter, cut into small pieces. (Some nuts may spill out.) Sprinkle fish with remaining 8 bay leaves (4 California bay leaves), 2½ teaspoons coriander seeds, and 2 teaspoons sea salt. Dot fish with remaining 2 tablespoons butter, cut into small pieces.

Put a rack in middle of oven and place fish in cold oven. Set oven temperature to 500°F and roast until fish is just cooked through, 40 to 45 minutes. Using two wide metal spatulas, transfer fish to a large platter. Reserve any pan juices.

MAKE THE SAUCE: Combine all ingredients in a small saucepan, bring to a boil, and boil for 1 minute. Stir in any pan juices, and pour over fish. Discard bay leaves.

Pan-Grilled Sardines with Fennel and Preserved Lemon

SERVES 3 TO 4 AS A MAIN COURSE, 6 AS A FIRST COURSE
ACTIVE TIME: 25 MINUTES ■ START TO FINISH: 25 MINUTES
(DOES NOT INCLUDE MAKING PRESERVED LEMONS)

■ A grill pan is a great tool for cooking sardines, those small but deliciously fatty saltwater fish. Their skins crisp up while their flesh stays sweet and moist. Their flavor is intense, so you don't need many to make a light meal—especially when they're served over a bed of warm, slightly caramelized fennel brightened with a smattering of preserved lemon. It's worth the (very minimal) effort to make your own preserved lemons. ■

FOR FENNEL

- 2 tablespoons extra-virgin olive oil
- 2 medium fennel bulbs (about 1½ pounds total), stalks discarded, bulbs halved lengthwise and cut into ½-inch-wide wedges
- ½ red onion, cut into ¼-inch-thick slices
- 4 teaspoons finely chopped rind (zest and pith) from Moroccan-Style Preserved Lemons (recipe follows) or store-bought preserved lemons (see Sources)
- ¼ teaspoon fennel seeds, crushed
- ½ teaspoon salt
- ¼ teaspoon freshly ground black pepper
- ½ cup water

FOR SARDINES

- 12 whole fresh sardines (2–3 ounces each), cleaned, heads and tails left intact, rinsed, and patted dry
- 3 tablespoons extra-virgin olive oil
- ½ teaspoon fine sea salt
- ¼ teaspoon fennel seeds, crushed
- ⅛ teaspoon freshly ground black pepper
- 2 teaspoons fresh lemon juice
- ⅓ cup coarsely chopped fresh dill

SPECIAL EQUIPMENT: a well-seasoned ridged grill pan

COOK THE FENNEL: Heat oil in a 10-inch heavy skillet over moderate heat until hot but not smoking. Add fennel, onion, preserved lemon, fennel seeds, salt, and pepper and cook, stirring occasionally, for 5 minutes. Add water, bring to a simmer, and simmer, covered, stirring occasionally, until fennel is very tender and slightly caramelized and water has evaporated, about 10 minutes. Remove from heat and cover to keep warm.

MEANWHILE, GRILL THE SARDINES: Spread sardines out on a platter. Drizzle with 1 tablespoon oil and sprinkle with sea salt, fennel seeds, and pepper.

Heat grill pan over moderately high heat until hot. Oil pan and grill sardines, in 2 batches if necessary, turning once, until just cooked through, 4 to 5 minutes per batch. Transfer to a clean platter with a slotted spatula.

Stir together lemon juice and remaining 2 tablespoons oil. Serve sardines on fennel mixture, sprinkled with dill and drizzled with lemon dressing.

COOK'S NOTE

■ The fennel can be braised up to 2 hours ahead and kept, uncovered, at room temperature. Reheat until warm before serving.

Moroccan-Style Preserved Lemons

MAKES 48 WEDGES
ACTIVE TIME: 15 MINUTES ■ START TO FINISH: 5 DAYS

■ Though you can buy preserved lemons in specialty foods shops, we prefer the clean taste of homemade. This technique, adapted from the Mediterranean authority Paula Wolfert's recipe, brings a multidimensional freshness to the lemons. Having a jar of this sparkly staple in your fridge makes it easy to liven up salads, dressings, soups, grilled fish, and even cocktails. There's no need to rinse them before using, but do discard the pulp—only the rind is eaten. ■

- 6 lemons
- ⅔ cup kosher salt
- 1–1½ cups fresh lemon juice (from 4–6 additional lemons)
- 2 tablespoons olive oil

SPECIAL EQUIPMENT: a 1½-quart jar with a tight-fitting lid

Blanch lemons in boiling water for 5 minutes; drain.

When lemons are cool enough to handle, cut each

one into 8 wedges; discard seeds. Toss lemons with salt in a bowl, then pack lemons, along with salt, tightly into jar. Add enough lemon juice to completely cover lemons. Seal jar and let lemons stand at room temperature, shaking gently once a day, for 5 days.

Add oil to jar and refrigerate.

COOK'S NOTE
■ The preserved lemons can be refrigerated, covered in their juices, for up to 1 year.

Bay Scallops Meunière

SERVES 2 AS A MAIN COURSE, 4 AS A FIRST COURSE
ACTIVE TIME: 20 MINUTES ■ START TO FINISH: 20 MINUTES

■ The best bay scallops are so sweet that you almost want to eat them raw and unembellished, but a quick turn in a hot pan with some butter and lemon juice teases out their succulence even more. When you come across fresh Nantucket bay scallops—about the size of miniature marshmallows—during their short autumn season, don't hesitate. They're worth every penny. ■

1 pound Nantucket bay scallops, tough ligament removed from side of each if necessary, rinsed, and patted dry
Salt and freshly ground black pepper
¼ cup all-purpose flour
1½ tablespoons olive oil
4½ tablespoons unsalted butter
2 teaspoons fresh lemon juice, or to taste
2 tablespoons chopped fresh flat-leaf parsley
ACCOMPANIMENTS: a baguette, warmed; lemon wedges
SPECIAL EQUIPMENT: 2 shallow 6-inch ramekins if serving as a main course or 4 large scallop shells (see Sources) or shallow ramekins if serving as a first course

SARDINES

Both fresh and canned sardines are delicious, but generally speaking, you can't substitute one for the other in a recipe. There is nothing like plump fresh sardines on the grill, for instance, but that technique won't work with the canned variety. Those are better suited to sandwiches, salads, or being served on crackers with a squeeze of lemon.

Fresh sardines, like other robust, oily fish such as bluefish and mackerel, must be very fresh indeed (the oils break down fairly quickly, so the fish don't travel well). Avoid them if they smell fishy, and cook them the same day you buy them. They're more common on the West Coast than on the East.

True sardines are in the herring family, and the tender little fishies in tins labeled "sardines" are often various types of small herring. The taste and quality of canned sardines, however, depend more on the care taken in handling than on species. In Norway, the smallest sprats (European herrings), called brislings, are lightly smoked, canned in oil, and steamed. The Norwegian brands King Roland and King Oscar are delicately smoky and balanced in flavor. Underwood sardines, from Scotland, are very salty but wonderful, and the brand Matiz, from Galicia, Spain, is also excellent.

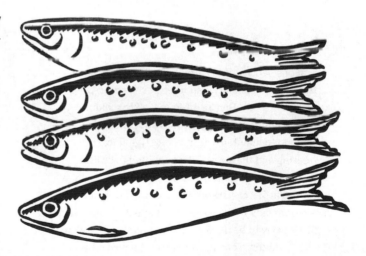

All sardines, whether fresh or canned, are full of omega-3 fatty acids. Canned sardines that include the bones are extremely rich in calcium as well. The canning process softens the bones, so you don't even notice them.

Put a rack in middle of oven and preheat oven to 250°F.

Warm ramekins or scallop shells (and baguette) on a baking sheet in oven while you cook scallops.

Sprinkle scallops with ½ teaspoon salt and ¼ teaspoon pepper. Toss with flour in a large bowl to coat lightly, then transfer to a colander and shake well over sink to remove excess flour.

Heat oil and 1½ tablespoons butter in a 12-inch nonstick skillet over moderately high heat until foam subsides. Add scallops and cook, turning occasionally, until golden and just cooked through, 3 to 4 minutes. Using a slotted spoon, divide scallops among warmed ramekins or shells (do not clean skillet).

Cut remaining 3 tablespoons butter into 6 pieces. Return skillet to moderately high heat, add lemon juice and butter, and heat, stirring occasionally, until butter is melted and foamy. Remove from heat and stir in parsley and salt and pepper to taste.

Pour sauce over scallops and transfer ramekins or shells to small plates. Serve with warm bread and lemon wedges.

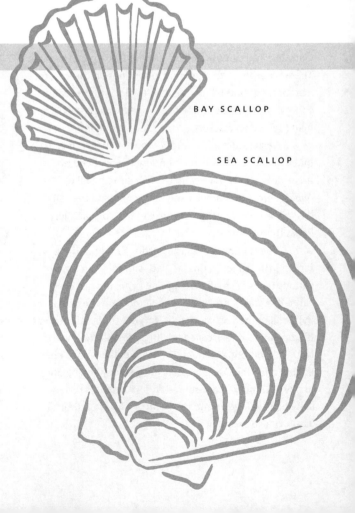

Scallops with Mushrooms and Sherry

SERVES 4
ACTIVE TIME: 30 MINUTES ■ START TO FINISH: 30 MINUTES

■ Cremini mushrooms prove a meaty foil for sweet scallops. Mushrooms benefit from the trinity of soy, sherry, and balsamic vinegar—the soy deepens their foresty flavor, while the sherry and vinegar add a caramel edge. ■

1¼ pounds sea scallops, tough ligament removed from side of each if necessary
    Salt
⅛ teaspoon freshly ground black pepper
 2 tablespoons olive oil
⅓ cup water

BAY SCALLOP

SEA SCALLOP

CAVEAT EMPTOR: SCALLOPS

Scallops perish quickly after being harvested, so they are almost always shucked at sea and iced down or frozen. They're often soaked in sodium tripolyphosphate (STP), which is added to frozen seafood to maintain the moisture that is lost in freezing and thawing. STP is supposed to be listed on the label, but unfortunately, it seldom is. Scallops soaked in STP can absorb much of their weight in water, which means you're paying for that extra water weight. STP is likely to be the reason those hunky sea scallops you sauté come out shriveled and steamed rather than seared. Scallops that have been treated with STP look unnaturally shiny, feel slippery and flabby, and, after cooking, have a soapy aftertaste. When shopping, look for scallops that are translucent and have a natural sheen, or "bloom," and avoid those sitting in milky-looking liquid. They should be firm, springy, and moist to the touch. The marketing term "dry-packed" on a label should signify that the scallops haven't been soaked in STP, but its use isn't regulated by the FDA.

½ stick (4 tablespoons) unsalted butter
1 pound cremini mushrooms, trimmed and quartered
⅓ cup finely chopped shallots
2 garlic cloves, finely chopped
⅔ cup medium-dry sherry
1 tablespoon balsamic vinegar
1 tablespoon soy sauce

Preheat oven to 200°F.

Pat scallops dry and sprinkle with ¼ teaspoon salt and pepper. Heat oil in a 12-inch nonstick skillet over moderately high heat until it begins to smoke. Add scallops and sear, turning once, until well browned and just cooked through, 4 to 6 minutes (scallops will continue to cook in oven). Transfer to a platter and keep warm, uncovered, in oven.

Pour off and discard any fat from skillet, then add water and simmer, scraping up any brown bits, for 1 minute. Add 2 tablespoons butter and heat until foam subsides. Add mushrooms and cook, stirring occasionally, until golden, about 8 minutes.

Add shallots and garlic and cook, stirring, for 2 minutes. Add sherry, vinegar, soy sauce, ¼ teaspoon salt, and any juices from platter and simmer, uncovered, stirring occasionally, for 3 minutes.

Cut remaining 2 tablespoons butter into small pieces. Remove skillet from heat and stir in butter until incorporated. Spoon mushrooms and sauce over scallops.

Seared Scallops with Brussels Sprouts and Bacon

SERVES 4
ACTIVE TIME: 30 MINUTES ■ START TO FINISH: 30 MINUTES

■ Essentially a one-dish dinner, this combination couldn't be tastier. Salty, smoky bacon is a natural with scallops, but you might be surprised by how the golden Brussels sprouts underscore the scallops' sweetness. ■

1 pound Brussels sprouts, trimmed and halved lengthwise
Salt

4 bacon slices, cut crosswise into ½-inch-wide pieces
1⅓ cups Chicken Stock (page 153) or store-bought reduced-sodium broth
5 tablespoons water
2 tablespoons unsalted butter
½ teaspoon sugar
Freshly ground black pepper
1¼ pounds sea scallops, tough ligament removed from side of each if necessary
2 teaspoons olive oil
1 teaspoon cornstarch
2 teaspoons fresh lemon juice

Preheat oven to 200°F.

Blanch Brussels sprouts in a 3- to 4-quart saucepan of boiling salted water (1 tablespoon salt), uncovered, for 2 minutes; drain.

Line a small bowl with a paper towel. Cook bacon in a 12-inch nonstick skillet over moderate heat, turning occasionally, until crisp. Transfer bacon with a slotted spoon to paper-towel-lined bowl; reserve rendered bacon fat in another small bowl.

Add ⅓ cup stock and ¼ cup water to skillet and bring to a simmer, scraping up any brown bits. Add butter, sugar, ¼ teaspoon salt, ⅛ teaspoon pepper, and Brussels sprouts and simmer, covered, for 4 minutes. Remove lid and cook over moderately high heat, stirring occasionally, until liquid has evaporated and sprouts are tender and golden brown, 8 to 12 minutes more.

Stir in bacon, transfer to a platter, and keep warm, covered, in oven.

Pat scallops dry and sprinkle with ¼ teaspoon salt and ⅛ teaspoon pepper. Heat oil with 2 teaspoons reserved bacon fat in cleaned skillet over moderately high heat until fat begins to smoke. Add scallops and sear, turning once, until golden brown and just cooked through, 4 to 6 minutes. Transfer to another platter and cover loosely with foil to keep warm.

Pour off any fat from skillet. Add remaining 1 cup stock, bring to a simmer, and simmer, stirring and scraping up brown bits, for 1 minute. Stir cornstarch into remaining 1 tablespoon water in a cup, then stir into sauce, along with any juices accumulated on scallop platter. Simmer, stirring, for 1 minute, remove from heat, and stir in lemon juice and salt and pepper to taste.

Top Brussels sprouts with scallops and sauce.

Scallops with Snail-Garlic Butter and Leeks

SERVES 4 AS A MAIN COURSE, 10 AS A FIRST COURSE
ACTIVE TIME: 30 MINUTES ■ START TO FINISH: 40 MINUTES

■ If you like garlicky escargots, you'll love how the French classic tastes with the addition of scallops. It boasts a perfect trio of savory, sweet, and garlic that makes you want to keep eating and eating. Crusty bread for soaking up the extra sauce is de rigueur. We adapted this recipe from one at L'Ardoise, a cozy Parisian bistro near the Louvre. ■

¾ stick (6 tablespoons) unsalted butter, softened
1½ pounds leeks (white and pale green parts only), halved lengthwise, cut into ¼-inch-wide slices, and washed well
Salt
1½ teaspoons minced garlic
3 tablespoons finely chopped fresh flat-leaf parsley
⅓ cup chopped rinsed canned snails (see Cook's Note)
Freshly ground black pepper
20 medium sea scallops (about 1 pound), tough ligament removed from side of each if necessary
1 tablespoon finely chopped fresh chives
SPECIAL EQUIPMENT: 4 large scallop shells if serving as a main course or 20 small scallop shells if serving as first course (see Sources), or a 2½- to 3-quart gratin or other shallow baking dish

Put a rack in middle of oven and preheat oven to 450°F.

Heat 2 tablespoons butter in a 12-inch heavy skillet over moderate heat until foam subsides. Stir in leeks with ¼ teaspoon salt, reduce heat to low, and cook, covered, stirring occasionally, until tender, about 10 minutes. Remove from heat and cover to keep warm.

Combine remaining ½ stick butter, garlic, 2 tablespoons parsley, snails, ⅛ teaspoon salt, and ⅛ teaspoon pepper in a food processor and puree until almost smooth.

Put 5 scallops in each large shell or 1 scallop in each small shell and arrange shells on a baking sheet.

(Alternatively, arrange scallops about 1 inch apart in gratin dish.) Sprinkle with ¼ teaspoon salt and ⅛ teaspoon pepper, then dot each with about 1 teaspoon snail-garlic butter. Bake until scallops are just cooked through, about 7 minutes (9 to 11 minutes if using gratin dish).

Meanwhile, reheat leeks over low heat.

Top scallops with leeks, and sprinkle them with chives and remaining tablespoon parsley.

COOK'S NOTES

■ Snails come in 7-ounce cans, so you'll have about 5 ounces left over. You can make more snail butter for future use to spread on toasts for a quick hors d'oeuvre. Combine 1 stick (8 tablespoons) butter, 1 tablespoon minced garlic, ¼ cup finely chopped fresh parsley, the snails, ¼ teaspoon salt, and ¼ teaspoon pepper in a food processor and puree until almost smooth. Form the butter into a log, wrap in plastic wrap and foil, and freeze for up to 1 month.

■ The snail-garlic butter can be made ahead and refrigerated, covered, for up to 2 days or frozen in an airtight container for up to 1 month.

Sea Scallops with Cilantro Gremolata and Ginger Lime Beurre Blanc

SERVES 4 AS A MAIN COURSE, 6 AS A FIRST COURSE
ACTIVE TIME: 35 MINUTES ■ START TO FINISH: 35 MINUTES

■ Gremolata, a traditional Italian garnish, is made with lemon zest, garlic, and parsley; we love this variation, which uses lime zest and cilantro. Fresh lime juice takes the place of the usual vinegar in the silky *beurre blanc,* or classic white butter sauce, and ginger adds extra zing. The result is an elegant contemporary dish that, despite its rather grand name, is remarkably straightforward to prepare. ■

FOR GREMOLATA
1½ tablespoons finely chopped fresh cilantro
1 small garlic clove, minced
¾ teaspoon finely grated lime zest

FOR *BEURRE BLANC*

- ¼ cup dry white wine
- 3 tablespoons fresh lime juice (from 1½ limes)
- 2 tablespoons minced shallot
- 1 tablespoon finely grated peeled fresh ginger
- ¾ stick (6 tablespoons) cold unsalted butter, cut into tablespoons
- ⅛ teaspoon salt
  Pinch of freshly ground white pepper

FOR SCALLOPS

- 24 medium sea scallops (1½ pounds), tough ligament removed from side of each if necessary
- ½ teaspoon salt
- ¼ teaspoon freshly ground black pepper
- 1 tablespoon olive oil

MAKE THE GREMOLATA: Stir together cilantro, garlic, and zest in a small bowl.

MAKE THE *BEURRE BLANC:* Combine wine, lime juice, shallot, and ginger in a 1- to 1½-quart heavy saucepan. Bring to a simmer, and simmer until liquid is reduced to about 2 tablespoons, about 6 minutes.

Whisk in butter 1 tablespoon at a time, adding each new piece before previous one has melted completely and occasionally lifting pan from heat to cool mixture. (Do not allow sauce to get too hot, or it will separate.) Pour sauce through a fine mesh sieve into a bowl (discard solids), then return to cleaned pan and stir in salt and white pepper. Cover to keep warm while you cook scallops.

COOK THE SCALLOPS: Pat scallops dry and sprinkle with salt and pepper. Heat oil in a 12-inch heavy nonstick skillet over moderately high heat until hot but not smoking. Add scallops and cook, turning once, until golden brown and just cooked through, 4 to 5 minutes.

Sprinkle with gremolata and serve with sauce.

Sea Scallops with Corn Coulis and Tomatoes

SERVES 6 AS A MAIN COURSE, 10 AS A FIRST COURSE
ACTIVE TIME: 35 MINUTES ■ START TO FINISH: 45 MINUTES

■ Thanks to a pureed sauce that makes the most of fresh corn's natural creaminess, this low-fat recipe is full of flavor. Tomatoes add a slight acidity, which balances the sweetness of the scallops and the corn. ■

- 1 teaspoon finely chopped shallot
- ¼ teaspoon finely chopped garlic
- 4 teaspoons olive oil
- ¾ cup corn kernels (from 2 large ears)
- 1 teaspoon finely chopped fresh basil
  Salt and freshly ground black pepper
- ½ cup whole milk
- ½ pound ripe tomatoes, seeded and cut into ¼-inch dice (1 cup)
- 1 tablespoon chopped fresh flat-leaf parsley
- 30 large sea scallops (2½ pounds), tough ligament removed from side of each if necessary

Cook shallot and garlic in 2 teaspoons oil in a small skillet over moderately low heat, stirring, until softened, about 1 minute. Add corn, basil, ¼ teaspoon salt, and ⅛ teaspoon pepper and cook, stirring occasionally, until corn is tender and beginning to lightly brown on edges, about 4 minutes. Add milk and scrape up any brown bits from bottom of skillet, then transfer corn mixture to a blender.

Puree mixture at medium speed until very smooth, about 1 minute. Force puree through a fine-mesh sieve into a small saucepan, pressing hard on solids; discard solids. Cover coulis until ready to serve.

Toss tomatoes with parsley and salt and pepper to taste in a bowl.

Pat scallops dry and season with salt and pepper. Heat remaining 2 teaspoons oil in a 12-inch heavy nonstick skillet over moderately high heat until hot but not smoking. Add half of scallops and cook, turning once, until golden and just cooked through, 4 to 5 minutes. Transfer to a platter and cover loosely with foil to keep warm. Cook remaining scallops in same manner.

Reheat coulis over low heat, covered. Spoon about 2 tablespoons coulis onto center of each plate. Arrange 5 scallops per plate (3 if serving as a first course) in a circle on coulis, then spoon tomatoes into center.

COOK'S NOTE

■ The coulis can be made up to 8 hours ahead and, once cooled, refrigerated, covered. Reheat the coulis over low heat, covered.

Garlic Shrimp

SERVES 4
ACTIVE TIME: 45 MINUTES ■ START TO FINISH: 1¼ HOURS

■ El Paso Taqueria, located in the vibrant Spanish Harlem neighborhood of Manhattan, serves some of the best Mexican food in the city. These garlicky shrimp, based on El Paso's recipe, get their deep flavor from guajillo chiles, which are fruity and only mildly hot. They are sautéed to impart a smoky flavor, then cooked with tomatoes to soften them. Soak up the flavorful sauce with rice or warm tortillas. ■

A BUYER'S GUIDE TO SHRIMP

Shrimp are cheaper and more plentiful than ever before, but the vast majority of those we eat today are no longer wild and netted from unpolluted ocean waters. Instead, they're raised in crowded, murky man-made ponds in developing countries—which may go a long way toward explaining why they often taste like bottom-feeding fish. Over the years, the shrimp industry has grown into one of the most environmentally destructive enterprises by which humans produce food. Despite recent improvements, securing sustainable shrimp can require some legwork. It can also be a little confusing, because there is no system of standards that applies to all shrimp.

If you are looking for a general rule of thumb, follow the advice of Seafood Watch (www.seafoodwatch.org), which says that domestic wild shrimp are generally a better alternative than imported shellfish. Pink shrimp from the West Coast (a small but flavorful "salad" species) and spot prawns (large orange-pink shrimp with white markings found from Southern California to Alaska) earn the organization's "Best" rating; shrimp from the Atlantic and the Gulf of Mexico are considered "Good." Imported shrimp, whether farmed or trawled, are listed under "Avoid."

An updated list of sources for certified wild American shrimp can be found at www.wildamericanshrimp.com. In the South and East, Wal-Mart and supermarkets such as A&P, Albertsons, Super One, and Kroger carry wild American shrimp, but they are not always available at all locations.

6 dried guajillo chiles (see Sources)
½ cup mild olive oil
1 medium onion, chopped
3 large garlic cloves, minced
2 medium tomatoes, seeded and cut into
⅓-inch dice
Salt
1½ pounds large shrimp in shells (21–25 per pound), peeled, leaving tail and last segment of shell intact, and deveined

Wipe chiles clean. Discard stems, seeds, and ribs. Cut into roughly ⅓-inch squares with kitchen shears.

Heat oil in a 12-inch heavy skillet over moderately high heat until hot but not smoking. Add chiles and cook, stirring, just until they turn a shade darker, about 1 minute (do not let mixture smoke, or chiles will blacken). Add onion and garlic and cook, stirring, until beginning to brown, 2 to 3 minutes. Add tomatoes and ¼ teaspoon salt and cook, stirring, for 5 minutes. Remove from heat and let stand for at least 30 minutes to soften chiles.

Toss shrimp with 1 teaspoon salt in a large bowl.

Bring tomato mixture to a simmer over moderately high heat. Add shrimp and cook, stirring, until just cooked through, about 5 minutes.

COOK'S NOTE
■ The tomato mixture can stand at room temperature for up to 2 hours. Reheat before adding the shrimp.

Thai Shrimp and Spinach Curry

SERVES 4
ACTIVE TIME: 35 MINUTES ■ START TO FINISH: 35 MINUTES

■ Combining bottled curry paste with coconut milk and a handful of supermarket ingredients makes Thai curry a weeknight dinner. If you're wary of overspicing the dish, start with the lower range of curry paste and keep tasting as you add more. The recipe is adapted from one by the cookbook author Faye Levy. ■

1 (13- to 14-ounce) can unsweetened coconut milk, chilled (do not stir or shake)
1½–2 teaspoons Thai green or red curry paste
1 pound medium shrimp in shells (31–35 per pound), peeled and deveined
2 tablespoons Asian fish sauce
2 carrots, thinly sliced
1 red bell pepper, cored, seeded, and thinly sliced
¾ pound spinach (1 large bunch), tough stems discarded
3 tablespoons chopped fresh cilantro

ACCOMPANIMENT: jasmine or basmati rice

Spoon about ⅓ cup of thick coconut cream from top of coconut milk (set remaining coconut milk aside) into a large heavy skillet and cook over moderate heat, stirring, until slightly thickened, 2 to 3 minutes. Add curry paste and cook, whisking, for 1 minute. Add shrimp and cook over moderately high heat, stirring, until they begin to turn pink, 1 to 2 minutes. Add remaining coconut milk and fish sauce, bring to a simmer, and simmer, uncovered, stirring occasionally, until shrimp are just cooked through, about 1 minute. Transfer shrimp with a slotted spoon to a bowl.

Add carrots and bell pepper to sauce and simmer for 5 minutes. Add spinach in batches, stirring until each batch is wilted. Return shrimp to skillet and simmer, stirring occasionally, for 1 minute.

Sprinkle curry with cilantro and serve with rice.

South Indian Shrimp Curry

SERVES 4
ACTIVE TIME: 30 MINUTES ■ START TO FINISH: 30 MINUTES

■ Here is a fast curry that can be pulled together on any weeknight and positively bursts with warm flavors. Cook the curry powder completely to eliminate any raw taste. Sometimes we throw in a handful of frozen peas during the last few minutes of cooking or sprinkle the final dish with chopped cashews. Complete the meal with a salad, sautéed greens, or, more traditionally, Indian Lentil Stew (page 286) and Indian-Spiced Cauliflower and Potatoes (page 588). ■

FISH AND SHELLFISH   367

- 1 large onion, quartered
- 1 (3-inch-long) piece fresh ginger, peeled and quartered
- 1 (3-inch) serrano chile, stemmed and quartered
- ¼ cup vegetable oil
  Salt
- ½ teaspoon sugar
- 2 teaspoons curry powder, preferably Madras
- 1 (13- to 14-ounce) can unsweetened coconut milk, well stirred
- 1 tablespoon fresh lime juice
- 1 pound large shrimp in shells (21–25 per pound), peeled and deveined
  Freshly ground black pepper
- 2 tablespoons chopped fresh cilantro

ACCOMPANIMENT: basmati rice; lime wedges

Pulse onion, ginger, and chile together in a food processor until finely chopped.

Heat oil in a 12-inch heavy skillet over moderate heat until hot but not smoking. Add onion mixture, ½ teaspoon salt, and sugar and cook, stirring frequently, until onion begins to brown, about 5 minutes. Stir in curry powder and cook, stirring frequently, until fragrant, about 2 minutes. Stir in coconut milk and lime juice, bring to a simmer, and simmer, stirring occasionally, until thickened, 3 to 5 minutes.

Season shrimp with salt and pepper. Add to sauce and simmer, stirring occasionally, until just cooked through, about 3 minutes. Season with salt to taste and sprinkle with cilantro. Serve with rice and lime wedges.

Vietnamese-Style Shrimp Curry

SERVES 4 TO 6
ACTIVE TIME: 1½ HOURS ■ START TO FINISH: 1½ HOURS

■ This colorful curry, redolent of coconut milk, tamarind, lemongrass, ginger, chiles, spices, and fresh herbs, is magnificent. Small amounts of the seasonings work together like a symphony. The curry itself cooks very quickly; it's the chopping and measuring that are somewhat time-consuming. ■

- 2 tablespoons tamarind (from a pliable block; see Sources)
- ¼ cup boiling water
- 2 stalks lemongrass
- 1 (13- to 14-ounce) can unsweetened coconut milk, well stirred
- 1½ pounds extra-large shrimp in shells (16–20 per pound), peeled (shells reserved), and deveined
- 2 tablespoons minced shallot
- 2 tablespoons minced peeled fresh ginger (from a 2-inch knob)

COCONUT MILK

The unsweetened coconut milk that comes in cans is not the sweet stuff used for piña coladas or the thin, clear, refreshing "water" that is found inside the shell (and, increasingly, in aseptic containers), but the aromatic liquid pressed from the meat of fresh coconuts. If left to stand, it separates into a layer of fat-rich cream and a layer of thinner "milk." Good canned brands are available in grocery stores across the land; you'll find them on the shelves with Asian ingredients, not with the drink mixers. Some have more cream on the top than others. If a recipe calls for just coconut cream (as on page 367, where the cream is used as the fat to fry the curry paste), refrigerate the can first to help separate the layers, and be gentle when opening. Otherwise, shake the can well before using to incorporate the cream into the milk.

2 teaspoons minced seeded red chile, or to taste

1 tablespoon coriander seeds, crushed
(see Cook's Note)

2 teaspoons cracked white pepper
(see Cook's Note)

1 teaspoon cumin seeds

1 teaspoon turmeric

¼ cup Asian fish sauce

½ cup plus 2 tablespoons water

¼ cup peanut oil

½ medium red onion, thinly sliced into rings

1 red bell pepper, cored, seeded, and cut into
½-inch pieces

1 (1- to 1½-pound) firm but ripe mango, peeled, pitted,
and cut into ½-inch pieces

3 tablespoons chopped fresh cilantro

3 tablespoons chopped fresh mint

3 tablespoons chopped fresh basil

ACCOMPANIMENT: white rice

Soak tamarind in boiling water in a small bowl, mashing gently, until softened. Force tamarind through a sieve into a bowl, pressing on solids; discard solids.

Trim root ends of lemongrass and discard tough outer layers. Mince enough of bottom third of stalks to measure 3 tablespoons.

Combine minced lemongrass, coconut milk, tamarind, and shrimp shells in a 1½ quart heavy saucepan. Bring to a simmer, and simmer, uncovered, until reduced by one third, about 10 minutes. Pour mixture through a sieve into a large bowl, pressing on solids; discard solids.

Combine shallot, ginger, chile, coriander, white pepper, cumin, turmeric, 2 tablespoons fish sauce, 2 tablespoons water, and 2 tablespoons oil in a blender and puree until smooth. Transfer spice paste to a small heavy skillet and cook over moderately low heat, stirring, for 10 minutes. Whisk into coconut milk mixture, along with remaining ½ cup water.

Heat 1 tablespoon oil in a deep 12-inch heavy skillet over moderately high heat until hot but not smoking. Add shrimp and cook, stirring, until almost cooked through, about 2 minutes. Add to coconut milk mixture.

Add remaining tablespoon oil to same skillet, reduce heat to moderate, and add onion, bell pepper, mango, and remaining 2 tablespoons fish sauce. Cook, stirring, until onion and pepper are softened, about 3

minutes. Add coconut milk mixture and shrimp and simmer, stirring occasionally, until shrimp are just cooked through, about 4 minutes.

Remove from heat, stir in herbs, and serve curry with rice.

COOK'S NOTES

- Use a mortar and pestle or the side of a large heavy knife to crush the coriander seeds and crack the white pepper.

- The coconut milk mixture, without the spice paste, can be made up to 1 day ahead. Cool, uncovered, then refrigerate, covered.

Shrimp and Avocado in Tamarind Sauce

SERVES 4
ACTIVE TIME: 40 MINUTES ■ START TO FINISH:
40 MINUTES

■ In this Southeast Asian–inspired recipe, sweet shrimp and buttery avocado come together in a tart, spicy tamarind sauce. The salty and sweet flavors of roasted peanuts and fried shallot help balance the whole dish. ■

¼ cup vegetable oil

1 large shallot, thinly sliced and separated into rings

¼ cup tamarind (from a pliable block; see Sources)

½ cup boiling water

2 tablespoons sugar

1 tablespoon soy sauce

1 tablespoon Asian fish sauce

3 tablespoons fresh lime juice (from 1½ limes)

2 large firm but ripe avocados

1 tablespoon minced peeled fresh ginger

1 garlic clove, minced

2 (1½- to 2-inch-long) fresh Thai chiles or 1 serrano
chile, minced, including seeds

¼ teaspoon salt

1 pound large shrimp in shells (21–25 per pound),
peeled, leaving tail and last segment of shell
intact, and deveined

⅓ cup roasted salted peanuts, chopped

GARNISH: fresh cilantro sprigs

ACCOMPANIMENT: jasmine rice

Heat oil in a 1-quart heavy saucepan over moderate heat until hot but not smoking. Add shallot and fry, stirring, until golden brown, about 2 minutes. Transfer with a slotted spoon to paper towels to drain (shallots will crisp as they cool). Reserve oil.

Soak tamarind in boiling water in a small bowl, mashing gently, until softened, about 5 minutes.

Force tamarind through a sieve into a bowl, pressing on solids; discard solids. Add sugar, soy sauce, fish sauce, and 1½ tablespoons lime juice and stir until sugar is dissolved.

Halve, pit, and peel avocados. Cut into 1½-inch chunks and toss with remaining 1½ tablespoons lime juice in a bowl.

Transfer reserved shallot oil to a 12-inch heavy skillet and heat over moderately high heat until hot but not smoking. Add ginger, garlic, chiles, and salt and cook, stirring constantly, until fragrant, about 30 seconds. Add shrimp and cook, turning once, for 2 minutes. Stir in tamarind mixture and simmer until shrimp are just cooked through, about 2 minutes more.

Spoon shrimp and avocado over rice and sprinkle with peanuts and fried shallots. Garnish with cilantro sprigs.

Shrimp and Tasso Gumbo

SERVES 6
ACTIVE TIME: 1¼ HOURS ■ START TO FINISH: 2¼ HOURS

■ Growing up in Abbeville, Louisiana, associate food editor Alexis Touchet spent many a day trawling for shrimp with her father. This deeply flavored gumbo was his favorite recipe. A traditional slow-cooked roux gives the dish its backbone, and that step cannot be rushed. Long cooking over low heat caramelizes the flour, adding color and rich, distinctive flavor. Tasso, Cajun smoked cured pork, adds even more depth. (You can substitute sausage.) Don't be tempted to add more tasso than is called for—a little of its particular smokiness goes a long way.

For best flavor, make the gumbo base a day ahead and add the okra and shrimp just before serving. ■

ALL ABOUT ROUX

As any Louisiana native will tell you, roux is one of the cornerstones of Cajun cooking. The simple combination of flour and fat has been a staple in French sauces for hundreds of years. Sometime back in the eighteenth century, the word *roux*—meaning "rouge"—was adopted into European culinary parlance to describe flour that had been cooked long enough to turn a reddish color. When the technique was brought to Louisiana, it instantly found its place in the cooking culture there and, after a little tinkering, became the base for the region's piquant sauces and lively gravies.

The flour for a roux is cooked in butter, oil, or rendered fat to get rid of its raw, pasty taste. The flour-to-fat ratio is typically 1 to 1, but it can vary according to the recipe and the cook's preference. For a classic French sauce, a liquid, usually stock, milk, or water, is then added, and the mixture is brought to a boil. As the heat increases, the starch molecules within each granule begin to move rapidly and absorb liquid. When the proper temperature is reached, the molecules have become so saturated that they explode and release their starches into the liquid, thus thickening it.

You might be startled by the fact that a Cajun roux cooks for 30 to 45 minutes, until it turns the color of milk chocolate. That long cooking is what gives a finished gumbo its deep, almost toasted flavor. The darker a roux gets, by the way, the less it thickens—the long exposure to heat breaks down the starch, so there aren't many molecules left to absorb liquid.

When making any roux, you'll want to keep the heat gentle and keep the mixture moving. After adding the flour and fat to the pan, immediately begin scraping the mixture back and forth with a whisk. Or, for a Cajun roux, use a flat metal or wooden spatula, which allows you to move more of the mixture at once, so that it browns more evenly and there is less chance of scorching.

2 pounds large shrimp in shells (21–25 per pound), peeled (shells reserved), and deveined

3½ quarts water

¼ cup vegetable oil

½ cup all-purpose flour

2 medium onions, chopped

2 celery ribs, chopped

1 large green bell pepper, cored, seeded, and chopped

½ pound fresh or frozen tasso (Cajun smoked cured pork; see Sources), thawed if frozen, trimmed of excess fat, and cut into ¼-inch pieces (see Cook's Note)

Salt

½ teaspoon cayenne

10 ounces fresh or frozen baby okra, thawed if frozen, trimmed, and cut into ¼-inch-thick rounds

¾ cup thinly sliced scallion greens

ACCOMPANIMENTS: white rice; hot pepper sauce

Combine shrimp shells and water in an 8-quart pot, uncovered, bring to a simmer, and simmer until liquid is reduced to about 3 quarts, 15 to 20 minutes. Pour stock through a sieve set over a large bowl; discard shells.

With a flat metal or wooden spatula, stir together oil and flour in a 10-inch heavy skillet, preferably cast-iron, and cook over moderately low heat, scraping (not stirring) back and forth constantly until roux is the color of milk chocolate, 30 to 45 minutes. (As roux cooks, it may be necessary to lower heat to prevent scorching.)

Add onions, celery, and bell pepper and cook, scraping back and forth occasionally, until onion is softened, about 8 minutes.

Scrape roux mixture into cleaned 8-quart pot, add shrimp stock, and bring to a boil, stirring occasionally. Reduce heat, add tasso, 1½ teaspoons salt, and cayenne, and simmer, uncovered, for 30 minutes.

Add okra and simmer until tender, 5 to 8 minutes. Stir in shrimp and simmer until just cooked through, 2 to 3 minutes. Stir in scallion greens and salt to taste. Serve gumbo over rice, with hot pepper sauce for additional seasoning as desired.

COOK'S NOTES

■ Andouille or another smoked pork sausage can be substituted for the tasso. Brown the cut-up sausage in

a heavy skillet over moderate heat, stirring occasionally, then transfer to paper towels to drain. Stir into the gumbo with the scallion greens.

■ The gumbo, without the okra, shrimp, and scallion greens, improves in flavor if made up to 1 day ahead. Cool completely, uncovered, then refrigerate, covered. Reheat before proceeding.

Brazilian Shrimp Stew

SERVES 6
ACTIVE TIME: 25 MINUTES ■ START TO FINISH: 45 MINUTES

■ *Feijoada*, a selection of sliced meats served with rice and black beans, may be the national dish of Brazil, but *moqueca de camarão* is a close second. A rich seafood stew from the coastal region of Bahia, it always includes three ingredients: coconut milk, *dendê* (palm) oil, and *malagueta* peppers. Every home cook there has his or her own recipe for *moqueca*. We've substituted black pepper for the *malagueta* pepper and have made the *dendê* oil optional. If you can find it, by all means use it—just a spoonful transforms the coconut milk with its shimmery deep orange color and boosts the tropical flavor of the shrimp. It is as perishable as it is seductive, so smell it before you use it. ■

1¼ pounds large shrimp in shells (21–25 per pound), peeled and deveined

2 garlic cloves, minced

¼ cup fresh lemon juice

Salt and freshly ground black pepper

1 (14- to 15-ounce) can whole tomatoes in juice

1½ tablespoons olive oil

1 medium onion, finely chopped

1 green bell pepper, cored, seeded, and finely chopped

½ teaspoon cayenne

5 tablespoons coarsely chopped fresh cilantro

1 cup well-stirred canned unsweetened coconut milk

1 tablespoon *dendê* (palm) oil (optional; see Sources)

ACCOMPANIMENT: white rice

Toss shrimp with garlic, lemon juice, ½ teaspoon salt, and ¼ teaspoon pepper in a bowl. Marinate, covered and refrigerated, for 20 minutes.

Puree tomatoes with juice in a blender until smooth.

Heat olive oil in a 12-inch heavy skillet over moderately low heat until hot but not smoking. Add onion and bell pepper and cook, stirring, until softened, 8 to 10 minutes. Add cayenne, 1 tablespoon cilantro, and 1 teaspoon salt and cook, stirring, for 1 minute. Add tomato puree, bring to a simmer, and simmer briskly, stirring occasionally, until mixture is very thick, 10 to 15 minutes.

Stir in coconut milk and bring to a boil, then add shrimp mixture and cook, stirring, until shrimp are just cooked through, 3 to 5 minutes.

Stir in *dendê* oil, if using, and remaining ¼ cup cilantro, and season with salt and pepper. Serve with rice.

Squid in Vinegar Sauce

SERVES 4
ACTIVE TIME: 25 MINUTES ■ START TO FINISH: 40 MINUTES

■ Filipino cuisine is an amalgam of many different influences. *Adobo*—meat or fish cooked with lots of garlic, soy sauce, and vinegar—is one of the country's few truly native dishes. Squid *adobo,* or *adobong pusit,* adds tomatoes and onions to the mix. Authentic Filipino *adobo* calls for coconut, palm, or sugarcane vinegar, but we use cider vinegar to good effect. ■

  ½ cup water
  ⅓ cup cider vinegar
  ¼ cup soy sauce
  ¼ cup thinly sliced garlic
  ½ teaspoon freshly ground black pepper
  1 pound cleaned medium squid, bodies cut into
      1-inch-wide rings, tentacles left whole
  2 tablespoons vegetable oil
  1 medium onion, halved lengthwise and thinly sliced
      lengthwise
  1 (14- to 15-ounce) can diced tomatoes in juice

ACCOMPANIMENT: white rice

Bring water, vinegar, soy sauce, garlic, and pepper to a boil in a 2-quart heavy saucepan. Add squid

(liquid will not cover it) and cook over moderately high heat, stirring constantly, just until opaque, 1 to 2 minutes. Immediately drain squid in a sieve set over a bowl; reserve liquid.

Heat oil in a 12-inch heavy skillet over high heat until hot but not smoking. Add onion and cook, stirring occasionally, until lightly browned, about 3 minutes. Add tomatoes with juice, bring to a boil, and boil, stirring occasionally, until most of liquid has evaporated, about 3 minutes. Add squid cooking liquid and boil, stirring occasionally, until reduced by half, about 8 minutes.

Stir in squid and simmer until cooked through, about 2 minutes. Serve with rice.

Squid and Swiss Chard Stew

SERVES 4 TO 6
ACTIVE TIME: 30 MINUTES ■ START TO FINISH: 1¼ HOURS

■ Here is a dish that exemplifies the Italian phrase *brutti ma buoni* ("ugly but good"), which is a poetic way of saying that it isn't a looker but tastes great. (Don't be tempted to use red chard, which will impart a swampy hue.) This Tuscan classic, adapted from one served at Cibrèo in Florence, is a great alternative to a traditional meaty stew on a chill winter's night. Make sure to have a loaf of country bread on hand for soaking up the flavorful broth. ■

  ⅓ cup extra-virgin olive oil
  1 cup minced onion
  ½ cup minced carrot
  ½ cup minced celery
  1 cup tomato sauce
  ½ cup dry red wine
  3 bottled pickled peperoncini, stemmed and chopped
  2 large garlic cloves, minced
  ½ teaspoon fine sea salt
  3 pounds green Swiss chard, coarse stems discarded,
      leaves cut into 2-inch pieces
  2 pounds cleaned squid, bodies cut into ½-inch-wide
      rings, rings of tentacles cut lengthwise in half if
      large

ACCOMPANIMENT: grilled or toasted crusty bread

Heat oil in a 5- to 6-quart wide heavy pot over moderate heat until hot but not smoking. Add onion, carrot, and celery and cook, stirring occasionally, until pale golden, 10 to 15 minutes.

Stir in tomato sauce, wine, peperoncini, garlic, and sea salt and bring to a simmer. Stir in half of Swiss chard and cook, covered, until wilted, about 2 minutes. Stir in remaining Swiss chard and cook, covered, for 2 minutes more.

Stir in squid and simmer gently, covered, over low heat, stirring occasionally, until squid is very tender, about 45 minutes.

Serve with grilled or toasted bread.

Salt and Pepper Squid

SERVES 4
ACTIVE TIME: 15 MINUTES ■ START TO FINISH: 30 MINUTES

■ This utterly simple version of fried squid will remind you what all the fuss is about. The secret is in dredging the squiggles in ultralight cornstarch and seasoning the batches only with salt and pepper. The glorious results will be snapped up as fast as you can fry them. ■

6–7 cups vegetable oil for deep-frying
  1 pound cleaned squid, preferably small, bodies cut into ¼-inch-wide rings, tentacles left whole
  ½ cup cornstarch
  ½ teaspoon salt
  ½ teaspoon freshly ground black pepper
SPECIAL EQUIPMENT: a deep-fat thermometer

Put a rack in middle of oven and preheat oven to 200°F.

Heat 2 inches oil in a 4- to 5-quart deep heavy pot over high heat until it registers 390°F on thermometer. Dredge one third of squid in one third of cornstarch, shaking off excess. Fry, stirring occasionally, until crisp and just barely beginning to turn pale golden, 1 to 2 minutes. Transfer with a slotted spoon to paper towels to drain, then transfer to a baking sheet and keep warm in oven. (Return oil to 390°F between batches.) Coat and fry remaining squid in 2 batches in same manner.

Toss squid with salt and pepper and serve immediately.

PERFECT FRYING

The secret to crisp, nongreasy fried food with even color is to heat the oil to the right temperature and maintain it. In our recipes, we take out the guesswork by calling for a deep-fat thermometer and reminding you not to crowd the pan. (An instant-read or a meat thermometer can't be substituted, because their gauges don't go up high enough for frying.) If you don't own a deep-fat thermometer, another way to gauge whether the oil is hot enough is to pinch off a tiny piece of whatever you're frying and add it to the oil. If it bubbles vigorously, you're ready to fry. Here are some other tips.

- Pat food completely dry before frying.

- Cut food into small pieces when possible so that it cooks through before the outside burns.

- Use an oil with a high smoke point (the stage at which the oil begins to burn and give food a bitter flavor), such as canola, vegetable, or peanut oil.

- If the food is enveloped in a batter or thicker coating, make sure that it adheres firmly and evenly. If bits of the coating break off, scoop them out of the hot oil with a slotted spoon before they burn.

- If you are deep-frying, turn or stir the pieces throughout the cooking; if shallow-frying, turn once or twice.

- If frying vegetables or other ingredients as well as fish, fry the stronger-tasting fish last.

- Let the oil cool after frying. If it wasn't heated to over 400°F, you can strain it and reuse it once if desired; otherwise, discard it.

Mussels in Zucchini Basil Broth

■ This oh-so-good broth gets its heady aroma from fresh basil, its body from zucchini, and sharpness and richness from olive oil. It's much like a soupy pesto, with zucchini taking the place of nuts and cheese. Be careful not to overcook it, so the broth doesn't lose its green brilliance. ■

- 1 pound zucchini (2–3 medium), coarsely chopped
- ¾ cup loosely packed fresh basil leaves
- 1 medium shallot, coarsely chopped
- 2 garlic cloves
- 1½ cups water
- ¾ teaspoon salt
- ¼ teaspoon freshly ground black pepper
- ⅓ cup extra-virgin olive oil
- 4 pounds mussels, preferably cultivated, scrubbed and beards removed

GARNISH: chopped fresh basil

Combine zucchini, basil, shallot, garlic, water, salt, pepper, and oil, in batches if necessary, in a blender and puree until smooth, 1 to 2 minutes (per batch).

Transfer puree to a 6- to 7- quart wide heavy pot and add mussels. Bring to a simmer, uncovered, over moderately high heat, then cover and cook, stirring occasionally, until mussels just open wide; check frequently after 4 minutes. (Discard any mussels that have not opened after 8 minutes.)

Divide mussels and broth among bowls and sprinkle with chopped basil.

Spicy Curried Mussels

■ Adding cream to the curry-spiced mussel cooking liquid turns this dish into a fast, gratifying meal. We like to mop up the golden sauce with bread, but the mussels are also excellent served over rice. Red pepper flakes offer a dash of extra heat; depending on how hot your curry powder is, you may want to adjust the amount. ■

- 2 tablespoons unsalted butter
- ⅔ cup finely chopped shallots
- 2½ teaspoons curry powder, preferably Madras
- ¼ teaspoon red pepper flakes, or to taste
- ¼ cup medium-dry sherry
- 4 pounds mussels, preferably cultivated, scrubbed and beards removed
- 1 cup heavy cream
- ⅓ cup water
- ¼ cup chopped fresh cilantro
  Salt

ACCOMPANIMENT: crusty bread

Melt butter in an 8-quart wide pot over moderate heat. Add shallots, curry powder, and red pepper flakes and cook, stirring frequently, until shallots are softened, 3 to 4 minutes. Add sherry, bring to a simmer, and simmer, stirring, for 1 minute.

Add mussels and cook, covered, over moderately high heat until they just open wide; check frequently after 4 minutes and transfer opened mussels to a bowl. (Discard any that have not opened after 8 minutes.)

Add cream and water to pot, bring to a simmer, and simmer for 1 minute. Add cilantro and salt to taste, pour over mussels, and toss gently. Serve with bread.

Seafood "Paella" with Israeli Couscous

■ As in traditional paella, chorizo, clams, mussels, scallops, and shrimp are bathed in a saffron glow, but the grain is Israeli couscous. Cooking the pearl-shaped orbs separately from the sausage and seafood is less fraught than making rice-based paella. We adapted this recipe from one by chef Robert Treviño of the Parrot Club in Puerto Rico. ■

¼ cup olive oil

1 large onion, chopped

¼ teaspoon crumbled saffron threads

2 cups Israeli couscous

2¾ cups plus ⅓ cup water

Salt

1 red bell pepper, cored, seeded, and cut into
    ¼-inch dice

¼ pound Spanish chorizo (cured spicy pork sausage),
    quartered lengthwise and cut into ¼-inch slices
    Freshly ground black pepper

12 small hard-shelled clams, such as littlenecks
    (1½–2 inches wide), scrubbed

12 mussels, preferably cultivated, scrubbed and beards
    removed

1 pound sea scallops, tough ligament removed from
    side of each if necessary

½ pound medium shrimp in shells (31–35 per pound),
    peeled and deveined

1 cup frozen peas, thawed

Heat 2 tablespoons oil in a 3-quart heavy sauce-pan over moderate heat. Add half of onion and ⅛ teaspoon saffron and cook, stirring occasionally, until onion is softened and golden, about 8 minutes.

Stir in couscous and cook until a shade darker, about 2 minutes. Add 2¾ cups water and 1 teaspoon salt, bring to a simmer, and simmer, covered, until liquid is absorbed and couscous is al dente, 12 to 15 minutes. Remove from heat and let stand, covered, for 10 minutes.

Meanwhile, heat remaining 2 tablespoons oil in a 12-inch heavy skillet over moderate heat. Add bell pepper, chorizo, remaining onion, remaining ⅛ tea-spoon saffron, ¼ teaspoon salt, and ¼ teaspoon pepper and cook, stirring occasionally, until vegetables are softened and golden, 10 to 12 minutes. Add remaining ⅓ cup water and increase heat to moderately high. Add clams and cook, covered, stirring occasionally, until they just open wide, about 6 minutes. (Discard any clams that have not opened after 10 minutes.) Transfer opened clams with tongs to a bowl. Add mussels to skillet and cook, covered, stirring occasionally, until mussels just open wide; check frequently after 4 minutes and transfer opened mussels to bowl. (Discard any that have not opened after 8 minutes.)

Pat scallops dry and season with ½ teaspoon salt and ¼ teaspoon pepper. Add scallops to skillet and cook, turning once, until just cooked through, about 6 minutes. Transfer to bowl with clams and mussels. Season shrimp with ¼ teaspoon salt, add to skillet, and cook, turning once, until just cooked through, about 3 minutes.

Reduce heat to moderate, return all seafood to skillet, and stir in couscous and peas. Cook until just warmed through, 2 to 3 minutes.

Seafood Fra Diavolo

SERVES 4 TO 6
ACTIVE TIME: 30 MINUTES ■ START TO FINISH: 1½ HOURS

■ Fra diavolo is a spicy, tomato-based pasta sauce. It's important to let the squid simmer gently until it becomes very tender before adding the other seafood. ■

¼ cup olive oil

3 garlic cloves, finely chopped

½ teaspoon red pepper flakes

1 (28-ounce) can whole tomatoes in juice,
    drained, juice reserved, and chopped

½ teaspoon salt

½ pound cleaned squid, preferably small,
    bodies cut into ¼-inch-wide rings, tentacles
    left whole

½ pound littleneck or Manila clams, scrubbed

½ pound mussels, preferably cultivated, scrubbed
    and beards removed

½ pound medium shrimp (31–35 per pound), peeled
    and deveined

½ cup finely chopped fresh flat-leaf parsley

1 pound dried linguine

Heat 2 tablespoons oil in a 5- to 6-quart heavy pot over moderately high heat until hot but not smoking. Add garlic and red pepper flakes and cook, stirring, until garlic is golden, about 30 seconds. Stir in tomatoes with juice and salt and bring to a boil. Add squid and return to a boil. Reduce heat to low and simmer, covered, until squid is just tender, about 30 minutes.

Remove lid and simmer until sauce is reduced slightly, about 10 minutes. Stir in clams and mussels and bring to a boil over high heat. Cook, covered, until clams and mussels open, 5 to 7 minutes. (Discard any that have not opened after 8 minutes.) Stir in shrimp and cook, uncovered, until just cooked through, about 2 minutes. Stir in ¼ cup parsley.

Meanwhile, cook pasta in a 6- to 8-quart pot of boiling salted water (3 tablespoons salt) until al dente; drain.

Add pasta to sauce and simmer, stirring, for 30 seconds. Serve drizzled with remaining 2 tablespoons oil and sprinkled with remaining ¼ cup parsley.

Cast-Iron Roasted Clams

SERVES 4
ACTIVE TIME: 20 MINUTES ■ START TO FINISH: 1 HOUR

■ If you've inherited your grandmother's large cast-iron skillet, now is the time to pull it out. (Or you can substitute a heavy roasting pan.) Chef Jody Adams, who shared this recipe, uses East Coast littlenecks when she makes this dish at her restaurant Rialto, in Cambridge, Massachusetts, but any small hard-shelled clam will do. The clam juices mix with the roasted tomatoes and garlic and flavor the tender potatoes and onions, which turn a deep golden brown in the pan. ■

  3 pounds medium (3- to 4-inch) red potatoes
 16 garlic cloves
  3 small red onions, quartered lengthwise, enough
      of root end left intact to hold onion quarters
      together
 ½ cup extra-virgin olive oil
  1 teaspoon salt
 ½ teaspoon freshly ground black pepper
1¾ pounds plum tomatoes (10–12), halved lengthwise
  4 pounds small hard-shelled clams (less than 2 inches
      wide), scrubbed
 ½ teaspoon red pepper flakes
 ¼ cup chopped fresh flat-leaf parsley
SPECIAL EQUIPMENT: a 14-inch cast-iron skillet with a lid (or
      heavy-duty foil) or a 17-by-12-inch heavy roasting
      pan (not aluminum, and preferably dark metal)
      and heavy-duty foil

Put a rack in middle of oven and preheat oven to 500°F.

Cut potatoes into ½-inch-thick slices. Toss with garlic, onions, oil, salt, and pepper in skillet (or roasting pan). Roast until potatoes begin to brown, about 15 minutes.

Add tomatoes, tossing to combine, and roast until skins wrinkle and split, about 10 minutes.

Add clams and red pepper flakes and roast, covered with lid (or tightly covered with foil), until clams are fully open, 6 to 10 minutes. (Discard any clams that have not opened after 10 minutes.)

Sprinkle with parsley and serve from skillet.

COOK'S NOTE
■ The clams can be scrubbed up to 1 hour ahead and refrigerated, uncovered.

ALL ABOUT CLAMS

Like oysters, scallops, and mussels, clams are bivalve mollusks: they have two symmetrical shells held together with a ligament and a hinge. Most clams live in sand or mud, and they are harvested with a rake, shovel, or dredge. The wild harvest of clams can't meet consumer demand and wouldn't be sustainable if depended upon, so most of the clams available in fish markets and supermarkets are cultivated. Since clams filter their food from the water, they actually improve water quality by removing excess nutrients. Happily, the farming of clams (and other bivalves) is well regulated and considered ecologically sound by the Monterey Bay Aquarium Seafood Watch and the Seafood Choices Alliance (for more on these organizations, see page 343).

ATLANTIC VARIETIES

ATLANTIC HARD-SHELL CLAM *(Mercenaria mercenaria)* Also known as a quahog (pronounced "*ko*-hog"), or hard clam, this clam is sold under other names according to size. A **littleneck**, the smallest, measures from 1 to 2½ inches in diameter, depending on the region. A **cherrystone** is a medium quahog that measures from 2 to 3½ inches in diameter. (In some areas, a 2- to 2½-inch quahog is sold as a **topneck**.) A **chowder clam**, the largest quahog, and the one identified as a quahog in New England, measures more than 3 inches across. The distinctive purple-scarred quahog shells, by the way, were used as wampum by Native Americans.

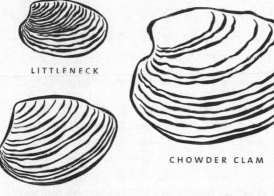

LITTLENECK

CHOWDER CLAM

CHERRYSTONE

ATLANTIC SOFT-SHELL CLAM *(Mya arenaria)* This is usually referred to as a steamer, longneck, or fryer. The term *soft shell* is confusing, because this clam actually has a hard shell, but it's thinner and more brittle than that of a quahog. Once a steamer is harvested, it can't close its shell completely because its long tubelike "neck" (anatomically speaking, two connected siphons used for respiration and feeding) protrudes; consequently, a soft-shell is more perishable than a hard-shell. (Check for freshness by touching the neck gently; it should retract slightly.)

ATLANTIC RAZOR (OR JACKKNIFE) CLAM *(Ensis directus)* This soft-shelled clam is instantly recognizable; its long, narrow shell looks like a straight razor and is almost as sharp. Like a steamer, it gapes even when closed if out of the water. Atlantic razor clams, not to be confused with the wider, meatier Pacific variety (see below) are popular in Chinese restaurants, where they are often steamed in black bean sauce (see page 378).

PACIFIC VARIETIES

MANILA CLAM *(Tapes philippinarum)* Native to the western Pacific Ocean (Japan, China, Korea, and the Philippines), this clam was accidentally introduced to the Pacific Coast of the United States and Canada in the early twentieth century and has become the hottest ticket in the clam world. The seafood guru Jon Rowley calls the little beauties a superfood: they're low in fat and chock-full of vitamins (especially B_{12}), minerals, amino acids, and omega-3 fatty acids. "Manila clams," he says, "served with parsley [high in vitamins A, C, and K] and garlic [vitamins C and B_6, calcium, thiamin, manganese, and phosphorus] could be one of the most nutritious dishes on the planet." Even though Manilas are small clams (1¼ to 2 inches in diameter), you get more meat per clam than from other hard-shells because their shells are thinner.

PACIFIC LITTLENECK *(Protothaca staminea)* This hard-shelled clam, native to the West Coast, is less expensive than the more popular Manila clam, which it resembles. Pacific littlenecks can be a challenge to cook because they won't all open at the same time. Freezing them in the shell briefly beforehand helps them cook more consistently, but they tend to be tougher in any case.

WEST COAST (OR PACIFIC) RAZOR CLAM *(Siliqua patula)* This wider, larger, meatier cousin of the Atlantic razor clam has a more pronounced flavor. Perhaps the most famous fan of this Pacific Northwest specialty was James Beard. "When I was a child and living near the Oregon coast," he wrote in *James Beard's New Fish Cookery*, "I used to dig them out by the bucketful in the early morning when the tide was out. My mother sautéed them in butter, cooked them as delicately light fritters, or made them into magnificent chowder." West Coast razor clams live in sand in the ocean surf. Today, most of the commercial supply comes from Alaska.

Razor Clams with Black Bean Sauce

SERVES 4 AS A MAIN COURSE
ACTIVE TIME: 25 MINUTES ▪ START TO FINISH: 25 MINUTES

▪ Because Pacific razor clams require more cleaning and prep work, make sure you use Atlantic razors here. This popular quick-cooking Chinese preparation is a wonderful introduction to these meaty bivalves. They're great paired with a stir-fried green vegetable like *gai lan* (Chinese broccoli) or bok choy. ▪

3 tablespoons Chinese rice wine, preferably Shaoxing, or medium-dry sherry
1 tablespoon light soy sauce (see Cook's Note)
1 teaspoon sugar
¼ teaspoon salt
¼ teaspoon cornstarch
1 (1-inch) piece fresh ginger, peeled, thinly sliced lengthwise, and cut into matchsticks
2 garlic cloves, very thinly sliced
1 fresh hot green chile, such as Thai or serrano, thinly sliced, including seeds
2 tablespoons Chinese fermented black beans, rinsed well and chopped (see Sources)
2 tablespoons peanut oil
2 pounds razor clams (see Cook's Note), shells scrubbed
1 teaspoon Asian sesame oil
¼ cup thinly sliced scallions

ACCOMPANIMENT: white rice

Stir together rice wine, soy sauce, sugar, salt, and cornstarch in a small bowl until sugar and salt are dissolved. Combine ginger, garlic, chile, and black beans in another small bowl.

Heat a 12-inch heavy skillet with a lid over high heat until hot, about 1 minute. Add peanut oil and swirl to coat bottom of pan. Add black bean mixture and cook, stirring, until fragrant, about 1 minute. Add clams, cover, and cook, shaking skillet occasionally, until clams open wide, 2 to 3 minutes. Remove skillet from heat and, with tongs, transfer clams, opened side up, to a platter.

Return clam cooking liquid to a simmer. Stir cornstarch mixture again, then whisk into cooking liquid and simmer sauce until slightly thickened, about 1 minute. Stir in sesame oil and half of scallions and pour over clams. Sprinkle with remaining scallions. Serve with rice.

COOK'S NOTES
▪ Light soy sauce refers to the first pressing. It is lighter in color and has a more delicate flavor than dark soy. "Lite" soy refers to a low-sodium alternative.
▪ You can also use Manila clams or littlenecks.
▪ The clams can be scrubbed up to 1 hour ahead and refrigerated, uncovered.

Scalloped Oysters

SERVES 6 AS A SIDE DISH
ACTIVE TIME: 20 MINUTES ▪ START TO FINISH: 1 HOUR

▪ Tender oysters layered with a buttery mix of bread crumbs and crushed oyster crackers are rich and delicious. Save this gratin for your nearest and dearest, perhaps as an accompaniment to an intimate holiday dinner—it is perfect with Thanksgiving turkey or Christmas goose. And if you buy the oysters already shucked, it couldn't be easier to make. ▪

3 ounces (about 1¾ cups) oyster crackers
½ cup fine dry bread crumbs
¾ stick (6 tablespoons) unsalted butter, melted
½ teaspoon freshly ground black pepper
1 quart shucked oysters (3–4 dozen), drained
⅓ cup heavy cream

Put a rack in middle of oven and preheat oven to 400°F.

Pulse crackers in a food processor until finely ground. Add bread crumbs, butter, and pepper and pulse to combine.

Sprinkle 1 cup cracker mixture evenly over bottom of a 2-quart gratin or shallow baking dish. Arrange oysters evenly over crumbs and drizzle cream over oysters. Top oysters with remaining crumb mixture, spreading it evenly.

Bake until top is golden and gratin is bubbling, about 40 minutes.

Creamed Oysters
on Toasted Corn Bread

SERVES 4 GENEROUSIY AS A MAIN COURSE,
8 AS A FIRST COURSE
ACTIVE TIME: 1¼ HOURS ■ START TO FINISH: 1¼ HOURS
(INCLUDES MAKING CORN BREAD)

■ Corn bread and briny oysters, two quintessential American products, have an affinity for each other. The tender crumb of the bread laps up the lush sauce but is sturdy enough to keep its shape. Chopped celery leaves add a clean, clear top note. ■

½ stick (4 tablespoons) unsalted butter, plus additional for buttering corn bread
½ cup finely chopped shallots
½ cup finely chopped celery, plus 3 tablespoons finely chopped celery leaves
3 tablespoons all-purpose flour
32 shucked oysters, 1¼ cups liquor reserved and strained
¼ cup whole milk
¼ cup heavy cream
8 (3-inch) squares Corn Bread (recipe follows)
2 teaspoons Worcestershire sauce
1 teaspoon ground celery seed
¼ teaspoon salt, or to taste
¼ teaspoon cayenne, or to taste

GETTING AT THE MEAT OF THE OYSTER

A short, sturdy oyster knife (available at cookware stores and most fish markets) and some sort of work glove are the only tools you need to shuck oysters. First, scrub them well with a stiff brush under cold running water. Then, holding the oyster flat side up (you don't want to spill any of its liquor, or briny juices), insert the knife into the narrow hinged end and twist until the shell loosens and pops open. Don't be afraid to put some muscle into it. If the shell crumbles and won't open, attack the wide end instead. Then slide the knife blade against the top shell to cut through the large muscle, freeing the oyster. After prying off the lid, so to speak, slide your knife along the bottom shell to release the oyster completely.

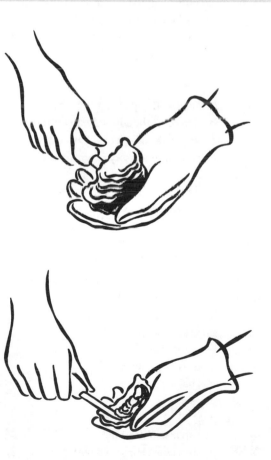

Although shucking your own oysters is the best way to ensure quality (water is often added to preshucked oysters and they absorb it, thus changing in flavor and texture), there are times when you can't beat the convenience of store-bought shucked fresh oysters. When shopping for them, look for bright, clear liquid—and, although it may sound obvious, check the "sell by" date. This date is 21 days after shucking in the winter and, depending on the company, from 14 to 17 days after shucking in summer. In other words, if you are buying oysters on December 2 and the sell-by date is December 21, you are buying very fresh oysters; if you're buying them on December 20, they will be three weeks old.

MAKE THE SAUCE: Melt butter in a 3- to 4-quart heavy saucepan over moderate heat. Add shallots and chopped celery and cook, stirring, until softened, about 5 minutes. Whisk in flour and cook over moderately low heat, whisking, for 3 minutes to make a roux. Whisk in reserved oyster liquor, milk, and cream and bring to a boil, whisking. Reduce heat and simmer, whisking, until thickened, about 3 minutes. Remove from heat.

TOAST THE CORN BREAD: Preheat broiler. Split corn bread squares horizontally in half with a serrated knife and arrange cut side up on a baking sheet. Broil corn bread, turning once, until lightly toasted, about 2 minutes. Butter cut sides of corn bread.

COOK THE OYSTERS: Reheat sauce over moderately low heat. Stir in Worcestershire sauce, celery seed, salt, cayenne, and oysters and simmer until edges of oysters curl, 1 to 2 minutes. Stir in celery leaves.

Arrange 2 bottom halves of a corn bread square on a plate (if serving 4) and top with some creamed oysters and top of corn bread square. Repeat with remaining corn bread squares and oysters.

COOK'S NOTE

■ The sauce can be made up to 1 day ahead. Cool, uncovered, then cover the surface with buttered wax paper and refrigerate. Reheat over low heat, whisking, adding more milk as necessary to reach the desired consistency.

Corn Bread

MAKES NINE 3-INCH SQUARES
ACTIVE TIME: 10 MINUTES ■ START TO FINISH: 30 MINUTES

■ Spread with butter, corn bread is an all-purpose side dish for soups, stews, and chilis. ■

    1 cup yellow cornmeal
    1 cup all-purpose flour
1½ teaspoons baking powder
    ½ teaspoon baking soda
    ½ teaspoon salt
    2 large eggs
1¼ cups well-shaken buttermilk
    ½ stick (4 tablespoons) unsalted butter,
        melted and cooled

Put a rack in middle of oven and preheat oven to 425°F. Generously grease a 9-inch square baking pan.

Whisk together cornmeal, flour, baking powder, baking soda, and salt in a bowl. Whisk together eggs, buttermilk, and butter in a small bowl, add to cornmeal mixture, and stir batter until just combined.

Heat baking pan in oven until very hot, 3 to 5 minutes. Pour in batter, spreading it evenly, and bake until top is pale golden and sides are beginning to pull away from edges of pan, about 15 minutes.

Cool corn bread in pan for 5 minutes, then turn out onto a rack to cool completely. Cut into 9 squares.

COOK'S NOTE

■ If you plan to toast the corn bread before serving it, you can make it up to 1 day ahead. Keep it, covered, at room temperature.

Thai-Style Crab Salad in Papaya

SERVES 4 AS A LIGHT MAIN COURSE
ACTIVE TIME: 20 MINUTES ■ START TO FINISH: 20 MINUTES

■ This lively lunch dish comes together in just 20 minutes, and you don't even have to turn on the stove. Look for gold or strawberry papayas. Their sweet flavor complements this tangy crab salad beautifully. ■

    ¼ cup rice vinegar (not seasoned)
    2 tablespoons water
    4 teaspoons Asian fish sauce
    3 tablespoons sugar
    ½ teaspoon salt
    ½ cup chopped green bell pepper
    ½ cup chopped red bell pepper
1½ teaspoons minced serrano chile, including
        seeds
    2 tablespoons chopped fresh cilantro
    ½ pound jumbo lump crabmeat (see Cook's Note),
        picked over for shells and cartilage
    2 ripe small papayas, halved lengthwise
        and seeded
ACCOMPANIMENT: lime wedges

Whisk together vinegar, water, fish sauce, sugar, and salt in a bowl until sugar and salt are dissolved. Add bell peppers, chile, cilantro, and crab and toss gently to combine.

Serve crab salad mounded in papaya halves, with lime wedges.

COOK'S NOTE
■ You can also use Dungeness crabmeat.

Kerala Boatmen's Crab Curry

SERVES 6
ACTIVE TIME: 30 MINUTES ■ START TO FINISH: 30 MINUTES

■ The cookbook author Laxmi Hiremath introduced us to this fabulous curry—sweet nuggets of lump crabmeat bathed in a rich coconut milk sauce punctuated by many bright spices. Kerala, whose name means "land of the coconuts," is located at the southwestern tip of India, facing the Arabian Sea, and is dotted and crisscrossed with lagoons, lakes, rivers, and canals. Seafood, understandably, makes up a large part of the diet, and this dish is styled on the ones that Kerala boatmen prepare for themselves. Despite its pedigree, though, these ingredients are simple to find. ■

- 2 tablespoons vegetable oil
- 1 teaspoon brown or black mustard seeds (see Sources)
- 1 medium onion, chopped
- 3 large garlic cloves, minced
- 1½ teaspoons minced peeled fresh ginger
- 2 (3-inch) dried hot red chiles, seeded, seeds reserved, and chiles crumbled
- ½ teaspoon black peppercorns
- 1 teaspoon ground cumin
- 1 teaspoon ground coriander
- ½ teaspoon turmeric
- 1½ pounds jumbo lump crabmeat (see Cook's Note), picked over for shells and cartilage
- 2 tablespoons chopped fresh cilantro

- 1 (13- to 14-ounce) can unsweetened coconut milk, well stirred
- 1½ teaspoons kosher salt, or to taste
GARNISH: sliced scallion greens
ACCOMPANIMENT: basmati rice

Heat oil in a 4- to 5-quart pot over moderately high heat until hot but not smoking. Add mustard seeds and cook until they begin to pop, about 30 seconds. Stir in onion, garlic, ginger, chiles with seeds, and peppercorns and cook, stirring, until onion is just browned, 3 to 4 minutes. Stir in cumin, coriander, and turmeric until well combined. Add crabmeat and cook, gently stirring occasionally (avoid breaking up crab), until heated through, about 4 minutes.

Stir in cilantro, coconut milk, and salt, bring to a simmer, and simmer, uncovered, stirring occasionally, until sauce is slightly thickened, 6 to 8 minutes.

Spoon curry over rice and garnish with scallion greens.

COOK'S NOTE
■ You can also use Dungeness crabmeat, or snow or king crab cut into ½-inch lengths.

Steamed Blue Crabs with Black Vinegar Dipping Sauce

SERVES 6
ACTIVE TIME: 20 MINUTES ■ START TO FINISH: 35 MINUTES

■ Teasing the meat out of blue crabs takes a little more work than larger crabs like Dungeness require, but their sweet flavor and delicate texture merit the extra effort. Blues are commercially harvested from New York to Florida—including, most famously, the Chesapeake Bay—as well as the Gulf Coast states, and the best are available in the late summer and early fall. We love them with this dipping sauce, which gets its remarkable depth from Chinese black vinegar. (Cider vinegar is an able substitute.) ■

½ cup coarsely chopped fresh cilantro stems

36 (4- to 6-ounce) live blue crabs, rinsed well

FOR DIPPING SAUCE

1½–2 tablespoons finely chopped peeled
fresh ginger (to taste)

½ cup soy sauce

¼ cup sugar

¼ cup water

3 tablespoons Chinese black vinegar, preferably
Chinkiang (see Sources), or cider vinegar

¼ teaspoon salt

SPECIAL EQUIPMENT: long-handled tongs

Bring 1½ inches water to a boil in a 6- to 8-quart wide heavy pot with a lid. Add cilantro stems, then carefully add half of crabs, using tongs, and return to a boil. Cook, covered, for 8 minutes (for 4-ounce crabs) to 10 minutes (for 6-ounce crabs) from time they enter water. (To determine doneness, remove a claw with tongs and crack it with the handle of a dinner knife; use knife to extract meat from claw. Crabmeat should be opaque.) Transfer crabs with tongs to a large platter and cover loosely with foil to keep warm. Cook remaining crabs in same manner.

MEANWHILE, MAKE THE SAUCE: Stir together all ingredients in a small bowl until sugar and salt are dissolved.

If necessary, dip crabs in cooking liquid to remove any external residue, then transfer to another large platter. Serve crabs hot with dipping sauce.

Crab Cakes with Wasabi Caper Sauce

SERVES 4

ACTIVE TIME: 45 MINUTES ■ START TO FINISH: 1¾ HOURS

■ Spiced with hot mustard and ginger, these lump crabmeat cakes, bound with egg and a bit of mayo, are dotted with leek and red bell pepper. A panko coating ensures they fry up crisp. The recipe comes from reader Peter Tulaney of Brooklyn, New York. For help in finding the Asian ingredients, see Sources. ■

FOR WASABI CAPER SAUCE

⅓ cup mayonnaise

2 tablespoons drained capers, chopped

2–3 teaspoons wasabi paste (to taste)

FOR CRAB CAKES

1 large egg

1 large egg yolk

1½ tablespoons mayonnaise

¾ teaspoon spicy Chinese mustard (see Cook's Note)

½ red bell pepper, finely chopped

2 tablespoons finely chopped leek (white part only),
washed well

½ teaspoon minced peeled fresh ginger

1½ cups panko (Japanese bread crumbs)

1 pound jumbo lump crabmeat (see Cook's Note),
picked over for shells and cartilage

About 2 cups vegetable oil for shallow-frying

MAKE THE WASABI CAPER SAUCE: Stir together all ingredients in a small bowl. Refrigerate, covered, until ready to serve.

MAKE THE CRAB CAKES: Whisk together egg, yolk, mayonnaise, and mustard in a large bowl. Stir in bell pepper, leek, ginger, and ¾ cup panko. Stir in crabmeat and refrigerate, covered, for 1 hour.

Divide crab mixture into 8 mounds and form into eight 1-inch-thick patties. Spread remaining ¾ cup panko in a shallow dish. Carefully coat patties, one at a time, in panko.

Heat ¾ inch oil in a 10-inch heavy skillet over moderately high heat until hot but not smoking. Fry crab cakes in 2 batches, turning once, until golden brown, 4 to 6 minutes per batch; transfer to several layers of paper towels to drain.

Serve crab cakes with sauce.

COOK'S NOTES

■ Colman's mustard mixed with water can be substituted for the Chinese mustard. Follow the instructions on the tin. The packets from Chinese takeout can also be used.

■ You can also use Dungeness crabmeat.

■ The crab cakes can be formed and breaded up to 3 hours ahead and refrigerated, covered.

Louisiana Seafood Boil

SERVES 6
ACTIVE TIME: 1 HOUR ■ START TO FINISH: 1¾ HOURS

■ Roll up your sleeves and put out the paper napkins—this is summer entertaining at its messy best. Traditional "boils" throw all the ingredients into the pot together to cook, but we prefer to stagger the crab, shrimp, potatoes, and corn so that everything cooks perfectly. Spread out on platters, the boil may look like a lot of food, but rest assured that guests won't be able to stop at just one or two crabs. Ice-cold beer is the beverage of choice. ■

- 24 live blue crabs
- 2 (3-ounce) packets Zatarain's Crab Boil (see Sources) or 5 tablespoons Old Bay seasoning
- ½ cup salt
- 1 tablespoon cayenne
- 3 lemons, quartered
- 2 onions, halved
- 1½ pounds small boiling potatoes (about 2 inches in diameter)
- 2 whole heads garlic
- 6 ears corn, shucked
- 3 tablespoons Old Bay seasoning, or to taste
- 2 pounds extra-large shrimp in shells (16–20 per pound)

ACCOMPANIMENTS: Horseradish Cocktail Sauce (recipe follows); French bread

SPECIAL EQUIPMENT: a 7- to 8-gallon kettle; long-handled tongs

Bring 5 gallons water to a boil in kettle. While water comes to a boil, rinse crabs in 2 or 3 changes of water in a sink, preferably deep. (Do not fill too full, or crabs may crawl out.)

Add crab boil, salt, cayenne, lemons, and onions to boiling water and boil, covered, for 5 minutes. Add potatoes and garlic and boil, uncovered, until potatoes are tender, about 20 minutes.

PRECOOKED DUNGENESS CRABS

Precooked Dungeness crabs, or "whole cooks," as they're called in the Pacific Northwest, are available in season—December 1 to mid-August—at high-end supermarkets and big-box stores as well as at fish markets. In a perfect world, we prefer to buy live crabs and cook them ourselves, but it's practically impossible to find live Dungeness on the East Coast.

Dungeness crabs have more meat than other crabs; an average-sized crab (about 2 pounds) will yield roughly 8 ounces of meat, mostly where the legs meet the body. Choose specimens that are heavy for their size, which means more meat inside the shell. Keep the crabs iced until ready to use, and crack them just before serving. If you do that in advance, the juices and flavor will escape. Whole crabs are at their best when not reheated, so serve the meat in a salad or with a sauce—Wasabi Caper (page 382) or Black Vinegar (page 381), for instance. Or make a sauce by brightening store-bought mayonnaise with curry powder, mustard, or minced herbs such as parsley, tarragon, or chervil and thinning it with a little lemon juice (and water if necessary), then toss the crab with the mayo.

Using a large sieve, transfer potatoes and garlic to a large platter and cover to keep warm. Add corn to boiling water and cook, covered, until tender, about 5 minutes. Transfer corn with tongs to platter and cover to keep warm.

Using tongs, carefully transfer crabs, one at a time, to boiling water. Return water to a boil and boil crabs, uncovered, until just cooked through, about 10 minutes. (To determine doneness, remove a claw with tongs and crack it with handle of a dinner knife; use knife to extract meat from claw. Crabmeat should be opaque.) Transfer crabs with tongs to another large platter and sprinkle with 1½ tablespoons Old Bay seasoning, or to taste.

Add shrimp to boiling water and boil, uncovered, until just cooked through, about 2 minutes. Transfer shrimp with sieve to platter with crabs and sprinkle with remaining 1½ tablespoons Old Bay seasoning, or to taste.

Serve seafood and vegetables with cocktail sauce and French bread.

Horseradish Cocktail Sauce

MAKES ABOUT 1⅔ CUPS
ACTIVE TIME: 5 MINUTES ■ START TO FINISH: 5 MINUTES

■ This mayonnaise-based version of the classic dipping sauce is a natural with shrimp, oysters, and clams. ■

⅔ cup mayonnaise
½ cup ketchup
2 tablespoons drained bottled horseradish, or to taste
Tabasco to taste
Salt to taste

Whisk together all ingredients in a bowl.

COOK'S NOTE
■ The cocktail sauce can be made up to 1 day ahead and refrigerated, its surface covered with plastic wrap.

Mini Lobster Rolls

SERVES 6
ACTIVE TIME: 20 MINUTES ■ START TO FINISH: 20 MINUTES

■ Quick and delicious, these delicate little rolls are stuffed with lobster and shrimp enveloped in a lemony herbal mayonnaise. We particularly like this salad in small dinner rolls, but you can use split-top hot dog buns to make larger sandwiches. ■

½ pound cooked lobster, finely chopped
½ pound cooked shrimp, finely chopped
½ cup mayonnaise
½ teaspoon finely grated lemon zest
1 tablespoon fresh lemon juice
1 tablespoon chopped fresh dill
2 teaspoons chopped fresh chives
¼ teaspoon salt
¼ teaspoon freshly ground black pepper
24 small soft dinner rolls (see headnote)

Stir together all ingredients except rolls in a bowl. Cut into tops of rolls to open without cutting all the way through. Fill each with seafood salad. Arrange 4 buns on each of six plates.

COOK'S NOTE
■ The lobster salad can be refrigerated, covered, for up to 1 hour.

Lobster Salad with Cellophane Noodles and Jicama

SERVES 6
ACTIVE TIME: 1¼ HOURS ■ START TO FINISH: 1¼ HOURS
PLUS 1 HOUR IF COOKING LOBSTER

■ The combination of slippery bean thread noodles with sweet lobster, tart dressing, herbs, and crisp matchsticks of jicama creates an explosion of refreshing tastes and textures in your mouth. If you don't want to tackle cooking and cleaning five lobsters, cooked lobster meat makes a fine alternative. ■

5 (1¼- to 1½-pound) live lobsters or 1¾–2 pounds
    cooked lobster meat
  Salt
½ cup fresh lime juice (from 4 limes)
1½ tablespoons packed light brown sugar
1 teaspoon dry mustard
⅓ cup canola oil
3–4 ounces bean thread (cellophane) noodles
    (see Sources)
3 tablespoons coarsely chopped fresh basil
3 tablespoons coarsely chopped fresh cilantro
2 tablespoons coarsely chopped fresh mint
1 (8-ounce) piece jicama, peeled and cut into
    ¹⁄₁₆-inch-thick matchsticks
  Flaky sea salt, such as Maldon

IF USING LIVE ONES, COOK THE LOBSTERS: Plunge 2 lobsters headfirst into a 10- to 12-quart pot of boiling salted water (3 tablespoons salt) and cook, covered, for 6 minutes for 1¼-pound lobsters, 7 minutes for 1½-pound lobsters, timing from when lobsters enter water. Transfer with tongs to sink to drain. Return water to a boil and cook remaining lobsters in 2 batches.

When lobsters are cool enough to handle, twist off tails (1). Break off claws at body. With kitchen shears, remove thin, hard membrane from underside of each tail by cutting just inside outer edge of shell on both sides (2). Firmly grasp lobster tail meat and pull it from shell (3). Cut claws open with shears and pull shells away to expose meat (4). Discard tomalley, any roe, and shells. Scrape off any coagulated white albumin from meat with point of a small knife. Cut meat into ¾-inch pieces and refrigerate, covered, for at least 1 hour.

MAKE THE DRESSING: Blend lime juice, brown sugar, mustard, and 1 teaspoon salt in a blender until combined. With motor running, add oil in a slow stream and blend until combined. Refrigerate, covered, until ready to use.

PREPARE THE NOODLES: Soak noodles in cold water until pliable, about 15 minutes; drain. Cut noodles in half with kitchen shears.

Cook noodles in a 4-quart pot of boiling salted water (1 teaspoon salt), stirring occasionally, until just tender, about 2 minutes. Drain in a colander and rinse under cold water until cool, then drain well.

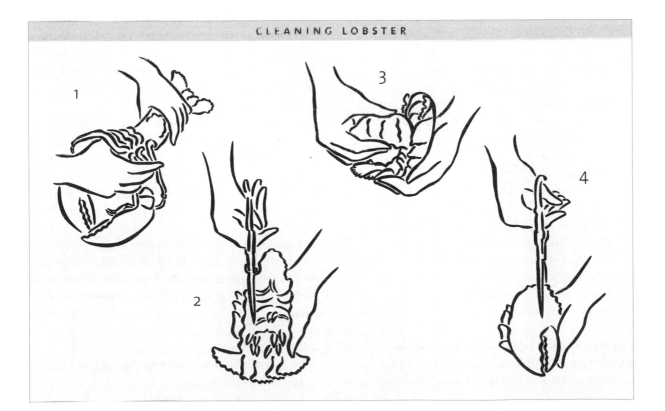

CLEANING LOBSTER

ASSEMBLE THE SALAD: Stir together lobster, herbs, and 6 tablespoons dressing.

Toss together noodles, jicama, remaining dressing, and salt to taste. Divide among six plates and top each serving with a mound of lobster salad. Sprinkle with sea salt.

COOK'S NOTES

- If using live lobsters, the lobsters can be cooked and the meat removed from the shells up to 1 day ahead.
- The dressing can be made up to 1 day ahead.

Lobster Cantonese

SERVES 4
ACTIVE TIME: 40 MINUTES ■ START TO FINISH: 45 MINUTES

■ The riot of lobster, ground pork, and Asian condiments in this Chinese restaurant classic is the kind of meal that guests will talk about for days afterward, but it's straightforward to prepare. ■

Salt
1 tablespoon cornstarch
¾ cup Chicken Stock (page 153) or store-bought reduced-sodium broth
¼ cup Chinese rice wine or dry sherry
3 tablespoons soy sauce
1 teaspoon sugar
¼ teaspoon freshly ground black pepper
2 (1½-pound) live lobsters
2 tablespoons vegetable oil
2 tablespoons Chinese fermented black beans, rinsed well and finely chopped (see Sources)
2 teaspoons finely chopped garlic
2 teaspoons finely chopped peeled fresh ginger
4 scallions, cut into 1½-inch pieces
¼ pound ground pork (not lean)
2 large eggs, lightly beaten
2 teaspoons Asian sesame oil

ACCOMPANIMENT: white rice

Bring 6 quarts salted water (3 tablespoons salt) to a boil in an 8- to 10-quart pot over high heat.

Meanwhile, stir together cornstarch, stock, rice wine, soy sauce, sugar, and pepper in a small bowl until sugar is dissolved.

Plunge lobsters headfirst into boiling water and cook, covered, for 2 minutes. Transfer lobsters with tongs to a large bowl of ice and cold water to stop the cooking (lobsters will not be cooked), then drain in a colander.

When lobsters are cool enough to handle, twist off tail and claws (including joints) of 1 lobster. Cut body lengthwise in half through shell with kitchen shears. Remove and discard sand sacs from inside head. Cut body crosswise in half. Halve tail lengthwise through shell with a cleaver or large heavy knife, then cut each half crosswise into 4 pieces. One at a time, wrap claws, with joints, in a kitchen towel and twist off claws from joints. Unwrap claws and crack open joints with a mallet or back of large heavy knife. Chop claws lengthwise in half, between pincers, with cleaver or large heavy knife. Transfer lobster pieces to a bowl, keeping meat in shells. Repeat with second lobster, putting pieces in another bowl.

Heat a well-seasoned 14-inch flat-bottomed wok (see Cook's Note) over high heat until a drop of water evaporates on contact. Pour 1 tablespoon vegetable oil down side of wok and swirl wok to coat sides. When oil begins to smoke, add pieces of 1 lobster and stir-fry just until meat starts to turn opaque, about 1½ minutes. Transfer cooked lobster with a slotted spoon to a large bowl. Repeat with second lobster, transferring cooked pieces to same bowl.

Add remaining tablespoon vegetable oil to wok, swirling to coat, then add black beans, garlic, ginger, scallions, and pork and stir-fry until pork is no longer pink, about 1 minute. Stir cornstarch mixture, add to wok, and bring to a boil. Add lobster and stir to coat, then cover wok, reduce heat, and simmer for 2 minutes.

Remove lid and pour eggs over lobster mixture in a thin circular stream. Cover wok and simmer just until eggs begin to set, 1 to 2 minutes. Drizzle with sesame oil, toss gently, and serve immediately over white rice.

COOK'S NOTE

- You can substitute a 12-inch heavy skillet, preferably cast-iron, for the wok.

Crawfish Étouffée

SERVES 4
ACTIVE TIME: 20 MINUTES ■ START TO FINISH: 35 MINUTES

■ Étouffée, a thick, spicy Cajun stew served over rice, is popular all over Louisiana. Locals use just-caught crawfish for their étouffée, but we take advantage of frozen crawfish tail meat, which is fairly readily available and saves loads of time. A roux, cooked to a rich peanut butter color, seasons and thickens the étouffée. ■

3 tablespoons unsalted butter
2 tablespoons all-purpose flour
1 medium onion, finely chopped
1 small green bell pepper, cored, seeded, and finely chopped
1¼ cups water
¾ teaspoon salt
½ teaspoon cayenne
¼ teaspoon freshly ground black pepper
1 pound crawfish tail meat (see Sources), thawed if frozen
½ cup thinly sliced scallion greens

ACCOMPANIMENT: white rice

Melt butter in a 10-inch heavy skillet over moderately low heat. Stir in flour with a flat-edged or wooden spatula and cook roux, stirring and scraping back and forth constantly, until the color of peanut butter, about 8 minutes.

Add onion and bell pepper and cook, stirring frequently, until vegetables are softened but not browned, 8 to 10 minutes.

Add water and bring to a boil, stirring, then reduce heat and simmer, stirring occasionally, until mixture is very thick, 5 to 8 minutes. Stir in salt, cayenne, and black pepper until combined, then stir in crawfish and cook over moderate heat, stirring occasionally, until crawfish is heated through, about 5 minutes. Stir in scallion greens.

Serve étouffée over rice.

POULTRY

"It tastes like chicken."

When I was growing up, that's what I was told about every unfamiliar food. And given that chicken was pretty much tasteless then, it was invariably true.

But it isn't anymore. With the increasing availability of all-natural, free-range, and organic poultry, American chicken once again has a definable flavor. This is wonderful news for poultry lovers like me. Unfortunately, those tasty birds have very little company; most of the other poultry that we once ate has vanished from the marketplace. When the very first *Gourmet Cookbook* was published in 1950, we were far more adventurous eaters. Recipes for wild birds of all sorts—ruffed grouse, pheasant, and geese—abounded, and I can't help wondering what they tasted like.

We still have adventures with poultry, but now the excitement is all about the ways in which we cook it. Looking through this chapter, you will find chicken dressed up in the flavors of almost every country of the world. One is accented with apricot-soy sauce, another with Middle Eastern tahini, a third with curry and cashews. Here is chicken dressed in Italian clothes (alla cacciatore) or with Cajun spices, or wrapped into a Mexican pozole, the great hominy-based stew. Some of these dishes have delightfully exotic names like *waterzooï* (a fancy name for the comfortingly creamy poached chicken of Belgium) or velvet chicken, which really is as tender as its name suggests.

But while we may no longer have much to do with grouse, our national admiration for turkey has increased enormously over the years. Although it was once relegated solely to the Thanksgiving table, we now eat the bird all year round; that is why this chapter offers turkey *mole* and turkey *chilaquiles,* for those days when you have a few hours to spend in the kitchen. And when time is tight, you can turn to the turkey burgers and several recipes for turkey cutlets. We also have turkey sloppy joes, a dish so popular in my own family that it now threatens the existence of the old familiar version made with beef.

There is good news for duck lovers as well: this once-beloved bird had gone out of fashion, only to return in triumph over the last decade. In this chapter, you will find everything from a seriously simple crisp roast duck to pan-grilled paillards that are not only elegant, but also so easy that they make a perfect weeknight supper. And should you be in the mood to take on a cooking project, I encourage you to consider classic French duck confit (it makes a terrific holiday gift that will never be forgotten).

Rabbits hop rather than fly, but on the theory that rabbit cooks very much like birds, we have included it in this chapter. If you are unaccustomed to cooking it, you won't want to miss the rabbit braised in red wine, which offers great flavor for a very small expenditure of time and money.

And while you will not find recipes for wild birds, you will find a few of our favorites for domesticated quail, poussin, guinea hen, Cornish hen, capon, and squab. That they are here at all is an early clue that our appetite for fowl is growing. If the number of wild turkeys that go strolling across my lawn in the Hudson Valley is any indication, by the time our next *Gourmet* cookbook rolls around, those rather amazing birds just might be considered fair game.

And I'll bet they don't taste anything like chicken.

POULTRY

Chicken

Chicken Parmesan Heros

SERVES 8
ACTIVE TIME: 1½ HOURS ■ START TO FINISH: 1½ HOURS

■ One bite of these heros—with crisp fried chicken cutlets, melted fresh mozzarella, and homemade tomato sauce—and your family will beg for them again. If you prepare the sauce ahead, they come together quickly. They're perfect for Super Bowl parties, but be sure to make lots; nobody can ever get enough. ■

    3 tablespoons olive oil
    1 small onion, finely chopped
    2 garlic cloves, chopped
    2 (28-ounce) cans whole tomatoes in puree, pureed in
        a blender until smooth
      Salt and freshly ground black pepper
    8 small skinless, boneless chicken breast halves (2⅔
        pounds total), rinsed and patted dry
    2 cups all-purpose flour
    5 large eggs
    3½ cups fine fresh bread crumbs (from about 10 slices
        firm white sandwich bread), lightly toasted
        (see Tips, page 912)
    1 cup finely grated Parmigiano-Reggiano (about
        3 ounces)
      About 2 cups vegetable oil
    4 (12-inch-long) loaves Italian bread, split lengthwise
    1 pound fresh mozzarella, thinly sliced

Heat olive oil in a 4- to 5-quart heavy pot over moderately high heat until hot but not smoking. Add onion and cook, stirring occasionally, until golden, about 5 minutes. Add garlic and cook, stirring, for 1 minute. Add tomato puree, ½ teaspoon salt, and ¼ teaspoon pepper, bring to a simmer, and simmer, uncovered, stirring occasionally, until sauce is slightly thickened, about 30 minutes. Remove from heat.

Meanwhile, using a flat meat pounder or a rolling pin, gently pound chicken breasts between two sheets of plastic wrap to ⅓-inch thick. Season with salt and pepper.

Stir together flour, ½ teaspoon salt, and ½ teaspoon pepper in a shallow bowl. Lightly beat eggs in a shallow bowl. Stir together bread crumbs and Parmigiano-Reggiano in another shallow bowl.

Dredge 1 chicken breast in flour, shaking off excess, then dip in egg, letting excess drip off, and dredge in bread crumbs until evenly coated. Transfer to a sheet of wax paper. Coat remaining chicken in same manner, arranging pieces in one layer on wax paper.

Put racks in upper and lower thirds of oven and preheat oven to 400°F.

Heat ¼ inch vegetable oil in a 12-inch deep heavy skillet over moderately high heat until hot but not smoking. Fry chicken 3 pieces at a time, turning once, until golden brown and just cooked through, about 6 minutes per batch. Transfer with tongs to paper towels to drain.

Arrange bottom halves of bread loaves on one large baking sheet and tops on another large baking sheet, cut side up. Spread ¼ cup tomato sauce on each bottom and top.

Divide chicken among 4 bottom halves and top each with ¼ cup tomato sauce and one quarter of mozzarella. Bake in lower third of oven until cheese melts, about 3 minutes.

Once cheese begins to melt, put tops of loaves in upper third of oven and bake until edges are golden, 3 to 4 minutes (watch tops closely; they burn easily). Put tops on bottoms to make sandwiches and slice into serving pieces.

COOK'S NOTE

■ The tomato sauce can be made up to 3 days ahead and refrigerated, covered. Reheat before using.

Chicken Burritos

SERVES 6
ACTIVE TIME: 45 MINUTES ■ START TO FINISH: 45 MINUTES

■ A complete meal—sliced rotisserie chicken warmed in a homemade salsa, black beans, creamy avocado, gooey cheese, all embraced by a soft, thin flour tortilla. What's not to love? The salsa has a moderate level of spice, which makes these burritos family-friendly. This is a knife-and-fork affair, but if you prefer handheld burritos, you can wrap them up in foil. ◼

1–2 serrano chiles, stemmed
1 medium white onion, halved
1 (14- to 15-ounce) can diced tomatoes in juice
1 garlic clove
½ cup fresh cilantro sprigs
Salt
¼ teaspoon freshly ground black pepper
1 tablespoon vegetable oil
1 (19-ounce) can black beans, rinsed and drained
3 tablespoons water
½ teaspoon ground cumin
¼ teaspoon dried oregano, crumbled
1 teaspoon fresh lime juice
1 (3-pound) rotisserie chicken, meat cut into
    bite-sized pieces, skin and bones discarded
6 (10-inch) flour tortillas
1½ cups coarsely shredded Monterey Jack
    cheese (about 6 ounces)
1 firm but ripe California avocado, halved, pitted, and
    cubed
6 tablespoons sour cream, or to taste

ACCOMPANIMENT: hot sauce or salsa

Preheat oven to 200°F.

Heat a dry 12-inch heavy skillet, preferably cast-iron, over moderately high heat for 5 minutes. Add whole chile(s) and 1 onion half, cut side down, and cook, turning chile and pressing on onion occasionally, until chile skin is charred on all sides and underside of onion is very well charred, about 10 minutes. Remove from heat and cool slightly.

Cut charred onion and chile into quarters (set skillet aside) and transfer to a blender. Add tomatoes with juice, garlic, cilantro, ¾ teaspoon salt, and pepper and blend until smooth.

Add oil to skillet and heat over moderate heat until hot but not smoking. Add tomato puree, bring to a simmer, and simmer, stirring occasionally, until slightly thickened, about 6 minutes.

Meanwhile, combine beans, water, cumin, oregano, and ½ teaspoon salt in a 1-quart saucepan and cook over moderately low heat, stirring, until beans are heated through. Mash beans with a potato masher or large fork. Remove pan from heat and stir in lime juice. Cover to keep warm.

Add chicken to tomato puree and cook until heated through, about 2 minutes. Remove from heat and cover to keep warm.

Finely chop remaining onion half.

Place a steamer rack in a 5- to 6-quart wide saucepan, add water to come to just below steamer rack, and bring to a simmer over moderate heat. Place 1 tortilla on steamer rack and sprinkle with ¼ cup cheese. Cover saucepan and steam until tortilla is softened and cheese is beginning to melt, about 45 seconds. Transfer tortilla to a work surface and top with one sixth of each filling: about 3 tablespoons beans, ⅔ cup chicken mixture, a rounded tablespoon chopped onion, 2 tablespoons avocado, and 1 tablespoon sour cream. Fold over opposite sides of tortilla to prevent contents from spilling, then fold bottom up and roll away from you. Transfer burrito to an ovenproof platter, seam side down, and keep warm in oven. Assemble 5 more burritos in same manner, transferring to platter in oven.

Serve burritos with hot sauce or salsa.

Chicken, Rice, and Mango Lettuce Wraps

SERVES 4
ACTIVE TIME: 40 MINUTES ◼ START TO FINISH:
40 MINUTES

◼ This do-it-yourself dish is perfect for a casual feast with friends. Do a demo for them—take a lettuce leaf, fill it with as much or as little of each of the fillings as you like, and fold it like a soft taco—then let your guests dig in. It's a little messy, yes, but very merry. The recipe makes more of the creamy ginger soy dressing than you'll need; use the leftovers for salad later in the week. ◼

FOR RICE
1 cup jasmine rice
1¾ cups water
¼ teaspoon salt
FOR DRESSING
½ cup seasoned rice vinegar
½ cup vegetable oil
6 tablespoons mayonnaise

¼ cup soy sauce

¼ cup finely chopped peeled fresh ginger
(from a 2-by-3-inch piece)

2 garlic cloves, chopped

½ teaspoon Asian sesame oil

FOR WRAPS

2 cups (10 ounces) shredded grilled chicken
or store-bought rotisserie chicken

2 heads Boston or Bibb lettuce, leaves separated

½ seedless cucumber (usually plastic-wrapped),
halved lengthwise, seedy center scooped out,
and cut into ⅛-inch-thick matchsticks

3 scallions, cut into 3-inch-long strips

1 (1-pound) firm but ripe mango, peeled, pitted,
and cut into ⅛-inch-thick matchsticks

½ cup chopped fresh cilantro

MAKE THE RICE: Wash rice in 3 or 4 changes of
cold water in a large bowl until water is clear; drain
in a sieve.

Bring water and salt to a boil in a 2- to 3-quart
saucepan. Add rice and cook, covered tightly, over
low heat until water is absorbed and rice is tender,
about 20 minutes. Remove from heat and let stand,
covered, for 10 minutes, then fluff rice with a fork
and transfer to a serving bowl to cool to warm.

MAKE THE DRESSING: Puree all ingredients in a
blender until smooth, about 1 minute. Transfer to a
serving bowl or small pitcher.

SERVE THE WRAPS: Put chicken, rice, and remaining wrap ingredients in separate bowls on a large
platter. Serve dressing on the side for drizzling.

Roast Chicken Breasts with Fennel, Potatoes, Tomatoes, and Olives

SERVES 4

ACTIVE TIME: 40 MINUTES ■ START TO FINISH: 1¼ HOURS

■ The heady flavors of Provence star in a one-dish meal
that's as suitable for company as it is for a family supper. Plum tomatoes, red-skinned potatoes, fennel,
black olives, and juicy chicken breasts roast together in
a garlicky lemon vinaigrette. ■

2 medium fennel bulbs

1½ pounds small red boiling potatoes (2 inches
in diameter), cut into 8 wedges each

6 tablespoons extra-virgin olive oil
Salt and freshly ground black pepper

14 garlic cloves (about 1 large head), peeled

4 teaspoons fresh lemon juice

4 chicken breast halves (with skin and bones;
3 pounds total), rinsed and patted dry

8 plum tomatoes, cored and cut lengthwise into
quarters

1 cup Kalamata olives

1½ tablespoons finely chopped fresh rosemary

Put a rack in middle of oven, put a roasting pan on
rack, and preheat oven to 450°F.

Cut off fennel stalks and discard. Quarter fennel
bulbs. Trim cores, leaving enough to keep layers intact, and cut fennel lengthwise into ¼-inch-thick
slices.

Toss fennel and potatoes with 2 tablespoons oil, ½
teaspoon salt, and ¼ teaspoon pepper in a bowl until well coated. Spread evenly in hot roasting pan and
roast for 20 minutes.

Meanwhile, mince 4 garlic cloves and mash to a
paste with ½ teaspoon salt, using side of a large heavy
knife. Transfer garlic paste to a small bowl and whisk
together with lemon juice, remaining ¼ cup oil, and
¼ teaspoon pepper. Brush chicken with about 2 tablespoons garlic mixture; set aside.

Thinly slice remaining 10 garlic cloves lengthwise.
Transfer to a bowl and toss with tomatoes, olives,
rosemary, and 2 tablespoons garlic mixture.

Remove roasting pan from oven, add tomato mixture, and stir to combine. Put chicken skin side up on
top of vegetables and roast for 15 minutes.

Brush chicken with remaining garlic mixture. Continue roasting chicken and vegetables until chicken is
just cooked through, about 20 minutes more.

Serve chicken with vegetables, spooning juices
over chicken.

A Buyer's Guide to Chicken

Rule of thumb: make sure that chicken is the last thing you put in your shopping cart and the first thing you put in your refrigerator. Even premium brands (including organic and kosher chicken) have tested positive for salmonella or campylobacter, two principal causes of food poisoning. Avoid cross-contamination by choosing chicken that is very well wrapped, and keep it separate from other foods. And always cook chicken thoroughly. Supermarkets and butchers respond to customer demand, so ask store managers to stock the chicken you want.

ANTIBIOTIC-FREE This term signifies that the birds were raised without antibiotics, but unless they are "certified organic," the claim hasn't been verified. Adding antibiotics to chicken feed to speed growth and prevent illness in large flocks (there can be 30,000 birds in an industrial chicken coop) is a widespread practice, and it contributes to the rapidly increasing rates of antibiotic resistance. Salmonella and campylobacter can now withstand not just individual antibiotics but whole classes of them. Unfortunately, antibiotic-resistant bacteria are found even in "antibiotic-free" chickens, because the pathogens are so widespread in the environment. Arsenic-based compounds are also added to chicken feed to speed growth, kill intestinal parasites, and improve the color of the meat. The amount used is considered safe by the decades-old USDA standards, but since chicken consumption has more than doubled since the 1960s (and since chicken manure used as fertilizer leaches vast amounts of the compounds into agricultural fields), some producers—including Tyson (the country's largest chicken producer), Bell & Evans, and Eberly—have stopped using it.

CERTIFIED HUMANE/FREE FARMED/ANIMAL COMPASSIONATE Humane Farm Animal Care oversees the "Certified Humane" program (www.certifiedhumane .com); the American Humane Association oversees the "Free Farmed" program (www.americanhumane.org);

and Whole Foods has its own "Animal Compassionate" program (www.animalcompassionfoundation.org). There are substantive differences between the programs, but all are stricter than poultry-industry guidelines.

CERTIFIED ORGANIC "Certified organic" poultry is raised under USDA standards that require, among other things, that it be fed 100 percent organic feed, not be given antibiotics or animal by-products, and have access to the outdoors, although the birds can be confined. Certified organic chickens are just as likely to pick up antibiotic-resistant salmonella and campylobacter as conventionally raised chickens: they peck at insects, manure, or water that harbors the bacteria. If you choose poultry that's certified organic, do so for reasons other than avoiding food-borne pathogens.

FREE-RANGE/FREE-ROAMING We would all like to think that free-range birds spend much of their lives in the open air, but, in reality, the USDA simply requires that they must have access to the outdoors for an "undetermined period each day"; 5 minutes is considered adequate. "Free-roaming" signifies that the birds aren't caged but are allowed to roam inside the chicken coop.

HORMONE-FREE Any poultry product that carries this claim is simply adhering to USDA standards, because the USDA prohibits the use of growth hormones in poultry and hogs (it allows them in beef); however, there is no independent organization that certifies the claim.

KOSHER Kosher poultry is slaughtered and processed (salting is required) according to Jewish dietary laws and under rabbinical supervision. At the time of slaughter, the bird should be free of additives such as antibiotics. Because kosher birds are cleaned with cold water (which closes up the follicles in the skin), feather removal is a little more difficult; remove any remaining feathers with needle-nose pliers or tweezers.

NATURAL All the fresh poultry in your supermarket is "natural," whether labeled so or not. Introduced by the USDA in the 1960s, the term indicates that the chicken has been minimally processed and contains no artificial flavors, added colors, or preservatives. It doesn't mean that the bird is certified organic or antibiotic-free. Some producers of "natural" meats follow some of the protocols that organic producers do, but they're not held accountable, and you have to take their claims on faith.

Roast Chicken and Asparagus with Tahini Sauce

SERVES 4
ACTIVE TIME: 30 MINUTES ■ START TO FINISH: 30 MINUTES

■ There's life beyond hummus for tahini, as this fast recipe deliciously proves. The Middle Eastern sesame seed paste is the basis for a velvety, nutty sauce sparkling with fresh lemon juice. ■

- 2 pounds asparagus, trimmed and cut into 2-inch pieces
- 3 tablespoons olive oil
  Salt and freshly ground black pepper
- 4 skinless, boneless chicken breast halves (2 pounds total), rinsed and patted dry
- ⅓ cup well-stirred tahini (Middle Eastern sesame paste)
- ⅓ cup water
- 2 tablespoons fresh lemon juice
- 1 teaspoon sugar
- 1 garlic clove, minced

Put racks in middle and lower thirds of oven and preheat oven to 450°F.

Toss asparagus with 1 tablespoon oil, ¼ teaspoon salt, and ¼ teaspoon pepper on a large baking sheet. Roast on bottom rack, shaking pan once or twice, until just tender, about 10 minutes.

Meanwhile, sprinkle chicken all over with ½ teaspoon salt and ¼ teaspoon pepper. Heat remaining 2 tablespoons oil in a 12-inch heavy ovenproof skillet over moderately high heat until hot but not smoking. Brown chicken, turning once, until golden, about 6 minutes.

Transfer skillet to middle of oven and roast until chicken is just cooked through, about 5 minutes.

Meanwhile, combine tahini, water, lemon juice, sugar, garlic, and ½ teaspoon salt in a blender and puree until smooth, about 1 minute. Add more water if sauce is too thick.

Serve chicken and asparagus drizzled with some of sauce, with remaining sauce on the side.

Apricot Chicken
with Almonds

SERVES 4
ACTIVE TIME: 10 MINUTES ■ START TO FINISH: 30 MINUTES

■ Creative use of a few choice pantry items turns chicken breasts into a memorable weekday meal. The whole-grain mustard saves the apricot preserves from becoming cloying. ■

> 4 (6-ounce) skinless, boneless chicken breast halves, rinsed and patted dry
> Salt and freshly ground black pepper
> ⅓ cup sliced almonds
> ½ cup apricot preserves
> 1½ tablespoons soy sauce
> 1 tablespoon whole-grain mustard
> 1 tablespoon unsalted butter
> SPECIAL EQUIPMENT: a 13-by-9-inch flameproof baking dish

Put a rack in lower third of oven and preheat oven to 400°F. Lightly oil baking dish.

Sprinkle chicken all over with ½ teaspoon salt and ¼ teaspoon pepper and arrange at least ¼ inch apart in baking dish. Roast for 10 minutes.

Meanwhile, toast almonds in a small baking pan in oven, stirring twice, until golden, 8 to 10 minutes. Set aside.

Combine apricot preserves, soy sauce, mustard, butter, ⅛ teaspoon salt, and ¼ teaspoon pepper in a small saucepan and cook over moderate heat, stirring, until preserves are melted.

Pour sauce over chicken and roast until just cooked through, about 10 minutes more.

Turn on broiler. Broil chicken 4 to 5 inches from heat, basting once, until glazed and browned in spots, about 3 minutes. Serve sprinkled with almonds.

Poached Chicken
with Tomatoes, Olives,
and Green Beans

SERVES 4
ACTIVE TIME: 40 MINUTES ■ START TO FINISH: 40 MINUTES

■ This quick summer supper is best served at room temperature, which shows off its fresh, bold flavors to best advantage. ■

> 4 skinless, boneless chicken breast halves (1¾ pounds total), rinsed and patted dry
> Kosher salt
> 5 cups water
> 1¾ cups Chicken Stock (page 153) or store-bought reduced-sodium broth
> 1 fresh thyme sprig
> ¾ pound haricots verts or other thin green beans, trimmed
> 5 tablespoons extra-virgin olive oil
> Freshly ground black pepper
> 1 pound tomatoes, cut into ¼-inch dice
> ½ cup mixed brine-cured green and black olives, such as Picholine and Kalamata, pitted and chopped
> 1 tablespoon torn fresh oregano leaves

Sprinkle chicken all over with 1 tablespoon salt. Set aside.

Bring water, stock, and thyme to a boil in a 4- to 6-quart heavy pot. Add beans and cook, uncovered, until crisp-tender, 3 to 6 minutes. Transfer beans with a wire skimmer or a slotted spoon to a bowl, toss with 1 tablespoon oil, and season with salt and pepper (keep stock mixture at a boil).

Add chicken to stock and cook at a bare simmer, uncovered, for 6 minutes. Remove pot from heat and let stand, covered, until chicken is cooked through, about 15 minutes.

Transfer chicken with tongs to a cutting board and let cool, about 5 minutes.

Meanwhile, stir together tomatoes, olives, oregano, ¼ teaspoon salt, ⅛ teaspoon pepper, and remaining ¼ cup oil in a bowl.

Cut chicken diagonally across the grain into 1-inch-thick slices. Divide green beans among four plates, arrange sliced chicken over beans, and top with tomato-olive mixture.

COOK'S NOTE

- The beans, chicken, and tomato-olive mixture can be made up to 2 hours ahead. Refrigerate separately, covered. Bring to room temperature before serving.

Spiced Chicken

SERVES 4
ACTIVE TIME: 10 MINUTES ■ START TO FINISH: 45 MINUTES

■ Fragrant and deeply savory, this spice rub balances the heat of chili powder and black pepper with the more floral notes of coriander and cinnamon. It jazzes up bland chicken breasts nicely, and legs give even juicier results. The quick pan sauce adds an extra shot of flavor. ■

- 2 teaspoons chili powder
- ½ teaspoon ground cumin
- ½ teaspoon ground coriander
- ½ teaspoon freshly ground black pepper
- ¼ teaspoon ground cinnamon
- 1½ teaspoons salt
- 3 tablespoons vegetable oil
- 4 chicken breast halves (with skin and bones) or 4 whole chicken legs, thighs and drumsticks separated if desired, rinsed and patted dry
- ½ cup water

Put a rack in middle of oven and preheat oven to 450°F.

Stir together spices, salt, and 1 tablespoon oil. Rub evenly all over chicken.

Heat remaining 2 tablespoons oil in a 12-inch ovenproof heavy skillet over moderately high heat until hot but not smoking. Brown chicken, turning once, 6 to 8 minutes.

Turn chicken skin side up, transfer skillet to oven, and roast until just cooked through, 16 to 18 minutes for breasts, about 25 minutes for legs. Transfer to a platter.

Add water to pan and deglaze by boiling over high heat, scraping up brown bits, for 1 minute. Transfer sauce to a bowl and skim off fat.

Serve chicken with sauce on the side.

Oven-Fried Panko Chicken

SERVES 4 TO 6
ACTIVE TIME: 20 MINUTES ■ START TO FINISH: 1 HOUR

■ For those with a fear of frying, this oven method has all of the crunch, thanks to crisp panko bread crumbs, with none of the mess. It's a great choice for an easy family dinner or casual entertaining. Even the most ardent fans of real fried chicken will be won over by the moist, flavorful meat. ■

- 2 cups panko (Japanese bread crumbs)
  Salt and freshly ground black pepper
- ½ teaspoon cayenne
- 1 stick (8 tablespoons) unsalted butter, softened
- 1 (3½- to 4-pound) chicken, rinsed, patted dry, and cut into 10 serving pieces (breasts cut crosswise in half)

Put a rack in middle of oven and preheat oven to 450°F.

Stir together panko, ½ teaspoon salt, ¼ teaspoon black pepper, and cayenne in a pie plate.

Stir together butter, ½ teaspoon salt, and ¼ teaspoon pepper in a small bowl, then rub all over chicken. Add chicken, 2 pieces at a time, to crumb mixture and coat evenly on both sides, pressing chicken into crumbs to help them adhere, then transfer, skin side up, to a shallow baking pan.

Bake chicken until well browned and cooked through, 30 to 40 minutes. Transfer pan to a rack and let chicken stand, uncovered, for 5 to 10 minutes to crisp.

Arroz con Pollo

Baked Cuban-Style Rice with Chicken

SERVES 4
ACTIVE TIME: 1¼ HOURS ▪ START TO FINISH: 2½ HOURS

▪ A festive one-dish dinner of flavorful rice and moist chicken, with exclamation points of tangy green olives, arroz con pollo has satisfied families for generations throughout Cuba and many of the Caribbean islands. The only "splurge" ingredient is saffron threads, which keep for a long time (only a pinch is called for). ▪

FOR CHICKEN

- 3 large garlic cloves, coarsely chopped
- 2 tablespoons fresh orange juice
- 2 tablespoons fresh lime juice
- 1½ teaspoons salt
- ¾ teaspoon freshly ground black pepper
- 1 (3½- to 4-pound) chicken, rinsed, patted dry, and cut into 8 serving pieces
- 1 tablespoon vegetable oil
- 1 tablespoon unsalted butter

FOR RICE

- 1 pound onions, chopped
- 2 green bell peppers, cored, seeded, and chopped
- 3 large garlic cloves, minced
- ¼ teaspoon crumbled saffron threads (see headnote)
- ¼ cup dry white wine
- 2 teaspoons ground cumin
- 2 teaspoons salt
- 1 Turkish bay leaf or ½ California bay leaf
- 1 (14- to 15-ounce) can diced tomatoes in juice
- 1½ cups Chicken Stock (page 153) or store-bought reduced-sodium broth
- 1½ cups water
- 2 cups long-grain white rice
- 1 cup frozen baby peas (not thawed)
- ½ cup small or medium pimiento-stuffed green olives, rinsed
- ¼ cup drained chopped pimientos, rinsed

PREPARE THE CHICKEN: Puree garlic with orange juice, lime juice, salt, and pepper in a blender until smooth. Put chicken pieces in a large bowl and pour puree over them, turning to coat. Cover and refrigerate, turning occasionally, for at least 1 hour.

Transfer chicken to paper towels, letting excess marinade drip back into bowl, and pat dry. Reserve marinade.

Heat oil and butter in 6- to 7-quart wide heavy pot over moderately high heat until foam subsides. Brown chicken in 2 or 3 batches, without crowding, turning occasionally, about 6 minutes per batch. Transfer chicken to a plate; reserve fat in pot.

PREPARE AND BAKE THE ARROZ CON POLLO: Add onions, bell peppers, and garlic to fat in pot and cook over moderately high heat, stirring occasionally and scraping up brown bits, until vegetables are softened, 6 to 8 minutes.

Meanwhile, toast saffron in a small dry skillet over low heat, shaking skillet, until fragrant, about 30 seconds. Add wine and bring to a simmer. Remove from heat.

Put a rack in middle of oven and preheat oven to 350°F.

Add cumin and salt to vegetables and cook over moderate heat, stirring, for 2 minutes. Stir in saffron mixture, bay leaf, tomatoes with juice, stock, water, and reserved marinade and bring to a boil. Add chicken, except breast pieces, skin side up, and simmer gently, covered, over low heat for 10 minutes. Stir in rice, add breast pieces skin side up, arranging chicken in one layer, and return to a simmer.

Cover pot tightly, transfer to oven, and bake until rice is tender and most of liquid is absorbed, about 20 minutes.

Scatter peas, olives, and pimientos over rice and chicken (do not stir). Cover pot with a kitchen towel and let stand until peas are heated through and any remaining liquid is absorbed by rice, about 5 minutes. Discard bay leaf.

COOK'S NOTE
▪ The chicken can marinate for up to 1 day.

Chicken Stir-Fry with Shiitakes, Snow Peas, and Watercress

SERVES 4
ACTIVE TIME: 30 MINUTES ■ START TO FINISH: 30 MINUTES

■ Many people are familiar with watercress as a garnish or as a salad ingredient; this fresh stir-fry is a wonderful introduction to it as a cooked vegetable. ■

1 large egg white
1 tablespoon cornstarch
¾ teaspoon salt
1 pound skinless, boneless chicken breast halves (about 2 large), rinsed, patted dry, and cut crosswise into very thin slices
5 tablespoons seasoned rice vinegar
3 tablespoons soy sauce
1 tablespoon sugar
6 tablespoons vegetable oil
1 tablespoon finely chopped peeled fresh ginger
2 medium garlic cloves, finely chopped
½ pound shiitake mushrooms, stems discarded, caps cut into ⅓-inch-wide strips
½ pound snow peas, trimmed
½ pound watercress (about 2 bunches), coarse stems discarded

ACCOMPANIMENT: white rice

Stir together egg white, cornstarch, and salt in a medium bowl. Add chicken and stir until well coated. Stir together vinegar, soy sauce, and sugar in another bowl until sugar is dissolved.

Heat a well-seasoned 14-inch flat-bottomed wok or a 12-inch heavy skillet over high heat until a drop of water evaporates on contact. Add 2 tablespoons oil and swirl pan to coat. Add chicken and stir-fry, separating pieces, until just cooked through, 2 to 3 minutes. Transfer chicken to a clean bowl.

Wipe pan clean with paper towels, heat pan, and add 2 tablespoons oil, swirling to coat. Add ginger and garlic and stir-fry for 30 seconds. Add mushrooms and stir-fry, drizzling with remaining 2 tablespoons oil, until they begin to soften, about 2 minutes. Add snow peas and stir-fry until crisp-tender, about 1 minute. Return chicken to pan, add vinegar mixture and wa-

tercress, and stir-fry until watercress is wilted, about 1 minute. Serve immediately with rice.

Garlicky Fried Chicken

SERVES 12
ACTIVE TIME: 2 HOURS ■ START TO FINISH: 14 HOURS
(INCLUDES MARINATING)

■ Few things sing of the South like crisp fried chicken. This version, soaked in a garlicky marinade before it is fried, will appeal to everyone. Don't be put off by the amount of salt called for in the marinade; think of it as a brine, which works to infuse the bird with flavor and keep it juicy. To ensure that everything cooks evenly, be sure to fry the white meat and dark meat separately. Fried chicken is definitely an endeavor, which is why this recipe makes so much, but it can be easily halved (you will still need the full 8 cups of oil for frying). And don't feel as if every piece has to arrive at the table smoking hot—this chicken is equally good served at room temperature. ■

2 medium onions, chopped
8 large garlic cloves, chopped
Salt and freshly ground black pepper
1 tablespoon cayenne
8 cups water
8 chicken breast halves, halved crosswise if large, 8 drumsticks, and 8 thighs (all with skin and bones; 8–9 pounds total), rinsed and patted dry
10 cups all-purpose flour
About 8 cups vegetable oil for deep-frying

SPECIAL EQUIPMENT: a deep-fat thermometer

MARINATE THE CHICKEN: Puree onions and garlic with ⅓ cup salt, 1 tablespoon black pepper, cayenne, and 1 cup water in a food processor until smooth. Pour into a large bowl and stir in remaining 7 cups water. Divide chicken and marinade among three 1-gallon sealable plastic bags, then seal, forcing out excess air. Refrigerate, turning bags a few times, for at least 12 hours. (If you're concerned about leaks, put bags in a large bowl.)

FRY THE CHICKEN: Whisk together flour, 2 teaspoons salt, and 1 tablespoon pepper in a large bowl. Divide between two large roasting pans. Drain chicken in a colander (discard marinade). Dredge each piece of chicken in seasoned flour and leave in flour. Let stand for 20 minutes.

Preheat oven to 250°F. Line two large baking sheets with paper towels and set a cooling rack on each.

Heat 2 inches oil in a 5- to 6-quart wide heavy pot, preferably cast-iron, or an electric deep fryer over moderately high heat until it registers 365°F on thermometer. Knocking off excess flour, transfer 4 pieces chicken to oil (keep batches all white meat or all dark) and fry, turning occasionally with tongs, until golden brown and cooked through, about 8 minutes for breasts, 10 to 12 minutes for drumsticks and thighs. Lift chicken from oil with tongs, letting excess oil drip back into pot, transfer to a rack on a baking sheet, and keep warm in oven. (Return oil to 365°F between batches.) Dredge and fry remaining chicken in same manner, keeping it warm in oven.

COOK'S NOTES

- You can use a mixture of your favorite chicken parts for this recipe, for a total weight of 8 to 9 pounds.
- The chicken can marinate for up to 1 day.

Puebla Chicken and Potato Stew

SERVES 4
ACTIVE TIME: 40 MINUTES ■ START TO FINISH: 1 HOUR

■ The town of Puebla, Mexico, is known for dishes full of complex flavors, especially red *mole poblano*, a rich sauce made from chiles, nuts, seeds, and spices. This chicken stew is much faster to prepare, but it boasts the depth of flavor for which Pueblan cooking is known. Toasting the onion and garlic in a dry skillet gives them a smoky edge, which adds another layer to the brick-red stew, spiced with chipotle chiles and chorizo and studded with meaty shreds of chicken and cubes of potato. Avocado and ivory crumbles of *queso fresco*, a Mexican fresh cheese that is creamy and lively tasting, offer cool contrast. ■

2 pounds chicken thighs, rinsed and patted dry
1 large white onion, quartered
6 cups water
  Salt
2 garlic cloves, left unpeeled
1 (14- to 15-ounce) can whole tomatoes in juice
4 teaspoons chopped canned chipotle chiles in adobo
1 teaspoon dried oregano, preferably Mexican
1 tablespoon vegetable oil
1 link (1½ ounces) mild Spanish chorizo (cured spicy pork sausage), finely chopped
1 pound boiling potatoes, peeled and cut into ¾-inch pieces
2 ounces *queso fresco* (Mexican fresh white cheese; see Sources) or ricotta salata, crumbled

ACCOMPANIMENTS: avocado slices; warm corn tortillas

Combine chicken, 2 onion quarters, water, and 1 teaspoon salt in a 4- to 5-quart pot and bring to a boil, covered, over moderately high heat. Boil for 10 minutes, then remove from heat and let stand, covered, until chicken is just cooked through, about 10 minutes. Transfer chicken to a plate; reserve broth with onion.

Meanwhile, heat a dry small cast-iron skillet over moderate heat until hot. Add garlic and remaining 2 onion quarters and brown on all sides, turning occasionally with tongs, about 5 minutes. Peel garlic and transfer to a blender. Add browned onion quarters, tomatoes with juice, chiles, and oregano and puree until smooth.

When chicken is cool enough to handle, coarsely shred, discarding skin and bones.

Heat oil in a deep 12-inch heavy skillet over moderately high heat until hot but not smoking. Add chorizo and cook, stirring, until fat is rendered, about 2 minutes. Carefully add puree (it will spatter and steam) and cook, stirring frequently, until thick, about 10 minutes.

Add potatoes and 1 teaspoon salt to reserved broth in pot, bring to a simmer, and simmer, covered, stirring occasionally, until potatoes are almost tender, about 10 minutes.

Add potatoes and onion to chorizo mixture, along with 2 cups broth (reserve remainder for another use if desired). Stir in chicken and simmer for 10 minutes.

Sprinkle stew with cheese and serve with avocado slices and corn tortillas on the side.

- The stew can be made up to 1 day ahead. Cool, uncovered, then refrigerate, covered.

Chicken with Shallots, Garlic, and Vinegar

SERVES 4
ACTIVE TIME: 1 HOUR ■ START TO FINISH: 1½ HOURS

■ During the 1960s and '70s, French chefs began to move away from their classic style of cooking, which often featured rich, heavy, cream-based and flour-thickened sauces, to a simpler, fresher mode, one that allowed ingredients to retain their native vibrancy. This elegant chicken, with its interplay of sweet and sour, is an excellent example of nouvelle cuisine at its best. The red wine and red wine vinegar, as well as a dab of tomato paste, provide acidity and brightness, but it's important to reduce the sauce thoroughly so their sharp flavors are not overpowering. ■

- 1 (3½- to 4-pound) chicken, rinsed, patted dry, and cut into 8 serving pieces
  Salt and freshly ground black pepper
- 1 tablespoon vegetable oil
- 3 tablespoons unsalted butter
- 4 large garlic cloves, finely chopped
- ⅓ cup finely chopped shallots
- 1 medium carrot, finely chopped
- 2 fresh thyme sprigs
- 2 Turkish bay leaves or 1 California bay leaf
- 1 tablespoon tomato paste
- 1 cup dry red wine
- ½ cup red wine vinegar
- 2 tablespoons sugar
- 1 cup Chicken Stock (page 153) or store-bought reduced-sodium broth

GARNISH: fresh thyme sprigs
SPECIAL EQUIPMENT: a 13-by-9-inch flameproof roasting pan

COOK THE CHICKEN: Put a rack in middle of oven and preheat oven to 350°F.

Sprinkle chicken with 1 teaspoon salt and ½ teaspoon pepper. Heat oil and 1 tablespoon butter in a 10- to 12-inch heavy skillet over moderately high heat until foam subsides. Brown chicken in 2 batches, turning once, 8 to 10 minutes per batch. Transfer chicken to roasting pan, arranging it in one layer.

Once all chicken is browned, transfer to oven (set skillet aside) and roast, uncovered, for 15 minutes.

MEANWHILE, MAKE THE SAUCE: Discard all but 2 tablespoons fat from skillet. Add garlic, shallots, carrot, thyme sprigs, and bay leaves and cook over moderately high heat, stirring and scraping up brown bits, until vegetables are browned, 3 to 6 minutes. Add tomato paste and cook, stirring, for 1 minute. Add wine, vinegar, sugar, 1 teaspoon salt, and ½ teaspoon pepper, bring to a boil, and boil, stirring occasionally, until reduced by half, 5 to 10 minutes.

FINISH THE SAUCE AND CHICKEN: Add stock to sauce and bring to a boil. Pour through a fine-mesh sieve onto chicken in roasting pan, pressing on solids; discard solids. Continue to roast chicken, uncovered, until just cooked through, about 15 minutes more.

Transfer chicken with tongs to an ovenproof serving dish and keep warm, uncovered, in turned-off oven.

Meanwhile, bring sauce in roasting pan to a boil over high heat and boil, stirring occasionally, until reduced to a scant cup. Remove from heat and swirl in remaining 2 tablespoons butter. Season with salt and pepper.

Pour sauce over chicken and garnish with thyme sprigs.

COOK'S NOTE

- The chicken can be roasted up to 1 day ahead. Cool the chicken in the liquid in the roasting pan and refrigerate until cold, uncovered, then cover. Reheat, covered, in a 350°F oven in the liquid in the roasting pan and proceed with the recipe.

Chicken Cacciatore

SERVES 6
ACTIVE TIME: 45 MINUTES ■ START TO FINISH: 1½ HOURS

■ *Alla cacciatora* means "cooked the hunter's way" in Italian, but we think of this dish as down-home American food of the best kind. The moist, tender meat takes on a deep tomatoey flavor and tastes as though it was slowly cooked for days. ∎

1 (3½- to 4-pound) chicken, rinsed, patted dry, and cut into 8 serving pieces
Salt and freshly ground black pepper
2 tablespoons olive oil
1 large onion, chopped
1 green bell pepper, cored, seeded, and chopped
4 garlic cloves, chopped
½ cup dry red wine
1 (28-ounce) can whole tomatoes in juice
½ cup Chicken Stock (page 153) or store-bought reduced-sodium broth

ACCOMPANIMENT: white rice or buttered noodles

Sprinkle chicken on all sides with 1¼ teaspoons salt and ¾ teaspoon pepper. Heat oil in a 12-inch deep heavy skillet over moderately high heat until hot but not smoking. Brown chicken in 2 batches, turning once, about 10 minutes per batch. Transfer to a plate.

Reduce heat to moderate and add onion, bell pepper, garlic, and ½ teaspoon salt to skillet. Cook, stirring occasionally and scraping up any brown bits, until onion and garlic are golden, 8 to 10 minutes. Add wine and deglaze by boiling, scraping up brown bits, for 1 minute, then boil until liquid is reduced by half. Add tomatoes with juice, bring to a simmer, and simmer, breaking up tomatoes with a wooden spoon, for 5 minutes.

Stir in stock and nestle chicken pieces in sauce. Simmer, partially covered, until chicken is cooked through, 35 to 45 minutes (see Cook's Note). Season with salt and pepper and serve with rice or noodles.

COOK'S NOTE
∎ For a thicker sauce, transfer the cooked chicken to a platter and cover to keep warm. Boil the sauce until it reaches the desired consistency.

Chicken and Corn Stew

SERVES 4
ACTIVE TIME: 30 MINUTES ∎ START TO FINISH: 45 MINUTES

∎ Using boneless chicken breasts and thighs makes this stew as easy to eat as it is to prepare. Don't omit the cream—the small amount called for makes all the difference. ∎

2 pounds skinless, boneless chicken breasts and thighs, rinsed, patted dry, and cut into 2-inch pieces
Salt and freshly ground black pepper
2 tablespoons unsalted butter
1 tablespoon vegetable oil
1 large onion, halved lengthwise and cut lengthwise into ¼-inch slices
1 garlic clove, minced
2 teaspoons chopped fresh thyme
2 tablespoons all-purpose flour
1¾ cups Chicken Stock (page 153) or store-bought reduced-sodium broth
¾ cup water
1 pound boiling potatoes, peeled and cut into 1-inch pieces
1½ cups fresh or frozen corn kernels
¼ cup heavy cream

Pat chicken dry and season with salt and pepper. Heat butter and oil in a 4- to 5-quart wide heavy pot over moderately high heat until foam subsides. Lightly brown chicken in 2 batches, turning occasionally with tongs, about 5 minutes per batch. Transfer chicken to a bowl.

Add onion, garlic, and 1 teaspoon thyme to pot and cook, stirring occasionally, until softened, 4 to 5 minutes. Add flour and cook, stirring, for 1 minute. Whisk in stock and water and bring to a boil, whisking. Add potatoes and corn, cover, and simmer over moderate heat, stirring occasionally, until potatoes are barely tender, about 10 minutes.

Stir in chicken, along with any juices accumulated in bowl, and cream and simmer, covered, until chicken is just cooked through and potatoes are tender, 5 to

10 minutes. Season stew with salt and pepper and sprinkle with remaining teaspoon thyme.

COOK'S NOTE
- The stew can be made up to 2 days ahead. Cool, uncovered, then refrigerate, covered.

Velvet Chicken

SERVES 6
ACTIVE TIME: 20 MINUTES ■ START TO FINISH: 1½ HOURS

■ Sophie Chou, the mother of *Gourmet* food editor Lillian Chou, shared this wonderful recipe with us. Reminiscent of her native Canton, China, it takes its name from the moist, velvety texture the chicken gets from being poached at a low temperature. It's a fascinating technique with a short preparation time—the chicken finishes cooking in the heat retained in the covered pot (make sure your chicken weighs between 3 and 3½ pounds, or it will not cook as the recipe indicates). And it's a recipe that keeps giving—the fragrant poaching liquid can be strained and refrigerated or frozen to be used again in soups and stir-fries.

Yellow rock sugar, a solidified mixture of honey and sugar, found in Asian markets, adds a distinctive sheen and sweetness, but brown sugar may be substituted. ■

3½ cups Chicken Stock (page 153) or store-bought
    reduced-sodium broth
1 cup soy sauce
1 cup dark soy sauce (see Cook's Note)
1 cup Chinese rice wine, preferably Shaoxing, or
    medium-dry sherry
¼ cup coarsely crushed yellow rock sugar (see
    headnote and Sources) or ¼ cup packed brown
    sugar
1 bunch scallions, cut into 3-inch pieces
6 (¼-inch-thick) slices fresh ginger
4 (3-by-1-inch) strips orange zest, removed with a
    vegetable peeler
1 tablespoon fine sea salt
2 whole cloves

2 whole star anise or 1½ teaspoons pieces
1 (2½-inch-long) dried red chile
½ teaspoon Sichuan peppercorns (see Sources)
    or black peppercorns
1 (3- to 3½-pound) chicken, rinsed and
    patted dry
GARNISH: fresh cilantro leaves
ACCOMPANIMENT: white rice or noodles

Combine all ingredients except chicken in a 4- to 6-quart heavy pot and bring to a boil.

Add chicken, breast side down (chicken may not be completely covered with liquid), and bring to a simmer. Simmer, covered, for 15 minutes.

Turn off heat and let chicken stand, covered, for 30 minutes. Turn chicken over, cover, and let stand for 15 minutes more to finish cooking.

Transfer chicken to a cutting board; reserve cooking liquid. Cut off drumsticks and thighs, then cut off wings; transfer pieces to a serving platter. Separate breast (with rib cage) from back; discard back. Using a cleaver or sharp heavy knife, split breast in half, then cut crosswise into 1-inch-thick slices; transfer to platter.

Spoon some of warm poaching liquid over chicken and sprinkle with cilantro. Chicken can be served warm, at room temperature, or chilled. Pour remaining poaching liquid through a sieve set into a bowl and serve some of liquid as a sauce if desired (reserve remaining liquid for another use if desired; see headnote). Serve chicken with rice or noodles.

COOK'S NOTES
- Dark soy sauce gives a deeper color to the dish. If it's unavailable, additional regular soy sauce is an acceptable substitute.
- The chicken keeps, covered and refrigerated, for 2 days.
- The leftover poaching liquid can be refrigerated, covered, for up to 1 week or frozen for up to 3 months. Thaw if necessary and bring to a boil before using.

Poached Chicken with Vegetables in Cream Sauce

SERVES 4

ACTIVE TIME: 40 MINUTES ■ START TO FINISH: 2 HOURS

■ *Waterzooï*, a delicately creamy stew of chicken (or sometimes fish) punctuated by bright strips of carrots and celery, is a Belgian dish with roots going back to the Renaissance. This version, adapted from one served at the restaurant Aux Armes de Bruxelles in Brussels, uses crème fraîche rather than the more classic combination of heavy cream and eggs. Boiled potatoes are the traditional accompaniment. ■

8 cups water
1 cup coarsely chopped onion
⅓ cup celery leaves
  Salt
1 (3- to 3½-pound) chicken, rinsed and patted dry
3 medium leeks (white and pale green parts only), trimmed
2 carrots, cut into long ⅛-inch-thick matchsticks
1 celery rib, cut into long ⅛-inch-thick matchsticks
½ stick (4 tablespoons) unsalted butter
¼ cup all-purpose flour
¾ cup crème fraîche
½ teaspoon freshly ground black pepper

ACCOMPANIMENT: boiled peeled potatoes

Combine water, onion, celery leaves, and 1 teaspoon salt in a 5-quart wide heavy pot with a tight-fitting lid. Add chicken, breast side down, and bring to a boil, covered, then reduce heat and simmer, covered, until chicken is cooked through, 45 to 50 minutes. Transfer chicken to a cutting board (leave cooking liquid in pot) to cool slightly.

Halve chicken lengthwise; discard backbone, rib bones, and skin (except for skin on wings). Cut thighs and drumsticks from breasts to get 4 pieces. Transfer chicken to a large shallow serving bowl or dish and cover loosely with foil to keep warm.

Reserve ⅔ cup cooking liquid and boil remaining liquid, uncovered, until reduced to about 3 cups, 30 to 40 minutes. Transfer to a large measuring cup or a bowl and skim off fat (set pot aside).

Meanwhile, cut leeks into 2- to 3-inch sections, then halve sections lengthwise and cut lengthwise into ⅛-inch-wide strips. Wash leek strips in a bowl of cold water, agitating them, lift out, and pat dry.

Bring reserved ⅔ cup broth to a simmer in a 12-inch heavy skillet over moderately high heat. Add vegetables and ¼ teaspoon salt and cook, covered, stirring occasionally, until just tender, 10 to 15 minutes. Spoon vegetables and any liquid over chicken and cover to keep warm.

Melt butter in pot over moderate heat, then whisk in flour and cook, whisking constantly, for 2 minutes to make a roux. Add reduced broth in a stream, whisking, and cook, whisking vigorously, until slightly thickened, 2 to 3 minutes. Remove from heat and whisk in crème fraîche, ¾ teaspoon salt, and pepper until smooth.

Pour sauce over chicken and vegetables and serve with potatoes.

Chicken Curry with Cashews

SERVES 4 TO 6

ACTIVE TIME: 45 MINUTES ■ START TO FINISH: 1½ HOURS

■ This easy curry, adapted from Charmaine Solomon's *Complete Asian Cookbook,* is one of our all-time most popular recipes. Warm hits of curry powder, cumin, and cayenne cooked with onions, garlic, and ginger infuse the dish, while tomatoes, cilantro, and yogurt add a tang and freshness. Ground cashews thicken the curry and give it a rich flavor. Though we call for a cut-up whole chicken, you can use an equivalent amount of chicken parts or all thighs. ■

½ stick (4 tablespoons) unsalted butter
2 medium onions, finely chopped
2 large garlic cloves, finely chopped
1 tablespoon finely chopped peeled fresh ginger
3 tablespoons curry powder
2 teaspoons salt
1 teaspoon ground cumin
½ teaspoon cayenne
1 (3½- to 4-pound) chicken, rinsed, patted dry,

and cut into 10 serving pieces (breasts cut
crosswise in half; see headnote)
1 (14- to 15-ounce) can diced tomatoes in juice
¼ cup chopped fresh cilantro
¾ cup cashews (toasted or raw)
⅔ cup whole-milk yogurt
GARNISH: chopped fresh cilantro
ACCOMPANIMENT: basmati or jasmine rice

Heat butter in a 5- to 6-quart wide heavy pot over moderately low heat until foam subsides. Add onions, garlic, and ginger and cook, stirring, until softened, about 5 minutes. Add curry powder, salt, cumin, and cayenne and cook, stirring, for 2 minutes. Add chicken and cook, stirring to coat, for 3 minutes.

Add tomatoes with juice and cilantro and bring to a simmer, then cover and simmer gently, stirring occasionally, until chicken is cooked through, about 40 minutes.

Just before serving, pulse cashews in a food processor or electric coffee/spice grinder until very finely ground (do not grind to a paste). Add to curry, along with yogurt, and simmer gently, uncovered, stirring, until sauce is thickened, about 5 minutes.

Serve chicken over rice, sprinkled with cilantro.

COOK'S NOTE

■ The curry, without the yogurt and cashews, can be made up to 5 days ahead. Cool, uncovered, then refrigerate, covered. Reheat over low heat before stirring in the yogurt and ground cashews.

Chicken Cashew Chili

SERVES 6 TO 8
ACTIVE TIME: 45 MINUTES ■ START TO FINISH: 1½ HOURS

■ A weeknight take on *mole* ("*moh*-leh"), the complex Mexican sauce whose most famous ingredient is chocolate, this chili gets much of its resonance from pureed ancho chiles, which lend a rich, sweet, and only mildly hot flavor to the dish. (For more heat, do not remove the ribs or seeds from the anchos.) The ground cashews help thicken the chile puree, while the whole nuts add another textural component. ■

4 dried ancho chiles
2½ cups Chicken Stock (page 153) or store-bought reduced-sodium broth
1 tablespoon canned chipotle chiles in adobo
1½ cups (7½ ounces) salted roasted cashews
¼ cup olive oil
2 large onions, coarsely chopped
6 garlic cloves, finely chopped
2 tablespoons ground cumin
2 teaspoons salt
1 (3½- to 4-pound) chicken, rinsed, patted dry, excess fat discarded, and cut into 8 serving pieces
½ cup chopped fresh cilantro
2 (14- to 15-ounce) cans diced tomatoes in juice
1 ounce bittersweet chocolate, chopped
1 (19-ounce) can kidney beans, rinsed and drained

MAKE THE CHILE PUREE: Heat a dry small heavy skillet (not nonstick) over moderate heat until hot. Toast dried chiles, one at a time, pressing down with tongs, for several seconds on each side to make them more pliable. Seed and devein dried chiles; discard stems. Tear dried chiles into pieces and transfer to a blender. Add stock, chipotles, and ½ cup cashews and puree until smooth.

MAKE THE CHILI: Heat oil in a 6- to 7-quart wide heavy pot over moderate heat until hot but not smoking. Add onions and garlic and cook, stirring, until softened, 5 to 7 minutes. Add cumin and salt and cook, stirring, for 1 minute. Add chicken and stir to coat with onion mixture. Stir in chile puree, ¼ cup cilantro, and tomatoes with juice. Bring to a simmer and simmer, covered, stirring occasionally to avoid sticking, until chicken is cooked through, about 45 minutes. Remove from heat and transfer chicken to a bowl.

Shred meat using two forks; discard bones and skin. Return chicken to pot and stir in chocolate, beans, remaining 1 cup cashews, and remaining ¼ cup cilantro. Cook over moderate heat, stirring, until chili is heated through and chocolate is melted.

COOK'S NOTE

■ The chili can be made up to 2 days ahead. Cool, uncovered, then refrigerate, covered.

Chicken with Tomatoes and Prunes

SERVES 4
ACTIVE TIME: 25 MINUTES ■ START TO FINISH: 1¼ HOURS

■ The simplicity and speed of this dish, adapted from one created by the chef and cookbook author Diane Kochilas, belie its deep, complex flavor—sweet, sour, spiced, and savory. It's emblematic of Greece's Epirus region, a rugged, mountainous area bordering Albania. Although the plums that once grew all over Epirus have been lost to more profitable crops, the fruit still appears in many of the region's dishes. Here tomatoes and prunes (dried plums) dance a jig with each other— the tomatoes offset the sweetness of the prunes, while the prunes balance the tomatoes' acidity. ■

    1 (3- to 3½-pound) chicken, rinsed, patted dry, and cut into 8 serving pieces
      Salt and freshly ground black pepper
  2½ tablespoons unsalted butter
    1 cup dry white wine
    ½ cup water
    ½ pound plum tomatoes (about 3), seeded and chopped
    1 (3- to 4-inch) cinnamon stick
  5½ ounces pitted prunes (16–18)
    2 tablespoons red wine vinegar
    2 teaspoons sugar

Sprinkle chicken with 1 teaspoon salt and ¼ teaspoon pepper. Heat butter in a 12-inch heavy skillet or a wide heavy pot over moderately high heat until foam subsides. Brown chicken in 2 batches, turning once with tongs, about 5 minutes per batch. Transfer to a plate.

Return chicken, skin side up, to skillet, along with any juices accumulated on plate. Add wine, bring to a boil, and boil until reduced by half, about 4 minutes. Add water, tomatoes, cinnamon stick, ¾ teaspoon salt, and a large pinch of pepper and bring to a boil. Reduce heat to moderately low, cover, and simmer for 20 minutes.

Stir in prunes, vinegar, and sugar and simmer, covered, until chicken is cooked through, about 10 minutes.

Transfer chicken with tongs to a shallow serving dish and cover with foil to keep warm. Boil cooking juices, stirring occasionally, until thickened and reduced to about 1½ cups, 8 to 10 minutes. Discard cinnamon stick and spoon sauce over chicken.

COOK'S NOTE

■ The chicken can be made up to 1 day ahead. Cool, uncovered, then refrigerate, covered.

Cajun Chicken Stew

SERVES 6
ACTIVE TIME: 1¼ HOURS ■ START TO FINISH: 1¾ HOURS

■ Many Cajun recipes begin with a roux, and it's a step that cannot be rushed. This roux, based on a mixture of chicken fat and vegetable oil, is cooked until it is a russet brown. The caramelized flour not only acts as a thickener but also creates deep, dark flavor, turning everyday ingredients—chicken, onion, bell pepper, and celery—into an extraordinarily rich and luscious stew. This recipe comes from Bettye Miller, the mother of *Gourmet*'s senior food editor Alexis Touchet, who recommends leaving any fat attached to the chicken for maximum flavor. ■

  3–6 tablespoons vegetable oil
    1 (3- to 3½-pound) chicken, rinsed, patted dry, and cut into serving pieces
      Salt
    ½ cup all-purpose flour
    1 medium onion, chopped
    1 medium green bell pepper, cored, seeded, and chopped
    1 celery rib, chopped
    3 cups water
    ¼ teaspoon cayenne, or to taste
    ¾ cup thinly sliced scallion greens
ACCOMPANIMENT: white rice

Heat 3 tablespoons oil in a 4- to 5-quart heavy pot, preferably cast-iron, over moderately high heat until hot but not smoking. Sprinkle chicken with 2½ teaspoons salt. Brown chicken in 4 batches, turning once with tongs, about 5 minutes per batch. Transfer to a large bowl.

Add enough of remaining oil to pot to total ¼ cup fat, then stir in flour with a flat-ended metal or wooden spatula and cook over moderately low heat, scraping back and forth constantly (not stirring; see page 370), until roux is the color of milk chocolate, 10 to 20 minutes.

Add onion, bell pepper, and celery and cook, scraping back and forth occasionally, until onion is softened, about 8 minutes. Add water and bring to a boil, stirring occasionally, until incorporated. (Roux will appear curdled initially, but it will come together as it reaches a boil.)

Add chicken and any juices accumulated in bowl, reduce heat, and simmer, partially covered, until chicken is cooked through, 30 to 35 minutes.

Stir in cayenne, scallion greens, and salt to taste and serve over rice.

COOK'S NOTE

- The stew improves in flavor if made up to 1 day ahead (without the scallion greens). Cool, uncovered, then refrigerate, covered. Reheat, then stir in the scallion greens.

Green Pozole with Chicken

SERVES 6 GENEROUSLY
ACTIVE TIME: 1½ HOURS ■ START TO FINISH: 2 HOURS

■ Pozole, a thick stew that is popular in Mexico, is generally made with pork or chicken, hominy, and chiles. This one is enlivened with a classic combination of tomatillos, pumpkin seeds, jalapeños, and cilantro. An array of chopped radish, onion, and avocado is served on the side. Tomatillos are available year-round in specialty markets, Latin grocery stores, and some supermarkets. Look for firm ones with tight-fitting husks. ■

9 cups water
1 Turkish bay leaf or ½ California bay leaf
1 large white onion, halved lengthwise and thinly sliced crosswise
6 garlic cloves, chopped
Salt
3 pounds skinless, boneless chicken thighs, rinsed and patted dry
½ cup green hulled pumpkin seeds (*pepitas*; see Cook's Note)
1 pound tomatillos, husked and rinsed under warm water
2 jalapeño chiles, quartered, including seeds
¾ cup chopped fresh cilantro
1 teaspoon dried epazote or oregano, preferably Mexican, crumbled
2 tablespoons vegetable oil
2 (15-ounce) cans white hominy, rinsed and drained

ACCOMPANIMENTS: diced radish; cubed avocado tossed with fresh lime juice; shredded romaine; chopped white onion; lime wedges; dried epazote or oregano

SPECIAL EQUIPMENT: an electric coffee/spice grinder

COOK THE CHICKEN: Combine 8 cups water, bay leaf, half of onion, half of garlic, and 1 teaspoon salt in a 6-quart heavy pot and bring to a boil, covered. Reduce heat and simmer for 10 minutes.

Add chicken and poach at a bare simmer, uncovered, skimming off any foam, until just cooked through, about 20 minutes. Transfer chicken to a cutting board to cool. Pour broth through a fine-mesh sieve into a large bowl; discard solids.

MEANWHILE, MAKE THE SAUCE: Cook pumpkin seeds in a dry small skillet over low heat, stirring occasionally, until puffed but not browned, 6 to 7 minutes. Transfer to a bowl and cool completely, then finely grind in coffee/spice grinder.

Combine tomatillos, remaining onion, and remaining cup water in a 3-quart saucepan. Bring to a simmer, and simmer, covered, until vegetables are tender, about 10 minutes; drain. Transfer vegetables to a blender, add jalapeños, ¼ cup cilantro, epazote, remaining garlic, and 1½ teaspoons salt, and puree.

When chicken is cool enough to handle, coarsely shred with your fingers.

Heat oil in a 4- to 5-quart heavy pot over moderately high heat until hot but not smoking. Add puree (use caution, as it will spatter and steam) and cook, uncovered, stirring frequently, until thickened, about 10 minutes. Stir in pumpkin seeds and 1 cup reserved broth and simmer for 5 minutes.

Stir in shredded chicken, hominy, and 3 more cups reserved broth, bring to a simmer, and simmer, partially covered, for 20 minutes.

Stir in remaining ½ cup cilantro. Serve pozole in deep bowls, with accompaniments.

COOK'S NOTES

- If you can only find toasted *pepitas,* do not toast them again.
- The chicken can be cooked and shredded up to 1 day ahead. Refrigerate it in 4 cups of the reserved broth, and measure out 1 cup broth before proceeding.

Steamed Chicken with Black Mushrooms and Bok Choy

SERVES 6
ACTIVE TIME: 30 MINUTES ■ START TO FINISH: 1¾ HOURS

■ Steamed chicken might sound ascetic, but this dish is brimming with flavor. The Chinese have been steaming meats and fish for thousands of years, and the technique invariably produces beautifully moist flesh infused with the flavors of whatever it is steamed with — in this case scallions, ginger, and soy sauce. Be sure to marinate the chicken for 30 minutes, so that it can fully soak up the marinade. ■

12 dried shiitake (Chinese black) mushrooms
      (see Sources)
2 cups boiling water
2½ pounds skinless chicken thighs (bone-in), rinsed and
      patted dry (see Cook's Note)
¼ cup soy sauce
2 tablespoons Chinese rice wine or medium-dry
      sherry
2 tablespoons cornstarch
1 teaspoon Asian sesame oil
½ teaspoon salt

3 scallions, cut into 1-inch pieces
1 tablespoon minced peeled fresh ginger
1½ pounds baby bok choy (6–8), trimmed, halved
      lengthwise, and washed well

GARNISH: thinly sliced scallions
ACCOMPANIMENT: white rice
SPECIAL EQUIPMENT: a well-seasoned 14-inch flat-
      bottomed wok with a lid and a 9-inch round
      metal cooling rack or a deep 12-inch skillet
      fitted with a steamer insert; a 9- to 9½-inch
      deep-dish pie plate

Soak shiitakes in boiling water in a bowl until softened, about 30 minutes.

Lift mushrooms from water and cut out and discard stems. Squeeze excess liquid from caps and discard soaking liquid.

With a heavy cleaver (see Cook's Note), hack each chicken thigh crosswise, through bone, into thirds.

Stir together soy sauce, rice wine, cornstarch, sesame oil, and salt in a large bowl until smooth. Add chicken, mushroom caps, scallions, and ginger and toss well to coat. Marinate at room temperature, stirring occasionally, for 30 minutes.

Put rack into wok (or steamer insert into skillet) and add enough water to reach just below it. Cover wok (or skillet) and bring water to a boil. Transfer chicken mixture to pie plate, put in wok (or skillet), and steam, covered, stirring once, until chicken is just cooked through, about 25 minutes.

Meanwhile, cook bok choy in a 4- to 6-quart pot of boiling (unsalted) water, uncovered, until just tender, 7 to 9 minutes. Drain.

Carefully remove pie plate from wok. Arrange bok choy around edges of a large deep platter and spoon chicken and sauce into center. Sprinkle chicken with scallions and serve with rice.

COOK'S NOTE

- If you don't have a cleaver, have your butcher hack the chicken thighs into 3 pieces each.

Chicken with Black Pepper–Maple Sauce

SERVES 4

ACTIVE TIME: 20 MINUTES ■ START TO FINISH: 40 MINUTES

■ Inspired by a recipe from chef Gray Kunz's *Elements of Taste,* this chicken is spatchcocked, which simply involves splitting it open by removing the backbone, then tucking the legs up and out of the way. The technique allows the bird to lie flat in the pan, ensuring that it cooks evenly. Weighting it with a second skillet produces wonderfully crisp skin. This is a great (and fast) alternative to roasting. The sauce—a hot and sweet melding of black peppercorns and robust Grade B maple syrup—is imaginative and comforting all at once. ■

1 (3- to 3½-pound) chicken, rinsed and patted dry
  Salt
¼ teaspoon freshly ground black pepper
5 tablespoons unsalted butter
2 (3-inch-long) fresh rosemary sprigs, plus
  1 (1-inch-long) sprig
1 tablespoon black peppercorns
¼ cup Grade B pure maple syrup
¾ cup Chicken Stock (page 153) or store-bought
  reduced-sodium broth
¼ cup cider vinegar

SPECIAL EQUIPMENT: parchment paper; two 10-inch heavy skillets (one well-seasoned cast-iron or heavy nonstick); 5 to 6 pounds weights, such as three 28-ounce cans of tomatoes

Remove backbone from chicken by cutting down each side of it with kitchen shears (1). Spread chicken skin side up on a cutting board. Cut a ½-inch slit on each side of chicken in center of triangle of skin between thigh and breast near drumstick and tuck bottom knob of each drumstick through slit (2). Tuck wing tips under breast (3). Sprinkle chicken all over with 1 teaspoon salt and ¼ teaspoon pepper.

Cut a 10-inch round of parchment paper. Heat 3 tablespoons butter in 10-inch cast-iron or heavy nonstick skillet over moderate heat until foam subsides. Add chicken, skin side down, and arrange larger rosemary sprigs over chicken. Cover with parchment round and second skillet, then top with weights. Cook until skin is browned, about 15 minutes.

Remove and reserve weights, top skillet, parchment, and rosemary. Carefully loosen chicken from skillet with spatula. Turn chicken over and replace rosemary sprigs, then re-cover with parchment, skillet, and weights. Cook until chicken is just cooked through, 15 to 20 minutes more.

Meanwhile, toast peppercorns in a dry 1-quart

SPATCHCOCKED CHICKEN

heavy saucepan over moderate heat, shaking pan occasionally, until fragrant, about 3 minutes. Transfer to a cutting board and coarsely crush with a rolling pin. Return peppercorns to saucepan, add maple syrup, ½ cup stock, and small rosemary sprig, and bring to a simmer. Reduce heat and simmer for 20 minutes.

Transfer chicken to platter and cover loosely with foil. Add vinegar to skillet and deglaze by boiling, scraping up brown bits, for 1 minute, then boil until liquid is reduced by half. Stir in maple mixture and remaining ¼ cup stock and boil until slightly syrupy, about 3 minutes. Reduce heat to low and swirl in remaining 2 tablespoons butter. Season sauce with salt and pour through a fine-mesh sieve into a bowl; discard solids.

Serve chicken with sauce.

Salt-Roasted Chicken

SERVES 4
ACTIVE TIME: 15 MINUTES ■ START TO FINISH: 13 HOURS
(INCLUDES OVERNIGHT SALTING)

■ One of the best—and easiest—roast chickens you'll ever taste. Though this recipe takes only 15 minutes of hands-on time, it does require planning ahead to salt the bird. Like a traditional wet brine, overnight salting helps tenderize and season the flesh, but it's easier and requires less fridge space. Rubbing the skin with butter and adding lemon slices to the cavity results in even more flavor for both the chicken and its pan juices. ■

    1 (3½-pound) chicken, rinsed and patted dry
 2¼ teaspoons fine sea salt
  ¼ teaspoon freshly ground black pepper
    1 tablespoon unsalted butter, softened
    3 (¼-inch-thick) lemon slices
SPECIAL EQUIPMENT: an instant-read thermometer

Sprinkle chicken inside and out with sea salt and pepper. Set in a shallow dish, cover loosely with plastic wrap, and refrigerate for at least 12 hours.

Put a rack in middle of oven and preheat oven to 500°F.

Pat chicken dry. Rub skin with butter and put lemon slices in cavity. Put chicken in a small roasting pan, transfer to oven, and reduce oven temperature to 425°F. Roast chicken, basting occasionally with pan juices, until thermometer inserted 2 inches into fleshy part of thigh (without touching bone) registers 170°F, about 50 minutes.

Let chicken stand for 15 minutes before carving.

COOK'S NOTE
■ The salted chicken can be refrigerated for up to 2 days.

Hainanese Chicken Rice

SERVES 6
ACTIVE TIME: 1 HOUR ■ START TO FINISH: 2½ HOURS

■ Almost every culture has its own version of chicken and rice. This three-in-one dish of chicken, rice, and soup is one of the zestier examples. It originated in Hainan, a tropical island off the southernmost coast of China, and has become a culinary staple in Singaporean and Malaysian cuisine. Some of the gingery broth left from poaching the bird is turned into a simple soup, while the rest is used to cook the rice. Sip the broth as you eat the chicken and shallot-flecked rice, customizing each bite with a dab of the tangy chile sauce or a nibble of cool cucumber. ■

    1 (3- to 3½-pound) chicken, rinsed and
      patted dry
      Salt
    4 quarts water
    4 (⅛-inch-thick) slices fresh ginger, smashed,
      plus 2 tablespoons chopped peeled fresh ginger
    6 (3- to 3½-inch-long) fresh hot red chiles, such as Thai
      or serrano, chopped, including seeds
    1 medium shallot, chopped, plus 4 small shallots,
      thinly sliced
    2 medium garlic cloves, chopped, plus 2 large garlic
      cloves, finely chopped
  ⅓ cup fresh lime juice (from about 3 limes)
    2 cups jasmine rice

About 1 tablespoon vegetable oil if necessary

1 seedless cucumber (usually plastic-wrapped)

1 bunch watercress, coarse stems discarded

1 tablespoon soy sauce

2 teaspoons Asian sesame oil

GARNISH: fresh cilantro leaves or sprigs

SPECIAL EQUIPMENT: a mini food processor

PREPARE THE CHICKEN AND BROTH: Remove fat from cavity of chicken and reserve for rice. Rub chicken inside and out with 1 teaspoon salt.

Bring water, 2 teaspoons salt, and slices of ginger to a boil in a 6- to 8-quart pot wide enough to hold chicken. Add chicken, breast side down, and return to a boil, covered. Reduce heat and simmer, partially covered, for 20 minutes.

Remove pot from heat and let chicken stand in hot broth, covered, until just cooked through, 15 to 20 minutes.

MEANWHILE, MAKE THE CHILE SAUCE: Combine chiles, chopped shallot, chopped ginger, chopped garlic (not finely chopped garlic), ½ teaspoon salt, and lime juice in mini food processor and pulse to a coarse paste.

Lift chicken out of pot by inserting handle of a long wooden spoon in cavity, allowing broth to drain from cavity back into pot, and transfer chicken to a bowl of ice and cold water. Cool completely, turning once.

Meanwhile, boil broth, uncovered, until reduced to 9 cups, about 30 minutes. Set aside.

Drain chicken and pat dry with paper towels. Cut into serving pieces, transfer to a platter, cover, and refrigerate.

MAKE THE RICE: Wash rice in a large medium-mesh sieve under cold running water until water runs clear; drain well.

Cook reserved chicken fat in a 3-quart heavy saucepan over moderate heat, stirring, until rendered; discard solids.

If necessary, add vegetable oil to pan to make 2 tablespoons fat. Cook sliced shallots in fat over moderate heat, stirring, until browned, 3 to 5 minutes. Add finely chopped garlic and cook, stirring, for 1 minute. Add rice and cook, stirring gently, for 1 minute. Add 3 cups reserved broth and bring to a boil. Boil until liquid on surface is evaporated and small bubbles ap-

pear in holes in rice, 3 to 4 minutes. Cover and cook over very low heat until rice is tender and liquid is absorbed, about 15 minutes more.

Remove rice from heat and let stand, covered, for 5 minutes, then fluff with a fork and cover again.

Remove chicken from refrigerator and pat dry.

ASSEMBLE THE DISH: Using a vegetable peeler, preferably a U-shaped one, make wide strips by shaving as many long ribbons as possible from cucumber and transfer to a bowl of ice and cold water. Refrigerate for 15 minutes; drain well.

Bring remaining 6 cups reserved broth and watercress to a boil in a 3-quart saucepan, uncovered, reduce heat, and simmer for 1 minute. Remove pan from heat and let stand, uncovered, until watercress is a shade darker, about 3 minutes.

Stir together soy sauce and sesame oil in a small bowl and brush all over chicken. Sprinkle chicken with cilantro and serve with cucumber ribbons and individual bowls of rice, soup, and chile sauce.

COOK'S NOTE

■ The chicken and broth can be prepared up to 1 day ahead. Cool the broth, uncovered, then refrigerate, covered; refrigerate the chicken separately, covered. Remove the chicken from the refrigerator up to 1 hour before brushing with the soy sauce and sesame oil and serving.

Roast Capon with Lemon, Thyme, and Onions

SERVES 8 TO 10
ACTIVE TIME: 1½ HOURS ■ START TO FINISH: 3½ HOURS

■ Weighing in somewhere between a small roaster and a turkey, a capon—a young, neutered male chicken—feeds a nice-sized group. In this recipe, the bird is complemented by a generous amount of onions and shallots, roasted until mellow and soft. Though you can find frozen capons in most supermarkets, we recommend ordering a fresh one from the butcher—the meat will be silkier and tastier. If you can't get a capon, you can substitute a large roasting chicken. ■

1 (8- to 9-pound) capon or roasting chicken,
   preferably not frozen, rinsed and patted dry
   (any excess fat from cavity discarded)
   Salt and freshly ground black pepper
1 stick (8 tablespoons) unsalted butter,
   softened
1½ tablespoons finely grated lemon zest
4 teaspoons chopped fresh thyme, plus
   10 fresh thyme sprigs
2 lemons, halved, plus ¼ cup fresh lemon
   juice
6 shallots, trimmed, leaving root ends intact,
   and halved lengthwise
4 medium red onions, trimmed, leaving root
   ends intact, and cut into 1-inch-thick
   wedges
4 medium yellow onions, trimmed, leaving root
   ends intact, and cut into 1-inch-thick wedges
2 cups Chicken Stock (page 153) or store-bought
   reduced-sodium broth
2 tablespoons all-purpose flour

GARNISH: lemon wedges and fresh thyme sprigs
SPECIAL EQUIPMENT: a 17-by-14-inch flameproof
   roasting pan; kitchen string; an instant-read
   thermometer

Sprinkle cavity of capon with ½ teaspoon salt and
½ teaspoon pepper. Put capon in roasting pan and let
stand at room temperature for 30 minutes.

Put a rack in middle of oven and preheat oven to
425°F.

Stir together butter, zest, 1 tablespoon chopped
thyme, 1 teaspoon salt, and ½ teaspoon pepper in a
small bowl.

Starting at neck cavity, gently slide your fingers
between skin and flesh of breast to loosen skin (be
careful not to tear skin). Push butter mixture evenly
under skin on both sides of breast, then massage skin
to distribute butter evenly. Tuck wings under. Put
thyme sprigs and lemon halves in (large) cavity and
tie legs together with string. Pour lemon juice all over
capon and sprinkle with 1 teaspoon salt and ½ teaspoon pepper.

Roast capon for 30 minutes.

Reduce oven temperature to 375°F and add shallots and red and yellow onions to pan, tossing with
pan juices. Continue roasting capon, basting with

pan juices and stirring shallots and onions every 30
minutes, until thermometer inserted 2 inches into
fleshy part of thigh (without touching bone) registers
170°F, about 1½ hours more.

Tilt capon so juices in cavity run into roasting
pan, and transfer capon to a cutting board (set roasting pan aside). Let stand, uncovered, for 20 to 30
minutes.

Meanwhile, transfer shallots and onions to a sieve,
holding it over roasting pan to drain any pan juices,
then transfer shallots and onions to a bowl. Stir in ¼
teaspoon salt and ¼ teaspoon pepper.

Pour pan juices into a 1-quart glass measure. Skim
off fat and reserve fat and juices separately.

Straddle roasting pan across two burners. Add 1
cup stock to pan and deglaze pan by boiling over high
heat, scraping up brown bits, for 1 minute. Add stock
mixture to glass measure with pan juices.

Cook flour in 2 tablespoons reserved fat in a
3-quart heavy saucepan over moderate heat, whisking, for 2 minutes to make a roux. Add remaining
cup stock in a stream, whisking constantly to prevent
lumps. Whisk in pan juice mixture, bring to a simmer, and simmer, whisking occasionally, until sauce
is reduced to about 1½ cups, 10 to 15 minutes.

Pour sauce through a fine-mesh sieve into a bowl.
Stir in remaining teaspoon chopped fresh thyme and
salt and pepper to taste.

Carve capon and garnish with lemon wedges and
thyme sprigs. Serve with shallots, onions, and sauce.

Turkey

Turkey Cutlets with Mustard Wine Sauce

SERVES 4
ACTIVE TIME: 25 MINUTES ■ START TO FINISH: 25 MINUTES

■ Turkey cutlets are one of our favorite convenience foods, especially in this delicious, French-inspired recipe, tangy with Dijon mustard and finished with fresh tarragon. ■

    4 (¼-inch-thick) turkey cutlets, rinsed and
       patted dry
    ½ teaspoon salt
    ¼ teaspoon freshly ground black pepper
    ½ stick (4 tablespoons) unsalted butter
    ½ cup finely chopped shallots
    ⅓ cup dry white wine
    1 tablespoon tarragon vinegar
    1 tablespoon Dijon mustard
    2 teaspoons finely chopped fresh tarragon

Sprinkle cutlets with salt and pepper and, if necessary, pound them between sheets of plastic wrap with flat side of a meat pounder or with a rolling pin until ¼ inch thick. Heat 1 tablespoon butter in a 12-inch heavy skillet over moderately high heat until foam subsides. Add 2 cutlets and cook, turning once, until golden and just cooked through, about 3 minutes. Transfer with tongs to a platter and cover loosely with foil to keep warm. Add 1 tablespoon butter to skillet and cook remaining 2 cutlets in same manner; transfer to platter.

Add 1 tablespoon butter to skillet and heat over moderately high heat until foam subsides. Add shallots and cook, stirring, until golden, about 5 minutes. Stir in any juices that have accumulated on turkey platter, then add wine, vinegar, and mustard and cook, whisking and scraping up brown bits, until sauce is slightly thickened, about 2 minutes. Remove from heat and whisk in tarragon and remaining tablespoon butter.

Pour sauce over turkey cutlets.

Hoisin Turkey Cutlets

SERVES 4
ACTIVE TIME: 15 MINUTES ■ START TO FINISH: 25 MINUTES

■ Because these savory cutlets, which are glazed with hoisin and showered with scallions, take just minutes to prepare, we turn to them often on busy weeknights. They are delicious with white rice and crisp steamed broccoli. Use the best-quality hoisin you can; we especially like Lee Kum Kee brand, available in many supermarkets. ■

    4 (¼-inch-thick) turkey cutlets, rinsed and
       patted dry
    ½ teaspoon salt
    ¼ teaspoon freshly ground black pepper
    2 tablespoons vegetable oil
    2 scallions, finely chopped
    2 teaspoons finely grated peeled fresh ginger
    1 garlic clove, finely chopped
    ¼ cup hoisin sauce
    1 tablespoon oyster sauce
    3 tablespoons water
    ½ teaspoon Asian sesame oil
GARNISH: chopped fresh cilantro and chopped scallion
       greens

Sprinkle cutlets with salt and pepper and, if necessary, pound them between sheets of plastic wrap with flat side of a meat pounder or with a rolling pin until ¼ inch thick. Heat vegetable oil in a 12-inch heavy skillet over moderately high heat until hot but not smoking. Add 2 cutlets and cook, turning once, until golden and just cooked through, about 3 minutes. Transfer with tongs to a platter and cover loosely with foil to keep warm. Cook remaining 2 cutlets in same manner and transfer to platter.

Add scallions, ginger, and garlic to skillet and cook, stirring, until golden, about 1 minute. Stir in hoisin sauce, oyster sauce, water, sesame oil, and any juices that have accumulated on turkey platter and boil, stirring and scraping up any brown bits, for 1 minute.

Return cutlets to skillet and turn to coat well with sauce.

Turkey Scaloppini with Capers and Lemon

■ Since turkey cutlets are easier to find and much less expensive than veal cutlets, they make a great substitute in this classic Italian dish. Capers and lemon contribute a frisson of flavor to the garlicky sauce, which is delicious sopped up with rice or crusty bread. ■

- 4 (¼-inch-thick) turkey cutlets, rinsed and patted dry
  Salt and freshly ground black pepper
- ½ cup all-purpose flour
- ¼ cup olive oil
- 2 garlic cloves, minced
- 1 cup Chicken Stock (page 153) or store-bought reduced-sodium broth
- 1–1½ tablespoons fresh lemon juice
- 2 tablespoons capers, rinsed
- 2 tablespoons chopped fresh flat-leaf parsley

Sprinkle cutlets with ½ teaspoon salt and ¼ teaspoon pepper and, if necessary, pound them between sheets of plastic wrap with flat side of a meat pounder or with a rolling pin until ¼ inch thick. Dredge 2 cutlets in flour, shaking off excess. Heat 1½ tablespoons oil in a 12-inch heavy skillet over high heat until hot but not smoking. Add floured cutlets and cook, turning once, until browned and just cooked through, about 4 minutes. Transfer with tongs to a platter and cover loosely with foil to keep warm. Dredge and cook remaining turkey in another 1½ tablespoons oil in same manner; transfer to platter.

Add remaining tablespoon oil to skillet and cook garlic over moderate heat, stirring, until fragrant, about 30 seconds. Add stock and deglaze pan by boiling over moderately high heat, scraping up brown bits, for about 1 minute, then boil until stock is reduced to about ¾ cup. Stir in lemon juice (to taste), capers, parsley, and salt and pepper to taste.

Return turkey to skillet, with any juices on platter, and simmer until heated through, about 1 minute.

Turkey Tonnato

■ Though it may sound improbable, the northern Italian dish *vitello tonnato*—poached veal with a creamy sauce of pureed canned tuna, anchovies, and lemon juice—is renowned for a reason. The delicate flavor of the meat is lifted by the ultrasavory tuna sauce. This version replaces the veal with a roast boneless turkey breast to great effect. Because it's served cold, it makes a good choice for a buffet table or any time you want a stunning meal that doesn't need last-minute cooking. ■

- 3 tablespoons tapenade (black olive paste)
- 1 tablespoon finely grated lemon zest
- 1 tablespoon finely chopped garlic
- 2 teaspoons finely chopped fresh rosemary
- 1 (4- to 4½-pound) boneless turkey breast half with skin, rinsed and patted dry
  Salt and freshly ground black pepper
- ½ cup plus 2 tablespoons extra-virgin olive oil
- 1 cup dry white wine
- 1 (6-ounce) can chunk light tuna in olive oil
- 2 tablespoons water
- 1 tablespoon fresh lemon juice
- 2 teaspoons anchovy paste

GARNISH: capers and chopped fresh flat-leaf parsley

ACCOMPANIMENTS: lemon wedges

SPECIAL EQUIPMENT: kitchen string; an instant-read thermometer

MAKE THE FILLING AND PREPARE THE TURKEY ROAST: Put a rack in middle of oven and preheat oven to 350°F.

Stir together tapenade, zest, garlic, and rosemary in a small bowl. Place turkey skin side up on a work surface with narrower, pointed end nearest you. Determine which long side of the breast is thickest and, starting from that side and holding knife parallel to work surface, cut breast horizontally almost in half, stopping 1 inch from other side. Open breast like a book. Sprinkle with 1 teaspoon salt and ½ teaspoon pepper. Spread tapenade mixture evenly over butterflied breast with back of a spoon, leaving a 1-inch border around edges. Starting from side without skin, roll up turkey, ending seam side down (skin will be on outside). Tie rolled turkey breast crosswise at 1-inch intervals with string. Sprinkle all over with 1 teaspoon salt and ½ teaspoon pepper.

COOK THE ROAST: Heat 2 tablespoons olive oil in a 12-inch heavy skillet until hot but not smoking. Add turkey and cook, turning occasionally, until browned all over, 8 minutes total.

Transfer turkey to a 13-by-9-inch roasting pan and add wine to pan. Roast turkey, uncovered, until thermometer inserted diagonally 2 inches into thickest part registers 160°F, about 1 hour.

Transfer roast to a platter; reserve pan juices. Cool roast completely, uncovered, then refrigerate, tightly wrapped in plastic wrap, for 2 hours.

MEANWHILE, MAKE THE SAUCE: Combine tuna, including oil, remaining ½ cup olive oil, water, lemon juice, anchovy paste, and ¼ cup reserved pan juices in a blender and puree, scraping down sides as necessary, until very smooth. Transfer to a bowl and season with salt and pepper. Cover with plastic wrap and refrigerate until cold, about 1 hour.

FINISH THE DISH: Cut cold turkey roast into ¼-inch thick slices, discarding string. Arrange on platter and top with cold sauce. Bring to room temperature, about 1 hour.

Sprinkle turkey with capers and parsley and serve with lemon wedges.

COOK'S NOTES

- You may need to order the turkey breast in advance from your butcher.
- The turkey roast and sauce can be refrigerated (separately) for up to 2 days.

Pepper Jack Turkey Burgers

SERVES 4
ACTIVE TIME: 20 MINUTES ■ START TO FINISH: 35 MINUTES

■ Tucking the cheese inside the burger guarantees extra-juicy results, especially if you seek out dark-meat ground turkey (see page 416). Any tasty melting cheese will work here, but we especially like the extra kick of pepper Jack. ■

FOR BURGERS
- ¼ cup finely chopped shallots
- 2 tablespoons olive oil
- ½ teaspoon salt
- ¼ teaspoon freshly ground black pepper
- 1½ pounds ground turkey (not labeled "all breast meat")
- 5 ounces pepper Jack cheese, cut into 4 (½-inch-thick) slices
- 4 hamburger or kaiser rolls

FOR SUN-DRIED TOMATO MAYONNAISE
- ¼ cup oil-packed sun-dried tomatoes, drained and coarsely chopped
- ¼ cup mayonnaise
- 1 tablespoon water
- 2 teaspoons cider vinegar
- ¼ teaspoon salt

ACCOMPANIMENT: lettuce leaves

MAKE THE BURGERS: Put a rack in middle of oven and preheat oven to 350°F.

Cook shallots in oil with salt and pepper in an 8-inch skillet over moderate heat, stirring occasionally, until golden, 2 to 3 minutes. Transfer to a bowl, add turkey, and mix gently but thoroughly.

Turn out turkey mixture onto a sheet of wax paper and divide into 8 equal mounds. Pat 1 mound into a 4-inch patty and top with 1 slice of cheese (trim cheese if necessary). Put a second mound on top, patting it down to enclose cheese, pinch edges together to seal, and shape into a single patty. Make 3 more burgers in same manner.

Heat an oiled well-seasoned ridged grill pan over moderately high heat until hot but not smoking. Grill burgers, turning once, until just cooked through (no longer pink), 10 to 12 minutes.

While burgers are cooking, heat rolls on a baking sheet in oven until crusty, about 5 minutes. Transfer rolls to a rack to cool slightly.

MEANWHILE, MAKE THE MAYONNAISE: Combine all ingredients in a blender or mini food processor and puree, scraping down sides as necessary.

Split rolls in half if necessary and spread cut sides with tomato mayonnaise. Serve burgers on rolls with lettuce.

Turkey Sloppy Joes on Cheddar Buttermilk Biscuits

SERVES 8
ACTIVE TIME: 40 MINUTES ■ START TO FINISH: 1¾ HOURS
(INCLUDES MAKING BISCUITS)

■ These zesty, messy sloppy joes on biscuits are perfect for a big family dinner or casual entertaining—all you need to complete the meal is a green salad. The drop biscuits are as tender as they are easy: the dough isn't rolled out, so there's no chance of overworking it. The amount of Parmesan may seem insignificant, but you'll be surprised how much it heightens the flavor of the cheddar. ■

  3 tablespoons olive oil
  1 large onion, chopped
  2 celery ribs, chopped
  1 red bell pepper, cored, seeded, and chopped
  4 garlic cloves, finely chopped
2½ pounds ground turkey (not labeled "all breast meat")
  1 teaspoon salt
  ½ teaspoon freshly ground black pepper
  1 (28-ounce) can whole tomatoes in juice
  ½ cup ketchup
  2 tablespoons molasses (not robust)
  2 tablespoons cider vinegar
1½ tablespoons Worcestershire sauce
1¼ teaspoons Tabasco, or to taste
    Cheddar Buttermilk Biscuits (recipe follows)

Heat oil in an 8-quart wide heavy pot over moderately high heat until hot but not smoking. Add onion, celery, bell pepper, and garlic and cook, stirring occasionally, until golden, 10 to 12 minutes. Add turkey and cook, stirring occasionally and breaking up large lumps with a wooden spoon, until meat is no longer pink, about 5 minutes. Stir in salt and pepper.

Meanwhile, combine tomatoes with juice, ketchup, molasses, vinegar, Worcestershire sauce, and Tabasco in a blender and puree until smooth.

Add tomato mixture to turkey and simmer, uncovered, stirring occasionally, until sauce is thickened, 25 to 30 minutes.

Serve sloppy joes on split biscuits.

COOK'S NOTE
■ The sloppy joe mixture can be made up to 2 days ahead. Cool, uncovered, then refrigerate, covered. Reheat before serving.

SHOPPING FOR GROUND TURKEY

If you've never met a turkey burger you liked, odds are it's been made entirely of white meat, turning it dry and crumbly. If you give the one on page 415 a try, though, you will be rewarded with plenty of moist succulence. (The same holds true of turkey sloppy joes.) Our burger is made with all dark meat, which has more fat, and thus more flavor, than white meat. (It's still lower in fat than lean ground beef.) Look for ground turkey that isn't labeled "all breast meat." That can sometimes be hard to find, so if you're not inclined to go the extra mile and grind the turkey yourself, ask the person behind the meat counter to grind it for you; in our experience, he or she is usually happy to oblige.

Cheddar Buttermilk Biscuits

MAKES 8 LARGE BISCUITS
ACTIVE TIME: 15 MINUTES ■ START TO FINISH: 40 MINUTES

■ Although these cheesy-buttery biscuits are ideal with sloppy joes, keep them in mind to serve with soup or chili too. We also like them with fried eggs and bacon to round out a hearty breakfast or brunch. ■

- 1¾ cups all-purpose flour
- ¾ cup cornmeal, preferably stone-ground (not coarse)
- 4 teaspoons baking powder
- 1 teaspoon baking soda
- 1 teaspoon salt
- ½ stick (4 tablespoons) cold unsalted butter, cut into ½-inch cubes
- 6 ounces extra-sharp cheddar, coarsely grated (about 1½ cups)
- 3 tablespoons finely grated Parmigiano-Reggiano
- 3 scallions, finely chopped
- 1⅓ cups well-shaken buttermilk

Put a rack in middle of oven and preheat oven to 450°F. Butter a large baking sheet.

Whisk together flour, cornmeal, baking powder, baking soda, and salt in a bowl. Blend in butter with your fingertips or a pastry blender until mixture resembles coarse meal. Stir in cheeses and scallions with a wooden spoon. Add buttermilk and stir until just combined.

Drop dough in 8 equal mounds about 2 inches apart on baking sheet. Bake until golden, about 15 minutes. Transfer to a rack and cool to warm, about 10 minutes, then split in half.

COOK'S NOTES

- You can use two small baking sheets instead of one large one. Bake the biscuits in the upper and lower thirds of the oven, switching the position of the baking sheets halfway through baking.
- The biscuits can be baked up to 1 day ahead. Cool, then keep in an airtight container at room temperature. Reheat in a preheated 350°F oven for 10 minutes.

Turkey Chilaquiles with Roasted Tomatillo Salsa

SERVES 6
ACTIVE TIME: 45 MINUTES ■ START TO FINISH: 1¼ HOURS

■ If you've ever searched for an inspired alternative to turkey tetrazzini for using up your Thanksgiving bird, this is it. In fact *chilaquiles*, a traditional Mexican peasant dish, was devised as a way to use up leftovers, namely day-old corn tortillas and meat. *Chilaquiles* are also delicious enough to make from scratch (you can also use the meat from a rotisserie chicken). The fried tortillas soften as they soak up the salsa, resulting in layers of textures from crisp and chewy to sweetly pliable. While the tortillas are the heart of the matter, the shredded meat adds backbone, and the accompaniments—fresh cilantro, crumbles of *queso fresco*, cool *crema*, and extra salsa—brighten everything up. ■

- 1¾ cups vegetable oil
- 2 (8-ounce) packages corn tortillas, cut into ½-inch-wide strips
- 1 large onion, chopped
- 1¾ cups Chicken Stock (page 153) or reduced-sodium broth
- 4 cups shredded cooked turkey (about 12 ounces)
  Roasted Tomatillo Salsa (recipe follows)
- 6 ounces Monterey Jack cheese, grated (about 1½ cups)
- ACCOMPANIMENTS: ½ cup *crema* (see Cook's Note and Sources); ¾ cup fresh cilantro sprigs; 6 ounces *queso fresco* (Mexican fresh white cheese; see Sources) or feta, crumbled (about 1½ cups)

Heat oil in a 12-inch heavy skillet over moderately high heat until it is hot but not smoking. Fry tortilla strips in 3 or 4 batches, turning occasionally with a slotted spoon, until golden, about 3 minutes per batch. Transfer to paper towels to drain. Carefully pour off and discard all but 1 tablespoon hot oil from skillet.

Meanwhile, put a rack in middle of oven and preheat oven to 375°F.

Cook onion in oil in skillet over moderately high

heat, stirring occasionally, until softened, about 5 minutes. Add stock and turkey, bring to a simmer, and simmer, uncovered, stirring occasionally, until liquid is reduced to about ½ cup, about 10 minutes.

Add 2¾ cups salsa and bring to a boil. Transfer to a bowl and stir in Monterey Jack and tortilla strips, then transfer tortilla mixture to a 2-quart shallow baking dish.

Bake, uncovered, until top is golden brown, about 15 minutes.

Serve *chilaquiles* with *crema*, cilantro, *queso fresco*, and remaining salsa.

COOK'S NOTES

- If you are unable to find *crema*, you can substitute ½ cup crème fraîche or sour cream mixed with 3 tablespoons milk.
- The *chilaquiles* can be made up to 1 day ahead. Cool, uncovered, then refrigerate, covered. Reheat to serve.

Roasted Tomatillo Salsa

MAKES ABOUT 5½ CUPS
ACTIVE TIME: 15 MINUTES ■ START TO FINISH: 15 MINUTES

■ You'll be happy that this recipe makes extra salsa. It's delicious over fried eggs and with chips, tacos, burritos (try it with Chicken Burritos, page 391), and much more. ■

2–3 serrano chiles
  4 garlic cloves, left unpeeled
  2 pounds fresh tomatillos, husked and rinsed under warm water, or 3 cups canned tomatillos (from three 11-ounce cans), drained
  ¾ cup fresh cilantro sprigs
  2 medium onions, coarsely chopped
2½ teaspoons kosher salt

Preheat broiler. Put chiles, garlic, and fresh tomatillos, if using, on rack of a broiler pan and broil 1 to 2 inches from heat, turning once or twice, until softened and partially charred, about 8 minutes.

Peel garlic. Discard stems of chiles. Puree tomatillos, garlic, and chiles with remaining ingredients, in 2 batches if necessary, in a blender until almost smooth.

COOK'S NOTE

- The salsa can be made up to 1 day ahead and refrigerated, covered.

Turkey Mole

SERVES 10 TO 12
ACTIVE TIME: 1¾ HOURS ■ START TO FINISH: 3½ HOURS

■ If you've never tasted the traditional Mexican specialty *mole poblano de guajolote*, you are in for a treat. *Moles* ("*moh*-lehs") can range from simple sauces made with a single chile and a few spices to this rich, smooth, complex concoction, adapted from a recipe by the late cookbook author Elisabeth Lambert Ortiz. It starts with the classic Mexican trinity of pasilla, ancho, and mulato chiles—each one contributes a distinct flavor and heat—and an array of spices. The sauce is sweetened with raisins and thickened with tortillas and nuts. A magical alchemy occurs when the deep flavors of unsweetened chocolate meld with chiles and nuts. This is a special-occasion dish, to be sure, but it's worth every minute of work. ■

  1 (10- to 12-pound) turkey, rinsed, patted dry, and cut into 10–12 serving pieces (see Cook's Note)
    Salt
  6 tablespoons lard or vegetable oil
3–4 quarts cold water
  6 dried ancho chiles (4 by 2½ inches; see Sources)
  4 dried mulato chiles (4 by 2½ inches; see Sources)
  4 dried pasilla chiles (about 6 by 1½ inches; see Sources)
  2 cups boiling water
  1 pound tomatoes (3 medium), peeled (see Tips, page 913), seeded, and coarsely chopped, or 1 (14- to 15-ounce) can whole tomatoes in juice, drained, juice reserved, and coarsely chopped
  1 pound white onions, chopped
  1 tablespoon chopped garlic
  2 (6- to 7-inch) corn tortillas, torn into pieces
  1 cup (about 5 ounces) blanched whole almonds
  ½ cup peanuts, preferably raw
  ½ cup raisins
  ½ teaspoon coriander seeds
  ½ teaspoon anise seeds

2 whole cloves

1 (½-inch) cinnamon stick, preferably Mexican canela, crumbled (see Cook's Note)

¼ cup sesame seeds, toasted (see Tips, page 911)

1½ ounces unsweetened chocolate, chopped

1 tablespoon sugar, or to taste

ACCOMPANIMENT: white rice

COOK THE TURKEY AND MAKE THE BROTH: Season turkey with 1½ teaspoons salt. Heat lard in a 12-inch heavy skillet over moderately high heat until hot but not smoking. Add turkey pieces in 3 or 4 batches and cook, turning, until browned on all sides, about 6 minutes per batch. Transfer to a 10-quart pot. Pour lard into a measuring cup and reserve.

Add enough cold water to just cover turkey, then add 2 tablespoons salt. Bring to a boil, skimming any foam, then reduce heat and simmer, uncovered, until turkey is cooked through, 1 to 1½ hours. Transfer turkey pieces to one bowl and pour broth into another bowl. Skim fat from surface of broth.

MEANWHILE, PREPARE THE CHILES: Discard stems, seeds, and ribs and tear all chiles into pieces. Soak chiles in boiling water in a large bowl, keeping them submerged with a sieve or plate, for 30 minutes.

MAKE THE MOLE: Working in 2 or 3 batches, puree chiles with soaking liquid, tomatoes with juice, onions, garlic, tortillas, and 2 cups turkey broth in a blender (use caution when blending hot liquids) until smooth, about 2 minutes per batch; transfer to a large bowl.

Combine almonds, peanuts, raisins, coriander seeds, anise seeds, cloves, cinnamon, and 2 table-spoons sesame seeds in a food processor and process until finely ground, about 2 minutes. Add ¼ cup turkey broth and process until mixture forms a paste, about 2 minutes more. Stir paste into chile puree.

Heat ¼ cup reserved lard in a wide 8- to 9-quart heavy pot over moderate heat until hot but not smoking. Carefully add chile mixture (mixture will spatter) and bring to a boil over high heat, stirring with a long-handled wooden spoon. Reduce heat to moderate and cook, stirring, until thickened, 8 to 10 minutes.

Stir in chocolate and enough turkey broth (about 4 cups) to thin *mole* to consistency of heavy cream and bring to a simmer, stirring until chocolate is melted. Stir in sugar and 2 teaspoons salt and simmer, partially covered (leave only a small gap), stirring occasionally, for 30 minutes.

Add turkey pieces to *mole* and simmer, covered, stirring occasionally, until heated through, 15 to 20 minutes. Season with salt and more sugar if desired and add more turkey broth as necessary; sauce should be thick enough to coat turkey, but not gloppy (sauce will continue to thicken as it stands).

Sprinkle with remaining 2 tablespoons sesame seeds and serve with rice.

COOK'S NOTES

- It's not easy to cut an uncooked turkey into serving pieces, so ask your butcher to do it for you. You will have 4 to 6 breast pieces (depending on how many people you are serving), 2 drumsticks, 2 thighs, and 2 wings.

- For *mole*, we prefer Mexican canela instead of regular supermarket cinnamon. Canela has a gentler flavor and is much softer. If you use regular stick cinnamon, you'll need to grind it in a coffee/spice grinder before adding it to the food processor.

- The turkey and broth can be cooked up to 1 day ahead. Cool the turkey in the broth, uncovered, then refrigerate in the broth, covered. Discard the solidified fat.

- The *mole*, without the turkey, can be prepared up to 1 day ahead. Cool, uncovered, then refrigerate, covered; refrigerate the turkey in the remaining broth. Add the turkey to the *mole* and gently reheat in a heavy pot over low heat, stirring frequently to prevent scorching and adding more broth to thin if necessary.

Simplest Roasted Turkey with Pan Gravy

SERVES 12 (WITH LEFTOVERS)
ACTIVE TIME: 30 MINUTES ■ START TO FINISH: 3¾ HOURS
(DOES NOT INCLUDE MAKING STOCK)

■ Imagine our surprise when this plain turkey, seasoned simply with salt and pepper and blasted in a 450°F oven, became the hands-down favorite of all the turkeys we've roasted. With its tender, juicy meat, crisp skin, and delicious gravy, it's the ultimate turkey lover's turkey. Plus, it's all done in under 4 hours, leaving you plenty of time to devote to side dishes.

An important note: To prevent smoking at this high heat, be sure to start with a clean oven. ■

1 (16-pound) turkey, neck and giblets removed and
    reserved for another use if desired, turkey left at
    room temperature for 1 hour
  Salt and freshly ground black pepper
  About 2 cups water
7–8 cups Turkey Stock (recipe follows)
  1 stick (8 tablespoons) unsalted butter
  ¾ cup all-purpose flour
1½–2 tablespoons cider vinegar
SPECIAL EQUIPMENT: 2 small metal skewers; kitchen string;
    a 17-by-14-inch flameproof roasting pan with a
    rack; an instant-read thermometer; a 2-quart
    measuring cup

ROAST THE TURKEY: Put a rack in lowest position
and preheat oven to 450°F.

Using needle-nose pliers or tweezers, remove any
feathers and quills from turkey. Rinse turkey inside
and out and pat dry. Season inside and out with 1
tablespoon salt and 1¾ teaspoons pepper. Fold neck
skin under body and secure with metal skewers. Tie
drumsticks together with kitchen string and tuck
wings under body.

Put turkey on rack in roasting pan. Add 1 cup
water to pan. Roast, without basting, adding water
to pan as necessary to maintain 1 cup and rotating
pan halfway through roasting, until thermometer inserted into fleshy part of thighs (test both thighs; do
not touch bones) registers 170°F, 2¼ to 2¾ hours.

Carefully tilt turkey so any juices from cavity run
into roasting pan, then transfer turkey to a platter;
reserve juices in roasting pan. Let turkey stand, uncovered, for 30 minutes (temperature of thigh meat
will rise to 180°F).

MEANWHILE, MAKE THE GRAVY: Pour pan juices
through a fine-mesh sieve into measuring cup (set
roasting pan aside) and skim off and discard fat. (Or,
if using a fat separator, pour pan juices through sieve
into separator and let stand until fat rises to top, 1 to
2 minutes. Carefully pour pan juices from separator
into measure; discard fat.)

Straddle roasting pan across two burners, add 1 cup
water, and deglaze pan by boiling over high heat, scraping up brown bits, for 1 minute. Pour liquid through
sieve into measuring cup containing pan juices. Add
enough turkey stock (if stock is congealed, heat to liquefy) to pan juices to make 8 cups.

Melt butter in a 4-quart heavy pot over moderate

heat. Whisk in flour and cook, whisking, for 5 minutes to make a roux. Add stock mixture in a stream,
whisking constantly to prevent lumps, and bring to a
boil, whisking occasionally. Stir in any turkey juices
accumulated on platter and simmer for 5 minutes.
Season gravy with salt and pepper and stir in cider
vinegar (to taste).

Carve turkey and serve with gravy.

Turkey Stock

MAKES A GENEROUS 3 QUARTS
ACTIVE TIME: 20 MINUTES ■ START TO FINISH: 4½ HOURS

■ Roasting the turkey and vegetables before simmering them results in a dark stock that is the corner-
stone of a rich brown gravy. If you don't have the time
to cosset a gently simmering stockpot on Thanksgiving morning, our senior food editor Alexis Touchet
has a solution. She suggests going to the supermarket
well in advance of the holiday and buying packages of
turkey wings, drumsticks, and thighs and premaking
the stock. This recipe yields more than enough for the
rich turkey gravy that accompanies Simplest Roasted
Turkey or for our Pomegranate Gravy (opposite page).
You'll be happy to have the extra when it comes time
to make soup. ■

  6 pounds turkey parts, such as wings, drumsticks, and
    thighs, rinsed and patted dry
  3 medium yellow onions, left unpeeled, halved
  3 celery ribs, cut into 2-inch lengths
  3 carrots, quartered
  5 quarts cold water
  6 fresh parsley stems
  1 Turkish bay leaf or ½ California bay leaf
 10 black peppercorns
1½ teaspoons salt
SPECIAL EQUIPMENT: a 17-by-14-inch flameproof
    roasting pan

Put a rack in lowest position in oven and preheat
oven to 500°F.

If using turkey wings, halve at joints with a cleaver
or large knife, then crack wing bones in several places
with back of cleaver or knife. Pat all turkey parts dry.
Put turkey skin side down in dry roasting pan and
roast, turning once, until well browned, about 45
minutes. Transfer turkey to an 8- to 10-quart stock-

pot using tongs; reserve fat in roasting pan. (Leave oven on.)

Add onions, cut side down, celery, and carrots to fat in roasting pan and roast, stirring halfway through roasting, until golden, about 20 minutes. Add vegetables to stockpot.

Straddle roasting pan across two burners, add 2 cups water, and deglaze by boiling over high heat, scraping up brown bits, for 1 minute. Add deglazing liquid to turkey and vegetables in stockpot, then add parsley stems, bay leaf, peppercorns, salt, and remaining 4½ quarts water. Bring just to a boil, then reduce heat and simmer gently, partially covered, for 3 hours, skimming as necessary.

Pour stock through a large fine-mesh sieve into a large bowl; discard solids. Measure stock: If there is more than 13 cups, boil in cleaned pot until reduced to 13 cups. If there is less, add enough water to make 13 cups. If using stock immediately, let stand until fat rises to top, 1 to 2 minutes, then skim off and discard. If not, cool completely, uncovered, then refrigerate, covered, before skimming fat (it will be easier to remove when cold).

COOK'S NOTES

- Using parsley stems (without leaves) will give great flavor to the stock without turning it green (the leaves contain lots of chlorophyll).

- The stock can be refrigerated for up to 1 week or frozen for up to 3 months.

Roasted Turkey with Pomegranate Gravy

MAKES ABOUT 8 CUPS
ACTIVE TIME: 40 MINUTES ■ START TO FINISH: 40 MINUTES
(DOES NOT INCLUDE MAKING STOCK OR COOKING TURKEY)

■ This beautifully rosy gravy with a pleasantly sweet-tart flavor is an exciting alternative to traditional gravy. Consider making the pomegranate syrup ahead. ■

Simplest Roasted Turkey (page 419; omit gravy
    ingredients)
⅔ cup sugar
1 cup fresh pomegranate juice (from about
    6 pomegranates; see page 434) or bottled
    pomegranate juice
7 cups Turkey Stock (opposite page)
2–3 tablespoons melted unsalted butter if needed
⅔ cup all-purpose flour
    Salt and freshly ground black pepper
1 tablespoon fresh lemon juice, or to taste, if using
    bottled pomegranate juice

Prepare roast turkey, without making turkey gravy.

While turkey roasts, cook sugar in a dry 1-quart heavy saucepan over moderate heat, undisturbed, until it begins to melt. Continue to cook, stirring occasionally with a fork, until sugar is melted into a deep golden caramel. Add pomegranate juice (use caution; mixture will bubble and steam vigorously) and simmer over low heat, stirring occasionally, until caramel is dissolved. Remove from heat.

While turkey stands, heat turkey stock in a 4-quart saucepan over low heat until hot; keep warm over very low heat. Straddle roasting pan across two burners, add 1 cup stock, and deglaze pan by boiling over high heat, scraping up brown bits, for 1 minute. Pour into a small bowl and let stand for 5 minutes to allow fat to rise to surface.

Skim off fat and transfer it to a glass measure. If you have less than ½ cup fat, add enough melted butter to make ½ cup. Pour pan juices through a fine-mesh sieve into hot stock.

Whisk together ½ cup fat and flour in a 3-quart heavy saucepan over moderately low heat to make a roux and cook, whisking constantly, until pale golden, 7 to 10 minutes. Add warm stock mixture in a stream, whisking constantly to prevent lumps, and bring to a boil, whisking. Whisk in pomegranate syrup, then reduce heat and simmer, whisking occasionally, until thickened, about 5 minutes. Stir in any turkey juices accumulated on platter and simmer for 1 minute.

Season gravy with salt and pepper and, if you used bottled pomegranate juice, add lemon juice to taste.

Carve turkey and serve with gravy.

COOK'S NOTE

- The pomegranate syrup can be made up to 1 day ahead and kept, covered, at room temperature.

LET'S TALK TURKEY

Of all the dishes that make up the Thanksgiving feast, the
big bird demands the most attention. But how best
to achieve turkey perfection—golden brown skin
with moist, tender white and dark meat? The
method that works best for us couldn't be
more straightforward. The bird is simply
seasoned with salt and pepper and
roasted in a 450°F oven—no brining, no
butter under the skin, no basting, no
foil tent, just blasted at high heat (see
page 419). The turkey cooks in record time,
only 2¼ to 2¾ hours for a 16-pound bird. (Starting
with a clean oven prevents smoking at high heat. Clean your oven again after roasting,
because of spatters.) Cookbook author Barbara Kafka popularized the high-heat method
for chickens and turkeys in her 1995 book *Roasting*. She cranked up her oven to 500°F, but
we lowered the temperature to 450°F to get the benefits of high heat while lessening the
risk of burning the pan juices.

CHOOSING THE BIRD

Fresh or frozen? Organic, conventional, or kosher? Using
the method outlined above, we had uniformly good
results, regardless of choice.

FRESH We're partial to a fresh turkey, because there's
no waiting for it to defrost—but that means there's less
flexibility as to when to buy it; the USDA recommends no
more than 2 days in advance. Keep it in the coldest part of
your refrigerator.

FROZEN Allow at least 3, preferably 4, days to thaw a
frozen turkey in the refrigerator.

ORGANIC The flavor of organic turkey is superior, but the
white meat tends to be a little tough—if you go organic,
you'll want gravy. We are also fans of locally raised turkeys
from small producers, as much for sustainability reasons
as for flavor.

KOSHER Because koshering involves salting, we've always
found the birds to be comparable in juiciness and flavor to
brined turkeys, which are soaked in a saltwater solution
for 10 to 24 hours before roasting. Because the birds are
processed using cold water (which tightens the follicles on
the skin), they usually do require a significant amount of
time for removal of stray feathers and quills.

TURKEY PREP—THE DAY BEFORE

TURKEY If you choose a kosher turkey, you will need to go over it and remove any remaining quills and feathers with needle-nose pliers or tweezers (see opposite).

TURKEY STOCK Do yourself a huge favor—make it the day before, or even a month or so before (see page 420). The stock takes longer than a fast-roasting turkey, and no one wants to wait for the gravy. Plus, it's always easier to remove solidified fat from a chilled stock than it is to skim it off a hot one.

Once your stock is made, let it cool completely, uncovered, then cover it and refrigerate. If covered while hot, it can turn sour. The shallower the container, the faster the stock loses its heat. The USDA recommends putting the shallow container of hot stock directly into the refrigerator to cool it quickly. You can also cool it at room temperature, but never for longer than 2 hours. We like to speed up the process by using an ice bath: put the container of stock in a large bowl (or sink) of ice and cold water and stir occasionally until cool.

EXTRA WHITE MEAT For white-meat-only types (and to have plenty for sandwiches), roast an extra turkey breast the day before as well, using the same high-heat method. A 6- to 8-pound breast should take 1¼ to 1½ hours to reach 160° to 170°F. Slice and reheat to serve.

EQUIPMENT CHECKLIST

NEEDLE-NOSE PLIERS These are useful for removing any remaining quills or feathers.

ROASTING PAN It should be heavy, to support the bird; flameproof, to go on top of the stove (that means no glass); and light-colored, to prevent burning. Make sure it's big enough to hold your turkey. We suggest a pan at least 17 by 14 inches and with sides no more than 2 to 2½ inches high— deeper pans prevent the sides of the bird from browning.

FLAT RACK A sturdy flat rack is preferable to a V-rack, because it helps the bird sit without tilting. A V-rack is ideal for a turkey breast, though, cradling it so it remains stable.

THERMOMETER We prefer instant-read thermometers to meat thermometers. They can be recalibrated easily (follow the manufacturer's instructions).

KITCHEN STRING Untreated cotton string is best; anything else may melt or impart an undesirable flavor to the meat. But if you don't have string, don't worry. While leaving the legs untied isn't as attractive, it does help the dark meat cook more evenly.

TURKEY LIFTERS Lifting up and landing a cooked bird on a platter is challenging. And if you didn't stuff your turkey, you'll need to pour out the flavorful juices that collect in the large cavity first. Silicone gloves let you work hands-on, but there are many gadgets for hoisting the turkey to suit your wallet and drawer space.

TURKEY PREP—THANKSGIVING DAY

TO STUFF OR NOT TO STUFF A stuffing that's baked separately has a crisp top and a moist, tender interior, and we love the contrasting textures. The bird also tends to cook faster unstuffed. But baking the stuffing inside the turkey has its fans. Before you stuff the turkey, make sure the stuffing is at room temperature; a hot stuffing will heat the cavity to a temperature at which bacteria thrive. The stuffing takes longer to heat to a safe temperature than the turkey itself does. To avoid overcooking the breast meat, remove the stuffed bird from the oven when the meat tests done (170°F), then test the stuffing in the large cavity; if it isn't done, immediately scoop it into a baking dish (test the temperature of the stuffing inside the smaller neck cavity too). Return the stuffing to the oven (covered for a moist stuffing, uncovered for a crisp top) to cook until it reaches at least 165°F, for reasons of food safety.

ROASTING TIPS

Position the oven rack so that the turkey will be in the center of the oven. Barbara Kafka recommends putting the turkey into the oven drumsticks first, so that the legs, which take the longest to cook, are in the back, usually the hottest part of the oven. In our 30-inch home-style ranges, though, turkeys fit best sideways, so we rotate them 180 degrees halfway through to allow the legs to cook more evenly.

Our fuss-free turkey comes out with gorgeous golden brown skin and a slight matte finish. If you prefer shinier skin, baste the bird just once, when you rotate it.

TESTING FOR DONENESS

A thermometer takes the guesswork out of knowing when the turkey is done, but where exactly should it go? It should measure the fleshiest part of both thighs, which take the longest time to cook. Insert the thermometer vertically between the drumstick and the tapered end of the breast and feel around with the tip; it should be near but not touching the bone. The temperature should register at least 165°F (according to the USDA, a whole turkey is safe when cooked to that internal temperature, but we prefer the texture of the dark meat when cooked to 170°F). If your turkey is especially large-breasted, you might want to take the temperature of the breast meat as well.

LETTING THE TURKEY STAND

Allowing the turkey to rest for 30 minutes after it comes out of the oven is essential. The juices in the bird need time to redistribute themselves, and the temperature will rise to 175° to 180°F.

Don't cover the turkey, or the skin will lose its crispness.

CARVING

How you carve the meat isn't just about aesthetics; proper carving enhances the tenderness and juiciness of each portion. If you remove each breast half from the bone in one piece and then slice it crosswise, each slice will contain both the slightly more well-done meat close to the skin as well as the velvety meat next to the bone.

STORAGE

A whole cooked turkey can take over your refrigerator, so break up the carcass before storing it. Cut off the legs, if you haven't already, and separate them into drumstick and thigh portions.

Put the wings, along with any picked-over bones, in a sealable plastic bag and freeze them for later use in soup.

Wrap leftovers in plastic wrap or sealable bags. The salt and iron from the turkey can cause foil to corrode, leaving smeary traces of aluminum on the meat.

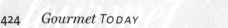

EVERYTHING YOU NEED TO KNOW ABOUT MAKING TURKEY GRAVY

CHOOSING THE BIRD As it roasts, the turkey contributes two important flavor components of delicious gravy—juices, with fat, and the brown bits that cling to the bottom of the pan. So the bird you use (see page 422) has a definite influence on the gravy you end up with. We don't brine our turkey, but if you like a brined bird, be aware that it will make the pan juices and brown bits salty—often too salty for gravy. (Kosher turkeys are also salted, but to a lesser degree.)

DEFATTING PAN JUICES Half our food editors use a fat separator: the fat floats to the top and the juices can be poured out through the spout located low on the vessel. The other editors simply skim the fat from the strained juices with a large shallow spoon.

DEGLAZING *Deglazing* is the culinary term for adding liquid to a hot pan and scraping up the brown bits left from the meat or vegetables—those caramelized nuggets pack a real flavor punch. You can simply add stock to the pan and scrape up the brown bits, but for another flavor component, substitute 1 cup dry white wine, port, medium-dry sherry, or Madeira for the water in the recipe on page 419.

THICKENING For the richest flavor, thicken your gravy, as we do, by making a roux, a mixture of fat and flour cooked together until the flour no longer tastes raw. An alternative is to stir cornstarch into room-temperature stock (check the package for quantities) until the cornstarch is dissolved, then whisk that mixture into hot stock combined with the pan drippings. The gravy won't have the depth of a roux-based one, but it will be glistening and translucent, with a light texture and clean taste. It will also be slightly lower in fat.

MAKING DARK BROWN GRAVY The most direct route to lustrous dark brown gravy is to start by thoroughly browning the turkey parts and vegetables that go into the stock. It doesn't pay to rush this step, because turkey parts and vegetables that are only golden won't produce a stock with the deep color that results in a dark brown gravy. Another option is to cook your roux (whisking constantly) until it becomes the color of peanut butter, about 20 minutes. But if you really need to fast-track things, add a little soy sauce (about 1½ teaspoons to 4 cups stock and drippings). You'll get the color, but no soy flavor.

VEGETARIAN GRAVY There's no need for your vegetarian guests to miss out on rich gravy to ladle over their mashed potatoes. The vegetarian gravy on page 330 is aromatic and delicious.

Porcini Onion Stuffing

SERVES 8 TO 10
ACTIVE TIME: 1 HOUR ■ START TO FINISH: 1¾ HOURS

■ Unlike many bread stuffings, which are cooked inside the turkey and/or include chicken broth, this wild mushroom version is completely vegetarian. A mix of dried porcini and fresh mushrooms is the secret behind the meaty, robust flavor. ■

- 1½ (1-pound) Pullman (sandwich) or round loaves, torn into 1-inch pieces (20 cups)
- 4½ cups boiling water
- 2 ounces (2 cups) dried porcini mushrooms
- 1 stick (8 tablespoons) unsalted butter
- 10 ounces white mushrooms, trimmed and cut into ½-inch-wide wedges
- 1 large onion, halved lengthwise and sliced crosswise ½ inch thick
- 4 large shallots, quartered
- 2 celery ribs, sliced ¼ inch thick
- 2 medium carrots, halved lengthwise and sliced ¼ inch thick
- 3 garlic cloves, minced
- 1½ teaspoons chopped fresh thyme
- 1½ teaspoons chopped fresh sage
- 2 tablespoons chopped fresh flat-leaf parsley
    Salt and freshly ground black pepper

Put racks in upper and lower thirds of oven and preheat oven to 350°F.

Spread bread on two large baking sheets. Bake, stirring occasionally and switching position of pans halfway through baking, until dry, 20 to 25 minutes. Transfer bread to a large bowl.

Increase oven temperature to 450°F. Butter a 13-by-9-inch baking dish.

Pour boiling water over porcini in a bowl and soak for 20 minutes. Drain porcini in a fine-mesh sieve set over a bowl; squeeze porcini over sieve and reserve soaking liquid. Rinse porcini under cold water to remove any grit, squeeze out excess water, and coarsely chop.

Meanwhile, heat butter in a 12-inch heavy skillet over moderately high heat until foam subsides. Add white mushrooms, onion, and shallots and cook, stirring occasionally, until golden, 15 to 20 minutes.

Add celery, carrots, garlic, and porcini to pan and cook, stirring, for 5 minutes. Stir in thyme, sage, parsley, 2¼ teaspoons salt, and ½ teaspoon pepper. Add vegetables to bread, tossing to combine.

Add 1 cup reserved porcini soaking liquid to skillet and deglaze by boiling over high heat, scraping up brown bits, for 1 minute. Add remaining soaking liquid and salt and pepper to taste and pour over bread mixture, tossing to moisten evenly.

Spread stuffing in baking dish. Cover tightly with buttered foil (buttered side down) and bake in upper third of oven until heated through, about 20 minutes. Remove foil and bake stuffing until top is browned, 10 to 15 minutes more.

COOK'S NOTES

- The stuffing can be made (but not baked) up to 2 days ahead. Refrigerate, covered.
- The stuffing can be baked up to 6 hours ahead and kept, uncovered, at room temperature. Reheat, uncovered, in a 350°F oven until hot, about 30 minutes (test the center with a toothpick or a metal skewer for warmth).

Miso-Rubbed Turkey with Gravy

SERVES 8 TO 10
ACTIVE TIME: 1¼ HOURS ■ START TO FINISH: 4½ HOURS

■ Rubbing miso butter under a turkey's skin is an intriguing way to ensure moist meat. The skin doesn't get as crisp as it would otherwise, but the succulence is well worth the tradeoff. The miso adds a rich meatiness to the gravy. Be sure not to use a brined or kosher turkey for this recipe, since miso has a high sodium content. ■

- 1 medium onion, left unpeeled, quartered
- ½ cup white or red miso (fermented soybean paste; see Sources)
- 1 stick (8 tablespoons) unsalted butter, softened, plus additional if necessary for making gravy
    Freshly ground black pepper
- 1 (12- to 14-pound) turkey, neck and giblets removed and reserved for another use if desired, turkey left at room temperature for 1 hour
    Salt

About 1 cup water

9 cups Turkey Stock (page 420)

¾ cup all-purpose flour

SPECIAL EQUIPMENT: 2 small metal skewers; kitchen string; a 17-by-14-inch flameproof roasting pan with a rack; an instant-read thermometer; a 2-quart measuring cup

MAKE THE MISO BUTTER: Peel and chop 1 onion quarter. Pulse in a food processor until finely chopped. Add miso and puree until smooth. Add ½ stick (4 tablespoons) softened butter and ½ teaspoon pepper and puree until combined (mixture will appear curdled).

ROAST THE TURKEY: Put an oven rack in lowest position and preheat oven to 350°F.

Using tweezers or needle-nose pliers, remove any feathers or quills from turkey. Rinse turkey inside and out, then pat dry. Working from large cavity end, gently run your fingers between skin and meat of breast and legs to loosen skin, being careful not to tear it. Push miso butter under skin, including thighs and drumsticks, and massage skin to spread butter evenly. Sprinkle cavity with ½ teaspoon salt and ½ teaspoon pepper. Fold neck skin under body and secure with metal skewers. Stuff cavity with remaining 3 onion quarters. Tie drumsticks together with string and tuck wings under body.

Put turkey on rack in roasting pan and roast for 30 minutes.

Melt remaining ½ stick butter and brush over turkey. Add 1 cup water to roasting pan. Tent turkey with foil and roast, basting every 30 minutes with pan juices and adding more water to pan if necessary to maintain 1 cup, until thermometer inserted into fleshy part of thighs (without touching bone) registers 170°F, 2 to 2½ hours more. Remove foil for last 30 minutes of roasting if turkey looks pale. Carefully tilt turkey so any juices from cavity run into roasting pan, then transfer turkey to a platter; reserve juices in roasting pan. Let turkey stand, loosely covered, for 25 minutes (temperature of thigh meat will rise to 180°F).

MEANWHILE, MAKE THE GRAVY: Pour pan juices through a fine-mesh sieve into measuring cup (set roasting pan aside) and skim off and reserve fat. If there is less than ½ cup fat, add enough melted butter to make ½ cup. Pour pan juices and 8 cups turkey stock into a 3-quart saucepan and bring to a simmer.

Meanwhile, straddle roasting pan across two burners, add remaining cup turkey stock, and deglaze pan by boiling over moderately high heat, scraping up brown bits, for 1 minute. Pour liquid through sieve into remaining stock and bring to a simmer. Remove from heat and cover to keep warm.

Whisk together flour and ½ cup reserved fat in a 4-quart heavy saucepan and cook over moderately low heat, whisking, for 5 minutes to make a roux. Add hot stock mixture in a fast stream, whisking constantly to prevent lumps, and simmer, whisking occasionally, until gravy is thickened, about 10 minutes. Stir in any turkey juices accumulated on platter and season with salt and pepper.

Carve turkey and serve with gravy.

COOK'S NOTES

- The miso butter can be made up to 4 days ahead and refrigerated, covered. Soften at room temperature before using.
- The miso butter can be pushed under the turkey skin up to 1 day ahead; refrigerate the bird on a rack in the roasting pan, covered with plastic wrap.

Duck

Crisp Roast Duck

SERVES 4
ACTIVE TIME: 15 MINUTES ■ START TO FINISH: 2¾ HOURS

■ A whole roasted duck doesn't have to be fussy. With hardly any work at all and just a few hours in the oven, you can have a juicy bird with crisp skin—the best of both textures. The trick is the water—not only does it keep the meat moist, it helps prevent the fat from spattering. ■

1 (5- to 6-pound) Pekin (Long Island) duck (see Sources)

2 cups boiling water

1 tablespoon kosher salt

1 teaspoon freshly ground black pepper

Put a rack in middle of oven and preheat oven to 425°F.

If necessary, cut off wing tips from duck with poultry shears or a sharp knife. Remove and discard excess fat from body cavity and neck and rinse duck inside and out. Prick skin all over with a sharp fork. Fold neck skin under body and put duck breast side up on a rack in a 13-by-9-inch roasting pan. Pour boiling water over duck (to tighten skin). Cool duck.

Pour any water from cavity into pan; leave water in pan. Pat duck dry inside and out, then rub inside and out with salt and pepper.

Roast duck breast side up for 45 minutes. Turn duck over using two wooden spoons and roast for 45 minutes more. Turn duck over again (breast side up), tilting duck to drain any liquid from cavity into pan. Continue to roast duck until skin is brown and crisp, about 45 minutes more (for a total roasting time of about 2¼ hours).

Tilt duck to drain any liquid from cavity into pan. Transfer duck to a cutting board (discard liquid in roasting pan) and let stand for 15 minutes before carving.

Pan-Grilled Duck Paillards

SERVES 4
ACTIVE TIME: 40 MINUTES ■ START TO FINISH: 40 MINUTES

■ The breast of a Moulard duck is immensely satisfying, with a steaklike texture and deep flavor that take well to this recipe's spice rub of ginger, curry, cinnamon, and pepper. Slicing the meat and pounding it into paillards, or thin cutlets, means it cooks in just minutes. The duck breast's thick layer of fat is too flavorful to go to waste, and the cracklings made from it

DUCK BREASTS

The beauty of duck breast—beside the fact that it has delicious, full-bodied flavor and lends itself to innumerable presentations—is that it is less hassle than a whole duck. You have a solid piece of meat without any bones, so it's easy to cook and even easier to slice. Duck breast is sometimes sold whole, but more typically what is sold as a breast (or as a "single breast") is one side of a boned whole breast, or a breast half. In general, all duck breast meat is lean; the fattiness of the skin depends on the variety of duck. Despite their differences, whatever type your market offers will work in our recipes.

The PEKIN breed (not to be confused with "Peking," a Chinese method for cooking duck) is the duck most available in our supermarkets. Although this species originated in China, it became a specialty of Long Island, New York, and it is also referred to as Long Island duck. The meat is mild and tender and the skin is moderately fatty, making it an ideal partner for any number of preparations and seasonings. Weighing in at 6 to 8 ounces, each breast is ideal for a single serving.

MUSCOVY DUCK BREASTS, available at butcher shops and specialty markets, have thinner (less fatty) skin than the Pekin, but the meat is just as tender and it has a deep, rich flavor. Each breast weighs a pound or more and serves 2.

The MOULARD DUCK, sometimes called Barbary, is the sterile offspring of a female Pekin and a male Muscovy. In Gascony, the Moulard is known as the foie gras duck because it is the breed that is fattened for foie gras production. The breasts (often labeled "magret") can be found at butcher shops, specialty foods markets, and many supermarkets. They have firmer flesh—more of a red-meat texture—and the half breasts range in size from 12 ounces to 1 pound (the larger ones usually serve two). The skin on a Moulard breast is fatty, and it is often scored in a crosshatch pattern so it renders its fat during cooking. Even if you don't use the rendered fat in the recipe, save it for sautéing potatoes, making an omelet, or swirling into soup or a white-bean stew.

For all of the varieties listed here, free-range birds that have been fed a natural diet are best. But whichever duck breast you choose, you will end up with a meat that takes beautifully to all sorts of flavors.

prove irresistible with the tender meat. Grilled orange slices add a little acidic counterpoint to the richness of the dish. ∎

2 (1-pound) boneless Moulard duck breast halves (also called *magrets*; see Cook's Note and Sources), rinsed and patted dry
2 tablespoons water
2 teaspoons ground ginger
Salt and freshly ground black pepper
1 teaspoon curry powder
1 teaspoon ground cinnamon
2 navel oranges, cut into ¼-inch-thick slices
SPECIAL EQUIPMENT: a well-seasoned large (2-burner) ridged grill pan

Pull skin off breasts and thinly slice skin. Cook skin in water in a 10- to 12-inch heavy skillet over moderately low heat, stirring occasionally, until fat is rendered and cracklings are browned and crisp, about 15 minutes. Drain in a sieve set over a bowl; reserve rendered fat. Spread cracklings on paper towels to drain.

Remove tender from underside of each breast half if attached and reserve for another use. Trim silver membrane from each breast half. Halve each breast half horizontally to make a total of 4 thin pieces. With flat side of a meat pounder or with a rolling pin, gently pound each piece between two sheets of plastic wrap to an even ¼ inch thickness.

Heat grill pan over moderately high heat until hot but not smoking. While pan is heating, stir together ginger, 2 teaspoons salt, 1 teaspoon pepper, curry powder, and cinnamon in a small bowl. Sprinkle each duck paillard with ½ teaspoon spice mixture per side (reserve remainder) and lightly brush with some rendered duck fat.

Grill duck, turning once, for 3 to 4 minutes for medium-rare. Transfer to a cutting board and let stand, loosely covered with foil.

While paillards stand, lightly brush orange slices with some rendered duck fat and sprinkle with remaining spice mixture. Grill orange slices, turning once, until slices are just warmed through and grill marks appear, about 1 minute.

Transfer duck and oranges to a platter. Season cracklings with salt and pepper and sprinkle over duck and oranges.

COOK'S NOTE
■ You can substitute 2 whole boneless Pekin (Long Island) duck breasts for the larger Moulard breasts. Remove the skin from the duck breasts, but do not halve or pound them. Cook for 2 minutes per side.

Duck Purloo

SERVES 6 TO 8
ACTIVE TIME: 45 MINUTES ■ START TO FINISH: 3 HOURS

■ Purloo is a traditional Low Country dish, made in the backyards of coastal South Carolina. Also spelled *perloo* or *pilau* (pronounced "pur-*low*"), it is more like a risotto than a pilaf, but a messy, stick-to-your-ribs one. This version, adapted from a recipe by home cook Dickie Reynolds of Florence, South Carolina, is chock-full of slow-poached duck meat, smoky kielbasa, breakfast sausage, peppers, and mushrooms. A minced habanero chile keeps things lively. ∎

2 (1 pound) boneless Moulard duck breast halves (also called *magrets*; see Cook's Note and Sources), rinsed and patted dry
4 cups Chicken Stock (page 153) or store-bought reduced-sodium broth
1 pound bulk breakfast sausage
½ pound kielbasa (not low-fat), cut into ¼-inch slices
Freshly ground black pepper
¼ teaspoon red pepper flakes
2 large onions, chopped
1 yellow bell pepper, cored, seeded, and chopped
1 red bell pepper, cored, seeded, and chopped
3 ounces shiitake mushrooms, stems discarded, caps sliced ¼ inch thick
1 habanero or Scotch bonnet chile (see Cook's Note), minced
Salt
1½ cups long-grain white rice
2 tablespoons chopped fresh flat-leaf parsley

Put duck breasts skin side up in a 6- to 8-quart heavy pot, add stock, and bring just to a boil over high heat. Reduce heat to low and simmer, covered, until duck is very tender when pierced with a fork,

2 to 3 hours. Transfer duck to a bowl with a slotted spoon; reserve stock in pot.

Meanwhile, crumble sausage into a deep 12-inch heavy skillet and cook over moderately high heat, breaking up lumps occasionally, until browned, about 5 minutes. Add kielbasa, ¼ teaspoon pepper, and red pepper flakes and cook, stirring occasionally, for 5 minutes. Skim off and discard all but about 2 tablespoons fat.

Add onions and bell peppers to sausage mixture, increase heat to high, and cook, stirring occasionally, until onions are softened, about 10 minutes. Add mushrooms and cook, stirring, until softened, about 3 minutes. Transfer sausage mixture to a large bowl. Cool to room temperature, then refrigerate, covered, until duck has finished cooking.

When duck is cool enough to handle, remove and discard skin. Shred meat with two forks. Skim off and discard fat from stock and return shredded duck to pot.

Add sausage mixture, chile, ½ teaspoon salt, and ¼ teaspoon pepper to pot. Stir in rice and bring to a rolling boil over high heat, then reduce heat and simmer, covered, stirring occasionally, until rice is tender and moist but not soggy, about 20 minutes. Remove from heat and let stand, covered, for 15 minutes.

Stir in parsley and season with salt and pepper.

COOK'S NOTES

- Two pounds of Pekin (Long Island) duck breasts can be substituted for the Moulard duck breast.
- Two serrano chiles can be substituted for the habanero or Scotch bonnet.
- The duck can be cooked and shredded up to 1 day ahead. Refrigerate, covered.
- The purloo can be made up to 3 days ahead. Cool, uncovered, then refrigerate, covered.

Confit Duck Legs

SERVES 6 AS A MAIN COURSE
ACTIVE TIME: 45 MINUTES ■ START TO FINISH: 2 DAYS
(INCLUDES MARINATING AND CHILLING)

■ *Confit* refers to the French method of cooking meat, traditionally goose, duck, or pork, in its own fat, then packing it tightly into a crock or bowl and covering it with the fat. It is one of the oldest preserving methods and produces unctuously flavorful meat. Reheated until the skin crisps up, confit duck legs are wonderful served whole with a salad of bitter greens. Or shred the meat and use in a terrine. It's also part of Smoky Tortilla Soup with Duck (page 143). ■

1 large garlic head, plus 4 large garlic cloves
¼ cup kosher salt
1 tablespoon finely chopped fresh thyme
1 teaspoon French Four-Spice Blend (recipe follows)
2 large shallots, finely chopped
2 Turkish bay leaves or 1 California bay leaf, crumbled
6 Moulard, Muscovy, or Pekin (Long Island) duck legs (about 5 pounds; see Sources), rinsed and patted dry
2 whole cloves
5 (7-ounce) containers rendered duck fat (see Sources)

SPECIAL EQUIPMENT: a deep-fat thermometer

Mince 4 garlic cloves and mash to a paste with a pinch of salt, using side of a large heavy knife. Stir together garlic paste, remaining salt, thyme, spice blend, shallots, and bay leaves in a large bowl. Add duck legs and toss to coat, then marinate, covered and refrigerated, for at least 1 day.

Trim off ¼ inch from top of garlic head and stick cloves into head. Melt duck fat in a large wide heavy pot over low heat. Wipe excess marinade from duck legs, add duck legs and garlic head to pot, and cook, uncovered, until fat registers approximately 190°F on thermometer, about 1 hour.

Continue to cook duck, maintaining a temperature of 190° to 210°F, until a wooden toothpick slides easily into thighs, 2 to 3 hours more.

Transfer duck with a slotted spoon to a large bowl. Pour duck fat through a fine-mesh sieve into a large crock or deep bowl, discarding any cloudy liquid or meat juices at bottom of pot. Pour strained fat over duck legs to cover completely. (If necessary, cut off 1 to 2 inches of drumsticks, using a large heavy knife, so legs fit more tightly in bowl.) Cool to room temperature, about 2 hours, then refrigerate, covered, for at least 8 hours.

To serve, remove duck from fat, scraping off most of it and reserving fat. Cook legs, skin side down, in a large heavy nonstick skillet over low heat, covered, until skin is crisp and duck is heated through, 15 to 20 minutes.

COOK'S NOTES

- The duck can be marinated for up to 2 days.
- The duck legs, completely covered in fat with a piece of parchment paper pressed against the surface, can be refrigerated for up to 1 month.
- The rendered duck fat remaining from the confit can be used for sautéing potatoes or cabbage.

French Four-Spice Blend
Quatre Épices

MAKES ABOUT 2 TABLESPOONS
ACTIVE TIME: 5 MINUTES ■ START TO FINISH: 5 MINUTES

■ This mixture of white pepper, cloves, ginger, and nutmeg (some variations include cinnamon or allspice) is traditionally used to season pâtés, terrines, and duck confit. Leftover *quatre épices* can be used as a rub for pork or other meats. ■

    1 tablespoon freshly ground white pepper
      Rounded ¼ teaspoon ground cloves
    1 teaspoon ground ginger
    1 teaspoon freshly grated nutmeg

Stir together all ingredients.

COOK'S NOTE

- The spice blend keeps in an airtight container for up to 6 months.

Small Birds

Cornish Hens with Roasted-Garlic Aïoli

SERVES 4
ACTIVE TIME: 20 MINUTES ■ START TO FINISH: 1¼ HOURS

■ Made with roasted garlic rather than raw, this version of aïoli is milder than the traditional kind (and it's a cinch to make, since it relies on jarred mayonnaise). Whenever we roast garlic, we like to make twice as much as is called for—kept in the fridge, roasted garlic cloves are a great flavor enhancer for soups or sauces. The aïoli is also excellent over vegetables, lamb, and fish. ■

    2 garlic heads
    2 teaspoons extra-virgin olive oil
    2 (1¼- to 1½-pound) Cornish hens, rinsed and patted
      dry
      Salt and freshly ground black pepper
    1 cup mayonnaise
    1 teaspoon finely grated lemon zest
    2 tablespoons fresh lemon juice
    2 tablespoons finely chopped fresh chives
SPECIAL EQUIPMENT: kitchen string; an instant-read
      thermometer

Put a rack in middle of oven and preheat oven to 500°F.

Trim off and discard about ¼ inch from top of garlic heads to expose cloves, and put heads on a sheet of foil. Spoon oil over garlic, then wrap up tightly in foil. Roast garlic, directly on oven rack, until very soft, about 40 minutes.

Meanwhile, season hens inside and out with 1 teaspoon salt and ¼ teaspoon pepper. Tie legs together with string and tuck wing tips under. Transfer to a 13-by-9-inch roasting pan and roast alongside garlic until hens are golden brown and thermometer inserted into thickest part of a thigh (without touching bone) registers 170°F, 30 to 40 minutes. Let hens stand, loosely covered with foil, for 15 minutes.

Carefully unwrap garlic and cool slightly, then squeeze pulp into a bowl. Add mayonnaise, lemon zest, juice, chives, ½ teaspoon salt, and ¼ teaspoon pepper, plus 2 tablespoons pan juices from hens if desired, and stir until aïoli is well combined.

Halve hens lengthwise. Serve with aïoli.

ASSORTED FOWL

When you're experiencing chicken fatigue (who hasn't?), it's time to try cooking other types of birds. Some of the fowl listed below are as rich and juicy as a great steak, others are as tender and succulent as veal. Each one has its own distinctive flavor, and all take well to a range of seasonings and cooking techniques. And the diminutive size of most of these birds makes for a lovely presentation.

The key to enjoying these fowl is to avoid overcooking. Game birds are, rather unfortunately, often associated with a strong liverlike flavor, which is the direct result of overcooking. Because their meat is lean, they cook very quickly. Following recipes carefully and checking the meat's temperature frequently will ensure perfectly cooked birds. We tested our recipes with farm-raised birds, which are increasingly available in supermarkets, making them a good alternative any night of the week.

CORNISH HENS, sometimes called game hens, are actually a hybrid of the large, meaty Plymouth Rock and Cornish chicken breeds (the former are often used for laying eggs and the latter are commonly sold as "broilers" in supermarkets). What differentiates game hens from other chickens is that they're slaughtered at 4 to 5 weeks, when they weigh 1 to 2 pounds, but they're still similar enough in flavor and texture to make them appealing to everyone. With these miniature birds, you get a "chicken" dinner in about half the time. Cornish hens are fun to stuff and roast, and they taste great when flattened and grilled.

CORNISH HEN

POUSSIN

GUINEA HEN

POUSSINS, or baby chickens (the name means "chicks" in French), are younger and smaller than Cornish hens; they are slaughtered at 3 to 4 weeks, when they weigh 12 to 18 ounces. In other words, they're an ideal serving size. Because most farm-raised poussins are allowed to roam and feed freely in their brief life spans, their extremely tender white meat is incredibly succulent. They have a clean, light flavor that evokes spring and pairs well with greens and brothy sauces. Poussins are not as readily available as Cornish hens, but they are worth seeking out at specialty markets or butcher shops.

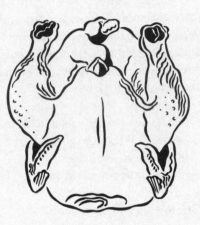

GUINEA HENS, also called guinea fowl, are native to Africa and have long been popular in Europe. They are similar in size to chickens, but they have longer breasts, supported by a prominent arching breastbone, and leaner, more sinewy legs. Though guinea hens are frequently compared to chicken, their tender meat actually has a deeper, more savory flavor reminiscent of pheasant. Traditionally hunted and served in the fall, guinea hens are often accompanied by grains, nuts, and mushrooms. (Chanterelles and guinea hens are a classic combination.) Just be sure to avoid overcooking these lean, thin-skinned birds. Guinea hens can be ordered online or from specialty markets and butcher shops.

QUAIL weigh only 6 to 8 ounces, but they are plump with meat that is a deep beige and reminiscent of high-quality dark-meat chicken in taste and appearance. Quail are usually sold whole or semiboneless (with the back, rib cage, and thigh bones removed, leaving only the drumstick and wing bones). Both types are easy to prepare, and the latter is ideal for stuffing. Because quail are quite lean and very small, they cook quickly.

QUAIL

SQUAB

SQUABS are farm-raised young pigeons. They have rich, juicy meat somewhat like steak, so they are best cooked to medium-rare. Their depth of flavor surpasses even that of duck: squabs are to other fowl what espresso is to regular coffee. The dark, intense meat is delicious enough to be served alone but is well complemented by robust sauces.

Roast Poussins or Cornish Hens with Lavender and Thyme

SERVES 4
ACTIVE TIME: 45 MINUTES ■ START TO FINISH: 1½ HOURS

■ Good-quality dried lavender has a fragrant bite and works beautifully with thyme and lemon to season these roasted poussins. The French dessert wine Sauternes adds a rich, honeyed sweetness to the quick pan sauce. ■

- ¾ stick (6 tablespoons) unsalted butter, softened
- 2 teaspoons dried untreated lavender flowers (see Sources), finely chopped
- 1 teaspoon fresh thyme leaves, minced
- ¼ teaspoon finely grated lemon zest
  Salt and freshly ground black pepper
- 4 (1-pound) poussins (young chickens; see opposite and Sources) or 4 (1¼-pound) Cornish hens, giblets discarded, necks cut off if necessary
- 1 small lemon, halved
- 1½ cups water
- ¼ cup Sauternes

GARNISH: dried lavender and fresh thyme leaves
SPECIAL EQUIPMENT: kitchen string; a 17-by-14-inch flameproof shallow roasting pan, with a rack; an instant-read thermometer

Stir together butter, lavender, thyme, zest, 1½ teaspoons salt, and ½ teaspoon pepper in a small bowl until well combined. Spoon butter onto a sheet of plastic wrap and form into a 4-inch-long log. Refrigerate, wrapped well in plastic wrap, until firm, at least 30 minutes.

Put a rack in middle of oven and preheat oven to 475°F.

Rinse birds inside and out and pat dry. Starting at neck end of each bird, slide your fingers between meat and skin to loosen skin (be careful not to tear skin). Cut butter into sixteen ¼-inch-thick slices and gently push 4 slices under skin of each bird, putting 1 slice over each breast half and each thigh. Sprinkle ⅛ teaspoon salt into cavity of each bird. Tie legs together with kitchen string and tuck wings under back.

Arrange birds on rack in pan. Gently rub birds with lemon halves, squeezing juice over them. Sprinkle with ½ teaspoon salt and ¼ teaspoon pepper. Pour water into pan and roast birds for 20 minutes.

Lift rack slightly with tongs and baste birds with pan drippings. Continue to roast until thermometer inserted in thickest part of a thigh (without touching bone) registers 170°F, 10 to 20 minutes more for poussins, 20 to 30 minutes more for Cornish hens. Transfer birds to a platter, baste with pan juices, and cover loosely with foil to keep warm.

Add Sauternes to pan and straddle over two burners. Deglaze pan by boiling over moderate heat, scraping up brown bits, for 3 minutes. Pour sauce through a fine-mesh sieve into a bowl.

Garnish birds with herbs and serve with sauce.

COOK'S NOTE
- The compound butter can be refrigerated for up to 3 days.

POMEGRANATE PROCEDURES

David Rakoff, a *Gourmet* contributor, offers an unusual method for extracting the juicy ruby-red seeds from a pomegranate, which he learned from a woman from the Republic of Georgia. First, cut the pomegranate crosswise in half. Working with one half at a time, hold it in the palm of your hand, cut side up, and make 4 deep cuts through the flesh and skin at 12, 3, 6, and 9 o'clock. Hold the fruit upside down over a large bowl and give it a couple of whacks with a large metal spoon—a rain of seeds will come pouring out, with a minimum of pith and spatter.

TO JUICE A POMEGRANATE Cut it crosswise in half and juice with a manual or electric juicer. Alternatively, remove the seeds from the pomegranate and pulse the seeds in a food processor until juicy, then transfer the seeds to a sieve and let drain, pressing on the solids; discard the solids.

SEMIBONELESS QUAIL

Plump, juicy quail are flavorful without being too gamy and very easy to cook. When shopping for quail, look for ones that are semiboneless. The term means that the backbone, rib cage, and thigh bones have been removed, leaving just the wing bones and drumsticks. Semiboned quail cook quickly and don't require carving skills.

Quail with Pomegranate Jus

SERVES 4 AS A MAIN COURSE, 8 AS A FIRST COURSE
ACTIVE TIME: 20 MINUTES ■ START TO FINISH: 3 HOURS
(INCLUDES MARINATING)

■ Semiboneless quail are elegant and easy to eat. The pomegranate marinade gives the birds a spicy sweetness, a nice foil for their mild gaminess. Best of all, once the quail marinate, it's less than 20 minutes to an impressive meal. ■

- ½ cup thinly sliced shallots
- 1 tablespoon Worcestershire sauce
- ¼ cup fresh or bottled pomegranate juice
- 1 tablespoon chopped fresh tarragon
  Salt
- ½ teaspoon freshly ground black pepper
- 8 semiboneless quail (see Sources), rinsed and patted dry
- ½ stick (4 tablespoons) unsalted butter
- ⅓ cup pomegranate seeds

Combine shallots, Worcestershire sauce, 2 tablespoons pomegranate juice, 2 teaspoons tarragon, ⅛ teaspoon salt, and pepper in a large bowl. Add quail, tossing gently to coat. Marinate, covered and refrigerated, for at least 2 hours.

Remove quail from marinade, scraping off shallots; reserve marinade. Pat quail dry with paper towels and sprinkle with ¼ teaspoon salt.

Heat 2 tablespoons butter in a 12-inch heavy nonstick skillet over moderately high heat until foam subsides. Add 4 quail and cook, turning once, until browned and just cooked through, about 5 minutes total. (Quail will still be rare.) Transfer quail to a serving dish and cover loosely with foil to keep warm. Cook remaining 4 quail in remaining 2 tablespoons butter in same manner; transfer to serving dish.

Add reserved marinade to skillet and cook over moderately high heat, scraping up any brown bits with a wooden spoon, until shallots are just softened, about 4 minutes. Stir in remaining 2 tablespoons pomegranate juice and season with salt.

Spoon sauce over quail. Sprinkle with pomegranate seeds and remaining teaspoon tarragon.

COOK'S NOTE
■ The quail can marinate for up to 4 hours.

Roast Quail with Grapes and Chestnuts

SERVES 4
ACTIVE TIME: 45 MINUTES ■ START TO FINISH: 1¼ HOURS

■ Utterly French and very refined, this dish is adapted from one served at Restaurant Nicholas Le Bec in Lyon. Quail's mild meat is ideal for this sauce, enriched with Cognac, crème fraîche, and meaty chestnuts. Green grapes dot the dish with fresh sweetness. ■

- 8 (6-ounce) whole quail (see Sources)
  Salt and freshly ground black pepper
- ¼ cup peanut or vegetable oil
- 1 tablespoon unsalted butter
- 1 medium carrot, finely chopped
- 1 medium onion, finely chopped
- 3 fresh thyme sprigs
- ½ cup Cognac or other brandy
- 2 cups Chicken Stock (page 153) or store-bought reduced-sodium broth
- ½ cup crème fraîche
- 1 cup seedless green grapes
- 18 bottled peeled cooked chestnuts (from a 7¼-ounce jar; see Sources)

Put a rack in middle of oven and preheat oven to 350°F.

Remove and discard any feathers from quail. If necessary, cut off necks with poultry shears and discard. Rinse quail inside and out and pat dry. Sprinkle all over with ¾ teaspoon salt and ¼ teaspoon pepper.

Heat oil and butter in a deep 12-inch heavy ovenproof skillet over moderate heat until foam subsides. Brown quail on all sides, 12 to 15 minutes. Transfer to a large plate.

Pour off all but 2 tablespoons fat from skillet. Add carrot, onion, and thyme and cook over moderately high heat, stirring and scraping up brown bits, for 2 minutes.

Return quail, breast side up, along with any juices on plate, to skillet. Transfer to oven and roast until just cooked through (cut into an inner thigh; meat should still be slightly pink), about 10 minutes. Transfer quail to a platter and cover loosely with foil to keep warm.

Add Cognac to vegetables in skillet, bring to a boil, and boil for 1 minute. Add stock, bring to a boil, and boil until liquid is reduced by half, about 6 minutes. Stir in crème fraîche and simmer until slightly thickened, 3 to 4 minutes.

Pour sauce through a fine-mesh sieve into a bowl, pressing hard on solids; discard solids. Pour back into skillet, add grapes and chestnuts, and simmer, stirring occasionally, until grapes turn a shade lighter, about 3 minutes. Transfer grapes and chestnuts to platter with quail and boil sauce until thick enough to lightly coat back of a spoon, about 10 minutes. Add salt and pepper to taste.

Spoon some sauce over quail and serve remainder on the side.

Roast Stuffed Squab

SERVES 4
ACTIVE TIME: 45 MINUTES ■ START TO FINISH: 1½ HOURS

■ The late chef Edna Lewis was an expert in Southern cooking and one of America's most resonant food writers. This recipe shows how she worked her magic on delicate squab, roasting it in the oven with plenty of butter, which plays up the contrast between the rich, tender, moist dark meat and the crisp skin. Miss Lewis, as she was always called, would never waste any part of such a luxurious bird, so she chopped up the livers and added them to the bread stuffing. This is a simple, elegant meal, one deserving of a wonderful Bordeaux. ■

5 (½-inch-thick) slices good-quality white sandwich bread, such as a Pullman loaf, crusts discarded
1 cup whole milk
1½ sticks (12 tablespoons) unsalted butter
4 (1-pound) squabs, livers reserved and coarsely chopped
1 teaspoon chopped fresh thyme
Salt and freshly ground black pepper
½ cup water

GARNISH: chopped fresh flat-leaf parsley
SPECIAL EQUIPMENT: kitchen string; an instant-read thermometer

Put a rack in middle of oven and preheat oven to 375°F.

Arrange bread in one layer in a shallow dish and pour milk over it. Soak bread, turning once, just until it has absorbed most of milk, about 2 minutes. Squeeze excess milk from each slice and tear bread into bite-sized pieces, dropping them into a bowl. Discard milk.

Melt ½ stick (4 tablespoons) butter and add to bread, along with livers, ½ teaspoon thyme, ½ teaspoon salt, and ¼ teaspoon pepper, stirring to combine.

Rinse squabs and pat dry. Chop off necks and wing tips and scatter them into a large baking pan. Divide stuffing among cavities of squabs and close openings with wooden toothpicks. Tie legs together with kitchen string and secure wings to sides with toothpicks.

Stir together ¾ teaspoon salt, ¼ teaspoon pepper, and remaining ½ teaspoon thyme in a small bowl. Rub all over squabs. Arrange squabs in baking pan (with necks and wing tips), without crowding. Cut remaining stick of butter into 8 slices and put 2 pieces on top of each bird.

Roast squabs, basting with melted butter from pan every 8 to 10 minutes, until thermometer inserted in thickest part of thigh (without touching bone) registers 160°F, about 1 hour. Transfer to a platter and let stand, covered loosely with foil to keep warm.

Discard necks and wing tips and pour pan juices into a bowl. Let stand for 2 minutes to allow fat to separate from juices, then skim off fat and transfer to a small bowl or a measuring cup. Reserve ¼ cup fat and discard the rest. Add water to baking pan and deglaze by boiling, scraping up brown bits, for 1 to 2 minutes. Transfer to a small saucepan, add pan juices and ¼ cup fat, and simmer, whisking, until well blended, about 1 minute.

Sprinkle squabs with parsley and serve with sauce.

Braised Guinea Hens with Black Bean Sauce

SERVES 6
ACTIVE TIME: 45 MINUTES ■ START TO FINISH: 2½ HOURS

■ Guinea hens are similar to chickens in size, but their meat is leaner and darker. Because they are so lean, they take well to long, moist cooking. This sauce gets its body from pureed black beans and its spice and fragrance from cumin, oregano, and orange peel. Making annatto oil for browning the hens intensifies the color of the dish and is a nod to its Latin inspiration. Be sure to serve this with lots and lots of fluffy white rice—you'll want to soak up every lick of sauce. ■

1 orange
2 tablespoons fresh lime juice
4 garlic cloves, minced
Salt and freshly ground black pepper
2 (3- to 3½-pound) guinea hens, rinsed, patted dry, cut into 6 serving pieces each, and excess fat removed
¼ cup olive oil
2 teaspoons annatto (achiote) seeds (see Sources)
1 (15-ounce) can black beans, rinsed and drained
¾ cup Chicken Stock (page 153) or store-bought reduced-sodium broth
1 medium onion, chopped
1 teaspoon ground cumin
¾ teaspoon dried oregano, crumbled
½ cup cream sherry

ACCOMPANIMENT: white rice

With a vegetable peeler, remove 4 strips of zest from orange, each about 3 inches long; set aside. Juice orange.

Stir together ¼ cup orange juice, lime juice, half of garlic, 1 teaspoon salt, and ½ teaspoon pepper in a large bowl. Add hen pieces, turning to coat. Marinate, covered, at room temperature, turning occasionally, for 1 hour.

Heat oil and annatto seeds in a very small saucepan over low heat, swirling pan frequently, until oil is bright red-orange and beginning to simmer, 1 to 2 minutes. Remove from heat and let stand for 10 minutes. Pour oil through a fine-mesh sieve into a 12-inch heavy skillet; discard seeds.

Puree beans with stock in a blender until smooth; set aside.

Put a rack in middle of oven and preheat oven to 350°F.

Pat hen pieces dry (discard marinade) and sprinkle with 1½ teaspoons salt. Heat annatto oil in skillet over moderate heat until hot but not smoking. Brown hens, skin side down, in 3 batches (without turning pieces except for drumsticks), 3 to 4 minutes per batch. Transfer with tongs to a large roasting pan, skin side up.

Pour off all but 2 tablespoons fat from skillet. Add onion and cook, stirring, until softened, about 6 minutes. Add cumin, oregano, orange zest, and remaining garlic and cook, stirring, for 1 minute. Add sherry and deglaze by boiling, scraping up any brown bits, for 1 minute, then boil until reduced by half. Add bean puree and bring to a simmer.

Pour sauce over hens. Cover tightly with foil, transfer to oven, and braise until hens are very tender, about 1 hour. Season with salt and pepper and serve with rice.

Rabbit Braised in Red Wine

SERVES 4
ACTIVE TIME: 30 MINUTES ■ START TO FINISH: 1½ HOURS

■ This homey dish will dissuade you from the notion that rabbit tastes just like chicken. Dry red wine takes the meat to a dark intriguing place, and creamy po-

lenta adds richness. Because polenta tastes best served immediately, start cooking it while the rabbit is simmering, timing it so that it will finish after you rewarm the rabbit in the thickened sauce. ■

- 2 tablespoons all-purpose flour
- 1 teaspoon salt
- 1 (3-pound) rabbit, giblets discarded, cut into 8 serving pieces
- 3 tablespoons olive oil
- 1 large onion, chopped
- 2 garlic cloves, minced
- 2 teaspoons minced fresh rosemary
- 1½ cups Chicken Stock (page 153) or store-bought reduced-sodium broth
- 1 cup dry red wine
- 2 tablespoons coarsely chopped fresh flat-leaf parsley

ACCOMPANIMENT: Buttered Polenta (page 272)

Stir together flour and salt in a large bowl. Add rabbit and toss to coat.

Heat 2 tablespoons oil in a 4-quart heavy pot over moderately high heat until hot but not smoking. Brown rabbit in 2 batches, turning occasionally, 3 to 4 minutes per batch. Transfer to a bowl.

Add onion with remaining tablespoon oil to pot and cook, stirring occasionally, until softened but not browned, about 2 minutes. Add garlic and rosemary and cook, stirring, for 1 minute. Add stock, wine, and rabbit, with any juices accumulated in bowl (rabbit will not be completely covered with liquid), bring to a simmer, and simmer, tightly covered, turning occasionally, until meat is tender, about 1 hour.

Transfer rabbit to a bowl with tongs. Simmer sauce, uncovered, until slightly thickened, 8 to 10 minutes.

Return rabbit to sauce and simmer, turning rabbit, until heated through, then stir in parsley. Serve rabbit over polenta, drizzled with some sauce. Serve remaining sauce on the side.

COOK'S NOTE

■ The rabbit can be braised and the sauce thickened (without adding the parsley) up to 1 day ahead. Cool, uncovered, then refrigerate, covered. Reheat the rabbit in the sauce, covered, over moderately low heat, and stir in the parsley.

BEEF, VEAL, PORK, AND LAMB

Say "comfort food" to some people, and they'll start dancing around the room telling tales of all the white foods that they love. They'll recite odes to mashed potatoes and sing songs about macaroni and cheese. But when I am yearning for a taste of home, I dream about the round, brown aroma of prime rib roasting in the oven, the Fourth of July sizzle of hamburgers on the grill, or the deep winter scent of a wine-rich stew slowly braising on the stove.

Meat is a pure and primal pleasure. It is also one of life's ultimate luxuries, and throughout human history, great cooks have devoted themselves to making the most of it. In my opinion, you can unearth more interesting and inventive recipes for meat than for any other foodstuff. So you can imagine my joy when it came time for us to test the recipes for this chapter.

There are many reasons to rejoice, and one of them is that the beginning of the twenty-first century has been kind to carnivores like me. After years of lamenting the loss of truly flavorful meat, we can now celebrate a sudden change. These days it is increasingly possible to buy heritage pork that tastes as delicious as the pigs our ancestors raised. This is meat that has enough fat for deep flavor, meat that tastes of the land on which the animals were bred, meat that can be cooked very simply. Many other meats have changed too; we are being reintroduced to the taste of steers that have been raised naturally and allowed to graze on grass. Ethical and environmental factors aside, there is also the simple fact that happy animals taste better.

With some of this meat, the major work is in the shopping. A tenderloin of beef or an aged prime rib offers the luxury of simplicity; these cuts are so elegant that they can stand naked on the table and turn an ordinary dinner into an instant party. But with the proper coddling, lesser cuts can also be turned into feast-day fare. The French taught us to make much out of very little when they braised short ribs with Dijon mustard, a classic that begins with a humble cut smothered in layers of flavor until it is utterly transformed. We figured out how to simplify the dish, using nothing more than wine, shallots, mustard, and tomatoes. Braised veal shoulder with bacon and thyme and lamb chili with masa harina dumplings are also impressive dishes that depend on the chemistry of cooking and yield much more than the sum of their parts.

All over the world, good cooks have done their best to honor animals by turning inexpensive cuts into impressive meals. We learned about Wuxi spareribs from Wang Haibo, a California master of the art of Shanghainese cooking. The ribs are a bit of work, but they will astonish you with their depth of flavor. Osso buco—braised veal shanks—is another kitchen magician's trick; Italians coax these meaty bones into giving up their flavor through long, slow cooking. And in the hands of a talented Indian cook, lashings of exotic spices turn an ordinary rack of lamb into an impossibly fragrant tandoori dish. But you don't have to go wandering around the globe to discover interesting ideas: if you have never tried the American classic chicken-fried pork with milk gravy, you have a treat in store. And if sausage making is new to you, you are about to discover one of the most fun—and most rewarding—things that you can do in a kitchen.

There's been another awakening as well. We are starting to expand our tastes, as buffalo, venison, and goat slowly start to find their way to our tables. But one thing has not changed. Despite a lot of talk about nose-to-tail eating, we have not become a nation of offal eaters. So while we have included an extraordinary recipe for veal tongue—it is, hands down, the most tender piece of meat you will ever eat—and a recipe for sweetbreads, surely the subtlest piece of flesh in the world, and a superb one for liver, the other innards will have to wait.

BEEF, VEAL, PORK, AND LAMB

Beef

Rib-Eye Steak au Poivre with Balsamic Reduction

SERVES 4 GENEROUSLY
ACTIVE TIME: 10 MINUTES ■ START TO FINISH: 30 MINUTES

■ Boneless rib-eye, also known as Delmonico, is a tremendously beefy cut. The syrupy, concentrated sweetness of reduced balsamic vinegar balances the steak's richness and piquancy and gives the pan sauce depth of flavor. ■

    4 (¾-inch-thick) boneless rib-eye steaks (12 ounces
        each)
    2 tablespoons black peppercorns
      Kosher salt
    3 tablespoons unsalted butter
    1 tablespoon vegetable oil
    ½ cup balsamic vinegar

Pat steaks dry. Coarsely crush peppercorns in a sealable plastic bag by pressing hard with a meat pounder or bottom of a heavy skillet. Press pepper evenly onto both sides of steaks and season with 1 tablespoon salt.

Heat 1 tablespoon butter and oil in a 12-inch heavy skillet over moderately high heat until hot but not smoking. Reduce heat to moderate, add 2 steaks, and cook, turning once, 6 to 8 minutes for rare. Transfer steaks to a platter. Cook remaining 2 steaks in fat remaining in pan in same manner; transfer to platter.

Pour off fat from skillet, add vinegar to skillet, and deglaze by boiling, scraping up brown bits, then boil until reduced to about ¼ cup. Remove from heat and whisk in remaining 2 tablespoons butter until melted. Lightly season sauce with salt and drizzle over steaks.

Blade Steaks with Mushrooms

SERVES 4
ACTIVE TIME: 25 MINUTES ■ START TO FINISH: 25 MINUTES

■ Top blade chuck steaks are an inexpensive cut, mainly because they have a thin line of cartilage running down the middle. But here's the secret: they are also extremely tender, with a big flavor. So while they may not be company fare, they make a wonderful weeknight supper, especially topped with this quick sauté of mushrooms. Since blade steaks are so lean, they are best cooked rare to medium-rare. ■

    4 (½-inch-thick) top blade chuck steaks (1¼ pounds
        total)
    ¼ teaspoon salt
    ⅛ teaspoon freshly ground black pepper
    1 tablespoon olive oil
    1 tablespoon unsalted butter
   10 ounces cremini or white mushrooms, trimmed and
        cut into ¾-inch-wide wedges
    1 tablespoon finely chopped shallot
    ¼ cup balsamic vinegar
    2 tablespoons soy sauce
    ½ cup plus 2 teaspoons Beef Stock (page 153) or store-
        bought reduced-sodium broth
    ¾ teaspoon cornstarch

Pat steaks dry. Cut three 1-inch-long slits, 1 inch apart, across center cartilage of each steak to keep meat from curling. Sprinkle with salt and pepper.

Heat oil in a 12-inch heavy skillet over moderately high heat until hot but not smoking. Add steaks and cook, turning once, until just medium-rare, 4 to 6 minutes. Transfer to a platter and cover loosely with foil to keep warm.

Add butter to skillet, then add mushrooms and shallot and cook, stirring frequently, until mushrooms are browned and tender, about 4 minutes. Transfer to platter with steaks.

Add vinegar and soy sauce to skillet and deglaze by boiling, scraping up brown bits, for 2 minutes. Add ½ cup beef stock and simmer for 2 minutes. Stir cornstarch into remaining 2 teaspoons stock in a cup, stir mixture into sauce, and simmer, stirring, for 1 minute.

Return steaks and mushrooms, along with any juices accumulated on platter, to skillet and simmer, turning steaks in sauce, until just heated through, about 1 minute.

Steak Pizzaiola

SERVES 4
ACTIVE TIME: 40 MINUTES ■ START TO FINISH: 45 MINUTES

■ *Pizzaiola* refers to the tomatoey sauce that the meat is cooked in, which gives it a tender consistency. We pound the blade steaks so that they cook more quickly, then simply spoon the sauce on top. The result is crisp, zesty, and satisfying. ■

4   (½-inch-thick) top blade chuck steaks (1¼ pounds total)
    Salt and freshly ground black pepper
¼   cup olive oil
1   medium onion, thinly sliced
1   yellow bell pepper, cored, seeded, and cut lengthwise into ¼-inch-wide strips
6   ounces white mushrooms, trimmed and thinly sliced
3   garlic cloves, finely chopped
3   tablespoons sweet vermouth
1   (14- to 15-ounce) can diced tomatoes in juice
3   tablespoons water

Pat steaks dry. Cut three 1-inch-long slits, 1 inch apart, across center cartilage of each steak to keep meat from curling. Put meat between two sheets of plastic wrap and pound to ¼ inch thick with flat side of a meat pounder or with a rolling pin. Sprinkle steaks with 1 teaspoon salt and ⅛ teaspoon pepper.

Heat 2 tablespoons oil in a 12-inch heavy skillet over moderately high heat until hot but not smoking. Add 2 steaks and cook, turning once, until just medium-rare, 2 minutes. Transfer steaks to a platter and cover loosely with foil to keep warm. Cook remaining 2 steaks in fat remaining in pan in same manner; transfer to platter.

Add remaining 2 tablespoons oil to skillet, then add onion and bell pepper and cook, stirring, until onion is golden, about 4 minutes. Add mushrooms and garlic and cook, stirring, until mushrooms are golden, about 4 minutes. Add vermouth and cook until evaporated, about 1 minute. Add tomatoes with juice and water, reduce heat, and simmer, covered, stirring occasionally, until tomatoes and onion are softened, about 5 minutes. Remove lid and simmer until most of liquid has evaporated, about 5 minutes.

Stir in ½ teaspoon salt and ¼ teaspoon pepper and add steaks to sauce. Simmer, turning steaks occasionally, until heated through, about 5 minutes. Serve steaks with sauce spooned on top.

Korean Marinated Beef

Bulgogi

SERVES 4
ACTIVE TIME: 20 MINUTES ■ START TO FINISH: 40 MINUTES

■ Hot and cool, fresh and crunchy, *bulgogi* is a seductive dish, and a staple at Korean restaurants. The flank steak is marinated in a soy and sesame mixture, panfried, and topped with accompaniments such as raw garlic slices, kimchi (assorted spicy pickles), and steamed white rice, then wrapped in lettuce and eaten out of hand. This is an ideal choice for a casual dinner party. ■

¼   cup soy sauce
1   tablespoon sugar
2   teaspoons Asian sesame oil
1   bunch scallions, minced, white and green parts kept separate
1   tablespoon minced garlic
1   tablespoon minced peeled fresh ginger
3   tablespoons sesame seeds, toasted (see Tips, page 911)
1   (1-pound) piece flank steak, cut across the grain into very thin slices (no more than ⅛ inch thick)
1   tablespoon vegetable oil
ACCOMPANIMENTS: Boston lettuce or other soft-leaf lettuce; thinly sliced garlic; packaged kimchi (assorted spicy pickles; see Sources); white rice

Stir together soy sauce, sugar, sesame oil, whites of scallions, garlic, ginger, and 2 tablespoons sesame seeds in a medium bowl until sugar is dissolved. Add steak, toss to coat, and marinate for 15 minutes.

Heat vegetable oil in a 12-inch heavy skillet over high heat until just smoking. Add steak in one layer and cook, turning occasionally, until browned and just cooked through, about 5 minutes. Transfer to a platter and sprinkle with scallion greens and remaining 1 tablespoon sesame seeds.

Serve with accompaniments.

Japanese Beef and Scallion Rolls
Negimaki

SERVES 4 AS A MAIN COURSE, 6 AS AN HORS D'OEUVRE
ACTIVE TIME: 40 MINUTES ■ START TO FINISH: 1 HOUR

■ This Japanese treat—tender flank steak wrapped around sweet scallions, seared, and cut into sushi-roll-sized pieces—works equally well as a main course and as a passed hors d'oeuvre. Pounding the steak very thin gives it an almost crepe-paper texture, but the rolls are cooked so quickly that they stay juicy, with a nice brown crust on the outside and a rarer interior. ■

- 12 small scallions, cut into 6-inch lengths
  Salt
- 1 (1-pound) piece flank steak (6–7 inches square)
- ¼ cup sake
- ¼ cup mirin (Japanese sweet rice wine)
- 3 tablespoons soy sauce
- 1 tablespoon sugar
- 1 tablespoon vegetable oil

SPECIAL EQUIPMENT: kitchen string

PREPARE THE SCALLIONS: Blanch scallions in a 5-quart pot of boiling salted water (2 tablespoons salt) for 45 seconds. Transfer with tongs or a slotted spoon to a bowl of ice and cold water to stop the cooking, then transfer to paper towels to drain and pat dry.

PREPARE THE BEEF: Holding a large knife at a 30-degree angle, cut flank steak with the grain into twelve ⅛-inch-thick slices (1½ to 2 inches wide). Arrange slices 1 inch apart on a very lightly oiled sheet of parchment paper or plastic wrap and cover with another very lightly oiled sheet of parchment or plastic wrap (oiled side down). Pound slices with flat side of a meat pounder or with a rolling pin to about ¹⁄₁₆ inch thick.

ASSEMBLE THE ROLLS: Arrange 3 beef slices side by side on a clean sheet of plastic wrap, with short ends of slices nearest you, overlapping slices slightly to form a 6-inch square. Sprinkle beef with a pinch of salt, then lay 3 scallions (2 going in one direction, 1 going in the other direction) across slices at end closest to you and tightly roll up meat around scallions to form a log, using plastic wrap as an aid. Remove plastic wrap and tie log with kitchen string at ends and where meat slices overlap. Make 3 more rolls in same manner.

MARINATE THE ROLLS: Stir together sake, mirin, soy sauce, and sugar in a small bowl until sugar is dissolved. Put rolls in a small baking dish and pour marinade over them, turning to coat. Marinate, turning occasionally, for 15 minutes.

COOK THE ROLLS: Heat a 10-inch heavy skillet over moderately high heat until hot, 1 to 2 minutes. Meanwhile, lift rolls out of marinade, letting excess drip off, and pat dry; reserve marinade.

Add oil to skillet, swirling to coat bottom, and cook rolls, turning with tongs, until well browned on all sides, 4 to 5 minutes for medium-rare. Transfer rolls to a cutting board. Add marinade to skillet and boil until reduced and slightly syrupy, 1 to 2 minutes. Remove from heat.

Cut off and discard strings and cut each roll into 6 slices. Pour sauce into a shallow serving dish and arrange *negimaki* in sauce.

COOK'S NOTE
■ The *negimaki* can be assembled (not marinated) up to 4 hours ahead and refrigerated, wrapped in plastic wrap.

Skirt Steak
with Red Wine Sauce

SERVES 4

ACTIVE TIME: 15 MINUTES ■ START TO FINISH: 20 MINUTES

■ Until fajitas popularized it, skirt steak was an economical cut of meat. That may be a thing of the past, but its phenomenal flavor and juiciness merit spending extra for it. This simple presentation highlights those characteristics to great effect. ■

- 1¼ pounds skirt steak, cut crosswise into 4 pieces
  Salt and freshly ground black pepper
- 1 tablespoon vegetable oil
- ¾ cup dry red wine
- 4 fresh thyme sprigs
- 1 Turkish bay leaf or ½ California bay leaf
- 1 teaspoon sugar
- ½ teaspoon Worcestershire sauce
- 2 tablespoons cold unsalted butter, cut into small pieces

Pat steak dry and sprinkle all over with ¾ teaspoon salt and ¼ teaspoon pepper. Heat oil in a 12-inch heavy skillet over moderately high heat until hot but not smoking. Add steak and cook, turning once, for 3 to 5 minutes for thin pieces, 5 to 7 minutes for thicker pieces, for medium-rare. Transfer to a platter.

Pour off fat from skillet. Add wine, thyme, bay leaf, sugar, and Worcestershire sauce and deglaze by boiling, scraping up brown bits, for 1 minute, then boil until sauce is reduced by half, 2 to 3 minutes.

Add any meat juices on platter, remove skillet from heat, and discard bay leaf and thyme. Stir in butter and salt and pepper to taste and serve with steak.

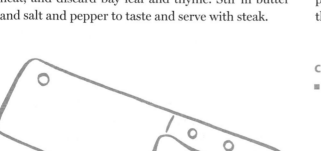

Skirt Steak
with Cilantro Garlic Sauce

SERVES 6

ACTIVE TIME: 20 MINUTES ■ START TO FINISH: 20 MINUTES

■ That this recipe is so quick and easy is a boon, but the real reason to make it is taste: the combination of rich skirt steak and the fresh, slightly acidic, assertive cilantro sauce is magical. ■

- 1 medium garlic clove
  Salt
- 1 cup coarsely chopped fresh cilantro
- ¼ cup olive oil
- 2 tablespoons fresh lemon juice
- ⅛ teaspoon cayenne
- 1 teaspoon ground cumin
- ½ teaspoon freshly ground black pepper
- 2 pounds skirt steak, cut crosswise into 3- to 4-inch pieces

SPECIAL EQUIPMENT: a well-seasoned ridged grill pan

Mince garlic and mash to a paste with ½ teaspoon salt, using side of a heavy knife. Transfer garlic paste to a blender, add cilantro, olive oil, lemon juice, and cayenne, and blend until smooth.

Stir together cumin, ½ teaspoon salt, and pepper in a small bowl. Pat steak dry and rub both sides with cumin mixture.

Heat grill pan over high heat until hot but not smoking. Brush pan with oil and grill steak in 2 batches, turning occasionally, for about 2 minutes per batch for thin pieces, 6 to 8 minutes per batch for thicker pieces, for medium-rare.

Serve steak drizzled with sauce.

COOK'S NOTE

■ Alternatively, the steak can be grilled outdoors on a charcoal or gas grill (see Grilling Basics, page 510).

BEEF BUYER'S GUIDE

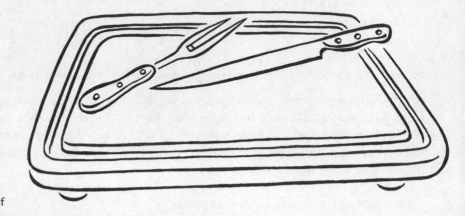

More and more of us are willing to pay a premium for beef that is "sustainable"—not only safe to eat, but raised humanely and in an environmentally responsible way. Selecting from the choices at the meat counter—if there are choices—can be confusing, though. If you can't find what you're looking for at stores near you, help create demand by asking for the kind of beef you want. Farmers markets and the Internet are two other options.

Most of the beef available to consumers comes from conventionally raised cattle. These animals have been raised on pasture for about 6 months, then sent to feedlots for "finishing," during which they're fed a calorie-dense diet (primarily processed corn and other grains) so that they gain intramuscular fat in the form of marbling—those snowy flakes of fat in the muscle—before slaughter. The USDA grades of "Prime," "Choice," and "Select" are based on the amount of marbling in a cut, Prime having the most. Grain finishing came into being after World War II, in large part because federally subsidized corn became cheap feed. It produces the tender, well-marbled meat that consumers are used to eating; it's consistent and available year-round. Nonetheless, grain is not a natural diet for cows—grass and other forage are—and most cattle confined in industrial feedlots have to be fed a steady course of antibiotics to prevent the illnesses that result from their grain diet. In addition, they are given hormones to stimulate growth, as well as plastic pellets for roughage. They live in conditions that are often overcrowded, unsanitary, and stressful.

NATURAL This term, introduced by the USDA in the 1960s, technically means that the beef has been minimally processed and contains no artificial flavors, added colors, or preservatives. All the fresh beef you'll see in your supermarket is "natural," whether labeled so or not. The issue is confused by the fact that some meat producers use the term to mean they raise their cattle without growth hormones and antibiotics. The term does not mean that the cattle are grass-finished or certified organic. Many "natural" cattle are kept in feedlots.

100 PERCENT VEGETARIAN DIET These words on a label don't guarantee that the animal was raised outdoors on pasture, only that it was fed strictly grasses (and grain), hay, silage, and other forage found in a field. The label is a response to concern about mad cow disease (bovine spongiform encephalopathy, or BSE), which is spread through the feeding of rendered material from diseased ruminants (cattle, sheep, deer, and goats) to other ruminants. In 1997 the FDA prohibited the feeding of these animal by-products to industrially raised livestock, but loopholes remain. (Cattle blood and blood products, poultry litter, plate waste, and salvaged pet food may all be used as ingredients in cattle feed.)

CERTIFIED ORGANIC These cattle must have been raised under standards set by the USDA, which require, among other things, that they be fed 100 percent organic feed and have access to pasture (how much pasture has not been defined). The USDA does not require the cattle to be grass-finished, though; they can be finished on organic grain in a feedlot. The producers must adhere to humane-treatment standards that are stronger than those in the cattle industry guidelines. The cattle can't be given growth hormones or antibiotics in the absence of illness (if a sick animal is treated with antibiotics, it's removed from the National Organic Program), but they can be vaccinated against diseases. For more information, visit the websites of the **Organic Farming Research Foundation** (http://ofrf .org) and **Sustainable Table** (www.sustainabletable.org).

GRASS-FED All cattle graze on pasture until they're ready for finishing, so in one respect all cattle are grass-fed, but today younger and younger cattle are being put into feedlots. In recent years, if you wanted a steak from a steer that had been fed a 100 percent pasture diet for its entire life, you wanted beef that had been grass-finished or pasture-finished, terms that described cattle that stayed home on the range until they were taken to the slaughterhouse. But in October 2007, after almost five years of discussion, the USDA issued standards for "grass (forage) fed" labeling claims, stating in part that "grass and/or forage shall be the feed source consumed for the life of the ruminant animal. . . . Animals cannot be fed grains or grain by-products and must have continuous access to pasture during the growing season." The seasonality of peak pasture determines when the best finishing time is in different parts of the country, so consumers shouldn't expect to see grass-finished beef in their supermarkets or, more likely, their natural foods stores year-round. Most grass-fed beef is available in the late spring and early summer. Grass-fed beef may or may not be certified organic. In general, the meat is leaner and less tender than conventional beef, so it's important not to overcook it. It's best when served rare or medium-rare.

In terms of flavor, grass-fed beef is cleaner-tasting than grain-finished, but it's not as consistent, because of the differences in pasture. Proper aging also seems to make a difference. Recent tastings have convinced us that quality is steadily improving: ranchers (some of whom are now calling themselves "grass farmers") are learning which cattle breeds finish best on grass, how to manage grazing lands to bring pasture to its peak, and how to modify aging techniques. People's palates are changing too—perhaps because of the increasing availability of the

renowned beef from Argentina, all of which is grass-fed. In the United States, grass-fed beef represents just a tiny fraction of the market, but health concerns are fueling growth: the meat is not only much lower in saturated fats, but it's also higher in healthy omega-3 fatty acids. And it's higher in the antioxidant vitamins A and E, as well as in CLA (conjugated linoleic acid, found in the fat), which, recent studies show, may help prevent breast cancer, diabetes, and other illnesses. Researchers have also found that cattle fed grass or hay for a short period before slaughter have a much lower incidence of *E. coli* 0157:H7, the virulent, relatively new strain of bacteria common in feedlot cattle.

For more information, visit the websites of **American Grassfed Association** (www.americangrassfed .org), **Eatwild** (www.eatwild.com), and the **Stockman Grass Farmer** (www.stockmangrassfarmer.net).

HUMANE TREATMENT There are substantive differences between these programs, but they are all stricter than cattle industry guidelines.

- Humane Farm Animal Care oversees the **"Certified Humane" program:** www.certifiedhumane.com
- The American Humane Association oversees the **"Free Farmed" program:** www.americanhumane.org/protecting-animals/ programs/farm-animals/
- The **Animal Welfare Institute** has its own protocols and label: www.awionline.org
- **Whole Foods** has its own standards for meat: www.wholefoodsmarket.com/pdfs/cattle.pdf

London Broil with Soy Citrus Mayonnaise

SERVES 6
ACTIVE TIME: 25 MINUTES ■ START TO FINISH: 5¼ HOURS
(INCLUDES MARINATING)

■ Marinating tough London broil in a citrus marinade (which is later used to flavor the accompanying mayonnaise), cooking it carefully, and cutting the steak very thin on a 45-degree angle against the grain ensures a tender result. This recipe is a reminder that mayonnaise is classically a sauce, not a sandwich spread; just a dollop adds a great deal of moisture to this cut. ■

- ¾ cup soy sauce
- ½ cup dry red wine
- ⅓ cup fresh orange juice
- ¼ cup fresh lemon juice
- 3 tablespoons olive oil
- 1 bunch scallions, cut into 3-inch lengths
- 5 garlic cloves, smashed
- ½ teaspoon freshly ground black pepper
  Pinch of cayenne
- 2½–3 pounds top-round London broil (1–1½ inches thick; see Cook's Note)
- 1 cup mayonnaise

SPECIAL EQUIPMENT: an instant-read thermometer

Combine soy sauce, red wine, citrus juices, 2 tablespoons oil, scallions, garlic, black pepper, and cayenne in a 1-gallon heavy-duty sealable plastic bag. Add steak and seal bag, pressing out air. Turn bag to coat steak and marinate, refrigerated, turning bag occasionally, for 2 to 4 hours.

Transfer steak to a plate. Pour 2 tablespoons marinade through a fine-mesh sieve into a 1-quart heavy saucepan; discard remainder. Bring steak to room temperature, about 30 minutes.

Heat remaining tablespoon oil in a 12-inch heavy skillet over moderately high heat until hot but not smoking. Add steak and cook until underside is browned, about 5 minutes. Turn steak, reduce heat to moderately low, cover skillet, and cook until thermometer inserted horizontally 2 inches into center of steak registers 120°F, 10 to 12 minutes. Transfer steak to a cutting board and let stand, uncovered, for 15 minutes (internal temperature of steak will rise about 10 degrees, for medium-rare).

Meanwhile, bring reserved marinade to a boil and boil for 1 minute. Pour into a bowl and cool completely, then whisk in mayonnaise until well combined. Refrigerate, covered, until ready to serve.

Holding knife at a 45-degree angle, cut steak across the grain into very thin slices. Transfer to a platter and drizzle with any juices accumulated on cutting board. Serve at room temperature or slightly chilled, with mayonnaise.

COOK'S NOTES

- London broil comes in different weights and thicknesses; it may be necessary to use 2 pieces to get the proper amount.
- The steak can marinate for up to 1 day.
- The soy citrus mayonnaise can be refrigerated for up to 5 days.

Chinese Beef with Broccoli

SERVES 4
ACTIVE TIME: 35 MINUTES ■ START TO FINISH: 1½ HOURS

■ Beef with broccoli, that staple of Chinese restaurants everywhere, is traditionally made by deep-frying the beef before adding it to the stir-fried broccoli. The Chinese cooking authority Nina Simonds simply stir-fries the meat. Do be sure to cook it in small batches so it browns rather than steams. ■

- 1 (1-pound) flank steak, trimmed of excess fat, halved lengthwise, and cut crosswise into ⅛-inch-thick slices
- ¼ cup soy sauce
- 2 tablespoons water
- 2 tablespoons Chinese rice wine or medium-dry sherry
- 2 teaspoons Asian sesame oil
- 3½ teaspoons cornstarch
- 1 tablespoon plus 2 teaspoons finely chopped garlic
- 2 teaspoons sugar
- 1 bunch broccoli (2 pounds), cut into small florets, stems peeled and cut into 2-by-¼-inch matchsticks

⅓ cup Chicken Stock (page 153) or store-bought
   reduced-sodium broth
3 tablespoons oyster sauce
½ cup peanut or vegetable oil
1 tablespoon finely chopped peeled fresh ginger
1 scallion, finely chopped

ACCOMPANIMENT: white rice

Put steak in a bowl, add 2 tablespoons soy sauce, water, 1 tablespoon rice wine, 1 teaspoon sesame oil, 2 teaspoons cornstarch, 2 teaspoons garlic, and 1 teaspoon sugar, and stir with a fork to combine. Cover with plastic wrap and marinate steak at room temperature for 1 hour.

Bring a 5- to 6-quart pot of salted water (1½ tablespoons salt) to a boil. Add broccoli florets and stems and blanch, stirring occasionally, until crisp-tender, about 2 minutes. Drain and transfer to a bowl of ice and cold water to stop the cooking; drain again.

Whisk together stock, oyster sauce, and remaining 2 tablespoons soy sauce, 1 tablespoon rice wine, 1 teaspoon sesame oil, 1 teaspoon sugar, and 1½ teaspoons cornstarch in a bowl.

Drain beef in a colander, gently pressing on beef.

Heat a well-seasoned 14-inch flat-bottomed wok over high heat until a drop of water evaporates on contact. Pour 3 tablespoons peanut oil down side of wok and swirl to coat sides. Working quickly, add one quarter of beef, spreading it in one layer on bottom and up sides of wok, and cook, undisturbed, until beef begins to brown, about 30 seconds, then stir-fry until meat is just browned on all sides but still pink in center, about 1 minute. Transfer meat and any juices to a plate. Wipe out wok with a paper towel and cook remaining beef in 3 batches in same manner, adding 1 tablespoon oil to wok for each batch.

Pour remaining 2 tablespoons peanut oil down side of wok and swirl to coat sides. Add ginger, scallion, and remaining 1 tablespoon garlic and stir-fry until golden, about 1 minute. Add broccoli and stir-fry for 30 seconds. Add beef, with any juices, and stock mixture and cook, stirring, until sauce boils and thickens, about 2 minutes. Serve immediately, with rice.

COOK'S NOTE
- You can substitute a 12-inch heavy skillet, preferably cast-iron, for the wok.

SOY SAUCE

Soy sauce has been a staple of Chinese, Japanese, and other Asian kitchens for thousands of years. Created in China, the savory, versatile flavoring agent was introduced to Japan by Buddhist monks in the eighth century. Generally speaking, Chinese soy sauces, which are made primarily or only from soybeans, are earthy and salty. Japanese soy sauces, which usually have equal amounts of soybeans and wheat, are sweeter, meatier, and more rounded in flavor. No matter what kind of soy sauce you buy (brands vary in intensity, color, and viscosity), read the label carefully to make sure it is naturally or traditionally brewed—produced, that is, through an alcoholic fermentation, a process that takes about 6 months. The high level of amino acids (mostly glutamic acid) in soy sauce heightens the flavors of other ingredients in a dish. Avoid synthetic (nonfermented) soy sauces that include hydrolyzed soy (or "vegetable") protein, corn syrup, caramel, and other additives; produced in a matter of days, they taste harsh and one-dimensional and will overpower rather than enhance other flavors. The dark Japanese soy sauce called tamari, made from the thick, rich concentrate that settles at the bottom of vats of soy sauce, is too robust to be a good substitute for naturally brewed soy sauce; it usually makes a better dipping sauce than an ingredient. Keep soy sauce in the refrigerator after opening.

Greek Beef Stew

SERVES 6 TO 8
ACTIVE TIME: 1 HOUR ■ START TO FINISH: 3½ HOURS

■ Walnuts and tangy feta add an unexpected accent to this satisfying beef and onion stew, which we adapted from one served at the former Hal's restaurant in Atlanta. We especially like it over orzo. ■

2 pounds boiling onions (1–1½ inches in diameter); left unpeeled
1 cup finely chopped fresh flat-leaf parsley
1 (6-ounce) can tomato paste
½ cup dry white wine
¼ cup red wine vinegar
2 teaspoons salt
1 teaspoon ground cumin
1 teaspoon ground cinnamon
1 teaspoon dried oregano, crumbled
1 Turkish bay leaf or ½ California bay leaf
3 pounds boneless beef chuck, cut into 1½-inch pieces
½ pound feta, crumbled (about 2 cups)
about 1 cup (3½ ounces) walnuts, coarsely chopped
ACCOMPANIMENT: orzo

Put a rack in middle of oven and preheat oven to 325°F.

To make peeling easier, blanch onions in a 5- to 6-quart pot of boiling unsalted water for 2 minutes; drain. When they are cool enough to handle, peel onions and transfer to a 6-quart heavy ovenproof pot.

Add all remaining ingredients except feta and nuts, toss well, and bring to a boil over moderate heat, stirring frequently. Cover, transfer pot to oven, and braise until meat and onions are very tender, about 2½ hours.

Skim fat from surface and discard bay leaf. Serve stew over orzo sprinkled with feta and walnuts.

COOK'S NOTE

■ The stew can be cooked up to 2 days ahead. Cool, uncovered, then refrigerate, covered. Reheat before serving with the feta and nuts.

Beef and Guinness Pies

SERVES 4
ACTIVE TIME: 1¼ HOURS ■ START TO FINISH: 6½ HOURS
(INCLUDES MAKING DOUGH)

■ For years Guinness promoted its stout with the slogan "Guinness is good for you," and tales abound from the 1920s of U.K. doctors prescribing the beer to postoperative patients, blood donors, and nursing mothers because of its high iron content. Its health benefits aside, Guinness is certainly good for these potpies, enriching and deepening the flavor of their meaty filling. Topped with an elegant puff pastry crust, they can be made in advance and are perfect for entertaining, served with a simple salad. Irish stouts produce a thick head when poured, so chill the can or bottle well before measuring to reduce the foam. ■

2 pounds boneless beef chuck, cut into 1-inch pieces
2 tablespoons all-purpose flour
1 teaspoon salt
½ teaspoon freshly ground black pepper
2 tablespoons vegetable oil
1 large onion, coarsely chopped
2 garlic cloves, chopped
¼ cup water
1½ tablespoons tomato paste
1 cup Beef Stock (page 153) or store-bought reduced-sodium broth
1 cup Guinness or other Irish stout
1 tablespoon Worcestershire sauce
2 teaspoons green peppercorns packed in brine, drained and coarsely chopped
2 fresh thyme sprigs
Quick Puff Pastry Dough (recipe follows)
1 large egg, lightly beaten
SPECIAL EQUIPMENT: four 14-ounce deep bowls or ramekins (4–5 inches wide; see Sources) or similar ovenproof dishes

Put a rack in middle of oven and preheat oven to 350°F.

Pat beef dry. Stir together flour, salt, and pepper in a shallow dish. Add beef, turning to coat, then shake off excess flour and transfer to a plate.

Heat oil in a 5- to 6-quart wide heavy ovenproof pot over moderately high heat until just smoking. Brown meat in 3 batches, turning occasionally, about 5 minutes per batch; transfer to a bowl.

Add onion, garlic, and 3 tablespoons water to pot and cook, scraping up any brown bits from bottom of pot and stirring frequently, until onion is softened, about 5 minutes. Add tomato paste and cook, stirring, for 1 minute.

Stir in beef with any juices accumulated in bowl, stock, stout, Worcestershire sauce, peppercorns, and thyme and bring to a simmer. Cover, transfer to oven, and braise until beef is very tender and sauce is thickened, 1¼ to 1½ hours. Discard thyme and cool stew completely, uncovered, about 30 minutes. (If stew is warm when you assemble pies, it will melt pastry tops.)

Divide cooled stew among bowls (they won't be completely full). Roll out pastry dough on a lightly floured surface with a lightly floured rolling pin into a 13-inch square, about ⅛ inch thick. Trim edges and cut dough into quarters. Stir together egg and remaining 1 tablespoon water and brush a 1-inch border of egg wash around each square. Invert 1 square over each bowl and drape, pressing sides lightly to help adhere. Brush pastry tops with some of remaining egg wash and freeze for 15 minutes to chill dough thoroughly.

Put a baking sheet on middle oven rack and preheat oven to 425°F.

Place pies on preheated baking sheet and bake until pastry is puffed and golden brown, about 20 minutes. Reduce oven temperature to 400°F and bake for 5 minutes more to fully cook dough.

COOK'S NOTE
- The stew (without the pastry) can be made up to 2 days ahead. Cool, then refrigerate, covered. Bring to room temperature before using.

Quick Puff Pastry Dough

MAKES ABOUT 1 POUND, ENOUGH FOR
FOUR 4- TO 5-INCH POTPIES
ACTIVE TIME: 30 MINUTES ■ START TO FINISH: 3½ HOURS
(INCLUDES CHILLING)

■ To produce the layers of buttery flakiness for which puff pastry is known, traditional methods incorporate the butter by spreading it across the rolled-out dough and then rolling and folding it multiple times. This easier version calls for simply grating frozen butter into the flour and mixing it like a pie dough, then rolling and folding the dough just three times. The dough can be used in any recipe that calls for puff pastry. ■

    1¼ cups all-purpose flour
    ¼ teaspoon salt
    1 stick (8 tablespoons) plus 5 tablespoons
       unsalted butter, frozen
    5–6 tablespoons ice water

Whisk together flour and salt in a chilled large metal bowl. Set a grater in flour mixture and coarsely grate frozen butter into flour, gently lifting flour and tossing to coat butter. Drizzle 5 tablespoons ice water evenly over flour mixture and gently stir with a fork until incorporated. Test mixture by gently squeezing a small handful: when it has the proper texture, dough will hold together without crumbling apart. If necessary, add another tablespoon water, stirring until just incorporated and testing again. (If you overwork dough or add too much water, pastry will be tough.)

Gather dough together and form into a 5-inch square (dough will be lumpy and streaky). Refrigerate, wrapped in plastic wrap, until firm, about 30 minutes.

Roll out dough on a floured surface with a floured rolling pin into a 15-by-8-inch rectangle. Position dough with a short side nearest you, then fold dough into thirds like a letter: bottom third up over center, top third down over dough. Rewrap dough and refrigerate until firm, about 30 minutes.

Position dough with a short side nearest you on a floured surface and repeat rolling out, folding, and refrigerating 2 times. Brush off any excess flour, wrap dough in plastic wrap, and refrigerate for at least 1 hour.

COOK'S NOTE
- The dough can be refrigerated for up to 1 day.

Sweet-and-Sour Stuffed Cabbage

SERVES 6
ACTIVE TIME: 1 HOUR ■ START TO FINISH: 3 HOURS

■ These tidy cabbage bundles and the gravylike tomato sauce they're cooked in are delicious served with mashed potatoes or noodles. Dried cherries and lemon juice contribute the "sour," balanced by brown sugar's "sweet." A small amount of rice helps keep the filling together. Make sure to buy a fattier grade of ground chuck (we prefer 80 percent lean), which will stay juicy. Savoy cabbage makes a prettier, more refined dish than regular green cabbage, which is fine too. ■

- 1 large Savoy or green cabbage (2–2¼ pounds)
- 3 tablespoons vegetable oil
- 2 medium onions (about 1 pound), halved lengthwise and thinly sliced crosswise, plus ¼ cup grated onion
- 1 (28-ounce) can whole tomatoes in juice
- 3 tablespoons fresh lemon juice
- 3 tablespoons packed dark brown sugar
- ½ cup dried sour cherries
  Salt and freshly ground black pepper
- 1 pound ground beef chuck (not lean)
- 3 tablespoons long-grain white rice
- 3 tablespoons water

SPECIAL EQUIPMENT: parchment paper

Core cabbage. Cook in an 8- to 10-quart pot of boiling salted water (3 tablespoons salt), uncovered, for 5 minutes. Transfer with a large slotted spoon to a shallow baking dish; leave water at a boil. When cabbage is cool enough to handle, remove 16 outer leaves. Return them to boiling water and cook until slightly softened, 3 to 4 minutes; drain.

Cut out thick ribs from drained leaves; set leaves aside. Thinly slice ribs and remaining cabbage.

Heat oil in a deep 12-inch heavy skillet over moderate heat until hot but not smoking. Add sliced onions and cook, stirring occasionally, until golden, 12 to 15 minutes. Add sliced cabbage, tomatoes with juice, lemon juice, brown sugar, cherries, 2 teaspoons salt, and ½ teaspoon pepper and bring to a simmer. Simmer, uncovered, breaking up tomatoes

with a wooden spoon and stirring occasionally, until cabbage is tender and sauce is thickened, about 30 minutes. Spread sauce in a 13-by-9-inch shallow baking dish.

Put a rack in middle of oven and preheat oven to 350°F.

Stir together grated onion, beef, rice, water, 2 teaspoons salt, and ¼ teaspoon pepper in a medium bowl until combined.

Lay out 1 cabbage leaf on a work surface with rounded edge nearest you. Put 2 tablespoons beef filling in center and fold rounded edge over filling. Then fold over sides and roll up tightly into a cylinder. Put cabbage roll seam side down in sauce. Stuff remaining cabbage leaves in same manner; transfer to sauce.

Cover stuffed cabbage with parchment paper and cover pan tightly with foil. Bake until cabbage is very tender, about 1½ hours.

COOK'S NOTE

■ The cabbage rolls can be baked up to 2 days ahead. Cool, uncovered, then refrigerate, covered. Reheat in a 350°F oven for about 30 minutes before serving.

ANNATTO

The hard, irregularly shaped, rusty red seeds of the small annatto tree (aka lipstick plant), native to tropical Central and South America, are sometimes called by their Aztec name, achiote. Either heated in oil or ground, the seeds give a mild but noticeable flavor and aroma—earthy and slightly astringent—to many South American dishes. Annatto has been used as a dye and natural food coloring since pre-Columbian times; today it's still used to color things like cheese, margarine, and microwave popcorn.

Jamaican Meat Patties

SERVES 4 TO 6
ACTIVE TIME: 1¼ HOURS ■ START TO FINISH: 2¾ HOURS
(INCLUDES CHILLING)

■ These spicy ground beef pies, bright yellow and half-moon-shaped, are found everywhere on the Caribbean island, as well as anywhere Jamaicans have settled in large numbers. Often eaten for lunch or on the run as a snack, they call out for a cold beer or an icy rum drink. Brushing the pastry with annatto oil gives the patties their distinctive color. ■

FOR PASTRY
3 cups all-purpose flour
1½ teaspoons baking powder
½ teaspoon salt
¾ cup vegetable shortening, preferably
    trans fat–free, chilled
½–¾ cup ice water

FOR FILLING AND ASSEMBLY
¼ cup vegetable oil
1 tablespoon annatto (achiote) seeds (see Sources)
1 pound ground beef chuck (not lean)
2 medium onions, chopped
2 scallions, chopped
2 large garlic cloves, chopped
1 teaspoon minced seeded Scotch bonnet or
    habanero chile
1½ teaspoons chopped fresh thyme
1 teaspoon salt, or to taste
½ teaspoon ground allspice
½ teaspoon freshly ground black pepper

1 large egg, lightly beaten for egg wash

MAKE THE PASTRY: Whisk together flour, baking powder, and salt in a large bowl (or pulse together in a food processor). Blend in shortening with your fingertips or a pastry blender (or pulse) just until mixture resembles coarse meal. Drizzle ½ cup water evenly over mixture and gently stir with a fork (or pulse) until incorporated. Squeeze a small handful of dough: if it doesn't hold together, add more ice water 1 tablespoon at a time, stirring (or pulsing) until just incorporated, then test again. Do not overwork mixture, or pastry will be tough.

Turn dough out onto a work surface and divide into 6 portions. With heel of your hand, smear each portion once or twice in a forward motion to help distribute fat. Gather dough together and form into 2 balls, then flatten each into a 5-inch disk. If dough is sticky, lightly dust with flour. Refrigerate, wrapped in plastic wrap, until firm, at least 1 hour.

MEANWHILE, MAKE THE FILLING: Heat oil and annatto seeds in a very small saucepan over low heat, swirling pan frequently, until oil is bright red-orange and beginning to simmer, 1 to 2 minutes. Remove from heat and let stand for 10 minutes, then pour oil through a fine-mesh sieve into a small bowl (discard annatto seeds).

Heat 2 tablespoons annatto oil (reserve remainder for brushing pastries) in a 12-inch heavy skillet over moderately high heat until hot but not smoking. Add beef and cook, stirring to break up clumps, until no longer pink, 3 to 5 minutes. Reduce heat to moderate, add remaining filling ingredients, and cook, stirring, until onions are softened, about 5 minutes.

Transfer meat mixture to a food processor and process until very finely ground. Transfer to a shallow dish to cool, then refrigerate, uncovered, until cold, about 1 hour.

ASSEMBLE AND BAKE THE PATTIES: Put racks in upper and lower thirds of oven and preheat oven to 400°F.

Roll out 1 disk of dough on a lightly floured surface with a floured rolling pin, lifting dough frequently to dust underneath with flour, into a 20-by-15-inch rectangle. Using a 5-inch cookie/pastry cutter (or use a 5-inch plate or lid as a guide), cut out as many rounds as possible, transferring rounds to a sheet of wax paper; reserve scraps. Repeat procedure with remaining disk of dough. Gather all scraps and reroll dough, then cut out enough rounds to make a total of 18.

Put about 2 tablespoons cold filling on one half of 1 round, spreading it slightly with your fingers to cover half, leaving a ¾-inch border around edge. Brush edge of dough with egg and fold other half of dough over filling to form a half-moon. Press edges together and crimp decoratively with tines of a fork. Repeat with remaining dough and filling.

Transfer patties to two baking sheets and brush

lightly with annatto oil. Bake, switching position of sheets halfway through baking, until golden brown, 25 to 30 minutes.

COOK'S NOTES

- The dough can be refrigerated for up to 1 day.
- The filling can be made up to 1 day ahead. Cool, uncovered, then refrigerate, covered.
- The patties can be assembled and brushed with the annatto oil up to 1 day ahead and refrigerated on the baking sheets, covered. They can also be frozen: freeze on the sheets, then transfer to sealable plastic bags and freeze for up to 1 week; bake without thawing.

Braised Short Ribs with Dijon Mustard

SERVES 4
ACTIVE TIME: 45 MINUTES ■ START TO FINISH: 3 HOURS

■ The rich, meaty taste of short ribs makes them the perfect choice for cooks who want full-bodied food with little fuss. We adapted this preparation from a recipe by chef Daniel Boulud, who begins by reducing a great deal of red wine for the rich sauce. For all its ease, the dish tastes as if many days—and ingredients—were required to produce it. ■

  1 (750-ml) bottle dry red wine
  4 pounds beef short ribs, cut into 2½-inch lengths by the butcher
    Salt and freshly ground black pepper
  2 tablespoons olive oil
 10 shallots, trimmed, leaving root ends intact, and halved lengthwise
  3 tablespoons whole-grain Dijon mustard
  6 plum tomatoes, halved lengthwise

Boil wine in a 2-quart heavy saucepan, uncovered, until reduced to about 1 cup, about 20 minutes.

Meanwhile, pat ribs dry and sprinkle with 1 tablespoon salt and ½ teaspoon pepper. Heat oil in a 5-quart heavy pot over moderately high heat un-

til hot but not smoking. Add ribs in 2 batches and cook, turning occasionally, until browned on all sides, about 8 minutes per batch. Transfer with tongs to a bowl.

Reduce heat to moderate, add shallots to fat remaining in pot, and cook, stirring occasionally, until browned, about 5 minutes. Transfer with a slotted spoon to another bowl.

Stir reduced wine and mustard into juices in pot. Add ribs, meat side down, cover tightly, and simmer for 1½ hours.

Gently stir shallots and tomatoes into braised rib mixture and continue to simmer, covered, without stirring, until meat is very tender, about 1 hour more.

Carefully transfer ribs, shallots, and tomatoes to a platter. Skim off fat from cooking liquid. Liquid should coat a spoon and measure about 1 cup; if necessary, boil to reduce.

Season sauce with salt and pepper and pour over short ribs.

COOK'S NOTE

- The shallots can be browned and the ribs braised in the wine and mustard up to 1 day ahead. Cool, uncovered, then refrigerate separately, covered. To finish the dish, skim off some of the fat from the surface of the braising liquid. Bring the rib mixture to a boil, covered, then gently stir in the shallots and tomatoes. Reduce the heat and simmer until the meat is very tender, about 40 minutes.

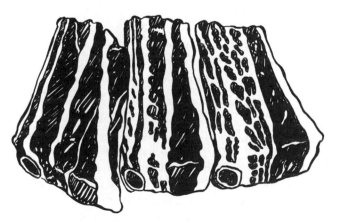

Prime Rib Roast with Red Wine Sauce

SERVES 8
ACTIVE TIME: 1 HOUR ▪ START TO FINISH: 3¾ HOURS

▪ Nothing says celebration like a perfectly cooked rib roast waiting to be carved at the head of the dining room table, and nothing smells so tempting as it cooks. Rubbing the roast with powdered dried porcini mushrooms imparts a savory woodsiness, which is enhanced by the small amount of dried porcini and the veal demi-glace in the velvety red wine sauce. ▪

FOR ROAST
- 1 (4-rib) standing rib roast (bone-in rib-eye roast, 9–10 pounds), at room temperature
- ½ ounce (2 tablespoons) dried porcini mushrooms, ground to a powder in a blender
- 1 tablespoon kosher salt
- ¾ teaspoon freshly ground black pepper

FOR SAUCE
- 2 small onions, 1 left unpeeled and halved lengthwise, 1 peeled and chopped
- ¾ stick (6 tablespoons) unsalted butter
- ⅔ cup chopped shallots
- 2 garlic cloves, smashed
- 1 carrot, finely chopped
- 1 celery rib, finely chopped
- 1 tablespoon tomato paste
- 2 sprigs fresh flat-leaf parsley
- 1 sprig fresh thyme
- 1 Turkish bay leaf or ½ California bay leaf
- 4 black peppercorns
- 1 (750-ml) bottle dry red wine, such as Côtes du Rhône
- ½ ounce (½ cup) dried porcini mushrooms
- 2 cups boiling water
- ⅔ cup veal demi-glace (see Sources)
- ½ teaspoon salt

ACCOMPANIMENT: Yorkshire Pudding (recipe follows)
SPECIAL EQUIPMENT: an instant-read thermometer

COOK THE ROAST: Put a rack in middle of oven and preheat oven to 450°F.

Trim all but a thin layer of fat from roast. Rub meat all over with porcini powder, salt, and pepper. Transfer to a rack set in a 13-by-9-inch roasting pan.

Roast beef for 20 minutes. Reduce oven temperature to 350°F and roast until thermometer inserted into center of meat registers 110°F, 1½ to 2 hours more. Transfer to a platter and let stand, uncovered, for 30 minutes (internal temperature of meat will rise to 130°F, for medium-rare).

MEANWHILE, PREPARE THE SAUCE: Cook halved onion, cut side down, in 1 tablespoon butter in a 2-quart heavy saucepan over moderate heat, undisturbed, until well browned, about 4 minutes. Add chopped onion, shallots, garlic, carrot, celery, and 2 tablespoons butter, reduce heat to moderately low, and cook, covered, stirring occasionally, until vegetables are softened, 8 to 10 minutes. Add tomato paste, herbs, bay leaf, peppercorns, and 2 cups wine, bring to a boil over moderately high heat, and boil, uncovered, until liquid is reduced to about ¼ cup, 25 to 30 minutes.

While wine reduces, soak porcini in boiling water in a bowl until softened, about 20 minutes. Drain porcini in a paper-towel-lined sieve set over a bowl; reserve soaking liquid. Rinse porcini and pat dry, then finely chop. Set aside.

Pour reduced wine mixture through a fine-mesh sieve into another 2-quart heavy saucepan, pressing down on solids; discard solids. Add porcini soaking liquid, demi-glace, and remaining 1¾ cups wine, bring to a boil over moderately high heat, and boil, uncovered, skimming off froth occasionally, until reduced to about 2 cups, 20 to 35 minutes.

Stir reserved porcini into sauce, reduce heat to low, and whisk in salt, any meat juices accumulated on platter, and remaining 3 tablespoons butter until incorporated.

Slice roast across the grain and serve with Yorkshire pudding, with sauce on the side.

COOK'S NOTE
▪ The sauce (without the cooked meat juices and 3 tablespoons butter) can be made up to 2 days ahead. Cool, uncovered, then refrigerate, covered. Reheat before finishing the sauce.

Yorkshire Pudding

SERVES 8
ACTIVE TIME: 15 MINUTES ■ START TO FINISH: 1¼ HOURS

■ The perfect Dickensian pairing: "an unctuous piece of roast beef and blisterous Yorkshire pudding, bubbling hot." Traditionally cooked in the hot drippings from the roast, these puddings instead get a level of deep flavor from nutty browned butter. Chilling the batter before pouring it into the piping-hot buttered tin helps produce the rapid rise and golden puff for which Yorkshire is known. ■

1½ cups all-purpose flour
1¼ teaspoons salt
3 large eggs
1½ cups whole milk
3 tablespoons unsalted butter, cut
   into pieces

Combine flour, salt, eggs, and milk in a blender and blend, scraping down sides occasionally, until just smooth. Refrigerate batter, covered, for at least 30 minutes.

Put a rack in middle of oven and preheat oven to 450°F.

Put butter in a 13-by-9-inch baking pan and heat in oven until solids separate and turn dark golden brown, 6 to 8 minutes (check frequently toward end).

Pour cold batter into hot baking pan (see Cook's Note) and bake, rotating pan once halfway through baking, until pudding is puffed and center is golden brown, 26 to 28 minutes. Cut into 8 pieces and serve immediately.

COOK'S NOTES

■ The batter can be refrigerated for up to 8 hours.
■ You can make individual Yorkshire puddings in a muffin pan with twelve ½-cup cups. Cut the 3 tablespoons butter into 12 pieces and put 1 piece in each muffin cup. Place the muffin pan in a shallow baking pan and brown the butter in the oven, about 5 minutes. Pour ¼ cup batter into each muffin cup and bake, rotating the pan halfway through cooking, until the puddings are puffed and golden brown, 23 to 25 minutes.

Rosemary Beef Fillet

SERVES 8 TO 10
ACTIVE TIME: 20 MINUTES ■ START TO FINISH: 1¼ HOURS

■ How can something so impressive be so easy? This perfect party dish, which can be served warm or at room temperature, gets a piney perfume from the fresh rosemary sprigs snuggled next to the roast. Whole-grain mustard offers a lively counterpoint to the meat's richness. ■

1 (3½-pound) trimmed and tied center-cut beef
   tenderloin roast, at room temperature
4 teaspoons kosher salt
1 teaspoon freshly ground black pepper
2 garlic cloves, finely chopped
6 (3- to 4-inch-long) fresh rosemary sprigs
3 tablespoons extra-virgin olive oil

ACCOMPANIMENT: whole-grain or Dijon mustard

SPECIAL EQUIPMENT: a 17-by-14-inch flameproof roasting
   pan; an instant-read thermometer

Put a rack in middle of oven and preheat oven to 350°F.

Pat tenderloin dry. Rub on all sides with salt, pepper, and garlic to coat. Tuck rosemary sprigs under strings around roast, leaving a few inches between each.

Straddle roasting pan over two burners, add oil, and heat over high heat until hot but not smoking. Brown tenderloin on all sides, about 10 minutes.

Transfer pan to oven and roast until thermometer inserted diagonally 2 inches into center of meat registers 120°F, 25 to 30 minutes. Transfer beef to a cutting board and let stand for 15 minutes (internal temperature of meat will rise to about 130°F, for medium-rare).

Discard string and rosemary sprigs and slice meat.

COOK'S NOTE

■ The tenderloin can be cooked up to 1 hour ahead. Bring the meat to room temperature and slice just before serving.

Tri-Tip Roast with Parsley–Cherry Tomato Sauce

SERVES 4 TO 6
ACTIVE TIME: 15 MINUTES ■ START TO FINISH: 55 MINUTES

■ The juicy tri-tip comes from the bottom sirloin and is very tender. Even better, it sings with deep basso flavor. The chunky, no-fuss sauce makes just the right partner; it mixes the sweetness and depth of roasted cherry tomatoes with the vitality of fresh parsley, garlic, and red wine vinegar. Because there are only two tri-tips per steer, you may have to order the roast in advance. ■

FOR ROAST
- 1 (2- to 2¼-pound) tri-tip beef roast (also called triangular roast; about 2 inches thick)
- 1½ teaspoons salt
- ¼ teaspoon freshly ground black pepper
- 1 tablespoon olive oil

FOR PARSLEY–CHERRY TOMATO SAUCE
- 1½ pounds (5 cups) cherry tomatoes
- ½ teaspoon salt
- ¼ teaspoon red pepper flakes
- 6 tablespoons extra-virgin olive oil
- 1 cup firmly packed fresh flat-leaf parsley leaves
- 1 garlic clove, sliced
- 1 tablespoon red wine vinegar

SPECIAL EQUIPMENT: an instant-read thermometer

COOK THE ROAST: Put racks in upper and lower thirds of oven and preheat oven to 425°F.

Pat roast dry and sprinkle with salt and pepper. Heat oil in a 10-inch heavy ovenproof skillet, preferably cast-iron, over moderately high heat until hot but not smoking. Sear roast until underside is browned, about 4 minutes.

Turn meat over, transfer skillet to upper rack of oven, and roast until thermometer inserted 2 inches into center of meat registers 120°F, 20 to 25 minutes. Transfer to a cutting board and let stand for 15 minutes (internal temperature of meat will rise to 130° to 135°F, for medium-rare).

MEANWHILE, MAKE THE SAUCE: Toss together tomatoes, salt, red pepper flakes, and ¼ cup oil in a 13-by-9-inch baking dish. Roast on lower oven rack until tomatoes burst and release their juices, about 30 minutes.

Pulse parsley and garlic with vinegar and remaining 2 tablespoons oil in a food processor until chopped. Transfer to a bowl.

Stir tomatoes, with juices, into parsley mixture. Slice roast across the grain and serve with sauce.

COOK'S NOTE
■ Any leftover sauce keeps, covered and refrigerated, for up to 5 days. It is equally tasty on chicken, fish, or pasta.

Wine-Braised Chuck Roast with Onions

SERVES 6
ACTIVE TIME: 40 MINUTES ■ START TO FINISH: 4¾ HOURS

■ This is one of our favorite recipes for weekend cooking: with little effort, you have one fabulous, homey meal and, with the leftovers, which are even better, the makings of another supper later in the week. (We shred any leftover cooked meat and use it for Beef Salad with Potatoes and Cornichons, page 197.) The sliced onions practically melt into the sauce, gently thickening it and infusing it with an allium sweetness. Avoid roasts that are already rolled and tied; they tend to come from the area closer to the neck and take longer to become tender. ■

- 1 (4-pound) boneless beef chuck roast
  Salt and freshly ground black pepper
- 2 tablespoons vegetable oil
- 2 pounds onions (4–6 medium), halved lengthwise and thinly sliced crosswise
- 2 large garlic cloves, finely chopped
- 1 tablespoon tomato paste
- 1 teaspoon chopped fresh thyme
- 1 teaspoon chopped fresh rosemary
- 1½ cups dry white wine
- 1 cup water

GARNISH: chopped fresh flat-leaf parsley
ACCOMPANIMENT: egg noodles

Put a rack in middle of oven and preheat oven to 325°F.

Pat beef dry and rub all over with 1½ teaspoons salt and ½ teaspoon pepper. Heat oil in a 5-quart wide heavy ovenproof pot over moderately high heat until hot but not smoking. Brown beef on all sides, about 15 minutes. Transfer to a plate.

Add onions to pot and cook, stirring frequently, until pale golden, about 10 minutes. Add garlic, tomato paste, thyme, rosemary, ½ teaspoon salt, and ¼ teaspoon pepper and cook, stirring, for 2 minutes. Add wine and water and bring to a boil.

Return beef to pot, cover tightly, and braise in oven, turning once after 1 hour, until beef is very tender, 2½ to 3 hours. Let beef stand, uncovered, in sauce for about 30 minutes.

Meanwhile, increase oven temperature to 350°F.

Transfer beef to a cutting board and cut across the grain into ½-inch-thick slices. Season with salt and pepper and return to sauce. Reheat in oven, covered, for 20 minutes.

Serve meat over noodles, sprinkled with parsley.

COOK'S NOTE

- The beef can be braised up to 5 days ahead. Let it cool in sauce to room temperature, then refrigerate it in the sauce in an airtight container. Slice the meat while still cold. Reheat the sliced beef in the sauce in a covered pot or an ovenproof serving dish covered with foil, in a 350°F oven for about 30 minutes.

BRAISING

When you take a tough, inexpensive cut of meat and braise it—cook it long and slow in a tightly covered pot with a small amount of liquid—it emerges transformed into something meltingly soft and unctuous. Browning the meat before braising creates a chemical change called the Maillard reaction, which produces rich, deep flavor and color. That intensity makes for a better sauce. (It's not the place to cut corners, so don't rush this step.) If you brown the meat in a different pan from the one you braise it in, always use some liquid to deglaze the pan and add it to the meat, since those brown bits in the bottom are full of flavor.

Most of our food editors prefer to braise in the oven rather than on top of the stove because it's easier to regulate the temperature. With the even, indirect heat of an oven, you can, for instance, put a pot roast (which isn't, in fact, roasted, but the most popular braise of all) and walk away for 3 hours. The heaviness of your pot isn't crucial if you are braising in the oven, but it is important on the stovetop; a heavy pot will give you the most even heat.

A fork is the best tool for assessing whether a braise has reached the requisite tender, almost-ready-to-fall-apart stage of doneness. With small cuts like short ribs, simply turn the fork on its side and see if you can cut the meat. When you slide a kitchen fork in and out of a larger cut, it should encounter absolutely no resistance. You will have to slice the piece of meat with a knife, but the slices themselves should be cuttable with a fork.

Oven-Braised Barbecued Brisket

SERVES 8
ACTIVE TIME: 25 MINUTES ■ START TO FINISH: 4 HOURS

■ We love brisket cooked over the smoke and smoldering heat of a barbecue fire, so we developed this oven-braised version, which makes homemade barbecue deliciously feasible. The trick is to use a shallow roasting pan, cover the brisket with parchment paper, and then cover the whole pan tightly with foil (the parchment prevents the foil from reacting with the tomatoey sauce, which would impart a metallic taste). The result is meat so tender it melts in your mouth. It tastes great with creamy coleslaw, corn on the cob, and a basket of hot, fluffy biscuits. For best flavor, make it at least a day in advance. ■

1 (4-pound) beef brisket, preferably "second cut"
1 tablespoon salt
¾ teaspoon freshly ground black pepper
2 tablespoons vegetable oil
1 large onion, halved lengthwise and thinly sliced lengthwise
1 cup Beef Stock (page 153) or store-bought reduced-sodium broth
1 cup tomato sauce
⅓ cup cider vinegar
⅓ cup packed light brown sugar
1 tablespoon Worcestershire sauce

SPECIAL EQUIPMENT: parchment paper

Put a rack in middle of oven and preheat oven to 325°F.

Pat brisket dry and rub salt and pepper all over it. Heat oil in a 12-inch heavy skillet over moderately high heat until hot but not smoking. Add brisket and cook, turning once, until browned on both sides, about 10 minutes. Transfer brisket to a 13-by-9-inch baking dish.

Add onion to skillet and cook over moderate heat, stirring frequently, until browned, 7 to 8 minutes. Add stock and deglaze skillet by boiling, scraping up brown bits, for 1 minute. Stir in remaining ingredients and bring to a simmer, stirring occasionally.

Pour sauce over brisket. Cover meat with a sheet of parchment and cover pan tightly with foil. Braise in oven, turning meat once, until fork-tender, 3 to 3½ hours.

Transfer brisket to a cutting board and slice across the grain. Skim off and discard fat from surface of sauce. Serve sauce spooned over meat.

COOK'S NOTE

■ The brisket is best when made at least 1 day ahead, and it can be made up to 4 days ahead. Cool, uncovered, in the sauce, then refrigerate, covered with parchment and foil. Remove and discard the fat from the surface of the sauce before reheating, covered, in a 350°F oven for 1 hour.

BEEF BRISKET

Brisket is a large flat cut that comes from the chest of a steer, just below the chuck. It's a tough, fatty piece that when cured in a brine is called corned beef. Because it's practically impossible to overcook, brisket has been a favorite of home cooks for generations. Any leftovers reheat well, and they make terrific sandwiches (try them on rye bread slathered with whole-grain mustard).

What's known as the "first cut," "thin cut," or "flat cut" is leaner than the less expensive "second cut," aka the "point cut," "thick cut," or "nose cut." We prefer the second cut because it's more flavorful and succulent. No matter which cut you buy, it should have at least ¼ inch of surface fat on one side. That is what will keep the meat moist during cooking, so don't be tempted to remove it.

Slice the cooked brisket crosswise—that is, against the grain. If you carve it with the grain, it will fall apart.

Veal

Wiener Schnitzel

SERVES 4
ACTIVE TIME: 30 MINUTES ■ START TO FINISH: 30 MINUTES

■ Whether made with the traditional veal or with pork, this Viennese classic is outrageously delicious. The trick is to keep an eagle eye on the cutlets while they're in the hot pan—they cook very quickly. A drizzle of lemony caper butter is the final touch. For the tenderest schnitzel, ask for scaloppine (which means "thinly cut") cut across the grain from the top round. ■

About 1 stick (8 tablespoons) unsalted butter
2 tablespoons capers, rinsed and patted dry
1 teaspoon fresh lemon juice
Salt
1½ pounds veal scaloppine (¼-inch-thick cutlets)
Freshly ground black pepper
3 large eggs
1½ cups fine dry bread crumbs
About 6 tablespoons vegetable oil
1½ teaspoons finely chopped fresh flat-leaf parsley
ACCOMPANIMENT: lemon wedges

Put a rack in middle of oven and preheat oven to 200°F. Line a baking sheet with wax paper.

Melt 3 tablespoons butter in a small saucepan. Stir in capers, lemon juice, and a pinch of salt. Remove from heat and cover loosely to keep warm.

Pat veal dry and season with 1¼ teaspoons salt and ¼ teaspoon pepper. Beat eggs with ¼ teaspoon salt in a pie plate or shallow bowl until combined. Put bread crumbs in another pie plate or bowl. Dip veal, 1 piece at a time, in egg, letting excess drip off, then coat in bread crumbs and place on wax-paper-lined baking sheet. (If it is necessary to stack meat, separate layers with another sheet of wax paper.)

Line a baking sheet with paper towels. Heat 1 tablespoon oil with 1 tablespoon butter in a 12-inch nonstick skillet over moderately high heat until foam subsides. Add 2 or 3 pieces of veal (do not crowd) and cook, turning once, until golden and just cooked through, 45 seconds to 1 minute per side. Transfer to paper-towel-lined baking sheet, in one layer, and keep warm in oven. Cook remaining veal in batches in same manner, adding 1 tablespoon each oil and butter for each batch.

Serve veal drizzled with caper butter and sprinkled with parsley, with lemon wedges alongside.

VARIATIONS

■ PORK SCHNITZEL: Substitute pork tenderloin (1½ pounds) for the veal. Cut the tenderloin into 1-inch-thick slices and pound the pieces between sheets of plastic wrap with the flat side of a meat pounder or with a rolling pin until ¼ inch thick.

■ SCHNITZEL HOLSTEIN: Omit the caper butter and lemon wedges. Mash together ½ stick (4 tablespoons) softened unsalted butter, 2 finely chopped anchovy fillets, 2 tablespoons finely chopped dill pickle, and ¼ teaspoon fresh lemon juice. Fry 4 eggs, sunny-side up, in 1 tablespoon unsalted butter in a 10-inch skillet. Serve each cutlet topped with an egg and a dollop of anchovy butter, sprinkled with the parsley.

Veal Bocconcini with Porcini and Rosemary

SERVES 4
ACTIVE TIME: 35 MINUTES ■ START TO FINISH: 1¾ HOURS

■ Though you may associate bocconcini with the tiny mozzarella balls sold at Italian markets, the word simply means "little bites"—the veal in this stew is cut into bite-sized pieces. Artist Wendy Artin shared this rich braised dish, which captures the unpretentious yet sophisticated flavors of Rome, her adopted home. Dried porcini mushrooms and rosemary offer rusticity, while a single chile casts its sparkle over the dish. Like all braises, this one is better made a day ahead. ■

1¼ ounces (1¼ cups) dried porcini mushrooms, rinsed
1½ cups warm water
1¾ pounds boneless veal shoulder, cut into 1-inch cubes
¼ cup extra-virgin olive oil

3 tablespoons all-purpose flour

1 cup dry white wine

½ cup heavy cream

½ cup whole milk

8 soft sun-dried tomatoes (not packed in oil), cut crosswise into ⅛-inch-thick slices

1 (1½-inch-long) fresh hot chile, such as Thai or serrano, halved crosswise

2 (4-inch-long) fresh rosemary sprigs

¾ teaspoon salt

Soak porcini in warm water in a small bowl until softened, about 20 minutes. Lift porcini out, squeezing excess liquid back into bowl, rinse (to remove any grit), and cut into ½-inch pieces. Pour soaking liquid through a sieve lined with a dampened paper towel into another small bowl.

Pat veal dry. Heat oil in a 4- to 5-quart heavy pot over moderately high heat until hot but not smoking. Toss one quarter of veal in flour, shake off excess flour, and brown veal, turning occasionally, until golden brown, about 3 minutes. Transfer with a slotted spoon to a bowl. Coat and brown remaining veal in 3 batches in same manner.

Add wine to pot and deglaze by boiling, scraping up brown bits, for 1 minute. Stir in veal, along with any juices accumulated in bowl, porcini, soaking liquid, cream, milk, tomatoes, chile, and rosemary sprigs, bring to a simmer, and simmer, partially covered, stirring occasionally, until veal is very tender, about 1¼ hours.

Discard rosemary sprigs and chile and stir in salt.

COOK'S NOTE

■ The stew can be made up to 1 day ahead. Cool, uncovered, then refrigerate, covered. Bring to room temperature before reheating over moderate heat, stirring occasionally.

Veal Chops with Radicchio, White Beans, and Rosemary

SERVES 2
ACTIVE TIME: 30 MINUTES ■ START TO FINISH: 30 MINUTES

■ Radicchio offers a welcome bite against the butteriness of tender veal chops, while white beans offer a welcome alternative to the usual mashed potatoes, rice, or noodles. Best of all, the dish takes just half an hour to pull together. ■

4 garlic cloves
Salt

¼ cup olive oil

1 teaspoon chopped fresh rosemary
Freshly ground black pepper

2 (½-inch-thick) veal loin chops (14 ounces total)

10 ounces radicchio, leaves torn into 2- to 3-inch pieces (about 6 cups)

⅔ cup canned small white beans, rinsed and drained

4 teaspoons red wine vinegar

1 cup Chicken Stock (page 153) or store-bought reduced-sodium broth

1 teaspoon cornstarch

Mince 2 garlic cloves and mash to a paste with ½ teaspoon salt, using side of a large heavy knife. Transfer to a shallow bowl and stir in 2 tablespoons oil, ½ teaspoon rosemary, and ½ teaspoon pepper. Add veal and turn to coat.

Finely chop remaining 2 garlic cloves. Heat remaining 2 tablespoons oil in a 12-inch heavy skillet over moderate heat until hot but not smoking. Add veal and cook, turning once, until golden and just cooked through, 5 to 6 minutes. Transfer to a plate and cover loosely with foil to keep warm.

Add chopped garlic to skillet and cook over moderate heat, stirring, until golden, about 30 seconds. Add radicchio and beans and cook, stirring, until radicchio begins to wilt, about 2 minutes. Stir in vinegar and cook until most of it is evaporated, about 1 minute.

Whisk together stock and cornstarch, add to bean mixture, and bring to a boil, scraping up brown bits from bottom of skillet, then boil until sauce is slightly thickened and liquid is reduced by about two thirds, 6 to 8 minutes. Remove from heat and stir in remaining ½ teaspoon rosemary, ¼ teaspoon salt, and ½ teaspoon pepper.

Serve veal with radicchio and beans.

COOK'S NOTE

■ The recipe can be doubled: Cook the chops in 2 batches and reduce the radicchio-broth mixture for 8 to 10 minutes.

Braised Veal Shoulder with Bacon and Thyme

SERVES 6
ACTIVE TIME: 25 MINUTES ■ START TO FINISH: 3 HOURS

■ Meaty, well-marbled, and full of flavor, veal shoulder is an ideal cut for braising. It's also very reasonably priced. This veal roast, cooked with a classic French mirepoix (a mixture of diced carrots, onions, celery, and herbs) and wine, is the epitome of tender comfort food. ■

1 (4-pound) boneless veal shoulder roast, rolled and tied
2 teaspoons salt
1 teaspoon freshly ground black pepper
1 tablespoon olive oil
2 bacon slices, chopped
2 carrots, quartered
2 celery ribs, quartered
1 medium onion, quartered
2 garlic cloves
3 fresh thyme sprigs
1 cup dry white wine
1 cup Beef Stock (page 153) or store-bought reduced-sodium broth
1 cup water

Put a rack in middle of oven and preheat oven to 350°F.

Pat veal dry and sprinkle on all sides with salt and pepper. Heat oil in a 5- to 6-quart wide heavy pot over moderately high heat until hot but not smoking. Add veal and cook, turning occasionally, until browned on all sides, about 10 minutes. Transfer to a platter.

Reduce heat to moderately low, add bacon to pot, and cook, stirring frequently, until fat is rendered, 3 to 4 minutes.

Meanwhile, pulse carrots, celery, onion, and garlic in a food processor until finely chopped.

Add vegetable mixture and thyme to bacon and cook, stirring occasionally, until vegetables are softened and beginning to brown, 8 to 10 minutes. Add wine and deglaze pot by boiling, scraping up any brown bits, for 1 minute, then boil until liquid is reduced by half, 5 to 7 minutes. Add veal, along with any juices accumulated on platter, stock, and water and return to a boil.

Tightly cover pot and braise veal in oven, turning twice, until very tender, 2½ to 3 hours.

Transfer meat to a cutting board. Discard thyme. Cut off and discard strings and cut meat across the grain into ½-inch-thick slices. Serve with sauce.

COOK'S NOTE

■ The veal can be braised up to 2 days ahead. Cool the sliced veal and the sauce, uncovered, then refrigerate the meat in the sauce in an airtight container. Reheat in a tightly covered pot in a 350°F oven for about 30 minutes.

Osso Buco with Mushroom Sauce

SERVES 6 TO 8
ACTIVE TIME: 1 HOUR ■ START TO FINISH: 4 HOURS

■ A nice change of pace from the usual osso buco, this version features a luxurious sauce made from portobello, cremini, and shiitake mushrooms. Served over egg noodles, rice, or mashed potatoes, the meaty veal shanks and their sauce are practically a one-dish dinner. ■

8 (12- to 16-ounce) meaty cross-cut veal shanks (osso buco; 6–8 pounds total), tied

Salt and freshly ground black pepper
¾ cup plus 1 tablespoon all-purpose flour
¾ stick (6 tablespoons) unsalted butter,
     1 tablespoon softened
5 tablespoons extra-virgin olive oil
1½ pounds onions, halved lengthwise and
     thinly sliced lengthwise
3 celery ribs, thinly sliced
3 (1-by-3-inch) strips lemon zest, removed
     with a vegetable peeler
2 cups dry vermouth
1 cup water
1 pound cremini or white mushrooms, trimmed
     and cut into ¼-inch-thick slices
¾ pound shiitake mushrooms, stems discarded,
     caps cut into ¼-inch-thick slices
¾ pound portobello mushrooms, stems discarded,
     caps cut into ¼-inch-thick slices
1 teaspoon dried thyme, crumbled
3 tablespoons fresh lemon juice
2 tablespoons finely chopped fresh flat-leaf
     parsley

ACCOMPANIMENT: egg noodles, rice, or mashed potatoes
SPECIAL EQUIPMENT: a 17-by-14-inch flameproof roasting
     pan; parchment paper

Put a rack in middle of oven and preheat oven to
325°F.

Pat shanks dry and sprinkle with 2 teaspoons salt
and 1 teaspoon pepper. Dredge shanks in ¾ cup flour
and shake off excess.

Heat 1 tablespoon butter and 1 tablespoon oil in a
12-inch heavy skillet over moderately high heat until foam subsides. Add 4 shanks and brown, turning
once, for 8 to 12 minutes. Transfer to roasting pan.
Wipe out skillet and brown remaining 4 shanks in 1
tablespoon butter and 1 tablespoon oil in same manner; transfer to roasting pan.

Wipe out skillet again and heat 1 tablespoon butter and 1 tablespoon oil until foam subsides. Add
onions, celery, and zest and cook, stirring occasionally, until vegetables are soft and pale golden, about
10 minutes. Stir in 1 cup vermouth and water, then
spoon mixture around veal shanks.

Cover shanks with parchment paper and cover
pan tightly with foil. Braise shanks in oven until very
tender, 2½ to 3½ hours.

Meanwhile, heat 2 tablespoons butter and remaining 2 tablespoons oil in a deep 12-inch skillet over
moderately high heat until foam subsides. Add mushrooms, thyme, 1 teaspoon salt, and ½ teaspoon pepper
and cook, stirring constantly, until mushrooms begin
to give off liquid, about 3 minutes. Stir in remaining
1 cup vermouth and 2 tablespoons lemon juice and
cook, stirring occasionally, until liquid is reduced to
about ½ cup, 8 to 10 minutes. Remove from heat.

Transfer shanks to a platter (reserve sauce in pan)
and cover loosely with foil to keep warm.

Rub together remaining 1 tablespoon softened
butter and 1 tablespoon flour in a small bowl to
form a paste (*beurre manié*). Straddle roasting pan
over two burners and bring sauce to a boil. Whisk
in *beurre manié*, then reduce heat and simmer for 1
minute. Stir in mushrooms, remaining 1 tablespoon
lemon juice, and parsley and simmer for 1 minute.
Season with salt and pepper.

Serve osso buco and sauce with noodles, rice, or
mashed potatoes.

COOK'S NOTES

- The shanks can be braised up to 3 days ahead.
  Cool in the sauce, uncovered, then refrigerate
  in the sauce, covered. Reheat the shanks before
  proceeding.
- The mushrooms can be cooked up to 1 day ahead. Cool,
  uncovered, then refrigerate, covered; simmer in the
  sauce until heated through.

Sweet-and-Sour
Veal Tongue

SERVES 6
ACTIVE TIME: 45 MINUTES ■ START TO FINISH: 4 HOURS

■ This is not the sticky sweet-and-sour sauce of Chi-
nese-American restaurants, but rather the thinner,
more complex sauce of Jewish tradition. The recipe was
adapted from one that *Gourmet*'s test kitchen director
Ruth Cousineau's grandmother Sadie Cutler cooked at
the kosher hotel in upstate New York that she and her
husband ran. Guests traveled from New York City and
beyond to relax in the sulfur springs, enjoy the fresh

mountain air, and invigorate their taste buds with seven-course kosher meals. The tender veal tongue is bathed in a sweet rosy sauce that has just the right amount of acidity. Be sure to seek out tangy California apricots for this dish—the pale, Turkish 'cots are cloying and will upset the dish's balance. ■

2 veal tongues (about 2½ pounds total)
8 cups cold water
1 medium onion, quartered
1 carrot, quartered
1 celery rib, quartered
 Salt
1 Turkish bay leaf or ½ California bay leaf
6 black peppercorns
1 cup tomato sauce
6 ounces dried California apricots
6 tablespoons sugar
2½ tablespoons fresh lemon juice, or to taste
¼ teaspoon freshly ground black pepper
GARNISH: finely chopped fresh flat-leaf parsley
SPECIAL EQUIPMENT: parchment paper

Put tongues in a 4- to 6-quart pot, add water, onion, carrot, celery, 1 teaspoon salt, bay leaf, and peppercorns, and bring to a boil. Reduce heat and simmer, covered, until meat is tender, about 1½ hours. Remove from heat and cool tongues in cooking liquid, uncovered, about 1 hour.

Transfer tongues to a cutting board; reserve cooking liquid. Peel skins from tongues and trim off any excess fat.

Pour cooking liquid through a sieve into a bowl; discard solids. Transfer 2¼ cups cooking liquid to a 2-quart heavy saucepan (discard remainder). Add tomato sauce, apricots, sugar, lemon juice, 1 teaspoon salt, and pepper. Bring to a simmer and simmer until apricots are very tender and sauce is slightly thickened, 20 to 30 minutes.

Put a rack in middle of oven and preheat oven to 350°F.

Cut tongues crosswise into ¼-inch-thick slices. Arrange meat in an even layer, overlapping slices, in an 11-by-7-inch shallow baking dish and cover with sauce. Cover meat directly with a piece of parchment, then cover baking dish tightly with foil. Braise in oven until tongue is very tender, about 45 minutes.

Serve tongue sprinkled with parsley.

COOK'S NOTE

■ The tongue can be made up to 2 days ahead. Cool in the sauce, uncovered, then refrigerate, covered with parchment and foil. Reheat, covered, in a 350°F oven for 30 minutes.

Offal

Calf's Liver with Bacon and Onions

SERVES 4
ACTIVE TIME: 35 MINUTES ■ START TO FINISH: 35 MINUTES

■ Classic liver and onions gets a lip-smacking twist with the addition of bacon. Ask the butcher for the freshest calf's liver available, since it can vary in quality. Soaking the liver in milk helps mellow and soften its flavor. ■

1 pound calf's liver (¼ inch thick), cut into 4 pieces
1 cup whole milk
8 bacon slices, halved crosswise
3 medium onions, halved lengthwise and cut lengthwise into ¼-inch-thick slices
 Salt and freshly ground black pepper
½ cup all-purpose flour

Soak liver in milk in a bowl for 20 minutes.

Meanwhile, cook bacon in a 12-inch nonstick skillet over moderate heat, turning occasionally, until crisp. Transfer bacon to paper towels to drain, and transfer all but 2½ tablespoons fat from skillet to a small bowl.

Add onions to fat remaining in skillet, season with salt and pepper to taste, and cook, stirring frequently, until golden brown, 12 to 15 minutes. Transfer to another bowl, add bacon, and cover to keep warm.

Drain liver (discard milk) and pat dry. Stir together flour, 1 teaspoon salt, and ½ teaspoon pepper on a sheet of wax paper. Dredge liver in flour, shaking off excess.

Add 1½ tablespoons reserved bacon fat to skillet and heat over moderately high heat until hot but not smoking. Add liver and cook, turning once, until browned but still pink inside, about 4 minutes. Serve liver topped with onions and bacon.

Sweetbreads Meunière

SERVES 4 AS A MAIN COURSE, 8 AS A FIRST COURSE
ACTIVE TIME: 1¾ HOURS ■ START TO FINISH: 3¾ HOURS
(INCLUDES SOAKING TIME)

■ Because sweetbreads—the lobed thymus gland (or sometimes the pancreas) of a calf, lamb, or cow—are so delicately flavored, they are a great introduction to organ meats. To make them firmer, sweetbreads are usually weighted, but here, just a quick sauté gives perfect results. The sweetbreads emerge tender but not wobbly, and the sherry and brown butter enhance their nuttiness. Adapted from a dish served during the 1970s at the Compound in Santa Fe, New Mexico, the sweetbreads pair well with broccolini and parsley potatoes. ■

2 pounds veal sweetbreads
1¼ sticks (10 tablespoons) unsalted butter, cut into tablespoons
1 medium onion, sliced
1 Turkish bay leaf or ½ California bay leaf
1 whole clove
Salt
8 cups water
½ pound chanterelle or cremini mushrooms, trimmed
Freshly ground black pepper
⅓ cup finely chopped shallots
⅓ cup dry sherry, or to taste
2 tablespoons fresh lemon juice, or to taste
¼ cup chopped fresh flat-leaf parsley

SOAK THE SWEETBREADS: Rinse sweetbreads well under cold running water. Soak in a large bowl of ice and cold water in the refrigerator, changing water once or twice if water becomes pink, for at least 2 hours; drain.

MAKE THE BROWN BUTTER: Melt 1 stick (8 tablespoons) butter in a 2-cup to 1-quart heavy saucepan over moderate heat. Cook, stirring occasionally, until butter is golden with a nutlike fragrance and flecks on bottom of pan turn a rich caramel brown, 10 to 20 minutes. Butter will initially foam, then subside, and a thicker foam will appear and cover the surface just before butter begins to brown; stir more frequently toward end of cooking. Pour brown butter through a fine-mesh sieve into a heatproof measuring cup (you will have 5 to 6 tablespoons).

COOK THE SWEETBREADS AND MUSHROOMS: Combine onion, bay leaf, clove, 1 tablespoon salt, and water in a 3- to 4-quart saucepan and bring to a simmer. Add sweetbreads and poach, uncovered, at a bare simmer for 20 minutes.

Transfer sweetbreads with a slotted spoon to a bowl of cold water to stop the cooking. Pour 1 cup poaching liquid through a sieve into a small bowl and reserve for sauce; discard remaining poaching liquid and solids.

Drain sweetbreads and pat dry. Using a paring knife, cut away any fat, then pull away as much membrane and connective tissue as possible while separating sweetbreads into roughly 2-inch pieces. Arrange sweetbreads on a tray lined with paper towels and blot tops with more paper towels.

Tear any large chanterelles lengthwise into 2 or 4 pieces (or quarter cremini lengthwise).

Put a rack in middle of oven and preheat oven to lowest temperature (175° to 200°F, or Warm).

Heat a 12-inch heavy skillet over high heat until a drop of water evaporates on contact, 2 to 3 minutes. Meanwhile, season half of sweetbreads on both sides with ¼ teaspoon salt and ¼ teaspoon pepper.

Add 2 tablespoons brown butter to skillet, swirling to cover bottom (butter will smoke), and add seasoned sweetbreads, without crowding. Reduce heat to moderately high and cook, undisturbed, until undersides are golden brown, 2 to 3 minutes. Turn sweetbreads and cook, undisturbed, until golden brown on second side, 2 to 3 minutes. Transfer browned sweetbreads with tongs to a baking sheet, arranging them in one layer, and keep warm in oven. Wipe skillet clean, season remaining sweetbreads, and brown in 2 more tablespoons brown butter in same manner. Transfer to baking sheet.

Add remaining brown butter to hot skillet, then add mushrooms and cook, stirring occasionally, until browned on edges, 3 to 5 minutes. Add shallots,

¼ teaspoon salt, and ¼ teaspoon pepper and cook, stirring, for 1 minute. Add sherry, lemon juice, and reserved poaching liquid, bring to a boil, scraping up brown bits, and boil until mushrooms are tender and liquid is reduced by half, about 5 minutes. Add parsley and remaining 2 tablespoons butter, remove from heat, and swirl or stir until butter is incorporated.

Serve sweetbreads topped with mushrooms and sauce.

COOK'S NOTES

- The sweetbreads can be soaked for up to 1 day.
- The sweetbreads can be poached and trimmed up to 1 day ahead. Refrigerate the sweetbreads, wrapped in plastic wrap; refrigerate the reserved poaching liquid separately.
- The brown butter can be made ahead and refrigerated, covered, for up to 2 weeks.

Pork

Chicken-Fried Pork with Milk Gravy

SERVES 4
ACTIVE TIME: 40 MINUTES ■ START TO FINISH: 1 HOUR

■ Inspired by a popular item served at the Rock Café in Stroud, Oklahoma, our chicken-fried pork is thin and juicy. A light coating of egg and flour produces a shatteringly crisp crust that softens ever so slightly under the savory milk gravy. Serve mashed potatoes on the side, and you'll be in diner heaven. ■

    4 (½-inch-thick) boneless pork rib chops (1½ pounds
       total)
       Salt and freshly ground black pepper
    2 cups plus 3 tablespoons all-purpose flour
    1 large egg
    3¼ cups whole milk
    2 cups vegetable oil for shallow-frying
SPECIAL EQUIPMENT: a meat pounder with a rough-
    textured side

Pound pork chops on both sides with meat pounder until ¼ inch thick. Season with salt and pepper and cut into 3-inch pieces.

Whisk together 2 cups flour, 1 teaspoon salt, and 1 teaspoon pepper in a shallow dish. Whisk together egg, ¾ cup milk, ¾ teaspoon salt, and ½ teaspoon pepper in another shallow dish. Dip pork pieces in egg mixture to coat, then dredge in flour and transfer to a large rack set on a baking sheet. Let pork stand, uncovered, at room temperature for 15 minutes.

Put a rack in middle of oven and preheat oven to 250°F.

Heat oil in a deep 10-inch heavy skillet, preferably cast-iron, over high heat until hot but not smoking. Fry pork in batches, without crowding, turning once, until golden, about 4 minutes per batch. Transfer to paper towels to drain, then keep pork warm on a clean baking sheet in oven.

Pour off all but 2 tablespoons oil into a heatproof bowl, leaving any brown bits in bottom of skillet. Whisk remaining 3 tablespoons flour into oil in skillet to make a roux and cook over moderate heat, whisking constantly, for 3 minutes. Bring to a boil and whisk in remaining 2½ cups milk, then reduce heat and simmer, whisking occasionally, until thickened, about 5 minutes.

Season gravy with salt and pepper and serve over pork.

Roasted Pork Chops with Hard Cider Jus

SERVES 8
ACTIVE TIME: 30 MINUTES ■ START TO FINISH: 45 MINUTES

■ One bite of these chops, and it will be easy to imagine yourself in the Gallic countryside on a brisk autumn evening. Look for a hard cider that's on the sweeter side and not too dry; it makes a fine counterpoint to the meaty chops and shallots. (If you can't get a French cider, Woodchuck Amber from Vermont works well.) ■

    8 (1-inch-thick) pork rib chops (4 pounds total)
       Salt and freshly ground black pepper

2½ tablespoons unsalted butter

1 pound large shallots (about 8), bulbs separated if necessary, halved lengthwise, and peeled, leaving root ends intact

1 cup hard cider

SPECIAL EQUIPMENT: an instant-read thermometer

Put a rack in lower third of oven and preheat oven to 450°F.

Pat pork chops dry and sprinkle on both sides with 1 teaspoon salt and 1¼ teaspoons pepper. Heat 1½ tablespoons butter in a 12-inch heavy skillet over moderately high heat until foam subsides. Brown chops in 3 batches, turning once, about 6 minutes per batch. Transfer with tongs to a large baking sheet.

Add shallots and remaining tablespoon butter to skillet and cook over moderate heat, turning occasionally, until shallots are golden brown and tender, 6 to 8 minutes. Add cider and bring to a boil, scraping up brown bits, then boil until reduced to about ¾ cup, about 3 minutes.

Spoon shallots and sauce around chops. Roast until thermometer inserted horizontally into center of 1 chop (without touching bone) registers 145° to 150°F, 5 to 9 minutes. Cover chops loosely with foil and let stand for 5 minutes (internal temperature of chops will rise to 155°F).

Serve chops with shallots and sauce.

Pork Chops with Gingered Plum Sauce

SERVES 4
ACTIVE TIME: 40 MINUTES ■ START TO FINISH:
40 MINUTES

■ Slices of plums zinged with a bit of ginger offer a sweet-tart accompaniment to pork chops. ■

4 (1-inch-thick) pork rib chops (about 2½ pounds total)

¾ teaspoon salt

½ teaspoon freshly ground black pepper

1 tablespoon vegetable oil

¼ cup soy sauce

2 tablespoons sherry vinegar or red wine vinegar

2 tablespoons packed light brown sugar

1 tablespoon finely grated peeled fresh ginger

1 tablespoon finely chopped garlic

1 pound firm but ripe black plums (about 4) or Italian prune plums (about 8), pitted and cut into 1-inch-wide wedges

¼ cup Chicken Stock (page 153) or store-bought reduced-sodium broth

1 tablespoon red currant jelly, or to taste

1 tablespoon cold unsalted butter

Put a rack in middle of oven and preheat oven to 300°F.

Pat pork dry and sprinkle with salt and pepper. Heat a 12-inch heavy skillet over moderately high heat until hot, 2 to 3 minutes. Add oil, swirling to coat bottom, then add pork and cook, turning once, until golden brown, about 6 minutes.

Transfer chops with tongs to a small baking pan (reserve fat in skillet) and bake until just cooked through, 8 to 12 minutes. Transfer to a platter (reserve any juices in baking pan).

Meanwhile, add soy sauce, vinegar, brown sugar, ginger, and garlic to skillet and bring to a boil over moderately high heat, scraping up brown bits. Add plums, reduce heat to moderate, and cook, uncovered, stirring frequently, until plums are tender but not falling apart and sauce is slightly thickened, 5 to 10 minutes.

Stir stock, jelly, and any meat juices from baking pan into sauce and bring to a simmer. Add butter, swirling skillet until butter is incorporated and sauce is slightly thickened.

Spoon sauce over chops.

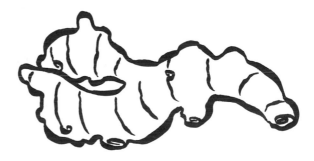

Balsamic-Glazed Pork Chops

SERVES 4
ACTIVE TIME: 25 MINUTES ■ START TO FINISH: 25 MINUTES

■ Here is an astonishing little recipe that shows what a power ingredient like balsamic vinegar can do. Caramelized shallots and the dark vinegar glaze give these chops intriguing sweet, sour, dark, and syrupy notes. ■

4 (¾-inch-thick) center-cut pork loin chops (about 2 pounds total)
Salt and freshly ground black pepper
2 tablespoons olive oil
8 small shallots, peeled, leaving root ends intact, and quartered
⅔ cup balsamic vinegar
1½ teaspoons sugar

Pat pork dry and sprinkle with ½ teaspoon salt and ¼ teaspoon pepper.

Heat oil in a 12-inch heavy skillet over moderately high heat until hot but not smoking. Cook pork, in 2 batches if necessary, with shallots, turning pork once and stirring shallots occasionally, until pork is browned and shallots are golden brown and tender, about 5 minutes. Transfer pork with tongs to a plate, leaving shallots in skillet.

Add vinegar, sugar, ½ teaspoon salt, and ¼ teaspoon pepper to skillet and cook, stirring, until sugar is dissolved and liquid has thickened slightly, about 1 minute. Reduce heat to moderate and return pork, along with any juices accumulated on plate, to skillet, turning 2 or 3 times to coat with sauce. Cook, turning once, until pork is just cooked through, about 3 minutes.

Transfer pork to a platter and boil sauce until thickened and syrupy, 1 to 2 minutes. Pour sauce over pork.

Pork Chops with Pomegranate and Fennel Salsa

SERVES 4
ACTIVE TIME: 40 MINUTES ■ START TO FINISH: 40 MINUTES

■ Pomegranates are available primarily from October to January, making this a chilly weather dish. The salsa is also tasty with lamb. ■

1 large fennel bulb (1 pound)
3 tablespoons vegetable oil
1 cup pomegranate seeds (from 1 large pomegranate; see page 434)
2 scallions, finely chopped
¼ cup chopped fresh cilantro
1 teaspoon seasoned rice vinegar
2 teaspoons mild honey
¼ teaspoon salt
4 (½- to ¾-inch-thick) pork chops (2 pounds total)
Freshly ground black pepper

Cut off and discard fennel stalks. Halve fennel bulb lengthwise, core it, and cut into ¼-inch pieces.

Heat 2 tablespoons oil in a 12-inch heavy skillet over moderate heat until hot but not smoking. Add fennel and cook, stirring, until just tender, 6 to 8 minutes. Transfer to a bowl and stir in pomegranate seeds, scallions, cilantro, vinegar, honey, and ¼ teaspoon salt (set skillet aside).

Pat pork chops dry and season with salt and pepper. Heat remaining tablespoon oil in skillet over moderately high heat until hot but not smoking. Add chops and cook, turning once, until deep golden and just cooked through, 7 to 9 minutes. Transfer chops to a platter and let stand, loosely covered with foil, for 5 minutes.

Serve chops topped with pomegranate and fennel salsa.

COOK'S NOTE
■ The salsa can be made up to 3 hours ahead and refrigerated, covered. Bring to room temperature before serving.

Carnitas

SERVES 4 TO 6
ACTIVE TIME: 45 MINUTES ■ START TO FINISH: 8¼ HOURS
(INCLUDES MARINATING)

■ Well-browned pieces of pork that have been simmered in a combination of lard and water, *carnitas* are served all over central Mexico. They're ridiculously good—full of flavor and tender, with beguiling crisp bits here and there. Adding a small amount of milk to the lard helps sweeten the meat and caramelize its edges. ■

FOR MARINADE AND PORK
1 navel orange
2 pounds boneless pork shoulder (not lean), cut into 1- to 1½-inch cubes
1 small onion, cut into 8 wedges and layers separated
2 garlic cloves, finely chopped
2 teaspoons kosher salt
½ teaspoon freshly ground black pepper
1 teaspoon chopped fresh thyme
2 Turkish bay leaves or 1 California bay leaf
FOR COOKING PORK
1 pound (2 cups) lard
2 cups water
½ cup whole milk
ACCOMPANIMENTS: warm corn tortillas; store-bought fresh tomato or tomatillo salsa or Roasted Tomatillo Salsa (page 418)

MARINATE THE PORK: Peel large wide strips of zest, including some white pith, from orange with a vegetable peeler. Halve orange and squeeze juice into a large bowl; add zest.

Add pork and remaining marinade ingredients and toss. Marinate, covered and refrigerated, for at least 6 hours.

COOK THE PORK: Melt lard in a 4- to 5-quart wide heavy pot over moderate heat. Add water, milk, and pork, with marinade, bring to a simmer, and simmer gently, uncovered, skimming foam, until pork is very tender, about 1¼ hours.

Increase heat to moderately high and boil pork (water and juices will evaporate and meat will start to brown), stirring occasionally, until meat is golden brown, 30 to 50 minutes.

With a slotted spoon, transfer pork, along with orange zest and onions, to paper towels to drain briefly; discard bay leaf and fat. Cut pork into bite-sized pieces if necessary and serve with tortillas and salsa.

COOK'S NOTE
■ The pork can marinate for up to 24 hours.

Pork and Tomatillo Stew

SERVES 6
ACTIVE TIME: 45 MINUTES ■ START TO FINISH: 2¾ HOURS

■ An easy recipe that delivers big results, this tasty stew of tender pork and black beans from editor in chief Ruth Reichl balances the heat of jalapeños with the tang of oranges, tomatillos, and tomatoes. Served with rice and lime-spiked sour cream, a big batch is perfect for an open-house party. You may need to order pork shoulder ahead from your butcher. ■

2 pounds boneless pork shoulder, trimmed and cut into 1½-inch cubes
Salt and freshly ground black pepper
¼ cup vegetable oil
8 large garlic cloves
1 (12-ounce) bottle dark beer
1½ cups fresh orange juice (from about 5 oranges)
1 pound tomatillos, husked, rinsed under warm water, and quartered
1 (28-ounce) can whole tomatoes in juice, drained, juice reserved, and chopped
2 large onions, coarsely chopped
1 bunch fresh cilantro, root ends discarded, leaves and stems chopped
2 jalapeño chiles, chopped, including seeds
1 (14- to 19-ounce) can black beans, rinsed and drained
2 tablespoons fresh lime juice
1 (8-ounce) container sour cream
ACCOMPANIMENT: white rice

Pat pork dry and season with 1 teaspoon salt and ½ teaspoon pepper. Heat oil in a 6- to 8-quart heavy pot over moderately high heat until hot but not smoking. Add garlic and cook, stirring, until golden, about

2 minutes. Add pork in batches, without crowding, and cook, turning occasionally, until browned on all sides; transfer to a large bowl.

Meanwhile, combine beer, orange juice, tomatillos, and tomatoes with juice in a 5- to 6-quart pot and bring to a boil. Reduce heat and simmer until tomatillos and tomatoes are soft, about 20 minutes. Remove from heat.

When pork is browned, pour off all but 1 tablespoon oil from pot. Add onions and cook over moderate heat, stirring occasionally, until soft, about 8 minutes. Add tomatillo mixture, pork, cilantro, jalapeños, 1 teaspoon salt, and ½ teaspoon pepper and cook, stirring and scraping up brown bits, until well combined. Bring to a boil, reduce heat, and simmer, partially covered, stirring occasionally, until meat is very tender, about 2 hours.

Season stew with salt and pepper. Add black beans and simmer, uncovered, stirring occasionally, for 10 minutes.

Stir lime juice into sour cream. Serve stew with rice, with sour cream on the side.

COOK'S NOTE

■ The stew can be made up to 2 days ahead. Cool, uncovered, then refrigerate, covered. Reheat over moderately high heat until warmed through, about 30 minutes.

TOMATILLOS

Native to Mexico and Guatemala, tomatillos bring a complex fruity tartness to Mexican salsas and stews. Although they are sometimes called Mexican green tomatoes (they're known as *tomates verdes* in much of Mexico), they're only distantly related to backyard beefsteaks. Like their first cousins, the Cape gooseberry and the decorative Chinese lantern, tomatillos are enclosed in papery husks. Choose specimens that have filled out their husks and are firm; stored in a plastic bag, they'll keep for a couple of weeks in the refrigerator. Pull the husks off before using and rinse the fruit under warm water to remove any stickiness.

Jungle Curry with Pork and Eggplant

SERVES 4
ACTIVE TIME: 30 MINUTES ■ START TO FINISH: 30 MINUTES

■ Sometimes known as "country" curries, jungle curries from the north of Thailand are traditionally made with game and whatever vegetables villagers can grow or find in the wild. They do not contain the coconut milk that's common to the dishes of southern Thailand. Although the ingredients for this version can be foraged from any supermarket, the combination of tender pork and eggplant, accented by green beans, baby corn, ginger, and basil, has the fiery taste of authenticity. If you prefer your food less spicy, use a smaller amount of curry paste. ■

6 tablespoons vegetable oil
1–1½ tablespoons Thai red curry paste
1½ pounds pork tenderloin, halved lengthwise and sliced crosswise ¼ inch thick
1 (1-pound) eggplant, cut into 1-inch cubes
⅓ cup small matchsticks peeled fresh ginger (from a 4-inch piece)
¼ pound green beans, trimmed and cut into 1-inch pieces
8 ears canned baby corn, rinsed, drained, and halved lengthwise
1½ cups Chicken Stock (page 153) or store-bought reduced-sodium broth
2 tablespoons Asian fish sauce
1 (5-inch-long) mild red chile, thinly sliced
Salt
1 cup loosely packed fresh basil leaves
ACCOMPANIMENT: jasmine rice

Heat 2 tablespoons oil in a well-seasoned 14-inch flat-bottomed wok or a 12-inch heavy skillet over moderate heat until warm, about 30 seconds. Add curry paste (to taste) and cook, stirring constantly, until fragrant and a shade darker, about 1 minute. Add pork and stir-fry over high heat until no longer pink on the outside, 2 to 3 minutes (pork will not be cooked through). Transfer pork and any juices to a bowl.

Add 2 tablespoons oil to wok and heat over moderately high heat until hot but not smoking. Add eggplant and stir-fry for 1 minute. Drizzle with remaining 2 tablespoons oil and stir-fry until eggplant is lightly browned, about 3 minutes. Add pork with any juices in bowl, ginger, beans, corn, and stock, bring to a simmer, and simmer, stirring, until eggplant is tender, 3 to 5 minutes.

Add fish sauce, chile, and salt to taste and bring to a boil, then remove from heat. Stir in half of basil and scatter remaining basil on top. Serve curry over rice.

Chipotle and Molasses Pork Tenderloin with Green Chile Stew

SERVES 4
ACTIVE TIME: 1 HOUR ■ START TO FINISH: 1¼ HOURS

■ An upscale version of New Mexico's traditional green chile stew, this features a verdant mélange of roasted poblano chiles, hominy, and vegetables topped with tender slices of savory pork tenderloin. A garnish of chopped toasted pumpkin seeds adds another textural dimension. We have Robert McGrath, formerly of the Roaring Fork in Scottsdale, Arizona, to thank for this elegant Southwestern dish. ■

FOR PORK
- 2 (12-ounce) boneless pork tenderloins, trimmed
- ½ teaspoon salt
- ¼ teaspoon freshly ground black pepper
- 2 tablespoons plus 2 teaspoons vegetable oil
- 2 tablespoons molasses (not robust)
- 2 tablespoons finely chopped canned chipotle chiles in adobo sauce

FOR GREEN CHILE STEW
- 1½ pounds poblano chiles (about 8 medium), roasted (see Tips, page 914), peeled, and seeded
- 2 cups Chicken Stock (page 153) or store-bought reduced-sodium broth
- 4 thick bacon slices, coarsely chopped
- ½ cup finely chopped carrot
- 1 cup finely chopped onion
- 2 tablespoons chopped garlic
- 2 cups canned hominy (from two 15-ounce cans), rinsed and drained

- ¾ teaspoon salt
- ¼ teaspoon freshly ground black pepper
- ¼ cup water

GARNISH: green (hulled) pumpkin seeds (*pepitas*), toasted (see Tips, page 911) and chopped
SPECIAL EQUIPMENT: a 17-by-14-inch flameproof roasting pan; an instant-read thermometer

ROAST THE PORK: Put a rack in middle of oven and preheat oven to 400°F. Oil roasting pan.

Pat pork dry and sprinkle with salt and pepper. Heat 2 tablespoons oil in a deep 12-inch heavy skillet over moderately high heat until hot but not smoking. Add pork and cook, turning, until browned on all sides, 6 to 7 minutes. Transfer to roasting pan.

Stir together molasses, chipotles, and remaining 2 teaspoons oil in a small bowl. Brush all over pork. Roast pork until thermometer inserted diagonally into center registers 145°F, about 15 minutes.

MEANWHILE, MAKE THE STEW: Puree poblanos with stock in a blender until smooth.

Cook bacon in cleaned skillet over moderately high heat, stirring, until browned, 2 to 3 minutes. Add carrot and onion and cook, stirring, until lightly browned, about 3 minutes. Add garlic and cook, stirring, until fragrant, about 30 seconds. Add poblano puree, hominy, salt, and pepper and simmer, uncovered, stirring occasionally, until slightly thickened, about 5 minutes.

FINISH THE DISH: Transfer cooked pork to a cutting board and let stand, loosely covered with foil, for 10 minutes.

Meanwhile, straddle roasting pan over two burners, add water, and deglaze by simmering over moderate heat, scraping up brown bits, for 1 minute. Remove from heat.

Cut pork into ½-inch-thick slices. Divide stew among four large shallow bowls and arrange pork on top. Drizzle pan juices over pork and sprinkle with pumpkin seeds.

COOK'S NOTES
- ■ If the pumpkin seeds you buy are toasted and salted, don't toast them again.
- ■ The stew can be made up to 2 days ahead. Cool, uncovered, then refrigerate, covered. Reheat over moderate heat, adding up to ¼ cup water to thin if necessary.

Pork Tenderloin in Paprika Cream

SERVES 4
ACTIVE TIME: 45 MINUTES ■ START TO FINISH: 1¼ HOURS

■ This rich dish gets its depth from *lecsó*, a sort of Hungarian *sofrito* made by sautéing onion, peppers, paprika, and tomatoes in lard. Though *lecsó* is often served on its own in Hungary, we add browned pork and sour cream. It's imperative to simmer the pork very gently so that it doesn't become tough. We like this served over egg noodles or buttered spaetzle. ■

    1½ pounds pork tenderloin, cut into 1½-inch-thick slices
        Salt
    ¼   teaspoon freshly ground black pepper
    ¼   cup lard or vegetable oil
    1   large onion, halved lengthwise and thinly sliced lengthwise
    2   garlic cloves, minced
    3   Italian frying peppers (12 ounces total), cored, seeded, and coarsely chopped
    2   teaspoons sweet paprika
    1   pound plum tomatoes, coarsely chopped
    1¾ cups water
    ½   cup sour cream
    1   tablespoon all-purpose flour

Pat pork dry and sprinkle with 1 teaspoon salt and pepper. Heat 1 tablespoon lard in a 12-inch heavy skillet over moderately high heat until hot but not smoking. Brown pork in 2 batches, turning once, 2 to 4 minutes per batch. Transfer to a plate.

Add remaining 3 tablespoons lard to skillet and reduce heat to moderate. Add onion, garlic, and peppers and cook, stirring frequently, until onion and peppers are beginning to brown, 7 to 8 minutes. Stir in paprika, tomatoes, and 1 teaspoon salt and cook, stirring frequently, until tomatoes have broken down and mixture is very thick, about 15 minutes.

Stir together water, sour cream, and flour in a bowl until smooth. Stir into tomato mixture, bring to a simmer, and simmer, stirring occasionally, until sauce is thickened, about 15 minutes.

Add pork, with any juices accumulated on plate, and simmer gently until meat is just cooked through, about 12 minutes.

Mustard Fennel Pork Loin with Cumberland Pan Sauce

SERVES 8
ACTIVE TIME: 20 MINUTES ■ START TO FINISH: 14¼ HOURS
(INCLUDES MARINATING)

■ Rubbed with mustard and salt seasoned with fennel seeds and bay leaves, this juicy pork loin is served with Cumberland sauce, a British classic that calls for port, red currant jelly, and orange juice and turns almost anything it touches into a celebration. Red currant jelly is a useful pantry item, and it's worth buying the best you can find; it's lovely added to vinaigrettes or brushed on pie shells as a flavorful seal. Wonderful all by itself, the pork becomes even more memorable when you accent it with the crisp cracklings. ■

FOR PORK
    4   Turkish bay leaves or 2 California bay leaves
    1½ tablespoons kosher salt
    1   tablespoon fennel seeds
    1   (4- to 4½-pound) center-cut boneless pork loin roast (3–4 inches in diameter)
    ¼   cup whole-grain mustard
    2   teaspoons olive oil
FOR SAUCE
    ½   cup plus 1 tablespoon water
    ⅓   cup ruby port
    ⅔   cup fresh orange juice (from 2 oranges)
    1½ tablespoons fresh lemon juice
    3   tablespoons red currant jelly
    ¼   teaspoon ground ginger
    ¼   teaspoon salt
    1   tablespoon cornstarch
    1   tablespoon unsalted butter
OPTIONAL ACCOMPANIMENT: Pork Cracklings (recipe follows)

ROAST THE PORK: Discard center vein from bay leaves. Crumble leaves into grinder and pulse with salt and fennel seeds until leaves are finely chopped.

Discard string from roast if tied. Place roast fat side up on a work surface. Holding a thin sharp knife with blade parallel to work surface, make a lengthwise cut about 1½ inches deep into a long side of loin (do not cut all the way through). Open roast at cut and pat dry inside and out. Rub 1 tablespoon mustard all over cut side and sprinkle with 1 teaspoon seasoned salt. Close roast and tie crosswise at 1-inch intervals with string. Rub olive oil evenly over roast, rub with remaining 3 tablespoons mustard, and sprinkle with remaining seasoned salt, pressing lightly to help it adhere.

Oil roasting rack and transfer pork, fat side up, to rack in roasting pan. Marinate, loosely covered and refrigerated, for at least 12 hours.

Let pork stand at room temperature for 30 minutes before roasting.

Meanwhile, put a rack in middle of oven and preheat oven to 450°F.

Roast pork for 25 minutes. Reduce oven temperature to 325°F and roast until thermometer inserted diagonally 2 inches into center of meat registers 145° to 150°F, 35 to 45 minutes. Transfer pork to a platter (set roasting pan aside) and let stand, uncovered, for 25 minutes (temperature of pork will rise 5 to 10 degrees as it stands).

MEANWHILE, MAKE THE SAUCE: Skim off all but 1 tablespoon fat from pan juices. Straddle pan across two burners, add ½ cup water, and deglaze pan by boiling over high heat, scraping up brown bits, for 1 minute. Add port and boil for 1 minute. Add orange and lemon juices, jelly, ginger, and salt and cook, whisking, until jelly is dissolved. Whisk together remaining tablespoon water and cornstarch in a cup, add to pan, whisking, and boil, whisking, for 1 minute. Remove from heat and whisk in butter, then pour sauce through a fine-mesh sieve into a bowl.

Discard string from pork. Slice pork and serve with sauce and cracklings, if desired.

COOK'S NOTE

■ The pork can marinate for up to 24 hours.

Pork Cracklings

SERVES 8
ACTIVE TIME: 20 MINUTES ■ START TO FINISH: 2 HOURS

■ Cracklings—pork fatback with skin, cooked until it becomes crunchy—add another layer of flavor and texture to a dish. They're also delicious to nibble on by themselves.■

  2 teaspoons kosher salt
1½ teaspoons fennel seeds
  1 (2-pound) piece pork fatback with skin, fat trimmed to ⅓ inch thick
  ¾ cup water

SPECIAL EQUIPMENT: an electric coffee/spice grinder

Pulse salt and fennel seeds in grinder until fennel is coarsely ground.

Place fatback skin side up on a work surface with a long side nearest you. With a sharp knife, score skin (¼ inch deep) crosswise at ⅓-inch intervals; do not cut through to fat. Pat skin completely dry with paper towels and rub fennel salt into skin. Let stand, loosely covered, at room temperature, for 1 hour.

Put a rack in bottom third of oven and preheat oven to 450°F.

Pat skin completely dry with paper towels again and cut fatback into strips, using scored cuts as a guide. Arrange strips close together on a large baking sheet and slowly pour water into pan (not over skin).

Roast, stirring twice (use caution, as fat may spatter), until strips are golden, blistered, and crisp, 30 to 35 minutes. Transfer with a slotted spoon to a paper-towel-lined plate to drain; discard fat remaining in pan.

COOK'S NOTE

■ The cracklings can be made up to 6 hours ahead, while the pork marinates or roasts. Cool, uncovered, and keep at room temperature, covered. While the pork rests, reheat in the upper third of a 425°F oven until hot, about 10 minutes.

Braised Pork Loin
with Prunes

SERVES 8

ACTIVE TIME: 40 MINUTES ■ START TO FINISH: 1½ HOURS

■ Years ago, all pork dishes were cooked until well done in order to kill the *Trichinella* parasite, and since pork was so fatty, it could hold up to long cooking. Today trichinosis has been pretty much eradicated, and pork can be served safely at much lower temperatures, but it is much leaner, so it needs greater attention during cooking. Browning the meat and then braising it preserves its tenderness. And it makes for a dramatic presentation—slicing reveals the gorgeous Armagnac-scented prunes running through the meat. ■

¼ cup olive oil

2 pounds onions (6–8 medium), halved lengthwise and thinly sliced lengthwise

1 garlic head, cloves separated and peeled
Salt and freshly ground black pepper

2 cups (14 ounces) pitted prunes

1 cup Armagnac or other brandy

1 (3- to 3½-pound) boneless center-cut pork loin roast (3–4 inches in diameter), tied

10 fresh parsley stems

2 large fresh thyme sprigs

1 large fresh sage sprig

2 Turkish bay leaves or 1 California bay leaf

¼ teaspoon black peppercorns

2 whole cloves

⅓ cup Dijon mustard

⅓ cup packed light brown sugar

1 cup dry white wine

1 cup Chicken Stock (page 153) or store-bought reduced-sodium broth

2–3 tablespoons red wine vinegar

SPECIAL EQUIPMENT: cheesecloth; kitchen string; an instant-read thermometer

Heat 2 tablespoons oil in a 5-quart heavy pot large enough to accommodate roast over moderate heat until hot but not smoking. Add onions, gar-lic, ½ teaspoon salt, and ¼ teaspoon pepper and cook, stirring occasionally, until onions are soft and golden, about 20 minutes. Transfer to a bowl; set pot aside.

Meanwhile, combine prunes and Armagnac in a 1- to 2-quart saucepan, bring to a simmer, and simmer for 5 minutes. Remove from heat and set aside.

To make a hole in roast, insert a long thin sharp knife into middle of one end toward center of loin, then repeat at opposite end to make an incision that runs lengthwise through roast. Enlarge incision with your fingers, working from both ends, to create a ¾-inch-wide opening. Pack about 20 prunes into pork, pushing them from both ends toward center (reserve remaining Armagnac and prunes). Pat pork dry and season with ½ teaspoon salt and ¼ teaspoon pepper.

Put a rack in middle of oven and preheat oven to 375°F.

Wrap parsley, thyme, sage, bay leaves, pepper-corns, and cloves in a square of cheesecloth and tie into a bundle with kitchen string.

Brush pork with mustard and coat evenly with brown sugar. Heat remaining 2 tablespoons oil in re-served pot over high heat until hot but not smoking. Brown meat on all sides, reducing heat if necessary to prevent burning, for about 6 minutes. Transfer pork with tongs to a plate. Add white wine and reserved Armagnac (not prunes) to pot and bring to a boil, then remove from heat.

Add stock, onion mixture, and cheesecloth bundle to pot, then add pork, along with any juices accumu-lated on plate, turning pork fat side up. Cover and bring to a boil over high heat, transfer to oven, and braise for 30 minutes.

Add remaining prunes to pot and braise until thermometer inserted diagonally 2 inches into meat (avoiding stuffing) registers 150°F, about 15 minutes. Transfer pork to a cutting board and cut off and dis-card string. Cover with foil (internal temperature of pork will rise as it stands).

While pork stands, skim fat from surface of sauce if necessary and discard cheesecloth bundle. Stir in vinegar (to taste), ¼ teaspoon salt, and pepper to taste.

Slice pork and serve with sauce.

Pork Loin Roast with Roasted Carrots and Onions

SERVES 6
ACTIVE TIME: 40 MINUTES ■ START TO FINISH: 2½ HOURS

■ A bone-in pork loin roast—the prime rib of the pig—is an impressive cut, yielding thick juicy chops when sliced (wow your guests by doing the honors at the table). A judicious application of chopped fresh rosemary and garlic subtly perfumes the meat and the vegetables that are cooked with it. Starting the roast in a hot oven and then turning the temperature down gives the meat a beautiful brown color (and the deep flavor that goes with it) without drying it out. ■

- 2 large garlic cloves, finely chopped
- 1 tablespoon finely chopped fresh rosemary
- 1 (8-rib) center-cut pork loin roast (about 4½ pounds), chine removed and bottom of ribs cracked (have the butcher do this), trimmed of all but a thin layer of fat
- 1 teaspoon vegetable oil
  Salt and freshly ground black pepper
- 2 pounds carrots, cut into 2½-inch-long ½-inch-thick sticks
- ¾ pound small white onions (1½ inches in diameter), halved lengthwise
- 3 bacon slices, chopped
- 1½ cups Chicken Stock (page 153) or store-bought reduced-sodium broth
- 1½ teaspoons cornstarch
- ¼ cup cold water
- 2 tablespoons chopped fresh flat-leaf parsley

SPECIAL EQUIPMENT: a 17-by-14-inch flameproof roasting pan; an instant-read thermometer

Put a rack in middle of oven and preheat oven to 450°F. Oil roasting pan.

Mix together garlic and rosemary. With a paring knife, make ½-inch-deep slits about 1 inch apart in top of roast. Push some herb mixture into each slit with your fingers, and rub any excess onto outside of

pork. Transfer pork to roasting pan and let stand at room temperature for 15 minutes.

Rub pork with oil and sprinkle with 1 teaspoon salt and ½ teaspoon pepper. Toss carrots, onions, and bacon with ½ teaspoon salt and ¼ teaspoon pepper and scatter around pork.

Roast pork for 30 minutes. Reduce oven temperature to 325°F and roast until thermometer inserted 2 inches into center of meat (without touching bone) registers 145° to 150°F, 30 to 45 minutes. Transfer pork to a platter and let stand, loosely covered with foil, for 25 minutes.

Meanwhile, stir vegetables in roasting pan, return to oven, and roast until carrots are tender, 15 to 20 minutes more. Transfer vegetables to a bowl with a slotted spoon and cover with foil to keep warm.

Straddle roasting pan across two burners, add stock, and deglaze pan by boiling, scraping up brown bits, for 1 minute. Pour stock mixture into a small saucepan. Stir together cornstarch and water in a small cup, add to stock mixture, bring to a boil, whisking, and boil, whisking, for 1 minute. Remove from heat and stir in parsley.

Cut pork roast into chops and serve with vegetables and sauce.

Garlic-Roasted Pork Shoulder

SERVES 8
ACTIVE TIME: 30 MINUTES ■ START TO FINISH: 1 DAY
(INCLUDES MARINATING)

■ We love it when an inexpensive cut of meat is coaxed into being a glorious showstopper, and this pork masterpiece is perhaps the best example we can think of. Some of the garlicky marinade is pushed into slits in the roast so it penetrates the meat, and the rest is smeared over the roast, forming a sticky crust of irresistible caramelization. Rubbed with salt, the skin becomes rich and crunchy and is cut into strips to make *chicarrones,* or cracklings, the last pieces of which everyone will fight over. ■

1 head garlic, separated into cloves and peeled

2 tablespoons plus 1 teaspoon kosher salt

1½ tablespoons dried oregano, crumbled

2 tablespoons distilled white vinegar

2 tablespoons fresh lemon juice

1 tablespoon freshly ground black pepper

1 (7- to 7½-pound) bone-in pork shoulder with skin

ACCOMPANIMENT: lime wedges

SPECIAL EQUIPMENT: a 17-by-14-inch flameproof roasting pan; parchment paper

Mince garlic and mash to a paste with 2 tablespoons salt, using a mortar and pestle or side of a large heavy knife. Transfer to a small bowl if using a knife, and stir in oregano, vinegar, lemon juice, and pepper.

Pat pork dry. Using a small sharp knife, gently loosen skin from fat at large end of roast to create a wide pocket, leaving skin attached at sides and stopping before roast narrows to bone. Make 1-inch-deep slits in pork under skin and on all meaty sides, twisting knife slightly to widen openings. Push some of garlic mixture into slits with your fingers. Rub remaining garlic mixture over roast (not skin). Wipe skin clean and rub with remaining teaspoon salt to help it crisp. Transfer pork to a shallow baking dish and marinate, covered and refrigerated, for at least 8 hours.

Put pork skin side up in roasting pan; discard marinade. Bring roast to room temperature, about 1 hour.

Put a rack in middle of oven and preheat oven to 350°F.

Cover pork with parchment paper and then tightly with foil. Roast for 2½ hours.

Remove and discard foil and parchment. Add ½ cup water to roasting pan and roast, uncovered, adding more water as liquid in pan evaporates (check about every 30 minutes), until skin is browned and crisp and meat is fork-tender, 2 to 2½ hours more. Transfer pork to a cutting board or platter and let stand for 30 minutes.

Meanwhile, pour pan juices through a sieve into a fat separator or bowl (set pan aside) and discard fat, then pour into a large glass measure. Straddle roasting pan across two burners, add ¾ cup water, and deglaze by boiling over medium-high heat, scraping

up brown bits, for 1 minute. Add liquid to pan juices, along with enough water to total 1½ cups.

Cut skin off pork. (If skin is not crisp, roast on a baking sheet in a 475°F oven until crisp, about 10 minutes.) Cut skin into serving pieces. Pull meat from roast in pieces, using a fork.

Serve meat with pan juices, skin, and lime wedges.

COOK'S NOTE

■ The pork can be marinated for up to 3 days.

Glazed Ham with Pineapple Mustard Sauce

SERVES 10
ACTIVE TIME: 35 MINUTES ■ START TO FINISH: 3¾ HOURS

■ There's a reason baked hams gussied up with pineapple rings and maraschino cherries became popular—the pineapple contributes sweetness and a little acidity to salty ham. Here the pineapple juice is concentrated into a syrup and combined with thyme and Dijon mustard, so the effect is subtler and less sweet. It's important to seek out a ham that is labeled "partially cooked," which means it has been cooked long enough to kill any bacteria but needs further time in the oven to become tender. Hold on to the bone for making soup. ■

1 (8- to 10-pound) partially cooked smoked shank-end ham

3 cups unsweetened pineapple juice

1 tablespoon sugar

¾ cup Dijon mustard

¼ teaspoon salt

¼ teaspoon freshly ground black pepper

1 tablespoon finely chopped fresh thyme

GARNISH: fresh thyme sprigs

SPECIAL EQUIPMENT: an instant-read thermometer

Put a rack in middle of oven and preheat oven to 325°F. Oil a large roasting pan.

If ham came wrapped in plastic, rinse it and pat dry. Cut away and discard any thick skin with a sharp paring knife, leaving a 1-inch band around shank end. Cut away all but about ⅛-inch-thick layer of fat where possible.

Put ham flat side down in roasting pan. Pour ¾ cup pineapple juice around ham. Cover pan tightly with foil and bake for 1 hour.

Meanwhile, combine sugar and remaining 2¼ cups pineapple juice in a 1½- to 2-quart heavy saucepan, bring to a boil, and boil gently, stirring occasionally, until reduced to ¾ cup, 12 to 15 minutes.

Transfer pineapple syrup to a bowl and cool for 5 minutes, then whisk in mustard, salt, and pepper. Pour ½ cup mustard mixture into a small bowl and stir in thyme. Reserve remaining mixture for serving.

Discard foil and brush ham with thyme-mustard mixture. Bake, basting occasionally with pan juices, until thermometer inserted into center of meat (without touching bone) registers 145° to 150°F, 1¼ to 1½ hours; if pan juices evaporate during baking, add ½ cup water. Transfer ham to a platter (discard pan juices) and let stand, uncovered, for 15 to 30 minutes before slicing.

Serve ham garnished with thyme sprigs, with reserved mustard mixture on the side.

COOK'S NOTES

- The ham can be trimmed up to 8 hours ahead and refrigerated, covered with plastic wrap. Let stand at room temperature for 30 minutes before baking.
- The pineapple-mustard mixture, without the thyme, can be made up to 1 day ahead and refrigerated, covered.

WHAT TO DO WITH LEFTOVER HAM

Leftover ham is a beautiful thing. Sandwiches are the first order of business: hearty ones made with thick-cut country bread and lashings of coarse mustard, or thinner, more mannerly ones spread with softened butter that's been mixed with a little chopped parsley. Tangy gherkins or cornichons are nice with both.

For a decorative effect, put ham and thin slices of Swiss cheese between slices of buttered white bread and cook in your waffle iron for 4 to 6 minutes. (Children love this, and it also might be the time to remember that Jack Benny once famously defined an hors d'oeuvre as a ham sandwich cut into 40 pieces.)

For a French café effect, make a croque monsieur (grilled ham and cheese gilded with a béchamel cheese sauce); top with a fried egg, and you have a croque madame.

Stir cubes of ham into macaroni and cheese or scalloped potatoes. And remember to save the bone, with some generous chunks of meat still on it. Put it in a sealable plastic bag and toss it into the freezer. What is just as much fun as the actual soup you will make with it on a rainy cold afternoon is conjuring up all the possibilities: Split Pea (page 134) is the obvious choice, but don't forget about Gascon White Bean Soup (page 133) or Gumbo Z'Herbes (page 118). Bolster it with good bread and butter, and you have one more satisfying meal.

Midwest Boiled Dinner

SERVES 6
ACTIVE TIME: 25 MINUTES ■ START TO FINISH: 1¾ HOURS

■ Old-fashioned? Yes. Delicious? Definitely. Salty, tender smoked pork butt adds oomph to boiled cabbage, potatoes, turnips, and carrots. We refine this classic by staggering the cooking time for the vegetables, so that each retains its distinct flavor, texture, and color. A drizzling of browned butter with horseradish and white vinegar further perks them up. A thrifty Midwestern cook would be sure to save the boiling liquid and use it in a hearty bean soup. ■

FOR BOILED DINNER

4½   quarts cold water
 1   (2-pound) boneless smoked pork butt (do not
       remove netting)
 2   Turkish bay leaves or 1 California bay leaf
10   black peppercorns
1¼   pounds small yellow-fleshed potatoes
       (about 2 inches in diameter)
 ¾   pound turnips
 ¾   pound carrots
 ½   green cabbage (about 1½ pounds)

FOR BROWN BUTTER–HORSERADISH SAUCE

 ¾   stick (6 tablespoons) unsalted butter,
       cut into bits
 2   tablespoons bottled horseradish
 1   tablespoon reserved cooking liquid from
       boiled dinner
 2   teaspoons distilled white vinegar
 ¼   teaspoon salt

ACCOMPANIMENT: brown mustard

MAKE THE BOILED DINNER: Combine water, pork butt, bay leaves, and peppercorns in a 5- to 6-quart pot (add more water if pork is not covered) and bring to a boil over moderately high heat. Reduce heat and simmer, uncovered, for 5 minutes.

Transfer pork with tongs to a cutting board and remove and discard netting, then return pork to pot. Simmer, partially covered (add boiling water as necessary to keep covered with liquid), for 1 hour.

Meanwhile, peel potatoes and put in a bowl of cold water. Peel turnips and cut into 1-inch-wide wedges (keep vegetables separate). Peel carrots and cut into 3-inch pieces. Cut cabbage into 6 wedges.

After pork has simmered for 1 hour, drain potatoes, add to pork, and simmer for 8 minutes. Add turnips and simmer for 5 minutes. Add carrots and simmer for 10 minutes. Add cabbage and simmer until vegetables are just tender, 7 to 10 minutes.

Transfer vegetables with a slotted spoon to a heated large platter; reserve 1 tablespoon cooking liquid for making sauce (discard remainder). Transfer pork with tongs to a cutting board. Thinly slice and transfer to platter with vegetables. Cover loosely with foil to keep warm.

MAKE THE SAUCE: Melt butter in a small heavy saucepan over moderately low heat and simmer until milk solids are golden brown and butter has a nutty aroma, about 5 minutes. Remove from heat and immediately whisk in remaining ingredients.

Drizzle sauce over vegetables and serve mustard on the side.

Cuban Roast Suckling Pig

SERVES 10 TO 12
ACTIVE TIME: 1 HOUR ■ START TO FINISH: 4¾ HOURS

■ Nothing is more festive and extravagant than a suckling pig. Roasted whole, it offers something for everyone: lots of crisp, crackly skin and heaps of falling-off-the-bone-tender meat. A traditional Cuban *mojo* of lime and orange juices and garlic is added to the pan drippings, and the resulting sauce is refreshingly tart—a wonderful antidote to the lush meat.

Suckling pig has been fed solely on its mother's milk and is slaughtered before it is six weeks old. Order it ahead from specialty butchers. ■

FOR PIG

 1   (12- to 15-pound) suckling pig (see Sources)
 ¼   cup distilled white vinegar
 2   tablespoons minced garlic
1½   teaspoons salt

2 teaspoons dried oregano, crumbled
½ teaspoon freshly ground black pepper
4 cups boiling water
   About ¼ cup vegetable oil

FOR *MOJO* SAUCE

1 cup fresh sour orange juice (from about 3 oranges;
   see Sources for sour oranges) or ½ cup fresh lime
   juice (from about 4 limes) plus ½ cup fresh orange
   juice (from about 2 oranges)
½ cup water
1 tablespoon minced garlic
1½ teaspoons dried oregano, crumbled
¼ teaspoon ground cumin
½ teaspoon salt, or to taste

SPECIAL EQUIPMENT: a flameproof 17-by-14-inch roasting
   pan

ROAST THE PIG: Put a rack in bottom third of oven
and preheat oven to 450°F.

Rinse pig and pat dry. Brush all over with vinegar.

Mince garlic and mash to a paste with salt, using
side of a large heavy knife. Mash in oregano and pepper. Rub mixture all over inside of pig. Fold stomach
flaps closed and arrange pig diagonally in roasting
pan resting on legs: straighten hind legs forward,
head resting between them, then fold front legs
back outside hind legs. Pour boiling water over pig
to tighten skin, then brush skin all over with some
of oil.

Roast pig, basting with oil every 20 minutes, for
40 minutes. Reduce heat to 350°F and continue to
roast pig, basting with oil every hour and adding 1
or 2 cups room-temperature water to pan as necessary (so you have 2 cups liquid for sauce), for 3 hours
more. If skin is not crisp after 2½ hours, increase
temperature to 400°F for last half hour.

MAKE THE *MOJO* SAUCE: Stir together all ingredients in a bowl.

Transfer pig to a large platter or serving board,
leaving drippings in pan.

Straddle roasting pan across two burners, add
mojo, and bring to a boil, stirring and scraping up
brown bits. Simmer *mojo* for 3 minutes, then season
with salt and transfer to a sauceboat.

Carve pig and serve sections of crisp skin with tender meat, moistened with sauce.

Red-Cooked Pork Belly

SERVES 6 TO 8
ACTIVE TIME: 40 MINUTES ■ START TO FINISH: 4 HOURS

■ With pork bred to be ever more lean, Americans are
thrilled to discover pork belly—fresh (unsmoked) bacon, with or without skin and bones—a cut so rich and
succulent that it has become popular on restaurant
menus everywhere. Bruce Cost, an authority on Chinese cuisine, introduced us to this traditional Shanghai
technique for cooking pork belly. "Red-cooking" refers
to the slow simmering of rich meats in a combination
of rice wine, yellow rock sugar (you can substitute dark
brown sugar), and dark soy sauce. When making the
sauce, resist the temptation to skim off the fat; you
need it for flavor and consistency. The green bouquets
of baby bok choy balance the pork's richness.

For the Asian ingredients, see Sources. ■

6 cups water
1 (2- to 2½-pound) piece fresh pork belly (unsmoked
   bacon), about 3 inches thick, with skin and bones
¼ cup Chinese rice wine, preferably Shaoxing, or
   medium-dry sherry
3 garlic cloves, smashed
6 (¼-inch-thick) slices peeled fresh ginger
1½ tablespoons soy sauce
1½ tablespoons dark soy sauce
½ cup coarsely crushed yellow rock sugar (sometimes
   labeled "yellow rock candy") or ½ cup packed dark
   brown sugar
1 teaspoon kosher salt
12 baby bok choy (2½ inches long), halved
   lengthwise

ACCOMPANIMENT: white rice

Bring water to a boil in a 3- to 4-quart heavy pot.
Add pork belly and return to a boil. Skim foam and
add rice wine, reduce heat to moderate, and briskly
simmer, partially covered, skimming occasionally, for
20 minutes.

Add remaining ingredients except bok choy, reduce heat to low, and simmer, partially covered, turning pork occasionally, until skin and meat are very
tender, about 3 hours.

Transfer pork with tongs and a spatula to a platter and cover with foil to keep warm.

Pour cooking liquid into a 12-inch heavy skillet (do not skim off fat) and boil until reduced to about 1 cup and syrupy, about 25 minutes. Pour through a fine-mesh sieve into a bowl; discard solids.

Cook bok choy in a large pot of boiling water until bright green and crisp-tender, about 2 minutes. Drain and pat dry with paper towels.

Arrange bok choy around pork and pour sauce over meat, drizzling a little over vegetables.

COOK'S NOTE

■ The pork belly can be made up to 3 days ahead. Cool, uncovered, in the (unreduced) cooking liquid, then refrigerate, covered.

Orange-Soy-Braised Pork Ribs

SERVES 4 TO 6
ACTIVE TIME: 30 MINUTES ■ START TO FINISH: 3 HOURS

■ This recipe is a reminder that you can make fabulous ribs in your oven in the middle of winter. A long, slow braise is the secret to the tender meat, which falls off the bone in sticky, melting chunks redolent of orange and ginger. Complete the meal with Chinese broccoli and steamed white rice with scallions. ■

    4 pounds country-style pork ribs
    ½ teaspoon salt
    1½ cups fresh orange juice (from about 5 oranges)
    ½ cup soy sauce
    2 tablespoons sugar
    2 tablespoons finely chopped peeled fresh ginger
    1 tablespoon minced garlic
    ½ teaspoon coarsely ground black pepper
SPECIAL EQUIPMENT: a 17-by-14-inch flameproof roasting
        pan

Put a rack in middle of oven and preheat oven to 325°F.

Sprinkle ribs with salt.

Straddle roasting pan over two burners. Add juice, soy sauce, sugar, ginger, garlic, and pepper and bring

to a boil over moderately high heat, stirring until sugar is dissolved.

Using tongs, add ribs in one layer, turning to coat. Cover pan tightly with foil and braise ribs in oven until very tender, about 2 hours.

Transfer ribs to a baking dish, arranging them in one layer. Reduce oven temperature to 200°F and keep ribs warm in oven.

Skim fat from cooking liquid if desired. Straddle roasting pan over two burners, bring liquid to a boil over moderately high heat, and boil, uncovered, stirring occasionally, until reduced to about ¾ cup and syrupy, about 15 minutes.

Brush glaze generously on ribs.

COOK'S NOTE

■ The ribs can be braised up to 5 days ahead. Cool in the cooking liquid, uncovered, then refrigerate in an airtight container. To reheat, return the ribs and cooking liquid to the roasting pan and cover tightly with foil. Straddle the pan over two burners and simmer, covered, turning once, until the ribs are heated through, about 15 minutes. Transfer them to a baking dish, arranging them in one layer, and keep warm in a 200°F oven. Make the glaze and brush on the ribs.

Wuxi Spareribs

SERVES 2
ACTIVE TIME: 30 MINUTES ■ START TO FINISH: 1¾ HOURS

■ These flavor-packed spareribs, adapted from a recipe by chef Wang Haibo of San Gabriel Valley, California, are one of the signature dishes of Wuxi ("woo-shee"), a bustling city about two hours outside of Shanghai. The blanched and knotted scallion adds just the right amount of onion flavor to the ribs. ■

    1 scallion, trimmed, plus 1 tablespoon chopped
        scallion
    1 pound pork spareribs, individual ribs cut crosswise
        into 2-inch pieces by butcher
    ⅓ cup Chinese rice wine, preferably Shaoxing, or
        medium-dry sherry
    1 tablespoon soy sauce
    1 tablespoon dark soy sauce

3 cups plus 1 tablespoon water
1 (½-inch) piece fresh ginger, peeled and cut into ⅛-inch-thick slices
1½ teaspoons pieces star anise
1 (3-inch) cinnamon stick
1½ tablespoons coarsely crushed yellow rock sugar (sometimes labeled "yellow rock candy"; see Sources) or 1½ tablespoons packed brown sugar
1 teaspoon coarsely ground black pepper
1 teaspoon cornstarch
1 teaspoon Asian sesame oil
1 tablespoon chopped fresh cilantro

ACCOMPANIMENT: white rice

Blanch whole scallion in a 4-quart pot of boiling water until softened, about 1 minute. Transfer scallion to a work surface. Add ribs to boiling water, return to a boil, and immediately drain ribs.

Transfer ribs to a 2½- to 3-quart wide heavy pot. Carefully tie blanched scallion into a knot and add to pot. Add wine, soy sauces, 3 cups water, ginger, star anise, cinnamon, sugar, and pepper, bring to a simmer, and simmer, covered, until meat is just tender, about 1 hour.

Remove lid and boil over moderately high heat, stirring occasionally, until sauce is reduced by three quarters and meat is very tender, about 20 minutes more.

Whisk together cornstarch and remaining tablespoon water in a cup. Reduce heat to moderate, add cornstarch mixture to ribs, and boil, stirring, until sauce is thickened, about 1 minute. Remove from heat and stir in sesame oil; discard knotted scallion and cinnamon.

Serve ribs with rice. Spoon sauce over ribs and sprinkle with chopped scallion and cilantro.

Pork "Osso Buco" with Sauerkraut

SERVES 6
ACTIVE TIME: 30 MINUTES ■ START TO FINISH: 4 HOURS

■ Less well known than veal shanks, pork shanks are a flavorful cut that becomes tender when cooked low and slow. It's well worth placing a special order for them with your butcher. Here we pair them with cara-way-flecked sauerkraut moistened with apple cider for a wonderful fall dish. ■

¼ cup firmly packed brown sugar (light or dark)
3 tablespoons vegetable oil
1 tablespoon sweet paprika, preferably Hungarian
2 teaspoons salt
½ teaspoon freshly ground black pepper
6 (¾- to 1-pound) cross-cut slices pork shank (or pork butt), tied
½ pound bacon, cut crosswise into ½-inch-wide pieces
1 pound onions, thinly sliced
½ cup dry white wine
2 teaspoons caraway seeds
2½ cups apple cider, preferably unfiltered
3 pounds packaged (not canned) sauerkraut, rinsed

Preheat broiler. Line a large baking sheet with heavy-duty foil.

Stir together brown sugar, oil, paprika, salt, and pepper in a bowl. Pat spice mixture all over pork and put on baking sheet. Broil pork about 4 inches from heat, turning every 3 to 5 minutes, until browned on all sides (use caution, as sugar can burn quickly). Remove from heat.

Put a rack in lower third of oven and preheat oven to 350°F.

Meanwhile, cook bacon in a 6- to 7-quart heavy pot over moderate heat until browned, about 10 minutes. Transfer with a slotted spoon to a plate. Add onions to bacon fat remaining in pot and cook, stirring occasionally, until soft and golden, 16 to 20 minutes. Add wine and caraway seeds, bring to a simmer, stirring and scraping up brown bits, and simmer until liquid has evaporated, about 6 minutes. Add cider and sauerkraut and bring to a simmer.

Nestle pork and any pan juices into sauerkraut mixture and sprinkle with bacon. Cover pot with aluminum foil and then the lid and braise pork in oven until meat is falling off the bone, about 3 hours.

Transfer pork and sauerkraut to a large deep platter.

COOK'S NOTE
■ The pork and sauerkraut can be made up to 2 days ahead. Cool, uncovered, then refrigerate in an airtight container. Reheat in a tightly covered pot in a 350°F oven for about 30 minutes.

Sweet Fennel Sausage

MAKES ABOUT 4 POUNDS
ACTIVE TIME: 2 HOURS ■ START TO FINISH: 11 HOURS
(INCLUDES CHILLING)

■ Making and stuffing your own pork sausage is no easy task, but the result—plump, juicy links resonating with fennel, black pepper, allspice, and white wine—is truly worth it. As a bonus, you know exactly what is going into your sausages, and unlike so many prepackaged supermarket varieties, these do not contain corn syrup and preservatives. If you don't want to make links, you can prepare these as patties (see Cook's Note). Please don't be put off by the amount of fat called for in this recipe; because today's pork is so lean, the sausages need the extra fat to keep from being dry and crumbly. Before you start to stuff the casings, test the meat's seasoning by frying up a small amount. ■

    2 pounds well-chilled pork fatback
    4 pounds boneless pork butt, trimmed of excess fat
    3 tablespoons fennel seeds, crushed using a mortar
        and pestle or a heavy skillet
    1 tablespoon kosher salt
    2 teaspoons freshly ground black pepper
    ¼ teaspoon ground allspice
    ½ cup dry white wine
    4 (32- to 35-ml) hog casings (see Sources)
SPECIAL EQUIPMENT: a manual meat grinder or a stand
        mixer with a food grinder attachment, fitted with
        a coarse-grind plate (holes ¼ inch in diameter);
        a sausage stuffer with funnel attachment (tip at
        least ½ inch in diameter; see Sources)

PREPARE THE SAUSAGE: Rinse salt from fatback and dry well with paper towels; remove and discard skin. Cut pork butt and fatback into chunks as necessary and put through meat grinder into a large bowl. Add fennel seeds, salt, pepper, allspice, and wine and blend with your hands until well combined.

Refrigerate mixture, covered, for at least 8 hours to allow flavors to blend.

MEANWHILE, SOAK THE CASINGS: Rinse casings well in a sieve under cold running water to remove salt. Transfer to a bowl and cover with cold water. Refrigerate, uncovered, for at least 8 hours.

FORM THE SAUSAGES: Drain casings in a sieve and rinse under cold running water. Gently slip one end of a casing onto tip of sausage funnel. Holding casing at tip of funnel, put funnel under kitchen faucet and rinse inside of casing with cold water. Turn off water and gently slide all of casing except last 3 inches onto throat of funnel. Tie a knot at end of casing. Attach funnel with casing to sausage stuffer and stuff casing with sausage meat, twisting casing 4 or 5 times every 3½ inches to form sausages about 1½ inches thick (do not pack too tightly). As you form each sausage, poke holes in casing with a wooden skewer to release any air bubbles. Tie a knot at end of casing, put sausages on a baking sheet, and refrigerate. Make more sausages with remaining casings and meat in same manner. Refrigerate sausages until cold, about 30 minutes.

COOK THE SAUSAGES: Cut apart 1 string of sausages with kitchen shears. Prick casings all over with a fork or skewer. Put sausages and ¼ cup water in a 12-inch heavy skillet and bring to a boil, covered. Reduce heat to moderate and cook for 3 minutes. Remove lid and cook, turning sausages frequently, until water is evaporated and sausages are well browned, about 12 minutes. Transfer to a platter. Cook remaining sausages in same manner, or store for future use (see Cook's Note).

COOK'S NOTES

■ The uncooked sausage mixture can be refrigerated for up to 24 hours.

■ The casings can be soaked for up to 24 hours.

■ The uncooked sausages can be refrigerated in a heavy-duty sealable plastic bag for up to 3 days or frozen for up to 1 month. Thaw if necessary before cooking.

■ The sausage mixture can be prepared as patties rather than links. Form the mixture into 3-inch round patties, ½ inch thick. Cook in a lightly oiled 12-inch heavy skillet over moderately high heat until well browned and cooked through, 2 to 3 minutes per side.

Parsley and Cheese Pork Sausages

MAKES ABOUT 4 POUNDS
ACTIVE TIME: 3 HOURS ■ START TO FINISH: 11 HOURS
(INCLUDES CHILLING)

■ A type of luganega, or mild Italian sausage, this gets its distinctive flavor from fresh parsley and two cheeses, Asiago and pecorino Romano. It is traditionally made with narrower casings than other sausages and not twisted into links, so the result is one long sausage that is then coiled. You can panfry the sausages, but we also like to insert skewers through the coils (see illustration) and grill them (the skewers keep the coil together and facilitate turning on the grill). Skewers and all, it looks great over a fresh arugula salad.

If you prefer, you can skip the casings and prepare the sausages as patties (see Cook's Note). ■

- 2 pounds well-chilled pork fatback
- 4 pounds boneless pork butt, trimmed of excess fat
- 2 cups coarsely grated Asiago (about 8 ounces)
- 1 cup finely grated pecorino Romano (about 3 ounces)
- 1½ cups coarsely chopped fresh flat-leaf parsley
- 1 tablespoon kosher salt
- 1 teaspoon freshly ground black pepper
- ¼ cup dry white wine
- 4 (29- to 32-ml) hog casings (see Sources)

SPECIAL EQUIPMENT: a manual meat grinder or a stand mixer with a food grinder attachment, fitted with a coarse-grind plate (holes ¼ inch in diameter); a sausage stuffer with funnel attachment (tip at least ½ inch in diameter; see Sources)

PREPARE THE SAUSAGE: Rinse salt from fatback and dry well with paper towels. Remove and discard skin from fatback. Cut pork butt and fatback into chunks as necessary and put through meat grinder into a large bowl. Add cheeses, parsley, salt, pepper, and wine and blend with your hands until well combined.

Refrigerate mixture, covered, for at least 8 hours to allow flavors to blend.

MEANWHILE, SOAK THE CASINGS: Rinse casings well in a sieve under cold running water to remove salt. Transfer to a bowl and cover with cold water. Refrigerate, uncovered, for at least 8 hours.

FORM THE SAUSAGE COILS: Drain casings in a sieve and rinse under cold running water. Gently slip one end of a casing onto tip of sausage funnel. Holding casing at tip of funnel, put funnel under kitchen faucet and rinse inside of casing with cold water. Turn off water and gently slide all of casing except last 3 inches onto throat of funnel. Tie a knot at end of casing. Attach funnel with casing to sausage stuffer and stuff casing with sausage meat to make one sausage that is 30 inches long and 1 inch thick (do not pack too tightly). As you form sausage, poke holes in casing using a wooden skewer to release any air bubbles. Tie a knot at end of casing, coil sausage on a baking sheet, and refrigerate. Make 3 more sausage coils with remaining casings in same manner. Refrigerate sausages until cold, about 30 minutes.

COOK THE SAUSAGES: Prick casing of 1 coil all over with a fork or skewer. Put 1 sausage and ¼ cup water in a 12-inch heavy skillet and bring to a boil, covered. Reduce heat to moderate and cook for 3 minutes. Remove lid and cook, turning sausage once, until water has evaporated and sausage is well browned, about 12 minutes total. Transfer to a platter. Cook remaining sausage coils in same manner, or store for future use (see Cook's Note).

COOK'S NOTES

- The uncooked sausage mixture can be refrigerated for up to 24 hours.
- The casings can be soaked for up to 24 hours.
- The uncooked sausage coils can be refrigerated in a heavy-duty sealable plastic bag for up to 3 days or frozen for up to 1 month. Thaw if necessary before cooking.
- The sausage mixture can be prepared as patties rather than links. Form the mixture into 3-inch round patties, ½ inch thick. Cook in a lightly oiled 12-inch heavy skillet over moderately high heat until well browned and cooked through, 2 to 3 minutes per side. (Lower the heat if the cheese begins to burn.)

Lamb

Lamb Chops with Salmoriglio Sauce

SERVES 4
ACTIVE TIME: 15 MINUTES ■ START TO FINISH: 15 MINUTES

■ Salmoriglio is a robust sauce of fresh oregano, thyme, lemon zest, and olive oil from Calabria and Sicily. When you taste it with these meaty shoulder lamb chops, you can almost feel the warm breezes blowing off the Mediterranean. Serve with a chopped tomato salad and some grilled bread for soaking up the sauce. ■

1½ tablespoons finely chopped fresh oregano
1½ tablespoons finely chopped fresh thyme
 2 teaspoons finely grated lemon zest
1½ tablespoons fresh lemon juice
   Kosher salt
 6 tablespoons extra-virgin olive oil
   Freshly ground black pepper
 4 (¾-inch-thick) lamb shoulder chops (about
    2 pounds total)

SPECIAL EQUIPMENT: a well-seasoned ridged grill pan

Grind herbs, zest, lemon juice, and 1⅛ teaspoons salt to a paste in mortar with pestle. (Or combine in a mini food processor and pulse until a paste forms.) Transfer to a bowl and add oil in a slow stream, whisking until well blended. Season with ⅛ teaspoon pepper.

Pat lamb dry and season with ¾ teaspoon salt and ¼ teaspoon pepper. Heat grill pan over moderately high heat until hot but not smoking. Grill lamb, turning once, about 8 minutes for medium-rare. Transfer to a platter and let stand, uncovered, for 5 minutes.

Serve sauce spooned over lamb.

COOK'S NOTE
■ The chops can be grilled outdoors on a charcoal or gas grill (see Grilling Basics, page 510).

Garlic-Rosemary-Marinated Lamb Chops

SERVES 4
ACTIVE TIME: 20 MINUTES ■ START TO FINISH: 1 HOUR

■ A quick rub of garlic and rosemary makes a tasty weeknight lamb chop, and adding a little lemon zest takes it to another dimension. ■

 2 garlic cloves
 1 teaspoon salt
 2 teaspoons finely grated lemon zest
 1 tablespoon chopped fresh rosemary
 2 tablespoons olive oil
 ½ teaspoon freshly ground black pepper
 8 (1¼-inch-thick) lamb loin chops (about 1 pound
    total)

SPECIAL EQUIPMENT: a well-seasoned ridged grill pan

Mince garlic and mash to a paste with salt, using side of a large heavy knife. Stir together garlic paste, zest, rosemary, olive oil, and pepper in a bowl. Rub paste onto both sides of chops and marinate at room temperature for 20 minutes.

Heat grill pan over high heat until hot. Brush with oil and grill chops, turning once, about 10 minutes for medium-rare. Let stand, uncovered, for 5 minutes before serving.

Lamb Chops with Cumin, Cardamom, and Lime

SERVES 4
ACTIVE TIME: 20 MINUTES ■ START TO FINISH: 40 MINUTES

■ Featuring a whiff of the exotic without being outré, this easy dish is ideal for a quick weeknight supper or a casual dinner party. ■

 ¾ teaspoon ground cumin
 ¾ teaspoon ground cardamom
1¼ teaspoons salt
 ¾ teaspoon freshly ground black pepper

8 (¾-inch-thick) lamb rib chops (2 pounds total),
    trimmed
2 tablespoons olive oil
6 garlic cloves, smashed and peeled
ACCOMPANIMENT: lime wedges

Stir together cumin, cardamom, salt, and pepper in a small bowl. Pat chops dry and rub both sides of each chop with scant ½ teaspoon spice mixture.

Heat 1 tablespoon oil in a 12-inch heavy skillet over moderate heat until hot but not smoking. Add 3 smashed garlic cloves and cook, stirring occasionally, until golden, about 3 minutes. Remove garlic with a slotted spoon and discard. Increase heat to moderately high, add 4 chops to skillet, and cook, turning once, for 6 to 8 minutes for medium-rare. Transfer chops to a platter and cover loosely with foil to keep warm. Wipe out skillet, add remaining 1 tablespoon oil, and heat over moderate heat until hot but not smoking. Cook remaining 3 garlic cloves in same manner and discard. Increase heat to moderately high and cook remaining 4 chops in same manner; transfer to platter and cover with foil.

Let chops stand for 5 minutes before serving with lime wedges.

Panfried Double Lamb Chops with Date Puree

SERVES 4
ACTIVE TIME: 1¼ HOURS ■ START TO FINISH: 1¾ HOURS

■ These double chops require a bit of coddling in the form of basting and frequent turning, but paired with a spiced date puree that subtly plays up the sweet meatiness, they are out of this world. We adapted this recipe from one by chef Nick Martschenko who, when he cooked at Manhattan's Gramercy Tavern, served the chops with Roasted Savoy Cabbage with Raisins (page 580).

This is easily halved for a special dinner for two. ■

FOR DATE PUREE
3 cups (about 14 ounces) pitted dates
1 (750-ml) bottle dry red wine
1 (3- to 4-inch-long) cinnamon stick
2 star anise

FOR LAMB CHOPS
2 (8-rib) racks of lamb (about 1½ pounds each),
    trimmed and frenched if desired, at room
    temperature
1½ teaspoons kosher salt
½ teaspoon freshly ground black pepper
1 tablespoon peanut oil
2 tablespoons unsalted butter
2 fresh thyme or rosemary sprigs
SPECIAL EQUIPMENT: parchment paper; an instant-read
    thermometer

MAKE THE DATE PUREE: Stir together dates, wine, cinnamon stick, and star anise in a 2-quart heavy saucepan and cover directly with a round of parchment paper. Bring to a simmer over moderate heat, then reduce heat and simmer until dates are tender, 15 to 20 minutes. Remove and discard spices.

Transfer dates with a slotted spoon to a food processor. Measure cooking liquid in a large measuring cup; if it measures more than about 1 cup, boil to reduce to 1 cup. Add to dates and puree until smooth (use caution when blending hot liquids). Force puree, a few tablespoons at a time, through a fine-mesh sieve into a small saucepan, pressing on dates with back of a wooden spoon; discard skins. Set aside.

COOK THE LAMB: Cut each rack into 4 double chops. Pat dry and sprinkle with salt and pepper.

Heat oil in a 12-inch heavy skillet over moderate heat until hot but not smoking. Add chops and brown on all sides, about 6 minutes. (Adjust heat so oil sizzles but does not spatter.) Add butter and thyme sprigs and cook, turning chops and basting occasionally, until thermometer inserted between ribs into center of a chop (without touching bone) registers 130°F for medium-rare, 16 to 20 minutes more. Transfer chops to a cutting board and let stand, loosely covered with foil, for 10 minutes.

Meanwhile, heat date puree over low heat, stirring occasionally.

If desired, cut each double chop into 2 chops. Serve lamb with date puree.

COOK'S NOTE
■ The date puree can be made up to 1 week ahead. Cool, uncovered, then refrigerate in an airtight container. Reheat over low heat.

Turkish-Style Lamb Burgers with Walnut Sauce

SERVES 4

ACTIVE TIME: 45 MINUTES ■ START TO FINISH: 45 MINUTES

■ The sauce for these juicy burgers, a combination of walnuts with garlic and lemon juice, is our take on a famous Turkish sauce, the pungent *tarator*. The burgers are seasoned with fresh herbs and spices and bound with a bit of bulgur. You'll want to serve them in toasted pita rounds. ■

FOR BURGERS
- ⅓ cup bulgur (not fine)
- Salt
- 1 cup boiling water
- 1 medium onion, quartered
- ¼ cup packed fresh cilantro leaves
- ¼ cup packed fresh flat-leaf parsley leaves
- 1 pound ground lamb (not lean)
- ½ teaspoon sweet paprika
- ¼ teaspoon ground allspice
- ¼ teaspoon freshly ground black pepper
- ¼ teaspoon cayenne

FOR SAUCE
- 1 small garlic clove
- ⅛ teaspoon salt
- ½ cup walnuts
- ¼ cup water
- 1 teaspoon fresh lemon juice
- ⅛ teaspoon cayenne

FOR PITAS
- 4 (4-inch) pita breads (with pockets)
- 1 tablespoon olive oil
- Sweet paprika
- Freshly ground black pepper

GARNISH: fresh cilantro leaves

SOAK THE BULGUR: Combine bulgur and ½ teaspoon salt in a small bowl. Pour boiling water over bulgur and soak for 15 minutes; drain in a sieve.

MEANWHILE, MAKE THE SAUCE: Mince garlic and mash to a paste with salt, using side of a large heavy knife. Transfer to a food processor, add remaining ingredients, and blend until smooth. Transfer to a bowl.

MAKE THE BURGERS: Preheat broiler. Pulse onion, cilantro, and parsley in cleaned processor until finely chopped. Transfer to a bowl and stir in bulgur, lamb, paprika, allspice, ¼ teaspoon salt, black pepper, and cayenne until just combined. Form lamb mixture into four 4-inch patties.

BROIL THE PITAS AND BURGERS: Arrange whole pitas on a baking sheet. Brush on both sides with oil, lightly dust with paprika, and season with pepper. Broil about 10 inches from heat until toasted, 1 to 3 minutes (watch to prevent burning). Cover loosely with foil to keep warm.

Oil rack of broiler pan and heat pan 4 inches from heat until hot, 3 to 5 minutes. Put burgers on broiler rack and broil, turning once, until cooked through, 5 to 7 minutes. Serve burgers on pitas, topped with sauce and garnished with cilantro leaves.

COOK'S NOTES

- The sauce can be made up to 1 day ahead and refrigerated in an airtight container.
- The burgers can be formed up to 2 hours ahead. Refrigerate, loosely covered with plastic.
- Instead of broiling the burgers, you can cook them on a charcoal or gas grill (see Grilling Basics, page 510) or in an oiled well-seasoned ridged grill pan on the stove.

Moroccan Lamb and Eggplant Matzo Pie with Spiced Tomato Sauce

SERVES 8

ACTIVE TIME: 1¼ HOURS ■ START TO FINISH: 1¾ HOURS

■ A sort of cross between lasagne and moussaka, this dish uses softened matzo in place of noodles or potatoes, making it a perfect Passover dish, yet it's too good to limit to that short season. ■

- ½ cup olive oil, plus additional for brushing matzo
- 1 medium onion, finely chopped

1½ pounds ground lamb (see Cook's Note)
3 garlic cloves, finely chopped
Salt
1½ teaspoons Ras el Hanout (recipe follows, or see Sources)
1 teaspoon dried oregano, crumbled
1 teaspoon dried mint, crumbled
½ teaspoon freshly ground black pepper
¼ teaspoon ground cinnamon
2 (28- to 32-ounce) cans whole tomatoes in juice, drained, juice reserved, and chopped
2 (1-pound) eggplants, peeled and cut into ⅓-inch-thick slices
6 matzos (about 6 inches square)
¼ teaspoon cayenne
¾ teaspoon sugar

MAKE THE LAMB FILLING: Heat 3 tablespoons oil in a deep 12-inch heavy skillet over moderately high heat until hot but not smoking. Add onion and cook, stirring occasionally, until golden, about 5 minutes. Add lamb and cook, stirring and breaking up lumps, until no longer pink, about 5 minutes.

Add two thirds of garlic, 1½ teaspoons salt, 1 teaspoon *ras el hanout*, oregano, mint, pepper, and cinnamon and cook, stirring, for 1 minute. Stir in 3 cups tomatoes with 1 cup juice (reserve remaining tomatoes and juice for sauce), bring to a simmer, and simmer, uncovered, stirring occasionally, until slightly thickened, 10 to 12 minutes. Remove from heat.

ROAST THE EGGPLANT: Preheat broiler. Toss eggplant slices with ¼ cup oil and ½ teaspoon salt in a bowl. Brush a large baking sheet generously with oil and arrange as many eggplant slices as possible in one layer. Broil eggplant 5 to 7 inches from heat, turning slices with a spatula as they brown (6 to 7 minutes), until golden brown, 12 to 15 minutes. Broil any remaining eggplant in same manner.

ASSEMBLE AND BAKE THE PIE: Put a rack in middle of oven and preheat oven to 350°F.

Soak matzos 1 or 2 at a time in a pan of warm water until they are slightly softened but still hold their shape, 1 to 1½ minutes. Let excess water drip off and transfer matzos to paper towels to drain.

Arrange 2 matzos side by side in a generously oiled 13-by-9-inch baking dish. Spread 3 cups lamb filling over matzos. Arrange 2 more matzos side by side on

top and spread remaining lamb filling over them. Arrange eggplant slices in one layer over filling, overlapping slices slightly if necessary. Arrange remaining 2 matzos on top and brush with oil.

Cover with foil and bake for 20 minutes. Remove foil and continue to bake until filling is hot, about 10 minutes more.

MEANWHILE, MAKE THE TOMATO SAUCE: Puree remaining chopped tomatoes with remaining juice in a blender.

Heat remaining tablespoon oil in a 10- to 12-inch heavy skillet over moderate heat. Add cayenne, remaining garlic, remaining ½ teaspoon *ras el hanout*, and ½ teaspoon salt and cook, stirring, until garlic is golden, about 1 minute. Add tomato puree and sugar, bring to a simmer, and simmer, uncovered, stirring occasionally, until slightly thickened, 4 to 6 minutes.

Top matzo pie with some tomato sauce and serve remaining sauce on the side.

COOK'S NOTES
■ Ground beef chuck can be substituted for the lamb. Drain off the fat after browning.
■ The meat filling, tomato sauce, and broiled eggplant can be made up to 1 day ahead. Cool, uncovered, then refrigerate separately, covered. Bring to room temperature before assembling the pie.

Ras el Hanout
Moroccan Spice Blend

MAKES 2 TABLESPOONS
ACTIVE TIME: 5 MINUTES ■ START TO FINISH: 5 MINUTES

■ This vibrant spice blend makes an excellent seasoning for lamb burgers or roasted chicken. It's wise to triple the recipe so you can have it on hand for grilled meats or for adding to lentil soup or a quick chili. ■

1 teaspoon ground cumin
1 teaspoon ground ginger
1 teaspoon salt
¾ teaspoon freshly ground black pepper
½ teaspoon ground cinnamon
½ teaspoon ground coriander
½ teaspoon cayenne
½ teaspoon ground allspice
¼ teaspoon ground cloves

Whisk together all ingredients in a small bowl until well combined.

COOK'S NOTE

- The *ras el hanout* keeps for up to 6 months in an airtight container in a cool, dark place.

Baked Kibbeh

SERVES 6

ACTIVE TIME: 40 MINUTES ■ START TO FINISH: 2 HOURS

■ Considered the national dish of Lebanon, kibbeh, a mixture of finely ground lamb, bulgur, pine nuts, and spices, may be served raw, baked, or fried. Because the meat and bulgur were traditionally pounded by hand in a mortar, the dish was reserved for special occasions, but with the advent of the food processor, kibbeh can be enjoyed any time. In this version, a savory "crust" of ground lamb and soaked bulgur surrounds a well-spiced filling of lamb, onion, and pine nuts. A few moments under the broiler gives the kibbeh a golden crown. ■

FOR FILLING
- 2 tablespoons olive oil
- 1 medium onion, finely chopped
- ½ pound ground lamb (not lean)
- ½ teaspoon ground allspice
- ¼ teaspoon ground cinnamon
- ½ teaspoon salt
- ¼ teaspoon freshly ground black pepper
- ⅓ cup pine nuts, toasted (see Tips, page 911)

FOR BULGUR MIXTURE
- 1 cup fine bulgur (see Cook's Note)
- 1 medium onion, coarsely chopped
- 1 pound ground lamb (not lean)
- 1 teaspoon ground allspice
- ½ teaspoon ground cinnamon
- 1 teaspoon salt
- ½ teaspoon freshly ground black pepper
- 2½ tablespoons olive oil

GARNISH: 2 tablespoons pine nuts, toasted (see Tips, page 911)

ACCOMPANIMENT: plain yogurt

SPECIAL EQUIPMENT: a 10-inch metal pie plate or a 10-inch cast-iron skillet

MAKE THE FILLING: Heat oil in a 12-inch heavy skillet over moderate heat until hot but not smoking. Add onion and cook, stirring occasionally, until golden, 8 to 10 minutes. Add lamb, allspice, cinnamon, salt, and pepper and cook, stirring and breaking up lumps, until lamb is no longer pink, about 5 minutes. Remove from heat and stir in pine nuts.

MAKE THE BULGUR MIXTURE: Put a rack in middle of oven and preheat oven to 400°F.

Cover bulgur with cold water by 1 inch in a bowl. When dust and chaff rise to surface, pour off water. Repeat rinsing twice. Cover rinsed bulgur with cold water by 1 inch and let stand for 10 minutes, then drain in a fine-mesh sieve, pressing hard on bulgur to remove excess liquid, and transfer to a large bowl.

Pulse onion in a food processor until finely chopped. Add lamb, allspice, cinnamon, salt, and pepper and pulse until onion is finely minced (meat will look smooth). Add to bulgur and mix with your hands until well combined.

ASSEMBLE AND BAKE THE KIBBEH: Grease pie plate (or skillet) with 1½ teaspoons olive oil. Press half of bulgur mixture evenly onto bottom and up sides of plate (1 inch up sides if using skillet). Spoon filling evenly over bulgur mixture. Spoon remaining bulgur mixture over filling and spread to cover, smoothing top. Brush top with remaining 2 tablespoons olive oil and score a crosshatch pattern with a paring knife. Bake kibbeh until cooked through, 35 to 40 minutes.

Preheat broiler. Broil kibbeh 5 to 7 inches from heat until top is golden brown and crusty, 3 to 5 minutes. Transfer to a rack and let stand for 5 minutes.

Sprinkle top with toasted pine nuts and serve with yogurt.

COOK'S NOTES

- Fine bulgur is available in most supermarkets, near the rice section, under the name Near East Taboule Wheat Salad Mix (you won't need the seasoning packet).
- The kibbeh can be made up to 1 day ahead. Cool, uncovered, then refrigerate, covered. Reheat in a 300°F oven.

Lamb Biryani

SERVES 8

ACTIVE TIME: 2 HOURS ■ START TO FINISH: 2¾ HOURS

■ *Biryani*, an elaborate layered Indian rice dish, is usually served at festive occasions such as weddings and other religious ceremonies. With its multiplicity of flavors, textures, and colors, it's a showstopper—each forkful overflows with basmati rice streaked gold with saffron, tender cubes of seasoned lamb, toasted almonds, pistachios, plump raisins, and fried onions. ■

FOR LAMB

- 3 pounds boneless lamb shoulder, cut into 1½-inch pieces
- 2 teaspoons salt
- ¾ cup Ghee (recipe follows) or vegetable oil
- 1 pound onions, halved lengthwise and thinly sliced crosswise
- 1 cup whole-milk yogurt
- 1 cup sour cream

FOR GINGER GARLIC PASTE

- 1 (3-by-1½-inch) piece fresh ginger, peeled and coarsely chopped
- 12 garlic cloves
- ⅓ cup water

FOR SPICE BLEND

- 1 (3-inch) cinnamon stick, broken into pieces
- ½ whole nutmeg
- 2 teaspoons black peppercorns
- 2 teaspoons cumin seeds
- 1½ teaspoons coriander seeds
- 1 teaspoon whole cloves
- 1 teaspoon cardamom seeds (from about 20 green cardamom pods; see Sources)
- ½ teaspoon crumbled mace pieces or ¼ teaspoon ground mace

FOR RICE

- ½ teaspoon crumbled saffron threads
- ¼ cup whole milk
- 3 cups basmati rice
- Salt

FOR TOPPINGS

- ⅓ cup shelled pistachios
- ¾ cup Ghee (recipe follows) or vegetable oil
- 1 small onion, thinly sliced crosswise and separated into rings
- ⅓ cup sliced blanched almonds
- ⅓ cup golden raisins

OPTIONAL ACCOMPANIMENTS: Zucchini Raita (page 490), Banana Tamarind Chutney (page 491), and/or lime pickle (see Sources)

SPECIAL EQUIPMENT: an electric coffee/spice grinder

PREPARE THE LAMB: Toss lamb with salt in a large bowl. Arrange in one layer on a paper-towel-lined large baking sheet. Let stand for 30 minutes, then pat dry.

MEANWHILE, MAKE THE GINGER GARLIC PASTE: With motor of a food processor running, drop ginger and garlic through feed tube to mince. With motor running, add water, then blend until a thin paste forms. Transfer to a small bowl.

MAKE THE SPICE BLEND: Combine all ingredients in grinder and grind to a powder.

COOK THE LAMB: Heat ghee in a deep (at least 2 inches deep) 12-inch heavy skillet or pot over moderately high heat until hot but not smoking. Brown lamb in 3 or 4 batches, without crowding, turning occasionally, about 4 minutes per batch. Transfer with a slotted spoon to a bowl.

Reduce heat to moderate, add onions to ghee remaining in skillet, and cook, stirring, until deep golden brown, about 15 minutes. Add ginger garlic paste and cook, stirring frequently, until liquid has evaporated and fat separates out from mixture, 3 to 5 minutes. Add spice blend and cook, stirring, until fragrant and several shades darker, 1 to 2 minutes (be careful not to burn spices). Add yogurt and sour cream and bring to a boil, stirring.

Stir in lamb, with any juices accumulated in bowl, reduce heat, and simmer, covered, stirring occasionally, until lamb is tender, about 45 minutes.

MEANWHILE, PREPARE THE RICE: Heat saffron in a very small heavy skillet or saucepan over low heat until just fragrant, about 1 minute. Add milk and heat until warm, about 1 minute. Remove skillet from heat and let milk stand until bright yellow, about 30 minutes.

Rinse rice in several changes of cold water in a large bowl until water runs clear when drained from bowl. Add enough cold water to bowl to cover rice by

1 inch and let soak for 30 minutes. Drain in a sieve.

Cook rice in a 6- to 8-quart pot of boiling salted water (1 tablespoon salt), stirring occasionally, just until it still has a slightly chalky center, about 5 minutes. Drain in sieve.

BAKE THE *BIRYANI*: Put a rack in middle of oven and preheat oven to 300°F.

Transfer lamb and sauce to a 13-by-9-inch baking dish and spread in one layer. Spread rice evenly over lamb. Drizzle saffron mixture over rice. Cover dish tightly with foil and bake until rice is tender, about 30 minutes.

MEANWHILE, PREPARE THE TOPPINGS: Cover pistachios with boiling water in a small bowl and let soak for 1 minute. Drain and transfer to a kitchen towel. Fold towel over nuts and rub to remove skins.

Heat ghee in a 10-inch heavy skillet over moderate heat until hot but not smoking. Add onion and cook, stirring, until golden brown, about 5 minutes. Transfer with a slotted spoon to paper towels to drain.

Add almonds to ghee and cook, stirring, until golden, about 30 seconds. Transfer with slotted spoon to paper towels to drain.

Add pistachios to ghee and cook, stirring, until a shade darker, about 30 seconds. Transfer with slotted spoon to paper towels to drain.

Add raisins to ghee and cook, stirring, until plump, about 30 seconds. Transfer with slotted spoon to paper towels to drain.

GARNISH THE *BIRYANI*: Sprinkle *biryani* with onions, almonds, pistachios, and raisins, and serve with accompaniments if desired.

COOK'S NOTES

- Using ghee instead of vegetable oil will give a richer flavor to the dish.
- The lamb and sauce can be cooked up to 1 day ahead. Transfer to the baking dish and cool, uncovered, then refrigerate, covered.
- The rice can be boiled up to 1 day ahead. Rinse under cold running water to stop the cooking, then refrigerate, covered. Fluff with a fork before topping the lamb with it. The *biryani* will take 5 to 10 minutes longer to bake with refrigerated ingredients.
- The pistachios can be soaked and skinned up to 1 day ahead and kept in a sealable plastic bag at room temperature.

Ghee
Indian Clarified Butter

MAKES ABOUT 1½ CUPS
ACTIVE TIME: 40 MINUTES ■ START TO FINISH:
40 MINUTES

■ Because clarified butter has a high smoke point (the stage at which it starts to smoke and taste acrid), it's useful for sautéing or frying; it also keeps for months. It's made by slowly heating butter until the water evaporates and the milk solids separate out and sink to the bottom of the pan. Ghee is similar to clarified butter but has more flavor. The butter is cooked for longer, until the milk solids turn light brown and the liquid becomes golden, translucent, and nutty-tasting. ■

1 pound unsalted butter, cut into
    1-inch pieces

Melt butter in a medium heavy saucepan over moderate heat and bring to a boil. Once foam completely covers butter, reduce heat to very low and cook, stirring occasionally, until a thin crust begins to form on surface and milky white solids fall to bottom of pan, about 8 minutes. Watching constantly to prevent burning, continue to cook, without stirring, until solids turn light brown and butter deepens to golden and becomes fragrant, about 30 minutes.

Pour ghee through a sieve lined with a dampened triple layer of cheesecloth or heavy paper towels into a heatproof jar. Discard solids.

COOK'S NOTE
■ Ghee keeps, covered and refrigerated, for up to 2 months.

Zucchini Raita

MAKES ABOUT 2½ CUPS
ACTIVE TIME: 15 MINUTES ■ START TO FINISH: 15 MINUTES

■ Flecked with zucchini and fresh herbs, this creamy yogurt sauce offers a cooling, tangy counterpoint to the *biryani*. It is delicious served with grilled lamb or even plain naans. ■

1 pound zucchini (3 medium)
1½ cups whole-milk yogurt
¼ cup chopped fresh mint
¼ cup chopped fresh cilantro

2 teaspoons fresh lime juice, or to taste
¾ teaspoon ground cumin
¾ teaspoon salt, or to taste

Grate zucchini on large holes of a box grater. Blanch in a 3- to 4-quart saucepan of boiling salted water (1 tablespoon) for 1 minute. Immediately drain zucchini in a sieve and rinse under cold running water to stop the cooking.

Squeeze zucchini dry by small handfuls, transferring to a bowl. Stir in remaining ingredients.

COOK'S NOTE

■ The raita can be made up to 2 days ahead and refrigerated, covered. Serve at cool room temperature.

Banana Tamarind Chutney

MAKES ABOUT 1 CUP
ACTIVE TIME: 15 MINUTES ■ START TO FINISH: 35 MINUTES

■ Instead of pureeing the banana for this quick chutney, you can slice it and stir it in with the cilantro. ■

½ cup boiling water
2 tablespoons tamarind (from a pliable block; see Sources)
½ teaspoon cumin seeds, toasted (see Tips, page 911)
1 ripe banana, cut into chunks
1½ tablespoons packed dark brown sugar
¾ teaspoon finely grated peeled fresh ginger
½ teaspoon salt, or to taste
1 tablespoon chopped fresh cilantro

SPECIAL EQUIPMENT: an electric coffee/spice grinder

Pour boiling water over tamarind paste in a small bowl and soak for 30 minutes. Mash paste into water, then force through a medium-mesh sieve into a bowl; discard solids.

Grind cumin seeds to a powder in grinder.

Combine tamarind puree, ground cumin, banana, brown sugar, ginger, and salt in a blender or food processor and puree until smooth. Transfer to a small serving bowl and stir in cilantro.

COOK'S NOTE

■ The chutney can be made up to 1 day ahead and refrigerated, covered. Bring to room temperature before serving.

Lebanese Lamb and Bean Stew

SERVES 8
ACTIVE TIME: 30 MINUTES ■ START TO FINISH: 2½ HOURS
PLUS SOAKING TIME FOR BEANS

■ Terre Haute, Indiana, may not be the place you'd expect to discover authentic Lebanese food. But alongside the selections of George's Downtown Café and Diner, run by Albert Issa, you'll find such specialties as falafel, tabbouleh, and this savory stew. It is seasoned with *baharat*, a Middle Eastern and African ground spice mixture that typically includes allspice, cinnamon, clove, cumin, Maras chile, and black pepper. (You can substitute a cinnamon stick.) *Baharat* also makes a great rub for grilled meats. ■

1 pound dried navy beans, picked over and rinsed
2 pounds boneless lamb shoulder, trimmed of excess fat and cut into 1½ inch pieces
4 teaspoons *baharat* (see Sources) or 1 (3-inch) cinnamon stick
9 cups water
2 tablespoons olive oil
2 medium onions, chopped
4 garlic cloves, finely chopped
Salt and freshly ground black pepper
3 tablespoons tomato paste

ACCOMPANIMENTS: Spiced Basmati Rice (page 256)

Soak beans in cold water to cover by 2 inches at room temperature (refrigerate if kitchen is very warm) for 8 to 12 hours (or see page 129 for quick-soaking procedure); drain.

Combine lamb, *baharat*, and water in a 6- to 8-quart heavy pot and bring to a boil. Reduce heat and simmer vigorously, covered, until meat is almost tender, 1¼ to 1½ hours.

Add beans and simmer, uncovered, until beans are tender, about 1 hour.

Meanwhile, heat oil in a 12-inch heavy skillet over moderate heat until hot but not smoking. Add onions, garlic, ½ teaspoon salt, and ¼ teaspoon pepper and cook, stirring, until onions are pale golden and tender, 8 to 10 minutes. Stir in tomato paste and cook, stirring, for 2 minutes. Remove from heat.

When beans are tender, stir in tomato onion mixture, 1½ teaspoons salt, and ½ teaspoon pepper and simmer until just heated through, about 5 minutes. Serve with rice.

COOK'S NOTE

- The stew can be made up to 3 days ahead. Cool, uncovered, then refrigerate, covered. Reheat over moderate heat.

Lamb Chili with Masa Harina Dumplings

SERVES 6 TO 8
ACTIVE TIME: 1¼ HOURS ■ START TO FINISH: 4¼ HOURS

■ Slowly cooking lamb with lard, spices, and a mix of smoky chipotle and mild New Mexico chiles creates a wonderfully complex chili. Topped with tender corn-flavored dumplings, the result is a sophisticated take on tamale pie, buzzing with a mellow heat. ■

FOR CHILI
- 10 dried mild New Mexico chiles (2½–3 ounces; see Sources)
- 5 cups water
- 3¼ pounds boneless lamb shoulder, trimmed of excess fat and cut into 1½-inch pieces
- Salt
- ½ teaspoon freshly ground black pepper
- 3 tablespoons lard or vegetable oil
- 1 large onion, chopped
- 4 garlic cloves, minced
- 2 Turkish bay leaves or 1 California bay leaf
- 2 teaspoons ground cumin
- 1½ teaspoons dried oregano, crumbled
- 3 tablespoons finely chopped canned chipotle chiles in adobo

FOR DUMPLINGS
- ¾ cup masa harina
- ¼ cup all-purpose flour
- 1 teaspoon baking powder
- ¼ teaspoon baking soda
- ¼ teaspoon salt
- ¼ cup lard or unsalted butter, cut into small pieces and chilled

- ¾ cup well-shaken buttermilk
- 2 tablespoons chopped fresh cilantro

MAKE THE CHILI: Simmer dried chiles in 2 cups water, covered, in a 2-quart heavy saucepan until very soft, about 20 minutes.

Reserve ¾ cup cooking liquid and drain chiles. Stem chiles (do not remove seeds) and puree in a blender with reserved cooking liquid until smooth (use caution when blending hot liquids). Force puree through a fine-mesh sieve into a bowl; discard solids.

Pat lamb dry and sprinkle with 1 teaspoon salt and pepper. Heat 2 tablespoons lard in a 6-quart wide heavy pot or a large 3-inch-deep skillet over moderately high heat until hot but not smoking. Brown lamb in 4 batches, without crowding, turning occasionally, about 5 minutes per batch. Transfer to a bowl.

Add remaining tablespoon lard to pot, add onion, garlic, bay leaves, and ¼ teaspoon salt, and cook over moderate heat, stirring occasionally, until onion is softened, 4 to 5 minutes. Add cumin and oregano and cook, stirring frequently, for 1 minute. Stir in chile puree and chipotles and simmer, stirring frequently and scraping up brown bits from bottom of pot, for 5 minutes. Add lamb, along with any juices accumulated in bowl, and remaining 3 cups water and bring to a boil. Reduce heat and simmer, covered, until lamb is tender, about 2½ hours.

MAKE THE DUMPLINGS: Stir together masa harina, flour, baking powder, baking soda, and salt in a bowl. Blend in lard with a pastry blender or your fingertips until mixture resembles coarse meal. Add buttermilk, stirring just until dough is moistened; do not overmix.

Skim fat off chili and discard bay leaves. Drop 8 or 9 heaping tablespoons of dough onto simmering chili, about 2 inches apart. Reduce heat to low, cover, and simmer gently until tops of dumplings are dry to the touch, 15 to 20 minutes.

Sprinkle dumplings with cilantro.

COOK'S NOTE

- The chili (without the dumplings and cilantro) is best when made at least 1 day ahead, and it can be made up to 2 days ahead. Cool, uncovered, then refrigerate, covered. Remove the fat from the surface and reheat before cooking the dumplings.

Lamb in Spiced Yogurt Sauce with Rice and Pita Bread

SERVES 6 TO 8
ACTIVE TIME: 1 HOUR ■ START TO FINISH: 3½ HOURS

■ This recipe, adapted from one contributed by Kathy Sullivan and Janine El Tal, international educators and longtime residents of Jordan, is a scaled-down version of that country's national dish, *mensaf,* which is usually served in large quantities at important gatherings. *Mensaf* is generally eaten standing up, using the right hand to form little balls of rice and meat. You'll wow your guests when you serve this. ■

    3 pounds bone-in lamb shoulder, cut into 6 large
       chunks by the butcher
    7 cups water
       Salt and freshly ground black pepper
    ¼ cup clarified butter (see Tips, page 914) or
       vegetable oil
    ¼ cup pine nuts
    1 large onion, chopped
 1½ teaspoons turmeric
    ½ teaspoon ground allspice
    2 green cardamom pods (see Sources), lightly cracked
    1 (2-inch) piece cinnamon stick
    2 cups whole-milk yogurt
    2 cups long-grain white rice
    4 (5-inch) pita breads (with pockets), halved

ACCOMPANIMENT: 3 small red onions, quartered

Combine lamb and 4 cups water in 5-quart wide heavy pot (add more water to just cover lamb if necessary) and bring to a boil over moderate heat, skimming all froth from surface. Add 1 teaspoon salt and ½ teaspoon pepper, reduce heat, cover, and simmer for 30 minutes.

Meanwhile, heat clarified butter in a 12-inch heavy skillet over moderate heat until hot. Add pine nuts and cook, stirring occasionally, until golden, about 5 minutes. Transfer with a slotted spoon to paper towels to drain. Add onion to skillet and cook, stirring occasionally, until softened and golden, about 12

minutes. Stir in turmeric, allspice, cardamom pods, and cinnamon and cook, stirring, until fragrant, about 2 minutes. Remove from heat.

When lamb has simmered for 30 minutes, add onion mixture and simmer, covered, for 1 hour.

Remove lid from pot and briskly simmer until liquid is reduced by half, about 1 hour more.

Add yogurt, gently shaking and swirling pot to incorporate. Simmer lamb over moderately low heat, uncovered, stirring occasionally in one direction only (or yogurt may curdle), until sauce is slightly thickened and meat is very tender, 30 to 40 minutes. Season sauce with salt and pepper if necessary and discard cinnamon stick.

While sauce simmers, bring remaining 3 cups water and 1 teaspoon salt to a boil in a 3-quart saucepan. Add rice and stir once, reduce heat to low, and cook, covered, for 20 minutes. Remove pan from heat and let stand, covered, for 5 minutes, then fluff rice gently with a fork.

Line a large deep platter with a single layer of pita halves (reserve remaining pita to serve alongside) and mound rice on top of bread. Spoon ½ cup sauce over rice to moisten and arrange meat on rice. Sprinkle with pine nuts and spoon ½ cup sauce over meat. Arrange reserved pita and red onions around edges of platter. Pour remaining sauce through a sieve into a small bowl and serve on the side.

COOK'S NOTE
■ The lamb and sauce can be made up to 1 day ahead. Cool, uncovered, then refrigerate, covered. Reheat over low heat and continue as directed.

Lamb and Vegetable Tagine

SERVES 8 TO 10
ACTIVE TIME: 1½ HOURS ■ START TO FINISH: 2½ HOURS
PLUS SOAKING TIME FOR CHICKPEAS

■ Tagine is the name for both an earthenware dish with a volcano-shaped top and the tender Moroccan stew that is slowly cooked in it. The heavy pot we use here isn't nearly as romantic, and the seasonings are from the supermarket rather than the *souk*, but the end result is full of deep, subtle flavors. Because we cut the vegetables into similar-sized pieces, this tagine is more handsome than most, making it a fantastic dish for entertaining. Serve it with couscous. ■

1½ cups (9 ounces) dried chickpeas, picked over and
    rinsed
1 teaspoon cumin seeds
½ teaspoon caraway seeds
5 tablespoons unsalted butter
1 pound onions, finely chopped
1 tablespoon minced garlic
1 Turkish bay leaf or ½ California bay leaf
1 tablespoon sweet paprika
1 teaspoon ground cinnamon
1 teaspoon ground ginger
1½ pounds boneless lamb shoulder, trimmed of excess
    fat and cut into 1½-inch pieces
6 cups water
2 medium tomatoes, peeled (see Tips, page 913),
    seeded, and chopped, or 1 (14- to 15-ounce)
    can whole tomatoes in juice, drained and
    chopped
    Salt
1 (2-pound) butternut squash, peeled, halved, seeded,
    and cut into 1-inch pieces
1 pound carrots, cut into 1-inch pieces
1 pound zucchini, quartered lengthwise and cut into
    1-inch pieces
1 pound turnips, peeled and cut into 1-inch pieces
½ cup raisins
2 tablespoons chopped fresh cilantro
2 tablespoons chopped fresh flat-leaf parsley
2 tablespoons chopped fresh mint
1–2 tablespoons harissa (see Sources)
1 teaspoon fresh lemon juice

ACCOMPANIMENT: COUSCOUS

SPECIAL EQUIPMENT: an electric coffee/spice grinder

Soak chickpeas in cold water to cover by 3 inches at room temperature (refrigerate if kitchen is very warm) for 8 to 12 hours (or see page 129 for quick-soaking procedure); drain.

Transfer chickpeas to a 3-quart heavy saucepan, cover with water by 3 inches, and bring to a simmer over moderate heat. Simmer, skimming froth, until chickpeas are almost tender, about 45 minutes.

Meanwhile, grind cumin and caraway seeds to a powder in grinder.

Drain chickpeas in a colander and rinse under cold running water to cool. Rub skins off chickpeas and discard. Cover chickpeas with a dampened paper towel and set aside.

Melt butter in a 6- to 8-quart heavy pot over moderately low heat. Add onions, garlic, and bay leaf and cook, stirring occasionally, until onions are softened, 6 to 7 minutes. Stir in spices (including cumin and caraway) and cook, stirring frequently, for 1 minute. Increase heat to moderately high, add lamb, and cook, stirring frequently, until well browned, 6 to 7 minutes.

Add water, tomatoes, and 2 teaspoons salt and bring to a boil, then reduce heat, cover, and simmer until lamb is almost tender, 40 to 60 minutes.

Add butternut squash, carrots, zucchini, turnips, raisins, and 1 tablespoon each cilantro, parsley, and mint, stir in chickpeas, cover, and simmer until vegetables and lamb are tender, about 20 minutes.

Ladle 1 cup cooking liquid into a bowl and whisk in harissa (to taste), lemon juice, and salt to taste.

Serve lamb and vegetables with broth over couscous, sprinkled with remaining herbs. Serve harissa sauce on the side.

COOK'S NOTES

■ The tagine (without the couscous) can be made up to 2 days ahead. Cool, uncovered, then refrigerate, covered. Reheat before serving with the couscous.
■ The harissa sauce can be made up to 2 days ahead. Cool, uncovered, then refrigerate, covered. Reheat before serving.

Provençal Rack of Lamb

SERVES 2
ACTIVE TIME: 45 MINUTES ■ START TO FINISH: 1¾ HOURS

■ A savory sauce of roasted tomatoes, black olives, shallots, anchovies, and white wine, thickened with roasted garlic, makes a sublime base for tender rack of lamb. It's the properly luxe treatment for this pricey cut of meat. Be sure to have some crusty bread on hand to mop up the sauce. ■

½ cup plus ⅓ cup dry white wine

2 tablespoons extra-virgin olive oil

1 garlic head, left whole, plus 2 cloves, smashed

¼ cup finely chopped shallots

2 teaspoons finely chopped fresh thyme

2 teaspoons finely chopped fresh rosemary

1 (8-rib) frenched rack of lamb (1½ pounds), trimmed of fat and silverskin

2 tablespoons plus ¼ teaspoon olive oil

1 pint (8 ounces) grape tomatoes, halved lengthwise
    Salt and freshly ground black pepper

1 tablespoon Dijon mustard

4 anchovy fillets

¼ cup Niçoise olives, pitted

¼ cup water

2 tablespoons chopped fresh flat-leaf parsley

SPECIAL EQUIPMENT: an instant-read thermometer

Put a rack in middle of oven and preheat oven to 450°F.

Combine ⅓ cup wine, extra-virgin olive oil, smashed garlic cloves, shallots, 1 teaspoon thyme, and 1 teaspoon rosemary in a sealable plastic bag. Add lamb, seal, squeezing out excess air, and marinate at room temperature for 1 hour.

Meanwhile, trim ¼ inch off top of head of garlic. Drizzle tops of cloves with ¼ teaspoon olive oil and wrap head in foil. Roast garlic until pale golden and tender when pierced with tip of a knife, about 45 minutes. (Leave oven on.)

While garlic roasts, toss tomatoes with 1 tablespoon olive oil, ¼ teaspoon salt, ⅛ teaspoon pepper, and remaining 1 teaspoon each thyme and rosemary in a bowl until coated. Arrange tomatoes, cut side up, on a foil-lined baking sheet and roast until beginning to brown, 25 to 30 minutes. Set aside. (Leave oven on.)

Remove lamb from marinade; reserve marinade. Discard smashed garlic cloves. Scrape shallots off meat and return them to marinade. Pat meat dry and

RACK OF LAMB

A rack of lamb is one of the most elegant, celebratory main courses imaginable for an intimate dinner. Cut from the lamb's rib section, the curved rack is tender and flavorful, and because it's so small, it can easily be seared on the stovetop before being roasted in the oven. Then it's carved into 7 or 8 individual chops (a rack may have 7 or 8 bones), which resemble fanciful meat lollipops, or 4 double chops.

Rack of lamb is also enormously versatile—it is just as delicious prepared with Indian spices (page 496) as it is with French herbs (above). It also takes well to a variety of cooking techniques and is virtually foolproof: cook the meat to medium-rare (it doesn't take long), and you're guaranteed a delicious main course.

All of these virtues, of course, come with a price. The main reason racks of lamb (or lamb rib chops) are so expensive is that there is lots of waste in breaking down this "subprimal" section into retail cuts. The butcher has to remove the thick, waxy "hard fat," which is strong and earthy in flavor. Often the bones are frenched—scraped clean of every iota of fat and meat—for a more formal presentation, which is as laborious and time-consuming as it sounds. Many butchers also remove the deckle (the

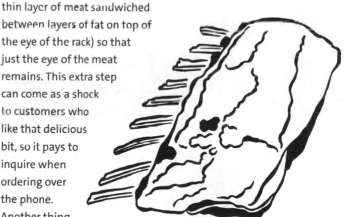

thin layer of meat sandwiched between layers of fat on top of the eye of the rack) so that just the eye of the meat remains. This extra step can come as a shock to customers who like that delicious bit, so it pays to inquire when ordering over the phone. Another thing to ask about is whether the chine bone (backbone) has been sawed off; it almost always is, but in the unlikely event that a sloppy butcher has left it intact, you will not be able to cut a rack into chops either before or after cooking.

Racks of lamb are generally much less expensive at big-box stores, but you will probably have to cut off the thick, hard fat yourself. Take it down to about ⅛ inch—especially if you are going to cut chops for grilling (pages 547 to 549), to help prevent flare-ups.

season with ½ teaspoon salt and ⅛ teaspoon pepper.

Heat remaining 1 tablespoon olive oil in a 10-inch heavy ovenproof skillet over moderately high heat until hot but not smoking. Add lamb and sear, turning once, until browned, about 4 minutes. Spread mustard over top and sides of lamb, using back of a spoon.

Turn lamb fat side down, transfer skillet to oven, and roast lamb until thermometer inserted 2 inches into center (without touching bone) registers 130°F for medium-rare, 16 to 20 minutes. Transfer lamb to a cutting board (set skillet aside) and let stand, loosely covered with foil, for 10 minutes.

Meanwhile, squeeze roasted garlic from skins into a bowl and mash with a fork.

Add reserved marinade to skillet and bring to a boil, stirring and scraping up any brown bits. Reduce heat to moderate, stir in remaining ½ cup wine and anchovies, and simmer, covered, until shallots are softened, about 5 minutes. Stir to blend anchovies into sauce, then add mashed garlic, tomatoes, olives, water, and parsley and stir until well combined. Stir in any meat juices accumulated on cutting board.

Cut lamb into chops. Spoon tomato and olive sauce onto two plates and arrange chops on top.

Tandoori Rack of Lamb with Raita

SERVES 4

ACTIVE TIME: 30 MINUTES ■ START TO FINISH: 1 HOUR

■ In the Middle East and India, a tandoor, or clay oven, is used to bake breads and cook meats at very high heats. A regular oven cranked up to 500°F does the job with this supremely flavorful rack of lamb. Bottled vindaloo paste adds a fiery note to the yogurt marinade, and the bright, herby raita mellows the lamb's incendiary heat. Our inspiration was a recipe from Jasper Schneider, executive chef of the Ritz-Carlton in St. Thomas. ■

FOR LAMB

1 cup thick yogurt, preferably Greek-style
¼ cup chopped fresh mint
¼ cup chopped fresh cilantro
2 tablespoons Patak's vindaloo paste (see Sources)
2 tablespoons grapeseed oil (see Sources) or vegetable oil
Salt and freshly ground black pepper
2 (8-rib) frenched racks of lamb (1¼ pounds each), trimmed of all but a thin layer of fat

FOR RAITA

½ cup thick yogurt, preferably Greek-style
½ cup loosely packed fresh cilantro leaves
½ cup loosely packed fresh mint leaves
1½ teaspoons fresh lemon juice
Salt
½ teaspoon freshly ground black pepper
½ teaspoon mild honey
½ teaspoon chopped serrano chile, including seeds
¼ seedless cucumber (usually plastic-wrapped)

SPECIAL EQUIPMENT: an instant-read thermometer

ROAST THE LAMB: Put a rack in middle of oven and preheat oven to 500°F. Line rack of a broiler pan with foil.

Stir together yogurt, mint, cilantro, vindaloo paste, oil, ¼ teaspoon salt, and ¼ teaspoon pepper in a bowl until well combined. Rub meaty part of lamb with ¾ teaspoon salt and ½ teaspoon pepper, then coat with yogurt mixture (avoid rib bones). Arrange lamb fat side up on broiler rack.

Roast lamb until thermometer inserted 2 inches into center (without touching bone) registers 130°F for medium-rare, 25 to 30 minutes. Transfer lamb to a cutting board and let stand, loosely covered with foil, for 10 minutes.

MEANWHILE, MAKE THE RAITA: Put yogurt, cilantro, mint, lemon juice, ½ teaspoon salt, pepper, honey, and chile in a food processor and pulse until combined. Transfer to a bowl. Grate cucumber using large holes of a box grater and stir into yogurt mixture, along with salt to taste. Set aside.

Cut each rack into double chops. Stir raita and serve on the side.

COOK'S NOTES

■ The lamb can be coated with the yogurt mixture up to 1 day ahead and refrigerated, covered.

■ The raita can be made up to 1 day ahead and refrigerated, covered. Bring to room temperature and stir before serving.

Leg of Lamb with Greens

SERVES 4
ACTIVE TIME: 30 MINUTES ■ START TO FINISH: 1 HOUR

■ A petite leg of lamb makes an elegant choice for a small dinner party. This stuffing of pungent, slightly bitter dandelion greens and sweet golden raisins tastes marvelous with the mild meat (substituting spinach results in a more subtle dish). The 2½-pound boned and butterflied leg we call for here is available at most supermarkets—it's a great convenience cut and extremely easy to work with. ■

8 cups loosely packed dandelion greens (stems discarded) or 10 ounces baby spinach (8 cups packed)
3 tablespoons extra-virgin olive oil
1 cup chopped onion
2 teaspoons finely chopped garlic
½ cup golden raisins, coarsely chopped
Salt and freshly ground black pepper
1 (2½-pound) boned and butterflied leg of lamb (see headnote)
⅓ cup water

SPECIAL EQUIPMENT: kitchen string; an instant-read thermometer

Put a rack in middle of oven and preheat oven to 350°F.

Blanch dandelion greens (do not blanch spinach if using) in a 5-quart pot of boiling salted water (2 tablespoons salt) for 2 minutes. Drain in a colander and rinse under cold water. Squeeze excess water from dandelion greens and coarsely chop.

Heat 2 tablespoons oil in a large heavy skillet over moderate heat until hot but not smoking. Add onion and garlic and cook, stirring, until just golden, about 5 minutes. Add chopped dandelion greens (or whole spinach leaves), raisins, ¼ teaspoon salt, and ¼ teaspoon pepper and cook, stirring, until dandelion greens are tender but still green (or until spinach is wilted and any liquid has evaporated), 2 to 3 minutes. Refrigerate greens for 5 minutes. If using spinach, transfer to a cutting board and coarsely chop filling.

Open out lamb and place fat side down on a work surface with a long side nearest you. Sprinkle with ¼ teaspoon salt. Spread greens over lamb. Fold lamb over to enclose stuffing and tie with string at 1-inch intervals. Pat lamb dry. Rub with remaining 1 tablespoon oil, ½ teaspoon salt, and ¾ teaspoon pepper.

Transfer lamb to a small flameproof roasting pan and roast until thermometer inserted diagonally 2 inches into meat registers 135°F for medium-rare, 45 to 55 minutes. (Test in several places.) Transfer lamb to a cutting board and let stand, loosely covered with foil, for 15 minutes.

Meanwhile, add water to roasting pan and deglaze by boiling, scraping up any brown bits, for 1 minute. Slice lamb (discard strings) and serve with pan juices spooned over slices.

Anchovy and Rosemary Roasted Lamb

SERVES 6
ACTIVE TIME: 30 MINUTES ■ START TO FINISH: 3½ HOURS
(INCLUDES MARINATING)

■ Lamb with anchovy paste is a classic Italian preparation. The anchovy blends beautifully with the meat and stealthily deepens the salsa verde. For guidelines on carving a leg of lamb, see page 498. ■

6 garlic cloves
9 anchovy fillets, patted dry
¼ cup olive oil
2½ tablespoons chopped fresh rosemary
1 (6- to 7-pound) semiboneless leg of lamb (aitchbone removed), trimmed of all but a thin layer of fat and tied
2 teaspoons salt
¾ teaspoon freshly ground black pepper

ACCOMPANIMENT: Salsa Verde (page 499)
SPECIAL EQUIPMENT: an instant-read thermometer

MARINATE THE LAMB: Mince garlic and anchovies and mash to a paste, using side of a large heavy knife. Transfer to a small bowl and stir in oil and rosemary.

Pat lamb dry and put fat side up on a rack in a 17-by-14-inch roasting pan. Make several small

1-inch-deep slits in lamb with a paring knife and rub marinade over entire surface of lamb, pushing some marinade into slits. Marinate lamb, loosely covered, at room temperature for 1 hour.

ROAST THE LAMB: Put a rack in middle of oven and preheat oven to 400°F.

Sprinkle lamb all over with salt and pepper. Roast until thermometer inserted into thickest part of lamb (almost to the bone but not touching it) registers 125°F for medium-rare, 1½ to 1¾ hours (temperature in thinner parts of leg may register up to 160°F). Let stand, uncovered, for 30 minutes.

Carve lamb and serve with salsa verde.

COOK'S NOTE

- The lamb can be marinated, covered, in the refrigerator for up to 5 hours. Bring to room temperature (about 1 hour) before roasting.

CARVING A LEG OF LAMB THE FRENCH WAY

The charm of slicing a leg of lamb the French way is that you end up with an ample selection of medium-rare to well-done meat, enough to satisfy a range of tastes. The method involves shaving slices lengthwise from the leg, cutting almost parallel to the bone (instead of crosswise, as with a smoked ham). The muscles in a leg of lamb go in all different directions, so that even though you may think you are committing a sacrilege by going with the grain, in fact you'll find you are slicing many of the muscles on a long diagonal slightly across the grain. The secret to achieving beautiful slices is to give your sharpest knife a fresh honing before you begin. Grabbing the leg by the shank end, lift the leg up to a level where it's comfortable for your other arm (specifically, your wrist) to carve on a downward slope. Tilting the knife blade at roughly a 20-degree angle to the meat, begin paring thin slices from the opposite end of the leg, just to one side of it (1). Start each slice above the previous one so that the slices lengthen and widen as you move up the leg. After you've made significant inroads on one side, rotate the leg a quarter turn and continue to carve, lifting each slice off with the knife and fluidly draping it over the previous slice (2). Keep turning and slicing the leg until you reach the bone (3).

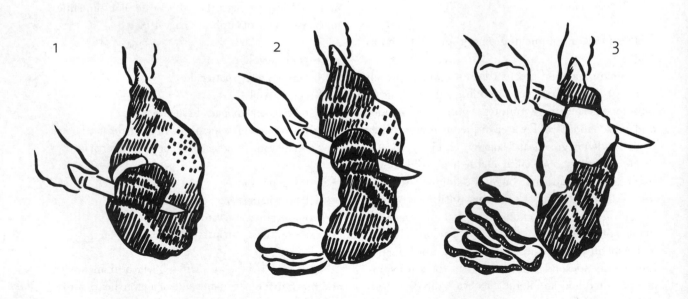

Salsa Verde

MAKES ABOUT ¾ CUP
ACTIVE TIME: 15 MINUTES ■ START TO FINISH: 15 MINUTES

■ Vividly green, given another flavor level by the anchovies and capers, this fresh sauce is also good on grilled steak, roast chicken, or even steamed vegetables. ■

½ cup extra-virgin olive oil
9 anchovy fillets, patted dry and minced
2½ tablespoons capers, preferably nonpareil, rinsed and finely chopped
6 tablespoons finely chopped fresh flat-leaf parsley
3 tablespoons finely chopped fresh mint
1 teaspoon white wine vinegar
⅛ teaspoon freshly ground black pepper

Stir together all ingredients in a bowl.

COOK'S NOTE

■ The salsa can be made up to 1 day ahead and refrigerated, covered.

Lamb Shanks with Ancho Chiles and Prunes

SERVES 4
ACTIVE TIME: 1 HOUR ■ START TO FINISH: 4 HOURS

■ In this braise, anchos contribute a mild heat, while prunes and a touch of balsamic vinegar add sweetness. We like to serve these shanks over grits. ■

3 dried ancho chiles
2 cups boiling water
1½ cups (about 9 ounces) loosely packed pitted prunes
1 large white onion, coarsely chopped
2 garlic cloves, smashed
2 tablespoons balsamic vinegar
1 teaspoon cumin seeds
½ teaspoon ground cinnamon
1 Turkish bay leaf or ½ California bay leaf
Salt and freshly ground black pepper
2 cups water
4 lamb shanks (4–4½ pounds total), trimmed of excess fat and silverskin
¼ cup olive oil
2 tablespoons chopped fresh cilantro

SPECIAL EQUIPMENT: parchment paper

Heat a dry heavy skillet over moderately low heat until hot. Toast chiles, turning once and pressing down with tongs, until slightly darker, 30 to 40 seconds. Halve chiles lengthwise and discard seeds, stems, and ribs. Transfer chiles to a bowl, add boiling water, and soak until softened, about 30 minutes.

Meanwhile, combine prunes, onion, garlic, vinegar, cumin seeds, cinnamon, bay leaf, 1½ teaspoons salt, ¼ teaspoon pepper, and 2 cups water in a 2- to 3-quart heavy saucepan, bring to a simmer, and cook, covered, over moderate heat until prunes fall apart, about 30 minutes.

Discard bay leaf and transfer prune mixture to a blender. Add chiles and soaking liquid and puree (use caution when blending hot liquids), in 2 batches if blender is small.

Put a rack in middle of oven and preheat oven to 350°F.

Pat shanks dry and season with ½ teaspoon salt and ½ teaspoon pepper. Heat 2 tablespoons oil in a 12-inch heavy skillet over moderately high heat until hot but not smoking. Add shanks and cook, turning occasionally, until browned, about 7 minutes. Transfer shanks to a 13-by-9-inch shallow baking dish.

Add remaining 2 tablespoons oil to skillet, carefully add prune puree (it will spatter and steam), and cook over moderate heat, stirring frequently, for 5 minutes. Pour sauce over shanks and cover shanks with parchment paper, then tightly cover dish with foil. Braise in oven, turning shanks after 1 hour, until meat is very tender, 2½ to 3 hours.

Skim fat from surface of sauce and sprinkle shanks with cilantro.

COOK'S NOTE

■ The shanks can be braised up to 2 days ahead. Cool, uncovered, then refrigerate, covered. Reheat before serving.

Buffalo, Venison, and Goat

Buffalo Tenderloin Steaks with Gorgonzola Butter

SERVES 8
ACTIVE TIME: 15 MINUTES ■ START TO FINISH: 35 MINUTES

■ Meaty buffalo steaks become even more luxurious topped with a dollop of gently tangy Gorgonzola butter. Be sure to use Gorgonzola dolce. This blue-veined cow's-milk cheese produced near Milan is not sweet, as its name suggests, but it is milder than regular Gorgonzola, whose pungency would overwhelm the meat's clean taste. Because buffalo can be very red even when cooked to medium-rare, it's important to use a thermometer to check the doneness. ■

- ¼ pound Gorgonzola dolce, softened
- ½ stick (4 tablespoons) unsalted butter, softened
- 2 tablespoons minced fresh flat-leaf parsley
- 8 (1¼-inch-thick) buffalo tenderloin steaks (about 4 pounds total; see Sources)
- Salt and freshly ground black pepper
- 2 tablespoons olive oil

SPECIAL EQUIPMENT: an instant-read thermometer

Put a rack in middle of oven and preheat oven to 450°F.

Cut off and discard rind from cheese. Stir together cheese, butter, and parsley in a bowl until well combined. Set aside, covered, at room temperature while you cook steaks.

Pat 4 steaks dry and season on both sides with salt and pepper. Heat 1 tablespoon oil in a 12-inch heavy skillet over high heat until hot and just beginning to smoke. Add seasoned steaks and sear, turning once, until browned, about 4 minutes. Transfer to a large baking sheet. Pat dry, season, and sear remaining 4 steaks in remaining tablespoon oil in same manner; transfer to baking sheet.

Roast steaks until thermometer inserted horizontally 2 inches into center of 2 or 3 steaks registers 130°F, 5 to 6 minutes. Transfer steaks to a platter, top each with a dollop of Gorgonzola butter, and let stand, tented with foil, for 5 minutes.

COOK'S NOTE

■ The Gorgonzola butter can be made up to 1 day ahead and refrigerated, covered. Bring to room temperature before using.

Portobello Buffalo Burgers with Celery Apple Slaw

SERVES 4
ACTIVE TIME: 20 MINUTES ■ START TO FINISH: 1 HOUR

■ More and more people are choosing ground buffalo over ground chuck, because it's lower in fat. That asset can turn into a liability if the meat is cooked too long, so we add sautéed chopped portobello mushrooms, which contribute moisture and flavor. Don't reach for the ketchup—the crisp slaw of celery and apples in a mustardy dressing is a tangy taste surprise. ■

FOR BURGERS
- 1 medium onion, chopped
- 10 ounces portobello mushrooms, trimmed and quartered
- 2 tablespoons plus 2 teaspoons olive oil
- ¾ teaspoon salt
- Rounded ¼ teaspoon freshly ground black pepper
- 1 pound ground buffalo

FOR SLAW
- 2 celery ribs
- ½ Granny Smith apple, cored (left unpeeled)
- 1 tablespoon mayonnaise
- 1½ teaspoons cider vinegar
- 1 teaspoon olive oil
- 1 teaspoon whole-grain mustard
- Rounded ¼ teaspoon sugar
- Rounded ⅛ teaspoon salt
- ⅛ teaspoon freshly ground black pepper

ACCOMPANIMENT: 4 hamburger buns or kaiser rolls, split and toasted

COOK THE VEGETABLES FOR THE BURGERS: Pulse onion and mushrooms in a food processor until finely chopped. Heat 2 tablespoons oil in a 10-inch heavy skillet over moderate heat until hot but not smoking. Add mushroom mixture, salt, and pepper and cook, stirring occasionally, until vegetables are beginning to brown and liquid has evaporated, 8 to 10 minutes. Transfer to a bowl and cool, stirring occasionally, until warm, about 15 minutes.

MEANWHILE, MAKE THE SLAW: Cut celery and apple into thin 2-inch-long matchsticks with a mandoline or other adjustable-blade vegetable slicer or with a knife.

Whisk together mayonnaise, vinegar, oil, mustard, sugar, salt, and pepper in a medium bowl. Add celery and apple, tossing to coat. Let stand for 15 minutes to develop flavors.

FINISH AND COOK THE BURGERS: Stir buffalo into cooled mushroom mixture with your hands until well combined. Form into four 4-inch patties.

Heat remaining 2 teaspoons oil in a 12-inch heavy skillet over moderately high heat until hot but not smoking. Cook burgers, turning once, for about 8 minutes for medium-rare.

Serve burgers on buns, topped with slaw.

Venison Steaks with Red Cabbage and Red Wine Sauce

SERVES 8
ACTIVE TIME: 1¼ HOURS ■ START TO FINISH: 2 HOURS

■ The flesh of deer, elk, moose, caribou, and pronghorn is all commonly referred to as venison, but we use farm-raised deer. In this dish, a tender tangle of red cabbage and currants makes a bed for the juniper-rubbed steaks. Using gin to deglaze the skillet subtly plays up the juniper on the meat and the wintry flavors. ■

BUFFALO

American buffalo—or, more correctly, bison—is significantly higher in protein and omega-3 fatty acids and lower in saturated fats and cholesterol than beef and, at its best, tastes sweeter and cleaner. Most of us cherish the thought of the massive creatures (at 6½ feet tall and 2,000 pounds, the largest land animal in North America) roaming free on the range, eating nothing but native grasses. Some ranchers do raise their herds this way, but in reality, most of the buffalo (especially the ground meat) available at supermarkets today is from animals grain-finished in ranch or commercial feedlots. Growth hormones and antibiotics, which are commonly given to beef cattle in feedlots, are not a factor with buffalo, though, since the feedlots are not overcrowded and the animals pass through them quickly.

If you prefer grass-finished buffalo, your best bet is to order from a regional rancher or supplier whose management protocols can be checked with the National Bison Association in Denver (see Directory of Sources).

Because buffalo has no intramuscular fat, it cooks more quickly than beef does, so keep an eye on the cooking time. And when you're testing for doneness, be aware that buffalo's high iron content will make it look rarer than it really is, so you may have to fight the urge to overcook. The meat is at its best when medium-rare.

FOR RED CABBAGE

- 8 cups thinly sliced red cabbage (about 2 pounds)
- 3 tablespoons unsalted butter
- 1 large onion, thinly sliced
- 2 garlic cloves, smashed
- 1 Turkish bay leaf or ½ California bay leaf
- 4 whole allspice, crushed
- 1 Granny Smith apple
- 1 cup dry red wine, preferably Zinfandel
- ¼ cup red wine vinegar
- 2 tablespoons sugar
- Salt and freshly ground black pepper
- ⅓ cup dried currants

FOR VENISON AND SAUCE

- 1¾ teaspoons juniper berries (see Sources)
- 8 (5- to 6-ounce) slices venison loin (preferably fallow deer; see page 503 and Sources)
- Salt
- 1 teaspoon freshly ground black pepper
- 2 tablespoons vegetable oil
- ½ cup finely chopped shallots
- 2 tablespoons dry gin
- 1 cup dry red wine, preferably Zinfandel
- 1 cup venison stock (see Sources), Beef Stock (page 153), or store-bought reduced-sodium beef broth
- ½ teaspoon mild honey
- 3 tablespoons unsalted butter, cut into tablespoons

GARNISH: finely chopped fresh chives

SPECIAL EQUIPMENT: an electric coffee/spice grinder; an instant-read thermometer

PREPARE THE CABBAGE: Cook cabbage in a 6- to 8-quart pot of boiling salted water (3 tablespoons salt) for 2 minutes; drain.

Heat butter in a 4- to 5-quart heavy pot over moderate heat until foam subsides. Add onion, garlic, bay leaf, and allspice and cook, stirring occasionally, until onion is pale golden, 6 to 8 minutes.

Meanwhile, peel and coarsely grate apple (discard core). Add apple, wine, vinegar, sugar, ¾ teaspoon salt, ½ teaspoon pepper, and cabbage to onion mixture, stirring to combine, then reduce heat to moderately low and simmer, covered, stirring occasionally, until cabbage is tender, 30 to 35 minutes.

Add currants and cook, covered, stirring occasionally, until plump, about 15 minutes. Season with salt and pepper. Remove pot from heat, discard bay leaf, and cover cabbage to keep warm.

COOK THE VENISON: Put a rack in middle of oven and preheat oven to 350°F.

Finely grind juniper berries in grinder. Sprinkle evenly over venison and sprinkle with 1¼ teaspoons salt and pepper. Heat 1 tablespoon oil in a 12-inch heavy skillet over moderate heat until it shimmers. Add 4 slices of venison and cook, turning once, until browned, about 8 minutes. Transfer to a large baking sheet. Wipe out skillet and cook remaining 4 slices of venison in remaining 1 tablespoon oil in same manner; transfer to baking sheet. Set skillet aside (do not wipe out).

Roast venison until thermometer inserted horizontally into a slice registers 120°F, 5 to 10 minutes for medium-rare. Transfer venison to a plate (reserve any meat juices in pan) and cover loosely with foil to keep warm.

MAKE THE SAUCE: Add shallots and gin to skillet and deglaze pan by boiling over moderate heat, scraping up brown bits, for 1 minute, then cook until shallots are softened, 2 to 3 minutes. Increase heat to moderately high, add wine, bring to simmer, and simmer until reduced by half, about 4 minutes. Add stock, bring to a simmer, and simmer until mixture is reduced to about 1 cup, about 5 minutes.

Stir in honey, ¼ teaspoon salt, and any pan juices. Remove from heat and whisk in butter 1 tablespoon at a time until incorporated.

Serve venison with cabbage and sauce, sprinkled with chives.

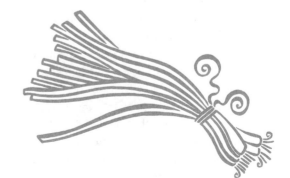

VENISON

Venison (from the Latin *venari,* "to hunt") used to be available only to hunters or those who bought it from specialty purveyors. Today it is farmed in Europe, Asia, New Zealand, and parts of the United States, making it both accessible and affordable year-round.

Venison is touted as a lean, low-fat alternative to other red meats, but its rich, earthy flavor is what makes it even more appealing. Farmed deer graze naturally on pasture or range without steroids or growth hormones. They are not domesticated, but they lead less rigorous lives than their wild counterparts and are slaughtered young (usually under 18 months), so their meat is marbled with more fat and is thus more tender. Because wild deer are not only more active but also have a more varied diet, their meat has a more complex flavor.

As far as cooking methods go, the leg is ideal for roasting, as is a whole saddle, or the chops, loin, and fillet cut from a saddle. A quick roast will ensure that the lean meat stays moist; overcooking results in dry, tough meat. The remainder of the deer—the shoulder, flank, and neck—is better suited to braising or stewing, or for grinding for burgers, sausage, and pasta sauces.

The most widely available farmed venison is CERVENA, which is raised in New Zealand. The term, which comes from *Cervidae* (the taxonomic family name for deer) and "venison," designates leg and saddle cuts

from red deer. It's mild, with a faint gaminess, and tender, with a slightly coarse-grained texture. Cervena, already a regular item at many butcher counters, is increasingly available at major supermarkets.

FALLOW DEER, native to Europe, was the species most likely used in traditional European venison dishes. Now farmed in the United States, fallow deer is available fresh from October through January or February; frozen fallow deer is available year-round (or as long as supplies last). Because fallow deer are smaller than other farmed deer, their muscles are more finely textured. This kind of venison is worth seeking out online (see Sources) or at specialty butcher stores—which is certainly easier than hunting and field-dressing your own.

Venison with Cranberry– Red Wine Sauce

SERVES 6
ACTIVE TIME: 45 MINUTES ■ START TO FINISH: 1 HOUR

■ Venison tenderloins taper at either end, offering a range of medium-rare to better-done meat, which should make all your guests happy. This sprightly sauce is a twist on a *gastrique,* a classic French sauce in which vinegar is added to caramelized sugar. We use tart fresh cranberries in place of the vinegar and combine it all with a heady reduction of red wine. ■

FOR RED WINE REDUCTION
- 1 tablespoon unsalted butter
- 2 celery ribs, chopped
- 2 carrots, chopped
- 1 onion, chopped
- 2 garlic cloves, smashed
- 1 (750-ml) bottle dry red wine
- 1 teaspoon black peppercorns, cracked with bottom of a heavy skillet
- 4 whole cloves
- 1 Turkish bay leaf or ½ California bay leaf
- 1 fresh thyme sprig

FOR CRANBERRY CARAMEL
- ½ cup sugar
- 3 tablespoons water
- 1 cup fresh or thawed frozen cranberries

FOR VENISON
- 1½ pounds venison tenderloin (preferably fallow deer; see page 503 and Sources), trimmed of silverskin
- ¾ teaspoon salt
- ½ teaspoon freshly ground black pepper
- 1½ tablespoons olive oil

FOR SAUCE
- ¼ cup finely chopped shallots
- ½ teaspoon finely grated orange zest
- ⅓ cup Cognac or other brandy
- 1½ teaspoons cornstarch
- 1 tablespoon water
- Salt and freshly ground pepper
- 1 tablespoon unsalted butter

SPECIAL EQUIPMENT: an instant-read thermometer

MAKE THE RED WINE REDUCTION: Melt butter in a 5-quart wide heavy pot over moderately high heat. Add celery, carrots, onion, and garlic and cook, uncovered, stirring occasionally, until vegetables are softened and golden brown, 10 to 12 minutes. Add wine, peppercorns, cloves, bay leaf, and thyme and bring to a boil, then reduce heat and simmer, uncovered, for 15 minutes. Set aside.

MEANWHILE, MAKE THE CRANBERRY CARAMEL: Bring sugar and water to a boil in a small heavy saucepan, stirring until sugar is dissolved and washing down any sugar crystals on sides of pan with a pastry brush dipped in cold water. Boil syrup, without stirring, gently swirling pan, until it is a deep golden caramel. Carefully stir in cranberries (mixture will steam vigorously and caramel will harden) and cook over low heat, stirring occasionally, until caramel is dissolved, 1 to 2 minutes. Set aside.

FINISH THE RED WINE REDUCTION: Pour reduction through a sieve (without pressing on solids) into a bowl; discard solids. Reduction should measure about 1¼ cups (if you have more, reduce to 1¼ cups in cleaned pot). Set aside.

COOK THE VENISON: Put a rack in middle of oven and preheat oven to 425°F.

Pat venison dry and sprinkle with salt and pepper. Heat oil in a 12-inch heavy ovenproof skillet over moderately high heat until hot but not smoking. Brown venison on all sides, turning occasionally, about 5 minutes.

Transfer skillet to oven and roast venison until thermometer inserted diagonally 2 inches into center registers 120°F, 3 to 6 minutes, depending on size of tenderloins. Transfer venison with tongs to a plate (set skillet aside) and let stand while you make sauce (interior temperature of meat will rise about 5 degrees, for medium-rare).

MAKE THE SAUCE: Add shallots to fat remaining in skillet and cook over moderately high heat, stirring, until softened, 1 to 2 minutes. Carefully add zest and Cognac (if Cognac ignites, shake skillet until flame dies down) and boil, stirring, until liquid is reduced to a glaze, about 2 minutes. Add red wine reduction and bring to a simmer. Stir together cornstarch and water in a small bowl until well combined, whisk into sauce, and simmer, whisking, for 1 minute. Stir in cranberry caramel and season with salt and pepper. Remove from heat and add butter, whisking until combined.

Slice venison and serve with sauce on the side.

COOK'S NOTES

- Venison tenderloins vary in size but are usually sold in 6- or 12-ounce pieces. Size variance dramatically affects cooking times, so check the temperature of the meat frequently after the first 3 minutes.
- The red wine reduction and cranberry caramel can be made up to 1 day ahead. Refrigerate separately, covered.

Goat Tacos

SERVES 8
ACTIVE TIME: 45 MINUTES ■ START TO FINISH: 5 HOURS

■ Adapted from a family recipe of Alexandro Garcia, the chef-owner of Blue Agave Club in Pleasanton, California, this dish combines the subtle perfume of bay leaves and cloves with the spice of dried chiles. It's a combination so compelling we find ourselves going back for seconds and even thirds. ■

- 3 dried guajillo or New Mexico chiles (see Sources), wiped clean
- 2 dried ancho chiles, wiped clean
- 3½–4 pounds bone-in goat, such as shoulder, neck, or leg (see Sources)
- Salt
- 1 pound tomatoes, peeled (see Tips, page 913) and coarsely chopped, juice reserved
- 3 garlic cloves
- 1½ teaspoons dried oregano, crumbled
- 1 teaspoon distilled white vinegar
- ½ teaspoon cumin seeds
- 5 black peppercorns
- 3 whole cloves
- 2 Turkish bay leaves or 1 California bay leaf
- 16–24 corn tortillas
- ACCOMPANIMENTS: sliced radishes; crumbled *queso fresco* (Mexican fresh white cheese); salsa verde; thinly sliced romaine or iceberg lettuce; chopped cilantro; chopped white onion; lime wedges

Slit chiles lengthwise, then stem and seed (leave in ribs for heat). Heat a dry large heavy skillet over moderate heat until hot. Toast chiles in batches, opening them out flat and turning and pressing with tongs, until more pliable and slightly changed in color, about 30 seconds per batch. Transfer to a bowl. Soak chiles in hot water to cover until softened, 20 to 30 minutes.

Put a rack in middle of oven and preheat oven to 350°F.

Cut goat into pieces at joints and put in a 13-by-9-inch baking dish. Sprinkle all over with 1½ teaspoons salt.

Drain chiles and transfer to a blender. Add tomatoes with juice, ¾ teaspoon salt, and remaining ingredients except tortillas and puree until very smooth, about 1 minute.

Pour sauce over meat, turning to coat. Cover dish tightly with a double layer of foil and braise in oven until meat is very tender, 3 to 3½ hours. Remove from oven and cool meat in liquid, uncovered, for 30 minutes. (Leave oven on.)

Coarsely shred meat, discarding bones, then mix into braising liquid in dish. Cover again, return to oven, and cook until sauce is simmering, about 30 minutes.

Meanwhile, 15 minutes before goat is done, make 2 stacks of tortillas and wrap each stack in foil. Heat in oven on rack alongside baking dish.

Serve goat with warm tortillas and accompaniments, arranged on a large platter or served separately in little bowls.

COOK'S NOTE

- The goat can be made up to 3 days ahead. Cool, uncovered, then refrigerate, covered. Reheat in a 350°F oven.

GRILLED DISHES

These days most Americans grill over gas; it makes the process so simple. You turn the knob, flip a piece of protein onto the grate, and a few minutes later, dinner is ready.

Still, I can't help thinking that those who take the easy way out are missing one of the truly great pleasures of being a cook. The first time you experience the joy of standing before a wood-filled grill watching the crackling flames as the comforting scent of smoke eddies through the air, you are hooked. And then, when you show up at the table with that gorgeously grilled morsel of meat or the perfect fillet of fish, you feel such a sense of triumph that you can't help wanting to try it again. It takes both technical knowledge and infinite patience to truly master an open fire, which makes this one occupation that is guaranteed to give you a sense of satisfied competence.

That is, I think, why so many men take such pleasure in getting out the grill. Playing with fire has long been considered the male prerogative, but that is finally starting to change. Why should men have all the fun? Grilling is such a companionable way to cook, such a perfect opportunity to stand by the fire with a glass of wine as you discuss the problems of the universe. There is a kind of communion that happens when you are outside together in the dark, and it is one that I would be very sorry to miss out on.

No wonder grilling has become America's favorite way to cook. At *Gourmet* we all get so much pleasure from grilling that we were determined to make this chapter reach far beyond the ordinary. I have to admit that it is hard to top the appeal of a thick Florentine-style steak, with its beautiful coat of char, and we have plenty of advice on that.

We also have a surprising version of veal involtini, which begins with breaded veal cutlets and ends on the grill; the result is something that is not only different from the classic Italian version, but, to my mind, a big improvement. And I don't think there is a better way to cook pork ribs than the wonderfully messy, sticky, spicy ones from our kitchen: they are so fragrant and appealing it's hard to wait long enough to keep from burning your fingers.

Once you start grilling, you begin to respect the wisdom of the many cultures that have made the grill their own. In India, where great cooks have been grilling over fire for thousands of years, yogurt is a secret ingredient, producing meat that is surprisingly soft and silken. Jamaicans know a thing or two about grilled food as well: jerk pork is absolutely addictive, especially when paired with a curried peach relish. Nobody does more exciting things with grilled lamb than the cooks of Turkey, and the Greeks are masters of simply grilled fish. When it comes to vegetables, our own American cooks have been particularly inventive. We began by burying potatoes in the ashes of the grill, as in the classic hobo pack, and we never looked back. In this chapter you'll find exciting ways to transform eggplants, onions, okra, peppers, and potatoes, which may well make you consider the grill in a whole new light.

But be warned: once you get the hang of cooking on an open fire, you're not likely to stop. I find myself looking at almost every food with new eyes, and no matter what I'm cooking, I suddenly wonder how it would taste if it spent a little time on the grill.

GRILLED DISHES

GRILLING BASICS

GAS OR CHARCOAL? Many people equip their "outdoor kitchen" with two options: a gas grill for weeknight suppers and a charcoal grill for the weekend, holidays, and the more leisurely evenings of, say, vacations. Each has its advantages.

Gas, obviously, is easy and convenient—no need to mess around with charcoal and matches to light the fire; no worries about the effect of wind on the flames; no necessity of fussing around to keep the fire temperature even as the cooking time wears on. Just turn the knob and start cooking.

A charcoal grill, on the other hand, provides the undeniable thrill of playing with fire, and because you are involved in every step of the process, from lighting the fire to dealing with the ashes when the cooking is done, it is the most interactive and involving cooking method of all. In other words, it's just plain fun. Many people also feel that charcoal fire provides a more intense version of the ineffable grill flavor.

COOKING ON A CHARCOAL GRILL When most people think of the fuel for live-fire cooking, charcoal briquettes are what comes to mind. Briquettes were an invention of Henry Ford in the early twentieth century, created to use up scrap wood left over from the forms used for car production. They're convenient and perfectly acceptable as a fuel, but they're not 100 percent charcoal: they are rather low-quality powdered charcoal mixed with binders and pressed into those plump little pillows. The next best thing to using wood itself (which is too inconsistent and difficult to deal with for most home grillers) is using hardwood charcoal. This is made by an age-old process of burning hardwood in a closed container with very little oxygen. Because it is almost pure carbon, hardwood charcoal lights more easily than briquettes, burns cleaner and slightly hotter, and responds more quickly to changes in the oxygen level—which means that you can regulate the heat through the bottom vents more easily.

Once you've chosen your fuel, you need to decide how to ignite it. In the old days, most people used lighter fluid, but for both environmental and taste reasons, it's better to avoid it. The best option, in our opinion, is a chimney starter, an inexpensive tool that's available at any hardware store. It's a sheet-metal cylinder that's open at both ends, with ventilation holes around the bottom, an inside grate a few inches from the bottom, and a handle. You simply fill the space under the grate with crumpled newspaper, put it in the middle of the grill, and fill the top with charcoal. When you light the paper, the flames sweep up through the chimney to ignite the charcoal. It works quickly, and it works every time. When the coals are red-hot, dump them out into the grill and put any additional charcoal called for on top or around them.

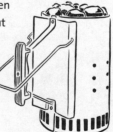

OILING THE GRILL RACK There's one more thing to do before you start cooking. Our recipes usually call for grilling food on a lightly oiled rack, which helps keep the food from sticking. The safest, most efficient way to go about this is to oil a paper towel and use tongs to rub the oiled towel on the grill rack. Along this same line, right after you are finished cooking but before the fire has died down, give the grill a brisk scrub with a wire brush; doing it at this time makes the chore as easy as it gets, and it will also help prevent sticking the next time you grill. Not to mention that you don't want those spareribs you just grilled to taste like last week's salmon steaks.

GETTING ORGANIZED Now that you've dealt with the fire and the grill itself, you need to be sure you are organized and set to go so you don't have to interrupt yourself mid-grilling. First, create a "staging area" on a large table near the grill so you have enough room to work, and make sure you have the essential tools at hand. This is easier if you have a sturdy baking sheet or jelly-roll pan that you can use as a tray to carry the food (don't forget salt and pepper) and tools you need from the kitchen to the grillside table.

The other tools you will need are

- **heavy-duty long-handled tongs** (one pair for handling raw food and another pair for handling cooked food, to prevent cross-contamination)
- **a large heavy-duty offset spatula** (ideal for handling burgers or fish)
- **a long-handled meat fork** for checking doneness and moving around some types of food
- **oiled paper towels** for oiling the grill rack (use tongs)
- **moistened paper towels** for cleaning hands
- **a stash of folded kitchen towels** for cleaning up spills and to use to move hot dishes
- **a heavy-duty wire brush** for cleaning the grill rack

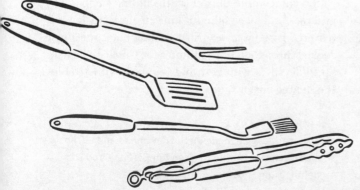

If you will often be grilling small or delicate foods such as asparagus or mushrooms, a perforated grill sheet—basically a flat piece of metal with holes in it for the heat of the fire to penetrate—is a handy thing to have. And if you're going to do lots of cooking at night, it's very helpful to have a lamp that attaches to the grill. Finally, there's one more tool that may actually be the most important of all, after tongs. Make sure you have a couple of disposable foil pans around for covering food on those occasions when you want something to finish cooking on the inside but not cook any more on the exterior. The pan creates a kind of oven effect, which makes for even, thorough cooking with no charring.

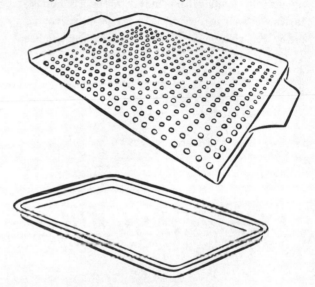

DIRECT VERSUS INDIRECT HEAT No matter whether you're cooking with charcoal or gas, there are times when you should use direct heat and times when indirect heat is best. Direct-heat grilling means cooking right over the source of heat, whether it's coals or flames; indirect heat means cooking off to the side of the heat source. Basically you use direct heat when you're cooking something like a boneless chicken breast or a thin pork chop that will cook all the way through before charring on the outside if put right over the heat source. Indirect heat is best when you're cooking something that, if cooked over the flames or coals, would burn on the outside before cooking on the inside—a bone-in chicken breast, say, or a really thick chop. You still usually start out directly over the heat so that you get a good sear on the food before moving it to the side.

Setting up a gas grill for indirect heat is straightforward: simply preheat all the burners for about 10 minutes, then turn all but one of the burners off. Setting up a charcoal grill for indirect heat is a little more complicated (see opposite).

TO PREPARE A CHARCOAL GRILL FOR DIRECT HEAT Open the vents in the bottom of the grill. Light a large chimney starter full of charcoal, preferably hardwood. When the coals are lit, dump them out across the bottom, leaving about a quarter of the bottom of the grill free of charcoal so you can move food there in case of flare-ups. When all the charcoal is grayish white (start checking the coals 15 minutes after lighting them), the grill will be at its hottest; then it will begin to cool off. You can gauge the heat of the fire by seeing how long you can comfortably hold your hand 5 inches above the rack directly over the coals:

HOT: 1 to 2 seconds

MEDIUM-HOT: 3 to 4 seconds

LOW: 5 to 6 seconds

TO PREPARE A CHARCOAL GRILL FOR INDIRECT HEAT Open the vents in the bottom of the grill. Light a large chimney starter full of charcoal, preferably hardwood. When the coals are lit, dump them out on two opposite sides of the bottom rack, leaving a space free of charcoal in the middle; it should be slightly larger than the size of the food you plan to grill. When all the charcoal is grayish white (start checking the coals 15 minutes after lighting them), the grill will be at its hottest; then it will begin to cool off. You can gauge the heat of the fire by seeing how long you can comfortably hold your hand 5 inches above the rack directly over the coals.

WHEN AND WHEN NOT TO COVER A CHARCOAL FIRE Although you need to cover a charcoal fire when you are cooking over indirect heat, it's not a good idea to cover the grill when the food is directly over the coals, because it tends to give it an off flavor. Although many sources recommend that you use the cover to bring a flare-up under control, don't. If you've set up the fire as suggested, you can just move the food away from the coals until the flames have died down.

Fish and Shellfish

Grilled Salmon with Lime Butter Sauce

SERVES 6
ACTIVE TIME: 20 MINUTES ■ START TO FINISH: 50 MINUTES

■ A sprinkle of lime zest and a drizzle of lime butter highlight the rich flavor of grilled salmon. The fantastic sauce takes only 5 minutes to prepare, and once you see how versatile it is—try it on grilled corn and other vegetables—you'll want to make it for a host of your summer favorites. ■

1 small garlic clove, chopped
2 tablespoons fresh lime juice (grate zest first)
   Salt and freshly ground black pepper
½ stick (4 tablespoons) unsalted butter, melted

6 (6-ounce) pieces center-cut salmon fillet, preferably wild, with skin
1½ teaspoons finely grated lime zest

If using a charcoal grill, prepare it for direct-heat cooking over medium-hot coals; if using a gas grill, prepare it for direct-heat cooking over medium heat (see above).

Meanwhile, combine garlic, lime juice, ½ teaspoon salt, and ¼ teaspoon pepper in a blender and blend until smooth. With motor running, add melted butter and blend until combined, about 30 seconds.

Season salmon all over with salt and pepper. Oil grill rack and place salmon skin side up on rack. Grill (covered if using a gas grill), turning once, until just cooked through, 8 to 10 minutes for 1-inch-thick fish. Sprinkle fillets with zest and top each with 1 tablespoon lime butter sauce.

COOK'S NOTE

■ The sauce can be made up to 1 day ahead and refrigerated, covered. Bring to room temperature and stir before using.

Grilled Salmon with Mustard Dill Sauce

SERVES 4

ACTIVE TIME: 20 MINUTES ■ START TO FINISH: 30 MINUTES

■ Salmon, cooked until its flesh is tender and moist and its skin is delightfully crisp, is paired with a cool, creamy, Scandinavian-style sauce flecked with dill and shallots. If you make the sauce while you're heating up the grill, you'll be eating dinner before you know it. ■

⅓ cup crème fraîche

⅓ cup sour cream

1 tablespoon finely chopped shallot

1 teaspoon whole-grain mustard

1 teaspoon fresh lemon juice

2–3 tablespoons finely chopped fresh dill

Salt and freshly ground black pepper

4 (6-ounce) pieces center-cut salmon fillet, preferably wild, with skin

If using a charcoal grill, prepare it for direct-heat cooking over medium-hot coals; if using a gas grill, prepare it for direct-heat cooking over medium-high heat (see Grilling Basics, page 512).

Stir together crème fraîche, sour cream, shallot, mustard, lemon juice, dill (to taste), ¼ teaspoon salt, and ¼ teaspoon pepper in a bowl.

Pat salmon dry and sprinkle all over with ½ teaspoon salt and ¼ teaspoon pepper. Oil grill rack and place salmon skin side up on rack. Grill (covered if using a gas grill), turning once, until just cooked through, 8 to 10 minutes for 1-inch-thick fillets.

Serve salmon with sauce.

COOK'S NOTE

■ The sauce can be made up to 3 days ahead and refrigerated, covered.

GRILLING FISH AND OTHER SEAFOOD

THE FIRE Since fish and other seafood are delicate, you'll need a fire that isn't quite as intense as you'd use for meat or poultry. Medium-hot is the proper temperature for most seafood.

WHAT TO GRILL **Firm-fleshed fish**—tuna, swordfish, pompano, mahimahi, halibut, and salmon, for instance— are ideal for the grill because they hold together beautifully. **Rich, oily fish** such as mackerel, bluefish, and fresh sardines are also excellent because they are forgiving and won't dry out quickly and thus overcook. (Although tuna is also oily, it has a denser texture, more like meat, and it will become tight and almost inedible if overdone.) Buy fish fillets with the skin on: the skin protects the flesh and keeps it from falling apart, and the layer of fat between skin and flesh adds flavor and moisture. You can easily remove the skin after grilling if desired. **Scallops** and **shrimp** are wonderful on the grill—they cook quickly, and the smoky edge that the fire adds to them provides the perfect complement to their rather mild flavors. Be sure to grill them only until just cooked through (4 to 5 minutes for scallops, 3 to 4 minutes for shrimp), or they will be tough. **Lobster** is best parboiled before grilling, since it tends to burn slightly on the exterior if cooked on a grill from raw to done (this also allows you to avoid having to kill the lobster before putting it on the grill).

PREVENTING STICKING To prevent fish from sticking, always start with a very clean grill. Although the fire should generally be medium-hot, preheat the grill rack so it is very hot and oil it just before you place the fish on it. Plan on turning the fish just once, since turning it often increases the likelihood that it will stick (and that it will fall apart). If it sticks when you try to turn it, wait a few seconds and try again; it will release more cleanly after it's cooked a bit longer and developed a little sear. A large offset spatula is our tool of choice for turning fish.

MARINADES A marinade can enhance the flavor of grilled fish, but don't let a fish sit in the marinade for longer than the recipe directs, or the flesh may turn mealy.

DON'T OVERCOOK It's particularly important not to overcook fish and seafood. Remember that thicker steaks or fillets or whole fish will continue to cook after you remove them from the grill, so take them off when they are still slightly less done than you want them to be when you eat them.

Grilled Chile-Lime Arctic Char

SERVES 4 GENEROUSLY
ACTIVE TIME: 40 MINUTES ▪ START TO FINISH:
40 MINUTES

▪ Arctic char's firmness makes it a great choice for the grill. Its pretty, rosy flesh takes well to marinades and sauces. Ground chipotle adds a hint of smoky heat to the quick garlicky marinade. We like to finish the skin on the grill for an extra minute or two; the crunch makes a fine contrast to the tender flesh. Because Arctic char is a rather oily fish, we use indirect heat to prevent flare-ups. ▪

    7 medium garlic cloves
    2 tablespoons salt
    ¼ cup fresh lime juice (from about 2 limes)
    2 tablespoons olive oil
  1¾ teaspoons sugar
  1¼ teaspoons ground chipotle chile (see
       Sources)
    2 (1-pound) Arctic char fillets with skin
       (see Cook's Note)

ACCOMPANIMENT: lime wedges

MARINATE THE FISH: Mince garlic and mash to a paste with salt, using side of a large heavy knife. Stir together garlic paste, lime juice, oil, sugar, and chile in a small bowl until sugar is dissolved.

Pat fish dry and place skin side down on a plastic-wrap-lined tray.

Rub chile mixture all over flesh side of fish. Wrap fish in plastic wrap and marinate at a cool room temperature for 15 minutes.

MEANWHILE, PREPARE THE GRILL: If using a charcoal grill, prepare it for indirect-heat cooking over medium-hot coals; if using a gas grill, prepare it for indirect-heat cooking over medium-high heat (see Grilling Basics, page 512).

GRILL THE FISH: Oil grill rack and place fish skin side down over area with no coals, or over turned-off burner. Grill, covered, for 4 minutes. Using two metal spatulas, loosen fish from rack and turn over. Grill, covered, until just cooked through, 3 to 5 minutes

more for 1¼-inch-thick fillets. Loosen from grill rack with spatulas and transfer to a platter.

If desired, lift skin from fish with tongs and cook skin on rack over coals or over hot burner, uncovered, turning occasionally, until lightly browned and crisp, 1 to 2 minutes. Lay skin over fish and serve with lime wedges.

COOK'S NOTE
▪ You can substitute 2 (1-pound) pieces wild salmon fillet. Grill, turning once, for about 12 minutes total for 1½-inch-thick fillets.

Grilled Halibut Steaks with Fennel Tzatziki

SERVES 6
ACTIVE TIME: 30 MINUTES ▪ START TO FINISH: 45 MINUTES

▪ Fennel flavors this dish in two ways: with toasted fennel seeds in the marinade and fresh fennel in the tzatziki, the Greek yogurt dip traditionally made with cucumber. This variation—tangy, creamy, and shot through with fronds of dill—is marvelous with these thick halibut steaks (it also makes a wonderful dip for grilled pita). ▪

    2 tablespoons fennel seeds, toasted (see Tips,
       page 911)
    6 tablespoons fresh lemon juice (from about 2
       lemons)
    4 garlic cloves, minced
       Salt
    2 tablespoons olive oil
    4 (8-ounce) halibut steaks, 1 inch thick (see
       Cook's Note)
    1 medium fennel bulb (about 12 ounces), stalks
       discarded, fronds reserved
    2 cups (about 16 ounces) thick yogurt, such as Greek
       (see Cook's Note)

SPECIAL EQUIPMENT: an electric coffee/spice grinder

If using a charcoal grill, prepare it for direct-heat cooking over medium-hot coals; if using a gas grill, prepare it for direct-heat cooking over medium-high heat (see Grilling Basics, page 512).

Grind fennel seeds in grinder. Stir together 4 teaspoons ground fennel (reserve remainder), ¼ cup lemon juice, half of garlic, 1 teaspoon salt, and oil in a small bowl. Put halibut in a large dish and pour marinade over it, turning to coat. Marinate, covered and refrigerated, for at least 10 minutes.

Quarter fennel bulb. Cut out and discard core and finely chop bulb. Finely chop reserved fennel fronds.

Mash remaining garlic to a paste with 1¼ teaspoons salt, using side of a large heavy knife. Transfer to a large bowl, add chopped fennel bulb and fronds, reserved ground fennel, yogurt, and remaining 2 tablespoons lemon juice, and mix well.

If using a gas grill, turn off one burner (middle one if there are three). Oil grill rack and grill halibut over hot coals or burner(s) (covered if using a gas grill), turning once and moving to cooler area of grill if flare-ups occur, until just cooked through, 10 to 13 minutes.

Serve halibut with tzatziki on the side.

COOK'S NOTES

- You can substitute mahimahi for the halibut.
- The fish can be marinated for up to 1 hour.
- If you can't find thick yogurt, buy regular whole-milk yogurt and drain it in a medium-mesh sieve lined with paper towels, refrigerated, for 12 hours. You will need 6 cups of whole-milk yogurt to yield 2 cups thick yogurt.

Grilled Halibut with Lima Bean and Roasted Tomato Sauce

SERVES 6
ACTIVE TIME: 1½ HOURS ■ START TO FINISH: 1¾ HOURS

■ Chef Jonathan Waxman cooks the same food at his Manhattan restaurant Barbuto that he likes to eat at home, finding the best seasonal ingredients and preparing them as simply as possible. Here he adds chopped lima beans to roasted tomatoes for an unusual sauce with body, which complements the sturdy halibut. ■

4 large tomatoes (2 pounds total), cored and halved crosswise
3 garlic cloves, cut lengthwise into slivers
  Salt and freshly ground black pepper
2 tablespoons olive oil
2 pounds fresh lima or fava beans in the pod, shelled, or 2 cups (10 ounces) frozen baby lima beans or shelled edamame (soybeans), not thawed
½ cup chopped fresh basil
1–2 tablespoons fresh lemon juice
6 (6-ounce) pieces halibut fillet

Put a rack in middle of oven and preheat oven to 450°F.

Stud cut side of each tomato half with garlic slivers, then sprinkle with ½ teaspoon salt and ¼ teaspoon pepper (total). Arrange tomatoes cut side up in a lightly oiled baking pan and drizzle with 1 tablespoon oil. Roast until just softened and wilted, 15 to 20 minutes.

Meanwhile, cook fresh or frozen beans in a 6- to 8-quart pot of boiling salted water (2 tablespoons salt), uncovered, until just tender, 5 to 8 minutes. Drain and cool slightly. When beans are cool enough to handle, gently slip off skins.

Coarsely chop beans. Coarsely chop roasted tomatoes. Toss beans and tomatoes with basil, remaining tablespoon oil, ½ teaspoon salt, ¼ teaspoon pepper, and lemon juice (to taste).

If using a charcoal grill, prepare it for direct-heat cooking over medium-hot coals; if using a gas grill, prepare it for direct-heat cooking over medium heat (see Grilling Basics, page 512).

Pat fish dry and season all over with salt and pepper. Oil grill rack and place fish skin side down on rack. Grill (covered if using a gas grill), turning once, until just cooked through, 6 to 8 minutes for 1¼- to 1½-inch-thick fillets.

Serve fish topped with bean and tomato sauce.

COOK'S NOTES

- The beans can be cooked and peeled up to 1 day ahead. Refrigerate in a sealable plastic bag.
- The bean and roasted tomato sauce can be made up to 1 day ahead and refrigerated, covered. Bring to room temperature before serving.
- Be aware that fava beans can cause a potentially fatal reaction in some people (see page 181).

Grilled Bass or Mahimahi with Green Tomato and Watermelon Salsa

■ The tartness of green tomato balances the sweetness of watermelon in this tasty, colorful salsa. You can use any kind of green tomato, from the unripe garden variety to the heirloom Green Zebra. The salsa is a delicious match with bass, and it is also great on chicken or pork. ■

1½ cups finely chopped green tomatoes
1½ cups finely chopped red watermelon
⅔ cup minced red onion
1 (2½- to 3-inch-long) fresh red or green chile, such as Thai or serrano, minced, including seeds
¼ cup chopped fresh cilantro
1 teaspoon fresh lime juice
Salt
6 (6-ounce) center-cut pieces striped bass or mahimahi fillet with skin
1½ tablespoons olive oil

If using a charcoal grill, prepare it for direct-heat cooking over medium-hot coals; if using a gas grill, prepare it for direct-heat cooking over medium-high heat (see Grilling Basics, page 512).

Toss together tomatoes, watermelon, onion, chile, cilantro, lime juice, and ¾ teaspoon salt in a medium bowl.

Pat fish dry, brush all over with oil, and season with salt. Oil grill rack and place fish skin side down on rack. Grill (covered if using a gas grill), turning once, until just cooked through, 8 to 9 minutes for 1-inch-thick fish.

Serve fish topped with salsa.

COOK'S NOTE
■ Do not make the salsa more than 1 hour ahead, or it will become watery.

Grilled Mahimahi with Pineapple Sambal

■ In Indonesia, Malaysia, and parts of India, the term *sambal* encompasses a wide range of condiments, relishes, and side dishes that add extra layers of flavor and often a touch of fiery heat. This version gets sweetness and spiciness from pineapple and chiles. Exotic doesn't have to mean difficult—once you've chopped the ingredients, the *sambal* takes less than 15 minutes to cook. ■

3 tablespoons vegetable oil
2 garlic cloves, finely chopped
3 ounces shallots, halved lengthwise and thinly sliced crosswise (⅔ cup)
2 (2- to 3-inch-long) fresh chiles, such as Thai or serrano, minced, including seeds
¾ pineapple (preferably not labeled "super sweet"; see Cook's Note), peeled, cored, and cut into ½-inch cubes (4 cups)
1½ tablespoons Asian fish sauce
1 teaspoon sugar
Salt
⅓ cup coarsely chopped fresh cilantro
6 (6-ounce) pieces mahimahi fillet with skin (see Cook's Note)

Heat 2 tablespoons oil in a 12-inch heavy skillet over moderate heat until hot but not smoking. Add garlic and shallots and cook, stirring, until softened, 3 to 5 minutes. Add chiles and pineapple and cook over moderately high heat, stirring occasionally, until pineapple is softened, 4 to 5 minutes. Add fish sauce, sugar, and ¼ teaspoon salt and cook, stirring, for 30 seconds. Cool *sambal* to room temperature, then stir in cilantro.

Meanwhile, if using a charcoal grill, prepare it for direct-heat cooking over medium-hot coals; if using a gas grill, prepare it for direct-heat cooking over medium heat (see Grilling Basics, page 512).

Brush fish all over with remaining tablespoon oil

and season with salt. Oil grill rack and place fish skin side down on rack. Grill (covered if using a gas grill) until skin is crisp, 4 to 5 minutes. Turn fish and grill until just cooked through, 4 to 5 minutes more for 1- to 1½-inch-thick fillets.

Serve fish with *sambal*.

COOK'S NOTES

- If you can only find pineapple labeled "super sweet," omit the sugar in the *sambal*.
- You can substitute halibut or swordfish for the mahimahi.
- The *sambal*, without the cilantro, can be made up to 4 hours ahead and refrigerated, covered. Bring to room temperature and stir in the cilantro before serving.

Grilled Pompano Fillets with Tomato-Lemon Salsa

SERVES 4
ACTIVE TIME: 30 MINUTES ■ START TO FINISH: 45 MINUTES

■ Prized for its firm flesh and delicate flavor, pompano swims in ocean waters from Brazil to Massachusetts but is caught primarily off the Atlantic and Gulf coasts of Florida. We would be happy eating it plain, but this simple salsa of cherry tomatoes and fresh lemon adds a bright note. ■

2 large lemons
1 tablespoon sugar
Salt
1 pound cherry or grape tomatoes, halved (or quartered if large)
3 tablespoons chopped fresh chives
2 tablespoons extra-virgin olive oil, plus additional for brushing fish
¼ teaspoon freshly ground black pepper
4 (4- to 6-ounce) pompano fillets with skin (see Cook's Note)

Finely grate 2 teaspoons zest from lemons. Cut off ends of both lemons to expose pulp. One at a time,

stand each lemon on a cutting board and remove peel, including all white pith, with a sharp paring knife. Cut segments free from membranes and cut crosswise into ¼-inch pieces.

Gently toss lemon segments with sugar and ½ teaspoon salt in a medium bowl. Stir in zest, tomatoes, chives, oil, and pepper and let stand, covered, at room temperature for 15 minutes to allow flavors to develop.

If using a charcoal grill, prepare it for direct-heat cooking over medium-hot coals; if using a gas grill, prepare it for direct-heat cooking over medium-high heat (see Grilling Basics, page 512).

With a sharp knife, slit skin of pompano lengthwise down center of each piece to keep skin from curling when grilling; be careful not to cut into flesh. Brush pompano all over with oil and sprinkle with 1 teaspoon salt. Oil grill rack and place pompano skin side down on rack. Grill (covered if using a gas grill), turning once—use a metal spatula to loosen fish if necessary before turning—until just cooked through, 5 to 6 minutes.

Transfer to a platter and spoon salsa over fish.

COOK'S NOTE

- You can substitute flounder for the pompano.

Grilled Swordfish Kebabs with Bacon and Cherry Tomatoes

SERVES 4
ACTIVE TIME: 45 MINUTES ■ START TO FINISH: 1¼ HOURS

■ We love bacon-wrapped anything. Here the bacon acts as benevolent protector, basting the swordfish within while imparting a smoky savor. The plump cherry tomatoes, brushed with a bit of bacon fat, sizzle and soften on the grill and provide a juicy counterpoint to the cubes of fish. Because this dish is quite rich, a leafy green salad is all you need to complete the meal. ■

1¼ pounds 1-inch-thick swordfish or mahimahi steaks

¼ cup fresh lemon juice

¼ cup olive oil

2 teaspoons sugar

2 garlic cloves, minced

1 teaspoon dried oregano, crumbled

12 bacon slices

24 cherry tomatoes (about 12 ounces)

Salt and freshly ground black pepper

ACCOMPANIMENT: lemon wedges

SPECIAL EQUIPMENT: eight 12-inch wooden skewers, soaked in water for 30 minutes

Trim fish, discarding any skin. Cut fish into 1-inch pieces (you will need 24 pieces).

Stir together lemon juice, oil, sugar, garlic, and oregano in a shallow dish until sugar is dissolved. Transfer half of marinade to a small bowl and set aside. Add swordfish to remaining marinade, turning to coat. Marinate at room temperature, turning once, for 20 minutes.

If using a charcoal grill, prepare it for direct-heat cooking over medium-hot coals; if using a gas grill, prepare it for direct-heat cooking over medium-high heat (see Grilling Basics, page 512).

Meanwhile, cook bacon in a 12-inch heavy skillet over moderate heat until pale golden but still soft and pliable, 2 to 3 minutes. Transfer to paper towels to drain; reserve fat in pan. When bacon is cool, cut each slice crosswise in half.

Drain fish (discard marinade). Tightly wrap each piece of fish in a piece of bacon, overlapping ends. Thread 6 wrapped pieces, leaving ¼ inch between them, onto each of four skewers; make sure skewer pierces bacon at overlap to keep bacon on fish during grilling. Thread 6 tomatoes onto each of remaining four skewers.

Brush fish and tomato kebabs with some reserved bacon fat. If using a gas grill, turn off one burner (middle one if there are three). Grill kebabs over hot coals or burner(s), turning frequently and moving to cool area of grill if flare-ups occur, until fish is just cooked through and tomatoes are blistered, 3 to 4 minutes.

SKEWERS: WOODEN OR METAL?

To help some foods cook more uniformly and to make them easier to turn on the grill, we use skewers. Although metal skewers are sturdier than wooden ones, we generally prefer the latter. Because food seems to cling to them better, wooden skewers are easier to turn over. (Soak them in water for 30 minutes beforehand so they don't burn.) If you want to use metal ones, buy skewers that are flat or twisted, so that when you turn them, the food won't spin around and end up with the same side down on the grill rack again.

Depending on the food you're grilling, you can use skewers in a variety of ways. For satés, shrimp, or cubes of meat, for instance, thread a few pieces onto each skewer, leaving ¼ inch between them. To keep long coils of sausages curled together (see page 546), crisscross the skewers; that technique can also keep a

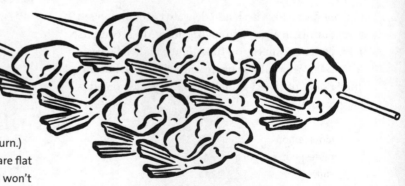

large, unwieldy piece of meat, such as a butterflied leg of lamb, under control if parallel skewers alone don't give you enough stability. And a raft effect, in which you run multiple skewers in the same direction crosswise through food, works brilliantly to keep small vegetables such as okra (page 555) or scallions (page 558) together and makes it easier to turn them.

Transfer kebabs to a platter and season with salt and pepper. Serve with reserved marinade and lemon wedges.

turning once, until just cooked through, 4 to 6 minutes.

Serve tuna satés with wasabi mayonnaise.

Grilled Tuna Satés with Wasabi Mayonnaise

SERVES 6
ACTIVE TIME: 30 MINUTES ■ START TO FINISH: 1½ HOURS
(INCLUDES MARINATING)

■ The secret to these satés—grilled skewers of marinated tuna—is an addictive sauce of wasabi paste, soy sauce, lemon juice, and mayonnaise. It's delicious with almost any kind of seafood, but it tastes especially good with the grilled tuna. The marinade caramelizes just enough on the grill that the tuna is seared on the outside but stays tender and moist inside. ■

1½ cups mayonnaise
2 tablespoons soy sauce
2 teaspoons sugar
1 tablespoon fresh lemon juice
1 tablespoon wasabi paste, or to taste
1½ pounds 1-inch-thick tuna steaks, cut into 1½-inch cubes

SPECIAL EQUIPMENT: six 10-inch wooden skewers, soaked in water for 30 minutes

Stir together mayonnaise, soy sauce, sugar, and lemon juice in a medium bowl. Transfer 1 cup mayonnaise to a small bowl and stir in wasabi paste. Toss tuna with remaining mayonnaise. Marinate, covered and refrigerated, for at least 1 hour. Cover and refrigerate wasabi mayonnaise.

If using a charcoal grill, prepare it for direct-heat cooking over medium-hot coals; if using a gas grill, prepare it for direct-heat cooking over medium-high heat (see Grilling Basics, page 512).

Thread about 8 tuna cubes onto each skewer. Oil grill rack and grill satés (covered if using a gas grill),

Grilled Whole Mackerel with Lemon, Oregano, and Olives

SERVES 4
ACTIVE TIME: 45 MINUTES ■ START TO FINISH: 1 HOUR

■ Mackerel's rich, meaty flesh stands up well to the licks of an open fire. Stuffing and wrapping the fish with lemon slices and fresh oregano sprigs ensures that the flavors permeate the flesh. A whole 3½-pound mackerel or bluefish is about 2 feet long, so you will just be able to fit it on a large grill by placing it at an angle; measure your grill before buying a fish to make sure you'll have enough room. The easy lemon vinaigrette, flavored with oregano and briny olives, complements the deep flavor of the fish. ■

½ teaspoon finely grated lemon zest
1½ tablespoons fresh lemon juice
Salt and freshly ground black pepper
⅓ cup extra-virgin olive oil
¼ cup pitted Kalamata olives, cut into slivers
3 tablespoons finely chopped fresh oregano, plus 6 large oregano sprigs
1 (3¼- to 3½-pound) whole Spanish mackerel or bluefish, cleaned, head and tail left intact
2 tablespoons vegetable oil
6 (¼-inch-thick) lemon slices

SPECIAL EQUIPMENT: kitchen string

Whisk together zest, lemon juice, ⅛ teaspoon salt, and ¼ teaspoon pepper in a small bowl. Add olive oil in a stream, whisking until well combined. Whisk in olives and chopped oregano.

With a sharp paring knife, make 1-inch-long slits at 2-inch intervals down middle of fish on both sides. Brush fish all over with vegetable oil and season with salt and pepper. Season fish cavity with salt and pepper and distribute 3 lemon slices and 3 oregano sprigs evenly in cavity. Close cavity and arrange remaining 3 lemon slices and 3 oregano sprigs evenly on top of fish. Tie fish closed with soaked string at 2-inch intervals, securing lemon slices and oregano sprigs.

If using a charcoal grill, prepare it for direct-heat cooking over medium-hot coals; if using a gas grill, prepare it for direct-heat cooking over medium heat (see Grilling Basics, page 512).

Oil grill rack and grill fish (covered if using a gas grill) for 15 minutes. Turn fish, using a metal spatula and tongs, and grill until just cooked through, about 15 minutes more. (If the fish tail begins to brown too much, wrap loosely in a small piece of foil.)

Transfer fish to a large platter using two metal spatulas, and cut off string. Serve with lemon sauce.

Grilled Scallops with Tomato Coulis

SERVES 4
ACTIVE TIME: 20 MINUTES ■ START TO FINISH: 1¼ HOURS

■ A chunky roasted tomato coulis casts sweet grilled scallops in a Mediterranean light. The coulis can be made in advance and reheated when the scallops hit the grill, so this is an almost effortless meal. ■

FOR COULIS
- 3 tablespoons olive oil
- 1½ pounds plum tomatoes (about 12), cut into ¼-inch-thick slices
- 2 teaspoons finely chopped fresh oregano
- 1 teaspoon sugar
- ¾ teaspoon salt
- ½ teaspoon freshly ground black pepper

HOW TO GRILL A WHOLE FISH

A whole fish hot and sizzling off the grill makes a dramatic presentation. It's best to buy relatively small fish—about 3 pounds or less—not only because they are easier to turn and more likely to cook through without burning on the outside, but also because larger ones won't fit on a standard grill. The simplest fish to grill are those that are on the oily side and rich in flavor—for instance, mackerel, bluefish, and salmon. Less oily fish such as striped bass and snapper work well too, but because their flesh and skin are more delicate, you'll need to take extra care to prevent the fish from sticking or breaking apart when turning it over. If the fish isn't oily, or if you've tucked herbs and lemon slices inside, tying it up with soaked kitchen string will make it easier to handle. (As a bonus, the string also holds more fragile fish together.) If the tail starts to burn, you can wrap it in foil. It's helpful to have two large offset spatulas, both for turning the fish and for transferring it to a platter when done, though using one spatula with a

small cookie sheet as an aid also does the trick. We don't call for a fish-grilling basket, because in our experience, the fish don't often fit in one perfectly, and if you need to cover the grill, you can't do so effectively over the handle.

4 garlic cloves, left unpeeled
2 teaspoons balsamic vinegar
1–2 tablespoons water
2 tablespoons chopped fresh basil

FOR SCALLOPS

24 sea scallops (about 1½ pounds), tough ligament
   removed from side of each if necessary
½ teaspoon salt
¼ teaspoon freshly ground black pepper

SPECIAL EQUIPMENT: six 12-inch wooden skewers, soaked
   in water for 30 minutes

ROAST THE TOMATOES AND GARLIC: Put a rack in
middle of oven and preheat oven to 450°F.

Brush a baking sheet with 1 tablespoon oil. Put tomatoes on pan in one layer. Drizzle with remaining
2 tablespoons oil and sprinkle with oregano, sugar,
salt, and pepper. Wrap garlic tightly in foil and put
on pan. Roast until tomatoes are lightly browned and
garlic is tender when pierced with a knife, 20 to 25
minutes.

MEANWHILE, PREPARE THE GRILL: If using a charcoal grill, prepare it for direct-heat cooking over
medium-hot coals; if using a gas grill, prepare it
for direct-heat cooking over medium-high heat (see
Grilling Basics, page 512).

MAKE THE COULIS: Carefully unwrap garlic, peel,
and transfer to a blender. Add tomatoes and vinegar
and puree until smooth, adding water if necessary to
reach desired consistency. Pour into a bowl, stir in
basil, and cover with foil to keep warm.

GRILL THE SCALLOPS: Pat scallops dry and sprinkle
with salt and pepper. Thread 4 scallops side by side
onto each skewer, leaving ¼ inch between them.

Oil grill rack and grill scallops (covered if using a
gas grill), turning once, until just cooked through, 4
to 5 minutes; transfer to a plate.

Serve scallops with coulis.

COOK'S NOTE

■ The coulis can be made up to 4 hours ahead and kept,
  covered, at room temperature. Reheat before serving.

Grilled Scallops Teriyaki

SERVES 4
ACTIVE TIME: 15 MINUTES ■ START TO FINISH: 45 MINUTES

■ In Japan, teriyaki—traditionally made with soy sauce,
sake, and mirin—isn't just a sauce. It's also a technique.
Teri is the word for "gloss" or "glaze," and *yaki* means
grilling or panfrying. Together, they refer to meat or
fish that is basted repeatedly while it cooks, to develop
layers of flavors and textures. As the sugars in the sauce
caramelize over the open flame, they give the scallops a
deep mahogany shine. Though dozens of bottled teriyaki sauces are available, it couldn't be easier to make
your own, and it won't be full of additives. ■

⅓ cup soy sauce
½ cup sake or dry sherry
⅔ cup mirin (Japanese sweet rice wine)
2 tablespoons sugar
24 sea scallops (about 1½ pounds), tough
   ligament removed from side of each if
   necessary

Combine soy sauce, sake, mirin, and sugar in
a 2-quart heavy saucepan and bring to a boil, then
reduce heat to moderately low and simmer until reduced to about ¾ cup, about 15 minutes. Pour into a
shallow bowl and cool glaze to room temperature.

If using a charcoal grill, prepare it for direct-heat
cooking over medium-hot coals; if using a gas grill,
prepare it for direct-heat cooking over medium-high
heat (see Grilling Basics, page 512).

Reserve ¼ cup glaze for drizzling over scallops.
Pat scallops dry and oil grill rack. Brush scallops generously with some of remaining glaze and grill (covered if using a gas grill), turning once and brushing
frequently with remaining glaze (do not brush with
glaze during last minute of cooking on either side),
until just cooked through, 4 to 5 minutes.

Transfer scallops to a plate and drizzle with reserved glaze.

COOK'S NOTE

■ The glaze can be made up to 5 days ahead and
  refrigerated, covered.

Grilled Jumbo Shrimp with Garlic and Oregano

SERVES 6
ACTIVE TIME: 45 MINUTES ■ START TO FINISH: 1¼ HOURS

■ A citrusy Greek-style marinade, which does double duty as a sauce, makes this dish a standout. Lemon juice, olive oil, and oregano come together with the help of garlic—a natural emulsifier—to create a dairy-free sauce that's creamy-looking. Cooking the shrimp in their shells keeps them juicy and tender. It's casual finger food that requires plenty of napkins, which is part of the fun. ■

  3 pounds jumbo shrimp in shells (7–8 per pound)
  4 large garlic cloves
  ¾ teaspoon salt
  5 tablespoons fresh lemon juice (from 1½ lemons)
  ½ teaspoon freshly ground black pepper
  ¾ cup olive oil
  ¼ cup finely chopped fresh oregano (from 1 bunch)
  3 lemons, cut into 6 wedges each

With kitchen shears, snip through shell of each shrimp down middle of back, leaving tail and last segment of shell intact. With a small sharp knife, make an incision down back and devein, leaving shells in place.

Mince garlic and mash to a paste with salt, using side of a large heavy knife. Transfer garlic paste to a blender, add lemon juice and pepper, and blend until smooth. With motor running, add oil in a slow stream, blending until well combined. Transfer sauce to a bowl and stir in oregano.

If using a charcoal grill, prepare it for direct-heat cooking over medium-hot coals; if using a gas grill, prepare it for direct-heat cooking over medium heat (see Grilling Basics, page 512).

Meanwhile, toss shrimp with ¼ cup sauce in a large bowl. Marinate for 10 to 15 minutes (texture of shrimp will become cottony if marinated longer).

Lightly brush lemon wedges with some of remaining sauce and grill, turning once, until grill marks appear, 3 to 5 minutes. Transfer to a large platter.

Pat shrimp dry and oil grill rack. Grill (covered if using a gas grill), turning once, until just cooked through, 7 to 8 minutes. Transfer to platter with lemon wedges.

Serve shrimp with remaining sauce on the side.

Grilled New Orleans–Style Shrimp

SERVES 4
ACTIVE TIME: 40 MINUTES ■ START TO FINISH:
40 MINUTES

■ Versions of this dish can be found all over the Crescent City. This one is based on the popular grilled shrimp served at Mr. B's Bistro in the French Quarter. The shrimp are tossed in an irresistible spicy, messy, buttery sauce after they come off the grill—make sure to have plenty of bread on hand for sopping it up. ■

  1½ pounds large shrimp in shells (21–25 per pound)
  2 tablespoons olive oil
  3 medium garlic cloves, minced
    Salt
  ¾ stick (6 tablespoons) unsalted butter
  4 teaspoons Worcestershire sauce
  2 teaspoons chili powder
  2 teaspoons freshly ground black pepper
  1 tablespoon fresh lemon juice
ACCOMPANIMENTS: a baguette; lemon wedges
SPECIAL EQUIPMENT: seven 12-inch wooden skewers,
    soaked in water for 30 minutes

With kitchen shears, snip through shell of each shrimp down middle of back, leaving tail and last segment of shell intact. With a small sharp knife, make an incision down back and devein, leaving shells in place. (Shells will prevent shrimp from toughening when grilled.) Toss shrimp with oil, garlic, and ½ teaspoon salt in a bowl. Marinate at a cool room temperature for 15 to 30 minutes.

Meanwhile, if using a charcoal grill, prepare it for direct-heat cooking over medium-hot coals; if using a gas grill, prepare it for direct-heat cooking over medium-high heat (see Grilling Basics, page 512).

Combine butter, Worcestershire sauce, chili powder, ¼ teaspoon salt, and pepper in a small heavy saucepan and heat over moderately low heat, stirring, until butter is melted. Remove from heat and stir in lemon juice.

Thread 4 or 5 shrimp onto each skewer. Oil grill rack and grill shrimp (covered if using a gas grill), turning once, until just cooked through, 3 to 4 minutes. Push shrimp off skewers into a bowl, pour butter mixture over them, and toss to coat.

Serve shrimp with bread and lemon wedges.

Grilled Lobster and Potatoes with Basil Vinaigrette

SERVES 4
ACTIVE TIME: 45 MINUTES ■ START TO FINISH: 45 MINUTES

■ Instead of the customary side of melted butter, this grilled lobster gets a lighter touch with a simple basil vinaigrette and a nudge from garlic and red pepper flakes. The grilled lobsters and potatoes are arranged on a platter of baby arugula and everything is drizzled with a bit of the dressing, making this a convenient and beautiful all-in-one meal. ■

- 4 (1¼- to 1½-pound) live lobsters
- 2 pounds small (1½- to 2-inch) boiling potatoes, preferably yellow-fleshed
- 3 tablespoons red wine vinegar
- 5 tablespoons fresh lemon juice (from 1½ lemons)
- 3 garlic cloves, minced
- ½ teaspoon red pepper flakes, or to taste
- 1 teaspoon sugar
- ½ teaspoon salt
- ⅔ cup extra-virgin olive oil
- ½ cup chopped fresh basil
- ½ pound baby arugula, tough stems discarded (10 cups loosely packed)

ACCOMPANIMENT: lemon wedges

Plunge lobsters headfirst into a 12-quart pot of boiling salted water (see Cook's Note). Cook, cov-

ered, over high heat for 4 minutes for 1¼-pound lobsters, 5 minutes for 1½-pound lobsters, from time they enter water. (Lobsters will not be fully cooked.) Transfer with tongs to a large colander to drain and cool.

Return cooking water to a boil, add potatoes, and simmer, uncovered, until just tender, 15 to 20 minutes. Drain.

When lobsters are cool enough to handle, twist off claws (including knuckles) and crack with a meat mallet or rolling pin. Halve lobsters lengthwise, using a large heavy knife. Discard green tomalley and any orange roe from lobster bodies.

If using a charcoal grill, prepare it for direct-heat cooking over hot coals; if using a gas grill, prepare it for direct-heat cooking over high heat (see Grilling Basics, page 512).

Meanwhile, whisk together vinegar, lemon juice, garlic, red pepper flakes, sugar, and salt in a bowl until sugar and salt are dissolved. Add oil in a slow stream, whisking until well blended, then stir in basil.

Halve potatoes. Oil grill rack and place potatoes cut side down on rack. Grill (covered if using a gas grill), turning once, until grill marks appear, about 4 minutes. Transfer to a bowl and toss with 2 tablespoons vinaigrette. Cover to keep warm.

Oil grill rack and place 4 lobster halves, cut side down, and all claws on rack. Grill (covered if using a gas grill), until grill marks appear on meat, about 4 minutes. Turn bodies and claws and grill for 4 minutes more. Transfer to a large bowl and toss with ¼ cup vinaigrette; cover to keep warm. Grill remaining lobster halves in same manner and add to bowl, tossing to coat.

Arrange arugula on a large platter and top with grilled lobster and potatoes. Drizzle with ½ cup vinaigrette and serve with lemon wedges and remaining vinaigrette on the side.

COOK'S NOTES
- The lobsters can be cooked in 2 batches in an 8- to 10-quart pot.
- The vinaigrette, without the basil, can be made up to 1 day ahead and refrigerated, covered. Stir in the basil just before using.

Poultry

❧
Grilled Cumin Chicken Breasts with Avocado Salsa

SERVES 6
ACTIVE TIME: 1 HOUR ■ START TO FINISH: 1 HOUR

■ A generous rub of cumin and a zesty salsa of ripe avocado and tomato give chicken breasts personality. It all comes together quickly in a perfect weeknight dinner. ■

FOR SALSA
- 3 medium tomatoes (about 1 pound total), finely chopped
- 2 California avocados, halved, pitted, peeled, and finely chopped
- ¾ cup finely chopped red onion
- 1 jalapeño or serrano chile, minced, including seeds
- ⅓ cup fresh lime juice (from about 3 limes)
- 1 tablespoon vegetable oil
- 1½ teaspoons salt

FOR CHICKEN
- 2 tablespoons ground cumin
- 1½ tablespoons vegetable oil
- 1 teaspoon salt
- ½ teaspoon freshly ground black pepper
- 6 chicken breast halves (with skin and bones; about 3¾ pounds total)

MAKE THE SALSA: Gently stir together all ingredients in a bowl.

PREPARE THE CHICKEN: Stir together cumin, oil, salt, and pepper in a small bowl. Pat chicken dry and rub all over with cumin oil.

PREPARE THE GRILL: If using a charcoal grill, prepare it for indirect-heat cooking over medium-hot coals; if using a gas grill, prepare it for indirect-heat cooking over medium heat (see Grilling Basics, page 512).

GRILL THE CHICKEN: Oil grill rack and place chicken skin side down on area of grill with no coals underneath, or over turned-off burner. Grill, partially covered if using a charcoal grill, completely covered if using a gas grill, turning occasionally, until browned and just cooked through, 25 to 30 minutes.

Serve chicken with salsa.

COOK'S NOTE
■ The salsa can be made up to 1 hour ahead and kept at room temperature.

❧
Grilled Lemon-Pepper Chicken Breasts

SERVES 6
ACTIVE TIME: 30 MINUTES ■ START TO FINISH: 30 MINUTES

■ Pounding skinless, boneless chicken breasts thin means they will cook quickly. In this recipe, the chicken gets a drizzle of a lemon-pepper vinaigrette. A sprinkling of gremolata, a garnish of chopped fresh herbs, garlic, and lemon zest, adds a jolt of fresh flavor to the grilled meat. ■

- 2 tablespoons fresh lemon juice (grate zest first)
- 6 tablespoons extra-virgin olive oil
  Salt and freshly ground black pepper
- 1½ tablespoons coarsely chopped fresh thyme
- 2 large garlic cloves, minced
- 1½ teaspoons finely grated lemon zest
- 6 skinless, boneless chicken breast halves (about 2¼ pounds total)

Whisk together lemon juice, ¼ cup oil, ½ teaspoon salt, and ½ teaspoon pepper in a bowl until well blended to make vinaigrette. Stir together thyme, garlic, and lemon zest in a small bowl to make gremolata.

If using a charcoal grill, prepare it for direct-heat cooking over hot coals; if using a gas grill, prepare it for direct-heat cooking over high heat (see Grilling Basics, page 512).

Meanwhile, with smooth side of a meat pounder or with a rolling pin, pound chicken to ¼ inch thick between sheets of plastic wrap. Pat chicken dry, rub both sides with remaining 2 tablespoons oil, and sprinkle with ½ teaspoon salt and ½ teaspoon pepper.

Oil grill rack and grill chicken (covered if using a gas grill), turning once, until just cooked through, about 2 minutes. Transfer to a platter.

Whisk vinaigrette and drizzle over chicken. Sprinkle with gremolata.

Grilled Chicken Breasts with Tomato and Bread Salad

SERVES 6
ACTIVE TIME: 1 HOUR ■ START TO FINISH: 1¼ HOURS

■ The accompaniment to this grilled chicken is based on panzanella, the Italian salad of cubes of bread, tomatoes, onion, and basil dressed with olive oil and vinegar. Panzanella is traditionally made with stale bread, which has the sturdy texture to soak up the tomato juices without disintegrating. Here we toast pieces from a fresh loaf and add some chopped celery for crunch, along with black olives and capers for brine and tang. ■

FOR SALAD
- ½ pound crusty peasant-style bread, cut into bite-sized pieces (about 6 cups)
- 3 large tomatoes (about 1½ pounds total), cut into ¾-inch pieces
- ¾ cup finely chopped pale green inner celery ribs and leaves
- ⅓ cup small brine-cured black olives, such as Niçoise or Gaeta, halved and pitted
- ¼ cup finely chopped red onion
- 2 tablespoons drained capers
- 2 garlic cloves
- ½ teaspoon salt
- 2–3 tablespoons red wine vinegar
- ⅓ cup extra-virgin olive oil
- ½ teaspoon freshly ground black pepper
- 1 cup packed fresh basil leaves, torn into pieces

FOR CHICKEN
- 6 skinless, boneless chicken breast halves (about 2¼ pounds total)
- 1 tablespoon extra-virgin olive oil

- ½ teaspoon salt
- ½ teaspoon freshly ground black pepper

GARNISH: celery leaves

MAKE THE SALAD: Preheat broiler. Spread bread in one layer on a large baking sheet and toast about 4 inches from heat, turning once, until golden, 4 to 5 minutes. Cool on pan on a rack.

Toss together bread, tomatoes, celery, olives, onion, and capers in a large bowl. Mince garlic and mash to a paste with salt, using side of a large heavy knife. Whisk together garlic paste, vinegar (to taste), oil, and pepper in a small bowl until well combined. Pour over salad and toss well. Let stand at room temperature while you grill chicken.

PREPARE THE GRILL: If using a charcoal grill, prepare it for direct-heat grilling over medium-hot coals; if using a gas grill, prepare it for direct-heat grilling over medium-high heat (see Grilling Basics, page 512).

GRILL THE CHICKEN: Pat chicken dry. Stir together oil, salt, and pepper in a small bowl and rub all over chicken. Oil grill rack and grill chicken (covered if using a gas grill), turning once, until just cooked through, about 8 minutes.

Transfer chicken to a cutting board and slice diagonally. Stir basil into salad and garnish salad with celery leaves. Serve with chicken.

COOK'S NOTE
■ The bread can be toasted up to 2 days ahead and, once cooled, kept in a sealable plastic bag at room temperature.

Grilled Chicken Paillards with Nectarine Chutney

SERVES 4
ACTIVE TIME: 15 MINUTES ■ START TO FINISH: 25 MINUTES

■ The sweet juiciness of nectarines matches well with tomatoes and curry powder in this summery chutney, a cheeky accompaniment to chicken breasts. Flattened into paillards, they cook in a flash. Unlike peaches, nectarines don't need to be peeled, so the chutney too is quick and fuss-free. ■

1 pound firm but ripe nectarines, pitted and cut into
    1-inch pieces
1 large tomato, coarsely chopped
1 small garlic clove, chopped
¼ cup cider vinegar
3 tablespoons packed light brown sugar
1 teaspoon curry powder, preferably Madras
    Salt
4 skinless, boneless chicken breast halves (about
    1½ pounds total)
1 tablespoon vegetable oil
    Freshly ground black pepper
GARNISH: fresh cilantro sprigs

Combine nectarines, tomato, garlic, vinegar, brown sugar, curry powder, and ¼ teaspoon salt in a 2-quart heavy saucepan and cook, uncovered, over moderate heat, stirring occasionally, until slightly thickened but still saucy, about 20 minutes.

Meanwhile, if using a charcoal grill, prepare it for direct-heat cooking over hot coals; if using a gas grill, prepare it for direct-heat cooking over high heat (see Grilling Basics, page 512).

While grill heats, with flat side of a meat pounder or with a rolling pin, pound chicken to ¼ inch thick between sheets of plastic wrap. Pat chicken dry and brush on both sides with oil. Season on both sides with salt and pepper.

Oil grill rack and grill chicken, turning once, until just cooked through, 2 to 3 minutes.

Garnish chicken with cilantro sprigs and serve with nectarine chutney.

COOK'S NOTE

- The chutney can be made up to 1 day ahead and refrigerated, covered. Reheat before serving.

Grilled Indian-Spiced Chicken

SERVES 4
ACTIVE TIME: 1¼ HOURS ■ START TO FINISH: 9½ HOURS
(INCLUDES MARINATING)

■ While on a research trip to India, two of our food editors tasted a version of this gently spiced grilled chicken at the Udai Bilas Palace in the Rajasthan city of Dungarpur. Thick yogurt helps the marinade cling to the chicken, so you get its full flavor—like a particularly fresh and zingy curry—in the final dish. The long marinating time and regular basting with ghee produce a tender, melt-in-your-mouth result. ■

1 cup chopped onion
3 tablespoons finely chopped garlic
2 tablespoons finely chopped peeled fresh ginger
1 small fresh hot green chile, such as Thai or serrano,
    coarsely chopped, including seeds
1¼ teaspoons salt
1 teaspoon distilled white vinegar
⅓ cup thick yogurt, such as Greek (see
    Cook's Note)
1½ tablespoons ground coriander
1 tablespoon vegetable oil
1 teaspoon turmeric
½ teaspoon cayenne
1 (3- to 3½-pound) chicken, quartered, backbone and
    skin (except on wings) removed and discarded
1 stick (8 tablespoons) unsalted butter

MARINATE THE CHICKEN: Combine onion, garlic, ginger, chile, salt, and vinegar in a food processor and blend to a smooth paste. Transfer to a large bowl and whisk in yogurt, coriander, oil, turmeric, and cayenne. Add chicken pieces and turn to coat generously. Marinate, covered and refrigerated, for at least 8 hours.

MAKE THE GHEE: Melt butter in a 1-quart heavy saucepan over moderate heat and bring to a boil. Once foam completely covers butter, reduce heat to very low and cook, stirring occasionally, until a very thin crust begins to form on surface and milky white solids fall to bottom of pan, about 8 minutes. Watching constantly to prevent burning, continue to cook, without stirring, until solids turn light brown and butter deepens to golden and becomes fragrant, 8 to 16 minutes. Remove from heat and let stand for 1 minute.

Pour ghee through a sieve lined with a dampened triple layer of cheesecloth or heavy-duty paper towel into a bowl; discard solids.

GRILL THE CHICKEN: Remove chicken from refrigerator and let stand at room temperature for 30 minutes.

Meanwhile, if using a charcoal grill, prepare it for indirect-heat cooking over medium-hot coals; if using a gas grill, prepare it for indirect-heat cooking over medium heat (see Grilling Basics, page 512).

Oil grill rack. Put chicken (still heavily coated with marinade) over area of grill with no coals underneath, or over turned-off burner, and drizzle with about 1 tablespoon ghee. Grill, covered, turning and drizzling with ghee every 5 minutes, until cooked through, 20 to 25 minutes.

Serve chicken drizzled with any remaining ghee.

COOK'S NOTES

- If you can't find thick yogurt, buy regular plain whole-milk yogurt and drain it in a medium-mesh sieve lined with a paper towel set over a bowl, refrigerated, for 12 hours. You will need 1 cup whole-milk yogurt to yield ⅓ cup thick yogurt.
- The chicken can be marinated for up to 3 days.
- The ghee keeps, covered and refrigerated, for up to 1 month. Melt before using.

USING YOGURT IN MARINADES

The tangy fermented-milk product called yogurt has been eaten for millennia from eastern Europe to India, an area that our contributing editor Anne Mendelson (a food historian who is also the author of a book on dairy products) calls "Yogurtistan." She's a big fan of what's commonly referred to as Greek yogurt, as are we. Incredibly thick, it has enough body to cling, which makes it great in marinades for chicken or lamb. Greek yogurt is becoming more widely available, but if you can't find it, buy a good whole-milk commercial yogurt and drain it in a paper-towel-lined medium-mesh sieve set over a bowl, refrigerated, for about 12 hours before using.

Grilled Chicken with Lemon, Garlic, and Oregano

SERVES 4
ACTIVE TIME: 50 MINUTES ■ START TO FINISH: 50 MINUTES

■ Chicken hot off the grill is tossed in a tart, garlicky dressing, which allows the meat to soak up all the flavors. ■

- 2 tablespoons fresh lemon juice
- 2½ tablespoons olive oil
- 2 tablespoons finely chopped fresh oregano
- 1 tablespoon minced garlic
  Salt and freshly ground black pepper
- 3½ pounds chicken parts (thighs, drumsticks, wings, and breast halves with skin and bone)
- 2 lemons, cut into ⅓-inch-thick slices

MAKE THE DRESSING AND PREPARE THE CHICKEN: Whisk together lemon juice, oil, oregano, garlic, ½ teaspoon salt, and ¼ teaspoon pepper in a large bowl.

Discard excess fat from chicken. Pat chicken dry and sprinkle with ¾ teaspoon salt and ½ teaspoon pepper.

PREPARE THE GRILL: If using a charcoal grill, prepare it for indirect-heat cooking over medium-hot coals; if using a gas grill, prepare it for indirect-heat cooking over medium-high heat (see Grilling Basics, page 512).

TO COOK THE CHICKEN ON A CHARCOAL GRILL: Oil grill rack and place chicken skin side down on area with no coals underneath. Grill, partially covered, turning occasionally, until browned and cooked through, 25 to 30 minutes. (Add more charcoal during grilling if necessary to maintain heat.)

Meanwhile, grill lemon slices on oiled rack directly over coals until grill marks appear, 3 to 4 minutes per side. Transfer to a plate.

TO COOK THE CHICKEN ON A GAS GRILL: Oil grill rack and place chicken skin side down over turned-off burner. Grill, covered, without turning, until browned on first side, about 8 minutes. Reduce heat to medium and grill (still over turned-off burner), turning occasionally, until just cooked through, 17 to 22 minutes more.

Meanwhile, grill lemon slices on oiled rack directly over lit burner(s) until grill marks appear, 3 to 4 minutes per side. Transfer to a plate.

Transfer chicken to bowl with lemon dressing and turn to coat, then transfer to a platter. Arrange lemon slices over chicken and serve with remaining lemon dressing on the side.

Brown Sugar Barbecued Chicken

SERVES 4
ACTIVE TIME: 1 HOUR ■ START TO FINISH: 1½ HOURS

■ This fork-tender chicken is worth making for the sauce alone. Ketchup and dark brown sugar contribute a sweetness that is underlined and balanced by Worcestershire sauce and mustard. As the chicken grills, the sauce becomes deliciously sticky, glossy, and caramelized—just the way you want it. Bonus: it's equally good with pork. ■

FOR SAUCE
¾ cup finely chopped onion
1 tablespoon vegetable oil
1½ cups Chicken Stock (page 153) or store-bought reduced-sodium broth
¾ cup ketchup
¼ cup packed dark brown sugar
1½ tablespoons Worcestershire sauce
2¼ teaspoons Dijon mustard
¼ teaspoon salt
½ teaspoon freshly ground black pepper

FOR CHICKEN
3½ pounds chicken parts (thighs, drumsticks, wings, and breast halves with skin and bone)
¾ teaspoon salt
½ teaspoon freshly ground black pepper

MAKE THE SAUCE: Cook onion in oil in a 2½- to 3-quart heavy saucepan over moderately low heat, stirring occasionally, until softened, about 10 minutes. Whisk in remaining ingredients, bring to a simmer, and simmer, uncovered, stirring occasionally,

until reduced to about 1¾ cups, 25 to 30 minutes.

PREPARE THE GRILL: If using a charcoal grill, prepare it for indirect-heat cooking over medium-hot coals; if using a gas grill, prepare it for indirect-heat cooking over medium-high heat (see Grilling Basics, page 512).

Meanwhile, discard excess fat from chicken. Pat dry and sprinkle all over with salt and pepper.

TO COOK THE CHICKEN ON A CHARCOAL GRILL: Oil grill rack and place chicken skin side down on area with no coals underneath. Grill, partially covered, turning occasionally, until browned and just cooked through, 25 to 30 minutes. (Add more charcoal during grilling if necessary to maintain heat.) Brush chicken all over with some of sauce and grill, turning once, for 2 to 4 minutes more.

TO COOK THE CHICKEN ON A GAS GRILL: Oil grill rack and place chicken skin side down over turned-off burner. Cook, covered, without turning, until browned on first side, about 8 minutes. Reduce heat to medium and grill (still over turned-off burner), turning occasionally, until just cooked through, 17 to 22 minutes. Brush chicken all over with some of sauce and grill, turning once, for 2 to 4 minutes more.

Serve chicken with remaining sauce on the side.

COOK'S NOTE
■ The sauce can be made up to 5 days ahead. Refrigerate, uncovered, until cool, then cover.

Chipotle Grilled Chicken Thighs

SERVES 6
ACTIVE TIME: 15 MINUTES ■ START TO FINISH: 35 MINUTES

■ Lime juice and mild honey partner up with chipotle hot sauce in this irresistible dish. The heartiness of the smoky hot sauce is a great match for the robust flavor of chicken thighs, which stay moist and juicy on the grill. ■

¼ cup fresh lime juice (from about 2 limes)
¼ cup olive oil
2½ tablespoons chipotle Tabasco
¾ teaspoon salt

6 large skinless, boneless chicken thighs (2½ pounds total)

2 teaspoons mild honey

If using a charcoal grill, prepare it for direct-heat cooking over medium-hot coals; if using a gas grill, prepare it for direct-heat cooking over medium heat (see Grilling Basics, page 512).

Meanwhile, stir together lime juice, oil, Tabasco, and salt in a glass measuring cup. Put chicken in a large sealable bag and add ⅓ cup marinade; reserve remainder in cup. Seal bag and marinate chicken at room temperature for 15 minutes. Stir honey into remaining marinade until dissolved to make sauce.

Remove chicken from marinade (discard marinade). If using a gas grill, turn off one burner (middle one if there are three). Oil grill rack and grill chicken over hot coals or burner(s) (covered if using a gas grill), turning occasionally and moving chicken to cooler area of grill if flare-ups occur, until just cooked through, 8 to 10 minutes. Brush both sides of chicken with some of sauce and grill, turning once, until lightly browned, about 1 minute more.

Serve chicken drizzled with remaining sauce.

COOK'S NOTE

■ The chicken can be marinated, refrigerated, for up to 24 hours.

Grilled Lemon-Lime Chicken Legs

SERVES 4 TO 6
ACTIVE TIME: 1 HOUR ■ START TO FINISH: 3 HOURS
(INCLUDES MARINATING)

■ A bit of sugar nicely balances the tart, citrusy marinade. ■

2 teaspoons finely grated lemon zest

2 teaspoons finely grated lime zest

½ cup fresh lemon juice (from about 2 lemons)

½ cup fresh lime juice (from about 4 limes)

1 tablespoon sugar

1 large garlic clove, finely chopped

¾ teaspoon cayenne

1¼ teaspoons salt

½ teaspoon freshly ground black pepper

¾ cup olive oil

6 whole chicken legs (about 4½ pounds total)

Whisk together zests, juices, sugar, garlic, ½ teaspoon cayenne, salt, pepper, and ¼ cup oil in a medium bowl. Pour ½ cup mixture into a small bowl to use as marinade. Whisk remaining ½ cup oil and ¼ teaspoon cayenne into remaining mixture to make citrus vinaigrette.

Divide chicken between two large sealable plastic bags. Pour half of marinade into each bag and seal bags, forcing out excess air. Turn chicken in bags to coat, put bags (in case of leaks) in a shallow pan, and refrigerate, turning once, for at least 2 hours.

If using a charcoal grill, prepare it for indirect-heat cooking over medium-hot coals; if using a gas grill, prepare it for indirect-heat cooking over medium heat (see Grilling Basics, page 512).

Pat chicken dry (discard marinade). Oil grill rack and place chicken skin side down on area of grill with no coals underneath, or over turned-off burner. Grill, partially covered if using a charcoal grill, completely covered if using a gas grill, turning occasionally, until browned and cooked through, 30 to 35 minutes. (If using a charcoal grill, add more charcoal during grilling if necessary to maintain heat.)

Transfer chicken to a platter. Whisk citrus vinaigrette and spoon over chicken.

COOK'S NOTE

■ The chicken can be marinated for up to 8 hours.

Grilled Lemon-Coriander Chicken

SERVES 4
ACTIVE TIME: 25 MINUTES ■ START TO FINISH: 1½ HOURS

■ Spreading a puree of fresh herbs, garlic, and chile under the skin of a whole chicken infuses the meat with flavor. This dish is terrific with basmati rice and a crunchy salad full of bright flavors, such as Tomato, Cucumber, and Pineapple Salad with Asian Dressing (page 172). ■

¾ cup loosely packed fresh cilantro sprigs

¼ cup olive oil

2 large shallots, chopped

1 large garlic clove, chopped

1 teaspoon finely grated lemon zest

2 teaspoons fresh lemon juice

1 serrano chile, minced, including seeds

1 teaspoon coriander

1 teaspoon sugar

Salt

1 (3- to 3½-pound) chicken, rinsed and patted dry

¼ teaspoon freshly ground black pepper

1 tablespoon unsalted butter, melted and cooled

SPECIAL EQUIPMENT: kitchen string; an instant-read thermometer

MAKE THE PUREE AND PREPARE THE CHICKEN: Combine cilantro, oil, shallots, garlic, lemon zest and juice, chile, coriander, sugar, and ½ teaspoon salt in a food processor and blend until a puree forms.

Leave any fat at opening of chicken cavity and sprinkle cavity with ¼ teaspoon salt and pepper. Starting at cavity end, gently slide your index finger between skin and flesh of breast and legs to loosen skin; be careful not to tear skin. Using a small spoon, slide cilantro puree under skin of breast and legs, pressing on skin with your fingers to push puree out of spoon and distribute it evenly. Tie legs together with kitchen string and tuck wing tips under. Brush chicken all over with butter.

PREPARE THE GRILL: If using a charcoal grill, prepare it for indirect-heat cooking over medium-hot coals; if using a gas grill, prepare it for indirect-heat cooking over medium heat (see Grilling Basics, page 512).

TO COOK THE CHICKEN USING A CHARCOAL GRILL: Oil grill rack and put chicken over area with no coals underneath. Cook, covered, until thermometer inserted into fleshy part of thigh (without touching bone) registers 170°F, 40 to 50 minutes. (Add more charcoal during grilling if necessary to maintain heat.)

TO COOK THE CHICKEN USING A GAS GRILL: Oil grill rack and put chicken over turned-off burner. Grill, covered, turning chicken around halfway through cooking if using a two-burner grill, until thermometer inserted into fleshy part of thigh (without touching bone) registers 170°F, 35 to 45 minutes.

Transfer chicken to a platter and let stand for 15 minutes before carving.

COOK'S NOTE

■ The chicken can be prepared up to 1 day ahead and refrigerated, covered. Let stand at cool room temperature for 30 minutes before grilling.

Grilled Peruvian Chicken

SERVES 4
ACTIVE TIME: 40 MINUTES ■ START TO FINISH: 9¾ HOURS
(INCLUDES MARINATING)

■ Few Peruvians would ever think of making *pollo a la brasa* at home—they buy it at the many take-out shops that specialize in this iconic regional dish. For the rest of us, it's good to know that the homemade version is very easy. An intensely flavored soy-lime marinade, heady with garlic, deeply seasons the meat, and the grill gives it a beautiful sear. The soy sauce is evidence of the strong influence of the Japanese and Chinese communities in Peru. ■

⅓ cup soy sauce

2 tablespoons fresh lime juice

2 tablespoons chopped garlic

2 teaspoons ground cumin

1 teaspoon sweet paprika

½ teaspoon dried oregano, crumbled

½ teaspoon freshly ground black pepper

1 tablespoon vegetable oil

1 (3½-pound) chicken, rinsed, patted dry, and quartered

ACCOMPANIMENT: lime wedges

MARINATE THE CHICKEN: Blend soy sauce, lime juice, garlic, cumin, paprika, oregano, pepper, and oil in a blender until smooth.

Put chicken in a large sealable plastic bag, add soy sauce mixture, and seal bag, pressing out excess air. Marinate chicken, refrigerated, turning once, for at least 8 hours.

GRILL THE CHICKEN: If using a charcoal grill, prepare it for indirect-heat cooking over medium-hot coals; if using a gas grill, prepare it for indirect-heat cooking over medium heat (see Grilling Basics, page 512).

Discard marinade and pat chicken dry. Oil grill rack and place chicken skin side down on area with no coals underneath, or over turned-off burner. Grill, covered, turning once, until cooked through, 30 to 35 minutes. (If using a charcoal grill, add charcoal during grilling if necessary to maintain heat.)

Serve chicken with lime wedges.

Southeast Asian Turkey Burgers

SERVES 4
ACTIVE TIME: 40 MINUTES ■ START TO FINISH: 1¾ HOURS
(INCLUDES CHILLING)

■ The bold flavors in this burger will definitely get guests talking. A paste of lemongrass, garlic, ginger, and serrano chile enlivens ground turkey while helping to keep it moist. If you don't have a mini food processor, don't worry. It takes longer, but you can finely chop the ingredients, then mash them to a paste using a mortar and pestle. A spicy lime sauce and a fluffy mix of fresh herbs take the place of traditional burger condiments and toppings. ■

2 stalks lemongrass, root ends trimmed and tough outer leaves discarded
2 garlic cloves, chopped
3 tablespoons chopped shallots
1 tablespoon finely chopped peeled fresh ginger
1 (3-inch) serrano or jalapeño chile, finely chopped, including seeds
1 teaspoon water
4 teaspoons Asian fish sauce
1½ pounds ground turkey (dark meat only)
¼ cup fresh lime juice (from about 2 limes)
¼ cup vegetable oil
½ teaspoon sugar
½ teaspoon red pepper flakes
⅛ teaspoon salt
4 kaiser rolls or hamburger buns, split and grilled
2 cups mixed fresh mint, basil, and cilantro leaves

SPECIAL EQUIPMENT: a mini food processor

Thinly slice lower 6 inches of lemongrass stalks; you should have ¼ cup (discard remainder). Combine lemongrass, garlic, shallots, ginger, chile, water, and 2 teaspoons fish sauce in mini food processor and grind, scraping down sides frequently, to a paste.

Mix paste and turkey with your hands until just combined; do not overmix. Form into four ¾-inch-thick patties, 4 inches in diameter. Transfer to a plate and refrigerate, covered with plastic wrap, for 1 hour to allow flavors to develop.

Whisk together lime juice, oil, sugar, red pepper flakes, salt, and remaining 2 teaspoons fish sauce in a small bowl until sugar and salt are dissolved.

If using a charcoal grill, prepare it for direct-heat cooking over medium-hot coals; if using a gas grill, prepare it for direct-heat cooking over medium heat (see Grilling Basics, page 519).

If using a gas grill, turn off one burner (middle one if there are three). Oil grill rack and grill patties over hot coals or burner(s) (covered if using a gas grill), turning once and moving to cooler area of grill if flare-ups occur, until just cooked through, 10 to 12 minutes.

Whisk lime juice sauce and drizzle bottom of each bun evenly with 1 tablespoon sauce. Top each with a patty and ½ cup mixed herbs. Drizzle herbs with 1 tablespoon sauce and cover with tops of buns.

Grilled Turkey

SERVES 8 TO 10
ACTIVE TIME: 3 HOURS ■ START TO FINISH: 3½ HOURS

■ Kitchen real estate is at such a premium during Thanksgiving that it makes sense to think outside the box. The day's big bird is a great candidate for the grill, freeing up valuable oven space for side dishes. But don't limit this recipe to Thanksgiving—like ham, turkey feeds a crowd and is great for a party. For this recipe, you'll want to fire up your gas grill: it's too labor-intensive to keep a charcoal grill at a constant high heat. ■

1 (14- to 16-pound) turkey
  Salt
1½ teaspoons freshly ground black pepper
ACCOMPANIMENT: Pan Gravy (page 419)
SPECIAL EQUIPMENT: a large gas grill with thermometer; kitchen string; a V-rack; a large disposable roasting pan; an instant-read thermometer

Prepare grill for indirect-heat cooking over high heat (see Grilling Basics, page 512).

Meanwhile, remove any remaining feathers and quills from turkey with needle-nose pliers or tweezers. Rinse turkey inside and out and pat dry. Mix 2½ teaspoons salt (2 teaspoons if using a kosher bird) and pepper in a small bowl. Sprinkle evenly in both turkey cavities and all over skin. Fold neck skin under body and secure with a small metal skewer if desired. Tuck wing tips under breast and tie drumsticks together with kitchen string.

Oil V-rack and put in roasting pan. Put turkey on V-rack and add 2 cups water to pan. Set pan over turned-off burner and immediately close lid. Grill turkey, adjusting heat of lighted burner(s) throughout cooking as necessary to maintain 450°F (resist opening lid often, because of rapid heat loss), for 1 hour.

Turn pan around and add 2 cups more water if pan juices have evaporated. Continue to grill until thermometer inserted in fleshy part of thighs (without touching bone; test both thighs) registers 170°F, 45 minutes to 1½ hours more (or longer in cold weather).

Transfer turkey to a platter and let turkey stand, uncovered, for 30 minutes before carving (temperature of thigh meat will rise to 180°F). Serve with gravy.

Grilled Cornish Hens with Coconut Curry Sauce

SERVES 8
ACTIVE TIME: 1 HOUR ∎ START TO FINISH: 14½ HOURS
(INCLUDES MARINATING)

∎ A rich coconut milk marinade spiked with red curry paste, ginger, garlic, shallots, and fish sauce puts a Malaysian spin on tender Cornish hens (some of the marinade is served as an accompaniment). Serve them with rice to soak up the sauce. ∎

¼ cup vegetable oil
½ cup finely chopped shallots
2 large garlic cloves, minced
2 teaspoons minced peeled fresh ginger
2 tablespoons Thai red curry paste
2 (13- to 14-ounce) cans unsweetened coconut milk, well stirred
1½ teaspoons packed light brown sugar
  Salt
2 teaspoons Asian fish sauce
4 (1¼- to 1½-pound) Cornish hens, split lengthwise
GARNISH: fresh cilantro sprigs

Heat oil in a 4- to 5-quart wide heavy pot over moderately low heat. Add shallots and cook, stirring occasionally, until softened, 4 to 5 minutes. Add garlic and ginger and cook, stirring occasionally, for 2 minutes. Add curry paste and cook, mashing paste to combine with oil and stirring constantly, for 3 minutes (paste will begin sticking to bottom of pot). Add coconut milk, brown sugar, and 1 teaspoon salt, bring to a simmer, and simmer, uncovered, stirring occasionally, until reduced to about 3 cups, 25 to 30 minutes.

Remove sauce from heat, stir in fish sauce, and cool to room temperature, stirring occasionally, about 30 minutes.

Transfer 1½ cups curry sauce (for serving) to a bowl and refrigerate, covered.

Trim off any excess fat from hens (to prevent flare-ups), then rinse and pat dry. Coat hens well with remaining curry sauce in a large bowl. Divide hens between two large sealable plastic bags and seal bags, pressing out excess air. Marinate hens, refrigerated, for at least 12 hours.

Remove hens from refrigerator and let stand at room temperature for 30 minutes before grilling.

Meanwhile, if using a charcoal grill, prepare it for direct-heat cooking over medium-hot coals; if using a gas grill, prepare it for direct-heat cooking over medium heat (see Grilling Basics, page 512).

Remove hens from marinade, shaking off excess (discard marinade). Season with salt.

If using a gas grill, turn off one burner (middle burner if there are three). Oil grill rack and place hens skin side down over hot coals or burner(s). Grill (covered if using a gas grill), turning occasionally and moving to cool area of grill if flare-ups occur, until cooked through, 25 to 30 minutes. (Add more charcoal during grilling if necessary to maintain heat.)

Meanwhile, heat reserved curry sauce in a small saucepan over moderate heat, stirring, until hot.

Scatter cilantro sprigs over hens and serve with curry sauce.

COOK'S NOTE
■ The hens can be marinated for up to 24 hours.

Grilled Duck Breast with Spiced Salt Rub

SERVES 4
ACTIVE TIME: 30 MINUTES ■ START TO FINISH: 1 HOUR

■ A rub of mixed peppercorns, fennel seeds, cumin seeds, and salt gives a nice crust of flavor to meaty duck breasts. The duck's skin and underlying fat provide a protective layer against the grill's heat. To help prevent flare-ups, the breasts are grilled over indirect low heat. If using a charcoal grill, be sure to allow enough time for the coals to cool down; adding extra charcoal when you lay the duck on the grill ensures that the coals won't die out completely before it is done. ■

2 teaspoons four-peppercorn blend (see Cook's Note)
2 teaspoons cumin seeds
1½ teaspoons fennel seeds
¾ teaspoon coarse sea salt
1 whole Moulard duck breast (1¾–2 pounds; see page 428 and Sources), split
Salt
SPECIAL EQUIPMENT: an electric coffee/spice grinder or a mortar and pestle

PREPARE THE DUCK: Coarsely grind peppercorns, seeds, and sea salt in grinder. Pat duck dry and score skin in a crosshatch pattern (½-inch diamonds) with a sharp knife, cutting through fat but not into meat. Rub spiced salt all over duck breasts. Let stand while grill heats.

PREPARE THE GRILL: If using a charcoal grill, prepare it for indirect-heat cooking over low coals; if using a gas grill, prepare it for indirect-heat cooking over low heat (see Grilling Basics, page 512).

TO COOK THE DUCK ON A CHARCOAL GRILL: Add 4 large pieces unlit charcoal to each side of grill. Grill duck skin side down on area with no coals underneath, partially covered, until skin is browned and crisp, about 12 minutes. Turn duck and grill for 3 minutes more for medium-rare.

TO COOK THE DUCK ON A GAS GRILL: Grill duck skin side down on rack above turned-off burner, covered, for 8 minutes. Increase heat to medium and grill until skin is browned and crisp, 4 to 5 minutes. Turn duck over, then increase heat to high and grill for 3 minutes for medium-rare.

Transfer duck to a cutting board and let stand, uncovered, for 5 minutes.

Thinly slice duck against the grain and season with salt.

COOK'S NOTE
■ The four-peppercorn blend is available in most supermarkets, but if you are not able to find it, you can substitute black peppercorns.

Grilled Charmoula Quail

SERVES 4
ACTIVE TIME: 30 MINUTES ■ START TO FINISH: 2¾ HOURS
(INCLUDES MARINATING)

■ Made up of peppercorns, cinnamon, cumin, cloves, coriander, and other spices with fresh cilantro, the North African spice mixture called *charmoula* is fragrant and robust. It makes a deliciously assertive rub for the flavorful meat of quail. ■

1 (3-inch-long) cinnamon stick, broken in half

1 tablespoon cumin seeds

1 tablespoon coriander seeds

¼ teaspoon black peppercorns

3 whole cloves

2 tablespoons sweet paprika

2 teaspoons ground ginger

½ teaspoon cayenne

Salt

2 cups coarsely chopped fresh cilantro

1 tablespoon finely chopped garlic

¼ cup extra-virgin olive oil

8 semiboneless quail (see page 434), necks cut off

ACCOMPANIMENT: lemon wedges

SPECIAL EQUIPMENT: an electric coffee/spice grinder;
　　　　eight 12-inch wooden skewers, soaked in water
　　　　for 30 minutes

Finely grind cinnamon, cumin, coriander, peppercorns, and cloves together in grinder. Transfer spice mixture to a large bowl and whisk in paprika, ginger, cayenne, 1 teaspoon salt, cilantro, garlic, and oil. Add quail, turning to coat. Transfer to a large sealable plastic bag. Marinate, refrigerated, for 2 hours.

If using a charcoal grill, prepare it for indirect-heat cooking over medium-hot coals; if using a gas grill, prepare it for indirect-heat cooking over medium heat (see Grilling Basics, page 512).

Meanwhile, place 2 quail breast side up, with ends of drumsticks nearest you, on a work surface. Thread one skewer horizontally through all 4 drumsticks and lower carcasses of birds. Thread a second skewer, parallel to the first, through wings and upper carcasses. Position skewered quail so that there is 1 inch of space between the birds. Repeat procedure with remaining quail. Sprinkle quail with ½ teaspoon salt (total).

Oil grill rack and place quail breast side down on area with no coals underneath, or over turned-off burner. Grill, partially covered if using a charcoal grill, completely covered if using a gas grill, turning once, until just cooked through, 6 to 8 minutes.

Serve quail with lemon wedges.

Beef

Grilled Rib-Eye Steaks with Warm Tomato and Corn Salad

SERVES 6

ACTIVE TIME: 40 MINUTES ■ START TO FINISH: 50 MINUTES

■ This is the dish you want to make when summer is in full swing. Rib eye pairs beautifully with the sweetness of ripe corn, the slight acidity of tomatoes, and a smattering of fresh basil and lime juice (though this salad tastes equally good with any steak). On a languid evening, you won't need anything else. ■

2 tablespoons unsalted butter

1 medium onion, chopped

1 Italian frying pepper, cored, seeded, and chopped

2 garlic cloves, finely chopped

1 teaspoon chili powder

2 cups corn (from 4 large ears)

½ pound cherry or grape tomatoes, halved

3 (1½-inch-thick) rib-eye steaks (about 1 pound each)

Salt

½ teaspoon freshly ground black pepper

¼ cup chopped fresh basil

1 tablespoon fresh lime juice

SPECIAL EQUIPMENT: an instant-read thermometer

If using a charcoal grill, prepare it for indirect-heat cooking over medium-hot coals; if using a gas grill, prepare it for indirect-heat cooking over medium-high heat (see Grilling Basics, page 512).

Meanwhile, heat butter in a 12-inch heavy skillet over moderately high heat until foam subsides. Add onion and frying pepper and cook, stirring occasionally, until onion begins to turn golden, about 6 minutes. Add garlic and chili powder and cook, stirring, for 1 minute. Stir in corn, cover skillet, and cook, stirring occasionally, until corn is just tender, about 3 minutes. Add tomatoes and cook, uncovered, stirring, until they just begin to soften, about 2 minutes. Remove from heat and partially cover to keep warm.

Pat steaks dry and sprinkle all over with ¾ teaspoon salt and pepper. Oil grill rack and sear steaks directly over hot coals or burner(s) (covered if using a gas grill), turning once, until grill marks appear, 2 to 3 minutes. Move steaks to cool area of grill (reduce other burner[s] to medium if using gas) and grill, covered, turning occasionally, until thermometer inserted horizontally 2 inches into meat registers 120°F, 12 to 15 minutes. Transfer steaks to a cutting board and let stand, loosely covered with foil, for 5 minutes (steaks will continue to cook as they stand, reaching medium-rare).

Cut steaks across the grain into ½-inch-thick slices.

Meanwhile, if necessary, reheat corn salad over moderate heat, stirring. Stir in basil, lime juice, any meat juices accumulated on cutting board, and salt to taste.

Serve steak with corn salad.

COOK'S NOTE

■ The corn salad, without the basil and lime juice, can be made up to 2 hours ahead and kept at room temperature. Stir in the basil, lime juice, meat juices, and salt before serving.

Grilled Steaks with Olive Oregano Relish

SERVES 4
ACTIVE TIME: 25 MINUTES ■ START TO FINISH: 30 MINUTES

■ The briny saltiness of black olives is a fine match for beef, and chopping them into a relish with red onion is a speedy way to give them pizzazz. The steaks' natural marbling may cause flare-ups, which is why a section of the grill is kept free of flames, in case you need to move the meat off the heat for a moment or two. Don't walk away from the grill—you don't want to torch an expensive cut of meat. ■

⅔ cup Kalamata or other brine-cured black olives, pitted and coarsely chopped
¼ cup finely chopped red onion
4 teaspoons minced fresh oregano
4 teaspoons extra-virgin olive oil
  Freshly ground black pepper
4 (¾-inch-thick) boneless beef top loin steaks (also known as strip steaks) or rib-eye steaks (about 8 ounces each)
1 teaspoon salt

Stir together olives, onion, oregano, oil, and ¼ teaspoon pepper in a bowl.

If using a charcoal grill, prepare it for direct-heat cooking over medium-hot coals; if using a gas grill, prepare it for direct-heat cooking over medium-high heat (see Grilling Basics, page 512).

Pat steaks dry and sprinkle all over with salt and 1 teaspoon pepper. If using a gas grill, turn off one burner (middle one if there are three). Oil grill rack and grill steaks over hot coals or burner(s) (covered if using a gas grill), turning once and moving to cool area of grill if flare-ups occur, 7 to 8 minutes for medium-rare. Transfer steaks to a platter and let stand, loosely covered with foil, for 5 minutes.

Serve steaks topped with olive relish.

Florentine-Style Porterhouse Steaks

SERVES 8
ACTIVE TIME: 35 MINUTES ■ START TO FINISH: 1 HOUR

■ It may not look like much—just steak, sea salt, and olive oil—but the success lies in the quality of the meat and the care in the cooking. *Bistecca fiorentina* is traditionally made from a favored Tuscan breed of cow called Chianina, a huge work animal prized for its complex, beefy flavor; here, a thick domestic porterhouse comes closest to that taste. As with most grilled meats, the standing time is vital—if you cut into the steak too early, you'll lose its precious juices. ■

2 (2-inch-thick) porterhouse steaks (about 2½ pounds each)
  Sea salt
2 tablespoons olive oil
ACCOMPANIMENT: lemon wedges
SPECIAL EQUIPMENT: an instant-read thermometer

If using a charcoal grill, prepare it for direct-heat cooking over medium-hot coals; if using a gas grill, prepare it for direct-heat cooking over high heat (see Grilling Basics, page 512).

Pat steaks dry and rub each all over with 1 teaspoon sea salt.

TO COOK THE STEAKS ON A CHARCOAL GRILL: Oil grill rack and sear steaks, turning once, until grill marks appear on both sides (rotate 90 degrees once on each side to make crosshatch marks), about 10 minutes. Move steaks to cool area of grill and grill, covered, turning occasionally, until thermometer inserted horizontally 2 inches into meat (without touching bone) registers about 110°F in larger section of meat and about 125°F in smaller (fillet) section for medium-rare, 12 to 15 minutes.

TO COOK THE STEAKS ON A GAS GRILL: Oil grill rack and sear steaks, covered, turning once, until grill marks appear (rotate 90 degrees once on each side to make crosshatch marks), about 10 minutes. Turn off one burner (middle one if there are three) and put steaks over turned-off burner. Reduce remaining burner(s) to medium heat. Grill steaks, covered, turning occasionally, until thermometer inserted horizontally 2 inches into meat (without touching bone) registers about 110°F in larger section of meat and about 125°F in smaller (fillet) section for medium-rare, 10 to 15 minutes.

Transfer steaks to a cutting board and let stand, uncovered, for 10 minutes (steaks will continue to cook as they stand).

Cut each section of meat off bone, slice meat crosswise against the grain, and arrange slices on a platter. Lightly sprinkle with sea salt and drizzle with oil. Serve with lemon wedges.

Garam Masala–Rubbed Flank Steak

SERVES 4
ACTIVE TIME: 35 MINUTES ■ START TO FINISH: 1 HOUR

■ This version of the aromatic North Indian spice blend called garam masala, from cookbook author Janie Hibler, is perfect for bold-flavored flank steak. ■

1½ tablespoons Garam Masala (recipe follows, or see Sources)
1½ teaspoons kosher salt
1 teaspoon freshly ground black pepper
1 (1½-pound) flank steak (1 inch at thickest part)

Stir together garam masala, salt, and pepper in a small bowl. Pat steak dry and rub all over with seasoning. Marinate steak, uncovered, at room temperature for 30 minutes.

If using a charcoal grill, prepare it for direct-heat cooking over medium-hot coals; if using a gas grill, prepare it for direct-heat cooking over medium-high heat (see Grilling Basics, page 512).

If using a gas grill, turn off one burner (middle one if there are three). Oil grill rack and grill steak over hot coals or burner(s) (covered if using a gas grill), turning once and moving to cool area of grill if flare-ups occur, 12 to 15 minutes for medium-rare. Transfer steak to a cutting board and let stand, loosely covered with foil, for 10 minutes.

Holding knife at a 45-degree angle, cut steak across the grain into very thin slices.

Garam Masala

MAKES ABOUT ½ CUP
ACTIVE TIME: 15 MINUTES ■ START TO FINISH: 15 MINUTES

■ *Garam* is the Hindi word for "hot" and *masala* means "spice blend," but this Indian rub is not so much spicy as deep and warming. ■

2 tablespoons coriander seeds
1 tablespoon cumin seeds
¼ teaspoon cardamom seeds (from about 10 green or white pods; see Sources)
2 teaspoons brown mustard seeds (see Sources)
2 teaspoons fenugreek seeds (see Sources)
2 teaspoons black peppercorns
1 rounded teaspoon whole cloves
1 (3-inch-long) cinnamon stick, broken in half
SPECIAL EQUIPMENT: an electric coffee/spice grinder

Heat a dry 10-inch heavy skillet, preferably cast-iron, over moderate heat until hot. Add all spices and toast, stirring frequently and covering skillet when mustard seeds begin to pop, until several shades darker and fragrant, 3 to 4 minutes (be careful not to burn spices). Transfer spices to a bowl and cool for 5 minutes.

Grind spices to a powder in grinder.

COOK'S NOTE
■ The garam masala keeps in an airtight container in a cool, dark place for up to 1 month.

Grilled Spicy Skirt Steak

SERVES 4
ACTIVE TIME: 25 MINUTES ■ START TO FINISH: 40 MINUTES

■ Who knew such a sultry spice rub could come straight from your pantry? ■

    2 large garlic cloves
    2 teaspoons salt
    2 tablespoons chili powder
    2 teaspoons ground cumin
    2 teaspoons sugar
 1¼ teaspoons freshly ground black pepper
  ½ teaspoon ground allspice
    4 teaspoons Worcestershire sauce
    2 tablespoons vegetable oil
    2 (¾- to 1-pound) skirt steaks, halved crosswise

Mince garlic and mash to a paste with salt, using side of a large heavy knife. Stir together garlic paste, chili powder, cumin, sugar, pepper, allspice, Worcestershire sauce, and oil in a small bowl until sugar is dissolved. Pat steaks dry, rub all over with spice paste, and marinate at room temperature for 30 minutes.

If using a charcoal grill, prepare it for direct-heat cooking over hot coals; if using a gas grill, prepare it for direct-heat cooking over high heat (see Grilling Basics, page 512).

Oil grill rack and grill steaks (covered if using a gas grill), turning occasionally to prevent overbrowning, for 4 to 5 minutes for thinner pieces, 5 to 7 minutes for thicker pieces, for medium-rare. Transfer steaks to a cutting board and let stand, loosely covered with foil, for 5 minutes.

Holding knife at a 45-degree angle, cut steaks across the grain into ¼-inch-thick slices.

COOK'S NOTE
■ The steaks can be marinated, covered and refrigerated, for up to 24 hours.

Grilled London Broil with Rum Molasses Sauce

SERVES 6
ACTIVE TIME: 45 MINUTES ■ START TO FINISH: 12¾ HOURS
(INCLUDES MARINATING)

■ Rum, syrupy molasses, lime juice, and allspice are the basis for a dark marinade that elevates the flavor of London broil to new heights. Marinating the meat for 12 hours allows the mix to work its way into the meat. ■

    6 tablespoons fresh lime juice (from about 3 limes)
  ⅓ cup olive oil
  ¼ cup dark rum
    2 tablespoons molasses (not robust)
    1 tablespoon habanero pepper sauce (see Sources)
    1 teaspoon salt
    1 teaspoon freshly ground black pepper
  ½ teaspoon ground allspice
 2½ pounds top-round London broil (1¼ inches thick)

SPECIAL EQUIPMENT: an instant-read thermometer

Whisk together lime juice, oil, rum, molasses, habanero sauce, salt, pepper, and allspice in a bowl until well combined. Put steak in a large sealable plastic bag, pour in marinade, and seal bag, pressing out excess air. Put steak in a shallow pan (in case of leaks) and marinate in refrigerator, turning several times, for 12 hours.

PREPARE THE GRILL: If using a charcoal grill, prepare it for direct-heat cooking over medium-hot coals; if using a gas grill, prepare it for direct-heat cooking over high heat (see Grilling Basics, page 512).

Meanwhile, lift steak from marinade, letting excess drip back into bag, and transfer to a tray. Pour marinade into a small saucepan, bring to a boil over moderately high heat, and boil, stirring occasionally, for 3 minutes. Reserve ¼ cup marinade for basting and set remaining marinade aside for serving with steak.

TO COOK THE STEAK ON A CHARCOAL GRILL: Oil grill rack. Pat steak dry and grill, uncovered, turning occasionally and moving to cool area of grill if flare-ups occur, for 15 minutes. Baste steak on both sides with reserved ¼ cup marinade and grill, turning once, until thermometer inserted horizontally 2 inches into meat registers 120°F, about 5 minutes more.

TO COOK THE STEAK ON A GAS GRILL: Oil grill rack. Pat steak dry and sear, covered, turning once, until grill marks appears on both sides, about 2 minutes total. Reduce heat to medium and grill steak, covered, turning occasionally, for 8 minutes more. Baste steak on both sides with reserved ¼ cup marinade and grill until thermometer inserted horizontally 2 inches into meat registers 120°F, about 5 minutes more.

Transfer steak to a cutting board and let stand, loosely covered with foil, for 5 minutes. (Steak will continue to cook as it stands, reaching medium-rare.)

Holding knife at a 45-degree angle, thinly slice steak. Serve with reserved sauce.

Flank Steak Pinwheels with Arugula Salad

SERVES 4
ACTIVE TIME: 45 MINUTES ■ START TO FINISH: 1 HOUR

■ These festive pinwheels take a bit of time to assemble, but you can do all the work ahead and the grilling is quick. Thin slices of prosciutto and provolone add flavor and juiciness. Have a larger crowd coming over? Double the recipe. ■

1 (1½-pound) flank steak
3 tablespoons olive oil
   Salt and freshly ground black pepper
¼ pound very thinly sliced prosciutto
¼ pound thinly sliced provolone
¾ pound arugula, tough stems discarded

ACCOMPANIMENT: lemon wedges
SPECIAL EQUIPMENT: eight to ten 6-inch wooden skewers, soaked in water for 30 minutes

Put steak on two overlapping sheets of plastic wrap, with a short end of steak nearest you. Butterfly steak: Anchoring meat with one hand, hold a sharp knife in other hand parallel to work surface and, starting on long side, begin to cut through meat horizontally. Lift top layer and continue to cut through meat, stopping about ½ inch from edge; do not cut all the way through. Open meat like a book. Cover steak with a double thickness of plastic wrap and, with flat side of a meat pounder or with a rolling pin, gently pound ¼ inch thick.

Discard top sheets of plastic wrap and turn steak on plastic wrap so grain of meat runs from left to right. Rub 1 tablespoon oil onto steak and sprinkle with ¼ teaspoon salt and ¼ teaspoon pepper. Arrange prosciutto in a slightly overlapping layer on steak, then cover with cheese. Beginning with side nearest you and using plastic wrap as an aid, tightly roll up steak, pressing slightly on filling. Skewer steak crosswise at 1-inch intervals. Using a sharp knife, cut between skewers to make 1-inch-thick pinwheels. (End pieces will be about 1½ inches thick; trim ends if desired.)

If using a charcoal grill, prepare it for direct-heat cooking over medium-hot coals; if using a gas grill, prepare it for direct-heat cooking over medium heat (see Grilling Basics, page 512).

Oil grill rack and grill pinwheels cut side down (covered if using a gas grill), turning once (use a metal spatula to loosen meat), until beef is well browned outside but still pink inside and cheese is beginning to melt, 6 to 8 minutes. Transfer to a large plate.

Toss arugula with remaining 2 tablespoons oil and ¼ teaspoon salt in a large bowl. Spread arugula on a platter and top with pinwheels. Serve with lemon wedges.

- The pinwheels can be formed up to 1 day ahead and refrigerated, loosely covered with plastic wrap.

Veal

Veal Involtini

SERVES 6
ACTIVE TIME: 2 HOURS ■ START TO FINISH: 2¼ HOURS

■ This Sicilian dish may seem an unconventional choice for the grill, but it's sensational. Veal cutlets are pounded thin and spread with a savory paste of parsley, garlic, and pecorino Romano, then rolled up, dredged in cheesy bread crumbs, and threaded onto skewers with pieces of onion. As the skewers grill, the filling bastes the veal and keeps it juicy, while the bread crumbs toast up. ■

- 4 cups fine fresh bread crumbs (from 10 slices firm white sandwich bread)
- 2 pounds veal cutlets (scaloppine; ¼ inch thick or less)
- ¼ cup chopped fresh flat-leaf parsley
- 5 garlic cloves, minced
- 1¼ cups finely grated pecorino Romano or Parmigiano-Reggiano (about 3½ ounces)
- 1¼ cups olive oil
  Freshly ground black pepper
  Salt
- 1 large white onion, cut into 8 wedges, layers separated

SPECIAL EQUIPMENT: seven 10- to 12-inch metal skewers

Put a rack in middle of oven and preheat oven to 350°F.

Spread bread crumbs on a baking sheet and toast in oven, stirring once or twice, until golden, 8 to 10 minutes.

With flat side of a meat pounder or with a rolling pin, gently pound veal cutlets to slightly less than ⅛ inch thick between two sheets of plastic wrap. Cut veal into about 20 roughly 4-by-3-inch pieces.

Stir together parsley, garlic, ¾ cup cheese, ¼ cup oil, and ½ teaspoon pepper in a bowl until a paste forms. Stir together bread crumbs, remaining ½ cup cheese, and ½ teaspoon pepper in a pie plate. Put remaining cup of oil in a shallow bowl.

Line a baking sheet with wax paper. Season cutlets lightly with salt and pepper. Spread 1 teaspoon parsley-garlic paste over each cutlet. Roll up veal pieces, starting from a short side. Dip each roll in oil to coat, letting excess drip off, then dredge in bread crumb mixture, pressing gently to help crumbs adhere, and transfer to lined baking sheet.

Thread 1 veal roll onto a skewer, then 1 piece of onion, leaving about ¼ inch between. Repeat 2 more times, then transfer skewer to baking sheet. Assemble 6 more skewers in same manner (last skewer may have only 2 rolls).

If using a charcoal grill, prepare it for direct-heat grilling over hot coals; if using a gas grill, prepare it for direct-heat cooking over medium-high heat (see Grilling Basics, page 512).

Oil grill rack and grill veal rolls (covered if using gas grill), turning once, until golden, about 6 minutes.

Remove veal and onion from skewers and serve immediately.

COOK'S NOTE

- The veal and onion can be threaded onto skewers up to 1 day ahead and refrigerated, loosely covered with plastic wrap.

Grilled Sweetbreads with Chimichurri Sauce

SERVES 4
ACTIVE TIME: 35 MINUTES ■ START TO FINISH: 35 MINUTES

■ Grilling sweetbreads gives them a crisp crust that contrasts with the creamy, tender interior. (Simmering them before they are skewered and grilled makes them firmer.) Although sweetbreads are delicate in flavor, their richness can stand up to bold sauces, like this chimichurri's vivacious mix of parsley, lemon, and garlic. The recipe came to us from Chris Schlesinger, the cookbook author and chef-owner of East Coast Grill in Cambridge, Massachusetts. ■

1 pound sweetbreads

1 cup distilled white vinegar

Salt

2 tablespoons extra-virgin olive oil

Freshly ground black pepper

ACCOMPANIMENT: Chimichurri Sauce (recipe follows)

SPECIAL EQUIPMENT: four 12-inch wooden skewers, soaked in water for 30 minutes

Rinse sweetbreads well. Transfer to a 6-quart pot, add 4 quarts cold water, vinegar, and 2 table-spoons salt, and bring to a boil over high heat. Reduce heat and simmer gently for 10 minutes. Drain sweetbreads and transfer to a bowl of ice and cold water to cool.

If using a charcoal grill, prepare it for direct-heat cooking over medium-hot coals; if using a gas grill, prepare it for direct-heat cooking over medium-high heat (see Grilling Basics, page 512).

Drain sweetbreads and gently pat dry. Separate into roughly 1½-inch pieces (about 20), using your fingers. Toss sweetbread pieces with oil in a bowl. Thread onto skewers (about 5 pieces on each) and season with salt and pepper.

If using a gas grill, turn off one burner (middle one if there are three). Oil grill rack and grill sweetbreads over hot coals or burner(s) (covered if using a gas grill), turning occasionally and moving to cool area of grill if flare-ups occur, until golden brown, 5 to 7 minutes. Transfer to a platter and let stand, loosely covered with foil, for 5 minutes.

Serve sweetbreads with chimichurri sauce.

Chimichurri Sauce

MAKES ABOUT ⅔ CUP
ACTIVE TIME: 15 MINUTES ■ START TO FINISH: 15 MINUTES

■ Originally from Argentina, this herb sauce is now popular throughout Central America. You'll want to serve it on everything from juicy steak to roasted sweet potatoes to grilled cherry tomatoes. ■

½ cup coarsely chopped fresh flat-leaf parsley

⅓ cup extra-virgin olive oil

¼ cup fresh lemon juice

2 tablespoons minced shallots

1 teaspoon minced garlic

1 teaspoon red pepper flakes

¼ teaspoon salt

Stir together all ingredients in a bowl.

COOK'S NOTE

■ The sauce can be made up to 3 hours ahead and refrigerated, covered. Bring to room temperature before serving.

Pork

Barbecued Pork Burgers with Slaw

SERVES 4
ACTIVE TIME: 30 MINUTES ■ START TO FINISH: 30 MINUTES

■ Spicing up store-bought barbecue sauce with cayenne and a splash of vinegar makes a big difference. Here, pork burgers get a triple hit of flavor: the sauce is mixed into the meat, slathered onto the cooked burgers for the last minute of grilling, and brushed on the buns. A cabbage slaw with a creamy dressing tops the patties off with just the right crunch. ■

½ pound green cabbage, cored

¼ cup mayonnaise

1 tablespoon whole milk

1½ tablespoons white wine vinegar

½ cup very finely shredded carrot

1 tablespoon thinly sliced fresh chives

Salt and freshly ground black pepper

½ cup bottled barbecue sauce

¼ teaspoon cayenne

1½ pounds ground pork

4 kaiser or soft rolls, split and grilled

If using a charcoal grill, prepare it for direct-heat cooking over medium-hot coals; if using a gas grill, prepare it for direct-heat cooking over medium-high heat (see Grilling Basics, page 512).

Thinly slice enough cabbage with a mandoline

or other adjustable-blade vegetable slicer or a sharp knife to measure 2 cups. Whisk together mayonnaise, milk, and 1½ teaspoons vinegar in a medium bowl until smooth. Add cabbage, carrot, chives, and salt and pepper to taste, tossing to coat. Let slaw stand, uncovered, at room temperature while you make burgers.

Stir together barbecue sauce, cayenne, ¼ teaspoon salt, and remaining tablespoon vinegar in a small bowl until well combined.

Mix together pork, ½ teaspoon salt, ¼ teaspoon pepper, and 2 tablespoons barbecue sauce mixture just until combined; do not overmix. Form into four ¾-inch-thick patties, 4 inches in diameter.

If using a gas grill, turn off one burner (middle one if there are three). Oil grill rack and grill patties over hot coals or burner(s) (covered if using a gas grill), turning occasionally and moving to cool area of grill if flare-ups occur, until just cooked through, about 6 minutes. Brush top of each patty with 1 tablespoon barbecue sauce mixture, turn over, and grill for 30 seconds. Brush top of each patty with another tablespoon barbecue sauce, turn over, and grill for 30 seconds more.

Brush cut sides of rolls with remaining barbecue sauce. Sandwich patties and coleslaw between rolls.

COOK'S NOTES
- The coleslaw can be made up to 8 hours ahead and refrigerated, covered.
- The patties can be formed up to 1 hour ahead and refrigerated, covered.

Grilled Monster Pork Chops with Tomatillo and Green Apple Salsa

SERVES 6
ACTIVE TIME: 50 MINUTES ■ START TO FINISH: 1½ HOURS

■ To keep these thick, succulent chops moist, we first sear them, then grill them, covered, over indirect heat, which allows the meat to cook gently without drying out. (You'll probably have to order the chops from a specialty butcher.) The crunchy tomatillo-apple relish is mild but addictive, melding sweet flavors (apples and honey) with tart (tomatillos and lime) and underscoring them with smoky chipotle. The relish also goes well with chicken or ham. ■

FOR PORK CHOPS
  3 tablespoons ground coriander
  3 tablespoons ground cumin
  1½ tablespoons kosher salt
  1½ tablespoons freshly ground black pepper
  3 tablespoons olive oil
  4 (2-inch-thick) loin pork chops (about 1 pound each; see headnote)

FOR TOMATILLO AND GREEN APPLE SALSA
  ½ pound tomatillos (about 5 medium), husks discarded, rinsed under warm water
  2 Granny Smith apples
  ½ cup loosely packed fresh cilantro sprigs
  1 garlic clove, minced
  1 teaspoon ground cumin
  ¼ cup apple juice
  1 tablespoon fresh lime juice
  1 tablespoon mild honey
  1 teaspoon minced canned chipotle chile in adobo

SPECIAL EQUIPMENT: a 17-by-12½-inch disposable aluminum roasting pan if using a charcoal grill; an instant-read thermometer

MARINATE THE CHOPS: Stir together coriander, cumin, salt, and pepper in a small bowl, then stir in oil. Pat chops dry and rub spice mixture all over them. Transfer to a plate and set aside.

MAKE THE SALSA: Put tomatillos in a 2½- to 3-quart saucepan, add 3 cups water, bring to a simmer, uncovered, and simmer, stirring occasionally, until tomatillos are just soft, 8 to 10 minutes. Drain and cool for 15 minutes.

Meanwhile, core apples and cut into ¼-inch pieces.

Puree tomatillos with remaining ingredients except apples in a food processor. Transfer to a bowl and stir in apples.

PREPARE THE GRILL: If using a charcoal grill, prepare it for indirect-heat cooking over medium-hot coals; if using a gas grill, prepare it for direct-heat cooking over high heat (see Grilling Basics, page 512).

TO COOK THE PORK ON A CHARCOAL GRILL: Oil grill rack and sear pork directly over coals, uncovered, turning once and moving to cool area of grill if flare-ups occur, until well browned, 10 to 12 minutes. Move pork to cool area of grill, cover with upside-down disposable roasting pan, and grill, turning once, until thermometer inserted diagonally into center of each chop (without touching bone) registers 145° to 150°F, 10 to 12 minutes.

TO COOK THE PORK ON A GAS GRILL: Oil grill rack and sear pork (over middle burner if there are three), covered, turning once, until well browned, 10 to 12 minutes. Turn off burner under pork, reduce other burner(s) to medium, and grill pork, covered, until thermometer inserted diagonally into center of each chop (without touching bone) registers 145° to 150°F, 12 to 16 minutes.

Transfer pork to a cutting board and let stand, loosely covered with foil, for 15 minutes. (The internal temperature will rise 5 to 10 degrees as the pork stands.)

Cut pork away from bone, thinly slice, and serve with salsa.

COOK'S NOTE

■ The salsa can be made up to 2 hours ahead and refrigerated, covered. Bring to room temperature before serving.

PORK TENDERLOIN

In many supermarkets, pork tenderloin is vacuum-packed in 1½- to 2½-pound bags and looks like a solid piece of meat. Slit open the plastic, though, and out come two tenderloins pressed together side by side, weighing ¾ to 1½ pounds each. Because a tenderloin narrows at the tail, you might want to double that end under and tie it with soaked kitchen string to even out the thickness before grilling.

Grilled Pork Tenderloin and Belgian Endive with Tomato Chile Jam

SERVES 4
ACTIVE TIME: 40 MINUTES ■ START TO FINISH: 45 MINUTES

■ Smoky and surprisingly quick, this dish marries juicy pork tenderloin with a boldly spiced tomato jam. The jam takes advantage of a handy kitchen technique—skinning a tomato by rubbing it on the large holes of a box grater. Halves of Belgian endive, their bitterness tamed by grilling, taste delicious with a dab of the jam and make this practically a one-dish dinner. ■

1 large garlic clove
  Salt
2 teaspoons minced fresh rosemary
¼ teaspoon freshly ground black pepper
2½ tablespoons olive oil
2 pork tenderloins (1½ pounds total)
2 pounds plum tomatoes, halved lengthwise
⅓ cup sugar
1 teaspoon red pepper flakes
4 Belgian endives, halved lengthwise

SPECIAL EQUIPMENT: an instant-read thermometer

Mince garlic and mash to a paste with 1 teaspoon salt, using side of a large heavy knife. Stir together garlic paste, rosemary, pepper, and 1 tablespoon oil in a small bowl. Pat pork dry and rub paste all over meat. Set aside to marinate, uncovered, at room temperature.

Set a box grater into a shallow dish and rub cut sides of tomatoes against large teardrop-shaped holes to remove as much tomato pulp as possible; discard skins. Combine tomato pulp, sugar, red pepper flakes, and ½ teaspoon salt in a 4-quart heavy pot, bring to a boil, and boil, uncovered, stirring occasionally, until reduced to about 1½ cups, 15 to 20 minutes. Transfer tomato jam to a bowl set in a larger bowl of ice and cold water and cool to room temperature, stirring occasionally.

Meanwhile, if using a charcoal grill, prepare it for direct-heat cooking over medium-hot coals; if using a gas grill, prepare it for direct-heat cooking over medium heat (see Grilling Basics, page 512).

Brush both sides of endive halves with remaining 1½ tablespoons oil and season with salt. If using a gas grill, turn off one burner (middle one if there are three). Oil grill rack and grill pork and endives over hot coals or burner(s) (covered if using a gas grill), turning occasionally and moving to cool area of grill if flare-ups occur, until thermometer inserted diagonally into center of pork registers 145° to 150°F and endives are tender, 10 to 20 minutes, depending on thickness of tenderloins. Transfer pork to a cutting board and let stand for 10 minutes. (Internal temperature will rise 5 to 10 degrees as pork stands.)

Slice pork and serve with endives and tomato chile jam.

Grilled Jerk Pork Tenderloin with Curried Peach Relish

SERVES 6
ACTIVE TIME: 50 MINUTES ■ START TO FINISH: 9½ HOURS
(INCLUDES MARINATING)

■ Keep this recipe in mind for late summer, when peaches are plentiful. The stone fruit's sweetness, combined with tomatoes, helps counteract the sting of the pork's jerk seasoning. Both the peach relish and the pork benefit from an overnight rest in the refrigerator; the relish mellows in flavor and the pork drinks up the spicy marinade. ■

FOR RELISH
- 1 tablespoon vegetable oil
- ½ cup chopped red onion
- 1 tablespoon minced peeled fresh ginger
- 1 teaspoon kosher salt
- 1½ teaspoons curry powder, preferably Madras
- 1½ pounds firm but ripe peaches, peeled (see Tips, page 913), halved, pitted, and cut into 1-inch pieces
- ½ pound tomatoes, peeled (see Tips, page 913) and chopped
- 2 tablespoons sugar
- 1 tablespoon fresh lime juice

FOR PORK
- 3 scallions, trimmed and cut into 2-inch pieces
- 1 tablespoon chopped fresh thyme
- 2 teaspoons kosher salt
- ½ teaspoon ground allspice
- ¼ teaspoon freshly ground black pepper
- 2 tablespoons fresh lime juice
- 1 tablespoon molasses (not robust)
- 1 teaspoon Scotch bonnet or habanero pepper sauce (see Sources), or to taste
- 2 pork tenderloins (2 pounds total)
- 2 tablespoons vegetable oil

SPECIAL EQUIPMENT: an instant-read thermometer

MAKE THE RELISH: Heat oil in a 3-quart heavy saucepan over moderate heat until hot but not smoking. Add onion, ginger, and salt and cook, stirring occasionally, until onion is softened, 3 to 4 minutes. Add curry powder and cook, stirring constantly, for 1 minute. Add peaches and tomatoes with any juices, sugar, and lime juice, bring to a simmer, and simmer, uncovered, stirring occasionally, until mixture is thick and peaches are tender but still hold their shape, about 8 minutes.

Transfer relish to a bowl and cool, uncovered, then refrigerate, covered, for at least 8 hours to allow flavors to develop.

MEANWHILE, MARINATE THE PORK: Combine scallions, thyme, salt, allspice, pepper, lime juice, molasses, and hot sauce in a blender and blend until smooth. Put pork in a glass or ceramic baking dish and rub all over with scallion marinade. Marinate, covered and refrigerated, turning occasionally, for 8 hours.

Remove the pork from refrigerator 30 minutes before grilling.

GRILL THE PORK: If using a charcoal grill, prepare it for direct-heat cooking over medium-hot coals; if using a gas grill, prepare it for direct-heat grilling over medium heat (see Grilling Basics, page 512).

Discard any marinade remaining in dish and brush pork lightly with oil. If using a gas grill, turn off one burner (middle one if there are three). Oil grill rack and grill pork over hot coals or burner(s) (covered if using a gas grill), turning occasionally, basting frequently with oil and moving to cool area of grill if flare-ups occur, until thermometer inserted diagonally into center of meat registers 145° to 150°F, 10 to 20 minutes, depending on thickness of tenderloin. Transfer pork to a cutting board and let stand, loosely covered with foil, for 10 minutes. (Internal temperature will rise 5 to 10 degrees as pork stands.)

Slice pork and serve with peach relish.

COOK'S NOTE

■ The relish can be made up to 1 week ahead and refrigerated, covered. Bring to room temperature before serving.

Sticky Spicy Ribs

SERVES 4
ACTIVE TIME: 1 HOUR ■ START TO FINISH: 5½ HOURS
(INCLUDES MARINATING)

■ These are some of the best grilled ribs we've tasted. The spice rub—a dark, complex base coat of cumin, chipotle, paprika, and brown sugar—infuses the meat while it parbakes, a step that ensures the meat is fall-off-the-bone tender. Finished by grilling over indirect heat, the ribs are basted with a sauce of onion, garlic, ginger, ketchup, vinegar, and soy sauce, which contribute tangy top notes to the meat. Pull out the paper napkins and dig in. ■

FOR RIBS
    2 (2-pound) racks baby back ribs
    2 tablespoons packed dark brown sugar
1½ teaspoons salt
    2 tablespoons sweet paprika
1½ teaspoons chipotle chile powder (see Sources)
1½ teaspoons ground cumin
    1 teaspoon ground allspice
    ½ teaspoon freshly ground black pepper
FOR SAUCE
    2 tablespoons vegetable oil
1½ cups chopped onions
    6 garlic cloves, finely chopped

1½ tablespoons finely chopped peeled fresh
    ginger
1½ cups ketchup
    ½ cup cider vinegar
    ½ cup water
    6 tablespoons soy sauce
    ¼ cup packed dark brown sugar
1½ teaspoons salt
    ¾ teaspoon freshly ground black pepper

MARINATE THE RIBS: Line a 17-by-12-inch heavy baking sheet with two sheets of foil, overlapping in center, and oil foil. Pat ribs dry and arrange on baking sheet. Whisk together brown sugar, salt, and spices in a small bowl. Rub ribs all over with spice mixture. Marinate, meaty sides up, covered and refrigerated, for 2½ hours.

Remove ribs from refrigerator and bring to room temperature, about 30 minutes.

Put a rack in middle of oven and preheat oven to 350°F.

Cover pan tightly with foil and bake ribs until meat is tender, about 1¼ hours. Remove foil.

MEANWHILE, MAKE THE SAUCE: Heat oil in a 2-quart heavy saucepan over moderate heat until hot but not smoking. Add onions, garlic, and ginger and cook, stirring occasionally, until softened, about 6 minutes. Add remaining ingredients and simmer, uncovered, stirring occasionally, for 15 minutes. Remove from heat.

Puree sauce in 2 or 3 batches in a blender until smooth (use caution when blending hot liquids). Set aside 1 cup sauce for serving with ribs.

GRILL THE RIBS: If using a charcoal grill, prepare it for indirect-heat cooking over medium-hot coals; if using a gas grill, prepare it for indirect-heat cooking over medium heat (see Grilling Basics, page 512).

Oil grill rack and place ribs on area with no coals underneath, or over turned-off burner; reserve juices. Grill ribs, covered, basting generously with pan juices and remaining sauce and turning and rotating ribs every 10 minutes (keeping ribs in cool area of grill), until tender and browned, 30 to 40 minutes; do not baste during last 5 minutes of grilling. (If using a charcoal grill, add more charcoal during grilling if necessary to maintain heat.)

Transfer ribs to a cutting board and let stand, uncovered, for 5 minutes.

Cut into individual ribs and serve with reserved sauce.

COOK'S NOTE

■ The sauce can be made up to 1 day ahead and refrigerated, covered. Bring to room temperature before using.

Grilled Country-Style Pork Ribs with Fennel Mustard Glaze

SERVES 4
ACTIVE TIME: 1 HOUR ■ START TO FINISH: 13 HOURS
(INCLUDES MARINATING)

■ Because country-style pork ribs are actually bone-in chops from the shoulder or blade end of the loin that have been halved through the loin, they are meatier than spareribs or baby backs. We grill them gently over indirect heat in order to keep the sweet-spicy marinade from burning and to achieve the tenderness the morsels deserve. A few minutes spent directly over the coals just before serving deepens their color. ■

2 tablespoons fennel seeds, toasted (see Tips, page 911)
4 garlic cloves
1 teaspoon salt
½ cup sweet orange marmalade
½ cup fresh lemon juice (from about 2 lemons)
½ cup olive oil
¼ cup Dijon mustard
4 teaspoons red pepper flakes
4½–5 pounds country-style pork ribs (10 ribs)
SPECIAL EQUIPMENT: an electric coffee/spice grinder or a mortar and pestle

MAKE THE MARINADE AND SAUCE: Grind fennel seeds to a powder in grinder or with mortar and pestle. Mince garlic and mash to a paste with salt, using side of a large heavy knife.

Combine marmalade, garlic paste, lemon juice, oil, mustard, red pepper flakes, and fennel powder in a blender and blend until smooth, about 1 minute. Transfer ¾ cup of mixture to a bowl and refrigerate.

Divide ribs between two large sealable plastic bags. Pour a scant ½ cup remaining mustard mixture over ribs in each bag. Seal bags, pressing out excess air, and set in a shallow dish (in case of leaks). Marinate in refrigerator, turning occasionally, for at least 12 hours.

Bring reserved mustard mixture to room temperature while you grill ribs.

GRILL THE RIBS: If using a charcoal grill, prepare it for indirect-heat cooking over medium-hot coals; if using a gas grill, prepare it for indirect-heat cooking over medium heat (see Grilling Basics, page 512).

Oil grill rack and transfer ribs, letting excess marinade drip back into bags (discard marinade), to area with no coals underneath, or to area over turned-off burner (ribs will be touching). Grill, covered, turning occasionally, until tender and lightly browned, about 40 minutes. (If using a charcoal grill, add more charcoal during grilling if necessary to maintain heat.)

Move ribs directly over coals or over hot burner(s) for darker browning and grill, turning occasionally, for 4 to 5 minutes.

Transfer ribs to a platter and brush with reserved mustard glaze.

COOK'S NOTE

■ The ribs can be marinated for up to 24 hours.

Grilled Italian Sausage with Warm Pepper and Onion Salad

SERVES 4
ACTIVE TIME: 45 MINUTES ■ START TO FINISH: 45 MINUTES

■ Street food fare, but even better. Luganega is a coiled slender Italian pork sausage that is often flavored with spices and cheese. If you can't find it, substitute any fresh Italian sausage. The colorful peppers and onions are cooked on an inexpensive perforated grill sheet, one of our favorite summer toys. It gives that unmistakable edge of smokiness to food that might otherwise slip through the rack and land in the coals. ■

3 large bell peppers of assorted colors, quartered lengthwise, seeded, and cored
1 large red onion, quartered lengthwise and separated into layers
3 tablespoons extra-virgin olive oil
1½ tablespoons red wine vinegar
½ teaspoon dried oregano, crumbled
½ teaspoon salt
⅛ teaspoon freshly ground black pepper
1 (1-pound) coil luganega or other fresh Italian sausage

SPECIAL EQUIPMENT: a perforated grill sheet (see page 511 and Sources); two 10- to 12-inch wooden skewers, soaked in water for 30 minutes, or metal skewers

If using a charcoal grill, prepare it for direct-heat cooking over medium-hot coals; if using a gas grill, prepare it for direct-heat cooking over medium-high heat (see Grilling Basics, page 512).

Toss peppers and onion with 1 tablespoon oil. Oil grill sheet. Grill vegetables on grill sheet set on grill rack (covered if using a gas grill), turning occasionally, until slightly softened and charred, 9 to 15 minutes (onion will cook faster). Transfer to a bowl.

Add vinegar, oregano, salt, pepper, and remaining 2 tablespoons oil to peppers and onion, tossing to coat.

Run skewers crisscrossed through sausage coil (to hold coil together and facilitate turning), securing ends. If using a gas grill, turn off one burner (middle one if there are three). Oil grill rack and grill sausage over hot coals or burner(s) (covered if using a gas grill), turning once and moving to cool area of grill if flare-ups occur, until cooked through, 10 to 12 minutes. (Thicker Italian sausages will take longer.)

Transfer vegetables to a platter and top with sausage.

Lamb

Grilled Lamb Burgers with Eggplant

SERVES 4
ACTIVE TIME: 45 MINUTES ■ START TO FINISH: 45 MINUTES

■ Tucked into toasted fluffy pocket pitas, these spiced lamb burgers offer a welcome change of pace from regular burgers. The tangy yogurt sauce sparkles with mint and lemon juice, and thin slices of grilled eggplant add smoky intrigue. ■

1¼ pounds ground lamb (not lean)
1 teaspoon ground cumin
Salt and freshly ground black pepper
2 garlic cloves, minced
½ cup thick yogurt, such as Greek (see Cook's Note)
2 teaspoons fresh lemon juice
¼ seedless cucumber (usually plastic-wrapped), halved lengthwise, seedy center scooped out, and chopped
3 tablespoons chopped fresh mint
4 (6-inch) pita breads (with pockets)
1 (1¼-pound) eggplant
¼ cup olive oil
1 cup thinly sliced romaine

If using a charcoal grill, prepare it for direct-heat cooking over medium-hot coals; if using a gas grill, prepare it for direct-heat cooking over medium heat (see Grilling Basics, page 512).

Meanwhile, mix lamb, cumin, ½ teaspoon salt, ½ teaspoon pepper, and garlic with your hands in a bowl until just combined (for juicier burgers, handle meat as little as possible). Form into four 4¼-inch patties, ½ inch thick.

Stir together yogurt, lemon juice, cucumber, mint, and salt to taste in a small bowl. Cut off one side of each pita bread to make a 5-inch opening and open bread.

Trim off bottom of eggplant and cut 8 (¼-inch-thick) rounds from eggplant; discard remainder. Brush both sides of slices with olive oil and sprinkle tops of slices with ¼ teaspoon salt and ¼ teaspoon pepper (total).

If using a gas grill, turn off one burner (middle one if there are three). Oil grill rack and grill eggplant rounds and lamb patties over hot coals or burner(s) (covered if using a gas grill), loosening patties with a metal spatula and turning occasionally, and moving to cool area of grill if flare-ups occur, until eggplant is very tender and patties are browned but still slightly pink in center, about 5 minutes. Transfer to a platter and cover with foil to keep warm.

Oil grill rack again and grill pitas, turning once, until grill marks just appear, 1 to 2 minutes. Transfer to platter with lamb and eggplant.

Spread yogurt mixture inside pita pockets and divide eggplant, lamb, and romaine among them.

COOK'S NOTES

- If you can't find thick yogurt, buy regular plain whole-milk yogurt and drain it in a medium-mesh sieve lined with a paper towel set over a bowl, refrigerated, for 12 hours. You will need 1½ cups whole-milk yogurt to yield ½ cup thick yogurt.

- The yogurt and cucumber mixture can be made up to 1 hour ahead and refrigerated, covered.

Grilled Chile-Rubbed Lamb Chops

SERVES 4 TO 6
ACTIVE TIME: 30 MINUTES ■ START TO FINISH: 1½ HOURS

■ We cover every inch of these lamb rib chops with the mixture of chile powder, cumin, allspice, and dried thyme; that way, guests who like to nibble on the bones get even more flavor. The small amount of sugar added to the rub balances the spice and salt and adds a touch of caramel flavor during grilling. ■

3 tablespoons medium-hot pure chile powder, such as New Mexico (see Sources)
1 tablespoon ground cumin
2 teaspoons dried thyme, crumbled
2 teaspoons sugar

1½ teaspoons salt
1 teaspoon freshly ground black pepper
¾ teaspoon ground allspice
16 (¾- to 1¼-inch-thick) lamb rib chops (cut from 2 racks), trimmed of excess fat

OPTIONAL ACCOMPANIMENT: hot pepper jelly

Stir together chile powder, cumin, thyme, sugar, salt, pepper, and allspice in a small bowl. Pat chops dry and rub all over with spice mixture. Transfer to a tray and marinate, covered, at room temperature for 1 hour.

If using a charcoal grill, prepare it for direct-heat cooking over medium-hot coals; if using a gas grill, prepare it for direct-heat cooking over medium-high heat (see Grilling Basics, page 512).

If using a gas grill, turn off one burner (middle one if there are three). Oil grill rack and grill chops over hot coals or burner(s) (covered if using a gas grill), turning occasionally and moving to cool area of grill if flare-ups occur, for 6 to 8 minutes, depending on thickness, for medium-rare. Transfer chops to a platter and let stand, loosely covered with foil, for 5 minutes.

Serve with hot pepper jelly if desired.

COOK'S NOTE

- The lamb chops can be marinated, covered and refrigerated, for up to 24 hours.

Grilled Lamb Chops with Balsamic Cherry Tomatoes

SERVES 4
ACTIVE TIME: 30 MINUTES ■ START TO FINISH: 1¾ HOURS

■ A marinade of honey, red wine vinegar, and garlic gives these quick lamb chops a Mediterranean bent. As the cherry tomatoes cook, their skins split and their juices mingle with the balsamic vinegar, so they become almost like a chunky sauce for the chops. If you buy one large cluster of tomatoes, simply cut it into four clusters before grilling and serving with the lamb. ■

- 2 tablespoons mild honey
- 2 tablespoons red wine vinegar
- 2 garlic cloves, finely chopped
- ½ teaspoon salt
- ¼ teaspoon freshly ground black pepper
- 8 (¾- to 1¼-inch-thick) lamb rib chops (cut from 1 rack), trimmed of excess fat
- 1½ pounds cherry tomatoes, preferably on the vine
- 1½ tablespoons balsamic vinegar

SPECIAL EQUIPMENT: a 12-by-8-inch disposable aluminum roasting pan

Stir together honey, vinegar, garlic, salt, and pepper in a small bowl. Transfer to a sealable plastic bag, add lamb, and seal bag, pressing out excess air and turning to distribute marinade. Marinate lamb at room temperature, turning occasionally, for 1 hour.

If using a charcoal grill, prepare it for direct-heat cooking over medium-hot coals; if using a gas grill, prepare it for direct-heat cooking over medium heat (see Grilling Basics, page 512).

Remove lamb from marinade; reserve marinade.

If using a gas grill, turn off one burner (middle one if there are three). Oil grill rack and grill chops over hot coals or burner(s) (covered if using a gas grill), turning occasionally and moving to cool area of grill if flare-ups occur, 6 to 8 minutes, depending on thickness, for medium-rare. Transfer to a platter and cover with foil to keep warm.

Grill tomatoes (see headnote) in disposable roasting pan, covered, carefully turning occasionally, until softened and just beginning to split, about 8 minutes. Drizzle balsamic vinegar over tomatoes, turning to coat, and cook, uncovered, until vinegar is reduced by about half, about 2 minutes. Remove from grill.

Bring reserved marinade, with any lamb juices accumulated on platter, to a boil in a small heavy saucepan, covered, then reduce heat and simmer for 1 minute.

Drizzle lamb with marinade and serve with tomatoes.

BALSAMIC VINEGAR

A true balsamic vinegar, which always bears the label *"aceto balsamico tradizionale,"* is made from the must (unfermented juice) of primarily the Trebbiano grape; other varieties used include Lambrusco, Ancellotta, Sauvignon, and Sgavetta. The process is overseen by the balsamic consortiums of Modena and Reggio Emilia, the only regions of Italy where the vinegar is produced. The vinegar is aged in a progression of barrels of different woods (each maker has its own combination, which might include chestnut, ash, oak, and juniper) for at least 12 years. Some balsamics are aged for 25 years or even longer; there is no upper limit, and bottles of 60- or 75-year-old vinegar, which cost hundreds of dollars, are not unheard-of. The vinegar just gets sweeter and creamier with age.

In Italy, you won't see the good stuff used in salad dressings, but rather as a condiment—drizzled sparingly over savory dishes or fresh fruit; the very old ones are sipped as a liqueur. There are plenty of balsamic vinegars in the $20 range that deliver the suave quality that you're looking for; two brands we like are Villa Manodori and Manicardi. Some inexpensive supermarket-brand balsamics, which don't bear the consortium seal, are not aged at all; others are aged for 6 months to a year in stainless steel tanks or for 2 to 12 years in wooden barrels. They're not as unctuous as older balsamics, but they work nicely as a marinade or seasoning.

Grilled Lemongrass Lamb Chops with Herbs

SERVES 4 TO 6
ACTIVE TIME: 45 MINUTES ■ START TO FINISH: 13 HOURS
(INCLUDES MARINATING)

■ Meaty loin lamb chops marinated overnight in a lemongrass paste are grilled, dressed with lime juice vinaigrette, and showered with fresh basil, mint, and cilantro leaves. ■

1½ teaspoons cumin seeds, toasted (see Tips, page 911)
3 stalks lemongrass, root ends trimmed and tough outer layers discarded
2 large shallots, chopped
4 garlic cloves, chopped
1½ tablespoons chopped peeled fresh ginger
1½ tablespoons sugar
Salt
½ teaspoon turmeric
¼ teaspoon cayenne
3 tablespoons water
¼ cup plus 3 tablespoons vegetable oil
6 (1¼-inch-thick) lamb loin chops
¼ teaspoon finely grated lime zest
1 tablespoon fresh lime juice
Freshly ground black pepper
½ cup small fresh basil leaves
¼ cup small fresh mint leaves
¼ cup fresh cilantro leaves

SPECIAL EQUIPMENT: an electric coffee/spice grinder or a mortar and pestle

Finely grind cumin seeds in grinder or with mortar and pestle.

Thinly slice bottom 6 inches of lemongrass; discard remainder. Combine lemongrass, shallots, garlic, ginger, cumin, sugar, 1 teaspoon salt, turmeric, cayenne, and water in a food processor and puree, scraping down sides occasionally, until as smooth as possible, about 2 minutes. (Paste will not be completely smooth.)

Heat 3 tablespoons oil in a 10-inch heavy skillet over moderate heat until hot but not smoking. Add lemongrass paste, reduce heat to moderately low, and cook, stirring constantly, until paste begins to stick to bottom of skillet and is very thick, 8 to 12 minutes. Transfer paste to a bowl and cool to room temperature.

Pat lamb chops dry and rub lemongrass paste all over them. Arrange in one layer in a 13-by-9-inch baking dish. Marinate, covered and refrigerated, for at least 12 hours.

If using a charcoal grill, prepare it for direct-heat cooking over medium-hot coals; if using a gas grill, prepare it for direct-heat cooking over medium heat (see Grilling Basics, page 512).

If using a gas grill, turn off one burner (middle one if there are three). Oil grill rack and grill chops over hot coals or burner(s) (covered if using a gas grill), loosening lamb from grill with a metal spatula and turning occasionally, and moving to cool area of grill if flare-ups occur, for 8 to 10 minutes for medium-rare (some of lemongrass paste will fall off). Transfer chops to a platter and let stand, loosely covered with foil, for 10 minutes.

Whisk together lime zest and juice, remaining ¼ cup oil, and salt and pepper to taste. Spoon over chops and sprinkle with herbs.

COOK'S NOTES

■ The lamb chops can be marinated for up to 24 hours.
■ Some lamb loin chops come with end flaps; secure them with toothpicks before grilling if desired.

Turkish Lamb Kebabs

SERVES 4
ACTIVE TIME: 45 MINUTES ■ START TO FINISH: 1 HOUR

■ These lamb kebabs, wrapped in squares of soft lavash flatbread, feature ground dried Urfa and Maras peppers, two linchpins of Turkish cooking. Urfa pepper flakes are almost purple in color, with a fruity, slightly smoky flavor. Maras pepper flakes are deep red and also rather fruity, but brighter. Both offer a mild heat. The kebabs won't be the same without them, but an equal amount of good-quality paprika plus a pinch of red pepper flakes makes a decent substitute. ■

1 medium red onion, finely chopped

½ cup coarsely chopped fresh flat-leaf parsley

1 medium tomato, diced

1 teaspoon dried oregano, crumbled

1½ teaspoons Urfa pepper (see headnote and Sources)

1½ teaspoons Maras pepper (see headnote and Sources)

6 tablespoons olive oil

Salt

1 (1½-pound) piece boneless leg of lamb, trimmed and cut into 32 (1-inch) cubes

½ teaspoon freshly ground black pepper

4 (10-inch) squares soft lavash bread (see Sources and Cook's Note)

SPECIAL EQUIPMENT: eight 10-inch wooden skewers, soaked in water for 30 minutes

If using a charcoal grill, prepare it for direct-heat cooking over medium-hot coals; if using a gas grill, prepare it for direct-heat cooking over medium heat (see Grilling Basics, page 512).

Meanwhile, stir together onion, parsley, tomato, oregano, Urfa and Maras peppers, 2 tablespoons oil, and ¼ teaspoon salt in a bowl.

Pat lamb dry and toss with ½ teaspoon salt, black pepper, and 1 tablespoon oil in a bowl. Thread 4 lamb cubes onto each skewer, leaving a little space between them. Brush lavash on both sides with remaining 3 tablespoons oil.

Oil grill rack and grill lamb (covered if using a gas grill), turning once, until medium-rare, 6 to 8 minutes. Transfer lamb skewers to a platter and cover with foil to keep warm.

Grill lavash (covered if using a gas grill), turning once, until just heated through and lightly browned but still soft, about 45 seconds total.

Remove lamb from skewers and divide among squares of lavash. Top lamb with tomato mixture and roll up lavash to enclose lamb. Serve immediately.

COOK'S NOTE

■ You can substitute warmed pita bread (with pockets) for the lavash.

Grilled Butterflied Leg of Lamb

SERVES 8
ACTIVE TIME: 30 MINUTES ■ START TO FINISH: 10 HOURS
(INCLUDES MARINATING)

■ The flavors of Greece—fresh lemon juice, pungent garlic, and heady oregano—infuse this leg of lamb. ■

½ cup extra-virgin olive oil

¼ cup fresh lemon juice

4 garlic cloves, minced

1 tablespoon dried oregano, preferably Greek, crumbled

2 teaspoons salt

1 teaspoon freshly ground black pepper

1 (4½- to 5-pound) butterflied leg of lamb (see Cook's Note), trimmed of excess fat

SPECIAL EQUIPMENT: three or four 10- to 12-inch metal skewers; an instant-read thermometer

Combine oil, lemon juice, garlic, oregano, salt, and pepper in a 2-gallon heavy-duty sealable plastic bag (see Cook's Note). Add lamb and seal bag, pressing out air. Turn bag to coat lamb and put in a shallow baking pan (in case of leaks). Marinate, refrigerated, turning bag occasionally, for at least 8 hours.

Remove lamb from refrigerator 1 hour before grilling.

If using a charcoal grill, prepare it for direct-heat cooking over medium-hot coals; if using a gas grill, prepare it for direct-heat cooking over medium heat (see Grilling Basics, page 512).

Remove lamb from marinade (discard marinade). Pat dry and run 3 or 4 skewers lengthwise through lamb about 2 inches apart.

If using a gas grill, turn off one burner (middle one if there are three). Oil grill rack and grill lamb over hot coals or burner(s) (covered if using a gas grill), turning occasionally and moving to cool area on grill if flare-ups occur, until thermometer inserted in thickest part of meat registers 125° to 128°F, 8 to 14 minutes, depending on thickness, for medium-rare.

Transfer lamb to a cutting board and remove skewers. Let stand, loosely covered with foil, for 20 minutes. (Internal temperature will rise to 135°F while meat stands.)

Slice lamb across the grain.

COOK'S NOTES

- If you can't find lamb that has already been butterflied, buy a 6½- to 7½-pound whole leg of lamb and ask your butcher to remove the bone, butterfly the meat, and trim as much fat as possible.
- If you don't have a 2-gallon sealable plastic bag, you can marinate the lamb in a large baking dish, covered tightly with plastic wrap, turning the lamb occasionally.
- The lamb can marinate for up to 24 hours.

Grilled Butterflied
Leg of Lamb
with Hoisin Lime Sauce

SERVES 8
ACTIVE TIME: 1 HOUR ■ START TO FINISH: 1¾ HOURS

■ Butterflying a boneless leg of lamb makes this ever-popular cut grill-friendly. The technique—slicing into the muscles so that the meat lies flat—promotes more even cooking, but it still offers different degrees of doneness, which can be a boon when you need to satisfy a range of tastes. Because there is sugar in hoisin sauce, we grill the lamb over indirect heat, to prevent charring. Leftovers, should you have any, make a great salad or sandwich. ■

  1 (4½- to 5½-pound) butterflied leg of lamb, trimmed of excess fat (see Cook's Note)
  ¼ cup finely chopped scallions, plus ¼ cup thinly sliced scallion greens
  1 tablespoon finely chopped garlic
  2½ tablespoons vegetable oil
  ⅔ cup hoisin sauce
  6 tablespoons rice vinegar (not seasoned)
  ¼ cup soy sauce
  1 tablespoon fresh lime juice
  1 teaspoon salt
  1 teaspoon freshly ground black pepper

SPECIAL EQUIPMENT: three or four 10- to 12-inch metal skewers; an instant-read thermometer

PREPARE THE LAMB AND SAUCES: Let lamb stand at room temperature for 30 minutes.

Meanwhile, cook chopped scallions and garlic in 1 tablespoon oil in a 2-quart heavy saucepan over moderately low heat, stirring occasionally, until softened, 2 to 3 minutes. Remove from heat and stir in ⅓ cup hoisin sauce, 3 tablespoons rice vinegar, and 2 tablespoons soy sauce. Transfer sauce to a serving bowl and cool to room temperature, then stir in lime juice and scallion greens.

Whisk together remaining ⅓ cup hoisin sauce, 3 tablespoons rice vinegar, and 2 tablespoons soy sauce in a small bowl to make basting sauce.

Rub lamb all over with remaining 1½ tablespoons oil and sprinkle all over with salt and pepper. Run skewers lengthwise through lamb about 2 inches apart to make it easier to handle and turn over.

PREPARE THE GRILL: If using a charcoal grill, prepare it for indirect-heat cooking over medium-hot coals; if using a gas grill, prepare it for direct-heat cooking over medium-high heat (see Grilling Basics, page 512).

TO COOK THE LAMB ON A CHARCOAL GRILL: Oil grill rack and sear lamb over hot coals, turning once, until browned, about 10 minutes. Move to cool area of grill and grill, covered with lid, turning occasionally, until thermometer inserted horizontally 2 inches into thickest part of meat registers 125° to 128°F, 20 to 30 minutes for medium-rare; brush with basting sauce during last 10 minutes of grilling. (Add more charcoal during grilling if necessary to maintain heat.)

TO COOK THE LAMB ON A GAS GRILL: Oil grill rack and sear lamb, covered, turning once, until browned, about 10 minutes. Turn off burner under lamb and reduce other burner(s) to medium. Cover and cook, turning occasionally, until thermometer inserted diagonally into thickest part of meat registers 125° to 128°F, 20 to 30 minutes for medium-rare; brush with basting sauce during last 10 minutes of grilling.

Transfer lamb to a cutting board (discard any remaining basting sauce) and let stand, loosely covered with foil, for 10 minutes. (Internal temperature will rise to 135°F while meat stands.)

Slice lamb across the grain and serve with hoisin lime sauce.

■ If you can't find lamb that has already been butterflied, buy a 6½- to 7½-pound whole leg of lamb and ask your butcher to remove the bone, butterfly the meat, and trim as much fat as possible.

Vegetables

Grilled Corn with Chipotle Mayonnaise

SERVES 6 TO 8
ACTIVE TIME: 1½ HOURS ■ START TO FINISH: 1½ HOURS

■ One taste of this Mexican-inspired corn, slathered with chipotle-spiked mayo and given a spritz of lime juice, and you may never go back to butter. ■

12 ears corn in the husk
1 cup mayonnaise
1½ tablespoons minced canned chipotle chiles in adobo
ACCOMPANIMENT: lime wedges

Pull back corn husks, leaving them attached at base, and discard silks. Wrap husks back around ears.

Stir together mayonnaise and chiles in a bowl.

If using a charcoal grill, prepare it for direct-heat cooking over medium-hot coals; if using a gas grill, prepare it for direct-heat cooking over medium-high heat (see Grilling Basics, page 512).

Grill corn (covered if using a gas grill), turning frequently, for 10 minutes. Transfer corn to a tray and cool for 5 minutes.

Holding corn with paper towels, pull off husks and discard. Grill corn, turning frequently, until browned and tender, 8 to 10 minutes more.

Serve corn with chipotle mayonnaise and lime wedges.

COOK'S NOTE
■ The silks can be discarded and the ears of corn reassembled up to 1 hour ahead. Keep, tightly covered with plastic wrap, on a tray.

Grilled Corn with Cumin Scallion Butter

SERVES 6 TO 8
ACTIVE TIME: 1¼ HOURS ■ START TO FINISH: 1¼ HOURS

■ Cumin and chopped scallion greens infuse melted butter with their toasty and bright flavors. Brushing the butter on the ears and then replacing the husks ensures tender, juicy kernels kissed by smoke. A big platter mounded high with the corn, still in its husks, crackling and blackened, is an impressive sight. Don't forget a bowl for the husks. ■

1 tablespoon cumin seeds, toasted (see Tips, page 911)
¾ teaspoon kosher salt
1½ sticks (12 tablespoons) unsalted butter, cut into pieces
⅓ cup finely chopped scallion greens
2 teaspoons fresh lemon juice
12 ears corn in the husk
SPECIAL EQUIPMENT: an electric coffee/spice grinder

Finely grind cumin seeds with salt in grinder.

Melt butter with cumin salt in a small saucepan over moderate heat, stirring. Stir in scallion greens and lemon juice. Remove from heat and cool.

Pull back corn husks, leaving them attached at base, and discard silks. Hold one ear at a time, tip of the ear pointing down, over pan of butter and brush with butter. Wrap husks back around ears.

If using a charcoal grill, prepare it for direct-heat cooking over medium-hot coals; if using a gas grill, prepare it for direct-heat cooking over medium-high heat (see Grilling Basics, page 512).

Grill corn (covered if using a gas grill), turning frequently, until kernels are tender, 18 to 20 minutes.

Serve with remaining cumin scallion butter.

COOK'S NOTES
■ The cumin butter, without the scallions, can be made up to 1 day ahead and refrigerated, covered. Reheat until melted and stir in scallion greens.
■ The corn can be brushed with the cumin scallion butter and reassembled up to 1 hour ahead. Keep, tightly covered with plastic wrap, on a tray.

Grilled Corn with Herbs and Lemon Butter

SERVES 6 TO 8
ACTIVE TIME: 1½ HOURS ■ START TO FINISH: 1½ HOURS

■ A big bowl of this herb-flecked corn with sliced ripe tomatoes and crusty bread on the side makes a heavenly late-summer dinner. Grilling the corn in its husk protects it from the heat so it stays tender. Cut from the ears, the kernels are tossed in a garlicky herbed butter. You can use almost any combination of herbs, or just one. ■

- 12 ears corn in the husk
- 2 large garlic cloves, chopped
- 6 tablespoons fresh lemon juice (from about 2 lemons)
- 1½ teaspoons salt
- 1 teaspoon freshly ground black pepper
- 1½ sticks (12 tablespoons) unsalted butter, melted
- 6 tablespoons chopped mixed fresh herbs, such as chives, parsley, basil, sage, and tarragon

Pull back corn husks, leaving them attached at base, and discard silks. Wrap husks back around ears.

If using a charcoal grill, prepare it for direct-heat cooking over medium-hot coals; if using a gas grill, prepare it for direct-heat cooking over medium-high heat (see Grilling Basics, page 512).

Meanwhile, puree garlic with lemon juice, salt, and pepper in a blender until smooth. With motor running, add melted butter and blend until combined, about 30 seconds.

Grill corn (covered if using a gas grill), turning frequently, until kernels are tender, 18 to 20 minutes. Remove from grill and let stand until cool enough to handle, about 10 minutes.

Pull off and discard husks. With a large knife, slice kernels off cobs into a bowl. Toss with herbs and lemon butter.

COOK'S NOTE

■ The silks can be discarded and the ears of corn reassembled up to 1 hour ahead. Keep, tightly covered with plastic wrap, on a tray.

Grilled Eggplant with Yogurt Mint Sauce

SERVES 6
ACTIVE TIME: 20 MINUTES ■ START TO FINISH: 50 MINUTES

■ Eggplant is a perfect vegetable for grilling—when cut into thick rounds, it's sturdy enough to take the heat yet supple enough to soak up that smoky flavor we love so much. ■

- 2 small garlic cloves
- Salt
- 1 cup thick yogurt, such as Greek (see Cook's Note)
- ⅓ cup finely chopped fresh mint
- 1–2 tablespoons water
- 2 medium eggplants (2 pounds total)
- ½ cup olive oil

If using a charcoal grill, prepare it for direct-heat cooking over medium-hot coals; if using a gas grill, prepare it for direct-heat cooking over medium heat (see Grilling Basics, page 512).

Meanwhile, mince garlic and mash to a paste with ¼ teaspoon salt, using side of a large heavy knife. Transfer garlic paste to a bowl and whisk in yogurt, mint, and enough water to thin sauce.

Cut eggplants into ¾-inch-thick rounds. Brush both sides of eggplant slices with oil and sprinkle with ¾ teaspoon salt.

Oil grill rack and grill eggplant (covered if using a gas grill), turning occasionally, until grill marks appear and eggplant is tender, 6 to 8 minutes.

Serve with yogurt sauce.

COOK'S NOTE

■ If you can't find thick yogurt, buy regular plain whole-milk yogurt and drain it in a medium-mesh sieve lined with a paper towel set over a bowl, refrigerated, for 12 hours. You will need 3 cups whole-milk yogurt to yield 1 cup thick yogurt.

Grilled Eggplant
with Spicy Peanut Sauce

SERVES 4 AS A SIDE DISH, 2 AS A MAIN COURSE
ACTIVE TIME: 30 MINUTES ■ START TO FINISH: 30 MINUTES

■ Grilled eggplant—smoky and custardy from the fire—is the base for a rich, spicy Indonesian peanut sauce and a scattering of chopped nuts. A worthy side dish, it would also satisfy any vegetarian as a main course. The peanut sauce, from reader Debbie White of Atlanta, is also great with grilled chicken. ■

FOR PEANUT SAUCE
- ¾ cup salted peanuts
- 2–3 (3-inch-long) fresh hot red chiles, such as Thai or serrano, chopped, including seeds
- 1 garlic clove, chopped
- ⅔ cup water
- 1 tablespoon distilled white vinegar
- 2½ teaspoons soy sauce
- 1 teaspoon brown sugar (light or dark)
- ¼ teaspoon salt, or to taste

FOR EGGPLANT
- 1 large eggplant (1¼ pounds)
- 2 tablespoons vegetable oil
- ¼ teaspoon salt

GARNISH: coarsely chopped salted peanuts

MAKE THE PEANUT SAUCE: Blend all ingredients in a blender until smooth. Transfer to a small heavy saucepan and bring just to a boil over moderate heat, stirring. Remove from heat and cool.

GRILL THE EGGPLANT: If using a charcoal grill, prepare it for direct-heat cooking over medium-hot coals; if using a gas grill, prepare it for direct-heat cooking over medium heat (see Grilling Basics, page 512).

Meanwhile, cut eggplant into ½-inch-thick rounds. Brush slices on both sides with oil and sprinkle with salt.

Oil grill rack and grill eggplant (covered if using a gas grill), turning occasionally, until grill marks appear and eggplant is tender, about 6 minutes.

Transfer to a platter and sprinkle with chopped peanuts. Serve with peanut sauce.

COOK'S NOTE
■ The peanut sauce can be made up to 1 week ahead and refrigerated, covered. Bring to room temperature before serving.

Grilled Fennel
with Lemon

SERVES 4
ACTIVE TIME: 20 MINUTES ■ START TO FINISH: 30 MINUTES

■ Fennel gains flavor depth when grilled, becoming sweeter and more mellow. (Steaming it first ensures that it will become fully tender on the grill without getting too dark.) Don't omit the lemon—it really lights up the dish. Fennel is compatible with any seafood, and this also goes nicely with grilled pork or lamb. ■

- 2 medium fennel bulbs (about 2 pounds total), stalks discarded, bulbs cut into 1-inch-wide wedges
- 2 tablespoons extra-virgin olive oil
- ½ teaspoon salt
- ½ teaspoon freshly ground black pepper
  Fresh lemon juice to taste

If using a charcoal grill, prepare it for direct-heat grilling over hot coals; if using a gas grill, prepare it for direct-heat cooking over high heat (see Grilling Basics, page 512).

Meanwhile, steam fennel in one layer on a large steamer rack set over boiling water, covered, until just tender, 8 to 10 minutes. Transfer to a platter, brush all over with oil, and sprinkle with salt and pepper.

Grill fennel (covered if using a gas grill), turning once, until grill marks appear, 4 to 6 minutes.

Serve fennel drizzled with lemon juice.

COOK'S NOTE
■ The fennel can be steamed and brushed with oil up to 8 hours ahead and refrigerated, covered. Let stand at room temperature for 1 hour before seasoning and grilling.

Grilled Shiitakes with Ginger and Scallions

SERVES 4
ACTIVE TIME: 30 MINUTES ■ START TO FINISH: 30 MINUTES

■ This marinade's classic Asian combination of soy sauce, sherry, ginger, and rice vinegar is a natural with the meaty, earthy flavor of shiitakes. The recipe, adapted from one by the Boston chef and cookbook author Chris Schlesinger, is good made with other mushrooms too, such as stemmed portobellos or cremini. Snack on them around the grill or serve with grilled meat. ■

1½ tablespoons dry sherry
1 tablespoon soy sauce
1 tablespoon minced peeled fresh ginger
1½ teaspoons rice vinegar (not seasoned)
½ teaspoon sugar
2½ tablespoons vegetable oil
1½ pounds large shiitake mushrooms (3 inches wide), stems discarded
½ teaspoon salt
½ teaspoon freshly ground black pepper
2 scallions, cut into very thin 2-inch-long strips

If using a charcoal grill, prepare it for direct-heat cooking over medium-hot coals; if using a gas grill, prepare it for direct-heat cooking over medium heat (see Grilling Basics, page 512).

Meanwhile, stir together sherry, soy sauce, ginger, vinegar, sugar, and 1½ teaspoons oil in a large bowl until sugar is dissolved. Toss mushrooms with salt, pepper, and remaining 2 tablespoons oil in another bowl.

Oil grill rack and grill mushrooms (covered if using a gas grill), turning occasionally, until lightly browned and tender, 4 to 6 minutes. Transfer mushrooms to bowl with sauce, add scallions, and toss until combined.

COOK'S NOTES

■ When shopping for shiitakes, look for mushrooms with solid, thick caps that are dry but not leathery. They can be stored, refrigerated in a bowl covered with a slightly damp towel, for up to 2 days. Use the stems in stock.

■ If you can't find large shiitakes, you can use smaller ones, but you will need to grill them on a lightly oiled perforated grill sheet.

Grilled Spiced Okra

SERVES 6
ACTIVE TIME: 30 MINUTES ■ START TO FINISH: 30 MINUTES

■ Tossed with a cumin-coriander mixture, okra emerges from the grill with slightly charred and crisp skins and nice moist insides. The pods take just minutes, which means they're the perfect thing to make while your grilled steak is resting. Skewering makes it easy to turn them. You can't help eating these with your fingers; in fact, they also make an excellent hors d'oeuvre. ■

2 teaspoons cumin seeds
2 teaspoons coriander seeds
½ teaspoon black peppercorns
¼ teaspoon turmeric
1 teaspoon kosher salt
1 tablespoon vegetable oil
1 pound okra (about 3 inches long)
SPECIAL EQUIPMENT: an electric coffee/spice grinder; twelve 12-inch wooden skewers, soaked in water for 30 minutes

If using a charcoal grill, prepare it for direct-heat cooking over medium-hot coals; if using a gas grill, prepare it for direct-heat cooking over medium heat (see Grilling Basics, page 512).

Meanwhile, toast cumin and coriander seeds in a dry small heavy skillet, preferably cast-iron, over moderately low heat, stirring constantly, until fragrant and a shade darker, about 3 minutes. Transfer to grinder (or use a mortar and pestle), add peppercorns, turmeric, and salt, and grind to a powder.

Stir together spice mixture and oil in a large bowl. Add okra and toss until evenly coated. Divide okra into 6 groups. Line up each group side by side on a work surface, aligning tops, and thread two parallel skewers (one at a time) crosswise through okra, leaving about ¼ inch between them (skewered okra will look like rafts).

Grill okra (covered if using a gas grill), turning occasionally, until browned and tender, 5 to 7 minutes.

COOK'S NOTE
■ The spice mixture can be made up to 4 hours ahead.

Grilled Red Onions with Balsamic Vinegar and Soy

SERVES 6
ACTIVE TIME: 30 MINUTES ■ START TO FINISH: 45 MINUTES

■ Serve these tender, floppy rings as an accompaniment to grilled steak or as a deluxe topping for hamburgers. The onions' sweetness intensifies during their time over the coals, and a quick dressing of balsamic vinegar, soy sauce, and Worcestershire deepens the sweetness. ■

  1 tablespoon balsamic vinegar
  1 tablespoon soy sauce
  1 teaspoon Worcestershire sauce
  3 large red onions (about 2 pounds total), cut into
      ½-inch-thick rounds
  2 tablespoons olive oil
    Salt and freshly ground black pepper
  ¼ cup finely chopped fresh flat-leaf parsley

SPECIAL EQUIPMENT: wooden toothpicks

If using a charcoal grill, prepare it for direct-heat cooking over medium-hot coals; if using a gas grill, prepare it for direct-heat cooking over medium heat (see Grilling Basics, page 512).

Meanwhile, stir together vinegar, soy sauce, and Worcestershire sauce in a medium bowl. Push a wooden toothpick into each onion slice to secure it for

grilling. Brush onions with oil on both sides and sprinkle with ½ teaspoon salt and ½ teaspoon pepper.

Grill onions (covered if using a gas grill), turning occasionally with a metal spatula, until lightly charred and softened, 10 to 12 minutes. Transfer to a tray and discard toothpicks.

Add onions to vinegar mixture, along with parsley and salt and pepper to taste, tossing to coat and separating onions into rings.

COOK'S NOTE
■ The onions can be secured with the toothpicks and brushed with oil up to 1 hour ahead; do not season them until just before grilling.

Grilled Bell Peppers with Caper Vinaigrette

SERVES 4
ACTIVE TIME: 50 MINUTES ■ START TO FINISH: 1½ HOURS

■ Peppers become meltingly supple when they are grilled and take on a smokiness that makes them even more seductive. This dish is especially beautiful with a mix of red, yellow, and orange bell peppers. The caper vinaigrette adds just the right note of piquancy. ■

  6 bell peppers of assorted colors (not green)
  1½ tablespoons white wine vinegar
  1 teaspoon salt
  ½ teaspoon freshly ground black pepper
  ¼ cup olive oil
  2 tablespoons drained capers, chopped

If using a charcoal grill, prepare it for direct-heat cooking over medium-hot coals; if using a gas grill, prepare it for direct-heat cooking over medium heat (see Grilling Basics, page 512).

Grill peppers (covered if using a gas grill), turning frequently with tongs, until skins are blackened and peppers are very tender, 25 to 30 minutes. (If using a charcoal grill, add more charcoal during grilling if necessary to maintain heat.) Transfer peppers to a large bowl, cover tightly with plastic wrap, and let steam until cool enough to handle.

Meanwhile, whisk together vinegar, salt, and pepper in a small bowl. Add oil in a slow stream, whisking until well blended. Whisk in capers.

Peel peppers, halve lengthwise, and discard stems and seeds. Toss peppers with vinaigrette.

COOK'S NOTE

■ The peppers and vinaigrette can be made up to 1 day ahead. Toss the peppers with the vinaigrette and refrigerate, covered. Bring to room temperature before serving.

Potato Hobo Packs

SERVES 6
ACTIVE TIME: 55 MINUTES ■ START TO FINISH: 2 HOURS

■ These foil-wrapped packages of potatoes, pearl onions, garlic, and sage, a longtime favorite of *Gourmet's* executive editor John Willoughby and his fellow cookbook author, chef Chris Schlesinger, are an impressive contribution to the pantheon of grilling. Taking advantage of the real estate under the grill rack, the goodie bags can be filled with all manner of vegetables, which become tender, smoky, and slightly charred in places, depending on their proximity to the coals (similar results can be achieved by cooking them over moderately low heat on a gas grill). Sour cream, crumbled bacon, and snips of fresh chives added after the packets are opened send the potatoes over the top. ■

½ pound pearl onions
1½ pounds fingerling or baby Yukon Gold potatoes (about 16), halved lengthwise
12 garlic cloves, peeled
2 tablespoons finely chopped fresh sage
¼ cup extra-virgin olive oil
1 teaspoon salt
1 teaspoon freshly ground black pepper
6 bacon slices
½ cup sour cream
¼ cup thinly sliced fresh chives
SPECIAL EQUIPMENT: 12-inch-wide heavy-duty foil

To make peeling easier, blanch pearl onions in a 3-quart pot of boiling water for 1 minute; drain. When cool enough to handle, peel.

Tear off eight 2-foot-long sheets of heavy-duty foil and arrange in two stacks. Divide potatoes between stacks and top with onions, garlic, and sage. Drizzle each with 2 tablespoons oil and sprinkle each with ½ teaspoon salt and ½ teaspoon pepper. Fold sides of top sheet of foil in one stack over potato mixture to enclose, turn package a quarter turn, and repeat folding and turning package with remaining pieces of foil. Make second hobo pack in same manner.

PREPARE THE GRILL: If using a charcoal grill, remove grill rack. Prepare grill for indirect-heat cooking over medium-hot coals; if using a gas grill, prepare it for direct-heat cooking over medium-low heat (see Grilling Basics, page 512).

TO COOK THE HOBO PACKS ON A CHARCOAL GRILL: Put packs folded side down on area of bottom rack with no coals (two sides of packages will be in direct contact with coals on either side) and cook, turning a half turn with tongs every 15 minutes, until potatoes are tender (poke a thin knife blade into 1 packet to test potatoes), about 1 hour. (Add more coals during grilling as necessary to maintain heat.)

TO COOK HOBO PACKS ON A GAS GRILL: Put hobo packs folded side down on grill rack and cook, covered, until potatoes are tender (poke a thin knife blade into 1 packet to test potatoes), about 45 minutes.

Meanwhile, during last 15 minutes of grilling, cook the bacon in a 12-inch heavy skillet over medium heat, turning occasionally, until crisp. Transfer to paper towels to drain, then crumble.

Carefully remove potato mixture from packages and serve with bacon, sour cream, and chives.

Grilled Potato Wedges
with Chili Salt

SERVES 4
ACTIVE TIME: 35 MINUTES ■ START TO FINISH: 35 MINUTES

■ Cooking thick potato wedges on the grill takes a bit of attention, but the smoky spears are well worth it. Tossed in a lively mixture of chili powder, paprika, and cayenne after they come off the heat, these spuds taste just right with burgers or grilled steak. ■

4 (8-ounce) russet (baking) potatoes
3 tablespoons olive oil
1 tablespoon chili powder
½ teaspoon paprika
¼ teaspoon salt
¼ teaspoon cayenne

If using a charcoal grill, prepare it for direct-heat cooking over medium-hot coals; if using a gas grill, prepare it for direct-heat cooking over medium heat (see Grilling Basics, page 512).

Meanwhile, cut each potato lengthwise into 4 wedges. Brush lightly all over with 2 tablespoons oil.

Oil grill rack and grill potatoes (covered if using a gas grill), turning frequently, until tender, 20 to 30 minutes.

Transfer potatoes to a large bowl and toss with chili powder, paprika, salt, cayenne, and remaining tablespoon oil.

Grilled Scallions with Lemon

SERVES 4
ACTIVE TIME: 10 MINUTES ■ START TO FINISH: 40 MINUTES

■ Scallions enter a new dimension when grilled; their sharpness and bite are transformed into sweet tenderness, and their slippery crunch gives way to a meaty, satisfying chew. Spritz them with lemon just before serving. ■

12 large scallions, trimmed, leaving most of greens attached
1 tablespoon olive oil
¼ teaspoon salt
⅛ teaspoon freshly ground black pepper
½ lemon
SPECIAL EQUIPMENT: two 8-inch wooden skewers, soaked in water for 30 minutes

If using a charcoal grill, prepare it for direct-heat cooking over medium-hot coals; if using a gas grill, prepare it for direct-heat cooking over medium-high heat (see Grilling Basics, page 512).

Meanwhile, toss scallions with oil, salt, and pepper in a large bowl. Line up scallions side by side on a work surface and thread two parallel skewers (one at a time),

about 2 inches from each end, crosswise through scallions (skewered scallions will look like a raft).

Oil grill rack and grill scallions (covered if using a gas grill), turning once or twice, until softened and charred in patches, 4 to 5 minutes.

Transfer scallions to a platter and squeeze lemon evenly over them; remove skewers.

Grilled Sweet Potatoes with Lime Cilantro Vinaigrette

SERVES 8
ACTIVE TIME: 35 MINUTES ■ START TO FINISH: 1¼ HOURS

■ Why save sweet potatoes for Thanksgiving when they're so good grilled and dressed up with a tart lime vinaigrette? Parboiling them first means they can be put on the grill to finish cooking after the meat comes off and is resting. Serve these with pork chops or jerk chicken. ■

4 sweet potatoes (2 pounds), preferably long ones
  Salt
2 tablespoons fresh lime juice
⅛ teaspoon freshly ground black pepper
¼ cup olive oil
2 tablespoons chopped fresh cilantro

Cover sweet potatoes with cold salted water (1½ tablespoons salt) in an 8-quart pot and bring to a boil. Reduce heat and simmer until just slightly resistant in center when pierced with a sharp small knife, 15 to 25 minutes, depending on size. Transfer to a large bowl of ice and cold water to stop the cooking, then drain well.

If using a charcoal grill, prepare it for direct-heat cooking over medium-hot coals; if using a gas grill, prepare it for direct-heat cooking over medium-high heat (see Grilling Basics, page 512).

Meanwhile, when potatoes are cool enough to handle, peel with a sharp small knife and quarter lengthwise.

Whisk together lime juice, ½ teaspoon salt, and pepper in a small bowl. Add oil in a slow stream, whisking, then whisk in cilantro.

Oil grill rack and grill potatoes in 2 batches (covered if using a gas grill), turning occasionally, loosening potatoes with a metal spatula if necessary, until grill marks appear and potatoes are just tender, 6 to 8 minutes. Transfer to a platter.

Serve potatoes warm or at room temperature, drizzled with vinaigrette.

COOK'S NOTES

- The potatoes can be boiled and peeled up to 1 day ahead and refrigerated, covered.
- The vinaigrette, without the cilantro, can be made up to 2 hours ahead and kept at room temperature. Stir in the cilantro just before serving.

Grilled Zucchini and Tomatoes with Feta Sauce

SERVES 4
ACTIVE TIME: 20 MINUTES ■ START TO FINISH: 40 MINUTES (INCLUDES SOAKING SKEWERS)

■ After taking a turn on the grill, two prolific summer vegetables are tossed with a lemony basil-flecked feta dressing. The feta loses its distinct crumbly texture when pureed with sour cream and olive oil but retains its creamy saltiness. ■

3 ounces mild feta cheese, preferably French, crumbled
¼ cup sour cream
2 tablespoons water
2 teaspoons fresh lemon juice
½ teaspoon minced garlic
2½ tablespoons extra-virgin olive oil
2 tablespoons finely chopped fresh basil
   Salt and freshly ground black pepper
2 medium zucchini
¾ pound cherry tomatoes (about 18)
SPECIAL EQUIPMENT: a mandoline or other adjustable-blade vegetable slicer; three 12-inch wooden skewers, soaked in water for 30 minutes

If using a charcoal grill, prepare it for direct-heat cooking over medium-hot coals; if using a gas grill, prepare it for direct-heat cooking over medium heat (see Grilling Basics, page 512).

Meanwhile, combine feta, sour cream, water,

lemon juice, and garlic in a food processor and puree until smooth. With motor running, add 1½ tablespoons oil in a slow stream. Add basil and salt and pepper to taste and pulse until just combined.

Using slicer, slice zucchini lengthwise just under ⅛ inch thick. Toss zucchini and tomatoes with ¼ teaspoon salt and remaining tablespoon oil in a large bowl. Thread tomatoes onto skewers.

Oil grill rack and grill vegetables (covered if using a gas grill), in batches if necessary, turning once, until just tender, 3 to 5 minutes per batch.

Serve vegetables with sauce.

Grilled Zucchini with Garlic and Lemon

SERVES 4
ACTIVE TIME: 25 MINUTES ■ START TO FINISH: 25 MINUTES

■ Slices of zucchini are brushed with garlic oil and grilled. The remaining garlic oil, mixed with lemon juice and zest, becomes a vinaigrette to dress the tender squash. ■

4 medium zucchini
1 small garlic clove
   Salt
¼ teaspoon freshly ground black pepper
3 tablespoons olive oil
½ teaspoon finely grated lemon zest
2 teaspoons fresh lemon juice

If using a charcoal grill, prepare it for direct-heat cooking over medium-hot coals; if using a gas grill, prepare it for direct-heat cooking over medium-high heat (see Grilling Basics, page 512).

Meanwhile, cut zucchini lengthwise into ¼-inch-thick slices. Mince garlic and mash to a paste with ¼ teaspoon salt, using side of a large heavy knife. Whisk together garlic paste, pepper, and oil in a medium bowl.

Brush both sides of zucchini lightly with some of garlic oil. Whisk zest and juice into remaining garlic oil.

Grill zucchini (covered if using a gas grill), turning occasionally, until grill marks form and zucchini is tender, 6 to 8 minutes.

Cut zucchini crosswise into ½-inch pieces and toss with lemon garlic oil and salt to taste.

VEGETABLES

Cardoons. Kohlrabi. Plantains. Bok choy. Jerusalem artichokes. Yuca. Seaweed. America, it seems, is no longer a peas-and-carrots country. In fact, one of the great joys of the new American food landscape has been the expansion of our vegetable repertoire over the past few years, and you will find recipes for all of these vegetables — and more — in this chapter.

Although they may seem exotic, the truth is that this is just a return to the way things once were. When *Gourmet* first hit the newsstand in the early 1940s, American farmers were growing a vast variety of vegetables, and American cooks who did not know what to do with them were eager for instruction. And so in those early days, you could find recipes like Chayote Soufflé (1942), Fried Plantain (1943), and Parsnip Croquettes (1944).

But over time our choices became increasingly narrow. What happened? Frozen food. When Americans began going to the freezer instead of the farmer, our choices became more limited. The frozen food manufacturers have had much the same effect on the American meal as Hollywood has had on the American movie: in their desire to cater to the broadest spectrum of people, they have eliminated everything but the most popular products. Walk along the freezer case someday, and you'll be stunned by how limited the offerings are. Small farmers, however, have no need to sell enormous quantities, and they like appealing to niche audiences. As farmers markets have begun to reappear, we have had the opportunity to rediscover forgotten flavors and learn entirely new ones.

So the corner of the plate that was once reserved for green beans or a stalk of broccoli has become a much more interesting place. These days it might be occupied by the elusive and beautiful cardoon, with its faint flavor of artichokes, or bok choy, with its sweet, subtle crispness. Watercress, once reserved for salads, is spectacularly different when it is sautéed. Seaweed, in all its varieties, is remarkably delicious (not to mention extremely nutritious), and our hijiki and carrots with sesame seeds will be a stunning addition to your table.

You will, of course, find all your old favorite vegetables here as well: irresistible braised eggplant with onion and tomato, a sumptuous leek and mushroom gratin, a fine rich cauliflower mousse, and red-wine-and-maple-glazed carrots that will make any meal a feast.

In sidebars throughout the chapter, we've also included basic methods of preparing common vegetables. So if you are looking forward to the pure, unadorned flavor of asparagus, you'll find out how to boil, steam, roast, or grill it. If you're eager to enjoy carrots and corn in all their natural sweetness, we'll tell you how to put them on your table quickly. With the enormous variety of vegetables now appearing in the American market, eating your vegetables has never been more fun.

VEGETABLES

ARTICHOKES

Like the plates on an armadillo, artichokes appear armored, secretive. And indeed, their thorny-edged, tightly packed leaves hide a delicious morsel of flesh at the base of each one, as well as the vegetable's tender heart. Braising is perhaps the easiest way to cook artichokes, and it concentrates their flavor beautifully. As a bonus, the cooking juices can be boiled down and used as a sauce. For extra-soft leaves, we turn to the pressure cooker. In just 10 minutes, the whole leaves become yielding enough to scrape with your teeth (with other methods, the base of the leaf may be tender while the rest remains tough). We usually serve these with melted butter seasoned with a good jolt of fresh lemon juice and salt. Should you want plain artichokes with a rich, flavorful dipping sauce like a vinaigrette or mustard mayonnaise, steaming is the way to go if you don't own a pressure cooker.

While it does take some time to trim artichokes, once you get the hang of it, you'll power through them. Removing the artichoke's inner yellow leaves and fuzzy choke before cooking results in an elegant, no-mess dish. But on weeknights, we find it easier to just cook them with the chokes in. Once you've eaten all the outer leaves and discarded the cone of soft inner leaves, the choke is easy to scrape out with the tip of a spoon, exposing the sweet, tender heart—one of our favorite parts.

To help artichokes stay upright in the pot, cut off the stems—but don't throw them out! Peeled and cooked along with the artichokes, they become a satisfying treat. Serve them with the whole artichokes or just nibble on them as you finish preparing the rest of dinner. Baby artichokes—small, young ones—are more difficult to find but well worth snapping up when they come into the market.

BEFORE COOKING To serve 4, buy four 8- to 10-ounce artichokes. Cut off the stems and trim and peel them with a sharp paring knife. Cut off the top inch of each artichoke if it is thorny, using a serrated knife, and snip about ½ inch off the remaining leaf tips with kitchen shears. Rub the cut leaves all over with a lemon half, and you are ready to cook.

TO BRAISE Combine 2 cups water, 2 tablespoons olive oil, and 1 teaspoon salt in a large pot, add the artichokes, standing upright, and stems, and bring to a boil. Reduce the heat to moderately low and braise the artichokes, covered, until the bottoms are tender when pierced with a knife, 25 to 30 minutes. Transfer the artichokes (and stems) to a platter and boil to reduce the juices for a few minutes, then drizzle over the artichokes.

TO COOK IN THE PRESSURE COOKER Combine 2 cups water, 2 tablespoons olive oil, and 1 teaspoon salt in a large pressure cooker and add the artichokes, standing upright, and the stems. Lock on the lid and cook over moderately high heat at high pressure, according to the manufacturer's instructions, for 10 minutes.

TO STEAM Add enough water to reach the bottom of a collapsible steamer set in a large pot and bring to a boil. Stand the artichokes upright in the steamer, add the stems, and steam over boiling water, covered, until the bottoms are tender when pierced with a knife, about 35 minutes.

Artichokes Braised with Garlic and Thyme

SERVES 6
ACTIVE TIME: 25 MINUTES ■ START TO FINISH: 1 HOUR

■ Rustic, caramelized, and browned in spots, artichokes braised in just a small amount of liquid become subtly infused with garlic and very tender. The dark pan sauce this cooking method yields is equally wonderful. Be sure to have lots of bread on hand for spreading the garlic on and mopping up the juices. This recipe comes from the prop stylist Betty Alfenito. ■

    6 medium artichokes (8 ounces each)
   18 fresh flat-leaf parsley sprigs
   ¼ cup olive oil
    8 fresh thyme sprigs
    1 head garlic, cloves separated but left unpeeled
    1 cup water
       Salt
   ¼ teaspoon freshly ground black pepper
    1 tablespoon extra-virgin olive oil
ACCOMPANIMENT: crusty bread
SPECIAL EQUIPMENT: a 6- to 8-quart heavy pot wide
       enough to hold the artichokes in a single layer
       (about 11 inches in diameter); a grapefruit spoon or
       a melon ball cutter

Cut off top inch of 1 artichoke with a serrated knife (1). Gently pull open center and scoop out sharp leaves and fuzzy choke with grapefruit spoon or melon ball cutter (2). Trim bottom ¼ inch of stem, if attached, and peel stem with a sharp paring knife. Put artichoke in a large bowl of cold water. Repeat with remaining artichokes.

Drain artichokes and push 3 parsley sprigs into center of each one. Heat olive oil in pot over moderate heat until hot but not smoking. Add artichokes (on their sides), thyme sprigs, garlic, ¼ cup water, ½ teaspoon salt, and pepper. Cover pot and braise artichokes, turning occasionally, until artichokes are browned in spots and bases are tender when pierced with a knife, about 35 minutes.

Transfer artichokes, thyme, and garlic to a plat-

ter. Add remaining ¾ cup water to pot and deglaze by boiling over high heat, scraping up brown bits, for 1 minute. Pour pan juices (they will be dark) into a small bowl and stir in extra-virgin olive oil and ½ teaspoon salt. Squeeze pulp from 2 of garlic cloves into juices and mash into sauce with a fork.

Serve sauce on the side for drizzling over artichokes. Remaining garlic cloves can be peeled and spread on crusty bread.

COOK'S NOTE
■ The artichokes can be trimmed up to 8 hours ahead and kept in the bowl of water in the refrigerator.

PREPARING ARTICHOKES

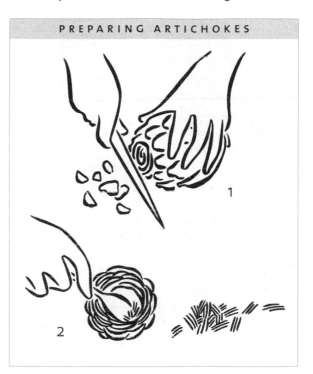

Braised Baby Artichokes and Shallots

SERVES 6
ACTIVE TIME: 50 MINUTES ■ START TO FINISH: 1 HOUR

■ Baby artichokes are much easier to prepare than the large ones, since they can be eaten choke and all; they also take a fraction of the time to cook. Here they are braised until tender with sweet shallots. ■

3 pounds baby artichokes (20–30; see Cook's Note)
2 lemon quarters
2 tablespoons olive oil
1 tablespoon unsalted butter
½ pound shallots (6 medium), peeled and halved
  lengthwise
½ cup Chicken Stock (page 153) or store-bought
  reduced-sodium broth
  Salt and freshly ground black pepper
½ cup dry white wine
1 tablespoon fresh lemon juice, or to taste
1 tablespoon chopped fresh flat-leaf parsley

Pull tough outer leaves (about 5 layers) from 1 artichoke until you reach inner leaves that are about two-thirds yellow and artichoke resembles a tight rosebud. Trim stem end and base and sides of artichoke, including any dark green bits, rubbing cut surfaces with a lemon quarter. Cut off top third of artichoke and discard. Halve artichoke lengthwise and rub cut surfaces with lemon quarter. Repeat with remaining artichokes.

Heat oil and butter in a 12-inch heavy skillet over moderately high heat until hot but not smoking. Add artichokes and shallots and cook, stirring occasionally, until golden, 3 to 5 minutes. Reduce heat to moderately low, add stock, ½ teaspoon salt, and ½ teaspoon pepper, and simmer, covered, stirring occasionally, until artichokes are tender when pierced with a knife, about 15 minutes.

Add wine, bring to a boil, and boil, uncovered, until liquid has evaporated, 2 to 3 minutes. Remove skillet from heat and add lemon juice, parsley, and salt and pepper to taste, tossing vegetables to coat.

COOK'S NOTES

- If only large artichokes are available, prepare them as shown for Artichokes Braised with Garlic and Thyme (page 565) and cut them into 8 wedges each.
- The vegetables can be simmered in the stock up to 1 hour ahead. Remove from the heat and keep, covered, in the skillet. Reheat before adding the wine and proceeding with the recipe.

Steamed Asparagus with Hollandaise Sauce

SERVES 4
ACTIVE TIME: 20 MINUTES ■ START TO FINISH: 20 MINUTES

■ The transformation of eggs, butter, and lemon juice into hollandaise sauce is culinary alchemy. The sunny emulsification is rich yet airy, and it lends a luxurious gloss to a variety of foods—fish, eggs Benedict, or tender spears of asparagus. ■

1½ pounds asparagus, trimmed
2 sticks (½ pound) unsalted butter, softened
3 large egg yolks
1 tablespoon fresh lemon juice
3–4 tablespoons warm water
¼ teaspoon salt
⅛ teaspoon freshly ground white pepper

Put a collapsible steamer in a deep 12-inch heavy skillet, add just enough water to reach bottom of steamer, and bring to a boil. Add asparagus and steam, covered, until just tender, about 7 minutes.

Meanwhile, melt butter in a 1-quart heavy saucepan over moderate heat. Remove from heat and let stand for 3 minutes, then skim off foam.

Blend yolks, lemon juice, and 1 tablespoon warm water in a blender for 2 seconds. With motor running at medium speed, add half of melted butter in a slow stream. Add 1 tablespoon warm water to thin sauce, then continue slowly adding butter, leaving milky solids in bottom of pan. Thin sauce to desired consistency by blending in additional warm water, then add salt and white pepper.

Serve asparagus with sauce on the side.

COOK'S NOTES

- The egg yolks in this recipe will not be cooked. If that is a concern, see page 915.
- The sauce can be made up to 1 hour ahead. Transfer to a 1-quart heavy saucepan and cover the pan with plastic wrap. Put the pan in a 4-quart saucepan of warm water (135°F; if the water is too hot, it will curdle the sauce). If the sauce thickens while sitting, whisk in 1 to 2 tablespoons warm water.

Asparagus

Although asparagus is found all year round in the grocery store, we still get a little thrill when, after a long, cold winter, the first vibrantly green locally grown spears show up at the farmers market. Because asparagus cooks so quickly and tastes delicious with nothing more than a little butter and salt, it truly is a busy cook's best friend. You can steam it, but boiling is the most straightforward approach, since cooking the spears, uncovered, in well-salted water seasons them and preserves their color.

It's easy to tell when they're done: pick up a spear in the middle with tongs, and if it gracefully bends slightly, without going limp, it's ready. Though we're very happy to eat asparagus plain, we also like it with a flavorful sauce, such as a vinaigrette or hollandaise (boiled asparagus is delicious served cold or at room temperature). Buttered toasted bread crumbs or sautéed chopped nuts mixed with finely grated lemon zest make a nice topping for boiled asparagus. Our other favorite methods—roasting and grilling—concentrate the vegetable's singular flavor, heightening its natural sweetness.

BEFORE COOKING If you're planning on boiling the asparagus, you'll need about 1½ pounds to serve 4. Because vegetables shrink when roasted or grilled, plan on about 1¾ pounds to serve 4. Trimming asparagus for cooking is quick and easy. For thin or medium stalks, gently bend the lower part of the stalk until it snaps; it will automatically break at the point where the tough part ends. For thick stalks, use a knife to cut off the tough white ends.

TO BOIL Put the asparagus in a 12-inch heavy skillet and cover with water. Bring to a boil, add 2 teaspoons salt, reduce the heat, and simmer, uncovered, until the asparagus is just tender, 6 to 8 minutes, depending on thickness. Drain.

TO ROAST Put a rack in the middle of the oven and preheat the oven to 450°F. Arrange the asparagus in one layer on a large baking sheet, drizzle with 2 tablespoons olive oil, and sprinkle with ¼ teaspoon salt and ⅛ teaspoon black pepper. Roll the spears around to coat them and roast, shaking the pan once or twice, until just tender, 10 to 15 minutes for medium spears.

TO GRILL (DO NOT USE PENCIL-THIN ASPARAGUS) Soak eight 6-inch wooden skewers in water for 30 minutes. Prepare a charcoal or gas grill for cooking over medium heat (see Grilling Basics, page 512). Divide the asparagus into 4 or 5 bunches. Lay the spears in each bunch side by side, aligning the bottoms, and thread two skewers crosswise through each bunch, about 2 inches apart. (The skewered asparagus will look like rafts.) Brush the asparagus with 2 tablespoons olive oil and sprinkle with salt. Lightly oil the grill rack and grill the asparagus, uncovered, turning once, until tender, 6 to 10 minutes.

Stir-Fried Asparagus with Oyster Sauce

SERVES 4
ACTIVE TIME: 15 MINUTES ■ START TO FINISH: 20 MINUTES

■ Oyster sauce—a thick concentration of oyster extract and soy sauce—adds a crucial depth of flavor to stir-fries and other Chinese dishes. Seek out thick, chubby asparagus spears for this speedy side dish. Cut into short pieces, they cook quickly to crisp-tender without becoming mushy and are a breeze to pick up with chopsticks. ■

½ cup Chicken Stock (page 153), store-bought reduced-sodium broth, or water
3 tablespoons oyster sauce
2 teaspoons Chinese rice wine, preferably Shaoxing, or medium-dry sherry
1½ teaspoons peanut or vegetable oil
2 tablespoons thinly sliced garlic
½ teaspoon salt
1½ pounds thick asparagus, trimmed and cut diagonally into 1½-inch-long pieces
2 teaspoons Asian sesame oil

Stir together stock, oyster sauce, and rice wine in a small bowl.

Heat a well-seasoned 14-inch flat-bottomed wok or 12-inch heavy skillet over high heat until a drop of water evaporates on contact, then add oil, swirling pan to coat. Add garlic and salt and stir-fry until garlic is fragrant, about 30 seconds. Add asparagus and stir-fry for 1 minute. Add stock mixture and cook, uncovered, stirring occasionally, until asparagus is crisp-tender, 3 to 6 minutes. Remove from heat and stir in sesame oil.

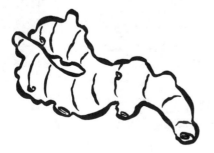

Green Beans with Ginger Butter

SERVES 6 TO 8
ACTIVE TIME: 30 MINUTES ■ START TO FINISH: 30 MINUTES

■ An unconventional pick-me-up for green beans, this combination of butter, fresh ginger, and lemon zest makes a refreshing counterpoint to a plate heaped with rich, heavy fare. ■

2 pounds haricots verts or other green beans, trimmed
Salt
1 (3-inch-long) piece fresh ginger
3 tablespoons unsalted butter
Finely grated zest of ½ lemon

Cook beans in an 8-quart pot of boiling salted water (2 tablespoons salt), uncovered, until just tender, 5 to 9 minutes, depending on thickness. Drain and transfer to a large bowl of ice and cold water to stop the cooking. Drain beans again and pat dry.

Peel ginger. Halve crosswise, then thinly slice lengthwise and cut into very thin matchsticks.

Heat butter in a 12-inch skillet over moderate heat until foam subsides. Add ginger and cook, stirring, until golden, about 3 minutes. Add beans and cook, stirring, until just heated through, about 2 minutes. Remove from heat and add zest and ½ teaspoon salt, tossing to combine.

COOK'S NOTE

■ The beans can be boiled up to 1 day ahead. Refrigerate, wrapped in paper towels in a sealable plastic bag.

Green Beans with Crisp Shallots, Chile, and Mint

SERVES 4
ACTIVE TIME: 30 MINUTES ■ START TO FINISH: 45 MINUTES

■ A Southeast Asian treatment casts green beans in a new light. Tossed with sweet fried shallots, fresh mint, and thin rings of fiery chile, they make a versatile side dish that complements nearly any meal. ■

- 1¼ pounds green beans, trimmed
  Salt
- ⅔ cup vegetable oil
- 6 ounces shallots (5 medium), thinly sliced and separated into rings
- 1 (2¼-inch-long) fresh hot chile, such as Thai or serrano, preferably red, thinly sliced
- ½ cup chopped fresh mint

Cook beans in a 4- to 5-quart pot of boiling salted water (1 tablespoon salt), uncovered, until just tender, about 5 minutes. Drain.

Heat oil in a 12-inch heavy skillet over moderate heat until hot but not smoking. Fry shallots in 3 batches, stirring frequently, until golden brown, 3 to 5 minutes per batch (watch carefully; shallots burn easily). Quickly transfer with a slotted spoon to paper towels to drain. (Shallots will crisp as they cool.)

Discard all but about 1 tablespoon oil from skillet. Add chile and cook, stirring, until softened, about 2 minutes. Add beans and ½ teaspoon salt and toss with tongs until beans are heated through. Remove from heat and add fried shallots and mint, tossing to combine.

BEANS (GREEN OR WAX)

The most common varieties of this familiar vegetable, sometimes labeled snap or string beans, are green beans and yellow wax beans, though a pretty purple variety is becoming more popular at farmers markets (these turn dark green when cooked). Look for specimens that are young and slender. Beans taste best when cooked in plenty of well-salted boiling water, which helps season them evenly, and it's important to cook them uncovered so that they stay a beautiful green. The color won't be as pretty if you roast them, but this method does concentrate their flavor nicely. For an easy dash of oomph, toss the cooked beans with vinaigrette or a few tablespoons of pesto.

BEFORE COOKING If you're planning on boiling the beans, you'll need about 1¼ pounds to serve 4. Because vegetables shrink somewhat when roasted, plan on about 1½ pounds to serve 4. Trim the stem ends, leaving the other (blossom) end alone if it's in good shape.

TO BOIL Fill a medium pot with well-salted water (1½ tablespoons per 4 quarts of water) and bring to a boil. Add the beans and boil, uncovered, until just tender, 5 to 7 minutes. Drain.

TO ROAST Put a rack in the middle of the oven and preheat the oven to 375°F. Toss the beans with 1 tablespoon olive oil and ¼ teaspoon salt on a baking sheet and spread out in one layer. Roast, stirring occasionally, until browned in places and tender, about 35 minutes.

Green Beans
with Parmesan Sauce

SERVES 4
ACTIVE TIME: 15 MINUTES ■ START TO FINISH: 15 MINUTES

■ Dressed in a light, clinging sauce, its flavor reminiscent of a zippy Caesar salad, these beans taste equally good warm, at room temperature, and cold, making them ideal for a buffet or picnic. ■

1¼ pounds green beans or a mixture of green and wax
    beans, trimmed
    Salt
⅓ cup finely grated Parmigiano-Reggiano
1½ tablespoons cream cheese, softened
1½ teaspoons Dijon mustard
1 garlic clove, minced
¼ teaspoon freshly ground black pepper
3 tablespoons olive oil
1 tablespoon white wine vinegar
1 tablespoon water

Cook beans in a 3-quart saucepan of boiling salted water (1 tablespoon salt), uncovered, until crisp-tender, 5 to 7 minutes. Drain and transfer to a bowl.

Meanwhile, blend Parmesan, cream cheese, mustard, garlic, ¼ teaspoon salt, and pepper in a blender until combined.

Bring oil, vinegar, and water just to a boil in a small saucepan. With blender on low speed, add hot oil mixture in a stream, stopping to scrape down sides of blender if necessary, then blend until thick and creamy.

Pour sauce over beans and toss to coat.

Roasted Beets
with Horseradish Cream

SERVES 6
ACTIVE TIME: 30 MINUTES ■ START TO FINISH: 1½ HOURS

■ When we buy fresh beets, we look for bunches that have fresh, healthy, abundant greens still attached—it's like getting two vegetables for the price of one. Sometimes we cook the tops with other greens such as collards or kale; at other times, as in this recipe, we serve them with the beets they came with. A dollop of horseradish cream adds a welcome pungency (serving the cream on the side prevents it from turning magenta). The beets go well with steak, as does the horseradish cream, which is one reason that this recipe makes a generous amount. ■

3 pounds medium beets (3½ pounds with greens)
1 cup sour cream
4½ tablespoons bottled horseradish (not drained)
    Salt and freshly ground black pepper
2 tablespoons extra-virgin olive oil

Put a rack in middle of oven and preheat oven to 350°F.

Cut greens from beets, leaving about 1 inch of stems attached to beets, and reserve greens. Scrub beets. Wrap tightly in three foil packages. (Match similar-sized beets in packages for even cooking.) Roast beets on a baking sheet until tender, 1 to 1½ hours. Unwrap beets carefully, discarding any liquid.

Meanwhile cut beet leaves from stems and discard stems. Coarsely chop leaves, wash well, and drain.

Stir together sour cream, horseradish, ½ teaspoon salt, and ½ teaspoon pepper in a small bowl.

When beets are cool enough to handle, slip off and discard skins and stems. Halve beets and cut into ¼-inch-thick slices.

Heat oil in a 12-inch heavy skillet over moderately high heat until hot but not smoking. Add greens and cook, stirring occasionally, until wilted and tender, 6 to 8 minutes. Add ¾ teaspoon salt, ¼ teaspoon pepper, and beets and cook, stirring occasionally, until beets are heated through.

Transfer beets and greens to a platter and serve with horseradish cream.

COOK'S NOTES

■ The beets can be roasted and peeled up to 1 day ahead; refrigerate, covered. The greens can be washed and chopped up to 1 day ahead; refrigerate separately from the beets.

■ The horseradish cream can be made up to 1 day ahead and refrigerated, covered.

BEETS

Earthy, sweet, and visually arresting, beets come in an array of colors, from deep purple-red to sunny gold to festive red-and-white stripes. Roasting is a neat and fuss-free method that accentuates their sweetness. Just wrap them in foil, stick them in a hot oven, and let them do their thing. The only downside is that roasting takes a long time (up to 1½ hours). But keep in mind that you can roast beets ahead of time. After they cool, peel, slice, and throw them in the fridge. When you're ready to eat, "refresh" the beets by tossing them in a skillet with butter or olive oil and seasonings (think minced fresh dill or chopped caraway seeds).

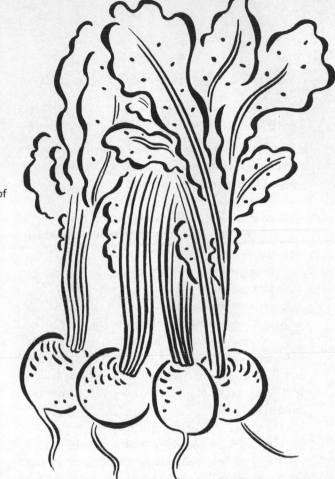

If time is of the essence, boiling is the way to go. Try not to pierce the beets to test for doneness too many times, or they'll lose some of their color to the water. Boiled beets can also be cooked ahead and then reheated with your favorite seasonings.

Bunches of beets can be frustratingly inconsistent. In a single bunch, there may be one enormous beet, a couple of medium ones, and some small ones. Adjust your cooking times accordingly, checking the smaller ones earlier and removing them as they are cooked.

BEFORE COOKING Buy beets with their tops still attached whenever possible. It's a good way to gauge freshness, and the greens give you a second vegetable. To serve 4, buy 2 pounds beets with greens (1½ pounds without greens). Trim stems to 1 inch. Do not peel. If planning to serve the greens later, wash them and dry in a salad spinner, then spread out in a thin layer on paper towels, loosely roll them up, put the roll in a plastic bag, and refrigerate.

TO ROAST Put a rack in the middle of the oven and preheat the oven to 425°F. Wrap the beets in a double layer of foil and roast on a baking sheet until tender, 1 to 1½ hours. Cool to warm, then peel and cut as desired.

TO BOIL Cover the beets with 2 inches cold unsalted water in a medium pot and bring to a boil, then reduce the heat and simmer the beets, covered, until tender, 35 to 45 minutes. Drain, peel, and cut as desired.

TO COOK BEET GREENS Cooked beet greens are silky, like spinach. To prepare them, first wash the leaves well, as they can be very sandy, but do not dry them. Cut the stems and center ribs from the leaves and chop the stems and leaves separately. Cook 1 small onion, finely chopped, in oil or butter until softened. Add the stems and stir to coat with oil, then add a couple of tablespoons of water and cook, covered, until just tender, about 5 minutes. Add the leaves and cook, covered, until tender, 3 to 5 minutes.

Balsamic-Glazed Beets

SERVES 8

ACTIVE TIME: 20 MINUTES ■ START TO FINISH: 1 HOUR

■ Beets take well to sweet-and-sour flavors. Here the sweet comes from maple syrup, the sour from balsamic vinegar. Leftovers reheat nicely. ■

3½ pounds beets (4 pounds with greens), stems
    trimmed to 1 inch (reserve greens for another use)
    Salt
3 tablespoons balsamic vinegar
2 tablespoons pure maple syrup or mild honey
1 tablespoon olive oil
¼ teaspoon freshly ground black pepper

Cover beets with salted water (1 tablespoon salt) by 1 inch in a 4-quart saucepan. Bring to a boil, reduce heat, and simmer, covered, for 35 to 45 minutes, or until tender.

Drain and cool beets until they can be handled, then slip off skins and stems. Cut into wedges.

Stir together vinegar, maple syrup, oil, ½ teaspoon salt, and pepper in a large skillet. Add beets and cook over moderate heat, stirring, until heated through and lightly coated, about 3 minutes.

COOK'S NOTE

■ The beets can be boiled and cut into wedges up to 2 days ahead. Refrigerate, covered; bring to room temperature before proceeding with the recipe.

Bok Choy Gratin

SERVES 6

ACTIVE TIME: 40 MINUTES ■ START TO FINISH: 1 HOUR

■ The most commonly found Chinese vegetable is also one of the oldest—bok choy has been cultivated in China since the fifth century A.D. You can find many kinds of bok choy at Asian markets, in different shapes and sizes; this recipe works well with any mature variety. Though it might seem odd to see a traditional Asian green served in a European-style gratin, it works brilliantly. This gratin pairs well with ham or beef tenderloin. ■

6 tablespoons fine dry bread crumbs
2½ pounds bok choy, tough stem ends trimmed
    Salt
5 tablespoons unsalted butter
1 shallot, finely chopped
2 tablespoons all-purpose flour
1¼ cups whole milk
⅛ teaspoon freshly grated nutmeg
    Freshly ground black pepper
½ cup coarsely grated Gruyère
¼ cup finely grated Parmigiano-Reggiano

SPECIAL EQUIPMENT: a 2-quart gratin dish or other shallow baking dish

Put a rack in upper third of oven and preheat oven to 425°F. Lightly butter gratin dish and dust with 2 tablespoons bread crumbs.

Remove bok choy stems and center ribs and cut into ½-inch pieces; set aside. Coarsely chop leaves. Cook stems and ribs in a large pot of boiling salted water (2 tablespoons salt) until just tender, about 5 minutes. Add leaves and cook for 30 seconds. Drain in a colander and rinse under cold water until cool enough to handle. Squeeze out excess water by handfuls.

Heat 1 tablespoon butter in a 12-inch heavy skillet over moderate heat until foam subsides. Add shallot and cook, stirring, until softened, about 2 minutes. Add bok choy and cook, stirring, until greens are coated with butter and shallot, 1 to 2 minutes. Spread bok choy in gratin dish.

Melt 2 tablespoons butter in a 2-quart heavy saucepan over moderately low heat. Add flour and cook, whisking, for 2 minutes to make a roux. Add milk in a slow stream, whisking constantly, and bring to a boil, whisking. Reduce heat and simmer, whisking, for 5 minutes. Add nutmeg, ½ teaspoon salt, and ¼ teaspoon pepper, then stir in Gruyère and 2 tablespoons Parmesan. Pour evenly over bok choy.

Toss remaining ¼ cup bread crumbs with remaining 2 tablespoons Parmesan in a small bowl. Blend in remaining 2 tablespoons butter with your fingertips until mixture resembles coarse meal. Season with ¼ teaspoon salt and ¼ teaspoon pepper. Sprinkle mixture evenly over gratin.

Bake until bubbly and golden brown, about 20 minutes.

BOK CHOY

One of the first Chinese vegetables to successfully cross over to mainstream America, bok choy is pretty and mild-tasting, with succulent stems and slightly bitter dark green leaves. The heads can be 10 to 20 inches in length. In addition to the easy-to-find regular bok choy, smaller varieties—Shanghai bok choy and baby bok choy—are becoming more available, and we love their slightly sweeter flavor. Baby bok choy is about 5 to 7 inches long and has white stems and dark green leaves. Though sometimes mislabeled baby bok choy, the Shanghai variety is pale green all over and has spoon-shaped stems.

Stir-frying bok choy is the natural choice; it highlights the vegetable's juicy crunch and preserves its contrasting colors. We like to add a little chopped garlic and/or ginger while stir-frying, as well as a teaspoon of soy sauce, along with a sprinkling of white or black sesame seeds. A teaspoon of Asian sesame oil added at the end of cooking makes a nice finish. Because of its mild flavor, bok choy takes well to more Western preparations, such as braising; it can also be boiled and baked in a gratin.

BEFORE COOKING To serve 4, buy 1½ pounds bok choy. Trim the tough ends and remove any bruised or withered outer leaves.

TO STIR-FRY Cut the bok choy crosswise into ¾-inch pieces. Heat a wok or a 10-inch cast-iron skillet over high heat until very hot. Add 2 tablespoons vegetable oil and swirl to coat. Add 3 garlic cloves, finely chopped, and 1 tablespoon very fine matchsticks of ginger and stir-fry until fragrant, about 15 seconds. Add the bok choy and stir-fry for 2 minutes (if using a cast-iron skillet, use tongs). Stir in 2 tablespoons Chinese rice wine or medium-dry sherry combined with 1 teaspoon sugar (if you have cream sherry, use that and skip the sugar) and ¼ teaspoon salt and cook, covered, for 2 minutes. Uncover and stir-fry until the bok choy is crisp-tender, about 2 minutes more. Transfer with a slotted spoon to a bowl. If desired, boil the pan juices, stirring, until thickened before pouring over the bok choy.

TO BRAISE Quarter the bok choy lengthwise. Combine 1½ cups water, 2 tablespoons unsalted butter, and ¼ teaspoon salt in a large deep skillet and bring to a boil. Add the bok choy in one layer and simmer, covered, until tender, 3 to 5 minutes. Transfer with a slotted spoon to a serving dish and cover to keep warm. Boil the cooking liquid, uncovered, until reduced to about ⅓ cup. Stir in salt and black pepper to taste and pour over the bok choy.

Stir-Fried Baby Bok Choy with Ginger

SERVES 4
ACTIVE TIME: 20 MINUTES ■ START TO FINISH: 20 MINUTES

■ In this recipe, adapted from one by the chef and Chinese cookbook author Grace Young, baby bok choy is quartered and quickly stir-fried with matchsticks of ginger. Although it is a traditional Cantonese recipe, it need not accompany a Chinese meal; try it with salmon or sautéed pork chops. ■

1 (2-inch) piece fresh ginger, peeled
¾ pound Shanghai bok choy or baby bok choy (5–8 heads)
¼ cup Chicken Stock (page 153) or store-bought reduced-sodium broth
1 teaspoon Chinese rice wine, preferably Shaoxing, or medium-dry sherry
1 teaspoon soy sauce
½ teaspoon cornstarch
½ teaspoon salt
¼ teaspoon sugar
1 tablespoon vegetable oil
½ teaspoon Asian sesame oil

Cut half of ginger into very fine matchsticks (less than ⅛ inch thick); set aside. Grate remaining ginger, then squeeze pulp with your fingers to yield 1 teaspoon liquid; discard pulp.

Trim ⅛ inch from bottom of each bok choy head and cut into quarters. Wash bok choy in several changes of cold water and dry in a colander or salad spinner.

Whisk together ginger juice, stock, rice wine, soy sauce, cornstarch, salt, and sugar in a small bowl until salt and sugar are dissolved.

Heat a well-seasoned 14-inch flat-bottomed wok or a 12-inch heavy skillet over high heat until a drop of water evaporates on contact. Add vegetable oil and swirl pan to coat. Add ginger matchsticks and stir-fry for 5 seconds. Add bok choy and stir-fry until leaves are bright green and just limp, 1 to 2 minutes. Stir stock mixture, pour into wok, and stir-fry until vegetables are crisp-tender and sauce is slightly thickened, about 1 minute. Remove from heat, drizzle with sesame oil, and stir to coat.

Steamed Broccoli with Olive Oil and Parmesan

SERVES 4
ACTIVE TIME: 10 MINUTES ■ START TO FINISH: 10 MINUTES

■ So quick and so good. Steaming the broccoli keeps it crisp and bright, and its residual heat melts the cheese ever so slightly, creating a sauce. We promise that you'll make this again and again. ■

1½ pounds broccoli
3 tablespoons extra-virgin olive oil
¾ cup finely grated Parmigiano-Reggiano
Salt and freshly ground black pepper

Cut stalks from broccoli and peel them with a paring knife, trimming any fibrous parts. Cut into ⅓-inch-thick matchsticks. Cut broccoli heads into 1½-inch-wide florets.

Steam broccoli in a steamer rack set over boiling water, covered, until tender, 5 to 6 minutes. Transfer to a bowl and toss with oil, cheese, and salt and pepper to taste.

Broccoli Spears in Garlic Sauce

SERVES 4
ACTIVE TIME: 25 MINUTES ■ START TO FINISH: 25 MINUTES

■ This is like the crisp, garlicky version from your favorite Chinese take-out place—but better, fresher, and faster. The smashed garlic cloves subtly season the oil and broccoli, while oyster sauce adds depth. ■

1½ pounds broccoli

1 tablespoon canola oil

4 garlic cloves, lightly smashed and peeled

3 tablespoons oyster sauce

½ cup Chicken Stock (page 153) or store-bought
reduced-sodium broth

1 teaspoon Asian sesame oil

Peel broccoli stalks with a paring knife. Halve broccoli crosswise. Cut bottom halves (stems) lengthwise into ½-inch-wide wedges. Cut top halves (stems with florets) lengthwise into ½-inch-wide wedges.

Heat a well-seasoned 14-inch flat-bottomed wok or a 12-inch heavy skillet over high heat until beginning to smoke. Add canola oil and swirl pan to coat. Add garlic and stir-fry until golden, about 30 seconds. Add broccoli and stir-fry for 5 minutes. Stir in oyster sauce and stock and cook, covered, until broccoli is crisp-tender, about 3 minutes. Remove from heat and toss with sesame oil.

BROCCOLI

Cooked until vibrant green and just tender, broccoli is one of our regular go-tos for its speed, ease, and ability to pair with almost everything. Overcooking is the enemy, resulting in the drab sulfurous sludge that gives the vegetable a bad name. Steaming is the best way to cook broccoli simply (we avoid boiling, which tends to bash the florets around, breaking off the delicate flower buds). It's important to steam it just until it is tender and then remove the lid immediately so that the vegetable keeps as much of its bright green color as possible. Transfer it gently to a bowl and toss with a little melted butter or olive oil and salt and black pepper to taste. It's also great with a sprinkling of Parmesan or a dollop of drained horseradish stirred in. Pan-roasting is easy and has the advantage of flavoring the broccoli as it cooks, so you don't have to add anything later. A classic addition is finely chopped garlic and/or hot red pepper flakes, stirred in as the oil gets hot.

BEFORE COOKING To serve 4, buy 1 large bunch of broccoli (about 1½ pounds). Cut off the stalks and peel them with a paring knife, trimming any fibrous parts, and cut crosswise into ¼-inch-thick slices. Cut the broccoli tops into 1½-inch-wide florets.

TO STEAM Pour enough water into a medium pot to reach the bottom of a collapsible steamer and bring to a boil. Add the broccoli to the steamer and steam, covered, over boiling water until crisp-tender, 5 to 6 minutes. Remove the lid immediately.

TO PAN-ROAST Heat 2 tablespoons olive oil in a large heavy skillet over high heat until hot. Stir in 2 or 3 garlic cloves, finely chopped, and ¼ teaspoon red pepper flakes. Add the broccoli and stir to coat with the oil (the broccoli will begin to turn bright green). Add ⅓ cup water and ¼ teaspoon salt, cover the skillet, lower the heat, and cook until the broccoli is crisp-tender, about 5 minutes, checking occasionally to make sure the water hasn't evaporated. Remove the lid immediately.

Broccoflower with Anchovies and Garlic

■ Many people assume that tightly crowned, pale jade broccoflower is a cross between broccoli and cauliflower, but it is actually descended from a type of green cauliflower grown in Italy. It's a natural with the Sicilian trinity of anchovies, pine nuts, and raisins, plus judicious amounts of golden garlic and red pepper flakes. Broccoflower is best when very fresh. The vegetable expert Elizabeth Schneider recommends sniffing your choice deeply—it should smell clean and sweet, not cabbagey. ■

- 1 (1½-pound) head broccoflower or cauliflower, cut into 2-inch-wide florets
  Salt
- ¼ cup olive oil
- 3 garlic cloves, thinly sliced
- 2½ teaspoons chopped anchovies, or to taste
- ¼ teaspoon red pepper flakes
- ¼ cup pine nuts, toasted (see Tips, page 911)
- ¼ cup golden raisins
- 2 tablespoons chopped fresh flat-leaf parsley

Add half of broccoflower to a 5- to 6-quart pot of boiling salted water (2 tablespoons salt) and cook until crisp-tender, about 5 minutes. Transfer with a wire skimmer or slotted spoon to a large bowl of ice and cold water to stop the cooking. Cook remaining broccoflower in same manner, drain, and transfer to ice water. Drain florets and pat dry with paper towels.

Heat oil in a 12-inch nonstick skillet over moderately high heat until hot but not smoking. Add garlic and cook, stirring, until pale golden, about 30 seconds. Add anchovies and red pepper flakes and cook, stirring, until anchovies are dissolved, about 1 minute. Add broccoflower and toss to coat. Add pine nuts, raisins, and ¼ teaspoon salt and cook, stirring, until heated through, about 2 minutes. Remove from heat and stir in parsley.

Garlicky Broccoli Rabe

■ A leisurely turn in a hot skillet renders chopped parboiled broccoli rabe positively silky. Golden slivers of garlic add bursts of toasty sweetness. Finely chopped and deep green, this side is terrific with almost anything from duck to pork, though we've been known to eat a big bowl all by itself, with just some crusty bread. ■

- 2 pounds broccoli rabe, bottom 2 inches trimmed off
  Salt
- 8 large garlic cloves, thinly sliced
- ⅓ cup extra-virgin olive oil
  Freshly ground black pepper

Cook broccoli rabe in an 8-quart pot of boiling salted water (2 tablespoons salt), uncovered, until tender, about 7 minutes. Immediately transfer with tongs to a bowl of ice and cold water to stop the cooking. Drain in a colander, pressing to extract excess water. Transfer to a cutting board and finely chop.

Cook garlic in oil in a 12-inch heavy skillet over moderate heat, stirring occasionally, until just golden, 2 to 3 minutes. Add broccoli rabe and cook, stirring frequently, until very soft, 20 to 30 minutes. Season with salt and pepper to taste.

COOK'S NOTE

■ The broccoli rabe can be boiled and chopped up to 1 day ahead. Refrigerate, covered; bring to room temperature before cooking in the oil with the garlic.

Sautéed Broccoli Rabe and Peas

■ Parboiling broccoli rabe softens its sturdy leaves and stems and mellows its bitterness. Sautéing the vegetable with sweet peas and garlic further tames its peppery bite. ■

1 (¾- to 1-pound) bunch broccoli rabe,
    bottom 2 inches trimmed off
1 (10-ounce) package frozen peas
    Salt
3 large garlic cloves, lightly smashed and peeled
¼ cup extra-virgin olive oil
½ teaspoon freshly ground black pepper

Cut broccoli rabe crosswise into 1½-inch pieces.

Cook broccoli rabe and peas in a 4- to 6-quart pot of boiling salted water (2 tablespoons salt) until leaves of broccoli rabe are wilted and stems are crisp-tender, 2 to 3 minutes Drain well in a colander.

Cook garlic in oil in a 12-inch heavy skillet over moderately high heat, turning frequently, until golden, 1 to 2 minutes; discard garlic. Add broccoli rabe, peas, ½ teaspoon salt, and pepper to skillet and cook, stirring, until vegetables are well coated with garlic oil, about 2 minutes.

Stir-Fried Chinese Broccoli with Garlic Sauce

SERVES 6
ACTIVE TIME: 25 MINUTES ■ START TO FINISH: 25 MINUTES

■ If you like broccoli rabe, you'll love Chinese broccoli. Also known as *gai lan*, this beautiful vegetable is one of the most popular greens in China and can be found at almost any Asian market. You'll recognize it by its round, solid, jade-colored stems, abundant collardlike leaves, and white flower buds. Its robust, slightly bitter flavor and great crunch make it a hit in stir-fries. The leaves alone are delicious floated in soups or chopped and added to dumplings. This simple Chinese preparation is a great introduction. ■

BROCCOLI RABE

Broccoli rabe has a natural bitterness that some people love and others prefer to tone down. If you are of the latter school, it's best to blanch the vegetable in boiling salted water first and then sauté it in olive oil. We often add finely chopped garlic and red pepper flakes to the hot oil before adding the rabe, and we sometimes throw in a little diced pancetta or bacon for even more flavor. Cooking the broccoli rabe first in the water and then in the oil until it is tender transforms it into a succulent, sweet, meaty green—a perfect complement to roasted poultry, pork, or beef. But if you crave broccoli rabe's distinctive bitterness, a quick braise is the best way to highlight that flavor while still getting tender greens.

BEFORE COOKING To serve 4, buy 1½ pounds broccoli rabe. Trim off the bottom 2 inches and cut the stalks into thirds.

TO BLANCH AND SAUTÉ Cook the broccoli rabe in a large pot of boiling salted water until the stems are crisp-tender, 2 to 3 minutes. Drain well and pat dry. Heat 2 tablespoons olive oil in a large skillet over medium-high heat. Add 1 garlic clove, minced, and a pinch of red pepper flakes and cook until fragrant, about 30 seconds. Add the broccoli rabe with ¼ teaspoon salt and cook, stirring, until well coated with oil, about 2 minutes.

TO BRAISE Heat ¼ cup olive oil in a large wide pot over moderately high heat until hot but not smoking. Add 1 garlic clove, minced, and a pinch of red pepper flakes and cook until fragrant, about 30 seconds. Add the broccoli rabe and cook, turning occasionally with tongs, until well coated with oil. Add ½ cup water and ½ teaspoon salt, bring to a simmer, and simmer, covered, stirring once or twice, until just tender, 3 to 5 minutes. Remove the lid and continue to cook, turning with tongs, until the broccoli rabe is tender and the liquid has nearly evaporated.

1½ pounds Chinese broccoli (also called *gai lan*) or broccolini

½ cup Chicken Stock (page 153) or store-bought reduced-sodium broth

1 tablespoon soy sauce

1 teaspoon cornstarch

½ teaspoon sugar

¼ teaspoon salt

1½ tablespoons peanut or vegetable oil

3 tablespoons chopped garlic

2 teaspoons Asian sesame oil

Discard any bruised or withered outer leaves from broccoli. Separate any lower branches from stalks and discard them. Trim and peel tough outer layer from lower portion of stalks; halve thick ones lengthwise. Cut stems and leaves crosswise into 2-inch pieces; keep leafy parts separate from thick stems.

Cook broccoli stems in a 6- to 8-quart pot of boiling unsalted water, uncovered, for 1 minute. Stir in leafy parts and cook, stirring occasionally, until bright green and barely crisp-tender, about 3 minutes. Drain and transfer to a bowl of ice and cold water to stop the cooking. Drain well and pat dry.

Stir together stock, soy sauce, cornstarch, sugar, and salt in a small bowl until sugar and salt are dissolved.

Heat a well-seasoned 14-inch flat-bottomed wok or a 12-inch heavy skillet over high heat until a drop of water evaporates on contact. Add peanut oil and swirl pan to coat. When oil just begins to smoke, add garlic and stir-fry until barely golden, 5 to 10 seconds. Add broccoli and stir-fry until heated through and crisp-tender, 3 to 4 minutes. Stir stock mixture again, add to broccoli, and boil, stirring, until slightly thickened, 2 to 3 minutes. Remove from heat, drizzle broccoli with sesame oil, and stir to combine.

CHINESE BROCCOLI

If you are lucky enough to live near an Asian market, you may already know how delicious *gai lan* is. Sweeter than familiar broccoli, Chinese broccoli has smooth, round stems and wide leaves dotted with florets, which open to reveal little white flowers. There's no reason you can't cook Chinese broccoli the same way you cook regular "American" broccoli, but we like it best stir-fried, which highlights its lovely jade color and tender crunch. Blanching Chinese broccoli before stir-frying yields slightly more tender results, but on busy weeknights we simply add the raw vegetable to the hot wok. Some recipes separate the leaves from the stems and start cooking the stems before adding the leaves, but we find that the dish doesn't suffer if you just cook them together. At the very least, we like to season the cooking oil with ginger and garlic, but it's also nice to top the finished dish with a drizzle of bottled oyster sauce or a sprinkling of finely chopped salted peanuts.

BEFORE COOKING To serve 4, buy 1½ pounds Chinese broccoli, seeking out bunches with slender stems. Discard any bruised or withered leaves and trim the stems. There's usually no need to peel the stems, but halve any thick ones lengthwise. Cut the stems and leaves crosswise into 2-inch pieces.

TO STIR-FRY Heat a wok over high heat until hot. Add 2 tablespoons vegetable oil and swirl to coat. (Alternatively, add oil to a large heavy skillet and heat over high heat until hot but not smoking.) Add 1 smashed garlic clove and a couple slices of peeled fresh ginger and stir-fry for 30 seconds to flavor the oil. Add the broccoli with ½ teaspoon salt and stir-fry for 2 minutes. Add ⅓ cup water and stir-fry until the broccoli is just tender, about 4 minutes more. Remove with a wire skimmer or slotted spoon.

Roasted Brussels Sprouts with Garlic and Pancetta

SERVES 4
ACTIVE TIME: 10 MINUTES ■ START TO FINISH: 35 MINUTES

■ Blasting halved Brussels sprouts in a hot oven caramelizes their edges, allowing their sweetness to emerge. That sweetness meets its match in the bits of salty pancetta strewn through the dish. ■

- 1 pound Brussels sprouts, trimmed and halved (or quartered if large)
- 2 ounces sliced pancetta (Italian unsmoked bacon), minced
- 1 garlic clove, minced
- 1 tablespoon extra-virgin olive oil
- ¼ teaspoon salt
- ⅛ teaspoon freshly ground black pepper
- ¼ cup water

Put a rack in upper third of oven and preheat oven to 450°F.

Toss together all ingredients except water in an 11-by-7-inch baking pan, then spread out in one layer. Roast, stirring once halfway through roasting, until sprouts are brown on edges and tender, about 25 minutes.

Stir in water to deglaze pan, over moderately high heat, scraping up brown bits. Serve warm.

BRUSSELS SPROUTS

When shopping for Brussels sprouts, buy the smallest, freshest specimens you can find. These will be sweeter and more tender than large ones, which can be woody. Although it's fun to buy them still attached to the stalk, the reality is that it's a heavy load to carry home from the market, and cutting off all those sprouts is tricky and time-consuming (plus, if you don't have a scale at home, you won't know the actual weight of your sprouts).

We favor roasting or sautéing Brussels sprouts, because those methods highlight the vegetable's sweet nuttiness. To speed things up, we generally halve or quarter the sprouts lengthwise. When sautéing, you can also try a completely different approach and separate the sprouts into individual leaves, or thinly shred the sprouts and cook them that way. If you have good knife skills and your knife is well honed, you can slice them by hand; otherwise, use an adjustable-blade vegetable slicer. If you like coleslaw, you can skip cooking the shredded sprouts altogether and simply toss them with a flavorful vinaigrette (see Shaved Brussels Sprout Slaw with Walnuts and Pecorino, page 175).

BEFORE COOKING If you are sautéing the sprouts, buy 1 pound to serve 4. Because roasting significantly shrinks them, plan on 1½ pounds for 4 people. No matter how you plan to cook them, trim the stems and discard any damaged or discolored leaves.

TO ROAST Put a rack in the middle of the oven and preheat the oven to 450°F. Depending on their size, halve or quarter the Brussels sprouts lengthwise. Toss with 2 tablespoons olive oil, a rounded ¼ teaspoon salt, and ¼ teaspoon black pepper on a baking sheet and spread out in one layer. Roast, stirring halfway through cooking, until tender and browned on the edges, 25 to 30 minutes. Season with salt and pepper to taste.

TO SAUTÉ Depending on their size, halve or quarter the Brussels sprouts lengthwise. Heat 2 tablespoons unsalted butter in a large skillet, preferably cast-iron, over moderately high heat until foam subsides. Add the Brussels sprouts, season with ¼ teaspoon salt and ¼ teaspoon black pepper, and cook, stirring occasionally and reducing the heat if the sprouts brown too quickly, until browned and just tender, 7 to 10 minutes. Season with salt and pepper to taste.

TO CHIFFONADE AND SAUTÉ If using an adjustable-blade slicer, hold the Brussels sprouts by their stem ends and finely shred. If using a knife, halve the sprouts lengthwise and cut crosswise into very thin slices. Heat 2 tablespoons butter or olive oil in a large heavy skillet over moderately high heat until hot. Add the sprouts, ¼ teaspoon salt, and ¼ teaspoon black pepper and cook, stirring occasionally, until the sprouts are bright green and crisp-tender, 2 to 3 minutes. Season with salt and pepper to taste.

Brussels Sprouts with Chestnuts

SERVES 8
ACTIVE TIME: 25 MINUTES ■ START TO FINISH: 35 MINUTES

■ A touch of cream transforms this vegetable into a positively luxurious holiday side dish. Crumbled chestnuts add a kiss of meaty sweetness to each bite. ■

    2 tablespoons unsalted butter
    ¾ teaspoon salt
    ½ teaspoon freshly ground black pepper
    1¼ cups water
    2 pounds Brussels sprouts, trimmed and halved
        lengthwise
    1 cup heavy cream
    ⅔ cup (4 ounces) bottled peeled cooked chestnuts,
        coarsely crumbled

Combine butter, salt, pepper, and 1 cup water in a deep 12-inch heavy skillet and bring to a boil over high heat. Add Brussels sprouts, reduce heat, and simmer, partially covered, stirring occasionally, until crisp-tender, 6 to 8 minutes. Remove lid and boil over moderately high heat, stirring occasionally, until water has evaporated and sprouts are lightly browned, 3 to 4 minutes.

Add cream and remaining ¼ cup water and bring to a boil, stirring. Add chestnuts, reduce heat, and simmer, stirring occasionally, until heated through, about 2 minutes.

Roasted Savoy Cabbage with Raisins

SERVES 4
ACTIVE TIME: 20 MINUTES ■ START TO FINISH: 1½ HOURS
(INCLUDES SOAKING TIME)

■ Cabbage might seem an unlikely candidate for roasting, but a hot oven renders it golden and wonderfully tender. Chef Nick Martschenko, formerly of Manhattan's Gramercy Tavern, pairs the ruffly savoy variety with plump golden raisins, which provide little sunbursts of sweetness. This is especially good with Panfried Double Lamb Chops with Date Puree (page 485). ■

    2 tablespoons golden raisins
    2½ tablespoons peanut oil
    1 large head savoy cabbage (about
        2½ pounds), quartered, cored, and torn
        into large pieces
    ¾ teaspoon kosher salt
    ¼ teaspoon freshly ground black pepper
    3 tablespoons unsalted butter
    2 fresh thyme sprigs

Soak raisins in very hot water to cover in a small bowl for 30 minutes, replacing hot water once or twice as it becomes tepid.

Put a rack in middle of oven and preheat oven to 400°F.

Heat oil in a 12-inch heavy ovenproof skillet or pot over moderately high heat until hot but not smoking. Add cabbage in 5 batches, adding some salt and pepper with each batch, stirring and adding next batch as previous batch begins to wilt. (Some cabbage will brown.) Add butter and thyme and cook, stirring frequently, until all cabbage is wilted, about 3 minutes. Drain raisins in a sieve and add to cabbage.

Transfer skillet to oven and roast, stirring every 10 minutes, until cabbage is tender, 30 to 40 minutes. Discard thyme sprigs.

Cabbage

Sturdy green, vibrant red, crinkly savoy, ruffled Napa—cabbage comes in a lovely array of shapes, sizes, and colors. All of them can be thinly sliced or shredded and turned into a slaw with a mayonnaise- or vinaigrette-style dressing. When making slaw, it's a good idea to toss the sliced cabbage with some salt and let it stand until it wilts slightly. The bit of liquid that the leaves release means that you won't need to add as much dressing to make the slaw moist.

GREEN and **SAVOY CABBAGES** take well to braising and sautéing. If you are sautéing, make sure to add handfuls of the cabbage in batches, letting each addition wilt (therefore making space in the pan) before adding the next. A spritz of lemon juice at the end of cooking is a nice addition.

RED CABBAGE is most commonly braised in broth or wine with sweet-and-sour accents of vinegar, chopped apples, and/or onions until it is very tender, which can take as long as 2 hours (see Braised Red Cabbage and Onions, page 582). If you like more texture to your red cabbage, start checking it after a half hour. When it's done to your taste, transfer the cabbage with tongs to a bowl; if there's a lot of liquid left in the pan, boil to reduce it, then add it to the cabbage.

NAPA CABBAGE is more tender than other cabbages. Because it cooks so quickly, it works well in a stir-fry (see Sweet-and-Sour Napa Cabbage, page 583). Be aware, however, that it is a juicy vegetable and releases its liquid when cooked, so it should be served immediately.

GREEN CABBAGE

SAVOY CABBAGE

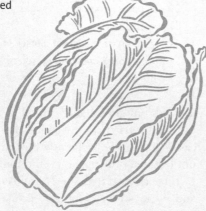

NAPA CABBAGE

BEFORE COOKING
To serve 4, buy one 2- to 2½-pound head of cabbage. Remove and discard any wilted outer leaves.

TO MAKE COLESLAW Quarter the cabbage (ordinary green, savoy, red, or Napa, or a mixture), cut out the core, and thinly slice the cabbage. Toss with ½ teaspoon salt in a large bowl. Let stand, uncovered, at room temperature, tossing occasionally, until wilted, about 30 minutes. Whisk together ⅓ cup mayonnaise, 3 tablespoons sour cream, 2 tablespoons cider vinegar, and ⅛ teaspoon black pepper until smooth. Add to the cabbage and toss well.

TO BRAISE Quarter a green, savoy, or red cabbage and cut out the core. Combine ¾ cup water, 3 tablespoons butter, ½ teaspoon salt, and ½ teaspoon sugar in a large wide pot and bring to a simmer. Arrange the cabbage cut side down in the pot and simmer, covered, until just tender, about 15 minutes (red cabbage will take longer). Remove the lid, add 1 tablespoon butter, and cook over moderately high heat until the water has evaporated, about 8 minutes. Continue to cook the cabbage, turning once, until it is well browned on both cut sides, about 5 minutes longer.

TO SAUTÉ Quarter the cabbage (ordinary green, savoy, red, or Napa, or a mixture), cut out the core, and thinly slice the cabbage. Melt 2 tablespoons unsalted butter with 2 tablespoons vegetable oil in large deep heavy skillet over moderately low heat. Add the cabbage by handfuls, letting each addition wilt before adding the next, then season with ¾ teaspoon salt and ¼ teaspoon black pepper, increase the heat to moderately high, and cook, stirring, until the cabbage is crisp-tender, 5 to 7 minutes.

Braised Red Cabbage and Onions

SERVES 8 TO 10
ACTIVE TIME: 1 HOUR ■ START TO FINISH: 3 HOURS

■ A long, slow simmer allows the cabbage and onions to drink up every drop of flavor from the red wine and spices. Think of this aromatic dish as the vegetable incarnation of mulled wine—beautiful, heady, and the perfect accompaniment to a warming winter meal. To round off the tastes, make the cabbage a day in advance. ■

¾ stick (6 tablespoons) unsalted butter
1½ pounds red onions, halved lengthwise and cut lengthwise into ¼-inch-thick slices
1 (3-pound) head red cabbage, cut into 8 wedges, wedges cut crosswise into ¼-inch-thick slices
2 cups dry red wine
2 cups water
¼ cup red wine vinegar
¼ cup balsamic vinegar
1 firm sweet apple, such as Honeycrisp, Gala, or Fuji, peeled and coarsely grated
1½ tablespoons sugar
Salt
10 black peppercorns
2 whole cloves
1 Turkish bay leaf or ½ California bay leaf
Freshly ground black pepper

SPECIAL EQUIPMENT: cheesecloth; kitchen string

Heat butter in a 6- to 8-quart wide heavy pot over moderately high heat until foam subsides. Add onions and cabbage and cook, stirring frequently, until wilted and lightly browned, about 20 minutes.

Add wine, water, vinegars, apple, sugar, and 1¼ teaspoons salt and bring to a boil.

Wrap peppercorns, cloves, and bay leaf in a 6-inch square of cheesecloth and tie with string. Add to cabbage mixture, cover cabbage directly with a round of parchment or wax paper, and cover pot with lid. Reduce heat and simmer until cabbage is very tender, about 2 hours.

Discard cheesecloth bundle and season cabbage with salt and pepper to taste.

COOK'S NOTE

■ The cabbage is best made 1 day ahead to allow the flavors to develop. Cool, uncovered, then refrigerate, covered. The cabbage can be refrigerated for up to 5 days.

Sweet-and-Sour Sauerkraut

SERVES 10
ACTIVE TIME: 20 MINUTES ■ START TO FINISH: 1½ HOURS

■ Tomatoes, brown sugar, toasted cumin seeds, and allspice lend a sweetly spicy depth to this sauerkraut, which is unlike any other we've tasted. It's delicious with smoked sausages, pork, or roast veal, and any leftovers keep and reheat well. Don't rush cooking the onions and garlic; caramelizing them until golden brown further accentuates the dish's sweetness. We much prefer the sauerkraut that is packaged in plastic bags and found in the refrigerated section of the supermarket. It is fresher-tasting and has a crisper texture than jarred or canned 'kraut. ■

1 large onion, halved lengthwise and thinly sliced crosswise
2 large garlic cloves, finely chopped
3 tablespoons vegetable oil
1 teaspoon cumin seeds, toasted (see Tips, page 911)
10 whole allspice, crushed
1 (28-ounce) can whole tomatoes in juice
½ cup packed dark brown sugar
1½ teaspoons salt
¼ teaspoon freshly ground black pepper
3 pounds packaged sauerkraut, rinsed well and drained

Cook onion and garlic in oil in a 3½- to 4-quart heavy saucepan over moderately low heat, stirring occasionally (more frequently toward end of cooking), until golden brown, about 30 minutes.

Increase heat to moderate, add cumin and allspice, and cook, stirring, for 30 seconds. Add tomatoes with juice, brown sugar, salt, and pepper, bring to a simmer, and simmer, stirring occasionally and breaking up tomatoes, for 10 minutes. Stir in sauerkraut and bring to a boil, then reduce heat and simmer, partially covered, stirring occasionally, until most of liquid is absorbed, about 30 minutes.

COOK'S NOTE

■ The sauerkraut can be cooked up to 2 days ahead. Cool, uncovered, then refrigerate, covered. Reheat in a saucepan with ½ cup water, covered, over low heat.

Sweet-and-Sour Napa Cabbage

SERVES 6
ACTIVE TIME: 25 MINUTES ■ START TO FINISH: 25 MINUTES

■ Pale frills of Napa cabbage and slender carrot matchsticks star in this dish, which is a great accompaniment to pork. The secret is white vinegar—its sharpness makes for a bold-tasting result. Be sure to serve it as soon as it is done; the cabbage will release water as it sits. ■

    2 tablespoons soy sauce
    1 tablespoon distilled white vinegar, or to taste
    2½ teaspoons sugar
    ½ teaspoon cornstarch
    ¼ teaspoon red pepper flakes
    2 tablespoons vegetable oil
    2 tablespoons finely chopped peeled fresh ginger
    1 tablespoon minced garlic
    ⅛ teaspoon salt
    3 medium carrots, cut into ⅛-inch-thick 2-inch-long matchsticks
    2 pounds Napa cabbage, cut crosswise into 1½-inch-wide pieces

Whisk together soy sauce, vinegar, sugar, cornstarch, and red pepper flakes in a bowl until sugar is dissolved.

Heat a well-seasoned 14-inch flat-bottomed wok or a 12-inch heavy skillet over high heat until a drop of water evaporates on contact. Add oil, swirling pan to coat. Add ginger and garlic with salt and stir-fry

until fragrant and pale golden, 20 to 30 seconds. Add carrots and stir-fry until crisp-tender, 1 to 2 minutes. Add cabbage and stir-fry until leaves are just wilted and ribs are crisp-tender, 3 to 4 minutes.

Whisk sauce again, add to pan, and stir-fry until vegetables are coated and sauce is slightly thickened, 1 to 2 minutes.

Fried Cardoons

SERVES 4
ACTIVE TIME: 45 MINUTES ■ START TO FINISH: 9 HOURS
(INCLUDES SOAKING TIME)

■ Cardoons are slowly becoming more common in the United States, keep an eye out for them in fall and winter at local farmers markets. Resembling a tall, flattened bunch of celery, cardoons are silvery gray and not as crisp as celery (when shopping, check the stalks to make sure they're not hollow). They have an intriguing flavor similar to artichokes and an almost custardy texture when cooked, which contrasts beautifully here with the crisp batter coating. Because cardoons can be quite bitter, they are often blanched before they are fried, added to a gratin, or stirred into a soup or stew. We find that a long soak in salted water works just as well and preserves the vegetable's texture. ■

    1 pound cardoons
       Salt
       About 4 cups vegetable oil for deep-frying
    ¼ cup all-purpose flour
    ⅛ teaspoon freshly ground black pepper
    1 large egg
    1 tablespoon water
    ¼ cup finely grated Parmigiano-Reggiano
SPECIAL EQUIPMENT: a deep-fat thermometer

Remove and discard any discolored outer stalks and small leaves from cardoons. Trim base, tips, and outermost stalks, removing strings from stalks with a vegetable peeler. Cut cardoons crosswise into 2-inch pieces.

Combine 8 cups water and 1 tablespoon salt in a large bowl, stirring until salt is dissolved. Add cardoons and soak, refrigerated, for at least 8 hours.

Drain cardoons, transfer to a 4-quart pot, and cover with salted cold water (1 tablespoon salt) by 2 inches. Bring to a boil, reduce heat, and simmer, uncovered, until cardoons are tender when pierced with a sharp knife, 20 to 25 minutes. Transfer with a slotted spoon to several layers of paper towels to drain and cool for 5 minutes. (Discard cooking water.)

Heat 1½ inches oil in a 3- to 4-quart heavy pot over moderate heat until it registers 360°F on thermometer. Meanwhile, whisk together flour and pepper in a shallow bowl. Whisk together egg, water, and cheese in another shallow bowl.

Toss one third of cardoons (all at once) with flour, shaking off excess, then transfer to egg mixture and turn with a fork to coat. Lift out coated cardoons 2 pieces at a time, letting excess drip off, carefully drop into hot oil, and fry, turning occasionally, until golden, 2 to 4 minutes. Transfer with a slotted spoon to dry paper towels to drain. (Return oil to 360°F between batches.) Coat and fry remaining cardoons in 2 batches. Sprinkle with salt to taste.

COOK'S NOTES

- The cardoons can be soaked and boiled up to 1 day ahead. Refrigerate, covered.
- The cardoons are best when fried just before serving, but they can be fried up to 4 hours ahead and reheated on a baking sheet in a 350°F oven for about 15 minutes.

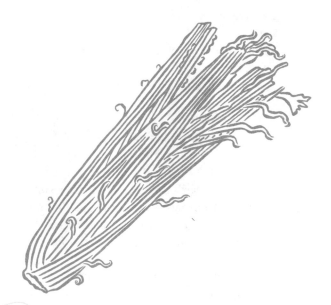

Roasted Carrots with Thyme and Garlic

SERVES 6
ACTIVE TIME: 20 MINUTES ■ START TO FINISH: 1¼ HOURS

■ To achieve the intense caramelization of these carrots, chef April Bloomfield of the Spotted Pig in Manhattan's West Village cooks them on the stovetop until they are golden brown, then roasts them, covered, until tender, uncovering them for the last few minutes so they become ever so crisp. The process concentrates the carrots' flavor and ratchets up their sweetness, but the roasted garlic and thyme keep the dish on the savory side. ■

- 2 tablespoons extra-virgin olive oil
- 2½ pounds large carrots, halved lengthwise diagonally
- 1 tablespoon unsalted butter
- 1 large head garlic, cloves separated but left unpeeled
- 3 fresh thyme sprigs
- ¼ teaspoon Maldon sea salt or other flaky sea salt
- ⅛ teaspoon freshly ground black pepper
- ½ cup water

Put a rack in middle of oven and preheat oven to 400°F.

Heat oil in a 12-inch heavy ovenproof skillet over moderately high heat until just beginning to smoke. Add half of carrots, cut side down, and cook, undisturbed, until they begin to brown, 12 to 15 minutes. Transfer to a plate. Brown remaining carrots in same manner, but leave in skillet. Add butter, stir once, and return carrots on plate to skillet. Continue to cook, turning frequently, until carrots are golden brown on edges, about 5 minutes more.

Add garlic, thyme, sea salt, pepper, and water, cover skillet tightly with foil, and transfer to oven. Roast until carrots are tender, about 20 minutes.

Remove foil and continue roasting, turning carrots occasionally with tongs, until edges are slightly crisp, 10 to 15 minutes more. Discard thyme and serve garlic unpeeled so guests can squeeze out pulp over carrots.

Red-Wine-and-Maple-Glazed Carrots

SERVES 6
ACTIVE TIME: 20 MINUTES ■ START TO FINISH: 45 MINUTES

■ You might think that all these different flavors—chili powder, maple syrup, red wine, vinegar, and dill—would create a cacophony, but they work beautifully together. Sweet, spicy, and completely unique, these carrots are the perfect accompaniment to simple roast chicken, turkey, or pork loin. ■

- 3 tablespoons unsalted butter
- ¾ cup thinly sliced shallots
- 1 teaspoon chili powder
- ¾ teaspoon salt
- ¼ teaspoon freshly ground black pepper
- 2 pounds carrots, cut diagonally into 3-inch pieces
- 1 cup dry red wine
- ⅓ cup pure maple syrup
- 2 teaspoons cider vinegar
- 2 tablespoons chopped fresh dill

Heat butter in a 12-inch heavy skillet over moderate heat until foam subsides. Add shallots and cook, stirring occasionally, until softened, about 4 minutes. Add chili powder, salt, and pepper and cook,

CARROTS

In their ubiquity, carrots can be overlooked in favor of more glamorous vegetables. That's a shame, because they are an irresistibly sweet, colorful addition to your dinner plate. Steaming is the most basic way to go (toss them with butter, fresh herbs, and salt and black pepper for a little lift). Although roasting takes longer, it intensifies carrots' natural sweetness and caramelizes them in spots. You can cut them into any size (bigger pieces, of course, will take longer to roast than smaller ones). If you are looking for flavor *and* speed, try braising. Sometimes we add a little honey, maple syrup, or sugar to the liquid.

BEFORE COOKING If you're planning on braising or steaming the carrots, you'll need about 1¼ pounds to serve 4. Because vegetables shrink somewhat when roasted, plan on about 1½ pounds to serve 4. Peel the carrots if desired and slice them into ½-inch-thick slices (for a prettier look, we usually slice them on the diagonal) or cut them into ½- to ¾-inch-wide sticks (cut them crosswise into 3 sections, then quarter each section lengthwise or, if the section is very thick, cut into sixths or eighths).

TO STEAM Pour enough water into a medium pot to reach the bottom of a collapsible steamer and bring to a boil. Steam the carrots over boiling water, covered, until just tender, 5 to 7 minutes.

TO ROAST Put a rack in the middle of the oven and preheat the oven to 450°F. Toss the carrots with 1½ tablespoons olive oil, ¼ teaspoon salt, and ¼ teaspoon black pepper on a baking sheet, then spread out in one layer. Roast, stirring occasionally, until just tender, 20 to 30 minutes. Season with salt and pepper if necessary.

TO BRAISE Combine the carrots with 1 cup water, 2 tablespoons olive oil or unsalted butter, 1 teaspoon sugar, ¼ teaspoon salt, and ¼ teaspoon black pepper in a 12-inch skillet and bring to a boil. Reduce the heat and simmer, covered, until just tender, 7 to 10 minutes. Uncover and cook until the liquid is reduced to a glaze and the carrots are tender, 3 to 5 minutes more.

stirring, until very fragrant, about 1 minute. Add carrots, wine, and maple syrup, bring to a simmer, and simmer, covered, stirring occasionally, until carrots are tender, about 20 minutes.

Add vinegar and boil, uncovered, until liquid is reduced to a glaze, 3 to 5 minutes. Remove from heat and stir in dill.

Carrot Puree
with Kalamata Olives

SERVES 4
ACTIVE TIME: 20 MINUTES ■ START TO FINISH: 35 MINUTES

■ Tender carrots pureed with cooked garlic until silky smooth, with inky Kalamata olives stirred in, make a dramatic presentation. The flavors are wild too—the garlic and salty olives add bright punctuation points to the sweet carrot mash. Try this with almost any lamb dish. ■

     2 pounds carrots, cut into ¼-inch-thick slices
     2 garlic cloves, peeled
       Salt
     2 tablespoons unsalted butter
     ½ cup Chicken Stock (page 153) or store-bought
       reduced-sodium broth
     ½ cup pitted Kalamata or other brine-cured black
       olives, sliced
       Freshly ground black pepper

Cover carrots and garlic with salted water (1 tablespoon salt) by 1 inch in a 2- to 3-quart saucepan. Bring to a boil, and boil, partially covered, until tender, about 15 minutes. Drain well.

Puree carrots and garlic with butter and stock in a blender or food processor until very smooth. Transfer puree to saucepan, add olives, and cook over low heat, stirring frequently, just until hot. Season with salt and pepper to taste.

COOK'S NOTE

■ The puree can be made up to 2 days ahead and refrigerated, covered. Reheat over low heat with a little water, stirring constantly until hot.

Hijiki and Carrots
with Sesame Seeds

SERVES 6
ACTIVE TIME: 15 MINUTES ■ START TO FINISH: 20 MINUTES

■ Delicate carrot matchsticks look dramatic when mixed with strands of hijiki, the color of India ink. This popular preparation of the calcium-and-iron-rich sea vegetable—the one most familiar to Americans—is often served as an appetizer in sushi restaurants. It also makes a wonderful companion to broiled salmon or mackerel. Take care not to soak the hijiki too long, or it will become too soft and lose valuable nutrients. ■

     1 cup (2 ounces) dried hijiki (Japanese dried black
       seaweed; see Sources)
     ¼ cup soy sauce
     ¼ cup water
    2½ tablespoons sugar
     2 tablespoons mirin (Japanese sweet rice wine)
     2 teaspoons vegetable oil
     1 teaspoon Asian sesame oil
     1 carrot, cut into thin matchsticks
     2 teaspoons sesame seeds, toasted (see Tips,
       page 911)

Soak hijiki in water to cover by 4 inches in a large bowl for 10 minutes (hijiki expands when soaked). Transfer with a slotted spoon to a sieve and drain well, pressing lightly on hijiki to remove excess liquid.

Stir together soy sauce, water, sugar, and mirin in a small bowl until sugar is dissolved.

Heat vegetable oil and sesame oil in a 12-inch heavy skillet over moderate heat until hot but not smoking. Add hijiki and carrot and cook, stirring occasionally, for 3 minutes. Add soy mixture, bring just to a simmer, and simmer gently, uncovered, stirring occasionally, until liquid has evaporated, 6 to 8 minutes. Cool to room temperature.

Serve sprinkled with sesame seeds.

COOK'S NOTE

■ The hijiki and carrots can be cooked up to 3 days ahead and refrigerated, covered. Bring to room temperature and sprinkle with sesame seeds before serving.

Whole Cauliflower with Brown Butter–Polonaise Topping

SERVES 4 TO 6
ACTIVE TIME: 25 MINUTES ■ START TO FINISH: 1½ HOURS

■ *Polonaise*, French for "in the style of Poland," is a mixture of crisp, buttery bread crumbs, chopped hard-boiled egg, and fresh parsley that is showered over cooked vegetables. Though it's delicious on asparagus or broccoli, we especially like it with cauliflower. Indeed, a beautifully roasted whole cauliflower à la polonaise makes a regal presentation. Don't worry if the toasty cauliflower looks dry—it will soak up the browned butter and be very moist inside. ■

- 1 stick (8 tablespoons) unsalted butter, cut into tablespoons
- 1 (2- to 2½-pound) head cauliflower, cored
  Salt

- 1 large hard-boiled egg (see Tips, page 915)
- ½ cup coarse white bread crumbs, preferably from a baguette
- ¼ teaspoon freshly ground black pepper
- ¼ cup chopped fresh flat-leaf parsley

Put a rack in middle of oven and preheat oven to 450°F. Lightly oil a 9-inch pie plate or shallow baking dish.

Melt butter in a 1- to 1½-quart heavy saucepan over moderate heat and bring to a boil. Once foam completely covers butter, reduce heat to moderately low and cook until solids turn light brown and butter deepens to golden and becomes translucent and fragrant, 5 to 10 minutes. Pour butter through a fine-mesh sieve into a heatproof measuring cup; discard solids. Keep in a warm spot.

Put cauliflower in oiled pie plate. Brush with about 2 tablespoons brown butter and sprinkle with

CAULIFLOWER

Once considered a little boring, a little skunky, a little *eh*, cauliflower comes into its own when roasted in an oven's high heat. Its snowy florets take on an appealing golden-brown crown, and a nutty sweetness overtakes its cabbagey undertones. In a word, delightful. For a quicker cauliflower fix, we turn to steaming, a gentler method than boiling, which tends to waterlog the florets. Be sure to season steamed cauliflower well before serving. Our favorite addition to roasted or steamed cauliflower is buttery toasted bread crumbs (rye bread is especially nice).

BEFORE COOKING To serve 4, buy 1 large cauliflower (about 2½ pounds). Core and cut into 1½-inch florets; discard stalk and leaves.

TO ROAST Put a rack in the middle of the oven and preheat the oven to 475°F. Toss the cauliflower florets with 3 tablespoons olive oil, ½ teaspoon salt, and ¼ teaspoon black pepper on a large baking sheet and spread out in one layer. Roast, stirring occasionally, until deep golden and just tender, 20 to 25 minutes.

TO STEAM Pour enough water into a medium saucepan to reach the bottom of a collapsible steamer and bring to a boil. Steam the cauliflower florets over boiling water, covered, until just tender, 6 to 8 minutes.

½ teaspoon salt. Roast, tenting cauliflower with foil once it browns, until tender, 1 to 1¼ hours.

Meanwhile, using back of a spoon, force hard-boiled egg through a medium-mesh sieve into a bowl.

Heat 2 tablespoons brown butter in an 8-inch skillet over moderate heat until hot but not smoking. Add bread crumbs and cook, stirring, until crisp and golden brown, 3 to 5 minutes. Sprinkle with ⅛ teaspoon salt, or to taste, and pepper.

Add bread crumbs and parsley to egg and toss gently to combine.

Transfer cauliflower to a serving dish and drizzle with remaining brown butter. Sprinkle bread crumb mixture over and around cauliflower.

Cauliflower Mousse

SERVES 6
ACTIVE TIME: 40 MINUTES ■ START TO FINISH: 1½ HOURS

■ This elegant mousse is adapted from a recipe in *Gourmet*'s own *Bouquet de France*, a classic written by Samuel Chamberlain, one of the magazine's earliest contributors and author of the delightful food memoir *Clémentine in the Kitchen*. The mousse has a sumptuous flavor and a flanlike airiness, but it is just sturdy enough to be cut into wedges. ■

    5 cups coarsely chopped cauliflower (from 1 large
        head)
      Salt
    1 tablespoon unsalted butter
    1 tablespoon all-purpose flour
    ½ cup whole milk
    ¼ teaspoon freshly ground white pepper
    ⅛ teaspoon freshly grated nutmeg
    3 large eggs, lightly beaten
    ¼ cup finely grated Parmigiano-Reggiano
SPECIAL EQUIPMENT: a 1-quart soufflé dish

Put a rack in middle of oven and preheat oven to 350°F. Butter soufflé dish, line bottom with a round of parchment or wax paper, and butter paper. Refrigerate dish.

Cook cauliflower in a 3- to 4-quart pot of boiling salted water (2 teaspoons salt), uncovered, until tender, 15 to 18 minutes. Drain cauliflower well, transfer to a food processor, and puree until smooth.

Melt butter in a 1-quart heavy saucepan over moderately low heat. Add flour and cook, whisking, for 3 minutes to make a roux. Add milk in a slow stream, whisking, then add ½ teaspoon salt, white pepper, and nutmeg, whisking. Bring to a boil over moderate heat, whisking, then reduce heat and simmer, whisking constantly, for 2 minutes. Remove béchamel from heat and cover surface with a piece of buttered wax paper (buttered side down). Let cool for 5 minutes.

Whisk cauliflower puree into béchamel. Add eggs, whisking until well combined.

Transfer mixture to soufflé dish and put dish in a 13-by-9-inch roasting pan. Add enough boiling water to pan to reach halfway up sides of soufflé dish. Bake until center of mousse is firm to the touch and mousse is beginning to pull away from sides of dish, 35 to 40 minutes.

Remove mousse from oven and water bath. Position rack so that top of unmolded mousse will be 4 to 6 inches from broiler and preheat broiler.

Run a knife around edge of soufflé dish, place a flameproof platter on top of soufflé dish, and invert mousse onto platter. Sprinkle cheese evenly over mousse and broil until cheese is melted and golden brown, about 2 minutes.

Indian-Spiced Cauliflower and Potatoes

SERVES 4
ACTIVE TIME: 30 MINUTES ■ START TO FINISH: 30 MINUTES

■ Warmly spiced cauliflower and potatoes are roasted until tender and browned, then stirred into a fragrant sauce. This is terrific with an Indian dish like Grilled Indian-Spiced Chicken (page 526), but we don't hesitate to pair it with plain roast chicken or grilled lamb chops. ■

1 medium head cauliflower (1¾ pounds), cored and
   cut into ¾-inch-wide florets
1¼ pounds Yukon Gold potatoes, peeled and cut into
   ½-inch cubes
5 tablespoons vegetable oil
½ teaspoon cumin seeds
   Salt
1 medium onion, finely chopped
2 garlic cloves, finely chopped
2 teaspoons minced jalapeño, including seeds
2 teaspoons minced peeled fresh ginger
1 teaspoon ground cumin
½ teaspoon ground coriander
¼ teaspoon turmeric
¼ teaspoon cayenne
½ cup water

ACCOMPANIMENT: lemon wedges

Put a rack in upper third of oven and put a baking sheet on rack. Preheat oven to 475°F.

Toss cauliflower and potatoes with 3 tablespoons oil, cumin seeds, and ¼ teaspoon salt in a bowl. Transfer to hot baking sheet, spread out in one layer, and roast, stirring occasionally, until potatoes are just tender and cauliflower is tender and browned in spots, about 20 minutes.

Meanwhile, heat remaining 2 tablespoons oil in a 12-inch heavy skillet over moderate heat until hot but not smoking. Add onion, garlic, jalapeño, and ginger and cook, stirring frequently, until very soft and beginning to turn golden, 8 to 10 minutes.

Add ground cumin, coriander, turmeric, cayenne, and ½ teaspoon salt to onion and cook, stirring constantly, for 2 minutes. Stir in water, scraping up any brown bits from bottom of skillet.

Stir roasted vegetables into onion mixture and cook, covered, stirring occasionally, for about 5 minutes, until flavors are blended. Serve with lemon wedges.

COOK'S NOTE

■ The dish can be made up to 1 day ahead and refrigerated, covered. Reheat in the microwave.

Cauliflower "Steaks" with Pancetta and Caper Berries

SERVES 4
ACTIVE TIME: 1 HOUR ■ START TO FINISH: 1½ HOURS

■ When a version of this recipe from Lucca restaurant in Boca Raton came our way, we were intrigued by the method of cutting the cauliflower into thick, meaty slices rather than florets. Pairing the beautifully browned cauliflower with a nicely finessed sauce of raisins, pancetta, capers, and caper berries seals the deal. This also makes a very impressive first course. Choose a head of cauliflower with a dense crown so that the "steaks" will hold together during cooking—but even if they separate a bit, the dish will still be fine. ■

½ cup salt-packed capers (see Sources), rinsed
5 (¼-inch-thick) slices pancetta (Italian unsmoked
   bacon), cut into ¼-inch dice
½ cup golden raisins
3 tablespoons fresh lemon juice
1 medium head cauliflower (1¾ pounds)
2 tablespoons extra-virgin olive oil
¾ stick (6 tablespoons) cold unsalted butter, cut into
   pieces
   Salt
2 pinches of sugar
   Freshly ground black pepper
2 tablespoons water
8 caper berries (see Sources), rinsed and drained

GARNISH: coarse sea salt, preferably sel gris; chopped fresh
   chives
SPECIAL EQUIPMENT: two 12-inch heavy ovenproof skillets
   (see Cook's Note)

Put capers in a small bowl, add water to cover by 2 inches, and soak for 30 minutes. Drain and repeat soaking. Drain, rinse, and pat dry.

Meanwhile, put racks in upper and lower thirds of oven and preheat oven to 350°F.

Cook pancetta in a dry 12-inch skillet over moderate heat, stirring occasionally, until crisp, about

10 minutes. Transfer with a slotted spoon to paper towels to drain. Pour off fat and wipe skillet clean; set aside.

Stir together raisins and lemon juice in a small bowl.

Trim cauliflower stalk flush with base of crown and trim any leaves. Put cauliflower stalk side down on a cutting board. Trim cauliflower to a rough rectangle by cutting a 1-inch-thick slice from two opposite sides of crown; discard. Cut remaining cauliflower length-wise into 4 "steaks" ¾ inch to 1 inch wide.

Heat 1 tablespoon oil, 1 tablespoon butter, ⅛ tea-spoon salt, and a pinch each of sugar and pepper in each 12-inch skillet over moderate heat, swirling pans occasionally, until butter begins to brown. Add 2 cau-liflower steaks to each skillet, season lightly with salt and pepper, and cook until undersides are golden, about 4 minutes.

Transfer skillets to oven and roast cauliflower (without turning), switching position of skillets half-way through roasting, until cauliflower is just tender and undersides are golden brown, 8 to 15 minutes, depending on thickness of slices.

Meanwhile, bring water just to a boil in a 1-quart heavy saucepan over moderate heat. Stir in pancetta, capers, raisins with lemon juice, and caper berries. Add remaining ½ stick butter and stir until melted. Remove from heat and season with pepper.

With a spatula, carefully invert cauliflower steaks onto a platter. Spoon sauce over them and sprinkle with sea salt and chives.

COOK'S NOTES

- If you have only one skillet, you can brown the cauli-flower in batches, then roast it on two baking sheets.
- If your sea salt is very coarse, lightly crush it with a mortar and pestle or the bottom of a heavy skillet.

Braised Celery Hearts

SERVES 4
ACTIVE TIME: 10 MINUTES ■ START TO FINISH: 30 MINUTES

■ Though celery serves as an essential aromatic in many soups, stews, and sauces, it's often overlooked as a veg-etable in its own right. That's too bad, because braising in particular transforms celery's crunchy blandness. As it soaks up the chicken stock, it becomes tender and delicately flavored, a foil to a rich and savory main course. ■

1 (1-pound) bag celery hearts (2 hearts)
2 tablespoons unsalted butter
1 cup Chicken Stock (page 153) or store-bought reduced-sodium broth
⅛ teaspoon salt
⅛ teaspoon freshly ground black pepper

Leaving celery ribs attached at base, peel strings from outer ribs of celery hearts with a vegetable peeler. Trim ends and halve each heart lengthwise.

Melt butter in a 12-inch heavy skillet over moderate heat. Add celery hearts and cook, turning occasionally with tongs, until pale golden on all sides, about 8 min-utes. Add stock, salt, and pepper, bring to a simmer, and simmer, covered, until liquid has evaporated and celery is tender and golden, about 20 minutes.

Celery Root and Apple Puree

SERVES 4
ACTIVE TIME: 20 MINUTES ■ START TO FINISH: 1¼ HOURS

■ Underneath its gnarly, sandy skin, celery root (or cele-riac) is a creamy white vegetable just waiting to woo you. The bulb has a delicate, ineffable flavor, reminiscent of parsley and celery but wholly its own, which is inten-sified when the vegetable is braised in butter. With its touch of apple sweetness, this soft, creamy puree makes a wonderful companion to pork or roast turkey. ■

2 pounds celery root (celeriac)
1 Gala, Empire, or McIntosh apple
2 tablespoons unsalted butter
½ teaspoon salt
⅓ cup heavy cream
⅛ teaspoon freshly ground white pepper
⅛ teaspoon freshly grated nutmeg
OPTIONAL GARNISH: celery leaves

Peel celery root with a sharp knife and cut into 1-inch cubes. Peel and core apple and cut into 1-inch pieces.

Melt butter in a 2- to 3-quart heavy saucepan over moderately low heat. Add celery root and apple with salt and stir to coat with butter. Cover with a tight-fitting lid and cook (without added liquid), stirring occasionally, until celery root is tender, 50 minutes to 1 hour.

Puree mixture in batches in a food processor until smooth, about 2 minutes per batch. Return puree to pot and stir in cream, white pepper, and nutmeg. Heat, covered, over moderate heat, stirring occasionally, until hot, about 5 minutes.

Sprinkle puree with celery leaves, if using.

COOK'S NOTE

- The puree can be made up to 1 day ahead. Cool, uncovered, then refrigerate, covered. Reheat, covered, over low heat, stirring occasionally, until hot, about 15 minutes.

CELERY ROOT

When peeled of its strange knobby skin, celery root reveals itself to be cream-colored and more pungently flavored than bunch celery. It's long been a favorite in France, in the forms of purees, soups, and salads such as the bracing *céleri rémoulade* (raw celery root dressed in a homemade mayonnaise flavored with Dijon mustard). Also known as celeriac, this vegetable deserves its growing fan base here in the United States. Don't be daunted by its appearance—with a good paring knife in hand, you'll quickly make your way to the heart of the matter (vegetable peelers are not up to the task). When boiled and pureed with a touch of heavy cream, celery root makes a welcome change from mashed potatoes and goes with almost anything (a dollop of truffle butter, if you have it, adds a luxe touch). When it is roasted, the vegetable's herbal sweetness comes to the fore. Cut into matchsticks, raw celery root makes a lovely addition to sharply dressed salads. Because its flesh is so dense, make sure to let the celery root marinate for a while in the dressing to soften it.

BEFORE COOKING To serve 4, buy 2½ pounds celery root. Peel it with a sharp paring knife.

TO PUREE Cut the celery root into ½-inch cubes. Put in a medium pot, fill three-quarters full with water, and add 2 teaspoons salt. Bring to a boil and boil the celery root until tender, about 15 minutes. Drain. Transfer the hot celery root to a food processor and puree with ⅓ cup heavy cream, ¼ teaspoon salt, ¼ teaspoon black pepper, and 3 tablespoons unsalted butter, cut into bits.

TO ROAST Put a rack in the middle of the oven and preheat the oven to 425°F. Cut the celery root into 1-inch pieces. Toss with ¼ cup olive oil and salt and black pepper to taste on a large baking sheet and spread out in one layer. Roast for 30 minutes. Stir the celery root, reduce the oven temperature to 375°F, and continue to roast, stirring after 30 minutes, until golden and tender, about 1 hour more.

TO MAKE CÉLERI RÉMOULADE Using an adjustable-blade vegetable slicer or a sharp knife, cut 1½ pounds celery root into matchsticks. Combine with ½ teaspoon salt and 2 tablespoons lemon juice in a bowl and marinate, covered and refrigerated, for 30 minutes to 1 hour. Meanwhile, whisk together 1 tablespoon Dijon mustard, 1½ teaspoons lemon juice, 1½ teaspoons white wine vinegar, a pinch of sugar, and salt and black pepper to taste in a bowl. Add 3 tablespoons olive oil in a slow stream, whisking until well blended. Drain the celery root and toss with the dressing. Refrigerate, covered, for 1 hour before serving. Sprinkle with chopped fresh chives or flat-leaf parsley before serving. (This recipe serves 4.)

Celery Root and Potato Latkes

SERVES 8 (MAKES ABOUT 32 LATKES)
ACTIVE TIME: 1¼ HOURS ■ START TO FINISH: 1¼ HOURS

■ Celery root adds a touch of sweetness to classic latkes. Crisp and flavorful, these are equally good as a first course served with applesauce or sour cream and as a side for roast fowl or fish. ■

    1 (1½-pound) celery root (celeriac), peeled with a knife
 1½ pounds russet (baking) potatoes (about 3 large)
    2 tablespoons fresh lemon juice
    1 pound onions, quartered
  ⅔ cup all-purpose flour
    4 large eggs, lightly beaten
 1¼ teaspoons salt
  ½ teaspoon freshly ground black pepper
  ½ teaspoon ground celery seed
    About 1½ cups vegetable oil

Put racks in upper and lower thirds of oven and preheat oven to 250°F.

Set a wire rack on each of two baking sheets.

Using the wide holes of a box grater, coarsely grate celery root into a bowl (see Cook's Note).

Peel potatoes and coarsely grate into a large bowl. Add lemon juice and toss. Coarsely grate onions into same bowl. Transfer to a kitchen towel (not terry cloth), gather up corners to form a sack, and twist tightly to wring out as much liquid as possible. Return potatoes and onions to cleaned bowl and stir in celery root, flour, eggs, salt, pepper, and celery seed until well combined.

Heat ⅓ inch oil in a 12-inch nonstick skillet over moderately high heat until hot but not smoking. Fill a ¼-cup measure with latke mixture (not tightly packed), carefully spoon it into skillet, and flatten to 3 inches in diameter with a slotted spatula. Form 3 more latkes and fry until undersides are deep golden, 1½ to 3 minutes. Turn over using two spatulas and fry until deep golden on second side, 1½ to 3 minutes more. (If latkes brown too quickly, lower heat to moderate.) Transfer to paper towels to drain briefly, then arrange (in one layer) on rack on one baking sheet and keep warm in oven. Make more latkes in same manner, using second baking sheet for last batches.

COOK'S NOTES

■ The celery root, potatoes, and onions can be shredded in a food processor with the shredding disk. In that case, use 5 eggs instead of 4, because the machine will grate them more coarsely and the mixture will require more binding.

■ The latkes can be fried up to 1 hour ahead.

Chayote with Cilantro, Chile, and Lime

SERVES 4
ACTIVE TIME: 20 MINUTES ■ START TO FINISH: 20 MINUTES

■ Chayote resembles a slightly flattened pear, so it's no surprise that it is also known as vegetable pear; other names include *mirliton* and *christophene*. Its light green flesh has a sweet, elusive flavor and an appealing crispness. With its tang of fresh lime juice and the serrano chile's sneaky heat, this simple dish is the ideal accompaniment to a juicy steak or grilled chicken. ■

    2 pounds chayote
      Salt
  ¼ cup chopped fresh cilantro
    1 large scallion, finely chopped
    1 teaspoon finely chopped serrano or jalapeño chile, including seeds, or to taste
    2 tablespoons extra-virgin olive oil
    1 tablespoon fresh lime juice

Peel chayote (see opposite page) with a sharp knife. Halve lengthwise, discard soft pits, and cut into ½-inch cubes.

Cook chayote in a 6- to 8-quart pot of boiling salted water (1 tablespoon salt) until crisp-tender, about 6 minutes.

Meanwhile, combine cilantro, scallion, chile, oil, and ½ teaspoon salt in a large bowl.

Drain chayote well and add to cilantro mixture (without mixing). Pour lime juice over chayote, then toss with cilantro mixture. Serve warm or at room temperature.

- The chayote can be cut up to 3 hours ahead and refrigerated, covered.

Corn with Bacon and Miso Butter

SERVES 4 TO 6
ACTIVE TIME: 35 MINUTES ■ START TO FINISH: 35 MINUTES

■ Momofuku Noodle Bar, in Manhattan's East Village, is known for its pork. This is chef-owner David Chang's riff on a northern Japanese dish of pork and miso broth topped with corn and butter. It reminds us of a hip version of our forebears' succotash. Chang swears by the bacon from Benton's Smoky Mountain Country Hams, a small operation run by the master pork man Allan Benton in Tennessee, and it's well worth seeking out (see Sources). ■

1 tablespoon unsalted butter, softened
1 tablespoon white miso (fermented soybean paste; see Sources)
¼ pound thick-sliced bacon (about 3 slices; see headnote)
1 small onion, halved lengthwise and thinly sliced crosswise
10 ears corn, shucked and kernels cut from cobs
Freshly ground black pepper
½ cup water
½ cup thinly sliced scallions
Salt

Stir together butter and miso in a small bowl; set aside.

Cut bacon crosswise into ⅛-inch-wide strips. Cook in a 12-inch heavy skillet over moderate heat, stirring occasionally, until browned and crisp, about 8 minutes. Transfer with a slotted spoon to paper towels to drain, leaving fat in skillet.

CHAYOTE

Native to North America and popular in Latino communities around the world, chayote (pronounced "chai-*oh*-teh"), a member of the gourd family, is finally becoming a fixture in American supermarkets. Sometimes called *mirliton* or *christophene*, most chayote available in the United States resembles a pear with pale apple-green skin and round, furrowed sides. It has a mild, subtle flavor and a crisp, fine texture, and it can be treated much as you would zucchini. In Latin American countries, it is often simmered and tossed with a lime-flavored dressing or stuffed and baked. We've found that roasting really brings this vegetable to life. It concentrates the chayote's natural sugars, highlighting its vegetal sweetness and its juiciness. Raw chayote, thinly sliced or julienned, adds a nice crunch to salads and salsas.

BEFORE COOKING When roasting chayote, buy 2 pounds (2 or 3 chayotes) to serve 4. Peel with a sharp knife. Because cut chayote exudes a sticky juice that some people find irritating, you may want to wear gloves when cutting it.

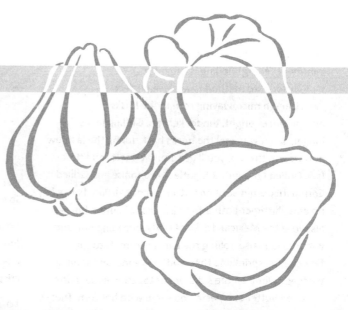

TO ROAST Put a rack in the middle of the oven and preheat the oven to 450°F. Halve the chayote lengthwise, discarding the soft pits, and cut into ¼-inch-thick slices. Toss the slices with 3 tablespoons olive oil and ½ teaspoon salt on a baking sheet and spread out in one layer. Roast, turning once halfway through cooking, until browned and tender, about 25 minutes.

Cook onion in bacon fat, stirring, until golden, 5 to 8 minutes. Add corn and ½ teaspoon pepper, increase heat to moderately high, and cook, stirring constantly, until some of kernels are pale golden, 3 to 4 minutes. Add water and butter mixture and cook, stirring, until corn is tender and coated with miso butter, about 4 minutes. Stir in bacon, ¼ cup scallions, and salt and pepper to taste.

Serve corn sprinkled with remaining ¼ cup scallions.

Corn and Tomato Gratin

SERVES 6 TO 8
ACTIVE TIME: 45 MINUTES ■ START TO FINISH: 1¾ HOURS

■ Fresh basil and Parmesan cheese give this hearty summer gratin an Italian accent. Serve it with anything hot off the grill. ■

1½ pounds red or yellow tomatoes (4 medium), cut into ½-inch-thick slices
  Salt and freshly ground black pepper
4 cups corn kernels (from 6–8 ears)
1 cup whole milk
½ cup heavy cream

CORN

Is there anything sweeter than fresh corn on the cob, enjoyed on a warm summer evening? Boiling is the most straightforward method to achieve perfect ears, though microwaving corn in the husks also produces bright, tender kernels. Grilling takes longer, and if you peel the husks back during the last few minutes on the fire, you'll get dramatic color and flavor (see Grilled Corn with Chipotle Mayonnaise and Grilled Corn with Cumin Scallion Butter, page 552). Purists need no embellishment other than a smear of butter, but we also love the Mexican trick of lightly spreading hot corn with mayonnaise, rolling the ears in crumbly *cotija* or feta cheese, sprinkling them with cayenne, and serving wedges of lime on the side. Or stir together equal parts softened butter and pesto and serve with hot corn. There's no reason the kernels always have to stay on the cob—cut off the cooked kernels and toss them with butter and salt and pepper to taste (see Grilled Corn with Herbs and Lemon Butter, page 553, for another idea). Or cook fresh kernels with a pat of butter and a little water in a saucepan and season with salt and pepper. When you cut the kernels from the cob, always scrape the cob with the back of your knife to extract as much of the delicious corn "milk" as possible.

BEFORE COOKING
To serve 4, buy 4 to 8 ears of corn.

TO BOIL Fill a 5-quart pot three-quarters full with water (don't add salt, which would toughen the corn) and bring to a boil. Shuck the corn, add to the boiling water, and boil until crisp-tender, 3 to 4 minutes. Transfer to a platter.

TO MICROWAVE Arrange the corn, in its husks, in one layer in a microwave (no more than 4 ears at a time) and microwave on high, allowing 2 minutes per ear (4 minutes if cooking 2 ears, etc.), turning each ear over halfway through cooking. Cool the corn slightly, then shuck.

2 cups fresh bread crumbs, preferably from an 8-inch piece of day-old baguette (including crust)

½ cup chopped fresh basil

½ cup finely grated Parmigiano-Reggiano

¾ stick (6 tablespoons) unsalted butter, cut into small pieces

Arrange tomato slices in one layer on a rack set on a baking sheet. Sprinkle on both sides with 1 teaspoon salt and ½ teaspoon pepper (total) and let drain for 30 minutes to concentrate flavor.

Meanwhile, combine corn, milk, cream, and ¼ teaspoon salt in a 2- to 3-quart heavy saucepan and bring to a simmer over high heat, then reduce heat and simmer, partially covered, until corn is tender, about 5 minutes. Remove from heat and cool slightly, uncovered.

Put a rack in upper third of oven and preheat oven to 375°F. Butter a shallow 2-quart baking dish.

Toss together bread crumbs, basil, cheese, ¾ teaspoon salt, and ½ teaspoon pepper in a bowl.

Arrange one third of tomato slices in baking dish, cover evenly with one third of bread crumb mixture, and dot with one third of butter. Spoon half of corn mixture over crumbs, then repeat layering with half of remaining tomatoes, crumbs, and butter and all of corn. Arrange remaining tomatoes over corn, top with remaining bread crumbs, and dot with remaining butter.

Bake, uncovered, until top is golden and gratin is bubbling all over, 40 to 45 minutes. Cool on a rack for about 15 minutes before serving.

COOK'S NOTE

■ The gratin can be assembled up to 4 hours ahead and refrigerated, covered. Let stand at room temperature for 30 minutes before baking.

South American Corn Packets

SERVES 8 TO 12
ACTIVE TIME: 2 HOURS ■ START TO FINISH: 2¾ HOURS

■ *Humitas*, fresh corn tamales popular in Chile and other Latin American countries, are made using every part of the ears. The grated kernels create a sweet fill-ing, the husks are used to form and tie the packages, and the cobs make a shelf on which to steam the *humitas*. We like serving these with a real hands-on main course, such as saucy spareribs or barbecued chicken, or as a first course. ■

6–8 ears corn in the husk

1 bunch scallions

3 tablespoons unsalted butter

⅓ cup diced (⅓-inch) green or red bell pepper

1–2 teaspoons minced serrano chile, including seeds

¾ teaspoon salt

⅛ teaspoon ground cinnamon

⅓ cup whole milk

2 large eggs

Shuck corn, removing each husk individually, keeping them as intact as possible and cutting at base as necessary to release them. Reserve husks. You will need 20 to 25 of the widest husks for making *humitas* and about 12 more for making ribbons and lining steamer. Remove and discard silks. Stand a box grater in a pie plate or wide shallow bowl and, using largest holes, grate enough corn to measure 2 cups, including liquid. Reserve cobs for steaming *humitas*.

Using tongs, submerge husks in a wide 6- to 8-quart pot of boiling water, then turn off heat and leave husks in water until ready to use.

Mince white and pale green parts of scallions. Mince 2 tablespoons of darker scallion greens, keeping them separate.

Heat butter in a 10-inch heavy skillet over moderately high heat until foam subsides. Add bell pepper, chile (to taste), and white and pale green parts of scallions and cook, stirring with a wooden spatula, until softened and pale golden, 3 to 5 minutes. Stir in salt, cinnamon, and grated corn, including liquid, and bring to a simmer, then reduce heat to low.

Whisk together milk and eggs in a small bowl, stir into corn mixture, and cook over low heat, stirring constantly, until mixture begins to hold its shape and resembles very loose scrambled eggs, 3 to 5 minutes. Transfer mixture to a bowl set in a larger bowl of ice and cold water and cool to room temperature. Stir in minced scallion greens.

Make about 25 ribbons from narrowest husks by tearing them lengthwise into long ½-inch-wide strips.

Pat 4 or 5 wide husks dry and arrange cupped side up on a kitchen towel, with wider ends of husks nearest you. Put about 2 tablespoons of corn filling in middle of 1 husk (1). Fold long sides over to enclose filling (2). Fold bottom end up over filling (3). Fold top end down over bottom; narrow end may reach around to back of package Tie package closed with a corn husk ribbon (4). Repeat with remaining husks, filling, and ribbons, making 4 or 5 *humitas* at a time.

Lay reserved corncobs in bottom of a 6- to 8-quart heavy pot (do not pack together tightly), cutting some in half if necessary to make an even shelf on which to steam *humitas*. Add enough water to almost cover cobs and arrange some of remaining husks in a layer over cobs. Stand *humitas* upright on husks and cover with another layer of husks. Bring water to a boil, cover pot, and steam *humitas,* adding more water if necessary, until filling is firm and separates easily from husks when opened (test one), about 40 minutes.

COOK'S NOTE

■ The *humitas* can be assembled up to 4 hours ahead and refrigerated, covered.

Cucumber Noodles

SERVES 4
ACTIVE TIME: 25 MINUTES ■ START TO FINISH: 25 MINUTES

■ If you like playing with your food, you'll love these slithery noodles made from cucumbers. When they're blanched, the cucumber strips are a brilliant green. They lose a touch of color when they hit the hot butter, so it's important not to overcook them. The noodles make a surprising bed for shrimp, fish, or chicken. ■

HISTORY IN A HUSK

You may think of tamales as Mexican, but in fact they are also quintessentially South American. All incarnations represent a blend of Indian and Spanish cuisines. The indigenous people boiled or steamed food—ground corn, perhaps sweet potatoes and squash—in packages made of leaves or corn husks. After the conquest of South America, the Spanish began adding embellishments such as chicken, eggs, pork, and even olives and raisins. Tamales have many aliases. In the Andean countries, they're called *humitas* (pronounced "ooh-*mee*-tahs"), which means "steamers." Unlike Mexican tamales—which are usually made with dried corn husks and earthy, starchy masa (the dough made from ground dried corn that's the backbone of cooking in Mexico)—*humitas* are made with fresh husks, which impart a green flavor to the subtly spiced, custardy corn filling. Fresh husks are easy to work with, although they need to be soaked in boiling water to make them more pliable before using. Choose the largest, widest husks for wrapping and save the others for making the long strips you'll need for tying the *humitas*.

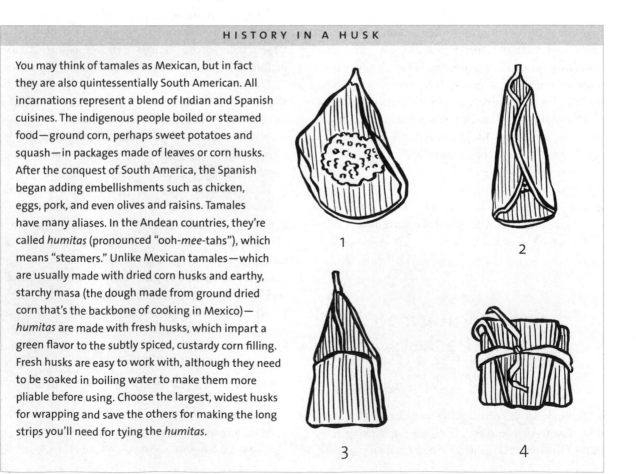

1

2

3

4

3 seedless cucumbers (usually plastic-wrapped),
   peeled
Salt
2 tablespoons unsalted butter
2 tablespoons finely chopped fresh mint
¼ teaspoon freshly ground black pepper
½ teaspoon finely grated lemon zest
1 teaspoon fresh lemon juice

SPECIAL EQUIPMENT: a mandoline or other adjustable-
   blade vegetable slicer with a ⅛-inch julienne blade

Adjust blade of slicer to ⅛-inch-wide setting. Using slicer, cut each cucumber lengthwise into long ⅛-inch-thick strips: slice until you reach seedy center, then rotate cucumber a quarter turn and continue slicing in same manner all around.

Blanch cucumber "noodles" in a 4-quart pot of boiling salted water (1 tablespoon salt) for 1 minute. Drain cucumbers in a colander and immerse colander in a large bowl of ice and cold water to stop the cooking. Drain again, transfer to a clean kitchen towel, and pat dry.

Heat butter in a 10-inch heavy skillet over moderate heat until foam subsides. Add cucumbers, mint, ½ teaspoon salt, pepper, zest, and lemon juice and cook, tossing to coat noodles, until just heated through, about 1 minute.

Braised Eggplant with Onion and Tomato

SERVES 6
ACTIVE TIME: 20 MINUTES ■ START TO FINISH: 1¾ HOURS

■ The Turkish dish *imam bayildi* translates as "swooning imam," but there are differing tales over what made the holy man faint. Some say that after eating this dish of tender stuffed eggplant, he collapsed in a delirium. Others contend that he passed out when he learned how much precious olive oil went into making it. Rest assured, this version of *imam bayildi* uses less oil than others, and your swooning will be due to ecstasy. In every bite, you can taste the Far Eastern, Central Asian, Iranian, Anatolian, and Mediterranean flavors that make up Turkish cuisine—each one reflecting a different stage in the country's complex history. ■

6 small Italian eggplants (2–2½ pounds total)
   Salt
¼ cup plus 3 tablespoons extra-virgin olive oil
2 medium onions, cut into ¼-inch-wide wedges
2 cups coarsely chopped ripe tomatoes (1½ pounds),
   with any juices, or 1 (28-ounce) can whole
   tomatoes in juice, drained, ¼ cup juice reserved,
   and coarsely chopped
⅓ cup chopped fresh flat-leaf parsley
⅓ cup chopped fresh basil
3 tablespoons fresh lemon juice
1 tablespoon plus 2 teaspoons sugar
⅓ cup water

Put a rack in middle of oven and preheat oven to 400°F.

Halve eggplants lengthwise. Score flesh ½ inch deep in a crosshatch pattern, making 1-inch squares (do not cut through skin). Arrange eggplant halves cut side up in a large roasting pan and sprinkle with 1 teaspoon salt.

Heat 3 tablespoons oil in a 12-inch skillet over moderate heat until hot but not smoking. Add onions and cook, stirring occasionally, until softened, about 10 minutes. Remove from heat and stir in tomatoes with juice, parsley, basil, lemon juice, 2 teaspoons sugar, and 1 teaspoon salt.

Divide onion mixture among eggplant halves, mounding it in center of each. Stir together water, remaining ¼ cup oil, and remaining tablespoon sugar until sugar is dissolved and add to roasting pan.

Cover pan tightly with foil and bake, basting eggplants every 15 minutes with cooking liquid, for 45 minutes. Uncover and bake until eggplants are tender (they will collapse and flatten slightly) and cooking liquid is reduced and beginning to caramelize, 30 to 40 minutes more.

Serve warm or at room temperature, drizzled with pan juices.

COOK'S NOTE
■ The dish can be made up to 1 day ahead. Cool, uncovered, then refrigerate, covered. Bring to room temperature before serving.

Marinated Eggplant with Mint

SERVES 4 TO 6
ACTIVE TIME: 30 MINUTES ■ START TO FINISH: 8¾ HOURS
(INCLUDES MARINATING)

■ Fried eggplant soaks up the flavors of this spirited marinade with red wine vinegar and mint. We love the tender slices as a side dish for grilled steak. Or consider serving as a make-ahead appetizer on crusty Italian bread spread with a mild fresh goat cheese. ■

1½ pounds small purple Italian or white eggplants (about 3), trimmed and cut lengthwise into ⅛-inch-thick slices
    Salt
5 tablespoons red wine vinegar
1 teaspoon sugar
1 garlic clove, thinly sliced
½ cup finely chopped fresh mint
⅔ cup extra-virgin olive oil

Toss eggplant with 1 teaspoon salt in a colander set over a bowl. Let drain for 30 minutes.

Rinse eggplant and drain well in colander, press-

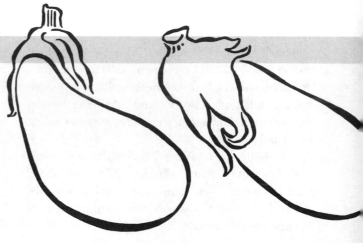

BEFORE COOKING To serve 4, buy 2 medium eggplants (about 12 ounces each).

TO ROAST Put a rack in the middle of the oven and preheat the oven to 400°F. Halve the eggplants lengthwise. Brush the cut sides with 2 tablespoons olive oil (total) and sprinkle with 1 teaspoon salt (total). Arrange the eggplants cut side up on a baking sheet and roast until very tender and browned, about 30 minutes.

TO BROIL Trim the eggplants and cut them into ½-inch-thick rounds. Arrange the rounds in one layer on two baking sheets, brush both sides with 3 to 4 tablespoons olive oil (total), and sprinkle with ½ teaspoon salt (total). Broil the rounds, one pan at a time, about 4 inches from the heat, moving the eggplant around in the pan as necessary for even browning and turning once, until browned and tender, about 9 minutes per batch.

EGGPLANT

Eggplants come in all shapes and sizes, from small green or white orbs to generous zaftig specimens to slender, graceful ones in shades of violet, ivory, and celadon. As for the glossy deep-purple-skinned variety that is easy to find in any supermarket, we prefer medium-sized eggplants, not whoppers, because they make such convenient serving sizes. Unfortunately, most eggplants' distinctive coloring cooks down to dun, but their silky texture and ability to soak up flavor more than make up for their appearance. Plus, they are remarkably versatile and equally at home with Mediterranean, Middle Eastern, Asian, and Indian seasonings and preparations.

For an easy weeknight side dish, roast or broil eggplant. Roasting is decidedly no-fuss, and the end result is wonderfully custardy; a bit of crumbled feta cheese, minced fresh flat-leaf parsley, and a spritz of lemon juice are good on top. Broiled eggplant is fast and so delicious that you'll be lucky if it makes it to the table without everyone nibbling on it. One of our favorite embellishments is to brush broiled eggplant during the last few minutes of cooking with a paste made of ¼ cup miso, 2 tablespoons rice vinegar (not seasoned), 1 tablespoon sugar, and 1 tablespoon water (if you brush it on too early, the sugars will burn before the eggplant fully cooks). Eggplant's sturdy texture also takes beautifully to grilling (see Grilled Eggplant with Yogurt Mint Sauce, page 553, and Grilled Eggplant with Spicy Peanut Sauce, page 554).

ing gently on eggplant to extract excess liquid, then pat dry.

Whisk together vinegar, sugar, and ¼ teaspoon salt in a small bowl until sugar and salt are dissolved. Stir in garlic and mint.

Heat oil in a 12-inch nonstick skillet over moderately high heat until hot but not smoking. Add eggplant, about 8 slices at a time, and fry until cooked through and pale golden, about 1 minute per side. Transfer eggplant to paper towels to drain, then transfer to a large shallow dish, overlapping slices slightly and spooning some of vinegar mixture over each batch.

Marinate eggplant, covered and refrigerated, for at least 8 hours. Bring to room temperature before serving, at least 30 minutes.

COOK'S NOTE

■ The eggplant can be marinated for up to 24 hours.

Braised Fennel

SERVES 4
ACTIVE TIME: 15 MINUTES ■ START TO FINISH: 25 MINUTES

■ Fennel's anise flavor fades somewhat when cooked, leaving just a whisper of licorice. That gentleness makes the braised vegetable a great accompaniment to almost any meat—pork, lamb, beef, or chicken—or fish. ■

  2 medium fennel bulbs with stalks and fronds
1½ tablespoons extra-virgin olive oil
  ¼ teaspoon salt
  ⅛ teaspoon freshly ground black pepper
  ½ cup Chicken Stock (page 153) or store-bought
     reduced-sodium broth
  ¼ cup water

Cut off stalks from fennel bulbs; reserve fronds and discard stalks. Chop enough fronds to make 1 tablespoon; discard remainder. Cut bulbs lengthwise into ½-inch-thick slices, leaving core intact.

Heat oil in a 12-inch heavy skillet over moderately

FENNEL

Sometimes mislabeled "anise" in the supermarket, fennel makes itself known by its compact round bulb, long stalks, feathery fronds—and its subtle yet distinct licorice-like aroma and flavor. In our opinion, roasting and braising bring out the best in fennel, softening its hearty crunch and playing up its sweetness. Raw fennel, cut into paper-thin slices, also works beautifully as a side-dish salad. Once dressed, it can be served immediately, but it will become more tender if allowed to sit for a while.

BEFORE COOKING To serve 4, buy 2 medium fennel bulbs (10 to 12 ounces each; look for fist-sized bulbs). Remove and discard stalks.

TO MAKE SHAVED FENNEL SALAD Quarter the fennel bulbs lengthwise, then, using a mandoline or other adjustable-blade slicer or a sharp knife, cut lengthwise into paper-thin slices. (Because the slices are so thin, there's no need to remove the core, and it helps hold the bulb together as you slice it.) Toss the fennel slices with 1 tablespoon lemon juice, 1 tablespoon olive oil, ½ teaspoon salt, and ¼ teaspoon black pepper.

TO ROAST OR BRAISE FENNEL See this page and page 600.

---

high heat until hot but not smoking. Add fennel slices and cook, turning once, until well browned, 3 to 4 minutes. Reduce heat to low, sprinkle fennel with salt and pepper, and add stock and water. Cook, covered, until fennel is tender, 10 to 12 minutes.

Sprinkle with chopped fennel fronds.

Roasted Fennel and Baby Carrots

SERVES 6
ACTIVE TIME: 15 MINUTES ■ START TO FINISH: 45 MINUTES

■ Don't confuse those supermarket bags of smooth orange nubs with true baby carrots; the packaged carrots are full-sized vegetables machine-cut to convenient snackable sizes. Real baby carrots, often sold with their plumed greens still attached, are simply cultivars that mature fully at a much smaller size. Because they don't store well, plan on using them soon after buying. This mix of roasted fennel and baby carrots—browned and caramelized in spots—is perfect alongside lamb. ■

> 6 bunches baby carrots, peeled and stems trimmed to ½ inch
> 2 medium fennel bulbs, stalks discarded, bulbs cut into ½-inch-thick wedges
> 3 tablespoons olive oil
> 3 tablespoons water
> 1 teaspoon fennel seeds
> ¾ teaspoon salt
> ¼ teaspoon freshly ground black pepper

Put a rack in middle of oven and preheat oven to 450°F.

Toss carrots and fennel with remaining ingredients on a large baking sheet and spread out in one layer.

Cover pan with foil and roast vegetables for 10 minutes. Uncover and roast, turning occasionally, until vegetables are tender and browned, about 20 minutes more.

Panfried Romaine

SERVES 8
ACTIVE TIME: 20 MINUTES ■ START TO FINISH: 50 MINUTES
(INCLUDES COOLING)

■ There is life beyond Caesar salad for romaine—and one bite of this dish will make you wonder why you never thought to cook it before. Briefly panfrying romaine

hearts in olive oil brings out their sweetness while preserving the crunch, an addictive combination. ■

> ¼ cup extra-virgin olive oil
> 6 hearts of romaine (two 18-ounce packages), trimmed and halved lengthwise
> Salt

Heat 1 tablespoon oil in a 12-inch heavy skillet over moderate heat until hot but not smoking. Add 3 romaine halves, cut side down, and sprinkle with a rounded ¼ teaspoon salt. Cook, turning once with tongs, until browned, about 2 minutes. Cover and cook until just crisp-tender, 2 to 3 minutes. Transfer to a platter.

Cook remaining romaine halves in oil in 3 batches in same manner and transfer to platter. Cool to room temperature before serving.

COOK'S NOTE
■ The romaine can be cooked up to 2 hours ahead and kept, loosely covered, at room temperature.

Braised Lacinato Kale with Pancetta and Caramelized Onions

SERVES 6
ACTIVE TIME: 1 HOUR ■ START TO FINISH: 2 HOURS

■ Cooking these greens covered with a round of parchment is the key to a truly tender result. Rich and meaty, they pair well with lighter main dishes, like chicken or fish. The leftovers make a delicious dinner all on their own: just have some crusty bread at the ready for mopping up the flavorful juices. This recipe comes from Jarrod Verbiak, the chef at Maison Boulud in Beijing. ■

> 2¼ pounds lacinato kale (also called Tuscan kale, *cavolo nero*, or dinosaur kale; 2–3 bunches), stems and center ribs discarded
> Salt
> 2 tablespoons extra-virgin olive oil

¼ pound sliced (¼-inch-thick) pancetta (Italian
   unsmoked bacon), cut into ¼-inch dice
2 fresh thyme sprigs
1 Turkish bay leaf or ½ California bay leaf
2 fresh flat-leaf parsley sprigs
2 large onions, finely chopped
1 head garlic, halved horizontally
   (left unpeeled)
½ stick (4 tablespoons) unsalted butter,
   cut into pieces
1¾ cups Chicken Stock (page 153) or store-bought
   reduced-sodium broth
¼ cup water
   Freshly ground black pepper

SPECIAL EQUIPMENT: parchment paper; kitchen string

Put a rack in middle of oven and preheat oven to
350°F.

Blanch kale in 2 batches in a 6- to 8-quart pot of
boiling salted water (2 tablespoons) for 2 minutes per
batch and transfer with tongs to a colander. Drain
well.

Heat oil in 5- to 6-quart pot over moderate heat
until warm. Add pancetta and cook, stirring frequently, until crisp, 10 to 15 minutes. Transfer pancetta with a slotted spoon to a plate; discard all but 3
tablespoons fat from pot.

Tie thyme, bay leaf, and parsley together with
kitchen string to make a bouquet garni and add to fat
in pot, along with onions and garlic. Cook over moderate heat, stirring frequently, until onions are golden
brown, about 20 minutes.

Return pancetta to pot, add butter, and cook, stirring occasionally, until melted. Stir in kale, stock, and
water, increase heat to high, and bring to a simmer.

Cover kale with a round of parchment paper,
transfer pot to oven, and braise, stirring once or
twice, until very tender, about 45 minutes.

Transfer pot to stovetop, discard parchment, and
boil, stirring occasionally, until almost all of liquid
has evaporated but kale is still moist, about 15 minutes. Discard bouquet garni and garlic and season
kale with salt and pepper.

COOK'S NOTE

■ The kale can be braised up to 1 day ahead. Cool, uncovered, then refrigerate, covered. Reheat before serving.

Sautéed Swiss Chard
with Onions

SERVES 4
ACTIVE TIME: 30 MINUTES ■ START TO FINISH: 50 MINUTES

■ Many recipes call for discarding chard stems and using only the broad leaves. That's a shame, because the
white stems (or fluorescent orange, yellow, and pink
ones if you get rainbow chard) are mellow and sweet.
Pairing the distinct textures and flavors of the leaves
and stems with sautéed onions makes for a multifac-
eted side dish with few ingredients. ■

1½ pounds Swiss chard (about 1 large bunch)
1 tablespoon olive oil
1 tablespoon unsalted butter
1 medium onion, halved lengthwise and thinly sliced
1 garlic clove, finely chopped
   Salt and freshly ground black pepper

Cut stems and center ribs from chard, discarding
any tough portions. Cut stems and ribs crosswise into
2-inch pieces. Stack chard leaves a few at a time, roll
up lengthwise into cylinders, and cut cylinders crosswise into 1-inch-wide pieces.

Heat oil and butter in a large heavy pot over medium heat until foam subsides. Add onion, garlic,
¼ teaspoon salt, and ⅛ teaspoon pepper and cook,
covered, stirring occasionally, until onion begins to
soften, about 8 minutes. Add chard stems and ribs, ¼
teaspoon salt, and ⅛ teaspoon pepper and cook, covered, stirring occasionally, until stems are just tender,
about 10 minutes.

Add chard leaves in batches, stirring and waiting until wilted before adding next batch, then cook,
covered, stirring occasionally, until tender, 4 to 6
minutes. Transfer with a slotted spoon to a serving
bowl.

COOK'S NOTES

■ The chard can be washed, dried, and cut up to 2 days
   ahead. Refrigerate wrapped in paper towels in a sealable plastic bag.
■ The chard can be cooked up to 4 hours ahead. Reheat
   over low heat or in a microwave oven.

CHARD

Greens

Although collard greens, kale, Swiss chard, beet greens, turnip greens, mustard greens, escarole, and dandelion greens all have their own particular look and taste, they can, with few exceptions, be prepared the same way. For instance, all greens are good cooked with garlic, bacon, and/or hot red pepper flakes, and very young, tender raw greens add a delicious bite to salads. Although we love the Southern tradition of long-cooked greens, we more often turn to the lighter, fresher taste of a quick sauté. Blanching the greens before sautéing has a couple of benefits. For one, greens such as mustard, escarole, and dandelion can have a bitter flavor that some people don't like (others love it); blanching helps reduce that bitterness. Also, blanching softens very sturdy greens such as collards and kale so that a quick sauté is all they need to finish cooking, and they'll still retain their color. Feel free to blanch and sauté different greens together for a dish with real character. Or try collard greens Miniera (opposite page), a Brazilian dish of thinly shredded collard greens quickly cooked in fat; the greens are crisp-tender and stay bright green.

   When shopping, look for fresh greens without any yellow spots or wilting. CHARD has shiny deep green leaves and tender flattish stems that, depending on the variety, can be white, red, orange, yellow, or pink. Both COLLARDS and KALE are a dull greenish gray, but collards have wide flat leaves, while kale has ruffled ones. LACINATO KALE, a favorite of ours, stands apart, with its long, crinkled, dark green leaves. ESCAROLE comes in large lettucelike heads and has thick flattish leaves that go from white at the base to green at the tips.

COLLARDS

KALE

ESCAROLE

DANDELION
LEAVES

DANDELION LEAVES are flat, narrow, and spiky; while they can grow to as long as 2 feet, shorter (younger) leaves will be more tender. Flat-leaved TURNIP GREENS have a spicy bite, but cooking tames their sharp assertiveness, as it does with ruffly bright green MUSTARD GREENS. If you are not sure if you have mustard greens, taste a small bit—the sharp radishlike flavor will let you know right away. Escarole and dandelion greens don't need their center ribs removed, but collards, kale, and mustard greens have particularly thick center ribs that should be cut out and discarded. BEET and chard stems, which are thick but tender, should be cut out, chopped into ½-inch pieces, and added to the pot 3 or 4 minutes before the leaves, so they can cook a little longer.

MUSTARD
GREENS

BEFORE COOKING To serve 4, for **chard, escarole, dandelion greens, turnip greens,** and **beet greens,** buy 1½ pounds of greens if you are planning to use the whole leaf. For **collards, kale,** and **mustard greens,** buy 2 pounds if the center ribs will be discarded. Wash the greens by swishing them gently in a large clean sink or bowl of cold water and letting any sand or silt drift to the bottom. Lift out the greens, being careful not to disturb sand at the bottom of the sink, and drain in a colander. (Slightly wilted greens can often be revived by soaking for 20 minutes in a large bowl of cool, not cold, water.)

TO BLANCH AND SAUTÉ Cut out the center ribs of **collards, kale,** and **mustard greens** and discard, then cut the leaves into 2-inch pieces. Cook in 2 batches in a large pot of boiling salted water (1 tablespoon salt per 6 quarts water), uncovered, for 2 minutes per batch (5 minutes per batch for **collards** and **kale**); transfer with a slotted spoon or tongs to a colander to drain. When they are cool enough to handle, squeeze the greens with your hands to remove the excess water. Heat 2 tablespoons olive oil in a large heavy skillet until it shimmers. Add 1 tablespoon minced garlic and cook, stirring, until fragrant, about 30 seconds. Add the greens and ¼ teaspoon salt and cook, stirring occasionally, until tender, 3 to 5 minutes. Season with salt and black pepper to taste.

TO MAKE COLLARD GREENS MINIERA Halve the leaves lengthwise and discard the center ribs. Stack the leaf halves a few at a time, roll lengthwise into a cigar shape, and cut crosswise into very thin slices (no wider than ⅛ inch) with a sharp knife. Chop 3 slices bacon and cook in a large nonstick skillet over moderate heat, stirring, until crisp. Add the collards, tossing to coat, and cook until just bright green, about 1 minute. Season with ¼ teaspoon salt and serve immediately.

Collard Greens and Turnips with Pepper Vinegar

SERVES 8 TO 10
ACTIVE TIME: 30 MINUTES ■ START TO FINISH: 2 HOURS

■ In England, collard greens are known as coleworts ("cabbage plant"). *Colewort* morphed to *collart* and eventually *collard* in the American South, where the popular vegetable is traditionally long-cooked with pork. Collards are also delicious with turnips, whose sweetness helps round out the greens' deep earthiness. With some pepper vinegar and a basket of corn bread on the side, you couldn't ask for anything more sustaining. ■

- 1 large ham hock (about 1½ pounds)
- 6 cups water
- 3 pounds collard greens
- 1½ pounds turnips, peeled if desired and cut into ½-inch cubes
- Salt
- ½ teaspoon freshly ground black pepper

ACCOMPANIMENT: Pepper Vinegar (recipe follows or see Cook's Note)

Combine ham hock and water in a 5- to 6-quart pot (water will not cover hock) and bring to a boil, then reduce heat and simmer, covered, turning hock halfway through cooking, for 1 hour.

Meanwhile, remove and discard stems and center ribs of collard greens. Cut leaves into 1-inch pieces.

Add half of collards to hock mixture and stir until wilted, then stir in remaining collards and simmer, partially covered, stirring occasionally, until collards are almost tender, about 35 minutes. Remove ham hock and cool slightly, then remove and coarsely chop meat. Discard bone and gristle.

Stir turnips into collard mixture and simmer, partially covered, stirring occasionally, until turnips are tender, 12 to 15 minutes.

Stir in ham and season mixture with salt and pepper. Using a slotted spoon, transfer to a bowl or plates. Serve with pepper vinegar.

COOK'S NOTES

■ The collards and turnips can be cooked up to 1 day ahead. Cool, uncovered, then refrigerate, covered. Reheat before serving.

■ Although there is no exact substitute for the pepper vinegar, you can use the liquid from a jar of store-bought pickled japaneños.

Pepper Vinegar

MAKES ABOUT 1¼ CUPS
ACTIVE TIME: 5 MINUTES ■ START TO FINISH: 3 WEEKS
(INCLUDES TIME FOR FLAVOR TO DEVELOP)

■ Pepper vinegar, the piquant liquid from pickled chiles, is a household staple in many parts of the South, used to liven up stews and vegetable dishes. Note that the vinegar needs to stand for at least 3 weeks for its flavor to develop. ■

- 6 ounces fresh red or green hot chiles, such as cayenne, serrano, or Thai, stems trimmed
- 1¼ cups distilled white vinegar
- ¼ teaspoon salt
- Pinch of cayenne

SPECIAL EQUIPMENT: a clear glass jar with a tight-fitting lid

Pat chiles dry and pack them into jar. Stir together remaining ingredients in a small bowl until salt is dissolved, then pour over chiles. Refrigerate pepper vinegar for at least 3 weeks before using.

COOK'S NOTE

■ The vinegar keeps, refrigerated, for up to 2 months.

Spicy Sautéed Dandelion Greens

SERVES 4
ACTIVE TIME: 30 MINUTES ■ START TO FINISH: 30 MINUTES

■ In Rome, cooks like to play up the natural verve of dandelion greens by sautéing them with garlic and hot pepper flakes. Although these greens can be found year-round in many places, they are at their most tender in the early spring. ■

 2 pounds dandelion greens, tough stems discarded,
    leaves cut crosswise into 4-inch pieces
    Salt
 ¼ cup extra-virgin olive oil
 2 large garlic cloves, smashed
 ½ teaspoon red pepper flakes

Cook greens in a 6- to 8-quart pot of boiling salted water (2 tablespoons salt) until ribs are tender, 4 to 5 minutes; drain in a colander. Rinse under cold water to stop the cooking and drain well, gently pressing out excess water.

Heat oil in a 12-inch heavy skillet over moderate heat until hot but not smoking. Add garlic and cook, stirring, until pale golden, about 30 seconds. Increase heat to moderately high, add greens, red pepper flakes, and ½ teaspoon salt, and cook, stirring, until liquid greens give off has evaporated, about 4 minutes.

COOK'S NOTE

■ If you are not able to find dandelion greens, escarole, broccoli rabe, or kale can be substituted. (You may need to cook the kale a little longer.)

Escarole with Pine Nuts

SERVES 4 TO 6
ACTIVE TIME: 20 MINUTES ■ START TO FINISH: 30 MINUTES

■ Think beyond the salad bowl: cooking escarole tempers its slight bitterness. Creamy pine nuts are a mellow complement. ■

 2 pounds escarole (about 2 heads), tough outer ribs
    discarded, leaves cut into 2-inch pieces
    Salt
 3 tablespoons extra-virgin olive oil
 3 tablespoons pine nuts
 3 large garlic cloves, finely chopped
 ⅛ teaspoon red pepper flakes
    Freshly ground black pepper

Wash escarole well in a sinkful of cold water, agitating it, then lift out and drain in a colander. Cook escarole in a 5- to 6-quart heavy pot of boiling salted water (1 tablespoon salt), uncovered, stirring occasionally, until tender, 5 to 10 minutes. Drain well in colander.

Dry pot, add oil, and heat over moderate heat until hot but not smoking. Add pine nuts and cook, stirring, until pale golden, about 1 minute. Add garlic and red pepper flakes and cook, stirring, until garlic and pine nuts are golden, 1 to 2 minutes.

Add escarole, stirring to coat with oil, increase heat to moderately high, and cook, stirring occasionally, until most of liquid has evaporated, 3 to 5 minutes. Season with salt and pepper to taste.

Smashed Roasted Jerusalem Artichokes

SERVES 4
ACTIVE TIME: 15 MINUTES ■ START TO FINISH: 1 HOUR

■ Jerusalem artichokes—small tubers with a sweet, nutty flavor faintly reminiscent of artichoke—belong to the sunflower family. Here they are roasted until softened, smashed, and roasted again. The insides stay moist, while the skin and irregular edges get browned and crisp, almost like potato skins. ■

1¼ pounds small to medium Jerusalem artichokes
       (sunchokes), scrubbed
 2 tablespoons extra-virgin olive oil
    Salt
½ teaspoon freshly ground black pepper

Put a rack in upper third of oven and preheat oven to 425°F.

Toss Jerusalem artichokes with oil, ¾ teaspoon salt, and pepper on a large baking sheet until coated, then spread out in one layer. Roast, turning occasionally, until just tender, about 30 minutes.

Flatten Jerusalem artichokes with a large heavy spatula or skillet to about ½ inch thick (use caution, since they contain hot juices). Continue roasting, turning once, until well browned, about 15 minutes more. Season with additional salt to taste.

Jicama and Watercress Stir-Fry

SERVES 4 TO 6
ACTIVE TIME: 30 MINUTES ■ START TO FINISH: 30 MINUTES

■ With a flavor and texture similar to water chestnuts, jicama is a natural addition to stir-fries; it soaks up the flavors of the sauce and stays crunchy even when cooked. In contrast, watercress is tender and has a peppy bite. Take care not to overcook it, or it will become stringy. ■

⅓ cup Chicken Stock (page 153) or store-bought
       reduced-sodium broth
 3 tablespoons Chinese rice wine, preferably Shaoxing,
       or medium-dry sherry

JERUSALEM ARTICHOKES

A member of the sunflower family, Jerusalem artichokes are sometimes labeled "sunchokes." These small knobby roots can resemble potatoes or, in their more gnarly guises, fresh ginger. Best in fall and winter, Jerusalem artichokes have a nutty, elusive flavor. They also have a reputation for being difficult to digest, so the adage "everything in moderation" is worth heeding here. Look for firm, light brown roots without any black spots. If possible, choose tubers that are of equal size, for even cooking, and relatively smooth; Jerusalem artichokes that are especially knobby or protuberant are difficult to clean and peel. Peeling makes a more refined dish (as you peel the tubers, drop them into lemon water to keep them from discoloring). Or leave the skins on for a more earthy flavor. We usually braise or roast Jerusalem artichokes, which plays up their unique texture and flavor. Peeled and sliced into rounds or matchsticks and tossed into salads, raw Jerusalem artichokes add a juicy crunch, similar to water chestnuts.

BEFORE COOKING Buy 1¼ pounds Jerusalem artichokes to serve 4 people. If leaving unpeeled, scrub carefully with a soft brush to remove dirt.

TO BRAISE Peel the artichokes if desired. Leave them whole if very small (¾ inch in diameter or less) or halve them lengthwise. Heat 1 tablespoon olive oil in a large heavy nonstick skillet over moderate heat. Add the Jerusalem artichokes cut side down and cook until golden on the first side, about 3 minutes. Add 1 cup chicken or vegetable stock, bring to a simmer, and simmer, covered, shaking the skillet occasionally, until the artichokes are very tender, about 20 minutes for peeled, up to 30 minutes for unpeeled, adding ¼ cup water at a time to the skillet if the stock evaporates too quickly. Uncover the skillet, season the artichokes with ½ teaspoon salt, and cook until any remaining liquid is almost evaporated. Toss with 1 tablespoon lemon juice if desired.

TO ROAST Put a rack in the middle of the oven and preheat the oven to 400°F. Peel the artichokes if desired. Leave them whole if very small (¾ inch in diameter or less) or halve them lengthwise. Toss them with 2 tablespoons olive oil and ½ teaspoon salt on a baking sheet, spread out in one layer, and roast, stirring occasionally, until very tender, 40 to 45 minutes.

2 tablespoons soy sauce

1½ teaspoons cornstarch

1 teaspoon sugar

⅛ teaspoon salt

2 tablespoons vegetable oil

¼ cup matchsticks peeled fresh ginger

1 tablespoon minced garlic

1 pound jicama, peeled and cut into matchsticks
¼ inch thick and 1 inch long

¾ pound watercress (about 2 bunches), tough stems
discarded, cut into 2-inch pieces

1 teaspoon Asian sesame oil

2 tablespoons sesame seeds, toasted (see Tips, page
911)

Whisk together stock, rice wine, soy sauce, cornstarch, sugar, and salt in a small bowl or measuring cup until sugar and salt are dissolved.

Heat a well-seasoned 14-inch flat-bottomed wok or a 12-inch heavy skillet over high heat until a drop of water evaporates on contact. Add vegetable oil, swirling to coat. Add ginger and stir-fry until crisp and golden, about 30 seconds. Stir in garlic, add jicama, and stir-fry until crisp-tender, about 3 minutes. Add watercress and stir-fry until just wilted, about 1 minute. Whisk sauce again, add to wok, and cook, tossing, until vegetables are coated and sauce is slightly thickened, 1 to 2 minutes. Stir in sesame oil.

Serve sprinkled with sesame seeds.

Roasted Kohlrabi and Butternut Squash

SERVES 4
ACTIVE TIME: 20 MINUTES ■ START TO FINISH: 1 HOUR

■ Shaped a bit like a UFO, with sturdy stems branching out from a pale green or deep purple orb, kohlrabi is an odd-looking vegetable. Sometimes those stems end in abundant collardlike leaves and sometimes they have been lopped off. The skin is easily peeled to reveal crisp, snow-white flesh that has a faintly turnipy bite. Cut into cubes and roasted, kohlrabi becomes sweeter and its texture more velvety. We add the squash to the baking sheet after the kohlrabi has roasted for 15 min-

utes, rather than tossing them together, so the vegetables' shapes and flavors stay distinct. ■

4 medium kohlrabi (2¼ pounds with greens; 1¾
pounds without greens), trimmed, peeled, and cut
into ¾-inch pieces

2 tablespoons extra-virgin olive oil

2 teaspoons finely chopped fresh thyme
Salt and freshly ground black pepper

2½ pounds butternut squash, peeled, halved
lengthwise, seeded, and cut into ¾-inch
pieces

SPECIAL EQUIPMENT: a 17-by-12-inch heavy baking sheet

Put a rack just below middle of oven and put baking sheet on rack. Preheat oven to 450°F.

Toss kohlrabi with 1 tablespoon oil, 1 teaspoon thyme, ¼ teaspoon salt, and ⅛ teaspoon pepper in a bowl. Transfer to preheated baking sheet and roast for 15 minutes (set bowl aside).

Toss squash with remaining 1 tablespoon oil, 1 teaspoon thyme, ¼ teaspoon salt, and ⅛ teaspoon pepper in same bowl.

Stir kohlrabi, turning it, and push it to one end of pan. Add squash to opposite end of pan. Roast, stirring and turning squash halfway through roasting, until vegetables are tender and lightly browned, about 30 minutes longer.

Toss vegetables to combine.

COOK'S NOTE

■ The kohlrabi and butternut squash can be cut up to
1 day ahead and refrigerated in separate sealable
plastic bags.

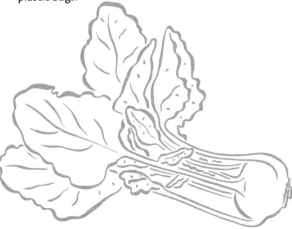

LEEKS

Often considered an ingredient rather than vegetables in their own right, leeks deserve more attention.

When halved lengthwise and braised or roasted, the results are downright sumptuous. Braising produces glossy, meltingly tender leeks, and using chicken or vegetable stock rather than water means even richer flavor. Roasting takes leeks to a meatier place, caramelizing their sweetness and crisping their edges a gorgeous golden brown; we like to serve them with steak in place of onion rings. Both braised and roasted leeks are delicious plain, but if you have a few extra minutes, sprinkle them with some fresh bread crumbs toasted in butter. You could even roast leeks earlier in the day and then serve them at room temperature with a drizzle of sprightly vinaigrette.

When buying leeks, choose ones with long stalks rather than a multitude of long green leaves (which are too tough and fibrous to eat). If the leaves cover much of the stalk, squeeze gently—if you can feel a thick stalk beneath the leaves, you will get a better yield. (Save the discarded green leaves to add to stock.) Thin and fat leeks are both delicious, but the fatter the leek, the longer it will take to cook. All leeks have sand between their layers—it can lurk in the bottom as well as high up in the leaves—so take washing very seriously. If you are chopping them for a dish, such as the Leek and Mushroom Gratin (opposite page), it's easiest to chop and then wash in large bowl of cold water; swish them around so the sand drifts to the bottom of the bowl, lift out, and drain in a colander (repeat if your leeks are particularly dirty). For braised and roasted leeks, see washing directions below.

BEFORE COOKING To serve 4, buy 1½ pounds leeks of uniform size. Or, if the leeks you find have lots of long dark-green leaves that will be discarded, buy 2 pounds. Trim the roots, keeping the ends of the leeks intact, and cut off the dark green parts. Peel off and discard the tough outer layers, then cut the leeks lengthwise in half. Wash the halves under running water, fanning the leaves to help remove sand and taking care to sluice water between each and every leaf near the root end, then swish them in a large bowl of water (or a half-filled sink) and let soak for a few minutes. Repeat with a bowl of fresh water. Lift the leeks from the water, being careful not to disturb any sand at the bottom of the bowl, and drain the leeks in a colander.

TO BRAISE Heat 2 tablespoons unsalted butter or olive oil in a large skillet over moderate heat until hot but not smoking. Add the leek halves and cook, turning occasionally, until golden brown, about 5 minutes. Add 1 cup chicken or vegetable stock to the skillet and simmer, covered, until the leeks are very tender, about 20 minutes. Remove the cover and cook until most of the liquid has evaporated but the leeks are still moist. Season with salt.

TO ROAST Put a rack in the middle of the oven and preheat the oven to 400°F. Combine the leek halves, ¼ cup olive oil, and ¼ teaspoon salt in a large roasting pan and toss to coat. Roast the leeks, turning them after 20 minutes, until very tender, 35 to 45 minutes.

Leek and Mushroom Gratin

SERVES 6
ACTIVE TIME: 40 MINUTES ■ START TO FINISH: 1 HOUR

■ This rich gratin employs one of our favorite techniques: the leeks are cooked in a skillet covered not with a lid but with a round of parchment paper placed directly on the vegetables. This low-tech method allows just enough steam to escape while keeping the vegetables perfectly moist. A bit of lemon zest helps balance the gratin's richness. This is delicious with roast chicken, squab, or pork chops. ■

¾ stick (6 tablespoons) unsalted butter
1 cup fine dry bread crumbs
¼ pound Gruyère, finely grated on small teardrop-shaped holes of a box grater (about 2 cups)
½ cup finely grated Parmigiano-Reggiano
2 teaspoons finely chopped garlic
1 tablespoon finely chopped fresh flat-leaf parsley
  Salt and freshly ground black pepper
3 pounds leeks, root ends trimmed
2 tablespoons all-purpose flour
1½ cups Chicken Stock (page 153) or store-bought reduced-sodium broth
⅛ teaspoon freshly grated nutmeg
½ teaspoon finely grated lemon zest
1 pound cremini mushrooms, trimmed and thinly sliced

SPECIAL EQUIPMENT: a 1½-quart gratin dish or shallow baking dish; parchment paper

Melt 2 tablespoons butter in a small saucepan over low heat; cool.

Toss melted butter with bread crumbs, cheeses, garlic, parsley, ¼ teaspoon salt, and ⅛ teaspoon pepper in a bowl until combined.

Trim each leek to an 8-inch length (reserve tops for another use if desired). Halve leeks lengthwise and cut crosswise into roughly 1-inch pieces. Wash leek pieces in a large bowl of cold water, agitating them, then lift out and transfer to another bowl. Repeat with fresh water and drain leeks well.

Melt 1 tablespoon butter in a 1- to 1½-quart heavy saucepan over moderate heat. Add flour and cook, whisking, for 1 minute to make a roux. Add stock in a slow stream, whisking, and bring to a boil, whisking. Add nutmeg and zest and boil, whisking, for 1 minute. Remove from heat.

Put a rack in middle of oven and preheat oven to 400°F. Butter gratin dish.

Melt 1 tablespoon butter in a 12-inch heavy skillet over moderately low heat. Add leeks, ¼ teaspoon salt, and ¼ teaspoon pepper, cover leeks directly with a round of parchment paper, and cook, stirring occasionally, until liquid is absorbed and leeks are tender and just beginning to brown, 10 to 15 minutes.

Meanwhile, heat remaining 2 tablespoons butter in a large heavy skillet over moderate heat until foam subsides. Add mushrooms, ¼ teaspoon salt, and ¼ teaspoon pepper and cook, stirring occasionally, until liquid is absorbed and mushrooms are just beginning to brown, about 15 minutes. Remove from heat.

Remove parchment from leeks and stir in mushrooms. Transfer mixture to gratin dish, spreading it evenly. Pour sauce over vegetables and top with crumb mixture. Bake until gratin is bubbling and topping is golden, about 15 minutes.

COOK'S NOTE
■ The gratin can be assembled, without the bread crumbs, up to 8 hours ahead. Cool, uncovered, then refrigerate, covered. Bring to room temperature, stir, and top with the bread crumbs before baking.

Greek-Style Lima Beans

SERVES 4
ACTIVE TIME: 10 MINUTES ■ START TO FINISH: 30 MINUTES

■ Europeans first tasted lima beans in Lima, Peru—hence their name. This preparation takes the creamy, pale green beans in a Mediterranean direction, and it couldn't be easier. Serve with bread to soak up the juices. ■

1 (10-ounce) package frozen baby lima beans
1 cup water
3 tablespoons extra-virgin olive oil
2 tablespoons chopped fresh flat-leaf parsley
1 tablespoon minced garlic
Salt and freshly ground black pepper

Combine lima beans, water, 2 tablespoons oil, 1 tablespoon parsley, garlic, and ½ teaspoon salt in a 2-quart heavy saucepan, bring to a brisk simmer, and cook over moderate heat, tightly covered, stirring occasionally, until beans are tender, 17 to 20 minutes. Season with salt and pepper.

Serve sprinkled with remaining tablespoon parsley and drizzled with remaining tablespoon oil.

Baby Lima Beans and Corn in Chive Cream

SERVES 6 TO 8
ACTIVE TIME: 15 MINUTES ■ START TO FINISH: 30 MINUTES

■ Fresh lima beans are hard to come by, and so we happily turn to frozen baby limas to get our fix—the quality is very good. Pairing the limas and frozen corn with chive cream produces an elegant succotash. ■

4 bacon slices, cut crosswise into ½-inch-wide pieces
1 medium onion, chopped
1 green bell pepper, cored, seeded, and cut into ½-inch dice
1 (10-ounce) package frozen baby lima beans
1 (10-ounce) package frozen corn kernels
1 cup water
  Salt
¼ teaspoon freshly ground black pepper
½ cup heavy cream
2 tablespoons chopped fresh chives
1 tablespoon chopped fresh flat-leaf parsley

Cook bacon in a 10-inch heavy skillet over moderate heat, stirring occasionally, until crisp. Transfer with a slotted spoon to paper towels to drain.

Cook onion and bell pepper in fat remaining in skillet, stirring frequently, until vegetables are softened, 5 to 6 minutes. Add lima beans, corn, water, ½ teaspoon salt, and pepper, bring to a simmer, and simmer, covered, for 8 minutes. Increase heat to high, add cream, and bring to a boil. Boil, uncovered, until liquid is reduced by half, 7 to 10 minutes.

Stir in herbs and salt to taste and serve sprinkled with bacon.

Fried Cornmeal-Coated Okra

SERVES 6
ACTIVE TIME: 40 MINUTES ■ START TO FINISH: 40 MINUTES

■ These irresistible okra nubbins are as much fun to eat as popcorn—we'd be in heaven if our local movie theater served them. We're also happy eating them with any kind of barbecued dish. ■

2 pounds okra, cut into ¼-inch-thick slices, tips and stems discarded
½ cup yellow cornmeal (not coarse)
½ teaspoon salt
¼ teaspoon cayenne
5–6 cups vegetable oil for deep-frying
SPECIAL EQUIPMENT: a deep-fat thermometer

Toss okra with cornmeal in a large bowl. Transfer, in batches if necessary, to a sieve and shake off excess cornmeal, then put on a plate. Toss together salt and cayenne in a small bowl.

Heat 1 inch oil in a deep 12-inch heavy skillet until thermometer registers 375°F. Fry okra in 4 or 5 batches, stirring occasionally, until golden, 3 to 4 minutes per batch; transfer with a slotted spoon to paper towels to drain and sprinkle with salt mixture to taste. (Return oil to 375°F between batches.)

OKRA

Emblematic of Southern cooking, where it is a vital component of gumbo, okra was brought here by African slaves; it also has been eaten for centuries in Arabia, Asia, and India. Much has been made of the fact that okra oozes a clear, viscous liquid, but that sliminess doesn't bother people who grew up with it and who use okra to thicken soups and stews (like gumbo). If you leave the okra whole and don't trim off the little caps, the ooze factor won't be much of an issue in any case. When we're not making gumbo, we love okra roasted (on top of the stove or in the oven) and grilled (see Grilled Spiced Okra, page 555). Both methods render the pods sweet, mellow, and very tender. Okra is positively addictive when pickled or fried. Though we are perfectly happy to eat cooked okra plain, it pairs well with acidic ingredients like tomato (see the braised version below), lemon, or vinegar. When shopping, choose small unblemished pods—the smaller the better, as larger ones tend to be seedy and tough, with fibrous strings running their length.

BEFORE COOKING If braising, buy 1 pound small okra (3 to 4 inches long) to serve 4. Buy 1¼ pounds to serve 4 if pan-roasting or oven-roasting. Rinse to remove any dirt and drain well in a colander. Trim the stems flush with the tops of the caps, being careful not to cut into the pods.

TO PAN-ROAST Heat a 10-inch cast-iron skillet over moderately high heat until hot but not smoking. Add 2 tablespoons olive oil and tilt to coat the bottom. Add the okra and ½ teaspoon salt and cook, covered, shaking the skillet occasionally, until well browned, about 5 minutes. Turn the okra, reduce the heat to moderately low, and cook, covered, gently stirring occasionally, until tender and browned all over, 10 to 15 minutes more. The okra will have shrunk somewhat, and any liquid in the pan should have evaporated.

TO OVEN-ROAST Put a rack in the middle of the oven and preheat the oven to 450°F. Stir together 2 tablespoons olive oil, 1½ teaspoons dried oregano, crumbled,

¼ teaspoon salt, and ⅛ teaspoon black pepper in a bowl, add the okra, and toss to coat. Transfer the okra to a large baking sheet and roast, shaking the pan occasionally, until tender, 10 to 15 minutes.

TO BRAISE Pulse 2 garlic cloves, coarsely chopped, and one 2-by-1½-inch piece peeled fresh ginger, coarsely chopped, in a food processor until finely chopped. Transfer to a large heavy skillet (don't wash the processor bowl), add 2 tablespoons vegetable oil and ¼ teaspoon red pepper flakes, and cook over moderate heat, stirring, until fragrant, about 1 minute. Pulse 2 large tomatoes, cored and quartered, with ¾ teaspoon salt and ¼ teaspoon black pepper in the processor until coarsely chopped, then stir into the garlic mixture. Cook, uncovered, stirring occasionally, until slightly thickened, about 10 minutes. Stir the okra into the sauce and simmer, covered, until just tender, about 10 minutes.

ONIONS

Onions play a crucial supporting role in so many recipes, helping to form a flavor base for soups, sauces, and stews. Rarely do we think to use them on their own and let their sweetness shine. Onion rings are, of course, the most notable exception, lightly breaded and fried until crisp and golden brown. Tiny pearl onions bathed in a rich cream sauce flavored with bay leaf and nutmeg are too good to serve only at Thanksgiving or Christmas—pair them with braised meat and roasted poultry throughout the year. And onion wedges roast beautifully. A mix of red and yellow onions tossed with a flavorful vinaigrette, cooked in a hot oven, and finished with a bit more dressing and herbs makes a perfect side dish for grilled or roasted meats. Cooled, the roasted onions are a great topping for mixed greens, especially when combined with grilled chicken and crumbled blue or goat cheese. They are also delicious alongside aged cheddar, apple or pear slices, and toasted bread.

BEFORE COOKING For onion rings, buy 1 very large onion, about 1 pound, to serve 4. For creamed onions, buy 1 pound pearl onions to serve 4. For roasted onions, buy 1½ pounds small to medium red and yellow onions (2 or 3 of each) to serve 4.

TO MAKE ONION RINGS Peel 1 very large onion and cut it crosswise into ¼-inch-thick slices. Separate the slices into rings. Heat 1 inch vegetable oil in a 5-quart pot over medium-high heat until it registers 360°F on a deep-fat thermometer. Meanwhile, stir together ⅔ cup flour, ½ teaspoon baking powder, and ½ teaspoon salt in a bowl. Whisk together 1 egg and 1 cup whole milk in another bowl. Spread 1 cup fine dry bread crumbs on a plate. Coat the rings in batches of 4: Dredge them in the flour mixture, shaking off the excess, dip them in the egg mixture, letting the excess drip off, then dredge them in the crumbs, shaking off the excess; transfer to sheets of wax paper. Fry the rings in batches of 4 to 6, without crowding, turning them once or twice, until golden brown, about 3 minutes per batch. Transfer the rings to paper towels to drain. (The onion rings can be made up to 1 week ahead and frozen. Once cooled, transfer them to wax-paper-lined baking sheets and freeze until firm, about 10 minutes, then put in a large sealable bag and freeze. Reheat the frozen rings on a large baking sheet in a preheated 425°F oven for about 8 minutes.)

TO MAKE
CREAMED ONIONS
To make peeling them easier, blanch the pearl onions in a saucepan of boiling salted water for 2 minutes, then transfer with a slotted spoon to a bowl of ice water; keep the cooking water hot. Peel the onions, leaving the root ends intact so the onions hold together. Return the water to a boil, add the onions, and simmer until tender, 8 to 12 minutes, depending upon size. Drain the onions, reserving about ⅓ cup of the cooking liquid. Melt 2 tablespoons unsalted butter with 1 bay leaf in a small heavy saucepan over moderately low heat. Whisk in 2 tablespoons flour and cook, whisking, for 3 minutes to make a roux. Pour in 1 cup whole milk (or ¾ cup milk and ¼ cup heavy cream), ½ teaspoon salt, ¼ teaspoon black pepper, and a pinch of freshly grated nutmeg. Bring the sauce to a boil, whisking, then reduce the heat and simmer, whisking, for 2 minutes. Add the onions and thin the sauce to the desired consistency with the reserved cooking liquid. Discard the bay leaf and stir in 2 tablespoons finely chopped fresh flat-leaf parsley and salt and pepper to taste.

TO ROAST Put a rack in the middle of the oven and preheat the oven to 400°F. Peel the red and yellow onions, leaving the root ends intact, and cut each into 6 wedges (if small onions) or 8 wedges (if larger onions). Whisk together 2 tablespoons balsamic vinegar, sherry vinegar, or fresh lemon juice, 1 teaspoon Dijon mustard, 1 large garlic clove, minced, 1 teaspoon salt, and ½ teaspoon black pepper in a small bowl. Add ¼ cup olive oil in a stream, whisking, and whisk the dressing until well combined. Toss the onion wedges with half of the dressing on a large baking sheet, spread them out in one layer, and roast, stirring occasionally, until golden and tender, 30 to 40 minutes. Transfer the onions to a bowl and toss with the remaining dressing and, if desired, 1 to 2 tablespoons chopped fresh flat-leaf parsley.

Balsamic-Roasted Onions

SERVES 6
ACTIVE TIME: 15 MINUTES ■ START TO FINISH: 1¾ HOURS

■ This nuanced dish elevates the humble yellow onion from its usual role as a behind-the-scenes workhorse. Halved and roasted with balsamic vinegar, cloves, and bay leaf until they become tender, these beauties are fabulous with steak. ■

    6 medium onions (2½ pounds)
    3 whole cloves
    1 Turkish bay leaf or ½ California bay leaf
    ⅔ cup balsamic vinegar
    2 tablespoons water
    1 teaspoon salt
    ¼ teaspoon freshly ground black pepper
    3 tablespoons olive oil

Put a rack in middle of oven and preheat oven to 375°F.

Trim ½ inch from top and bottom of each onion, then peel and halve crosswise. Arrange onions cut side down in one layer in 3-quart shallow glass or ceramic baking dish. Remove a layer from some of onions if necessary to fit them into dish. Add cloves and bay leaf.

Whisk together remaining ingredients until combined and pour over onions.

Cover dish with foil and roast for 30 minutes.

Remove foil, discard bay leaf, and roast, uncovered, for 30 minutes. Turn onions over and roast until very tender and liquid is reduced to a syrup, 20 to 25 minutes more. Discard cloves.

Serve warm or at room temperature.

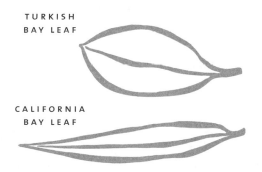

TURKISH
BAY LEAF

CALIFORNIA
BAY LEAF

Molasses-Baked Onions

SERVES 8
ACTIVE TIME: 30 MINUTES ■ START TO FINISH: 3½ HOURS

■ Rich and sweet, these onions are adapted from Angela Shelf Medearis's recipe for Honey-Baked Onions in *The African-American Kitchen*. With a flavor reminiscent of New England baked beans, they're great with ham, roast pork, or broiled chicken. ■

    4 large sweet onions, such as Vidalia, Walla Walla, or Oso Sweet (3–4 pounds total), peeled, trimmed, leaving root ends intact, and halved lengthwise
    1½ cups tomato juice
    1½ cups water
    2 tablespoons unsalted butter
    2 tablespoons molasses (not robust)
    ½ teaspoon salt, or to taste
    8 bacon slices, halved crosswise

Put a rack in middle of oven and preheat oven to 400°F.

Arrange onion halves cut side up in one layer in a 13-by-9-inch glass baking dish or other 2½-quart shallow baking dish.

Combine tomato juice, water, butter, molasses, and salt in a 2-quart heavy saucepan and bring to a boil, stirring occasionally. Pour over onions.

Bake onions, uncovered, basting with pan juices every 30 minutes, until tender, about 2 hours.

Lay 2 pieces of bacon side by side over each onion half and continue to bake, basting onions once with juices after 30 minutes, until onions are very tender, bacon is browned, and juices are thickened, about 1 hour more.

COOK'S NOTE
■ The onions can be baked up to 1 day ahead. Cool, uncovered, then refrigerate, covered. Reheat, covered with foil, in a 350°F oven for 20 to 30 minutes.

Parsnips

Resembling a large cream-colored carrot, the underappreciated parsnip has a buttery, slightly nutty flavor that shines no matter what the preparation—steamed, boiled, glazed, roasted, or blended to an almost fluffy puree. Look for firm, unblemished, medium-sized parsnips with smooth skin. Avoid very large specimens (their inner cores are usually woody), as well as any that are flabby or split, which are signs of age and developing bitterness. Embellishments can be as simple as butter and salt, a bit of sugar for glazing, or fresh or crumbled dried rosemary added before roasting. Try sprinkling grated aged Gruyère over plain roasted parsnips and returning them to the oven for a quick melt. A grating of fresh nutmeg works well in pureed parsnips, as does a hint of curry powder. For brighter color and flavor, we like to substitute carrots for half the amount of parsnips when steaming or boiling. Sometimes we even cook a chopped apple or pear along with the parsnips and puree them together for added sweetness.

BEFORE COOKING Buy 1½ pounds medium parsnips for 4 people. Peel, then cut them in half where the thinner bottom meets the wider top portion. Halve or quarter the top portions (removing any woody cores) to ensure pieces of uniform size and thickness.

TO STEAM Prepare the parsnips as above and cut crosswise into ½-inch-thick pieces. Add enough water to reach the bottom of a collapsible steamer set in a 3- to 4-quart saucepan and bring to a boil. Steam the parsnips over boiling water, covered, until tender, 7 to 10 minutes. Toss with 2 tablespoons melted (or browned) unsalted butter and salt and black pepper to taste. Sprinkle with chopped fresh flat-leaf parsley or chives if desired.

TO PUREE Steam the parsnips as above until very tender, 10 to 15 minutes. Transfer to a food processor, add 2 tablespoons unsalted butter, about ½ cup whole milk, half-and-half, or heavy cream, and salt and black pepper to taste, and puree until very smooth.

TO BRAISE AND GLAZE Prepare the parsnips as above and cut crosswise into ½-inch-thick pieces. Melt 2 tablespoons unsalted butter in a 3- to 4-quart heavy saucepan. Add the parsnips, 1 cup chicken stock or water, 1 teaspoon sugar, ½ teaspoon salt, and ¼ teaspoon black pepper. Bring to a boil, then reduce the heat and simmer, covered, until tender, 7 to 10 minutes. Transfer the parsnips to a bowl with a slotted spoon, then boil the remaining cooking liquid until it is reduced to a glaze of 3 to 4 tablespoons. Return the parsnips to the saucepan and heat until just heated through. Season with salt and pepper and sprinkle with chopped fresh flat-leaf parsley.

TO ROAST Put a rack in the middle of the oven and preheat the oven to 425°F. Prepare the parsnips as above and cut the thinner bottom portions into 2-inch pieces. Cut the top portions into 2-inch pieces. Toss with 2 tablespoons olive oil, ¾ teaspoon salt, and ¼ teaspoon black pepper on a large baking sheet until well coated and spread out in one layer. Roast, stirring every 10 to 15 minutes, until tender and golden, 20 to 30 minutes.

Balsamic-Glazed Parsnips

SERVES 8
ACTIVE TIME: 20 MINUTES ■ START TO FINISH: 40 MINUTES

■ The complex acidity of balsamic vinegar makes a great match for parsnips. In this easy *agrodolce*, or sweet-and-sour dish, the parsnips become caramelized and infused with an intriguing sweetness. ■

  1 tablespoon sugar
  2 tablespoons unsalted butter
  2 pounds parsnips, peeled, cored (see opposite page), and cut crosswise into ¼-inch pieces
  ¼ cup balsamic vinegar
  ½ cup water
  ¾ teaspoon salt
  ¼ teaspoon freshly ground black pepper

Put sugar in center of a 12-inch heavy skillet and heat over medium heat until it starts to melt, then cook, tilting skillet occasionally so it melts and caramelizes evenly, until it is a golden brown caramel. Stir in butter, add parsnips, and cook, stirring, for 2 minutes. Add remaining ingredients, reduce heat to low, and simmer, covered, until parsnips are just tender, 10 to 15 minutes.

Remove lid and simmer, stirring occasionally, until liquid is reduced to a glaze and parsnips are caramelized, about 5 minutes. Serve warm or at room temperature.

COOK'S NOTE
■ The parsnips can be cut up to 1 day ahead and refrigerated in a sealable plastic bag.

Parsnip-Leek-Potato Mash

SERVES 6
ACTIVE TIME: 20 MINUTES ■ START TO FINISH: 50 MINUTES

■ The haunting sweetness of parsnips adds a hint of complexity to a coarse mash of potatoes and leeks. This dish is a great alternative to plain old mashed spuds. ■

  5 tablespoons unsalted butter
  1½ pounds leeks (white and pale green parts only), chopped, washed well, and patted dry
  2 pounds parsnips, peeled, cored (see opposite page), and cut crosswise into ½-inch pieces
  1 pound russet (baking) potatoes, peeled and cut into 1-inch pieces
  2 cups water
  1½ teaspoons salt
  ¼ teaspoon freshly ground white pepper
  ⅛ teaspoon freshly grated nutmeg
  1 tablespoon finely chopped fresh flat-leaf parsley

Melt 4 tablespoons butter in a 4- to 5-quart heavy pot over moderate heat. Add leeks and cook, stirring occasionally, until slightly softened, 5 to 7 minutes.

Add parsnips, potatoes, water, salt, white pepper, and nutmeg to leeks and bring to a boil, stirring occasionally. Reduce heat and simmer, covered, stirring occasionally, until vegetables are very tender and most of liquid is absorbed, about 30 minutes.

Coarsely mash potatoes and parsnips with a potato masher and transfer to a serving bowl. Sprinkle with parsley and top with remaining tablespoon butter.

COOK'S NOTE
■ The mash can be made up to 1 day ahead and refrigerated, covered. Reheat in a heavy saucepan over low heat, stirring to prevent scorching; serve sprinkled with the parsley and topped with the remaining tablespoon butter.

Three Pea Stir-Fry

SERVES 4
ACTIVE TIME: 30 MINUTES ■ START TO FINISH: 30 MINUTES

■ This unusual stir-fry showcases the crisp succulence of sugar snaps, the tender bite of snow peas, and the sweet pop of green peas. Frozen green peas are superior to most fresh ones, which are usually starchy by the time they reach the supermarket. ■

PEAS

One of spring's earliest crops, peas are a harbinger of all the good things to come from the farm stand. The best way to enjoy shell peas, bar none, is to eat them out of hand from your own garden. Unfortunately, their delectable crunchy sweetness quickly converts to starch after harvesting, so always look for peas that are as fresh as possible, with crisp pale green pods that are full but not bulging (peas that are too big often signify starchiness). Because good shell peas are so elusive, we most often turn to frozen, which we love for their ease and consistent good flavor. Frozen peas have been blanched prior to freezing, but they still need a bit of cooking (though not as much as the package recommends). Happily, snow peas and sugar snaps retain their sweetness a bit longer than shell peas and are easier to prepare, since they are eaten pod and all.

Peas are incredibly versatile. Shell peas are delicious raw in a salad of butter lettuce and thin-sliced radishes, while sliced raw snow peas or sugar snaps add a fresh crispness to rice or grain salads. All peas are tasty sautéed in a little butter and water, then tossed with chopped fresh herbs or scallions and a sprinkling of salt, or added to a stir-fry during the last few minutes. Fresh and frozen shell peas make an excellent addition to hot or cold soups, and we also love them sautéed quickly with shredded lettuce; see below.

BEFORE COOKING Buy 1 pound of snow peas or sugar snaps to serve 4. You'll get slightly less than 1 cup of shelled peas per pound in the pod, so plan on 2 pounds of shell peas to serve 4; a 10-ounce package of frozen peas serves 4. String snow peas or sugar snaps by snapping the stem end without breaking it off, then pulling toward the blossom of the pea. If the peas are large, repeat on the outer side. For shell peas in the pod, press gently on the pod to open it and push out the peas with your thumb.

SHELL PEAS

TO BLANCH Add the snow peas or sugar snaps to a pot of well-salted boiling water and cook until bright green and crisp-tender (they will lose their raw fibrous quality but retain some of their crispness), 1 to 2 minutes. Or add the shelled fresh peas or frozen peas to a medium saucepan of well-salted boiling water and cook until bright green and just tender, 30 seconds to 1 minute. Drain in a colander. To serve cold, rinse with cold water to stop the cooking.

TO SAUTÉ ALL TYPES OF PEAS Bring 3 tablespoons water and 1 tablespoon unsalted butter to a simmer in a large skillet. Add the peas and cook, uncovered, stirring occasionally, until the water evaporates and the peas are bright green and crisp-tender, 3 to 4 minutes.

TO SAUTÉ SHELL PEAS WITH LETTUCE Heat 1 tablespoon unsalted butter in a medium skillet over moderately high heat. Add the white parts of 2 scallions, thinly sliced, and cook until tender, about 1 minute. Stir in 1 cup shredded green lettuce and cook, stirring occasionally, for 1 minute. Add the shelled fresh peas or frozen peas and ¼ cup chicken stock and simmer, uncovered, until most of the liquid has evaporated, about 3 minutes. Stir in the sliced scallion greens and season with salt.

SNOW PEAS

1 tablespoon vegetable oil

1 large garlic clove, minced

1 tablespoon finely chopped peeled fresh ginger

¼ teaspoon red pepper flakes

6 ounces sugar snap peas, trimmed and cut diagonally into 1-inch pieces

6 ounces snow peas, trimmed and cut diagonally into 1-inch pieces

1 cup frozen green peas

1 teaspoon soy sauce

1 teaspoon Asian sesame oil

1 tablespoon sesame seeds, toasted (see Tips, page 911)

Salt

Heat vegetable oil in a well-seasoned 14-inch flat-bottomed wok or a 12-inch heavy skillet over moderately high heat until hot but not smoking. Add garlic, ginger, and red pepper flakes and stir-fry until fragrant, about 1 minute. Add sugar snaps and snow peas and stir-fry until crisp-tender, about 3 minutes. Add green peas and stir-fry until hot, about 2 minutes.

Remove from heat and stir in soy sauce and sesame oil. Sprinkle with sesame seeds and season with salt to taste.

Pureed Peas with Mint Butter

SERVES 8
ACTIVE TIME: 20 MINUTES ■ START TO FINISH: 30 MINUTES

■ Pulsing peas in a food processor gives them an appealingly chunky texture. An easy mint butter makes the dish sophisticated enough for entertaining. ■

4 (10-ounce) packages frozen peas (not thawed)

⅔ cup water

Salt

5 tablespoons unsalted butter, softened

⅓ cup finely chopped fresh mint

3 tablespoons finely chopped fresh flat-leaf parsley

½ teaspoon coarsely ground black pepper

Cook peas in water with ½ teaspoon salt in a 5-quart heavy pot over moderate heat, covered, stirring occasionally, until tender, about 8 minutes.

Meanwhile, stir together butter, mint, parsley, ¾ teaspoon salt, and pepper in a small bowl until well combined.

Working in 2 batches, pulse peas with cooking water in a food processor until coarsely pureed; transfer to a large bowl. Stir in herb butter until melted.

HOW TO STRING SUGAR SNAP OR SNOW PEAS

Sugar snap and snow peas don't require much cooking to bring out their sweet flavor and crisp texture, but it's important to string them beforehand, because their seams are tough and fibrous. To do so, simply pinch or cut the stem end of each pod toward the inner curved side with a sharp small knife and pull it to remove the string on that side of the pod. If the peas are on the mature side, you will probably need to string the outer side as well.

Roasted Peppers with Almond-Garlic Bread Crumbs

SERVES 4 TO 6
ACTIVE TIME: 25 MINUTES ■ START TO FINISH: 1 HOUR

■ When they meet the heat of the broiler, bell peppers trade their crunchy succulence for an unctuous meatiness. Sprinkled with golden brown bread crumbs and toasted almond slivers, the peppers are then roasted, so they release their juices into some of the crumbs while the rest of the topping becomes nicely crisped. ∎

2 pounds mixed red and yellow bell peppers
½ cup slivered almonds, lightly toasted (see Tips, page 911)
1 (5-inch) section baguette, cut into 1-inch cubes
1 large garlic clove
3 tablespoons chopped fresh flat-leaf parsley
5 tablespoons extra-virgin olive oil
Salt and freshly ground black pepper

Preheat broiler. Halve peppers lengthwise and discard stems and seeds. Put peppers cut side down on broiler pan and broil about 2 inches from heat until skins are blistered and charred, about 15 minutes. Transfer peppers to a bowl, cover (to trap steam), and let stand until cool enough to handle.

Peel peppers.

Put a rack in middle of oven and preheat oven to 400°F.

Pulse almonds, bread, and garlic in a food processor until finely chopped. Transfer to a bowl and stir in parsley, oil, ½ teaspoon salt, and ⅛ teaspoon pepper.

Arrange half of peppers, alternating colors, in an oiled 9-inch glass or ceramic pie plate and sprinkle with ¼ teaspoon salt and ⅛ teaspoon pepper. Sprinkle with half of almond mixture. Arrange remaining peppers on top and sprinkle with remaining almond mixture.

Bake until peppers are hot and crumbs are golden, 20 to 25 minutes.

Peppers Stuffed with Cherry Tomatoes and Basil

SERVES 8
ACTIVE TIME: 30 MINUTES ∎ START TO FINISH: 1¼ HOURS

∎ Pretty and colorful, these stuffed peppers are best served warm or at room temperature, not hot. They are great with fillet of beef or with grilled steak or fish, or at a buffet or cookout. Letting the stuffed peppers sit for a while

after roasting allows some of the vegetables' moisture to be reabsorbed and all of the flavors to come together. ∎

4 red bell peppers
3 tablespoons extra-virgin olive oil
1 pint (about 10 ounces) cherry or grape tomatoes, halved (or quartered if large)
1 medium onion, finely chopped
3 large garlic cloves, finely chopped
1 cup packed fresh basil leaves, chopped
1 teaspoon salt
½ teaspoon freshly ground black pepper

Put a rack in middle of oven and preheat oven to 425°F. Lightly oil a large baking sheet.

Halve bell peppers lengthwise through stems and discard seeds and ribs. Arrange cut side up on baking sheet and brush cut edges and stems with 1 tablespoon oil.

Toss together tomatoes, onion, garlic, basil, salt, pepper, and remaining 2 tablespoons oil in a large bowl. Divide mixture among peppers. Cover loosely with foil and roast for 15 minutes.

Remove foil and continue to roast until peppers are tender, 20 to 25 minutes more.

COOK'S NOTE
∎ The stuffed peppers can be made up to 3 hours ahead and kept, covered, at room temperature.

Twice-Fried Green Plantains

Tostones

SERVES 4 TO 6
ACTIVE TIME: 40 MINUTES ∎ START TO FINISH: 40 MINUTES

∎ Plantains originated in Southeast Asia, but they have become so thoroughly absorbed by Latin American cultures that we think of them as being native to that region. This staple starch can be prepared in a myriad of ways throughout its various stages of ripeness, but *tostones*—thick slices of green plantains that are fried, flattened, and then fried again—might be the most recognizable. The first frying cooks the plantains through; frying them again after they have been flattened ensures lots of crisp, crunchy edges. Dipping the flattened plantains into warm salted water before frying a second time helps ensure a soft interior. ∎

2 pounds large unripe (green) plantains (about 3)
2–3 cups vegetable oil for shallow-frying
2 cups warm water
  Salt

Preheat oven to 250°F.

Cut ends from plantains with a sharp small knife, then cut a lengthwise slit through peels of each. Cut plantains crosswise into 1-inch-thick pieces and, beginning at slit, pry off peels.

Heat ½ inch oil in a deep 10- to 12-inch heavy skillet over moderate heat until just hot enough to sizzle when a piece of plantain is added. Fry plantains in 2 batches, turning occasionally with tongs, until tender and just golden, 5 to 6 minutes per batch. Transfer plantains to paper towels to drain. Reserve oil in pan.

With bottom of a heavy saucepan, flatten each plantain to ¼ inch thick. Stir together warm water and ½ teaspoon salt in a bowl.

Heat reserved oil over moderate heat until hot but not smoking. Dip a flattened plantain in salted water and, without patting dry, gently place in hot oil (plantain will not spatter). Repeat with several more pieces, without crowding, and fry, turning occasionally, until golden, about 3 minutes. Transfer *tostones* with tongs to clean paper towels to drain, then season with salt, transfer to a baking sheet, and keep warm in oven while you cook remaining *tostones* in batches. Serve hot.

Braised Plantains with Cilantro and Lime

SERVES 4 TO 6
ACTIVE TIME: 10 MINUTES ∎ START TO FINISH: 25 MINUTES

∎ Ripe plantains are simmered in spiced chicken broth until tender and then tossed with chopped cilantro, fresh lime juice, and salt. This tropical, sunny-tasting comfort food is the right companion for almost anything from a roast to homey black beans and rice. Note that the plantains need to be just ripe for the recipe; seek out yellow-skinned ones with just a few brown, not black, spots. ∎

2 tablespoons olive oil
1 medium onion, chopped
1 garlic clove, finely chopped
½–1 teaspoon finely chopped serrano chile, including seeds, to taste
  Salt
¼ teaspoon freshly ground black pepper
4 yellow plantains, peeled and cut into 8 pieces each
1 cup Chicken Stock (page 153) or store-bought reduced-sodium broth
3 tablespoons chopped fresh cilantro
1 tablespoon fresh lime juice

Heat oil in a 3-quart heavy saucepan over moderately high heat until hot but not smoking. Add onion, garlic, chile, 1 teaspoon salt, and pepper and cook, stirring occasionally, until onion is softened and golden, 6 to 8 minutes. Add plantains and stock and bring to a simmer. Cover pan and simmer until plantains are very tender, 12 to 15 minutes.

Gently stir in cilantro, lime juice, and salt to taste.

COOK'S NOTE

∎ The plantains can be braised in the stock up to 1 day ahead and refrigerated, covered. Reheat over medium heat until heated through, then gently stir in the cilantro, lime juice, and salt to taste.

POTATOES

Think of potatoes as a canvas—the possibilities are practically endless. Different varieties lend themselves particularly well to certain cooking methods. Happily, mashed potatoes, a perennial favorite, can be made with almost any kind. Some swear by the creaminess of boiling potatoes, particularly Yukon Golds, while others like the light fluffiness of baking (russet) potatoes. Combining an equal proportion of russets and Yukon Golds can be a nice compromise. As for the mashing itself, we usually use an old-fashioned potato masher, though some prefer a ricer or food mill for a silkier, lump-free mash (avoid electric mixers and food processors—they will turn your spuds into glue). A simple mash needs only a bit of butter, milk, and salt and pepper. For a lighter and/or nondairy version, substitute olive oil for the butter and some of the potato cooking water or chicken stock for the milk. Buttermilk or sour cream can replace the milk for added tang, while half-and-half or heavy cream instead of milk makes for a richer mash. For added verve, stir in chopped fresh herbs, roasted garlic puree, sautéed onions or leeks, freshly grated Parmesan, or crumbled goat cheese—you almost can't go wrong.

A baked potato is a fuss-free classic, a standby that can be dressed up (twice-baked with basil and sour cream) or down (slathered in sweet cream butter), depending on the occasion. Russets, or Idahos, as they are sometimes called, are the traditional baking potato; their starchiness and low moisture content mean they bake up fluffy. We recommend an 8-ounce potato per person, which makes a very generous serving (bagged russets are generally a little smaller than ones that are sold loose). If you like to eat the skins—one of the true joys of a good baked potato—buy organic so you can indulge with fewer worries about pesticides and fungicides, which concentrate in the skin. Steer clear of any potatoes with a greenish cast, a sign that they contain solanine, a potentially toxic alkaloid. Some people swear by rubbing the potatoes with oil or butter before baking, but we don't—it doesn't do much for the potato, producing a soft rather than crisp skin. Don't forget to prick the potatoes several times with a fork (they are likely to explode if you don't). And while the microwave has a time and a place in our kitchen, this is not one of them. It steams instead of bakes, leaving you with moist, dense spuds.

Roasting works with almost any type of potato, from your basic russet or boiling potato to any of the smaller (often organic) varieties, such as fingerlings, Russian Bananas, or red- or yellow-skinned creamers. Cutting up the potatoes speeds the roasting time and increases the ratio of crisp golden-brown skin to creamy flesh, but smaller spuds look lovely when left whole. For added flavor, stir a minced large garlic clove and a

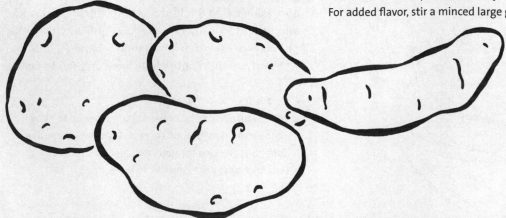

teaspoon of crumbled dried rosemary into the oil before tossing it with the potatoes and roasting them.

Then, of course, there is the sweet simplicity of steamed potatoes. For steaming, stick with the smaller boiling varieties, which can be left whole or halved. All steamed potatoes need is a knob of softened butter or a drizzle of olive oil, plus salt and pepper. A handful of chopped fresh herbs such as parsley, chives, or dill adds color and a fresh hit of flavor.

A couple of tricks guarantee a spectacular, full-flavored potato salad. First, always use boiling potatoes (which hold together better than baking ones) and boil them whole, in their skins. Let them cool slightly, then peel and cut. While they are still warm, toss the cut potatoes with vinegar and salt and let them cool further. This step ensures that the tart flavor penetrates the potatoes and enlivens the finished salad. Once the potatoes have reached room temperature, dress with your favorite mayonnaise dressing or vinaigrette and embellish as desired.

BEFORE COOKING Buy 2 pounds potatoes for 4 people (if you are making baked potatoes, buy four 8-ounce potatoes). Wash and pat dry if baking or roasting.

TO SIMMER AND MASH Peel the potatoes and cut into 1½- to 2-inch pieces. Combine with 1 teaspoon salt and cold water to cover by 1 inch in a medium pot and bring to a simmer. Simmer, uncovered, until very tender, 15 to 20 minutes. Drain the potatoes well and return to the pot. Add 3 tablespoons unsalted butter, ½ to ¾ cup whole milk, and salt and black pepper to taste and mash with a potato masher until smooth and well combined.

TO BAKE Put a rack in the middle of the oven and preheat the oven to 425°F. Prick each potato several times with a fork, place them directly on the rack, and bake until tender when pierced with a sharp knife, about 1 hour. If you like more crisp, chewy skin in contrast to creamy flesh, bake the potatoes a bit longer.

TO ROAST Put a rack in the middle of the oven and preheat the oven to 425°F. Cut the potatoes into 1½- to 2-inch pieces. (If using small potatoes such as fingerlings or creamers, cut in half if larger than 1½ inches in diameter; otherwise, leave them whole.) Toss the potatoes with 2 to 3 tablespoons olive oil, 1 teaspoon salt, and ¼ teaspoon black pepper and arrange cut side down in one layer on a large baking sheet. Roast for 20 minutes. Gently shake the potatoes, or toss them with a spatula, and roast for another 15 to 20 minutes, until golden brown and tender.

TO STEAM Peel small boiling potatoes if desired, and cut them in half if they are larger than 1½ inches in diameter. Add enough water to reach the bottom of a collapsible steamer in a 3- to 4-quart saucepan and bring to a boil. Steam the potatoes over boiling water, covered, until tender, 15 to 20 minutes. Transfer the potatoes to a bowl and toss them with 2 to 3 tablespoons olive oil or softened unsalted butter and salt and black pepper to taste.

TO MAKE POTATO SALAD Combine 2 pounds whole potatoes with well-salted cold water to cover by 2 inches in a 3-quart saucepan and bring to a boil. Reduce the heat and simmer, uncovered, until the potatoes are just tender, 15 to 25 minutes, depending on size. Drain and cool slightly. Meanwhile, whisk together 3 tablespoons cider vinegar and 1 teaspoon salt in a large bowl until the salt is dissolved. When the potatoes are just cool enough to handle, peel and cut them into 1-inch pieces, adding them to the vinegar mixture as they are cut and tossing them gently with a rubber spatula to coat. Cool to room temperature. Add ¾ cup chopped celery, ½ chopped white onion, 3 hard-boiled eggs, chopped, 1 cup mayonnaise, and salt and pepper to taste to the potatoes and stir gently to combine. (This salad will serve 6.)

Salt-Baked Potatoes

SERVES 4

ACTIVE TIME: 5 MINUTES ■ START TO FINISH: 1 HOUR

■ Encrusting potatoes in kosher salt results in a dry, fluffy interior and an intense potato flavor—in other words, the baked potato of your dreams. Choose russets, or Idahos: their starchiness and low moisture content make them the classic baking potato. ■

4 (8-ounce) russet (baking) potatoes
1 large egg white, lightly beaten
½ cup kosher salt

Put a rack in middle of oven and preheat oven to 425°F.

Prick each potato in several places with a fork. Coat potatoes with egg white, then crust completely in salt.

Put potatoes in a shallow baking pan and bake until tender when pierced with a sharp knife, about 1 hour. Crack off as much salt as desired from skin before serving.

Olive Oil–Glazed Potatoes

SERVES 4

ACTIVE TIME: 15 MINUTES ■ START TO FINISH: 25 MINUTES

■ Braising sliced potatoes in a tiny amount of water and olive oil results in a truly luxurious dish. The braising liquid thickens, thanks to the potatoes' natural starches, and forms a glossy glaze. Though you can use any type of potato for this recipe, we love it with fingerlings—they hold their shape beautifully and gleam like gold doubloons. ■

1½ pounds potatoes
1 cup water
2 tablespoons extra-virgin olive oil
1 garlic clove, minced
¾ teaspoon salt

Peel potatoes. Halve lengthwise if using a large variety such as russets. Cut potatoes crosswise into ⅛-inch-thick slices.

Combine potatoes, water, oil, garlic, and salt in a 10-inch heavy skillet and bring to a simmer. Cover skillet and simmer briskly, shaking skillet occasionally, until potatoes are tender but not falling apart and most of water is absorbed, 10 to 12 minutes.

Remove lid and boil, uncovered, until liquid has evaporated. If necessary, continue to cook, shaking skillet, until potatoes are glazed, 1 to 2 minutes.

COOK'S NOTE

■ The potatoes can be cut up to 2 hours ahead and kept in a bowl of water in the refrigerator (drain before adding to skillet).

Chinese Stir-Fried Potatoes

SERVES 4

ACTIVE TIME: 25 MINUTES ■ START TO FINISH: 25 MINUTES

■ When this dish was introduced in the early 1980s at David Keh and Ed Schoenfeld's Szechuan restaurant Auntie Yuan, it took New York by storm. Like the restaurant itself, these slender sticks of stir-fried potato were homey yet elegant. The dish was revolutionary in two ways: first, it introduced Americans to the unique camphor heat of Sichuan peppercorns; and second, the potatoes retained a bit of their crunch, which still seems radical today. ■

1¼ pounds russet (baking) potatoes (2 large)
2 tablespoons peanut or vegetable oil
1 tablespoon Sichuan peppercorns (see Sources)
¾ teaspoon salt, or to taste
1½ tablespoons distilled white vinegar
1 tablespoon Chinese rice wine or medium-dry sherry
1 tablespoon finely chopped scallion greens
½ teaspoon Asian sesame oil

Peel potatoes. Cut lengthwise into ⅛-inch-thick slices with a mandoline or other adjustable-blade vegetable slicer or a sharp knife. Transfer slices to a cutting board and cut lengthwise into very thin matchsticks. Rinse potatoes in a colander to remove excess starch and pat dry with paper towels.

Set a fine-mesh sieve over a heatproof bowl. Heat a well-seasoned 14-inch flat-bottomed wok or a 12-inch heavy skillet over high heat until just smoking. Add oil, swirling pan to coat, and heat until hot but not smoking. Add peppercorns and stir-fry until slightly darkened, about 10 seconds, then immediately pour oil through sieve into bowl; discard peppercorns.

Reheat wok over high heat until just smoking. Add strained oil, swirling to coat pan, and heat until just smoking. Add potatoes and salt and stir-fry until potatoes are slightly softened, about 3 minutes. Add vinegar, rice wine, and scallion greens and stir-fry until liquid has evaporated and potatoes are crisp-tender, 2 to 3 minutes. Stir in sesame oil and serve.

Potato and Cheese Puree with Horseradish Cream

SERVES 6
ACTIVE TIME: 35 MINUTES ■ START FINISH: 1¼ HOURS

■ Peasant ingenuity triumphs in this simple, soul-satisfying dish from France's mountainous Auvergne region. It's the perfect foil for grilled or roasted meat. Whether you use the more traditional Cantal or Gruyère, which gives the dish a similar consistency but a milder flavor, it's important to beat the potatoes and cheese together vigorously until the mix begins to form long, taffylike strands when lifted with a spoon. ■

6 medium Yukon Gold potatoes (2 pounds total)
  Salt
4 garlic cloves
3 tablespoons unsalted butter, softened
¾ cup whole milk
¾ pound Cantal or Gruyère cheese, coarsely grated
  (about 5 cups)
½ teaspoon freshly ground black pepper
⅔ cup very cold heavy cream
2 tablespoons drained bottled horseradish

SPECIAL EQUIPMENT: a potato ricer or a food mill fitted

with a medium disk; a shallow 2-quart flameproof baking dish or baking pan or six 1-cup gratin dishes

Cover potatoes with salted water (1 tablespoon salt) by 2 inches in a 4- to 5-quart heavy pot, bring to a simmer, and simmer until very tender, about 40 minutes. Drain.

Meanwhile, mince garlic and mash to a paste with 1 teaspoon salt, using side of a large heavy knife.

When potatoes are cool enough to handle, peel and force through ricer into cleaned saucepan. Add butter, garlic paste, and milk and heat over moderately low heat, stirring vigorously with a wooden spoon, until fluffy and heated through, about 2 minutes. Add cheese and pepper and cook, stirring vigorously with a heatproof rubber spatula or wooden spoon, until cheese is melted and puree is smooth and almost taffylike, about 10 minutes. Remove from heat.

Preheat broiler. Butter baking dish. (If using individual gratin dishes, butter and put on a baking sheet.) Transfer potato mixture to baking dish (or dishes), smoothing top.

Beat cream in a bowl with an electric mixer until it holds soft peaks. Beat in horseradish and ¼ teaspoon salt. Spread horseradish cream over potato mixture. Broil 4 to 5 inches from heat, rotating gratin if it isn't browning evenly, until golden, 1 to 2 minutes.

Chestnut and Potato Puree

SERVES 10 TO 12
ACTIVE TIME: 30 MINUTES ■ START TO FINISH: 1¾ HOURS

■ Plain chestnut puree can be almost unbearably rich, while plain mashed potatoes can be a little ho-hum. This recipe combines the two into one silky dish that highlights each ingredient's most lovable attributes. The meaty chestnuts enrich the potatoes, contributing a distinctive sweetness and tinting them the color of café au lait, and the potatoes temper their companions' forceful flavor. This holiday side is terrific with beef, turkey, or rack of lamb. ■

3 pounds medium yellow-fleshed potatoes, such as
 Yukon Gold (about 8)
1 stick (8 tablespoons) unsalted butter
3 cups (16 ounces) bottled peeled cooked whole
 chestnuts (see Sources)
4 cups half-and-half
1 Turkish bay leaf or ½ California bay leaf
 Salt and freshly ground black pepper
SPECIAL EQUIPMENT: heavy-duty foil; a potato ricer or a
 food mill fitted with a medium disk

Put a rack in middle of oven and preheat oven to
450°F.

Prick each potato in a few places with a fork. Divide potatoes into 3 groups and wrap each group in
foil. Bake until tender when pierced with a sharp
knife, 1¼ to 1½ hours.

Meanwhile, melt butter in a 4- to 5-quart heavy
pot over moderately low heat. Add chestnuts and
cook, stirring, for 5 minutes. Add half-and-half, bay
leaf, 2½ teaspoons salt, and ¾ teaspoon pepper,
bring to a simmer, and simmer gently, covered, until
chestnuts are very tender, 15 to 20 minutes.

Discard bay leaf and transfer chestnuts with a slotted spoon to a blender. Add enough cooking liquid to
puree chestnuts easily and puree (use caution when
blending hot liquids) until smooth. Return puree to
pot with remaining liquid and stir together. Keep
warm over very low heat.

Using a kitchen towel to protect your hands, carefully unwrap potatoes and peel, then push through
ricer, a few at a time, into chestnut mixture. Stir to
combine (mixture will continue to thicken) and season with salt and pepper.

COOK'S NOTE

- The puree can be made ahead and kept at room temperature for 1 hour or refrigerated for up to 1 day, the
 surface covered with a piece of wax paper or parchment. Bring to room temperature before reheating,
 covered, over very low heat, stirring occasionally and
 adding more half-and-half if necessary.

Matchstick Potatoes

SERVES 6
ACTIVE TIME: 20 MINUTES ■ START TO FINISH: 50 MINUTES

■ Keep three things in mind when making this recipe:
1) Don't use a small pot for frying the potatoes, or the
oil will bubble up and overflow. 2) Don't try to cook
the potatoes in fewer than 6 batches, or they won't get
crisp enough. 3) Don't eat all of the *pommes allumettes*
yourself! We also recommend that you make the potatoes ahead—they are just as delicious at room temperature as they are when hot. ■

2 large russet (baking) potatoes (1½ pounds total)
 About 6 cups vegetable oil for deep-frying
 Salt
SPECIAL EQUIPMENT: a mandoline or other adjustable-
 blade vegetable slicer; a deep-fat thermometer

Peel potatoes. Cut lengthwise into ⅛-inch-thick
slices with mandoline. Transfer slices to a cutting
board and cut lengthwise into very thin matchsticks
with a sharp knife. Transfer to a bowl of ice and cold
water. Soak for at least 30 minutes.

Heat 1¼ inches oil in a 6- to 7-quart heavy pot
over moderately high heat until thermometer registers 375°F.

Drain potatoes and pat completely dry between
several layers of paper towels.

Fry potatoes in 6 batches, gently stirring once or
twice with a slotted spoon or skimmer, until golden
and crisp, 1 to 1½ minutes per batch; transfer with
slotted spoon to paper towels to drain and season
with salt. (Return oil to 375°F between batches.)

COOK'S NOTES

- The julienned potatoes can be soaked in the water in
 the refrigerator for up to 4 hours.
- The potatoes can be fried and salted up to 6 hours
 ahead. Keep, uncovered, at room temperature.

Provençal Tomato Potato Gratin

SERVES 6
ACTIVE TIME: 25 MINUTES ■ START TO FINISH: 1¼ HOURS

■ Juicy ripe tomatoes and creamy red-skinned potatoes make a timeless summer match, roasted separately, then arranged in one overlapping layer and topped with herby bread crumbs. The beauty of this dish is that it can be assembled before your guests arrive, then quickly broiled after the meat comes off the grill and rests. ■

½ cup plus 2 tablespoons extra-virgin olive oil
2 pounds medium tomatoes, cut into ½-inch-thick slices
　Salt and freshly ground black pepper
2 pounds medium red potatoes, scrubbed and cut into ¼-inch-thick slices
1 garlic clove
½ cup fine dry bread crumbs
¼ cup finely chopped fresh basil
1½ teaspoons chopped fresh thyme

SPECIAL EQUIPMENT: a 3-quart gratin dish or shallow flameproof casserole dish (about 2 inches deep; not glass)

Put a rack in middle of oven and preheat oven to 425°F.

Brush a large baking sheet with 2 tablespoons oil. Arrange tomato slices in one layer on pan and sprinkle with a scant ½ teaspoon salt and ¼ teaspoon pepper. Roast tomatoes until just tender, not falling apart, about 20 minutes.

Meanwhile, toss potatoes with 5 tablespoons oil in a large bowl.

Remove tomatoes from oven and put racks in upper and lower thirds of oven. Transfer tomatoes to platters with a spatula, and clean baking sheet.

Arrange half of potato slices in one layer on cleaned baking sheet and arrange remaining potatoes on a second large baking sheet. Sprinkle potatoes on each pan with a scant ½ teaspoon salt and ¼ teaspoon pepper. Roast potatoes, switching position of pans halfway through roasting, until tender, about 16 minutes.

Meanwhile, mince garlic and mash to a paste with a pinch of salt, using side of a large heavy knife. Transfer garlic paste to a bowl, add bread crumbs, basil, thyme, remaining 3 tablespoons oil, ¼ teaspoon salt, and ¼ teaspoon pepper, and mix well.

Preheat the broiler. Arrange tomatoes and potatoes in one layer in gratin dish, alternating slices and overlapping them. Spoon any juices from tomatoes into dish. Sprinkle with bread crumbs and broil 5 to 7 inches from heat, checking frequently after 1 minute (crumbs can brown quickly), until golden brown, about 2 minutes.

Serve warm or at room temperature.

COOK'S NOTE

■ The gratin can be assembled up to 1 hour ahead and kept at room temperature.

Potato and Parmesan Gratin

SERVES 8
ACTIVE TIME: 35 MINUTES ■ START TO FINISH: 2¼ HOURS

■ This sumptuous dish just may be the ideal marriage of potatoes and cheese. The recipe comes from Oriana Neri of Bologna, a cook who opens her kitchen to guests as part of Home Food, a program that invites members to dine in private homes all across Italy. ■

4 pounds medium boiling potatoes
1½ teaspoons fine sea salt or table salt
1 cup heavy cream
1 cup whole milk
3 tablespoons unsalted butter, softened
7 ounces Parmigiano-Reggiano, finely grated (about 2⅓ cups)

Put a rack in middle of oven and preheat oven to 350°F.

Peel potatoes. Cut into ⅛-inch-thick slices with mandoline or other adjustable-blade vegetable slicer or a sharp knife, spreading slices out on a large kitchen towel. Sprinkle with sea salt.

Stir together cream and milk. Dot bottom of a 13-by-9-inch baking dish with 1½ tablespoons butter and pour in ⅓ cup cream mixture. Divide potatoes into 5 piles (don't rinse or dry them). Layer potatoes in baking dish, one pile per layer, drizzling ⅓ cup cream mixture and sprinkling one quarter of cheese over each layer. Drizzle remaining cream mixture over final layer of potatoes and dot with remaining 1½ tablespoons butter.

Bake, uncovered, until potatoes are very tender and top is browned, about 2 hours. Let stand at room temperature for 10 minutes before serving.

Sautéed Radishes and Watercress

SERVES 4 TO 6
ACTIVE TIME: 25 MINUTES ■ START TO FINISH: 30 MINUTES

■ Sautéing radishes in butter and oil softens their rosy color to a pale pink and mellows their sharpness into sweetness. They are delicious paired with wilted watercress, which has a little bite. This dish is exceptionally pretty—like Easter eggs peeking out of the grass. ■

- 2 tablespoons unsalted butter
- 1 tablespoon olive oil
- 2 bunches radishes (2 pounds total with greens), greens discarded, radishes halved lengthwise and sliced crosswise ¼ inch thick

RADISHES

The world of radishes encompasses much more than the peppery crimson globes that are so familiar in salads. We love the French custom of spreading them with sweet butter and sprinkling them with coarse sea salt. Braising them whole transforms them into tender little nubbins whose color and pungency are pleasantly mellowed; a healthy dose of vinegar in the braising liquid plays up their newfound sweetness. Roasting retains the vegetable's vivid color and juicy crunch. Sautéing similarly tempers radishes' bite and is quick to boot.

BEFORE COOKING Buy 1 pound radishes without greens or 2 pounds radishes with greens to serve 4. Discard any greens, scrub the radishes well, and trim the ends.

TO BRAISE Separate the radishes into 2 groups by size for even cooking. Combine 2½ tablespoons sugar, ½ cup water, ⅓ cup raspberry vinegar or red wine vinegar, 1 tablespoon unsalted butter, ½ teaspoon salt, and the larger radishes in a medium skillet or saucepan just large enough to hold them in one layer, cover, and bring

to a boil. Add the smaller radishes, reduce the heat, and simmer, covered, for 10 minutes. Remove the lid and simmer, stirring occasionally, just until all the radishes are tender, 5 to 10 minutes more. With a slotted spoon, transfer the radishes to a bowl and cover to keep warm. Boil the braising liquid until slightly thickened and reduced to about ¼ cup, about 1½ minutes. Return the radishes to the skillet, add salt and black pepper to taste, and swirl the skillet to coat the radishes thoroughly with the glaze. Garnish with chopped fresh chives if desired.

TO ROAST Put a rack in the middle of the oven and preheat the oven to 450°F. Quarter medium radishes lengthwise, cut larger ones into sixths, or halve smaller ones—aim for ¾- to 1-inch-wide wedges. Toss the radishes with 1 tablespoon olive oil, ½ teaspoon salt, and ¼ teaspoon black pepper in a bowl. Arrange the radishes in one layer on a large baking sheet and roast, stirring once or twice, until crisp-tender, 10 to 20 minutes, depending on size.

¾ teaspoon salt

¼ teaspoon freshly ground black pepper

½ cup water

2 bunches watercress (10 ounces total), coarse stems discarded and cut into 2-inch lengths

Heat butter with oil in a 12-inch heavy skillet over moderately high heat until foam subsides. Add radishes, salt, and pepper and cook, stirring occasionally, for 6 minutes. Add water and cook, covered, until radishes are crisp-tender, about 2 minutes. Remove lid and cook, stirring occasionally, until liquid has evaporated, 2 to 4 minutes.

Add watercress and cook, stirring, until wilted, about 1 minute.

Butter-Braised Salsify

SERVES 4
ACTIVE TIME: 35 MINUTES ■ START TO FINISH: 1½ HOURS

■ Salsify's pearly color and delicate flavor are said to be reminiscent of oysters (hence its nickname "oyster plant"), but its mild taste is actually more akin to artichoke hearts or Jerusalem artichokes. When scrubbed, peeled, and braised in butter, the scraggly white root becomes refined indeed. A brief soak in acidulated water keeps the salsify's color bright as it cooks. ■

4 teaspoons fresh lemon juice

2 pounds salsify, scrubbed

2 cups water

3 tablespoons unsalted butter

½ teaspoon salt

⅛ teaspoon freshly ground black pepper

1 tablespoon chopped fresh flat-leaf parsley

Fill a large bowl with cold water and stir in 1 tablespoon lemon juice. Peel salsify. Cut into 1½-inch pieces and immediately drop into acidulated water. Let stand for 10 minutes.

Drain salsify and transfer to a 3-quart saucepan. Add water, butter, salt, pepper, and remaining 1 teaspoon lemon juice, bring to a simmer, and simmer,

covered, until salsify is tender, 50 to 60 minutes (check thicker pieces for tenderness). Remove lid and boil until liquid is reduced to about ¼ cup, about 10 minutes. Stir in parsley.

Sautéed Spinach with Peanuts

SERVES 4
ACTIVE TIME: 15 MINUTES ■ START TO FINISH: 15 MINUTES

■ This super-fast dish punctuated with peanuts pairs nicely with steak. Make sure to serve it immediately; the spinach will get watery if it sits too long. ■

2 tablespoons vegetable oil

2 pounds spinach, coarse stems discarded

½ cup unsalted dry-roasted peanuts, chopped

⅛ teaspoon red pepper flakes

1 tablespoon soy sauce, or to taste

Heat oil in a 12-inch skillet over moderately high heat until hot but not smoking. Add spinach by handfuls, tossing with tongs and adding more as previous handful wilts. When all of spinach is in skillet, add remaining ingredients and cook, stirring, until spinach is tender, 1 to 2 minutes more.

Serve spinach with a slotted spoon. (Spinach will continue to exude liquid as it stands.)

SPINACH

Because fresh spinach is so readily available and cooks in a flash, we turn to it often. A simple sauté, flavored with garlic, hot pepper flakes, and fresh lemon juice, takes just minutes and makes a great accompaniment to almost anything. Steaming is just as easy. We usually toss steamed spinach with butter and salt or a drizzle of olive oil or dark sesame oil. For a rich, comforting side dish, stir chopped steamed spinach into a quick, velvety cream sauce (see below). Or, if you really want to gild the lily, spoon the creamed spinach into a shallow buttered baking dish, top generously with grated Gruyère, and bake in a hot oven until the sauce is bubbling and the cheese is melted.

Regular spinach usually comes in 8- or 12-ounce bunches and has coarse stems that need to be trimmed. We prefer to buy bunched spinach (flat or curly), because the leaves tend to be fresher and in better shape. Baby spinach, which generally does not need to be trimmed, is sold loose or in 5-ounce bags. If you do buy bagged spinach, comb through it to remove any damaged leaves, and ignore the "prewashed" label. All spinach needs extra-careful washing; it is grown in fine, sandy soil that splashes up when it rains and hides in the leaves. Try a few washed leaves to make sure they are free of grit.

BEFORE COOKING Buy 2 pounds bunched spinach or ¾ pound baby spinach for 4 people. Trim and discard any coarse stems. Wash the spinach by swishing the leaves gently in a large clean sink or bowl of cold water, letting any sand or silt drift to the bottom of the sink. Remove the leaves, being careful not to disturb the sand at the bottom of the basin, and drain in a colander. Spin dry if sautéing.

TO SAUTÉ Heat 2 tablespoons olive oil in a large heavy skillet or pot over moderately high heat until hot but not smoking. Add 2 garlic cloves, minced, and ¼ teaspoon red pepper flakes and cook, stirring, until the garlic is softened but not browned, 30 seconds to 1 minute. Add the spinach and cook, covered, for 2 minutes. Uncover and cook, stirring occasionally, until the spinach is just wilted and tender, 1 to 2 minutes more. Season with salt and black pepper and sprinkle with fresh lemon juice if desired.

TO STEAM Combine the spinach and 1 inch of water in a large pot and bring to a boil. Cover and steam the spinach until just wilted and tender, 2 to 3 minutes. Drain well in a colander.

TO MAKE CREAMED SPINACH Steam the spinach as above and drain it well. When cool, squeeze as much liquid as possible from the spinach, then chop it. Melt 2 tablespoons unsalted butter in a small heavy saucepan over moderate heat. Add ⅓ cup very finely chopped onion and cook, stirring, until very soft but not golden, 3 to 4 minutes. Whisk in 2 tablespoons all-purpose flour and cook over moderately low heat, whisking, for 3 minutes to make a roux. Whisk in ¾ cup whole milk, ½ cup heavy cream, ¾ teaspoon salt, ¼ teaspoon black pepper, and a pinch of freshly grated nutmeg and bring to a boil, whisking occasionally. Reduce the heat and simmer, whisking occasionally, for 2 minutes. Stir in 3 tablespoons freshly grated Parmigiano-Reggiano, the spinach, and additional salt and pepper to taste. Thin with additional heavy cream if desired.

Japanese Sesame Spinach

SERVES 4
ACTIVE TIME: 30 MINUTES ■ START TO FINISH: 30 MINUTES

■ The Bay Area chef and sake connoisseur Christian Geideman makes the most delicious sesame spinach we've ever tasted. His secret ingredient? Sake. It's amazing how just a tablespoon smooths out the dish's flavors. We also love his method of blanching spinach in bundles—it makes squeezing the excess water from it very easy. ■

4 (10- to 12-ounce) bunches flat-leaf spinach, preferably with root ends intact
¼ cup plus 1 teaspoon sesame seeds, toasted (see Tips, page 911)
1½ teaspoons sugar
1 tablespoon sake
1 tablespoon light soy sauce

SPECIAL EQUIPMENT: kitchen string

Wash spinach well under cold water. Gather spinach into 4 equal bunches and tie each bunch tightly around middle of stems with kitchen string.

Blanch spinach, 1 or 2 bunches at a time, in a 6- to 8-quart pot of boiling unsalted water until just wilted, 15 to 30 seconds per batch, then transfer with tongs to a large bowl of ice and cold water to stop the cooking.

Drain spinach in a colander. Holding each bunch by root end, firmly squeeze out excess water, keeping bunch intact. Cut off string and cut spinach crosswise into 1-inch sections, including inch of stems closest to leaves; discard stem ends. Squeeze sections of spinach by handfuls to remove remaining water and transfer to a bowl, separating clumps.

Combine ¼ cup sesame seeds with sugar in a food processor and pulse until coarsely chopped (some sesame seeds will remain whole). Add sake and soy sauce and pulse until mixture forms a coarse paste.

Toss spinach with sesame mixture and sprinkle with remaining teaspoon sesame seeds. Serve at room temperature or slightly chilled.

COOK'S NOTE

■ The spinach can be made up to 3 days ahead and refrigerated, covered.

Roasted Acorn Squash with Chile Vinaigrette

SERVES 4
ACTIVE TIME: 15 MINUTES ■ START TO FINISH: 45 MINUTES

■ A hot oven coaxes out the natural sugars of acorn squash, which is then drizzled with an equatorial vinaigrette of citrus juice, chile, and cilantro. The golden wedges with their dark green skins look beautiful on a serving platter. ■

2 (1½- to 1¾-pound) acorn squash
   Salt
½ teaspoon freshly ground black pepper
6 tablespoons olive oil
1 garlic clove
1½ tablespoons fresh lime juice, or to taste
1–2 teaspoons finely chopped fresh hot red chile, such as Thai or serrano, including seeds (to taste)
2 tablespoons chopped fresh cilantro

Put racks in upper and lower thirds of oven and preheat oven to 450°F.

Halve squash lengthwise. Cut off and discard stem ends. Scoop out seeds and cut squash lengthwise into ¾-inch-wide wedges. Toss with ¾ teaspoon salt, pepper, and 2 tablespoons oil in a bowl and arrange cut side down on two large baking sheets.

Roast, switching position of pans halfway through roasting, until squash is tender and undersides of wedges are golden brown, 25 to 35 minutes.

Meanwhile, mince garlic and mash to a paste with ¼ teaspoon salt, using side of a large heavy knife. Transfer garlic paste to a small bowl and whisk in lime juice, chile, cilantro, and remaining ¼ cup oil until combined.

Transfer squash, browned side up, to a platter and drizzle with vinaigrette.

Butternut Squash with Shallots and Sage

SERVES 4
ACTIVE TIME: 20 MINUTES ■ START TO FINISH: 25 MINUTES

■ Fresh sage and balsamic vinegar are the perfect balancing touches to sweet cubes of butternut squash. ■

2 tablespoons olive oil
3 large shallots, halved lengthwise and cut crosswise into ¼-inch-thick slices
1 (¾-pound) butternut squash, peeled, halved lengthwise, seeded, and cut into ½-inch cubes
½ cup Chicken Stock (page 153), store-bought reduced-sodium broth, or water
1 tablespoon packed brown sugar (light or dark)
½ teaspoon finely chopped fresh sage
 Salt
1 teaspoon balsamic vinegar
¼ teaspoon freshly ground black pepper

Heat oil in a 12-inch heavy skillet over moderate heat until hot but not smoking. Add shallots and squash and cook, stirring, until shallots are softened, about 5 minutes. Add stock, brown sugar, sage, and ½ teaspoon salt, stirring until sugar is dissolved. Bring to a simmer and simmer, covered, stirring occasionally, until squash is tender, 8 to 10 minutes.

Remove from heat and stir in vinegar, salt to taste, and pepper.

Butternut Squash and Creamed Spinach Gratin

SERVES 8 TO 10
ACTIVE TIME: 1¼ HOURS ■ START TO FINISH: 2 HOURS

■ This gratin is layered like a lasagne, with long, thin slices of butternut squash alternating with creamed spinach. The rich, bubbling result is unusual but homey, and it fits very well in a buffet alongside any kind of meat. ■

3 pounds spinach, coarse stems discarded, or 3 (10-ounce) packages frozen leaf spinach, thawed
5 tablespoons unsalted butter
¾ cup finely chopped onion
3 garlic cloves, minced
1½ teaspoons salt
¾ teaspoon freshly ground black pepper
 Rounded ¼ teaspoon freshly grated nutmeg
1 cup heavy cream
2 large butternut squash (4 pounds), peeled, quartered lengthwise, and seeded
¼ cup finely grated Parmigiano-Reggiano

SPECIAL EQUIPMENT: a mandoline or other adjustable-blade vegetable slicer

If using fresh spinach, bring 1 inch water to a boil in a 6- to 8-quart pot over high heat. Add spinach a few handfuls at a time and cook, turning with tongs, until wilted, 3 to 5 minutes. Drain in a colander and rinse under cold water. Thoroughly squeeze cooked fresh or thawed frozen spinach in small handfuls to remove excess moisture. Coarsely chop and transfer to a bowl.

Melt 3 tablespoons butter in an 8-inch heavy skillet over moderately low heat. Add onion and garlic and cook, stirring, until softened, 3 to 5 minutes. Add onion mixture to spinach, along with salt, pepper, nutmeg, and cream, and stir to combine.

Put a rack in upper third of oven and preheat oven to 400°F. Butter a 13-by-9-inch or other 3-quart shallow baking dish.

Cut bulb sections from neck sections of squash. Cut bulb and neck pieces lengthwise into ⅛-inch-thick slices with slicer.

Layer about one fifth of squash slices in baking dish and cover with one quarter of spinach mixture. Repeat layering 3 more times, ending with a layer of squash. Sprinkle top evenly with cheese and dot with remaining 2 tablespoons butter. Cover top directly with a sheet of parchment or wax paper.

Bake until squash is tender and filling is bubbling, 25 to 30 minutes. Remove paper and bake gratin until browned in spots, 10 to 15 minutes.

COOK'S NOTE
■ The gratin can be assembled up to 1 day ahead. Cover with parchment, then plastic wrap, and refrigerate. Let stand at room temperature for 1 hour before baking.

WINTER SQUASH

Notable for their beautiful shapes and colors and sweet, flavorful flesh, winter squashes come in many varieties, but acorn and butternut are the most widely available. The thick skins and odd shapes of these vegetables help determine their most suitable cooking methods. Acorn squash, for example, has deep furrows that make peeling difficult and flesh that can be a bit stringy, so it's best simply halved or cut into wedges (carefully, with a large heavy knife or cleaver) and roasted with its skin on. Its natural sweetness can be enhanced with maple syrup or brown sugar. Butternut squash and other smooth-skinned varieties are easier to peel and thus more versatile in the kitchen. We most often roast butternuts, but we also steam them and then blend them into a velvety puree. The vibrant orange squash's mellow sweetness and smooth texture meld happily with both sweet and savory seasonings. When roasting, keep things basic — just olive oil, salt, pepper, and perhaps a touch of maple syrup or brown sugar. A sprinkling of fresh herbs at the end is always nice.

When pureeing butternut squash, sweet additions such as maple syrup, brown sugar, and honey work well, mixed with a pinch of ground cinnamon, ginger, or nutmeg. We often top a simply seasoned puree with sautéed mushrooms, caramelized onions, a crumble of a sharp blue cheese such as Roquefort, fresh shavings of Parmigiano-Reggiano, or a handful of chopped toasted walnuts. At its most basic—roasted or pureed—winter squash is deliciously earthy and sweet, one of nature's brightest comfort foods.

BEFORE COOKING Buy two 1- to 1½-pound acorn squash or one 2- to 2½-pound butternut squash for 4 people.

TO ROAST ACORN SQUASH Put a rack in the middle of the oven and preheat the oven to 425°F. Halve each squash lengthwise and discard the seeds. Brush the cavities and cut edges with 1 tablespoon softened unsalted butter and sprinkle with ¾ teaspoon salt and ¼ teaspoon black pepper. Arrange the squash halves cut side down on a large baking sheet and roast for 30 minutes. Stir together 1 tablespoon melted unsalted butter and 1 tablespoon maple syrup, brown sugar, or honey. Turn the squash cut side up and brush evenly with the butter mixture. Roast for 15 to 20 minutes more, or until very tender.

TO ROAST BUTTERNUT SQUASH Put a rack in the middle of the oven and preheat the oven to 425°F. Peel and seed the squash and cut into 1½- to 2-inch pieces. Toss the pieces with 2 tablespoons olive oil, ¾ teaspoon salt, ¼ teaspoon black pepper, and perhaps a sprinkling of fresh herbs and arrange them in one layer on a large baking sheet. Roast for 25 to 35 minutes, stirring every 15 minutes, until golden and tender.

As an alternative, halfway through roasting, combine 1 tablespoon maple syrup or brown sugar, ½ teaspoon grated orange zest, and 1 tablespoon melted unsalted butter. Pour over the squash pieces, and toss. Continue roasting until tender.

TO STEAM AND PUREE BUTTERNUT SQUASH Peel and seed the squash and cut into 1½- to 2-inch pieces. Pour enough water in a medium pot to reach the bottom of a collapsible steamer and bring to a boil. Add the squash and steam, covered, until very tender, 10 to 15 minutes. Transfer the squash to a food processor. Add 2 tablespoons unsalted butter, 3 to 4 tablespoons whole milk, half-and-half, heavy cream, or sour cream, ¾ teaspoon salt, and ¼ teaspoon black pepper and puree until very smooth.

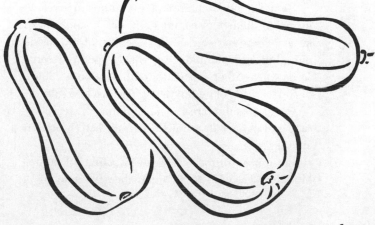

Roast Pumpkin
with Cheese "Fondue"

SERVES 8
ACTIVE TIME: 25 MINUTES ▪ START TO FINISH: 2 HOURS

▪ Editor in chief Ruth Reichl introduced us to the glories of this special dish. As the pumpkin roasts, its skin becomes gorgeously burnished, while inside, slices of baguette, Gruyère, and Emmental coalesce into a rich, velvety concoction that is utterly fabulous scooped up with spoonfuls of the tender pumpkin flesh. We tested several kinds of pumpkin and found that a plain old round jack-o'-lantern pumpkin produces the best results—sweet, creamy, and not at all fibrous. If you have a double oven, this makes an impressive Thanksgiving side dish. ▪

> 1 (15-inch) section of baguette (7 ounces), cut into
>   ½-inch slices
> 1 (7-pound) orange pumpkin
>   Salt
> 1½ cups heavy cream
> 1 cup Chicken Stock (page 153) or store-bought
>   reduced-sodium broth
> ½ teaspoon freshly grated nutmeg
> ½ teaspoon freshly ground black pepper
> 6 ounces Gruyère, coarsely grated (2½ cups)
> 6 ounces Emmental, coarsely grated (2½ cups)
> 1 tablespoon olive oil

Put a rack in lower third of oven and preheat oven to 450°F.

Arrange baguette slices in one layer on a baking sheet and toast in oven until tops are crisp (bread will still be pale), about 7 minutes. Transfer to a rack to cool.

Remove top of pumpkin by cutting a circle 3 inches in diameter around stem with a small sharp knife. Scrape out seeds and loose fibers from inside pumpkin and pumpkin top with a spoon (reserve seeds for another use if desired; see Cook's Note). Sprinkle inside of pumpkin with ½ teaspoon salt.

Whisk together cream, stock, nutmeg, 1 teaspoon salt, and pepper in a bowl. Mix together cheeses in another bowl.

Put a layer of toasted bread in bottom of pumpkin and cover with about 1 cup cheese and about ½ cup cream mixture. Continue layering bread, cheese, and cream mixture until pumpkin is filled to about ½ inch from top, using all of cream mixture (you may have some bread and cheese left over).

Cover pumpkin with top and put in an oiled small roasting pan. Brush pumpkin all over with olive oil. Bake until pumpkin is tender and filling is puffed, 1¼ to 1½ hours.

To serve, scoop out into bowls or onto plates, making sure to include some cheese, bread, and tender pumpkin flesh in each serving.

COOK'S NOTES
▪ The pumpkin can be filled up to 2 hours before baking and kept refrigerated.
▪ For a snack, pan-roast the seeds in a cast-iron skillet over moderately high heat, stirring, until they puff, then drizzle with olive oil and sprinkle with sea salt.

Baked Sweet Potatoes
with Bitters

SERVES 6 TO 8
ACTIVE TIME: 15 MINUTES ▪ START TO FINISH: 1½ HOURS

▪ The unusual combination of bitters and orange marmalade adds counterpoint and depth to sweet potatoes. These baked wedges aren't sticky and sweet; rather, they are just slightly candied and very sophisticated. We adapted this recipe from one by David Pasternack, the chef de cuisine at New York City's Esca, who learned it from his Russian grandmother. ▪

>   Unsalted butter, softened, for greasing baking dish
> 1 cup bitter orange marmalade
> 1 cup fresh orange juice (from about 3 oranges)
> 1 tablespoon Angostura bitters
> 1 teaspoon salt
> ½ teaspoon freshly ground black pepper
> 3 pounds sweet potatoes (4 large), peeled and cut
>   lengthwise into 6 wedges each

Put a rack in middle of oven and preheat oven to 450°F. Generously butter a 13-by-9-inch glass baking dish.

Heat marmalade and orange juice in a 1-quart heavy saucepan over moderately low heat, stirring, until marmalade melts. Stir in bitters, salt, and pepper and remove from heat.

Put potatoes in a large bowl, pour marmalade mixture over, and toss gently to coat. Arrange in one layer in baking dish. Bake, uncovered, turning potatoes once or twice, for 30 minutes. Then bake, without turning, until potatoes are tender and tops are slightly caramelized, about 30 minutes more.

Let stand for 10 minutes before serving, to allow glaze to thicken.

Baked Sweet Potatoes with Scallions and Cilantro

SERVES 4
ACTIVE TIME: 5 MINUTES ■ START TO FINISH: 40 MINUTES

■ Rummage around in the supermarket bin for slender sweet potatoes for this recipe—they're elegant-looking, and when slit lengthwise, their tender orange flesh happily laps up the herb butter. Though you can experiment with all kinds of herbs, scallions and cilantro really wake up this dish. ■

    4 small sweet potatoes (about 2 pounds total)
    3 tablespoons unsalted butter, softened
    2 scallions, finely chopped
    2 tablespoons finely chopped fresh cilantro
    ½ teaspoon salt
    ¼ teaspoon freshly ground black pepper

Put racks in middle and lower third of oven and put a sheet of foil on lower rack, to catch any drips. Preheat oven to 450°F.

Prick each potato several times with a fork and put on middle oven rack. Bake until soft when squeezed, 30 to 35 minutes.

Meanwhile, mash together remaining ingredients.

Slit potatoes lengthwise and put some butter mixture in center of each.

Sweet Potato Puree with Smoked Paprika

SERVES 6 TO 8
ACTIVE TIME: 15 MINUTES ■ START TO FINISH: 1½ HOURS

■ Innocent this puree may look, but it packs a ton of flavor. The secret is the paprika, which adds a dark mystique. It's critical that you use smoked—not regular—paprika here. No matter whether the smoked paprika is sweet or hot, you will end up with an irresistible dish, one that goes well with almost any meat. It's especially tasty with Thanksgiving turkey. ■

    3 pounds sweet potatoes (4 large)
    ½ stick (4 tablespoons) unsalted butter, cut into
        ½-inch cubes, softened
    ⅓ cup heavy cream
    ¼ teaspoon sweet or hot *pimentón* (Spanish smoked
        paprika; see Sources)
    ¼ teaspoon salt, or to taste
    ⅛ teaspoon cayenne, or to taste

Put a rack in middle of oven and preheat oven to 400°F. Line a baking sheet with foil.

Prick each potato several times with a fork. Bake on a baking sheet until tender, about 1 hour. Remove from oven. When potatoes are cool enough to handle, peel and cut away any eyes or dark spots. Puree potatoes with remaining ingredients in a food processor until smooth.

COOK'S NOTE

■ The puree can be made up to 1 day ahead and refrigerated in an airtight container. Reheat in a double boiler or metal bowl set over a saucepan of simmering water, stirring occasionally.

Sweet Potatoes

First things first: sweet potatoes are not in any way related to yams (or potatoes), though they are often mistakenly labeled so. Yams are actually a separate tropical vegetable, most often found in Latin or Asian markets. That said, sweet potatoes are one of the most popular vegetables on the planet, and they come in many varieties, with skins ranging from tan to orange to purple, and flesh from the palest yellow to the brightest orange. Their incredible versatility means they are equally sublime baked whole, roasted, and mashed or pureed, and they marry well with a wide range of flavors, from sweet spices, fruits, and nuts to garlic, chiles, and herbs.

Split and topped with butter and salt, baked sweets are a treat. While the insides can be easily scooped out and mashed, we prefer steaming sweet potatoes for a quicker and lighter-textured puree that can be flavored in a multitude of ways. Some of our favorites include infusing the milk or cream with a bit of minced garlic (strain before using to thin the mash) and substituting orange juice for the usual milk or cream. Take that idea a step further and simmer a handful of dried apricots in orange juice until very tender, then puree along with the sweet potatoes and a bit of grated orange zest for a delicious dish that goes well with baked ham or roast pork. Maple syrup and brown sugar are naturals with mashed sweet potatoes—combine them with minced candied ginger or a pinch of cinnamon or nutmeg. A topping of chopped toasted pecans or crumbled bacon adds a salty, crunchy counterpoint. Or add minced canned chipotle chiles in adobo (a bit at a time, adding them to taste) and some lime juice for a wonderfully spicy, slightly smoky puree.

Wedges of sweet potatoes also roast well, as their moist flesh softens beneath a golden exterior. Try whisking about 1 teaspoon chili powder, along with the salt and pepper, into the olive oil before tossing them and roasting, and finish with a sprinkle of chopped fresh cilantro.

BEFORE COOKING
For baking, buy
4 small (6 to 8 ounces
each) or 2 large (12 ounces
each) sweet potatoes to serve 4 people.
For mashing or roasting, buy 1½ pounds to serve 4. Sweet potatoes bruise easily, so choose firm, smooth, heavy tubers free of soft spots.

TO BAKE Put a rack in the middle of the oven and preheat the oven to 400°F. Poke each sweet potato a few times with a fork or cut a thin slice from both ends of each potato (to prevent an explosion). Put the sweet potatoes on a foil-lined baking sheet and bake until very tender when pierced with a knife, 45 minutes to 1 hour, depending upon size.

TO STEAM AND PUREE Peel the sweet potatoes and cut them into 1-inch pieces. Add enough water to reach the bottom of a collapsible steamer set in a 3- to 4-quart saucepan and bring to a boil. Steam the sweet potatoes over boiling water, covered, until very tender, 15 to 20 minutes. Transfer the sweet potatoes to a food processor, add 2 tablespoons unsalted butter, about ½ cup whole milk, half-and-half, or cream, and salt and black pepper to taste, and puree. Alternatively, mash the sweet potatoes with a potato masher or electric mixer, or pass through a ricer or food mill.

TO ROAST Put a rack in the middle of the oven and preheat the oven to 425°F. Peel the sweet potatoes and halve them crosswise. Cut the halves lengthwise into 1-inch-thick wedges and toss them with 2 tablespoons olive oil, ¾ teaspoon salt, and ¼ teaspoon black pepper until evenly coated. Arrange the wedges on a large baking sheet. Roast for 20 minutes, then turn and roast until tender and golden, 15 to 20 minutes more.

Roasted Sweet Potato Spears with Bacon Vinaigrette

SERVES 8
ACTIVE TIME: 40 MINUTES ■ START TO FINISH: 1¾ HOURS

■ Tossing these sweet potato spears in bacon fat assures that they'll brown up beautifully as they roast. But the coup de grâce is the vinaigrette, the nutty aroma of its sherry vinegar accented with scallions and crisp bits of smoky bacon. ■

½ pound bacon, cut crosswise into ½-inch-wide strips
4 pounds medium sweet potatoes (about 7)
   Salt and freshly ground black pepper
¼ cup extra-virgin olive oil
3 scallions, thinly sliced, white and green parts kept separate
2 tablespoons sherry vinegar
1 tablespoon water

Put a rack in upper third of oven and preheat oven to 450°F.

Cook bacon in a 10-inch heavy skillet over moderate heat, stirring, until browned and crisp, 10 to 15 minutes.

Meanwhile, peel sweet potatoes and cut each lengthwise into 6 spears. Cut spears in half crosswise if desired, and arrange in one layer on a large baking sheet.

Transfer bacon with a slotted spoon to paper towels to drain. Pour bacon fat through a fine-mesh sieve onto potato spears and toss with two spatulas to coat. Sprinkle spears with ½ teaspoon salt and ¼ teaspoon pepper. Roast, turning every 15 to 20 minutes, until potatoes are tender and edges are browned, 45 minutes to 1 hour. Transfer to a serving dish.

Return bacon to cleaned skillet, add oil, and heat over moderate heat until hot but not smoking. Stir in white parts of scallions and remove from heat. Stir in vinegar, water, ½ teaspoon salt, and ¼ teaspoon pepper.

Pour bacon mixture over potato spears and sprinkle with scallion greens.

COOK'S NOTE

■ The bacon can be cooked and the sweet potatoes cut and tossed with the bacon fat (but not the salt and pepper) up to 1 day ahead. Cool the potatoes, uncovered, then refrigerate, covered with plastic wrap. Refrigerate the bacon separately, covered. Sprinkle the potatoes with salt and pepper and bring to room temperature before proceeding with the recipe.

Slow-Roasted Tomatoes

SERVES 4 TO 6
ACTIVE TIME: 15 MINUTES ■ START TO FINISH: 3¼ HOURS

■ When summer draws to a close and fresh tomatoes have begun to lose some of their allure, turn to this easy recipe from chef Jody Adams of Rialto in Cambridge, Massachusetts. The plum tomatoes are cooked, uncovered, low and slow in olive oil, almost like a confit. Though they hold their shape, their flesh becomes melting and their flavor intensifies. The leftover oil is extremely savory. You can toss it with pasta, use it in dressings, or do as we do and serve it with crusty bread as an appetizer. ■

About 1 cup plus 2 tablespoons extra-virgin olive oil
1 medium white onion, chopped
3 garlic cloves, smashed
9 fresh basil leaves
⅛ teaspoon red pepper flakes
12 small plum tomatoes (2 pounds), halved lengthwise
1 teaspoon sugar
½ teaspoon kosher salt

Put a rack in middle of oven and preheat oven to 250°F.

Heat 2 tablespoons oil in a 12-inch heavy skillet over moderate heat until hot but not smoking. Add onion and garlic and cook, stirring occasionally, until softened, 5 to 7 minutes. Remove from heat and stir in basil and red pepper flakes.

Toss tomatoes with sugar and salt in a bowl. Arrange cut side down in a 13-by-9-inch baking dish.

Spoon onion mixture over tomatoes and add remaining 1 cup olive oil, or enough oil to reach halfway up tomatoes.

Roast, stirring gently halfway through cooking, until tomatoes are very tender but not falling apart, 2½ to 3 hours. Transfer with a slotted spoon to a serving dish.

COOK'S NOTE

■ The leftover tomato oil can be strained (discard the solids) and kept, refrigerated in an airtight container, for up to 1 month. Toss it with pasta or use it in dressings.

Rutabaga and Carrot Puree

SERVES 8
ACTIVE TIME: 15 MINUTES ■ START TO FINISH: 50 MINUTES

■ People who malign rutabaga probably have never made it. It's pleasantly turnipy, especially when purchased very fresh in the fall from a farmers market (off-season supermarket ones can have a stronger flavor). When cooked, its gorgeous pumpkin-colored

TOMATOES

Beautiful tomatoes need nothing. In the height of summer, they are best sliced or cut into wedges and eaten perfectly plain, or seasoned simply with salt, pepper, and olive oil. Unfortunately, not all tomatoes are created equal. When craving a tomato fix out of season, we turn to plum, cherry, or grape tomatoes, which tend to have better flavor and color. We either sauté them quickly or oven-roast them slowly, which concentrates their flavor (if making sauce or soup, we are always happy to use good-quality canned tomatoes). Because they cook so quickly and hold together nicely, easy-to-find grape or cherry tomatoes are the best candidates for sautéing. Cherry tomatoes sold on the vine, which tend to be larger than loose ones, are becoming more available and also work well. For a sauté, we like to add a pinch of red pepper flakes and a finish of chopped fresh herbs, such as parsley, basil, mint, or dill, or a combination. Available year-round, plum tomatoes are excellent for roasting. Their meatiness means they don't give off much liquid, and roasting allows for flavor enhancement from garlic, balsamic vinegar, and a touch of sugar, resulting in a very satisfying, full-flavored side dish. Regular vine-ripened tomatoes can also be roasted, but they will exude more liquid and cook more quickly than plum tomatoes. We often top roasted tomatoes with shavings of Parmigiano-Reggiano or fresh bread crumbs pan-toasted in olive oil, seasoned with salt and pepper, and tossed with chopped fresh herbs.

BEFORE COOKING Buy 1 pint (2 cups) cherry or grape tomatoes or 1½ pounds (about 6 large plum or 6 small vine-ripened) tomatoes for 4 people.

TO SAUTÉ Heat 2 tablespoons olive oil in a large heavy skillet until hot but not smoking. Add the cherry or grape tomatoes and cook, shaking the pan occasionally, for 1 minute. Reduce the heat to moderate and cook, covered, until the skins just start to split, 1 to 2 minutes more. Season with salt and black pepper.

TO ROAST Preheat the oven to 425°F. Halve the plum tomatoes lengthwise, or regular tomatoes crosswise, and arrange them cut side up on a baking sheet. Whisk together 2 tablespoons olive oil, 2 teaspoons balsamic vinegar, 1 garlic clove, minced, ¾ teaspoon sugar, ½ teaspoon salt, and ¼ teaspoon black pepper in a bowl and drizzle evenly over the tomatoes. Roast the tomatoes until they are beginning to caramelize but still hold their shape, 25 to 30 minutes.

flesh becomes quite tender. Pairing it with carrots and a bit of brown sugar heightens this lowly vegetable's earthy sweetness.

Rutabagas are very dense, which can making cutting them difficult. The vegetable expert Elizabeth Schneider suggests using a heavy cleaver, then peeling them once they are in smaller chunks. But be very careful—rutabaga's violet skin is often heavily waxed, making the vegetable slippery. ◾

2½ pounds rutabaga, peeled and cut into 1-inch pieces
    (see headnote)
  5 carrots, cut into 1-inch pieces
     Salt
  3 tablespoons unsalted butter
  3 tablespoons packed light brown sugar
     Freshly ground black pepper

Cook rutabagas and carrots in boiling salted water (2 teaspoons salt) to cover by 1 inch in a 5- to 6-quart pot until tender, about 30 minutes.

Drain and transfer to a food processor. Add butter, brown sugar, and 1 teaspoon salt and puree until very smooth. If necessary, transfer puree back to pot and reheat. Season with additional salt if needed and pepper to taste.

COOK'S NOTE
◾ The puree can be made up to 3 days ahead and refrigerated, covered. Reheat over moderate heat until warmed through.

Mashed
Root Vegetables
with Horseradish

SERVES 4
ACTIVE TIME: 15 MINUTES ◾ START TO FINISH: 45 MINUTES

◾ It may look like an ordinary bowl of mashed potatoes, but one bite reveals something more beguiling: the earthy sweetness of parsnips, turnips, and potatoes set off by horseradish. Combined, these three stalwarts taste like a whole new—and wholly delicious—root vegetable. ◾

¾ pound turnips, peeled and cut into ½-inch
    pieces
¾ pound parsnips, peeled, quartered lengthwise,
    woody cores discarded, and cut crosswise
    into ½-inch pieces
   Salt
 2 large russet (baking) potatoes (1 pound
    total)
¼ cup heavy cream
½ stick (4 tablespoons) unsalted butter
2–3 tablespoons finely grated peeled fresh horseradish
    or drained bottled horseradish
   Freshly ground black pepper

Cook turnips and parsnips in a 4-quart pot of boiling salted water (2 teaspoons salt) for 10 minutes.

Meanwhile, peel potatoes and cut into ½-inch pieces.

Add potatoes to pot and boil until all vegetables are tender, 10 to 12 minutes more.

Meanwhile, heat cream, butter, and horseradish (to taste) in a small saucepan over low heat, stirring occasionally, until butter is melted and mixture is hot. Remove from heat and cover to keep warm.

Drain vegetables, return to pot, and heat over high heat, shaking pot, until any excess liquid has evaporated, about 30 seconds. Remove from heat and pour cream mixture through a fine-mesh sieve into vegetables; press hard on solids for more horseradish flavor if desired. Add ½ teaspoon salt and ¼ teaspoon pepper and mash vegetables with a potato masher until smooth, with some small pieces remaining. Season with additional salt and pepper if needed.

Glazed Summer Turnips
with Miso

SERVES 4
ACTIVE TIME: 15 MINUTES ◾ START TO FINISH: 30 MINUTES

◾ Dainty summer turnips have pristine white bulbs the size of a baby's fist. They are addictively tasty, especially when cooked until just tender and nestled in their own vivid greens. Miso butter adds a creamy savor, with mirin bolstering the vegetable's own sweetness. ◾

3 pounds small white summer turnips (also called Japanese turnips or *hakurei*) with greens (about 2 bunches)
1⅓ cups water
2 tablespoons mirin (Japanese sweet rice wine)
 Pinch of salt
3 tablespoons unsalted butter, softened
3 tablespoons white miso (fermented soybean paste)

Cut greens from turnips, discarding stems, and coarsely chop leaves; set aside. Cut turnips into quarters (or in half if tiny) and arrange in one layer in a 12-inch heavy skillet. Add water, mirin, salt, and 1 tablespoon butter, bring to a boil over moderately high heat, and boil, covered, for 10 minutes. Add chopped greens in batches, stirring until wilted before adding a new batch, then cover and cook for 1 minute. Remove lid and continue boiling, stirring occasionally, until turnips are tender and liquid is reduced to a glaze, about 5 minutes.

Meanwhile, stir together miso and remaining 2 tablespoons butter in a small bowl.

Stir miso butter into turnips and cook for 1 minute.

TURNIPS AND RUTABAGAS

Too often served overboiled and underseasoned, turnips and rutabagas are woefully mistreated. However, when they are in season and prepared well, their sweetness comes to the fore, while their peppery bite mellows. Look for the freshest ones you can find (having the greens still attached is always a good sign); avoid any that are very large or shriveled. Turnips are especially delicious when they are braised and their cooking liquid is reduced to a flavorful glaze. Boiled rutabagas, on the other hand, make a vibrant puree. Just be aware that pureed rutabaga can exude liquid (we add a bit of plain white rice during cooking to absorb it). Any type of medium apple, peeled, cored, and chopped, can also be cooked along with the rutabaga. Just as a bit of sugar aids in the glazing of turnips, the apple's hint of sweetness helps round out the rutabaga's flavor. Not surprisingly, both vegetables benefit from roasting, which caramelizes their natural sugars and concentrates their flavor.

BEFORE COOKING Buy 1½ pounds turnips (about 5 large) or 1 small rutabaga for 4 people.

TO BRAISE AND GLAZE TURNIPS Peel the turnips and cut into 8 wedges each. (If using smaller turnips, cut them into quarters.) Melt 2 tablespoons unsalted butter in a heavy saucepan, add the turnips, 1 cup chicken stock or water, 1 teaspoon sugar, ½ teaspoon salt, and ¼ teaspoon black pepper, and bring to a boil. Reduce the heat and simmer, covered, until the turnips are tender, 10 to 15 minutes. Transfer the turnips to a bowl with a slotted spoon and boil the cooking liquid until reduced to a glaze, about 3 to 4 tablespoons. Return the turnips to the pan and simmer until just heated through. Season with salt and pepper and sprinkle with fresh flat-leaf parsley.

TO BOIL AND PUREE RUTABAGAS Peel the rutabaga and cut into 1- to 1½-inch pieces. Combine with cold water to cover by 1 inch in a medium pot, add 3 tablespoons white rice and 1 teaspoon salt, and bring to a boil, then reduce the heat and simmer, partially covered, until the rutabaga is very tender, 30 to 35 minutes. Drain well and transfer to a food processor. Add 2 tablespoons unsalted butter, 3 to 4 tablespoons whole milk, half-and-half, or heavy cream, and salt and black pepper to taste and puree until smooth.

TO ROAST TURNIPS OR RUTABAGAS Put a rack in the middle of the oven and preheat the oven to 425°F. Peel the turnips or rutabaga and cut into 1½- to 2-inch pieces. Toss with 2 tablespoons olive oil, ¾ teaspoon salt, and ¼ teaspoon black pepper until well coated and arrange in one layer on a baking sheet. Roast, stirring occasionally, until golden and tender, 20 to 30 minutes for turnips, 30 to 40 minutes for rutabaga. (Rutabagas take longer to cook because they are starchier and drier-fleshed.)

Turnip and Caraway Gratin Dauphinoise

SERVES 4 TO 6
ACTIVE TIME: 20 MINUTES ■ START TO FINISH: 1 HOUR

■ Most people rarely encounter caraway seeds outside of rye bread, so it comes as a surprise to find what an aromatic edge they contribute to this gratin. A single potato helps keep the turnips' flavor in check, while the turnips themselves add moisture, which means you can get away with using less cream than usual. ■

1½ pounds turnips
1 large russet (baking) potato (8–10 ounces)
1½ teaspoons salt
1 cup heavy cream
2 teaspoons caraway seeds

SPECIAL EQUIPMENT: a 1½-quart gratin dish or other flameproof baking dish (not glass); a mandoline or other adjustable-blade vegetable slicer

Put a rack in upper third of oven and preheat oven to 400°F. Butter gratin dish.

Peel turnips and potato and halve lengthwise. Cut vegetables into ⅛-inch-thick half-moon slices with slicer. Toss with salt in a large bowl. Arrange about one quarter of slices in gratin dish, overlapping them slightly and making sure to include both potato and turnip slices. Drizzle ¼ cup cream over slices and sprinkle with ½ teaspoon caraway seeds. Make 3 more layers in same manner with remaining turnip and potato slices, cream, and caraway seeds.

Cut a piece of parchment or wax paper that fits just inside top of gratin dish, butter one side, and cover gratin with paper, buttered side down. Put gratin dish on a baking sheet (to catch any drips) and bake until gratin is bubbling all over and vegetables are tender when pierced with a knife, 30 to 40 minutes.

Discard paper and bake gratin until top is golden, about 10 minutes more. Let stand for 5 minutes before serving.

COOK'S NOTE

■ The gratin can be assembled up to 4 hours ahead and refrigerated, covered with the parchment or wax paper.

Watercress Puree

SERVES 4
ACTIVE TIME: 10 MINUTES ■ START TO FINISH: 30 MINUTES

■ This bright puree is one of editor in chief Ruth Reichl's favorite side dishes. It has loads of flavor and stands up beautifully to meaty main courses, like lamb chops. The watercress should stay bright green. It's important to discard any thick or woody stems before boiling so the tender greens don't overcook. ■

1 (6-ounce) boiling potato, peeled and cut into 1-inch pieces
Salt
4 bunches watercress (1–1½ pounds total), tough stems discarded
½ stick (4 tablespoons) unsalted butter
Freshly ground black pepper

Cook potato pieces in a 6- to 8-quart pot of boiling salted water (1 tablespoon salt) until tender, about 20 minutes.

Add watercress, return water to a boil, and cook, stirring occasionally, until watercress stems are just tender, 1 to 2 minutes. Drain in a colander, pressing on vegetables to extract as much water as possible.

Transfer vegetables to a food processor and puree, scraping down sides of bowl as needed, until fairly smooth, about 1 minute. Add butter and pulse until incorporated. Season with salt and pepper.

Yuca Gratin

SERVES 8
ACTIVE TIME: 20 MINUTES ■ START TO FINISH: 1 HOUR

■ Also known as cassava or manioc, yuca is a dense, starchy root that is a staple in many Latin American, Caribbean, and African countries. Although you can increasingly find fresh yuca in American markets, it is difficult to peel and it spoils quickly—it is, after all, a root, not a tuber meant for long storage. We prefer to buy it frozen. Yuca is toxic when eaten raw, so it must always be cooked. Its starchiness and buttery, slightly sweet blandness make it absorb flavor readily. This gratin, a delicious introduction to yuca, makes a nice change of pace for a Sunday dinner, served with roast pork or rack of lamb. ■

1 (24-ounce) bag frozen peeled yuca (see Sources)
Salt
2 cups heavy cream
2 garlic cloves, finely chopped
¼ teaspoon freshly ground black pepper

Put a rack in middle of oven and preheat oven to 400°F.

Cook yuca in a 4- to 5-quart pot of boiling salted water (1 tablespoon salt) until fork-tender, about 25 minutes (thinner pieces may need less time and can be removed early with a slotted spoon). Drain.

YUCA

Although Americans have been eating yuca ("*yoo*-ka") all along without realizing it, in the form of tapioca, the fresh tuber is finally moving from Latin, Caribbean, and African markets to mainstream supermarkets, where it may also be called cassava or manioc. This tropical root vegetable has a stubborn dark brown, barklike covering that is usually waxed and must be peeled. Look for firm specimens with no mold or soft spots; if cut, the cross-section should be pure white, without any black veins. Although yuca looks as though it would keep well, it actually spoils quickly, so refrigerate and use it within a few days.

We prefer to use frozen peeled yuca pieces, which are increasingly available in supermarkets. The pieces are already peeled, cook beautifully (freezing seems to tenderize them), and work in any recipe, with the exception of the yuca chips. Whether you use fresh or frozen yuca, you may need to remove the vegetable's fibrous core, which can be tough, after its initial simmer.

You'll find that yuca tastes somewhat like a potato, but its flesh is denser, a little sweeter, and almost waxy. It makes a wonderfully comforting mash (see Mashed Yuca with Coconut, opposite page), and great fries (wedges or chips). We like to serve fried wedges with the unorthodox accompaniments of lemon wedges and barbecue sauce (just try it!), while the sturdy, crunchy chips make great scoops for dips or a side to burgers.

BEFORE COOKING Buy 1 pound yuca to serve 4 or more. To peel the yuca, first cut it into roughly 3-inch lengths, then make a lengthwise slit in each piece through the bark and the thin pink layer underneath. Loosen these outer layers by prying them away from the flesh with the knife and then, with the knife wedged between the outer layers and the flesh, continue to pry and peel your way around each piece.

TO MAKE CHIPS Using a mandoline or other adjustable-blade vegetable slicer, cut the peeled yuca (do not use frozen) crosswise into ⅟₁₆-inch-thick slices. Heat 1½ inches vegetable oil in a large wide heavy pot over moderate heat until it registers 375°F on a deep-fat thermometer. Fry the yuca in 4 batches until pale golden, 1½ to 2 minutes per batch; transfer the chips with tongs to paper towels to drain. (Return the oil to 375°F between batches.) Season the chips with ½ teaspoon salt. Serve immediately.

TO MAKE FRIES Combine the peeled yuca (fresh or frozen) with cold well-salted water to cover by 1 inch in a 3-quart saucepan and bring to a boil, then reduce the heat and simmer briskly until the yuca is tender when tested with a wooden toothpick, 15 to 20 minutes. Drain in a colander and cool slightly. When it is cool enough to handle, gently pat the yuca dry with paper towels and cut lengthwise into ¾-inch-wide wedges (discard the thin woody core). Heat 2 inches vegetable oil in a large wide heavy pot over moderate heat until it registers 360°F on a deep-fat thermometer. Fry the yuca in 3 batches, turning once, until golden brown, 3 to 4 minutes per batch; transfer with a slotted spoon to paper towels to drain. (Return oil to 360°F between batches.) Sprinkle the fries with coarse salt.

Meanwhile, combine cream, garlic, ¾ teaspoon salt, and pepper in a 2-quart saucepan and bring just to a boil over moderate heat. Remove from heat.

When yuca is cool enough to handle, halve lengthwise and cut out thin fibrous cores if necessary. Cut yuca crosswise into ¼-inch-thick slices. Layer slices evenly in a 2- to 2½-quart shallow baking dish.

Pour cream mixture over yuca. Bake gratin until cream is thickened and top is golden brown in spots, about 30 minutes.

COOK'S NOTE
■ The gratin can be baked up to 1 hour ahead and kept, loosely covered with foil, at room temperature.

Mashed Yuca with Coconut

SERVES 4 TO 6
ACTIVE TIME: 10 MINUTES ■ START TO FINISH: 30 MINUTES

■ Tapioca is the best-known by-product of yuca, and you'll recognize tapioca's pleasantly glutinous quality in this rich mash. With its hint of coconut, it makes a delicious alternative to potatoes or rice. The puree is a natural with the traditional Brazilian Shrimp Stew on page 371, but it is also good alongside jerk pork or even duck. Make sure to reserve some of the cooking liquid to thin the dish if necessary—it thickens considerably as it sits. ■

1 tablespoon olive oil
1 medium onion, chopped
1 garlic clove, finely chopped
  Salt
1 (24-ounce) bag frozen peeled yuca (not thawed; see Sources)
½ cup well-stirred canned unsweetened coconut milk

Heat oil in a 3- to 4-quart heavy saucepan over moderate heat until hot but not smoking. Add onion, garlic, and ½ teaspoon salt and cook, stirring occasionally, until onion is softened, about 6 minutes. Add yuca and 8 cups water, bring to a boil, and boil, partially covered, until yuca splits open, about 20 minutes.

Remove yuca with a slotted spoon and quarter it lengthwise; cut off any tough center cores. Return yuca to pan and boil until translucent and very tender, about 10 minutes more.

Reserve ¼ cup cooking water and drain yuca mixture. Transfer to a bowl and add coconut milk and ¾ teaspoon salt. Mash with a potato masher until yuca is coarsely mashed and coconut milk is absorbed. For a looser consistency, add some or all of reserved cooking water. Serve immediately.

Zucchini in Pecan Brown Butter

SERVES 4 TO 6
ACTIVE TIME: 15 MINUTES ■ START TO FINISH: 15 MINUTES

■ There's hardly anything that pecan butter doesn't improve, and it works wonders on bland zucchini. The secret to this dish, inspired by an appetizer served at the Red Cat in New York City, lies in barely cooking the matchsticks of zucchini—they should still have plenty of snap. Pair this with fish or chicken, or let it shine alone as a first course. ■

2 tablespoons unsalted butter
¼ cup pecans, coarsely chopped
1 pound zucchini, cut into matchsticks 2½ inches long and ⅛ inch thick
½ teaspoon salt
¼ teaspoon freshly ground black pepper
¾ cup Parmigiano-Reggiano shavings (from a 6- to 8-ounce piece)

Melt butter in a 12-inch heavy skillet over moderately high heat. Add pecans and cook, stirring, until nuts are golden brown and butter is browned, 1 to 2 minutes. Add zucchini and cook, tossing with tongs, until coated in butter and just tender, about 1 minute. Add salt and pepper and cook, tossing, for 30 seconds.

Serve zucchini topped with Parmesan shavings.

Smothered Yellow Squash with Basil

SERVES 4 TO 6
ACTIVE TIME: 15 MINUTES ■ START TO FINISH: 25 MINUTES

■ *Smothering* is a Cajun cooking term that refers to browning anything from meat to vegetables in oil, then braising in a little liquid, tightly covered, until tender. The method gives a complexity of flavor to even simple vegetables like summer squash. A handful of chopped basil added at the end of cooking contributes a fresh, herbal note. This is delicious with grilled chicken or steak. ■

2 tablespoons olive oil
1½ pounds medium yellow squash, halved lengthwise and cut crosswise into ⅛-inch-thick slices
2 garlic cloves, finely chopped
½ cup water
¼ teaspoon salt
⅛ teaspoon freshly ground black pepper
¼ cup finely chopped fresh basil

Heat 1 tablespoon oil in a 12-inch heavy skillet over moderately high heat until hot but not smoking. Add half of squash and cook, stirring occasionally, until browned, about 5 minutes. Transfer squash to a bowl, heat remaining tablespoon oil, and cook remaining squash in same manner. Return squash in bowl to skillet, add garlic, and cook, stirring occasionally, for 1 minute.

Add water, salt, and pepper, bring to a simmer, and simmer briskly, covered, until squash is tender and most of liquid has evaporated, 6 to 7 minutes. Stir in basil.

Yellow Squash Casserole

SERVES 12
ACTIVE TIME: 1 HOUR ■ START TO FINISH: 1½ HOURS

■ Sweet and golden, yellow squash is a summery pick-me-up. Roasting the thin slices first adds a deeper note to the finished casserole. Be sure to toss the squash together with the oil, salt, and pepper in batches just before roasting it; otherwise, the salt will draw out too much liquid as the raw squash stands, and the casse-role will be soupy. This crowd-pleaser makes a great addition to a cookout. We doubt you'll have leftovers, but if you do, they reheat beautifully. ■

4 pounds yellow squash (10 medium), trimmed, halved lengthwise, and cut crosswise into ⅛-inch-thick slices
¼ cup vegetable oil
Salt and freshly ground black pepper
2 medium onions, chopped
1 green bell pepper, cored, seeded, and chopped
1 red bell pepper, cored, seeded, and chopped
7 tablespoons unsalted butter
2¼ cups coarse fresh bread crumbs (from about 4 slices firm white sandwich bread, with crusts)
¼ cup all-purpose flour
1¾ cups Chicken Stock (page 153) or store-bought reduced-sodium broth
1 cup sour cream

Put a rack in lower third of oven, put a large baking sheet on rack, and preheat oven to 475°F.

Toss one third of squash with 1 tablespoon oil, ½ teaspoon salt, and ½ teaspoon pepper in a bowl. Arrange in one layer on hot baking sheet and roast, stirring once, until tender, 12 to 15 minutes. Transfer squash to a large bowl. Roast remaining squash in 2 batches in same manner, tossing with 1 tablespoon oil, ½ teaspoon salt, and ½ teaspoon pepper per batch; transfer to bowl. Set baking sheet aside.

Toss onions and bell peppers with remaining tablespoon oil, ½ teaspoon salt, and ½ teaspoon pepper in a large bowl. Transfer to baking sheet and roast, stirring once, until onions are golden, 8 to 10 minutes. Transfer to bowl with squash. Move rack to middle of oven and reduce oven temperature to 400°F.

Melt 3 tablespoons butter in a small saucepan. Remove from heat and add bread crumbs and a pinch of salt, tossing to coat crumbs. Spread evenly on a large baking sheet and toast in oven, without stirring, until pale golden, about 5 minutes. Set aside.

Melt remaining 4 tablespoons butter in a 3-quart heavy saucepan over moderately low heat. Whisk in flour and cook, whisking constantly, for 3 minutes to make a roux. Add stock, whisking, and bring to a boil, whisking. Reduce heat and simmer, whisking occasionally, for 3 minutes. Remove from heat and cool for 5 minutes, whisking occasionally. Whisk sour cream and salt and pepper to taste into sauce. Pour over squash mixture and stir gently until well combined.

Butter a 13-by-9-inch glass or ceramic baking dish. Spread squash mixture evenly in dish and sprinkle with bread crumbs. Bake until golden and bubbling, 15 to 20 minutes.

ZUCCHINI AND YELLOW SQUASH

Although called summer squash, zucchini and yellow squash are reliably available year-round in supermarkets. Some of their more intriguing brethren—the pale ribbed cocozelle, the cute pattypan, the roly-poly globe squash—can still be had only in the summer at farmers markets or in family gardens. Tender and quick-cooking, summer squashes are versatile. Sauté, steam, roast, grill (see Grilled Zucchini with Garlic and Lemon, page 559), or stuff them (see Bulgur-Stuffed Tomatoes, Zucchini, and Bell Peppers, page 321). They also make a wonderful addition to soups, stews, pastas, frittatas, and salads.

We usually slice zucchini into rounds or cut it into chunks or matchsticks, but using an adjustable-blade slicer to cut long ribbons is a neat trick too. We sometimes serve these ribbons raw in a salad (see Ribboned Zucchini Salad, page 168) or sauté them gently and then toss them with a handful of chopped fresh mild herbs, such as basil, parsley, chives, or mint. When shopping for summer squash, choose firm, smallish ones, about 5 to 7 inches long, with bright, shiny, unblemished skin. Avoid overly large ones, which tend to be spongy and full of seeds and are sometimes bitter.

BEFORE COOKING For sautéing or steaming, buy 1¼ pounds zucchini or yellow squash to serve 4. Because squash shrinks when roasted, plan on buying 1½ pounds zucchini or yellow squash to serve 4. Rinse the skins well, as they can be sandy, and trim the ends.

TO SAUTÉ Quarter the squash lengthwise and cut crosswise into ¾-inch chunks. Heat 1 tablespoon olive oil in a large nonstick skillet until hot but not smoking. Add the squash and cook, undisturbed, until golden brown on the bottom, about 2 minutes. Continue to cook, stirring occasionally, until tender, 2 to 3 minutes longer. Season with ¼ teaspoon salt.

TO SAUTÉ SQUASH RIBBONS Using a mandoline or other adjustable-blade vegetable slicer, cut the squash lengthwise into ¹⁄₁₆-inch-thick ribbons. Heat 1½ tablespoons olive oil in a large nonstick skillet over medium-high heat

COOK'S NOTE

■ The casserole, without the bread crumbs, can be assembled up to 1 day ahead. Cool, uncovered, then refrigerate, covered. Let stand at room temperature for 1 hour before sprinkling with the bread crumbs and baking.

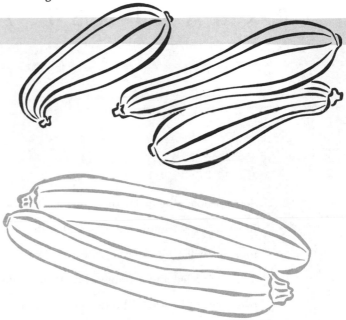

until hot but not smoking. Add the squash ribbons and cook, occasionally gently tossing with tongs, until just tender, 2 to 3 minutes. Season with ¼ teaspoon salt. Toss the squash with chopped mild herbs if desired.

TO STEAM Quarter the squash lengthwise and cut crosswise into ¾-inch chunks. Add enough water to reach the bottom of a collapsible steamer set in a 3- to 4-quart saucepan and bring to a boil. Steam the squash over boiling water, covered, until just tender, about 5 minutes. Transfer the squash to a serving bowl and season with ¼ teaspoon salt, then toss with 1 tablespoon unsalted butter and 1 tablespoon chopped fresh mild herbs. Or, to serve steamed squash cold as a salad, plunge it into a bowl of ice and cold water to stop the cooking, then drain well and pat dry. When ready to serve, toss with 2 tablespoons vinaigrette.

TO ROAST Put a rack in the middle of the oven and preheat the oven to 450°F. Quarter squash lengthwise and cut crosswise into ¾-inch chunks. Toss the squash with 1 tablespoon olive oil and ¼ teaspoon salt and arrange in one layer on a large baking sheet. Roast the squash, without stirring, until tender and golden on the bottom, 15 to 20 minutes.

BREAKFAST AND BREADS

Some people go to bed with a smile. They are already anticipating breakfast, rejoicing in the knowledge that the first moments of morning will bring their favorite meal. While others make do with a cup of coffee and a mingy slice of toast, they linger dreamily over piles of pancakes, butter-toasted oatmeal with sticky apple topping, and deep-fried poached eggs set on a creamy heap of spinach. They sit down and drink their juice, knowing that no matter what the day may bring, they will be fortified against misfortune.

This chapter will delight all true breakfast lovers. And should you not be among their number, it will do its best to remind you of the many delights of the morning meal. It will whisper about the magic of eggs, which can, with the flick of a wrist, turn into hearty frittatas or light and fluffy omelets or simply scramble up into sunny golden mounds. Give them a little more encouragement, and baked eggs become gorgeous breakfast soufflés, oozing Cantal cheese and impossible to resist.

Here too are the many delights of pancakes, waffles, and French toast, each a magnificent way to start the day. Some, like the shatteringly crisp seltzer waffles, are happiest when drizzled with

maple syrup, but a few, like raspberry–chocolate chip pancakes, require no embellishment at all. Want to get a different sort of start? Ricotta cornmeal crêpes with fresh corn topping begin the day on a delightfully savory note.

For the creative cook, breakfast is the ultimate challenge. It is, on the one hand, an opportunity to make the true breakfast lover deliriously happy. A chance to make a babka so rich that it leaves your fingers slightly stained with chocolate after every bite. Or figgy scones so short and flaky that each bite is accompanied by a little shower of crumbs. Or to take on the challenge of doughnuts—real doughnuts—that are still warm when you set them on the table, so that their fragrance wafts up into the air.

On the other hand, these wonderful dishes give you a chance to show the I-never-eat-breakfast crowd just how much they are missing. And if they insist on eschewing the morning meal, that's fine too. Who says breakfast has to be eaten in the morning? With recipes this good, you may very well want to eat breakfast all day long.

BREAKFAST AND BREADS

Breakfast

Butter-Toasted Oatmeal with Sticky Apple Topping

SERVES 4
ACTIVE TIME: 25 MINUTES ■ START TO FINISH: 50 MINUTES

■ You'll wake up early for this one. The nuttiness of steel-cut oats is heightened by a quick toasting in butter, and their pleasant chewiness pairs beautifully with a topping of tender caramelized apples. ■

FOR OATMEAL
    2½ tablespoons unsalted butter
    1 cup steel-cut oats
    4¼ cups boiling water
      Scant ¼ teaspoon salt

FOR TOPPING
    ½ stick (4 tablespoons) unsalted butter
    2 Gala or Fuji apples, peeled, cored, and cut
      lengthwise into ⅛-inch-thick slices
    ½ cup packed light brown sugar
    ⅛ teaspoon salt
    ¼ cup half-and-half

MAKE THE OATMEAL: Heat butter in a 3-quart heavy saucepan over moderate heat until foam subsides. Add oats and cook, stirring, until oats are pale golden and have a nutty fragrance, about 4 minutes. Carefully add boiling water and salt and boil, stirring occasionally, until oats swell and oatmeal thickens slightly, about 10 minutes.

Reduce heat and simmer, stirring occasionally, until oatmeal is soft and thickened, 20 to 30 minutes.

MEANWHILE, MAKE THE TOPPING: Melt butter in a 10-inch heavy skillet over moderately high heat. Add apples and cook, stirring occasionally, until beginning to brown. Reduce heat to moderate, add brown sugar and salt, and cook, stirring gently, until sugar is melted. Simmer topping, stirring occasionally, until apples are very tender and almost translucent, about 15 minutes.

Stir in half-and-half and simmer until thickened, about 5 minutes.

Divide oatmeal among bowls and spoon topping over it.

COOK'S NOTES

■ The topping can be made up to 2 days ahead and refrigerated, covered. Reheat gently before serving.
■ Any leftover oatmeal keeps in an airtight container, refrigerated, for up to 3 days. Reheat in a microwave or over low heat.

ALL ABOUT OATS AND OATMEAL

With a sweet, nutty flavor that makes them a breakfast table favorite, oats (*Avena sativa*) are packed with nutrition. They're a great source of energy-giving carbohydrates, and they have more protein than many other grains, which is nice to know if you don't eat much meat. They are also rich in essential vitamins, minerals, fatty acids, disease-fighting phytochemicals, and fiber. Even if you are reduced to racing through a cup of the instant stuff on your way out the door in the morning, you're still getting the benefits of the whole grain, because, unlike other grains, oats almost never have their bran and germ removed in processing. The bran, endosperm, and germ are all present.

Steel-cut oats are whole oats that have been cut crosswise into a few pieces after processing. They are what's commonly used in traditional Scottish and Irish preparations, and they're sometimes called Scotch oats, Irish oats, or pinhead oats. They take the longest to cook (up to 40 minutes, depending on the brand), but the payoff is deep flavor and a satisfyingly chewy texture. Rolled oats (aka "old-fashioned" oatmeal) are steamed to soften them, then flattened between rollers into flakes. They've got less flavor and chew, but they cook in about 5 minutes. Quick-cooking oats and instant oatmeal are rolled into thinner flakes, so they cook even faster. In North America, oats are heat-treated (kilned) after their hulls are removed, which deactivates the enzymes that can cause rancidity. But if you don't eat oats often, you might want to store yours in the refrigerator to be on the safe side.

Fruit and Spice Granola

MAKES ABOUT 8 CUPS
ACTIVE TIME: 15 MINUTES ■ START TO FINISH: 2¼ HOURS
(INCLUDES COOLING)

■ This granola, from the Governor's Inn in Rochester, New Hampshire, is one of the best we've ever tasted. Nutty, nubbly, and warm with cinnamon and nutmeg, it's delicious with milk, over yogurt, or all by itself as an afternoon snack. ■

- 4 cups old-fashioned rolled oats
- 1 cup unsweetened dried coconut
- 1 cup (about 3½ ounces) sliced almonds
- 1 cup (about 3¾ ounces) pecans
- 1½ teaspoons ground cinnamon
- ½ teaspoon freshly grated nutmeg
- ¼ teaspoon salt
- 1 stick (8 tablespoons) unsalted butter
- ½ cup mild honey
- 2 cups (about 9 ounces) mixed dried fruit, such as cranberries, cherries, currants, golden raisins, apricots, prunes, and/or dates, coarsely chopped if large

Put racks in upper and lower thirds of oven and preheat oven to 300°F.

Stir together oats, coconut, nuts, spices, and salt in a large bowl.

Melt butter with honey in a small saucepan over low heat, stirring occasionally. Pour butter mixture over oat mixture and toss to combine well.

Spread granola evenly on two baking sheets and bake, stirring frequently and switching position of pans halfway through baking, until golden brown, about 30 minutes.

Transfer granola to a large bowl, add dried fruit, and toss to mix. Cool, stirring occasionally, about 1½ hours.

COOK'S NOTE

■ The granola keeps in an airtight container, refrigerated, for up to 1 month.

Rolled Omelet with Arugula–Goat Cheese Filling

SERVES 6
ACTIVE TIME: 20 MINUTES ■ START TO FINISH: 35 MINUTES

■ We adapted this velvety omelet filled with goat cheese and fresh arugula from a dish at the Gostilna Devetak restaurant (*gostilna* is Slovenian for "trattoria") in Friuli, Italy, which borders the northern end of the Adriatic Sea. Ripe fresh tomatoes or juicy roasted ones add a nice counterpoint to the omelet's richness. ■

- 6 large eggs
- 2 cups heavy cream
  Salt
- ½ pound (about 1 cup) soft mild goat cheese, at room temperature
- 1 cup chopped arugula
  Freshly ground black pepper

SPECIAL EQUIPMENT: **parchment paper**

Put a rack in middle of oven and preheat oven to 325°F. Butter a 17-by-14-inch baking sheet, line bottom and sides with parchment paper, and butter parchment.

Whisk together eggs, cream, and ½ teaspoon salt in a large bowl just until well combined. Pour into baking pan and bake until set, 15 to 20 minutes.

Meanwhile, beat together goat cheese and arugula in a bowl with an electric mixer. Season with salt and pepper.

Remove omelet sheet from oven. Dot goat cheese mixture on top, leaving a 1-inch border on all sides, then spread evenly with an offset spatula or heatproof rubber spatula (leaving some border). With a long side nearest you, using the parchment paper as an aid, roll up omelet sheet. Put a long platter alongside baking sheet and, using parchment paper as an aid, carefully flip omelet onto platter. Cut omelet diagonally into 6 slices and serve.

Summer Vegetable Frittata

SERVES 6
ACTIVE TIME: 35 MINUTES ■ START TO FINISH: 40 MINUTES

■ Angelo Pellegrini, an English professor who emigrated as a young boy from Tuscany to Washington state, was wild about food—growing it, cooking it, and enjoying it with friends and family. He put that passion into words with *The Unprejudiced Palate*, which was published in 1948 to long standing admiration. "When the garden yields its abundance of fresh vegetables and the hens drop their eggs with reckless abandon, the entire family will enjoy an occasional frittata," he wrote. You will indeed. ■

    6 large eggs
    6 large fresh basil leaves, chopped
    1 tablespoon chopped fresh flat-leaf parsley
    ¼ teaspoon salt
    ¼ teaspoon freshly ground black pepper
    1 tablespoon olive oil
    1 ounce thinly sliced prosciutto, finely chopped
    1 pound medium zucchini (about 3), halved
        lengthwise and cut into ¼-inch-thick slices
    5 medium Swiss chard leaves, stems and center ribs
        discarded, leaves finely chopped
   12 scallions, finely chopped
    5 zucchini blossoms (optional; see Sources)
    1 cup finely grated Parmigiano-Reggiano (about
        3 ounces)

Preheat broiler. Whisk together eggs, basil, parsley, salt, and pepper in a bowl.

Heat oil in a 12-inch ovenproof nonstick skillet over moderate heat until hot but not smoking. Add prosciutto and cook, stirring, until edges begin to crisp, about 2 minutes. Add zucchini and chard and cook, covered, stirring occasionally, until vegetables are just tender, about 8 minutes. Add scallions and zucchini blossoms, if using, and cook, uncovered, stirring occasionally, until just wilted, 1 to 2 minutes.

Pour egg mixture into skillet and cook, lifting up cooked egg around edges using a heatproof rubber spatula to let as much raw egg as possible flow underneath, until edges are set, about 2 minutes (top and center will still be very loose).

Sprinkle cheese evenly over top and broil frittata about 6 inches from heat until set, slightly puffed, and golden, 2 to 2½ minutes.

Cool frittata for 5 minutes, then loosen edges with a clean spatula and slide onto a large plate. Cut into wedges. Serve warm or at room temperature.

Parsley-Crouton Omelets with Gruyère

SERVES 4
ACTIVE TIME: 30 MINUTES ■ START TO FINISH: 45 MINUTES

■ *Persillade* ("pear-see-*yahd*"), a French garlic and parsley mixture, and Gruyère pair up in this classic omelet, while fresh croutons offer a crunchy surprise. ■

FOR FILLING
    2 cups ½-inch cubes firm white bread
    3 tablespoons unsalted butter, melted
    ¼ teaspoon salt
    ½ cup finely chopped fresh flat-leaf parsley
    1 small garlic clove, finely chopped
   3½ ounces Gruyère, coarsely grated (about 1 cup)
FOR OMELETS
   12 large eggs
    4 teaspoons water
       Scant 1 teaspoon salt
    ½ teaspoon freshly ground black pepper
    ½ stick (4 tablespoons) unsalted butter
SPECIAL EQUIPMENT: a well-seasoned 9½-inch carbon-
       steel French omelet pan (see Sources) or a 10-inch
       nonstick skillet with sloping sides

MAKE THE FILLING: Put a rack in middle of oven and preheat oven to 350°F.

Toss bread cubes with butter on a small baking sheet and bake until golden and crisp, 10 to 15 minutes. Sprinkle with salt.

Stir together parsley and garlic in a small bowl.

MAKE THE OMELETS: Beat together 3 eggs, 1 teaspoon water, scant ¼ teaspoon salt, and ⅛ teaspoon pepper in a bowl with a fork until combined.

Heat omelet pan over moderately high heat until hot. Add 1 tablespoon butter and heat, swirling pan, until foam subsides and butter begins to brown near edges of pan. Pour beaten eggs into skillet and cook, shaking pan back and forth quickly while stirring eggs in a circular pattern with a heatproof rubber spatula, until eggs begin to set. Quickly spread set eggs evenly in skillet, sprinkle with about ¼ cup cheese and 1 tablespoon parsley-garlic mixture, and cook until omelet is just set, 30 seconds to 1 minute. Scatter one quarter of croutons (about ⅓ cup) across center of omelet. Using a rubber spatula, lift edge of omelet closest to handle and fold one third of omelet over croutons. Holding handle from underneath (see opposite page), tilt pan over plate until unfolded part of omelet slides onto plate, then immediately invert skillet, as if trying to cover plate, to make omelet fold over itself onto plate. Make 3 more omelets in same manner.

Fluffy Egg White Omelets with Basil and Tomatoes

SERVES 4
ACTIVE TIME: 25 MINUTES ■ START TO FINISH: 25 MINUTES

■ Most egg white omelets are anemic-looking, but this one, flecked with chopped basil and topped with a quick cherry tomato sauté, is stunning, tender, and delicious. This recipe serves 4, but we also offer directions for making the omelet for fewer people; see Cook's Note. Save any leftover topping for another omelet, or serve with pasta. ■

FOR SAUTÉED TOMATOES
- 1½ tablespoons extra-virgin olive oil
- 1 cup halved cherry tomatoes (about 6 ounces)
- 4 scallions, chopped, white and green parts reserved separately
- ¼ teaspoon salt
- ⅛ teaspoon freshly ground black pepper

FOR OMELET
- 16 large egg whites or 2 cups (16 ounces) packaged liquid egg whites (see Cook's Note)
- ½ teaspoon salt
- ¼ cup chopped fresh basil
- ¼ teaspoon freshly ground black pepper
- 2 tablespoons extra-virgin olive oil

MAKE THE TOMATOES: Heat oil in a 10-inch heavy skillet over moderately high heat until hot but not smoking. Add tomatoes and white parts of scallions and cook, stirring, until tomatoes are wilted, 2 to 3 minutes. Remove from heat and stir in scallion greens, salt, and pepper. Cover to keep warm.

MAKE THE OMELETS: Whisk egg whites with salt in a large bowl until very foamy. Whisk in basil and pepper.

Heat oil in a 12-inch nonstick skillet over moderate heat until moderately hot. Add egg white mixture and cook, stirring with a heatproof rubber spatula, until eggs start to set, about 3 minutes. Spread egg whites out to cover bottom of skillet. Tilt skillet slightly and immediately begin to roll up omelet little by little with spatula, starting at edge closest to handle and letting any uncooked egg flow underneath to cook. Holding handle of skillet from underneath (with your palm facing up; see opposite page), align far edge of skillet with center of a platter, tilt handle up, and tip skillet up and over platter to turn out omelet. Blot platter with a paper towel to remove any liquid.

Spoon tomatoes over omelet and cut into 4 servings.

COOK'S NOTES
- The omelet ingredients are divisible by 4, so it is easy to make an omelet for 1, 2, or 3 people, reducing the skillet size accordingly. For an omelet for 1 person, use a 7- to 8-inch skillet and 1½ teaspoons oil (it will cook in about half the time); for 2 people, use a 9-inch skillet and 1 tablespoon oil; for 3 people, use a 10-inch skillet and 1½ tablespoons oil.
- Packaged liquid egg whites are available in most supermarkets.

ABOUT OMELETS

An omelet is a cook's best friend. Once you get the hang of making one (and it is entirely a matter of practice, as Julia Child famously said, because there is no time at all to stop in the middle and pore over the recipe), you will never want for a fast, nourishing, inexpensive meal again. Cook omelets to order, and don't limit them to morning hours. They are an excellent reason to invite friends for a light late-night supper. Seat them around your kitchen table and open a bottle of rosé (one of the most egg-friendly wines). To make the best omelets, buy a traditional 24-centimeter (9½-inch) carbon-steel French pan with gently sloping sides; the sloping sides encourage the omelet to roll in on itself and thus help you form the classic omelet shape (see Sources). Be aware that omelet pans have to be seasoned; because manufacturers are notoriously sketchy when it comes to seasoning instructions, we offer a short tutorial. A nonstick pan with sloping sides works fine too, but the texture of the cooked egg will be a little tougher and not as light — the fact that you can't get a nonstick surface as hot as steel or iron makes a difference.

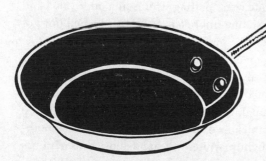

HOW TO SEASON AN OMELET PAN

1. Wash the pan well (do not use abrasives) and dry it.

2. Generously sprinkle the bottom of the pan with coarse salt, then cover it with a ½-inch layer of vegetable oil. Let the pan sit at room temperature for 12 hours.

3. Heat the pan over moderately low heat until the oil is very hot and just beginning to smoke. Pour out the oil and wipe the pan dry.

4. Use the pan only for omelets. Never wash it; simply wipe it out after using with salt and a paper towel.

Eggs Baked in Pipérade

SERVES 4

ACTIVE TIME: 35 MINUTES ■ START TO FINISH: 45 MINUTES

■ Pipérade, a saucy tomato and pepper mixture from the Basque region of France, is often paired with eggs. We love this with fried ham and crusty bread. ■

- 3 tablespoons extra-virgin olive oil
- 1 large onion, coarsely chopped
- 2 red bell peppers, cored, seeded, and coarsely chopped
- ½ teaspoon hot paprika
- 1 teaspoon minced garlic
- 2 (14- to 15-ounce) cans diced tomatoes, with juice
- 8 large eggs
  Salt and freshly ground black pepper
- ¾ cup crumbled feta

Put a rack in middle of oven and preheat oven to 450°F.

Heat oil in a 12-inch heavy skillet over moderately high heat until hot but not smoking. Add onion and bell peppers and cook, stirring occasionally, until softened, 7 to 8 minutes. Add paprika and garlic and cook, stirring, for 1 minute. Add tomatoes, with juice, and cook, uncovered, stirring occasionally, until vegetables are tender, 5 to 9 minutes.

Meanwhile, warm eggs, still in shells, in a bowl of hot water for 5 minutes; drain (warming the eggs before baking helps them cook more evenly).

Transfer vegetables to a 3-quart shallow baking dish or gratin dish. Make 8 indentations in mixture with back of a large spoon. Crack an egg into each indentation and season with salt and pepper. Bake until egg whites are set but yolks are still runny, 8 to 10 minutes.

Sprinkle with feta and serve immediately.

COOK'S NOTES

- The yolks in this recipe will not be fully cooked. If that is a concern, see page 915. Alternatively, bake the eggs until the yolks are completely set.
- The vegetable mixture can be made up to 1 day ahead. Cool, uncovered, then refrigerate, covered. Reheat before proceeding with the recipe.

Baked Eggs with Cheese

SERVES 6

ACTIVE TIME: 25 MINUTES ■ START TO FINISH: 40 MINUTES

■ Made with airy whipped egg whites and strategically placed yolks, this is like having a cheese soufflé for breakfast. The Cantal cheese melts beautifully, adding richness and structure to the fluffy whites. Keeping the yolks in a bowl of water makes it easy to scoop them out with your fingers. When transferring the yolks to the baking dish, take care not to drip too much water onto the beaten egg whites (a couple of drops aren't a problem). ■

- 6 large eggs
- ¼ teaspoon salt
- ¼ teaspoon freshly ground black pepper
- ⅛ teaspoon freshly grated nutmeg
- ⅛ teaspoon cream of tartar
- 4 ounces Cantal or Gruyère cheese, grated (about 1⅓ cups)
- 6 tablespoons crème fraîche
- 1 tablespoon chopped fresh herbs, such as chives, flat-leaf parsley, chervil, or tarragon

Put a rack in middle of oven and preheat oven to 350°F. Butter six 8-ounce ramekins or a 13-by-9-inch glass or ceramic baking dish.

Separate eggs, putting whites in a large bowl and carefully sliding unbroken yolks into a small bowl of cold water.

Using an electric mixer at high speed, beat whites with salt, pepper, nutmeg, and cream of tartar until they just hold stiff peaks, about 1 minute. Gently but thoroughly fold in half of cheese. Divide mixture among ramekins or transfer to baking dish, smoothing top slightly (whites will stand above rims of ramekins). Make an indentation in centers of whites in each ramekin, or make 6 evenly spaced indentations in whites in baking dish, with back of a spoon. With your fingers, carefully remove yolks from water, one at a time, and place 1 in each indentation.

Stir crème fraîche and spoon 1 tablespoon on top of each yolk. Sprinkle eggs with remaining cheese. Transfer ramekins, if using, to a large shallow baking pan.

Bake until whites are puffed and pale golden, 10 to 14 minutes; yolks will still jiggle in center. Sprinkle with herbs and serve immediately.

COOK'S NOTE

■ The eggs in this recipe will not be fully cooked. If that is a concern, see page 915. Alternatively, cook the eggs until fully set.

Baked Eggs with Roasted Vegetable Hash

SERVES 6
ACTIVE TIME: 15 MINUTES ■ START TO FINISH: 45 MINUTES

■ Nothing could be easier than this brunch dish. The eggs are whisked together with milk and cheese and baked at high heat to make them delightfully puffy, then topped with a sophisticated hash of roasted cremini mushrooms and sweet potatoes. ■

10 large eggs
1 cup whole milk
  Salt and freshly ground black pepper
5 ounces Swiss cheese, coarsely grated (about 1½ cups)
10 ounces cremini mushrooms, trimmed and chopped into ¼-inch pieces
1 large sweet potato (8–10 ounces), peeled and chopped into ¼-inch pieces
1 large shallot, halved lengthwise and thinly sliced crosswise
3 tablespoons olive oil

Put racks in upper and lower thirds of oven and preheat oven to 450°F. Butter an 11-by-7-inch or other shallow 2-quart baking dish.

Whisk together eggs, milk, ¾ teaspoon salt, and ¼ teaspoon pepper in a large bowl until smooth. Whisk in cheese. Pour into baking dish.

Bake in upper third of oven until puffed, golden, and set, about 20 minutes.

Meanwhile, toss together mushrooms, sweet potato, and shallot with oil, ¾ teaspoon salt, and ¼

teaspoon pepper on a large baking sheet. Spread vegetables out in an even layer and roast in lower third of oven, stirring twice after 10 minutes, until tender and golden brown, about 18 minutes.

Serve eggs with roasted vegetables spooned on top.

Poached Eggs with Tomato Cilantro Sauce

SERVES 4
ACTIVE TIME: 30 MINUTES ■ START TO FINISH: 35 MINUTES

■ In Mexico, this dish is called *huevos ahogados*, meaning "drowned eggs," since the eggs are served in soup bowls with lots of sauce. If you like *huevos rancheros*, you'll love this—it's cleaner and lighter, and the serrano chile offers a similar buzz on the tongue. You might find yourself making it for breakfast, lunch, *and* dinner. ■

1 teaspoon distilled white vinegar
2 pounds tomatoes, coarsely chopped, or 1 (28-ounce) can tomatoes in juice, drained, juice reserved, and coarsely chopped
2 large garlic cloves, coarsely chopped
1 small green serrano chile, coarsely chopped
  Salt
½ teaspoon sugar, plus additional to taste
1 cup water (if using fresh tomatoes)
5 tablespoons olive oil
¼ cup chopped fresh cilantro, plus additional for sprinkling
8 (½-inch-thick) slices baguette
  Freshly ground black pepper
8 large eggs

Put a rack in middle of oven and preheat oven to 350°F.

Fill a deep 12-inch skillet with 1½ inches cold water, add vinegar, and bring to a simmer.

Meanwhile, combine tomatoes, with juice if using canned tomatoes, garlic, chile, 1 teaspoon salt, and ½ teaspoon sugar in a blender until smooth. Add 1 cup water if using fresh tomatoes and puree. Pour through a medium-mesh sieve into a bowl, pressing hard on solids; discard solids.

Heat ¼ cup oil in another 12-inch heavy skillet over moderately high heat until hot but not smoking. Carefully pour in tomato puree (it will spatter). Stir in cilantro, bring to a simmer, and simmer briskly, uncovered, stirring occasionally, until sauce is slightly thickened, about 10 minutes. Stir in salt and sugar to taste and reduce heat to low.

Meanwhile, put baguette slices on a baking sheet, brush with remaining tablespoon oil, and season lightly with salt and pepper. Bake until just crisp on top, about 10 minutes. Keep toasts warm in turned-off oven.

While bread toasts, break eggs two at a time into a cup and slide into simmering water, spacing pairs of eggs evenly in skillet. Poach at a bare simmer until whites are firm but yolks are still runny, 4 to 5 minutes.

Carefully transfer eggs with a slotted spoon to soup bowls and season with salt. Spoon sauce generously over eggs and sprinkle with cilantro. Serve with toasts.

COOK'S NOTES

- The eggs in this recipe will not be fully cooked. If that is a concern, see page 915. Alternatively, cook the eggs until fully set.
- The tomato sauce can be made up to 2 hours ahead. Cool, uncovered, then refrigerate, covered.

Deep-Fried Poached Eggs with Creamed Spinach

SERVES 4
ACTIVE TIME: 1 HOUR ■ START TO FINISH: 1¼ HOURS

■ Eggs Florentine rise to a whole new level in this witty adaptation, which causes rapturous sighs. Yes, deep-frying a poached egg is a case of gilding the lily, but it adds an incredible layer of texture and flavor to the creamy spinach and crisp shards of serrano ham. When you dredge each poached egg in flour and bread crumbs, handle it as though it were a baby bird—you want to cup it gently so that it will neither break nor get away. These eggs also taste great with a classic frisée salad instead of the creamed spinach.

It's worth a trip to the farmers market to make these beauties: the fresher the egg, the sturdier the membrane that keeps the yolk together and the thicker the white. ■

- 1 teaspoon vinegar (any kind)
- 5 large eggs
- 1 cup heavy cream, plus additional if needed (optional)
- ½ cup plus 2 teaspoons all-purpose flour
- 2 tablespoons finely chopped shallot
- 1 tablespoon unsalted butter
- 1 (10-ounce) package frozen chopped spinach, thawed and squeezed dry
- ⅛ teaspoon freshly grated nutmeg
  Salt and freshly ground black pepper
- ¼ teaspoon water
- 1½ cups coarse fresh bread crumbs (from firm white bread)
- 7–8 cups vegetable oil for deep-frying
- 3 ounces thinly sliced serrano ham or prosciutto, cut crosswise into ¼-inch-wide strips

SPECIAL EQUIPMENT: a deep-fat thermometer

Pour 1½ inches water into a 3-quart wide heavy saucepan (preferably about 9 inches wide), stir in vinegar, and bring to a simmer.

Break 1 egg into a small bowl or cup and slide into water. Repeat with 3 more eggs, spacing them evenly in pan. Poach at a bare simmer until whites are firm but yolks are still runny, 2 to 3 minutes. Transfer eggs to paper towels with a slotted spoon.

Whisk together cream and 2 teaspoons flour in a small bowl until just combined.

Cook shallot in butter in a 9- to 10-inch heavy skillet over moderately low heat, stirring occasionally, until softened, about 3 minutes. Add spinach, nutmeg, ½ teaspoon salt, and ¼ teaspoon pepper and cook, stirring constantly, until excess liquid has evaporated, about 2 minutes. Stir cream mixture, add to spinach, and cook, stirring occasionally, until cream is slightly thickened, about 2 minutes. Remove from heat.

Spread remaining ½ cup flour on a plate. Lightly beat remaining egg with water in a small bowl. Stir together bread crumbs, ¼ teaspoon salt, and ⅛ teaspoon pepper in a shallow bowl.

Gently blot any water from top of poached eggs with paper towels and sprinkle with ¼ teaspoon salt and ⅛ teaspoon pepper.

Carefully dredge 1 poached egg in flour, dusting off excess, and transfer to beaten egg, spooning it over egg to coat completely. Transfer with a slotted spoon to bread crumbs, letting excess egg drip off, coat with crumbs, and transfer to a plate. Repeat with remaining poached eggs.

Heat 1½ inches oil in a 3- to 4-quart heavy saucepan over high heat until thermometer registers 375°F. Fry ham, stirring with a slotted spoon to separate strips, until crisp, 15 to 20 seconds. Transfer to paper towels to drain.

Return frying oil to 375°F. Using slotted spoon, lower 2 eggs, one at a time, into oil and fry until golden brown, 15 to 20 seconds. Transfer to paper towels to drain. Repeat with remaining 2 eggs.

Reheat spinach over low heat, stirring constantly and adding more cream or water to loosen mixture if necessary, for about 1 minute. Divide creamed spinach among four plates and top with poached eggs and ham.

COOK'S NOTES

- The poached eggs can be refrigerated overnight. Transfer the eggs as they are cooked to a bowl of cold water, then refrigerate. To reheat, lower the eggs into simmering water with a slotted spoon and simmer for 20 to 30 seconds. Transfer to paper towels.
- The eggs in this recipe will not be fully cooked. If that is a concern, see page 915.

Breakfast Burritos

SERVES 4
ACTIVE TIME: 30 MINUTES ■ START TO FINISH: 30 MINUTES

■ Our inspiration for these handheld burritos came from those served at the Santa Fe Farmers Market in New Mexico, where they are truly the early bird's reward—feasting on this portable breakfast while scoring the pick of the produce gives a magical start to the day. Though either Mexican or Spanish chorizo would work, we prefer the smooth richness of the Mexican sausage and the way its flavor soaks into the potatoes. Avocado adds a fresh, bright note. ■

- 1 large boiling potato (8 ounces), peeled and cut into ⅓-inch dice
- Salt
- 4 (9- to 11-inch) flour tortillas
- 7–8 ounces Mexican chorizo (spicy raw pork sausage; see Cook's Note and Sources), removed from casings
- 4 large eggs
- 1 teaspoon water
- ⅛ teaspoon freshly ground black pepper
- 1 tablespoon olive oil
- 1 cup coarsely grated Monterey Jack cheese (about 4 ounces)
- 1 California avocado, halved, pitted, peeled, and sliced
- About ¼ cup fresh or bottled salsa

Put a rack in middle of oven and preheat oven to 350°F. Cut four 12-by-8-inch sheets of foil.

Cook potato in a small pot of boiling salted water (1½ teaspoons salt) until just tender, about 5 minutes. Drain in a sieve.

Wrap tortillas tightly in a large sheet of foil and warm in oven until heated through, 10 to 15 minutes.

Meanwhile, cook chorizo in an 8-inch heavy skillet over moderate heat, stirring and breaking it up, until just cooked through, 3 to 5 minutes. Add potatoes and cook over moderately low heat, stirring until tender and lightly browned, 3 minutes. Remove from heat and cover to keep warm.

Whisk together eggs, water, ¼ teaspoon salt, and pepper in a medium bowl. Heat oil in a small nonstick skillet over moderate heat until hot but not smoking. Add egg mixture and cook, stirring to scramble, until just cooked through. Remove from heat.

Put a tortilla on one sheet of foil. Spoon one quarter of chorizo mixture, one quarter of eggs, one quarter of cheese, one quarter of avocado, and then salsa to taste in vertical rows across center, leaving room to fold over bottom and sides. Fold bottom of tortilla over most of filling, then fold over sides, overlapping them. If desired, fold top down; filling can be left exposed. Wrap foil around burrito, leaving top exposed. Make 3 more burritos in same manner and serve hot.

COOK'S NOTE

■ If you can't find Mexican chorizo, you can use Spanish chorizo (see Sources). Peel off the casings and finely chop the chorizo. Cook in the small skillet over moderate heat until the chorizo is warmed through and some of the fat is rendered, about 2 minutes. Add the potato and proceed with the recipe.

Breakfast Stack

SERVES 4
ACTIVE TIME: 25 MINUTES ■ START TO FINISH: 1½ HOURS

■ From the culinary crossroads of the Asian breakfast experience and the American Egg McMuffin comes this unique dish. We started with a panfried rice cake, made from pearl-like sushi rice, which Japanese schoolchildren love to snack on. Then we added a few of our own breakfast staples—Canadian bacon and fried eggs—to come up with a morning meal that's at once fanciful and familiar. ■

    1 cup sushi rice (see Sources)
 1¼ cups water
    Salt
    3 tablespoons unsalted butter
    8 slices Canadian bacon (6–8 ounces total)
    4 large eggs
  ⅛ teaspoon freshly ground black pepper
    1 scallion, cut diagonally into very thin slices

Rinse rice in a large fine-mesh sieve under cold running water, then drain well, tapping sieve.

Combine rice, water, and ¼ teaspoon salt in a 2-quart heavy saucepan and bring to a boil. Reduce heat to low and cook, covered, for 15 minutes. Remove pan from heat and let stand, covered, for 10 minutes.

Stir rice from bottom to top. Butter a plate. Lightly butter a metal 1-cup measure. Using a rubber spatula, firmly pack enough rice into measure to fill measure halfway. (If spatula becomes sticky, dip in water.) Invert measure onto buttered plate and tap measure to unmold rice. Repeat with remaining rice, rebuttering measure each time, to make 3 more disks. Refrigerate disks, uncovered, until firm, at least 15 minutes.

Heat 1 tablespoon butter in a 12-inch nonstick skillet over moderately low heat until foam subsides. Add rice disks and cook, rotating them for even browning, until undersides are golden, 8 to 10 minutes. Turn cakes over, add ½ tablespoon butter to skillet, swirling to melt it, and cook, rotating each cake once, until golden, about 5 minutes more. Transfer to plates.

Increase heat to high and add ½ tablespoon butter to skillet, then add bacon and brown it, turning once, about 2 minutes. Place 2 slices bacon on each rice cake.

Wipe out skillet with a paper towel and heat remaining tablespoon butter over moderately high heat until foam subsides. Crack eggs one by one into skillet, sprinkle with ⅛ teaspoon salt and pepper, and fry until whites are cooked and yolks are beginning to set, 2 to 4 minutes.

Place an egg on each rice cake stack and sprinkle with scallion.

COOK'S NOTES

■ When forming the rice disks, be sure to use a 1-cup measure; using a ½-cup measure will result in narrower, taller disks, which would be too small for the eggs.

■ The rice cakes can be shaped up to 1 day ahead. Refrigerate, uncovered, until firm, then loosely cover. Cook directly from the refrigerator, allowing an additional 2 to 5 minutes.

■ The eggs in this recipe will not be fully cooked. If that is a concern, see page 915. Alternatively, cook the eggs until fully set.

Cowboy Christmas Breakfast

SERVES 12 (OR 8 COWBOYS)
ACTIVE TIME: 30 MINUTES ■ START TO FINISH: 1¼ HOURS

■ Reader Tracy Jones of Midland, Texas, shared this recipe with us, and it's a delicious way to feed a crowd. Every year, her family assembles the dish on Christmas Eve and then bakes it in the morning while opening presents. Two dozen eggs and thick slices of garlicky bread are transformed into a custardy bread pudding, which makes a savory base for crumbled breakfast sausage and grated cheddar cheese. ■

1 (1-pound) package bulk breakfast sausage (not links)
1 (15-inch-long) loaf Italian bread (about 4 inches wide)
½ stick (4 tablespoons) unsalted butter, softened
1 garlic clove, coarsely chopped
24 large eggs
1 cup whole milk
2 teaspoons salt
1 teaspoon freshly ground black pepper
1 large bunch scallions, chopped
4 ounces sharp cheddar, coarsely grated (about 1 cup)

Put a rack in middle of oven and preheat oven to 375°F. Generously butter a 13-by-9-inch baking dish.

Cook sausage in a 12-inch heavy skillet over moderately high heat, stirring frequently and breaking up large lumps with a fork, until browned, about 10 minutes. Pour off fat from skillet and cool sausage to room temperature.

Cut 1-inch-thick slices from half of loaf; reserve remaining half and end piece for another use.

Pulse butter and garlic in a food processor until smooth. Spread a thin layer of garlic butter on both sides of each slice of bread, arranging bread tightly in one layer in baking dish. Sprinkle sausage on top.

Whisk together eggs, milk, salt, and pepper in a large bowl until frothy. Whisk in scallions and half of cheese. Pour egg mixture over sausage (bread will float to the top) and push down on bread with a spatula to help it absorb liquid. Sprinkle with remaining cheese.

Cover with a large sheet of buttered foil (buttered side down) and bake for 30 minutes. Carefully remove foil and bake until top is slightly puffed and eggs are cooked through in center, about 20 minutes more.

Let casserole cool for 10 minutes, then cut into 12 squares.

COOK'S NOTE

■ The dish can be assembled up to 12 hours ahead and refrigerated, covered with buttered foil. Bake as directed.

Buttermilk Pancakes

SERVES 4 (MAKES ABOUT TWELVE 3-INCH PANCAKES)
ACTIVE TIME: 15 MINUTES ■ START TO FINISH: 15 MINUTES

■ These buttermilk pancakes are the best we've ever had—as terrific topped with sweet butter and dark maple syrup as with sour cream and caviar (see next recipe). ■

1 cup all-purpose flour
1 teaspoon baking soda
½ teaspoon salt
1 large egg, lightly beaten
1 cup well-shaken buttermilk
Vegetable oil for brushing griddle

Preheat oven to 200°F.

Whisk together flour, baking soda, salt, egg, and buttermilk in a bowl until smooth.

Heat a griddle or large heavy skillet over moderate heat until hot enough to make drops of water scatter over its surface. Brush with oil. Working in batches, using a ¼-cup measure filled halfway for each pancake, pour batter onto griddle and cook pancakes, turning once, until golden, about 2 minutes per batch. Transfer to a heatproof platter and keep warm, covered, in oven while you cook remaining batches.

COOK'S NOTE

■ The batter keeps, covered and refrigerated, for up to 3 days. Thin as necessary with additional buttermilk or water, 1 tablespoon at a time, before using.

Caviar Pancakes

SERVES 4
ACTIVE TIME: 45 MINUTES ■ START TO FINISH: 45 MINUTES
(INCLUDES MAKING PANCAKES)

■ Patty Early, the mother of former executive food editor Zanne Stewart, used to make these colorful stacks for her daughter as a special treat, and they are good even with supermarket roe. The caviar pancakes also make a festive first course; use only 2 pancakes per serving, to serve 6. ■

- ½ stick (4 tablespoons) unsalted butter
- 12 Buttermilk Pancakes (page 657), kept warm
  About ¾ cup sour cream
- ¼ cup caviar (from a 2-ounce jar)
- 2 hard-boiled large egg yolks, forced through a medium-mesh sieve
- 1 scallion, minced

Cook butter in a very small saucepan over moderate heat, swirling pan occasionally, until golden brown (be careful not to let it burn). Remove from heat and keep warm.

Spread each pancake with about 1 tablespoon sour cream, or to taste, and top with a scant teaspoon caviar. Sprinkle with some of yolks and scallion. Stack 3 pancakes on each of four plates and drizzle with brown butter.

Blueberry Corn Hotcakes

SERVES 4 (MAKES ABOUT SIXTEEN 3½-INCH PANCAKES)
ACTIVE TIME: 30 MINUTES ■ START TO FINISH: 30 MINUTES

■ The nuttiness of stone-ground cornmeal makes these blueberry pancakes irresistible. We adapted them from the ones served at Tutti's off Main Street in Ventura, California. ■

- 1 cup all-purpose flour
- ¾ cup stone-ground cornmeal (not coarse)
- ¼ cup sugar

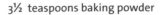

- 3½ teaspoons baking powder
- ½ teaspoon baking soda
- ½ teaspoon salt
- 2 large eggs
- 1¼ cups well-shaken buttermilk
- 3 tablespoons unsalted butter, melted
- 1 cup fresh or frozen blueberries
  Vegetable oil for brushing griddle

Preheat oven to 200°F.

Whisk together flour, cornmeal, sugar, baking powder, baking soda, and salt in a large bowl. Whisk together eggs, buttermilk, and butter in a bowl until combined. Whisk into flour mixture until just combined. Fold in berries (batter will be lumpy and will thicken as it stands).

Brush a 12-inch nonstick griddle or skillet with oil and heat over moderate heat until hot but not smoking. Working in batches of 3 or 4, drop ¼-cup measures of batter onto griddle and cook until bubbles appear on surface and undersides are lightly browned, 1 to 2 minutes. Flip hotcakes with a spatula and cook until edges are light brown and cakes are cooked through, 1 to 2 minutes more. Transfer to a heatproof platter and keep warm, uncovered, in oven while you cook remaining hotcakes. Brush griddle with oil between batches and adjust heat as necessary.

Lemon Soufflé Pancakes

SERVES 6 TO 8
(MAKES ABOUT THIRTY 3- TO 3½-INCH PANCAKES)
ACTIVE TIME: 1 HOUR ■ START TO FINISH: 1 HOUR

■ Airy and zinged with lemon, these pancakes need no embellishment (though a scattering of fresh berries and slivered almonds wouldn't hurt). They get their lightness from cake flour, while fresh lemon zest and juice enhance the tangy undertone of buttermilk. This recipe is adapted from one served at Mirbeau Inn and Spa in the Finger Lakes region of New York. ■

- 2¼ cups cake flour (not self-rising)
- ¾ cup sugar

- 1 tablespoon baking powder
- 1 teaspoon salt
- ½ teaspoon freshly grated nutmeg
- 2 tablespoons finely grated lemon zest (from about 3 large lemons)
- 5 large eggs, separated
- 1½ cups whole-milk ricotta
- 1½ sticks (12 tablespoons) unsalted butter, melted and cooled slightly
- ¼ cup fresh lemon juice
- ¾ cup well-shaken buttermilk
- ½ teaspoon vanilla extract
- Vegetable oil for brushing griddle
- Confectioners' sugar for dusting

Preheat oven to 200°F.

Whisk together flour, sugar, baking powder, salt, nutmeg, and zest in a medium bowl. Whisk together yolks, ricotta, butter, lemon juice, buttermilk, and vanilla in a large bowl until combined. Whisk in flour mixture until incorporated.

Beat egg whites in a large bowl with an electric mixer at medium speed until they just hold soft peaks.

Fold one third of whites into batter to lighten it, then fold in remaining whites gently but thoroughly.

Heat a griddle or 12-inch heavy skillet over moderate heat until hot enough to make drops of water scatter over surface, and brush with oil. Drop ¼ cup batter per pancake onto griddle and cook until bubbles appear on surface and undersides are golden, 1 to 2 minutes. Flip pancakes with a spatula and cook until undersides are golden brown and pancakes are cooked through, 1 to 2 minutes more. Transfer to a heatproof platter and keep warm, uncovered, in oven while you cook remaining pancakes. Brush griddle with oil as needed.

Dust pancakes with confectioners' sugar before serving.

COOK'S NOTES

- The batter can be made up to 1 hour ahead and refrigerated, covered. Bring to room temperature before using.
- The pancakes can be frozen for up to 1 week. Cool completely and wrap in paper towels in stacks of 4, then put in sealable plastic bags. To heat, microwave pancakes, wrapped in paper towels, until heated through.

BUTTERMILK

Buttermilk was originally a by-product of butter making: the liquid left after the cream was churned. Especially popular in the American South, it was enjoyed as a refreshing drink, but it was also a necessary ingredient in biscuits, corn bread, and cakes.

Today commercial buttermilk is made by culturing (fermenting) low-fat or skim milk with lactic acid–producing bacteria, which are also used to make sour cream. The culture's acidity is what gives buttermilk its characteristic tangy flavor, thickness, and tenderizing ability. Some brands use added thickeners, so check the label before buying; the fewer additives, the better. We use it to enliven and enrich a wide range of things, including Banana Nut Bread (page 666), Buttermilk Coffee Cake (page 669), and Ginger Doughnut Rounds (page 668). If you're the kind of cook who's always making pancakes, waffles, or biscuits, you probably already have buttermilk in the refrigerator, but if you're not, pick up a can of powdered buttermilk—essentially, dried buttermilk—the next time you're at the grocery store. It keeps for ages (refrigerate after opening), which means you can bake that coffee cake without a last-minute shopping trip. (In our experience, though, only liquid buttermilk gives corn bread the body it needs, and that's because of its texture, thick with emulsifying phospholipids. Many of these molecules are destroyed during the manufacturing of powdered buttermilk.)

TO MAKE YOUR OWN BUTTERMILK SUBSTITUTION

- Thin ⅔ cup yogurt with ⅓ cup water to equal 1 cup buttermilk.
- Add 1 tablespoon fresh lemon juice or distilled white vinegar to 1 cup whole milk (it will curdle).

Raspberry–Chocolate Chip Pancakes

SERVES 4 (MAKES ABOUT FOURTEEN 4-INCH PANCAKES)
ACTIVE TIME: 30 MINUTES ■ START TO FINISH: 30 MINUTES

■ *This* is what you make the morning after a slumber party. Kids—and adults—can't resist the classic combination of raspberries and chocolate, so make sure you get enough of each in every scoop of batter. ■

About 1 stick (8 tablespoons) unsalted butter
1¾ cups plus 2 tablespoons whole milk
2 large eggs
2¼ cups all-purpose flour
4 teaspoons baking powder
½ teaspoon salt
2 cups (about 8 ounces) raspberries
1 cup (about 6 ounces) semisweet chocolate chips

ACCOMPANIMENT: warm pure maple syrup

Heat 4 tablespoons butter with milk in a small saucepan over moderately low heat, stirring, until butter is just melted. Transfer to a bowl, add eggs, and whisk together.

Whisk together flour, baking powder, and salt in another bowl. Stir in egg mixture until just combined. Gently stir in raspberries and chocolate chips.

Preheat oven to 200°F.

Heat a griddle or 12-inch heavy skillet over moderate heat until hot enough to make drops of water scatter over surface. Add 2 teaspoons butter and spread over griddle with a wide metal spatula. Drop ⅓ cup batter per pancake onto griddle and cook until bubbles appear on surface and undersides are golden, 1 to 2 minutes. Flip pancakes with spatula and cook until undersides are golden brown and pancakes are cooked through, 1 to 2 minutes more. Transfer to a heatproof platter and keep warm, uncovered, in oven while you cook remaining pancakes; add 2 teaspoons butter to griddle before each batch.

Serve pancakes with syrup.

MAPLE SYRUP

Pure maple syrup is great on a short stack or French toast, and we also use it to impart a deep, complex sweetness to everything from salad dressings to pork loin. The grade of the syrup—based on USDA regulations—depends on its color and flavor. Some states and Canada use slightly different terminology: Grade A Light Amber maple syrup is sometimes called Fancy Grade, for instance, and in Canada it's called Number 1 Extra Light. Generally speaking, lighter syrup is made early in the spring, when it's colder, and darker Grade B syrup is made later. But producers would be the first to tell you that they have little control over what grade they make: it depends on the weather and the chemical and metabolic changes the trees go though as they progress from the dormancy of winter to the new growth of spring.

As a rule, we prefer the robust flavor of Grade B to the light Grade A, but both are about as far away from artificial-tasting commercial table syrup brands (which are based on high-fructose corn syrup and have little or no maple content) as you can possibly get. Refrigerate maple syrup after opening, or it will turn moldy.

Granulated maple sugar is essentially maple syrup without any sticky mess, and it's handy for baking recipes because it's dry. Produced by boiling maple sap past the syrup stage until the liquid has almost completely evaporated, it's an ingredient in the delectable ragamuffins on page 667; our guess is that you'll prefer it to the refined white or brown stuff on your breakfast cereal as well.

For help finding Grade B maple syrup and maple sugar, see Sources.

Ricotta Cornmeal Crêpes with Fresh Corn Topping

SERVES 6

ACTIVE TIME: 40 MINUTES ▪ START TO FINISH: 1¼ HOURS

▪ Hot pepper jelly lends an unexpected jolt to these pillowy crêpes—it plays off the sweetness of the corn and cornmeal while adding a touch of heat. Great taste aside, this is also one of the prettiest brunch dishes we know. Because it can take one or two tries to get the hang of making crêpes, the batter in the recipe yields a couple more than you need—choose the 12 best to fill and bake. ▪

FOR CRÊPES

- 1½ cups all-purpose flour
- 1 cup yellow cornmeal (not coarse)
- ½ teaspoon salt
- 2½ cups whole milk
- 4 large eggs
- 3 tablespoons unsalted butter, melted, plus additional for brushing skillet

FOR FILLING

- 4¼ cups (about 2 pounds) whole-milk ricotta, preferably fresh (for homemade, see page 231)
- 1 large egg, lightly beaten
- ¾ teaspoon salt
- ½ teaspoon coarsely ground black pepper
- ⅔ cup hot pepper jelly

FOR TOPPING

- ½ stick (4 tablespoons) unsalted butter
- 8 scallions, thinly sliced on a slight diagonal
- 3 cups corn kernels (from about 4 ears)
- ½ teaspoon salt
- ¼ teaspoon freshly ground black pepper
- ⅓ cup chopped fresh basil

SPECIAL EQUIPMENT: a 15-by-10-inch shallow baking dish

MAKE THE CRÊPES: Whisk together flour, cornmeal, salt, milk, eggs, and butter in a bowl until smooth. Let batter stand, refrigerated, for 30 minutes.

Lightly brush a 10-inch nonstick skillet with butter and heat over moderately high heat until hot but not smoking. Working quickly, stir batter, then lift skillet off heat and pour in ⅓ cup batter, tilting and rotating skillet to cover bottom. (If batter sets before bottom is coated, reduce heat slightly for next crêpe.) Return skillet to heat and cook until crêpe is just set and bottom is golden brown in spots, about 30 seconds. Loosen edge of crêpe with a heatproof rubber spatula and flip over, using your fingertips. Cook crêpe until bottom is set and golden brown, about 30 seconds more. Slide crêpe onto a plate. Continue making crêpes in same manner, brushing skillet lightly with butter for each and stacking crêpes on plate.

MAKE THE FILLING AND BAKE THE CRÊPES: Put a rack in middle of oven and preheat oven to 375°F. Lightly butter baking dish.

Stir together ricotta, egg, salt, and pepper in a bowl until combined. Put 1 crêpe paler side up on a work surface and spread 2 teaspoons pepper jelly in a horizontal line just below center of crêpe, leaving a 1-inch border at each end. Spoon ⅓ cup ricotta filling over jelly. Fold sides of crêpe to cover filling, fold bottom up over filling, and roll up to enclose. Place crêpe seam side down in baking dish; you will be forming 2 rows of 6 crêpes each. Fill 11 more crêpes in same manner, arranging them in baking dish.

Cover with foil and bake until filling is hot, about 30 minutes.

JUST BEFORE SERVING, MAKE THE TOPPING: Heat butter in a 10- to 12-inch heavy skillet over moderate heat until foam subsides. Add scallions, corn, salt, and pepper and cook, stirring occasionally, until scallions are wilted and corn is crisp-tender, about 4 minutes. Remove from heat and stir in basil.

Spoon topping over crêpes.

COOK'S NOTE

▪ The crêpes can be filled (but not baked) up to 1 day ahead and refrigerated, covered. Bring to room temperature before baking.

Crispy Seltzer Waffles

SERVES 4 TO 6 (MAKES ABOUT TEN 4-INCH BELGIAN WAFFLES; SEE HEADNOTE)

ACTIVE TIME: 25 MINUTES ▪ START TO FINISH: 25 MINUTES

▪ Seltzer might seem like an odd addition to your Sunday morning waffles, but consider the pivotal role fizzy beer plays in beer-battered fish or vegetables, resulting in a coating with unparalleled crunch. The bubbles in seltzer work similar wonders for waffles, producing a crisp shell and a tender, fluffy interior. Although we make these waffles in a Belgian waffle iron, you can also use a standard one; your yield will depend on its size. ∎

> 2 cups all-purpose flour
> 2 tablespoons sugar
> 2 teaspoons baking powder
> Slightly rounded ½ teaspoon salt
> ½ stick (4 tablespoons) unsalted butter, melted and cooled
> 2 large eggs
> 1¾ cups seltzer or club soda (from a new bottle)
> Vegetable oil for brushing waffle iron

ACCOMPANIMENTS: butter; pure maple syrup
SPECIAL EQUIPMENT: a well-seasoned or nonstick Belgian waffle iron or a standard waffle iron

Preheat waffle iron. Put a rack in middle of oven and put a large cooling rack on it. Preheat oven to 200°F.

Whisk together flour, sugar, baking powder, and salt in a large bowl. Add butter, eggs, and seltzer and whisk until smooth.

Brush waffle iron lightly with oil. Spoon batter into iron, using ⅓ cup batter for each 4-inch Belgian waffle, and cook according to manufacturer's instructions. Transfer waffles to rack in oven to keep warm; keep waffles in one layer, uncovered, so they stay crisp. Make more waffles in same manner.

Serve with butter and maple syrup.

Almond French Toast

SERVES 4
ACTIVE TIME: 25 MINUTES ∎ START TO FINISH: 25 MINUTES

∎ Here's a French toast reminiscent of the almond-flavored brioche pastries found in so many French bakeries. It's very good made with challah, and even better with brioche—stash a loaf of this wonder bread in your freezer so you can have French toast whenever the whim strikes. ∎

> 4 large eggs
> 1⅓ cups half-and-half
> 4 teaspoons sugar
> ⅛ teaspoon salt
> ½ teaspoon vanilla extract
> 1¼ cups (about 4½ ounces) sliced almonds
> 8 (¾-inch-thick) slices brioche or challah (from a 4- to 5-inch-wide loaf)
> 3 tablespoons unsalted butter

ACCOMPANIMENTS: pure maple syrup; confectioners' sugar (optional)

Put a rack in middle of oven and preheat oven to 275°F.

Whisk together eggs, half-and-half, sugar, salt, and vanilla in a large shallow dish until well combined. Spread almonds on a large plate.

Soak 4 slices of bread in egg mixture, turning once, until saturated. Remove bread one slice at a time, letting excess egg mixture drip off, and dredge in almonds to coat both sides, gently pressing to help adhere; transfer to a plate or wax paper. Repeat procedure with remaining 4 slices.

Heat 1½ tablespoons butter in a 12-inch heavy skillet over moderate heat until foam subsides. Cook 4 slices bread, turning once, until almonds and bread are golden brown, 5 to 6 minutes. Transfer to a baking sheet and keep warm in oven. Add remaining 1½ tablespoons butter to pan and cook remaining 4 slices in same manner.

Served drizzled with maple syrup and, if desired, sprinkled with confectioners' sugar.

Baked Butter-Pecan French Toast with Blueberry Syrup

SERVES 6
ACTIVE TIME: 30 MINUTES ∎ START TO FINISH: 8¾ HOURS
(INCLUDES SOAKING TIME)

∎ You don't have to be in the kitchen at the crack of dawn to prepare a terrific breakfast. This French toast is soaked overnight, like bread pudding. In the morning, all you need to do is add the pecan topping and pop it into the oven. The sticky bun–like result, lavished with warm fresh blueberry maple syrup, is a glorious reason to get out of bed. ∎

FOR FRENCH TOAST

    1   (24-inch-long) baguette
    6   large eggs
    2   cups whole milk
    1   cup packed light brown sugar
    ½   teaspoon freshly grated nutmeg
    1   teaspoon vanilla extract
    ½   stick (4 tablespoons) unsalted butter
    ¼   teaspoon salt
    ½   cup heavy cream
    1   cup (about 3¾ ounces) pecans, lightly toasted
        (see Tips, page 911) and coarsely chopped

FOR SYRUP

    1   cup blueberries
    ½   cup pure maple syrup
    1   tablespoon fresh lemon juice

MAKE THE FRENCH TOAST: Generously butter a 13-by-9-inch baking dish. Cut twenty 1-inch-thick slices from baguette and arrange in one layer in baking dish.

Whisk together eggs, milk, ¾ cup brown sugar, nutmeg, and vanilla in a large bowl until well combined and pour evenly over bread. Let bread soak for 10 minutes. Turn slices over and cover surface with a large sheet of plastic wrap, leaving a 3-inch overhang on each end of baking dish. If necessary, place a smaller baking dish on top to keep bread submerged. Refrigerate mixture until all liquid is absorbed, at least 8 hours.

Put a rack in middle of oven and preheat oven to 350°F.

Combine butter, remaining ¼ cup brown sugar, salt, and cream in a small saucepan and bring just to a boil, stirring until sugar is dissolved. Stir in pecans.

Spoon pecan mixture evenly over bread. Bake until bread is puffed, edges are lightly browned, and liquid is absorbed, 40 to 45 minutes.

MEANWHILE, MAKE THE SYRUP: Combine blueberries and maple syrup in a small saucepan and cook over moderate heat until berries burst, about 3 minutes. Stir in lemon juice.

Serve French toast with syrup.

COOK'S NOTES

■ The bread can be soaked for up to 24 hours.
■ The syrup can be made up to 1 day ahead and refrigerated, covered. Reheat before serving.

Pain Perdu with Mushrooms and Thyme

SERVES 6
ACTIVE TIME: 35 MINUTES ∎ START TO FINISH: 35 MINUTES

■ In France, day-old bread dipped in milk and eggs and fried until golden is known as *pain perdu,* or "lost bread." This rich, savory version of French toast is as welcome at dinnertime as it is for brunch. Cremini and white mushrooms make a good base for the creamy sauce, while dried porcini give it depth. ∎

FOR TOPPING

    ½   ounce (½ cup) dried porcini mushrooms
    1   cup boiling water
    3   bacon slices, chopped
    ½   cup finely chopped shallots
    ⅓   pound cremini mushrooms, trimmed and sliced
    ¼   pound white mushrooms, trimmed and sliced
    1   teaspoon chopped fresh thyme
    ⅓   cup crème fraîche
    ½   teaspoon salt
    ¼   teaspoon freshly ground black pepper
    2   tablespoons finely chopped fresh flat-leaf parsley

FOR PAIN PERDU

    1½ cups whole milk
    3   large eggs
    ½   teaspoon salt
    ¼   teaspoon freshly ground black pepper
    6   (1-inch-thick) slices brioche or challah (from a 4- to
        5-inch-wide loaf)
    ½   stick (4 tablespoons) unsalted butter

MAKE THE TOPPING: Cover porcini mushrooms with boiling water in a small bowl and soak until softened, about 10 minutes. Agitate mushrooms to dislodge grit, then lift from water, squeezing liquid from mushrooms back into bowl. Pour mushroom liquid through a sieve lined with a dampened coffee filter or paper towel into another bowl; reserve.

Cook bacon in a 12-inch heavy skillet over moderate heat, stirring occasionally, until browned and crisp, about 5 minutes. Transfer with a slotted spoon to paper towels to drain.

Add shallots to fat remaining in skillet and cook, stirring occasionally, until softened and golden, about 3 minutes. Add porcini mushrooms, fresh mushrooms, and thyme and cook, stirring occasionally, until liquid mushrooms give off has evaporated and mushrooms are golden, about 15 minutes.

Transfer mushroom mixture to a 1½- to 2-quart saucepan. Stir in reserved mushroom soaking liquid, crème fraîche, salt, and pepper until combined, then stir in parsley. Cover and keep warm over low heat, stirring occasionally.

MAKE AND COOK THE PAIN PERDU: Put a rack in middle of oven and preheat oven to 250°F.

Whisk together milk, eggs, salt, and pepper in a large shallow dish until well combined. If using challah, cut slices in half. Soak 3 slices of bread (6 half-slices if using challah) in egg mixture, turning once, just until saturated.

Heat 2 tablespoons butter in cleaned skillet over moderate heat until foam subsides. Remove bread from egg mixture with a slotted spatula, letting excess drip back into bowl, add to pan, and cook, turning once, until golden brown on both sides, 5 to 6 minutes. With a clean spatula, transfer to a baking sheet and keep warm in oven. Wipe out skillet if necessary, then soak and cook remaining bread in remaining 2 tablespoons butter in same manner.

Divide pain perdu among six plates, top with mushroom topping, and sprinkle with bacon.

Breads

Raisin Bran Muffins

MAKES ABOUT 32 MUFFINS
ACTIVE TIME: 25 MINUTES ■ START TO FINISH: 1¼ HOURS

■ Made with good-for-you wheat bran and whole wheat flour, these muffins are moist and light. This recipe yields a generous number of muffins, which makes it perfect for holiday weekends or family reunions. Or make the batter and bake just six or a dozen muffins instead of the whole batch, then stow the remainder in the fridge for the next time the urge for a muffin strikes. ■

  2 cups wheat bran
1½ cups whole wheat flour
1½ cups all-purpose flour
 ½ cup sugar
  1 tablespoon baking soda
  2 teaspoons baking powder
1¼ teaspoons salt
  1 teaspoon ground cinnamon
1⅓ cups raisins
  4 large eggs
  1 stick (8 tablespoons) unsalted butter, melted and cooled
  2 cups well-shaken buttermilk
1½ cups unsweetened applesauce
 ½ cup mild honey
  1 teaspoon vanilla extract

SPECIAL EQUIPMENT: a muffin pan with twelve ½-cup muffin cups (see Cook's Note)

Put a rack in middle of oven and preheat oven to 400°F. Generously butter muffin cups or line with paper liners.

Spread wheat bran on a large shallow baking sheet and bake until golden brown, about 5 minutes. Cool completely on pan on a rack.

Stir together wheat bran, flours, sugar, baking soda, baking powder, salt, cinnamon, and raisins in a large bowl.

Whisk together eggs in another large bowl until well combined. Add butter a little at a time, whisking until mixture is creamy. Stir in buttermilk, applesauce, honey, and vanilla, then fold in flour mixture until well combined.

Spoon about ¼ cup batter into each muffin cup. Bake until puffed and golden and a wooden toothpick or skewer comes out clean, 18 to 20 minutes. Cool in pan on a rack for 5 minutes, then remove muffins from pan and cool slightly on rack. Bake more muffins in same manner. Serve warm or at room temperature.

- If you have two muffin pans and a large oven, you can bake two pans of muffins side by side on the middle rack.
- The batter can be refrigerated in an airtight container for up to 2 weeks (it may darken slightly); the batter will expand somewhat, so make sure your container has ample room. Stir the batter before using and bake as many muffins as desired. If you're not baking a full pan of muffins, fill the empty muffin cups three-quarters full with water.
- The muffins, once cooled completely, can be stored in an airtight container at room temperature for up to 1 day.

Linzer Muffins

MAKES 12 MUFFINS
ACTIVE TIME: 30 MINUTES ■ START TO FINISH: 1¼ HOURS

■ These unassuming-looking almond-flavored muffins hide a surprise—a dollop of raspberry jam, just like classic linzer cookies. It's a delightful treat to wake up to on the weekend. ■

  1 cup (about 5¼ ounces) unblanched whole almonds, toasted (see Tips, page 911)
  ¾ cup sugar
  ½ teaspoon finely grated lemon zest
  1½ cups all-purpose flour
  2 teaspoons baking powder
  ½ teaspoon salt
  ¼ teaspoon ground cinnamon
  1 cup whole milk
  ¾ stick (6 tablespoons) unsalted butter, melted and cooled
  1 large egg
  ⅛ teaspoon almond extract
    About ⅓ cup seedless raspberry jam
    Confectioners' sugar for dusting
SPECIAL EQUIPMENT: a muffin tin with twelve ½-cup muffin cups

Put a rack in middle of oven and preheat oven to 400°F. Butter muffin cups.

Pulse almonds with sugar and zest in a food processor until finely ground.

Whisk together flour, almond mixture, baking powder, salt, and cinnamon in a large bowl. Whisk together milk, butter, egg, and almond extract in a small bowl, then stir into dry ingredients until just combined.

Spoon a scant ¼ cup batter into each muffin cup. Top each with 1 rounded teaspoon jam. Divide remaining batter among cups. Bake until muffins are golden and pull away from sides of cups, about 20 minutes. Cool in pan on a rack for 5 to 10 minutes, then turn out onto rack to cool completely.

Dust with confectioners' sugar before serving.

COOK'S NOTE

- Once cooled completely, the muffins can be stored in an airtight container at room temperature for up to 1 day.

Orange Raisin Scones

MAKES 8 SCONES
ACTIVE TIME: 15 MINUTES ■ START TO FINISH: 1 HOUR

■ Scones, teatime favorites, are perhaps even better at breakfast. Perfumed with orange zest and studded with soft, plump raisins, these are especially tasty. You'll be tempted to tuck into them as soon as they come out of the oven, but resist the urge—they taste best after cooling for about 15 minutes, when they will still be warm enough to melt any butter you spread on them. ■

  2 cups all-purpose flour
  3 tablespoons sugar
  2½ teaspoons baking powder
  ¾ teaspoon salt
  1 stick (8 tablespoons) cold unsalted butter, cut into tablespoons
  1 cup raisins
  ¾ cup whole milk
  1 large egg, separated
  1 tablespoon finely grated orange zest
  ½ teaspoon vanilla extract

Put a rack in middle of oven and preheat oven to 375°F.

Pulse together flour, 2 tablespoons sugar, baking powder, and salt in a food processor. Add butter and pulse until mixture resembles coarse meal with some small (roughly pea-sized) lumps. Transfer to a large bowl and stir in raisins.

Stir together milk, yolk, zest, and vanilla in a small bowl. Add to flour mixture, stirring with a fork just until a dough forms.

Turn dough out onto a lightly floured surface and gently knead until it just comes together. Transfer to an ungreased baking sheet and pat into a 7½-inch round. Lightly beat egg white in a small bowl and brush top of round with it. Sprinkle round with remaining 1 tablespoon sugar and cut into 8 wedges, but do not separate them.

Bake scones until undersides are browned, 30 to 35 minutes. Transfer to a rack and cool for 15 minutes, then pull apart wedges.

Serve warm or at room temperature.

COOK'S NOTE

- The scones can be made up to 2 hours ahead.

Figgy Scones

MAKES 20 SCONES
ACTIVE TIME: 25 MINUTES ■ START TO FINISH: 1 HOUR

■ Most scone doughs are either patted into a round and sliced into wedges or cut into circles with a biscuit cutter, but this tender batter is simply dropped by the spoonful onto baking sheets. The scones are dotted with diced amber-colored Calimyrna figs, which are grown in California (the same type of fig is called Smyrna if grown in Turkey or Greece); the dried fruit lends a pleasing complicated sweetness to this recipe. ■

- ¾ cup well-shaken buttermilk
- ¼ cup pure maple syrup
- ½ cup plus 2 tablespoons heavy cream
- 3½ cups all-purpose flour
- ¾ cup sugar
- 1 teaspoon salt
- 1 teaspoon baking powder
- ½ teaspoon baking soda
- 2 sticks (½ pound) unsalted butter, cut into ½-inch cubes
- ½ pound dried Calimyrna figs, stems discarded, cut into ½-inch pieces (about 1½ cups)
- 2 large egg yolks

SPECIAL EQUIPMENT: parchment paper

Put racks in upper and lower thirds of oven and preheat oven to 400°F. Line two large baking sheets with parchment paper.

Whisk together buttermilk, syrup, and ½ cup cream in a small bowl. Combine flour, sugar, salt, baking powder, and baking soda in bowl of a stand mixer and mix with paddle attachment at low speed (or whisk together in a large bowl) until combined. Add butter and mix (or blend with your fingertips or a pastry blender) until mixture resembles coarse meal with some small (roughly pea-sized) lumps. Mix in figs, then add buttermilk mixture and mix until just combined; do not overmix.

Drop ten ¼-cup mounds of batter onto each lined baking sheet, leaving 1 inch between mounds.

Whisk together yolks and remaining 2 tablespoons cream and brush over tops of scones (use all of egg wash).

Bake, switching position of baking sheets halfway through baking, until scones are puffed and golden, 20 to 25 minutes. Transfer to a rack and cool to warm.

COOK'S NOTE

- The scones are best eaten the day they're made.

Banana Nut Bread

MAKES ONE 9-BY-5-INCH LOAF
ACTIVE TIME: 25 MINUTES ■ START TO FINISH: 2¼ HOURS
(INCLUDES COOLING)

■ Muriel Reisman, the mother of *Gourmet* food editor Ruth Cousineau, made a version of this loaf often, buying extra bananas for it and letting them go almost black. A toasted slice of the moist bread topped with vanilla ice cream and chocolate sauce makes a fine impromptu dessert. ■

2½ cups sifted cake flour (not self-rising; sift before measuring)
1 teaspoon baking powder
½ teaspoon baking soda
¾ teaspoon salt
½ teaspoon ground cinnamon
½ teaspoon freshly grated nutmeg
1 stick (8 tablespoons) unsalted butter, softened
⅔ cup sugar
2 large eggs
3 very ripe medium bananas
⅔ cup well-shaken buttermilk
1 cup (about 3½ ounces) walnuts or pecans, toasted (see Tips, page 911) and chopped

SPECIAL EQUIPMENT: a 9-by-5-inch loaf pan

Put a rack in middle of oven and preheat oven to 350°F. Butter loaf pan, line bottom with wax paper or parchment, and butter paper.

Stir together flour, baking powder, baking soda, salt, cinnamon, and nutmeg in a bowl.

Beat together butter and sugar in a large bowl with an electric mixer at high speed until pale and fluffy, about 2 minutes. Reduce speed to medium and add eggs one at a time, beating until combined, then beat in bananas until combined (mixture will look curdled). Reduce speed to low and add flour mixture in 3 batches alternately with buttermilk, beginning and ending with flour mixture and mixing just until batter is smooth. Stir in nuts.

Scrape batter into loaf pan and bake until a wooden toothpick or skewer inserted into center of bread comes out clean, 1 to 1¼ hours. Cool bread in pan on a rack for 2 minutes. Invert bread onto rack and remove paper, then invert again and cool completely.

COOK'S NOTE

■ The bread keeps, wrapped in plastic wrap, at room temperature, for up to 4 days. It can also be frozen, well wrapped, for up to 1 month.

Maple Sugar Ragamuffins

MAKES 12 PASTRIES
ACTIVE TIME: 25 MINUTES ■ START TO FINISH: 1 HOUR

■ Maple sugar lends its distinctive sweetness and crunch to these quick sticky buns. The simple biscuit dough makes them a snap to pull together on a weekend morning. Granulated maple sugar keeps well in an airtight container in a cool, dark spot; it's a great staple to have on hand for adding to oatmeal or coffee. ■

FOR DOUGH
2 cups all-purpose flour
1 tablespoon granulated maple sugar (see Cook's Note and Sources)
1 tablespoon baking powder
½ teaspoon salt
5 tablespoons cold unsalted butter, cut into small pieces
¾ cup whole milk

FOR FILLING
¾ stick (6 tablespoons) unsalted butter, well softened
1 cup granulated maple sugar

SPECIAL EQUIPMENT: parchment paper

Put a rack in middle of oven and preheat oven to 400°F. Line a 17-by-14-inch baking sheet with parchment.

MAKE THE DOUGH: Whisk together flour, maple sugar, baking powder, and salt in a large bowl. Blend in butter with a pastry blender or your fingertips until most of mixture resembles coarse meal with some small (roughly pea-sized) lumps. Add milk and stir with a fork until a shaggy dough forms. Turn dough out onto a lightly floured surface and gently knead 8 to 10 times with floured hands.

ROLL OUT AND FILL THE DOUGH: Roll out dough on lightly floured surface with a floured rolling pin into a 13-by-11-inch rectangle. Spread softened butter evenly over dough and sprinkle all over with maple sugar, pressing firmly to help adhere. Beginning at one long side, roll up dough snugly, jelly-roll style. Cut roll into 12 slices with a sharp knife.

Arrange slices cut side down 2 inches apart on baking sheet. Gather any maple sugar from work surface and sprinkle on top of rolls. Bake until rolls are puffed and golden, 18 to 20 minutes. Transfer to a rack to cool until warm, about 15 minutes.

COOK'S NOTES

- If your maple sugar is in large granules, pulse it in a blender until it is finely ground.
- The ragamuffins are best eaten immediately, but they can be made up to 1 day ahead. Cool, uncovered, then store in an airtight container at room temperature. Reheat in a 350°F oven before serving.

Ginger Doughnut Rounds

MAKES ABOUT 42 SMALL DOUGHNUTS
ACTIVE TIME: 40 MINUTES ■ START TO FINISH: 40 MINUTES

■ Zesty yet sophisticated, whisper-light mini cake doughnuts make an elegant breakfast treat or a surprise ending to a meal, served with a cup of espresso. ■

 4 cups all-purpose flour
 4 teaspoons baking powder
 2 teaspoons baking soda
 1½ teaspoons salt
 1½ teaspoons ground ginger
 1¾ cups sugar
 2 ounces crystallized ginger, coarsely chopped
 ¾ cup well-shaken buttermilk
 ½ stick (4 tablespoons) unsalted butter, melted and cooled slightly
 2 large eggs
 About 3 quarts vegetable oil for deep-frying

SPECIAL EQUIPMENT: a 1¾-inch round cookie cutter; a deep-fat thermometer

Whisk together flour, baking powder, baking soda, salt, and ¾ teaspoon ground ginger in a large bowl.

Whisk together 1 cup sugar and remaining ¾ teaspoon ground ginger in a shallow bowl, to use for coating doughnuts after they're fried.

Pulse crystallized ginger with remaining ¾ cup sugar in a food processor until finely chopped. Transfer to a bowl and whisk in buttermilk, butter, and eggs until smooth. Add buttermilk mixture to flour

mixture and stir until a dough forms (dough will be sticky).

Turn dough out onto a well-floured surface and knead gently 10 to 12 times, until it just comes together. Form into a ball. Lightly dust work surface and dough with flour and roll out dough into a 13-inch round with a floured rolling pin. Cut out rounds with floured cutter and transfer to a lightly floured baking sheet. Gather scraps, reroll, and cut out more rounds. (Reroll scraps only once.)

Heat 3 inches oil in a 5-quart wide heavy pot until it registers 375°F on thermometer. Fry doughnuts in batches of 7 or 8, turning once with a wire skimmer or a slotted spoon, until golden brown, 1½ to 2 minutes per batch. Transfer to paper towels to drain. (Return oil to 375°F between batches.)

Serve doughnuts warm, dredged in ginger sugar.

COOK'S NOTE

- The doughnuts can be fried (but not dredged in ginger sugar) up to 4 hours ahead. Cool, then transfer to an airtight container. Reheat on a baking sheet in a 250°F oven for 10 to 15 minutes, cool slightly, and dredge in ginger sugar.

Coffee-Glazed Doughnuts

MAKES ABOUT 12 DOUGHNUTS
ACTIVE TIME: 45 MINUTES ■ START TO FINISH: 3¾ HOURS
(INCLUDES RISING)

■ For these doughnuts, an ethereal yeast dough is fried and then coated with a bracing coffee glaze. The result is a bit like having your morning cup of joe and a pastry in one incredible bite. Let the dough rise overnight in the refrigerator, and you'll wake up to something truly special. ■

FOR DOUGHNUTS
 1 (¼-ounce) package (2½ teaspoons) active dry yeast
 2 tablespoons warm water (105°–115°F)
 3¼ cups all-purpose flour, plus additional for sprinkling
 1 cup whole milk, at room temperature
 ½ stick (4 tablespoons) unsalted butter, softened
 3 large egg yolks

2 tablespoons granulated sugar

1½ teaspoons salt

½ teaspoon ground cinnamon

About 10 cups vegetable oil for deep-frying

FOR GLAZE

¼ cup boiling water

5 teaspoons instant espresso powder, such as
Medaglia d'Oro, or instant coffee granules

1½ cups confectioners' sugar

1 tablespoon light corn syrup

¼ teaspoon pure vanilla extract

¼ teaspoon salt

About ¼ cup sanding sugar (see Sources) or
turbinado sugar, such as Sugar in the Raw
(optional)

SPECIAL EQUIPMENT: stand mixer fitted with a paddle
attachment; a 3-inch round cookie cutter; a 1-inch
round cookie cutter; a deep-fat thermometer

MAKE THE DOUGH: Stir together yeast and warm water in a small bowl until yeast is dissolved. Let stand until foamy, about 5 minutes. (If yeast doesn't foam, discard and start over with new yeast.)

Combine flour, milk, butter, yolks, sugar, salt, and cinnamon in mixer bowl, add yeast mixture, and mix at low speed until a soft dough forms. Increase speed to medium-high and beat for 3 minutes.

Scrape dough from sides of bowl into center and sprinkle lightly with flour, to keep a crust from forming. Cover bowl with a kitchen towel (not terry cloth) and let dough rise in a warm draft-free place until doubled in bulk, 1½ to 2 hours. (Alternatively, let dough rise in refrigerator for 8 to 12 hours.)

Turn dough out onto a lightly floured surface. Roll out with a lightly floured rolling pin into a 12-inch round. Cut out as many rounds as possible with 3-inch cutter, cut a hole in center of each round with 1-inch cutter, and transfer doughnuts to a lightly floured large baking sheet. (Do not reroll scraps.) Cover doughnuts with a kitchen towel (not terry cloth) and let rise in a warm draft-free place until slightly puffed, about 30 minutes (45 minutes if dough was refrigerated).

Heat 2½ inches oil in a 4-quart deep heavy pot until it registers 350°F on thermometer. Fry doughnuts 2 at a time, turning occasionally with a wire skimmer or a slotted spoon, until puffed and golden brown, about 2 minutes per batch. Transfer to paper towels to drain. (Return oil to 350°F between batches.)

MAKE THE GLAZE: Stir together boiling water and espresso powder in a medium bowl until espresso powder is dissolved. Stir in confectioners' sugar, corn syrup, vanilla, and salt until smooth.

Set a rack on a baking sheet. Dip doughnuts into glaze, turning to coat well, and put on rack. If using sanding (or turbinado) sugar, sprinkle doughnuts with sugar while glaze is still wet; let stand until glaze is set, about 20 minutes.

COOK'S NOTE

■ The doughnuts are best eaten right after they're fried, but they are still great several hours later and very good for the rest of the day.

Buttermilk Coffee Cake

SERVES 10 TO 12
ACTIVE TIME: 45 MINUTES ■ START TO FINISH: 4 HOURS
(INCLUDES COOLING)

■ This streusel-swirled cake is what we dream of when we dream about coffee cake. Underneath a nice crisp crust, ribbons of buttery sugared walnuts run through the moist, golden cake. ■

FOR STREUSEL

¾ cup walnuts

¾ cup sugar

1 teaspoon ground cinnamon

FOR CAKE

3⅓ cups all-purpose flour

1½ teaspoons salt

2 teaspoons baking powder

1 teaspoon baking soda

1½ cups well-shaken buttermilk

2 teaspoons vanilla extract

1½ sticks (12 tablespoons) unsalted butter, softened

1¾ cups sugar

3 large eggs

SPECIAL EQUIPMENT: a 10-by-4-inch (12-cup) tube pan with
a removable bottom

MAKE THE STREUSEL: Pulse walnuts with sugar and cinnamon in a food processor until finely chopped.

MAKE THE CAKE: Put a rack in middle of oven and preheat oven to 350°F. Butter and flour tube pan, knocking out excess flour.

Whisk together flour, salt, baking powder, and baking soda in a bowl. Stir together buttermilk and vanilla in a 2-cup glass measuring cup or small bowl until combined.

Beat together butter and sugar in a large bowl with an electric mixer at medium-high speed until pale and fluffy, about 5 minutes in a stand mixer, 10 minutes with a handheld. Add eggs one at a time, beating well after each addition. Reduce speed to low and add flour mixture in 4 batches, alternating with buttermilk mixture, beginning and ending with flour mixture and beating until just combined.

Spoon one quarter of batter into tube pan and spread evenly with offset spatula or rubber spatula. Sprinkle evenly with ⅓ cup streusel mixture. Repeat with remaining batter and streusel mixture in 3 additions, ending with streusel on top.

Bake cake until a wooden skewer inserted into center comes out clean, about 1 hour and 5 minutes. Cool in pan on a rack for 10 minutes. Run a thin sharp knife around edges and center tube of pan to loosen cake. Lift cake, still on bottom of pan, and run a knife under bottom of cake to loosen it. Invert cake onto rack and turn cake right side up to cool completely.

COOK'S NOTE

■ The cake keeps, well wrapped in plastic wrap, at room temperature for up to 2 days.

Breakfast Jam Cake

SERVES 6 TO 8
ACTIVE TIME: 1 HOUR ■ START TO FINISH: 20 HOURS
(INCLUDES RISING TIME AND CHILLING)

■ This showpiece is similar to monkey bread, in which small balls of sweet yeast dough are layered in a pan and baked. The plain-looking exterior conceals pockets of jam filling ready to burst when the buttery, briochelike bread is separated. Letting the dough rest overnight is an important step, giving its flavor time to develop. ■

FOR STARTER
    1 teaspoon sugar
    ¼ cup warm milk or water (105°–115°F)
    2¼ teaspoons active dry yeast
    ½ cup sifted all-purpose flour (sift before measuring)
FOR DOUGH
    3 tablespoons sugar
    ¾ teaspoon salt
    1 tablespoon hot milk or water
    3 large eggs
    1½ cups sifted all-purpose flour (sift before measuring), plus additional for dusting
    1½ sticks (12 tablespoons) unsalted butter, cut into tablespoons, at room temperature, plus additional for brushing mold
FOR CAKE
    Rounded ½ cup thick jam or marmalade (see Cook's Note)
    1 tablespoon unsalted butter, melted
    ¼ cup pecans, finely chopped
SPECIAL EQUIPMENT: a stand mixer with whisk attachment and dough hook; an 8½-by-2¾-inch aluminum ring mold (see Sources); a 2-inch round cookie cutter

MAKE THE STARTER: Stir together sugar, warm milk, and yeast in a bowl and let stand until foamy, about 5 minutes. (If mixture doesn't foam, discard and start over with new yeast.)

Stir flour into yeast mixture until a soft dough forms. Cut a deep X in top with sharp kitchen shears. Cover bowl with plastic wrap and let rise in a warm draft-free place until almost doubled in volume, about 1 hour.

MAKE THE DOUGH: Stir together sugar, salt, and hot milk in a small bowl until well combined.

Fit mixer with whisk attachment and beat 2 eggs at medium-low speed until foamy. Add sugar mixture and beat until well combined. With motor running, add, beating well after each addition, ½ cup flour, remaining egg, ½ cup flour, 3 tablespoons butter, and remaining ½ cup flour. Beat for 1 minute.

Switch to dough hook. Scrape starter onto dough

with a rubber spatula and beat at medium-high speed until dough is smooth and elastic, about 6 minutes. Add remaining 9 tablespoons butter and beat until incorporated, about 1 minute.

Lightly butter a large bowl. Scrape dough into bowl with rubber spatula (dough will be very sticky). Lightly dust dough with flour to prevent a crust from forming. Cover bowl with plastic wrap and let dough rise in a warm draft-free place until doubled in bulk, 2 to 3 hours.

Stir down dough with rubber spatula and lightly dust with flour (dough will still be very sticky). Cover bowl with plastic wrap and refrigerate dough, stirring it once after the first hour, for at least 12 hours.

MAKE THE CAKE: Generously brush softened butter over bottom and up sides of ring mold.

Using a rubber spatula, scrape dough onto a well-floured surface. Dust dough with flour. Roll out dough into a 10½-inch disk with a well-floured rolling pin. Cut out 20 rounds, as close together as possible, with floured cutter. Gather scraps and knead once or twice, then roll out into a 5½-inch disk. Wrap in plastic wrap and refrigerate.

Flatten 2 rounds of dough to 2½ inches wide with floured fingertips. Make an indentation in center of 1 round with your thumb and place 1 level teaspoon jam in indentation, keeping edges of round clean. Cover with second flattened round and gently pinch edges with floured fingers to seal completely. Gently roll between floured palms to smooth side seams and form a flat circular pouch. Repeat with remaining rounds. (If rounds become too soft to work with, refrigerate on a plate, covered.)

Cut out 8 more rounds from chilled disk of dough and make 4 more pouches in same manner, for a total of 14 pouches.

Brush tops of pouches with some melted butter. With floured fingers, carefully arrange 7 pouches buttered side down in ring mold, evenly spaced and barely touching. Brush pouches with more butter and sprinkle pecans evenly on top. Make another layer with remaining 7 pouches, placing each pouch over edges of 2 pouches underneath, to cover gaps. Brush with remaining melted butter.

Loosely cover with plastic wrap and let pouches rise in a warm draft-free place until doubled in bulk, 1 to 2 hours (they will rise slightly above edge of ring mold).

Put a rack in middle of oven and preheat oven to 375°F.

Carefully remove plastic wrap. Put ring mold on a baking sheet and bake until top is golden brown, about 30 minutes. Invert cake onto a rack, remove mold, and cool to warm, 20 to 30 minutes, or room temperature.

Turn cake right side up just before serving, and serve intact, allowing guests to pull off their own pouches.

COOK'S NOTES
- Use your favorite jam or marmalade, but be sure to cut any large pieces of fruit into small pieces.
- The dough can be refrigerated for up to 3 days. Stir it down with rubber spatula once a day.
- The cake can be frozen for up to 1 week. Cool completely, then return to the ring mold and freeze, wrapped well in plastic wrap. Reheat, the top covered with foil, in a 350°F oven until heated through, 20 to 30 minutes.

Oatmeal Wheat Bread

MAKES TWO 8½-BY-4½-INCH LOAVES
ACTIVE TIME: 30 MINUTES ■ START TO FINISH: 5¼ HOURS
(INCLUDES RISING TIME AND COOLING)

■ This wheat loaf is soft, delicate, and slightly sweet from the oats—ideal for toast or sandwiches. ■

2 cups whole milk
1 cup old-fashioned rolled oats (not quick-cooking), plus additional for topping
½ cup warm water (105°–115°F)
2 tablespoons active dry yeast (from three ¼-ounce packages)
½ cup mild honey
½ stick (4 tablespoons) unsalted butter, melted and cooled
3 cups stone-ground whole wheat flour
About 2 cups unbleached all-purpose flour
1 tablespoon salt
1 large egg, lightly beaten with 1 tablespoon water for egg wash

SPECIAL EQUIPMENT: two 8½-by-4½-inch loaf pans

Heat milk in a 1½- to 2-quart saucepan over low heat until hot but not boiling. Remove pan from heat and stir in oats. Let stand, uncovered, stirring occasionally, until cooled to warm.

Stir together warm water, yeast, and 1 teaspoon honey in a small bowl and let stand until foamy, 5 minutes. (If mixture doesn't foam, discard and start over with new yeast.)

Stir yeast mixture, melted butter, and remaining honey into oatmeal.

Stir together whole wheat flour, 1½ cups white flour, and salt in a large bowl. Add oat mixture, stirring with a wooden spoon until a soft dough forms. Turn out onto a well-floured surface and knead with floured hands, adding just enough additional white flour to prevent sticking, until dough is smooth, soft, and elastic, about 10 minutes (dough will be slightly sticky).

Form dough into a ball and transfer to an oiled large bowl, turning to coat. Cover bowl loosely with plastic wrap and a kitchen towel and let dough rise in a warm draft-free place until doubled in bulk, 1 to 1½ hours.

Lightly butter loaf pans. Turn dough out onto a lightly floured surface and knead several times to remove air pockets. Divide dough in half and pat each half into a 10-by-6-inch rectangle. Starting from a long side, roll up each rectangle tightly, jelly-roll style. Pinch seam to seal and put dough seam side down in pans, gently tucking ends under to fit. Cover loaf pans loosely with a kitchen towel (not terry cloth) and let dough rise in a warm draft-free place until doubled in bulk, about 1 hour.

Put a rack in middle of oven and preheat oven to 375°F.

Lightly brush tops of loaves with egg wash and sprinkle with oats. Bake until bread is golden and loaves sound hollow when tapped on bottom, 35 to 40 minutes (run a knife around edge of one pan to loosen and remove loaf to test). Remove bread from pans and transfer to a rack to cool completely.

COOK'S NOTE

■ The bread keeps, wrapped in plastic wrap, at room temperature for up to 4 days.

Anadama Bread

MAKES TWO 8½-BY-4½-INCH LOAVES
ACTIVE TIME: 20 MINUTES ■ START TO FINISH: 4¼ HOURS
(INCLUDES RISING TIME AND COOLING)

■ Where did this New England specialty get its wacky name? Most speculations involve an irate, hungry Yankee cursing his culinarily challenged wife with an "Anna, damn her!" She must have eventually gotten it right, because this fragrant bread is a keeper. Stone-ground corn grits and molasses contribute distinctive flavor and moistness, without making it heavy. It makes great toast. ■

1½ cups whole milk, plus 1 tablespoon for brushing
½ cup corn grits (preferably stone-ground; see Sources), plus 1 tablespoon for sprinkling
½ cup molasses (not robust)
½ stick (4 tablespoons) unsalted butter
  Salt
1 tablespoon active dry yeast (from two ¼-ounce packages)
1 teaspoon sugar
1 cup warm water (105°–115°F)
5 cups unbleached all-purpose flour

SPECIAL EQUIPMENT: a stand mixer with a dough hook; two 8½-by-4½-inch loaf pans

Combine milk, grits, molasses, butter, and 1 teaspoon salt in a 2- to 3-quart heavy saucepan and bring to a boil, stirring frequently. Reduce heat and simmer, stirring frequently, until very thick, 10 to 12 minutes. Transfer to a bowl and cool, stirring occasionally, until just warm, about 15 minutes.

Stir together yeast, sugar, and ¼ cup warm water in bowl of mixer and let stand until foamy, about 5 minutes. (If mixture doesn't foam, discard and start over with new yeast.)

Add grits mixture, 2 cups flour, and 1 teaspoon salt to yeast mixture and mix with dough hook at low speed until combined. Add remaining 3 cups flour and remaining ¾ cup water and mix until combined. Increase speed to medium and beat until dough pulls away from sides of bowl and is smooth and elastic, 6 to 8 minutes.

Transfer dough to an oiled bowl and turn to coat. Cover bowl with plastic wrap and let dough rise in a warm draft-free place until doubled in bulk, about 1 hour.

Grease loaf pans. Punch down dough and divide in half. Pat each half into a 10-by-6-inch rectangle. Starting from a long side, roll up each rectangle tightly, jelly-roll style. Pinch seams to seal and put dough seam side down in pans, tucking ends under slightly to fit. Cover pans with plastic wrap and let rise in a warm draft-free place until dough has filled pans, 1½ to 2 hours.

Put a rack in middle of oven and preheat oven to 375°F.

Brush loaves with remaining tablespoon milk and sprinkle with remaining tablespoon grits. Bake until loaves are golden brown and bottoms sound hollow when tapped (run a knife around edges of one pan to loosen and remove loaf to test), about 30 minutes. Turn loaves out onto a rack to cool completely.

COOK'S NOTE

■ The bread keeps, wrapped in plastic wrap, at room temperature for up to 2 days. It can also be frozen, well wrapped, for up to 1 month.

Portuguese Honey Bread

MAKES 6 SMALL LOAVES
ACTIVE TIME: 40 MINUTES ■ START TO FINISH: 2½ HOURS
(INCLUDES COOLING)

■ Dense with dried fruit and nuts, this makes a wonderful addition to the morning bread basket. It's sweet but not overly so, and it requires neither butter nor jam. The little loaves are great for holiday gift giving. You'll notice that the recipe calls for both yeast and baking soda—that's because honey and molasses are very acidic, which can affect the leavening; the soda neutralizes that acid. ■

¾ cup dried cranberries or dried sour cherries
¾ cup chopped mixed fine-quality candied fruit, such as pear, citron, and candied orange peel (see Sources)

¼ cup port
1 tablespoon active dry yeast (from two ¼-ounce packages)
¼ cup warm water (105°–115°F)
1¼ cups (about 4 ounces) walnuts
4½ cups all-purpose flour
1 teaspoon salt
1 teaspoon baking soda
½ teaspoon ground ginger
½ teaspoon ground cinnamon
¼ teaspoon ground cloves
2½ sticks (1¼ cups) unsalted butter, softened
1 cup sugar
3 large eggs
¾ cup molasses (not robust)
½ cup mild honey

SPECIAL EQUIPMENT: six 6-by-3¼-by-2-inch loaf pans (2- to 2¼-cup capacity; see Cook's Note)

Put a rack in middle of oven and preheat oven to 325°F. Butter loaf pans.

Combine cranberries, candied fruit, and port in a small saucepan and bring to a simmer. Remove from heat and set aside, covered.

Stir together yeast and warm water in a small bowl and let stand until foamy, about 5 minutes. (If mixture doesn't foam, discard and start over with new yeast.)

Meanwhile, pulse walnuts in a food processor just until coarsely chopped. Add flour, salt, baking soda, and spices and pulse to combine.

Beat together butter and sugar in a large bowl with an electric mixer at medium-high speed until pale and fluffy, about 4 minutes in a stand mixer, 6 with a handheld. Add eggs one at a time, beating well after each addition. Add one third of flour mixture and mix at low speed until combined. Add molasses and mix until incorporated. Add half of remaining flour mixture and mix until combined, then add honey and mix until incorporated. Add yeast mixture and remaining flour mixture and mix until combined. Stir in candied fruit mixture.

Divide batter among pans, smoothing tops. Bake until a wooden toothpick or skewer inserted in centers of loaves comes out clean, 50 to 60 minutes. Cool in pans on a rack for 10 minutes, then remove loaves from pans and cool completely on rack.

- Disposable foil mini loaf pans are available in many supermarkets.
- The breads keep, wrapped tightly in plastic wrap and then foil, at room temperature for up to 1 week.

Mexican Sweet Buns

Pan Dulce

MAKES 12 BUNS
ACTIVE TIME: 1 HOUR ■ START TO FINISH: 4¼ HOURS
(INCLUDES RISING TIME AND COOLING)

■ Anyone who has traveled to Mexico—or to Mexican bakeries in the United States—will recognize these squat round yeast buns; they are eagerly snapped up by hungry patrons and eaten with coffee or hot chocolate. *Pan dulce* is the generic term—there are dozens of different kinds. They are traditionally crowned with a sugar-butter topping and impressed with a special cutter to form a shell-like or crosshatched pattern on top; a sharp knife works just as well. Using a stand mixer allows the dough to remain slightly sticky, which is crucial for moist, fluffy buns. ■

FOR DOUGH
- ⅔ cup plus 1 teaspoon sugar
- 2 tablespoons warm water (105°–115°F)
- 1 (¼-ounce) package (2½ teaspoons) active dry yeast
- ⅓ cup warm whole milk (105°–115°F)
- 1½ teaspoons vanilla extract
- 4 large eggs
- 2 large egg yolks
- 1 stick (8 tablespoons) unsalted butter, cut into tablespoons, softened
- 1 teaspoon salt
- 4½–5 cups all-purpose flour

FOR TOPPING
- ½ cup all-purpose flour
- ½ cup sugar
- 2 teaspoons ground cinnamon
- ¾ stick (6 tablespoons) unsalted butter, cut into tablespoons

FOR EGG WASH
- 1 large egg yolk
- 1 tablespoon water

SPECIAL EQUIPMENT: a stand mixer with paddle attachment and dough hook

MAKE THE DOUGH: Stir together 1 teaspoon sugar, warm water, and yeast in bowl of mixer and let stand until foamy, about 5 minutes. (If mixture doesn't foam, discard and start over with new yeast.)

Add milk, vanilla, and remaining ⅔ cup sugar to yeast mixture and beat with paddle attachment at medium speed until well combined. Beat in eggs and yolks one at a time, then add butter, salt, and 1 cup flour, beating until butter is in small lumps.

Switch to dough hook and beat in 3½ cups flour at medium speed until a slightly sticky dough forms, adding up to ½ cup more flour if necessary. Beat until dough is smooth and elastic, 5 to 6 minutes.

Turn dough out onto an unfloured surface, form into a loose ball, and transfer to a lightly buttered large bowl, turning to coat. Cover bowl tightly with plastic wrap and let dough rise in a warm draft-free place until doubled in bulk, 1½ to 2 hours.

MEANWHILE, MAKE THE TOPPING: Blend all ingredients in a food processor until a ball forms. Turn out onto a work surface and divide into 12 rounded tablespoons. Roll tablespoons into balls and arrange 3 inches apart in rows on a wax-paper-lined large baking sheet. Cover balls with a second sheet of wax paper and flatten each ball into a 3-inch round with bottom of a glass. Chill rounds until firm, about 1 hour.

MAKE THE EGG WASH: Whisk together yolk and water in a small bowl.

MAKE THE BUNS: Butter two large baking sheets. Divide dough into 12 equal pieces. Roll 1 piece into a ball on an unfloured work surface and flatten into a 3½-inch disk with your fingers. Carefully transfer to one of baking sheets, reshaping it if necessary. Brush top of disk lightly with egg wash and place 1 round of topping on disk, pressing lightly to help it adhere. With back of a small paring knife, score topping in a crosshatch pattern. Make more buns with topping in same manner, arranging 6 buns on each sheet. Let rise, uncovered, in a warm draft-free place until slightly puffed, 1½ to 2 hours.

Put a rack in middle of oven and preheat oven to 375°F.

Bake buns one sheet at a time until bottom edges are pale golden, about 12 minutes per batch. (Topping will not turn golden.) Transfer buns to racks to cool.

COOK'S NOTES

■ The topping rounds can be made and flattened up to 1 day ahead. To make an airtight package, fold the rows of wax-paper-wrapped rounds on top of one another (like a business letter) and wrap tightly in plastic.

■ The buns can be baked up to 1 day ahead. Cool completely, then store in airtight containers at room temperature. Reheat in the middle of a 350°F oven to recrisp the topping before serving, about 5 minutes.

Chocolate Babka

MAKES TWO 8½-BY-4½-INCH LOAVES
ACTIVE TIME: 1 HOUR ■ START TO FINISH: 6½ HOURS
(INCLUDES RISING TIME AND COOLING)

■ Babka fills your kitchen with an enticing aroma as it bakes. The rich yeast bread from Eastern Europe may be filled with raisins, nuts, cinnamon, or cheese, but this version—generously laced with dark bittersweet chocolate—is our hands-down favorite. It's best served warm so that the babka's buttery nature reasserts itself and the chocolate melts ever so slightly. ■

FOR DOUGH

    ¾ cup warm milk (105°–115°F)
    ½ cup plus 2 teaspoons sugar
    1 tablespoon active dry yeast (from two ¼-ounce packages)
  3¼ cups all-purpose flour
    2 large eggs
    1 large egg yolk
    1 teaspoon vanilla extract
    ¾ teaspoon salt
  1¼ sticks (10 tablespoons) unsalted butter, cut into tablespoons, softened

FOR EGG WASH

    1 large egg yolk

    1 tablespoon heavy cream or whole milk

FOR CHOCOLATE FILLING

    5 tablespoons unsalted butter, softened
    2 (3½- to 4-ounce) bars bittersweet chocolate (no more than 60% cacao; see page 705), finely chopped
    ¼ cup sugar

SPECIAL EQUIPMENT: a stand mixer with a paddle attachment; two 8½-by-4½-inch loaf pans; parchment paper

MAKE THE DOUGH: Stir together warm milk, 2 teaspoons sugar, and yeast in bowl of mixer and let stand until foamy, about 5 minutes. (If mixture doesn't foam, discard and start over with new yeast.)

Add ½ cup flour to yeast mixture and beat with paddle attachment at medium speed until combined. Add eggs, yolk, vanilla, salt, and remaining ½ cup sugar and beat until combined. Reduce speed to low and mix in remaining 2¾ cups flour about ½ cup at a time. Increase speed to medium and beat in butter a few pieces at a time. Continue to beat until dough is shiny and forms strands running from paddle to sides of bowl, about 4 minutes. (Dough will be very soft and sticky.)

Scrape dough into a lightly oiled bowl and cover bowl with plastic wrap. Let dough rise in a warm draft-free place until doubled in bulk, 1½ to 2 hours.

SHAPE AND FILL THE BABKAS: Line each loaf pan with two pieces of parchment paper (one running lengthwise and one crosswise).

Push down dough with a lightly oiled rubber spatula. Halve dough. Roll out 1 piece of dough on a well-floured surface with a lightly floured rolling pin into an 18-by-10-inch rectangle. Turn dough so a long side is nearest you.

Beat together yolk and cream for egg wash. Spread 2½ tablespoons softened butter on dough, leaving a ½-inch border all around. Brush some of egg wash on long border nearest you. Sprinkle half of chocolate evenly over buttered dough, then sprinkle with 2 tablespoons sugar. Starting with long side farthest from you, roll dough into a snug log and pinch seam firmly to seal. Bring ends of log together to form a ring, pinching to seal. Twist entire ring twice to form a double figure eight, and fit into one of lined loaf pans.

Make another babka with remaining dough, some of egg wash, and remaining butter and chocolate in same manner; refrigerate remaining egg wash, covered. Loosely cover pans with buttered plastic wrap (buttered side down) and let babkas rise in a warm draft-free place until dough reaches top of pans, 1 to 2 hours. (Alternatively, let dough rise in pans in refrigerator for 8 to 12 hours; bring to room temperature, 3 to 4 hours, before baking.)

Put a rack in middle of oven and preheat oven to 350°F.

Brush tops of dough with reserved egg wash. Bake until tops are deep golden brown and bottoms sound hollow when tapped (remove 1 loaf from pan to test), about 40 minutes. Transfer loaves to a rack and cool to room temperature.

COOK'S NOTE

- The babkas can be frozen, wrapped in plastic wrap and then foil, for up to 3 weeks. Reheat by wrapping tightly in foil and warming for 10 to 15 minutes in a 350°F oven.

Panettone

MAKES 2 LOAVES
ACTIVE TIME: 45 MINUTES ■ START TO FINISH: 7¾ HOURS
(INCLUDES RISING TIME AND COOLING)

- Christmas in Milan means panettone, delightful dome-shaped yeast breads studded with sultana raisins and candied citron. (Citron is a citrus fruit with sour flesh and a thick, gnarled skin that is perfect for candying.) A slice of this moist, slightly sweet loaf is just as good with a glass of dessert wine after dinner as it is with a mug of morning coffee. The store-bought version can't compare to the rich, subtle sweetness of this one. ■

FOR DOUGH
- 1 cup golden raisins
- ½ cup sweet Marsala
- ½ cup warm milk (105°–115°F)
- ⅔ cup plus 2 teaspoons sugar
- 4 teaspoons active dry yeast (from two ¼-ounce packages)

- 3¼ cups unbleached all-purpose flour
- 3 large eggs, left at room temperature for 30 minutes
- 1 large egg yolk
- 1 tablespoon finely grated lemon zest
- 1 tablespoon fresh lemon juice
- ¾ teaspoon salt
- 1 stick (8 tablespoons) unsalted butter, cut into tablespoons, softened
- 1 cup diced fine-quality candied citron (see Cook's Note and Sources)

FOR EGG WASH
- 1 large egg yolk
- 1 tablespoon water

SPECIAL EQUIPMENT: a stand mixer with a paddle attachment; two 10- to 15-ounce clean coffee cans (paper or plastic labels removed); parchment paper

MAKE THE DOUGH: Simmer raisins in Marsala in a small saucepan for 2 minutes. Remove from heat and let cool to room temperature.

Meanwhile, stir together warm milk, 2 teaspoons sugar, and yeast in bowl of mixer and let stand until foamy, about 5 minutes. (If mixture doesn't foam, discard and start over with new yeast.)

Add ¼ cup flour to yeast mixture and beat with paddle attachment at medium speed until combined. Add eggs, yolk, zest, lemon juice, salt, and remaining ⅔ cup sugar and beat until incorporated. Reduce speed to low and mix in remaining 3 cups flour ½ cup at a time. Increase speed to medium-high and gradually beat in butter, a few pieces at a time. Continue to beat until dough is shiny and forms strands running from paddle to sides of bowl, 4 to 6 minutes. (Dough will be very soft and sticky.) Drain raisins (discard Marsala), add to dough, along with candied citron, and mix at low speed until incorporated.

Scrape dough into a lightly oiled bowl and cover bowl with plastic wrap. Let dough rise in a warm draft-free place until doubled in bulk, 2 to 3 hours.

Generously butter coffee cans. Line bottom and sides of each with parchment (use a round for bottom and a rectangle for sides).

Punch down dough with lightly floured hands and turn out onto a lightly floured surface. Halve dough and scoop one half into each can, pressing gently to remove any air bubbles. Loosely cover cans with lightly buttered plastic wrap and let rise in a warm draft-free place until dough reaches top of cans, 2 to 3 hours. (Alternatively, let dough rise in refrigerator for 8 to 12 hours; bring to room temperature, 3 to 4 hours, before baking.)

MAKE THE EGG WASH AND BAKE THE PANETTONE: Put a rack in lower third of oven and preheat oven to 375°F.

Beat together yolk and water and lightly brush tops of dough with egg wash. Bake until tops are deep golden brown and bottoms sound hollow when tapped (firmly thump bottom of inverted can and remove 1 loaf from can to test; return to can if necessary), 35 to 40 minutes. Transfer loaves to a rack (discard parchment) and cool to room temperature.

COOK'S NOTES

- Supermarket candied citron, often made with inferior ingredients and preservatives, should not be used.
- The panettone can be frozen, wrapped tightly in plastic wrap and then foil, for up to 3 weeks.

COOKIES, BARS, AND CONFECTIONS

I once sat down and attempted to calculate how many cookies *Gourmet* has invented in its long history. To begin with, there were those sixty-seven Christmas articles to factor in, not to mention showers, Super Bowl parties, back-to-school specials . . . Over the years, it has added up to hundreds and hundreds of cookies.

And yet, when we began gathering our recipes, we discovered there were a few holes. The sudden comeback of the s'more, a treat ordinarily made with supermarket ingredients, gave us pause. What would happen, we wondered, if we tried making them with homemade graham crackers? Into the kitchen we went, only to be startled by the results: these graham crackers are superb!

This led us to a consideration of marshmallows. Making our own seemed slightly crazy until we discovered that they are remarkably easy, great fun, and so much tastier than the store-bought kind. On top of that, you can add any flavor that you like; we opted for coconut, which gives them a kind of magical fluffiness. Pair them with graham crackers and chocolate if you like, but they're so good on their own that they're likely to be gone long before the campfire is built.

We tend to think of cookies and candies as enduring classics, and many certainly are. But they are also an excellent indication of the ways in which our tastes have changed. Consider hazelnut biscotti: ten years ago, they would have seemed exotic. Today they occupy a new position in the American culinary repertoire, and cooks vie to see who makes them best. (Ours are guaranteed winners.) Or think about pistachio cranberry icebox cookies, whose extraordinary beauty comes from the dried cranberries that have only recently become a supermarket staple. And *alfajores*, the fabulous caramel sandwich cookies of Peru, would have seemed strange and mysterious until a few years ago, when dulce de leche became a pantry staple in American homes.

We've included some things old and some things new. A few are sturdy after-school treats, like peanut butter and jelly cookies or the straightforwardly delicious (and extremely comforting) cornmeal sugar cookies. Others are classics—bittersweet chocolate brownies, superbly silly and utterly irresistible whoopie pies, and elegant sand tarts. If these don't strike you as sufficiently sophisticated, you have only to whip up fleur de sel caramels or some jewel-like passion fruit gelées to add instant elegance to your table.

These cookies and confections share one other important attribute: they all make great gifts. So when you're faced with one of those people who already owns absolutely everything, turn to the stove. You can bet that they don't have any of these — and you can also be sure that they'd like to.

COOKIES, BARS, AND CONFECTIONS

Oatmeal Cookies with Dried Fruit

MAKES 2½ DOZEN COOKIES
ACTIVE TIME: 20 MINUTES ■ START TO FINISH: 1 HOUR

■ It may seem heretical to make an oatmeal cookie without raisins, but you'll never miss them after one bite of these moist cookies, loaded with dried apricots, prunes, and sour cherries. The combination volleys between sweet and tart, all in a familiar context. ■

    1 stick (8 tablespoons) unsalted butter, softened
    ¾ cup packed dark brown sugar
    1 large egg, lightly beaten
    ½ teaspoon baking soda, dissolved in 1 tablespoon
       warm water
    ⅔ cup all-purpose flour
    ½ teaspoon salt
    1 teaspoon vanilla extract
    1½ cups old-fashioned rolled oats
    ½ cup chopped dried apricots
    ½ cup chopped pitted prunes
    ½ cup dried sour cherries or dried cranberries

Put a rack in middle of oven and preheat oven to 350°F. Butter two large baking sheets.

Beat together butter and brown sugar in a large bowl with an electric mixer until pale and fluffy. Beat in egg, baking soda mixture, flour, salt, and vanilla until combined. Stir in oats, apricots, prunes, and cherries until well combined.

Drop slightly rounded tablespoons of dough about 3 inches apart onto baking sheets. Flatten and spread into 2-inch rounds with a fork dipped in cold water. Bake cookies in batches until golden, about 12 minutes. Cool cookies on sheets for 5 minutes, then transfer to racks to cool completely.

COOK'S NOTE

■ The cookies keep in an airtight container at room temperature for up to 5 days.

Chocolate Chunk Oatmeal Coconut Cookies

MAKES ABOUT 2 DOZEN LARGE COOKIES
ACTIVE TIME: 20 MINUTES ■ START TO FINISH: 1 HOUR

■ When it comes to cookies, we prefer chunks of chocolate to chips. The irregular shapes and sizes of hand-chopped chocolate mean that some pieces melt and ooze while others hold their shape. Throw in some toasted almonds, sweet tendrils of coconut, and nubby old-fashioned oats, and you have what just may be the ultimate oatmeal cookie. ■

    2 sticks (½ pound) unsalted butter, softened
    1 cup packed brown sugar (light or dark)
    6 tablespoons granulated sugar
    2 large eggs
    1½ teaspoons vanilla extract
    ½ teaspoon baking soda
    ½ teaspoon salt
    1 cup all-purpose flour
    2¼ cups old-fashioned rolled oats
    1½ cups finely shredded unsweetened dried coconut
    12 ounces semisweet or bittersweet chocolate, cut into
       ½-inch chunks (about 2 cups; see Cook's Note)
    ¾ cup unblanched whole almonds, toasted (see Tips,
       page 911) and chopped

Put racks in upper and lower thirds of oven and preheat oven to 375°F. Lightly butter two large baking sheets.

Beat together butter and sugars in a large bowl with an electric mixer until pale and fluffy. Beat in eggs. Beat in vanilla, baking soda, and salt. Beat in flour at low speed. Stir in oats, coconut, chocolate, and almonds.

Place ¼-cup mounds of dough about 3 inches apart on baking sheets (about 8 cookies per sheet), then gently pat down each mound to about ½ inch thick. Bake cookies in batches, switching position of sheets halfway through baking, until golden, 15 to 18 minutes. Cool cookies on sheets for 1 minute, then transfer to racks to cool completely.

- You can use packaged chocolate chunks instead of cutting up the chocolate yourself.
- The cookies keep in an airtight container at room temperature for up to 5 days.

Chocolate Cookies with Gin-Soaked Raisins

MAKES ABOUT 1 DOZEN LARGE COOKIES
ACTIVE TIME: 40 MINUTES ■ START TO FINISH: 10 HOURS
(INCLUDES SOAKING RAISINS)

■ Maida Heatter, the doyenne of American desserts and a renowned cookbook author, came up with the brilliant idea of soaking golden raisins in gin and then adding them to a rich, chocolaty dough. The glorious result is crusty on the outside, gooey on the inside, and just wicked enough to save until the kids go to bed. ■

½ cup golden raisins
⅓ cup gin
3 cups sifted confectioners' sugar (sift before measuring)
⅔ cup sifted unsweetened cocoa powder, preferably Dutch-process (sift before measuring)
1 teaspoon instant espresso powder, such as Medaglia d'Oro
2 tablespoons all-purpose flour
⅛ teaspoon salt
3 large egg whites
½ teaspoon vanilla extract
2 cups (about 7½ ounces) pecans, toasted (see Tips, page 911) and coarsely chopped

Combine raisins and gin in a cup and let macerate for at least 8 hours (see Cook's Note).

Put a rack in middle of oven and preheat oven to 350°F. Butter and flour two large baking sheets, knocking off excess flour.

Mix confectioners' sugar, cocoa, espresso powder, flour, and salt in a bowl with an electric mixer at low speed. Add egg whites and vanilla and mix until smooth.

Drain raisins in a sieve, without pressing on them,

and add to dough, along with pecans. Stir until thoroughly mixed. (Dough will be thick and sticky.)

Working quickly, drop ¼-cup mounds of dough at least 3 inches apart onto baking sheets. Gently pat down to about ½ inch thick.

Bake cookies in batches, rotating sheet halfway through baking, until cookies appear cracked and centers are just set, 15 to 17 minutes. Cool cookies on sheets for 1 minute, then carefully transfer to racks to cool completely.

COOK'S NOTES

- You can soak the raisins in the gin for up to 1 week.
- The cookies keep in an airtight container at room temperature for up to 5 days.

Toasted-Coconut Cookies

MAKES ABOUT 6 DOZEN COOKIES
ACTIVE TIME: 30 MINUTES ■ START TO FINISH: 1 HOUR

■ Soft, buttery, and very coconutty, these old-fashioned cookies were made to go with a glass of cold milk. The recipe makes a lot, but you'll be happy to have a jar full of them. ■

1½ cups sweetened flaked coconut
1¼ cups all-purpose flour
1 teaspoon baking soda
½ teaspoon salt
1¼ sticks (10 tablespoons) unsalted butter, softened
½ cup packed light brown sugar
¼ cup granulated sugar
1 large egg
1 teaspoon vanilla extract

Put a rack in middle of oven and preheat oven to 375°F.

Spread coconut evenly on a baking sheet and lightly toast in oven, stirring once, until pale golden, about 7 minutes. Cool.

Sift together flour, baking soda, and salt into a small bowl.

Beat together butter and sugars in a large bowl with an electric mixer until pale and fluffy. Beat in egg and vanilla. Reduce speed to low and mix in flour mixture and coconut until well combined.

Place level teaspoons of dough about 1½ inches apart on ungreased baking sheets. Bake cookies in batches until golden, 8 to 10 minutes. Cool cookies on sheets for 1 minute, then transfer to racks to cool.

COOK'S NOTE

■ The cookies keep in an airtight container at room temperature for up to 1 week.

Drop heaping teaspoons of dough about ½ inch apart onto lined baking sheets. Gently squeeze each one with your fingers to form a rough cone shape.

Bake cookies in batches until barely browned and still moist in center, 12 to 15 minutes. Cool cookies for 5 minutes on sheet, then transfer to a rack to cool completely.

COOK'S NOTE

■ The cookies keep in an airtight container at room temperature for up to 1 week.

Brutti-Boni

MAKES ABOUT 4 DOZEN COOKIES
ACTIVE TIME: 45 MINUTES ■ START TO FINISH: 1 HOUR

■ *Brutti ma buoni*—"ugly but good" cookies—are found in many regions of Italy, usually made from finely ground almonds in a meringue base. But the Mattei bakery in Prato, near Florence, makes (and spells) them in the typical Tuscan style. The egg whites are only lightly beaten, and the nuts, which include a handful of pine nuts that add a more complex, creamy flavor, are coarser. These crisp, chewy cookies were shared with us by the authority on Italian cooking Faith Heller Willinger. ■

2 cups (10½ ounces) unblanched whole almonds, toasted (see Tips, page 911)
¼ cup pine nuts, lightly toasted (see Tips, page 911)
1⅓ cups sugar
2–3 large egg whites
2 tablespoons cake flour (not self-rising)
⅛ teaspoon salt
SPECIAL EQUIPMENT: parchment paper

Put a rack in middle of oven and preheat oven to 350°F. Line two baking sheets with parchment paper.

Pulse almonds and pine nuts with sugar in a food processor until coarsely chopped. Lightly beat 2 egg whites with a whisk and add to nuts, along with flour and salt. Process until evenly moist. (Dough should be slightly sticky but firm enough to hold together. If it is too dry, lightly beat remaining egg white and blend into dough 1 teaspoon at a time.)

Ginger Honey Cookies

MAKES ABOUT 3 DOZEN COOKIES
ACTIVE TIME: 15 MINUTES ■ START TO FINISH: 1¾ HOURS

■ Lots of crystallized ginger contributes a peppery bite to these easy drop cookies. Their deep sweetness comes from a combination of honey and brown sugar. ■

2½ cups all-purpose flour
2 teaspoons baking soda
½ teaspoon salt
½ cup finely chopped crystallized ginger
2 sticks (½ pound) unsalted butter, softened
1 cup packed light brown sugar
2 large eggs
½ cup mild honey

Put racks in upper and lower thirds of oven and preheat oven to 350°F.

Whisk together flour, baking soda, salt, and ginger in a bowl.

Beat together butter and brown sugar in a large bowl with an electric mixer at medium-high speed until pale and fluffy. Beat in eggs and honey until combined. Reduce speed to low and mix in flour mixture.

Drop heaping tablespoons of dough 2 inches apart onto two ungreased baking sheets. Bake cookies in batches, switching position of sheets halfway through baking, until golden, 10 to 14 minutes (cookies will spread flat). Cool cookies completely on sheets on racks.

COOK'S NOTE

■ The cookies keep in an airtight container at room temperature for up to 3 days.

Molasses Crinkles

MAKES ABOUT 6 DOZEN COOKIES
ACTIVE TIME: 35 MINUTES ■ START TO FINISH: 1½ HOURS

■ This molasses crinkle cookie, from reader Jane Booth Vollers of Chester, Connecticut, stands out from the others we've tasted. It has just the right amount of molasses sweetness, balanced by a generous combination of cinnamon, ginger, allspice, and cloves. As the cookies bake, they develop a crackly pattern, which is highlighted by the glittering sugar. When fresh, these cookies have a slight crunch on the outside and are tenderly chewy within; over time, they will soften. ■

2¼ cups all-purpose flour
2 teaspoons baking soda
1 teaspoon ground cinnamon
¾ teaspoon ground ginger
½ teaspoon ground allspice
½ teaspoon ground cloves
½ teaspoon salt
½ cup vegetable shortening, preferably trans fat–free, at room temperature
½ stick (4 tablespoons) unsalted butter, softened
1 cup packed dark brown sugar
1 large egg
½ cup molasses (not robust)
About ⅓ cup sanding sugar (see Sources) or granulated sugar

Put racks in upper and lower thirds of oven and preheat oven to 375°F.

Whisk together flour, baking soda, cinnamon, ginger, allspice, cloves, and salt in a bowl.

Beat together shortening, butter, and brown sugar in a large bowl with an electric mixer at medium-high speed until pale and fluffy. Add egg and molasses, beating until combined. Reduce speed to low and mix in flour mixture.

With wet hands, roll heaping teaspoons of dough into 1-inch balls, then dip bottom of each ball in sanding sugar and arrange balls, sugared side up, 2 inches apart on two ungreased baking sheets.

Bake cookies in batches, switching position of sheets halfway through baking, until bottoms are golden brown, 10 to 12 minutes. Cool cookies on sheets for 1 minute, then transfer to racks to cool completely.

COOK'S NOTE
■ The cookies keep, layered between sheets of wax paper or parchment, in an airtight container at room temperature for up to 2 weeks.

MOLASSES

Molasses—a traditional sweetener used in cookies, gingerbread, shoofly pie, barbecue sauces, and dishes such as baked beans—is the thick concentrated syrup that remains after all the readily crystallizable sucrose (granulated sugar) has been extracted from boiled sugarcane juices. (The molasses made from sugar beets is extremely bitter and is primarily used in cattle feed.) In order to remove as much sucrose as possible from the juices, the crystallization is done in three different steps, each one of which produces a different grade of molasses. In general, the darker the molasses, the less sweet and more bitter it is, because its sugars have been chemically transformed by caramelization and browning reactions. LIGHT MOLASSES (sometimes labeled "original" or "mild"), which is a product of the first boiling, is mild and mellow in flavor. Most of the light molasses sold in supermarkets is labeled "UNSULFURED." Sulfured molasses has had sulfur dioxide added as a preservative and bleaching agent, and it isn't as mellow as the unsulfured type. ROBUST MOLASSES (also labeled "full" or "full-flavored" molasses) is what's left behind after the second boiling. It's not as sweet as light molasses, but it's more complex and suave in flavor. BLACKSTRAP MOLASSES (from the Dutch word *stroop*, meaning "syrup") comes from the third and last boiling. It's too harsh and bitter for most recipes, but because of its high mineral content, it's often sold as a nutritional supplement.

Peanut Butter and Jelly Cookies

MAKES ABOUT 2 DOZEN COOKIES
ACTIVE TIME: 25 MINUTES ■ START TO FINISH: 1 HOUR

■ When you cross the classic flavors of a PB and J with a thumbprint cookie, this is the delicious result. ■

¾ cup all-purpose flour
½ teaspoon salt
½ teaspoon baking soda
⅓ cup creamy peanut butter (regular or natural-style)
½ stick (4 tablespoons) unsalted butter, softened
⅓ cup packed light brown sugar
1 large egg
½ teaspoon vanilla extract
⅓ cup granulated sugar
3 tablespoons grape jelly

Put a rack in middle of oven and preheat oven to 375°F.

Whisk together flour, salt, and baking soda in a bowl.

Whisk together peanut butter, butter, and brown sugar in a medium bowl until smooth. Whisk in egg and vanilla. Add flour mixture and stir until blended. If dough is very soft, refrigerate, covered, until firm.

Put granulated sugar in a small bowl. Roll pieces of dough into 1-inch balls, roll in sugar, and arrange 2 inches apart on a large ungreased baking sheet. Bake for 10 minutes. Working quickly, make an indentation about ½ inch in diameter in center of each cookie with back of a ¼-teaspoon measuring

MAKING COOKIES: TIPS FOR SUCCESS

TOOLS

- A HANDHELD MIXER allows you to use bowls of any size. A HEAVY DUTY STAND MIXER is helpful for large batches of batter. (It also zips through dense almond paste and whips up a meringue in minutes.)
- ALUMINUM BAKING SHEETS should be light-colored and light- to medium-weight to promote even browning. NONSTICK BAKING SHEETS are easier to clean, but their darker color can cause cookies to burn on the bottom.
- SMALL OFFSET SPATULAS are perfect for smoothing the surface of bar cookie batter and for applying icing.
- MESH COOLING RACKS with tightly spaced wires prevent cookies from falling through the cracks.
- A SMALL ICE CREAM SCOOP forms even, round drop cookies.
- A DISPOSABLE PASTRY BAG (or a sealable plastic bag with a corner snipped off) works well for decorating with icing and is easy to use.
- PLAIN ROUND WRITING TIPS in all sizes are good for outlining ("tracing") cookies with icing.

TEMPERATURE

- All ingredients (butter, eggs, shortening, melted chocolate, etc.) should be at room temperature for proper aeration and volume, unless otherwise noted.
- Always cool baking sheets between batches to prevent cookies from spreading too much as they bake.

TECHNIQUES

- When rolling out dough, don't overflour the work surface or dough, or your cookies will be tough.
- For slice-and-bake cookies, shape the dough into a rough log in a sheet of plastic wrap or wax paper, leaving the ends open, and press and smooth the plastic or paper with your hands to remove any air bubbles. Then twist the ends of the wrap or paper to help compact the log, so it is easier to slice.

TIMING

- Check for doneness a minute or so before the time indicated, unless you know your oven is correctly calibrated.

spoon. Fill each indentation with a slightly heaping ¼ teaspoon jelly. Bake cookies until golden, about 10 minutes more. Transfer to racks to cool. Make more cookies in the same manner.

COOK'S NOTE

■ These cookies are best eaten the day they are baked.

Bake until firm and golden brown, 18 to 20 minutes. Transfer crisp, still on parchment, to a rack to cool completely.

Remove crisp from paper, breaking into pieces.

COOK'S NOTE

■ The crisps keep in an airtight container at room temperature for up to 1 day (after that, they will lose their crispness).

Pistachio–Dark Chocolate Crisps

SERVES 8
ACTIVE TIME: 25 MINUTES ■ START TO FINISH: 1 HOUR

■ This variation on spice cookies will beguile with its unlikely ingredients: a little curry powder provides a base note for flat brown sugar tuiles studded with pistachios and chocolate chunks. These are the least fussy of cookies—just spread the batter, sprinkle with chocolate and nuts, and break up into pieces after baking. ■

- ½ stick (4 tablespoons) unsalted butter, softened
- ½ cup packed light brown sugar
- 6 tablespoons all-purpose flour
- ⅛ teaspoon salt
- ⅛ teaspoon curry powder
- ¼ teaspoon vanilla extract
- 1 large egg white
- 2 ounces bittersweet chocolate, chopped
- ½ cup roasted shelled pistachios, chopped

SPECIAL EQUIPMENT: parchment paper

Put a rack in middle of oven and preheat oven to 350°F. Line a large baking sheet with parchment paper.

Combine butter, brown sugar, flour, salt, curry powder, vanilla, and egg white in a food processor and blend until smooth.

Glue parchment to baking sheet with a dab of batter in each corner. Spread remaining batter evenly into a 14-by-10-inch rectangle on parchment with an offset spatula or a rubber spatula. Scatter chocolate and nuts evenly over batter.

Almond Spice Cookies

MAKES ABOUT 4 DOZEN COOKIES
ACTIVE TIME: 35 MINUTES ■ START TO FINISH: 5 HOURS
(INCLUDES CHILLING)

■ Basic butter cookies are transformed by adding cinnamon, nutmeg, cloves, and ginger, plus a good amount of slivered almonds. The result—warm, fragrant, and nutty—is perfect with a cup of tea or cocoa. ■

- 2 cups all-purpose flour
- 1½ teaspoons ground cinnamon
- ¼ teaspoon freshly grated nutmeg
- ¼ teaspoon ground cloves
- ¼ teaspoon ground ginger
- ½ teaspoon baking powder
- ½ teaspoon salt
- 1½ sticks (12 tablespoons) unsalted butter, softened
- 1 cup sugar
- 1 large egg
- ½ teaspoon vanilla extract
- 1 cup (4 ounces) slivered almonds

Whisk together flour, cinnamon, nutmeg, cloves, ginger, baking powder, and salt in a bowl.

Beat together butter and sugar in a large bowl with an electric mixer at medium-high speed until pale and fluffy. Beat in egg and vanilla. Reduce speed to low, add flour mixture, and mix until just combined. Stir in almonds.

Form dough into a 12-by-2-inch rectangular log (1½ inches thick) and wrap in plastic wrap. Refrigerate on a baking sheet until firm, at least 4 hours.

Put racks in upper and lower thirds of oven and preheat oven to 375°F.

Cut enough ⅛- to ¼-inch-thick slices from log with a heavy knife to fill two ungreased large baking sheets, arranging slices about 1 inch apart (refrigerate remainder of log, wrapped in plastic wrap). Bake cookies, switching position of sheets halfway through baking, until edges are golden, 12 to 15 minutes. Cool cookies on sheets for 3 minutes, then transfer to racks to cool completely. Make more cookies in same manner with remaining dough.

COOK'S NOTES

- The dough log can be refrigerated for up to 5 days or frozen, wrapped in a double layer of plastic wrap, for up to 1 month. Thaw frozen dough in the refrigerator just until it can be sliced.
- The cookies keep, layered between sheets of parchment paper, in an airtight container at room temperature for up to 1 week.

Sand Tarts

MAKES 4 TO 6 DOZEN COOKIES
ACTIVE TIME: 30 MINUTES ■ START TO FINISH: 5 HOURS
(INCLUDES CHILLING)

■ Thin and crisp, these icebox cookies sparkle with a glittery topping of cinnamon and sugar. They come from former staffer James Humphrey, *Gourmet*'s director of media relations for advertising, who continues his grandmother's tradition of baking them for the Christmas holidays. ■

1½ sticks (12 tablespoons) salted butter, softened
  1 cup plus 2 tablespoons sugar
  1 large egg, lightly beaten
  ½ teaspoon vanilla extract
  2 cups all-purpose flour
  ½ teaspoon ground cinnamon
  1 large egg white, lightly beaten

SPECIAL EQUIPMENT: parchment paper

With a wooden spoon, stir together butter and 1 cup sugar vigorously in a large bowl until well com-bined. Stir in egg and vanilla until smooth. Add flour and stir just until incorporated.

Transfer dough to a 20-inch-long sheet of parchment paper. Using sheet as an aid, roll dough into a 12-inch-long log (2 inches wide). Refrigerate, wrapped in parchment, until firm, at least 4 hours.

Put racks in upper and lower thirds of oven and preheat oven to 375°F. Lightly butter two large baking sheets.

Stir together cinnamon and remaining 2 tablespoons sugar in a small bowl.

Cut chilled log into ⅛- to ¼-inch-thick slices and arrange about 1 inch apart on baking sheets (refrigerate remainder of log, wrapped in parchment paper). Lightly brush cookies with egg white and sprinkle with some of cinnamon sugar.

Bake cookies, switching position of sheets halfway through baking, until edges are golden, 12 to 15 minutes. Cool cookies on sheets for 3 minutes, then transfer to racks to cool completely. Make more cookies in same manner with remaining dough.

COOK'S NOTES

- The dough log can be refrigerated for up to 5 days or frozen, wrapped in the parchment paper and then foil, for up to 1 month. Thaw frozen dough in the refrigerator just until it can be sliced.
- The cookies can be kept in an airtight container at room temperature for up to 1 week.

Pistachio Cranberry Icebox Cookies

MAKES ABOUT 3 DOZEN COOKIES
ACTIVE TIME: 20 MINUTES ■ START TO FINISH: 2½ HOURS
(INCLUDES CHILLING)

■ With their atypical square shape and glittering sugar edges, these cookies look labor-intensive, but they're actually a host's best friend: keep the dough in your fridge, and you can bake and serve them in half an hour, so they're ready at short notice. Sparkles of flavor come from cinnamon and threads of fragrant orange zest. ■

1½ cups all-purpose flour

½ teaspoon ground cinnamon

¼ teaspoon salt

1½ sticks (12 tablespoons) unsalted butter, softened

6 tablespoons granulated sugar

½ teaspoon finely grated orange zest

½ cup unsalted shelled pistachios

⅓ cup dried cranberries

1 large egg, lightly beaten

¼ cup decorating sugar, preferably coarse

SPECIAL EQUIPMENT: parchment paper

Whisk together flour, cinnamon, and salt in a bowl.

Beat together butter, granulated sugar, and zest in a large bowl with an electric mixer until pale and fluffy. Reduce speed to low and add flour mixture in 3 batches, mixing until dough just comes together in clumps. Mix in pistachios and cranberries.

Gather and press dough together, then divide into 2 equal pieces. Using a sheet of plastic wrap or parchment paper as an aid, form each piece of dough into a log about 1½ inches in diameter. Square off sides of each log to form a bar with 4 equal sides, then refrigerate, wrapped in plastic wrap, until very firm, at least 2 hours.

Put racks in upper and lower thirds of oven and preheat oven to 350°F. Line two large baking sheets with parchment paper.

Brush egg over all sides of bars (not ends). Sprinkle decorative sugar onto a sheet of parchment or wax paper and press sides of bars into sugar, coating well.

Cut each bar into ¼-inch-thick slices, rotating bar after each slice to help keep square shape, and arrange cookies about ½ inch apart on baking sheets. (If dough gets too soft, freeze briefly until firm.)

Bake cookies in batches, switching position of sheets halfway through baking, until edges are pale golden, 15 to 18 minutes. Transfer cookies to racks to cool completely.

COOK'S NOTES

- The dough can be refrigerated for up to 3 days or frozen, wrapped in plastic wrap and then in foil, for up to 1 month. Thaw frozen dough in the refrigerator just until it can be sliced.

- The cookies keep in an airtight container at room temperature for up to 5 days.

Number Sixteen
Sugar Cookies

MAKES ABOUT 6 DOZEN COOKIES
ACTIVE TIME: 30 MINUTES ■ START TO FINISH: 6 HOURS
(INCLUDES CHILLING)

■ These golden, sandy cookies, adapted from a recipe from Number Sixteen, a London hotel in South Kensington, may be unprepossessing to look at, but you won't be able to stop eating them. ■

2¾ cups all-purpose flour

1 cup cornstarch

½ teaspoon salt

2½ sticks (10 ounces) unsalted butter, softened

¾ cup sugar

1 teaspoon finely grated lemon zest

¾ teaspoon vanilla extract

SPECIAL EQUIPMENT: parchment paper; a 2-inch fluted or plain round cookie cutter

Whisk together flour, cornstarch, and salt in a bowl.

Beat together butter and sugar in a large bowl with an electric mixer until pale and fluffy. Mix in zest and vanilla at low speed. Add flour mixture and mix until ingredients come together; dough will be crumbly.

Gather dough into a ball and wrap in plastic wrap, then flatten into a 7-inch disk. Refrigerate until firm, 2 to 4 hours.

Bring dough to cool room temperature before rolling out, about 1 hour.

Put a rack in middle of oven and preheat oven to 400°F.

Roll out dough ¼ inch thick between sheets of parchment paper. Cut out as many cookies as possible with cutter and transfer to two ungreased large baking sheets, arranging cookies about 1 inch apart. Gather scraps into a ball, flatten into a disk, and refrigerate until firm enough to roll.

Bake cookies in batches until pale golden, 10 to 12 minutes. Transfer cookies to racks to cool.

Roll out chilled dough, cut out more cookies, and transfer to a cooled baking sheet, then bake in same manner.

- The dough can be refrigerated for up to 24 hours.
- The cookies keep in an airtight container at room temperature for up to 1 week.

- The cookies keep in an airtight container at room temperature for up to 3 days.

Cornmeal Sugar Cookies

MAKES 1½ DOZEN COOKIES
ACTIVE TIME: 20 MINUTES ■ START TO FINISH: 45 MINUTES

■ Cornmeal gives these crisp rounds a sturdy texture that makes them ideal for dunking in cold milk or hot coffee. They're also great all by themselves. ■

- ⅔ cup all-purpose flour
- ¼ cup yellow cornmeal
- 2 tablespoons cornstarch
- ¼ teaspoon salt
- 1 stick (8 tablespoons) unsalted butter, softened
- ⅓ cup confectioners' sugar
- ½ teaspoon vanilla extract
- 1 teaspoon grated lemon zest
- Granulated sugar for sprinkling

SPECIAL EQUIPMENT: a 2-inch round cookie cutter

Put a rack in middle of oven and preheat oven to 350°F.

Whisk together flour, cornmeal, cornstarch, and salt in a bowl.

Combine butter, confectioners' sugar, vanilla, and zest in a food processor and blend until creamy, about 30 seconds. Scrape down sides of bowl, add flour mixture, and pulse until dough just begins to come together.

Roll out dough on a well-floured surface with a well-floured rolling pin to ⅓ inch thick. Cut out as many rounds as possible with cutter and transfer to an ungreased large baking sheet, arranging cookies about 1 inch apart. Reroll scraps and cut out more rounds. Sprinkle tops with granulated sugar.

Bake until bottoms are pale golden, 12 to 14 minutes. Transfer cookies to a rack to cool.

Anise Sesame Cookies

MAKES ABOUT 3 DOZEN COOKIES
ACTIVE TIME: 30 MINUTES ■ START TO FINISH: 4 HOURS
(INCLUDES CHILLING)

■ The pleasant bite of anise makes these cookies, decorated with toasted sesame seeds, stand out. Plumping the anise seeds in hot water softens them, allowing their gentle licorice flavor to perfume the dough. The recipe is from reader and lifelong baker Mary McAvoy of Willow Grove, Pennsylvania. ■

- 1 tablespoon anise seeds
- 2 tablespoons boiling water
- 2 cups all-purpose flour
- ⅛ teaspoon baking soda
- ½ teaspoon salt
- 1½ sticks (12 tablespoons) unsalted butter, softened
- ⅔ cup sugar
- 2 large eggs
- 1 tablespoon water
- ¼ cup sesame seeds, lightly toasted (see Tips, page 911)

SPECIAL EQUIPMENT: a 2½-inch fluted round cookie cutter

Soak anise seeds in boiling water in a small bowl until most of water is absorbed, about 15 minutes.

Whisk together flour, baking soda, and salt in a bowl.

Beat together butter and sugar in a large bowl with an electric mixer until pale and fluffy. Beat in 1 egg and anise seeds, with any remaining soaking liquid, until combined. Mix in flour mixture on low speed until just combined.

Divide dough into 4 pieces. Shape each one into a ball, flatten into a 4-inch disk, and wrap in plastic wrap. Refrigerate until firm, about 3 hours.

Put racks in upper and lower thirds of oven and preheat oven to 350°F.

Roll out 1 piece of dough (keep remaining dough

refrigerated) on a well-floured surface with a well-floured rolling pin into a 7-inch round (if dough becomes too soft to roll out, refrigerate on a baking sheet until firm). Cut out as many cookies as possible from dough with cutter and transfer to two ungreased large baking sheets, arranging cookies about 1 inch apart. Gather scraps together and refrigerate until firm enough to roll.

Beat remaining egg in a small bowl with water to make an egg wash. Brush cookies lightly with egg wash, then sprinkle with some of sesame seeds.

Bake cookies, switching position of sheets halfway through baking, until bottoms are golden, 10 to 12 minutes. Transfer to racks to cool completely.

Roll out chilled dough (reroll scraps only once), cut out more cookies, brush with egg wash, and sprinkle with sesame seeds. Bake on cooled sheets.

COOK'S NOTE

■ The cookies keep, layered between sheets of parchment or wax paper, in an airtight container at room temperature for up to 1 week.

Tea and Honey Crisps

MAKES ABOUT 6 DOZEN COOKIES
ACTIVE TIME: 1½ HOURS ■ START TO FINISH: 1½ HOURS

■ Earl Grey tea lends a sophisticated note of bergamot and a handsome speckled look to these crisp, buttery cookies, which are wonderful with ice cream or your afternoon cuppa. As you spread the thin batter over homemade stencils, let your imagination run wild. We like making long, irregular, ribbony shapes, but any configuration will do. You could also drape the warm cookies over a rolling pin to make gently curved tuiles. ■

   1 stick (8 tablespoons) unsalted butter, softened
   1 cup confectioners' sugar
  ¼ cup mild honey
 2¼ teaspoons Earl Grey tea leaves (from 2–3 tea bags; see Cook's Note)
   2 large egg whites
   1 cup all-purpose flour

SPECIAL EQUIPMENT: Styrofoam plates; a small sharp knife such as an X-Acto; a 17-by-11-inch nonstick baking sheet liner, such as a Silpat

Draw desired shape of cookie in center of a Styrofoam plate. Cut out shape with X-Acto knife and discard shape, then trim away enough of plate so you have a 1-inch border around stencil. Make more stencils with more plates as desired.

Put a rack in middle of oven and preheat oven to 350°F. Line a large baking sheet with nonstick liner.

Beat together butter, confectioners' sugar, honey, and tea leaves in a large bowl with an electric mixer until well combined. Add egg whites one at a time, beating well after each addition. Reduce speed to low and mix in flour until just combined.

Place stencil on liner and spread batter evenly in stencil with a small offset spatula or a rubber spatula. Carefully lift stencil from liner and make more cookies in same manner, spacing them about 1 inch apart.

Bake cookies in batches until edges are deep golden brown, 6 to 9 minutes. Cool cookies for 1 minute on sheet, then transfer with spatula to a rack to cool completely. (To curl cookies, drape over rolling pins or thick wooden dowels as soon as you remove them from oven and let cool.)

COOK'S NOTES

■ If using loose tea, finely crush it before measuring.
■ The cookies keep in an airtight container at room temperature for up to 1 week.

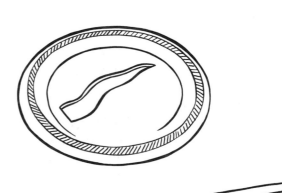

Five-Spice Gingersnaps

MAKES ABOUT 3 DOZEN COOKIES
ACTIVE TIME: 1 HOUR ■ START TO FINISH: 10 HOURS
(INCLUDES CHILLING)

■ Most gingersnaps lean toward the soothingly plain. These are the opposite—spicy with chewy crystallized ginger and aromatic with Chinese five-spice powder. The stealth ingredient is Lyle's Golden Syrup, which is found in many supermarkets and lends a rich sweetness. When iced, these rolled cookies make wonderful Christmas ornaments. Left unadorned, they will continue to crisp over time. ■

2 cups all-purpose flour
1¾ teaspoons Chinese five-spice powder
1½ teaspoons baking soda
¼ teaspoon salt
3 tablespoons finely chopped crystallized ginger
1 cup sugar
¼ cup Lyle's Golden Syrup (see headnote and Sources)
1½ sticks (12 tablespoons) unsalted butter, melted and cooled
1 large egg
Decorative Icing (optional; recipe follows)
Food coloring (optional)

SPECIAL EQUIPMENT: parchment paper; a 2½-inch round cookie cutter; a piping tip with a ¼-inch plain round opening if making cookies into ornaments; pastry bags fitted with small piping tips or several small heavy-duty sealable plastic bags if decorating cookies (see Cook's Note)

Whisk together flour, five-spice powder, baking soda, and salt in a bowl.

Pulse ginger with ¼ cup sugar in a food processor until finely ground. Add syrup, butter, egg, and remaining ¾ cup sugar to processor and blend until mixture is thick and creamy, about 3 minutes. Add flour mixture and pulse just until a dough forms.

Shape dough into a disk, wrap in plastic wrap, and refrigerate for at least 2 hours to allow flavors to develop (see Cook's Note).

Put a rack in middle of oven and preheat oven to 325°F. Line two large baking sheets with parchment paper.

Cut dough into quarters. Keeping remaining 3 pieces wrapped in plastic wrap and refrigerated, roll out 1 piece of dough on a lightly floured sheet of parchment paper with a lightly floured rolling pin to ⅛ inch thick. (If dough becomes too soft to roll out, refrigerate on parchment paper until firm.) Cut out rounds with cutter and transfer to one lined baking sheet, arranging cookies about 2 inches apart; reserve dough scraps.

Bake cookies until slightly puffed and a shade darker, 10 to 12 minutes. Cool for 5 minutes on sheet. If desired, make holes with piping tip near one edge to hang cookies. Transfer cookies, still on parchment, to a rack to cool completely.

While first batch is baking, roll out and cut another batch, arranging cookies on second lined sheet. Gather scraps and refrigerate until dough is firm enough to roll, 15 to 20 minutes. Bake cookies in same manner, then make more cookies with remaining pieces of dough and scraps (reroll scraps only once), cooling sheets and lining them with parchment before using.

If using icing and coloring it, transfer small batches to small bowls, one for each color, and tint with food coloring. Spread icing on cookies with an offset spatula or spoon each color of icing into a pastry bag, pressing out excess air (if using plastic bags, see Cook's Note). Twist bag firmly just above icing, then decoratively pipe icing onto cookies. Let icing dry completely, about 1 hour, before serving or storing cookies.

COOK'S NOTES

■ The cookies are best when the dough is refrigerated for 8 hours to allow the flavors to develop, but if you're in a hurry, the dough can be refrigerated for just 2 hours. The dough can be refrigerated for up to 3 days.

■ Using pastry bags fitted with piping tips results in cleaner lines of icing, but sealable plastic bags also work. Spoon each color of icing into a separate bag, seal, pressing out the excess air, and snip a ⅛-inch opening in one bottom corner of the bag.

■ The cookies keep, layered between sheets of parchment if iced, in an airtight container at room temperature for up to 5 days.

Decorative Icing

MAKES ABOUT 3 CUPS
ACTIVE TIME: 15 MINUTES ■ START TO FINISH: 15 MINUTES

■ This dead-simple icing is a cinch to decorate with—it pipes and spreads very neatly. It works well with any cut-out cookie. ■

    1 (1-pound) box confectioners' sugar
    4 teaspoons powdered egg whites, such as Just
       Whites
    ⅓ cup water
    1 tablespoon fresh lemon juice
    1 teaspoon vanilla extract

Beat together all ingredients in a large bowl with an electric mixer at medium speed until just combined, about 1 minute. Increase speed to high and beat until icing holds stiff peaks, about 3 minutes in a stand mixer, 10 minutes with a handheld. If not using icing immediately, cover surface with a dampened paper towel and cover bowl with plastic wrap.

Moravian Crisps

MAKES ABOUT 8½ DOZEN COOKIES
ACTIVE TIME: 1 HOUR ■ START TO FINISH: 1 DAY PLUS
1½ HOURS (INCLUDES CHILLING)

■ Beginning in the 1700s, members of the Moravian church left what is now the Czech Republic and settled in the United States, notably in North Carolina. They brought these delicious, paper-thin spice cookies to their new home, and even now, no Moravian Christmas is complete without them. The secret to getting the dough to its necessary thinness is to use a rolling pin cover, a fabric sleeve that keeps the dough from sticking, and a pastry cloth (sometimes called a "flour sack") for rolling them out. ■

    1½ cups all-purpose flour, plus additional if necessary
    1¼ teaspoons baking soda
    1 teaspoon ground cinnamon
    1 teaspoon ground ginger
    ¾ teaspoon ground cloves
    ¼ teaspoon salt
    ¼ cup vegetable shortening, preferably trans fat–free
    ⅓ cup packed light brown sugar
    ½ cup molasses (not robust)

SPECIAL EQUIPMENT: parchment paper; a pastry cloth and a rolling pin cover (see Sources); a 2-inch fluted cookie cutter; a small offset spatula

Whisk together flour, baking soda, spices, and salt in a bowl.

Blend shortening, brown sugar, and molasses in a food processor until smooth. Add flour mixture and blend just until combined.

Turn dough out onto a floured surface and knead just until smooth, incorporating a little more flour if dough is sticky. Divide dough in half, form each piece into a 3-inch square, and wrap in plastic wrap. Refrigerate for at least 24 hours to allow flavors to develop.

Put a rack in middle of oven and preheat oven to 325°F. Line two large baking sheets with parchment paper.

Using a rolling pin with floured cover, roll out 1 piece of dough (keep remaining dough refrigerated) as thin as possible into an approximately 15-inch square on floured pastry cloth. Cut out cookies with cutter and arrange about ½ inch apart on lined baking sheets, using a spatula to transfer them if necessary; reserve scraps.

Bake cookies in batches for 10 minutes. Cool on sheet for 1 minute, then loosen cookies with offset spatula and transfer, on parchment paper, to a rack to cool and crisp, about 10 minutes. If first batch doesn't crisp, return to baking sheet and bake for 1 minute, then bake remaining batches for 1 minute more.

Repeat procedure with remaining square of dough, arranging cookies on cooled baking sheets lined with parchment paper. Knead together dough scraps and roll out for additional cookies.

Once cookies are completely cooled, remove from parchment paper.

COOK'S NOTES

■ The dough can be refrigerated for up to 3 days.
■ The crisps keep in an airtight container at room temperature for up to 2 weeks.

Whoopie Pies

MAKES 8 WHOOPIE PIES
ACTIVE TIME: 30 MINUTES ■ START TO FINISH: 1 HOUR

■ The generally accepted story of whoopie pies is that they evolved from little individual cakes mothers would make their children from leftover chocolate batter and frosting—the "whoopie" is said to be the kids' happy shout. Though whoopie pies can be served on the same day they're made, we think they are much better a day after baking, when the cake and the marshmallow filling have had time to mingle a bit. ■

FOR CAKES

    2 cups all-purpose flour
    ⅔ cup unsweetened Dutch-process cocoa powder, preferably Droste or Valrhona
    1¼ teaspoons baking soda
    1 teaspoon salt
    1 cup well-shaken buttermilk
    1 teaspoon vanilla extract
    1 stick (8 tablespoons) unsalted butter, softened
    1 cup packed brown sugar, preferably dark
    1 large egg

FOR FILLING

    1 stick (8 tablespoons) unsalted butter, softened
    1¼ cups confectioners' sugar
    2 cups marshmallow cream, such as Marshmallow Fluff
    1 teaspoon vanilla extract

MAKE THE CAKES: Put racks in upper and lower thirds of oven and preheat oven to 350°F. Butter two large baking sheets.

Whisk together flour, cocoa, baking soda, and salt in a bowl. Stir buttermilk and vanilla together in a small bowl.

Beat together butter and brown sugar in a large bowl with an electric mixer until pale and fluffy. Add egg, beating well. Reduce speed to low and add flour mixture and buttermilk alternately in 3 batches, beginning and ending with flour, scraping down sides of bowl occasionally and mixing until smooth.

Spoon ¼-cup mounds of batter about 2 inches apart onto baking sheets. Bake, switching position of sheets halfway through baking, until tops are puffed and cakes spring back when touched, 11 to 13 minutes. Transfer to a rack to cool completely.

MAKE THE FILLING AND ASSEMBLE THE PIES: Beat together all filling ingredients in a bowl with an electric mixer until smooth, about 3 minutes.

Spread a rounded tablespoon filling on flat sides of half of cakes and top with remaining cakes.

COOK'S NOTE

- The pies keep, layered between sheets of parchment paper, in an airtight container at room temperature for up to 1 day.

Almond Macaroons with Buttercream Filling

MAKES 16 SANDWICH COOKIES
ACTIVE TIME: 1½ HOURS ■ START TO FINISH: 2¼ HOURS

■ All over Paris, tiny macaroons in every color and flavor fill bakery windows, like rows and rows of candy dots. Almond is one of the classic flavors of these exquisite sandwich cookies. As you bite into them, your teeth shatter the macaroon's crisp shell, sink through to moist, sugary airiness inside, and then settle into the silky buttercream. ■

FOR MACAROONS
 ¾ cup unblanched whole almonds, toasted
   (see Tips, page 911)
1½ cups confectioners' sugar
 3 large egg whites, left at room temperature
   for 30 minutes
 ¼ teaspoon salt
 ⅓ cup granulated sugar
 ¼ teaspoon vanilla extract
 ⅛ teaspoon almond extract
FOR BUTTERCREAM
 2 large egg whites, left at room temperature
   for 30 minutes

 ½ cup granulated sugar
 ⅛ teaspoon salt
 2 sticks (½ pound) unsalted butter, cut into
   tablespoons, softened
 ¼ teaspoon vanilla extract
 ⅛ teaspoon almond extract

SPECIAL EQUIPMENT: parchment paper; a pastry bag fitted with a ¼-inch plain tip

MAKE THE MACAROONS: Put racks in upper and lower thirds of oven and preheat oven to 300°F. Line two large baking sheets with parchment paper.

Finely grind almonds with confectioners' sugar in a food processor.

Beat whites with salt in bowl of a stand mixer fitted with the whisk attachment at medium-high speed or in a large bowl with a handheld mixer until they just hold soft peaks. Reduce speed to medium and add granulated sugar a little at a time, then continue to beat until whites hold stiff, glossy peaks. Fold in almond mixture in 2 batches until just combined, then fold in vanilla and almond extracts.

Transfer meringue to pastry bag and pipe sixteen 1½-inch-wide mounds 1 inch apart on each lined baking sheet (32 total). Smooth tops of mounds with a wet fingertip.

Bake, switching position of sheets halfway through baking, until macaroons are puffed and tops appear dry, 15 to 17 minutes. (Macaroons should be crisp on the outside and chewy on the inside.) Slide parchment with macaroons onto racks and cool for 10 minutes, then peel macaroons from parchment, transferring them to a rack to cool completely.

MAKE THE BUTTERCREAM: Vigorously whisk together whites, sugar, and salt in cleaned mixer bowl (or cleaned large bowl if using a hand mixer) set over a 4-quart pot of barely simmering water, until sugar is dissolved and mixture is warm. Remove bowl from pot and beat with cleaned whisk attachment or beaters at medium-high speed until whites hold stiff, glossy peaks. Continue to beat, scraping down sides of bowl with a rubber spatula, until meringue is completely cool to the touch, about 5 minutes.

With mixer at medium speed, add butter 1 piece at a time, beating well after each addition. (If buttercream looks soupy at any point, meringue is still too warm; briefly chill bottom of bowl in a large bowl filled with ice water for a few seconds before beating in remaining butter.) Continue beating until butter-cream is smooth. (Mixture may look curdled before all of butter is added, but it will come back together by the time you finish beating.) Add vanilla and almond extracts and beat for 1 minute more.

ASSEMBLE THE COOKIES: Transfer buttercream filling to cleaned pastry bag and pipe about 1 tablespoon onto flat sides of 16 macaroons. Top with remaining macaroons.

COOK'S NOTES

- The egg whites in the buttercream are not fully cooked. If that is a concern, see page 915.
- The buttercream can be made up to 1 week ahead and refrigerated, covered. Bring to room temperature (this may take up to 3 hours; do not use a microwave) and beat with an electric mixer until smooth before using.
- The filled macaroons keep, refrigerated in an airtight container, layered between sheets of parchment paper, for up to 2 days. Bring to room temperature before serving.

Butter Cookies with Dulce de Leche
Alfajores

MAKES 16 SANDWICH COOKIES
ACTIVE TIME: 25 MINUTES ■ START TO FINISH: 50 MINUTES

■ Cornstarch gives these tiny butter cookies ("al-fa-*hor*-es") a crisp, delicate texture; the caramel-sweet dulce de leche filling puts them over the top. In some Latin American countries, the cookies are made with pisco—brandy distilled from white Muscat grapes grown in Peru, Chile, and Bolivia—but regular brandy works fine. ■

⅓ cup cornstarch
¾ cup all-purpose flour, plus additional if necessary
¼ teaspoon baking powder
⅛ teaspoon salt
¾ stick (6 tablespoons) unsalted butter, softened
¼ cup granulated sugar
2 large egg yolks
1 tablespoon pisco or regular brandy
¼ teaspoon vanilla extract

About ¼ cup dulce de leche (see Sources)
Confectioners' sugar for dusting
SPECIAL EQUIPMENT: a 1½-inch round cookie cutter

Put a rack in middle of oven and preheat oven to 350°F. Butter a large baking sheet.

Whisk together cornstarch, flour, baking powder, and salt in a small bowl.

Beat together butter and sugar in a large bowl with an electric mixer until pale and fluffy. Beat in egg yolks, pisco, and vanilla. Stir in flour mixture until combined, adding 1 to 2 tablespoons more flour if dough is sticky. (Dough should be soft.)

Form dough into a disk. Roll out into an 11-inch round on a lightly floured surface with a lightly floured rolling pin. Cut out 32 rounds with cutter and transfer to baking sheet, arranging rounds ½ inch apart (reroll scraps once if necessary).

Bake until firm and pale golden around edges, 12 to 15 minutes. Transfer cookies to a rack to cool completely.

Spread about ½ teaspoon dulce de leche on flat sides of half of cookies and top with remaining cookies. Dust with confectioners' sugar.

COOK'S NOTE

- The unfilled cookies, once cooled, can be kept in an airtight container at room temperature for up to 3 days.

DULCE DE LECHE

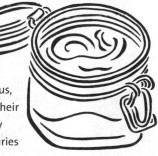

Both Argentina and Uruguay claim dulce de leche ("*dool*-sey deh *leh*-cheh")—cow's and/or goat's milk and sugar cooked down to a luscious, caramel-like consistency—as their own, but the Latin classic likely came from Spain or Italy centuries ago, and similar products exist across Latin America. We use it as a filling for sandwich butter cookies and in cheesecake squares (page 703), but you can also spoon it onto ice cream or use it as you would Nutella, spreading it on crepes or hot buttered toast. To find it, see Sources.

Inside-Out Carrot Cake Cookies

MAKES ABOUT 1 DOZEN SANDWICH COOKIES
ACTIVE TIME: 20 MINUTES ■ START TO FINISH: 45 MINUTES

■ The ingredients of a favorite cake are transformed into delectable handheld treats. Two moist carrot cookies surround honeyed cream cheese. ■

FOR COOKIES
- 1 cup plus 2 tablespoons all-purpose flour
- 1 teaspoon ground cinnamon
- ½ teaspoon baking soda
- ½ teaspoon salt
- 1 stick (8 tablespoons) unsalted butter, softened
- ⅓ cup plus 2 tablespoons packed light brown sugar
- ⅓ cup plus 2 tablespoons granulated sugar
- 1 large egg
- ½ teaspoon vanilla extract
- 1 cup coarsely grated carrots (2 medium)
- 1 cup (about 3¼ ounces) walnuts, chopped
- ½ cup raisins

FOR FILLING
- 1 (8-ounce) package cream cheese
- ¼ cup honey

MAKE THE COOKIES: Put racks in upper and lower thirds of oven and preheat oven to 375°F. Butter two large baking sheets.

Whisk together flour, cinnamon, baking soda, and salt in a bowl.

Beat together butter, sugars, egg, and vanilla in a large bowl with an electric mixer until pale and fluffy. Mix in carrots, nuts, and raisins at low speed. Add flour mixture and beat until just combined.

Drop 1½ tablespoons of batter 2 inches apart onto baking sheets. Bake, switching position of sheets halfway through baking, until cookies are lightly browned and springy to the touch, 12 to 16 minutes. Cool cookies on sheets on racks for 1 minute, then transfer to racks to cool completely.

MAKE THE FILLING AND ASSEMBLE THE COOKIES: Blend cream cheese and honey in a food processor until smooth.

Spread a generous tablespoon of cream cheese fill-ing on flat sides of half of cookies and top with remaining cookies.

COOK'S NOTE
■ The cookies keep, refrigerated in an airtight container, for up to 1 day.

Sicilian Fig Cookies

MAKES ABOUT 5½ DOZEN COOKIES
ACTIVE TIME: 1 HOUR ■ START TO FINISH: 10 HOURS
(INCLUDES CHILLING)

■ A Christmas tradition in Sicily, *cuccidati* are cookies made with a pastry dough and filled with a heady combination of dried figs, raisins, nuts, spices, and honey. Though the *cuccidati* at bakeries are always garnished with colorful nonpareils, they are equally pretty with nothing but the icing. Because these are a bit of a production, we like breaking up the work: consider making the filling one day and the pastry dough the next, then assembling and baking them on the third day. ■

FOR FILLING
- 1 cup (8 ounces) packed soft dried Black Mission figs, hard stems discarded
- ¾ cup raisins
- ¾ cup mild honey
- ¼ cup brandy
- 1½ teaspoons finely grated orange zest
- 1 teaspoon finely grated lemon zest
- 1 tablespoon ground cinnamon
- ¼ teaspoon ground cloves
- ¼ teaspoon freshly grated nutmeg
- ¾ cup whole almonds (blanched or unblanched), toasted (see Tips, page 911) and coarsely chopped
- ¾ cup walnuts, toasted (see Tips, page 911) and coarsely chopped

FOR PASTRY DOUGH
- 4 cups all-purpose flour
- 1 cup plus 2 tablespoons sugar
- 1 tablespoon baking powder
- 1 teaspoon salt
- 2 sticks (½ pound) cold unsalted butter, cut into ½-inch cubes
- 2 large eggs, lightly beaten

½ cup whole milk

1½ teaspoons vanilla extract

1 teaspoon finely grated orange or lemon zest

FOR ICING

1 cup confectioners' sugar

½ teaspoon vanilla extract

1½–2 tablespoons fresh orange juice

OPTIONAL GARNISH: multicolored nonpareils (tiny pellets of colored sugar)

MAKE THE FILLING: Pulse figs and raisins in a food processor until finely chopped. Stir together with remaining ingredients in a bowl. Refrigerate, covered, for at least 8 hours to firm up.

MAKE THE DOUGH: Whisk together flour, sugar, baking powder, and salt in a large bowl. Add butter and blend with your fingertips or a pastry blender just until mixture resembles coarse meal with some small (roughly pea-sized) butter lumps. Add eggs, milk, vanilla, and zest and stir with a fork until a soft dough forms.

Halve dough. Gather each half into a ball and flatten into a rough 6-by-4-inch rectangle between sheets of plastic wrap. Refrigerate, wrapped in plastic, until firm, at least 8 hours.

BAKE THE COOKIES: Put a rack in middle of oven and preheat oven to 350°F. Butter two large baking sheets.

Roll out 1 rectangle of dough (keep remaining dough refrigerated) into a 15-by-14-inch rectangle on a well-floured surface with a floured rolling pin. Trim to a 13-by-10-inch rectangle (refrigerate trimmings). Cut crosswise into four 10-by-3¼-inch strips. Put ⅓ cup filling in a 1-inch-wide log lengthwise down center of each strip and fold sides of strip up over filling to enclose it, pinching edges together to seal. Turn rolls seam side down and press gently to flatten seams. With a floured sharp knife, cut logs into 1½-inch-wide slices and arrange ½ inch apart on baking sheets. Make more cookies in same manner with remaining dough and scraps (reroll scraps only once) and filling.

Bake cookies in batches until golden around edges, 16 to 20 minutes. Transfer cookies to racks and cool until warm, about 10 minutes.

WHILE THE FIRST BATCH OF COOKIES BAKES, MAKE THE ICING: Whisk together confectioners' sugar, va-

nilla, and enough orange juice to make a pourable icing in a bowl.

Brush icing on warm cookies. Decorate with nonpareils if using, and cool completely.

COOK'S NOTES

- The filling can be made up to 1 week ahead.
- The dough can be refrigerated, wrapped in the plastic wrap and then in foil, for up to 3 days.
- The cookies keep, layered between sheets of parchment paper, in an airtight container at room temperature for up to 1 week.

Lemon Vanilla Madeleines

MAKES ABOUT 3 DOZEN MADELEINES
ACTIVE TIME: 25 MINUTES ■ START TO FINISH: 45 MINUTES

■ The crisp edges of these delightful lemon-scented cookies, adapted from Bouley Bakery in Manhattan's TriBeCa neighborhood, set them apart from the other madeleines we've tasted. They're most sublime when freshly baked, so make the batter ahead. Then pop the pan into the oven after dinner, and the madeleines will be ready to eat by the time the dishes are cleared and the coffee is made. ■

1¾ sticks (14 tablespoons) unsalted butter, melted and cooled, plus additional for brushing molds

1⅔ cups all-purpose flour

1 tablespoon baking powder

2 teaspoons finely grated lemon zest

1 vanilla bean, halved lengthwise

¾ cup sugar

3 large eggs

¼ cup whole milk

1½ tablespoons mild honey

SPECIAL EQUIPMENT: 2 nonstick madeleine pans with twelve 2-tablespoon molds each

Put racks in upper and lower thirds of oven and preheat oven to 350°F. Brush molds with melted butter.

Sift together flour and baking powder into a large bowl, then whisk in zest.

Scrape seeds from vanilla bean into another bowl with tip of a paring knife (discard bean). Add sugar and rub between your fingertips until vanilla is well dispersed. Whisk in eggs, milk, honey, and melted butter. Fold into flour mixture until just combined.

Spoon a rounded tablespoon of batter into each mold, filling it about two-thirds full. Bake, switching position of pans halfway through baking and rotating them, until madeleines are golden around edges and a wooden toothpick inserted into center comes out clean, 10 to 12 minutes. Turn madeleines out onto a rack. Make more madeleines in same manner, brushing cooled mold with melted butter. Serve slightly warm.

COOK'S NOTES

■ The madeleines are best eaten when freshly baked.
■ The batter can be made up to 3 hours ahead and refrigerated, covered.

Rugelach

MAKES ABOUT 3½ DOZEN COOKIES
ACTIVE TIME: 40 MINUTES ■ START TO FINISH: 9¾ HOURS
(INCLUDES CHILLING)

■ These rugelach are, hands down, the best we've ever tasted. They're also incredibly easy to make. Instead of shaping each cookie individually, you simply roll the tender cream cheese dough into a rectangle, add the filling, roll up into a log, and cut into pieces. Feel free to get creative with your fillings: any kind of dried fruit, nuts, and jam (as long as it's not too runny) will work. We've experimented with blueberry jam and toasted pecans, as well as with exotic rose petal jam and pistachios. Phyllis Roberts, the mother of *Gourmet* food editor Melissa Roberts, got her inspiration for these traditional Jewish cookies from her great-grandmother, who owned a small Catskills hotel. ■

2 cups all-purpose flour
½ teaspoon salt
2 sticks (½ pound) unsalted butter, softened
1 (8-ounce) package cream cheese, softened
½ cup plus 4 teaspoons sugar

1 teaspoon ground cinnamon
1 cup apricot preserves or raspberry jam
1 cup loosely packed golden raisins, chopped
1¼ cups (about 4 ounces) walnuts, finely chopped
Milk for brushing cookies

SPECIAL EQUIPMENT: parchment paper

Whisk together flour and salt in a bowl.

Beat together butter and cream cheese in a large bowl with an electric mixer until well combined. Add flour mixture and stir with a wooden spoon until a soft dough forms.

Gather dough into a ball and wrap in plastic wrap, then flatten into a roughly 7-by-5-inch rectangle. Refrigerate until firm, at least 8 hours.

Put a rack in middle of oven and preheat oven to 350°F. Line a large baking sheet with parchment paper.

Cut dough into 4 pieces. Keeping remaining dough wrapped and refrigerated, roll out 1 piece into a 12-by-8-inch rectangle on a well-floured surface with a floured rolling pin. Transfer dough to a sheet of parchment, transfer to a tray, and refrigerate while you roll out remaining dough in same manner; transfer each rectangle to another sheet of parchment and stack on tray.

Whisk ½ cup sugar together with cinnamon.

Arrange 1 dough rectangle, still on parchment, on a work surface with a long side nearest you. Spread ¼ cup preserves evenly over dough with an offset spatula or back of a spoon. Sprinkle ¼ cup raisins and a rounded ¼ cup walnuts over jam, then sprinkle with 2 tablespoons cinnamon sugar. Using parchment as an aid, roll up dough tightly into a log. Place seam side down on lined baking pan, then pinch ends closed and tuck underneath. Make 3 more logs in same manner, arranging them 1 inch apart on pan.

Brush logs with milk and sprinkle each with 1 teaspoon of remaining sugar. With a sharp large knife, make ¾-inch-deep crosswise cuts in dough logs (not all the way through) at 1-inch intervals. (If dough is too soft to cut, refrigerate for 20 to 30 minutes.)

Bake logs until golden, 45 to 50 minutes. Cool logs until warm in pan on a rack, about 30 minutes.

Transfer logs to a cutting board and slice cookies all the way through.

- The dough can be chilled for up to 24 hours.
- The logs can be frozen, wrapped in parchment and then in foil, for up to 1 month. Thaw, still wrapped, at room temperature or overnight in the refrigerator before baking.
- These cookies are best the day they are baked.

Bake more cookies in same manner on cooled sheet and liner.

COOK'S NOTE
- The cookies keep in an airtight container at room temperature for up to 1 week.

Lemon Almond Tuiles

MAKES ABOUT 1½ DOZEN COOKIES
ACTIVE TIME: 15 MINUTES ■ START TO FINISH: 45 MINUTES

■ Potato starch is the secret ingredient of these tuiles, which are perfect for Passover. They are very delicate, with a soft lemon perfume. If you make them with olive oil, be sure to choose a mild oil, one whose flavor will not overpower the batter. We love them with an after-dinner espresso or alongside a bowl of ripe berries and whipped cream. ■

- ¼ cup sugar
- 1 large egg white
- 6 tablespoons potato starch
- ½ stick (4 tablespoons) unsalted butter, melted, or ¼ cup olive oil
- ¾ teaspoon finely grated lemon zest
- ¼ teaspoon salt
- ¼ teaspoon almond extract

SPECIAL EQUIPMENT: a 17-by-11-inch nonstick baking sheet liner, such as a Silpat

Put a rack in middle of oven and preheat oven to 375°F. Line a large baking sheet with liner.

Whisk together sugar and egg white in a medium bowl until sugar is dissolved. Whisk in remaining ingredients until smooth.

Spoon ½ tablespoon of batter for each cookie, 2 inches apart and in staggered rows, on baking sheet (about 6 cookies), spreading with a small offset spatula or back of a small spoon into 4-inch-long cookies (straight or curvy). Bake until pale golden, 7 to 8 minutes. Transfer cookies with a spatula to a rack to cool completely, or curl cookies by draping them over a rolling pin to cool (if the cookies become too crisp to curl, return to oven to soften for 1 minute).

Hazelnut Biscotti

MAKES ABOUT 2½ DOZEN COOKIES
ACTIVE TIME: 20 MINUTES ■ START TO FINISH: 2 HOURS

■ These crunchy biscotti are made without butter. The natural fat in the hazelnuts, released when the nuts are ground with the sugar, stands in, and every bite is imbued with their flavor. Dipping the biscotti into strong espresso or a luscious Vin Santo will transport you to a Tuscan piazza. ■

- 1½ cups (about 7½ ounces) hazelnuts
- ¾ cup sugar
- 2 cups self-rising cake flour
- 2 large eggs
- 1 teaspoon vanilla extract

SPECIAL EQUIPMENT: parchment paper

Put a rack in middle of oven and preheat oven to 350°F. Line a large baking sheet with parchment paper.

Toast hazelnuts on an unlined baking sheet in oven until nuts are lightly colored and skins are blistered, 10 to 15 minutes. Wrap nuts in a clean kitchen towel (leave oven on) and let steam for 1 minute, then rub off loose skins with towel while nuts are still warm (don't worry about skins that don't come off). Cool nuts completely, then very coarsely chop.

Pulse ½ cup chopped hazelnuts with sugar in a food processor until finely ground. Transfer to a bowl, add flour, and beat with an electric mixer until well combined. Add eggs and vanilla and beat just until a dough forms. Reduce speed to low, add remaining chopped hazelnuts, and mix until incorporated. Knead in any loose hazelnuts with your hands.

Halve dough. With dampened hands, form each half into a roughly 10-by-2-by-1-inch log on lined baking sheet, arranging logs 3 inches apart.

Bake until golden and set but still soft to the touch, 25 to 30 minutes. Cool logs on baking sheet on a rack for 10 minutes. (Leave oven on.)

Transfer logs to a cutting board (discard parchment). With a serrated knife, cut logs on a slight diagonal into ½-inch-thick slices. Arrange slices cut side down in one layer on (unlined) baking sheet. Bake slices, turning once, until golden and crisp, 20 to 25 minutes.

Cool biscotti completely on sheet on rack.

COOK'S NOTE

- The biscotti keep in an airtight container at room temperature for up to 2 weeks.

Toasted Anise Seed Cake Slices

MAKE 12 SLICES
ACTIVE TIME: 30 MINUTES ■ START TO FINISH: 2 HOURS

■ Baked first as a loaf, then sliced and baked until golden and crisp, these cookies are similar to biscotti. Their haunting anise flavor and crunchy texture make them the perfect complement to a lemony custard or sorbet. ■

    1¾ cups all-purpose flour
    1¾ teaspoons baking powder
    ¼ teaspoon salt
    3 jumbo eggs
    ¾ cup sugar
    5 tablespoons unsalted butter, melted and cooled
    1½ teaspoons anise seeds, finely crushed (with a
        mortar and pestle or side of a heavy knife)
SPECIAL EQUIPMENT: an 8½-by-4½-inch loaf pan; a stand
        mixer with a whisk attachment

Put a rack in middle of oven and preheat oven to 350°F. Lightly butter and flour loaf pan.

Sift together flour, baking powder, and salt.

Beat together eggs and sugar in mixer bowl at high speed until tripled in volume and thick enough to form a ribbon that takes 2 seconds to dissolve when beater is lifted, 12 to 18 minutes.

Sift flour mixture over egg mixture in 3 batches and fold in each batch. Gently stir in butter and anise seeds. Immediately pour batter into loaf pan and smooth top.

Bake until top is golden brown and a wooden toothpick inserted in center of loaf comes out clean, 35 to 45 minutes. Cool loaf for 5 minutes, then invert onto a cutting board, turn right side up, and cool for 30 minutes.

Preheat oven to 400°F.

Trim ends of loaf and cut loaf into ½-inch-thick slices. Arrange slices cut side down on a baking sheet. Bake until undersides are golden brown, about 7 minutes. Turn toasts over and bake until second sides are golden brown, about 5 minutes more. Serve warm or at room temperature.

COOK'S NOTE

- The loaf, once cooled, can be kept, wrapped in foil, at room temperature for up to 2 days or frozen for up to 1 month. Thaw, still wrapped, in the refrigerator or at room temperature. Slice and toast just before serving.

Mixed Nut Shortbread

MAKES 18 BARS
ACTIVE TIME: 15 MINUTES ■ START TO FINISH: 45 MINUTES

■ Mixed cocktail nuts give these buttery shortbread bars a lovely salty crunch. You can put them together in just 15 minutes. ■

    1 stick (8 tablespoons) unsalted butter, softened
    ⅓ cup plus 1 tablespoon sugar
    ½ teaspoon vanilla extract
    1 cup all-purpose flour
    ¾ cup salted roasted mixed cocktail nuts, coarsely
        chopped (see Cook's Note)

Put a rack in middle of oven and preheat oven to 375°F. Lightly butter a baking sheet.

Stir together butter and ⅓ cup sugar in a medium bowl with a wooden spoon until smooth and creamy. Stir in vanilla. Add flour and mix with your hands just until a dough forms.

Transfer dough to baking sheet and spread evenly

with your fingers into an 8-inch square. Sprinkle nuts evenly over dough, pressing down to help them adhere. Sprinkle remaining tablespoon sugar over nuts.

Bake until shortbread is deep golden, 20 to 25 minutes. Cool on baking sheet on a rack for 10 minutes. Cut into 18 bars and let cool completely.

COOK'S NOTE
■ If you use unsalted nuts, sprinkle them with a generous ¼ teaspoon salt along with the 1 tablespoon sugar.

Graham Crackers

MAKES 3½ DOZEN CRACKERS
ACTIVE TIME: 25 MINUTES ■ START TO FINISH: 2 HOURS
(INCLUDES CHILLING)

■ One taste will persuade you of the superiority of homemade graham crackers. They are light and crisp, with a sweetly wheaty flavor—delightful with a glass of milk. Or make s'mores. ■

- 2 cups whole wheat flour
- ¼ cup all-purpose flour
- 1 tablespoon cornmeal
- ¼ cup granulated sugar
- ¼ cup packed light brown sugar
- 2 tablespoons molasses (not robust)
- 2 tablespoons mild honey
- 1 teaspoon baking powder
- ½ teaspoon baking soda
- ½ teaspoon salt
- ¼ teaspoon ground cinnamon
- 1 stick (8 tablespoons) cold unsalted butter, cut into ½-inch pieces
- ¼ cup cold water

SPECIAL EQUIPMENT: parchment paper

Combine flours, cornmeal, sugars, molasses, honey, baking powder, baking soda, salt, and cinnamon in a food processor and pulse until combined. Add butter and pulse until mixture resembles coarse meal. Drizzle water over mixture and pulse until dough forms a ball, about 30 seconds.

Divide dough in half. Roll out 1 piece between two sheets of parchment paper into a 15-by-10-inch rect-

angle and put on a large baking sheet. Roll out remaining dough in same manner and put on another large baking sheet. Refrigerate until firm, about 1 hour.

Put racks in upper and lower thirds of oven and preheat oven to 350°F.

Remove top sheets of parchment from dough. Using a sharp knife or pizza cutter, trim edges of dough, then cut into approximately 3-by-2-inch rectangles, wiping knife clean between cuts (do not separate rectangles). Prick each rectangle several times with a fork.

Bake, switching position of sheets halfway through baking, until edges are golden brown, 15 to 20 minutes. Transfer crackers, on parchment paper, to a rack to cool completely.

COOK'S NOTE
■ The crackers keep in an airtight container at room temperature for up to 5 days.

Bittersweet Chocolate Brownies

MAKES 2 DOZEN BROWNIES
ACTIVE TIME: 20 MINUTES ■ START TO FINISH: 1½ HOURS

■ The antithesis of the heavy, fudgy bricks found at so many bakeries nowadays, these brownies are downright elegant—smooth, moist, and quite delicate. Their deep chocolate flavor comes from a combination of bittersweet chocolate and cocoa powder. ■

- 8 ounces bittersweet chocolate, coarsely chopped
- 2 sticks (½ pound) unsalted butter
- 1½ cups sugar
- 6 large eggs
- 2 teaspoons vanilla extract
- ½ cup all-purpose flour
- ½ cup unsweetened cocoa powder (not Dutch-process)
- ½ teaspoon salt

Put a rack in middle of oven and preheat oven to 375°F. Butter and flour a 13-by-9-inch baking pan, knocking out excess flour.

Melt chocolate and butter in a metal bowl set over

a saucepan of barely simmering water, stirring until smooth. Remove bowl from heat and whisk in sugar. Whisk in eggs one at a time until well combined. Stir in vanilla. Sift flour, cocoa powder, and salt over chocolate mixture and whisk until just combined.

Pour batter into baking pan and bake until a wooden toothpick inserted in center comes out clean, about 30 minutes. Cool completely in pan on a rack, then cut into 24 bars.

COOK'S NOTE

■ The brownies keep in an airtight container at room temperature for up to 3 days.

Chockfull Blondies

MAKES 20 SQUARES
ACTIVE TIME: 30 MINUTES ■ START TO FINISH: 2 HOURS
(INCLUDES COOLING)

■ Loaded with dried fruit, toasted almonds, and chocolate, these bars make a terrific addition to any holiday cookie platter. Or serve with vanilla ice cream. ■

- 1 cup boiling water
- 1 cup dried cranberries
- 1 cup dried sour cherries
- 1 cup golden raisins
- 2½ cups all-purpose flour
- 1½ teaspoons baking soda
- 1 teaspoon salt
- ¾ teaspoon ground cinnamon
- 2 sticks (½ pound) unsalted butter, melted and cooled
- 2 cups sugar
- 3 large eggs
- 1½ teaspoons vanilla extract
- 1 cup (about 5¼ ounces) unblanched whole almonds, toasted (see Tips, page 911) and very coarsely chopped
- 8 ounces bittersweet chocolate, coarsely chopped

Pour boiling water over dried fruit in a small bowl and soak for 20 minutes, then drain well in a sieve.

Put a rack in middle of oven and preheat oven to 325°F. Butter and flour bottom and sides of a 17-by-12-inch baking sheet, knocking out excess flour.

Whisk together flour, baking soda, salt, and cinnamon in a bowl.

Beat together butter, sugar, eggs, and vanilla in a large bowl with an electric mixer until creamy. Mix in flour mixture at low speed until just combined. Stir in dried fruit, almonds, and chocolate.

Spread batter evenly in baking sheet. Bake until golden brown and a wooden toothpick inserted in center comes out clean, 25 to 30 minutes. Cool blondies completely in pan on a rack.

Run a thin knife around edges of pan to loosen blondies, then cut into roughly 3-inch squares.

COOK'S NOTE

■ The blondies can be baked (but not cut into squares) up to 2 days ahead. Once cooled, wrap well in plastic wrap and keep at room temperature.

Jam Walnut Streusel Bars

MAKES 15 BARS
ACTIVE TIME: 35 MINUTES ■ START TO FINISH: 2¼ HOURS

■ With a perfect balance of rich shortbread crust, jam, and crumbly topping, these bars are homey and addictive. ■

FOR CRUST AND FILLING
- 1½ sticks (12 tablespoons) unsalted butter, cut into ½-inch cubes
- 2 cups all-purpose flour
- ½ cup packed light brown sugar
- ¼ teaspoon salt
- ⅔ cup raspberry, blackberry, or apricot jam or preserves
FOR STREUSEL
- ¾ cup all-purpose flour
- ¾ cup chopped walnuts, toasted (see Tips, page 911)
- ⅓ cup packed light brown sugar
- ¾ teaspoon ground cinnamon

¼ teaspoon salt

½ stick (4 tablespoons) cold unsalted butter, cut into ½-inch cubes

MAKE THE CRUST: Put a rack in middle of oven and preheat oven to 350°F. Line a 9-inch square baking pan with two crisscrossed sheets of foil, leaving a 2-inch overhang on two opposite sides, and butter foil.

Combine butter, flour, brown sugar, and salt in a food processor and pulse until mixture begins to look crumbly with some small (roughly pea-sized) lumps of butter. Press into bottom of baking pan.

Bake until crust is pale golden and beginning to set, 20 to 25 minutes. Cool in pan on a rack for 10 minutes, then spread jam over warm crust.

MEANWHILE, MAKE THE STREUSEL: Stir together flour, walnuts, brown sugar, cinnamon, and salt in a bowl until combined. Work in butter with your fingertips until mixture comes together in clumps. Sprinkle streusel evenly over jam.

Bake until crumbs and edges of crust are golden, 30 to 35 minutes. Cool completely in pan on rack.

Lift bars out of pan using foil overhang, peel off foil, and cut into 15 bars.

COOK'S NOTE

■ The bars keep in an airtight container at room temperature for up to 2 days.

Dulce de Leche Cheesecake Squares

MAKES 64 SQUARES
ACTIVE TIME: 45 MINUTES ■ START TO FINISH: 9¾ HOURS
(INCLUDES CHILLING)

■ Dreamy dulce de leche adds a deep, dark sweetness and a tawny, elegant look to these bite-sized cheesecake squares. A glossy topping of bittersweet chocolate is just the right finishing touch. The wheat-meal crackers used for the crust are a bit more sophisticated-tasting than graham crackers and have a more nubbly texture. ■

FOR CRUST

3½ ounces wheat-meal crackers (see Cook's Note), crumbled (1 cup)

2 tablespoons sugar
Pinch of salt

3 tablespoons unsalted butter, melted

FOR FILLING

1 teaspoon unflavored gelatin

¼ cup whole milk

1 (8-ounce) package cream cheese, softened

2 large eggs

⅜ teaspoon salt

1 cup (12½ ounces) dulce de leche (see page 695 and Sources)

FOR GLAZE

3 ounces bittersweet chocolate, coarsely chopped

½ stick (4 tablespoons) unsalted butter, cut into small pieces

2 teaspoons light corn syrup

MAKE THE CRUST: Put a rack in middle of oven and preheat oven to 325°F. Line an 8-inch square baking pan with two crisscrossed sheets of foil, leaving a 2-inch overhang on all sides.

Finely grind crackers with sugar and salt in a food processor. With motor running, add butter and process until combined.

Press mixture evenly onto bottom of baking pan. Bake for 10 minutes, then cool in pan on a rack for 5 minutes.

MEANWHILE, MAKE THE FILLING: Sprinkle gelatin over milk in a small bowl and let stand for 2 minutes to soften.

Beat together cream cheese, eggs, salt, and gelatin mixture in a bowl with an electric mixer until well combined. Gently but thoroughly stir in dulce de leche. Pour filling over crust, smoothing top.

Put pan in a roasting pan and add enough boiling water to reach halfway up sides of baking pan. Bake cheesecake until center is just set, about 45 minutes. Cool completely in pan on rack, about 2 hours, then refrigerate, covered, for at least 6 hours.

WITHIN 2 HOURS OF SERVING, GLAZE THE CAKE: Melt chocolate and butter with corn syrup in a small metal bowl set over a saucepan of barely simmering water, stirring until smooth. Pour over cheesecake, tilting baking pan to cover top evenly. Refrigerate, uncovered, for 30 minutes.

Lift cheesecake from pan using foil overhang. Cut into 1-inch squares with a thin knife, wiping knife clean after each cut.

COOK'S NOTES

- Wheat-meal crackers are sometimes called digestive biscuits. For this recipe, we prefer Carr's wheat-meal crackers, which are available at supermarkets and labeled as "whole wheat crackers." (Don't use Carr's Wheatolos, which are too sweet.)
- The cheesecake, without the glaze, can be refrigerated for up to 3 days.

Crispy Chocolate Marshmallow Squares

MAKES ABOUT 5 DOZEN SQUARES
ACTIVE TIME: 30 MINUTES ■ START TO FINISH: 3 HOURS

■ Dark chocolate ganache with a tiny jab of coffee flavor turns classic Rice Krispie squares into sophisticated treats. Using bittersweet chocolate of different cacao levels results in a ganache that has just the right intensity without being overpowering. ■

FOR GANACHE

- 5 ounces bittersweet chocolate (no more than 60% cacao; see page 705), chopped
- 3 ounces bittersweet chocolate (70% cacao; see page 705), chopped
- ¾ cup heavy cream
- 2 tablespoons Tía Maria, Kahlúa, or other coffee-flavored liqueur
- 1 tablespoon instant espresso powder, such as Medaglia d'Oro, or instant coffee granules

FOR MARSHMALLOW SQUARES

- ¼ pound marshmallows (15 large marshmallows or 2 cups small marshmallows)
- 2 tablespoons unsalted butter
- 2 tablespoons sugar
- 2 tablespoons unsweetened cocoa powder
- ⅛ teaspoon salt
- 3 cups puffed rice cereal, such as Rice Krispies

MAKE THE GANACHE: Melt chocolates with cream, liqueur, and espresso powder in a metal bowl set over a saucepan of barely simmering water, whisking occasionally, until smooth. Remove from heat and let stand at room temperature until thickened, about 2 hours.

MAKE THE MARSHMALLOW SQUARES: Line a 13-by-9-inch baking pan with foil, leaving a 1-inch overhang on each end.

Melt marshmallows and butter with sugar, cocoa powder, and salt in a 2½- to 3-quart heavy saucepan over low heat, stirring frequently until smooth. Remove from heat and gently stir in cereal.

Transfer mixture to lined baking pan and press evenly onto bottom with dampened fingertips. Cool to room temperature, about 20 minutes.

Carefully lift mixture from pan using foil overhang, peel off foil, and cut into 1-inch squares.

Spread about ½ teaspoon ganache each onto half of squares, then top with remaining squares. Reheat remaining ganache in bowl over barely simmering water, whisking occasionally, until loosened, then drizzle over tops of squares (you will have some ganache left over; see Cook's Note).

Let squares stand until set, about 15 minutes.

COOK'S NOTES

- The marshmallow squares, with the ganache, can be made up to 1 day ahead and refrigerated, covered with plastic wrap after the ganache is set. Bring to room temperature, uncovered, before serving.
- The leftover ganache keeps, covered and refrigerated, for up to 1 week. Reheat as above and serve over ice cream.

Fruit and Nut Chocolate Chunks

MAKES 3 DOZEN CANDIES
ACTIVE TIME: 15 MINUTES ■ START TO FINISH: 1¼ HOURS

■ These candies are among the easiest you can make—simply melt good-quality bittersweet chocolate, stir in a combination of dried fruit and nuts, and pour into a pan to firm up. Once set, the mixture can be cut into squares that make a fine addition to a cookie tray. ■

A Chocolate Primer

The famed wit and woman of letters Marie de Sévigné wrote to her daughter, Françoise-Marguerite, Comtesse de Grignan, in February 1671: "If you are not feeling well, if you have not slept, chocolate will revive you. But you have no chocolate pot! I think of that again and again. How will you manage?"

Centuries before the marquise ever sipped the exotic drink, the peoples of Mesoamerica had turned the cacao tree—*Theobroma cacao* (*Theobroma* meaning "food of the gods")—into a valuable crop. Today chocolate is one of life's most affordable luxuries, and a vast (some would say dizzying) array of fine chocolates is available to the home cook.

CHOCOLATE FOR COOKING

The flavor of chocolate depends on the cacao beans used, where they're cultivated, and how they're roasted. The percentage of chocolate liquor (the technical term for unsweetened chocolate, or cocoa solids, often called simply "cacao"), now listed on many chocolate labels, also makes a big difference. In the United States, only chocolate with more than 35 percent cacao content can be labeled **semisweet** or **bittersweet**; fine-quality dark chocolate generally has 50 percent or greater. For most baking, it's fine to use any in the 50 to 60 percent range, but be aware that some manufacturers don't list the percentages on labels until it's 60 percent or more. A higher percentage of chocolate liquor indicates more intense (and correspondingly less sweet) chocolate, which is why we specify "not more than 60%" in some of our recipes. Our tried-and-true favorites include Lindt (the regular bittersweet, not the 71 percent), Ghirardelli, and Valrhona. Lindt and Ghirardelli are both available at supermarkets (look for Lindt in the candy aisle and Ghirardelli in the baking aisle), while Valrhona can be found at specialty foods shops, high-end supermarkets, and online. (The chocolate liquor percentage varies on Valrhona, but it's marked on the package.) And even though cooking chocolate and snacking chocolate are frequently interchangeable, don't reject a chocolate for cooking if you don't like the way it tastes straight out of the wrapper. Its flavor may well improve when bolstered by other ingredients.

So what's the difference between semisweet and bittersweet chocolate? Sometimes not much, as it turns out. The chocolate industry puts the two in the same category, and one brand's semisweet may well have the same percentage of chocolate liquor as another brand's bittersweet. As a general rule, though, semisweet chocolate tends to contain more sugar than bittersweet.

Cocoa powder is what's left after cocoa butter has been extracted from chocolate liquor. It's generally not a good idea to substitute American-style (sometimes labeled "natural") unsweetened cocoa (such as Hershey's regular or Ghirardelli) for European-style Dutch-process cocoa (such as Valrhona or Droste) or vice versa in baking: the two types don't always behave the same way in a recipe. ("Dutched" cocoa powder differs from regular in that an alkaline solution is added to the beans during roasting, thus mellowing their acidity.) If our recipe doesn't specify which kind to use, either will work.

GETTING THE BEST OUT OF CHOCOLATE

MELT IT GENTLY. Finely chop the chocolate and melt it slowly in a metal bowl set over a pan of barely simmering water, stirring often. (Don't let the bottom of the bowl touch the water; that will raise the temperature, and the chocolate might scorch.) An alternative is to use a microwave oven at low to medium power for short intervals (start with 30 seconds and adjust the time as you go). Be aware that microwaved chocolate tends to hold its shape until stirred, so it may be more fluid than it looks. Stir between intervals and check its consistency.

KEEP IT DRY. Be sure that your bowl and utensils are absolutely dry, and don't let any drops of water or other liquid get into your melting chocolate. Moisture—including steam—can make it harden and become grainy, a process called seizing.

STORE IT CAREFULLY. Keep chocolate tightly wrapped and in a cool, dry place (out of the sunlight and away from the stove). Chocolate that has been exposed to excessive heat and humidity may "bloom," becoming streaked and gritty. Although bloom will affect flavor and texture, you can still cook with it successfully.

1¼ pounds bittersweet chocolate (no more than 70% cacao; see page 705), broken into small pieces
⅔ cup dried cranberries
⅔ cup raisins
⅔ cup salted roasted shelled pistachios
⅔ cup salted roasted cashews

Line an 8-inch square baking pan with two criss-crossed sheets of foil, leaving a 2-inch overhang on all sides, then lightly oil foil.

Melt chocolate in a metal bowl set over a saucepan of barely simmering water, stirring occasionally, until smooth.

Remove chocolate from heat and stir in fruit and nuts. Spread evenly in baking pan. Refrigerate until firm, about 1 hour.

Lift candy from pan using foil overhang and transfer to a cutting board. Peel off foil and cut candy into 36 pieces with a long heavy knife.

COOK'S NOTE

■ The candy keeps, wrapped well in foil and refrigerated, for up to 2 weeks.

Line an 8-inch square baking pan with parchment paper.

Stir together all ingredients in a metal bowl. Set bowl over a saucepan of barely simmering water, and heat until chocolate appears to be melted, 5 to 8 minutes. Gently stir with a rubber spatula occasionally, letting chocolate rest for a few minutes if it appears to stiffen, until smooth.

Pour mixture into baking pan and refrigerate, uncovered, until firm, about 4 hours.

Run a knife around edges of pan, invert fudge onto a cutting board, peel off paper, and cut fudge into 1-inch squares. Serve cold.

COOK'S NOTE

■ The fudge keeps, refrigerated, layered between sheets of parchment paper, in an airtight container for up to 1 week.

VARIATION

MILK CHOCOLATE FUDGE: Substitute 1 pound high-quality milk chocolate, finely chopped, for the bittersweet chocolate.

Truffle Fudge

MAKES 64 PIECES
ACTIVE TIME: 15 MINUTES ■ START TO FINISH: 4½ HOURS
(INCLUDES CHILLING)

■ With just three ingredients (plus a pinch of salt), this is the easiest fudge you'll ever whip up. And it doesn't even require a candy thermometer. Made with good bittersweet chocolate, it is smooth and creamy but still unquestionably fudgy. If you use milk chocolate (see Variation below), the result will be sweeter and more kid-pleasing. ■

¾ pound bittersweet chocolate (no more than 60% cacao; see page 705), finely chopped
½ stick (4 tablespoons) unsalted butter, cut into tablespoons, softened
1 (14-ounce) can sweetened condensed milk
⅛ teaspoon salt
SPECIAL EQUIPMENT: parchment paper

Chocolate Raspberry Truffles

MAKES ABOUT 4 DOZEN TRUFFLES
ACTIVE TIME: 50 MINUTES ■ START TO FINISH: 2 HOURS
(INCLUDES CHILLING)

■ Ripe raspberries cloaked in bittersweet chocolate make a delightful little indulgence. Although there are many tempting bittersweet chocolates available these days, you need one that is sweet enough to soften the berries' tartness, so choose a brand that has no more than 60% cacao. ■

¼ cup heavy cream
7 ounces bittersweet chocolate (no more than 60% cacao; see page 705), finely chopped
1½ tablespoons framboise (raspberry eau-de-vie) or brandy
6 ounces raspberries
¾ cup unsweetened cocoa powder

SPECIAL EQUIPMENT: parchment paper; a large sealable plastic bag

Line a tray with parchment paper.

Bring cream just to a simmer in a 1- to 2-quart heavy saucepan over moderate heat. Remove from heat, add chocolate, and stir gently with a heat-proof rubber spatula until ganache is smooth. Stir in framboise.

Pat raspberries dry if necessary. Add 6 to 8 raspberries to ganache and gently fold to coat, using rubber spatula. Remove each chocolate-covered raspberry with two forks, shifting it from one fork to the other to let excess ganache drip off, and transfer to tray. Coat remaining raspberries in same manner, working in batches of 6 to 8.

Refrigerate truffles on tray until set, at least 1 hour.

Loosen truffles from parchment. Put cocoa in large sealable plastic bag and add all of truffles. Seal bag and shake to coat. Empty bag into a shallow bowl. Transfer coated truffles to a platter with your fingers, shaking off excess cocoa. Keep refrigerated.

COOK'S NOTE

- The truffles can be refrigerated, covered after 1 hour, for up to 2 days. Coat with cocoa powder no more than 1 hour before serving

2 teaspoons loose Earl Grey tea leaves (see Cook's Note)
6 ounces bittersweet chocolate (no more than 60% cacao; see page 705), finely chopped
1 cup unsweetened cocoa powder

Bring cream and butter to a boil in a 1- to 2-quart heavy saucepan. Stir in tea leaves, remove from heat, and let steep for 5 minutes.

Put chocolate into a bowl. Pour cream mixture through a fine-mesh sieve over chocolate, pressing on and then discarding tea leaves, and whisk until ganache is smooth. Refrigerate, covered, until firm, about 2 hours.

Spoon level teaspoons of ganache onto a baking sheet. Put cocoa in a bowl. Dust your palms lightly with cocoa and roll each teaspoon of ganache into a ball (wash your hands and redust as they become sticky). Drop several balls at a time into bowl of cocoa and turn to coat, then transfer to an airtight container, separating layers with parchment paper. Refrigerate until ready to serve.

COOK'S NOTES

- Loose tea leaves have a fresher, more distinctive flavor than the leaves in tea bags.
- The truffles can be refrigerated for up to 1 week or frozen for up to 1 month.

Chocolate Earl Grey Truffles

MAKES ABOUT 3 DOZEN TRUFFLES
ACTIVE TIME: 45 MINUTES ■ START TO FINISH: 2¾ HOURS
(INCLUDES CHILLING)

■ Bergamot is a small, sour orange grown primarily for the fragrant oil in its peel. It perfumes Earl Grey tea, which lends these truffles their haunting, citrusy flavor. ■

⅔ cup heavy cream
2 tablespoons unsalted butter, cut into 4 pieces, softened

Peppermint Patties

MAKES ABOUT 4 DOZEN CANDIES
ACTIVE TIME: 1½ HOURS ■ START TO FINISH: 2½ HOURS
(INCLUDES SETTING)

■ A bracing peppermint filling enrobed in bittersweet chocolate is one of the best—and most refreshing—candy combinations going, and homemade versions of these popular patties are leagues better than anything you'll find in a foil wrapper. Here we temper, or stabilize, the chocolate to give it a beautiful sheen and to prevent the coating from developing gray streaks at room temperature. All tempering involves is carefully melting, cooling, and gently reheating the chocolate. ■

2½ cups confectioners' sugar, plus extra for dusting

1½ tablespoons light corn syrup

1½ tablespoons water

½ teaspoon peppermint extract

1 tablespoon vegetable shortening, preferably trans fat–free

Pinch of salt

10 ounces bittersweet chocolate (70% cacao; see page 705), coarsely chopped

SPECIAL EQUIPMENT: parchment paper; a 1-inch round cookie cutter; a digital instant-read thermometer

MAKE THE FILLING: Combine 2¼ cups confectioners' sugar, corn syrup, water, peppermint extract, shortening, and salt in a large bowl and beat with an electric mixer at medium speed until just combined. Turn out onto a work surface dusted with remaining ¼ cup confectioners' sugar and knead until smooth.

Roll mixture out between sheets of parchment paper on a large baking sheet into a 7- to 8-inch round (less than ¼ inch thick). Freeze until firm, about 15 minutes.

Remove top sheet of paper and sprinkle round with confectioners' sugar. Replace top sheet, flip round over, and repeat sprinkling on other side. Cut out as many rounds as possible with cutter and transfer to a parchment-lined baking sheet. Freeze until firm, at least 10 minutes. Meanwhile, gather scraps, reroll, and freeze, then cut out more rounds and freeze.

TEMPER THE CHOCOLATE AND MAKE THE PATTIES: Melt three quarters of chocolate in a metal bowl set over a saucepan of barely simmering water, stirring occasionally, until smooth. Remove bowl from pan, add remaining chocolate, and stir until smooth. Cool until thermometer inserted at least ½ inch into chocolate registers 80°F.

Return water in pan to a boil, then remove from heat. Set bowl with cooled chocolate over pan and reheat, stirring, until thermometer registers 88° to 91°F. Remove bowl from pan.

Balance 1 peppermint round on a fork and submerge in melted chocolate, then return patty to sheet, letting excess drip off and scraping back of fork against rim of bowl if necessary (to make decorative ridges on patty, immediately press back of fork lightly on top of patty, then lift fork straight up). Coat re-

maining rounds, rewarming chocolate to 88° to 91°F as necessary. Let patties stand until chocolate is set, about 1 hour.

COOK'S NOTE

■ The patties keep, refrigerated, layered between sheets of parchment paper in an airtight container, for up to 1 month. Bring to room temperature before serving.

Toasted-Coconut Marshmallow Squares

MAKES ABOUT 4 DOZEN CANDIES
ACTIVE TIME: 1 HOUR ■ START TO FINISH: 3¼ HOURS
(INCLUDES SETTING)

■ You may never go back to store-bought marshmallows after a bite of these dreamy treats, especially when you see how easy they are. A flurry of toasted coconut surrounds each square, adding a counterpoint of crunch to the sweet, pillowy insides. And since the marshmallows keep for a month, they can be made well in advance. ■

2 cups finely shredded unsweetened dried coconut

2 (¼-ounce) envelopes unflavored gelatin

1 cup water

1½ cups sugar

1 cup light corn syrup

¼ teaspoon salt

2 teaspoons vanilla extract

½ teaspoon coconut extract

SPECIAL EQUIPMENT: a stand mixer with a whisk attachment; a candy thermometer

Put a rack in middle of oven and preheat oven to 350°F.

Toast coconut on a baking sheet in oven, stirring occasionally, until golden, 7 to 10 minutes. Remove from oven.

Lightly oil a 9-inch square baking pan. Sprinkle bottom with ½ cup toasted coconut.

Sprinkle gelatin over ½ cup water in bowl of mixer and let soften while you make syrup.

Combine sugar, corn syrup, remaining ½ cup water, and salt in a 1- to 2-quart heavy saucepan and heat over low heat, stirring, until sugar has dissolved. Bring to a boil over medium heat, without stirring, washing down any sugar crystals from sides of pan with a pastry brush dipped in cold water. Insert thermometer and boil, without stirring, until it registers 240°F (soft-ball stage). Remove from heat and let stand until bubbles dissipate.

With mixer at low speed, pour hot syrup into gelatin in a thin stream down side of bowl, being careful to avoid beater. Increase speed to high and beat until very thick, about 15 minutes. Add vanilla and coconut extracts and beat for 1 minute more.

Spoon marshmallow mixture over toasted coconut in baking pan and press evenly with dampened fingertips to smooth top (it will be very sticky). Sprinkle top evenly with ½ cup toasted coconut. Let stand, uncovered, at room temperature until firm, about 2 hours.

Run a sharp knife around edges of marshmallow and invert onto a cutting board. Cut into ¾-inch-wide strips, then cut each strip into ¾-inch squares.

Put remaining toasted coconut in a small bowl and dredge marshmallows in it to coat completely.

COOK'S NOTES

- To avoid stickiness, make the marshmallows on a dry day.
- The marshmallow squares keep, layered between sheets of parchment paper in an airtight container, in a cool, dry place for up to 1 month.

Passion Fruit Gelées

MAKES ABOUT 10½ DOZEN CANDIES
ACTIVE TIME: 45 MINUTES ■ START TO FINISH: 13 HOURS
(INCLUDES SETTING)

■ These delicate gelées are wonderful for company—the passion fruit puree gives them a golden color and a heady tropical flavor. As a bonus, they keep beautifully. ■

- 4 (¼-ounce) envelopes unflavored gelatin
- 1 cup water
- 2 cups sugar, plus additional for coating
- 1 teaspoon fresh lemon juice
- ¾ cup thawed unsweetened passion fruit puree, such as Goya

SPECIAL EQUIPMENT: an 8-inch square nonstick baking pan

Lightly oil baking pan.

Sprinkle gelatin over water in a 2-quart heavy saucepan and let stand for 4 minutes to soften.

Heat gelatin over medium-low heat, stirring, until dissolved. Stir in sugar until dissolved, then stir in lemon juice. Bring to a boil over medium-high heat, washing down any sugar crystals from sides of pan with a pastry brush dipped in cold water. Reduce heat to medium-low and boil, uncovered, without stirring, for 13 minutes (watch carefully so that mixture does not boil over). Remove from heat and let stand for 5 minutes for bubbles to dissipate.

Skim any foam on surface of gelatin mixture that remains after 5 minutes, then stir in passion fruit puree (do not scrape bottom of pan; leave any dark bits that stick). Pour into oiled baking pan and let stand at room temperature until set, at least 12 hours.

Run a sharp knife around edges of gelée and invert onto a cutting board. Cut into ½-inch-wide strips, then cut strips into 1-inch pieces.

Just before serving, gently toss gelées in a bowl of sugar to coat, brushing off excess.

COOK'S NOTE

- The gelées, without the sugar coating, keep in an airtight container at a cool room temperature for up to 2 weeks.

Chocolate-Covered Nut Toffee

MAKES ABOUT 3½ POUNDS
ACTIVE TIME: 45 MINUTES ■ START TO FINISH: 1¾ HOURS
(INCLUDES CHILLING)

■ Combining two kinds of nuts (almonds and walnuts) and two kinds of chocolate (milk and bittersweet) makes this crunchy toffee doubly irresistible. It comes from reader Joe Miller of Glasgow, Montana, who says that the sweet snack is a family tradition. We understand why—one bite, and we were hooked. ■

1 cup (about 4 ounces) slivered or sliced almonds,
    toasted (see Tips, page 911)
3 cups (about 9¾ ounces) walnuts
2 (3½- to 4-ounce) bars milk chocolate
2 (3½- to 4-ounce) bars bittersweet chocolate
    (no more than 60% cacao; see page 705)
1 pound salted butter
2 cups sugar
2 tablespoons water
SPECIAL EQUIPMENT: two large (17-by-13-inch) baking
    sheets; a candy thermometer; parchment paper

Pulse almonds in a food processor until coarsely chopped and transfer to a small bowl. Pulse walnuts in processor until finely chopped; set aside.

Finely chop 1 bar of milk chocolate and 1 bar of bittersweet chocolate with a large knife and combine in a bowl. Finely chop remaining 2 chocolate bars and combine in another bowl.

Butter one baking sheet and put on a heatproof work surface. Combine butter, sugar, and water in a 5-quart pot and bring to a boil over moderately high heat, whisking until smooth. Insert thermometer and boil, stirring occasionally, until mixture is golden and registers 300°F on thermometer, 20 to 30 minutes.

Immediately stir in almonds, then carefully pour toffee onto center of prepared baking sheet. Spread into a 15-by-12-inch rectangle (¼ inch thick) with a heatproof rubber spatula, smoothing top. Let stand for 1 minute, then sprinkle 1 bowl of chopped chocolate evenly on top of hot toffee. Let stand until chocolate is melted, 4 to 5 minutes. Spread chocolate evenly

using heatproof spatula or an offset metal spatula. Sprinkle half of walnuts evenly over melted chocolate, then cover with a sheet of parchment paper.

Wearing oven mitts, invert second baking sheet over toffee and carefully invert toffee and sheet. If toffee does not release, use a spatula to loosen it. Sprinkle remaining chocolate on top to melt, then spread (as before) and sprinkle with remaining walnuts. Put a sheet of parchment paper on top and press lightly to help nuts adhere.

Freeze toffee on baking sheet until chocolate is set, about 30 minutes. Break toffee into pieces.

COOK'S NOTE

■ The toffee keeps in an airtight container at cool room temperature for up to 2 weeks.

Fleur de Sel Caramels

MAKES 64 CANDIES
ACTIVE TIME: 45 MINUTES ■ START TO FINISH: 2¾ HOURS

■ As shops devoted to fine candies continue to open up everywhere, salted caramels have become wildly popular—and are priced as extravagantly as they taste. These buttery caramels, whose flavor is rounded out with French sea salt, won't break the bank. That they are truly easy to make can be your little secret. ■

1 cup heavy cream
5 tablespoons unsalted butter, cut into pieces
1 teaspoon fleur de sel (see Sources)
1½ cups sugar
¼ cup light corn syrup
¼ cup water
SPECIAL EQUIPMENT: parchment paper; a candy
    thermometer

Line bottom and sides of an 8-inch square baking pan with parchment paper and lightly oil parchment.

Bring cream, butter, and fleur de sel to a boil in a small saucepan. Remove from heat.

Bring sugar, corn syrup, and water to a boil in a 3- to 4-quart heavy saucepan, stirring until sugar is dissolved. Insert thermometer and boil, without stirring but gently swirling pan, until mixture is a light golden caramel. Carefully stir in cream mixture (mixture will bubble up) and simmer, stirring frequently, until caramel registers 248°F on thermometer.

Pour mixture into baking pan, transfer to a rack, and let stand until cool and set, about 2 hours.

Invert caramel slab onto a cutting board; discard parchment. Cut into 1-inch pieces and wrap each piece in a 4-inch square of parchment paper, twisting ends to close.

COOK'S NOTE

■ The caramels keep in an airtight container at room temperature for up to 2 weeks.

Pumpkin Seed Brittle

MAKES ABOUT 12 OUNCES
ACTIVE TIME: 30 MINUTES ■ START TO FINISH: 30 MINUTES

■ Most nut brittle recipes call for toasting the nuts and then stirring them into the caramel at the last minute. But this one borrows from a method that we discovered in *Los Postres de El Bulli* (*The Desserts of El Bulli*), by Albert Adrià, pastry chef and brother of the renowned Spanish chef Ferran Adrià. Instead of nuts, our food editor Ruth Cousineau used raw *pepitas* (green pumpkin seeds). Added to the sugar syrup when it reaches the soft-ball stage, before it caramelizes, the seeds toast as the sugar syrup continues to cook. This method requires some effort—you must stir constantly with a wooden spoon until the sugar crystallizes—and you shouldn't panic when the mixture becomes cloudy and grainy and looks as if it's ruined. Just keep cooking and stirring, and you will be rewarded with a gorgeous deep-golden caramel and the intoxicating aroma of roasty-toasty *pepitas*. ■

1 cup sugar
½ cup water
⅛ teaspoon fine sea salt
¾ cup green (hulled) pumpkin seeds (*pepitas*; not toasted)
SPECIAL EQUIPMENT: parchment paper; a candy thermometer

Cut two 24-by-12-inch sheets of parchment paper. Put one sheet on a work surface and anchor corners with pieces of tape.

Bring sugar, water, and salt to a boil in a 2-quart heavy saucepan over moderate heat, stirring until sugar is dissolved. Insert thermometer and cook mixture, without stirring, washing down any sugar crystals from sides of pan with a pastry brush dipped in cold water, until syrup registers 238°F (soft-ball stage). Remove from heat and stir in seeds with a wooden spoon, then continue stirring until syrup crystallizes, 3 to 4 minutes.

Return pan to moderate heat and cook, stirring constantly, until sugar melts completely (sugar will become grainy before melting) and turns a deep caramel color, 4 to 5 minutes more.

Carefully pour hot caramel mixture onto parchment paper and carefully cover with second sheet of parchment (1). Immediately roll out mixture between parchment sheets, pressing firmly with a large wooden rolling pin, until as thin as possible (2). Remove top sheet of parchment and immediately cut brittle into pieces with a sharp heavy knife or pizza cutter. Cool brittle completely, then peel paper from bottom. (Alternatively, break brittle into pieces once cool.)

COOK'S NOTE

■ The brittle keeps in an airtight container, layered between sheets of parchment paper, at room temperature for up to 1 month.

ROLL THE BRITTLE

CAKES

Why do you bake?

Sometimes it is because you have the urge to produce something so spectacular that everyone stops talking when it shows up at the table. You want people to stare at your creation, and then stare some more. You want someone to say incredulously, "Did you really make that?"... and not quite believe your answer.

But other times you bake for entirely different reasons. Cakes are a reminder of how it felt to be a child eagerly awaiting the opening of the oven door. The magic of that moment, when what went in as gooey batter emerged as a solid cake, never disappears. When you find yourself in need of simple comfort, baking always does the trick. Whether you are looking to feel good or feel proud—or both—you will find the perfect solution in this chapter.

For those show-off moments, little is as satisfying as a fresh coconut layer cake. I make one every year for Christmas, and I'll admit that there is always a point when I find myself muttering imprecations as I attempt to hit the coconut with a hammer, only to watch it roll away. I mutter a few more as I beat the frosting, watching the sweet white clouds billow up as I stand, face flushed, over the hot stove. And even more when I grate the fresh coconut, watching it fall onto the frosting in a shower of soft white flakes. But the minute I take the cake to the table, all that is forgotten. It is a towering white snowball of a cake, an impressive diva, a fashion statement. And the flavor is so spectacular that it invariably renders the entire table momentarily mute.

There are plenty of other showstoppers here, from an elegant Opera cake enrobed in a sleek layer of chocolate frosting, to a double chocolate layer cake, to a chocolate-glazed hazelnut mousse cake—all absolutely guaranteed to elicit oohs and ahs. And should there be a child in your life, you must bake the ice cream cone cake, if only to see the glow in his eyes when he realizes that you've created something so special just for him.

Baking for comfort, however, calls for an entirely different approach. For those moments, nothing works so well as a caramel buttermilk cake. It is a flat but amazingly fluffy square that looks completely humble until you cover it with a soft pillow of warm caramel. One bite of the cake's extraordinarily delicate texture can make me feel fine on even the bleakest day.

And then there is Elvis's favorite pound cake. The first time I tasted it, I took a tiny bite. Then I took a bigger one. Then I cut out the recipe and put it in the special file that I keep for the dishes I know I am going to make over and over again. This is simply the best pound cake ever. (The secret is seven eggs, half a pound of butter, and a cup of cream.) But it's not the kind of cake you save for special occasions; it is one you bake when you want to make someone very, very happy.

And in the end, isn't that the real reason that we bake? A cake is not just another recipe. A cake is special. A cake is a declaration of love.

CAKES

Applesauce Pecan Cake

SERVES 8
ACTIVE TIME: 25 MINUTES ■ START TO FINISH: 2 HOURS
(INCLUDES COOLING)

■ This homespun cake is the quintessential after-school snack. Laced with pecans and moist with applesauce, it couldn't be easier. And there's no need to stand on ceremony—the cake is just as delicious served straight from the pan as it is presented on a cake plate, dusted with confectioners' sugar. ■

- 1¼ cups all-purpose flour
- 1 teaspoon baking powder
- ½ teaspoon baking soda
- ½ teaspoon salt
- 1 teaspoon ground cinnamon
- ½ teaspoon ground ginger
- ¼ teaspoon freshly grated nutmeg
  Pinch of ground cloves
- 1 stick (8 tablespoons) unsalted butter, softened
- 1 cup packed light brown sugar
- 2 large eggs, left at room temperature for 30 minutes
- 1 teaspoon vanilla extract
- 1 cup unsweetened applesauce
- 1 cup coarsely chopped pecans (about 4¼ ounces)

GARNISH: confectioners' sugar
SPECIAL EQUIPMENT: a 9-inch square baking pan

Put a rack in middle of oven and preheat oven to 350°F. Butter baking pan.

Sift together flour, baking powder, baking soda, salt, and spices.

Beat together butter and brown sugar in a large bowl with an electric mixer (fitted with paddle attachment if using a stand mixer) at medium speed until pale and fluffy, about 3 minutes. Add eggs one at a time, beating well after each addition. Beat in vanilla and applesauce, then scrape down sides of bowl (mixture will look curdled). At low speed, add flour mixture and mix, scraping down sides of bowl, just until flour is incorporated. Stir in pecans.

Spread batter evenly in baking pan. Bake until a wooden toothpick inserted in center of cake comes out clean, 25 to 30 minutes. Cool cake in pan on a rack for 30 minutes.

Run a thin knife around sides of pan. Turn cake out of pan, if desired, and dust with confectioners' sugar.

COOK'S NOTE

■ The cake can be made up to 1 day ahead and kept in an airtight container at room temperature.

Crumble Cake

SERVES 6 TO 8
ACTIVE TIME: 30 MINUTES ■ START TO FINISH: 2 HOURS
(INCLUDES COOLING)

■ *La torta sbrisolona,* or "crumbly cake," is a specialty of Mantua, in northern Italy. Originally a peasant dish made with cornmeal and lard, it was later adopted by noblemen, whose cooks replaced the lard with butter and added flour, almonds, and sugar. These ordinary ingredients come together into a cake that resembles the top of a fruit crumble (without the fruit); it resists being cut into neat wedges and is traditionally just broken into pieces. It's wonderful with a cup of coffee or a glass of wine, and you'll find yourself reaching for just one more crumb, then just one more . . . ■

- 2 cups (7 ounces) sliced almonds, toasted (see Tips, page 911)
- ¾ cup sugar
- 1 cup all-purpose flour
- 1 cup stone-ground cornmeal
- 1 tablespoon finely grated lemon zest
  Scant ½ teaspoon salt
- 1½ sticks (12 tablespoons) unsalted butter, cut into tablespoons
- 2 large egg yolks, lightly beaten with 2 teaspoons water

SPECIAL EQUIPMENT: a 9-inch springform pan

Put a rack in middle of oven and preheat oven to 350°F. Butter pan.

Pulse 1¾ cups almonds and ¼ cup sugar in a food processor until finely ground. Add flour, cornmeal, remaining ½ cup sugar, zest, and salt and pulse until combined. Add butter and pulse until most of mixture resembles coarse meal with some small (roughly pea-sized) lumps. Add yolk mixture and pulse until incorporated and dough begins to form a ball.

Press three quarters of dough into bottom of pan. Crumble remaining dough evenly over top and sprinkle with remaining ¼ cup almonds.

Bake until top is golden, 30 to 35 minutes. Cool in pan on a rack for 10 minutes.

Remove side of pan and cool cake completely. Cut or break into pieces to serve.

COOK'S NOTE
- The cake can be made up to 1 week ahead and kept in an airtight container at room temperature.

Banana Chocolate Walnut Cake

SERVES 8
ACTIVE TIME: 20 MINUTES ■ START TO FINISH: 2 HOURS
(INCLUDES COOLING)

■ Make this crowd-pleasing cake with those overripe bananas you wouldn't consider eating. Collect them in the freezer, unpeeled, until you have enough to make the cake, then thaw and peel. You'll be rewarded with a moist snack cake threaded with cinnamon-scented bittersweet chocolate and punctuated with toasted walnuts. ■

2¼ cups all-purpose flour
1 teaspoon baking soda
½ teaspoon salt
1 stick (8 tablespoons) unsalted butter, softened
1 cup sugar
2 large eggs, left at room temperature for 30 minutes
1¼ cups mashed overripe bananas (about 3 medium)
⅔ cup whole-milk yogurt
1 teaspoon vanilla extract
1 (3½- to 4-ounce) bar bittersweet chocolate (70% cacao; see page 705), coarsely chopped
1 cup (about 3¼ ounces) walnuts, toasted (see Tips, page 911) and coarsely chopped
½ teaspoon ground cinnamon
2 tablespoons unsalted butter, melted and cooled

SPECIAL EQUIPMENT: a 9-inch square baking pan

Put a rack in middle of oven and preheat oven to 375°F. Butter baking pan.

Stir together flour, baking soda, and salt in a small bowl.

Beat together softened butter and ¾ cup sugar in a medium bowl with an electric mixer (fitted with paddle attachment if using a stand mixer) at medium speed until pale and fluffy. Beat in eggs one at a time until blended. Beat in bananas, yogurt, and vanilla (mixture will look curdled). At low speed, add flour mixture, beating just until flour is incorporated.

Toss together chocolate, nuts, cinnamon, melted butter, and remaining ¼ cup sugar in a small bowl. Spread half of batter in cake pan and sprinkle with half of chocolate mixture. Spread remaining batter evenly over filling and sprinkle remaining chocolate mixture on top.

Bake until cake is golden and a wooden toothpick inserted in center of cake comes out dry, 35 to 40 minutes. Cool cake in pan on a rack for 30 minutes.

Run a thin knife around sides of pan, invert cake onto rack, turn right side up, and cool completely.

COOK'S NOTE
- The cake can be made up to 1 day ahead and kept in an airtight container at room temperature.

WHAT "SOFTENED BUTTER" MEANS

"Softened butter" is malleable but not so soft that it oozes from the wrapper. It can be mixed thoroughly with other ingredients (so the fat disperses evenly), and when beaten, it aerates (holds air bubbles, thus helping the leavening) more easily. To soften butter, let it sit out at room temperature for 30 minutes or so, less if the kitchen is very warm. (To speed things along, cut it into pieces.) If it gets too soft, simply rechill it.

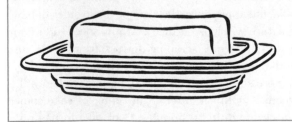

Hawaiian Sweet-Rice-Flour Coconut Cake

MAKES 24 SQUARES
ACTIVE TIME: 15 MINUTES ■ START TO FINISH: 3¾ HOURS
(INCLUDES COOLING)

■ This chewy snack cake, adapted from a recipe in Rachel Laudan's cookbook *The Food of Paradise*, gets its name—*mochi*—and distinctive texture from mochiko, a sweet rice flour that's commonly used in Hawaii. Coconut milk and butter add rich creaminess. Be prepared for guests to fight over the crisp browned edges. ■

    3 cups (1 pound) mochiko (sweet rice flour; see
         Sources)
  2½ cups sugar
    2 teaspoons baking powder
    ¼ teaspoon salt
    2 (14-ounce) cans unsweetened coconut milk (not
         low-fat)
    5 large eggs
    ½ stick (4 tablespoons) unsalted butter, melted and
         cooled
    1 teaspoon vanilla extract
SPECIAL EQUIPMENT: a 13-by-9-inch baking pan

Put a rack in middle of oven and preheat oven to 350°F.

Whisk together mochiko, sugar, baking powder, and salt in a large bowl.

Whisk together coconut milk, eggs, butter, and vanilla in another bowl. Add coconut mixture to flour mixture, whisking until combined.

Pour batter into ungreased baking pan, smoothing top. Bake until top is golden and cake is beginning to pull away from sides of pan, about 1½ hours. Cool cake completely in pan on a rack.

Cut cake into 24 squares before serving.

COOK'S NOTE

■ The cake can be made up to 3 days ahead and refrigerated, covered.

MOCHIKO

Mochiko is a very soft flour made from *mochigome*, a sweet short-grained Japanese rice with an extremely high starch content. (The Japanese word *mochi* refers to sweet confections made from the pounded rice.) It's mochiko that gives the Hawaiian Sweet-Rice-Flour Coconut Cake its appealingly chewy texture.

Elvis Presley's Favorite Pound Cake

SERVES 10 TO 12
ACTIVE TIME: 20 MINUTES ■ START TO FINISH: 3½ HOURS
(INCLUDES COOLING)

■ This pound cake, rumored to be the King's favorite, is truly heavenly. Its tender appeal comes from cake flour and cream and from beating the batter for an extra 5 minutes at the end. ■

    3 cups sifted cake flour (not self-rising; sift before
         measuring)
    ¾ teaspoon salt
    2 sticks (½ pound) unsalted butter, softened
    3 cups sugar
    7 large eggs, left at room temperature for 30 minutes
    2 teaspoons vanilla extract
    1 cup heavy cream
SPECIAL EQUIPMENT: a 10-inch tube pan (4½ inches deep;
         not with a removable bottom) or a 12-cup Bundt
         pan

Generously butter pan and dust with flour, knocking out excess flour.

Sift together sifted flour and salt. Sift again (flour will have been sifted 3 times).

Beat together butter and sugar in a large bowl with an electric mixer (fitted with paddle attachment if using a stand mixer) at medium-high speed until pale and fluffy, about 5 minutes in a stand mixer, 6 to 8 minutes with a handheld. Add eggs one at a time, beating well after each addition, then beat in vanilla. Reduce speed to low and add half of flour mixture, then all of cream, and then remaining flour, mixing well after each addition. Scrape down sides of bowl and beat at medium-high speed for 5 minutes; batter will become creamier and satiny.

Spoon batter into pan and rap pan against work surface once or twice to eliminate air bubbles. Put a rack in middle of oven, place pan in oven, and turn oven temperature to 350°F. Bake until top is golden and a wooden toothpick inserted in center of cake comes out with a few crumbs adhering, 1 to 1¼ hours. Cool cake in pan on a rack for 30 minutes.

Run a thin knife around sides of pan and center tube and invert cake onto rack to cool completely.

COOK'S NOTE

■ The cake can be made up to 5 days ahead and kept in an airtight container at room temperature.

Aunt Rose's Pound Cake

SERVES 10 TO 12
ACTIVE TIME: 15 MINUTES ■ START TO FINISH: 1¼ HOURS

■ The unconventional addition of cream cheese yields an exemplary pound cake—rich and moist, with a nice crust. It comes from reader Barbara Chazan of Manhattan. ■

2 sticks (½ pound) unsalted butter, softened
1 (8-ounce) package cream cheese, softened
2⅓ cups self-rising cake flour, sifted
2 cups sugar
2 teaspoons vanilla extract
6 large eggs, left at room temperature for 30 minutes

SPECIAL EQUIPMENT: a 12-cup Bundt pan

Put a rack in middle of oven and preheat oven to 350°F. Butter and flour Bundt pan, knocking out excess flour.

Beat together butter and cream cheese in a large bowl with an electric mixer (fitted with paddle attachment if using a stand mixer) until pale and fluffy. Add flour, sugar, and vanilla and beat on low speed until just combined (mixture will be dry and crumbly). Add eggs one at a time, beating well after each addition.

BAKING PANS

If you like to bake, you undoubtedly have a number of different-sized cake pans in your kitchen. But if you don't have a pan with the exact dimensions called for, you needn't panic. For most recipes, you can substitute a larger pan; simply adjust the cooking time accordingly. The layers will not be quite as high and they'll bake in less time: if the recipe specifies that 8-inch square layers will take 25 to 30 minutes and you have 9-inch round pans, check the cake at 15 minutes. If you don't have two 8-inch round pans but do have a 13-by-9-inch one, make a sheet cake instead. A good rule of thumb, no matter what size pans you use, is to fill them about two-thirds full.

We usually prefer cake pans that are 2 inches deep because they have straight sides and cakes baked in them have a neater appearance. Pans that are 1½ inches deep often have slightly flared sides, which need to be evened out with extra frosting.

For basic baking, the following will take you a long way:

■ Two 8-by-2-inch round pans
■ Two 9-by-2-inch round pans
■ One 8-inch square pan

Pour batter into pan and smooth top. Bake until top is golden and a wooden toothpick inserted in center of cake comes out clean, about 50 minutes. Cool cake in pan on a rack for 15 minutes.

Run a thin knife around sides of pan and center tube and invert cake onto a rack to cool completely.

COOK'S NOTE
■ The cake can be made up to 5 days ahead and kept in an airtight container at room temperature.

Cardamom Apple Almond Cake

SERVES 8
ACTIVE TIME: 35 MINUTES ■ START TO FINISH: 2½ HOURS
(INCLUDES COOLING)

■ Shredded apples add moistness and natural sweetness to this perfect Passover cake, whose plain good looks also make it an ideal accompaniment to a midday cup of tea. Ground cardamom contributes a whiff of spice and warmth. ■

1 cup (about 4 ounces) slivered almonds, toasted (see Tips, page 911)
½ cup matzo meal (not matzo cake meal)
Salt
Scant ½ teaspoon ground cardamom
5 large eggs, separated, left at room temperature for 30 minutes
1 cup sugar
2 Granny Smith apples, peeled and coarsely grated

GARNISH: Passover Powdered Sugar (recipe follows)
SPECIAL EQUIPMENT: a 9-inch springform pan; an electric coffee/spice grinder

Put a rack in middle of oven and preheat oven to 350°F. Oil springform pan and dust with matzo meal, knocking out excess.

Pulse almonds with matzo meal, ¼ teaspoon salt, and cardamom in a food processor until finely ground. (Be careful not to pulse to a paste.)

Beat yolks in a large bowl with an electric mixer at medium-high speed until smooth. Beat in ¾ cup sugar 1 tablespoon at a time, then beat until mixture is very thick and pale, 2 to 3 minutes. Stir in nut mixture, then apples.

Beat whites and ¼ teaspoon salt in a large bowl with cleaned beaters at medium speed until whites hold soft peaks. Beat in remaining ¼ cup sugar a little at a time, and continue to beat until whites just hold stiff peaks. Stir one quarter of whites into yolk mixture to lighten it, then fold in remaining whites gently but thoroughly.

Scrape batter into pan and rap pan once on work surface to eliminate any large air bubbles. Bake until cake is puffed and browned and top springs back when touched, 40 to 45 minutes. Transfer to a rack and cool completely in pan (cake will sink slightly in center).

Run a thin knife around side of pan, then remove side of pan.

Sift some of powdered sugar over cake before serving and reserve remainder for another use.

COOK'S NOTE
■ The cake can be made up to 1 day ahead and kept, covered with foil, at room temperature.

Passover Powdered Sugar

MAKES ABOUT ½ CUP
ACTIVE TIME: 5 MINUTES ■ START TO FINISH: 5 MINUTES

■ Confectioners' sugar contains cornstarch, which is forbidden during Passover. We whir granulated sugar in a spice grinder and mix it with potato starch for a similar result. ■

⅓ cup sugar
½ teaspoon potato starch

SPECIAL EQUIPMENT: an electric coffee/spice grinder

Grind sugar with potato starch in grinder until powdery.

COOK'S NOTE
■ The powdered sugar keeps in an airtight container at room temperature for up to 1 month.

Caramel Cake

SERVES 9
ACTIVE TIME: 45 MINUTES ■ START TO FINISH: 3 HOURS
(INCLUDES COOLING)

■ This little square cake topped with a tawny gloss of creamy caramel looks modest, but its moist, tender crumb, buttermilk tang, and rich caramel glaze are winning. Happily, it's a snap to make. ■

FOR CAKE
- 2 cups sifted cake flour (not self-rising; sift before measuring)
- 1 teaspoon baking powder
- ¾ teaspoon baking soda
- ½ teaspoon salt
- 1 stick (8 tablespoons) unsalted butter, softened
- 1 cup sugar
- 1 teaspoon vanilla extract
- 2 large eggs, left at room temperature for 30 minutes
- 1 cup well-shaken buttermilk

FOR CARAMEL GLAZE
- 1 cup heavy cream
- ½ cup packed light brown sugar
- 1 tablespoon light corn syrup
- Pinch of salt
- 1 teaspoon vanilla extract

SPECIAL EQUIPMENT: an 8-inch square baking pan; parchment paper; a candy thermometer

MAKE THE CAKE: Put a rack in middle of oven and preheat oven to 350°F. Butter baking pan, line with a square of parchment paper, and butter paper.

Sift together flour, baking powder, baking soda, and salt.

Beat butter and sugar in a large bowl with an electric mixer (fitted with paddle attachment if using a stand mixer) at medium speed until pale and fluffy. Beat in vanilla. Add eggs one at a time, beating well after each addition. At low speed, beat in buttermilk until just combined (mixture may look curdled). Add flour mixture in 3 batches, mixing until each addition is just incorporated.

Spread batter evenly in cake pan, then rap pan on counter several times to eliminate air bubbles. Bake until top is golden and a wooden toothpick inserted in center of cake comes out clean, 35 to 40 minutes. Cool in pan on a rack for 10 minutes.

Run a thin knife around sides of pan, invert cake onto rack, and discard paper. Cool completely.

MAKE THE GLAZE: Bring cream, brown sugar, corn syrup, and salt to a boil in a 1-quart heavy saucepan over medium heat, stirring until sugar is dissolved. Insert thermometer and boil until glaze registers 210° to 212°F, 12 to 14 minutes. Remove from heat and stir in vanilla.

Put rack with cake on a baking sheet and pour hot glaze over top of cake, allowing it to run down sides. Cool until glaze is set, about 30 minutes, and serve.

COOK'S NOTE
■ The cake, without the glaze, can be made up to 1 day ahead and kept in an airtight container at room temperature.

Walnut Date Torte

SERVES 8
ACTIVE TIME: 30 MINUTES ■ START TO FINISH: 1½ HOURS
(INCLUDES COOLING)

■ In this moist, chewy torte made with ground walnuts, pureed dates take the place of butter or oil, and orange zest and cardamom add a warm fragrance. The matzo meal makes it perfect for Passover, but don't pigeonhole this dessert—it's healthful and delicious any time of year. ■

- ¼ cup boiling water
- 1½ cups (8 ounces) pitted dates, finely chopped
- 1½ cups (about 6½ ounces) walnuts, toasted (see Tips, page 911)
- ¾ cup sugar
- ⅔ cup matzo meal (not matzo cake meal)
- 1 tablespoon grated orange zest
- ½ teaspoon ground cardamom
- Salt
- 4 large eggs, separated, left at room temperature for 30 minutes

GARNISH: Passover Powdered Sugar (page 719)
ACCOMPANIMENT: unsweetened whipped cream
SPECIAL EQUIPMENT: a 9-by-2-inch round cake pan

Pour boiling water over dates in a large bowl and let stand for 15 minutes to soften.

Put a rack in middle of oven and preheat oven to 350°F. Generously grease cake pan with butter or vegetable oil and dust with matzo meal, knocking out excess.

Pulse walnuts in a food processor until chopped. Add ¼ cup sugar and pulse until nuts are finely ground. Add matzo meal, zest, cardamom, and ¼ teaspoon salt and pulse until combined.

Beat egg whites with a pinch of salt in a large bowl with an electric mixer (fitted with whisk attachment if using a stand mixer) at medium-high speed until they just hold soft peaks. Add remaining ½ cup sugar in a slow stream and continue to beat until whites hold stiff, glossy peaks.

Whisk yolks into date mixture. Fold one third of whites into yolk mixture to lighten it, then fold in remaining whites gently but thoroughly. Fold in nut mixture.

Spoon batter into pan and bake until cake is golden, springy to the touch, and just beginning to pull away from sides of pan, 35 to 40 minutes. Cool in pan on a rack for 30 minutes.

Run a thin knife around sides of pan and invert cake onto rack. Turn cake right side up to cool completely.

Just before serving, dust cake with powdered sugar. Serve with whipped cream.

COOK'S NOTE

■ The cake can be made up to 2 days ahead and kept in a sealable bag or wrapped tightly in plastic wrap at room temperature.

Lemon Cakes
with Basil Lemon Syrup

SERVES 8
ACTIVE TIME: 30 MINUTES ■ START TO FINISH: 2 HOURS
(INCLUDES COOLING)

■ Here's an elegant ending to any Passover feast: delicate little cakes are served in shallow bowls pooled with fragrant basil lemon syrup and topped with fluffs of whipped cream. Surprisingly, you don't need any special equipment, just regular muffin tins. If you want to make these cakes for an occasion other than Passover, you can substitute cake flour for the matzo cake meal (you'll need ¼ cup more). ■

FOR CAKES
1½ tablespoons unsalted butter, melted
1 stick (8 tablespoons) unsalted butter, softened
⅔ cup plus ¼ cup sugar
Salt
3 large eggs, separated, left at room temperature for 30 minutes
1 tablespoon finely grated lemon zest
2 tablespoons fresh lemon juice
¾ cup matzo cake meal or 1 cup sifted cake flour (not self-rising; sift before measuring)

FOR SYRUP
1¼ cups sugar
1½ cups water
1 (4-by-1-inch) strip lemon zest, removed with a vegetable peeler
½ cup fresh lemon juice (from about 2 lemons)
8 large fresh basil sprigs
GARNISH: small fresh basil leaves
ACCOMPANIMENT: unsweetened whipped cream
SPECIAL EQUIPMENT: a muffin pan with twelve ½-cup muffin cups

MAKE THE CAKES: Put a rack in middle of oven and preheat oven to 350°F. Lightly brush eight muffin cups with some of melted butter and refrigerate for 2 minutes. Butter cups again and refrigerate for 1 minute more. Dust buttered cups with matzo meal or flour, knocking out excess.

Beat together softened butter, ⅔ cup sugar, and ⅛ teaspoon salt in a large bowl with an electric mixer (fitted with paddle attachment if using a stand mixer) at medium-high speed until pale and fluffy. Add yolks one at a time, beating well after each addition. Beat in 2 teaspoons zest and lemon juice until combined. At low speed, add matzo cake meal and mix until just combined.

Beat whites with ⅛ teaspoon salt in another bowl with cleaned beaters (or with whisk attachment) until they hold soft peaks. Beat in 2 tablespoons sugar a little at a time and continue to beat until whites just hold stiff peaks. Stir one quarter of whites into yolk mixture to lighten it, then fold in remaining whites gently but thoroughly. Spoon batter into prepared muffin cups.

Blend remaining 2 tablespoons sugar and 1 teaspoon zest with your fingertips and sprinkle over batter. Bake until cakes are puffed, edges are golden, and a wooden toothpick inserted in center of cakes comes out clean, 20 to 25 minutes. Cool cakes in pan on a rack for 15 minutes.

Lift cakes out carefully (tops break easily) and cool completely on rack.

MAKE THE SYRUP: Bring all ingredients to a boil in a 3-quart heavy saucepan, covered, over moderate heat, stirring occasionally to dissolve sugar. Remove lid and boil for 10 minutes. Pour syrup through a sieve into a bowl, pressing on solids; discard solids. Cool to room temperature.

ASSEMBLE THE DESSERT: Spoon ¼ cup syrup into each of eight shallow bowls and top with cakes. Spoon whipped cream on top of cakes and garnish with basil leaves.

COOK'S NOTES

- The cakes can be made up to 1 day ahead and kept in an airtight container at room temperature.
- The syrup can be made up to 1 day ahead and refrigerated, covered.

Small Pear and Almond Cakes

SERVES 12
ACTIVE TIME: 45 MINUTES ■ START TO FINISH: 1½ HOURS

■ Individual almond cakes crowned with tiny Muscat-poached Seckel pears make a charming end to a holiday meal. The pears, often available at farmers markets, have a short autumn season, and Thanksgiving is the perfect time to showcase them. This is a fruity, floral dessert. ■

FOR POACHED PEARS
12 firm small Seckel pears (2–3 inches long; see Cook's Note)

1 tablespoon fresh lemon juice
2 cups Essencia or other Muscat wine
½ tablespoon unsalted butter

FOR CAKES
1½ cups (about 10½ ounces) whole blanched almonds
1 cup plus 1 tablespoon sugar
2 sticks (½ pound) unsalted butter, softened
1 teaspoon vanilla extract
4 large eggs, left at room temperature for 30 minutes
⅔ cup all-purpose flour
⅜ teaspoon salt

SPECIAL EQUIPMENT: twelve 4-ounce ramekins or 2 muffin pans with six large (1-cup) muffin cups each

POACH THE PEARS: Peel pears, leaving stems intact, then remove core from bottom with a melon ball cutter or the tip of a paring knife; toss pears with lemon juice in a bowl as you peel them. Arrange pears on their sides in a 10-inch heavy skillet, add wine, butter, and lemon juice from bowl (liquid will not cover pears), and bring to a boil. Reduce heat and simmer, covered, until pears are just tender, 10 to 20 minutes. Transfer pears with a slotted spoon to a dish.

Boil poaching liquid, uncovered, until just syrupy and reduced to about ¼ cup, 12 to 15 minutes. Spoon syrup over pears and cool to room temperature, stirring occasionally.

MAKE THE CAKES: Put a rack in middle of oven and preheat oven to 400°F. Lightly butter and flour ramekins (or muffin cups), knocking out excess flour. If using ramekins, arrange on a large baking sheet.

Pulse almonds with ½ cup sugar in a food processor until finely ground. Transfer to a bowl (do not clean processor).

Blend butter with ½ cup sugar in processor until pale and creamy, then pulse in vanilla. Add eggs one at a time, blending well after each addition. Pulse in almond mixture, flour, and salt until just combined.

Divide batter among ramekins (about a slightly rounded ¼ cup per ramekin). Gently nestle a pear, leaning it slightly and pressing on it very lightly, into batter in center of each cake. (Cakes will rise around pears as they bake.) Reserve reduced poaching liquid for another use if desired. Sprinkle pears and tops of cakes with remaining tablespoon sugar.

Bake, rotating pan halfway through baking, until cakes are just firm and pale golden with slightly darker edges, about 20 minutes. Transfer ramekins to a rack and cool for 10 minutes.

Run a thin knife around sides of each cake and invert onto a plate. Turn cakes right side up and serve warm or at room temperature.

COOK'S NOTES

- If you can only find Forelle pears, which are slightly larger than Seckels, use 6 of them, peeled, cored, and halved lengthwise.
- The pears can be poached up to 2 days ahead and refrigerated, covered.
- The cakes can be baked up to 8 hours ahead. Cool, uncovered, then keep, covered with plastic wrap, at room temperature.

Brown Sugar Spice Cake with Whipped Cream and Caramelized Apples

SERVES 9
ACTIVE TIME: 45 MINUTES ■ START TO FINISH: 1¾ HOURS

■ Simple pantry ingredients come together in a homey cake that's so tender and moist that your guests will fight over the last piece. Maple syrup adds a robust bottom note to the cake's spices. A topping of caramelized apples and cream whipped with sour cream makes it extra-special. ■

FOR CARAMELIZED APPLES
8 Gala or Fuji apples
¾ stick (6 tablespoons) unsalted butter, softened
¾ cup packed light brown sugar
FOR CAKE
1½ cups all-purpose flour
1½ teaspoons baking powder
½ teaspoon baking soda
½ teaspoon salt
½ teaspoon ground allspice
½ teaspoon freshly grated nutmeg
⅛ teaspoon ground cloves
1 stick (8 tablespoons) unsalted butter, softened
⅓ cup packed light brown sugar
1 large egg, left at room temperature for 30 minutes

½ cup Grade B pure maple syrup
½ cup sour cream
1 teaspoon vanilla extract
FOR CREAM
1¼ cups very cold heavy cream
½ cup sour cream
2 tablespoons granulated sugar
SPECIAL EQUIPMENT: an 8-by-2-inch square baking pan (not nonstick)

Put a rack in middle of oven and preheat oven to 350°F. Lightly butter and flour baking pan, knocking out excess flour.

MAKE THE CARAMELIZED APPLES: Peel and core apples, then cut into ½-inch-thick wedges.

Spread softened butter in an even layer over bottom of a 12-inch heavy skillet and sprinkle with brown sugar. Add apple wedges and cook over moderate heat, without stirring, until sugar is melted and apples start to give off liquid, about 10 minutes. Cook, stirring occasionally, until apples are just tender and juices become syrupy, about 30 minutes more.

Pour syrup from skillet into a small heatproof bowl. Cook apples, stirring occasionally, until caramelized and very tender, about 30 minutes more. Return syrup to apples and cook until heated through, about 2 minutes.

MEANWHILE, MAKE THE CAKE: Whisk together flour, baking powder, baking soda, salt, and spices in a bowl.

Beat together butter and brown sugar in a large bowl with an electric mixer (fitted with paddle attachment if using a stand mixer) at medium speed until pale and fluffy. Beat in egg until combined. Add maple syrup, sour cream, and vanilla and beat until well combined. At low speed, add flour mixture and mix until just combined.

Spread batter in prepared pan. Bake until cake is golden brown and a wooden toothpick inserted in center comes out clean, 35 to 40 minutes. Cool in pan on a rack for 10 minutes.

JUST BEFORE SERVING, MAKE THE CREAM: Beat cream with sour cream and sugar in a large bowl with an electric mixer at high speed until it just holds soft peaks.

Run a thin knife around sides of pan and invert cake onto a plate. Cut into squares and serve warm or at room temperature, topped with warm apple mixture and cream.

Norwegian Almond Caramel Cake

SERVES 8 TO 12
ACTIVE TIME: 35 MINUTES ■ START TO FINISH: 2½ HOURS
(INCLUDES COOLING)

■ Versions of this wonderfully buttery, fine-crumbed cake abound throughout Scandinavia, where it is referred to as Tosca cake. Its crowning glory is a caramel glaze with toasted almond slices that is spooned over the moist cake. A quick run under the broiler bestows extra crunch on the nuts. ■

FOR CAKE
    2 cups all-purpose flour
    2 teaspoons baking powder
    ¼ teaspoon salt
    4 large eggs, left at room temperature for 30 minutes
    1½ cups superfine sugar
    2 sticks (½ pound) unsalted butter, melted and cooled
    ⅓ cup whole milk
    1½ teaspoons vanilla extract
FOR TOPPING
    1 cup (about 3½ ounces) sliced almonds, preferably unblanched
    ½ cup heavy cream
    ⅓ cup granulated sugar
    ½ stick (4 tablespoons) unsalted butter, cut into tablespoons
SPECIAL EQUIPMENT: a 10-inch tube pan (4½ inches deep) (see Cook's Note)

MAKE THE CAKE: Put a rack in middle of oven and preheat oven to 350°F. Generously butter cake pan.

Whisk together flour, baking powder, and salt in a bowl.

Beat together eggs and superfine sugar in a large bowl with an electric mixer (fitted with whisk attachment if using a stand mixer) at high speed until pale and thick, 5 to 7 minutes. Beat in butter, milk, and vanilla until combined. Reduce speed to low and add flour mixture, mixing until just combined.

Pour batter into pan and gently rap pan on counter to eliminate any air bubbles. Bake until cake pulls away from sides of pan and a wooden toothpick inserted in center comes out clean, 35 to 45 minutes. Cool cake completely in pan on a rack, about 1¼ hours.

If using a two-piece pan, lift out cake with tube and invert onto a baking sheet; otherwise, simply invert pan to unmold cake onto baking sheet.

MAKE THE TOPPING: Preheat oven to 350°F (with rack still in middle).

Spread almonds in one layer on a baking sheet and toast in oven until pale golden, 8 to 10 minutes. Transfer to a plate.

With oven mitts, position oven rack so that top of cake will be 4 inches from heat and preheat broiler. Bring cream and sugar to a boil in a 10-inch heavy skillet over moderate heat, stirring until sugar is dissolved. Add butter and stir until melted. Boil mixture, stirring occasionally, until slightly thickened, about 3 minutes. Stir in toasted almonds and remove from heat.

Spoon mixture evenly over top of cake and broil, turning cake as necessary, until almonds are golden, 1 to 2 minutes. Transfer cake to a serving plate using two spatulas and serve warm or at room temperature.

Coconut Rum Cake

SERVES 8
ACTIVE TIME: 45 MINUTES ■ START TO FINISH: 2½ HOURS

■ Cream of coconut, the sweet concoction sold in cans in the drink-mixes aisle of the supermarket, brings just the right note of tropical sweetness to this cake, contributing a definite but surprisingly subtle coconut flavor. Shavings of fresh coconut dusted with confectioners' sugar scattered over the top add a final, sophisticated touch. ■

FOR CAKE
1¼ cups all-purpose flour
1½ teaspoons baking powder
¼ teaspoon salt
4 large eggs
3 large egg yolks
1½ cups granulated sugar
1 teaspoon vanilla extract
1½ sticks (12 tablespoons) unsalted butter, melted and cooled
¾ cup well-stirred canned cream of coconut, such as Coco López

FOR COCONUT SLIVERS
1 medium coconut (see Cook's Note)
2 teaspoons confectioners' sugar

FOR ICING
3 tablespoons cream cheese, softened
3 tablespoons well-stirred canned cream of coconut
1 tablespoon dark rum
⅛ teaspoon vanilla extract
2–3 tablespoons heavy cream
½ cup confectioners' sugar

SPECIAL EQUIPMENT: a 9-by-2-inch round cake pan; parchment paper; a mandoline or other adjustable-blade vegetable slicer

MAKE THE CAKE: Put a rack in middle of oven and preheat oven to 350°F. Lightly butter cake pan and line bottom with a round of parchment paper. Lightly butter parchment, then flour pan, knocking out excess.

Whisk together flour, baking powder, and salt in a bowl.

Whisk together eggs, yolks, sugar, and vanilla in a large bowl. Gradually whisk in flour mixture until combined, then whisk in butter until just combined.

Pour batter into cake pan and rap pan on counter to eliminate air bubbles. Bake until cake is golden brown and starting to pull away from sides of pan, about 45 minutes. Cool in pan on a rack for 10 minutes. (Leave oven on.)

Run a thin knife around sides of pan, invert cake onto rack (discard parchment), and cool for 10 minutes.

Generously brush top and sides of warm cake with cream of coconut, allowing it to soak in each time before brushing on more. Cool completely.

MEANWHILE, MAKE THE COCONUT SLIVERS: Pierce softest eye of coconut with a small screwdriver, then drain and discard liquid. Bake coconut in a shallow baking pan for 15 minutes. Remove from oven. (Leave oven on.)

Break coconut shell with a hammer and remove flesh with a butter knife, prying it out carefully. Thinly shave enough coconut with slicer to measure 2 cups. Toss with confectioners' sugar and spread in one layer on a baking sheet. Bake until just dry but not golden (some tips may color), 5 to 10 minutes. (If desired, shave and bake remaining coconut with more confectioners' sugar to serve on the side, or freeze for another use.) Cool coconut completely. (It will crisp as it cools.)

MAKE THE ICING: Beat together cream cheese, cream of coconut, rum, vanilla, and 2 tablespoons cream in a small bowl with a handheld mixer until smooth. Beat in confectioners' sugar. Icing should be smooth and slightly runny; stir in remaining tablespoon cream if necessary.

Spread icing over top of cake, allowing some to drip down sides. Top with coconut slivers.

COOK'S NOTES
■ Coconuts are sometimes rancid—you may want to buy an extra one.
■ The cake can be baked and soaked with the cream of coconut up to 1 day ahead and kept in an airtight container at room temperature. It can be iced up to 2 hours ahead.
■ The coconut slivers can be made up to 1 day ahead and kept in an airtight container at room temperature.

Rhubarb Strawberry Pudding Cake

SERVES 6 TO 8
ACTIVE TIME: 15 MINUTES ■ START TO FINISH: 50 MINUTES

■ Tart rhubarb and juicy strawberries unite in a moist cake. This is a classic no-hassle mix-and-bake dessert. Any ripe, luscious fruit—raspberries, cherries, peaches, apricots, nectarines, and plums—will work. We especially love it with summery blueberries (see Variation). ■

¼ cup water
1½ teaspoons cornstarch
½ cup plus ⅓ cup sugar
2 cups chopped rhubarb stalks
1 cup chopped strawberries
1 cup all-purpose flour
1¾ teaspoons baking powder
½ teaspoon salt
1 large egg
½ cup whole milk
1 stick (8 tablespoons) unsalted butter, melted and cooled slightly
1 teaspoon vanilla extract

SPECIAL EQUIPMENT: an 8-inch square glass or ceramic baking dish

Put a rack in middle of oven and preheat oven to 400°F. Butter baking dish.

Stir together water, cornstarch, and ⅓ cup sugar in a small saucepan, then stir in rhubarb. Bring to a simmer, stirring constantly, and simmer, stirring occasionally, for 3 minutes. Remove from heat and stir in strawberries.

Whisk together flour, baking powder, salt, and remaining ½ cup sugar in a bowl.

Whisk together egg, milk, butter, and vanilla in a large bowl. Whisk in flour mixture until just combined.

Reserve ½ cup fruit mixture and add remainder to baking dish. Pour batter over fruit, spreading it evenly. Spoon reserved ½ cup fruit mixture over batter. Bake until a wooden toothpick inserted into center of cake (not fruit) comes out clean, 25 to 30 minutes. Cool in pan on a rack for 5 minutes before serving.

VARIATION

■ BLUEBERRY PUDDING CAKE: Substitute 2 cups (10 ounces) blueberries for the rhubarb and strawberries. Reduce the cornstarch to 1 teaspoon and add 1 tablespoon fresh lemon juice to the cornstarch mixture.

Lemon Pudding Cake

SERVES 6
ACTIVE TIME: 20 MINUTES ■ START TO FINISH: 1½ HOURS

■ Half pudding, half cake, all easy. As it bakes, the batter separates, and the top becomes a tender, delicate-crumbed cake, while the bottom turns into a saucy pudding—both fragrant with lemon. ■

2 large lemons
¼ cup all-purpose flour
Rounded ¼ teaspoon salt
¾ cup plus 2 tablespoons sugar
3 large eggs, separated, left at room temperature for 30 minutes
1⅓ cups whole milk

SPECIAL EQUIPMENT: a 1½-quart gratin dish or shallow glass or ceramic baking dish

Put a rack in middle of oven and preheat oven to 350°F. Butter gratin dish.

Finely grate 1 tablespoon zest from lemons, then squeeze 6 tablespoons juice.

Whisk together flour, salt, and ½ cup plus 2 tablespoons sugar in a large bowl. Whisk together yolks, milk, zest, and juice in a small bowl and add to flour mixture, whisking until just combined.

Beat whites in another large bowl with an electric mixer (fitted with whisk attachment if using a stand mixer) until they hold soft peaks. Beat in remaining ¼ cup sugar a little at a time and continue to beat until whites hold stiff, glossy peaks. Whisk about one quarter of whites into batter to lighten it, then fold in remaining whites gently but thoroughly (batter will be thin).

Pour batter into gratin dish. Put dish in a small roasting pan and put pan in oven. Add enough boiling water to pan to reach halfway up sides of gratin dish. Bake until cake is puffed and golden, 45 to 50 minutes. Transfer to a rack.

Serve warm or at room temperature.

Silky
Chocolate-Pudding Cakes

SERVES 4
ACTIVE TIME: 15 MINUTES ■ START TO FINISH: 1 HOUR
(INCLUDES COOLING)

■ These luxurious flourless chocolate cakes are deeply chocolaty and outrageous with coffee ice cream. Lindt's original bittersweet chocolate (which has a cacao content of about 50%, although that is not marked on the label) produces a pudding with an irresistibly smooth texture. If you use a chocolate with more than 60% cacao, the pudding may taste tannic and be a little grainy. ■

7 ounces bittersweet chocolate, preferably Lindt (no more than 60% cacao; see page 705), finely chopped
½ stick (4 tablespoons) unsalted butter, cut into pieces
2 large eggs, separated, left at room temperature for 30 minutes
Pinch of salt
2 tablespoons sugar
ACCOMPANIMENT: coffee ice cream
SPECIAL EQUIPMENT: four 5- to 6-ounce ovenproof glass or ceramic bowls or ramekins

Put a rack in middle of oven and preheat oven to 350°F. Butter bowls.

Melt chocolate and butter in a metal bowl set over a saucepan of barely simmering water, stirring until smooth. Remove bowl from heat and cool, stirring occasionally, for 5 minutes. Whisk in egg yolks and salt until combined.

Beat egg whites in a bowl with an electric mixer (fitted with whisk attachment if using a stand mixer) at medium-high speed until they hold soft peaks. Gradually beat in sugar and continue to beat until whites just hold stiff, glossy peaks.

Whisk about one quarter of whites into chocolate mixture to lighten it, then fold in remaining whites gently but thoroughly.

Divide batter among bowls. Cover each bowl with a small square of foil and crimp foil tightly around rim. Put bowls in a baking dish, then put dish in oven and add enough boiling water to dish to reach halfway up side of bowls, making sure that water is below foil. Bake until cakes are just set, about 30 minutes.

Transfer bowls to a rack and cool cakes, uncovered, for about 30 minutes.

To serve, unmold cakes into serving bowls and add a scoop of ice cream to each bowl.

COOK'S NOTE

■ The cakes can be made up to 4 hours ahead and kept (in bowls) at warm room temperature. Dip in hot water for 10 to 15 seconds to unmold.

Chocolate Whiskey
Bundt Cake

SERVES 12 TO 14
ACTIVE TIME: 30 MINUTES ■ START TO FINISH: 3¼ HOURS
(INCLUDES COOLING)

■ This rich, moist cake is perfect for entertaining—it feeds a crowd and its taste even improves if made ahead. Most of the alcohol cooks off, but a distinct whiskey flavor remains, which adds a smooth, adult note to the cake. ■

1 cup unsweetened cocoa powder (not Dutch-process), plus 3 tablespoons for dusting pan
1½ cups brewed coffee
½ cup American whiskey
2 sticks (½ pound) unsalted butter, cut into 1-inch pieces
2 cups sugar
2 cups all-purpose flour
1¼ teaspoons baking soda
½ teaspoon salt
2 large eggs, left at room temperature for 30 minutes
1 teaspoon vanilla extract
GARNISH: confectioners' sugar
ACCOMPANIMENT: lightly sweetened whipped cream
SPECIAL EQUIPMENT: a 12-cup Bundt pan

Put a rack in middle of oven and preheat oven to 325°F. Butter Bundt pan well, then dust with 3 tablespoons cocoa powder, knocking out excess.

Combine coffee, whiskey, butter, and remaining 1 cup cocoa powder in a 3-quart heavy saucepan and heat over moderate heat, whisking, until butter is melted. Remove from heat, add sugar, and whisk until dissolved, about 1 minute. Transfer mixture to a large bowl and cool for 5 minutes.

Meanwhile, whisk together flour, baking soda, and salt in a bowl.

Whisk together eggs and vanilla in a small bowl, then whisk into warm chocolate mixture until well combined. Add flour mixture and whisk until just combined (batter will be thin and bubbly).

Pour batter into Bundt pan. Bake until a wooden toothpick inserted in center comes out clean, 40 to 50 minutes. Cool cake completely in pan on a rack.

Run a thin knife around sides of pan, then invert cake onto rack. Sift confectioners' sugar over cake and serve with whipped cream.

COOK'S NOTE

■ This cake improves in flavor if made at least 1 day ahead. It can be kept in a cake keeper or wrapped well in plastic wrap at cool room temperature for up to 1 day or refrigerated for up to 5 days. Bring to room temperature before serving.

Mexican Chocolate Cake

SERVES 10 TO 12
ACTIVE TIME: 35 MINUTES ■ START TO FINISH: 2 HOURS

■ The hint of cinnamon in the batter of this cake is a nod toward Mexican chocolate, which contains cinnamon and other spices. Glazed with a rich concoction of bittersweet chocolate and toasted pecans, it is a great choice for a party. The recipe comes from chef Rebecca Rather, the owner of Rather Sweet Bakery & Café in Fredericksburg, Texas. At her bakery, Rather makes both cupcakes and Bundt cakes with this recipe. ■

FOR CAKE
    2 sticks (½ pound) unsalted butter
    ½ cup unsweetened Dutch-process cocoa powder
    ¾ cup water
    2 cups granulated sugar
    2 large eggs
    ½ cup well-shaken buttermilk
    2 tablespoons vanilla extract
    2 cups all-purpose flour
    1 teaspoon baking soda
    ½ teaspoon ground cinnamon
    ¼ teaspoon salt

WHISKEY

Whiskey is made by cooking a variety of grains—including corn, wheat, rye, and barley—in water to make a mash, adding yeast to make the mixture ferment, and distilling the result. All American whiskeys are made by the sour-mash method, which entails adding fermented mash from a previous batch—much like a starter for sourdough bread or a mother for vinegar—but few distillers put the term "sour mash" on the label. If the flavor of the whiskey is a major component of the recipe, as in the Bundt cake above, it's important to choose one you like. A good bourbon such as Maker's Mark or Wild Turkey (the 80 proof) or a Tennessee whiskey such as Jack Daniel's will work well. (Unlike bourbon, Tennessee whiskey is filtered through sugar-maple charcoal before being put into casks for aging.)

FOR GLAZE

    2 cups (about 8½ ounces) chopped pecans
    ½ stick (4 tablespoons) unsalted butter
    ½ cup half-and-half
    ½ cup confectioners' sugar
    5 ounces bittersweet chocolate (no more than 60%
        cacao; see page 705), finely chopped
    ¼ teaspoon salt
SPECIAL EQUIPMENT: a 9-inch tube pan (4 inches deep) or a
    12-cup Bundt pan

MAKE THE CAKE: Put a rack in middle of oven and
preheat oven to 350°F. Butter cake pan well and dust
with flour, knocking out excess.

Melt butter in a 3-quart heavy saucepan over
moderately low heat. Whisk in cocoa, add water, and
whisk until smooth. Remove from heat and whisk in
sugar, then eggs, and then buttermilk and vanilla.

Sift together flour, baking soda, cinnamon, and
salt, then sift again into cocoa mixture and whisk
until just combined (don't worry if there are some
lumps).

Pour batter into cake pan. Bake until a wooden
toothpick comes out with a few crumbs adhering, 45
to 55 minutes. Cool cake in pan on a rack for 20 minutes. (Leave oven on.)

Run a thin knife around sides of pan and invert
cake onto a plate.

MEANWHILE, MAKE THE GLAZE: Spread pecans in
one layer on a baking sheet and toast in oven until
fragrant and a shade darker, 6 to 8 minutes. Cool pecans slightly on pan on a rack, about 5 minutes.

Meanwhile, melt butter in a 2-quart heavy saucepan over low heat. Stir in half-and-half and confectioners' sugar, add chocolate, and cook, stirring,
until smooth. Remove from heat and stir in pecans
and salt. Cool glaze until slightly thickened, about 5
minutes.

Spoon glaze over top and sides of warm cake and
spread with a small offset spatula or knife to cover
completely.

COOK'S NOTE

■ The cake (with the glaze) can be made up to 2 days
  ahead and kept at room temperature in a cake keeper
  or covered with an inverted bowl.

CINNAMON

Cinnamon was one of the first spices to reach the
Mediterranean: a find excavated at the sanctuary of
Hera on the Greek island of Samos was dated to the
seventh century B.C. In the Middle East and India, the
spice has long been used in meat and vegetable dishes,
and medieval European cooks followed the lead. These
days in the United States, cinnamon appears primarily
in baked goods.

The spice comes from the aromatic bark of
several different species of a tropical Asian tree (genus
Cinnamomum). After workers cut wafer-thin sheets of
bark from the young shoots, they furl them into long
quills and dry them in the shade.

There are two main types of cinnamon:
cassia and canela. What's labeled "cinnamon" in
U.S. supermarkets is usually *C. cassia*. It's preferred
in this country because of its assertive flavor, which
comes from the hot, spicy phenolic compound called
cinnamaldehyde. Cassia quills are thick, hard (and thus
a little difficult to grind), and dark. Today most cassia,
which originated in Assam and northern Burma, is
imported from China and Vietnam (the best quality
comes from northern Vietnam).

Canela (*C. zeylanicum*), often called "true"
cinnamon, originated in Sri Lanka, which still produces
the finest quality of the spice. It is mainly imported by
Mexico and was first brought there by Spanish settlers
(*canela* is Spanish for "cinnamon"). Canela is softer
than cassia, and its shaggy, brittle quills are pale brown,
with a delicately woodsy, citrusy fragrance. There's
a hint of clove, too, which comes from the phenolic
compound eugenol, an essential oil not found in cassia.

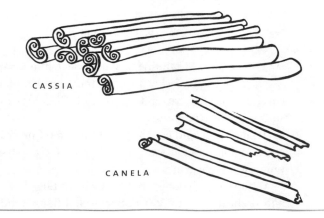

CASSIA

CANELA

Pecan Fig Bourbon Cake

SERVES 12 TO 16
ACTIVE TIME: 1 HOUR ■ START TO FINISH: 3½ HOURS
(INCLUDES COOLING)

■ Plenty of figs, bourbon, and brown sugar make this crowd-pleasing Bundt cake very moist. Vegetable oil, rather than butter, also helps ensure that the cake is a good keeper. An easy bourbon-spiked glaze gives it extra kick. Pleasantly plump dried Black Mission figs have deep purple, almost black skins and lend the cake a complex sweetness. ■

FOR CAKE
- 1 pound dried Black Mission figs, hard tips discarded
- 2 cups water
- ½ cup bourbon
- 1 teaspoon vanilla extract
- 3 cups sifted cake flour (not self-rising; sift before measuring)
- 2 teaspoons baking powder
- ¾ teaspoon baking soda
- ¾ teaspoon salt
- ½ teaspoon ground cinnamon
- ½ teaspoon freshly grated nutmeg
- 1¾ cups (about 7½ ounces) pecans
- 2 cups packed light brown sugar
- 1 cup vegetable oil
- 3 large eggs, left at room temperature for 30 minutes

FOR ICING
- 1 cup confectioners' sugar
- 4½ tablespoons heavy cream
- 2 teaspoons bourbon
- ¼ teaspoon vanilla extract

SPECIAL EQUIPMENT: a 12-cup Bundt pan

MAKE THE CAKE: Combine figs and water in a heavy 2-quart saucepan, bring to a simmer, and simmer, covered, until figs are tender and most of liquid is absorbed, 35 to 40 minutes.

Transfer figs and cooking liquid to a food processor, add bourbon and vanilla, and process to a coarse puree. Cool to warm.

While figs are cooling, put a rack in middle of oven and preheat oven to 350°F. Butter and flour Bundt pan, knocking out excess flour.

Sift together flour, baking powder, baking soda, salt, cinnamon, and nutmeg.

Lightly toast pecans on a baking sheet in oven, 8 to 10 minutes. Cool and coarsely chop. (Leave oven on.)

Beat together brown sugar, oil, and eggs in a large bowl with an electric mixer (fitted with paddle attachment if using a stand mixer) until thick and creamy, about 3 minutes. Stir in fig mixture. At low speed, mix in flour mixture until just incorporated. Fold in pecans.

Pour batter into pan. Bake until a wooden toothpick inserted in center comes out clean, 1 to 1¼ hours. Cool cake completely in pan on a rack, then invert onto a plate.

MAKE THE ICING: Sift confectioners' sugar into a bowl. Whisk in remaining ingredients until smooth.

Drizzle icing over cake.

COOK'S NOTE

■ The cake improves in flavor if made (but not iced) at least 1 day, or up to 5 days, ahead, and kept in an airtight container at room temperature.

Pear Johnnycake

SERVES 8
ACTIVE TIME: 15 MINUTES ■ START TO FINISH: 1¼ HOURS

■ Thought originally to be called "journey cake" (for the circuit preachers who packed it for sustenance as they rode throughout New England), this Rhode Island specialty—a cross between corn bread and a pancake—is too delicious to travel much farther than from your fork to your mouth. We have dressed it up a bit with pears, yet it remains a simple, comforting cake, equally appropriate for breakfast, brunch, and dinner. ■

- 1 stick (8 tablespoons) unsalted butter
- 2 tablespoons sugar
- 4 firm but ripe Anjou pears, peeled, halved lengthwise, and cored
- ½ teaspoon freshly grated nutmeg
- 1 cup all-purpose flour
- ¾ cup stone-ground cornmeal, preferably white
- 2 teaspoons baking powder

½ teaspoon baking soda
½ teaspoon salt
¾ cup whole milk
¼ cup pure maple syrup, preferably Grade B
2 large eggs, lightly beaten

ACCOMPANIMENTS: pure maple syrup and sour cream
SPECIAL EQUIPMENT: a 9-by-2-inch round cake pan

Put a rack in middle of oven and preheat oven to 400°F.

Melt butter in a 10-inch nonstick skillet. Remove from heat and brush cake pan with 1 tablespoon butter, then transfer 6 tablespoons butter to a small bowl. Sprinkle sugar evenly over remaining tablespoon butter in skillet. Arrange pears cut side up in skillet and sprinkle with ⅛ teaspoon nutmeg.

Cook pears over medium heat for 5 minutes. Carefully turn pears over, sprinkle with ⅛ teaspoon nutmeg, and cook until liquid evaporates and cut sides of pears begin to brown, 8 to 10 minutes. Transfer pears, cut side down, to baking pan, arranging them in a circle with stem ends toward center.

Whisk together flour, cornmeal, baking powder, baking soda, salt, and remaining ¼ teaspoon nutmeg in a bowl. Whisk in milk, syrup, eggs, and reserved 6 tablespoons butter just until smooth, then pour over pears.

Bake until top is golden and a wooden toothpick inserted in center comes out dry, 25 to 30 minutes. Cool cake in pan on a rack for 15 minutes.

Run a thin knife around sides of pan and invert cake onto a platter. Serve wedges drizzled with syrup and dolloped with sour cream.

Pear Gingerbread Upside-Down Cake

SERVES 6
ACTIVE TIME: 30 MINUTES ■ START TO FINISH: 1½ HOURS

■ Gingerbread topped with sweet, buttery pears makes a wonderful ending to a casual dinner party. A scoop of vanilla ice cream is all the gilding this warm, spicy cake needs. ■

FOR TOPPING
2½ firm pears, preferably Bosc
½ stick (4 tablespoons) unsalted butter
¾ cup packed light brown sugar

FOR CAKE
2½ cups all-purpose flour
1½ teaspoons baking soda
1 teaspoon ground cinnamon
1 teaspoon ground ginger
½ teaspoon ground cloves
¼ teaspoon salt
1 cup molasses (not robust)
1 cup boiling water
1 stick (8 tablespoons) unsalted butter, softened
½ cup packed light brown sugar
1 large egg, lightly beaten

ACCOMPANIMENT: vanilla ice cream
SPECIAL EQUIPMENT: a well-seasoned 10-inch cast-iron skillet or a deep 12-inch nonstick skillet (handle wrapped with a double layer of foil if not ovenproof)

MAKE THE TOPPING: Peel, halve, and core pears. Cut each pear half into 4 wedges.

Heat butter in skillet over moderate heat until foam subsides. Reduce heat to low, sprinkle brown sugar over butter, and cook, undisturbed, for 3 minutes (not all sugar will be melted). Arrange pears decoratively over sugar and cook, undisturbed, for 2 minutes. Remove from heat.

MAKE THE CAKE: Put a rack in middle of oven and preheat oven to 350°F.

Whisk together flour, baking soda, cinnamon, ginger, cloves, and salt in a bowl. Whisk together molasses and boiling water in a small bowl.

Beat together butter, brown sugar, and egg in a large bowl with an electric mixer (fitted with paddle attachment if using a stand mixer) at medium speed until creamy, about 2 minutes. Reduce speed to low and add flour mixture alternately with molasses in 3 batches, beginning and ending with flour, and mixing until smooth.

Pour batter over pears in skillet, spreading it evenly but being careful not to disturb pears. Bake until a wooden toothpick inserted in center comes out clean, 40 to 50 minutes. Cool cake in skillet on a rack for 5 minutes.

Run a thin knife around sides of skillet, invert

a large plate with a lip over skillet, and, using pot holders to hold skillet and plate tightly together, invert cake onto plate. Replace any pears that stuck to skillet. Serve warm or at room temperature, with ice cream.

Blackberry Upside-Down Cake

SERVES 6
ACTIVE TIME: 20 MINUTES ■ START TO FINISH: 45 MINUTES

■ Pints of chubby blackberries line produce shelves all year round, and they are surprisingly good, even when out of season. So while this buttermilk cake is sublime at the height of blackberry season, it's also very tasty in the depths of winter. Be sure to line the cake pan with a double layer of parchment, as called for; without it, the blackberries tend to take on a tinny flavor. ■

> 2½ cups (12 ounces) blackberries
> ½ cup plus 1½ tablespoons sugar
> 1 cup all-purpose flour
> ½ teaspoon baking soda
> ¼ teaspoon salt
> ½ stick (4 tablespoons) unsalted butter, softened
> 1 large egg, left at room temperature for 30 minutes
> 1 teaspoon vanilla extract
> ½ cup well-shaken buttermilk

ACCOMPANIMENT: vanilla ice cream
SPECIAL EQUIPMENT: an 8-by-2-inch round cake pan; parchment paper

Put a rack in middle of oven and preheat oven to 350°F. Butter cake pan and line bottom with two rounds of parchment paper, then butter top piece of parchment. Dust pan with flour, knocking out excess.

Arrange blackberries in one layer in pan. Sprinkle with 1½ tablespoons sugar and shake pan to help distribute sugar.

Whisk together flour, baking soda, and salt in a bowl.

Beat together butter and remaining ½ cup sugar in a large bowl with an electric mixer (fitted with paddle attachment if using a stand mixer) at high speed until pale and fluffy, about 2 minutes. Add egg and vanilla and mix at low speed until just incorporated. Add flour mixture and buttermilk alternately in 3 batches, scraping down sides of bowl between batches, mixing until just incorporated.

Spoon batter evenly over berries, smoothing top. Bake until top is golden and a wooden toothpick inserted in center comes out clean, 35 to 40 minutes. Cool cake in pan for 5 minutes.

Run a thin knife around sides of pan, invert a large plate over pan, and, using pot holders to hold plate and pan tightly together, flip cake onto plate. Peel off parchment and serve cake with ice cream.

Peach Spice Upside-Down Cake

SERVES 8 TO 10
ACTIVE TIME: 30 MINUTES ■ START TO FINISH: 2 HOURS (INCLUDES COOLING)

■ An Indian-style blend of spices gives this summery cake its intriguing warmth and fragrance. Just a small amount contributes a layer of flavor that plays beautifully against the sweet peaches cloaked in caramel. The spice mix recipe makes enough for three cakes, so hold on to it (see Cook's Note). Even without the spice mix, the recipe produces a perfectly delicious upside-down cake. ■

FOR SPICE MIX
> 4 whole cloves
> ½ cinnamon stick
> ¼ teaspoon coriander seeds
> ¼ teaspoon cardamom seeds (see Sources)
> ¼ teaspoon black peppercorns
> ¼ teaspoon freshly grated nutmeg
> ⅛ teaspoon red pepper flakes
> ⅛ teaspoon cumin seeds

FOR CAKE
> 1⅔ cups sugar
> 4 firm but ripe medium peaches (1 pound total)
> 2 teaspoons fresh lemon juice

1⅔ cups all-purpose flour

1½ teaspoons baking powder

¼ teaspoon baking soda

¼ teaspoon salt

1 stick (8 tablespoons) unsalted butter, softened

1 teaspoon vanilla extract

2 large eggs, left at room temperature for 30 minutes

⅔ cup well-shaken buttermilk

SPECIAL EQUIPMENT: an electric coffee/spice grinder; a
    9-by-2-inch round cake pan

MAKE THE SPICE MIX: Finely grind all ingredients together in grinder.

MAKE THE CAKE: Heat 1 cup sugar in a small heavy saucepan over moderate heat, stirring with a fork to heat sugar evenly, until it starts to melt. Stop stirring and cook, swirling pan occasionally so sugar melts and cooks evenly, until caramel is dark amber. Carefully pour caramel into cake pan and tilt to coat bottom of pan. Cool on a rack.

Blanch peaches in a 3-quart saucepan of boiling water for 30 seconds. With a slotted spoon, transfer peaches to a bowl of ice and cold water to cool. Peel and pit peaches and cut them into ½-inch-thick wedges. Toss with lemon juice in a bowl.

Put a rack in middle of oven and preheat oven to 350°F.

Sift together flour, baking powder, baking soda, salt, and 1 teaspoon spice mix; reserve remaining spice mix for another use.

Beat together butter, remaining ⅔ cup sugar, and vanilla with an electric mixer (fitted with paddle attachment if using a stand mixer) at medium speed until pale and fluffy, about 2 minutes. Add eggs one at a time, beating well after each addition. At low speed, add flour mixture alternately with buttermilk in 3 batches, beginning and ending with flour and mixing just until batter is smooth.

Drain peaches and arrange over hardened caramel, starting in center of pan and overlapping slices slightly.

Spread batter evenly over peaches. Bake until a wooden toothpick inserted in center comes out clean, 40 to 45 minutes. Cool in pan on a rack for 15 minutes.

Run a thin knife around sides of pan and invert cake onto plate. Cool to room temperature.

COOK'S NOTES

■ The cake can be made up to 6 hours ahead and kept, uncovered, at room temperature.

■ The extra spice mix keeps, frozen in an airtight container, for up to 6 months.

Plum Kuchen

SERVES 8 TO 10
ACTIVE TIME: 30 MINUTES ■ START TO FINISH: 4¼ HOURS
(INCLUDES RISING TIME)

■ A kuchen ("*koo*-khehn") is a buttery yeast-raised cake filled with fruit or cheese. It originated in Germany, and it goes so well with coffee that it is sometimes called a *Kaffeekuchen,* or coffee cake. This version, topped with fragrant prune plums, tastes best the day it is baked. ■

FOR DOUGH

1½ teaspoons active dry yeast

2 tablespoons lukewarm water

2 cups all-purpose flour

⅓ cup sugar

½ teaspoon salt

½ cup warm whole milk (105°–110°F)

2 large eggs

1½ teaspoons finely grated lemon zest

1 teaspoon vanilla extract

1 stick (8 tablespoons) unsalted butter, cut into
    tablespoons, softened

FOR TOPPING

1 pound small firm but ripe prune plums (12–14),
    halved lengthwise and pitted

3 tablespoons granulated sugar

GARNISH: confectioners' sugar

SPECIAL EQUIPMENT: a 13-by-9-inch baking pan

MAKE THE DOUGH: Stir together yeast and water in a small bowl and let stand until foamy, about 5 minutes. (If mixture doesn't foam, discard and start over with new yeast.)

Combine 1¾ cups flour, sugar, salt, milk, eggs, zest, vanilla, and yeast mixture in a large bowl and beat with an electric mixer (fitted with paddle attachment if using a stand mixer) at medium-low speed until batter is smooth. Beat in butter 1 tablespoon at a time. Scrape down sides of bowl and sprinkle batter with remaining ¼ cup flour.

Cover bowl with a clean kitchen towel (not terry cloth) and let batter rise in a warm draft-free place until doubled in bulk, 45 minutes to 1 hour.

Butter baking pan. Stir batter until flour is incorporated, then scrape into pan, spreading evenly. Cover pan with plastic wrap, then kitchen towel. Let batter rise in a warm place until almost doubled in bulk, about 45 minutes.

MEANWHILE, PREPARE THE TOPPING: Put each plum half cut side down on a cutting board and, holding knife parallel to board, cut it into 3 thin slices. Transfer plum slices to a bowl, toss with 2 tablespoons sugar, and let macerate for 1 hour at room temperature.

Put a rack in middle of oven and preheat oven to 375°F.

Drain plums, discarding liquid, and arrange slices on batter, slightly overlapping. Sprinkle with remaining tablespoon sugar. Bake until kuchen is golden brown and plums are tender, 30 to 35 minutes. Cool kuchen in pan on a rack.

Serve warm or at room temperature, dusted with confectioners' sugar.

Lollie's Lemon Fruitcake

MAKES 2 LOAVES; SERVES 16
ACTIVE TIME: 25 MINUTES ■ START TO FINISH: 6¼ HOURS
(INCLUDES COOLING)

■ Those who don't generally like fruitcake may change their minds after one bite of this light version from reader Jennifer Minifie of Seattle, whose mother, Lollie, always made it around the holidays. Slow baking in a low oven ensures that the cake, loaded with golden raisins and pecans, stays moist. It gets even better with age, so it's a perfect make-ahead gift. The recipe does indeed call for an entire 1-ounce bottle of lemon extract, but don't worry—the lemony flavor is surprisingly subtle. ■

3 cups (1 pound) golden raisins
4½ cups (about 1 pound) pecan halves
3 cups all-purpose flour
½ teaspoon salt
1 pound unsalted butter, softened
2 cups sugar
6 large eggs, separated, left at room temperature for 30 minutes
1 teaspoon baking soda
1 tablespoon lukewarm water
1 (1-ounce) bottle pure lemon extract

SPECIAL EQUIPMENT: two 9-by-5-inch loaf pans; parchment paper

Put a rack in middle of oven and preheat oven to 250°F. Line bottom and sides of loaf pans with parchment paper.

Toss raisins and pecans with 1 cup flour in a large bowl until well coated. Set aside.

Whisk salt into remaining 2 cups flour in a small bowl.

Beat butter in a large bowl with an electric mixer (fitted with paddle attachment if using a stand mixer) at medium-high speed until pale and fluffy. Add sugar and beat until pale and fluffy. Add yolks and beat until incorporated. Add flour and mix at low speed until just combined.

Stir baking soda into lukewarm water in a small bowl until dissolved. Add to butter mixture, along with lemon extract, and stir until smooth. Stir in raisins and nuts (including flour remaining in bowl) until raisins and nuts are coated and no visible traces of flour remain.

Beat egg whites in a clean bowl with cleaned beaters (or whisk attachment) until they just hold stiff peaks. Fold into batter until combined. (Batter will be thick and very lumpy from raisins and nuts.)

Divide batter between loaf pans and smooth tops by gently rapping bottom of each pan against counter. Bake until tops of cakes are golden and a wooden toothpick inserted in center of each cake comes out clean, about 2¾ hours. Cool cakes in pans on racks for 10 minutes.

Turn cakes out onto racks. Peel off and discard parchment paper, turn cakes right side up, and cool completely.

- The fruitcake is best when made at least 1 day ahead to allow the flavors to develop. It can be kept, wrapped in plastic wrap, in an airtight container at room temperature for up to 2 weeks or frozen for up to 1 month.

Christmas Fruitcake

SERVES 12
ACTIVE TIME: 45 MINUTES ■ START TO FINISH: 5½ HOURS
(INCLUDES COOLING)

■ You'll be proud to give this handsome fruitcake as a gift, though it's so delicious it may be hard to part with. It's filled with a bountiful mix of dried apricots, cranberries, golden raisins, and currants macerated in Cognac and baked in a springform pan for an elegant look. It improves with age, stays moist without being at all heavy, and is perfect with a cup of coffee. ■

- ¾ cup Cognac or other brandy
- ⅔ cup golden raisins
- ⅔ cup dried currants
- ⅔ cup dried apricots, finely chopped
- ⅔ cup dried cranberries
- ¾ cup plus ⅓ cup blanched whole almonds (about 5½ ounces total)
- 1 cup sugar
- 2 cups all-purpose flour
- 1 teaspoon baking powder
- ¾ teaspoon salt
- 2½ sticks (10 ounces) unsalted butter, softened
- 4 large eggs
- 1 teaspoon vanilla extract
- 1 tablespoon finely grated orange zest
- 3 tablespoons sweet orange marmalade or apricot preserves
- 1 tablespoon Grand Marnier, Cointreau, or other orange-flavored liqueur

SPECIAL EQUIPMENT: a 9-inch springform pan

Heat brandy in a 1-quart saucepan over low heat until warm. Remove from heat, stir in dried fruit, cover, and let stand until fruit is softened, about 30 minutes.

Put a rack in middle of oven and preheat oven to 325°F. Invert bottom of springform pan (to make it easier to slide cake off pan bottom) and lock on side. Generously butter pan and dust with flour, knocking out excess.

Finely grind ¾ cup almonds with ¼ cup sugar in a food processor. Whisk together with flour, baking powder, and salt in a bowl.

Beat together butter and remaining ¾ cup sugar in a large bowl with an electric mixer (fitted with paddle attachment if using a stand mixer) at medium-high speed until pale and fluffy, about 5 minutes. Add eggs one at a time, beating well after each addition (batter will appear curdled). Add vanilla, zest, and fruit with brandy and beat until thoroughly combined, about 2 minutes. Reduce speed to low and mix in flour mixture until incorporated.

Spoon batter into springform pan, spreading it evenly. Scatter remaining ⅓ cup almonds over top. Bake until a wooden toothpick inserted in center of cake comes out clean, 1½ to 1¾ hours. Run a thin knife around side of pan and cool cake in pan on a rack for 10 minutes.

Meanwhile, melt marmalade with liqueur in a small heavy saucepan over moderate heat, stirring. Pour glaze through a sieve into a small bowl; discard solids.

Loosen sides of cake with thin knife again, remove side of pan, and loosen cake from bottom of pan. Transfer cake to rack and brush glaze over top of cake. Cool completely.

- The cake improves in flavor if made at least 1 day ahead. It keeps, wrapped in parchment paper, then foil, and put in a sealable bag, at room temperature for up to 5 days. It can also be frozen for up to 2 weeks; thaw and bring to room temperature (still wrapped) before serving.

Panforte

MAKES ONE 9-INCH CAKE (ABOUT 24 SMALL PIECES)
ACTIVE TIME: 40 MINUTES ■ START TO FINISH: 4 HOURS
(INCLUDES COOLING)

■ A cross between a cake and a candy and traditionally served in small pieces, panforte is a classic Italian Christmas treat. It's a dense, rich confection loaded with nuts, dried fruit, and spices (hence its name, which means "strong bread") that is best made ahead (see Cook's Note). This recipe yields a generous amount, but panforte keeps so well that you'll have delicious leftovers long after the holiday season. ■

⅔ cup all-purpose flour

1 teaspoon ground cinnamon

½ teaspoon ground ginger

⅛ teaspoon ground cloves

¼ teaspoon salt

4 teaspoons unsweetened Dutch-process cocoa powder

1 cup (about 5¼ ounces) whole almonds, toasted (see Tips, page 911)

1 cup (about 4¾ ounces) unblanched hazelnuts, toasted (see Tips, page 911) and loose skins rubbed off

1 cup soft pitted prunes, quartered

1 cup soft dried figs, preferably Black Mission, cut into 6 pieces each

1 cup soft raisins

¾ cup sugar

⅔ cup honey

SPECIAL EQUIPMENT: a 9-inch springform pan; parchment paper; a candy thermometer

Put a rack in middle of oven and preheat oven to 300°F.

Butter springform pan and line with parchment paper, using a round for bottom and a long strip for side. Butter paper well and dust with cocoa powder, knocking out excess.

Whisk together flour, spices, salt, and 4 teaspoons cocoa in a large bowl. Stir in nuts and fruit.

Bring sugar and honey to a boil in a 2-quart heavy saucepan over moderate heat, stirring until sugar is dissolved. Boil without stirring until thermometer registers 238° to 240°F.

Immediately pour honey over fruit mixture and quickly stir until combined (mixture will be very thick and sticky). Quickly spoon mixture into springform pan, spreading it evenly with back of spoon. Dampen your hands and press mixture firmly and evenly into pan to compact it as much as possible.

Bake until edges start to rise slightly and have a matte look, 50 to 55 minutes. Cool panforte completely in pan on a rack.

Remove side of pan and invert panforte onto a plate; peel off paper. If making ahead, wrap panforte well. To serve, cut into small pieces with a serrated knife.

COOK'S NOTE

■ Because the flavors of panforte deepen over time, this is best made at least 1 week, or up to 1 month, ahead. Refrigerate, wrapped in parchment paper, in a sealable plastic bag.

Cannoli Roll

SERVES 12
ACTIVE TIME: 1 HOUR ■ START TO FINISH: 2 HOURS
(INCLUDES COOLING)

■ The beloved hallmarks of Sicily's great dessert—creamy ricotta, chocolate shavings, and pistachios—are transformed into a tender rolled sponge cake. The sheet cake is brushed with Grand Marnier syrup and slathered with a fresh ricotta filling before being rolled and frosted with fluffy whipped cream. A shower of chocolate and pistachios completes the show. Sophisticated, with a nicely balanced sweetness, it will feed a houseful of friends. ■

FOR CAKE

5 large eggs, separated, left at room temperature for 30 minutes

¼ teaspoon salt

¼ teaspoon cream of tartar

½ cup plus 2 tablespoons granulated sugar

¾ cup cake flour (not self-rising), sifted

¼ cup confectioners' sugar

1½ cups (about 12 ounces) fresh or regular ricotta

4 ounces cream cheese, softened

⅓ cup confectioners' sugar

1 teaspoon finely grated orange zest

¼ teaspoon ground cinnamon

¼ teaspoon vanilla extract

¼ teaspoon orange-flower water (see Sources)

2 ounces bittersweet chocolate, coarsely grated
   (about ½ cup)

FOR SYRUP

3 tablespoons sugar

3 tablespoons water

1 tablespoon Grand Marnier or Cointreau

FOR ASSEMBLY

1 cup very cold heavy cream

2 tablespoons confectioners' sugar

1 tablespoon Grand Marnier or Cointreau

½ teaspoon vanilla extract

⅓ cup shelled pistachios, finely chopped

1 tablespoon shaved or coarsely grated bittersweet
   chocolate

SPECIAL EQUIPMENT: a 15-by-10-by-1-inch baking sheet
(jelly-roll pan); parchment paper

MAKE THE CAKE: Put a rack in middle of oven and preheat oven to 350°F. Lightly butter baking sheet and line bottom and sides with parchment paper (paper may hang over ends), then butter paper. Dust with flour, knocking out excess.

Beat whites with salt and cream of tartar in a large bowl with an electric mixer (fitted with whisk attachment if using a stand mixer) at medium speed until they just hold soft peaks. Beat in 5 tablespoons sugar a little at a time, then increase speed to high and beat until whites hold stiff, glossy peaks. (Transfer to another bowl if using a stand mixer.)

Beat yolks and remaining 5 tablespoons sugar until very thick and pale, about 5 minutes with a stand mixer, longer with a handheld. Gently but thoroughly fold whites into yolks in 2 batches. Fold in flour until just combined.

Spread batter evenly in baking sheet with an offset spatula or rubber spatula. Bake until top of cake springs back when gently pressed with your finger, about 8 minutes.

Sprinkle a clean kitchen towel (not terry cloth) with confectioners' sugar and immediately invert hot cake onto towel, then carefully peel off paper and discard. With a long side nearest you, roll up cake using towel as an aid, jelly-roll style, keeping it wrapped in towel. Cool cake completely, seam side down, on a rack.

MEANWHILE, MAKE THE FILLING: Combine all ingredients except chocolate in a food processor and blend until smooth. Transfer to a bowl and stir in chocolate. Refrigerate for at least 30 minutes.

MAKE THE SYRUP: Stir together all ingredients in a small heavy saucepan and bring to a boil over high heat, stirring until sugar is dissolved, then boil for 1 minute. Remove from heat and cool to room temperature.

ASSEMBLE THE CAKE: Unroll cake and brush top with syrup. Spread filling evenly over cake, leaving a ¼-inch border on all sides. Starting from a long side, roll up cake and carefully transfer, seam side down, to a platter.

Beat cream with confectioners' sugar, liqueur, and vanilla in a medium bowl with electric mixer until it holds soft peaks.

Spread cream over roll, covering it completely. Sprinkle with pistachios and chocolate.

COOK'S NOTES

■ The filling can be refrigerated, its surface covered with plastic wrap, for up to 1 day.

■ The cake can be filled and iced up to 4 hours ahead and refrigerated, uncovered. Sprinkle with the pistachios and chocolate just before serving.

Maple Walnut Bûche de Noël

SERVES 8
ACTIVE TIME: 1¼ HOURS ■ START TO FINISH: 3½ HOURS
(INCLUDES MAKING BUTTERCREAM AND BRITTLE)

■ Decorated with marzipan woodland animals and meringue mushrooms, cakes resembling Yule logs are popular at Christmastime in France and the French-speaking parts of Canada. This one has a simpler, more elegant look—think beautiful young sapling rather than dark log. In a nod to our neighbors to the north, it replaces the traditional chocolate and coffee flavoring with maple and walnuts. The classic foundation for a bûche is a sheet cake—usually a génoise whipped up from whole eggs or a sponge cake made with separately beaten yolks and whites—that rolls up neatly, without breaking. Each step of the dessert is very straightforward. ∎

1¼ cups (about 4 ounces) walnuts, toasted (see Tips, page 911)
¼ cup cake flour (not self-rising)
Salt
¼ teaspoon ground cinnamon
⅓ cup plus ¼ cup sugar
4 large eggs, separated, left at room temperature for 30 minutes
1½ tablespoons Canadian whiskey (rye)
½ teaspoon vanilla extract
½ stick (4 tablespoons) unsalted butter, melted and cooled
Maple Meringue Buttercream (recipe follows)
Walnut Brittle (page 740)
SPECIAL EQUIPMENT: a 15-by-10-by-1-inch baking sheet (jelly-roll pan); parchment paper

Put a rack in middle of oven and preheat oven to 350°F. Butter baking sheet and line bottom with parchment paper. Butter paper and dust with flour, knocking out excess.

Pulse walnuts with flour, ½ teaspoon salt, cinnamon, and 2 tablespoons sugar in a food processor until finely chopped.

Beat together yolks, whiskey, vanilla, and ⅓ cup sugar in a large bowl with an electric mixer (fitted with whisk attachment if using a stand mixer) at high speed until mixture is thick and pale and forms a ribbon that dissolves slowly into mixture when beaters are lifted, 5 to 8 minutes in a stand mixer, 8 to 12 minutes with a handheld. Fold in nut mixture in 4 batches.

Beat whites with a pinch of salt in another bowl with cleaned beaters (or whisk attachment) at medium speed until they just hold soft peaks. Beat in remaining 2 tablespoons sugar ½ tablespoon at a time and continue to beat until whites just hold stiff peaks.

Fold one quarter of whites into yolk mixture to lighten it, then fold in remaining whites gently but thoroughly. Stir ½ cup batter into butter in a small bowl until combined, then fold butter mixture into batter gently but thoroughly.

Spread batter evenly in baking sheet and rap once on counter to help eliminate air bubbles. Bake cake until firm to the touch, pale golden, and beginning to pull away from sides of pan, 12 to 16 minutes. Cool cake in pan on a rack for 15 minutes.

Run a thin knife around sides of pan, then put a sheet of foil over cake, invert a rack over foil, and flip cake onto rack; discard parchment paper. Cool completely.

Slide cake, on foil, onto a work surface. Spread 1¼ cups buttercream evenly over cake. Sprinkle with chopped brittle. Using foil as an aid, beginning with a short end, roll up cake jelly-roll style (**1**). Carefully transfer cake with a long metal spatula to a platter, seam side down, and remove foil.

Frost cake with about 1½ cups buttercream and refrigerate until frosting is firm, about 30 minutes. (If you plan to finish assembling cake within 1 hour, keep remaining buttercream at room temperature; if not, refrigerate, covered; see Cook's Note.)

Cut a thin slice from both ends of log to even ends. Starting about ½ inch in from one cut edge, cut a diagonal piece from end of cake (**2**). Arrange piece on side of cake to resemble a cut branch, using a bit of remaining buttercream to glue piece to log (**3**). Spackle remaining buttercream around it to mask the joint. Arrange shards of walnut brittle decoratively on cake.

COOK'S NOTE

∎ The frosted cake (uncut, and without the topping of brittle shards) can be made up to 3 days ahead and refrigerated, covered; bring to room temperature before serving. Refrigerate the remaining buttercream, covered, and bring to room temperature before using; if the buttercream seems lumpy, beat with an electric mixer until smooth.

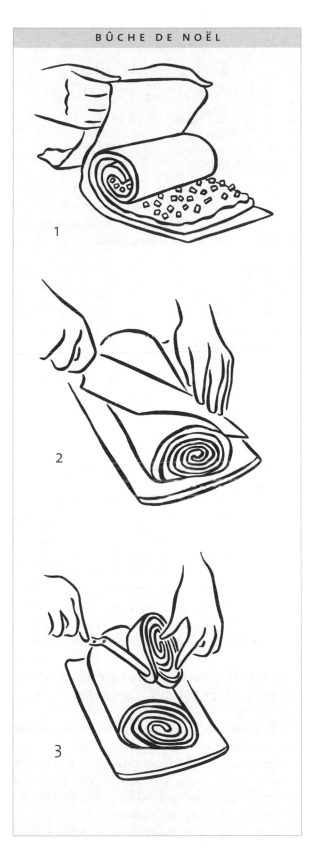

BÛCHE DE NOËL

1

2

3

Maple Meringue Buttercream

MAKES ABOUT 3 CUPS
ACTIVE TIME: 20 MINUTES ■ START TO FINISH: 35 MINUTES

■ A combination of maple syrup and maple sugar gives this frosting a deep, rich taste. ■

> 2 large egg whites, left at room temperature for
>   30 minutes (see Cook's Note)
>   Scant ¼ teaspoon cream of tartar
> ⅛ teaspoon salt
> 2 tablespoons maple sugar (see Sources)
> ⅔ cup pure maple syrup, preferably Grade A dark
>   amber
> 2 sticks (½ pound) unsalted butter, cut into
>   tablespoons, softened

SPECIAL EQUIPMENT: a candy thermometer

Beat egg whites with cream of tartar and salt in a large bowl with an electric mixer (fitted with whisk attachment if using a stand mixer) at medium speed until they just hold soft peaks. Beat in maple sugar 1 teaspoon at a time and continue to beat until whites just hold stiff peaks.

Boil syrup in a small heavy saucepan over moderate heat, undisturbed, until it reaches 238° to 242°F on thermometer, 3 to 7 minutes. Immediately remove from heat.

With mixer at high speed, slowly pour hot syrup in a thin stream down side of bowl into egg whites, then continue to beat meringue, scraping down sides of bowl with a rubber spatula as necessary, until cool to the touch, about 6 minutes. It's important to cool meringue before proceeding.

With mixer at medium speed, add butter one piece at a time, beating until incorporated after each addition. (If meringue is too warm and buttercream looks soupy after some of butter is added, chill bottom of bowl in a larger bowl filled with ice and cold water for a few seconds, then beat in remaining butter.) Continue beating until buttercream is smooth. (Mixture may look curdled before all butter is added, but it will come back together before beating is finished.)

COOK'S NOTES

■ The buttercream can be made up to 1 week ahead and refrigerated, covered. It can also be frozen in an airtight container for up to 1 month. Bring to room temperature (do not use a microwave) and beat with an electric mixer until smooth before using.

- The egg whites in this recipe may not be fully cooked. If that is a concern, see page 915. Alternatively, substitute pasteurized liquid egg whites or reconstituted powdered egg whites, such as Just Whites.

Walnut Brittle

MAKES ABOUT 2 CUPS (½ CUP CHOPPED PLUS SHARDS)
ACTIVE TIME: 15 MINUTES ■ START TO FINISH: 30 MINUTES

■ This brittle adds a sweet, nutty crunch to the bûche de Noël, and it also is delicious sprinkled over ice cream. We like to make extra to have on hand for just such a treat. ■

½ cup walnuts, toasted (see Tips, page 911) and finely chopped
1 cup sugar
¼ cup water

Line a baking sheet with a nonstick baking sheet liner, such as a Silpat, or with an oiled sheet of foil.

Shake nuts in a sieve to remove nut powder (this will make for a clearer brittle); set aside.

Bring sugar and water to a boil in a 10-inch heavy skillet, stirring until sugar is dissolved and washing down any sugar crystals on sides of skillet with a pastry brush dipped in cold water. Boil syrup, without stirring, gently swirling skillet, until mixture is a golden caramel. Stir in walnuts, then immediately pour caramel onto baking sheet, tilting sheet to spread caramel as thinly as possible. Cool brittle completely at room temperature.

If using brittle for bûche de Noël, coarsely chop enough brittle to measure ½ cup, then break remainder into shards for decorating.

COOK'S NOTE

- The brittle can be made up to 1 week ahead and kept in an airtight container at room temperature.

Carrot Cupcakes with Molasses Cream Cheese Icing

MAKES 12 CUPCAKES
ACTIVE TIME: 30 MINUTES ■ START TO FINISH: 1½ HOURS

■ Fragrant with cinnamon and nutmeg, these moist cupcakes are textured with coconut and toasted walnuts, but their traditional cream cheese frosting gets added depth from a touch of molasses. ■

FOR CUPCAKES
1½ cups all-purpose flour
1 teaspoon baking soda
¼ teaspoon salt
1½ teaspoons ground cinnamon
½ teaspoon freshly grated nutmeg
¾ cup vegetable oil
1 cup packed light brown sugar
2 large eggs
½ teaspoon vanilla extract
1¾ cups finely shredded carrots (about 4 medium)
⅓ cup walnuts, finely chopped and lightly toasted (see Tips, page 911)
½ cup sweetened flaked coconut, lightly toasted (see Tips, page 912)
FOR ICING
4 ounces cream cheese, softened
½ stick (4 tablespoons) unsalted butter, softened
1 tablespoon molasses (not robust)
2 tablespoons confectioners' sugar
SPECIAL EQUIPMENT: a muffin pan with twelve ½-cup muffin cups; 12 paper muffin cup liners

MAKE THE CUPCAKES: Put a rack in middle of oven and preheat oven to 350°F. Line muffin cups with paper liners.

Whisk together flour, baking soda, salt, cinnamon, and nutmeg in a bowl.

Whisk together oil, brown sugar, eggs, and vanilla in a large bowl. Beat in flour mixture with a wooden spoon until well combined. Add carrots, walnuts, and coconut, stirring until just combined.

Divide batter among muffin cups. Bake until a

wooden toothpick inserted in center of a cupcake comes out clean, 25 to 30 minutes. Turn cupcakes out onto a rack and cool completely.

MAKE THE ICING: Beat together all ingredients in a bowl with a wooden spoon until fluffy.

Spread icing on cupcakes.

COOK'S NOTES

- The cupcakes, without the icing, can be made up to 2 days ahead and kept in an airtight container at room temperature. Ice just before serving.
- The icing can be made up to 2 days ahead and refrigerated, covered. Bring to room temperature before using.

Vanilla Cupcakes

MAKES 36 CUPCAKES
ACTIVE TIME: 30 MINUTES ■ START TO FINISH: 1½ HOURS

■ These cupcakes are rich, golden, and deliciously buttery. ■

    3 cups all-purpose flour
    1 tablespoon baking powder
  1¾ teaspoons salt
    3 sticks (¾ pound) unsalted butter, softened
  1¾ cups sugar
    4 large eggs, left at room temperature for 30 minutes
  1½ teaspoons vanilla extract
  1½ cups whole milk
SPECIAL EQUIPMENT: 3 muffin pans with twelve ½-cup
       muffin cups each; 36 paper muffin cup liners

Put racks in upper and lower thirds of oven and preheat oven to 350°F. Line muffin cups with liners.

Sift together flour, baking powder, and salt.

Beat together butter and sugar in a large bowl with an electric mixer (fitted with paddle attachment if using a stand mixer) at medium-high speed until pale and fluffy, about 5 minutes with a stand mixer, longer with a handheld. Add eggs one at a time, beating well after each addition, then add vanilla and beat until thoroughly incorporated. Reduce speed to low and add flour mixture and milk alternately in 3 batches,

beginning and ending with flour mixture and mixing just until batter is smooth.

Divide batter among muffin cups, filling them two-thirds full. Bake cupcakes, switching position of pans halfway through baking, until a wooden toothpick inserted in center of a cupcake comes out clean, 18 to 22 minutes. Cool cupcakes in pans on racks for 5 minutes, then invert onto racks, turn right side up, and cool completely before frosting.

COOK'S NOTE

- The cupcakes are best eaten the day they're made.

Vanilla Mini Cupcakes

MAKES 24 MINI CUPCAKES
ACTIVE TIME: 1 HOUR ■ START TO FINISH: 1¾ HOURS
(INCLUDES MAKING BUTTERCREAM)

■ A great workhorse recipe to keep on hand, this yields a manageable number of small cupcakes, so you can make and frost them quickly. Decorated in various colors, they top Chocolate Cake with Vanilla Buttercream (page 756), and they are delicious with almost any kind of icing. ■

    1 cup all-purpose flour
    1 teaspoon baking powder
   ¼ teaspoon salt
   ⅓ cup whole milk
   ½ teaspoon vanilla extract
   ¾ stick (6 tablespoons) unsalted butter, softened
   ½ cup plus 1 tablespoon sugar
    1 large egg
  1¾ cups Vanilla Buttercream (page 757) or other
       frosting as desired
       Various food colorings (optional)
SPECIAL EQUIPMENT: 2 mini muffin pans with twelve
       1¾-inch muffin cups each; 24 foil or paper mini
       muffin liners

Put a rack in middle of oven and preheat oven to 350°F. Line muffin cups with liners.

Whisk together flour, baking powder, and salt in a bowl. Stir together milk and vanilla in a small bowl.

Beat together butter and sugar in a large bowl with

an electric mixer (fitted with paddle attachment if using a stand mixer) at medium-high speed until pale and fluffy, about 4 minutes in a stand mixer, longer with a handheld. Add egg and beat until just combined. Reduce speed to low and add flour and milk mixtures alternately in 3 batches, beginning and ending with flour and mixing until just combined.

Divide batter among muffin cups, filling them two-thirds full. Bake until tops are pale golden and a wooden toothpick inserted in center of a cupcake comes out clean, about 15 minutes. Turn cupcakes out onto a rack and cool completely.

If using buttercream and food colorings, divide buttercream among several small bowls and tint with food coloring. Frost cupcakes with buttercream.

COOK'S NOTE
■ The cupcakes are best eaten the day they're made.

Chocolate Soufflé Cake with Orange Caramel Sauce

SERVES 8 TO 10
ACTIVE TIME: 1 HOUR ■ START TO FINISH: 2½ HOURS

■ You won't believe such a sophisticated dessert can result from just six ingredients. The citrusy caramel sauce teases out the deep flavors of the cake, whose success lies in its contrasting textures: its unctuous chocolate center is veiled by a crisp, crackly crust. When making the cake, take it easy when you fold the egg whites into the batter—the gentler the folding, the airier the cake. It tastes best if made a day ahead, so plan accordingly. ■

2 sticks (½ pound) unsalted butter, cut into pieces

9 ounces bittersweet chocolate (no more than 60% cacao; see page 705), chopped

6 large eggs, separated, left at room temperature for 30 minutes

⅔ cup plus ½ cup superfine sugar

½ teaspoon salt

3 oranges

SPECIAL EQUIPMENT: a 10-inch springform pan; parchment paper

MAKE THE CAKE: Put a small roasting pan filled halfway with hot water on a rack in bottom third of oven (to provide moisture during baking). Position another rack in middle of oven and preheat oven to 325°F. Invert bottom of springform pan (to make it easier to slide cake off bottom) and lock on side. Butter pan and line bottom with a round of parchment paper. Butter paper.

Melt butter and chocolate in a 2-quart heavy saucepan over low heat, stirring until smooth. Remove from heat.

Beat together yolks, ⅓ cup sugar, and salt in a large bowl with an electric mixer (fitted with paddle attachment if using a stand mixer) at medium-high speed until mixture is pale and thick enough to form a ribbon that dissolves slowly into mixture when beaters are lifted, 6 to 8 minutes in a stand mixer, longer with a handheld. Stir in warm chocolate mixture until well combined.

Beat whites in another large bowl with cleaned beaters (or whisk attachment) at medium speed until they just hold soft peaks. Gradually beat in ⅓ cup sugar and continue to beat until whites just hold stiff peaks. Stir one quarter of whites into chocolate mixture to lighten it, then fold in remaining whites gently but thoroughly.

Pour batter into springform pan. Bake until a wooden toothpick inserted in center of cake comes out with a few crumbs adhering, about 1 hour (a crust will form on top of cake and crack). Transfer to a rack and cool for 10 minutes (cake will deflate as it cools).

MEANWHILE, MAKE THE SAUCE: Remove zest from 2 oranges with a vegetable peeler. Trim any white pith from zest with a paring knife. Cut enough very thin strips of zest to measure ¼ cup. Squeeze juice from all 3 oranges and pour through a fine-mesh sieve into a bowl. Measure out 1 cup juice; reserve remainder for another use.

Heat remaining ½ cup sugar in a dry 1- to 2-quart heavy saucepan over moderate heat, stirring with a fork to heat sugar evenly, until it begins to melt. Stop stirring and cook, without stirring, swirling pan occasionally so sugar melts and caramelizes evenly, until it is a dark amber caramel. Add zest and cook, stirring, until fragrant, about 15 seconds. Tilt pan and carefully pour in juice (caramel will harden and steam vigorously). Cook over moderately low heat, stirring, until caramel is dissolved. Remove sauce from heat and let cool.

Carefully run a thin knife around edges of cake, then remove side of pan. Cool cake on bottom of pan for 30 minutes.

Invert cake onto rack, remove bottom of pan, and carefully peel off paper. Invert a serving plate over cake and invert cake onto plate.

Serve cake with caramel sauce.

COOK'S NOTES

- The cake improves in flavor if made a day ahead. Cool completely, then refrigerate, covered with plastic wrap. Bring to room temperature before serving.
- The sauce can be made up to 1 day ahead and kept at a cool room temperature.

Devil's Food Cake with Marshmallow Frosting

SERVES 8
ACTIVE TIME: 30 MINUTES ■ START TO FINISH: 2½ HOURS
(INCLUDES COOLING)

■ Topped with swirls of fluffy white frosting, this cocoa cake will take you back to those "devil dog" snack cakes of your childhood—but it's much better. Baked in a brownie pan, it's easy to pull together on a weeknight, and it is just the thing for a homey family celebration. ■

FOR CAKE
- 2 cups all-purpose flour
- ¾ cup unsweetened cocoa powder (not Dutch-process)
- 1¼ teaspoons baking soda
- ¾ teaspoon salt
- 2 sticks (½ pound) unsalted butter, softened
- 1½ cups packed dark brown sugar
- 2 large eggs, left at room temperature for 30 minutes
- 1 teaspoon vanilla extract
- 1⅓ cups water

FOR FROSTING
- 2 large egg whites, left at room temperature for 30 minutes
- ½ cup granulated sugar
- Pinch of salt
- ¼ cup light corn syrup
- 2 tablespoons water
- 1 teaspoon vanilla extract

GARNISH: unsweetened cocoa powder
SPECIAL EQUIPMENT: an 8-inch square baking pan

MAKE THE CAKE: Put a rack in middle of oven and preheat oven to 350°F. Butter baking pan and dust with flour.

Whisk together flour, cocoa powder, baking soda, and salt in a bowl.

Beat together butter and brown sugar in a large bowl with an electric mixer (fitted with paddle attachment if using a stand mixer) until pale and fluffy. Add eggs one at a time, beating well after each addition, then beat in vanilla. Add flour mixture and water alternately in 3 batches, beginning and ending with flour and mixing until just combined.

Pour batter into cake pan and smooth top. Bake until a wooden toothpick inserted in center of cake comes out clean, 45 to 55 minutes. Cool in pan on a rack for 1 hour.

Run a thin knife around sides of pan and invert cake onto rack, then reinvert onto a cake plate.

MAKE THE FROSTING: Combine all ingredients in a metal bowl set over a saucepan of simmering water and beat with a handheld electric mixer at high speed until frosting is thick and fluffy, 6 to 7 minutes. Remove bowl from heat and continue to beat until slightly cooled.

Mound frosting on top of cake. Dust with cocoa powder.

COOK'S NOTES

- The cake improves in flavor if made up to 1 day ahead. Cool, uncovered, then keep, wrapped in plastic wrap, at room temperature. Frost the cake just before serving.
- The egg whites in the frosting are not fully cooked. If that is a concern, see page 915. Alternatively, substitute pasteurized liquid egg whites or reconstituted powdered egg whites, such as Just Whites.

Chocolate-Glazed Hazelnut Mousse Cake

SERVES 6 TO 8
ACTIVE TIME: 45 MINUTES ■ START TO FINISH: 4½ HOURS
(INCLUDES CHILLING)

■ Not a cake in the traditional sense of the word, this decadent dessert features a crisp hazelnut shortbread crust topped with smooth, airy mousse and enrobed in glistening ganache. Nutella—that silky chocolate hazelnut spread and guilty pleasure—both echoes and enhances the marriage of the hazelnut crust and the mousse. Because the dessert is simple to prepare, can be made ahead of time, and doesn't require any last-minute fussing, it's an ideal choice for entertaining. ■

FOR SHORTBREAD BASE
- 2 tablespoons hazelnuts, toasted (see Tips, page 911), loose skins rubbed off
- 3 tablespoons sugar
- ½ cup all-purpose flour
- ½ stick (4 tablespoons) unsalted butter, softened
- 2 tablespoons unsweetened Dutch-process cocoa powder
- ⅛ teaspoon salt

FOR MOUSSE
- 1 teaspoon unflavored gelatin
- 3 tablespoons cold water
- ½ cup chocolate hazelnut spread, such as Nutella
- ½ cup mascarpone
- 1½ cups very cold heavy cream
- 2 tablespoons unsweetened Dutch-process cocoa powder
- 3 tablespoons sugar

FOR GANACHE
- 5 tablespoons heavy cream
- 3½ ounces bittersweet chocolate (no more than 60% cacao; see page 705), finely chopped

SPECIAL EQUIPMENT: an 8-inch springform pan; parchment paper

MAKE THE SHORTBREAD BASE: Put a rack in middle of oven and preheat oven to 350°F. Invert bottom of springform pan (to make it easier to slide shortbread base off bottom), lock on side of pan, and line bottom with a round of parchment paper.

Pulse hazelnuts with sugar in a food processor until finely chopped. Add flour, butter, cocoa powder, and salt and pulse just until a dough forms.

Press dough evenly onto bottom of springform pan. Prick all over with a fork and bake until just dry to the touch, 18 to 20 minutes. Transfer pan to a rack to cool completely.

MEANWHILE, MAKE THE MOUSSE: Sprinkle gelatin over water in a 1- to 1½-quart heavy saucepan and let stand until softened, about 2 minutes.

Heat gelatin mixture over low heat, stirring, just until gelatin is melted, about 2 minutes. Whisk in chocolate hazelnut spread until combined, then transfer to a large bowl. Whisk mascarpone into chocolate hazelnut mixture.

Beat together cream, cocoa powder, and sugar in another large bowl with an electric mixer (fitted with whisk attachment if using a stand mixer) at low speed until just combined, then increase speed to high and beat until cream just holds soft peaks. Whisk one third of whipped cream into mascarpone mixture to lighten it, then fold in remaining whipped cream until well combined.

Remove side of springform pan and carefully slide out parchment from under cooled shortbread, then reattach side of pan to shortbread base. Spoon mousse onto shortbread base, gently smoothing top. Refrigerate, covered, for at least 3 hours.

MAKE THE GANACHE AND GLAZE THE CAKE: Bring cream to a simmer in a small heavy saucepan. Remove from heat, add chocolate, and let stand for 1 minute, then gently whisk until completely melted and smooth. Transfer ganache to a small bowl and cool, stirring occasionally, until slightly thickened but still pourable, about 20 minutes.

Run a warmed thin knife around side of springform pan and remove side. Slide cake off bottom of pan onto a serving plate. Pour ganache onto top of cake and spread, allowing it to drip down sides.

COOK'S NOTES

- The cake, without the glaze, can be refrigerated for up to 2 days.
- The cake can be glazed up to 6 hours ahead and refrigerated, uncovered.

Double Chocolate Layer Cake

SERVES 12 TO 14
ACTIVE TIME: 1¼ HOURS ■ START TO FINISH: 3¾ HOURS
(INCLUDES COOLING)

■ We adore this old-fashioned chocolate cake, adapted from one served at the Engine Co. No. 28 restaurant in Los Angeles. It's ultramoist, as only a cake made with oil (rather than butter) can be, and the rich ganache frosting ups the ante even more. The cake will serve a crowd. ■

FOR CAKE LAYERS

3 ounces semisweet chocolate (no more than 60% cacao; see page 705), finely chopped
1½ cups hot brewed coffee
3 cups sugar
2½ cups all-purpose flour
1½ cups unsweetened cocoa powder (not Dutch-process)
2 teaspoons baking soda
¾ teaspoon baking powder
1¼ teaspoons salt
3 large eggs
¾ cup vegetable oil
1½ cups well-shaken buttermilk
¾ teaspoon vanilla extract

FOR FROSTING

1 cup heavy cream
2 tablespoons sugar
2 tablespoons light corn syrup
1 pound semisweet chocolate (no more than 60% cacao; see page 705), finely chopped
½ stick (4 tablespoons) unsalted butter, cut into cubes and chilled

SPECIAL EQUIPMENT: two 10-by-2-inch round cake pans; parchment paper

MAKE THE CAKE LAYERS: Put a rack in middle of oven and preheat oven to 300°F. Grease pans, line bottoms with rounds of parchment paper, and grease paper.

Put chocolate in a bowl, pour hot coffee over it, and let stand, stirring occasionally, until chocolate is melted and mixture is smooth.

Sift together sugar, flour, cocoa powder, baking soda, baking powder, and salt.

Beat eggs in a large bowl with an electric mixer (fitted with whisk attachment if using a stand mixer) at high speed until slightly thickened and pale, about 3 minutes in a stand mixer, longer with a handheld. Reduce speed to medium and slowly add oil, then add buttermilk, vanilla, and melted chocolate mixture, beating until well combined. Add sugar mixture and beat just until well combined.

Divide batter between pans. Bake until a wooden toothpick inserted in center of each cake comes out clean, 1 hour and 10 minutes to 1 hour and 20 minutes. Cool cakes in pans on racks for 1 hour.

Run a thin knife around sides of pans and invert cakes onto racks. Carefully remove paper and cool cakes completely.

MAKE THE FROSTING: Bring cream, sugar, and corn syrup to a boil in a 1½- to 2-quart saucepan over moderate heat, whisking until sugar is dissolved. Remove from heat and add chocolate, whisking until melted. Add butter, whisking until melted and smooth. Transfer frosting to a bowl and cool, stirring occasionally, until spreadable, about 1 hour. (Depending on chocolate you use, it may be necessary to chill frosting to spreadable consistency.)

ASSEMBLE THE CAKE: Put 1 cake layer rounded side up on a cake stand or platter and spread with about ¾ cup frosting. Top with remaining cake layer, rounded side down, and frost top and sides of cake with remaining frosting.

COOK'S NOTES

■ The cake layers can be made up to 1 day ahead and kept, tightly wrapped in plastic wrap, at room temperature.

■ The frosted cake keeps, covered and refrigerated, for up to 3 days. Bring to room temperature before serving.

Chocolate Sour Cream Layer Cake

SERVES 10 TO 12
ACTIVE TIME: 1 HOUR ■ START TO FINISH: 3½ HOURS
(INCLUDES COOLING)

■ This four-layer triumph is as easy as it is stunning. A generous amount of sour cream keeps the cake layers tender, and the frosting is rich and glossy. It's perfect for everything from a birthday celebration to an elegant dinner party. ■

FOR CAKE LAYERS

- 5 ounces fine-quality unsweetened chocolate, chopped
- 2¼ sticks (9 ounces) unsalted butter, softened
- 2¾ cups sifted cake flour (not self-rising; sift before measuring)
- ¼ cup unsweetened cocoa powder (not Dutch-process)
- 2 teaspoons baking soda
- 1 teaspoon baking powder
- ½ teaspoon salt
- 4 large eggs, left at room temperature for 30 minutes
- 1 cup granulated sugar
- 1 cup packed light brown sugar
- 1½ teaspoons vanilla extract
- 2 cups sour cream

FOR FROSTING

- 1 cup sugar
- 6 tablespoons all-purpose flour
- 6 tablespoons unsweetened cocoa powder (not Dutch-process)
- Pinch of salt
- 1½ cups whole milk
- 4 ounces fine-quality unsweetened chocolate, finely chopped
- 1 tablespoon vanilla extract
- 6 sticks (1½ pounds) unsalted butter, softened

SPECIAL EQUIPMENT: two 8-by-2-inch round cake pans; parchment paper

MAKE THE CAKE LAYERS: Put a rack in middle of oven and preheat oven to 350°F. Butter cake pans, line bottom of each with a round of parchment paper, and butter paper. Flour pans, knocking out excess.

Melt chocolate with butter in a metal bowl set over barely simmering water, stirring; cool.

Sift together flour, cocoa powder, baking soda, baking powder, and salt.

Beat eggs, sugars, and vanilla in a large bowl with an electric mixer (fitted with whisk attachment if using stand mixer) at medium speed until pale and thick, 3 to 5 minutes. Reduce speed to low and mix in melted chocolate until incorporated. Add flour mixture in 3 batches alternately with sour cream, beginning and ending with flour mixture and mixing until each addition is just incorporated.

Spread batter evenly in pans and rap pans several times on work surface to eliminate air bubbles. Bake until a wooden toothpick inserted in center of each cake comes out clean and cakes pull away from sides of pans, 40 to 50 minutes. Cool in pans on a rack for 10 minutes.

Run a thin knife around sides of pans and invert cakes onto racks. Remove paper and cool cakes completely.

MAKE THE FROSTING: Whisk together sugar, flour, cocoa powder, and salt in a 1-quart heavy saucepan. Whisk in milk and cook over medium heat, whisking constantly, until mixture boils and is smooth and thick, 3 to 5 minutes. Remove from heat and whisk in chocolate and vanilla until smooth. Transfer to a bowl, cover surface with parchment paper to prevent a skin from forming, and cool to room temperature.

Beat butter in a large bowl with an electric mixer (fitted with paddle attachment if using a stand mixer) until creamy. Add chocolate mixture a little at a time, beating until frosting is fluffy and spreadable.

ASSEMBLE THE CAKE: Cut each cake horizontally into 2 layers with a long serrated knife. Put 1 layer on a cake stand or large plate, cut side up, and spread top with 1¼ cups frosting. Place a second layer over frosting, cut side down, and spread with 1¼ cups frosting. Top with a third layer, cut side up, and spread with 1¼ cups frosting. Add remaining layer, cut side down, and spread top and sides of cake with remaining frosting.

COOK'S NOTES

■ The cake layers can be made up to 2 days ahead (but not split) and kept, tightly wrapped in plastic wrap, at room temperature.

- The frosting can be made up to 2 days ahead and refrigerated, covered. Bring to room temperature (about 1 hour) and beat until fluffy before using.
- The cake can be frosted up to 1 day ahead and refrigerated, covered.

SPLITTING CAKE LAYERS

Working with one layer at a time, insert long wooden skewers horizontally into it, halfway up the side, in about 8 places. Rest the blade of an 11- to 12-inch-long serrated knife on the skewers and use a long sawing motion to cut the cake layer in two. Lift off the top layer with two wide metal spatulas (or with the removable bottom of a tart pan) so that it doesn't crack or break. Remember that frosting can cover a multitude of imperfections: if the top layer of the cake does crack or break, gently piece it back together on top of the filling and slather it with frosting.

Strawberry and Cream Cake with Cardamom Syrup

SERVES 10
ACTIVE TIME: 1 HOUR ■ START TO FINISH: 2½ HOURS

■ A tall take on shortcake, this confection alternates moist cardamom-scented sponge cake with gently whipped cream and sweet berries. A syrup made of Muscat de Beaumes-de-Venise, a French dessert wine prized for its summery notes of honey and or-

anges (domestic Essensia makes a fine substitute), brushed on the layers proves to be the perfect enhancement for the strawberries. A little sour cream brings substance, complexity, and a light tang to the whipped cream. ■

FOR CAKE LAYERS
- 4 large eggs, separated, left at room temperature for 30 minutes
- 4 large egg yolks, left at room temperature for 30 minutes
- 1½ cups sugar
- ¼ cup whole milk
- 1 teaspoon vanilla extract
- ½ teaspoon finely grated lemon zest
- 1 cup all-purpose flour
- Salt

FOR SYRUP
- 1½ cups Muscat de Beaumes-de-Venise or Essensia (orange-flavored Muscat wine; see headnote)
- ¼ cup sugar
- ¾ teaspoon ground cardamom

FOR FILLING
- 2 cups very cold heavy cream
- ½ cup sour cream
- 2 tablespoons sugar
- 1 teaspoon vanilla extract
- 1½ pounds strawberries, 5 left whole, remainder hulled and cut lengthwise into ¼-inch-thick slices

SPECIAL EQUIPMENT: three 9-by-2-inch round cake pans; parchment paper

MAKE THE CAKE LAYERS: Put racks in upper and lower thirds of oven and preheat oven to 350°F. Butter cake pans. Line bottom of each with a round of parchment paper, butter parchment, and dust pans with flour, knocking out excess.

Whisk together 8 yolks, 1 cup sugar, milk, vanilla, and zest in a large bowl until smooth. Whisk in flour and ½ teaspoon salt until combined (batter will be thick).

Beat whites with a pinch of salt in a large bowl using an electric mixer (fitted with whisk attachment if using a stand mixer) at medium-high speed until they just hold soft peaks. Beating at medium speed, add remaining ½ cup sugar a little at a time and continue to beat until whites hold stiff, glossy peaks, about 2 minutes more. Fold about one third of whites into batter to lighten it, then fold in remaining whites gently but thoroughly.

Divide batter among cake pans, smoothing tops. Bake, switching position of cake pans halfway through baking, until cakes are springy to the touch and a wooden toothpick inserted in center of each comes out clean, 20 to 25 minutes. Cool cakes in pans on racks for 10 minutes.

Run a knife around sides of pans and invert cakes onto racks. Carefully peel off parchment and cool cakes completely.

MEANWHILE, MAKE THE SYRUP: Bring wine, sugar, and cardamom to a boil in a 1-quart heavy saucepan, stirring until sugar is dissolved, then boil until reduced to about 1 cup, 6 to 8 minutes. Strain syrup through a fine-mesh sieve and cool completely.

MAKE THE FILLING: Beat together heavy cream, sour cream, sugar, and vanilla in a large bowl with electric mixer until cream just holds stiff peaks.

ASSEMBLE THE CAKE: Prick cake layers all over with toothpick and brush or pour syrup, little by little, evenly over each layer, letting it be absorbed each time before adding more.

Transfer 1 layer flat side up to a cake stand or plate and spread with a rounded cup of cream filling. Arrange some sliced strawberries in one layer over cream filling. Turn second layer right side up and spread a thin layer of cream over top, then place it, with the aid of a spatula, cream side down over strawberries. Make one more layer with cream, strawberries, and cake in same manner. Spread top with remaining cream and decorate with remaining strawberries, including reserved whole berries.

COOK'S NOTES

- The layers (without the syrup) can be made up to 2 days ahead and kept, tightly wrapped in plastic wrap, at room temperature.
- The syrup can be made up to 1 day ahead and refrigerated, covered. Bring to room temperature before using.
- The cake can be assembled up to 1 hour ahead and kept at room temperature.

Walnut Meringue Cake with Strawberry Sauce

SERVES 10 TO 12
ACTIVE TIME: 30 MINUTES ■ START TO FINISH: 2 HOURS

■ The picturesque Simon Pearce restaurant in Quechee, Vermont, is the home of this decidedly unpicturesque but devastatingly good cake. It's made of two crackly, craggy meringue layers sandwiched around a deep drift of freshly whipped cream, and is served with a fresh strawberry sauce. The result is sweet and nutty and chewy. In a word, irresistible. ■

     8 large egg whites, left at room temperature
          for 30 minutes
        Pinch of salt
  2½ cups sugar
     2 teaspoons vanilla extract
     1 teaspoon distilled white vinegar
     2 cups (about 8 ounces) chopped walnuts
     2 cups very cold heavy cream
     2 pints (about 1¼ pounds) strawberries, hulled
  1–2 teaspoons fresh lemon juice
SPECIAL EQUIPMENT: two 9-inch round cake pans;
          parchment paper

Put a rack in middle of oven and preheat oven to 350°F. Butter bottoms of cake pans and line with rounds of parchment paper. Butter paper and dust pans with flour, knocking out excess.

Beat egg whites with salt in a large bowl with an electric mixer (fitted with whisk attachment if using a stand mixer) until they hold soft peaks. Beat in 2¼ cups sugar 1 tablespoon at a time and continue to beat until meringue holds stiff, glossy peaks, 10 to 15 minutes. Slowly beat in vanilla and vinegar, then beat meringue at high speed for 30 seconds. Fold in walnuts.

Divide meringue between pans, smoothing tops. Bake until puffed and golden, about 45 minutes. Cool meringues completely in pans on racks. (The meringues will crack and collapse as they cool; they will be moist on the inside and crisp on the outside.)

Beat cream in a chilled bowl with electric mixer until it holds soft peaks.

Run a thin knife around edge of 1 meringue layer and carefully invert it onto a rack. Discard paper and reinvert meringue onto a serving plate. Spread with whipped cream, leaving a ½-inch border all around. Invert remaining meringue carefully onto whipped cream; discard paper. Pat layers into a cake shape as much as possible. (Layers will be cracked and crumbly.)

Puree strawberries (see Cook's Note) with remaining ¼ cup sugar and lemon juice (to taste) in a food processor. Force through a fine-mesh sieve into a bowl.

Cut cake into wedges and spoon strawberry sauce over it.

COOK'S NOTE
- Instead of strawberry sauce, the cake can be served with sliced strawberries tossed with a little sugar and fresh lemon juice.

Fresh Coconut Layer Cake

SERVES 8 TO 10
ACTIVE TIME: 1¼ HOURS ■ START TO FINISH: 4 HOURS
(INCLUDES COOLING)

■ A towering white coconut cake is the quintessential Southern layer cake. This version is both breathtaking and delicious. Brushing each layer with a syrup made from coconut water and sugar syrup ensures that each bite is incredibly moist, and the fresh coconut lends a delicate flavor that is much finer than what you'd get from the packaged kind. ■

CRISP MERINGUES

Meringue layers or shells combine shattering crispness with melt-in-your-mouth tenderness. Here are some tips for success.

- ■ USE A SPOTLESSLY CLEAN BOWL AND BEATERS. Even a trace of fat—from an oily residue or a drop of egg yolk, for instance—will ruin an egg white foam.

- ■ SEPARATE THE EGGS WHEN COLD, then bring to room temperature. If you let the whole eggs come to room temperature before separating them, the yolks will be more fragile and thus more liable to break.

- ■ INCORPORATE THE SUGAR GRADUALLY INTO THE BEATEN WHITES so it has a chance to dissolve. If you put too much in at once, it will weigh the whites down, and you won't get the volume you're after.

- ■ AVOID MAKING MERINGUES ON A RAINY OR HUMID DAY, and don't let them stand before baking. Meringues are high in sugar, and because sugar absorbs moisture from the atmosphere, they can take longer to bake to the desired crispness if allowed to stand.

FOR COCONUT

2 (1½-pound) coconuts (see Cook's Note)
¼ cup sugar
Pinch of salt

FOR CAKE LAYERS

3⅓ cups sifted cake flour (not self-rising; sift before measuring)
1 tablespoon baking powder
1 teaspoon salt
1½ cups whole milk
1½ teaspoons vanilla extract
¾ teaspoon almond extract
2½ sticks (10 ounces) unsalted butter, softened
1¾ cups sugar
7 large egg whites, left at room temperature for 30 minutes

FOR FROSTING AND FILLING

3 large egg whites, left at room temperature for 30 minutes
2¼ cups sugar
¾ cup water
1½ tablespoons light corn syrup
½ teaspoon cream of tartar
¾ teaspoon salt
1 teaspoon vanilla extract

SPECIAL EQUIPMENT: three 9-by-2-inch round cake pans; parchment paper

PREPARE THE COCONUT: Put racks in upper and lower thirds of oven and preheat oven to 350°F.

Pierce softest eye of each coconut with a small screwdriver and collect liquid in two separate bowls. Taste it, and if either one tastes rancid, discard that coconut and liquid. Pour liquid from 2 coconuts through a dampened-paper-towel-lined sieve into a 1-cup measure (you should have about ¾ cup liquid; if not, add water to make ¾ cup). Set coconuts aside.

Combine coconut water, sugar, and salt in a small saucepan and bring to a simmer, stirring until sugar is dissolved. Remove from heat and let syrup cool.

Bake coconuts on lower oven rack for 15 minutes. Remove from oven. (Leave oven on.)

Break coconut shells with a hammer and remove flesh with a butter knife, prying it out carefully. Peel brown skin from flesh with a vegetable peeler. Coarsely grate enough coconut on large holes of a box grater to measure 5 cups; reserve any remaining coconut for another use.

MAKE THE CAKE: Butter cake pans, line bottom of each with a round of parchment paper, and butter paper. Flour pans, knocking out excess.

Sift together flour, baking powder, and salt. Stir together milk and extracts in a small bowl.

Beat butter and 1½ cups sugar in a large bowl with an electric mixer (fitted with paddle attachment if using a stand mixer) at medium speed until pale and fluffy, 2 to 3 minutes. At low speed, add flour mixture in 3 batches alternately with milk mixture, beginning and ending with flour mixture and mixing until just incorporated.

Beat egg whites in another large bowl with cleaned beaters (or whisk attachment) at medium speed until they just hold soft peaks. Beat in remaining ¼ cup sugar 1 tablespoon at a time and continue to beat until whites just hold stiff, glossy peaks. Stir one third of whites into batter to lighten it, then fold in remaining whites gently but thoroughly.

Divide batter among pans, spreading it evenly, and rap pans on counter several times to eliminate air bubbles. Put two pans on upper oven rack and one pan on lower rack and bake for 20 minutes. Switch position of pans and bake until tops are golden and a wooden toothpick inserted in center of each cake comes out clean, 10 to 15 minutes more. Cool cakes in pans on racks for 5 minutes.

Run a thin knife around sides of pans and invert cakes onto racks; discard paper. Cool completely.

MAKE THE FROSTING AND FILLING: Beat together egg whites, sugar, water, corn syrup, cream of tartar, and salt in a large deep metal bowl with a handheld mixer until combined. Set bowl over a pot of simmering water and beat mixture at high speed until it holds stiff, glossy peaks, 5 to 7 minutes. (Humid weather may require additional beating time.) Remove bowl from heat, add vanilla, and beat until frosting has cooled and is very thick, 6 to 10 minutes.

Transfer 2⅓ cups frosting to a bowl and stir in 2 cups coconut to make filling.

ASSEMBLE THE CAKE: Put 1 cake layer on a cake stand or large plate, rounded side down. Brush top with one third of coconut syrup and spread with half of coconut filling. Repeat with another layer, more syrup, and remaining coconut filling. Top with third layer, rounded side down, and brush top with remaining syrup. Cover top and sides of cake with remaining frosting and coat cake with remaining coconut, gently pressing to help it adhere.

- Coconuts are sometimes rancid—you may want to buy an extra one.
- The egg whites in the frosting may not be fully cooked. If that is a concern, see page 915. Alternatively, substitute pasteurized liquid egg whites or reconstituted powdered egg whites, such as Just Whites.
- The cake layers can be made up to 3 days ahead and refrigerated, wrapped tightly in plastic wrap.
- The cake can be assembled up to 4 hours ahead and kept at room temperature.

CAKE FLOUR VERSUS ALL-PURPOSE FLOUR

Cake flour is made from finely milled low-protein flour that's been strongly bleached with chlorine. The chlorine causes the starch granules in the flour to swell when liquid is added and the fat to bind more easily to the starch. The result is a thicker batter and a fine-crumbed cake with maximum volume; cake flour is ideal for ultrawhite angel food cakes or other white cakes.

Because all-purpose flour is made from a blend of hard-wheat flour, which has a high protein (gluten) content, and soft-wheat flour, which has a lower protein content, a cake made from all-purpose flour will be a bit coarser in texture than one made with cake flour. All-purpose flour is enormously versatile: home bakers rely on it for everything from pastry doughs to breads and cakes. We haven't noticed any appreciable difference between bleached and unbleached flour when it comes to finished baked goods, so we use unbleached.

Both cake flours and all-purpose flours are available in "self-rising" varieties that include measured amounts of salt and baking powder. Because it's not possible to know how old the leavening is in a self-rising flour and because more or less leavening may be needed in a cake depending on the recipe, we usually avoid these.

Ambrosia Layer Cake

SERVES 10 TO 12
ACTIVE TIME: 1 HOUR ■ START TO FINISH: 2 HOURS

■ Ambrosia may sound exotic, but it's simply chilled fruit (typically oranges or bananas) tossed with coco-

nut and sugar. Here, we riff on this Southern classic by bringing four layers of tender yellow cake into the picture, putting orange juice and zest into the filling, and pressing lots of toasted coconut into the frosting. ■

FOR CAKE LAYERS
2¾ cups sifted cake flour (not self-rising; sift before measuring)
2½ teaspoons baking powder
½ teaspoon salt
1½ sticks (12 tablespoons) unsalted butter, softened
1½ cups sugar
4 large eggs, left at room temperature for 30 minutes
1 tablespoon finely grated orange zest
1½ teaspoons vanilla extract
1 cup whole milk

FOR FILLING
2 large eggs
¾ cup sugar
¼ cup cornstarch
Pinch of salt
¾ cup water
½ cup fresh orange juice (from about 1½ oranges; grate zest first)
¼ cup fresh lemon juice
3 tablespoons unsalted butter
2 teaspoons finely grated orange zest

FOR FROSTING
1 (7-ounce) bag (2⅔ cups) sweetened flaked coconut
2 large egg whites
1 cup sugar
¼ cup water
2 teaspoons light corn syrup
Pinch of salt
1 teaspoon vanilla extract
1 teaspoon fresh lemon juice

SPECIAL EQUIPMENT: two 9-by-2-inch round cake pans

MAKE THE CAKE LAYERS: Put a rack in middle of oven and preheat oven to 350°F. Butter and flour cake pans, knocking out excess flour.

Sift together flour, baking powder, and salt.

Beat together butter and sugar in a large bowl with an electric mixer (fitted with paddle attachment if using a stand mixer) at medium-high speed until pale and fluffy, 3 to 5 minutes. Beat in eggs one at a time, beating well after each addition. Beat in zest and vanilla and continue beating for 5 minutes more.

At low speed, add flour mixture and milk alternately in 4 batches, beginning with flour mixture and mixing until batter is just smooth.

Divide batter between cake pans, spreading it evenly. Bake until a wooden toothpick inserted in centers comes out clean and cakes are beginning to pull away from sides of pans, 20 to 25 minutes. Cool for 5 minutes in pans on racks.

Run a thin knife around sides of pans, invert cake layers onto racks, and cool completely. (Leave oven on.)

MEANWHILE, MAKE THE FILLING: Whisk together eggs in a medium heatproof bowl until well combined. Whisk together sugar, cornstarch, and salt in a 1½- to 2-quart heavy saucepan, then whisk in water and juices until smooth. Bring to a boil over moderate heat, whisking, then reduce heat and cook at a bare simmer, whisking constantly, for 2 minutes (mixture will be thick).

Add half of hot juice mixture to eggs in a slow stream, whisking. Whisk egg mixture into juice in saucepan and cook over moderately low heat, whisking, just until it reaches a boil. Remove pan from heat and add butter and zest, whisking until butter is melted.

Refrigerate filling, its surface covered with a buttered round of wax paper (buttered side down), until cold, about 30 minutes.

MAKE THE FROSTING: Spread coconut on a baking sheet and toast in oven, stirring occasionally, until golden, 12 to 15 minutes. Set aside to cool.

Beat together egg whites, sugar, water, corn syrup, and salt in a large metal bowl with a handheld electric mixer until combined. Set bowl over a saucepan of simmering water and beat mixture at high speed until it holds stiff, glossy peaks, 5 to 7 minutes. (Humid weather may require additional beating time.) Remove bowl from heat, add vanilla and lemon juice, and continue beating until frosting is cooled and very thick, 6 to 10 minutes.

ASSEMBLE THE CAKE: Halve each cake horizontally with a long serrated knife (see page 747). Put 1 layer cut side up on a cake stand or large plate. Spread with about ¾ cup filling. Stack a second cake layer over filling, cut side down. Spread with about ¾ cup filling. Top with third layer, cut side up, and spread with remaining filling. Top with remaining cake layer, cut side down. Spread top and sides of cake with frosting and coat cake with coconut, pressing gently to help it adhere.

COOK'S NOTES

- The cake layers (not split) can be made up to 3 days ahead and refrigerated, tightly wrapped in plastic wrap.
- The filling can be refrigerated for up to 8 hours. Stir before using.
- The frosting can be made up to 4 hours ahead and refrigerated, covered.
- The cake can be assembled up to 2 hours ahead.

Apricot Almond Layer Cake

SERVES 6
ACTIVE TIME: 45 MINUTES ■ START TO FINISH: 2½ HOURS
(INCLUDES COOLING)

■ The crisp tiers of this magnificent almond macaroon cake are a fabulous foil to the amaretto-tinged mascarpone and tangy apricot compote. California dried apricots (rather than Turkish varieties, which are sometimes labeled "Mediterranean") are essential—they have the tartness needed to balance the sweet filling and macaroon layers. Don't assemble the cake ahead of time, or the macaroon layers will get soggy. ■

FOR MACAROON LAYERS
- ¾ pound sliced blanched almonds (3½ cups) or slivered almonds (3 cups)
- 3⅓ cups confectioners' sugar
- 6 large egg whites
- ¼ teaspoon salt
- 6 tablespoons granulated sugar

FOR APRICOT COMPOTE
- 1½ cups (6 ounces) dried California apricots (see Sources), finely chopped
- 1½ cups water
- 3 tablespoons apricot preserves

FOR PRALINE ALMONDS
- 1 cup (about 3½ ounces) sliced blanched almonds
- ½ cup confectioners' sugar

FOR MASCARPONE CREAM

1½ cups (10 ounces) imported Italian mascarpone cheese

¼ cup very cold heavy cream

¼ cup amaretto or other almond-flavored liqueur

SPECIAL EQUIPMENT: parchment paper

MAKE THE MACAROON LAYERS: Line two baking sheets with parchment paper. Trace two 8-inch circles on one sheet of paper and a third circle on second sheet, then turn sheets over.

Pulse almonds with 1⅓ cups confectioners' sugar in a food processor until very finely ground (mixture should resemble sand), 2 to 3 minutes. Transfer to a large bowl and sift in remaining 2 cups confectioners' sugar. Stir until well combined.

Beat egg whites with salt in a large bowl with an electric mixer (fitted with whisk attachment if using a stand mixer) at medium speed until they just hold soft peaks. Beat in granulated sugar a little at a time, then increase speed to high and continue to beat until whites hold stiff, glossy peaks, about 3 minutes.

Gently stir whites into almond mixture until completely incorporated (batter will be thick). Divide batter evenly among traced circles on baking sheets (about 1⅔ cups per circle), smoothing it into ⅛-inch-thick rounds. Let rounds stand, uncovered, at room temperature until tops are no longer sticky and a light crust forms, about 30 minutes.

Put racks in upper and lower thirds of oven and preheat oven to 300°F.

Bake macaroon layers, switching position of baking sheets halfway through baking, until macaroons are crisp and edges are just barely pale golden, about 25 minutes. Turn off oven and let macaroons stand in oven for 10 minutes.

Cool macaroons completely on baking sheets on racks.

MEANWHILE, MAKE THE COMPOTE: Combine dried apricots and water in a 2- to 3-quart heavy saucepan, bring to a simmer over moderate heat, and simmer, uncovered, stirring occasionally, until apricots are very soft and most of liquid has evaporated, about 15 minutes. Stir in preserves, remove from heat, and cool completely.

MAKE THE PRALINE ALMONDS: Put a large sheet of foil on countertop. Heat almonds in a 12-inch dry heavy skillet over moderate heat, stirring frequently, until they are hot but not colored, about 2 minutes. Add confectioners' sugar and cook, stirring and tossing, until almonds are lightly toasted and sugar glaze is caramelized, about 3 minutes.

Immediately transfer almonds to foil and spread into one layer with a fork. Cool completely.

JUST BEFORE SERVING, MAKE THE MASCARPONE CREAM: Beat together mascarpone, cream, and amaretto in a large bowl (fitted with whisk attachment if using stand mixer) at medium speed until thick and smooth, about 2 minutes. Reserve ¼ cup praline almonds and fold remainder into cream.

ASSEMBLE THE CAKE: Put 1 macaroon layer on a platter and spread with one third of apricot compote (about ½ cup), then spread one quarter of mascarpone cream (about ¾ cup) on top. Make another layer with second macaroon in same manner. Top with remaining macaroon, remaining compote, and remaining cream. Sprinkle with reserved praline almonds.

COOK'S NOTES

- The macaroon layers can be made up to 2 days ahead and kept in an airtight container, layered between sheets of parchment paper, at room temperature.

- The apricot compote can be made up to 5 days ahead and refrigerated, covered.

- The praline almonds can be made up to 1 week ahead and kept in an airtight container at room temperature.

Opera Cake

SERVES 6 TO 8
ACTIVE TIME: 2 HOURS ■ START TO FINISH: 3½ HOURS
(INCLUDES CHILLING)

■ It's impossible to say whether the *gâteau Opéra*, sometimes known as Clichy cake, is more famous for its decadent appearance or its incredible taste, but it is one showstopping dessert. The low cake's unfrosted sides reveal stripes of almond sponge cake soaked with Cognac-spiked espresso syrup and layered with smooth coffee buttercream and rich bittersweet chocolate ganache. A layer of glossy ganache, spread over a thin coat of buttercream, crowns the affair. Many believe that Louis Clichy was the cake's creator, because he premiered it, with his name written across the top, at the 1903 Exposition Culinaire in Paris, and it became the signature dessert at his shop on Boulevard Beaumarchais. Another pastry shop, Dalloyau, sold a similar cake, known as L'Opéra, in honor of the Paris Opera, which some claim was the original. Whatever you call it, your guests will be mightily impressed. ■

FOR SPONGE CAKE

- 2 large eggs, left at room temperature for 30 minutes
- 1 cup (3½ ounces) almond flour or ⅔ cup blanched whole almonds (see Cook's Note)
- ½ cup confectioners' sugar, sifted
- 3 tablespoons cake flour (not self-rising), sifted
- 2 large egg whites, left at room temperature for 30 minutes
- ⅛ teaspoon cream of tartar
- ⅛ teaspoon salt
- 1 tablespoon granulated sugar
- 2 tablespoons unsalted butter, melted, foam discarded, and cooled

FOR COFFEE SYRUP

- 1 teaspoon instant espresso powder, such as Medaglia d'Oro
- ½ cup plus 1 tablespoon water
- ½ cup granulated sugar
- ¼ cup Cognac or other brandy

FOR BUTTERCREAM

- 2 teaspoons instant espresso powder, such as Medaglia d'Oro
- 5 tablespoons water
- 6 tablespoons granulated sugar
- 2 large egg yolks
- 1 stick (8 tablespoons) unsalted butter, cut into ½-inch cubes, softened

FOR CHOCOLATE GLAZE

- ¾ stick (6 tablespoons) unsalted butter
- 7 ounces bittersweet chocolate (preferably 70% cacao; see page 705), coarsely chopped

SPECIAL EQUIPMENT: a 15-by-10-by-1-inch baking sheet (jelly-roll pan); parchment paper; a candy thermometer; a small sealable plastic bag

MAKE THE SPONGE CAKE: Put a rack in middle of oven and preheat oven to 425°F. Butter baking sheet and line bottom with a sheet of parchment paper, leaving a 1-inch overhang on short sides. Generously butter paper. Dust pan with cake flour, knocking out excess.

Beat whole eggs in a large bowl with an electric mixer (fitted with whisk attachment if using a stand mixer) at high speed until eggs are pale, have tripled in volume, and form a ribbon when beaters are lifted, 2 to 3 minutes. Reduce speed to low, add almond flour and confectioners' sugar, and mix until just combined. Transfer mixture to a wide shallow bowl, sift cake flour over batter, and gently fold in.

Beat egg whites in a medium bowl with cleaned beaters (or whisk attachment) at medium speed until foamy. Add cream of tartar and salt and beat until whites just hold soft peaks. Slowly add granulated sugar, increase speed to high, and beat until whites just hold stiff peaks. Fold one third of whites into almond mixture to lighten it, then fold in remaining whites gently but thoroughly. Fold in butter.

Pour batter evenly into baking sheet, spreading it gently with an offset spatula or a rubber spatula, being careful not to deflate it (batter will be only about ¼ inch thick). Bake until very pale golden, 8 to 10 minutes. Cool in pan on a rack for 10 minutes.

Run a thin knife around edges of pan, then carefully slide cake, on paper, using ends of parchment as handles, to a cutting board. Cut cake crosswise in half, cutting though paper lining. Cut off a 3¼-inch-wide strip from the bottom of each half so you have 2 roughly 7-inch squares and 2 roughly 3-by-7-inch rectangles (opposite page). Trim outside edges slightly. Carefully peel paper from strips and squares and set cake back on paper.

MAKE THE COFFEE SYRUP: Stir together espresso powder and 1 tablespoon water in a small cup until espresso powder is dissolved.

Bring sugar and remaining ½ cup water to a boil in a 1- to 2-quart heavy saucepan, stirring until sugar is dissolved. Reduce heat and simmer, without stirring, for 5 minutes. Remove syrup from heat and stir in Cognac and coffee mixture.

MAKE THE BUTTERCREAM: Stir together espresso powder and 1 tablespoon water in a small cup until espresso powder is dissolved.

Bring sugar and remaining ¼ cup water to a boil in a small heavy saucepan, stirring until sugar is dissolved. Boil, without stirring, washing down any sugar crystals on sides of pan with a pastry brush dipped in cold water, until syrup registers 238°F on thermometer.

Meanwhile, beat yolks in a large bowl with electric mixer (fitted with whisk if using stand mixer) at medium speed for 1 minute.

Add hot syrup to yolks in a slow stream (avoiding beaters and side of bowl), beating. Add coffee mixture and beat until completely cool, 3 to 5 minutes. Beat in butter one piece at a time, then beat until buttercream is thickened and smooth.

MAKE THE GLAZE: Reserve 2 tablespoons chopped chocolate. Melt butter and remaining chocolate in a metal bowl set over a saucepan of barely simmering water, stirring occasionally until smooth. Remove bowl and stir in reserved 2 tablespoons chocolate until smooth. Cool glaze to room temperature; it should still be liquid.

ASSEMBLE THE CAKE: Put 1 cake square on a plate and brush generously with one third of coffee syrup. Spread half of buttercream evenly over top, preferably with an offset spatula, spreading it to edges. Arrange cake strips side by side on top of first layer (the seam will be covered by next layer) and brush with half of remaining coffee syrup. Spread half of glaze evenly over top, spreading it just to edges. Top with remaining cake square and brush with remaining coffee syrup. Spread remaining buttercream evenly over top, spreading it just to edges. Refrigerate cake until buttercream is firm, about 30 minutes.

Reheat remaining glaze over barely simmering water just until shiny and spreadable but not warm to the touch, about 1 minute. Pour all but 1 tablespoon glaze over top of cake and spread evenly just to edges. Scrape remaining tablespoon glaze into sealable plastic bag and twist bag so glaze is in one bottom corner. Snip a tiny hole in corner and decorate cake with a design or written message (leave a ½-inch border around edges). Refrigerate cake until glaze is set, about 30 minutes. Trim edges of cake slightly with a sharp serrated knife to even them.

COOK'S NOTES

■ If you can't find almond flour, you can pulse whole almonds with the confectioners' sugar in a food processor until powdery (be careful not to grind to a paste).

■ The cake can be made up to 2 days ahead. Cover the sides with strips of plastic wrap and cover the top loosely with plastic wrap, once the glaze is set, and

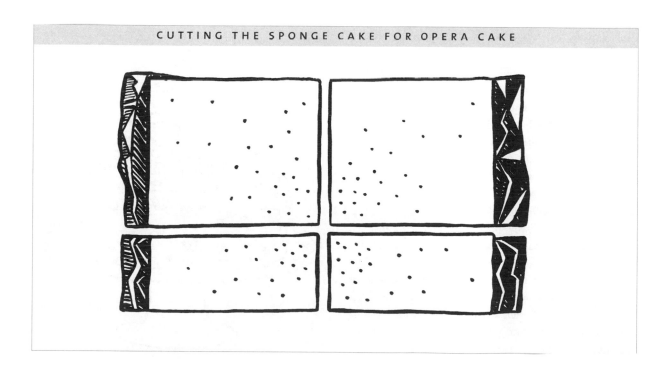

CUTTING THE SPONGE CAKE FOR OPERA CAKE

refrigerate the cake. Remove the plastic wrap from the top as soon as you remove the cake from the refrigerator and bring the cake to room temperature, 30 minutes to 1 hour.

Chocolate Cake with Mini Cupcakes and Vanilla Buttercream

SERVES 10 TO 14
ACTIVE TIME: 1 HOUR ■ START TO FINISH: 3 HOURS
(INCLUDES MAKING BUTTERCREAM BUT NOT CUPCAKES)

■ This layer cake's moist crumb, deep chocolaty flavor, and rich buttercream will win everyone over, but its festive good looks—including a mile-high pyramid of gaily decorated miniature cupcakes—will make kids stop dead in their tracks. And isn't that exactly what a great birthday cake should do? We like to frost the cupcakes in lots of different colors and then decorate the cake with polka dots using the leftover frostings, a look that is very easy to achieve using a couple of sealable plastic bags. ■

 1 cup boiling water
 ¾ cup unsweetened cocoa powder
 ½ cup whole milk
 1 teaspoon vanilla extract
 2 cups all-purpose flour
 1½ teaspoons baking soda
   Rounded ½ teaspoon salt
 2 sticks (½ pound) unsalted butter, softened
 2 cups packed dark brown sugar
 4 large eggs, left at room temperature for 30 minutes
 6 cups Vanilla Buttercream (recipe follows)
   Various food colorings
GARNISH: Vanilla Mini Cupcakes (page 741)
SPECIAL EQUIPMENT: two 9-by-2-inch round cake pans; parchment paper; small sealable plastic bags

MAKE THE CAKE LAYERS: Put a rack in middle of oven and preheat oven to 350°F. Butter cake pans and line bottom of each with a round of parchment paper. Butter paper and dust pans with flour, knocking out excess.

Whisk together boiling water and cocoa powder in a bowl until smooth, then whisk in milk and vanilla.

Whisk together flour, baking soda, and salt in another bowl.

Beat together butter and brown sugar in a large bowl with an electric mixer (fitted with paddle attachment if using a stand mixer) at medium-high speed until pale and fluffy, 3 to 5 minutes. Add eggs one at a time, beating well after each addition. Reduce speed to low and add flour and cocoa mixtures alternately in 3 batches, beginning and ending with flour mixture (batter may look curdled).

Divide batter between cake pans, smoothing tops. Bake until a wooden toothpick inserted in centers comes out clean and cakes are beginning to pull away from sides of pans, 25 to 35 minutes. Cool layers in pans on racks for 10 minutes.

Run a thin knife around sides of pans and invert cakes onto racks. Discard paper and cool completely.

ASSEMBLE THE CAKE: Put 1 cake layer rounded side up on a cake stand or platter and spread top with about 1 cup buttercream. Top with remaining cake layer, rounded side down, and frost sides and top of cake with 2 cups buttercream.

FROST THE CUPCAKES AND DECORATE THE CAKE: Divide remaining 3 cups buttercream among several small bowls (up to five) and tint with food coloring.

Frost cupcakes with buttercream. Transfer each color of remaining buttercream to a bag, pressing out excess air, then snip off one corner of each plastic bag to create a ¼-inch opening. Twist each bag firmly just above buttercream and pipe buttercream decoratively onto cake, making polka dots. Refrigerate cake and cupcakes until buttercream is set, about 30 minutes. Bring cake to room temperature before serving.

Just before serving, arrange 6 to 8 mini cupcakes on top of cake in one layer, and stack remaining cupcakes on top.

COOK'S NOTES

- The cake layers can be made up to 2 days ahead and kept, tightly wrapped in plastic wrap, at room temperature. They can also be frozen for up to 2 weeks.
- The cake can be assembled up to 4 hours ahead and kept at cool room temperature.

Vanilla Buttercream

MAKES ABOUT 6 CUPS
ACTIVE TIME: 30 MINUTES ■ START TO FINISH: 1 HOUR

■ Vanilla buttercream dresses up any cake, but this phenomenal no-fail frosting goes especially well with chocolate birthday cake. ■

   4 large egg whites, left at room temperature
      for 30 minutes
      Rounded ¼ teaspoon salt
  ⅔ cup water
1⅓ cups plus 2 tablespoons sugar
   4 sticks (1 pound) unsalted butter, cut into
      tablespoons, softened
   2 teaspoons vanilla extract

SPECIAL EQUIPMENT: a candy thermometer

Combine whites and salt in a large bowl (or mixer bowl).

Stir together water and 1⅓ cups sugar in a 3- to 4-quart heavy saucepan until sugar is dissolved. Bring to a boil over moderate heat, without stirring, brushing down any sugar crystals on sides of pan with a pastry brush dipped in water.

When syrup reaches a boil, start beating egg whites with an electric mixer (fitted with whisk attachment if using stand mixer) at medium-high speed until frothy. Gradually add remaining 2 tablespoons sugar and beat at medium speed until whites just hold soft peaks. (Do not beat again until sugar syrup is ready.)

Meanwhile, put thermometer into sugar syrup and continue boiling until syrup registers 238° to 242°F. Immediately remove from heat.

With mixer at high speed, slowly pour hot syrup in a thin stream down side of bowl into whites, beating constantly, then continue to beat meringue, scraping down sides of bowl with a rubber spatula as necessary, until cool to the touch, about 10 minutes in a stand mixer, 15 with a handheld. It's important to cool meringue before proceeding.

With mixer at medium speed, add butter one piece at a time, beating until incorporated after each addition. (If meringue is too warm and buttercream looks soupy after some of butter is added, chill bottom of bowl in a larger bowl filled with ice and cold water for a few seconds, then beat in remaining butter.) Continue beating until buttercream is smooth. (Mixture may look curdled before all of butter is added, but it will come back together before beating is finished.) Add vanilla and beat for 1 minute more.

COOK'S NOTES

- The egg whites in this recipe are not cooked. If that is a concern, see page 915. Alternatively, substitute pasteurized liquid egg whites or reconstituted powdered egg whites, such as Just Whites.
- The buttercream can be made up to 1 week ahead and refrigerated, covered. It can also be frozen in an airtight container for up to 1 month. Bring to room temperature (this may take up to 3 hours; do not microwave) and beat with an electric mixer until smooth before using.

Ice Cream Cone Cake

SERVES 20
ACTIVE TIME: 3 HOURS ■ START TO FINISH: 4½ HOURS

■ This fantasy dessert will produce cries of joy from kids and adults alike—and that's before they take a bite. A dozen trompe-l'oeil soft-serve ice cream cones encircle a tall, golden, buttery layer cake frosted with vanilla buttercream. The ice cream cones are actually cupcakes baked in store-bought crisp wafer cones, then halved lengthwise, attached to the sides of the cake, and crowned with swirls of vanilla and chocolate frosting. Some guests will go straight for the cones, while others will beg for cake, especially when they see that the layers are bound with vanilla buttercream mixed with crushed chocolate cookies. Think cookies and cream, and you get the idea. ■

FOR CAKE AND CONES

- 3 cups all-purpose flour
- 1 tablespoon baking powder
- 1¾ teaspoons salt
- 3 sticks (¾ pound) unsalted butter, softened
- 1¾ cups sugar
- 4 large eggs, left at room temperature for 30 minutes
- 1½ teaspoons vanilla extract
- 1½ cups whole milk
- 7 flat-bottomed wafer cones

FOR CUSTARD BUTTERCREAM

- 1½ cups whole milk
- 9 large egg yolks
- ¾ cup sugar
- ¼ teaspoon salt
- 3½ ounces bittersweet chocolate, chopped
- 6 sticks (1½ pounds) unsalted butter, softened
- 1 tablespoon vanilla extract
- 2 cups coarsely crushed chocolate wafers (28 small cookies)

SPECIAL EQUIPMENT: two 8-by-2-inch round cake pans; parchment paper; a 12-cup muffin pan; an instant-read thermometer; 2 small sealable plastic bags; a large pastry bag fitted with ⅓-inch star tip, such as Ateco 824

MAKE THE CAKE AND CONES: Put racks in upper and lower thirds of oven and preheat oven to 350°F. Butter cake pans and line bottoms with rounds of parchment paper, then butter and flour pans, knocking out excess flour.

Sift together flour, baking powder, and salt.

Beat together butter and sugar with an electric mixer (fitted with paddle attachment if using a stand mixer) at medium-high speed until pale and fluffy, about 5 minutes in a stand mixer, 10 with a handheld. Add eggs one at a time, beating well after each addition, then add vanilla and beat until thoroughly incorporated, about 5 minutes. At low speed, add flour mixture in 4 batches alternately with milk, beginning and ending with flour mixture and mixing just until batter is smooth.

Stand cones up in muffin pan and fill cones two-thirds full with batter. Divide remaining batter between cake pans.

Bake cones in upper third of oven and cakes in lower third until a wooden toothpick inserted in center of cake comes out clean, 15 to 22 minutes for cones, 25 to 35 minutes for cakes. Cool cones completely on a rack. Cool cakes for 5 minutes in pans on a rack, then run a thin knife around edges of pans, invert cakes onto rack, and cool completely.

MAKE THE BUTTERCREAM: Bring milk just to a boil in a medium saucepan.

Meanwhile, whisk together yolks, sugar, and salt in a bowl until well combined. Add milk to yolks in a slow stream, whisking constantly. Return mixture to saucepan and cook over medium-low heat, stirring constantly with a wooden spoon, until custard is thickened and registers 175°F on thermometer, 5 to 10 minutes; do not let boil.

Strain custard through a fine-mesh sieve into a heatproof bowl. Refrigerate, covered, until cold, at least 1 hour (see Cook's Note).

Melt chocolate in a medium metal bowl set over a saucepan of barely simmering water, stirring until smooth. Remove bowl from heat and cool to warm.

Beat butter with electric mixer (fitted with whisk attachment if using stand mixer) at high speed until light and fluffy, about 2 minutes in a stand mixer, 4 minutes with a handheld. Reduce speed to medium and gradually beat in cold custard. Add vanilla, increase speed to high, and beat until buttercream is smooth, about 2 minutes in a stand mixer, 4 with a handheld.

To make chocolate buttercream, transfer 1¼ cups buttercream to a bowl and stir in warm melted chocolate. To make cookies-and-cream filling, transfer 2 cups buttercream to another bowl and fold in cookies.

ASSEMBLE THE CAKE: Halve cakes horizontally with a long serrated knife (see page 747). Put 1 cake layer cut side up on a cake stand or plate. Spread top with 1 cup cookies-and-cream buttercream. Top with another cake layer, cut side down, and spread with 1 cup cookies-and-cream buttercream. Top with another cake layer, cut side up, and spread with remaining cookies-and-cream buttercream. Top with remaining cake layer, cut side down. Spread sides and top of cake with about 2½ cups vanilla buttercream.

Spoon chocolate buttercream into a small sealable plastic bag. Spoon remaining vanilla buttercream into another small sealable plastic bag. Snip ½ inch from a bottom corner of each bag, then put both bags into pastry bag.

Halve each ice cream cone lengthwise with serrated knife. Press flat sides of cones against sides of cake to attach them, with top edges of cones touching (there is an extra cone in case one gets damaged). Holding pastry bag vertically, pipe about 2 tablespoons buttercream on top of each cone (touching top of cake) to resemble soft-serve ice cream.

COOK'S NOTES

- The cake and cones can be baked up to 1 day ahead and kept, wrapped in plastic wrap, at room temperature.
- To quick-chill the custard for the buttercream, set the bowl in a larger bowl of ice and cold water and stir until cold, about 5 minutes.
- The buttercream, without the chocolate and cookies, can be made up to 2 days ahead and refrigerated, covered. Bring to room temperature and beat before using.

Mascarpone Cheesecake

SERVES 10 TO 12
ACTIVE TIME: 30 MINUTES ■ START TO FINISH: 12 HOURS
(INCLUDES CHILLING)

■ This cheesecake manages to be both ultra-creamy and deceptively light, and it owes it all to mascarpone, the thick, buttery cow's-milk cream cheese that originated in Italy's Lombardy region. A topping of sour cream adds a slight tang, but the overall effect is of gentle sweetness. We have the restaurant Syrah in Santa Rosa, California, to thank for this marvelous recipe. ■

FOR CRUST
8½ ounces vanilla wafers (70 cookies), finely ground in a
    food processor (2⅓ cups)
1 stick (8 tablespoons) unsalted butter, melted and
    cooled
FOR FILLING
2½ (8-ounce) packages cream cheese, softened
1 cup (8 ounces) imported Italian mascarpone cheese,
    at room temperature
¾ cup sugar
3 large eggs
1 teaspoon vanilla extract
1 teaspoon fresh lemon juice
¼ teaspoon salt
FOR TOPPING
1 cup sour cream
¼ cup sugar
1 teaspoon vanilla extract
1 teaspoon fresh lemon juice
⅛ teaspoon salt
SPECIAL EQUIPMENT: a 9-inch springform pan

MAKE THE CRUST: Put a rack in middle of oven and preheat oven to 350°F. Invert bottom of springform pan (to make it easier to slide cake off bottom), then lock on side. Butter bottom and side of pan.

Stir together cookie crumbs and butter in a bowl. Reserve ¼ cup crumb mixture for sprinkling over cheesecake. Pat remainder onto bottom and 1½ inches up side of springform pan (about ⅛ inch thick). Bake crust until golden, about 10 minutes. Transfer to a rack to cool completely. (Leave oven on.)

MEANWHILE, MAKE THE FILLING: Beat cream cheese, mascarpone, and sugar in a large bowl with an electric mixer (fitted with paddle attachment if using a stand mixer) at medium-high speed until fluffy, 3 to 5 minutes. Add eggs one at a time, beating well after each addition. Add vanilla, lemon juice, and salt and mix at low speed until combined.

Pour filling into cooled crust. Bake until cake is set and puffed around edges but still trembles slightly when pan is shaken gently, 25 to 30 minutes (cheesecake will continue to set as it cools). Cool slightly in springform pan on rack for 20 minutes. (Leave oven on.)

MAKE THE TOPPING: Stir together sour cream, sugar, vanilla, lemon juice, and salt in a small bowl. Spoon topping over cheesecake, spreading gently and evenly, leaving a ¼-inch border all around. Bake until topping is set, about 10 minutes. Run a thin knife around edges of cheesecake to help prevent cracking. Sprinkle top with reserved crumbs and cool completely in pan on rack.

Refrigerate cheesecake, loosely covered, for at least 8 hours before serving.

COOK'S NOTES

- The cheesecake can be refrigerated, loosely covered, for up to 3 days.
- Cut the cake with a long thin sharp knife dipped in a tall glass of hot water and wiped dry.

Sour Cherry Cheesecake

SERVES 8 TO 10
ACTIVE TIME: 30 MINUTES ■ START TO FINISH: 6½ HOURS
(INCLUDES CHILLING)

■ Cherry cheesecakes look seductive. Too bad that one bite often breaks the spell—many are loaded with cloying, gooey canned cherries. This one tastes as good as it looks. The sour cherry topping is held together with just a smidgen of gelatin, and its tang acts as a wonderful counterpoint to the cheesecake's cool creaminess. Fresh and frozen sour cherries work equally well in this recipe. ■

FOR CRUST
- 1⅓ cups graham cracker crumbs (from ten 4¾-by-2¼-inch crackers)
- ¼ cup sugar
- 5 tablespoons unsalted butter, melted

FOR FILLING
- 3 (8-ounce) packages cream cheese, softened
- ¾ cup sugar
- 3 large eggs
- 1 teaspoon vanilla extract
- 1½ teaspoons finely grated lemon zest

FOR CHERRY TOPPING
- 1 teaspoon unflavored gelatin
- 1 tablespoon water
- 3 cups pitted sour cherries (1 pound), not thawed if frozen (see Sources)
- ⅓ cup sugar
- 1 tablespoon fresh lemon juice

SPECIAL EQUIPMENT: a 9-inch springform pan

MAKE THE CRUST: Put a rack in middle of oven and preheat oven to 350°F. Invert bottom of springform pan (to make it easier to slide cake off bottom), then lock on side.

Stir together crust ingredients in a bowl and press onto bottom and 1 inch up side of pan. Put springform pan in a baking pan and bake crust for 10 minutes.

Transfer springform pan to a rack to cool completely. Reduce oven temperature to 300°F.

MAKE THE FILLING AND BAKE THE CAKE: Beat together cream cheese and sugar in a large bowl with an electric mixer (fitted with paddle attachment if using a stand mixer) at medium speed until smooth. Scrape down sides and bottom of bowl. Reduce speed to low and add eggs one at a time, mixing well after each addition. Scrape down sides and bottom of bowl and mix in vanilla and zest until combined.

Pour filling into crust, smoothing top. Put springform pan back in baking pan and bake until cake is set 2 inches from edges but center trembles slightly when pan is gently shaken, about 50 minutes (cheesecake will continue to set as it cools). Transfer springform pan to a rack and immediately run a thin knife around edges of cake to loosen it and prevent cracking. Cool completely.

MEANWHILE, MAKE THE TOPPING: Sprinkle gelatin over water in a small bowl and let stand for about 1 minute to soften.

Bring cherries and sugar to a simmer in a 2-quart heavy saucepan, stirring until sugar is dissolved. Remove pan from heat and stir in softened gelatin until it is dissolved, then stir in lemon juice. Set pan in a large bowl of ice and cold water and let stand, stirring every 5 to 10 minutes, until gelatin begins to set, 40 to 45 minutes.

Spread topping evenly over cake and refrigerate, loosely covered, for at least 3 hours.

Run a knife around side of pan and remove side.

SOUR CHERRIES

Sour, or tart, cherries aren't as common as sweet varieties at farmers markets; being more perishable, they're most often frozen, dried, or canned right after harvest. For this cheesecake, you can use fresh cherries or IQF (Individually Quick Frozen) cherries, which are available at supermarkets, natural food stores, or by mail-order (see Sources). If you're lucky enough to have a surfeit of fresh ones, you can freeze them yourself. Pit them (they're softer than sweet cherries, so you can simply squeeze out the pits) and freeze in a single layer on trays lined with paper towels to absorb any juice. Once they're hard, double-bag them in sealable freezer bags and put them in the coldest part of your freezer. Next winter, celebrate George Washington's birthday with a pie or make a sauce for pork, lamb, or venison.

Transfer cake to a serving plate and bring to room temperature (about 1 hour) before serving.

COOK'S NOTE
■ The cheesecake can be refrigerated, loosely covered with foil, for up to 3 days.

Marbled Lemon Curd Cheesecake

SERVES 10
ACTIVE TIME: 30 MINUTES ■ START TO FINISH: 8 HOURS
(INCLUDES CHILLING)

■ Homemade lemon curd cuts a serpentine swirl through this ultracreamy cheesecake, so you get a bit of jammy lemon flavor with every bite. Expect a line to form when you unveil this stunning dessert. ■

FOR LEMON CURD
- 1 teaspoon finely grated lemon zest
- ½ cup fresh lemon juice (from about 2 lemons)
- ½ cup sugar
- 3 large eggs
- ½ stick (4 tablespoons) unsalted butter, cut into small pieces

FOR CRUST
- 1⅓ cups finely ground graham cracker crumbs (from ten 4¾-by-2¼-inch crackers)
- ⅓ cup sugar
- ⅛ teaspoon salt
- 5 tablespoons unsalted butter, melted

FOR FILLING
- 3 (8-ounce) packages cream cheese, softened
- 1 cup sugar
- 3 large eggs
- ¾ cup sour cream
- 1 teaspoon vanilla extract

ACCOMPANIMENT: blueberries

SPECIAL EQUIPMENT: a 9-inch springform pan

MAKE THE LEMON CURD: Whisk together zest, juice, sugar, and eggs in a 2-quart heavy saucepan. Add butter and cook over moderately low heat, whisking frequently, until curd is thick enough to hold marks of whisk and first bubbles appear on surface, about 6 minutes.

Force lemon curd through a fine-mesh sieve into a wide shallow dish; scrape curd from bottom of sieve into bowl. Cover surface with wax paper to prevent a skin from forming and cool completely, stirring occasionally.

MAKE THE CRUST: Put a rack in middle of oven and preheat oven to 350°F. Invert bottom of springform pan (to make it easier to slide cake off bottom), then lock on side.

Stir together crust ingredients in a bowl, then press onto bottom and 1 inch up side of springform pan. Place springform pan on a baking sheet and bake for 10 minutes. Transfer springform pan to a rack to cool completely. Reduce oven temperature to 300°F.

MAKE THE FILLING AND BAKE THE CHEESECAKE: Beat together cream cheese and sugar in a large bowl with an electric mixer (fitted with paddle attachment if using a stand mixer) at medium speed until smooth, 1 to 2 minutes. At low speed, add eggs one at a time, beating well after each addition. Beat in sour cream and vanilla until combined.

Pour two thirds of cream cheese filling into crust. Spoon half of lemon curd over filling and swirl curd into filling with a small knife. (Avoid touching crust with knife, to prevent crumbs from getting into filling.) Repeat with remaining filling and curd.

Bake cheesecake until filling is set 1½ inches from edges but center trembles when pan is gently shaken, 45 minutes to 1 hour (cheesecake will continue to set as it cools). Transfer springform pan to a rack and immediately run a knife around edges of cake to prevent cracking. Cool completely.

Refrigerate cheesecake, uncovered, for at least 4 hours. Remove side of pan before serving with blueberries.

COOK'S NOTES

■ The lemon curd can be made up to 1 week ahead and refrigerated, covered.

■ The crust can be made up to 1 day ahead and kept, covered, at room temperature.

■ The cheesecake can be refrigerated, loosely covered, for up to 2 days. (Chill the cheesecake completely before covering to prevent condensation on its surface.)

Lemon Vanilla Cheesecake

SERVES 8 TO 10
ACTIVE TIME: 30 MINUTES ■ START TO FINISH: 5 HOURS
(INCLUDES COOLING)

■ This cheesecake makes an indulgent end to a Seder or any springtime celebration. A crumb crust made of toasted almonds and matzo cake meal grounds it in buttery goodness. Fresh lemon zest perfumes the filling and tempers its richness. ■

FOR CRUST
¾ cup sliced blanched almonds, toasted (see Tips, page 911)
⅔ cup sugar
⅔ cup matzo cake meal
⅓ teaspoon salt
1 stick (8 tablespoons) unsalted butter, melted and cooled slightly

FOR FILLING
3 (8-ounce) packages cream cheese, softened
¾ cup sugar
3 large eggs
2 teaspoons grated lemon zest
1 teaspoon vanilla extract

SPECIAL EQUIPMENT: a 9-inch springform pan

MAKE THE CRUST: Put a rack in middle of oven and preheat oven to 350°F. Invert bottom of springform pan (to make it easier to slide cake off bottom), then lock on side.

Pulse almonds with sugar, matzo cake meal, and salt in a food processor until finely ground. Transfer to a bowl and stir in butter until well combined.

Press onto bottom and 1 inch up side of springform pan. Bake until crust is firm and a shade darker, 12 to 15 minutes. Cool crust completely in pan on a rack. Reduce oven temperature to 300°F.

MAKE THE FILLING AND BAKE THE CHEESECAKE: Beat together cream cheese and sugar in a large bowl with an electric mixer (fitted with paddle attachment if using a stand mixer) at medium speed until smooth, 1 to 2 minutes. Reduce speed to low and add eggs one at a time, mixing well after each addition. Mix in zest and vanilla.

Put springform pan in a shallow baking pan and pour filling into cooled crust. Bake until filling is set 1½ inches from edges but center trembles when pan is gently shaken, 45 to 50 minutes (cheesecake will continue to set as it cools). Transfer cake to a rack and immediately run a knife around edges of cake, then remove side of pan. Cool completely before serving.

COOK'S NOTE

- The cheesecake can be made up to 2 days ahead and refrigerated, loosely covered. Bring to room temperature before serving.

Chocolate Orange Cheesecakes

MAKES 12 INDIVIDUAL CAKES
ACTIVE TIME: 35 MINUTES ■ START TO FINISH: 45 MINUTES

■ These bite-sized cheesecakes make happy little treats. The only baking required is the 5 minutes to set the chocolate wafer crumb crusts. A cream cheese filling, perfumed with orange zest, is lightened with whipped cream for a cool, airy contrast to the crisp chocolate shells. Though it's simple enough to spoon the filling into the chocolate shells, taking an extra moment to pipe it in using a pastry bag adds a touch of elegance. ■

½ cup finely ground chocolate wafers, such as Nabisco Famous (12 wafers)
2 tablespoons unsalted butter, softened
⅓ cup packed light brown sugar
4 ounces cream cheese, softened
    Rounded ¼ teaspoon finely grated orange zest
½ cup very cold heavy cream
GARNISH: bittersweet chocolate shavings (made with a vegetable peeler)
SPECIAL EQUIPMENT: a nonstick mini muffin pan with twelve ⅛-cup muffin cups

Put a rack in middle of oven and preheat oven to 350°F. Butter muffin cups.

Mix together wafer crumbs, butter, and 2 tablespoons brown sugar in a bowl with a rubber spatula until well combined. Divide crumbs among muffin cups and firmly press onto bottom and a little up sides of each cup with your fingertips or with bottom of an ⅛-cup measure, twisting measure.

Bake for 5 minutes. Transfer to a rack and cool crusts in muffin pan for 10 minutes. Gently rotate crusts with your fingertips to loosen, and turn out onto rack.

Beat together cream cheese, zest, and remaining brown sugar in a medium bowl with a handheld electric mixer at medium-high speed until fluffy.

Beat cream in another bowl with cleaned beaters until it just holds stiff peaks. Stir about one third of whipped cream into cream cheese mixture to lighten it, then gently fold in remaining whipped cream until just combined.

Mound filling into crusts with a spoon (or pipe filling into crusts with a pastry bag) and serve, or refrigerate, covered, until ready to serve.

Just before serving, top cheesecakes with chocolate shavings.

COOK'S NOTE

- The cheesecakes can be made up to 2 hours ahead.

PIES, TARTS, AND PASTRIES

Nothing makes me happier than baking a pie. It is a seriously sensual activity, and I prefer to do it all by hand so I can feel the butter as it slips and slides, insinuating itself into the softness of the flour. I enjoy flinging the icy drops of water into that dusty mixture, watching as they collect daintily on the surface like little gems. There is always that tiny hesitation before the flour finally gives in, gathers those drops into itself, and absorbs them with the faintest sigh.

I enjoy the slight danger of this operation, the knowledge that one inattentive moment will ruin the crust. Too much water, and it becomes a tough ruffian. Too little, and it cracks and breaks as you attempt to roll it out.

The feeling of the fork in your hand as it gently coaxes the morsels into joining into a cohesive whole is another distinct pleasure. Gathering this ragged mass into a ball, I always stop to appreciate the smooth feel of the dough beneath the palms of my hands as I give it a final massage.

When at last it is time to roll out the dough, there is such pleasure in the way your body leans into the motion, substituting speed and confidence for pressure as these few simple ingredients—flour, shortening, salt, and water—spin themselves into a silken round at the touch of the rolling pin. And, at the end, there is the pure textural delight of the cool, smooth dough beneath your fingers as you place it into the pan and crimp the edges.

Wandering through the market to seek out the finest fillings is delight of a different sort. You never know what you will find. Perhaps there will be gorgeous raspberries, bright with promise, or the sweet, smooth nectarines of summer waiting to surrender their skins. Perhaps the strawberries will be ripe, tasting of gathered sunshine, or the first plump plums of the year will have arrived, bursting with juice.

The pastries here offer as much pleasure as pie, from the complexity of hazelnut Paris-Brest and Sicilian cannoli to the voluptuous joy of a chocolate truffle tart. And if there is a way to have more fun in the kitchen than making peaches-and-cream éclairs with bourbon caramel sauce, I have yet to encounter it.

Unless, of course, it is the ultimate joy of eating the result.

PIES, TARTS, AND PASTRIES

Pies

Rum-Raisin Apple Pie

SERVES 8
ACTIVE TIME: 35 MINUTES ■ START TO FINISH: 4¼ HOURS
(INCLUDES MAKING DOUGH AND COOLING)

■ Raisins steeped in dark rum mingle with apples in this update of an American favorite. Using a combination of sweet and tart apples results in a well-balanced pie. ■

  3 tablespoons dark rum
  ⅓ cup raisins
  ⅔ cup packed light brown sugar
  3 tablespoons all-purpose flour
  1 teaspoon finely grated lemon zest
  ½ teaspoon ground cinnamon
  ⅛ teaspoon freshly grated nutmeg
  ⅛ teaspoon salt
  6 medium apples (2½ pounds), ranging from sweet to tart (see Cook's Note)
    Basic Pastry Dough for a double-crust pie (page 781)
  1 tablespoon unsalted butter, cut into small pieces
    About 2 teaspoons whole milk
  1 tablespoon sanding sugar (see Sources) or granulated sugar

SPECIAL EQUIPMENT: a 9-inch pie plate

Bring rum and raisins to a boil in a 1-quart heavy saucepan. Remove from heat and let stand, covered, for 1 hour.

Put a rack in middle of oven and put a large baking sheet on rack. Preheat oven to 425°F.

Rub together brown sugar, flour, zest, cinnamon, nutmeg, and salt in a large bowl with your fingertips until no lumps remain. Peel and core apples and cut into ½-inch-wide wedges. Add to sugar mixture, tossing gently to coat. Add raisins, with any liquid, and toss until combined.

Roll out larger piece of dough on a lightly floured surface with a lightly floured rolling pin into a 13-inch round (keep remaining piece refrigerated). Fit into

pie plate. Trim edges, leaving a ½-inch overhang. Refrigerate while you roll out dough for top crust.

Roll out remaining piece of dough in same manner into an 11-inch round.

Spoon filling into shell and dot with butter. Brush pastry overhang with some of milk and cover filling with pastry round. Press edges together to seal, then crimp decoratively. Lightly brush top of pie with milk and sprinkle with sanding sugar. Cut 3 steam vents in top crust with a small sharp knife.

Put pie on hot baking sheet and bake for 20 minutes. Reduce oven temperature to 375°F and bake until crust is golden and filling is bubbling, 45 to 50 minutes more.

Cool pie to warm or room temperature on a rack, about 1½ hours.

COOK'S NOTES

■ To achieve an ideal balance of tart and sweet apples, use 2 Golden Delicious or Gala, 2 Winesap or Granny Smith, and 2 McIntosh or Northern Spy.

■ The raisins can be soaked in the rum up to 1 day ahead and, once cooled, kept in an airtight container at room temperature.

■ The pie can be made up to 8 hours ahead and kept, uncovered, at room temperature.

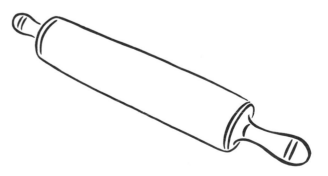

Pie Plates and Tart Pans

Pie plates are made of metal (usually aluminum), heatproof glass, or earthenware. The latter two choices are the nicest for serving; glass is especially convenient because you can (very carefully) look at the bottom crust to gauge doneness.

When choosing a tart pan, opt for one that has a removable bottom (unlike a pie, a tart is never served in the pan, and the loose bottom makes easy work of liberating it) and is made of shiny tinned steel; a dark, or "blued," metal pan can bake too fast, resulting in an overly dark crust.

As for nonstick finish, you don't need it: pastry dough has enough fat to prevent sticking. Any serious baker will tell you that "it's a poor crust that doesn't grease its own pan."

A quick perusal of kitchenware stores or websites reveals a bewildering array of different-sized pans for sale, but you really only need a few basics. An inexpensive Pyrex 9-inch pie plate and 9½-inch deep-dish pie plate will get you through any pie-baking endeavor.

In the case of tart pans, many of them have been (inconsistently) converted from the metric system: that's why you may see them marked variously 9 inches, 9½ inches, 10 inches, 10¼ inches, and so on. And, depending on the manufacturer, they may also be measured from the outside of the fluted rim or the inside. If you buy one that's marked 9 to 9½ inches in diameter and one that's 10 to 10¼ inches in diameter, you will be able to make a wide range of tarts. The pastry isn't a problem (the dough will fit a whole host of pans), but the amount of filling will make a difference. If all you have is a 9-inch tart pan, for instance, and the recipe is for a 10-inch tart, then you will have a little filling left over. Alternatively, if you're putting the filling for a 9-inch tart into a larger pan, start checking the tart for doneness about 10 minutes before the end of the specified cooking time (visual cues are given in each recipe).

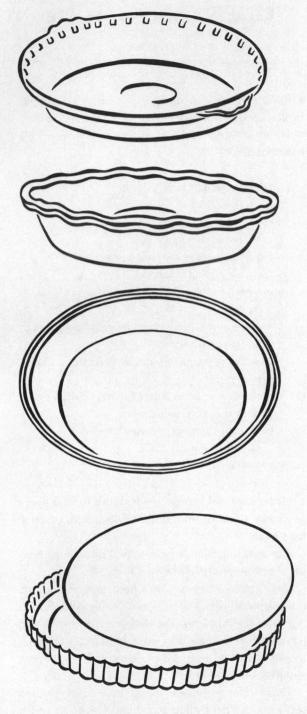

Lattice-Crust Pear Pie

SERVES 8
ACTIVE TIME: 1 HOUR ■ START TO FINISH: 5½ HOURS
(INCLUDES MAKING DOUGH AND COOLING)

■ It seems novel to bake pears into a pie, but one bite will convince you that this deserves a place of honor on every fall table. The fruit takes on a lovely golden color as it bakes, and it boasts a honeylike taste. The pastry, woven into a beautiful lattice, shatters into crisp, buttery flakes under your fork. The overall effect is gilded autumnal abundance. ■

3 tablespoons all-purpose flour
¼ teaspoon freshly grated nutmeg
⅛ teaspoon salt
⅔ cup plus 1 tablespoon sugar
2½ pounds firm but ripe Bartlett or Anjou pears, peeled, cut into 8 wedges each, and cored
1 tablespoon fresh lemon juice
   Basic Pastry Dough for a double-crust pie (page 781)
1 tablespoon milk

SPECIAL EQUIPMENT: a 9½-inch deep-dish pie plate

Put a rack in middle of oven and put a large baking sheet on rack. Preheat oven to 425°F.

LATTICE CRUSTS

ABOUT LATTICE CRUSTS

Not only are lattice pie crusts decorative, they also allow steam to escape easily. The simplest way to fashion a lattice is to place half of the pastry strips across the pie, then lay the remaining strips across them, working on the diagonal if you like for a diamond or crisscross effect. But the traditional lattice is woven, giving the result a certain elegance. You can weave the lattice separately on a flat surface (such as a cardboard cake round, and slide it onto your pie, but we find it easier to weave the crust directly on top of the filling, especially if it's not too wet. The key to success is to keep the pastry cold and work as quickly as possible. If the strips get too soft to handle, put them on a wax-paper-lined baking sheet and pop them into the refrigerator for 15 minutes.

TO MAKE A WOVEN LATTICE CRUST

Set aside half of the pastry strips on a wax-paper-lined baking sheet in the refrigerator. Arrange the remaining strips over the filling parallel to each other, spacing them evenly (1). Gently flip back every other strip, then place 1 chilled strip of dough across the center of the pie, perpendicular to the other strips (2). Unfold the strips, so they lie over the perpendicular strip. Flip back the strips that weren't flipped before, lay a second strip across the pie below and parallel to the first, and then unfold the strips back over it. Repeat the process, flipping back alternate strips, placing a third strip parallel to the other two near the bottom edge of the pie, and then unfolding the strips over it. Continuing in the same manner, working away from the center toward the top of the pie, place the remaining 3 strips over the pie (3).

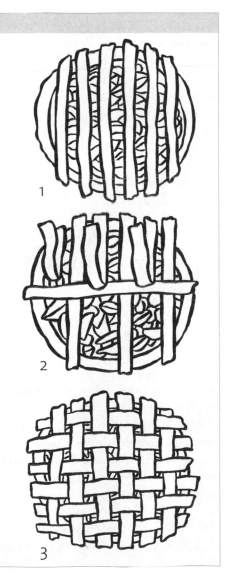

Whisk together flour, nutmeg, salt, and ⅔ cup sugar in a large bowl. Add pears and lemon juice, tossing gently.

Roll out larger piece of dough (keep remaining piece refrigerated) on a lightly floured surface with a lightly floured rolling pin into a 13-inch round. Fit it into pie plate. Trim edges, leaving a ½-inch overhang. Refrigerate while you roll out dough for top crust.

Roll out remaining piece of dough in same manner into a roughly 16-by-11-inch rectangle. Cut crosswise into twelve 1-inch-wide strips with a pastry wheel or a sharp knife.

Spoon filling into shell. Weave a lattice pattern over pie with pastry strips (see page 769). Trim edges of all strips close to edge of pie plate. Fold bottom crust up over edges of lattice and crimp edges. Brush lattice with milk and sprinkle with remaining tablespoon sugar.

Put pie on hot baking sheet and bake for 20 minutes. Reduce oven temperature to 375°F, cover edges of pie with a pie shield or foil, and bake until crust is golden brown and filling is bubbling, 50 to 60 minutes more.

Cool pie on a rack to warm or room temperature, at least 2 hours.

Deep-Dish Wild Blueberry Pie

SERVES 8
ACTIVE TIME: 40 MINUTES ■ START TO FINISH: 7¼ HOURS
(INCLUDES MAKING DOUGH AND COOLING)

■ If you've never had pie made from wild blueberries, you'll be bowled over by the intensity of this one. The light, tender crust provides a sublime foil for the deeply flavorful fruit. But take heart if you can't find fresh wild blueberries in your area—frozen wild berries also yield excellent results (so do regular blueberries; if they are exceptionally sweet, though, reduce the brown sugar to 1 cup). ■

1¼ cups packed light brown sugar
5 tablespoons quick-cooking tapioca (see Cook's Note)
6 cups (30 ounces) fresh wild blueberries, 3 (10-ounce) packages frozen wild blueberries (not thawed), or 6 cups fresh regular blueberries (see headnote)
1 tablespoon fresh lemon juice
Basic Pastry Dough for a double-crust pie (page 781)
1 tablespoon unsalted butter, cut into small pieces
1 large egg, beaten with 1 tablespoon water for egg wash

SPECIAL EQUIPMENT: a 9½-inch deep-dish pie plate

Put a rack in middle of oven and put a large baking sheet on rack. Preheat oven to 425°F.

Whisk together brown sugar and tapioca in a large bowl. Add blueberries and lemon juice, tossing gently.

Roll out larger piece of dough (keep remaining piece refrigerated) on a lightly floured surface with a lightly floured rolling pin into a 13-inch round. Fit into pie plate. Trim edges, leaving a ½-inch overhang. Refrigerate while you roll out dough for top crust.

Roll out remaining dough in same manner into an 11-inch round. Cut out 5 or 6 small holes in dough with small decorative cookie cutters, or use a small knife to slash steam vents toward center.

Spoon filling, with any accumulated juices, into shell and dot with butter. Cover with pastry round and trim edges, leaving a ½-inch overhang. Press edges together to seal, then crimp decoratively. Brush top of pie with egg wash.

Put pie on hot baking sheet and bake for 30 minutes. Cover edges with a pie shield or foil to prevent overbrowning, reduce oven temperature to 375°F, and bake until crust is golden and filling is bubbling, 45 to 50 minutes more.

Cool pie completely on a rack, about 4 hours (filling will be runny if pie is still warm).

COOK'S NOTE

■ We like our fruit filling on the soft side. If you prefer a firmer set, increase the tapioca to 6 tablespoons.

Nectarine Raspberry Pie

SERVES 8
ACTIVE TIME: 1¼ HOURS ■ START TO FINISH: 6 HOURS
(INCLUDES MAKING DOUGH AND COOLING)

■ Nestled in a flaky double crust, nectarines and raspberries tease the best out of each other: this pie is fragrant and floral, sweet and tart, and instantly tastes like a classic. ■

    3 pounds nectarines, halved, pitted, and cut into
         ½-inch-wide wedges
    1½ cups raspberries
    1½ tablespoons fresh lemon juice
    2 tablespoons quick-cooking tapioca
    2 tablespoons cornstarch
    ⅛ teaspoon salt
    ¾ cup plus 1 tablespoon sugar
       Basic Pastry Dough for a double-crust pie
         (page 781)
    1 tablespoon whole milk

SPECIAL EQUIPMENT: a 9-inch pie plate

Put a rack in lower third of oven and put a large baking sheet on rack. Preheat oven to 425°F.

Toss nectarines with raspberries and lemon juice in a large bowl.

Grind tapioca to a powder in an electric coffee/spice grinder or mini food processor. Whisk together with cornstarch, salt, and ¾ cup sugar in a small bowl; set aside.

Roll out larger piece of dough (keep remaining piece refrigerated) on a lightly floured surface with a lightly floured rolling pin into a 13-inch round. Fit into pie plate (do not trim edges) and refrigerate while you roll out dough for top crust.

Roll out remaining dough in same manner into an 11-inch round.

Gently toss fruit with sugar mixture and spoon into pie shell. Cover with pastry round and trim edges, leaving a ½-inch overhang. Press edges together to seal, then crimp decoratively. Brush top of pie with milk and sprinkle with remaining tablespoon sugar. Cut several steam vents in top of pie with a small sharp knife.

Put pie on hot baking sheet and bake for 20 minutes. Reduce oven temperature to 375°F and bake, checking occasionally and covering edges of pie with a pie shield or foil if they are browning too fast, until crust is golden brown and filling is bubbling, about 40 minutes more.

Cool pie on a rack to warm or room temperature, at least 2 hours.

Cherry Pie

SERVES 8
ACTIVE TIME: 1 HOUR ■ START TO FINISH: 8 HOURS
(INCLUDES MAKING DOUGH AND COOLING)

■ Too tart to eat raw, sour cherries were born to be baked into a pie. Sweet cherries would be too cloying, but tender, juicy sour ones taste just right, especially when you serve the pie with vanilla ice cream. This all-American version gets added sophistication from an unexpected hint of cinnamon. ■

    3 tablespoons quick-cooking tapioca
    1 vanilla bean, halved lengthwise, or 1½ teaspoons
         vanilla extract
    2 tablespoons cornstarch
    ½ teaspoon ground cinnamon
    ¼ teaspoon salt
    1¼ cups plus 1 tablespoon sugar
    6 cups (2 pounds) fresh or frozen (not thawed) pitted
         sour cherries
       Basic Pastry Dough for a double-crust pie
         (page 781)
    1 tablespoon whole milk

ACCOMPANIMENT: vanilla ice cream
SPECIAL EQUIPMENT: a 9-inch pie plate

Finely grind tapioca in an electric coffee/spice grinder or mini food processor.

If using a vanilla bean, scrape seeds into a large bowl with a small knife. (If using extract, add with cherries.) Add tapioca, cornstarch, cinnamon, salt, and 1¼ cups sugar and whisk together. Add cherries and toss well. Let stand for 30 minutes to allow cherries to release some juices.

PIES, TARTS, AND PASTRIES   771

Put a rack in middle of oven and put a large baking sheet on rack. Preheat oven to 425°F.

Roll out larger piece of dough (keep remaining piece refrigerated) on a lightly floured surface with a lightly floured rolling pin into a 13-inch round. Fit it into pie plate. Trim edges, leaving a ½-inch overhang. Refrigerate while you roll out dough for top crust.

Roll out remaining dough in same manner into a 11-inch round.

Toss cherries well again and spoon into shell. Cover with pastry round and trim edges, leaving a ½-inch overhang. Press edges together to seal, then crimp decoratively. Brush top of pie with milk. Cut five 1-by-½-inch teardrop-shaped steam vents 1 inch from center and sprinkle crust with remaining tablespoon sugar.

Put pie on hot baking sheet and bake for 30 minutes. Cover edges with a pie shield or foil, reduce oven temperature to 375°F, and bake until crust is deep golden and filling is bubbling in center, 50 minutes to 1 hour more.

Cool pie completely on a rack, at least 4 hours. Serve with ice cream.

Blackberry Hand Pies

MAKES 12 INDIVIDUAL PIES
ACTIVE TIME: 40 MINUTES ■ START TO FINISH: 3 HOURS
(INCLUDES MAKING DOUGH AND COOLING)

■ There's something special about individual pies like these. Maybe it's the childlike delight of getting a whole pie to yourself and eating it out of hand. Or maybe it's the perfect proportion of crisp pastry, sparkling with sugar, to inky blackberry filling. Grated apple and a smidge of semolina flour help thicken the filling, without muting the fresh flavor of the berries. ■

2 cups (12 ounces) blackberries
1 large Golden Delicious apple, peeled and coarsely grated
2 tablespoons plus 1 teaspoon semolina flour (see Sources)
¼ teaspoon ground cinnamon
½ cup sugar

Basic Pastry Dough for a double-crust pie (page 781)
2 tablespoons whole milk
SPECIAL EQUIPMENT: parchment paper

Combine blackberries, apple, semolina flour, cinnamon, and 6 tablespoons sugar in a 2-quart heavy saucepan and cook over moderate heat, stirring frequently, until mixture just boils and has thickened, about 5 minutes. Transfer to a shallow bowl to cool.

Put racks in upper and lower thirds of oven and preheat oven to 375°F. Line two large baking sheets with parchment paper.

Roll out half of dough on a lightly floured surface with a lightly floured rolling pin into a 16-by-11-inch rectangle. Trim to a 15-by-10-inch rectangle. Cut into six 5-inch squares. Place a heaping tablespoon of fruit filling in center of 1 square, moisten edges of square with milk, and fold over into a triangle, pressing edges to seal. Transfer to a lined baking sheet and press tines of a fork around edges of triangle. Make 5 more triangles in same manner, arranging them 1 inch apart on baking sheet. Repeat with remaining dough and filling, to make 12 triangles total.

Brush triangles with milk and sprinkle with remaining 2 tablespoons sugar. Bake, switching position of pans halfway through baking, until pies are golden, about 30 minutes.

Transfer pies to racks to cool.

COOK'S NOTE

■ The blackberry filling can be made up to 1 day ahead and refrigerated, covered. Bring to room temperature before using.

Sour Cream Apple Pie

SERVES 6 TO 8
ACTIVE TIME: 35 MINUTES ■ START TO FINISH: 3 HOURS
(INCLUDES MAKING DOUGH AND COOLING)

■ Sour cream is the basis for an extremely easy custard whose silky tang nicely complements the tartness of Granny Smith apples. Adapted from a recipe from Gold Hill Inn in Gold Hill, Colorado, this pie is finished with a streusel topping that adds a home-spun crunch. ∎

Basic Pastry Dough for a single-crust pie
  (page 781)
2 large eggs
1½ cups sour cream
1½ teaspoons vanilla extract
1⅓ cups sugar
⅓ cup plus 3 tablespoons all-purpose flour
¼ teaspoon freshly grated nutmeg
  Salt
1 pound Granny Smith apples
1 teaspoon ground cinnamon
½ stick (4 tablespoons) cold unsalted butter,
  cut into ½-inch cubes

SPECIAL EQUIPMENT: a 9-inch pie plate

Roll out dough on a lightly floured surface with a lightly floured rolling pin into a 13-inch round. Fit into pie plate. Trim edges, leaving a ½-inch over-hang. Fold overhang under and press against rim of pie plate, then crimp decoratively. Refrigerate until firm, about 30 minutes.

Put a rack in middle of oven and preheat oven to 400°F.

Whisk together eggs, sour cream, vanilla, 1 cup sugar, 3 tablespoons flour, nutmeg, and ¼ teaspoon salt in a bowl until smooth. Peel and core apples and cut into wedges slightly less than ¼ inch thick.

Arrange apples in shell and pour sour cream mix-ture evenly over them, coating all apples. Bake pie for 15 minutes. Reduce oven temperature to 350°F and bake until filling is puffed and golden and apples are tender, 45 to 50 minutes more.

Meanwhile, stir together remaining ⅓ cup sugar, remaining ⅓ cup flour, cinnamon, and a pinch of salt in a bowl. Blend in butter with your fingertips until mixture forms small clumps.

Remove pie from oven and increase oven temperature to 400°F. Crumble topping evenly over top and bake until sugar is melted, about 10 minutes.

Cool pie on a rack for at least 45 minutes. Serve warm or at room temperature.

Caramel Pumpkin Pie

SERVES 8
ACTIVE TIME: 45 MINUTES ∎ START TO FINISH: 6 HOURS
(INCLUDES MAKING DOUGH AND COOLING)

∎ Caramelizing the sugar deepens the flavor of the pumpkin filling and makes it slightly less sweet. The result is a light, delicately spiced pie, with a sensuous richness. ∎

Basic Pastry Dough for a single-crust pie
  (page 781)
⅔ cup sugar
¼ cup water
1⅓ cups heavy cream
1¼ cups solid-pack pumpkin (not pumpkin pie filling)
  Scant 1 teaspoon ground ginger
  Scant 1 teaspoon ground cinnamon
⅛ teaspoon freshly grated nutmeg
  Pinch of ground cloves
¼ teaspoon salt
3 large eggs, lightly beaten

ACCOMPANIMENT: lightly sweetened whipped cream
SPECIAL EQUIPMENT: a 9-inch pie plate

MAKE THE PIE SHELL: Roll out dough on a lightly floured surface with a lightly floured rolling pin into a 13-inch round. Fit into pie plate. Trim edges, leaving a ½-inch overhang. Fold overhang under and press against rim of pie plate, then crimp decoratively. Re-frigerate until firm, about 30 minutes.

Put a rack in middle of oven and preheat oven to 375°F.

Lightly prick bottom of shell all over with a fork. Line with foil and fill with pie weights or dried beans. Bake shell until edges are pale golden and bottom is set, about 20 minutes. Carefully remove foil and weights and bake shell until bottom and sides are golden, about 10 minutes more.

Cool shell completely on a rack, about 25 minutes. (Leave oven on.)

MEANWHILE, MAKE THE FILLING: Bring sugar and water to a boil in a 3- to 3½-quart heavy saucepan, stirring until sugar is dissolved. Boil, without stir-ring, washing down sides of pan occasionally with a pastry brush dipped in cold water and gently swirling pan for even cooking, until mixture is a deep golden caramel, about 10 minutes.

Reduce heat to moderate and carefully add half of cream (mixture will bubble vigorously), stirring until caramel is dissolved. Stir in remaining cream and bring just to a simmer. Remove from heat.

Whisk together pumpkin, spices, and salt in a large bowl. Whisk in hot cream mixture, then eggs, whisking until well combined.

Pour filling into cooled pie shell. Bake until filling is puffed 1½ inches from edges and center is loosely set, 40 to 45 minutes.

Cool pie completely on a rack, about 2 hours. (Filling will continue to set as it cools.) Serve with whipped cream.

COOK'S NOTES

- The pie shell can be baked up to 1 day ahead and kept, wrapped in plastic wrap, at room temperature.
- The pie is best the day it is made, but it can be baked up to 1 day ahead and refrigerated, covered. Bring to room temperature before serving.

BLIND BAKING

If you are making a pie or tart with a custard filling or other filling that will already be cooked, blind baking (prebaking) the empty crust guarantees that it will be thoroughly and evenly cooked until crisp. To minimize shrinkage of the baked crust, fit, rather than stretch, the dough into the pie plate or tart pan, then refrigerate the pastry shell until it's firm. (One of our most experienced pie bakers always saves her dough scraps. If a tear somehow occurs during blind baking, she can patch it, and no one will ever know.) Lightly prick the shell all over with a fork, line it with foil, and spread weights evenly over the bottom to prevent the shell from bubbling up as it bakes. Pie weights—ceramic or metal pellets made specifically for the task—are available at cookware shops (see Sources), but dried beans are fine. (You can keep and reuse them like pie weights, but don't cook them.) It's not necessary to fill the shell completely, but if you have enough of them, bank the weights around the sides for support. The pricking keeps the dough from billowing up once the foil and weights are removed.

Sour Cream Pumpkin Pie

SERVES 8
ACTIVE TIME: 40 MINUTES ■ START TO FINISH: 5½ HOURS
(INCLUDES MAKING DOUGH AND COOLING)

■ The filling of this pumpkin pie has a very silken texture. Sour cream tempers the sweetness of the rich custard, which is lightened with egg whites. Dark brown sugar deepens both the flavor and the color. ■

All-Butter Pastry Dough for a single-crust pie (page 782)
1½ cups sour cream
1½ cups solid-pack pumpkin (not pumpkin pie filling)
3 large eggs, separated
1 cup packed dark brown sugar
¾ teaspoon ground cinnamon

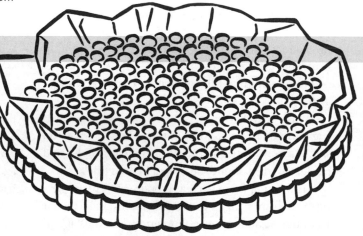

Blind baking generally involves baking the shell until the sides are golden and the bottom is set, then removing the foil and its cargo and continuing to bake until the bottom and sides of the shell are golden. Sometimes this may take a little longer than you think, so be patient; if the shell still looks raw in places, give it a few more minutes. If the edges begin to get too brown, cover with a pie shield (see Sources) or foil for protection. If any little bubbles appear once you've removed the foil and weights, prick them with a fork. Don't put your filled blind-baked shell on a hot baking sheet in the oven, or the crust may overbake.

¼ teaspoon freshly grated nutmeg

¼ teaspoon ground ginger

¼ teaspoon salt

ACCOMPANIMENT: lightly sweetened whipped cream

SPECIAL EQUIPMENT: a 9-inch pie plate; an instant-read thermometer

Roll out dough on a lightly floured surface with a lightly floured rolling pin into a 13-inch round. Fit into pie plate. Trim edges, leaving a ½-inch overhang. Fold overhang under and press against rim of pie plate, then crimp decoratively. Refrigerate until firm, about 30 minutes.

Put a rack in middle of oven and preheat oven to 375°F.

Lightly prick shell all over with a fork. Line shell with foil and fill with pie weights or dried beans. Bake until edges are pale golden and bottom is set, about 20 minutes. Carefully remove foil and weights and bake shell until bottom and sides are pale golden, about 10 minutes more.

Cool shell completely on a rack, about 25 minutes. (Leave oven on.)

MEANWHILE, MAKE THE FILLING: Heat 1 cup sour cream in a large metal bowl set over a large wide pot of boiling water (heating it over a pan of water helps prevent curdling) until warm, stirring occasionally.

Whisk together pumpkin, yolks, brown sugar, cinnamon, nutmeg, ginger, salt, and remaining ½ cup sour cream in a bowl until combined. Whisk into hot sour cream and cook over simmering water, stirring constantly with a wooden spoon, until custard is thickened and registers 170°F on thermometer, about 6 minutes.

Remove bowl from pot and cool pumpkin mixture in bowl set in a larger bowl of ice and cold water, stirring occasionally, about 15 minutes.

Beat egg whites in a large bowl with an electric mixer until they just hold stiff peaks. Fold one third of whites into pumpkin mixture gently but thoroughly, then fold in remaining whites.

Pour filling into cooled shell, smoothing top. Bake until filling is set and puffed around edges, 40 to 50 minutes.

Cool pie to room temperature on a rack, about 2 hours. Serve with whipped cream.

COOK'S NOTE

■ The pie can be made up to 1 day ahead and refrigerated, covered. Serve chilled or at room temperature.

Sweet Potato Meringue Pie

SERVES 8
ACTIVE TIME: 1 HOUR ■ START TO FINISH: 4½ HOURS
(INCLUDES MAKING DOUGH AND COOLING)

■ Piped stars of meringue make a festive topping for this suave pie, warmly spiced with cinnamon, allspice, and nutmeg. The lull between the main course and dessert is the best time to make the meringue and brown it (if you do it too far ahead, the meringue will weep). ■

FOR FILLING

1¾ pounds sweet potatoes (about 3 medium)

1⅓ cups half-and-half

½ cup sugar

2 large eggs

1¼ teaspoons ground cinnamon

¼ teaspoon ground allspice

¼ teaspoon freshly grated nutmeg

½ teaspoon salt

FOR PIE SHELL

Basic Pastry Dough for a single-crust pie (page 781)

FOR MERINGUE

3 large egg whites

¾ cup sugar

SPECIAL EQUIPMENT: a 9-inch pie plate; a pastry bag fitted with a large star tip

BAKE THE SWEET POTATOES: Put a rack in middle of oven and preheat oven to 400°F.

Prick sweet potatoes, put on a foil-lined baking sheet, and bake until very soft, 1 to 1¼ hours.

MEANWHILE, MAKE THE PIE SHELL: Roll out dough on a lightly floured surface with a lightly floured rolling pin into a 13-inch round. Fit into pie plate. Trim edges, leaving a ½-inch overhang. Fold overhang under and press against rim, then crimp decoratively. Refrigerate until firm, about 30 minutes.

MAKE THE FILLING: When sweet potatoes are done, remove from oven and cool slightly. Reduce oven temperature to 375°F.

Halve sweet potatoes and scoop out enough flesh to measure 2 cups (reserve any remaining potato for another use). Puree potatoes with remaining ingredients in a blender or food processor until smooth. Set aside.

BAKE THE PIE SHELL: Lightly prick bottom of shell all over with a fork. Line with foil and fill with pie weights or dried beans. Bake shell until edges are pale golden and bottom is set, about 20 minutes. Carefully remove foil and weights and bake shell until bottom and sides are golden, about 10 minutes more.

Cool shell completely on a rack, about 25 minutes. (Leave oven on.)

ASSEMBLE AND BAKE THE PIE: Pour filling into shell. Bake until filling is set but center still trembles slightly, about 1 hour.

Cool pie completely on a rack, about 1 hour. (Filling will continue to set as pie cools.)

MAKE THE MERINGUE AND GARNISH THE PIE: Preheat oven to 450°F.

Stir together whites and sugar in a metal bowl set over a saucepan of simmering water until sugar is dissolved. Remove bowl from pan and beat meringue with an electric mixer at high speed until it holds stiff, glossy peaks.

Transfer meringue to pastry bag and pipe tall, pointed mounds close together over pie, covering filling.

Bake pie on middle oven rack until meringue is golden brown, 4 to 5 minutes. Serve warm or at room temperature.

COOK'S NOTES

- The filling can be made up to 1 day ahead and refrigerated, loosely covered. Bring to room temperature before proceeding.
- The pie, without the meringue topping, can be made up to 1 day ahead and refrigerated, loosely covered. Bring to room temperature before topping with the meringue.

Banoffee Pie

SERVES 8
ACTIVE TIME: 45 MINUTES ■ START TO FINISH: 3½ HOURS
(INCLUDES MAKING DOUGH AND CHILLING)

■ An easy take on bananas with toffee (hence the name), this pie made its debut at the Hungry Monk, a pub in Jevington, England, in 1972. Traditional recipes involve boiling unopened cans of sweetened condensed milk until the milk caramelizes, but since that sometimes results in explosions (!), we prefer slowly cooking the milk in a water bath. The results are just as delectable. ■

    2 cups (from two 14-ounce cans) sweetened
       condensed milk
       Generous pinch of salt
       Basic Pastry Dough for a single-crust pie
       (page 781)
    3 large bananas
  1½ cups very cold heavy cream
    1 tablespoon packed light brown sugar
SPECIAL EQUIPMENT: a 9½-inch deep-dish pie plate

Put a rack in middle of oven and preheat oven to 425°F.

Pour condensed milk into pie plate and stir in salt. Cover pie plate with foil and crimp foil tightly around rim. Put in a roasting pan, put roasting pan in the oven, and add enough boiling water to reach halfway up sides of pie plate, making sure that water doesn't reach foil. Bake, refilling pan with water about every 40 minutes, until milk is thick and a deep golden caramel color, about 2 hours.

Remove pie plate from water bath and transfer toffee to a bowl. Refrigerate, uncovered, until cold, about 1 hour.

Meanwhile, roll out dough on a lightly floured surface with a lightly floured rolling pin into a 13-inch round. Fit dough into cleaned pie plate and trim edges, leaving a ½-inch overhang. Fold underhang under and press against rim of pie plate, then crimp decoratively. Refrigerate until firm, about 30 minutes.

Preheat oven to 375°F.

Lightly prick shell all over with a fork. Line shell with foil and fill with pie weights or dried beans. Bake until edges are pale golden and bottom is set, about 20 minutes. Carefully remove foil and weights and bake shell until bottom and sides are golden, about 15 minutes more.

Cool shell completely on a rack, about 25 minutes.

Spread toffee evenly in shell. Refrigerate, uncovered, for 15 minutes.

Cut bananas into ¼-inch-thick slices and pile over toffee.

Beat cream with brown sugar in a large bowl with an electric mixer until it just holds soft peaks. Mound over top of pie.

COOK'S NOTES

- The toffee can be refrigerated for up to 2 days (cover after 1 hour).
- The toffee-filled crust can be refrigerated for up to 3 hours.

Butterscotch Chiffon Pie

SERVES 8
ACTIVE TIME: 45 MINUTES ■ START TO FINISH: 6 HOURS
(INCLUDES MAKING DOUGH AND CHILLING)

■ Homemade butterscotch sauce, glossy beaten egg whites, and freshly whipped cream combine to make a lighter-than-air filling for this pie, a delicious throwback to the glory days of icebox desserts. Think butterscotch pudding that's been dressed up for a dinner party, complete with a sprinkling of salty, buttery toasted pecans. ■

FOR PIE SHELL
    Basic Pastry Dough for a single-crust pie
        (page 781)
FOR FILLING
    3 tablespoons light corn syrup
    ¾ cup plus 1 tablespoon sugar
    ¼ cup water
    ½ stick (4 tablespoons) unsalted butter
    1 teaspoon cider vinegar
        Salt
    1⅓ cups very cold heavy cream
    1½ teaspoons vanilla extract

    2 teaspoons unflavored gelatin
    3 large egg whites
FOR TOPPING
    1 cup (about 3½ ounces) chopped pecans
    1 tablespoon unsalted butter
    ⅛ teaspoon salt
SPECIAL EQUIPMENT: a 9-inch pie plate

MAKE THE PIE SHELL: Roll out dough on a lightly floured surface with a lightly floured rolling pin into a 13-inch round. Fit it into pie plate. Trim edges, leaving a ½-inch overhang. Fold overhang under and press against rim of pie plate, then crimp decoratively. Refrigerate until firm, about 30 minutes.

Put a rack in middle of oven and preheat oven to 375°F.

Lightly prick shell all over with a fork. Line with foil and fill with pie weights or dried beans. Bake until edges are pale golden and bottom is set, about 20 minutes. Carefully remove foil and weights and bake shell until bottom and sides are golden, about 10 minutes more.

Cool shell completely on a rack, about 25 minutes.

MEANWHILE, MAKE THE BUTTERSCOTCH FILLING: Bring corn syrup, ¾ cup sugar, and 2 tablespoons water to a boil in a 1½- to 2-quart heavy saucepan over moderate heat, stirring until sugar is dissolved. Boil, without stirring, swirling pan occasionally, until mixture is a deep golden caramel, 7 to 9 minutes.

Remove saucepan from heat and add butter, vinegar, and a pinch of salt, swirling pan until butter is melted. Add ⅓ cup cream and vanilla, return to heat, and simmer, stirring, for 1 minute. Cool sauce to warm.

While sauce cools, sprinkle gelatin over remaining 2 tablespoons water in a small saucepan and let stand for 1 minute to soften. Heat over low heat, stirring, until gelatin is dissolved. Stir gelatin mixture into butterscotch sauce and cool to room temperature.

Beat egg whites with a pinch of salt in a large bowl with an electric mixer until they hold soft peaks. Add remaining tablespoon sugar and beat until whites just hold stiff, glossy peaks. Fold in butterscotch sauce gently but thoroughly.

Beat remaining 1 cup cream in a medium bowl with cleaned beaters until it just holds stiff peaks. Fold into butterscotch mixture gently but thoroughly.

Gently pour filling into cooled pastry shell, letting it mound. Refrigerate, uncovered, until set, at least 2 hours.

MAKE THE TOPPING: Cook pecans in butter with salt in a small heavy skillet over moderate heat, stirring frequently, until golden, about 5 minutes. Remove from heat and cool completely.

Remove pie from refrigerator and let stand at room temperature for 30 minutes before serving. Sprinkle nuts over top of pie.

COOK'S NOTES
- The egg whites in this recipe are not cooked. If that is a concern, see page 915.
- The pie, without the nut topping, can be made up to 1 day ahead and refrigerated, loosely covered once set. Let stand at room temperature for 30 minutes before sprinkling with the nuts and serving.

Bittersweet Chocolate Pecan Pie

SERVES 8
ACTIVE TIME: 40 MINUTES ■ START TO FINISH: 4 HOURS
(INCLUDES MAKING DOUGH AND COOLING)

■ Pecan pie can be overly sweet, and you might think that adding a layer of chocolate to this classic would only make it sweeter. But bittersweet chocolate contributes a hint of darkness, a complexity that is boosted by using dark rather than light corn syrup in the filling. ■

　　All-Butter Pastry Dough for a single-crust pie (page 782)
1　(3½- to 4-ounce) bittersweet chocolate bar (no more than 70% cacao; see page 705), melted and cooled slightly
2　cups (8 ounces) pecan halves, toasted (see Tips, page 911)
3　large eggs
⅓　cup packed light brown sugar
1　teaspoon vanilla extract
¼　teaspoon salt
¾　cup dark corn syrup
ACCOMPANIMENT: lightly sweetened whipped cream
SPECIAL EQUIPMENT: a 9-inch pie plate

Roll out dough on a lightly floured surface with a lightly floured rolling pin into a 13-inch round. Fit into pie plate. Trim edges, leaving a ½-inch overhang. Fold overhang under and press against rim of pie plate, then crimp decoratively.

Spread chocolate in bottom of pie shell with back of spoon and refrigerate until firm, about 30 minutes.

Put a rack in middle of oven and preheat oven to 375°F.

Scatter pecans evenly over bottom of pie shell. Whisk together eggs, brown sugar, vanilla, and salt in a bowl. Whisk in corn syrup and pour over pecans.

Bake pie until filling is puffed and crust is golden, 50 to 60 minutes. (If pie is browning too fast after 30 minutes, loosely cover with foil.)

Cool pie on a rack to warm or room temperature. Serve with whipped cream.

COOK'S NOTE
- The pie can be baked up to 1 day ahead. Once cooled, refrigerate, uncovered, until cold, then cover. Reheat in a 350°F oven until warm before serving, about 10 minutes.

Lemon Chess Pie with Blackberry Compote

SERVES 8
ACTIVE TIME: 45 MINUTES ■ START TO FINISH: 3 HOURS
(INCLUDES MAKING DOUGH AND COOLING)

■ One of the great Southern desserts, chess pie boasts a firm, smooth filling made of eggs, butter, and a small amount of some kind of thickener (in this case, cornmeal). This version, from the pastry chef Sol Schott of the Morrison-Clark Hotel and Restaurant in Washington, D.C., gets its resounding tang from lemon and buttermilk. The rich coconut piecrust adds a decadent accent. The result is sublime, especially with a drizzle of blackberry compote. ■

FOR COCONUT CRUST
¾　cup all-purpose flour
⅓　cup unsweetened dried coconut
1　teaspoon sugar
⅛　teaspoon salt

5 tablespoons plus 1 teaspoon cold unsalted butter, cut into pieces

2½ tablespoons ice water

FOR LEMON FILLING

6 large eggs

1½ cups sugar

⅛ teaspoon salt

6 tablespoons well-shaken buttermilk

3 tablespoons yellow cornmeal

4 teaspoons finely grated lemon zest

6 tablespoons fresh lemon juice (from about 1½ lemons)

Pinch of freshly grated nutmeg

1 stick (8 tablespoons) unsalted butter, melted

ACCOMPANIMENT: Blackberry Compote (recipe follows)

SPECIAL EQUIPMENT: a 9-inch pie plate

MAKE THE CRUST: Pulse flour, coconut, sugar, and salt in a food processor until combined. Add butter and pulse until most of mixture resembles coarse meal with some small (roughly pea-sized) butter lumps. Add water and pulse just until mixture forms a dough. Do not overwork, or pastry will be tough.

Turn dough out, press into a ball, and flatten into a disk. Wrap tightly in plastic wrap and refrigerate until firm, about 30 minutes.

BAKE THE CRUST: Put a rack in middle of oven and preheat oven to 350°F.

Roll out dough on a lightly floured surface with a lightly floured rolling pin into a 12-inch round. Fit into pie plate. Trim edges, leaving a ½-inch overhang. Fold overhang under and press against rim of pie plate, then crimp decoratively.

Lightly prick shell all over with a fork. Line with foil and fill with pie weights or dried beans. Bake until edges are pale golden and bottom is set, about 15 minutes. Carefully remove foil and weights and bake shell until bottom and sides are pale golden, 5 to 10 minutes more. Transfer shell to a rack to cool for 5 minutes. Reduce oven temperature to 325°F.

MAKE THE FILLING AND BAKE THE PIE: Whisk together eggs, sugar, and salt in a medium bowl until well blended. Whisk in buttermilk, cornmeal, zest, juice, and nutmeg. Gradually whisk in butter until smooth.

Pour filling into pie shell. Cover edges of piecrust with a pie shield or foil to prevent overbrowning.

Bake until custard is just set, about 40 minutes.

Cool pie completely on a rack. Serve with compote.

COOK'S NOTE

■ This pie tastes best the day it is made.

Blackberry Compote

MAKES ABOUT 2 CUPS

ACTIVE TIME: 20 MINUTES ■ START TO FINISH: 40 MINUTES

■ Some of the blackberries are pureed into a super-smooth syrup, while others are folded in whole. The compote is also excellent on ice cream. ■

⅔ cup water

⅓ cup sugar

1¼ tablespoons fresh lemon juice

3–4 whole allspice

3 cups (1½ pints) fresh or thawed frozen blackberries

Bring water, sugar, juice, and allspice to a boil in a small saucepan over moderate heat, stirring until sugar is dissolved. Boil until reduced to about ¼ cup. Cool syrup to lukewarm; discard allspice.

Puree 2 cups blackberries with syrup in a blender. Force puree through a fine-mesh sieve into a bowl to remove seeds. Stir remaining cup berries into sauce.

COOK'S NOTE

■ The blackberry puree can be made up to 4 days ahead and refrigerated, covered. Stir in the berries just before serving.

Kiwi-Pomegranate Angel Pies

SERVES 10

ACTIVE TIME: 45 MINUTES ■ START TO FINISH: 4½ HOURS

■ These little pies are almost too pretty to eat. They're both delicate and decadent, the airy puffs of crisp meringue giving way to rich, vanilla-flavored pastry cream and a festive mix of ruby red pomegranate seeds and wedges of fresh kiwi. ■

FOR MERINGUES

4 large egg whites, left at room temperature
   for 30 minutes
¼ teaspoon cream of tartar
¼ teaspoon salt
1 cup superfine sugar
1 teaspoon confectioners' sugar

FOR PASTRY CREAM

1½ tablespoons all-purpose flour
2 teaspoons cornstarch
   Pinch of salt
¼ cup granulated sugar
4 large egg yolks
1 cup whole milk
1 tablespoon unsalted butter, softened
½ teaspoon vanilla extract
½ cup very cold heavy cream

FOR FRUIT TOPPING

1½ pounds (8–10) kiwifruit, peeled and cut into
   8 wedges each
½ cup pomegranate seeds (from 1 pomegranate;
   see page 434)

SPECIAL EQUIPMENT: parchment paper

MAKE THE MERINGUES: Put racks in upper and lower thirds of oven and preheat oven to 200°F. Line two large baking sheets with parchment paper.

Beat egg whites in a bowl with an electric mixer at medium-high speed until foamy. Add cream of tartar and salt and continue beating until whites hold soft peaks. Beat in ½ cup superfine sugar 1 tablespoon at a time, then increase mixer speed to high and beat until whites hold stiff, glossy peaks, about 5 minutes. Fold in remaining ½ cup superfine sugar gently but thoroughly.

With back of a spoon, spread meringue into ten 4-inch rounds, 5 on each lined baking sheet. Make a 3-inch-wide depression in center of each round (shape and smooth outside of each round with a butter knife if desired). Using a fine-mesh sieve, lightly dust confectioners' sugar evenly over meringues.

Bake meringues, with oven door propped open about ½ inch with handle of a wooden spoon, until crisp, about 2½ hours.

Turn oven off and leave meringues in oven, with door still propped open, until dry, at least 1 hour. Carefully peel off parchment paper.

MAKE THE PASTRY CREAM: Whisk together flour, cornstarch, salt, and 2 tablespoons sugar in a small bowl. Whisk together yolks in a medium bowl, then whisk in flour mixture until smooth.

Bring milk and remaining 2 tablespoons sugar just to a boil in a 1½- to 2-quart heavy saucepan, stirring until sugar is dissolved. Remove from heat and whisk half of milk mixture into egg mixture in a slow stream. Pour custard back into pan, whisking, bring to a boil over moderate heat, whisking constantly and vigorously, and boil, whisking, for 2 minutes. Remove from heat and whisk in butter and vanilla.

Using a rubber spatula, force pastry cream through a medium-mesh sieve into a shallow bowl. Refrigerate pastry cream, its surface covered with parchment paper, until cold, about 2 hours.

Whisk heavy cream vigorously (or beat with an electric mixer) in a medium bowl until it just holds stiff peaks. Whisk pastry cream briefly to loosen it, then gently fold in whipped cream. Refrigerate, covered, until cold, about 30 minutes.

JUST BEFORE SERVING, ASSEMBLE THE PIES: Fill each meringue shell with about 3 tablespoons pastry cream, smoothing top with back of a spoon. Divide kiwi wedges evenly among shells and sprinkle pomegranate seeds over tops.

COOK'S NOTES

■ The meringues are best baked on a dry day; humidity can cause them to be sticky.

■ The baked meringues can be left to dry in the turned-off oven for up to 12 hours.

■ The meringues can be baked up to 1 day ahead and kept in an airtight container at room temperature.

■ The pastry cream, without the whipped cream, can be refrigerated for up to 1 day. The whipped cream can be folded into the pastry cream up to 4 hours ahead.

■ The kiwis can be cut up to 3 hours ahead and refrigerated, covered.

■ The pomegranate seeds can be refrigerated, covered, for up to 3 days.

Basic Pastry Dough

MAKES ENOUGH FOR A 9-INCH SINGLE- OR DOUBLE-CRUST
PIE OR A 9- OR 10-INCH TART
ACTIVE TIME: 15 MINUTES ■ START TO FINISH: 1¼ HOURS
(INCLUDES CHILLING)

■ There's a reason that we use this recipe for almost all our pies—it results in a flaky pastry that we think is the best. The final step of smearing portions of dough across the work surface is called *fraisage*. It's a French technique that ensures the fat is distributed evenly throughout the dough. ■

FOR A SINGLE-CRUST PIE

- 1¼ cups all-purpose flour
- ¾ stick (6 tablespoons) cold unsalted butter, cut into ½-inch cubes
- 2 tablespoons cold vegetable shortening, preferably trans fat–free
- ¼ teaspoon salt
- 3–4 tablespoons ice water

FOR A DOUBLE-CRUST PIE

- 2½ cups all-purpose flour
- 1½ sticks (12 tablespoons) cold unsalted butter, cut into ½-inch cubes
- ¼ cup cold vegetable shortening, preferably trans fat–free
- ½ teaspoon salt
- 5–7 tablespoons ice water

Blend together flour, butter, shortening, and salt in a bowl with your fingertips or a pastry blender (or pulse in a food processor) just until mixture resembles coarse meal with some small (roughly pea-sized) butter lumps.

FOR A SINGLE-CRUST PIE: Drizzle 3 tablespoons ice water evenly over mixture. Gently stir with a fork (or pulse) until incorporated. Squeeze a small handful of dough: if it doesn't hold together, add more ice water ½ tablespoon at a time, stirring (or pulsing) until incorporated. Do not overwork, or pastry will be tough.

Turn dough out onto a work surface. Divide dough into 4 portions. With heel of your hand, smear each portion once or twice in a forward motion to help distribute fat. Gather all dough together, press into a ball, and flatten into a 5-inch disk. If dough is sticky, dust lightly with additional flour. Wrap tightly in plastic wrap and refrigerate until firm, at least 1 hour.

FOR A DOUBLE-CRUST PIE: Drizzle 5 tablespoons ice water evenly over mixture. Gently stir with a fork (or pulse) until incorporated. Squeeze a small handful of dough: if it doesn't hold together, add more ice water ½ tablespoon at a time, stirring (or pulsing) until incorporated. Do not overwork dough, or pastry will be tough.

Turn dough out onto a work surface. Divide dough into 8 portions. With heel of your hand, smear each portion once or twice in a forward motion to help distribute fat. Gather all dough together. Divide dough into 2 portions, one slightly larger than the other, form each one into a ball, and flatten into a 5-inch disk. If dough is sticky, dust lightly with additional flour. Wrap each disk tightly in plastic wrap and refrigerate until firm, at least 1 hour.

COOK'S NOTE

■ The dough can be refrigerated for up to 2 days. It can also be frozen, well wrapped, for up to 1 month.

VARIATION

SWEET PASTRY DOUGH: Add 2 tablespoons sugar to the flour mixture for a single crust.

All-Butter Pastry Dough

MAKES ENOUGH FOR A 9- OR 10-INCH SINGLE-CRUST PIE
ACTIVE TIME: 15 MINUTES ■ START TO FINISH: 1¼ HOURS
(INCLUDES CHILLING)

■ Make this rich pie dough once or twice, and you'll have the recipe memorized. It's that simple. ■

1¼ cups all-purpose flour
¼ teaspoon salt
1 stick (8 tablespoons) cold unsalted butter, cut into ½-inch cubes
3–4 tablespoons ice water

Whisk together flour and salt in a large bowl. Blend in butter with your fingertips or a pastry blender (or pulse in a food processor) until most of mixture resembles coarse meal with some small (roughly pea-sized) butter lumps. Drizzle 3 tablespoons ice water evenly over mixture and gently stir with a fork (or pulse in processor) until incorporated. Squeeze a small handful of dough: if it doesn't hold together, add more ice water ½ tablespoon at a time, stirring (or pulsing) until just incorporated. Do not overwork, or pastry will be tough.

Turn dough out onto a lightly floured surface and divide into 4 portions. With heel of your hand, smear each portion once or twice in a forward motion to help distribute fat. Gather all dough together, press into a ball, and flatten into a 5-inch disk. Wrap tightly in plastic wrap and refrigerate until firm, at least 1 hour.

COOK'S NOTE

■ The dough can be refrigerated for up to 1 day. It can also be frozen, well wrapped, for up to 1 month.

Tarts

Blueberry Lemon Cream Tart

SERVES 6 TO 8
ACTIVE TIME: 30 MINUTES ■ START TO FINISH: 1¼ HOURS

■ A quick alternative to cheesecake, this tart pairs pristine summery berries with a no-cook cream cheese filling and an easy graham cracker crust (use packaged crumbs to save time). If your brown sugar contains lumps, force it through a sieve before using. Otherwise, it won't dissolve in the filling. ■

FOR CRUST
1½ cups graham cracker crumbs (from about twelve 4¾-by-2¼-inch crackers)
2 tablespoons granulated sugar
¾ stick (6 tablespoons) unsalted butter, melted
FOR FILLING
3 tablespoons packed light brown sugar
⅓ cup sour cream
½ teaspoon vanilla extract
1 (8-ounce) package cream cheese, softened
1 teaspoon finely grated lemon zest
2 cups (about 10 ounces) blueberries
GARNISH: confectioners' sugar
SPECIAL EQUIPMENT: a 9- to 9½-inch fluted tart pan with a removable bottom

MAKE THE CRUST: Put a rack in middle of oven and preheat oven to 350°F.

Stir together graham cracker crumbs, sugar, and butter in a bowl with a fork until well combined. Using your fingers and back of a spoon, press crumb mixture evenly and firmly over bottom and up sides of tart pan.

Bake crust until slightly darker, about 10 minutes. Cool completely on a rack.

MEANWHILE, MAKE THE FILLING: Whisk together brown sugar, sour cream, and vanilla in a small bowl until sugar is dissolved.

Beat cream cheese in a medium bowl with an electric mixer until smooth and fluffy, about 2 minutes.

Add sour cream mixture and zest, beating until just combined.

Spread cream cheese filling in cooled tart shell and top with blueberries.

Just before serving, dust tart with confectioners' sugar.

Citrus Tart

SERVES 8
ACTIVE TIME: 40 MINUTES ■ START TO FINISH: 3½ HOURS
(INCLUDES COOLING)

■ At her restaurant, Magnolia Grill in Durham, North Carolina, the pastry chef Karen Barker serves this wondrous tart with fresh raspberries and whipped cream. It's also perfect all by itself. ■

FOR TART SHELL

    1 large egg, separated
    1 tablespoon whole milk
  1¼ cups plus 2 tablespoons all-purpose flour
    4 teaspoons sugar
    ⅛ teaspoon salt
    1 stick (8 tablespoons) cold unsalted butter, cut
       into ½-inch cubes

FOR FILLING

    4 large eggs
  1½ cups sugar
    2 teaspoons finely grated orange zest
  1½ teaspoons finely grated lemon zest
    ½ cup fresh orange juice
    ½ cup fresh lemon juice (from about 2 lemons)
    ¼ cup heavy cream

OPTIONAL ACCOMPANIMENTS: raspberries and whipped
       cream
SPECIAL EQUIPMENT: a 9- to 9½-inch fluted tart pan with a
       removable bottom

MAKE THE TART SHELL: Lightly beat yolk with milk in a small bowl.

Pulse together flour, sugar, and salt in a food processor. Add butter and pulse until mixture resembles coarse meal with some small (roughly pea-sized) butter lumps. Alternatively, make dough in a bowl, blending in butter with your fingers or a pastry blender. Add yolk mixture and pulse just until dough begins to gather into a ball (or stir in yolks with a fork). Turn dough out, form into a ball, and flatten into a 6-inch disk. Wrap tightly in plastic wrap and refrigerate until firm, about 1 hour.

Let dough soften slightly at room temperature before rolling out.

Roll out dough between sheets of plastic wrap into a 12-inch round. Discard top sheet, invert dough into tart pan, and remove plastic wrap. Fit dough into pan and push edges of dough to ⅛ inch above rim. Trim dough to even edges; save scraps to repair any cracks in partially baked shell.

Freeze shell until firm, about 10 minutes.

Meanwhile, put a rack in middle of oven and preheat oven to 350°F.

Prick shell all over with a fork. Line shell with foil and fill with pie weights or dried beans. Bake until edges are golden and bottom is set, about 20 minutes. Carefully remove foil and pie weights. Bake until bottom is pale golden, 10 to 15 minutes more. Transfer tart pan to a rack. (Leave oven on.)

Lightly beat egg white with a fork in a small bowl. Quickly repair any cracks in shell with reserved scraps and immediately brush hot pastry all over with some egg white.

MAKE THE FILLING AND BAKE THE TART: Whisk together all ingredients in a bowl until well combined. Put tart pan on a baking sheet, transfer to oven, and carefully pour filling into shell. Cover edges with a pie shield or foil to prevent overbrowning. Bake tart until filling is barely set and still trembles slightly in center when gently shaken, 20 to 25 minutes.

Cool completely in pan on a rack, about 45 minutes. (Filling will continue to set as it cools.) Serve with raspberries and whipped cream, if desired.

- The filling can be made up to 1 day ahead and refrigerated, covered. Bring to room temperature before using.
- The tart can be baked up to 3 hours ahead and kept at room temperature.

Summer Berry Mint Cream Tart

SERVES 8
ACTIVE TIME: 30 MINUTES ■ START TO FINISH: 3½ HOURS
(INCLUDES CHILLING)

■ A rich pastry cream infused with mint and lightened with whipped cream sets off a jumble of fresh berries. A crisp, cookielike crust holds it all together. This tart embodies summer's best flavors. ■

FOR MINT CREAM
    1 cup whole milk
    ⅓ cup coarsely chopped fresh mint
    3 large egg yolks
    ½ cup sugar
    1½ tablespoons cornstarch
    1 teaspoon vanilla extract
    ½ cup very cold heavy cream
FOR TART SHELL
    1 stick (8 tablespoons) unsalted butter, softened
    ⅓ cup sugar
    ¼ teaspoon salt
    ½ teaspoon vanilla extract
    1¼ cups all-purpose flour
FOR TOPPING
    1 quart strawberries, hulled
    2 cups (about 10 ounces) blueberries
    1 cup raspberries
SPECIAL EQUIPMENT: a 10- to 10½-inch fluted tart pan with a removable bottom

MAKE THE MINT CREAM: Bring milk and mint to a boil in a small saucepan. Remove from heat and let steep, covered, for 30 minutes.

Pour milk through a fine-mesh sieve into a bowl, pressing hard on mint; discard mint. Whisk together yolks, sugar, cornstarch, and vanilla in cleaned pan, whisk in milk, and bring to a boil over moderate heat,

whisking constantly. Boil, whisking, for 2 minutes. Pour pastry cream through a fine-mesh sieve into a bowl. Refrigerate, surface covered with wax paper, until cold, about 3 hours.

MEANWHILE, MAKE THE TART SHELL: Beat together butter, sugar, salt, and vanilla in a bowl with an electric mixer at medium speed. Reduce speed to low and add flour, blending until mixture forms crumbs that hold together when pressed.

Turn crumbs out into tart pan and press evenly over bottom and up sides of pan. Refrigerate for 30 minutes.

Put a rack in lower third of oven and preheat oven to 375°F.

Prick shell all over with a fork. Line with foil and fill with pie weights or dried beans. Bake shell until edges are golden and bottom is set, about 25 minutes. Carefully remove foil and weights and bake until bottom and sides are golden, about 10 minutes more. Cool shell in pan on a rack for 5 minutes, then remove side of pan and cool completely.

ASSEMBLE THE TART: Beat heavy cream in a bowl with electric mixer until it holds stiff peaks. Whisk pastry cream to loosen, then whisk in half of whipped cream. Fold in remaining whipped cream gently but thoroughly.

Put tart shell on a serving plate and fill with mint cream. Stand strawberries in mint cream and scatter blueberries and raspberries over and around strawberries. Refrigerate, loosely covered with plastic wrap, for 1 hour (no longer) before serving.

COOK'S NOTES
- The tart shell can be baked up to 1 day ahead and kept, tightly wrapped in plastic wrap, at room temperature.
- The mint cream, without the whipped cream, can be made up to 1 day ahead and refrigerated, covered.

Pear and Almond Tart

SERVES 6 TO 8
ACTIVE TIME: 1 HOUR ■ START TO FINISH: 3 HOURS
(INCLUDES COOLING)

■ In the Alsace region of France, versions of this dessert are typically made with apples, but we love it with pears. Their delicate flavor goes well with the tart's easy crème fraîche custard and crunchy sugared almond topping. Fruit brandies, or eaux-de-vie, are specialties of the area, and the Poire Williams teases out the essence of the fruit. ∎

FOR TART SHELL

1¼ cups all-purpose flour
1½ tablespoons sugar
¼ teaspoon salt
7 tablespoons cold unsalted butter, cut into bits
1 large egg yolk
2½ tablespoons cold water

FOR FILLING

2 firm but ripe Anjou or Bartlett pears
2½ tablespoons Poire Williams (pear brandy) or Cognac
2 large eggs
1 large egg yolk
2 tablespoons sugar
¼ teaspoon vanilla extract
⅔ cup crème fraîche or heavy cream
Pinch of salt

FOR TOPPING

1 cup (about 3½ ounces) sliced unblanched almonds
¼ cup sugar
1 large egg white

SPECIAL EQUIPMENT: a 9- to 9½-inch fluted tart pan with a removable bottom

MAKE THE DOUGH: Whisk together flour, sugar, and salt in a large bowl (or pulse together in a food processor). Blend in butter with your fingertips or a pastry blender (or pulse in food processor) until mixture resembles coarse meal with some small (roughly pea-sized) butter lumps. Beat together yolk and water in a small bowl with a fork and stir (or pulse) into flour mixture until well combined. Knead mixture gently in bowl with floured hands just until a dough forms.

Turn dough out onto a lightly floured surface and knead gently 4 or 5 times. Form dough into a ball and flatten into a 5-inch disk. Wrap tightly in plastic wrap and refrigerate until firm, about 1 hour.

MAKE THE TART SHELL: Roll out dough on a lightly floured surface with a floured rolling pin into a 13-inch round. Slide bottom of tart pan under dough and set into rim of tart pan. Trim edges, leaving a ½-inch overhang, and fold overhang over. Press dough against sides of pan, pushing dough to ¼ inch above rim. Lightly prick bottom of shell all over with a fork. Refrigerate until firm, 10 to 15 minutes.

Meanwhile, put a rack in middle of oven and preheat oven to 350°F.

Line shell with foil and fill with pie weights or dried beans. Bake until edges are pale golden and bottom is set, 20 to 25 minutes. Carefully remove foil and weights and bake shell until bottom and sides are golden, 15 to 20 minutes more. Transfer to a rack. Put a large baking sheet on middle oven rack.

MAKE THE FILLING AND BAKE THE TART: Peel pears, halve, core, and cut lengthwise into ¼-inch-wide slices. Toss pears with 1 tablespoon pear brandy in a bowl. Arrange pears, overlapping, in tart shell.

Cover edges with a pie shield or foil to prevent overbrowning, put pie pan on hot baking sheet, and bake just until pears are barely tender, 10 to 12 minutes.

Meanwhile, whisk together eggs, yolk, sugar, vanilla, crème fraîche, salt, and remaining 1½ tablespoons pear brandy in a bowl until smooth.

Pour crème fraîche mixture over pears and bake until custard is just set 2 inches from edges, about 18 minutes.

MEANWHILE, MAKE THE TOPPING: Stir together all ingredients. Remove tart from oven and remove pie shield. Gently sprinkle topping over custard and bake until top is pale golden, about 15 minutes more.

Cool tart to warm or room temperature on rack.

COOK'S NOTES

■ The dough can be refrigerated for up to 2 days.
■ The tart shell can be baked up to 1 day ahead. Cool, uncovered, then wrap tightly in plastic wrap and keep at room temperature.
■ The tart can be baked up to 8 hours ahead, cooled completely, and refrigerated, covered. Bring to room temperature before serving.

Raspberry Crumble Tart

SERVES 8 TO 10
ACTIVE TIME: 30 MINUTES ■ START TO FINISH: 3½ HOURS
(INCLUDES COOLING)

■ To make this stunning tart, we turn half of the pastry ingredients into a nutty streusel topping. In between the streusel and the bottom crust, loads of ripe raspberries bake into a juicy filling. ■

2½ cups all-purpose flour
1½ sticks (12 tablespoons) cold unsalted butter, cut into ½-inch cubes
¼ cup cold vegetable shortening, preferably trans fat–free
½ teaspoon salt
4–7 tablespoons ice water
¾ cup unblanched whole almonds, chopped
¾ cup sugar
4 (6-ounce) containers raspberries (6 cups)
SPECIAL EQUIPMENT: a 10- to 10½-inch fluted tart pan with a removable bottom

MAKE THE DOUGH: Blend together flour, butter, shortening, and salt in a bowl with your fingertips or a pastry blender (or pulse in a food processor) just until mixture resembles coarse meal with some small (roughly pea-sized) butter lumps.

Transfer 2 cups mixture to a medium bowl (reserve remaining mixture in bowl, or transfer it from processor to a bowl), drizzle ¼ cup ice water evenly over it, and stir gently with a fork until incorporated. Squeeze a small handful of dough: if it doesn't hold together, add more ice water ½ tablespoon at a time, stirring until incorporated. (Do not overwork dough, or pastry will be tough.)

Turn dough out onto a work surface and divide into 4 portions. With heel of your hand, smear each portion once or twice in a forward motion to help distribute fat. Gather all dough together and press into a ball, then flatten into a 5-inch disk. If dough is sticky, dust lightly with additional flour. Wrap disk tightly in plastic wrap and refrigerate until firm, about 1 hour.

MEANWHILE, MAKE THE TOPPING: Add almonds and sugar to reserved dough mixture and rub together until some large clumps form.

ASSEMBLE AND BAKE THE TART: Put a rack in lower third of oven and put a large baking sheet on it. Preheat oven to 375°F.

Roll out dough on a lightly floured surface with a lightly floured rolling pin into a 13-inch round. Fit into tart pan and trim edges, leaving a ½-inch overhang. Fold overhang under pastry and press against rim of pan to reinforce sides.

Fill shell with berries and sprinkle evenly with topping. Bake on hot baking sheet until topping and crust are golden and filling is bubbling, 55 to 60 minutes; loosely cover with a sheet of foil after 30 minutes to prevent overbrowning.

Cool tart on a rack for 20 minutes, then remove side of pan and cool completely, about 45 minutes.

Cranberry Eggnog Tart

SERVES 8
ACTIVE TIME: 45 MINUTES ■ START TO FINISH: 5¼ HOURS
(INCLUDES MAKING JAM AND CHILLING)

■ This tart is a beautiful addition to any holiday table. Its glory lies in the thin layers of sparkling cranberry jam that sandwich the creamy eggnog filling spiked with bourbon. The jam isn't just for decoration; the tangy fruit helps balance the richness. A chunky compote of cranberries and candied orange is a lively finishing touch. ■

FOR CRUST
1¼ cups all-purpose flour
¼ cup sugar
½ teaspoon salt
7 tablespoons unsalted butter, softened
1 large egg
FOR FILLING
1½ (8-ounce) packages cream cheese, softened
2 tablespoons crème fraîche or heavy cream
½ cup plus 2 tablespoons sugar
2 large eggs
2 large egg yolks
3 tablespoons bourbon

1 teaspoon vanilla extract
Scant ½ teaspoon freshly grated nutmeg
Scant ¼ teaspoon salt
Cranberry Jam (recipe follows)
¼ cup water

ACCOMPANIMENT: Candied Orange and Cranberry Compote (page 788)

SPECIAL EQUIPMENT: a 10-inch fluted quiche pan (2 inches deep) with a removable bottom or a 9-inch springform pan

MAKE THE CRUST: Pulse together all ingredients in a food processor just until a dough forms.

If using a springform pan, invert bottom of pan (to make it easier to slide tart off bottom) and lock on side. Turn crust mixture out into quiche or springform pan and press evenly over bottom and up sides of pan (2 inches up sides if using springform pan) with floured fingers. Refrigerate until firm, about 30 minutes.

Put a rack in middle of oven and preheat oven to 350°F.

Line shell with foil and fill with pie weights or dried beans. Bake until edges are pale golden and bottom is set, 20 to 25 minutes. Carefully remove foil and pie weights and bake shell until edges are golden and bottom is pale golden, 15 to 20 minutes more. Cool completely on a rack. Reduce oven temperature to 300°F.

MAKE THE FILLING: Blend cream cheese, crème fraîche, and sugar in food processor until creamy, about 1 minute. Add eggs, yolks, bourbon, vanilla, nutmeg, and salt and process until smooth.

Melt jam with water in a small heavy saucepan over moderately low heat, stirring until smooth. Spread half of jam evenly over bottom of shell (leave remaining jam in saucepan). Let stand until jam is set, about 5 minutes. Gently pour cream cheese mixture over jam.

BAKE THE TART: Cover edges of tart shell with a pie shield or foil and bake until filling is set but still trembles slightly in center when shaken, 35 to 40 minutes. Cool tart completely in pan on a rack. (Filling will continue to set as it cools.)

GLAZE THE TART: Reheat remaining jam over low heat, stirring, until pourable. Pour over filling and spread evenly with an offset spatula or back of a spoon. Refrigerate tart, uncovered, until cold, at least 2 hours.

Remove side of pan before serving tart with cranberry compote.

COOK'S NOTES

■ The tart shell can be baked up to 3 days ahead and kept, wrapped in plastic wrap, at cool room temperature.

■ The tart can be refrigerated for up to 2 days (cover after 2 hours).

Cranberry Jam

MAKES ABOUT 2 CUPS
ACTIVE TIME: 15 MINUTES ■ START TO FINISH: 1 HOUR

■ It takes no time at all to make this glittering, ruby-hued jam, and it's worth making extra. Spread it on buttered toast or put it in a turkey sandwich. ■

1 (12-ounce) bag fresh or frozen cranberries (not thawed)
1 cup sugar
½ cup fresh orange juice (from about 1½ oranges)
1 cup water

Bring all ingredients to a boil in a 2-quart heavy saucepan over moderate heat, stirring occasionally. Reduce heat and simmer, uncovered, stirring occasionally, until slightly thickened, about 20 minutes (jam will continue to thicken as it cools).

Force jam through a fine-mesh sieve into a bowl, pressing on solids; discard solids. Cool, stirring occasionally.

COOK'S NOTE

■ The jam can be made up to 4 days ahead and refrigerated, covered.

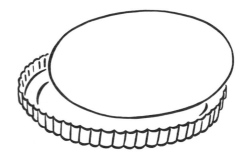

Candied Orange and Cranberry Compote

MAKES ABOUT 2 CUPS
ACTIVE TIME: 30 MINUTES ■ START TO FINISH: 2 HOURS
(INCLUDES CHILLING)

■ Consider doubling the recipe: this sweet compote is also delicious with vanilla ice cream or plain yogurt. ■

- ¾ cup water
- ¾ cup sugar
- 1 large navel orange, quartered lengthwise and sliced crosswise paper-thin (including peel; see Cook's Note)
- ¼ cup fresh or frozen cranberries (not thawed), thinly sliced
- 1 tablespoon Grand Marnier, Cointreau, or other orange-flavored liqueur

Bring water and sugar to a boil in a 2-quart heavy saucepan over moderate heat, stirring until sugar is dissolved. Add orange and gently simmer over moderately low heat, stirring occasionally, until peel begins to turn translucent and syrup is reduced to about ⅔ cup, 25 to 35 minutes. Transfer to a heatproof bowl and cool.

Stir in cranberries and Grand Marnier and refrigerate, covered, until cold, about 1 hour.

COOK'S NOTES
- It's important that the orange be sliced very thin, so the peel releases all its bitterness. An extremely sharp thin-bladed knife is best for the task.
- The compote can be refrigerated for up to 4 days.

Ricotta Tart with Dried Fruit Compote

SERVES 8 TO 10
ACTIVE TIME: 1 HOUR ■ START TO FINISH: 1 DAY
(INCLUDES CHILLING)

■ After a rich holiday meal, this gently sweet ricotta and cream cheese tart hits all the right notes. Lighter than a cheesecake and very refined, it becomes unforgettable with the addition of a rich compote of dried fruit. Figs, sour cherries, and apricots (we much prefer the tangy California kind over Turkish apricots) cooked in a white wine syrup flavored with vanilla bean and lemon zest provide a nice contrast to the tart's creaminess. The dessert is equally good chilled and at room temperature. ■

FOR TART SHELL
- 1 cup all-purpose flour
- 3 tablespoons sugar
- ½ teaspoon salt
- 1 stick (8 tablespoons) cold unsalted butter, cut into ½-inch cubes
- 1 teaspoon finely grated lemon zest
- 1 large egg yolk
- ½ teaspoon vanilla extract
- 1 tablespoon water

FOR RICOTTA FILLING
- 3 ounces cream cheese, softened
- ¼ cup sugar
- ⅛ teaspoon ground cinnamon
- ¾ pound (generous 1⅓ cups) ricotta, preferably fresh (for homemade, see page 231)
- 1 large egg, plus 1 large egg white, lightly beaten
- ⅛ teaspoon salt

FOR FRUIT COMPOTE
- 2½ cups water
- 2½ cups dry white wine
- ½ cup plus 2 tablespoons sugar
- ½ vanilla bean, halved lengthwise
- 3 (3-by-½-inch) strips lemon zest, removed with a vegetable peeler
- 1 cup (5 ounces) dried Calimyrna figs, trimmed and halved lengthwise
- ½ cup dried California apricots
- ¼ cup dried sour cherries

SPECIAL EQUIPMENT: an 8- to 8½-inch fluted tart pan with a removable bottom

MAKE THE TART SHELL: Generously butter tart pan.

Pulse flour, sugar, and salt in a food processor until combined. Add butter and zest and pulse until mixture resembles coarse meal with some small (roughly pea-sized) butter lumps. Or make dough in a bowl, blending in butter with your fingertips or a pastry blender. Add yolk, vanilla, and water and pulse (or toss with a fork) until just incorporated and dough begins to form large clumps.

Turn dough out onto a work surface and divide into 4 pieces. Smear each piece once with heel of your hand in a forward motion to help distribute fat. Gather all dough together, form into a ball, and flatten into a disk.

Press dough evenly over bottom and up sides of pan with well-floured fingers. Refrigerate shell for 45 minutes.

Put a rack in middle of oven and preheat oven to 375°F.

Lightly prick shell all over with a fork. Line with foil and fill with pie weights or dried beans. Bake shell until edges are golden and bottom is set, about 20 minutes. Carefully remove foil and weights and bake until bottom and sides are golden, about 15 minutes more. Cool shell completely in pan on a rack. (Leave oven on.)

MAKE THE FILLING: Beat together cream cheese, sugar, and cinnamon in a bowl with an electric mixer at medium-high speed until pale and fluffy, about 2 minutes. Reduce speed to low and mix in ricotta, egg and egg white, and salt until just combined.

Pour filling into cooled tart shell. Bake until slightly puffed around edges and just set in center, 15 to 20 minutes; center should tremble when tart is gently shaken. Transfer tart to a rack and cool completely.

Loosely cover tart with plastic wrap and refrigerate until filling is firm, at least 8 hours.

MEANWHILE, MAKE THE COMPOTE: Combine water, wine, sugar, vanilla bean, and zest in a 3- to 4-quart heavy saucepan and bring to a boil over medium heat, stirring until sugar is dissolved. Stir in figs and simmer, uncovered, until tender, 5 to 10 minutes.

Transfer figs with a slotted spoon to a bowl. Stir apricots into syrup and simmer until tender, about 3 minutes.

Transfer apricots with slotted spoon to bowl with figs. Stir cherries into syrup and simmer until just tender, about 1 minute. Add to fruit using slotted spoon.

Boil syrup until reduced to about 1 cup, 10 to 15 minutes.

Discard lemon zest and vanilla bean, pour syrup over fruit, and cool to room temperature.

Serve tart with compote.

COOK'S NOTES
- The tart can be refrigerated for up to 2 days (cover tightly after 8 hours). Bring to room temperature before serving if desired.
- The compote can be made up to 3 days ahead and kept in an airtight container at room temperature.

Macadamia Coconut Tart

SERVES 8 TO 10
ACTIVE TIME: 25 MINUTES ■ START TO FINISH: 5½ HOURS
(INCLUDES MAKING DOUGH AND COOLING)

■ Think of this attractive tart as a tropical version of pecan pie. The sweet, buttery filling bakes up like a custard, and each slice is packed with macadamia nuts and sweetened flaked coconut. ■

Basic Pastry Dough for a single-crust pie (page 781)
3 large eggs
1¼ cups packed light brown sugar
½ teaspoon vanilla extract
¼ teaspoon salt
½ stick (4 tablespoons) unsalted butter, melted and cooled slightly
1½ cups (7 ounces) dry-roasted macadamia nuts, toasted (see Tips, page 911) and coarsely chopped
1 cup sweetened flaked coconut
SPECIAL EQUIPMENT: a 10- to 10½-inch fluted tart pan with a removable bottom

Roll out dough on a lightly floured surface with a lightly floured rolling pin into a 13-inch round. Fit into tart pan and trim edges flush with rim. Refrigerate until firm, about 30 minutes.

Put a rack in middle of oven and preheat oven to 375°F.

Lightly prick bottom of shell all over with a fork. Line with foil and fill with pie weights or dried beans. Bake until edges are pale golden and bottom is set, about 20 minutes. Remove foil and weights and bake until bottom and sides are deep golden, 10 to 15 minutes more. Transfer to a rack to cool. (Leave oven on.)

Whisk together eggs, brown sugar, vanilla, and salt in a bowl until combined. Whisk in melted butter, nuts, and coconut. Pour filling into tart shell.

Bake until set in center, 25 to 30 minutes. Cool tart on a rack for 30 minutes.

Remove side of pan and cool to room temperature, 1½ to 2 hours.

COOK'S NOTES

- The tart can be made up to 1 day ahead and kept, covered loosely with foil, at room temperature.
- Macadamias' very high oil content makes them perishable; if possible, smell or taste them before you buy.

Chocolate Truffle Tart

SERVES 10
ACTIVE TIME: 20 MINUTES ■ START TO FINISH: 7 HOURS
(INCLUDES CHILLING)

■ This silky tart celebrates chocolate. A foolproof crisp chocolate cookie crust cozies up to a voluptuous, almost puddinglike ganache filling. Adding eggs and butter to a classic ganache and using bittersweet chocolate results in a well-rounded flavor and super-creamy texture. A dusting of unsweetened cocoa powder completes the truffle effect. ■

FOR CRUST
1½ cups finely ground chocolate wafers, such as
     Nabisco Famous (28 wafers)
¾   stick (6 tablespoons) unsalted butter, melted and
     cooled

FOR FILLING
½   pound bittersweet chocolate (no more than 60%
     cacao; see page 705), coarsely chopped
¾   stick (6 tablespoons) unsalted butter, cut into
     ½-inch cubes
2   large eggs, lightly beaten
⅓   cup heavy cream
¼   cup sugar
¼   teaspoon salt
1   teaspoon vanilla extract

GARNISH: unsweetened cocoa powder
SPECIAL EQUIPMENT: an 8-inch springform pan

MAKE THE CRUST: Put a rack in middle of oven and preheat oven to 350°F. Lightly butter side of pan.

Stir together ground wafers and butter in a bowl until combined. Pat mixture evenly over bottom of pan and 1½ inches up side.

Bake until crust is slightly puffed, about 10 minutes. Cool completely on a rack, about 15 minutes. (Leave oven on.)

MEANWHILE, MAKE THE FILLING: Melt chocolate and butter in a 2-quart heavy saucepan over low heat, stirring until smooth. Remove from heat and cool for 5 minutes.

Whisk together eggs, cream, sugar, salt, and vanilla in a bowl. Whisk in chocolate mixture until well combined.

ASSEMBLE AND BAKE THE TART: Pour filling into cooled crust and rap pan once on counter to eliminate any air bubbles. Bake until filling 1 inch from edges is set and slightly puffed but center still trembles slightly when pan is gently shaken, 20 to 25 minutes.

Cool tart completely in pan on a rack, about 2 hours. (Center will continue to set as it cools.)

Refrigerate tart, uncovered, until center is firm, about 4 hours. Remove side of pan and sprinkle with cocoa before serving.

COOK'S NOTES

- The crust can be made up to 1 day ahead and kept, covered, at room temperature.
- The tart can be refrigerated for up to 3 days (cover loosely after it's completely chilled).

Cranberry Almond Crostata

SERVES 8
ACTIVE TIME: 1 HOUR ■ START TO FINISH: 4½ HOURS
(INCLUDES COOLING)

■ The Italian sweet tarts known as crostatas are made with *pasta frolla*, a rich, crumbly pastry dough, and filled with anything from jam to chocolate to ricotta. The proportion of filling to pastry is our idea of perfection, and crostatas make an ideal Thanksgiving dessert.

This one gets its zest from fresh cranberries cooked down and paired with a sweet, almondy crust. ■

FOR PASTRY DOUGH
- ¾ cup unblanched whole almonds, toasted (see Tips, page 911)
- 2 cups all-purpose flour
- 1¼ sticks (10 tablespoons) unsalted butter, softened
- ½ cup packed light brown sugar
- 1 large egg, lightly beaten
- ½ teaspoon vanilla extract
- ⅛ teaspoon almond extract
- 2 teaspoons finely grated lemon zest
- ½ teaspoon salt

FOR FILLING AND ASSEMBLY
- 2½ cups fresh or frozen (not thawed) cranberries
- ¼ cup fresh orange juice
- ½ cup sweet orange marmalade
- ½ cup packed light brown sugar
- ¼ teaspoon salt
- 1 tablespoon granulated sugar

SPECIAL EQUIPMENT: a 9-inch springform pan

MAKE THE DOUGH: Pulse almonds with ¼ cup flour in a food processor until finely ground (be careful not to grind to a paste).

Beat together butter and brown sugar in a medium bowl with an electric mixer at medium speed until pale and fluffy, about 3 minutes. Reserve 1 tablespoon beaten egg, refrigerated, for egg wash. Beat remaining egg into butter mixture, mixing well. Beat in vanilla and almond extracts. At low speed, mix in almond mixture, zest, salt, and remaining 1¾ cups flour just until a dough forms.

Turn dough out, divide in half, and press each half into a ball. Form each ball into a 5- to 6-inch disk. Wrap each one tightly in plastic wrap and refrigerate until firm, at least 30 minutes.

MAKE THE FILLING: Combine cranberries, orange juice, marmalade, brown sugar, and salt in a 3- to 4-quart heavy pot and bring to a boil, stirring, then reduce heat and simmer, uncovered, until some of cranberries burst and mixture is slightly thickened, about 5 minutes. Spread filling in a shallow baking pan, for quicker cooling, and refrigerate it until lukewarm, about 15 minutes.

BAKE THE CROSTATA: Put a rack in middle of oven and put a foil-lined large baking sheet on rack. Preheat oven to 375°F. Invert bottom of springform pan (to make it easier to slide crostata off bottom) and lock on side. Generously butter pan.

Roll out 1 piece of dough between sheets of parchment or wax paper into a 12-inch round (dough will be very tender). Remove top sheet of paper and invert dough into springform pan. (Dough may tear, but it can be patched together with your fingers.) Remove paper and press dough over bottom and up side of pan. Trim dough to ½ inch up side of pan. Refrigerate.

Roll out remaining dough into a 12-inch round in same manner. Remove top sheet of paper. Cut dough into ten ⅓-inch-wide strips with a pastry wheel or sharp knife and slide, still on paper, onto a tray. Freeze strips until firm, about 10 minutes.

Spread filling in chilled shell. Arrange 5 strips 1 inch apart on filling. Arrange remaining 5 strips 1 inch apart diagonally across first strips to form a diamond-shaped lattice. Trim edges of all strips flush with edges of shell. Brush lattice with reserved beaten egg and sprinkle crostata with sugar.

Put crostata on hot baking sheet and bake until pastry is golden and filling is bubbling, 50 to 60 minutes. (If pastry is too brown after 30 minutes, loosely cover crostata with foil.)

Cool crostata completely on a rack, 1½ to 2 hours (to allow juices to thicken).

COOK'S NOTES
- The dough can be refrigerated for up to 8 hours.
- The crostata is best the day it is baked, but it can be made up to 1 day ahead and kept, covered with foil, at room temperature.

Fig Crostata

SERVES 8
ACTIVE TIME: 1 HOUR ■ START TO FINISH: 3¼ HOURS
(INCLUDES MAKING DOUGH AND COOLING)

■ This tart is a bit like a glorified Fig Newton, but it's much more subtle, with a beguiling orange perfume and a generous proportion of fig to tender crust. Peeping out from under a crosshatch of sweet pastry dough, the jammy fig filling sparkles like amber and garnet. The recipe comes from the Italian food expert and cookbook author Michele Scicolone. ∎

Italian Sweet Pastry Dough (recipe follows)
1 pound dried Calimyrna figs, trimmed and
    chopped (3 cups)
1 cup water
½ cup fresh orange juice (from about 1½ oranges)
¼ cup sugar
1 egg yolk, lightly beaten with 1 teaspoon water
    for egg wash
SPECIAL EQUIPMENT: a 9- to 9½-inch fluted tart pan with
    a removable bottom; parchment paper

Roll out larger piece of dough (keep remaining piece refrigerated) on a well-floured surface with a floured rolling pin into an 11-inch round. Fit dough into tart pan and trim edges flush with rim of pan. Refrigerate until firm, about 30 minutes.

Meanwhile, line a large baking sheet with parchment paper. Roll out smaller disk of dough into a 10-inch round in same manner. Transfer (rolled up on rolling pin) to lined baking sheet. Unroll and cut into ½-inch-wide ribbons with a pastry wheel or sharp knife. Refrigerate until firm, about 30 minutes.

Stir together figs, water, orange juice, and sugar in a heavy 3- to 4-quart saucepan and bring to a boil, stirring to dissolve sugar. Reduce heat and simmer, covered, stirring occasionally, until figs are tender and most of liquid has been absorbed, about 15 minutes. (If softened figs are still very moist, uncover pan and continue to simmer.) Spread fig filling on a platter and refrigerate, uncovered, until cooled completely, about 30 minutes.

Put a rack in lower third of oven and put a large baking sheet on rack. Preheat oven to 375°F.

Spread filling evenly in chilled tart shell. Arrange half of dough strips 1 inch apart on filling. Brush strips with some of egg wash. Arrange remaining dough strips (1 inch apart) across first strips to form a lattice. Trim all strips flush with side of pan and press them into edges of shell. Brush lattice with egg wash.

Put tart on hot baking sheet and bake until crust is golden brown and filling is bubbling all over, 35 to 45 minutes.

Cool tart on a rack for 10 minutes, then remove side of pan and cool completely.

COOK'S NOTE
∎ The crostata can be made up to 8 hours ahead and kept loosely covered, at room temperature.

Italian Sweet Pastry Dough
Pasta Frolla

MAKES ENOUGH FOR A 9-INCH DOUBLE-CRUST TART
ACTIVE TIME: 15 MINUTES ∎ START TO FINISH: 1½ HOURS
(INCLUDES CHILLING)

∎ *Pasta frolla* translates as "tender pastry," and this rich dough is just that. Made with flour, butter, eggs, and sugar and flavored with citrus zest, it is similar to a cookie dough and takes well to traditional jam or nut fillings. ∎

2⅓ cups all-purpose flour
⅓ cup sugar
½ teaspoon salt
    Finely grated zest of 1 orange
1½ sticks (12 tablespoons) cold unsalted butter,
    cut into bits
1 large egg
1 large egg yolk
1 teaspoon vanilla extract

Whisk together flour, sugar, salt, and zest in a large bowl. Blend in butter with your fingertips or a pastry blender (or pulse in a food processor) until mixture resembles coarse meal with some small (roughly pea-sized) butter lumps. Whisk together egg, yolk, and vanilla in a small bowl, add to flour mixture, and toss with a fork (or pulse) until incorporated.

Turn dough out onto a work surface and knead it lightly with heel of your hand to distribute egg. Divide dough into 2 portions, one slightly larger than the other. Form each one into a ball and flatten into a 5-inch disk. Wrap each disk tightly in plastic wrap and refrigerate for at least 1 hour.

COOK'S NOTE
∎ The dough can be refrigerated for up to 8 hours. Let stand at room temperature if necessary until softened but still firm before rolling out.

Peach Blueberry Torte

SERVES 8
ACTIVE TIME: 25 MINUTES ■ START TO FINISH: 3½ HOURS
(INCLUDES COOLING)

■ The base of this luscious dessert is an easy-to-make pastry that bakes up moist and crumbly, with a texture that's a cross between a biscuit and a cake. It cooks for a long time at a moderate temperature, which helps keep the ripe blueberries in the filling from bursting and releasing their juices. Note that it is important to make this in a standard light-colored springform pan; baking in a dark metal pan (including nonstick) will make it brown too quickly—the crust's high sugar content makes it more susceptible to burning. ■

FOR PASTRY
  1½ cups all-purpose flour
  ½ cup sugar
  1 teaspoon baking powder
  ¼ teaspoon salt
  1 stick (8 tablespoons) cold unsalted butter, cut into ½-inch cubes
  1 large egg
  1 teaspoon vanilla extract
FOR FILLING
  ½ cup sugar
  2 tablespoons all-purpose flour
  1 tablespoon quick-cooking tapioca
  2 pounds firm but ripe large peaches (4), halved lengthwise, pitted, and each half cut into 4 wedges
  1 cup blueberries
  1 tablespoon fresh lemon juice
SPECIAL EQUIPMENT: a 9-inch springform pan; an electric coffee/spice grinder

MAKE THE PASTRY: Pulse together flour, sugar, baking powder, and salt in a food processor until combined. Add butter and pulse just until mixture resembles coarse meal with some small (roughly pea-sized) butter lumps. Add egg and vanilla and pulse just until dough clumps and begins to form a ball.

Turn dough out and press evenly over bottom

(about ¼ inch thick) and all the way up side of springform pan with floured fingertips. Refrigerate pastry until firm, about 10 minutes.

MEANWHILE, MAKE THE FILLING: Put a rack in middle of oven and preheat oven to 375°F.

Grind 2 tablespoons sugar with flour and tapioca in grinder until tapioca is powdery. Transfer to a large bowl and stir in remaining 6 tablespoons sugar. Add peaches and blueberries with lemon juice and gently toss to coat.

Spoon filling into pastry shell. Bake, loosely covered with foil, until filling is bubbling in center and crust is golden, about 1¾ hours. Transfer in pan to a rack and cool, uncovered, for 20 minutes.

Carefully remove side of pan and cool to barely warm or room temperature.

COOK'S NOTE
■ The pastry can be made and pressed into the pan up to 1 day ahead. Refrigerate, tightly wrapped in plastic wrap. Remove from the refrigerator 30 minutes before filling.

Apricot Galette

SERVES 6
ACTIVE TIME: 20 MINUTES ■ START TO FINISH: 50 MINUTES

■ This thin, pretty, free-form tart is fast and foolproof. Using frozen puff pastry means there's no fuss making or rolling pie dough. Any fresh apricots will work, including tart underripe ones. ■

  ¼ cup sliced almonds
  ¼ cup confectioners' sugar
  1 sheet frozen puff pastry (from a 17.3-ounce package), thawed
  5 apricots, halved, pitted, and cut into ⅛-inch-thick wedges
  1 tablespoon granulated sugar

Put a rack in middle of oven and preheat oven to 425°F. Butter a large baking sheet.

Pulse almonds with confectioners' sugar in a food processor until finely ground.

Unfold pastry sheet on a lightly floured work surface and cut out a 9-inch round (discard scraps). Transfer round to baking sheet and prick all over with a fork. Spoon almond mixture evenly over pastry, leaving a ¼-inch border all around. Arrange apricot wedges decoratively, overlapping them, on top of almond mixture and sprinkle with granulated sugar.

Bake galette until edges are golden brown, about 25 minutes. Transfer with a metal spatula to a rack to cool.

Serve warm or at room temperature.

Apple "Pizza"

SERVES 6 TO 8
ACTIVE TIME: 20 MINUTES ■ START TO FINISH: 1½ HOURS

■ The playful name of this dessert refers to both its looks and the fact that it contains cheese. The cheese is cheddar—a nod to the all-American combination. Homey, rich, and not too sweet, this is one tasty dessert. ■

    1 sheet frozen puff pastry (from a 17.3-ounce package),
        thawed
    2 tablespoons fine dry bread crumbs
  1½ pounds Golden Delicious apples (3 medium),
        peeled, halved lengthwise, cored, and thinly sliced
        crosswise
  1½ tablespoons unsalted butter
    ¼ cup sugar
    ⅛ teaspoon salt
    1 cup grated sharp or extra-sharp white cheddar
        (about 4 ounces)

SPECIAL EQUIPMENT: parchment paper

Put a rack in middle of oven and preheat oven to 400°F. Line a baking sheet with parchment paper.

Unfold pastry sheet and roll out on a lightly floured surface with a floured rolling pin into a 15-by-12-inch rectangle. Transfer to lined baking sheet and prick all over with a fork. Sprinkle bread crumbs over pastry.

Put apples in a bowl. Heat butter in a small saucepan over moderate heat, swirling pan, until golden brown, about 1 minute. Pour butter over apples, add sugar and salt, and toss to coat.

Spread apples evenly over pastry, leaving a 1-inch

border on all sides. Fold edges over apples, pressing down firmly on folded corners and sides. Bake until apples are tender, 35 to 40 minutes.

Sprinkle cheese over apples and bake until cheese is golden and bubbling, 5 to 9 minutes. Serve warm.

Plum Galette

SERVES 8
ACTIVE TIME: 45 MINUTES ■ START TO FINISH: 3 HOURS
(INCLUDES MAKING DOUGH AND COOLING)

■ The beauty of plums is on display in this galette. It's accompanied by sweetened Armagnac-scented crème fraîche. ■

      Basic Pastry Dough for a single-crust pie
        (page 781)
    2 tablespoons semolina flour (see Sources)
    ½ cup granulated sugar
    5 large black or red plums, halved, pitted, and cut into
        8 wedges each
    1 tablespoon confectioners' sugar
    ¾ cup crème fraîche or sour cream
    1 tablespoon Armagnac, Cognac, or other brandy
        (optional)

SPECIAL EQUIPMENT: parchment paper

Put a rack in middle of oven and preheat oven to 375°F. Line a 17-by-12-inch baking sheet with parchment paper.

Roll out dough on a lightly floured surface with a lightly floured rolling pin into a 13-inch round. Transfer to baking sheet (edges will hang over sides of sheet).

Stir together semolina flour and 2 tablespoons sugar in a small cup and spread evenly over dough, leaving a 1-inch border all around. Arrange plums skin side down in one layer on top of sugar mixture. Sprinkle plums with 3 tablespoons sugar. Fold over edges of dough to cover outer rim of plums, pleating dough as necessary.

Bake galette, loosely covered with foil, for 40 minutes. Remove foil and bake until fruit is tender and juices are bubbling, about 5 minutes more.

Transfer baking sheet to a rack and immediately brush hot juices from galette over plums using a pastry brush. Dust galette with confectioners' sugar (sugar will melt and help glaze galette). Cool to warm, about 30 minutes, or room temperature.

Meanwhile, stir together crème fraîche, Armagnac (if using), and remaining 3 tablespoons sugar in a bowl until sugar is dissolved.

Serve galette with crème fraîche.

Nana's Almond Butter Galette

SERVES 8 TO 10
ACTIVE TIME: 30 MINUTES ■ START TO FINISH: 2½ HOURS
(INCLUDES COOLING)

■ Reader Armelle Curley of Smithtown, New York, shared this recipe with us. Her French mother traditionally made it for Easter, but it's delicious any time of the year. It features a filling of cinnamon-scented almond paste between two layers of buttery pastry. Be sure to use almond paste, not marzipan. Though they have the same ingredients, almond paste has more nuts and less sugar than marzipan and therefore has a more pronounced almond flavor. ■

    2 cups all-purpose flour
    ¾ cup sugar
    1 teaspoon baking powder
       Salt
    1½ sticks (12 tablespoons) unsalted butter, softened
    3 large eggs, 1 left whole, 2 separated
    ⅓ cup pure almond paste (not marzipan; see Sources)
    1 teaspoon ground cinnamon
    ¼ cup warm water

SPECIAL EQUIPMENT: a 9-inch springform pan

Put a rack in middle of oven and preheat oven to 350°F.

Whisk together flour, sugar, baking powder, and ¼ teaspoon salt in a bowl. Blend in butter with your fingertips or a pastry blender until mixture resembles coarse meal. Add whole egg and 2 yolks and knead in bowl until a soft dough forms, about 5 minutes.

Put ¾ cup dough between two sheets of plastic wrap and roll out into a 9½-inch round. Slide onto a baking sheet and refrigerate for 15 minutes.

Transfer remaining dough to springform pan, cover it with a large sheet of plastic wrap, and press evenly onto bottom of pan. Discard plastic wrap.

Blend almond paste with cinnamon and 1 tablespoon water in a food processor until crumbled (paste may be hard). Add remaining 3 tablespoons water a little at a time, processing until paste is smooth.

Beat together whites and ⅛ teaspoon salt in a medium bowl with an electric mixer at medium-high speed until whites just hold stiff peaks. Fold in almond paste mixture gently but thoroughly.

Spread almond mixture on top of dough in pan and tap side of pan gently to smooth surface.

Remove top sheet of plastic from dough round and cut twelve ½-inch-wide strips from center portion of dough round (reserve scraps for patching dough if necessary). Arrange 6 strips 1 inch apart over almond mixture. Trim ends of strips flush with side of pan. Arrange 6 remaining strips 1 inch apart diagonally across first strips to form a diamond-shaped lattice. (If dough becomes too soft as you work, refrigerate until firm.) Repair any broken strips by carefully pressing them together, then trim ends of strips flush with side of pan. Discard remaining dough.

Bake galette until pale golden, about 45 minutes. Cool in pan on a rack for 10 minutes.

Run a thin knife around edges of galette to loosen it if necessary, remove side of pan, and cool galette completely, about 30 minutes.

COOK'S NOTE
■ The galette can be made up to 1 day ahead and kept, covered with foil, at room temperature.

Pecan Praline Torte

SERVES 12
ACTIVE TIME: 1 HOUR ■ START TO FINISH: 2 HOURS

■ Beautifully elegant and wickedly tasty, this torte is from Nancy Brewer of the Kitchen Shop in Grand Coteau, Louisiana, where it is known as Gâteau

Na-Na. The sweet pastry dough, fragrant with orange zest, melts in your mouth. Like most praline desserts, this one is quite sweet. We like the crunch and sparkle that turbinado sugar adds to the top of the torte, but feel free to omit it. ■

FOR PECAN PRALINE FILLING
- ½ stick (4 tablespoons) unsalted butter
- ½ cup packed light brown sugar
- ⅓ cup mild honey
- 2 cups (about 7½ ounces) pecans, coarsely chopped

FOR DOUGH
- 2 sticks (½ pound) unsalted butter, softened
- 1 cup granulated sugar
- 4 large egg yolks
- 1 teaspoon finely grated orange zest
- 1 teaspoon vanilla extract
- 3 cups sifted all-purpose flour (sift before measuring)
- 1 tablespoon unsalted butter, melted
- 1½ tablespoons turbinado sugar, such as Sugar in the Raw (optional)

SPECIAL EQUIPMENT: parchment paper; a 9-inch round cake pan; a 10-inch round cake pan

MAKE THE FILLING: Cut one 11-inch round and two 10-inch rounds of parchment paper. Butter 9-inch cake pan and line with 11-inch parchment round, folding and pleating parchment as necessary to fit up sides of pan.

Bring butter, brown sugar, and honey to a boil in a 2- to 2½-quart heavy saucepan over moderate heat, stirring until butter is melted. Boil for 3 minutes. Remove from heat and quickly stir in pecans. Immediately pour mixture into parchment-lined pan and press evenly into bottom of pan with back of a large metal spoon. Cool filling on a rack.

MAKE THE DOUGH: Put a rack in middle of oven and preheat oven to 350°F. Butter 10-inch cake pan and line bottom with a 10-inch parchment round.

Beat together butter and sugar in a large bowl with an electric mixer until pale and fluffy. Add yolks one at a time, beating well after each addition, and continue to beat until mixture is light and fluffy. Beat in zest and vanilla. Add flour 1 cup at a time, beating just until well combined; do not overwork, or pastry will be tough.

Turn dough out, divide into 2 portions, one slightly larger than the other, and form each one into a ball. Dampen your fingertips and pat larger ball of dough evenly over bottom of 10-inch cake pan and halfway up sides.

Remove praline filling from pan and place smooth side up on dough in pan. Dampen your fingers and pat out smaller ball of dough evenly on remaining 10-inch parchment round (all the way to edges), then invert onto praline. Gently peel off parchment and press dough together at edges. Gently make a crosshatch pattern on top of torte with a fork.

Brush top of torte with butter and sprinkle with turbinado sugar, if using.

Bake torte until golden brown, 40 to 50 minutes. Cool on a rack for 5 minutes, then run a thin knife around edges to loosen torte if necessary, carefully invert torte onto another rack, and remove parchment. Invert again, onto a platter. Serve warm.

COOK'S NOTE
■ The torte can be made up to 5 days ahead and kept, covered, at cool room temperature. Reheat in a 350°F oven before serving, about 10 minutes.

Portuguese Cream Tarts

MAKES 24 INDIVIDUAL TARTS
ACTIVE TIME: 40 MINUTES ■ START TO FINISH: 1½ HOURS

■ Served blistered and warm from the oven and sprinkled liberally with confectioners' sugar and cinnamon, these rich egg custard tarts, called *pastéis de nata*, are a national obsession in Portugal. Because they are meant to be eaten in just a few bites, they are best when baked in ⅓-cup muffin cups. Since many manufacturers have increased the size of their pans, we also tested the tarts in easier-to-find ½-cup muffin cups. The pastry dough doesn't reach the tops of these cups, making the tarts rather squat, but they are still delicious. ■

FOR PASTRY
- 1 (17.3-ounce) package frozen puff pastry
- 1 tablespoon unsalted butter, melted

FOR CUSTARD FILLING
  1 cup granulated sugar
  2 tablespoons all-purpose flour
  2½ cups heavy cream
  1¼ teaspoons finely grated lemon zest
  8 large egg yolks
  ¼ teaspoon salt
  1 teaspoon vanilla extract
FOR TOPPING
  1 tablespoon confectioners' sugar
  ½ teaspoon ground cinnamon
SPECIAL EQUIPMENT: 2 muffin pans with 12 muffin cups
  each, preferably ⅓-cup (see headnote)

SHAPE THE TART SHELLS: Thaw pastry just until sheets can be unfolded but are still quite stiff. Gently unfold 1 sheet and cut along folds into 3 equal strips. Stack strips and cut lengthwise into twelve ¼-inch-wide strips, leaving strips stacked. Repeat with remaining pastry sheet.

Turn each triple strip on its side and coil tightly to form a flat 2- to 2½-inch-wide spiral. On a lightly floured surface, press each spiral with heel of your hand to flatten it into a 3-inch round.

Lightly grease muffin cups with melted butter. Place rounds in muffin cups and press into bottom and up sides, lining cups to within ⅛ inch of top if using ⅓-cup cups (if using larger muffin cups, dough will not reach all the way up sides).

MAKE THE FILLING: Whisk together sugar and flour in a 3-quart heavy saucepan, whisk in remaining filling ingredients, and cook over moderate heat, stirring constantly, until first bubble appears on surface, about 10 minutes. (Custard will be thick.) Transfer custard to a bowl and cool, whisking occasionally, until just warm, about 15 minutes.

Meanwhile, put a rack in upper third of oven and preheat oven to 450°F.

Fill pastry cups with custard, about 2 tablespoons each. Bake tarts until pastry is deep golden, 10 to 12 minutes (filling may brown).

Cool tarts slightly in pans on a rack, about 10 minutes, then lift from pans onto rack using a small offset spatula or table knife. Sift confectioners' sugar and cinnamon over tarts. Serve warm or at room temperature.

Almond Cream Puff Pastry Galette

SERVES 8
ACTIVE TIME: 20 MINUTES ■ START TO FINISH: 55 MINUTES

■ Since the Middle Ages, it has been traditional in parts of France to serve this flaky, buttery galette filled with rich almond cream on January 6, the Feast of the Epiphany, twelve days after Christmas. Its name, *galette des rois*, means galette "of kings." Whoever finds the bean (called a *fève* for the fava bean that was originally used and said to symbolize the Baby Jesus) in a slice is crowned king (or queen) for the day. ■

  ¼ cup pure almond paste (not marzipan; see Sources)
  ¼ cup granulated sugar
  3 tablespoons unsalted butter, softened
    Pinch of salt
  2 large eggs
  ¼ teaspoon vanilla extract
  ¼ teaspoon almond extract
  2 tablespoons all-purpose flour
  1 (17.3-ounce) package frozen puff pastry, thawed
  1 dried bean, such as a lima bean (optional)
  1½ teaspoons confectioners' sugar

Put racks in upper and lower thirds of oven and preheat oven to 450°F. Butter a large baking sheet (not dark metal).

Blend almond paste, granulated sugar, butter, and salt in a food processor until smooth. Blend in 1 egg, vanilla, and almond extract. Add flour and pulse until incorporated.

Roll out 1 puff pastry sheet on a lightly floured surface with a floured rolling pin into an 11½-inch square. Brush off excess flour from both sides. Cut an 11-inch round from pastry sheet by tracing with tip of a paring knife, using an inverted plate or pan lid as a guide. Transfer round to buttered baking sheet (discard trimmings) and refrigerate. Repeat procedure with second pastry sheet; leave round on floured surface.

Beat remaining egg with a fork and brush some over top of second round. Score round decoratively all over using tip of knife. Make several small slits through pastry at about 2-inch intervals for steam vents.

Brush some of egg in a 1-inch-wide border around edges of chilled pastry round. Mound almond cream in center of chilled round, spreading it slightly. Bury bean, if using, in cream. Cover with decorated round and press edges together with tines of a fork.

Bake galette in lower third of oven until puffed and pale golden, 13 to 15 minutes. Dust galette with confectioners' sugar and bake in upper third of oven until edges are deep golden brown and shiny, 12 to 15 minutes more.

Transfer to a rack to cool slightly, 5 to 10 minutes. Serve warm.

Pastries

Sweet Blini

SERVES 8
ACTIVE TIME: 45 MINUTES ■ START TO FINISH: 1¾ HOURS

■ Stuffed with fruit preserves, these sweet blini, adapted from those served at Café Pushkin in Moscow, make an ideal dessert. The batter is made with yeast, which gives the blini a wonderful lightness. ■

  1 teaspoon active dry yeast
  2 tablespoons plus 1 teaspoon sugar
  ¼ cup warm water (105°–115°F)
  1 cup all-purpose flour
  ½ teaspoon salt
  1 cup warm whole milk (105°–115°F)
  3 large eggs
  ½ stick (4 tablespoons) unsalted butter, melted
      and cooled
  1 cup apricot preserves
  1 tablespoon fresh lemon juice
GARNISH: confectioners' sugar

MAKE THE BATTER: Stir together yeast, 1 teaspoon sugar, and warm water in a small bowl and let stand until foamy, about 5 minutes. (If mix-

ture doesn't foam, discard and start over with new yeast.)

Transfer yeast mixture to a blender, add flour, salt, milk, and remaining 2 tablespoons sugar, and blend until combined. Pour into a bowl and cover with a kitchen towel. Let stand in a warm draft-free place until almost doubled in bulk, about 1 hour.

Return mixture to blender and add eggs and 2 tablespoons butter. Blend until smooth.

MAKE THE BLINI: Lightly brush a 10-inch nonstick skillet with some melted butter and heat over moderately high heat until hot but not smoking. Holding skillet off heat, pour in ⅓ cup batter, immediately tilting and rotating skillet to coat bottom. (If batter sets before skillet is coated, reduce heat slightly.) Return skillet to heat and cook crêpe until underside and edges are just set and golden, about 1½ minutes. (Loosen edge of crêpe with a heatproof rubber spatula to check.) Carefully flip crêpe over with your fingertips and cook until other side is golden, about 1 minute more. Transfer crêpe to a plate. Brush skillet with more melted butter and make 7 more crêpes in same manner, stacking them and brushing skillet between crêpes.

Puree preserves with lemon juice in a food processor until smooth.

Spread 1½ teaspoons preserves on a crêpe and fold in eighths (fold in half, fold in half again, and then again) to form a triangle. Repeat with remaining crêpes and preserves.

Brush a 12-inch heavy skillet with remaining butter. Arrange crêpes in 1 layer in pan, with points at center of skillet. Cook over moderate heat until crêpes just begin to brown, 1 to 2 minutes. Flip crêpes over with a spatula and cook for 1 minute more.

Transfer to a platter and dust with confectioners' sugar.

Raspberry Crème Fraîche Puffs

MAKES 9 PUFFS
ACTIVE TIME: 20 MINUTES ■ START TO FINISH: 40 MINUTES

■ Napoleons juxtapose creamy filling with shatteringly crisp pastry. This casual variation introduces a little tang to the mix by using crème fraîche, which goes well with the ripe raspberries glistening with liqueur. Best of all, the dessert takes just minutes to make. ■

1 sheet frozen puff pastry (from a 17.3-ounce package), thawed
3 cups (about 14 ounces) raspberries
3 tablespoons framboise or other raspberry-flavored eau-de-vie or Chambord
5 tablespoons granulated sugar
1¼ cups crème fraîche
¾ teaspoon vanilla extract
GARNISH: confectioners' sugar

Put a rack in upper third of oven and preheat oven to 400°F.

Unfold pastry sheet and cut into nine 3-inch squares with a sharp knife.

Put pastry squares on an ungreased baking sheet and bake until golden brown, 15 to 20 minutes. Transfer pastry to a rack and cool completely.

Meanwhile, stir together raspberries, eau-de-vie, and 1 tablespoon sugar in a bowl. Let macerate at room temperature for 30 minutes.

Stir together crème fraîche, remaining ¼ cup sugar, and vanilla in another bowl until sugar is dissolved.

Halve each pastry square horizontally.

Just before serving, top bottom halves of pastry with crème fraîche mixture, then raspberries and juices. Cover with top halves and dust with confectioners' sugar.

Mandarin Orange Napoleons

MAKES 4 NAPOLEONS
ACTIVE TIME: 20 MINUTES ■ START TO FINISH: 35 MINUTES

■ Canned mandarin oranges and packaged phyllo dough come together in an easy rendition of a traditionally time-consuming dessert. The Chinese five-spice powder adds a hint of spice to the sugar sprinkled on the phyllo sheets. ■

½ teaspoon Chinese five-spice powder
¼ cup granulated sugar
4 (17-by-12-inch) sheets phyllo, thawed if frozen
3 tablespoons unsalted butter, melted
1 (8-ounce) package cream cheese, softened
1½ teaspoons fresh lemon juice
½ teaspoon vanilla extract
2 (11-ounce) cans mandarin oranges in light syrup, drained, syrup reserved
GARNISH: confectioners' sugar

Put a rack in middle of oven and preheat oven to 375°F.

Whisk together five-spice powder and 2 tablespoons sugar in a small bowl.

Unfold phyllo and cover with plastic wrap and a dampened kitchen towel. Transfer 1 phyllo sheet to a large baking sheet, brush with some butter, and sprinkle with one third of spiced sugar. Make 2 more layers in same manner. Top with remaining phyllo sheet and brush with remaining butter. (For a corrugated look, invert a large rectangular wire rack on top of phyllo before baking.)

Bake until golden, 12 to 15 minutes. Carefully remove wire rack, if you used it, and transfer phyllo with two metal spatulas to a rack to cool.

Meanwhile, blend together cream cheese, lemon juice, vanilla, 2 tablespoons reserved orange syrup (discard remainder), and remaining 2 tablespoons sugar in a food processor until smooth. Transfer to a bowl and fold in oranges.

Break phyllo into 12 pieces or cut into pieces with a serrated knife. Arrange 1 piece of phyllo on a plate and top with a dollop of orange cream. Repeat layering and top with another piece of phyllo. Make 3 more napoleons in same manner. Dust with confectioners' sugar.

COOK'S NOTE
■ The phyllo can be baked up to 1 day ahead and kept, tightly wrapped, at room temperature.

Fig and Gingered Mascarpone Napoleons

MAKES 7 NAPOLEONS
ACTIVE TIME: 30 MINUTES ■ START TO FINISH: 1¼ HOURS

■ An impressive dessert that is also impressively easy: chopped fresh figs and crystallized ginger add a bit of zing to mascarpone cheese, the not-too-sweet filling. The crisp puff pastry is layered with sliced juicy figs and the mascarpone. ■

    1 sheet frozen puff pastry (from a 17.3-ounce package),
        thawed
   26 firm but ripe fresh figs (1½ pounds)
    1 cup (8½ ounces) mascarpone
    1 tablespoon finely chopped crystallized ginger, or
        to taste
   2½ tablespoons sugar
    ⅛ teaspoon vanilla extract
      Confectioners' sugar for dusting

Unfold pastry and roll out on a lightly floured surface with a floured rolling pin into a 15-by-12-inch rectangle. Trim edges. Halve pastry lengthwise with a pastry wheel or a large knife, then cut each strip crosswise into 7 equal rectangles (for a total of 14). Arrange rectangles in one layer on two large baking sheets and refrigerate for 20 minutes.

Put a rack in upper third of oven and preheat oven to 400°F.

Trim and chop 4 figs. Stir together with mascarpone, ginger, sugar, and vanilla in a bowl. Refrigerate filling, covered.

Cover pastry rectangles on one baking sheet with an inverted large wire rack to lightly weight them and bake until golden and cooked through, 15 to 18 minutes. Carefully remove rack and transfer baked pastry to a rack to cool completely. Bake remaining rectangles, weighted with rack (make sure it's cooled), in same manner.

Meanwhile, cut remaining figs lengthwise into ¼-inch-thick slices.

Spread filling over 7 pastry rectangles and top with half of sliced figs, overlapping them. Dust with confectioners' sugar. Cover figs with remaining pastry rectangles and top with remaining figs, overlapping them. Dust with confectioners' sugar.

Hazelnut Paris-Brest

SERVES 10 TO 12
ACTIVE TIME: 1½ HOURS ■ START TO FINISH: 3½ HOURS
(INCLUDES COOLING)

■ This classic French creation—a large ring of delicate choux pastry split and filled with rich pastry cream sweetened with homemade praline—makes a stunning end to a holiday meal. Think of it as an oversized éclair. The golden pastry crackles on top with sliced almonds and then gives way to a light, airy interior, a nice juxtaposition to the cool, creamy filling. As for the name, the wheel-shaped dessert was created in 1891 in honor of a bicycle race from Paris to Brest and back again that was the precursor of the Tour de France. ■

FOR PRALINE
   ½ cup granulated sugar
   1 cup (about 4¾ ounces) hazelnuts,
       toasted (see Tips, page 911), loose skins
       rubbed off
   ¼ cup sliced almonds, toasted (see Tips,
       page 911)
FOR CREAM FILLING
   1 cup whole milk
   3 large egg yolks
   ⅓ cup granulated sugar
   3 tablespoons cornstarch
   ¼ teaspoon salt
   2 tablespoons unsalted butter
   ½ teaspoon vanilla extract
   ¾ cup very cold heavy cream
FOR CHOUX PASTRY
   1 cup water
   1 stick (8 tablespoons) unsalted butter, cut into
       ½-inch cubes
   1 teaspoon granulated sugar
   ½ teaspoon salt
   1 cup all-purpose flour
   4 large eggs

1 large egg yolk, lightly beaten with 1 tablespoon
water for egg wash

3 tablespoons sliced almonds

1 tablespoon confectioners' sugar

GARNISH: confectioners' sugar

SPECIAL EQUIPMENT: parchment paper; a pastry bag; a
⅝-inch plain tip; a ½-inch open star tip

MAKE THE PRALINE: Lightly grease a baking sheet. Heat sugar in a 10-inch heavy skillet over moderate heat, stirring with a fork to heat sugar evenly, until it starts to melt. Stop stirring and cook, swirling skillet occasionally, so sugar melts evenly, until it is a dark amber caramel.

Remove from heat and, working quickly, stir in nuts to coat. Transfer mixture to greased baking sheet, spreading it slightly. Let stand until hardened and cooled, about 30 minutes.

Transfer praline to a heavy-duty sealable plastic bag and seal, pressing out excess air. Coarsely crush praline using a rolling pin or bottom of a heavy skillet. Transfer three quarters of praline to a food processor and blend to a smooth, creamy paste, 3 to 4 minutes. Reserve remaining crushed praline for garnish.

MAKE THE FILLING: Bring milk to a simmer in a 2½- to 3-quart heavy saucepan over moderate heat.

Meanwhile, whisk together yolks, sugar, cornstarch, and salt in a heatproof bowl. Add hot milk to yolk mixture in a stream, whisking. Transfer mixture to saucepan and bring to a simmer over moderate heat, whisking (mixture will become thick and lumpy). Simmer, whisking constantly, for 3 minutes (mixture will become smooth). Remove from heat and stir in butter and vanilla until butter is melted.

Transfer to a clean bowl and refrigerate pastry cream, surface covered with parchment or wax paper, until cold, at least 1 hour.

Beat heavy cream in a bowl with an electric mixer until it just holds stiff peaks. Beat pastry cream in a large bowl until smooth. Add praline paste and beat until incorporated. Gently but thoroughly fold in whipped cream one third at a time. Refrigerate, surface covered with parchment paper, until ready to use.

MAKE THE PASTRY: Put a rack in middle of oven and preheat oven to 425°F. Trace a 9-inch circle on a 12-inch square of parchment paper, then trace a 5-inch circle inside it. Turn paper over and put on a large baking sheet.

Bring water, butter, granulated sugar, and salt to a boil in a 3-quart heavy saucepan over high heat, stirring until butter is melted. Reduce heat to moderate, add flour all at once, and cook, stirring vigorously with a wooden spoon, until mixture pulls away from sides of pan, about 1 minute. Continue to cook and stir vigorously (to dry out mixture) for 3 minutes more.

Remove pan from heat and cool mixture, stirring occasionally, until warm to the touch, 5 to 10 minutes. Add eggs one at a time, stirring vigorously after each addition until dough is smooth.

Transfer dough to pastry bag fitted with plain tip. Pipe 3 concentric rings to fill space between traced circles on parchment paper. Pipe 2 more rings on top to cover seams between bottom rings. Lightly brush pastry with egg wash, scatter almonds over pastry, and dust with 1 tablespoon confectioners' sugar.

Bake pastry until golden and well puffed, 20 to 25 minutes. Reduce oven temperature to 375°F and continue to bake until deep golden and firm to the touch, about 25 minutes more.

Prick top of pastry in 8 to 10 places with tip of a small sharp knife (to release steam) and continue to bake until golden brown, about 10 minutes more. Transfer pastry, on parchment paper, to a rack and cool completely.

Halve pastry horizontally with a serrated knife and carefully invert top onto work surface. Remove and discard any wet dough from interior of top and bottom.

Transfer hazelnut cream to pastry bag fitted with star tip and pipe cream decoratively into bottom half of pastry. Carefully reinvert top half over it, sprinkle with reserved praline, and dust with confectioners' sugar.

COOK'S NOTES

- The praline and praline paste can be made up to 2 days ahead. Refrigerate the praline paste in an airtight container and keep the remaining praline in an airtight container at room temperature.

- The pastry cream (without the praline paste and whipped cream) can be refrigerated, its surface covered

- with wax paper and the bowl covered with plastic wrap, for up to 2 days.
- The cream filling can be refrigerated for up to 4 hours.
- The choux ring can be baked (but not split) up to 8 hours ahead and kept, loosely covered with foil (not plastic wrap), at room temperature. It can also be frozen, tightly wrapped in plastic wrap, for up to 1 week. Thaw completely in the wrapping and recrisp in a 350°F oven for 10 minutes. Cool to room temperature before proceeding.
- The Paris-Brest can be assembled up to 2 hours before serving and kept at cool room temperature.

Peaches-and-Cream Éclairs with Bourbon Caramel Sauce

MAKES 8 ÉCLAIRS
ACTIVE TIME: 50 MINUTES ■ START TO FINISH: 1½ HOURS

■ Choux dough is fast, the ingredients are kitchen basic (eggs, flour, butter, and salt), and you can leave your rolling pin tucked away in a drawer. Here the pastry is the basis for outrageous éclairs filled with peaches and cream and drizzled with caramel. ■

FOR CHOUX PASTRY
    ¾ stick (6 tablespoons) unsalted butter
    ¾ cup water
    ¼ teaspoon salt
    ¾ cup all-purpose flour
    3 large eggs
FOR CARAMEL SAUCE
    1 cup sugar
    ½ cup water
    ⅛ teaspoon salt
    ½ stick (4 tablespoons) unsalted butter, cut into tablespoons
    2 tablespoons bourbon or dark rum
FOR PEACHES-AND-CREAM FILLING
    1 pound firm but ripe peaches or nectarines, halved, pitted, and cut into thin wedges
    2 tablespoons sugar

    1¼ cups very cold heavy cream
    1 teaspoon bourbon or dark rum
SPECIAL EQUIPMENT: a large pastry bag fitted with a ¾-inch plain tip

MAKE THE PASTRY: Put a rack in upper third of oven and preheat oven to 425°F. Butter a large baking sheet.

Bring butter, water, and salt to a boil in a small heavy saucepan over high heat, stirring until butter is melted. Reduce heat to moderate, add flour all at once, and cook, stirring vigorously with a wooden spoon, until mixture pulls away from sides of pan and forms a ball, about 30 seconds. Transfer mixture to a large bowl and cool slightly, about 5 minutes.

Beat in eggs one at a time with an electric mixer at high speed, beating well after each addition.

Transfer dough to pastry bag. Pipe eight 5-inch-long strips (about 1 inch wide) onto baking sheet, spacing them at least 1 inch apart.

Bake éclairs for 15 minutes. Reduce oven temperature to 400°F and bake until golden, puffed, and crisp, about 15 minutes more. Pierce side of each éclair with tip of a paring knife (to release steam) and return to oven to dry, propping door slightly ajar, for 5 minutes. Halve an éclair horizontally: if it is still moist inside, return éclairs to oven and dry for 5 minutes more.

Cool éclairs completely on a rack.

MEANWHILE, MAKE THE CARAMEL SAUCE: Heat sugar in a 10-inch heavy skillet over moderate heat, stirring with a fork to heat sugar evenly, until it starts to melt. Stop stirring and cook, swirling skillet occasionally so sugar melts evenly, until it is a dark amber caramel. Remove from heat and immediately spoon about 1 teaspoon caramel down top of each éclair, spreading it with back of spoon.

Add water and salt to caramel remaining in skillet and simmer, stirring occasionally, until all caramel is dissolved. Add butter and bourbon, swirling skillet to incorporate. Remove from heat and cover sauce to keep warm.

MAKE THE FILLING: Toss peaches with 1 tablespoon sugar in a bowl. Let stand until sugar is dissolved, about 5 minutes.

Beat cream with bourbon or dark rum and remaining tablespoon sugar with electric mixer until it just holds stiff peaks.

ASSEMBLE THE ÉCLAIRS: Halve all éclairs horizontally. Put bottom halves on plates, top with whipped cream and peaches, and cover with top halves. Drizzle plates with caramel sauce.

COOK'S NOTE

■ The éclairs can be baked (but not glazed or filled) up to 1 day ahead and kept in an airtight container at room temperature. Recrisp on a baking sheet in a 375°F oven, about 5 minutes, then cool before glazing with the caramel.

Persian Baklava

SERVES 8 TO 10
ACTIVE TIME: 50 MINUTES ■ START TO FINISH: 2½ HOURS
(INCLUDES STANDING TIME)

■ This uniquely Persian baklava mingles the exotic flavors of almond, pistachio, cardamom, and rose water. Don't be put off by the homemade dough; it's easier to work with than fragile sheets of store-bought phyllo and tastes more authentic. The recipe is adapted from one in Najmieh Batmanglij's cookbook *From Persia to Napa: Wine at the Persian Table.* ■

FOR SYRUP
  2⅓ cups sugar
  1½ cups water
  ½ cup Middle Eastern rose water (see Sources)
  2 tablespoons fresh lime juice
FOR FILLING
  4 cups (about 22 ounces) blanched whole almonds
  2 cups sugar
  2 tablespoons ground cardamom
FOR DOUGH
  ¼ cup whole milk
  ¼ cup Middle Eastern rose water
  1 large egg
  ¾ cup canola or vegetable oil
  2½ cups unbleached all-purpose flour
GARNISH: chopped or slivered shelled pistachios; dried (untreated) rose petals (see Sources; optional)
SPECIAL EQUIPMENT: a 17-by-11-inch baking sheet

MAKE THE SYRUP: Bring sugar and water to a boil in a 2-quart heavy saucepan, stirring until sugar is dissolved. Stir in rose water and lime juice, remove from heat, and cool.

MAKE THE FILLING: Pulse almonds in a food processor until finely ground (be careful not to grind to a paste). Add sugar and cardamom and pulse to combine.

MAKE THE DOUGH: Put a rack in middle of oven and preheat oven to 350°F. Lightly oil baking sheet.

Whisk together milk, rose water, egg, ½ cup oil, and 1 tablespoon rose water syrup in a large bowl. Add flour, stirring until a dough forms. Turn out onto a dry work surface and knead for 8 minutes.

Divide dough in half and form into 2 balls. Wrap 1 ball in plastic wrap. Roll out remaining ball on a lightly floured surface into a 19-by-13-inch rectangle. Roll up dough on rolling pin, then unroll over baking sheet, letting edges hang over rim slightly.

Spread filling evenly over dough, patting it down firmly with your hands or an offset spatula.

Roll out remaining dough in same manner and drape over filling, letting excess hang over rim. Press edges of dough together, then fold in edges to form a rim and crimp decoratively.

Lay a ruler diagonally across top corner of pastry and use as a guide to carefully cut through pastry with a large knife, cutting all the way through bottom layer of dough. Continue to make parallel cuts about 1 inch apart down pastry, then repeat procedure on opposite diagonal to create diamond shapes (be careful not to lift up dough).

Drizzle pastry with remaining ¼ cup oil. Bake until golden, 35 to 40 minutes. Transfer pan to a rack and pour 2 cups rose water syrup evenly over pastry. Sprinkle top with pistachios and rose petals, if using, cover tightly with foil, and let stand at room temperature for at least 1 hour before serving. (Refrigerate additional syrup, covered, to add later if baklava becomes too dry.)

COOK'S NOTE

■ The baklava keeps, covered, at room temperature for up to 1 day (add more syrup as desired). It can also be covered and refrigerated for up to 1 week or frozen, well wrapped, for up to 2 weeks. Serve at room temperature.

Cannoli

MAKES ABOUT 10 CANNOLI
ACTIVE TIME: 2 HOURS ■ START TO FINISH: 3 HOURS

■ Cannoli, the king of Sicilian pastries—delicate fried shells filled with the freshest sheep's-milk ricotta mixed with pistachios and chocolate—offers multiple textures and flavors in a single bite. And although it's quite a production, no one will ever forget this home-made version. The dough for the shells is made with lard, traditional in Sicily, and is very stiff (the Sicilian fortified wine known as Marsala helps tenderize it), but rolling it out is easy with a pasta machine. For the filling, we use a combination of fresh cow's-milk ricotta and goat cheese to mimic the tangy flavor of sheep's-milk ricotta, which can be hard to find here. If you don't like goat cheese, use additional ricotta instead. ■

FOR CANNOLI SHELLS
1 cup all-purpose flour
3 tablespoons granulated sugar
1 teaspoon unsweetened cocoa powder
   (not Dutch-process)
¼ teaspoon ground cinnamon
¼ teaspoon salt
⅛ teaspoon baking soda
1 pound cold lard
2 tablespoons sweet Marsala
1 large egg, separated
About 3 cups vegetable oil for deep-frying

FOR FILLING
1 pound (2 cups) fresh ricotta (for homemade, see
   page 231)
2 ounces soft mild goat cheese
¼ cup confectioners' sugar
1 tablespoon minced candied orange peel
   (see Sources)
½ teaspoon orange-flower water (see Sources)
¼ teaspoon ground cinnamon
⅓ cup unsalted shelled pistachios, chopped
2 ounces bittersweet chocolate, chopped

GARNISH: confectioners' sugar

SPECIAL EQUIPMENT: a pasta maker; a 4- to 4¼-inch round
   cookie cutter; a deep-fat thermometer; 6 metal

cannoli tubes; a pastry bag fitted with a ¾-inch plain tip

MAKE THE DOUGH: Whisk together flour, sugar, co-coa, cinnamon, salt, and baking soda in a bowl. Add 2 tablespoons lard and blend with your fingertips or a pastry blender until combined. Add wine and yolk and stir until a dough forms.

Turn dough out onto a lightly floured surface and knead until smooth and elastic, 5 to 7 minutes. Form dough into a disk and wrap tightly in plastic wrap. Let stand at room temperature for 1 hour.

MEANWHILE, MAKE THE FILLING: Beat together ricotta, goat cheese, confectioners' sugar, orange peel, orange-flower water, and cinnamon in a bowl with an electric mixer at medium speed for 1 minute, just until combined (do not overbeat). Fold in nuts and chocolate until combined. Refrigerate.

MAKE THE SHELLS: Line a baking sheet with plas-tic wrap. Set rollers of pasta maker at widest setting. Unwrap dough and cut in half. Lightly flour 1 piece (keep remaining dough covered with plastic wrap), flatten into an oval, and feed through rollers. Turn dial down 2 notches and feed dough through rollers again. Continue to feed dough through rollers, turn-ing dial down 2 notches each time and finishing on second-to-narrowest setting.

Transfer dough to a lightly floured surface and cut out 4 or 5 rounds with floured cutter. Transfer rounds to lined baking sheet and cover with plas-tic wrap. Roll out remaining dough and cut rounds in same manner. Gather scraps and let stand for 10 minutes, then roll out scraps and cut in same manner.

Melt remaining lard in a 4-quart heavy pot, add enough oil to reach 1¼ inches up sides of pot, and heat over moderate heat until fat registers 350°F on thermometer.

Meanwhile, lightly oil cannoli tubes. Lightly beat egg white and brush bottom edge of 1 dough round with egg white. Wrap dough around a tube, over-lapping ends (with egg-white edge on top), and press edges together to seal. Make 5 more shells in same manner (keep remaining rounds covered with plastic).

Fry dough on tubes one at a time, turning with tongs, until a shade darker, about 45 seconds.

Wearing oven mitts, clamp end of each hot tube with tongs and, holding tube vertically, allow shell to slide off tube onto paper towels, gently shaking tube and wiggling shell as needed to loosen. (If you allow shell to cool, it will stick to tube and shatter when you try to remove it.) Transfer shells to paper towels to drain and cool tubes before reusing. Wrap remaining dough around tubes and fry in same manner.

Spoon filling into pastry bag and pipe some into 1 end of a cannoli shell, filling shell halfway, then pipe into other end. Repeat with remaining shells. Dust with confectioners' sugar.

COOK'S NOTES

- The dough can be made up to 1 day ahead and refrigerated. Let stand at room temperature for 1 hour before rolling.
- The shells can be fried up to 2 days ahead and cooled completely, then kept, layered between paper towels, in an airtight container at room temperature.

FRUIT DESSERTS

When it comes to dessert, there are basically two kinds of people: chocolate lovers and fruit eaters.

Personally, I'll go for fruit every time. For me the arrival of the first spring berries is one of the happiest moments of each year. I pounce on them in the market and rush home to make strawberries in orange caramel sauce. Only after I have swallowed that first fragrant spoonful do I really believe that winter is gone. The arrival of apricots makes me even happier: I can't wait to make the first apricot cobbler of the year, and I savor each sweet-tart bite, knowing that it is just a harbinger of the season's bounty. Summer is on its way, bringing the possibility of amaretti-stuffed peaches, raspberry clafoutis, and plum berry crisp.

At my table, fall means rum-raisin poached pears; figs with balsamic vinegar, mascarpone, and walnuts; and, of course, apples, turned into everything from brown Bettys to old-fashioned dumplings. I have a special fondness for apples — so versatile, so sturdy, so easy to keep during the fall months. I always have them on hand, ready to become an apple "Tatin" cobbler if I'm feeling ambitious, or simple baked apples with candied walnuts if

I'm not. No matter what I choose, I know that cooking apples will fill the house with the fine scent of warm, sugared fall fruit.

Winter may not be high fruit season in most of the United States, but it has its compensations. Those of us who try to eat local foods in season find ourselves succumbing to the lure of fruits from faraway places when the snow is on the ground. Even on the darkest day, oranges in Marsala are a reminder that somewhere in the world the sun is shining. Flambéed bananas with rum sauce bring the tropics right to your table. And now that grapes have become a year-round staple, there is no season in which you can't end a meal with a beautiful red and green grape crisp.

Fruit desserts tend to come together easily, but that is not their primary charm. They splash the seasons across your table and turn an ordinary weeknight dinner into a harvest celebration.

FRUIT DESSERTS

Baked Apples with Candied Walnuts

SERVES 4
ACTIVE TIME: 15 MINUTES ■ START TO FINISH: 35 MINUTES

■ This recipe perks up one of the easiest desserts in the world by adding thick yogurt and a drizzle of honey at the very end. ■

- 2 Gala or Golden Delicious apples
- ½ tablespoon unsalted butter
- 4½ tablespoons sugar
- ¼ teaspoon salt
- ½ cup walnut pieces, toasted (see Tips, page 911)
- ¼ cup thick yogurt, preferably Greek, sour cream, or crème fraiche
- 2 teaspoons honey, plus (optional) additional for drizzling

Put a rack in middle of oven and preheat oven to 450°F. Oil a baking sheet.

Halve apples lengthwise and remove cores with a melon ball cutter or a paring knife.

Melt butter in a 10-inch ovenproof skillet over moderate heat and sprinkle with 1½ teaspoons sugar. Arrange apple halves cut side down in pan and cook, undisturbed, until sugar begins to caramelize, 3 to 5 minutes. Transfer skillet to oven and bake apples until tender, about 15 minutes.

Meanwhile, heat remaining ¼ cup sugar with salt in a dry 7- to 8-inch heavy skillet over moderate heat, stirring with a fork to heat sugar evenly, until it starts to melt. Stop stirring and cook, swirling pan occasionally so sugar melts evenly, until it is a dark amber caramel. Remove from heat and add walnuts, stirring to coat. Pour onto prepared baking sheet. Cool for 10 minutes, then break nuts into small pieces if necessary.

Stir together yogurt and honey in a bowl.

Serve apples cut side up in bowls, topped with yogurt and candied nuts. Drizzle with additional honey if desired.

COOK'S NOTE

■ The walnuts can be candied up to 3 days ahead and kept in an airtight container at room temperature.

Apple Prune Brown Betty

SERVES 6
ACTIVE TIME: 45 MINUTES ■ START TO FINISH: 2 HOURS

■ Bettys—baked desserts with layers of spiced fruit and buttered bread crumbs—date back to Colonial times. They are most often made with apples, but we love the sweet nudge prunes add to the dish. ■

- 6 cups ½-inch cubes bread (from a day-old baguette)
- ¾ cup pitted prunes
- 1¼ pounds Gala, Fuji, or Golden Delicious apples (3 medium), peeled, halved, cored, and cut into ⅓-inch-thick slices
- 2 tablespoons fresh lemon juice
- ¾ stick (6 tablespoons) unsalted butter, melted
- ¾ cup packed dark brown sugar
- ¾ teaspoon ground cinnamon
- ¼ teaspoon salt

ACCOMPANIMENT: heavy cream

Put a rack in middle of oven and preheat oven to 375°F.

Grind baguette cubes to coarse crumbs in 3 batches in a food processor. Spread evenly on a large baking sheet and bake, stirring once, until golden and crisp, 15 to 18 minutes. Transfer pan to a rack to cool. Reduce oven temperature to 350°F.

Meanwhile, cover prunes with boiling water in a bowl and let stand for 15 minutes.

Drain prunes and quarter them. Toss with apples and lemon juice.

Stir together 2 cups crumbs (reserve remainder for another use) and butter in a bowl. Stir together brown sugar, cinnamon, and salt in another bowl.

Spread one third of crumb mixture in a 9-inch pie plate. Cover with half of apple mixture and sprinkle with half of sugar mixture. Sprinkle with half of remaining crumbs and cover with remaining apples, then sprinkle with remaining sugar mixture. Top with remaining crumbs.

Cover with foil and bake until apples are tender, about 40 minutes. Increase oven temperature to 425°F, remove foil, and bake until top is golden brown, about 10 minutes more. Serve warm with cream.

How to Store Fruits

When it comes to storing fruit, overall rules are no substitute for your own observations. How long any fruit keeps after purchase depends on the condition it was in when picked and the way it was handled and stored. Most apples and pears, for instance, are picked when they are mature but not ripe. (When a fruit's seeds have developed enough to germinate and the fruit is large enough to attract the animals that will scatter the seeds, the fruit is considered mature.) Cherries, on the other hand, are picked when actually ripe. Generally, organic fruit in perfect condition when picked will keep longer than nonorganic fruit. The reasons why are complicated and various, but a primary one is that the skins of fruits (and vegetables) fertilized with chemicals tend to be thinner. That, coupled with their higher water content (because they're forced to grow more quickly), means they spoil more readily. If you buy fruit that is especially delicate—burstingly ripe berries come to mind—pick it over and remove any bruised specimens, for they'll become moldy in no time flat. In this day and age, it's a good idea to wash fruit, like any produce, before serving. If you do so days beforehand, though, you'll destroy the natural protective coating that keeps many of them—for example, apples, blueberries, and plums—from losing moisture, so it's best to wash the fruit just before eating.

APPLES If apples are left out at room temperature, they'll turn mealy. Keep them in the refrigerator in a plastic bag with a few holes poked in it. (The plastic maintains high humidity so the apples won't shrivel; the perforations prevent excessive moisture accumulation.) Some varieties, though, keep better than others. Early varieties such as McIntosh and Rome tend to be "cookers"—they are often soft-fleshed and consequently bruise easily. They're more perishable than the sturdier midseason and late-season "storing" varieties such as Empire and Gala. In general, large apples don't keep as well as small ones. And before putting apples in the refrigerator, remove any that are bruised, refrigerate them separately, and use them as soon as you can, because one bad apple really *can* spoil the whole bunch.

APRICOTS, PEACHES, AND NECTARINES Store at a cool room temperature.

BANANAS Store at a cool room temperature. (Refrigerated bananas will turn black on the outside, although they will be perfectly fine inside.)

BERRIES Pick them over and discard any bruised or broken berries. If they came in a wooden or cardboard container, gently return them to it; put it, in turn, in a brown paper bag; and refrigerate. If they came in a perforated plastic clamshell container, there's no need to slip the container into a paper bag. Or spread the berries out in a single layer on a baking sheet or in a shallow dish lined with paper towels and refrigerate. Berries like raspberries and strawberries are so fragile that you should keep them as dry as possible. Simply give them a brief rinse and pat them dry before using. Blueberries keep nicely in a plastic container or sealable plastic bag; they can also be frozen.

CHERRIES Store in a paper bag in the refrigerator.

CITRUS FRUITS Store in a plastic bag (to prevent them from drying out) in the refrigerator.

DATES Store fresh dates in a plastic bag in the refrigerator. Store dried dates in an airtight container at room temperature.

FIGS If not eating figs within a day, refrigerate them in a perforated plastic bag.

MANGOES Ripen at cool room temperature if necessary. Keep ripe fruit in the refrigerator.

MELONS Ripen at room temperature if necessary. Refrigerate ripe melons.

PEARS Buy pears when they're hard and ripen them at room temperature until they yield to gentle pressure at the stem end. (Because pears ripen from the inside out, if you wait until they're soft all over, they will be overripe and mushy.) If you want to keep them longer, store the unripened fruit in a perforated plastic bag in the refrigerator and remove them about a week before you plan to eat them. Pears for cooking can be underripe.

PINEAPPLES Pineapples will rot at room temperature; they prefer the dark humidity of a refrigerator drawer.

PLUMS Ripen at room temperature if necessary until the fruit loses its shine. Store ripe plums in the refrigerator.

POMEGRANATES Store at room temperature. Pomegranate seeds can be frozen.

Old-Fashioned Apple Raisin Dumplings

SERVES 6
ACTIVE TIME: 45 MINUTES ■ START TO FINISH: 1¼ HOURS

■ After we tasted these dumplings in our test kitchens, there wasn't a crumb of pastry or a drop of cider syrup left. Some apple dumplings use pie dough, but an easy biscuit dough produces even better results. Rolled very thin, it creates a light, flaky wrapper that is sturdy enough to contain the chopped apple and raisin filling. Served with vanilla ice cream, this is the best kind of comfort food. ■

FOR FILLING
    2 small tart apples, such as Granny Smith (8 ounces total), peeled, cored, and cut into ½-inch pieces
    ⅓ cup raisins
    ⅓ cup coarse fresh bread crumbs
    ¼ cup packed light brown sugar
    1½ tablespoons unsalted butter, melted
    ¼ teaspoon ground cinnamon
FOR DOUGH
    2 cups all-purpose flour
    2 teaspoons baking powder
    ½ teaspoon salt
    3 tablespoons plus 1½ teaspoons granulated sugar
    3 tablespoons cold unsalted butter, cut into pieces
    2 tablespoons cold vegetable shortening, preferably trans fat–free
    ½ cup plus 1½ teaspoons whole milk
FOR SYRUP
    1½ cups unfiltered apple cider
    1 cup packed light brown sugar
ACCOMPANIMENT: vanilla ice cream

MAKE THE FILLING: Toss together all ingredients in a bowl.

MAKE THE DOUGH: Put a rack in middle of oven and preheat oven to 425°F. Generously butter a 13-by-9-inch baking dish.

Sift together flour, baking powder, salt, and 3 tablespoons sugar into a bowl. Blend in butter and shortening with a pastry blender or your fingertips just until mixture resembles coarse meal with a few small (roughly pea-sized) butter lumps. Add ½ cup milk and stir with a fork just until mixture is moistened.

Turn dough out onto a floured work surface and gently knead 7 or 8 times, until a soft dough forms (do not overwork, or dumplings will be tough). Roll out dough on a well-floured surface with a floured rolling pin into a rough 16-by-11-inch rectangle. Trim to a 15-by-10-inch rectangle. Halve dough lengthwise, then cut crosswise in thirds (to form 6 squares).

ASSEMBLE THE DUMPLINGS: Divide filling among centers of squares. Bring 4 corners of each dumpling together over filling and pinch together to seal. Transfer dumplings to buttered baking dish, arranging them about 1 inch apart. Brush tops with remaining 1½ teaspoons milk and sprinkle with remaining 1½ teaspoons granulated sugar.

MAKE THE SYRUP AND BAKE THE DUMPLINGS: Bring cider and brown sugar to a boil in a 2-quart saucepan, stirring until sugar is dissolved.

Pour syrup around dumplings. Bake until dumplings are golden brown and syrup is bubbling, 20 to 25 minutes. Serve immediately, with ice cream.

COOK'S NOTE
■ The filling and the apple syrup can be made up to 1 day ahead and refrigerated (separately), covered. Bring to room temperature before using.

Apple "Tatin" Cobbler

SERVES 8
ACTIVE TIME: 35 MINUTES ■ START TO FINISH: 1¾ HOURS
(INCLUDES STEEPING TIME)

■ In this take on a classic tarte Tatin (but without the messy inverting of a hot pan), the apples are enlivened with Calvados-soaked raisins and topped with biscuit rounds instead of pastry. Served warm from the skillet and drizzled with cream, the sugar-dusted biscuits are the perfect foil to all the sweet, bubbling apple goodness. ■

FOR APPLES
  ½ cup golden raisins
  ½ cup Calvados or other apple brandy

  ½ stick (4 tablespoons) unsalted butter
  ¾ cup granulated sugar
  3½ pounds Gala apples (7–8), peeled, cored, and cut into 1-inch pieces
  1½ tablespoons fresh lemon juice
FOR BISCUITS
  1½ cups all-purpose flour
  2 teaspoons baking powder
    Rounded ¼ teaspoon salt
  ¾ cup plus 1 tablespoon heavy cream
  1½ tablespoons turbinado sugar, such as Sugar in the Raw
ACCOMPANIMENT: heavy cream
SPECIAL EQUIPMENT: a 2¼-inch round cookie cutter

MAKE THE APPLES: Bring raisins and Calvados to a simmer in a small saucepan over medium heat and simmer until liquid is reduced to 3 tablespoons, about 4 minutes. Remove from heat and let stand, covered, for 30 minutes.

Put a rack in middle of oven and preheat oven to 425°F.

Melt butter in an ovenproof 10-inch heavy skillet over medium heat and sprinkle evenly with sugar. Toss apples with lemon juice and add to skillet, along with raisins and Calvados (pan will be full). Cook apples over moderately high heat, without stirring, until juices are deep golden and bubbling, 18 to 23 minutes. (Don't worry if juices color unevenly.)

Transfer skillet to oven and bake, uncovered, for 20 minutes.

MEANWHILE, MAKE THE BISCUITS: Stir together flour, baking powder, and salt in a medium bowl. Stir in ¾ cup cream just until a dough forms. Gather dough into a ball and turn out onto a lightly floured surface.

Gently knead dough 6 times, then pat dough into an 8-inch round. Cut out as many rounds as possible with lightly floured cutter. Gather scraps, pat out dough, and cut more rounds. (You will need 12.)

ASSEMBLE AND BAKE THE COBBLER: Arrange biscuits about ½ inch apart on apples. Brush tops with remaining tablespoon cream and sprinkle with turbinado sugar. Bake until biscuits are puffed and golden, about 15 minutes. Cool in skillet for 20 minutes.

Serve cobbler with cream.

COOK'S NOTE

■ The cobbler tastes best when just made, but it can be baked up to 3 hours ahead and kept at room temperature, covered. Reheat in a 350°F oven before serving.

Apricot Cobbler

SERVES 4
ACTIVE TIME: 25 MINUTES ■ START TO FINISH: 1½ HOURS

■ Summer's first apricots are reason to rejoice, and there's no better way to celebrate than baking up this cobbler. It is absolutely delicious hot from the oven, but we've also been known to sneak leftovers for breakfast. The topping, a classic buttermilk drop biscuit dough, couldn't be easier to make (have fun experimenting with other fruits too, such as blueberries, peaches, or sour cherries). ■

FOR FILLING
- 1½ pounds apricots, pitted and quartered
- ½ cup sugar
- 1 tablespoon cornstarch
- 1¼ teaspoons fresh lemon juice
- ⅛–¼ teaspoon almond extract (to taste)

FOR TOPPING
- 1 cup all-purpose flour
- 1 teaspoon baking powder
- ¼ teaspoon baking soda
- ¼ teaspoon salt
- 1 tablespoon sugar
- 5 tablespoons cold unsalted butter, cut into bits
- ⅓ cup well-shaken buttermilk

SPECIAL EQUIPMENT: a 9-inch glass or ceramic pie plate

MAKE THE FILLING: Toss together all ingredients in pie plate and let stand until juicy, about 30 minutes.

MAKE THE TOPPING AND BAKE THE COBBLER: Put a rack in middle of oven and preheat oven to 400°F.

Whisk together flour, baking powder, baking soda, salt, and 1 teaspoon sugar in a medium bowl. Blend in butter with your fingertips or a pastry blender until mixture resembles coarse meal with a few small (roughly pea-sized) butter lumps. Stir in buttermilk with a fork until just combined (do not overmix).

Drop rounded tablespoons of dough over filling, leaving some space in between to allow topping to expand. Sprinkle with remaining 2 teaspoons sugar.

Bake cobbler until fruit is tender when pierced with a knife and topping is golden, 30 to 35 minutes. Cool slightly, about 15 minutes, and serve warm.

COOK'S NOTE

■ The cobbler tastes best when just made, but can be baked up to 3 hours ahead and kept at room temperature, covered. Reheat in a 350°F oven before serving.

MEET THE COBBLER FAMILY

Cobblers, crisps, buckles, and brown Bettys all arrange fruit and dough in various delightful ways. Simple and old-fashioned, they capture fruits at the height of their season.

■ Think of a COBBLER— fruit topped with a crust and baked—as a fruit potpie. Most cobblers have a thick biscuit crust, which may be cut into rounds ("cobbles") or left intact. Cobblers found in the American South often sandwich the fruit filling between a top and bottom crust made of pie dough.

■ In a CRISP, the fruit is sprinkled with a streusel-like mixture of butter, sugar, flour, and, often, oatmeal or nuts that is rubbed together or pulsed in a food processor.

■ In a BUCKLE, the fruit is generally folded into (or sprinkled over) cake batter and covered with a topping similar to that found on a crisp; the cake batter will "buckle" as it bakes.

■ A BROWN BETTY is also similar to a crisp, but bread crumbs are used in place of streusel and layered with the fruit rather than scattered on top.

Vanilla-Poached Apricots with Zabaglione

SERVES 6
ACTIVE TIME: 25 MINUTES ■ START TO FINISH: 2 HOURS
(INCLUDES COOLING)

■ Silky, still-warm zabaglione, a gently cooked custard made from egg yolks, sugar, and wine, cloaks vanilla-scented fruit with a heady richness. It's normally made with Marsala, but this more subtle white wine version gives fresh apricots a chance to shine. ■

FOR APRICOTS
- ½ vanilla bean, halved lengthwise
- 1½ cups water
- 1 cup sugar
- 3 (4-by-1-inch) strips lemon zest, removed with a vegetable peeler
- ⅛ teaspoon salt
- 1¼ pounds firm but ripe apricots, halved lengthwise and pitted

FOR ZABAGLIONE
- 3 large egg yolks
- ⅓ cup sugar
- 2 tablespoons dry white wine

POACH THE APRICOTS: Scrape seeds from vanilla bean into a 2-quart saucepan, then add pod. Add water, sugar, zest, and salt. Bring to a boil over high heat, stirring to dissolve sugar, and boil for 1 minute. Carefully add apricots, reduce heat, and poach at a bare simmer, turning fruit once, until apricots are tender but still hold their shape and skins are still intact, 2 to 6 minutes.

Transfer apricots and syrup to a large shallow bowl and cool to room temperature.

JUST BEFORE SERVING, MAKE THE ZABAGLIONE: Beat together yolks, sugar, and wine in a 4-quart deep metal bowl with a handheld electric mixer at medium speed until well combined. Set bowl over a pot of barely simmering water and beat mixture until it has tripled in volume and forms a thick ribbon when beaters are lifted, 6 to 8 minutes. Remove bowl from heat.

Spoon 2 or 3 apricot halves into each of six glasses and top with zabaglione. Serve immediately.

COOK'S NOTES
- The apricots can be poached up to 2 days ahead and refrigerated, covered. Bring to room temperature before serving.
- The eggs in this recipe may not be fully cooked. If that is a concern, see page 915.

Chai-Poached Apricots and Plums

MAKES ABOUT 4 CUPS
ACTIVE TIME: 5 MINUTES ■ START TO FINISH: 1 HOUR
(INCLUDES COOLING)

■ This refined fruit compote that evokes the flavors of India goes with almost anything, from creamy yogurt and granola to cheese and crackers. Notable for their rosy skins and tart sweetness, dried Angelino plums hold their shape beautifully when cooked, but if you can't find them, just use more dried apricots. ■

- ½ vanilla bean, halved lengthwise
- ¾ cup sugar
- 3 cups water
- 1¼ cups (6 ounces) dried Angelino plums (see Cook's Note and Sources)
- 1¼ cups (6 ounces) dried California apricots
- 2 chai tea bags

Scrape seeds from vanilla bean into a 3- to 4-quart saucepan, then add pod. Add sugar and water and bring mixture to a boil, stirring occasionally until sugar is dissolved.

Add plums and simmer, uncovered, for 3 minutes. Add apricots and tea bags and return to a simmer. Cook fruit, gently stirring once or twice, for 5 minutes. Remove from heat and allow to steep for 15 minutes.

Remove tea bags, gently squeezing liquid from them into syrup. Transfer compote to a bowl or jar and cool, gently stirring occasionally.

COOK'S NOTES
- If you can't find dried Angelino plums, you can omit them and double the quantity of dried apricots.
- The compote keeps, covered and refrigerated, for up to 2 weeks.

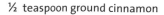

Banana Gratins

SERVES 4
ACTIVE TIME: 15 MINUTES ■ START TO FINISH: 15 MINUTES

■ Made with ingredients almost everyone has on hand, these tasty individual gratins offer a quick dessert fix. Turbinado sugar adds a sparkly crunch to bananas lavished with sour cream. ■

    2 firm but ripe bananas, thinly sliced
    1 cup sour cream
    2 teaspoons vanilla extract
    ¼ cup turbinado sugar, such as Sugar in the Raw
SPECIAL EQUIPMENT: four 5- to 6-ounce gratin dishes or
    one 1- to 1½-quart gratin dish

Preheat broiler. Divide bananas among gratin dishes (or put in gratin dish). Stir together sour cream and vanilla in a bowl, then spoon over bananas, covering them and smoothing top. Sprinkle each gratin with 1 tablespoon sugar (or sprinkle ¼ cup sugar over large gratin).

Put individual gratin dishes (if using) on a baking sheet. Broil 3 to 5 inches from heat until sugar is melted but not caramelized, about 3 minutes. Serve warm.

Flambéed Bananas with Rum Sauce

SERVES 4
ACTIVE TIME: 10 MINUTES ■ START TO FINISH: 10 MINUTES

■ A splash of rum offers a sexy grace note to flambéed bananas, whose buttery, caramelly sweetness is terrific with vanilla ice cream. ■

    ½ stick (4 tablespoons) unsalted butter
    3 firm but ripe bananas, halved crosswise and then
        lengthwise
    ⅓ cup dark rum
    ¼ cup packed brown sugar (light or dark)
    2 tablespoons water

    ½ teaspoon ground cinnamon
    ¼ teaspoon freshly grated nutmeg
    ⅛ teaspoon salt
    ½ cup chopped walnuts or pecans, toasted (see
        Tips, page 911)
ACCOMPANIMENT: vanilla ice cream

Heat butter in a 12-inch heavy skillet over moderately high heat until foam subsides. Add bananas cut side down and cook, shaking skillet, until lightly browned, about 2 minutes. Reduce heat, add rum, and increase heat to moderately high. Carefully tilt skillet over gas burner to ignite, or ignite with a long match (use caution, as flames may shoot up high). Cook, shaking skillet gently once or twice, until flames subside.

Sprinkle brown sugar, water, spices, and salt around bananas and cook, shaking skillet gently, until sugar has dissolved and sauce is slightly thickened, 1 to 2 minutes. Serve warm over vanilla ice cream, sprinkled with nuts.

Sweet Plantain Fritters

SERVES 6
ACTIVE TIME: 30 MINUTES ■ START TO FINISH: 30 MINUTES

■ Slices of creamy plantains dipped in an easy batter and fried until crisp and puffy make a delicious dessert or snack. A toss of cinnamon sugar adds a light, glittery crunch. Make sure the skins of your plantains are completely black, since the fruit becomes sweeter as it ripens. (Yellow or mottled brown plantains are very starchy, and they will usually take about a week to reach that stage.) ■

1 cup all-purpose flour
2 tablespoons light brown sugar
1 teaspoon baking powder
⅛ teaspoon salt
½ cup water
1 large egg, lightly beaten
4 very ripe (completely black) plantains
½ cup granulated sugar
½ teaspoon ground cinnamon
About 2 cups vegetable oil for shallow-frying

Whisk together flour, brown sugar, baking powder, and salt in a large bowl. Add water and egg and whisk until batter is smooth.

Peel plantains and cut on a slight diagonal into ½-inch pieces. Stir into batter to coat well.

Stir together sugar and cinnamon in a shallow bowl.

Heat ½ inch oil in a 10-inch heavy skillet over moderate heat until hot but not smoking. Fry plantain slices, in batches of 6 (don't crowd them), until bottoms are golden, about 45 seconds. Turn and fry until other sides are golden, 30 to 45 seconds more. Transfer with a slotted spoon to paper towels to drain, then, while still warm, toss each batch in cinnamon sugar until coated and transfer to a platter.

Serve fritters hot or warm.

Blueberries in Gin Syrup

SERVES 6
ACTIVE TIME: 10 MINUTES ■ START TO FINISH: 45 MINUTES
(INCLUDES COOLING)

■ An aromatic gin syrup amplifies the flavor of fresh blueberries. Serve these gorgeous sapphire berries with shortbread or spoon them over ice cream or yogurt. ■

1 cup water
¾ cup sugar
15 juniper berries, crushed (see Cook's Note)
1 (4-inch) rosemary sprig
Pinch of salt

2 pints (1½ pounds) blueberries
¼ cup dry gin
GARNISH: mint sprigs

Combine water, sugar, juniper berries, rosemary, and salt in a small saucepan and bring to a boil, stirring until sugar is dissolved. Boil syrup, without stirring, until reduced to about ¾ cup, 10 to 12 minutes.

Put blueberries in a heatproof bowl. Pour syrup through a sieve onto berries. Stir in gin. Let stand until completely cooled, about 30 minutes.

Serve berries garnished with mint sprigs.

COOK'S NOTES
■ Juniper berries can be found in the spice section of natural foods stores and large supermarkets. Also see Sources.
■ The gin can be omitted if desired.
■ The blueberries in gin syrup, once cooled, can be refrigerated, covered, for up to 1 day.

Raspberry Clafoutis

SERVES 4
ACTIVE TIME: 20 MINUTES ■ START TO FINISH: 1½ HOURS

■ Traditionally made with black cherries, clafoutis are also delicious with other small fruits. This version, with raspberries, boasts a perfect proportion of sweet, almondy custard to fruit. It couldn't be easier to pull together, and it effortlessly straddles the line between homey and elegant. ■

¼ cup blanched whole almonds
2 tablespoons all-purpose flour
¾ cup whole milk
⅓ cup plus 2 tablespoons sugar
2 large eggs
2 tablespoons unsalted butter, melted and cooled slightly
⅛ teaspoon salt
⅛–¼ teaspoon almond extract
6 ounces (about 1¼ cups) raspberries
GARNISH: confectioners' sugar

Put a rack in middle of oven and preheat oven to 400°F. Butter a shallow 1½-quart baking dish.

Pulse almonds with flour in a blender until finely ground. Add milk, ⅓ cup sugar, eggs, butter, salt, and almond extract (to taste) and blend until smooth.

Scatter raspberries in baking dish, pour batter over berries, and sprinkle with remaining 2 tablespoons sugar.

Bake clafoutis until puffed and golden, 35 to 40 minutes. Cool slightly on a rack (clafoutis will deflate slightly as it cools) and serve warm, dusted with confectioners' sugar.

Strawberries in Orange Caramel Sauce

SERVES 4 TO 6
ACTIVE TIME: 30 MINUTES ■ START TO FINISH: 30 MINUTES

■ Fresh strawberries cloaked with a Grand Marnier–spiked caramel sauce are delicious on their own or served over mascarpone or thick Greek yogurt. ■

- 1 large navel orange
- ½ stick (4 tablespoons) unsalted butter, cut into tablespoons
- ¼ cup Grand Marnier, Cointreau, or other orange-flavored liqueur
  Pinch of salt
- ½ cup sugar
- 1 pound (3 cups) small strawberries, hulled

Grate zest from orange into a small bowl, then squeeze juice into bowl. Add butter, liqueur, and salt.

Heat sugar in a dry 10-inch heavy skillet over medium heat, stirring with a fork to heat evenly, until it starts to melt. Stop stirring and cook, swirling skillet occasionally so sugar melts evenly, until it is a dark amber caramel. Remove from heat and immediately add orange juice mixture (caramel will harden and steam vigorously). Return to heat and boil, stirring until caramel has dissolved and sauce is slightly thickened, about 2 minutes. Add strawberries and cook, stirring, until heated through, about 1 minute.

Oranges in Marsala

SERVES 4
ACTIVE TIME: 20 MINUTES ■ START TO FINISH: 50 MINUTES
(INCLUDES MACERATING)

■ Sweet Marsala wine gives navel oranges a jolt of the exotic in this simple, elegant finale. ■

- 4½ navel oranges
- ½ cup sugar
- ½ cup sweet Marsala

Squeeze enough juice from ½ orange to measure 2 tablespoons. Cut off tops and bottoms of remaining 4 oranges to expose fruit. Stand each orange on a cutting board and remove peel, including all white pith, by cutting it off in vertical strips with a paring knife. Cut oranges crosswise into ¼-inch-thick slices.

Heat sugar in a dry small heavy saucepan over moderate heat, stirring with a fork to heat evenly, until it starts to melt. Stop stirring and cook, swirling pan occasionally so sugar melts evenly, until it is a dark amber caramel. Carefully add orange juice and wine (caramel will harden and steam vigorously) and cook over moderately low heat, stirring, until caramel is dissolved, about 5 minutes. Remove sauce from heat.

Arrange orange slices, overlapping, in four shallow bowls and spoon sauce over fruit. Let macerate for at least 30 minutes before serving.

COOK'S NOTE

■ The orange slices, with the sauce, can be prepared up to 4 hours ahead and kept, covered, at room temperature.

Ambrosia

■ For many Southerners, ambrosia is the "fruit of the gods." Southern chef Scott Peacock's version relies on a simple approach and the very best ingredients—fresh coconut and juicy oranges united by a whisper of sweet cream sherry. Ambrosia is equally good as a light dessert and as a side dish, offering a cool counterpoint to a rich Southern meal. You can leave out the sherry if you prefer. ■

    1 medium coconut (see Cook's Note)
    8 large navel oranges
    2 tablespoons sugar
      Pinch of kosher or sea salt
    3 tablespoons cream sherry (optional)

Put a rack in middle of oven and preheat oven to 400°F.

Pierce softest eye of coconut with a small screwdriver, drain liquid, and discard. Bake coconut in a shallow baking pan until it cracks, about 20 minutes. Remove from oven.

When coconut is cool, wrap in a towel and break shell with a hammer. Pry flesh from shell with a butter knife and remove brown skin with a vegetable peeler.

Coarsely grate coconut on large holes of a box grater, using light pressure and long strokes to produce long, feathery ribbons.

Cut off tops and bottoms of oranges to expose fruit. Stand each orange on a cutting board and remove peel, including all white pith, by cutting it off in vertical strips with a sharp paring knife. Working over a large bowl, cut segments free from membranes, letting them drop into bowl; squeeze juice from membranes into bowl.

Gently toss oranges with coconut, sugar, salt, and sherry (if using). Refrigerate, covered, for at least 1 hour.

COOK'S NOTES

■ Coconuts can sometimes be rancid—you may want to buy an extra one.

■ The oranges can be cut up to 1 day ahead and refrigerated, covered.

■ The ambrosia can be refrigerated for up to 2 hours.

Grapefruit Sabayon Gratin

■ The fluffy smoothness of this sabayon, a light custard made of egg yolks, sugar, and sweet wine, tames the spiky acidity of grapefruit. The visual contrast of Ruby Red grapefruit and the golden sabayon, browned in spots from its pass under the broiler, makes for a beautiful wintertime dessert. ■

    2 Ruby Red grapefruit, at room temperature
    2 large egg yolks
    ¼ cup sugar
    ¼ cup sweet dessert wine, such as Essensia (orange Muscat)
SPECIAL EQUIPMENT: four 5- to 6-ounce individual gratin dishes or a 1-quart gratin dish

Cut off tops and bottoms of grapefruit to expose fruit. Stand each grapefruit on a cutting board and remove peel, including all white pith, by cutting it off in vertical strips with a sharp paring knife. Cut segments free from membranes. Divide segments among individual gratin dishes (or put in gratin dish).

Preheat broiler. Combine yolks, sugar, and wine in a large metal bowl set over a saucepan of barely simmering water and beat with a handheld mixer at medium-high speed until mixture has tripled in volume and forms a thick ribbon when beaters are lifted, 8 to 9 minutes. Remove bowl from heat.

Put individual gratin dishes (if using) on a baking sheet. Spoon sabayon over grapefruit segments. Broil 4 to 6 inches from heat just until sabayon is browned, about 30 seconds. Serve immediately.

COOK'S NOTE

■ The eggs in this recipe may not be fully cooked. If that is a concern, see page 915.

Dates with Coffee and Cardamom

SERVES 4
ACTIVE TIME: 10 MINUTES ■ START TO FINISH: 1 DAY
(INCLUDES STEEPING)

■ The traditional Arabian flavors of dates, coffee, and cardamom are delicious steeped together and served over creamy, tangy yogurt. This recipe comes from Samuel and Samantha Clark, the chef-owners of Moro in London, who prefer Medjool dates—they tend to be sweeter and will make the espresso more syrupy. ■

- 2 cups (about 14 ounces) whole or pitted Medjool dates
- 2 cups freshly made espresso, or 5 rounded teaspoons instant espresso powder, such as Medaglia d'Oro, dissolved in 2 cups boiling water
- 1 teaspoon sugar
- 20 green cardamom pods (see Sources), lightly crushed
- 1 (3-inch) cinnamon stick, broken in half
- 1 cup thick whole-milk yogurt, preferably Greek

If necessary, pit dates: slit each date down one side and remove and discard pit. Put dates in a heatproof bowl.

Bring espresso, sugar, cardamom pods, and cinnamon stick just to a boil in a small saucepan. Pour over dates and cool to room temperature, then steep covered and refrigerated, overnight.

If using a regular supermarket brand of yogurt (not Greek), drain in a paper-towel-lined sieve set over a bowl for 1 hour. Discard liquid.

Serve chilled dates with some syrup and yogurt.

COOK'S NOTE

■ The dates can steep for up to 2 days.

DATES AND FIGS

DATES—which are the fruit of a tall, long-lived palm tree (*Phoenix dactylifera*) native to the hot, arid regions of North Africa and the Middle East—have been cultivated since prehistoric times and remain an important staple in those parts of the world. There are 1,500 known varieties.

If you are of a certain age and remember the deeply wrinkled, piercingly sweet dried **Deglet Noor** dates sold in a little cardboard box, the variety of fresh dates—both domestic and imported—in stores these days might surprise you. **Medjool** dates are widely available; large and tender, with a moist, meaty sweetness, they are a great all-around choice for baking or eating out of hand. Other varieties you might see include the small, golden brown **Halawy** and the pleasingly fibrous **Zahidi**.

The powdery layer sometimes seen on the surface of some dates is actually sugar; it simply indicates that they are losing moisture.

FIGS, like dates, have been cultivated for thousands of years in the Middle East and around the Mediterranean. Hundreds of varieties are eaten both fresh and dried. One of the most popular is the **Black Mission**. First grown in the Canary Islands, off the southern coast of Spain, it was brought to California by Spanish missionaries, along with dates. Its deep purple skin turns black when dried. The **Calimyrna** variety—a light brown whether fresh or dried—is a California-grown **Smyrna** fig, a variety that's been cultivated in the Middle East for 2,000 years. **Adriatic**, a greenish yellow fig grown in northern California and the Pacific Northwest, is a good all-purpose variety, as is the richly flavored greenish white **Kadota,** which is more common in the Southwest and parts of the South.

Dried Figs with Balsamic Vinegar, Mascarpone, and Walnuts

SERVES 6

ACTIVE TIME: 15 MINUTES ■ START TO FINISH: 1 HOUR

■ With a little finessing, supermarket balsamic vinegar can become a vital addition to many dishes, even dessert. Here it combines with red wine and sugar to make a poaching liquid for dried Black Mission figs. As the figs slurp up the fragrant liquid, they soften and swell. Crunchy toasted walnuts and a dollop of mascarpone contrast nicely with the full-flavored fruit. ■

1 cup dry red wine
⅓ cup balsamic vinegar
½ cup sugar
1 pound dried Black Mission figs, stems discarded
¾ cup walnut pieces, toasted (see Tips, page 911)
½ cup mascarpone

Put a rack in middle of oven and preheat oven to 350°F.

Bring wine, vinegar, and sugar to a boil in a 3-quart heavy saucepan over moderate heat, stirring until sugar is dissolved. Add figs and gently simmer, uncovered, for 5 minutes.

Pour figs, with liquid, into an 8-inch square or other 2-quart shallow baking dish and sprinkle with walnuts. Bake, uncovered, until figs are softened and have absorbed about two thirds of liquid, about 30 minutes. Cool figs slightly, about 15 minutes.

Serve figs with sauce, dolloped with mascarpone.

Red and Green Grape Crisp

SERVES 6

ACTIVE TIME: 30 MINUTES ■ START TO FINISH: 2 HOURS

■ So many crisp- and cobbler-type desserts rely on summer and fall fruits, but good grapes are readily available year-round. Here the fruit is cooked until it bursts, tossed with a syrup perfumed by Cognac and cinnamon, and topped with a buttery streusel. The result, from Chris Schlesinger, the chef of East Coast Grill in Cambridge, Massachusetts, is definitely out of the ordinary. ■

FOR FILLING
3 pounds seedless grapes, preferably a mix of red and green
6 tablespoons granulated sugar
2 tablespoons fresh lemon juice
½ teaspoon ground cinnamon
2 tablespoons Cognac or other brandy
1½ tablespoons cornstarch

FOR TOPPING
6 tablespoons all-purpose flour
6 tablespoons packed light brown sugar
6 tablespoons old-fashioned rolled oats
½ stick (4 tablespoons) cold unsalted butter, cut into bits
⅛ teaspoon ground cinnamon
⅛ teaspoon salt
½ cup coarsely chopped pecans

ACCOMPANIMENT: vanilla ice cream or lightly sweetened whipped cream

MAKE THE FILLING: Toss grapes with sugar, lemon juice, and cinnamon in a 3- to 4-quart wide heavy pot and bring to a boil, covered, over moderate heat, stirring occasionally. Continue to boil, covered, stirring occasionally, until grapes begin to burst, 20 to 30 minutes.

With a slotted spoon, transfer grapes to a colander set over a bowl and drain for 15 minutes. (Set pot aside.)

Return juices from drained grapes to pot. Bring to a boil and boil juices, uncovered, until syrupy and reduced to about 1 cup, about 15 minutes.

Meanwhile, put a rack in middle of oven and preheat oven to 425°F.

Stir together Cognac and cornstarch in a small cup until smooth and whisk into grape syrup. Boil, whisking constantly, for 1 minute. Stir grapes into syrup and spoon filling into an 8-inch square or other 2-quart shallow baking dish.

MAKE THE TOPPING: Pulse together flour, brown sugar, oats, butter, cinnamon, and salt in a food processor until mixture resembles coarse meal. Transfer to a bowl and stir in pecans.

ASSEMBLE AND BAKE THE CRISP: Sprinkle topping evenly over filling. Bake until topping is golden brown and filling is bubbling, about 20 minutes.

Serve warm with vanilla ice cream or whipped cream.

Mango Fool

SERVES 6
ACTIVE TIME: 15 MINUTES ■ START TO FINISH: 9¼ HOURS
(INCLUDES CHILLING)

■ Cool, creamy, yet ethereally light, fools are usually made by combining pureed fruit with whipped cream. This version, which begins with a simple custard, is a little richer than most, a trait that pairs well with the voluptuous nature of mango. One of the most popular and widely exported Indian cultivars is the Alphonso mango, renowned for its bright orange flesh and intense flavor. Canned sliced Alphonsos work best for this dessert. ■

1¼ teaspoons unflavored gelatin
1 cup whole milk
1 large egg
½ cup sugar
1 (30-ounce) can Alphonso mango slices in syrup (see Sources), drained
1½ tablespoons fresh lime juice
1 cup very cold heavy cream

SPECIAL EQUIPMENT: an instant-read thermometer

Sprinkle gelatin over 3 tablespoons milk in a small bowl and set aside to soften.

Meanwhile, bring remaining milk just to a boil in a small heavy saucepan; remove from heat. Whisk together egg and ¼ cup sugar in a bowl until well combined. Add hot milk in a slow stream, whisking. Pour mixture into saucepan and cook over moderately low heat, stirring constantly with a wooden spoon, until thermometer registers 170°F and custard coats back of spoon (do not boil), about 2 minutes. Stir in gelatin mixture and cook over low heat, stirring, until dissolved, about 1 minute (do not boil). Pour custard through a sieve into a bowl and cool, stirring occasionally.

Puree mangoes with remaining ¼ cup sugar and lime juice in a blender until very smooth. Force through a fine-mesh sieve, using a rubber spatula, into custard; discard solids. Stir until well combined, then refrigerate until cold but not set, about 1 hour.

Beat cream with an electric mixer until it just holds stiff peaks. Fold into mango custard gently but thoroughly. Refrigerate, covered, until very cold, at least 8 hours.

To serve, spoon fool into six dishes.

COOK'S NOTE

■ The fool can be refrigerated for up to 1 day.

Ginger Fruit Salad

SERVES 6
ACTIVE TIME: 15 MINUTES ■ START TO FINISH: 35 MINUTES

■ Lime syrup and little nuggets of crystallized ginger give this fruit salad plenty of zing. ■

2 limes
⅓ cup water
⅓ cup sugar
2 large mangoes (2½ pounds total), peeled, pitted, and cut into 1-inch pieces
3 cups (12 ounces) blueberries
¼ cup finely chopped crystallized ginger

Remove zest from 1 lime in strips with a vegetable peeler. Cut any white pith from strips with a sharp knife. Squeeze 3 tablespoons juice from limes.

Combine zest, water, and sugar in a 1-quart saucepan and bring to a boil, stirring until sugar is dissolved. Boil, without stirring, for 3 minutes. Remove from heat and stir in lime juice. Let syrup stand for 20 minutes for flavors to blend.

Remove zest from syrup with a slotted spoon and discard. Toss together mangoes, blueberries, and syrup in a large bowl. Sprinkle with ginger.

COOK'S NOTE

■ The salad, without the crystallized ginger, can be made up to 4 hours ahead and refrigerated, covered. Bring to room temperature and sprinkle with the ginger before serving.

Cantaloupe Curls
with Spiced Wine

SERVES 4
ACTIVE TIME: 20 MINUTES ▪ START TO FINISH: 30 MINUTES

▪ Got an ice cream scoop and a few minutes to spare? That's all it takes to create this colorful dessert. Infusing the wine with pink peppercorns and mustard seeds adds a kick to curls of ripe melon. A lever-type ice cream scoop will give you compacted balls instead of beautiful curls, so use a simple, no-frills scoop for this recipe. ▪

    1 cup dry red wine
    2 tablespoons sugar
    1 Turkish bay leaf or ½ California bay leaf
    1 teaspoon mustard seeds
    1 teaspoon pink peppercorns, crushed (optional)
    2 ripe cantaloupes, chilled
SPECIAL EQUIPMENT: an ice cream scoop (not a lever-type;
    see headnote and Cook's Note)

Combine all ingredients except cantaloupes in a 1-quart heavy saucepan, bring to a simmer, stirring to dissolve sugar, and simmer until liquid is reduced to about ¼ cup, 10 to 15 minutes. Remove from heat and cool in saucepan set in a bowl of ice and cold water. Discard bay leaf.

Halve each cantaloupe and discard seeds. Scoop out curls from melon halves with ice cream scoop and divide, along with any juices, among four bowls. Drizzle each serving with about 1 tablespoon cooled spiced wine.

COOK'S NOTES
▪ The spiced wine can be made up to 1 week ahead and refrigerated in an airtight container. Serve chilled.
▪ The cantaloupes can simply be cut into cubes or chunks with a knife.

Honeydew Melon
in Coconut Milk

SERVES 8
ACTIVE TIME: 25 MINUTES ▪ START TO FINISH: 35 MINUTES

▪ Fruit such as bananas or mangoes served in sweetened coconut milk is a popular homey dessert in Thailand. We especially like this version made with ripe melon. Its juicy crunch makes a nice contrast to the creamy coconut milk perfumed with fresh lime juice. It's just the thing on a sultry summer evening. ▪

    1 (13- to 14-ounce) can unsweetened coconut milk,
        well stirred
    3 tablespoons sugar
    1½ teaspoons fresh lime juice, or to taste
    1 large honeydew melon, chilled
GARNISH: thinly slivered lime zest
SPECIAL EQUIPMENT: a melon ball cutter (see Cook's Note)

Stir together coconut milk, sugar, and lime juice in a small metal bowl until sugar is dissolved. Set bowl in a larger bowl of ice and cold water and chill, stirring occasionally, until cold, about 6 minutes.

Meanwhile, halve melon and discard seeds. Scoop melon into balls with cutter and divide among eight serving dishes.

Pour coconut milk over melon and sprinkle with zest.

COOK'S NOTE
▪ The melon can simply be cut into cubes or chunks with a knife.

Amaretti-Stuffed Peaches

SERVES 8
ACTIVE TIME: 15 MINUTES ▪ START TO FINISH: 1½ HOURS

▪ Buttery amaretti crumbs fill tender peach halves with a sweet, intriguing crunchiness. Simple concept, delicious results. ▪

½ stick (4 tablespoons) unsalted butter, softened
1 cup coarsely crumbled amaretti (Italian almond macaroons; see Sources)
2½ tablespoons all-purpose flour
2 tablespoons sugar
⅛ teaspoon salt
1 large egg
8 firm but ripe small peaches (about 2 pounds total), halved and pitted

ACCOMPANIMENT: mascarpone or crème fraîche

Put a rack in middle of oven and preheat oven to 350°F.

Melt 2 tablespoons butter and pour into a 13-by-9-inch baking dish.

Pulse ¾ cup crumbled amaretti in a food processor until finely chopped. Add flour, sugar, salt, and remaining 2 tablespoons butter and blend until butter is incorporated. Add egg and blend until smooth.

Scoop out just enough peach pulp from center of each peach half with a melon ball cutter or a small spoon to create a 1-inch-deep cavity. Arrange peaches cut side down in baking dish and brush skins with melted butter from dish. Flip peaches over, cut sides up. Divide amaretti mixture among cavities and sprinkle remaining ¼ cup crumbled amaretti over filling.

Bake until filling is puffed and crisp, 40 to 50 minutes. Serve warm or at room temperature, with dollops of mascarpone.

COOK'S NOTE
■ The amaretti mixture can be made up to 2 hours ahead and refrigerated, covered.

Balsamic Peaches with Peach Sabayon

SERVES 4
ACTIVE TIME: 20 MINUTES ■ START TO FINISH: 35 MINUTES

■ Egg yolks, a bit of sugar, and a little wine turn into a silky, frothy custard when beaten over barely simmering water. This sabayon is the coda to a bowl of ripe peaches softened under the teasingly sweet tang of balsamic vinegar. ■

3 medium peaches, halved, pitted, and each half cut into 6 wedges
2 teaspoons balsamic vinegar
¼ cup sugar
4 large egg yolks
⅓ cup dry white wine
3 tablespoons peach brandy (see Cook's Note)

Gently toss peaches with vinegar and 1 tablespoon sugar in a bowl. Let macerate for 30 minutes.

Meanwhile, after peaches have macerated for 15 minutes, combine yolks, wine, brandy, and remaining 3 tablespoons sugar in a large metal bowl set over a saucepan of barely simmering water and beat with a handheld electric mixer at medium-high speed until sabayon has tripled in volume and forms a thick ribbon when beaters are lifted, about 11 minutes. Remove bowl from saucepan.

Divide peaches and their juice among four bowls and top with sabayon. Serve immediately.

COOK'S NOTES
■ If you don't have peach brandy on hand, use a little more white wine instead.
■ The eggs in this recipe may not be fully cooked. If that is a concern, see page 915.

Pears

Although the carbonized remains of wild pears, which originated in central Asia, have been unearthed at Neolithic (around 4000 B.C.E.) sites in Europe, pears, like apples, were in the second wave of fruits to be cultivated in the Near East, long after grapes, figs, dates, and pomegranates. The first varieties were probably brought to the Aegean region from the Fertile Crescent around 1000 B.C.E., during the time of Homer, who called them "the fruit of the gods." The grafting technique—essential to the propagation of edible fruit—was understood by then, and by the first century C.E. the list of cultivars had grown to thirty-five. Today there are more than 3,000 pear varieties grown around the world, but only a handful are cultivated in the United States. Of those, we use the following.

ANJOU This plump, generally lopsided yellow-green pear was developed in France or Belgium in the nineteenth century as Beurré d'Anjou. The standard commercial variety because it's such a good producer and keeper, it's much better for cooking than for eating out of hand. Although the texture is smooth, with juicy, firm flesh, the flavor is bland and not especially sweet.

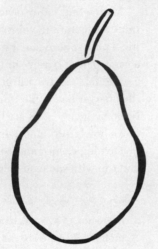

BARTLETT No pear is slurpier than a Bartlett, the most widely grown variety in the world. This large, golden, bell-shaped fruit is called Williams' Bon Chrétien, or simply Williams, in Europe. Harvested from late July through September, it's the standard summer pear and is not a good keeper. In addition to its renowned musky flavor and aroma, it has creamy, very juicy flesh. It's delicious eaten out of hand, made into a sauce or sorbet, or cooked in a pie or tart.

BOSC This pear, developed in Belgium as the Beurré Bosc in 1807, has a graceful, gourdlike neck and bronze, russeted skin. Look for a yellow rather than a green undertone to the skin—that's an indication that the pear wasn't harvested too early. Bosc is considered a winter pear (it matures in October), and it needs cold storage to ripen. Its flesh is rich, sweet, and syrupy and, because of its firm texture, even a ripe Bosc holds its shape beautifully when cooked.

SECKEL Discovered near Philadelphia in the eighteenth century, this very small green- to russet-colored pear is sometimes called a honey or sugar pear. The fruit matures in late summer and early fall. The Seckel has juicy, almost syrupy, firm flesh, a complex sweetness, and a rich, spicy flavor, making it a superb dessert pear. It can be eaten out of hand or cooked.

Pear Fool

SERVES 4
ACTIVE TIME: 25 MINUTES ■ START TO FINISH: 1½ HOURS
(INCLUDES CHILLING)

■ For her take on this cool, fluffy British dessert, April Bloomfield, the chef of New York City's Spotted Pig, starts by poaching pears in white wine with vanilla and lemon zest. She then layers the pureed fruit with whipped cream that has been sweetened with the reduced poaching liquid. The result is a little bit playful and a little bit sophisticated, with a pure pear flavor. ■

    1 cup dry white wine
    2 tablespoons superfine sugar or 1 tablespoon plus
        2 teaspoons granulated sugar
    ¼ vanilla bean, halved lengthwise
    2 (3-by-1-inch) strips lemon zest, removed with a
        vegetable peeler
    3 firm but ripe Bartlett pears, peeled, quartered
        lengthwise, and cored
    ¾ cup very cold heavy cream
    1 tablespoon confectioners' sugar

Combine wine, superfine sugar, vanilla bean, and zest in a 1½- to 2-quart heavy saucepan and bring to a boil, stirring to dissolve sugar. Add pears and gently simmer, turning and basting occasionally, until just tender, 10 to 15 minutes. Using a slotted spoon, transfer pears and zest to a blender (reserve poaching liquid and vanilla bean) and puree until smooth. Transfer puree to a metal bowl and chill in a larger bowl of ice and cold water, stirring occasionally, until cool, about 20 minutes.

Meanwhile, boil poaching liquid until reduced to about ¼ cup, about 5 minutes. Transfer to a glass measure (discard vanilla bean) and cool to room temperature.

Beat cream in a medium bowl with an electric mixer until it just holds soft peaks. Add confectioners' sugar and 3 tablespoons cooled pear syrup (reserve remaining syrup) and beat until just combined.

Divide half of pear puree among four 6- to

8-ounce juice glasses or small bowls and top with half of whipped cream mixture. Repeat layering with remaining pear puree and whipped cream. Drizzle each serving with a little of remaining poaching liquid. Refrigerate, covered, for 1 hour (no longer) before serving.

COOK'S NOTE

■ The pear puree can be made up to 1 day ahead and kept refrigerated, covered; stir the puree before serving. Make the syrup from the poaching liquid and refrigerate, covered. Bring the syrup to room temperature before using; if it is too thick, reheat gently to a pourable consistency.

Rum-Raisin Poached Pears

SERVES 4
ACTIVE TIME: 10 MINUTES ■ START TO FINISH: 35 MINUTES

■ Dotted with soft, sweet raisins, these pears are an elegant conclusion to any meal. As the dark rum cooks down to a syrup, it infuses them with deep, dusky flavor. They're mighty fine served over vanilla ice cream too. ■

    ⅓ cup plus 1 tablespoon dark rum
    ⅓ cup plus 1 tablespoon water
    1½ pounds firm but ripe Bosc or Anjou pears (3 large),
        peeled, halved, cored, and each half cut into
        4 wedges
    ⅓ cup raisins
    2 tablespoons sugar
    1 tablespoon unsalted butter

Combine ⅓ cup rum with remaining ingredients in a 10-inch heavy skillet and bring to a boil, stirring occasionally. Reduce heat and simmer, covered, until pears are just tender, about 10 minutes.

Remove lid and boil, stirring occasionally, until liquid is reduced to a syrup, 5 to 10 minutes.

Stir in remaining tablespoon rum and serve warm or at room temperature.

Roasted Pears
with Almond Crunch

SERVES 6
ACTIVE TIME: 15 MINUTES ■ START TO FINISH: 1 HOUR

■ Almonds and pears: one of those simple but utterly right combinations. Here almonds complement the fruit in two ways: infusing it as it roasts and covering it with a crisp, sugary crust. ■

FOR ALMOND CRUNCH
  1 large egg white
  3 tablespoons sugar
  ¾ cup sliced almonds, preferably unblanched
FOR PEARS
  3 firm but ripe Bosc pears
  1 tablespoon unsalted butter, softened
  ¼ cup sugar
  2 tablespoons amaretto or other almond-flavored liqueur
  ½ cup water
    Pinch of salt

SPECIAL EQUIPMENT: a 9-inch square baking pan

MAKE THE ALMOND CRUNCH: Put a rack in middle of oven and preheat oven to 350°F. Butter a baking sheet.

Whisk together egg white and sugar in a bowl. Add almonds, stirring until coated. Spread in a thin layer on baking sheet. Bake until golden, 15 to 25 minutes. Transfer baking sheet to a rack to cool. Increase oven temperature to 425°F.

ROAST THE PEARS: Halve pears lengthwise and core, preferably with a melon ball cutter. Spread butter over bottom of baking pan and sprinkle with sugar. Arrange pears cut side up in pan and brush cut sides with 1 tablespoon amaretto.

Roast pears, uncovered, until barely tender, about 25 minutes. Add water, remaining tablespoon amaretto, and salt to baking pan and baste pears with pan juices. Roast pears, basting twice with pan juices, until tender, about 15 minutes more.

Break cooled almond crunch into pieces.

Serve pears warm or at room temperature, drizzled with pan juices and topped with almond crunch.

COOK'S NOTES
■ The almond crunch can be made up to 4 days ahead and kept in an airtight container at room temperature.
■ The pears can be roasted up to 1 hour ahead and kept, covered, at room temperature.

Roasted Pears
with Candied Celery

SERVES 8
ACTIVE TIME: 15 MINUTES ■ START TO FINISH: 2 HOURS
(INCLUDES COOLING)

■ This recipe from the chef, cookbook author, and TV personality Lidia Bastianich is a most elegant marriage of the classic with the unexpected. The combination of shimmering pears, sweet celery, and candied lemon zest makes a refined finale to a rich meal. As the dish cooks, the celery soaks up the complex flavors of the wine mixture and becomes a crisp accent to the tender roasted pears. ■

  2 lemons
  1 cup Moscato (Italian dessert wine), Muscat, or Sauternes
  ¾ cup sugar
  ¼ cup apricot jam
  4 firm but ripe Bosc pears
  8 large celery ribs, peeled and cut diagonally into ½-inch pieces

Put a rack in middle of oven and preheat oven to 375°F.

Remove zest from lemons in long strips with a vegetable peeler. Cut off any white pith from zest with a sharp knife. Put zest and 2 cups cold water in a 1-quart saucepan and bring to a boil. Drain and rinse under cold water. Repeat blanching one more time. Pat zest dry.

Squeeze ⅓ cup juice from lemons into a medium bowl. Whisk in wine, sugar, and jam until sugar is dissolved.

Halve pears lengthwise and core. Spread celery out in a 13-by-9-inch baking dish and add wine mixture. Nestle pears cut side up in celery and scatter zest around them. Bake, uncovered, basting pears once or twice with pan juices, until tender, 50 to 60 minutes.

Transfer pears to a shallow serving dish using a slotted spoon. Pour cooking liquid, zest, and celery into a 10-inch skillet and boil until liquid is reduced to about 1 cup and syrupy, about 15 minutes.

Spoon sauce over pears and celery and cool, uncovered, to room temperature.

COOK'S NOTE

- The pears, with the celery, can be made up to 2 hours ahead. Cool uncovered, then keep, covered, at room temperature.

Plum Berry Crisp

SERVES 4
ACTIVE TIME: 15 MINUTES ■ START TO FINISH: 50 MINUTES

- This simple dessert takes sweet summer fruits and cooks them until everything good about them becomes even better, then adds a buttery brown sugar and oat topping. ■

FOR FILLING

1½ pounds purple plums, pitted and cut into ½-inch wedges
1 cup blueberries
1 cup blackberries
⅓–½ cup packed light brown sugar (depending on sweetness of fruit)

FOR TOPPING

1 cup old-fashioned rolled oats
¼ cup all-purpose flour
⅓ cup packed light brown sugar
½ stick (4 tablespoons) unsalted butter, cut into pieces, softened
¼ teaspoon salt

Put a rack in upper third of oven and preheat oven to 425°F.

MAKE THE FILLING: Toss together all ingredients in an 8-inch square or other 2-quart shallow baking dish. Bake until sugar dissolves and plums soften, about 10 minutes.

MEANWHILE, MAKE THE TOPPING: Blend together all ingredients in a bowl with your fingertips until butter is evenly distributed and mixture is crumbly.

Stir fruit filling, then sprinkle topping over it. Bake until topping is crisp and golden and fruit is bubbling, about 30 minutes. Serve warm or at room temperature.

COOK'S NOTE

- The topping can be made up to 3 hours ahead and refrigerated, covered.

PUDDINGS, CUSTARDS, MOUSSES, AND SOUFFLÉS

On the other side of the Atlantic, puddings are a much-exalted food, so well regarded that the word stands for the entire family of desserts. An English "pudding" is the final course, which might turn out to be a cake, a tart, or an ice cream concoction. But if one is very lucky, it is the real thing, perhaps an irresistible sticky toffee pudding swathed in an elegant Armagnac sauce.

On this side of the Atlantic, pudding was kidnapped and held for ransom by industrial food manufacturers, who turned it into a packaged food. But judging by the contents of this chapter, the time of the pudding may finally be coming to America.

Consider, for example, the resurrection of rice pudding, surely one of the great desserts of the world. (You will find that it is available here in either deep black or creamy white.) Or contemplate the return of butterscotch pots de crème, which are, in their finest expression, the ultimate marriage of sugar and cream.

The reentry of custards, mousses, and soufflés into the American pantheon of desserts is cause for celebration for three important reasons. The first is that they can, for the most part, be created out of ingredients that are already sitting in your

cupboard. The second is that they are, of all desserts, the least expensive, since they rarely rely on exotic ingredients. And the third is that while they give the appearance of being technically tricky, most are incredibly easy; there is nothing so simple as cherries in the snow, and few desserts require so little effort for such great effect as blackberry buttermilk panna cotta.

In this chapter you will find sophisticated desserts like lemon soufflé, a sassy creature that rises high and offers an instant pucker. You'll find rich desserts like crème brûlée, along with desserts that do very well for a diet, such as the beautiful dark-roast coffee gelée. You will find homey plain-Jane desserts like old-fashioned vanilla cup custards, ready to offer instant comfort. And you'll find dazzlers like the pistachio rhubarb trifle, which resembles a Florentine paperweight and lends elegance to any evening.

Every one of these desserts is a joy to cook and a pleasure to eat, and each one is a powerful argument for restoring the pudding to its rightful place at the table.

PUDDINGS, CUSTARDS, MOUSSES, AND SOUFFLÉS

Rich Chocolate Pudding

SERVES 6
ACTIVE TIME: 30 MINUTES ■ START TO FINISH: 3½ HOURS
(INCLUDES CHILLING)

■ This recipe comes from the City Limits Diner in Stamford, Connecticut, where the cooks use Valrhona bittersweet chocolate with a 61% cacao content. The recipe, which calls for more whole milk than heavy cream, yields a wonderful pudding—rich but not cloying, with a fine, silky texture. ■

½ vanilla bean, halved lengthwise
1½ cups whole milk
½ cup heavy cream
⅓ cup sugar
4½ ounces finely chopped bittersweet chocolate
        (61% cacao; see page 705), preferably Valrhona
5 large egg yolks
SPECIAL EQUIPMENT: 6 (4-ounce) ramekins or custard cups

Put a rack in middle of oven and preheat oven to 275°F.

Scrape seeds from vanilla bean into a 2- to 3-quart heavy saucepan, then add pod, milk, cream, and sugar, and bring just to a boil, stirring until sugar is dissolved. Add chocolate and cook over moderately high heat, stirring gently with a whisk, until chocolate is melted and mixture just comes to a boil.

Pour mixture into a metal bowl, set bowl in a large bowl of ice and cold water, and cool to room temperature, stirring occasionally, about 5 minutes.

Whisk yolks into chocolate mixture, then pour through a fine-mesh sieve into a 1-quart measure or a bowl with a pour spout; discard vanilla pod. Skim off any foam with a spoon.

Divide mixture among ramekins. Arrange ramekins in a small roasting pan, put pan in oven, and add enough boiling water to pan to reach halfway up sides of ramekins. Bake until puddings are just set but still wobbly in center, about 1 hour. Cool puddings in water bath for 1 hour.

Remove puddings from water and refrigerate, uncovered, until cold, at least 1 hour.

COOK'S NOTE
■ The puddings can be refrigerated, covered with a sheet of plastic wrap after 4 hours, for up to 2 days. Blot very gently with paper towels before serving.

Butterscotch Pots de Crème

SERVES 6
ACTIVE TIME: 25 MINUTES ■ START TO FINISH: 1¾ HOURS
(INCLUDES COOLING)

■ These pots de crème, from the chef M. J. Adams of the Corn Exchange in Rapid City, South Dakota, win raves for their wonderful butterscotch flavor and creamy texture. Adams replaces the customary brown sugar with a combination of muscovado and Demerara sugars, which gives the custard its deep, sophisticated flavor. Because these sugars aren't subjected to industrial processing like refined white and brown sugar, they retain their natural complexity and offer much more than simple sweetness. ■

1½ cups heavy cream
6 tablespoons dark muscovado sugar (see Sources)
¼ teaspoon salt
6 tablespoons water
2 tablespoons Demerara sugar (see Sources)
4 large egg yolks
½ teaspoon vanilla extract
ACCOMPANIMENTS: whipped cream; chocolate shavings or
        fresh berries
SPECIAL EQUIPMENT: 6 (4-ounce) ramekins or custard cups

Put a rack in middle of oven and preheat oven to 300°F.

Bring cream, muscovado sugar, and salt just to a simmer in a small heavy saucepan over moderate heat, stirring until sugar is dissolved. Remove from heat.

Meanwhile, bring water and Demerara sugar to a boil in a 2-quart heavy saucepan over moderate heat, stirring until sugar is dissolved. Continue to cook, stirring occasionally, until browned and bubbly. Remove from heat and carefully add cream mixture (mixture will bubble up and steam), whisking until combined.

Whisk together yolks and vanilla in a large bowl. Add hot cream mixture in a stream, whisking. Pour custard through a fine-mesh sieve into a 1-quart glass measure or a bowl with a pour spout. Skim off any foam with a spoon.

Divide custard among ramekins. Arrange ramekins in a small roasting pan, put pan in oven, and add enough boiling water to pan to reach halfway up sides of ramekins. Bake, uncovered, until custards are just set but still wobbly in center, about 40 minutes. Transfer ramekins to a rack and cool to warm or room temperature. (Pots de crème will continue to set as they cool.)

Top with dollops of whipped cream and chocolate shavings or fresh berries.

COOK'S NOTE

■ The custard can be cooked up to 2 days ahead and refrigerated, covered, in the glass measure or bowl. Bring to room temperature before pouring into ramekins and baking.

CUSTARDS: WHY WOBBLE?

Something about custard makes us think of the late Laurie Colwin, the novelist and food writer whose columns graced our pages in the 1990s. She once wrote that "at the end of the day, what a person wants in the way of dessert is something consoling and uncomplicated. The cook wants that too."

The recipes in this chapter are exactly the sort of thing she meant. Note that we say to bake custards until they are set around the edges but still wobbly in the center. Keep a close eye on them toward the end of baking. When you remove them from the oven, they'll continue to cook from the residual heat, so if you let them bake until they're set all the way through, the result will be overdone—tough and rubbery.

Vanilla Cup Custards

SERVES 8
ACTIVE TIME: 15 MINUTES ■ START TO FINISH: 1½ HOURS

■ These homey, old-fashioned cup custards are a taste of childhood. Creamy and smooth, they sing with deep vanilla flavor. Though the custard is delicious made with either vanilla extract or vanilla bean, only freshly grated nutmeg will do for dusting on the top—it adds a bit of extra warmth. Covering the custards with foil while they bake keeps a skin from forming. ■

3 cups whole milk
1 teaspoon vanilla extract or 1 vanilla bean, halved lengthwise
3 large eggs
3 large egg yolks
¾ cup sugar
  Pinch of salt
  Freshly grated nutmeg

SPECIAL EQUIPMENT: eight 6-ounce ramekins or custard cups

Put a rack in middle of oven and preheat oven to 325°F.

Pour milk into a 1-quart heavy saucepan. If using vanilla bean, scrape seeds into milk and add pod. Bring milk to a simmer, then remove from heat. If using vanilla bean, let milk mixture steep for 5 minutes.

Whisk together eggs, yolks, sugar, salt, and vanilla extract, if using, in a medium bowl. Add hot milk in a slow stream, whisking. Pour through a fine-mesh sieve into a 1-quart glass measure or a bowl with a pour spout. Skim off any foam with a spoon.

Divide mixture among custard cups and sprinkle with nutmeg to taste. Arrange custard cups in a small roasting pan. Put pan in oven, add enough boiling water to pan to reach halfway up sides of cups, and loosely cover pan with foil. Bake custards until just set around edges but still wobbly in center, 35 to 40 minutes. Transfer custard cups to a rack. Serve warm or chilled.

COOK'S NOTE

■ The custards can be made up to 2 days ahead. Cool, then refrigerate, covered with plastic wrap.

BAVARIAN CREAM A delicate, light mousse (see below) that has been fortified with gelatin and folded into whipped cream, Bavarian cream is usually used as a filling for cakes or charlottes, but it is wonderful on its own as well.

CRÈME BRÛLÉE Literally meaning "burned cream," the name describes an eggy custard that is baked and chilled, then sprinkled with sugar that is caramelized until it forms a thin, crunchy topping.

CUSTARD One of the world's great comfort foods, a custard is a smooth, soft, egg-based, puddinglike dish that can be sweet or savory, hot or cold or—in the case of ice cream—frozen. Gentle, even heat is the secret to the satiny texture. "Stirred custards," those cooked on the stovetop, are usually made in a double boiler; custards cooked in the oven are baked in a water bath. As a rule, stirred custards are softer and looser than baked custards; they are often used as a base for a sauce or ice cream. Crème brûlée, flan, and pots de crème are all examples of baked custards.

FLAN This Spanish custard is baked in a caramel-coated mold and chilled. When it's turned out of the mold, the liquefied caramel becomes a sauce for the custard. It's similar to a crème caramel, but denser and eggier.

GELÉE A gelée, or jelly (Jell-O, in other words), is light and refreshing.

MOUSSE The French word for "foam," *mousse* is a general term for a rich yet airy dish. Dessert mousses are usually made with chocolate or fruit purees; their lightness comes from whipped cream or beaten egg whites, and they sometimes include gelatin, as in Bavarian cream.

PANNA COTTA A very light, eggless cream custard (the Italian term literally means "cooked cream"), panna cotta is set with a little gelatin and typically chilled in small molds or ramekins.

POTS DE CRÈME Rich baked custards, "pots of cream" are made and served in small cups or ramekins.

PUDDING Thick, soft, and spoonable, like custards and mousses, puddings are thickened with flour, rice, cornstarch, or eggs and can be either light (chocolate pudding) or satisfyingly dense, even cakelike (sticky-toffee pudding).

SOUFFLÉ A soufflé can be sweet or savory, hot or cold. The airy mixture generally starts with a thick egg-yolk-based sauce or a puree lightened by egg whites that have been beaten to stiff peaks. Baked soufflés are more fragile than cold or frozen soufflés because the hot air trapped inside them starts to escape as soon as they are removed from the oven. Cold or frozen soufflés have the added heft and richness of whipped cream.

Maple Cup Custards

SERVES 6
ACTIVE TIME: 15 MINUTES ■ START TO FINISH: 1½ HOURS
(INCLUDES COOLING)

■ Maple syrup and maple sugar infuse a simple vanilla custard. When cooking with maple syrup (or pouring it over a short stack), we prefer the robust flavor of Grade B to the light, smooth taste of Grade A. The lower grade is essential for imparting the deep sweetness of these custards (don't even think about using a commercial table syrup, most of which contain little or no maple syrup). ■

    2 large eggs
    2 large egg yolks
 1½ cups whole milk
  ½ cup heavy cream
  ¼ cup Grade B pure maple syrup
    2 tablespoons granulated maple sugar (see
       Cook's Note and Sources)
  ½ teaspoon vanilla extract
  ¼ teaspoon salt
SPECIAL EQUIPMENT: 6 (6-ounce) ramekins or
       custard cups

Put a rack in middle of oven and preheat oven to 325°F.

Whisk together all ingredients in a large bowl until sugar is dissolved. Pour through a fine-mesh sieve into a 1-quart glass measure or a bowl with a pour spout. Skim off any foam with a spoon.

Divide custard evenly among cups. Arrange cups in a roasting pan, put pan in oven, and add enough boiling water to pan to reach halfway up sides of cups. Cover pan loosely with foil and bake until custards are just set around edges but still wobbly in center, about 1 hour. Transfer cups to a rack and cool to warm, about 30 minutes.

COOK'S NOTES

■ Maple sugar is usually sold granulated. If you get a brand with very large granules, pulse the sugar in a blender until it is more finely ground.
■ The custards are best when still warm, but they can be made up to 1 day ahead and refrigerated, covered.

Ginger Custards

SERVES 6
ACTIVE TIME: 15 MINUTES ■ START TO FINISH: 3¾ HOURS
(INCLUDES CHILLING)

■ Fresh ginger perfumes these custards with a hint of spice. You'll be surprised at how little time it takes to create such a sophisticated treat. ■

  ½ cup sugar
  ¼ cup finely chopped fresh ginger (not peeled)
  ¼ cup water
 1¾ cups whole milk
    2 large eggs
    2 large egg yolks
       Pinch of salt
SPECIAL EQUIPMENT: six 5- to 6-ounce ramekins or
       custard cups

Put a rack in middle of oven and preheat oven to 325°F.

Bring sugar, ginger, and water to a boil in a 1-quart heavy saucepan, stirring until sugar is dissolved. Add milk, return just to a boil, and remove from heat. Let stand, covered, for 15 minutes.

Whisk together eggs, yolks, and salt in a medium bowl. Gently whisk in hot milk mixture. Pour through a fine-mesh sieve into a 1-quart glass measure or a bowl with a pour spout, pressing on solids; discard solids. Skim off any foam with a spoon.

Divide custard among ramekins and cover each one tightly with foil. Arrange ramekins in a roasting pan, put pan in oven, and add enough boiling water to pan to reach halfway up sides of ramekins. Bake until custards are just set around edges but still wobbly in center, 35 to 40 minutes. Transfer ramekins to a rack and cool, uncovered, to room temperature.

Refrigerate cooled custards, uncovered, for at least 2 hours.

COOK'S NOTE

■ The custards can be refrigerated for up to 1 day.

Lemon Crème Brûlée

SERVES 8
ACTIVE TIME: 20 MINUTES ■ START TO FINISH: 5½ HOURS
(INCLUDES CHILLING)

■ Lemon zest adds a bright, floral perfume to classic crème brûlée. ■

  2 large lemons
  3 cups heavy cream
     About 10 tablespoons turbinado sugar, such as
       Sugar in the Raw
     Pinch of salt
  6 large egg yolks
  ½ teaspoon vanilla extract

SPECIAL EQUIPMENT: eight 4-ounce flameproof ramekins;
    a small blowtorch (see Sources)

Put a rack in middle of oven and preheat oven to 325°F.

Finely grate 2 tablespoons zest from lemons. Squeeze 1 teaspoon juice from 1 lemon.

Combine zest and cream in a 2- to 3-quart heavy saucepan, stir in 7 tablespoons turbinado sugar and salt, and heat over moderately low heat, stirring occasionally to dissolve sugar, until mixture is almost boiling. Remove from heat.

Lightly beat yolks in a medium bowl, then gradually whisk in hot cream. Pour custard through a fine-mesh sieve into a 1-quart glass measure or a bowl with a pour spout. Skim off any foam with a spoon. Stir in vanilla and lemon juice.

Divide custard among ramekins. Arrange ramekins in a roasting pan, put pan in oven, and add enough boiling water to pan to reach halfway up sides of ramekins. Bake until custards are just set around edges but still wobbly in center, 30 to 35 minutes. Cool custards in water bath for 20 minutes.

Remove custards from pan and refrigerate, uncovered, for at least 4 hours. (Custards will set completely as they chill.)

Just before serving, sprinkle about 1 teaspoon turbinado sugar evenly over each custard. Move blowtorch flame evenly back and forth close to sugar until it is caramelized. Let stand until caramel is hardened, 3 to 5 minutes.

COOK'S NOTE

■ The custards (without the sugar topping) can be refrigerated for up to 2 days (cover tightly once cold). Blot very gently with paper towels before sprinkling with the sugar and caramelizing.

Coffee Crème Brûlée

SERVES 8
ACTIVE TIME: 15 MINUTES ■ START TO FINISH: 6 HOURS
(INCLUDES CHILLING)

■ Coffee and Kahlúa give a wake-up call to crème brûlée, adding a note of bittersweet complexity. You won't need to brew a pot of coffee to get that jolt—instant espresso powder does the job effortlessly. ■

  1¾ cups heavy cream
  1¾ cups whole milk
  1½ tablespoons instant espresso powder, such as
        Medaglia d'Oro
   2 tablespoons Kahlúa
   1 large egg
   6 large egg yolks
   ⅔ cup granulated sugar
   ⅛ teaspoon salt
   ¼ cup turbinado sugar, such as Sugar in the Raw

SPECIAL EQUIPMENT: eight 4-ounce flameproof ramekins,
    a small blowtorch (see Sources)

Put a rack in middle of oven and preheat oven to 325°F.

Heat cream and milk in a heavy saucepan over moderately high heat until mixture just reaches a boil. Add espresso powder and Kahlúa, stirring until espresso powder is dissolved. Remove from heat.

Whisk together egg, yolks, granulated sugar, and salt in a bowl. Add milk mixture in a stream, whisking. Skim off any foam with a spoon.

Divide custard among ramekins. Arrange ramekins in a roasting pan, put pan in oven, and add enough boiling water to pan to reach halfway up sides of ramekins. Bake custards until just set around edges but still wobbly in center, 30 to 40 minutes. Transfer ramekins to a rack to cool.

Refrigerate custards, loosely covered with plastic wrap, for at least 4 hours.

Just before serving, sprinkle 1½ teaspoons turbinado sugar evenly over each custard. Move blowtorch flame evenly back and forth close to sugar until it is caramelized. Let stand until caramel is hardened, 3 to 5 minutes.

COOK'S NOTE

■ The custards (without the sugar topping) can be refrigerated for up to 2 days (cover tightly once cold). Blot very gently with paper towels before sprinkling with the sugar and caramelizing.

Rhubarb Crème Brûlée

SERVES 6
ACTIVE TIME: 25 MINUTES ■ START TO FINISH: 6 HOURS
(INCLUDES CHILLING)

■ Like fruit-on-the-bottom yogurts, these crème brûlées hide a colorful surprise—rosy roasted rhubarb is layered beneath the cool custard, allowing a bit of tart flavor to swirl into each creamy spoonful. ■

FOR RHUBARB FILLING
    2 pounds fresh rhubarb stalks
    6 tablespoons granulated sugar, or to taste
FOR CUSTARD
    5 large egg yolks
    ½ cup granulated sugar
    1¾ cups heavy cream
    1 teaspoon minced peeled fresh ginger
    2 tablespoons turbinado sugar, such as Sugar in
       the Raw
SPECIAL EQUIPMENT: six 6-ounce flameproof ramekins;
    a small blowtorch (see Sources)

MAKE THE FILLING: Put a rack in middle of oven and preheat oven to 375°F. Butter a 13-by-9-inch baking dish.

Cut enough rhubarb into ¼-inch slices to measure 6 cups. Arrange in one layer in baking dish

(reserve any remaining rhubarb for another use).

Bake rhubarb, uncovered, until very tender and falling apart, about 1¼ hours. Transfer rhubarb to a bowl and stir in sugar until well combined. Cool. Reduce oven temperature to 325°F.

MAKE THE CUSTARD: Whisk together yolks and sugar in a medium bowl. Heat cream with ginger in a small heavy saucepan over moderately high heat until it just reaches a simmer, then pour through a fine-mesh sieve into egg mixture in a stream, whisking. Skim off any foam with a spoon.

Divide filling among ramekins. Top with custard. Arrange ramekins in a small roasting pan. Put pan in oven, add enough boiling water to pan to reach halfway up sides of ramekins, and cover pan loosely with foil. Bake custards until just set around edges but still wobbly in center, 50 minutes to 1 hour. Transfer ramekins to a rack to cool.

Refrigerate custards, loosely covered with plastic wrap, for at least 4 hours.

Just before serving, sprinkle 1 teaspoon turbinado sugar evenly over each custard. Move blowtorch flame evenly back and forth close to sugar until it is caramelized. Let stand until caramel is hardened, 3 to 5 minutes.

COOK'S NOTES

■ The rhubarb filling can be made up to 2 days ahead and refrigerated, covered. Bring to room temperature before proceeding with the recipe.
■ The custards (without the sugar topping) can be refrigerated for up to 2 days (cover tightly once cold). Blot very gently with paper towels before sprinkling with the sugar and caramelizing.

Pistachio Rhubarb Trifle

SERVES 8
ACTIVE TIME: 1¼ HOURS ■ START TO FINISH: 12½ HOURS
(INCLUDES CHILLING)

■ Trifles are special-occasion desserts from England, in which pieces of sponge cake are soaked in spirits, usually sherry, layered with jam and custard, and topped with whipped cream. In our version, fresh rhubarb puree replaces the traditional jam and keeps the flavor lively, with an assist from pistachios. Because the colors are so pretty—pale pistachio green, golden sponge, and soft rhubarb pink—be sure to assemble this trifle in your nicest glass bowl. Don't use a dark sherry for the syrup or topping—it would muddy the beautiful green-gold color of the cake and tint the cream topping brown. ∎

FOR CAKE
    ½ cup all-purpose flour
    1½ cups sugar
    ½ cup unsalted shelled pistachios
      Salt
    4 large eggs, separated
    4 large egg yolks
    3 tablespoons whole milk
    1 teaspoon vanilla extract
    ½ teaspoon almond extract
FOR ASSEMBLING TRIFLE
      Sherry Syrup (page 838)
      Vanilla Custard (page 838)
      Rhubarb Puree (page 838)
FOR TOPPING
    1 cup very cold heavy cream
    1 tablespoon sugar
    1 tablespoon fino sherry (see headnote)
    2 tablespoons unsalted shelled pistachios,
      chopped

SPECIAL EQUIPMENT: a 15-by-10-by-1-inch baking sheet (jelly-roll pan); parchment paper

MAKE THE CAKE: Put a rack in middle of oven and preheat oven to 350°F. Butter bottom and sides of baking sheet, line bottom with parchment paper, and butter paper. Dust pan with flour, knocking out excess.

Pulse together flour, 1 cup sugar, pistachios, and ½ teaspoon salt in a food processor until pistachios are very finely ground (mixture will resemble slightly grainy flour). Transfer mixture to a large bowl and whisk in 8 yolks, milk, and extracts.

Beat egg whites with a pinch of salt in a large bowl with an electric mixer at medium-high speed until they hold soft peaks. Reduce speed to low and add remaining ½ cup sugar a little at a time.

Increase speed to high and beat until whites hold stiff, glossy peaks. Fold one third of whites into batter to lighten it, then fold in remaining whites gently but thoroughly.

Pour batter into baking sheet, spreading it evenly, and rap pan against counter to release any air bubbles. Bake cake until golden and springy to the touch, 20 to 25 minutes. Cool cake in pan on a rack for 20 minutes.

Remove pan from rack. Cover rack with a sheet of parchment paper, invert rack over cake, and flip cake onto rack. Carefully peel off parchment paper from bottom of cake and cool completely.

ASSEMBLE THE TRIFLE: Slide cake, on parchment, onto a work surface, with a long side nearest you. Trim cake with a serrated knife to a 12-by-9-inch rectangle; reserve trimmings. Brush cake and trimmings with sherry syrup. Halve cake crosswise, then cut each half lengthwise into thirds and crosswise into thirds to make eighteen 3-by-2-inch pieces. Halve each piece of cake diagonally to form 2 triangles.

Spoon ½ cup custard into bottom of 3- to 3½-quart glass trifle dish, soufflé dish, or bowl. Arrange half of triangles over custard in 2 layers, pressing short ends of triangles against sides of dish (there should be small spaces in between slices to allow custard to run through). Arrange half of trimmings in center, cutting them as needed to fit. Spread 1½ cups custard over cake pieces, then spread 1 cup rhubarb puree over custard. Cover with remaining cake and trimmings in same manner, then spread remaining custard over top. Spread remaining rhubarb puree over custard, leaving a 1-inch border around edges.

Refrigerate trifle, tightly covered with plastic wrap, for at least 8 hours.

JUST BEFORE SERVING, MAKE THE TOPPING: Beat cream with sugar and sherry in a medium bowl with electric mixer until it just holds soft peaks.

Spoon cream over top of trifle and sprinkle with pistachios.

COOK'S NOTES
∎ Each component of the trifle (see page 838) can be made well ahead.
∎ The trifle can be refrigerated for up to 2 days.

Sherry Syrup

MAKES ABOUT ¾ CUP
ACTIVE TIME: 5 MINUTES ■ START TO FINISH: 1¼ HOURS
(INCLUDES COOLING)

■ As it soaks into the trifle's sponge cake, this syrup infuses it with a boozy warmth. ■

½ cup water
½ cup sugar
6 tablespoons fino sherry

Bring water, sugar, and sherry to a boil in a small heavy saucepan, stirring until sugar is dissolved. Boil until reduced to about ¾ cup, about 5 minutes. Cool syrup completely before using.

COOK'S NOTE

■ The syrup can be refrigerated in an airtight container for up to 1 week.

Vanilla Custard

MAKES ABOUT 4 CUPS
ACTIVE TIME: 20 MINUTES ■ START TO FINISH: 3¼ HOURS
(INCLUDES CHILLING)

■ This custard isn't meant to be eaten on its own—it has a much looser consistency than most so it can soak into the trifle's cake layers. ■

3 cups whole milk
8 large egg yolks
⅔ cup sugar
¼ cup cornstarch
¼ teaspoon salt
1 tablespoon unsalted butter, softened
1 teaspoon vanilla extract

SPECIAL EQUIPMENT: an instant-read thermometer

Heat milk in a 2½- to 3-quart heavy saucepan over moderate heat until hot but not boiling; remove from heat. Whisk together yolks, sugar, cornstarch, and salt in a heatproof bowl until smooth. Add 1 cup hot milk to yolk mixture in a stream, whisking, then add remaining milk, whisking constantly. Transfer mixture to saucepan and cook over moderately low heat, stirring constantly, until custard is thickened and registers 170°F on thermometer, 6 to 10 minutes (do not boil).

Immediately pour custard through a fine-mesh sieve into a clean bowl, scraping sieve with a rubber spatula to force it through. Stir in butter and vanilla.

Refrigerate custard, its surface covered with parchment or wax paper, until cold and thickened, at least 3 hours.

COOK'S NOTES

■ The custard can be cooled quickly by setting the bowl in a larger bowl of ice and cold water and stirring occasionally.

■ The custard can be refrigerated, its surface covered with parchment paper and the bowl covered tightly with plastic wrap, for up to 2 days.

Rhubarb Puree

MAKES ABOUT 2 CUPS
ACTIVE TIME: 15 MINUTES ■ START TO FINISH: 1¾ HOURS
(INCLUDES COOLING)

■ An easy rhubarb puree adds tartness and color to the trifle. Straining the puree through a sieve removes any stringiness, resulting in a silky blend. ■

2 pounds fresh rhubarb stalks, cut into 1-inch pieces
⅔ cup confectioners' sugar

Put a rack in middle of oven and preheat oven to 375°F. Lightly oil a large shallow baking pan.

Arrange rhubarb in one layer in pan and sift confectioners' sugar evenly over top. Bake, stirring occasionally, until rhubarb is very tender, 25 to 30 minutes.

Transfer rhubarb to a food processor and puree (use caution when blending hot mixtures) until smooth. Force puree through a medium-mesh sieve into a bowl, pushing on solids; discard solids. Cool completely (see Cook's Note).

COOK'S NOTES

■ The puree can be cooled quickly by setting the bowl in a larger bowl of ice and cold water and stirring occasionally.

■ The puree can be refrigerated in an airtight container for up to 3 days.

Pumpkin Flan with Spiced Pumpkin Seeds

SERVES 8
ACTIVE TIME: 40 MINUTES ■ START TO FINISH: 8 HOURS
(INCLUDES CHILLING)

■ This flan is fragrant with pumpkin pie spices. A topping of toasted pumpkin seeds seasoned with cayenne creates a play of sweet and heat. ■

FOR CARAMEL AND FLAN
2 cups sugar
1½ cups heavy cream
1 cup whole milk
5 large eggs
1 large egg yolk
1 (15-ounce) can solid pack pumpkin (not pumpkin pie filling)
1 teaspoon vanilla extract
1½ teaspoons ground cinnamon
1 teaspoon ground ginger
¼ teaspoon freshly grated nutmeg
¼ teaspoon salt

FOR SPICED PUMPKIN SEEDS
1 cup (4 ounces) green (hulled) pumpkin seeds (pepitas; not toasted)
1 teaspoon vegetable oil
½ teaspoon salt
⅛ teaspoon cayenne

SPECIAL EQUIPMENT: a 2-quart soufflé dish or round casserole dish

MAKE THE CARAMEL: Put a rack in middle of oven and preheat oven to 350°F. Heat soufflé dish in oven while you make caramel.

Heat 1 cup sugar in a dry 2-quart heavy saucepan over moderate heat, stirring with a fork to heat sugar evenly, until it starts to melt. Stop stirring and cook, swirling pan occasionally so sugar melts evenly, until it is a dark amber caramel. Wearing oven mitts, remove hot dish from oven and immediately pour caramel into dish, tilting it to cover bottom and sides. Keep tilting as caramel cools and thickens enough to coat, then transfer to a rack and let harden. (Leave oven on.)

MAKE THE FLAN: Bring cream and milk to a bare simmer in a 2-quart heavy saucepan over moderate heat; remove from heat. Whisk together eggs, yolk, and remaining cup sugar in a large bowl until well combined. Whisk in pumpkin, vanilla, spices, and salt until well combined. Add hot cream mixture in a slow stream, whisking.

Pour custard through a fine-mesh sieve into a bowl, scraping sieve with a rubber spatula to force it through, and stir to combine well. Pour custard into soufflé dish. Put dish in a roasting pan, put pan in oven, and add enough boiling water to pan to reach halfway up sides of dish. Bake until flan is golden brown on top and a knife inserted in center comes out clean, about 1¼ hours. Transfer dish to a rack to cool.

Refrigerate flan, covered, for at least 6 hours.

MAKE THE SPICED PUMPKIN SEEDS: Toast pumpkin seeds in oil in a 10- to 12-inch heavy skillet, preferably cast-iron, over moderately low heat, stirring constantly, until puffed and golden, 8 to 10 minutes. Transfer to a bowl and toss with salt and cayenne until coated.

TO SERVE: Run a thin knife around sides of flan to loosen it. Shake dish gently from side to side until flan moves freely in dish. Invert a large platter with a lip over dish and, holding dish and platter securely together, quickly invert and turn out flan onto platter. (Caramel will pour out over and around flan.) Sprinkle flan with spiced pumpkin seeds just before serving.

COOK'S NOTES
■ The flan can be refrigerated for up to 1 day.
■ The spiced pumpkin seeds keep in an airtight container at room temperature for up to 3 days.

Cheese Flan

SERVES 8
ACTIVE TIME: 25 MINUTES ■ START TO FINISH: 1¾ HOURS

■ Unlike the custardy flan served in Mexican restaurants, this version, baked in individual ramekins, will remind you of a light, perfectly baked cheesecake. The unexpectedly rich, creamy texture comes from cream cheese. The flan has the familiar caramel topping and milky flavor, along with a gentle hint of cinnamon and vanilla. It's delicious warm or at room temperature, which means you don't have to take time to chill it. ∎

1 cup sugar
¼ cup water
2½ cups whole milk
1 (3-inch) cinnamon stick
1 (14-ounce) can sweetened condensed milk
1 (8-ounce) package cream cheese, softened
5 large eggs
1 teaspoon vanilla extract
⅛ teaspoon salt

SPECIAL EQUIPMENT: eight 7- to 8-ounce ramekins

MAKE THE CARAMEL: Heat sugar and water in a small heavy saucepan over moderate heat, stirring until sugar is dissolved. Wash down any sugar crystals from sides of pan with a pastry brush dipped in cold water, bring to a boil, and boil, without stirring, swirling pan occasionally so caramel colors evenly, until it is dark amber. Immediately pour caramel into ramekins and swirl to coat bottom and partway up sides of each.

MAKE THE FLAN: Put a rack in middle of oven and preheat oven to 350°F.

Bring milk and cinnamon stick just to a simmer in a small heavy saucepan. Remove from heat and let steep, covered, for 5 minutes. Remove cinnamon stick.

Meanwhile, blend condensed milk and cream cheese in a food processor until smooth. Add eggs, vanilla, and salt and blend until smooth. Transfer to a large bowl, preferably with a pour spout, and whisk in hot milk.

Divide mixture among ramekins. Arrange ramekins in a roasting pan, put pan in oven, and add enough boiling water to pan to reach halfway up sides of ramekins. Cover pan loosely with a sheet of foil and bake until custards are just set but still slightly wobbly in center, 45 to 55 minutes. Transfer ramekins to a rack and let stand for at least 15 minutes (flan will continue to set).

Serve flan warm or at room temperature. Just before serving, run a thin knife around each flan to loosen it, then invert onto a plate.

COOK'S NOTE

∎ The flan can be made up to 2 days ahead. Refrigerate in the ramekins, uncovered, until cool, then cover with plastic wrap. Let stand at room temperature for about 1 hour before serving. To serve warm, put the ramekins in a roasting pan of hot water, straddle over two burners on low, and heat for about 20 minutes.

Rich Chocolate Mousse

SERVES 8
ACTIVE TIME: 15 MINUTES ∎ START TO FINISH: 30 MINUTES

∎ Trends may come and go, but chocolate mousse never fails to impress. It manages to convey both decadence and comfort, yet it couldn't be easier to make. This version is a true classic, in that the eggs are not cooked (see Cook's Note), and it's unbelievably smooth and voluptuous. ∎

8 ounces bittersweet chocolate (no more than 60% cacao; see page 705), chopped
¾ stick (6 tablespoons) unsalted butter, cut into tablespoons
3 large eggs, separated
1 tablespoon Cognac or other brandy
1 cup very cold heavy cream
⅛ teaspoon salt

Melt chocolate and butter in a large metal bowl set over a saucepan of barely simmering water, gently stirring occasionally until melted and smooth. Remove from heat.

Meanwhile, beat yolks in a small bowl with an electric mixer until thick enough to form a ribbon that takes a few seconds to dissolve when beaters are lifted, 2 to 4 minutes. Whisk into chocolate mixture, along with Cognac. Let mixture cool to warm.

Beat cream in a medium bowl with cleaned beaters until it just holds stiff peaks.

Beat whites and salt in another bowl with cleaned beaters until they just hold soft peaks.

Add cream and egg whites to chocolate mixture and fold together gently but thoroughly. Transfer to stemmed glasses, 4-ounce ramekins, or a serving dish and serve immediately, or refrigerate. (If mousse has been chilled, let stand at room temperature for at least 30 minutes before serving.)

COOK'S NOTES

- The eggs in this recipe will not be cooked. If that is a concern, see page 915.
- The mousse can be refrigerated, its surface covered with parchment paper, for up to 2 days.

Lemon Curd Mousse

SERVES 8 TO 10
ACTIVE TIME: 30 MINUTES ■ START TO FINISH: 10¾ HOURS
(INCLUDES CHILLING)

■ Just what you want after a hearty meal, this mousse refreshes your palate with its lemon tang. Making your own lemon curd is a snap. The mousse is delicious with almost anything—fresh berries, poached pears, and shortbread are some of our favorite accompaniments. ■

- 1 tablespoon finely grated lemon zest
- 1 cup fresh lemon juice (from about 4 lemons)
- 1 cup sugar
- 6 large eggs
- ⅛ teaspoon salt
- 1½ sticks (12 tablespoons) unsalted butter, cut into pieces
- 1 cup very cold heavy cream

Whisk together zest, juice, sugar, eggs, and salt in a 3-quart heavy saucepan until combined. Add butter and cook over moderately low heat, whisking frequently, until mixture is thick enough to hold marks of whisk and just starts to boil, 6 to 8 minutes.

Pour lemon curd through a fine-mesh sieve into a bowl. Refrigerate, surface covered with parchment or wax paper, until cold, 3 to 4 hours (see Cook's Note).

Beat cream in a bowl with an electric mixer until it holds stiff peaks. Fold one third of cream into curd, then fold in remaining cream gently but thoroughly. Refrigerate, covered, for at least 6 hours.

Let mousse stand at room temperature for about 15 minutes before serving.

COOK'S NOTES

- You can quick-chill the curd by setting the bowl in a

larger bowl of ice and cold water, stirring occasionally, until cold.

- The mousse can be refrigerated for up to 2 days.

Yogurt Mousse with Apricot Sauce

SERVES 8
ACTIVE TIME: 45 MINUTES ■ START TO FINISH: 2¼ HOURS

■ Made with thick Greek yogurt and lemon zest, this mousse is luscious, airy, and tangy. It's delicious with the apricot sauce, but it's remarkably versatile; serve it with a drizzle of honey and a scattering of toasted walnuts, or with Rhubarb Puree (page 838) or Blackberry Compote (page 843). ■

FOR MOUSSE
- 1½ teaspoons unflavored gelatin
- 1 cup whole milk
- ½ vanilla bean, halved lengthwise
- ½ cup sugar
- 1 (4-by-1-inch) strip lemon zest, removed with a vegetable peeler
- 1½ cups Greek yogurt (see Cook's Note)
- ¾ cup very cold heavy cream

FOR SAUCE
- ½ vanilla bean, halved lengthwise
- ½ cup sugar
- ¼ cup water
- 1 pound apricots, quartered and pitted
- 1–1½ teaspoons fresh lemon juice

MAKE THE MOUSSE: Sprinkle gelatin over ¼ cup milk in a small bowl and let stand for 1 minute to soften.

Meanwhile, scrape seeds from vanilla bean into remaining ¾ cup milk in a 1-quart heavy saucepan, then add pod, sugar, and zest and bring to a simmer over moderate heat, stirring until sugar is dissolved. Stir in gelatin mixture until dissolved. Pour mixture through a fine-mesh sieve into a metal bowl; discard solids. Set bowl in a larger bowl of ice and cold water and cool, stirring frequently, for about 10 minutes.

Gradually add milk mixture to yogurt in a medium bowl, whisking.

Beat cream in a medium bowl with an electric

mixer at high speed until it just holds soft peaks. Fold into yogurt mixture gently but thoroughly. Cover and refrigerate, folding it twice again in first 20 minutes, until set, about 2 hours.

MEANWHILE, MAKE THE SAUCE: Scrape seeds from vanilla bean into a 2-quart heavy saucepan, then add pod, sugar, water, apricots, and 1 teaspoon lemon juice. Cook, uncovered, over moderate heat, stirring frequently and skimming off any foam, until fruit is tender, 8 to 12 minutes. Cool to room temperature.

Add more lemon juice to taste to sauce, and discard vanilla pod. Spoon sauce into bowls and top with mousse.

COOK'S NOTES

- You can substitute one 32-ounce container whole-milk yogurt, well stirred, for the Greek yogurt. Drain it in a paper-towel-lined sieve set over a bowl, refrigerated, for 8 hours; pour off the liquid occasionally.
- The mousse can be refrigerated for up to 1 day.
- The sauce can be made up to 3 days ahead. Cool, uncovered, then refrigerate, covered. Bring to room temperature before serving.

Dark-Roast Coffee Gelée

SERVES 10
ACTIVE TIME: 20 MINUTES ■ START TO FINISH: 8½ HOURS
(INCLUDES CHILLING)

■ Forgo after-dinner coffee in favor of these softly set, seriously sophisticated little gelées, topped with sweetened whipped cream. The darker and richer the coffee, the better. We make the gelée with cone-filtered coffee; it's equally delicious with plunged coffee. Curry powder may seem like a strange addition to the whipped cream topping, but when combined with the brown sugar, it lends fullness and depth. ■

FOR GELÉE
6 tablespoons finely ground (for filter) dark-roast coffee
2 cups boiling water
½ cup granulated sugar
5 tablespoons cold water

1½ teaspoons unflavored gelatin
2 teaspoons vanilla extract
FOR TOPPING
¼ cup packed dark brown sugar
1 cup very cold heavy cream
Scant ¼ teaspoon curry powder
SPECIAL EQUIPMENT: ten 2- to 4-ounce cups, such as espresso cups

MAKE THE GELÉE: Brew ground coffee in a filter-style coffee maker (not electric) using boiling water; or put coffee in a sieve lined with a paper filter and pour boiling water over it.

Meanwhile, bring sugar and ¼ cup water to a boil in a small saucepan, stirring until sugar is dissolved. Remove sugar syrup from heat.

Sprinkle gelatin over remaining 1 tablespoon water in a small cup and let soften for 1 minute.

Stir together hot coffee, sugar syrup, and vanilla in a bowl, then add gelatin mixture, stirring until dissolved. Refrigerate, covered, until softly set, about 8 hours.

MAKE THE TOPPING: Force brown sugar through a sieve into a medium bowl. Add cream and curry powder and beat with an electric mixer until cream just holds soft peaks.

Divide gelée among cups and top with dollops of whipped cream.

COOK'S NOTE

- The gelée can be refrigerated for up to 1 day.

Yogurt and Brown Sugar
Panna Cotta
with Grape Gelée

SERVES 6
ACTIVE TIME: 30 MINUTES ■ START TO FINISH: 8½ HOURS
(INCLUDES CHILLING)

■ Flavored with dark brown sugar and tangy yogurt, this panna cotta is crowned with a glittering wine-colored layer of gelatin in which thin slices of red and green grapes are suspended. It makes for a stunning presentation, and each bite offers rich creaminess juxtaposed with the refreshing grape gelée. ■

FOR GELÉE

- 1 teaspoon unflavored gelatin
- 1 cup all-natural Concord grape juice
- 1 tablespoon fresh lemon juice
- 1 cup mixed red and green seedless grapes, thinly sliced crosswise
- 1 tablespoon grappa (optional)

FOR PANNA COTTA

- 2 teaspoons unflavored gelatin
- 1 cup heavy cream
- ½ cup packed dark brown sugar
- 2 cups plain low-fat yogurt
- 2 tablespoons grappa
- ⅛ teaspoon salt

SPECIAL EQUIPMENT: six 8-ounce ramekins or custard cups

MAKE THE GELÉE: Sprinkle gelatin over ¼ cup grape juice in a 1-quart heavy saucepan and let stand for 1 minute to soften.

Bring grape juice to a simmer, stirring until gelatin is dissolved. Remove from heat and stir in remaining ¾ cup grape juice, along with lemon juice, grapes, and grappa (if using).

Lightly oil ramekins. Divide grape mixture among ramekins, put in a shallow baking pan, and chill in freezer until just set, about 30 minutes.

MEANWHILE, MAKE THE PANNA COTTA: Stir together gelatin and ¼ cup cream in a 1-quart heavy saucepan and let stand for 1 minute to soften.

Bring cream to a simmer over moderate heat, stirring until gelatin is dissolved. Add remaining ¾ cup cream, along with brown sugar, and return to a simmer, stirring until sugar is dissolved. Remove from heat.

Whisk together yogurt, grappa, and salt until smooth in a 1-quart glass measure or a bowl with a pour spout. Pour in cream mixture and whisk until well combined. Pour mixture into ramekins. Refrigerate, covered, until firm, at least 8 hours.

To unmold, run a thin sharp knife around sides of each ramekin to loosen panna cotta, dip briefly in a small bowl of very warm water, about 10 seconds, then invert panna cotta (with gelée) onto a plate; gently lift off ramekin.

COOK'S NOTE

- The panna cotta can be refrigerated for up to 2 days.

Blackberry Buttermilk Panna Cotta with Blackberry Compote

SERVES 6
ACTIVE TIME: 30 MINUTES ■ START TO FINISH: 8½ HOURS
(INCLUDES CHILLING)

■ Plump, juicy blackberries in a rich crème de cassis syrup glisten over lush, lilac-colored panna cotta. A generous amount of buttermilk complements the flavor of the blackberries. ■

FOR PANNA COTTA

- ¾ pound (about 3 cups) blackberries
- 1¼ cups well-shaken buttermilk
- 2¾ teaspoons unflavored gelatin (from two ¼-ounce envelopes)
- ¼ cup water
- 1½ cups heavy cream
- ⅔ cup sugar
- 2 tablespoons blackberry syrup, store-bought or homemade (see Cook's Note)

FOR BLACKBERRY COMPOTE

- ½ pound (about 2 cups) blackberries
- ½ cup water
- ½ cup crème de cassis
- 2 tablespoons sugar
- 1½ tablespoons fresh lemon juice

SPECIAL EQUIPMENT: six 6-ounce molds (see Cook's Note), ramekins, or custard cups

MAKE THE PANNA COTTA: Puree blackberries with buttermilk in a blender until very smooth. Pour through a fine-mesh sieve into a bowl, pressing on solids; discard solids.

Sprinkle gelatin over water in a small bowl and let stand for 1 minute to soften.

Meanwhile, heat cream and sugar in a 1-quart saucepan over moderate heat until hot, stirring until sugar is dissolved. Remove from heat and add gelatin mixture, stirring until dissolved. Stir cream mixture and syrup into blackberry puree, then pour through cleaned sieve into a bowl with a spout.

Pour mixture into molds. Refrigerate, covered, until firm, at least 8 hours.

MEANWHILE, MAKE THE BLACKBERRY COMPOTE:
Put blackberries in a bowl; set aside. Combine water, crème de cassis, and sugar in a small saucepan, bring to a boil, stirring occasionally to dissolve sugar, and boil until syrupy and reduced to about ⅓ cup, 10 to 12 minutes. Stir in lemon juice.

Pour syrup over blackberries and gently stir to combine.

To serve, run a thin knife around sides of molds to loosen panna cotta. Dip each mold in a small bowl of warm water for 3 to 5 seconds, then invert panna cotta onto a plate and gently lift off mold. Spoon berries and syrup over and around panna cotta.

COOK'S NOTES

- To make blackberry syrup, heat ¼ cup blackberry jam with 1 tablespoon water in a small saucepan over moderately low heat, stirring, until jam is dissolved. Pour the mixture through a fine-mesh sieve into a small bowl, pressing on the solids; discard the solids.
- We have the best luck making these desserts with molds made of nonreactive materials such as stainless steel, glass, and ceramic. If you're using reactive molds for your panna cottas, make sure there are no rust spots—the acid in the buttermilk and the fruit will react to the rust and cause the panna cotta to discolor.
- The panna cotta can be refrigerated for up to 1 day.
- The compote can be made up to 2 hours ahead and kept at room temperature.

Cherries in the Snow

SERVES 6
ACTIVE TIME: 15 MINUTES ■ START TO FINISH: 1¼ HOURS
(INCLUDES CHILLING)

■ Here's a poetic version of a traditional Chinese almond-milk gelatin. Whipping the milk gives the top layer the appearance and texture of snow. As cappuccino fans can attest, fat-free or low-fat milk will create the most foam. The port-plumped cherries make an especially elegant pairing. ■

FOR ALMOND-SNOW GELATIN
- 2¼ teaspoons unflavored gelatin
- ½ cup cold water
- 1 cup 1% or skim milk
- ⅓ cup sugar
- ¼ teaspoon almond extract

FOR CHERRIES IN PORT
- ⅓ cup dried sour cherries
- 1 tablespoon sugar
- 1 cup ruby port

MAKE THE ALMOND-SNOW GELATIN: Lightly oil an 8-inch square glass baking dish; wipe out any excess with a paper towel.

Sprinkle gelatin over water in a large heatproof bowl and let stand for 1 minute to soften.

Meanwhile, bring milk and sugar just to a boil in a 1-quart saucepan, stirring until sugar is dissolved. Remove from heat and whisk into gelatin mixture. Add almond extract and whisk briskly until milk is foamy, about 5 minutes.

Pour into baking dish and freeze for 15 minutes to set foam.

Refrigerate, uncovered, until firm, at least 45 minutes.

MAKE THE CHERRIES: Combine cherries, sugar, and port in a 1-quart heavy saucepan, bring to a simmer, and simmer, uncovered, until liquid is reduced to about ½ cup, about 10 minutes. Set pan in a bowl of ice and cold water and refrigerate, stirring occasionally, until sauce is syrupy, about 15 minutes.

ASSEMBLE THE DESSERT: Cut gelatin into 1-inch squares using a knife dipped in hot water and wiped dry between cuts. Remove squares from dish with a spatula and arrange, frothy side up, on six chilled plates.

Spoon cherries and sauce over squares.

COOK'S NOTES

- The gelatin can be refrigerated for up to 2 days (cover after 45 minutes).
- The cherries in port can be refrigerated (without cooling in ice water), covered, for up to 1 week.

Tangerine Bavarian Cream with Tangerine Caramel Sauce and Candied Peel

SERVES 8
ACTIVE TIME: 25 MINUTES ∎ START TO FINISH: 4½ HOURS
(INCLUDES CHILLING)

∎ This lighter-than-air version of Bavarian cream is spooned into a springform pan and chilled until set, so that it can be served in neat slices. Tangerines have perhaps the most complex qualities of all the citrus fruits: floral and gently sweet, with an underlying tartness—like three fruits in one. ∎

6 tight-skinned tangerines
1 (¼-ounce) envelope unflavored gelatin
8 large egg yolks
¼ cup sugar
1 tablespoon fresh lemon juice
1 cup very cold heavy cream

ACCOMPANIMENTS: Candied Tangerine Peel (page 846); Tangerine Caramel Sauce (recipe follows)

SPECIAL EQUIPMENT: an 8-inch springform pan

Remove side of springform pan and invert bottom (to make it easier to slide Bavarian off bottom of pan), then lock on side. Lightly oil pan.

Remove peel, including a little pith, from 5 tangerines in 2-by-1-inch strips with a sharp vegetable peeler, preferably Y-shaped; reserve for making Candied Tangerine Peel (page 846). Grate enough zest from remaining tangerine to measure 1 teaspoon. Juice tangerines; you need 1¼ cups juice.

Sprinkle gelatin over ¼ cup tangerine juice in a small bowl and let stand for about 1 minute to soften.

Meanwhile, whisk together yolks, sugar, lemon juice, and remaining cup tangerine juice in a medium heavy saucepan and cook over moderately low heat, whisking constantly, until mixture just comes to a simmer (do not let boil). Remove from heat and whisk in gelatin mixture until completely dissolved. Transfer to a metal bowl and chill in a bowl of ice cubes and cold water, stirring frequently, until mixture has thickened to consistency of raw egg whites. Remove from bowl of ice water.

Beat cream with zest in a medium bowl with an electric mixer until it just holds soft peaks. Stir one third of whipped cream into yolk mixture to lighten it, then fold in remaining cream gently but thoroughly.

Spoon into springform pan and refrigerate until set, at least 4 hours. To serve, top Bavarian with candied tangerine peel and spoon sauce all around.

COOK'S NOTE

∎ The Bavarian can be refrigerated for up to 24 hours.

Tangerine Caramel Sauce

MAKES ABOUT 1½ CUPS
ACTIVE TIME: 25 MINUTES ∎ START TO FINISH: 35 MINUTES

∎ The bright perfume of tangerine juice brings intensity to the sauce. ∎

6 tight-skinned tangerines
1½ cups sugar
¼ cup water
2 Turkish bay leaves or 1 California bay leaf
1 tablespoon fresh lemon juice
Pinch of salt

Remove three 2-by-1-inch strips zest from 1 tangerine with a sharp vegetable peeler, preferably Y-shaped, and scrape off any white pith. Remove peel, including a little of pith, from 3 more tangerines in 2-by-1-inch strips and reserve for making Candied Tangerine Peel (page 846). Juice tangerines; you need 1¼ cups juice.

Bring sugar, water, bay leaves, and zest to a boil in a small heavy saucepan over moderate heat, stirring until sugar is dissolved. Wash down any sugar crystals from sides of pan with a pastry brush dipped in cold water and boil, without stirring, until caramel is a deep amber.

Remove from heat and carefully add tangerine juice (mixture will bubble and steam vigorously), then return to heat and simmer, stirring, until caramel is dissolved, 1 to 2 minutes. Stir in lemon juice and salt, remove from heat, and cool.

Refrigerate sauce, covered, until ready to serve (it will thicken slightly). Discard bay leaf and zest.

COOK'S NOTE

∎ The sauce can be refrigerated for up to 3 days.

Candied Tangerine Peel

MAKES ABOUT 3 CUPS

ACTIVE TIME: 30 MINUTES ■ START TO FINISH: 2¼ HOURS

■ This candied peel delivers a straight shot of sweet-tart tangerine flavor. ■

> Peel, including a little pith, from 8 tangerines (reserved from previous recipes)
> 2 cups granulated sugar
> 2 cups water
> Superfine sugar for coating

Cut peel into ⅛-inch-wide matchsticks. Cover matchsticks with cold water in a medium saucepan and bring to a boil. Drain in a sieve and repeat procedure 2 times.

Bring sugar, water, and peel to a boil in a heavy medium saucepan, stirring until sugar is dissolved, then simmer until peel is translucent and syrup has thickened, 45 to 50 minutes. Remove from heat.

Lightly oil a large rack and set over a wax-paper-lined baking sheet. Transfer candied peel to rack with a fork, separating strips. (Discard syrup or reserve for another use, such as sweetening tea, a dessert sauce, or fruit salad.)

When peel is cool but not completely dry, toss with superfine sugar in a bowl to coat. Return to rack and let stand until dry to the touch, about 30 minutes.

COOK'S NOTE

■ The candied peel keeps in an airtight container at room temperature for up to 2 days.

Mango Puddings

SERVES 8

ACTIVE TIME: 30 MINUTES ■ START TO FINISH: 9 HOURS
(INCLUDES CHILLING)

■ Fresh mango takes the spotlight in these softly set Malaysian-inspired puddings. Because the ingredients of this recipe are so straightforward, it's extremely important to use very ripe mangoes. ■

> 2¼–2¾ pounds very ripe mangoes (4–5)
> 1 (¼-ounce) envelope unflavored gelatin
> 1¼ cups water
> ½ cup sugar
> ¾ cup evaporated milk
> GARNISH: 1 mango, peeled, pitted, and diced

Peel and pit mangoes. Puree in a food processor until smooth (you should have 2⅓ cups puree). Force through a medium-mesh sieve into a bowl to remove any fibers; with a rubber spatula, scrape puree from bottom of sieve into bowl.

Sprinkle gelatin over ¼ cup water in a small bowl and let stand for 1 minute to soften.

Heat sugar and remaining cup water in a small saucepan over moderately high heat, stirring until sugar is dissolved. Add gelatin mixture and stir until dissolved. Add mango puree and heat, stirring, just until mixture reaches a bare simmer. Remove from heat and stir in evaporated milk until well combined. Cool to room temperature, stirring occasionally.

Divide pudding among eight 4-ounce goblets or small bowls and refrigerate, covered, for at least 8 hours to allow flavors to develop (puddings will be softly set).

Serve puddings topped with diced mango.

COOK'S NOTE

■ The puddings can be refrigerated for up to 24 hours.

Apple Budino

SERVES 6

ACTIVE TIME: 20 MINUTES ■ START TO FINISH: 1 HOUR

■ This budino ("pudding" in Italian) is a refined take on bread pudding. Cubes of buttery croissants suspended in a rich custard hide a layer of caramelized apples scented with cinnamon. It is adapted from a recipe by Walter Manzke, who served it when he was the chef at Bouchée in Carmel, California. ■

> ½ tablespoon unsalted butter
> 1 large Granny Smith apple, peeled, cored, and cut into ¼-inch dice

1 (3-inch) cinnamon stick, broken into thirds
2 tablespoons packed light brown sugar
½ cup apple juice
3 croissants, cut into ½-inch cubes (5 cups)
1 cup heavy cream
2 large eggs
5 tablespoons granulated sugar

ACCOMPANIMENT: cinnamon or vanilla ice cream

Put a rack in middle of oven and preheat oven to 375°F.

Melt butter in a 10-inch heavy skillet over moderate heat. Add apples and cinnamon stick and cook over moderately high heat, stirring occasionally, until apples are pale golden, about 3 minutes. Add brown sugar and cook, stirring, until sugar is dissolved and apples are slightly caramelized, about 2 minutes. Add apple juice and cook over moderate heat, stirring occasionally, until apples are tender and juice has evaporated, 3 to 4 minutes. Discard cinnamon stick.

Transfer apples to an ungreased 9-inch square baking dish or other 2½-quart shallow baking dish, spreading them evenly. Scatter croissant cubes evenly over apples.

Whisk together cream, eggs, and ¼ cup sugar in a bowl and pour mixture evenly over croissant cubes, pressing them down slightly to moisten them. Sprinkle top evenly with remaining tablespoon sugar.

Bake, uncovered, until custard is set and top is lightly browned, 25 to 30 minutes. Transfer baking dish to a rack to cool for 10 minutes.

Serve warm with ice cream.

Individual Bread Puddings with Banana Sauce

SERVES 6
ACTIVE TIME: 30 MINUTES ■ START TO FINISH: 1½ HOURS

■ Many a New Orleans meal ends with bread pudding, but the revered restaurant Galatoire's offers a particularly tempting version, individual puddings paired with a rummy banana sauce kissed with brown sugar. ■

FOR BREAD PUDDINGS
6 large eggs
½ cup sugar
½ teaspoon salt
2 cups whole milk
1 tablespoon vanilla extract
2 teaspoons ground cinnamon
12 (¾-inch-thick) slices baguette

FOR BANANA SAUCE
2 firm but ripe medium bananas
1 stick (8 tablespoons) unsalted butter, cut into pieces
¼ cup packed light brown sugar
¼ cup light or gold rum

SPECIAL EQUIPMENT: a nonstick muffin pan with 6 large (1-cup) muffin cups

MAKE THE BREAD PUDDINGS: Butter the muffin cups. Whisk together eggs, sugar, and salt in a large bowl. Whisk in milk, vanilla, and cinnamon.

Place 2 slices of bread in each muffin cup and divide custard among cups. Let stand, gently pressing down on bread occasionally, until bread is soft and some of custard is absorbed, about 30 minutes.

Put a rack in middle of oven and preheat oven to 350°F.

Bake bread puddings until golden on top and a toothpick inserted in center comes out clean, 30 to 35 minutes. Transfer to a rack to cool slightly, about 5 minutes (puddings will sink slightly in center).

Remove puddings from pan and cool on rack until warm, about 10 minutes more.

MEANWHILE, MAKE THE SAUCE: Cut bananas into ⅓-inch-thick slices.

Melt butter in a 1-quart heavy saucepan over moderate heat, add brown sugar, and cook, whisking, until smooth and well combined, about 1 minute. Add rum and bananas and simmer, stirring occasionally, for 2 minutes. Remove from heat.

Serve puddings warm, with sauce spooned over them.

Pumpkin Bread Pudding

SERVES 6

ACTIVE TIME: 15 MINUTES ■ START TO FINISH: 45 MINUTES

■ Full of the same spices you find in pumpkin pie, this creamy, custardy bread pudding is a satisfying dessert for a chilly evening. ■

   1 cup heavy cream
   ½ cup whole milk
   ¾ cup canned solid-pack pumpkin (not pumpkin
        pie filling)
   ½ cup sugar
   2 large eggs
   1 large egg yolk
   ¼ teaspoon salt
   ½ teaspoon ground cinnamon
   ¼ teaspoon ground ginger
   ⅛ teaspoon ground allspice
        Pinch of ground cloves
   5 cups cubed (1-inch) day-old baguette or
        crusty bread
   ¾ stick (6 tablespoons) unsalted butter,
        melted

Put a rack in middle of oven and preheat oven to 350°F.

Whisk together cream, milk, pumpkin, sugar, eggs, yolk, salt, and spices in a bowl.

Toss bread cubes with butter in a large bowl, then add pumpkin mixture and toss to coat. Spread in an ungreased 8-inch square baking dish and bake until custard is set, 25 to 30 minutes.

Serve warm or at room temperature.

COOK'S NOTE

■ The pudding can be made up to 2 days ahead. Cool, un-covered, then refrigerate, covered. Reheat, uncovered, in a 350°F oven.

The place: Minneapolis. The year: 1950. Rose Joshua, a young housewife and mother, mentioned to the other members of her Hadassah chapter that she wanted to bake the flavorful, dense cakes called *Bundkuchen* that she remembered from her native Germany. She knew that a heavy cake needs a heavy pan, but hers was made out of cast iron and difficult to lift. Mrs. Joshua became a woman with a mission: she took her pan to H. David Dalquist, the owner of Northland Aluminum in Minneapolis and a keen entrepreneur, and asked if he could make something similar in a more manageable weight. Dalquist set to making a hefty, curvaceous mold that turned out to be just what Mrs. Joshua had in mind, although he made the shape elegant by alternating large scallops with small flutes. That would be the cake's decoration, he reasoned; no frosting was needed, and even the most inexpert hostess could cut attractive slices.

BUNDT PAN

The women liked the BUNDT PANS so much that Northland started marketing them to depart-ment stores. (*Bund* means "alliance" in German—Dalquist added the "t" because that's how the word sounded to him.) The pans were slow to take off nationally, however; in fact, the company thought of discontinuing them. But then, in 1966, a Texan, Ella Helfrich, used one to create what she called a Tunnel of Fudge Cake, which took second prize in the Pillsbury Bake-Off. By the time Dalquist died in 2005, his company had sold almost fifty million Bundt pans.

Dalquist (who struck gold again with a portable turntable for microwave ovens) based his Bundt pan on a tall, fluted, seventeenth-century ceramic tube pan for

KUGELHOPF PAN

a coffee cake known as K U G E L H O P F, or "turban cake." (It was created, the story goes, after the Turks were defeated at the gates of Vienna in 1683 and bakers made a victory cake modeled on the sultan's turban.)

What Bundt, Kugelhopf, and plain T U B E P A N S have in common is the center tube, which allows heat to reach the middle of the cake and cook a heavy batter evenly. You can usually use the pans interchangeably, but make sure they are of comparable volume; in other words, measure by cups, not inches, and allow enough room for the cake to rise. Kugelhopf pans are generally taller than Bundt pans, and the design more deeply impressed; if you need to butter and flour the pan before baking, be sure you get into all the nooks and crannies. Also keep in mind that a dark pan will absorb more heat than a reflective shiny pan, and a cake baked in a dark pan may cook too fast on the outside and overbrown. Cakes need a certain amount of time to develop their structure, so shortening the cooking time won't fix the problem; it's better to lower the temperature by 25 degrees if using a dark pan.

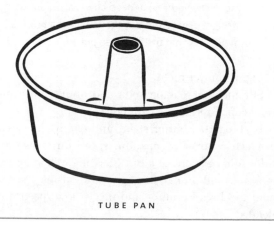

TUBE PAN

Prune Kumquat Sticky-Toffee Pudding with Armagnac Toffee Sauce

SERVES 12
ACTIVE TIME: 1 HOUR ■ START TO FINISH: 3½ HOURS
(INCLUDES COOLING)

■ Sticky-toffee pudding has a devoted following, and for good reason—its dark, rich flavors and moist crumb are irresistible, and even more so when lavished with a buttery toffee sauce. Kumquats and prunes make this version extra-special, punctuating the cake with tangy nuggets of sweetness. It's just the finale you want after a grand wintry meal. A tall Kugelhopf pan produces a cake with a regal bearing, but a regular Bundt pan also works. Decorate it with a handful of kumquats with their leaves attached. The Armagnac toffee sauce—a natural with the prunes—makes a wickedly festive partner. ■

1¾ cups (11–12 ounces) packed pitted prunes, halved
½ cup Armagnac or other brandy
1¼ cups water
6 kumquats
1½ cups granulated sugar
3 cups all-purpose flour
1¼ teaspoons baking soda
1 teaspoon ground ginger
½ teaspoon ground allspice
¾ teaspoon salt
2 sticks (½ pound) unsalted butter, softened
1¼ cups packed light brown sugar
4 large eggs
1 teaspoon vanilla extract

ACCOMPANIMENT: Armagnac Toffee Sauce (recipe follows)
OPTIONAL GARNISH: kumquats, preferably with leaves
SPECIAL EQUIPMENT: a 12-cup Kugelhopf pan (see Sources) or Bundt pan

Put a rack in middle of oven and preheat oven to 350°F. Generously butter Kugelhopf pan.

Combine prunes, Armagnac, and ¾ cup water in a 1-quart heavy saucepan, bring to a simmer, and simmer, uncovered, for 5 minutes. Drain prunes in a sieve set over a large measuring cup, then transfer prunes to a shallow dish. If liquid measures more than ¼ cup, return to pan and boil to reduce to ¼ cup. Add liquid to prunes.

Halve kumquats lengthwise and thinly slice crosswise, discarding any seeds. Bring remaining ½ cup water and ¼ cup sugar to a simmer in a small heavy saucepan, stirring until sugar is dissolved. Add kumquats and simmer, uncovered, for 10 minutes. Drain kumquats (discard liquid) and add to prunes. Cool to room temperature.

Sift together flour, baking soda, ginger, allspice, and salt. Resift mixture (to lighten it).

Beat together butter, brown sugar, and remaining 1¼ cups sugar in a large bowl with an electric mixer at medium-high speed until pale and fluffy. Add eggs one at a time, beating well after each addition. Beat in vanilla. Reduce speed to low and add flour mixture and prune mixture alternately in batches, beginning and ending with flour mixture and beating until just combined.

Spoon batter into pan (batter will come to about 1 inch from top). Put pan on a baking sheet and bake, rotating pan halfway through baking, until a wooden toothpick inserted in several places comes out clean, 1¼ to 1½ hours. Cool pudding in pan on a rack for 15 minutes.

Turn pudding out onto rack and cool for at least 1 hour.

Serve pudding warm or at room temperature with warm toffee sauce, garnished with kumquats if using.

COOK'S NOTE

- The pudding can be kept, wrapped in plastic wrap once completely cooled, at room temperature for up to 3 days. If desired, reheat in foil (sliced or whole) in a 350°F oven for 15 to 30 minutes.

Armagnac Toffee Sauce

MAKES ABOUT 2¼ CUPS
ACTIVE TIME: 5 MINUTES ■ START TO FINISH: 10 MINUTES

- Sticky toffee pudding is unthinkable without a rich, buttery toffee sauce. ■

- 1½ cups heavy cream
- 1½ sticks (12 tablespoons) unsalted butter, cut into small pieces
- ¾ cup packed light brown sugar
- 3 tablespoons Armagnac or other brandy

Combine cream, butter, and brown sugar in a heavy 2-quart saucepan, bring to a simmer, stirring, and simmer, stirring, until slightly thickened, 3 to 4 minutes. Remove from heat and stir in Armagnac.

COOK'S NOTE

- The sauce can be refrigerated, covered, for up to 1 week. Reheat before serving.

Steamed Orange Pudding

SERVES 6
ACTIVE TIME: 20 MINUTES ■ START TO FINISH: 2½ HOURS

- Old-fashioned steamed puddings taste just right on a winter's night. This one's sweet, tangy flavor comes from a combination of orange marmalade and fresh orange juice. The pudding pairs beautifully with custard sauce or crème fraîche. ■

- ¾ teaspoon baking soda
- 1½ tablespoons fresh orange juice
- ½ cup golden raisins
- 1 tablespoon all-purpose flour
- ½ stick (4 tablespoons) unsalted butter, softened
- ¼ cup sugar
- ⅛ teaspoon salt
- 2 large eggs
- ½ cup sweet orange marmalade
- 1½ cups fresh whole wheat bread crumbs

ACCOMPANIMENT: Orange Custard Sauce (recipe follows) or crème fraîche

SPECIAL EQUIPMENT: a 6-cup metal or ceramic pudding mold (see Sources) or deep bowl with a lip; kitchen string if using a mold without a lid or a bowl; a metal rack that fits in a deep pot

Lightly butter mold.

Stir together baking soda and orange juice in a small cup. Toss raisins with flour.

Beat together butter, sugar, and salt in a bowl with an electric mixer at medium speed until pale and fluffy. Add eggs one at a time, beating well after each addition. Add orange juice mixture, raisins, marmalade, and bread crumbs and mix at low speed until blended.

Spoon batter into mold. Cover mold with lid, or cover with a sheet of foil and secure it tightly with kitchen string. Put mold on a metal rack in a deep pot. Add enough boiling water to pot to reach halfway up sides of mold, cover pot, set over heat, and steam pudding in simmering water, adding more boiling water as needed, until surface of pudding feels dry and firm, about 2 hours. Carefully remove from pot and cool on a rack for 5 minutes.

Loosen edges of pudding with a thin knife and invert onto a serving plate. Serve warm with custard sauce or crème fraîche.

Orange Custard Sauce

MAKES ABOUT 1½ CUPS
ACTIVE TIME: 25 MINUTES ■ START TO FINISH: 2½ HOURS
(INCLUDES CHILLING)

■ Try this sauce spooned over chocolate mousse or pudding, or with slices of pound cake. ■

1¼ cups whole milk
1 (4-by-1-inch) strip orange zest, removed with a
    vegetable peeler
3 large egg yolks
¼ cup sugar
  Pinch of salt
½ teaspoon vanilla extract
SPECIAL EQUIPMENT: an instant-read thermometer

Bring milk and zest to a simmer in a small heavy saucepan over moderate heat. Remove from heat and let stand, covered, for 20 minutes.

Whisk together yolks, sugar, and salt in a bowl. Whisk in milk, with zest, then pour mixture into cleaned saucepan. Cook over moderate heat, stirring constantly with a wooden spoon, until custard thickens enough to coat back of spoon and registers 170°F on thermometer.

Immediately pour sauce through a fine-mesh sieve into a bowl; discard zest and stir in vanilla. Cool to room temperature, stirring occasionally.

Refrigerate custard, its surface covered with parchment or wax paper (to prevent a skin from forming), until cold, at least 1 hour.

COOK'S NOTE
■ The sauce can be refrigerated, covered with plastic
  wrap (and parchment), for up to 3 days.

Christmas Rice Pudding

SERVES 8
ACTIVE TIME: 25 MINUTES ■ START TO FINISH: 1 HOUR

■ Magnus Ek, the chef of Oaxen Skärgårdskrog on the picturesque island of Oaxen, south of Stockholm, uses Arborio rice for this rich rice pudding, which has a consistency that's creamier than most. It's barely sweetened, and it's delicious with Ek's warm dried cherry compote. Or you can stir warm milk into the pudding and sprinkle it with sugar and cinnamon. ■

1½ cups short-grain white rice, such as Arborio
1½ cups water
1 (2-inch) piece cinnamon stick
⅛ teaspoon salt
4 cups whole milk
2 tablespoons heavy cream
2 tablespoons sugar
ACCOMPANIMENT: Dried Cherry Compote (recipe follows)
    or warm milk, sugar (preferably turbinado), and
    ground cinnamon

Bring rice, water, cinnamon stick, and salt to a simmer in a 4- to 5-quart heavy pot. Reduce heat to low and gently simmer, covered, until water is absorbed, 8 to 10 minutes.

Add 2 cups milk, cream, and sugar to rice, bring back to a simmer, and simmer, uncovered, stirring occasionally, until rice has absorbed most of milk but is still creamy, about 10 minutes. Add 1 cup milk and simmer, stirring occasionally, for 10 minutes. Add remaining cup milk and simmer, stirring constantly, until rice is tender, 10 to 15 minutes. Remove from heat, cover, and let stand for 15 minutes; discard cinnamon stick.

Serve pudding warm with cherry compote or with warm milk, sugar, and cinnamon.

Dried Cherry Compote

MAKES ABOUT 1⅔ CUPS
ACTIVE TIME: 5 MINUTES ■ START TO FINISH: 30 MINUTES

■ Because fresh fruit was once scarce in Sweden during the winter, compotes stewed from dried fruits are traditional at Christmastime. Here, dried cherries simmered with red wine and port are subtly spiced with cinnamon and black pepper. The compote also makes a fine addition to a cheese plate. ■

  1½ cups (9 ounces) dried sour cherries
  ¾ cup dry red wine
  ⅔ cup ruby port
  6 tablespoons sugar
  1 (2- to 3-inch) cinnamon stick
    Pinch of salt
  ⅛ teaspoon freshly ground black pepper
  2 teaspoons cornstarch
  2 teaspoons red wine vinegar

Combine cherries, wine, port, sugar, cinnamon stick, salt, and pepper in a 1-quart heavy saucepan and bring to a boil over moderate heat. Stir together cornstarch and vinegar in a cup until smooth, then stir into boiling liquid and boil for 1 minute. Remove from heat, cover, and let stand for 15 minutes.

Serve compote warm.

COOK'S NOTE

■ The compote can be made up to 2 days ahead. Cool, uncovered, then refrigerate, covered. Bring to room temperature before serving.

Black Rice Pudding

SERVES 4
ACTIVE TIME: 10 MINUTES ■ START TO FINISH: 2 HOURS
(INCLUDES COOLING)

■ You'll never look at rice pudding the same way again once you try these dark, nutty grains infused with the richness of coconut milk and sugar. The ingredients are typically Asian, but the flavors are universally appealing. Serve after any kind of comforting meal, from *pho* to meat loaf. Leftovers make a great alternative to breakfast oatmeal. Chinese black rice, sometimes called forbidden rice, works well, but if you live near a Southeast Asian market, you can use traditional Thai black sticky rice. ■

  1 cup black rice, preferably Thai black sticky rice
    (see Sources)
  3 cups water

    Scant ¼ teaspoon salt
  ½ cup sugar
  1 (13- to 14-ounce) can unsweetened coconut milk,
    well stirred

Bring rice, water, and salt to a boil in a 3- to 4-quart heavy saucepan. Reduce heat to low and simmer, covered tightly, for 45 minutes (rice will be cooked but still wet).

Stir in sugar and 1½ cups coconut milk and bring to a boil over high heat, then reduce heat to low and simmer, uncovered, stirring occasionally, until mixture is thick and rice is tender but still slightly chewy, about 30 minutes. Remove from heat and cool to warm, stirring occasionally, about 30 minutes.

Stir pudding and divide among four bowls. Stir remaining coconut milk and drizzle over pudding.

COOK'S NOTE

■ The rice pudding, once completely cooled, can be refrigerated, covered, for up to 5 days.

Lemon Soufflé

SERVES 8
ACTIVE TIME: 30 MINUTES ■ START TO FINISH: 2 HOURS
(INCLUDES COOLING)

■ Because of its French pedigree, you might think a soufflé should be saved for tony affairs, but it's the perfect dessert for a casual dinner party—just bake it and then get it on the table immediately for everyone to admire. Though its glorious pouf is fleeting, this soufflé continues to stun long after it's been served. If you can find Meyer lemons, use them. Their unique flavor is more sweet and floral than that of regular lemons. ■

  1 cup whole milk
  4 large eggs, separated
  ½ cup plus 2 tablespoons sugar, plus additional for
    coating dish
  ½ teaspoon vanilla extract
  2 tablespoons cornstarch
  1½ teaspoons finely grated lemon zest, preferably from
    Meyer lemons (see Sources)

⅓ cup fresh lemon juice, preferably from Meyer
   lemons (from 2 lemons)
2 large egg whites
½ teaspoon salt
½ teaspoon cream of tartar

SPECIAL EQUIPMENT: a 7-inch soufflé dish; parchment
   paper

Bring milk just to a simmer in a 1½- to 2-quart heavy saucepan; remove from heat.

Beat together yolks, sugar, and vanilla in a medium bowl with an electric mixer at high speed until thick and pale, 3 to 6 minutes. Reduce speed to low and add cornstarch, mixing until incorporated. Add hot milk in a slow stream, mixing until smooth, then pour custard into saucepan and bring to a boil, whisking constantly. Reduce heat and simmer, whisking constantly, for 2 minutes. (Custard will be thick.)

Transfer to a large bowl and whisk in zest and juice. Cover surface with a round of parchment paper (to prevent a skin from forming) and cool to room temperature.

Put a rack in lower third of oven and preheat oven to 375°F.

Butter soufflé dish and sprinkle with sugar, turning to coat sides and knocking out excess.

Beat egg whites with salt in a large bowl with electric mixer at medium-high speed until foamy. Add cream of tartar, increase speed to high, and beat until egg whites just hold stiff peaks.

Stir one quarter of whites into custard to lighten it, then fold in remaining whites gently but thoroughly. Pour mixture into prepared soufflé dish. Wrap a 32-by-8-inch strip of parchment paper tightly around soufflé dish, forming a collar that extends at least 4 inches above rim, and tape overlapping ends together.

Bake soufflé until puffed and golden in spots, 35 to 45 minutes. Remove collar and serve immediately.

COOK'S NOTE

■ The lemon custard, without the egg whites, can be refrigerated, covered with parchment, for up to 1 day.

Salzburger Nockerl

SERVES 4 TO 6
ACTIVE TIME: 15 MINUTES ■ START TO FINISH: 30 MINUTES

■ Created in Salzburg (*nockerl* means "dumpling") but popular all over Austria, this delicate soufflé quickly transforms pantry items into an addictive delight. It features clouds of melt-in-your-mouth meringue baked over berry preserves. We use tart lingonberry sauce, but any preserves or jam would be good. ■

¼ cup heavy cream
¼ cup bottled lingonberry sauce (see Sources) or any
   fruit preserves or jam
3 large eggs, separated, left at room temperature for
   30 minutes
2 large egg whites, left at room temperature for
   30 minutes
⅛ teaspoon salt
½ cup granulated sugar
1 tablespoon all-purpose flour
1 teaspoon vanilla extract

GARNISH: Confectioners' sugar
SPECIAL EQUIPMENT: 9-inch pie plate or 1- to 1½-quart
   gratin dish

Put a rack in middle of oven and preheat oven to 400°F.

Pour cream into pie plate or gratin dish and spoon lingonberry sauce into cream in dollops (it will be sparse).

Beat egg whites with salt in a large bowl with an electric mixer at high speed until they just form soft peaks. Beat in sugar 1 tablespoon at a time, and continue beating until whites just hold stiff, glossy peaks.

Sprinkle flour over meringue and fold in gently but thoroughly. Whisk together egg yolks and vanilla in a small bowl, then fold into whites gently but thoroughly.

Spoon large dollops of meringue into pie plate or gratin dish. Bake until golden brown and set, 13 to 15 minutes. (For a less creamy soufflé, bake for 5 minutes more.)

Dust lightly with confectioners' sugar and cool for 5 minutes before serving.

FROZEN DESSERTS AND SWEET SAUCES

When I first came to *Gourmet*, I asked Zanne Stewart, who was then the executive food editor, why we published so many recipes for ice cream, gelato, and sorbet. "You can buy perfectly good ice cream in the store," I said. "Why would anyone bother to make their own?"

In response, Zanne offered me a spoonful of just-made hazelnut gelato, and I understood. There is nothing—absolutely nothing—like the taste of freshly churned ice cream or gelato. And if you decide to make it with some unusual ingredient—basil ice cream comes to mind—you have a dessert that you couldn't buy in any store.

Each and every one of these frozen desserts had to pass the much-better-than-store-bought test in order to be included in this chapter.

Some are unexpected, like the cinnamon toast ice cream that tastes disconcertingly familiar and yet is like nothing you've ever tried before. Some are combinations that are simply superb, like the watermelon sundae, a concoction so delicious you'll

never want to eat watermelon without ice cream again. And some are surprising riffs on familiar creations, like the irresistible praline ice cream sandwiches and the raspberry chocolate ice pops.

There are sauces here too, each one guaranteed to dress up ordinary store-bought ice cream into something really special. From a superb hot fudge sauce to the best butterscotch sauce you've ever tasted to the surprisingly sophisticated stout crème anglaise, these are recipes that are going to make your life easier—and much more delicious.

FROZEN DESSERTS AND SWEET SAUCES

Frozen Desserts

Dulce de Leche Ice Cream

MAKES ABOUT 1½ QUARTS
ACTIVE TIME: 15 MINUTES ■ START TO FINISH: 6 HOURS
(INCLUDES CHILLING AND FREEZING)

■ Long a popular sweet throughout Latin America, dulce de leche—milk and sugar cooked down to a luscious consistency—has taken the United States by storm. Who can resist its creamy caramel siren call? This version, adapted from one created by Mariana Crespo of Tienda del Encuentro in Buenos Aires, is not just the best dulce de leche ice cream we've ever had, it's one of the best ice creams we've ever had, period. Blissfully, its delicate caramel essence isn't obscured by too much sugar. And since it's not a custard-based ice cream, it's easy to make. ■

- 2 cups whole milk
- 1 cup heavy cream
- 1 (16-ounce) jar (about 1⅔ cups) dulce de leche (see Sources)
- ⅛ teaspoon vanilla extract
- ¾ cup chopped pecans, toasted (see Tips, page 911)

SPECIAL EQUIPMENT: an ice cream maker

Bring milk and cream just to a boil in a 3- to 4-quart heavy saucepan over moderate heat. Remove from heat and whisk in dulce de leche until dissolved. Whisk in vanilla and transfer to a metal bowl. Refrigerate, uncovered, stirring occasionally, until cool, about 1 hour, then cover and refrigerate until very cold, 3 to 6 hours.

Freeze mixture in ice cream maker until almost firm. Fold in pecans, transfer ice cream to an airtight container, and put in freezer to harden for at least 1 hour.

COOK'S NOTE

■ The ice cream keeps for up to 1 week.

Halvah Vanilla Ice Cream

MAKES ABOUT 1 QUART
ACTIVE TIME: 10 MINUTES ■ START TO FINISH: 4½ HOURS
(INCLUDES CHILLING AND FREEZING)

■ The best known version of halvah is a Middle Eastern–style confection made of ground sesame seeds and honey. With its unique nutty taste and sandy texture, it's an intriguing addition to homemade vanilla ice cream. Though the ice cream is delicious on its own, a drizzle of fragrant orange honey syrup renders it unforgettable. ■

- 1½ cups whole milk
- 1½ cups heavy cream
- 3 large egg yolks
- ½ cup sugar
- 1 tablespoon cornstarch
- 1 teaspoon vanilla extract
- ¼ pound halvah (see Sources), coarsely crumbled

ACCOMPANIMENT: Orange Honey Syrup (recipe follows)
SPECIAL EQUIPMENT: an instant-read thermometer; an ice cream maker

Bring milk and cream just to a boil in a 2- to 3-quart heavy saucepan; remove from heat.

Whisk together yolks, sugar, and cornstarch in a large bowl. Add milk mixture in a slow stream, whisking, and pour back into saucepan. Bring to a boil over moderate heat, stirring constantly with a wooden spoon, and boil, stirring constantly, until custard is thick enough to coat back of spoon and registers 170°F on thermometer, about 2 minutes.

Pour custard through a fine-mesh sieve into a metal bowl and stir in vanilla. Refrigerate, uncovered, stirring occasionally, until cool, about 1 hour, then cover and refrigerate until very cold, 3 to 6 hours. (Custard will become very thick.)

Freeze custard in ice cream maker until almost firm. Fold in halvah, transfer ice cream to an airtight container, and put in freezer to harden for at least 2 hours. Drizzle with syrup and serve.

COOK'S NOTE

■ The ice cream keeps for up to 1 week.

Orange Honey Syrup

MAKES ABOUT 1⅓ CUPS
ACTIVE TIME: 15 MINUTES ■ START TO FINISH: 1¼ HOURS
(INCLUDES COOLING)

■ The next time you need a dessert in a flash, drizzle this over vanilla ice cream or plain yogurt. ■

    1   cup mild honey
  1¼   teaspoons minced orange zest
    ½   cup fresh orange juice (from about 1½ oranges)
    ½   cup water

Combine honey, zest, juice, and water in a small heavy saucepan. Bring to a simmer, and simmer, stirring occasionally, until reduced to 1⅓ cups, about 20 minutes. (Do not reduce syrup too much, or it will be too thick and too sweet.) Transfer to a bowl and cool to room temperature.

COOK'S NOTE

■ The syrup keeps, covered, at room temperature for up to 1 week.

Rocky Road Ice Cream

MAKES ABOUT 1 QUART
ACTIVE TIME: 30 MINUTES ■ START TO FINISH: 8 HOURS
(INCLUDES CHILLING AND FREEZING)

■ The story goes that after the great stock market crash in 1929, William Dreyer, of Dreyer's Grand Ice Cream, whipped up a new flavor, mixing miniature marshmallows and nuts into milk chocolate ice cream. He named his creation Rocky Road, in hopes of making people smile during those dark days. It makes us smile still. In our version, generous amounts of toasted pecans and marshmallows are swirled into a rich chocolate ice cream. We prefer to chop regular marshmallows into bite-sized pieces rather than use minis, because the larger puffs have a softer texture. ■

    2   cups half-and-half
    ½   cup sugar
    3   ounces bittersweet chocolate (no more than 60%
         cacao; see page 705), finely chopped

    ⅓   cup unsweetened cocoa powder
    4   large egg yolks
    ⅛   teaspoon salt
    1   teaspoon vanilla extract
  1½   cups chopped marshmallows (about 15)
    1   cup (about 3¾ ounces) pecans, toasted (see Tips,
         page 911) and chopped
SPECIAL EQUIPMENT: an instant-read thermometer;
         an ice cream maker

Bring half-and-half and sugar just to a boil in a 2- to 3-quart heavy saucepan. Remove from heat, add chocolate and cocoa powder, and let stand for 1 minute, then whisk until smooth.

Whisk together egg yolks and salt in a bowl. Add hot chocolate mixture in a slow stream, whisking constantly, and pour back into pan. Cook over moderately low heat, stirring constantly with a wooden spoon, until custard is thick enough to coat back of spoon and registers 170°F on thermometer; do not let boil. Remove from heat and stir in vanilla.

Pour custard through a fine-mesh sieve into a metal bowl. Refrigerate, uncovered, stirring occasionally, until cool, about 1 hour, then cover and refrigerate until very cold, 3 to 6 hours. (Custard will become very thick.)

Freeze in ice cream maker until almost firm. Fold in marshmallows and pecans, transfer to an airtight container, and put in freezer to harden for at least 3 hours.

COOK'S NOTE

■ The ice cream keeps for up to 1 week.

Mango Coconut Ice Cream

MAKES ABOUT 1½ QUARTS
ACTIVE TIME: 45 MINUTES ■ START TO FINISH: 7 HOURS
(INCLUDES CHILLING AND FREEZING)

■ If you have trouble getting your hands on good mangoes, you'll be happy to see that this pleasing tropical ice cream is made from canned mango puree, which delivers the best flavor. The sweetness and acidity of the puree are balanced by the smooth creaminess of coconut milk. ■

1¼ cups canned mango puree (see Cook's Note)
¾ cup well-stirred canned unsweetened coconut milk
½ cup heavy cream
2 tablespoons light corn syrup
1 tablespoon fresh lemon juice
¼ teaspoon vanilla extract
1 cup whole milk
2 large egg yolks
½ cup sugar
  Large pinch of salt
SPECIAL EQUIPMENT: an instant-read thermometer;
  an ice cream maker

Stir together mango puree, coconut milk, cream, corn syrup, lemon juice, and vanilla in a bowl until well combined.

Bring milk just to a boil in a 2- to 3-quart heavy saucepan; remove from heat.

Whisk together yolks, sugar, and salt in a bowl. Add hot milk in a stream, whisking. Pour back into saucepan and cook over moderately low heat, stirring with a wooden spoon, until custard is thick enough to coat back of spoon and registers 170° to 175°F on thermometer; do not let boil. Remove from heat and stir in mango mixture until well combined.

Pour custard through a fine-mesh sieve into a large metal bowl; discard solids. Refrigerate, uncovered, stirring occasionally, until cool, about 1 hour, then cover and refrigerate until very cold, 3 to 6 hours.

Freeze custard in ice cream maker. Transfer ice cream to an airtight container and put in freezer to harden for at least 2 hours.

COOK'S NOTES

- Because many brands of canned mangoes taste more like peaches, we recommend seeking out brands that use Alphonso mangoes, an Indian cultivar renowned for its bright orange flesh and intense flavor.
- The ice cream keeps for up to 1 week.

Basil Ice Cream

MAKES ABOUT 3 CUPS
ACTIVE TIME: 25 MINUTES ■ START TO FINISH: 6 HOURS
(INCLUDES CHILLING AND FREEZING)

■ Though basil is usually considered a savory ingredient, its clean, almost aniselike taste is a natural churned into ice cream, and its leaves give it a pretty pale jade color. This ice cream is beyond elegant and makes an alluring alternative to vanilla—try it with a summery fruit crisp or pie. ■

2 cups whole milk
3 tablespoons chopped fresh basil
½ cup sugar
  Pinch of salt
4 large egg yolks
½ cup very cold heavy cream
SPECIAL EQUIPMENT: an instant-read thermometer;
  an ice cream maker

Combine milk, basil, ¼ cup sugar, and salt in a 2-quart heavy saucepan and bring just to a boil, stirring. Remove from heat and let steep for 30 minutes.

Transfer milk mixture to a blender (set saucepan aside) and blend until basil is finely chopped, about 1 minute.

Beat together yolks and remaining ¼ cup sugar in a medium bowl with an electric mixer until thick and pale, about 1 minute. Add milk mixture in a stream, beating until well combined. Pour mixture back into saucepan and cook over moderate heat, stirring constantly with a wooden spoon, until custard is thick enough to coat back of spoon and registers 175°F on thermometer; do not let boil.

Pour custard through a fine-mesh sieve into a metal bowl. Refrigerate, uncovered, stirring occasionally, until cool, about 1 hour, then cover and refrigerate until very cold, 2 to 5 hours.

Stir cream into custard and freeze in ice cream maker. Transfer ice cream to an airtight container and put in freezer to harden for at least 2 hours.

COOK'S NOTE

- The ice cream keeps for up to 2 days.

Cinnamon Toast Ice Cream

MAKES ABOUT 5 CUPS
ACTIVE TIME: 40 MINUTES ■ START TO FINISH: 8 HOURS
(INCLUDES CHILLING AND FREEZING)

■ The warm, buttery sweetness of cinnamon toast flavors this ice cream in two ways. First, the milk is infused with bread crumbs that have been drizzled with butter, brown sugar, and cinnamon and toasted. Second, lots of cinnamon-sweet croutons are folded into the ice cream itself, punctuating the rich coolness. Extreme? Maybe. Unforgettable? You bet. Contributor Celia Barbour gave us this outstanding recipe. ■

    2   cups whole milk
    2   (3-inch) cinnamon sticks
    5   slices firm white sandwich bread
    ½   stick (4 tablespoons) unsalted butter, melted
    2   tablespoons packed light brown sugar
    ½   teaspoon ground cinnamon
    6   large egg yolks
    ½   cup granulated sugar
    ¼   teaspoon molasses (not robust)
        Pinch of salt
    1   cup heavy cream

SPECIAL EQUIPMENT: an instant-read thermometer;
        an ice cream maker

Bring milk and cinnamon sticks just to a boil in a 2-quart heavy saucepan. Remove from heat and let steep, covered, for 30 minutes.

Meanwhile, put racks in upper and lower thirds of oven and preheat oven to 300°F.

Cut 3 slices bread into ¼-inch cubes and transfer to a bowl. Quarter remaining 2 slices and pulse in a food processor to make crumbs.

Whisk together butter, brown sugar, and ground cinnamon in a bowl. Drizzle 3 tablespoons butter mixture over bread cubes, stirring to coat lightly, and spread in one layer on a baking sheet. Add bread crumbs to remaining butter mixture and stir to coat evenly. Spread crumbs evenly on another baking sheet.

Bake bread cubes and crumbs, stirring occasionally and switching position of pans halfway through baking, until golden brown and crisp, about 25 minutes. Cool on pans on racks.

Transfer bread crumbs to a bowl. Return milk to a boil, pour over bread crumbs, and let stand for 10 minutes.

Pour milk through a fine-mesh sieve into same saucepan, pressing hard on solids; discard solids.

Whisk together yolks, sugar, molasses, and salt in a bowl.

Return milk to a boil and add half of hot milk to yolk mixture in a slow stream, whisking until well combined. Add yolk mixture in a slow stream to milk in saucepan, whisking, and cook over low heat, stirring constantly with a wooden spoon, until custard is thick enough to coat back of spoon and registers 170° to 175°F on thermometer; do not let boil.

Remove from heat and stir in cream. Pour custard through cleaned fine-mesh sieve into a metal bowl. Refrigerate, uncovered, stirring occasionally, until cool, about 1 hour, then cover and refrigerate until very cold, 3 to 6 hours.

Freeze custard in ice cream maker until almost firm. Fold in bread cubes, transfer to an airtight container, and put in freezer to harden for at least 2 hours.

COOK'S NOTE
■ The ice cream keeps for up to 1 week, but the toast is crunchiest the first 2 days after it's made.

Pistachio and Cardamom Ice Cream

MAKES ABOUT 1 QUART
ACTIVE TIME: 1 HOUR ■ START TO FINISH: 6 HOURS
(INCLUDES CHILLING AND FREEZING)

■ The Indian ice cream *kulfi* is made with slowly reduced milk, and the result, which is flavored with a variety of spices and nuts, is luscious. Here cardamom and just a pinch of saffron contribute a subtle warmth, while pistachios add sweet nuttiness. This *kulfi* is churned rather than stirred by hand intermittently, as many traditional versions are. We like the creamy smoothness that results from using the ice cream maker. ■

6 cups whole milk

15 green cardamom pods (see Sources)

1 cup heavy cream

½ cup sugar

Pinch of saffron threads, crumbled

½ cup unsalted shelled pistachios

SPECIAL EQUIPMENT: an ice cream maker

Bring 4 cups milk to a boil in a large nonstick skillet and boil over moderate heat, stirring frequently (so milk solids don't caramelize), until reduced to about 1 cup, 20 to 25 minutes.

Cook, stirring constantly, until milk is reduced to about ⅓ cup and is the consistency of a thick batter, about 10 minutes more. Transfer to a small bowl.

Crush cardamom pods using a mortar and pestle or side of a large heavy knife.

Bring remaining 2 cups milk, cream, sugar, carda-

mom, and saffron to a simmer in a 2-quart saucepan over moderate heat, stirring until sugar is dissolved. Whisk in thickened milk until dissolved, remove from heat, and let stand for 10 minutes.

Pour milk mixture through a fine-mesh sieve into a metal bowl, pressing on solids; discard solids. Refrigerate, uncovered, stirring occasionally, until cool, about 1 hour, then cover and refrigerate until very cold, 3 to 6 hours.

Meanwhile, blanch pistachios in a 1-quart saucepan of boiling water for 1 minute. Drain and rub off skins.

Coarsely chop pistachios and add to milk mixture.

Freeze mixture in ice cream maker. Transfer ice cream to an airtight container and put in freezer to harden for at least 1 hour.

COOK'S NOTES

- The thickened milk can be made up to 1 day ahead and refrigerated, its surface covered with plastic wrap.
- The ice cream keeps for up to 1 day.

Hazelnut Gelato

MAKES ABOUT 1 QUART
ACTIVE TIME: 30 MINUTES ■ START TO FINISH: 6 HOURS
(INCLUDES CHILLING AND FREEZING)

■ Rarely will you see a gelateria in Italy that doesn't have a line snaking out the door. Italians are passionate for this frozen treat, and hazelnut, or *nocciola*, is among the most popular flavors. This version, in which toasted hazelnuts are steeped in milk and heavy cream, is heady with their seductive, nutty flavor and rich with beaten egg yolks. The silky texture is beyond compare. ■

5 ounces (about 1 cup) hazelnuts, toasted (see Tips, page 911), loose skins rubbed off

½ cup plus 2 tablespoons sugar

Pinch of salt

2½ cups whole milk

⅓ cup heavy cream

4 large egg yolks

SPECIAL EQUIPMENT: an instant-read thermometer; an ice cream maker

SAFFRON

Saffron, the name given to the fragrant, flavorful orange-red stigmas of a purple fall-flowering crocus (*Crocus sativus*), is the world's most expensive spice (by weight), because it is so labor-intensive to harvest. To yield 1 pound of saffron, about 70,000 flowers must be hand-picked; each bloom has three delicate stigmas, or threads, which must then also be hand-picked. That said, saffron is actually economical to use—because it is so potent, a few dollars' worth will perfume and flavor an Indian curry, a bouillabaisse worthy of Marseilles, a risotto Milanese, or the Indian ice cream *kulfi*.

Always buy whole saffron threads; the powdered version may have been cut with turmeric or other additives. Spanish saffron (the Arabs were cultivating saffron in that country by A.D. 960) is of excellent quality and is widely available. Deep red Kashmiri saffron, considered by many connoisseurs to be the finest in the world, is available through spice merchants such as Penzeys (see Sources).

Pulse hazelnuts with ¼ cup sugar and salt in a food processor until finely chopped.

Transfer to a 3-quart saucepan, add milk and cream, and bring just to a simmer over moderate heat, stirring occasionally. Remove from heat and let steep, covered, for 1 hour.

Pour milk mixture through a fine-mesh sieve into a bowl, pressing hard on solids; discard solids.

Beat together yolks and remaining 6 tablespoons sugar in a bowl with an electric mixer at medium speed until thick and pale, 2 to 3 minutes. Beat in milk mixture and pour into cleaned saucepan. Cook over moderately low heat, stirring constantly with a wooden spoon, until custard is thick enough to coat back of spoon and thermometer registers 175°F; do not let boil.

Pour custard through cleaned sieve into a metal bowl. Refrigerate, uncovered, stirring occasionally, until cool, about 1 hour, then cover and refrigerate until very cold, 3 to 6 hours.

Freeze custard in ice cream maker. Transfer gelato to an airtight container and put in freezer to harden for about 1 hour.

COOK'S NOTE

- The gelato keeps for up to 1 week.

Cherry Gelato

MAKES ABOUT 5 CUPS
ACTIVE TIME: 20 MINUTES ■ START TO FINISH: 6¾ HOURS
(INCLUDES CHILLING AND FREEZING)

■ Sweet Bing cherries have a rich, almost meaty quality. They add both summery sweetness and texture to this gelato, from reader Viviane Banquet Farre. The almond extract complements the juicy cherries perfectly. ■

FOR GELATO
½ vanilla bean, halved lengthwise
3½ cups whole milk
Pinch of salt
½ cup turbinado sugar, such as Sugar in the Raw
2 tablespoons cornstarch

FOR CHERRIES
½ pound (1½ cups) Bing cherries (do not use frozen), pitted
2 tablespoons turbinado sugar
1 teaspoon vanilla extract
1 teaspoon almond extract
SPECIAL EQUIPMENT: an ice cream maker

MAKE THE GELATO BASE: Scrape seeds from vanilla bean into a small heavy saucepan. Add milk and salt and bring just to a boil; remove from heat.

Whisk together sugar and cornstarch in a small bowl. Add ½ cup hot milk mixture to sugar mixture, whisking until smooth, and whisk into remaining milk mixture in saucepan. Bring to a simmer, whisking, and simmer, whisking, for 3 minutes.

Pour mixture through a fine-mesh sieve into a metal bowl. Refrigerate, uncovered, stirring occasionally, until cool, about 1 hour, then cover and refrigerate until very cold, 3 to 6 hours.

MEANWHILE, PREPARE THE CHERRIES: Pulse cherries with sugar and extracts in a food processor until finely chopped. Transfer to a bowl and refrigerate, covered, for 1 hour.

MAKE THE GELATO: Stir cherries, with their juices, into gelato base. Freeze in ice cream maker. Transfer gelato to an airtight container and put in freezer to harden for at least 2 hours.

COOK'S NOTE

- The gelato keeps for up to 1 week.

Pomegranate Gelato

MAKES ABOUT 1 QUART
ACTIVE TIME: 15 MINUTES ■ START TO FINISH: 6½ HOURS
(INCLUDES CHILLING AND FREEZING)

■ Pomegranates come into season in fall and winter, and this gelato makes an irresistible cool-weather dessert. Refreshing without being heavy, it has a beautiful blush pink color, and the tanginess of the fruit cuts the richness of the dairy. The liqueur underscores the flavor of the pomegranate juice, and it also gives the gelato a creamier texture. ■

1½ cups heavy cream
½ cup whole milk
¾ cup sugar
1½ tablespoons cornstarch
⅛ teaspoon salt
1¼ cups bottled pomegranate juice
⅓ cup pomegranate liqueur, such as PAMA
1 teaspoon fresh lemon juice

GARNISH: pomegranate seeds
SPECIAL EQUIPMENT: an ice cream maker

Whisk together cream, milk, sugar, cornstarch, and salt in a 2½- to 3-quart heavy saucepan. Bring to a boil over moderate heat, whisking occasionally, and boil, whisking, for 2 minutes. Remove from heat and whisk in remaining ingredients.

Transfer mixture to a metal bowl and refrigerate, uncovered, stirring occasionally, until cool, about 1 hour, then cover and refrigerate until very cold, 3 to 6 hours.

Freeze mixture in ice cream maker. Transfer gelato to an airtight container and put in freezer to harden for at least 2 hours.

Soften gelato slightly in refrigerator, about 20 minutes, before serving, garnished with pomegranate seeds.

COOK'S NOTE
■ The gelato keeps for up to 1 week.

Grape Sorbet

MAKES ABOUT 1 QUART
ACTIVE TIME: 20 MINUTES ■ START TO FINISH: 7½ HOURS
(INCLUDES CHILLING AND FREEZING)

■ Almost any kind of seedless grape will work for this refreshing sorbet, which tastes of pure grape essence. Keep it in mind as a delightful intermezzo or a light ending to an autumn meal. If you're feeling ambitious, make a few batches, each with a different kind of grape—the color combination will be outrageously gorgeous. ■

FROZEN DESSERTS

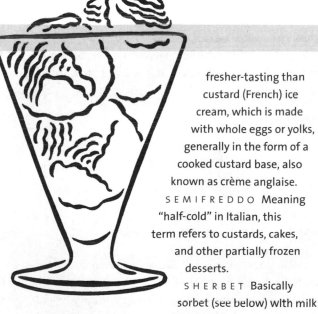

GELATO This Italian ice cream can be made with just milk or a combination of milk and cream; depending on the recipe, it may or may not contain eggs, egg whites, or cornstarch. Because gelato has a lower percentage of milk fat (sometimes called butterfat) than ice cream, it incorporates less air during the freezing process, which results in a dense, soft, very silky product. The lower fat content also gives more intense flavors the chance to shine, since fat tends to mask the true flavor of ingredients. In Italy, the term *gelato* includes SORBETTO as well; it is also churned, but it contains no dairy and is made primarily of fruit.
GRANITA Usually made with fruit juice, coffee, or wine, granita is stirred infrequently during the freezing process, so that coarse, flaky ice crystals form.
ICE CREAM There are two main styles. "Standard" ice cream (sometimes called Philadelphia-style or plain) is a frozen mixture of sweetened cream lightened with milk; it doesn't contain eggs. Standard ice cream is generally fresher-tasting than custard (French) ice cream, which is made with whole eggs or yolks, generally in the form of a cooked custard base, also known as crème anglaise.
SEMIFREDDO Meaning "half-cold" in Italian, this term refers to custards, cakes, and other partially frozen desserts.
SHERBET Basically sorbet (see below) with milk and/or cream added to it, sherbet usually has less dairy than ice cream but is sweeter.
SORBET Similar to a granita, a sorbet has a much finer, lighter texture because it's churned rather than still-frozen.

6 cups (about 2¼ pounds) seedless green grapes, chilled
¾ cup superfine sugar
¼ cup fresh lemon juice
SPECIAL EQUIPMENT: an ice cream maker

Combine all ingredients in a blender and puree until smooth, about 3 minutes. Strain through a fine-mesh sieve into a bowl, pressing on solids; discard solids. Refrigerate, covered, until very cold, 6 to 8 hours.

Freeze sorbet in ice cream maker. Transfer to an airtight container and put in freezer to harden for at least 1 hour.

COOK'S NOTE

■ The sorbet keeps for up to 1 week.

Chocolate Sorbet

MAKES ABOUT 1 QUART
ACTIVE TIME: 15 MINUTES ■ START TO FINISH: 12¼ HOURS
(INCLUDES CHILLING AND FREEZING)

■ Deep, dark, and richly chocolaty, this sorbet makes a perfect Valentine's Day dessert—it tastes naughty, but it's free of fat. The first step of making a caramel not only lends a complexity to the sorbet but gives it creaminess. ■

1¼ cups sugar
3 cups water
¾ cup unsweetened cocoa powder, preferably Dutch-process
¼ teaspoon salt
1 teaspoon vanilla extract
SPECIAL EQUIPMENT: an ice cream maker

Heat sugar in a small heavy saucepan over moderate heat, stirring with a fork to heat sugar evenly, until it starts to melt. Stop stirring and cook, swirling pan occasionally so sugar melts evenly, until it is a dark amber caramel. Add water (caramel will harden and steam vigorously) and cook over moderately low heat, stirring, until caramel is dissolved.

Add cocoa and salt, whisking until dissolved. Transfer to a bowl and cool, stirring occasionally.

Stir vanilla into sorbet base and refrigerate, uncovered, stirring occasionally, until cool, about 1 hour, then cover and refrigerate until very cold, 6 to 8 hours.

Freeze sorbet in ice cream maker. Transfer to an airtight container and put in freezer to harden for at least 5 hours.

COOK'S NOTE

■ The sorbet keeps for up to 1 week.

Lychee Coconut Sorbet with Mango and Lime

SERVES 4 (MAKES ABOUT 1 PINT)
ACTIVE TIME: 15 MINUTES ■ START TO FINISH: 7½ HOURS
(INCLUDES CHILLING AND FREEZING)

■ The delicate but distinct perfume of lychees is evocative of the tropical climates from which they come. The fruit has a natural affinity for coconut, and here the two combine in a creamy, sunny sorbet that pairs perfectly with slices of juicy mango. Canned lychees are a great treat to keep on hand, and the leftover syrup makes a delicious sweetener for iced tea. ■

1 (15- to 20-ounce) can lychees in syrup, chilled
½ cup well-stirred cream of coconut, preferably Coco López brand, chilled
3–3½ tablespoons fresh lime juice (from about 2 limes; grate zest first)
1 firm but ripe large mango (1 pound), peeled, pitted, and sliced
1 teaspoon finely grated lime zest
SPECIAL EQUIPMENT: an ice cream maker

Drain lychees, reserving syrup. Puree lychees with cream of coconut, ¼ cup reserved syrup, and 2½ tablespoons lime juice in a blender until smooth. Refrigerate, covered, until very cold, 6 to 8 hours.

Freeze in ice cream maker. Serve immediately, or transfer to a metal bowl and freeze for 1 hour to harden.

Toss together mango, zest, and remaining ½ to 1 tablespoon lime juice (to taste).

Serve scoops of sorbet over mango slices.

Guanabana Sherbet with Tropical Fruit

SERVES 8 (MAKES ABOUT 1½ QUARTS)
ACTIVE TIME: 30 MINUTES ■ START TO FINISH: 8½ HOURS
(INCLUDES CHILLING AND FREEZING)

■ This lush dessert radiates the sensuality of the tropics. As the guanabana (also known as soursop) sherbet melts on the tongue, it releases exotic flavors that are complemented by the fresh fruits. ■

1½ cups water

1¼ cups sugar

1 teaspoon unflavored gelatin

¾ cup very cold whole milk

2 (14-ounce) packages frozen guanabana (soursop) puree, such as Goya, thawed in refrigerator (3 cups)

2 small to medium papayas, peeled, halved, seeded, and cut into bite-sized pieces

2 firm but ripe mangoes, peeled, pitted, and cut into bite-sized pieces

½ cup pomegranate seeds (see page 434)

2 teaspoons fresh lime juice

SPECIAL EQUIPMENT: an ice cream maker

Bring 1¼ cups water and sugar to a boil in a small saucepan, stirring until sugar is dissolved. Transfer syrup to a metal bowl and quick-chill by putting bowl in another bowl of ice and cold water, stirring occasionally, until cold, about 5 minutes.

Add remaining ¼ cup water to cleaned saucepan, sprinkle gelatin over it, and let stand for 1 minute to soften. Bring water to a bare simmer, stirring until gelatin is dissolved.

Add gelatin mixture to syrup, along with milk and guanabana puree. Refrigerate, uncovered, stirring occasionally, until cool, about 1 hour, then cover and refrigerate until very cold, 6 to 8 hours.

Freeze mixture in ice cream maker. Transfer to an airtight container and put in freezer to harden for at least 2 hours.

Toss papayas and mangoes with pomegranate seeds and lime juice.

Soften sherbet slightly at room temperature, 3 to 10 minutes, and serve with fruit.

Gewürztraminer Peach Sorbet

MAKES ABOUT 1 QUART
ACTIVE TIME: 20 MINUTES ■ START TO FINISH: 7½ HOURS
(INCLUDES CHILLING AND FREEZING)

■ Imagine the best white sangria you've ever had, then turn it into a sorbet. The flavors of wine, peaches, and star anise sparkle, and the frosty taste ricochets all over your mouth. Reader Mary N. Lannin of Geyserville, California, shared this recipe with us. ■

1 pound peaches (3 large), peeled (see Tips, page 913), halved, pitted, and cut into 1-inch-thick wedges (see Cook's Note)

½ teaspoon fresh lemon juice

½ cup superfine sugar

1 whole star anise or 1 teaspoon star anise pieces

1½ cups Gewürztraminer, Riesling, or other slightly sweet white wine

2 tablespoons light corn syrup

SPECIAL EQUIPMENT: an ice cream maker

Toss peaches with lemon juice in a 4-quart heavy pot. Stir in sugar, star anise, and 1 cup wine, bring to a simmer, and simmer, covered, until peaches are tender, about 5 minutes.

Discard star anise. Working in batches, transfer mixture to a blender and puree (use caution when blending hot liquids). Force puree through a medium-mesh sieve into a metal bowl, pressing hard on solids; discard solids. Stir in corn syrup and remaining ½ cup wine. Refrigerate, uncovered, stirring occasionally, until cool, about 1 hour, then cover and refrigerate until very cold, 6 to 8 hours.

Freeze sorbet in ice cream maker. Transfer to an

airtight container and put in freezer to harden for at least 1 hour.

COOK'S NOTES

- You can substitute 1 pound frozen peach slices (not thawed) for the fresh peaches.
- The sorbet keeps for up to 1 week.

Port-and-Spice-Poached Pears with Granita

SERVES 4
ACTIVE TIME: 45 MINUTES ■ START TO FINISH: 10 HOURS
(INCLUDES STEEPING AND FREEZING)

■ As the poached pears cook, they take on the deep, jewel-like autumn tones of port, cinnamon, and cardamom, becoming floral, winey, and spicy all at once. The poaching liquid is then transformed into granita and served with the pears and a dollop of crème fraîche. ■

- 2 cups unsweetened white grape juice
- 2 cups ruby port
- ¼ cup sugar
- 6 green or white cardamom pods (see Sources), smashed
- 1 (1-inch) piece cinnamon stick
- 2 whole cloves
- 1¼ cups water
- 4 firm but ripe Bosc pears, peeled, stems left intact
- 3 tablespoons fresh lemon juice
- ⅔ cup crème fraîche, well stirred

SPECIAL EQUIPMENT: parchment paper

Cut a round of parchment paper to fit inside a wide 4-quart heavy pot.

Combine grape juice, port, sugar, spices, and 1 cup water in a 4-quart heavy pot and bring to a boil over moderate heat, stirring until sugar is dissolved. Add pears, arranging them on their sides (pears will not be covered by liquid), cover pears directly with round of parchment paper, reduce heat to low, and poach pears, turning occasionally, until just tender when pierced with a sharp knife, about 25 minutes.

Remove from heat and let pears steep in liquid,

covered with parchment, turning occasionally, for 2 to 3 hours.

Carefully transfer pears with a slotted spoon to a shallow dish; reserve poaching liquid. Let pears stand at room temperature or refrigerate, covered with parchment.

Meanwhile, pour poaching liquid through a fine-mesh sieve into a bowl; discard solids. Return liquid to pot, bring to a boil, and boil, uncovered, until reduced to about 2½ cups, 25 to 30 minutes. Remove from heat and stir in lemon juice and remaining ¼ cup water.

Pour liquid into an 8- to 9-inch square baking pan (not nonstick). Cool to room temperature, about 1 hour, then freeze until partially frozen, about 1½ hours.

Scrape and stir mixture with a fork, crushing any lumps. Repeat, scraping every hour, until evenly frozen, about 4 hours more.

Bring chilled pears to room temperature before serving, about 30 minutes.

Cut a thin slice from bottom of each pear and stand pears on chilled plates. Scrape granita up with a fork and serve pears with granita and crème fraîche alongside.

COOK'S NOTE

- The pears and granita can be made up to 2 days ahead. Scrape the granita up with a fork before serving.

Cantaloupe Granita

SERVES 4
ACTIVE TIME: 20 MINUTES ■ START TO FINISH: 3 HOURS
(INCLUDES FREEZING)

■ Simple to make and so very good, this granita offers icy shards of flavor that hit your tongue and immediately soften and dissolve, leaving behind the taste of pure melon. ■

- 2 cups coarsely chopped cantaloupe
- ¼ cup sugar, or to taste
- 1½ teaspoons fresh lemon juice, or to taste
- 1 cup ice cubes

Combine all ingredients in a blender and puree until smooth. Pour into a 13-by-9-inch baking pan (not nonstick) and freeze until mixture becomes a firm slush, at least 40 minutes.

Scrape and stir mixture with a fork, crushing any lumps. Repeat, scraping every hour, until evenly frozen, about 2 hours more.

Scrape granita up with a fork and serve in chilled glasses.

COOK'S NOTE

■ The granita can be made up to 2 days ahead. Scrape the granita up with a fork before serving.

Peach Praline Semifreddo with Amaretti

SERVES 8
ACTIVE TIME: 1¼ HOURS ■ START TO FINISH: 5½ HOURS
(INCLUDES FREEZING)

■ This creamy semifreddo in an amaretti crust captures the heady flavor of ripe summer peaches. It's an elegant showpiece that's perfect for entertaining, since it can be made well in advance. ■

FOR CRUST
  1 (7-ounce) box (16 paper-wrapped packets) amaretti (Italian almond macaroons; see Sources), finely ground in a food processor
  ½ stick (4 tablespoons) unsalted butter, melted
FOR PRALINE
  ¼ cup coarsely chopped unblanched almonds
  ¼ cup sugar
FOR SEMIFREDDO
  1¼ pounds firm but ripe peaches
  1 (500-mg) vitamin C tablet (ascorbic acid), crushed to a powder with a spoon (see Cook's Note)
  ½ cup plus 2 tablespoons sugar
  ⅛ teaspoon salt
  6 large egg yolks
  ⅜ teaspoon almond extract
  1 cup heavy cream

FOR PEACH TOPPING
  1 pound firm but ripe peaches
  1 (500-mg) vitamin C tablet, crushed to a powder
  ¼ cup sugar, or to taste
SPECIAL EQUIPMENT: a 9-inch round springform pan

MAKE THE CRUST: Put a rack in middle of oven and preheat oven to 350°F. Invert bottom of springform pan (to make it easier to slide semifreddo off bottom), lock on side, and oil pan.

Stir together amaretti and butter in a bowl until well combined. Press evenly over bottom and up side of springform pan.

Bake until crust is firm and a shade darker, about 10 minutes. Cool completely on a rack. (Leave oven on.)

MEANWHILE, MAKE THE PRALINE: Spread nuts on a baking sheet and toast in oven, stirring once or twice, until fragrant and golden, about 10 minutes. Transfer to a bowl. Cool baking sheet slightly, then lightly oil it; set aside.

Cook sugar in a heavy medium skillet over medium heat, stirring with a fork to heat sugar evenly, until it starts to melt. Stop stirring and cook, swirling skillet occasionally so sugar melts evenly, until it is a dark amber caramel. Immediately stir in nuts. Pour mixture onto oiled baking sheet. Let harden and cool completely, about 15 minutes.

Break praline into pieces and pulse in food processor until finely chopped.

MAKE THE SEMIFREDDO: Peel peaches if desired (see below), then halve, pit, and coarsely chop.

Puree peaches in food processor with crushed vitamin C, ½ cup sugar, and salt. Force through a medium-mesh sieve into a large metal bowl, pressing on solids; discard solids.

Stir yolks into puree, set bowl over a saucepan of barely simmering water, and beat with an electric mixer until mixture has tripled in volume and forms a thick ribbon when beaters are lifted, about 7 minutes.

Remove bowl from saucepan and set in a larger bowl of ice and cold water. Add almond extract and beat until cold, about 6 minutes.

Beat cream with remaining 2 tablespoons sugar in a medium bowl with cleaned beaters until it just holds soft peaks. Fold one third of cream into peach mixture. Fold in praline and remaining cream gently but thoroughly.

Pour mixture into cooled crust. Freeze, covered with plastic wrap, until firm, at least 3 hours. Let stand in refrigerator for 30 minutes to 1 hour before serving.

MEANWHILE, MAKE THE PEACH TOPPING: Cut an X in bottom of each peach and blanch in a medium saucepan of boiling water for 10 seconds. Transfer with a slotted spoon to a bowl of ice and cold water to stop the cooking. Peel peaches and cut into ½-inch wedges.

Toss peaches with crushed vitamin C and sugar and let stand, stirring occasionally, until sugar is dissolved, about 10 minutes.

Remove side of springform pan. Slide semifreddo onto a plate and spoon peaches over with a slotted spoon.

COOK'S NOTES

- The vitamin C will prevent the peaches from turning brown. Ascorbic acid is available in powdered form at pharmacies and natural foods stores; to equal 1 tablet, use ¼ teaspoon.
- The eggs in this recipe may not be fully cooked. If that is a concern, see page 915.
- The semifreddo, without the peach topping, can be frozen for up to 2 days.

Pistachio Semifreddo

MAKES ABOUT 2 QUARTS
ACTIVE TIME: 20 MINUTES ■ START TO FINISH: 4½ HOURS
(INCLUDES FREEZING)

■ Its name is Italian for "half-cold," and this semifreddo is a cross between ice cream and mousse, but more effortlessly elegant than either. Lush and airy, it contains ground salted pistachios folded into a whipped cream–meringue mixture. ■

- 1½ cups (about 6½ ounces) salted shelled pistachios
- 1 cup sugar
- 6 large egg whites
- 2 cups very cold heavy cream
- ¼ teaspoon almond extract

Pulse 1 cup pistachios with ½ cup plus 2 tablespoons sugar in a food processor until very finely ground. Add remaining ½ cup pistachios and pulse until just coarsely ground.

Beat egg whites in a large bowl with an electric mixer at medium speed until they just hold soft peaks. Beat in remaining ¼ cup plus 2 tablespoons sugar a little at a time, then increase speed to high and beat until meringue just holds stiff, glossy peaks.

Beat cream with almond extract in a large wide bowl with mixer at high speed until it just holds soft peaks.

Fold meringue into cream gently but thoroughly. Fold in nut mixture in same manner. Spoon into a serving dish.

Freeze, covered, until firm enough to scoop, about 4 hours.

Let semifreddo soften slightly before serving.

COOK'S NOTES

- The egg whites in this recipe are not cooked. If that is a concern, see page 915.
- The semifreddo keeps for up to 1 week.

Frozen Apricot Soufflé

SERVES 8
ACTIVE TIME: 40 MINUTES ■ START TO FINISH: 8¾ HOURS
(INCLUDES FREEZING)

■ Rising high above the rim, dusted with cocoa powder and confectioners' sugar, this dessert will make you do a double take—you'll swear it just came out of the oven. But one bite, and you'll discover cool creaminess whipped to an airy froth, wonderfully chewy nuggets of dried apricots, and a hint of almond. ■

- ½ pound dried California apricots
- 1 cup water
- 1 cup sugar
- 6 large egg whites, left at room temperature for 30 minutes
- 2 cups very cold heavy cream

½ teaspoon almond extract

¼ teaspoon vanilla extract

GARNISH: unsweetened cocoa powder and confectioners' sugar

SPECIAL EQUIPMENT: a 1½-quart soufflé dish; kitchen string; a candy thermometer

Wrap a collar of parchment paper or foil around soufflé dish so it extends about 3 inches above rim of dish, and secure with kitchen string.

Combine apricots and water in a small saucepan, bring to a simmer, and simmer, covered, over low heat until apricots are tender, 6 to 8 minutes. Drain, reserving ½ cup liquid.

Transfer apricots to a food processor and pulse until finely chopped (not pureed). Transfer to a large bowl.

Cook sugar and reserved apricot liquid in a small heavy saucepan over low heat, stirring, until sugar is dissolved. Boil syrup, without stirring, washing down sugar crystals from sides of pan with a pastry brush dipped in cold water, until it registers 238°F on thermometer, about 10 minutes.

Meanwhile, beat egg whites in a large bowl with an electric mixer at low speed until stiff peaks form. Beating constantly at high speed, gradually pour hot syrup in a thin stream down side of bowl into whites (being careful to avoid beaters) and continue to beat until meringue is cooled to room temperature, about 5 minutes.

Beat cream with almond and vanilla extracts in a large bowl with cleaned beaters until soft peaks form.

Whisk one third of meringue into apricots. Fold in remaining meringue, then fold in whipped cream gently but thoroughly.

Transfer to soufflé dish, smoothing top. Cover surface with plastic wrap and freeze for at least 8 hours.

Let soufflé stand at room temperature for 15 minutes to soften slightly before serving.

Remove collar and plastic wrap and dust top thoroughly with a thin layer of cocoa powder, then dust very lightly with confectioners' sugar.

COOK'S NOTE

■ The soufflé, without the garnish, can be frozen for up to 2 days.

Brandied Peach Parfaits

SERVES 4
ACTIVE TIME: 20 MINUTES ■ START TO FINISH: 1½ HOURS

■ In a dessert that manages to be both sophisticated and homey, tender peaches bathed in caramel alternate with layers of store-bought vanilla ice cream. A dram of brandy highlights the fruit's sweet muskiness. Be picky when buying the fruit for these parfaits: a ripe peach will have an intense aroma and give slightly to the touch. ■

1 pound firm but ripe peaches, peeled (see Tips, page 913), halved, pitted, and cut into 1-inch pieces

1 tablespoon fresh lemon juice

3 tablespoons brandy

½ cup sugar

1 pint vanilla ice cream, slightly softened

SPECIAL EQUIPMENT: 4 parfait glasses or other tall narrow glasses

Toss peaches with lemon juice and 2 tablespoons brandy in a bowl.

Heat sugar in a dry 9- to 10-inch heavy skillet over moderately low heat, stirring with a fork to heat sugar evenly, until it starts to melt. Stop stirring and cook, swirling pan occasionally so sugar melts evenly, until it is a dark amber caramel.

Carefully add peach mixture (caramel will harden and steam vigorously) and cook, stirring frequently, until caramel is dissolved and peaches are tender, about 5 minutes. Transfer to a bowl and cool to room temperature, stirring occasionally.

Stir remaining tablespoon brandy into peaches.

Spoon 2 tablespoons peach mixture into each glass and top with a small scoop of ice cream. Repeat with another layer of peaches and ice cream, and spoon remaining peaches on top.

COOK'S NOTE

■ The brandied peaches can be made ahead and refrigerated, covered, for up to 1 week.

Watermelon Sundae

SERVES 8
ACTIVE TIME: 15 MINUTES ■ START TO FINISH: 3¾ HOURS
(INCLUDES FREEZING)

■ Most homemade ice creams use eggs as the thickening base for a custard, but in this no-cook version, ricotta and cream cheese do the work instead. The result? Ice cream whose extra-silky texture makes a wonderful contrast to the crispness of watermelon. To top things off, we add shavings of bittersweet chocolate. It's an easy-to-prepare dessert that's out of this world. ■

  1 (15-ounce) container (1⅔ cups) whole-milk ricotta or
      1⅔ cups fresh ricotta (see page 231), well chilled
  3 ounces cream cheese, softened
  1 cup whole milk
  1 cup sugar
  2 tablespoons dark rum
  1 teaspoon finely grated lemon zest
  ½ teaspoon vanilla extract
  ⅛ teaspoon salt
  ⅓ cup very cold heavy cream
  1 (4½- to 5-pound) wedge watermelon, cut into
      1-inch-thick slices and chilled
  1 ounce bittersweet chocolate, shaved with a
      vegetable peeler

SPECIAL EQUIPMENT: an ice cream maker

Combine cheeses, milk, sugar, rum, zest, vanilla, and salt in a blender and blend until smooth, about 1 minute. Add cream and blend until just combined, about 5 seconds.

Freeze mixture in ice cream maker. Transfer to an airtight container and put in freezer to harden for at least 3 hours.

Put watermelon slices on plates, top with scoops of ice cream, and sprinkle with chocolate shavings.

COOK'S NOTE
■ The ice cream keeps for up to 2 days.

Caramel Espresso Float

SERVES 4
ACTIVE TIME: 20 MINUTES ■ START TO FINISH: 30 MINUTES

■ This very grown-up float was inspired by the Italian dessert *affogato al caffè*, a scoop of ice cream "drowned" in hot coffee. We added caramelized sugar to the coffee and capped it with whipped cream, toasted nuts, and chocolate shavings. ■

  6 tablespoons granulated sugar
  2 cups water
  ¼ cup instant espresso powder, such as Medaglia
      d'Oro
  2 cups ice cubes
  ½ cup very cold heavy cream
  3 tablespoons confectioners' sugar
  4 generous scoops vanilla ice cream (from 1 pint)
  2 tablespoons chopped nuts, such as almonds or
      hazelnuts, toasted (see Tips, page 911)
  3 tablespoons bittersweet chocolate shavings (made
      with a vegetable peeler, from a 3½-ounce bar)

Heat sugar in a 3- to 4-quart heavy saucepan over moderate heat, stirring with a fork to heat sugar evenly, until it starts to melt. Stop stirring and cook, swirling pan occasionally so sugar melts evenly, until it is a dark amber caramel. Remove from heat and carefully add 1 cup water (caramel will harden and steam vigorously), then cook over high heat, stirring, until caramel is dissolved.

Remove pan from heat, add espresso powder, and stir until dissolved. Add remaining cup water and ice cubes and stir until espresso is cold; remove any unmelted ice cubes.

Beat cream with confectioners' sugar in a bowl with an electric mixer until it just holds soft peaks.

Divide ice cream among four 8-ounce glasses, pour ½ cup espresso mixture over each serving, and top with whipped cream, nuts, and chocolate.

Frozen Mango, Blackberry Cassis, and Vanilla Mosaic

SERVES 10 TO 12
ACTIVE TIME: 20 MINUTES ■ START TO FINISH: 4¼ HOURS
(INCLUDES FREEZING)

■ If you're searching for a showstopping finale, stop right here. Each delicious slice of this tricolored frozen terrine is a canvas of decorative swirls: vibrant orange, deep purple, and creamy white. It's easy to make and it will only take 20 minutes of your time. ■

    2 pints mango sorbet
    1 pint vanilla ice cream
    1½ cups (6 ounces) blackberries (fresh or thawed
        frozen)
    ¼ cup sugar
    2 tablespoons crème de cassis
SPECIAL EQUIPMENT: a 9-by-5-by-3-inch loaf pan or other
        7- to 8-cup mold; parchment paper

Put sorbet and ice cream in refrigerator until evenly softened, 45 minutes to 1 hour.

Meanwhile, puree blackberries with sugar and cassis in a blender until smooth. Strain through a fine-mesh sieve into a bowl, pressing on solids; discard solids. Freeze to thicken slightly until ice cream is ready, 20 to 40 minutes.

Lightly oil loaf pan. Line bottom and long sides of pan with a piece of parchment, leaving at least a 3-inch overhang on each side.

Stir chilled blackberry puree until smooth. Fill loaf pan with spoonfuls of sorbet and ice cream, pressing down on them and filling in empty spaces with blackberry puree as you go. Smooth top, pressing down with back of spoon to eliminate air spaces, fold parchment flaps over top, and freeze until solid, about 3 hours.

To unmold, run a thin knife along short ends of pan to loosen mosaic, open flaps of parchment, and invert onto a flat serving dish; discard parchment. Cut mosaic into ½-inch-thick slices.

COOK'S NOTE

■ The mosaic can be frozen, covered with plastic wrap, for up to 5 days.

Chocolate-Covered Mint Ice Cream Terrine

SERVES 6 TO 8
ACTIVE TIME: 1 HOUR ■ START TO FINISH: 9 HOURS
(INCLUDES CHILLING AND FREEZING)

■ Once you've tried ice cream made with fresh mint leaves—a far cry from the artificial green stuff—you'll never go back. Here it's completely surrounded by a thick robe of rich bittersweet chocolate. The technique of coating the terrine in chocolate is not especially difficult, but the effect is sophisticated. ■

FOR ICE CREAM
    1½ cups heavy cream
    ⅔ cup whole milk
    1 cup packed fresh mint leaves
    4 large egg yolks
    ⅔ cup sugar
FOR CHOCOLATE COATING
    3½ ounces bittersweet chocolate (preferably 70% cacao;
        see page 705)
    ⅓ cup water
    ¼ cup heavy cream
    3 tablespoons sugar
    ¼ cup unsweetened Dutch-process cocoa powder
    1 tablespoon crème de menthe or 1 tablespoon sugar
SPECIAL EQUIPMENT: an instant-read thermometer; an ice
        cream maker; a 3-cup loaf pan (about 7¼ by 4 by
        2 inches; see Cook's Note); parchment paper

MAKE THE ICE CREAM: Blend together cream, milk, and mint in a blender just until mint is finely chopped.

Pour cream mixture into a heavy medium saucepan and bring to a boil. Remove from heat and let stand for 5 minutes.

Whisk together egg yolks and sugar in a bowl and slowly add cream mixture, whisking. Return mixture to saucepan and cook over medium heat, stirring constantly with a wooden spoon, until custard thickens enough to coat back of spoon and registers 175°F on thermometer; do not let boil.

Pour custard through a fine-mesh sieve into a metal bowl, pressing on solids; discard solids. Refrigerate, uncovered, stirring occasionally, until cool, about 1 hour, then cover and refrigerate until very cold, 3 to 6 hours.

Freeze custard in ice cream maker.

Lightly oil loaf pan and line bottom and long sides with a sheet of parchment paper, leaving at least 2 inches of overhang on each side. Pack ice cream into pan, smoothing top. Cover with parchment overhang and freeze terrine until completely firm, at least 3 hours.

MEANWHILE, MAKE THE CHOCOLATE COATING: Finely chop chocolate, preferably in a food processor.

Bring water, cream, sugar (including additional 1 tablespoon sugar if not using crème de menthe), and cocoa to a boil in a small heavy saucepan, whisking until sugar is dissolved. Remove from heat, add crème de menthe (if using) and chopped chocolate, and whisk gently until chocolate is melted and mixture is smooth. Cool to room temperature (chocolate should still be liquid—do not chill), about 20 minutes.

Put a 12-by-8-inch piece of parchment on a small baking sheet, anchoring it with a dab of chocolate under each corner. Spread chocolate evenly over parchment with an offset spatula or long narrow spatula, leaving a ½-inch border on all sides. Refrigerate until set, about 1 hour.

COAT THE TERRINE: Remove terrine from freezer and open flaps of parchment paper. Run a hot knife along short ends to loosen them, then invert ice cream onto a sheet of plastic wrap; discard parchment paper. Invert ice cream lengthwise across center of set chocolate; discard plastic. Lift chocolate coating (with parchment) around ice cream, pressing to help it adhere, until edges of chocolate meet, then press them together so that excess chocolate and parchment paper are standing up like a seam (you will trim it off later). Freeze terrine until chocolate is firm, at least 1 hour.

Starting from seam, peel parchment paper off both sides of terrine. Trim excess chocolate from seam with kitchen shears, and trim open ends with a knife to even them. Invert terrine onto a platter and peel off parchment paper.

COOK'S NOTES

- The ice cream can be made up to 2 days ahead.
- The terrine can be frozen for up to 1 day. Cover with

plastic wrap once the chocolate is firm. Let soften for 5 to 10 minutes before slicing.

- If using a loaf pan or terrine with different dimensions, you'll need to adjust the size of the parchment paper for the chocolate coating so that the chocolate will wrap around the ice cream. The piece of parchment paper should be ½ inch longer than the length of the pan and the width 1 inch more than the measure around the terrine.

Raspberry Chocolate Ice Pops

MAKES 8 ICE POPS
ACTIVE TIME: 25 MINUTES ■ START TO FINISH: 4½ HOURS
(INCLUDES FREEZING)

■ These beautifully layered ice pops, made with chocolate ice and a fruity puree of fresh raspberries and framboise liqueur, are surprisingly light. They make a handsome dessert after an alfresco meal or a refreshing snack on a hot afternoon. ■

FOR RASPBERRY ICE
- 1¼ cups (6 ounces) raspberries
- ⅓ cup water
- ¼ cup light corn syrup
- 3 tablespoons sugar
- 1 tablespoon framboise (raspberry eau-de-vie; optional)
- 2 teaspoons fresh lemon juice, or to taste

FOR CHOCOLATE ICE
- ¾ cup water
- ¼ cup corn syrup
- 3 tablespoons sugar
- ⅓ cup unsweetened cocoa powder, preferably Dutch-process
- Pinch of salt
- ½ teaspoon vanilla extract

SPECIAL EQUIPMENT: eight 3-ounce ice pop molds and sticks (see Sources)

MAKE THE RASPBERRY ICE MIXTURE: Combine all ingredients in a blender and blend until smooth.

Force through a fine-mesh sieve into a bowl, pressing on solids; discard solids.

MAKE THE CHOCOLATE ICE MIXTURE: Bring water, corn syrup, and sugar to a boil in a small saucepan, stirring until sugar is dissolved. Whisk in cocoa and salt, then whisk in vanilla. Transfer to a metal bowl and quick-chill by setting bowl in a large bowl of ice and cold water and stirring occasionally until cold, about 15 minutes. Refrigerate until ready to use.

MAKE THE ICE POPS: Divide half of raspberry puree among molds and freeze until partially frozen, about 20 minutes.

Divide chocolate mixture among molds (layers may run into each other a little) and freeze until partially frozen (not hard), about 30 minutes.

Fill molds with remaining raspberry puree, place cover on molds, and insert sticks at least through middle layer, making sure they are straight (to make it easy to remove top when unmolding). Freeze until completely firm, about 3 hours.

UNMOLD THE ICE POPS: Put molds in a container of room-temperature water that comes to ¼ inch from top of molds and let stand for 30 seconds, then remove cover and pull out pops. Serve immediately, or wrap individually in plastic wrap and freeze until ready to serve.

COOK'S NOTES

- Feel free to vary the order and amounts of flavors when making the layers.
- The ice pops can be frozen for up to 1 week.

Frozen Chocolate Peanut Butter Bars

MAKES 8 BARS
ACTIVE TIME: 35 MINUTES ■ START TO FINISH: 3 HOURS
(INCLUDES FREEZING)

■ These frozen bars top flourless chocolate cake with a layer of creamy peanut butter frosting and a drizzle of gooey hot fudge sauce. The hot fudge sauce recipe makes more than you'll need, but you'll be happy to have it on hand for impromptu sundaes. ■

FOR CHOCOLATE LAYER
- 7 ounces bittersweet chocolate, chopped
- 1 stick (8 tablespoons) cold unsalted butter, cut into pieces
- ¼ cup granulated sugar
- ¼ teaspoon salt
- 3 large eggs, lightly beaten
- 1 teaspoon vanilla extract
- 1 cup (about 5 ounces) salted dry-roasted peanuts

FOR PEANUT BUTTER LAYER
- 4 ounces cream cheese, softened
- ½ cup creamy peanut butter (not "natural")
- ¾ cup confectioners' sugar
- ¼ teaspoon salt
- ½ cup very cold heavy cream
- 1 teaspoon vanilla extract

ACCOMPANIMENT: Hot Fudge Sauce (page 877)

MAKE THE CHOCOLATE LAYER: Put a rack in middle of oven and preheat oven to 350°F. Line a 9-inch square baking pan with foil, leaving a 2-inch overhang on two opposite sides, and lightly brush foil with oil.

Melt chocolate and butter with sugar and salt in a large metal bowl set over a pan of barely simmering water, whisking occasionally until smooth. Remove bowl from heat and whisk in eggs and vanilla. Stir in peanuts.

Pour batter into baking pan and bake until it is set and edges are slightly puffed, about 15 minutes. Transfer pan to a rack to cool completely.

MAKE THE PEANUT BUTTER LAYER: Beat cream cheese, peanut butter, confectioners' sugar, and salt in a bowl with an electric mixer at medium speed until well combined, about 4 minutes.

Beat cream with vanilla in a bowl with cleaned beaters at medium-high speed until it just holds stiff peaks. Gently fold into peanut butter mixture until just combined.

Spread mixture evenly on top of chocolate layer, cover pan with foil, and freeze until firm, about 2 hours.

Carefully lift cake from pan using foil overhang. Pull back foil and trim ¼ inch from edges of cake. Cut into 8 bars and peel off foil. Serve with sauce.

COOK'S NOTE

- Any leftover bars can be frozen, individually wrapped in plastic wrap, for up to 4 days.

Praline
Ice Cream Sandwiches

MAKES 24 SANDWICHES
ACTIVE TIME: 45 MINUTES ■ START TO FINISH: 3 HOURS
(INCLUDES FREEZING)

■ Tell yourself you're making these for the kids, but you won't mean it. The sweet, slightly salty cookie layers become a little chewy as they absorb the ice cream. This recipe is delightfully easy; you simply make one big sandwich and cut it into small pieces. ■

FOR PRALINE
　　1 cup (about 3½ ounces) pecans, coarsely chopped
　1½ teaspoons salt
　　1 cup sugar
FOR SANDWICH LAYERS
　1½ cups all-purpose flour
　　1 teaspoon baking powder
　　¼ teaspoon baking soda
　　½ teaspoon salt
　1½ sticks (12 tablespoons) unsalted butter, softened
　1¼ cups packed dark brown sugar
　　2 large eggs
　　1 teaspoon vanilla extract
FOR FILLING
　　2 pints vanilla ice cream, slightly softened
SPECIAL EQUIPMENT: two 15½-by-10½-inch baking sheets
　　　(jelly-roll pans); parchment paper

MAKE THE PRALINE: Line a large baking sheet with foil. Stir together pecans and salt in a small bowl.

Heat sugar in a 10-inch heavy skillet over moderate heat, stirring with a fork to heat sugar evenly, until it starts to melt. Stop stirring and cook, swirling pan occasionally so sugar melts evenly, until it is a dark amber caramel, about 8 minutes. Add pecans, stirring until well coated, then spread on foil and cool completely.

Peel praline off foil and finely chop with a large heavy knife.

MAKE THE SANDWICH LAYERS: Put racks in upper and lower thirds of oven and preheat oven to 375°F. Draw a large X with butter from corner to corner on each baking sheet and line bottom of each pan with parchment paper, leaving a 1-inch overhang

on each short end, pressing to help parchment adhere to X.

Whisk together flour, baking powder, baking soda, and salt in a medium bowl.

Beat together butter and brown sugar in a large bowl with an electric mixer at medium-high speed until pale and fluffy, about 3 minutes. Add eggs one at a time, beating well after each addition. Beat in vanilla. Reduce speed to low and add flour mixture in 2 batches, mixing until just combined.

Divide batter between baking sheets (about 1½ cups for each) and spread into thin even layers with an offset spatula or rubber spatula. Sprinkle with praline. Bake, switching position of pans halfway through baking, until layers are golden brown but still tender, about 10 minutes. Cool in pans for 10 minutes, then transfer, on parchment, to racks and cool completely.

ASSEMBLE THE SANDWICHES: Line cleaned baking sheet with parchment, leaving a 1-inch overhang on each short end. Invert sandwich layers onto work surface and carefully peel off and discard parchment. Trim edges. Transfer 1 sandwich layer, praline side down, to baking sheet and spread evenly with ice cream. Top with second sandwich layer, praline side up, pressing gently to form an even sandwich.

Wrap baking sheet in plastic wrap and freeze ice cream sandwich until firm, about 1 hour.

Cut into 24 sandwiches to serve.

COOK'S NOTE
■ The ice cream sandwich can be frozen, wrapped in plastic wrap and then in foil, for up to 1 week; cut before serving.

Banana
Ice Cream Sandwiches

SERVES 4
ACTIVE TIME: 10 MINUTES ■ START TO FINISH: 2 HOURS
(INCLUDES FREEZING)

■ Crisp tortillas sandwich a quick, homemade "ice cream" flavored with dulce de leche and ripe banana for a great make-ahead dessert that requires very little work. ■

½ cup very cold heavy cream
¼ cup dulce de leche (see Sources)
1 ripe medium banana
½ teaspoon fresh lime juice
4 (7-inch) flour tortillas (not low-fat)
1 tablespoon unsalted butter, melted

ACCOMPANIMENT: chocolate sauce, such as Dark Chocolate Sauce (page 877)

Put a rack in middle of oven and preheat oven to 350°F.

Beat cream with an electric mixer in a metal bowl until it just holds stiff peaks. Reduce speed to low and beat in dulce de leche, banana, and lime juice until combined.

Freeze until firm but not frozen hard, at least 45 minutes.

Meanwhile, brush tortillas on both sides with butter. Arrange in one layer on a baking sheet and toast, turning once, until golden, 12 to 16 minutes. Cool completely.

Divide cream mixture between 2 tortillas and top with remaining 2 tortillas. Freeze on baking sheet, loosely covered with foil, until firm, about 1 hour.

Cut ice cream sandwiches in half and serve with sauce.

COOK'S NOTE

■ The ice cream sandwiches can be frozen for up to 1 day.

Espresso and Mascarpone Icebox Cake

SERVES 12
ACTIVE TIME: 30 MINUTES ■ START TO FINISH: 9½ HOURS (INCLUDES CHILLING)

■ On sultry summer nights, leave the oven off and serve a cool treat that's elegant enough for grown-ups and fun enough for kids. Echoing the flavors of tiramisù, this dessert of cream, mascarpone cheese, chocolate, and espresso is perfect after any meal. ■

3 cups very cold heavy cream
½ cup plus 1 tablespoon sugar
1 cup (about 9 ounces) mascarpone cheese, at room temperature
1 (9-ounce) box chocolate wafers, such as Nabisco Famous
1 tablespoon instant espresso powder, such as Medaglia d'Oro

SPECIAL EQUIPMENT: a 10-inch springform pan

Beat 2 cups cream with 6 tablespoons sugar in a large bowl with an electric mixer at medium speed until it just holds soft peaks, 2 to 4 minutes. Reduce speed to low, add mascarpone, and mix until combined.

Spread 1¼ cups mascarpone mixture evenly in bottom of springform pan. Cover with 14 wafers, slightly overlapping them if necessary. Spread with another 1¼ cups mascarpone mixture, followed by 14 more wafers arranged in same manner. Spread remaining mascarpone mixture on top, smoothing top. Cover pan with foil and freeze until firm, about 1 hour.

Transfer cake to refrigerator and let stand, covered, until a sharp knife inserted into center cuts through softened wafers easily, about 8 hours.

Pulse remaining chocolate wafers in a food processor until finely ground.

Beat remaining cup cream, remaining 3 tablespoons sugar, and espresso powder in a bowl with electric mixer at medium speed until cream just holds stiff peaks, about 3 minutes.

Remove foil and side of pan. Frost top and sides of cake with espresso cream. Sprinkle edges of top lightly with wafer crumbs. Serve cold.

COOK'S NOTES

■ The cake, without the espresso cream, can be refrigerated for up to 2 days.
■ The cake can be frosted up to 4 hours ahead and refrigerated, loosely covered with foil.

Frozen Passion Fruit Meringue Cake

SERVES 8 TO 10
ACTIVE TIME: 1½ HOURS ■ START TO FINISH: 7 HOURS
(INCLUDES FREEZING)

■ Passion fruit is irresistible, its taste halfway between mango and lemon with a floral perfume. Fresh fruits are tricky to work with and expensive to boot, so frozen pulp is the way to go (it may be labeled with its Spanish name, *maracuyá*). For this impressive dessert, the pulp is made into a rich curd, which is then transformed into an airy pale orange mousse, layered with crisp-chewy layers of meringue, and frozen. The result is as delicious as it is gorgeous. ■

FOR MERINGUE LAYERS
    4 large egg whites, left at room temperature for
        30 minutes
       Pinch of salt
    1 cup sugar
FOR PASSION FRUIT MOUSSE AND CREAM
    1 stick (8 tablespoons) unsalted butter, cut into pieces
    ½ teaspoon cornstarch
    ¾ cup thawed frozen passion fruit pulp (see Sources)
    ¾ cup plus 2 tablespoons sugar
    1 large egg
    6 large egg yolks
    1½ cups very cold heavy cream
SPECIAL EQUIPMENT: parchment paper; a pastry bag; a
    ⅓-inch plain tip; an ⅛-inch plain tip; a long narrow
    platter or a foil-wrapped cardboard rectangle (at
    least 15 by 4 inches)

MAKE THE MERINGUE LAYERS: Put a rack in middle of oven and preheat oven to 275°F.

Trace three 14-by-3-inch rectangles about ¾ inch apart on a 15-by-12-inch sheet of parchment paper. Turn paper over and put it on a lightly oiled large baking sheet.

Beat whites with salt in a large bowl with an electric mixer (fitted with whisk attachment if using a stand mixer) at medium speed until they hold soft peaks. Beat in sugar 1 tablespoon at a time, then increase speed to high and beat until whites hold stiff, glossy peaks, about 4 minutes with a stand mixer, 8 to 10 minutes with a handheld.

Transfer meringue to pastry bag fitted with ⅓-inch tip and fill in traced rectangles completely. Gently smooth tops. Bake until firm and very pale golden, 45 to 60 minutes.

Slide meringue layers, on parchment, onto a large rack and cool completely, then carefully peel off parchment.

MEANWHILE, MAKE THE MOUSSE: Combine butter, cornstarch, passion fruit pulp, and ¾ cup sugar in a 2-quart heavy saucepan and cook over moderately low heat, stirring, until butter is melted and sugar is dissolved. Remove from heat.

Whisk together egg and yolks in a large bowl until combined. Add butter mixture in a stream, whisking. Return mixture to saucepan and cook over moderately low heat, whisking constantly, until thick enough to hold mark of whisk and first bubble appears on surface, 3 to 5 minutes. Immediately transfer curd to a metal bowl set in a larger bowl of ice and cold water to quick-chill, stirring occasionally, until cold.

Beat cream with remaining 2 tablespoons sugar in a large bowl with electric mixer until it just holds stiff peaks. For mousse, fold 2 cups whipped cream into curd gently but thoroughly. Transfer ¾ cup whipped cream to a small bowl and reserve, refrigerated, for cream layer. Fold ½ cup mousse into remaining whipped cream for decorative icing, transfer to pastry bag fitted with ⅛-inch tip, and refrigerate.

ASSEMBLE AND FREEZE THE CAKE: Arrange 1 meringue layer, flat side down, on platter and spread evenly with ¾ cup mousse. Cover with another meringue layer and spread evenly with reserved whipped cream. Cover with remaining meringue layer, flat side up, and spread remaining mousse evenly over top and sides of cake. Pipe cream mixture decoratively on top of cake. Freeze, uncovered, until firm, about 3 hours.

Put cake in refrigerator to soften slightly, about 1 hour, before serving.

COOK'S NOTE
■ The cake can be frozen for up to 2 days. Once it is firm, cover with plastic wrap; remove the plastic wrap before softening it in the refrigerator.

Sweet Sauces

Hot Fudge Sauce

MAKES ABOUT 2 CUPS
ACTIVE TIME: 10 MINUTES ■ START TO FINISH: 20 MINUTES

■ When this sauce hits cold ice cream, it becomes chewy and seriously fudgy. It's wonderful over any type of ice cream and with the Frozen Chocolate Peanut Butter Bars (page 873). ■

⅔ cup heavy cream
6 tablespoons light corn syrup
6 tablespoons packed brown sugar
¼ cup unsweetened Dutch-process cocoa powder
½ teaspoon salt
7 ounces bittersweet chocolate, chopped
1 teaspoon vanilla extract

Combine cream, syrup, brown sugar, cocoa, salt, and chocolate in a 1-quart heavy saucepan and bring to a boil over moderate heat, stirring until chocolate is melted. Reduce heat and simmer, stirring frequently, until thickened, about 3 minutes.

Remove from heat and stir in vanilla. Cool sauce to warm, stirring occasionally.

COOK'S NOTE

■ The sauce keeps for up to 1 week in the refrigerator. Cool, uncovered, then refrigerate, covered. Reheat before serving.

Dark Chocolate Sauce

MAKES ABOUT ¾ CUP
ACTIVE TIME: 5 MINUTES ■ START TO FINISH: 15 MINUTES

■ It's 11 o'clock on a Tuesday night—and you've got a craving. If you have 5 minutes and some cocoa powder, you're in luck. This quick pantry chocolate sauce has a deep flavor that will more than satisfy your need. ■

⅓ cup water
½ cup packed dark brown sugar
½ cup unsweetened Dutch-process cocoa powder
⅛ teaspoon salt
2 tablespoons unsalted butter, cut into pieces
½ teaspoon vanilla extract

Heat water with brown sugar in a heavy saucepan over moderate heat, whisking, until sugar is dissolved. Add cocoa powder and salt, whisking until smooth. Add butter and vanilla and whisk until butter is melted. Serve warm.

COOK'S NOTE

■ The sauce keeps for up to 1 week in the refrigerator. Cool, uncovered, then refrigerate, covered. Reheat before serving.

VARIATION

MOCHA SAUCE: Substitute ⅓ cup brewed coffee for the water.

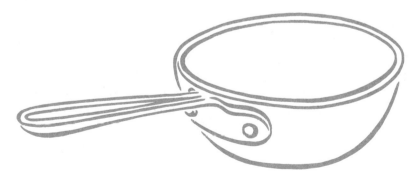

Chocolate Hazelnut Sauce

MAKES ABOUT 1¾ CUPS
ACTIVE TIME: 15 MINUTES ■ START TO FINISH: 45 MINUTES
(INCLUDES COOLING)

■ Blended with cream and bittersweet chocolate, Nutella, that beloved hazelnut spread found in many supermarkets, becomes a silky, easy-to-pour sauce. It's imperative to use 70% bittersweet chocolate for this recipe; its high cocoa content helps balance the sweet Nutella. For a killer sundae, pour the sauce over vanilla ice cream and top with some toasted hazelnuts. ■

    1 ounce bittersweet chocolate (70% cacao;
        see page 705), finely chopped
    1 cup heavy cream
    ½ cup chocolate hazelnut spread, such as Nutella
        Pinch of salt

Put chocolate in a bowl. Bring cream to a boil in a small saucepan, pour over chocolate, and gently whisk until smooth. Add chocolate hazelnut spread and salt, stirring until smooth. Serve warm or at room temperature.

COOK'S NOTE

■ The sauce keeps for up to 2 weeks in the refrigerator. Cool, uncovered, then refrigerate, covered. Bring to room temperature or heat in a microwave or in a metal bowl set over a saucepan of simmering water, stirring occasionally, before serving.

Butterscotch Sauce

MAKES ABOUT 1⅓ CUPS
ACTIVE TIME: 15 MINUTES ■ START TO FINISH: 45 MINUTES
(INCLUDES COOLING)

■ Making butterscotch sauce is almost a lost art, and finding a well-balanced recipe for it is difficult. Look no further. This is smooth, buttery, and rich, with a slight hint of bitterness. For a special do-it-yourself dessert, set out pitchers of butterscotch and Hot Fudge Sauce (page 877), an array of ice creams, and a tray of brownies and let everyone make their own sundaes. ■

    1 cup sugar
    ¼ cup light corn syrup
    3 tablespoons water
    ½ stick (4 tablespoons) unsalted butter, cut into
        tablespoons
    1 teaspoon cider vinegar
        Pinch of salt
    ½ cup heavy cream
    2 teaspoons vanilla extract

Bring sugar, corn syrup, and water to a boil in a 1- to 2-quart heavy saucepan over moderate heat, stirring until sugar is dissolved. Boil, without stirring, swirling pan occasionally, until mixture becomes a golden caramel, about 8 minutes.

Remove from heat and add butter, vinegar, and salt, swirling pan until butter is melted. Add cream and vanilla, return to heat, and simmer, stirring, for 1 minute. Serve warm or at room temperature (sauce will thicken as it cools).

COOK'S NOTE

■ The sauce keeps for up to 3 weeks in the refrigerator. Cool, uncovered, then refrigerate, covered. Bring to room temperature or heat in a metal bowl set over a saucepan of simmering water, stirring occasionally, before serving.

Marshmallow Sauce

MAKES ABOUT 1½ CUPS
ACTIVE TIME: 25 MINUTES ■ START TO FINISH: 1½ HOURS
(INCLUDES CHILLING)

■ Fluffy and light, this sauce tastes of pure marshmallow, not like the jarred fluff. It has a wonderfully velvety consistency and a snowy white color, and it just begs to be poured over chocolate ice cream. ■

- ¾ cup sugar
- 2 tablespoons light corn syrup
- Pinch of salt
- ⅓ cup plus ¼ cup cold water
- ½ teaspoon unflavored gelatin
- ½ teaspoon vanilla extract

SPECIAL EQUIPMENT: a candy thermometer

Bring sugar, corn syrup, salt, and ¼ cup water to a boil in a small heavy saucepan over moderate heat, stirring until sugar is dissolved. Insert thermometer and boil, without stirring, until thermometer registers 260°F.

Meanwhile, sprinkle gelatin over remaining ⅓ cup cold water in a large deep heatproof bowl and let stand until softened, about 1 minute.

Beating constantly with an electric mixer at medium speed, gradually add hot syrup to gelatin mixture in a thin stream (be careful not to let syrup touch beaters and sides of bowl when pouring, or it will spatter and harden). Increase speed to high and beat until mixture is cool, tripled in volume, and very thick, about 10 minutes.

Add vanilla and beat until incorporated. Refrigerate sauce, uncovered, for 1 hour, then cover and keep refrigerated until ready to use.

COOK'S NOTE
■ The sauce keeps for up to 1 month.

Stout Crème Anglaise

MAKES ABOUT 1½ CUPS
ACTIVE TIME: 20 MINUTES ■ START TO FINISH: 1½ HOURS
(INCLUDES CHILLING)

■ The malty flavor of stout is a welcome contrast to the sweetness of this creamy dessert sauce, which makes a sophisticated topping for a bowl of vanilla ice cream or fresh fruit. It's also wonderful over toasted slices of pound cake. ■

- ½ cup stout, such as Mackeson or Guinness (pour beer slowly into measuring cup; do not measure foam)
- 5 large egg yolks
- ¾ cup packed light brown sugar
- Pinch of salt
- ¼ cup heavy cream
- 1 teaspoon vanilla extract

SPECIAL EQUIPMENT: an instant-read thermometer

Bring beer just to a boil in a small heavy saucepan; remove from heat.

Whisk together yolks, brown sugar, and salt in a medium bowl until well combined. Whisk in cream and vanilla, then add hot beer in a slow stream, whisking constantly. Pour into saucepan and cook over moderately low heat, stirring constantly with a wooden spoon, until custard thickens enough to coat back of spoon and registers 175°F on thermometer; do not let boil.

Strain sauce through a fine-mesh sieve into a bowl and cool to room temperature, then refrigerate, covered, until cold, at least 1 hour.

COOK'S NOTE
■ The sauce keeps for up to 2 days.

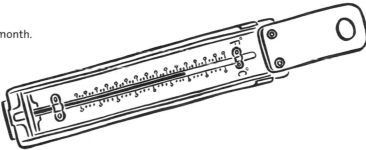

Raspberry Zing Syrup

■ This zippy take on a Colonial-era shrub—a drink of fruit juice, sugar, and vinegar—is great drizzled over ice cream, added to a cocktail, or stirred into a tall glass of sparkling water for a refreshing cooler. The raspberry vinegar boosts the fruit's beautiful color and adds a floral top note. ■

> 4½ cups (1 pound 2 ounces) raspberries
> ¾ cup sugar
> 2½ tablespoons raspberry vinegar
> 2 tablespoons water

Combine all ingredients in a medium heavy saucepan and bring to a boil, stirring until sugar is dissolved. Reduce heat and simmer, uncovered, stirring occasionally, for 20 minutes.

Strain syrup through a fine-mesh sieve into a bowl, pressing gently on solids; discard solids. You should have about 1 cup syrup. If you have more, boil it until reduced. Cool, uncovered, stirring occasionally, to room temperature. Serve at room temperature or chilled.

COOK'S NOTE

■ The syrup keeps, covered and refrigerated, for up to 1 week.

Blackberry Syrup

■ Nowadays it's easy to get your hands on blackberries all year round, and this deeply flavored, wine-colored syrup is a great showcase for the fruit. We love it over coffee ice cream. ■

> 4½ cups (1½ pounds) blackberries
> 1 cup sugar
> ½ cup water

Combine all ingredients in a 2- to 3-quart heavy saucepan and bring to a boil over moderately high heat, stirring until sugar is dissolved. Reduce heat and simmer, uncovered, stirring occasionally, until fruit is soft, about 30 minutes.

Strain syrup through a fine-mesh sieve into a bowl, pressing gently on solids; discard solids. Serve at room temperature.

COOK'S NOTE

■ The syrup keeps, covered and refrigerated, for up to 1 week.

Warm Sour Cherry Compote

■ The season of sour cherries is fleeting. That's why we stock up when the fruit hits the market and freeze as much as we can to get us through the dead of winter. Deepened by a caramel base and enlivened with kirsch, the saucy cherries taste wonderful with a scoop of vanilla ice cream and a shortbread cookie or two. ■

> 1 cup sugar
> 1 teaspoon fresh lemon juice
> 1 tablespoon unsalted butter
> 1½ pounds (2½ cups) fresh or thawed frozen sour cherries, pitted
> 2 tablespoons kirsch

Rub together sugar and lemon juice in a 12-inch heavy skillet with your fingertips until mixture resembles wet sand. Cook over moderately high heat, swirling skillet slowly, until sugar is melted and pale golden, 5 to 6 minutes.

Add butter and swirl skillet until incorporated, about 30 seconds (caramel will bubble up). Add cherries, swirling skillet to coat, and bring to a boil (cherries will exude liquid and caramel will harden). Cook cherries, swirling skillet, until caramel is dissolved, 5 to 8 minutes.

Drain cherries in a medium-mesh sieve set over a bowl, then return liquid to skillet and boil until reduced to about ¾ cup, 6 to 8 minutes.

Remove from heat and add cherries and kirsch, then return to heat and boil for 30 seconds. Serve warm.

COOK'S NOTE
■ The cherries can be cooked up to 3 hours ahead and kept, covered, at room temperature. Bring to a boil just before serving.

MENUS

TIPS AND TECHNIQUES

GLOSSARY

SOURCES

DIRECTORY OF SOURCES

INDEX

MENUS

Quick Weeknight Dinners

Spring #1
SERVES 4

Roast Chicken and Asparagus with Tahini Sauce (page 395)
Bulgur Pilaf (page 274)

Spring #2
SERVES 4

Garlic-Rosemary-Marinated Lamb Chops (page 484)
Roasted Fennel and Baby Carrots (page 600)
Green salad

Spring #3
SERVES 4

Thai Shrimp and Spinach Curry (page 367)
Boiled rice noodles

Spring #4
SERVES 4

Grilled Steaks with Olive Oregano Relish (page 535)
Grilled Eggplant with Yogurt Mint Sauce (page 553)
Green salad

Spring #5
SERVES 4

Apricot Chicken with Almonds (page 396)
Cucumber Noodles (page 596)
Steamed couscous

Spring #6
SERVES 4

Lamb Chops with Salmoriglio Sauce (page 484)
Quinoa and Bulgur Salad with Feta (page 188)
Steamed carrots (page 585)

Late Spring/Early Summer #7
SERVES 6

Salmon with Soy Glaze (page 339)
Kohlrabi Slivers and Pea Shoots with Sesame Dressing (page 176)
Steamed white rice

Summer #1

SERVES 4

Grilled Spicy Skirt Steak (page 537)
Smothered Yellow Squash with Basil (page 642)
Crusty bread

Summer #2

SERVES 4

Poached Chicken with Tomatoes, Olives, and Green Beans (page 396)
Herbed Jasmine Rice (page 256)

Summer #3

SERVES 4

Shrimp and Avocado in Tamarind Sauce (page 369)
Steamed white rice
Boiled green beans (page 569)

Summer #4

SERVES 4

Fettuccine with Arugula Puree and Cherry Tomato Sauce (page 208)

Green salad and crusty bread

Summer #5

SERVES 4

Barbecued Pork Burgers with Slaw (page 540)

Grilled Mexican corn with mayonnaise and *cotija* or feta cheese (page 594)

Summer #6

SERVES 4

Grilled Chicken Paillards with Nectarine Chutney (page 525)

Grilled Fennel with Lemon (page 554)

Barley with Toasted Cumin and Mint (page 273)

Summer #7

SERVES 6

Grilled Bass or Mahimahi with Green Tomato and Watermelon Salsa (page 516)

Fresh Corn Spoon Bread (page 272)

Sautéed zucchini (page 643)

Fall #1
SERVES 4
Spaghetti with Olive and Pine Nut Salsa (page 206)
Steamed Broccoli with Olive Oil and Parmesan (page 574)
Green salad

Fall #2
SERVES 4
Grilled Cheddar and Fennel Sandwiches with Curry Mayo
   (page 294)
Baby Spinach Soup with Croutons (page 124)

Fall #3
SERVES 4
Balsamic-Glazed Pork Chops (page 468)
Baked Sweet Potatoes with Scallions and Cilantro (page 633)
Green salad

Fall #4
SERVES 4
Pan-Glazed Mackerel with Citrus and Soy (page 354)
Sweet-Hot Mustard Green and Avocado Salad (page 174)
Steamed white rice

Fall #5
SERVES 4
Grilled Duck Breast with Spiced Salt Rub (page 533)
Farro Tricolore (page 186)

Fall #6
SERVES 4
Spiced Chicken (page 397)
Steamed Broccoli with Olive Oil and Parmesan (page 574)
Minted Green Salad (page 159)

Fall #7
SERVES 6
Skirt Steak with Cilantro Garlic Sauce (page 445)
Roast sweet potato fries (page 634)
Green salad

Winter #1
SERVES 4
Wiener Schnitzel (page 460)
Steamed small boiling potatoes (page 621)
Cucumber, Mustard, and Dill Salad (page 171)

Winter #2
SERVES 4
Seared Scallops with Brussels Sprouts and Bacon (page 363)
Herbed Jasmine Rice (page 256)
Braised carrots (page 585)

Winter #3
SERVES 4
Blade Steaks with Mushrooms (page 442)
Salt-Baked Potatoes (page 622)
Boiled green beans (page 569)

Winter #4

SERVES 4

Chicken with Black Pepper–Maple Sauce (page 409)
Butternut Squash with Shallots and Sage (page 630)
Sautéed Brussels sprouts (page 579)

Winter #5

SERVES 4

Lamb Chops with Cumin, Cardamom, and Lime (page 484)
Mashed Yuca with Coconut (page 641)
Pan-roasted broccoli (page 575)

Winter #6

SERVES 4

Rice Noodles with Duck and Spicy Orange Sauce (page 244)
Braised broccoli rabe (page 577)

Winter #7

SERVES 4

Creamless Clam Chowder (page 136)
Minted Green Salad (page 159) and crusty bread

Vegetarian Menus

Spring Vegetarian #1
SERVES 8

Tempeh Burgers (page 298)
Panfried Romaine (page 600)
Blackberry Upside-Down Cake (page 732)

Spring Vegetarian #2
SERVES 4 TO 6

Spinach Stracciatella Soup (use vegetable broth or water; page 125)
Herb and Cheese Phyllo Pie (*Tiropita;* page 309)
Artichokes Braised with Garlic and Thyme (page 565)
Rhubarb Crème Brûlée (page 836)

Spring Vegetarian #3
SERVES 4

Easy Carrot Soup with Toasted Pecans (page 114)
Vegetable Casserole with Tofu Topping (page 318)
Spinach Salad with Strawberry Vinaigrette (page 160)
Chocolate Sorbet (page 864)
Brutti-Boni (page 683)

Spring Vegetarian #4
SERVES 4

Asparagus Quiche (page 304)
Shaved fennel salad (page 599)
Spicy Sautéed Dandelion Greens (page 604)
Cardamom Apple Almond Cake (page 719)

Summer Vegetarian #1

SERVES 4

Peach and Tomato Gazpacho (page 109)

Tomato, Goat Cheese, and Onion Tart (page 305)

Green Beans with Crisp Shallots, Chile, and Mint (page 568)

Watermelon Sundae (page 870)

Summer Vegetarian #2

SERVES 4

Smooth Chayote Soup (page 115)

Grilled Zucchini Salad with Purslane and Tomatoes (page 169)

Hummus and Vegetable Lavash Wraps (page 295)

Cornmeal Sugar Cookies (page 689)

Summer Vegetarian #3

SERVES 4 TO 6

Broiled Tofu with Cilantro Pesto (page 327; omit rice)

Spicy Soba Noodles with Lacquered Eggplant (page 239)

Lemon Cakes with Basil Lemon Syrup (page 721)

Summer Vegetarian #4
SERVES 4
- Bulgur-Stuffed Tomatoes, Zucchini, and Bell Peppers (page 321)
- Grilled Eggplant with Spicy Peanut Sauce (page 554)
- Green salad
- Amaretti-Stuffed Peaches (page 822)

Fall Vegetarian #1
SERVES 4
- Chunky Butternut Squash, White Bean, and Tomato Soup (use vegetable broth or water; page 123)
- Mushroom Strudels (page 61)
- Green salad
- Cranberry Almond Crostata (page 790)

Fall Vegetarian #2
SERVES 6
- Fennel, Taleggio, and Cardamom Tart (page 307)
- Wheat Berry Waldorf Salad (page 186)
- Pear Gingerbread Upside-Down Cake (page 731)

Fall Vegetarian #3
SERVES 6
- Curried Lentil Stew with Vegetables (page 288)
- Rice or quinoa
- Roasted cauliflower (page 587)
- Ginger Custards (page 834)

Fall Vegetarian #4
SERVES 4
- Spaghetti with Pecorino Romano and Black Pepper (double recipe; page 206)
- Italian Vegetable Stew (*Ciambotta;* page 332)
- Crusty bread and green salad
- Crumble Cake (page 715)

Winter Vegetarian #1

SERVES 4

Poblano Tortilla Gratin (page 318)
Three-Bean Salad with Cilantro-Chile Dressing (page 191)
Mexican Chocolate Cake (page 728)

Winter Vegetarian #2

SERVES 8

Eggplant Parmesan (page 319)
Sautéed Broccoli Rabe and Peas (double recipe; page 576)
Caramel Cake (page 720)

Winter Vegetarian #3

SERVES 6 TO 8

Roasted Red Peppers with Walnuts and Raisins (page 178)
Roasted Vegetable Panzanella (page 178)
Banoffee Pie (page 776)

Winter Vegetarian #4

SERVES 6 TO 8

Curried Potato and Leek Soup with Spinach (use vegetable stock or water; page 122)
Vegetable Potpie with Cheddar Biscuit Topping (page 320)
Green Leaf Lettuce, Pomegranate, and Almond Salad (page 161)
Frozen Chocolate Peanut Butter Bars with Hot Fudge Sauce (pages 873 and 877)

Holiday Menus

Thanksgiving #1
SERVES 10

Smoked Trout Spread (page 46), with crackers or toasts
Pumpkin Soup with Red Pepper Mousse (page 123)
Simplest Roasted Turkey with Pan Gravy (page 419)
Porcini Onion Stuffing (page 426)
Parsnip-Leek-Potato Mash (double recipe; page 615)
Green Beans with Ginger Butter (page 568)
Shaved Brussels Sprout Slaw with Walnuts and Pecorino (double recipe; page 175)
Caramel Pumpkin Pie (page 773)
Pecan Praline Torte (page 795)

Thanksgiving #2
SERVES 8

Dried Apricots with Goat Cheese and Pistachios (page 43)
Onion and Fennel Bisque (page 121)
Grilled Turkey (page 531)
Pan Gravy (page 419)
Roast Pumpkin with Cheese "Fondue" (page 632)
Garlicky Broccoli Rabe (double recipe; page 576)
Sour Cream Pumpkin Pie (page 774)
Rum-Raisin Apple Pie (page 767)

Cozy, Untraditional Thanksgiving #3

SERVES 8

Bacon and Cheddar Toasts (page 58)
Tuscan Yellow Pepper Soup (page 122)
Cornish Hens with Roasted-Garlic Aïoli (double recipe; page 431)
Wild Rice with Roasted Peppers and Toasted Almonds (page 259)
Roasted Cauliflower, Romaine, and Radicchio Salad (page 176)
Ricotta Tart with Dried Fruit Compote (page 788)
Ginger Honey Cookies (page 683)

Vegetarian Thanksgiving #4

SERVES 6

Roasted Red Peppers with Walnuts and Raisins (page 178)
Fall Vegetables with Broiled Polenta Sticks, Frizzled Onions, and Vegetable Gravy (page 329)
Pumpkin Flan with Spiced Pumpkin Seeds (page 839)
Lattice-Crust Pear Pie (page 769)

Christmas Dinner

SERVES 8

Stone Crab Claws with Parsley Sauce (page 79)
Rosemary Beef Fillet (page 456)
Sautéed Swiss Chard with Onions (double recipe; page 601)
Mashed potatoes (page 621)
Clementine, Olive, and Endive Salad (page 167)
Kiwi-Pomegranate Angel Pies (page 779)
Chocolate Earl Grey Truffles (page 707)

Intimate Christmas Dinner

SERVES 4

Shrimp Gribiche (page 93)
Crisp Roast Duck (page 427)
Green Beans with Ginger Butter (page 568)
Olive Oil–Glazed Potatoes (page 622)
Norwegian Almond Caramel Cake (page 724)

Christmas Breakfast

SERVES 10 TO 12

Mimosas (double recipe; page 23)
Figgy Scones (page 666)
Cowboy Christmas Breakfast (page 657)
Chai-Poached Apricots and Plums
    (double recipe; page 814), with yogurt

Hanukkah

SERVES 8

Celery Root and Potato Latkes (page 592)
Winter Salad (double recipe; page 174)
Striped Bass in Agrodolce (page 346)
Couscous with Dates (double recipe; page 236)
Roasted Carrots with Thyme and Garlic (page 584)
Chocolate Truffle Tart (page 790)

Hanukkah Brunch

SERVES 6

Browned Onion Kugels (page 239)
Rolled Omelet with Arugula–Goat Cheese Filling (page 648)
Clementine, Olive, and Endive Salad (page 167)
Ginger Doughnut Rounds (page 668)
Mexican Hot Chocolate (page 32)

New Year's Eve Cocktail Party

SERVES 12

Ruby Red Sea Breezes (multiply recipe by 6; page 8)
Spicy Cashews (double recipe; page 37)
Hunan Scallion Pancakes (page 55)
Rice-Studded Chinese Meatballs (page 82)
Anchovy Puffs (page 53)
Pork Belly Buns (page 83)
Grilled Chicken Wings with Two Asian Sauces (page 79)
Mini Shrimp Cornets (page 67)

Easter Dinner

SERVES 8

Caviar Tart (page 47)
Grilled Butterflied Leg of Lamb (page 550)
Egg Noodles with Brown Butter and Feta (page 238)
Grilled asparagus (page 567)
Lemon Soufflé (page 852)

Easter Brunch

SERVES 6

Bellinis (page 23)
Glazed Ham with Pineapple Mustard Sauce (page 476)
Baked Eggs with Cheese (page 652)
Green salad
Ambrosia (page 818)
Buttermilk Coffee Cake (page 669)

Passover

SERVES 8

Classic Matzo Ball Soup (page 141)
Oven-Braised Barbecued Brisket (page 459; if necessary, omit Worcestershire sauce and increase cider
    vinegar to ½ cup)
Sautéed Broccoli Rabe and Peas (double recipe; page 576; if necessary, omit peas)
Olive Oil–Glazed Potatoes (double recipe; page 622)
Walnut Date Torte (page 720)

Party Menus

Summer Cocktail Party
SERVES 10 TO 12

Strawberry Frozen Daiquiris (multiply recipe as needed; page 14)

Caipirinhas (multiply recipe as needed; page 24)

Tom Collins (multiply recipe as needed; page 10)

Spicy Cashews (double recipe; page 37) and Marinated Green Olives (double recipe; page 37)

Lobster Salad Cucumber Canapés (page 57)

Crostini (page 40) with Tomato and Basil Topping (page 41)

Wasabi Shrimp Crackers (page 57)

Clams with Ponzu and Panko (page 76)

Sweet-and-Spicy Beef Skewers (page 81)

Chocolate Raspberry Truffles (page 706)

Winter Birthday Party
SERVES 8

Kir Royales (multiply recipe by 8; page 24)

Crostini (page 40) with Chicken Liver, Sage, and Onion Topping (page 42)

Provençal Fish Soup with Croûtes and Saffron Rouille (page 140)

Braised Pork Loin with Prunes (page 474)

Steamed small boiling potatoes (page 621)

Green salad

Chocolate Sour Cream Layer Cake (page 746)

Fourth of July Picnic

SERVES 8

Peach–White Wine Sangria (page 22)

Classic Lemonade (page 29)

Baba Ghanouj (page 44), with pita, chopped tomato, red onion, and Kalamata olives

Prosciutto-wrapped steamed asparagus (page 49)

Grilled Butterflied Leg of Lamb with Hoisin Lime Sauce (page 551)

Peppers Stuffed with Cherry Tomatoes and Basil (page 618)

Cherry Pie (page 771)

Raspberry Chocolate Ice Pops (page 872)

New Year's Day Open House

SERVES 10 TO 12

Sun-Dried Tomato Dip (page 45)

Crostini (page 40) with Chicken Liver, Sage, and Onion Topping (page 42)

Pork and Tomatillo Stew (double recipe; page 469)

White rice

Winter Salad (triple recipe; page 174)

Chockfull Blondies (page 702)

Vanilla ice cream with Butterscotch Sauce (page 878)

Irish Coffee (multiply recipe as needed; page 28)

Fancy Buffet Party

SERVES 10 TO 12

Kir Royales (multiply recipe as needed; page 24)

Planter's Punch (multiply recipe as needed; page 12)

Terrine de Campagne (page 102), with bread, cornichons,
    and mustard

Spicy Cashews (page 37)

Rosemary Beef Fillet (page 456),
    at room temperature

Provençal Tomato Potato Gratin (page 625),
    at room tempertature

Butternut Squash and Creamed Spinach Gratin (page 630)

Roasted Cauliflower, Romaine, and Radicchio Salad (page 176)

Cannoli Roll (page 736)

Dulce de Leche Cheesecake Squares (page 703)

Tea Party
SERVES 6 TO 8

Spiced Milk Tea (*Masala Chai;* multiply recipe as needed; page 32)
  or black tea
French Kisses (multiply recipe as needed; page 24)
Stilton Cheese Puffs (page 52)
Chicken Salad with Grapes and Walnuts (double recipe; page 196)
Creamy Tofu Salad Sandwiches (double recipe; page 298)
Elvis Presley's Favorite Pound Cake (page 717)
Almond Macaroons with Buttercream Filling (page 694)
Truffle Fudge (page 706)

Weekend Entertaining Menus

Spring #1
SERVES 4

Tom Collins (double recipe; page 10)
Caramelized Onion Tartlets (page 55)
Leg of Lamb with Greens (page 497)
Carrot Puree with Kalamata Olives (page 586)
Lemon Crème Brûlée (page 835)

Spring #2
SERVES 6

Strawberry Frozen Daiquiris (double recipe; page 14)
Salt and Pepper Shrimp (page 71)
Mushroom Risotto (page 261)
Green salad
Frozen Apricot Soufflé (page 868)

Late Spring/Early Summer #3
SERVES 8

Mint Juleps (page 19)
Chive and Pine Nut Dip with Sourdough Toasts (page 45)
Slow-Roasted Glazed King Salmon (page 340)
Pureed Peas with Mint Butter (page 617)
Steamed small boiling potatoes (page 621)
Frozen Passion Fruit Meringue Cake (page 876)

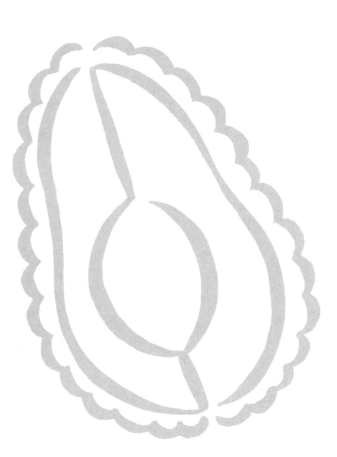

Summer #1
SERVES 4

Summer #2
SERVES 6

Summer #3
SERVES 8

Fall #1

SERVES 4

Gin Rickeys (quadruple recipe; page 9)
Baba Ghanouj (page 44), with warm pita
Roasted Striped Bass with Pistachio Sauce (page 357)
Winter Tabbouleh (page 185)
Pear Fool (page 825)

Fall #2

SERVES 6

French Kisses (page 24)
Marinated Green Olives (page 40)
Roasted Tomato Soup with Parmesan Wafers (page 126)
Osso Buco with Mushroom Sauce (page 462)
Creamy Stone-Ground Grits (page 271)
Green salad
Old-Fashioned Apple Raisin Dumplings (page 811)

Fall #3

SERVES 8

Moscow Mules (quadruple recipe; page 5)
Deviled Crab (page 96)
Oven-Braised Barbecued Brisket (page 459)
Coleslaw (page 581)
Cheddar Buttermilk Biscuits (page 417)
Green salad
Butterscotch Chiffon Pie (page 777)

Winter #1

SERVES 4

Manhattans (double recipe; page 20)
Roasted Grape Relish with Cheddar Crisps (page 51)
Pan-Grilled Duck Paillards (page 428)
Mashed Root Vegetables with Horseradish (page 637)
Garlicky Broccoli Rabe (page 576)
Silky Chocolate-Pudding Cakes (page 727)

Winter #2

SERVES 6

Kir Royales (multiply recipe by 6; page 24)
Beet Chips with Curried Sour Cream (page 43)
Braised Veal Shoulder with Bacon and Thyme (page 462)
Mashed potatoes (page 621)
Boiled green beans (page 569)
Marbled Lemon Curd Cheesecake (page 761)

Winter #3

SERVES 8

Gimlets (quadruple recipe; page 9)
Wasabi Shrimp Crackers (page 57)
Pumpkin Soup with Red Pepper Mousse (page 123)
Rosemary Beef Fillet (page 456)
Yorkshire Pudding (page 456)
Brussels Sprouts with Chestnuts (page 580)
Cucumber, Mustard, and Dill Salad (double recipe; page 171)
Chocolate Soufflé Cake with Orange Caramel Sauce (page 742)

Brunch Menus

Spring/Summer Brunch #1
SERVES 4

Mexican Fruit Coolers (page 30)
Poached Eggs with Tomato Cilantro Sauce (page 653)
Sliced mangoes
Mexican Sweet Buns (*Pan Dulce;* page 674)

Spring/Summer Brunch #2
SERVES 6

Pimm's Cup (multiply recipe by 6; page 25)
Asparagus with Roasted Potatoes and Fried Eggs (page 330)
Oatmeal Wheat Bread (page 671)
Rhubarb Strawberry Pudding Cake (page 726)

Spring/Summer Brunch #3
SERVES 6 TO 8

Fizzy Sour Cherry Lemonade (page 7)
Wild Rice Salad with Smoked Fish and Snap Peas (page 184)
Walnut Meringue Cake with Strawberry Sauce (page 748)

Summer Brunch #4
SERVES 6

Bellinis (page 23)
Ricotta Cornmeal Crêpes with Fresh Corn Topping (page 661)
Green salad
Honeydew Melon in Coconut Milk (page 822)

Fall/Winter Brunch #1
SERVES 4

Mimosas (page 23)
Roasted Butternut Squash and Caramelized Onion Tart (page 306)
Green salad
Rum-Raisin Poached Pears (page 825)

Fall/Winter Brunch #2
SERVES 6

Bloody Marys (page 5)
Baked Eggs with Roasted Vegetable Hash (page 653)
Fresh fruit
Breakfast Jam Cake (page 670) or Orange Raisin Scones (page 665)

Fall/Winter Brunch #3

SERVES 6 TO 8

Kirs (multiply recipe as needed; page 23)
Lemon Soufflé Pancakes (page 658)
Bacon or breakfast sausage
Ambrosia Layer Cake (page 751)

Fall/Winter Brunch #4

SERVES 6

Negronis (quadruple recipe; page 10)
Pain Perdu with Mushrooms and Thyme (page 663)
Frisée and Celery Salad with Toasted Fennel Seed Dressing (page 162)
Red and Green Grape Crisp (page 820)

International Menus

Chinese Feast

SERVES 6

Shrimp and Pork Pot Stickers (page 73)
Chinese Hot-and-Sour Soup (page 149)
Steamed Bass with Ginger and Scallions (page 346)
Red-Cooked Pork Belly (page 479)
Broccoli Spears in Garlic Sauce (double recipe; page 574)
Steamed white rice
Cherries in the Snow (page 844)

Cuban

SERVES 8

Cuban Roast Suckling Pig (page 478)
Yellow Rice (*Arroz Amarillo;* double recipe; page 254)
Black Beans with Garlic, Cumin, and Cilantro (double recipe; page 281)
Twice-Fried Green Plantains (*Tostones;* double recipe; page 618)
Coconut Rum Cake (page 725)

French #1

SERVES 8

    Miniature Camembert Walnut Pastries (page 53)
    Salmon and Scallop Terrine with Frisée Salad (page 99)
    Roasted Pork Chops with Hard Cider Jus (page 466)
    Rutabaga and Carrot Puree (page 636)
    Almond Cream Puff Pastry Galette (page 797)

French #2

SERVES 6

    Mushroom Consommé Topped with Puff Pastry (page 120)
    Confit Duck Legs (page 430)
    Cauliflower Mousse (page 588)
    Green salad
    Opera Cake (page 753)

French #3

SERVES 4

    Shrimp Gribiche (page 93)
    Chicken with Shallots, Garlic, and Vinegar (page 401)
    Potato and Cheese Puree with Horseradish Cream (page 623)
    Roasted Carrots with Thyme and Garlic (page 584)
    Pear and Almond Tart (page 784)

Indian

SERVES 8

    Samosas with Potato and Pea Filling (page 64)
    Lamb Biryani (page 489)
    Zucchini Raita (page 490)
    Banana Tamarind Chutney (page 491)
    Store-bought naan or flatbread
    Pistachio and Cardamom Ice Cream (page 860)

Italian #1
SERVES 4

Mixed olives
Campanelle with Squid, Tomatoes, and Capers (page 211)
Veal Bocconcini with Porcini and Rosemary (page 460)
Green salad
Port-and-Spice-Poached Pears with Granita (page 866)

Italian #2
SERVES 4

Stuffed Artichokes (page 86)
Rabbit Braised in Red Wine (page 437)
Buttered Polenta (page 272)
Sautéed Broccoli Rabe and Peas (page 576)
Fig Crostata (page 791)

Italian #3
SERVES 6

Asparagus Flan with Cheese Sauce (page 85)
Florentine-Style Porterhouse Steaks (page 535)
White Beans with Roasted Tomatoes (page 280)
Tuscan Kale and Ricotta Salata Salad (page 178)
Cherry Gelato (page 862)
Brutti-Boni (page 683)

Italian #4 (Sicilian)
SERVES 8 TO 10

Marinated Green Olives (page 40)
Sicilian Fried Stuffed Rice Balls (*Arancini;* page 104)
Spaghetti with Olive and Pine Nut Salsa (page 206)
Sicilian Tuna (double recipe; page 356)
Cannoli (page 804)
Oranges in Marsala (double recipe; page 817)

Mediterranean

SERVES 6

Taramasalata (page 46)

Greek Egg and Lemon Soup (*Soupa Avgolemono;* page 125)

Grilled Butterflied Leg of Lamb (page 550)

Orzo with Feta and Cherry Tomatoes (page 182)

Grilled Zucchini with Garlic and Lemon (double recipe; page 559)

Yogurt and Brown Sugar Panna Cotta with Grape Gelée (page 842)

Mexican #1

SERVES 4 TO 6

Mexican Shrimp Cocktail (page 92)

Carnitas (page 469)

Pickled Onions (double recipe; from Arepas with Black Beans and Feta, page 62)

Roasted Tomatillo Salsa (page 418)

Warm corn tortillas and sliced avocados

Green Rice (*Arroz Verde;* page 253)

Dulce de Leche Ice Cream (page 857)

Mexican #2

SERVES 8 TO 12

Mexican Black Bean Soup with Ancho Chiles (page 131)

Turkey Mole (page 418)

Steamed white rice or corn tortillas

Chayote with Cilantro, Chile, and Lime (double recipe; page 592)

Steamed white rice

Cheese Flan (page 839)

Middle Eastern

SERVES 6

Dried Apricots with Goat Cheese and Pistachios (page 43)
Lamb in Spiced Yogurt Sauce with Rice and Pita Bread (page 493)
Braised Eggplant with Onion and Tomato (page 597)
Persian Baklava (page 803)

Spanish Tapas

SERVES 6 TO 8

Mussels with Serrano Ham (page 76)
Salt Cod in Tomato Garlic Confit (page 89)
Chicken Empanada with Chorizo, Raisins, and Olives (page 103)
Hot Pepper and Garlic Shrimp (page 93)
Roasted Peppers with Almond-Garlic Bread Crumbs (double recipe; page 617)
Mixed olives and crusty bread
Pumpkin Seed Brittle (page 711)

Thai

SERVES 4 TO 6

Ground Beef Salad with Shallots, Lemongrass, Cilantro, and Mint (page 199) or
    Vegetables with Thai Pork-Chile Dipping Sauce (page 50)
Thai-Style Chicken and Rice Soup (page 142)
Catfish with Red Curry Sauce (page 353)
Foolproof Thai Sticky Rice (double recipe; page 258)
Lychee Coconut Sorbet with Mango and Lime (double recipe; page 864)

Vietnamese

SERVES 4

Vietnamese Summer Rolls (page 94)
Vietnamese Chicken and Pineapple Soup (page 144)
Vietnamese Caramelized Grilled Pork and Rice Noodle Salad (page 201)
Daikon and Carrot Pickle (page 201)
Black Rice Pudding (page 852)

TIPS AND TECHNIQUES

Unless otherwise specified, we tested the recipes with regular table salt. We don't recommend substituting another kind of salt since the amounts when measured by volume differ.

When we call for ground black or white pepper, we mean freshly ground pepper from a pepper mill, not ground pepper from a jar. Like other spices, pepper is far more aromatic and flavorful when freshly ground.

TO MEASURE LIQUIDS AND FLOUR

Use the appropriate measuring cup for each ingredient: measure liquids in glass or clear plastic liquid-measuring cups, and measure dry ingredients in nesting dry-measuring cups (usually made of metal or plastic) that can be leveled off with a knife.

Spoon flour (don't scoop it) into a dry-measuring cup, letting it mound slightly on top, then level it off with the straight edge of a knife. Don't be tempted to tap or shake the cup to level the flour, because that will increase the amount the cup holds.

Do not sift flour before measuring it unless the recipe tells you to. If sifted flour is called for (as it is in many recipes using cake flour), sift the flour before spooning it into a dry-measuring cup. (Many brands say "presifted" on the label; disregard this.)

CHOOSING AND MEASURING PANS

Measure skillets and baking pans across the top, not across the bottom.

Use light-colored metal pans for baking unless otherwise specified. If you use dark metal pans, including nonstick ones, your baked goods will probably brown more and the cooking times may be shorter. Lower the oven temperature 25°F to compensate.

Use nonreactive cookware — stainless steel, glass, or enameled cast iron — when cooking with acidic ingredients. Avoid pure aluminum and uncoated iron, which can impart an unpleasant taste and color to such recipes.

TO TOAST SPICES

Toast whole spices in a dry heavy skillet over moderate heat, stirring, until they are fragrant and a shade darker, usually 3 to 5 minutes.

TO TOAST SEEDS

You can toast most seeds either in a dry heavy skillet (not nonstick) over medium heat or on a baking sheet in a preheated 350°F oven. One exception is sunflower seeds; they are best toasted in the oven. Some seeds, such as mustard seeds, pop when cooked on top of the stove, so it is best to toast them in a skillet with a lid. Be sure to shake the skillet to keep the seeds moving.

TO TOAST NUTS

Spread nuts out on a baking sheet and toast them in the middle of a preheated 350°F oven until they are golden and aromatic, 5 to 15 minutes. If the nuts are dark to begin with, like almonds with skins and hazelnuts, you may need to cut one open to check the interior color.

Recipes using hazelnuts often specify rubbing off any loose skins after toasting. To do this, wrap the nuts in a clean kitchen towel while they are still hot and rub them together to flake off the papery brown skins. Some patches of skin will probably remain on the nuts, but that is not a problem. Occasionally hazelnuts won't part with any of their skin, no matter how much they are rubbed.

TO TOAST COCONUT

Spread the coconut evenly on a baking sheet and toast it in the middle of a preheated 350°F oven, stirring occasionally, until golden, 10 to 12 minutes. Cool it on the pan on a rack, stirring occasionally.

TO MAKE FRESH BREAD CRUMBS

Tear or cut bread into 1-inch pieces and pulse in a food processor or in small batches in a blender until they are coarse or fine crumbs. Because brands of bread vary, it's difficult to give exact equivalents; use the following yields as a guide. (Bread crumbs freeze beautifully, so you may want to make extra.)

- **TO GET 1 CUP COARSE CRUMBS,** use 2 slices of firm white sandwich bread or a 4-inch-long piece of baguette (any tough bottom crust removed).
- **TO GET 1 CUP FINE CRUMBS,** use about 3 slices of firm white sandwich bread or a 5-inch-long piece of baguette (remove any tough bottom crust).

TO MAKE DRY BREAD CRUMBS

Spread fresh bread crumbs on a baking sheet and bake in the middle of a preheated 250°F oven, stirring once, until they are dry and very pale golden, about 10 minutes for fine crumbs, 15 minutes for coarse crumbs. Cool the crumbs on the pan on a rack.

The volume of crumbs shrinks when they are dried.

- **TO GET 1 CUP DRY COARSE CRUMBS,** use 1¼ cups fresh coarse crumbs.
- **TO GET 1 CUP DRY FINE CRUMBS,** use 1⅓ cups fresh fine crumbs.

TO GRATE CHEESE

The volume measure (cups) of grated cheeses can differ depending on a number of variables, including the kind of cheese and its temperature, the choice of grater, and the way the cheese is put into the measuring cup (loosely or firmly). Weight is a more precise measure, but since many people do not have kitchen scales, we usually give just the cup measure. For measures of 1 cup or more, we provide the weight as well, so you know how much you'll need to buy (allow for more if the cheese has an inedible rind). For the recipes in this book, assume, unless we tell you otherwise, that the cheese is cold from the refrigerator (since room-temperature cheese, being slightly softer, will pack down more in the cup).

To coarsely grate firm cheeses such as cheddar and Gruyère, use the large (¼-inch) teardrop-shaped holes of a box grater or other handheld grater, then loosely pack the cheese into dry-measuring cups. The shredding disk of a food processor produces thicker shreds of cheese and can give you a slightly different cup-weight ratio, as can purchased grated cheese.

To finely grate Parmigiano-Reggiano and similar cheeses, use the small (⅛-inch) teardrop-shaped holes (not the ragged-edged holes) of a box grater or other handheld grater, such as a rotary grater, unless otherwise specified. Be aware that rasplike graters (such as Microplane) result in a significantly larger volume because they shave the cheese so fine. Pregrated cheese tends to be denser, and the same weight will yield a lower volume.

TO PREPARE PRODUCE

Wash and dry all produce before you use it. Before chopping herbs, remove the leaves or fronds from the stems and discard the stems (the exception is cilantro, which has tender stems).

To wash greens, submerge them in a large bowl or clean sink full of cold water and agitate them with your hands to loosen any dirt. Lift them from the water and transfer them to a salad spinner. If a noticeable amount of dirt is visible in the wash water, wash the greens again in clean water (spinach, arugula, and basil often need two or three washings). When spinning greens dry in a salad spinner, spin them several times, stopping to pour off the collected water occasionally and redistribute the greens in the basket. Alternatively, you can drain the washed greens well in a colander and then pat them dry with a kitchen towel.

TO PEEL FRESH TOMATOES OR PEACHES

Using a very sharp paring knife and being careful not to cut deeply into the flesh, cut an X through the skin in the bottom of each tomato or peach. Bring a large pot of water to a boil and have an ice bath ready. Working in batches of 2 or 3, lower the tomatoes or peaches one by one into the boiling water with a slotted spoon, or carefully drop them in. Blanch them for 10 seconds, then transfer them to the ice water with the slotted spoon. (Barely ripe or out-of-season tomatoes or peaches will take 15 to 20 seconds.) When they are cool enough to handle, pull or slip off the skins, beginning at the X; use the paring knife to remove any stubborn spots.

TO SEED TOMATOES

Cut each tomato horizontally in half, then squeeze the halves gently, cut sides down, to extract the seeds.

TO HANDLE CHILES

You may want to wear protective gloves when handling chiles. Avoid touching your face, particularly your eyes.

TO ROAST AND PEEL BELL PEPPERS OR POBLANO CHILES

If using a gas stove, lay the bell peppers or chiles on their sides on the burner grates and turn the flames on high. Char the peppers or chiles, turning them with tongs, until the skins are blackened on all sides, 3 to 8 minutes.

If using a (preheated) broiler, put the peppers or chiles on the rack of the broiler pan and broil about 2 inches from the heat, turning them frequently, until the skins are blistered and charred, about 5 minutes for chiles, about 15 minutes for bell peppers.

Transfer the roasted peppers or chiles to a bowl, cover it tightly (to trap the steam), and let them stand until they are cool enough to handle. Peel them, cut off the stems, and remove and discard the seeds and ribs.

TO ZEST CITRUS FRUITS

Remove the colored part of the rind only, avoiding the bitter white pith. For strips, use a vegetable peeler; we prefer the swivel-bladed kind. Peelers vary in how deeply they cut, so some strips may include some white pith. If so, trim it away with a paring knife. For grating zest, we prefer to use a rasplike zester (such as a Microplane), which results in fluffier zest. If you use one, pack the zest to measure it.

TO MELT CHOCOLATE

Coarsely chop the chocolate. Put it in a metal bowl, set the bowl over a saucepan of barely simmering water, and let the chocolate melt, stirring occasionally. Or, put the chocolate in a microwave-safe bowl and microwave it at low to medium power for short intervals (30 seconds or less), stirring after each interval to check the consistency.

TO CLARIFY BUTTER

Cut the butter into 1-inch pieces and melt it in a small heavy saucepan over low heat. Remove the pan from the heat and let stand for 3 minutes. Skim the froth, then slowly pour the butter into a measuring cup, leaving the milky solids in the bottom of the pan (discard them).

TO QUICK-SOAK DRIED BEANS

Put the beans in a saucepan, cover them with cold water by 2 inches, and bring to a boil. Boil for 2 minutes, then remove from the heat, cover, and let the beans soak for 1 hour; drain.

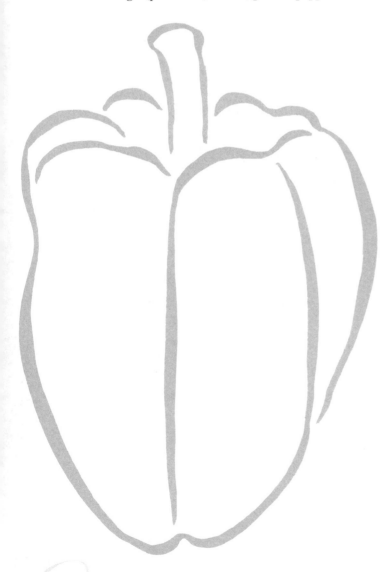

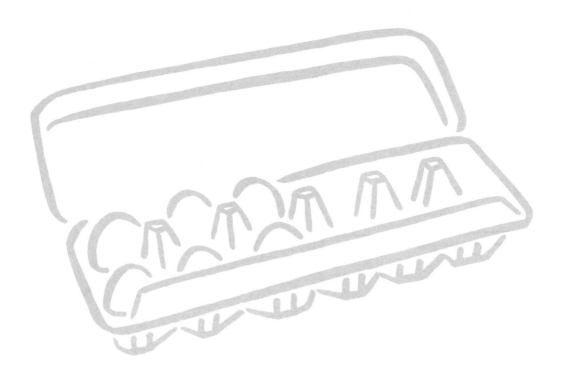

TO HARD-BOIL EGGS

Put the eggs (at least 1 week old) in a heavy saucepan and cover them with cold water by 1½ inches. Partially cover the pan and bring the water to a rolling boil, then reduce the heat to low, cover the pan completely, and cook the eggs for 30 seconds. Remove the pan from the heat and let the eggs stand in the water, covered, for 15 minutes. Transfer the eggs to a colander and run under cold running water for about 5 minutes — this stops the cooking and helps prevent yolk discoloration.

EGG SAFETY

We are all more aware of egg safety these days because salmonella (specifically *Salmonella enteritidis*) can be a problem, even in organic or free-range eggs. The risk of egg-borne salmonella is minimized by proper handling. Keep eggs cold until you cook them unless otherwise specified in the recipe. Wash your hands and any utensils that have come in contact with them. If you are preparing meals for young children, the elderly, pregnant women, or anyone with a compromised immune system, always cook eggs fully, which will kill any bacteria. As an alternative, you may be able to find pasteurized egg products (including eggs in the shell) at some markets. Be aware that pasteurized egg whites do not whip in the same way that unpasteurized eggs do; whipping may take up to three times as long.

GLOSSARY

For information about obtaining the following ingredients, see Sources.

ALEPPO PEPPER — These dried flakes of a Syrian chile are relatively mild compared to regular red pepper flakes but give depth and a fruity sweetness to many Middle Eastern dishes. **MARAS** or **URFA PEPPER FLAKES** are a good alternative; you could also use dried red pepper flakes or paprika.

AMCHOOR (GROUND DRIED MANGO) — Green (unripe) mango is a popular souring agent in India; it has a sweet-tart complexity. To make *amchoor,* green mangoes are dried in the sun and then ground to a fine, slightly fibrous powder.

ANNATTO SEEDS — Also called achiote ("ah-chee-oh-teh"), brick-red annatto seeds, harvested from a tropical shrub, lend a subtle, earthy flavor and aroma to many South American dishes. They have been used as a natural food coloring and a dye for centuries. The seeds are sold whole, crushed, or in a paste. Avoid dull brown seeds; they are old. Keep annatto seeds in a cool, dry, dark place.

ARAME ("ah-*rah*-may") — This brown sea vegetable, which grows in deep waters, is similar to **HIJIKI** in flavor and texture, but it is sweeter, milder, and softer. It's also known as sea oak, because its large, thick, irregular fronds look like oak leaves.

Dried arame is sold in thin brown strips that turn black when cooked.

AREPA FLOUR ("ah-*reh*-pa") — *Arepa* flour is made from corn (usually white but sometimes yellow) that has been dried, cracked, precooked with steam, pressed into flakes, and ground. It is used extensively in Venezuela and Colombia for the round corn cakes called *arepas*. Unlike Mexican masa, it is not treated with mineral lime, and it has a more neutral, less earthy taste. Store *arepa* flour in doubled sealable plastic bags in the refrigerator.

ASIAN CHILE PASTE — Lots of different Asian chile pastes are available; they vary in thickness, but they are all hot, so use them sparingly. Once opened, jars of these pastes keep for about a month, stored in the refrigerator. Some pastes come in cans; if that's what you find, transfer the paste to a small jar and refrigerate it.

ASIAN CHILE SAUCE — The seasonings in this sauce — a blend of chiles, vinegar, salt, and sugar that may also include tomato, dried shrimp, garlic, and/or ginger — depend on the country of origin, and the sauces range from mildly to very hot and from thin to thick. In general, Southeast Asian chile sauces are sweeter and more garlicky than Chinese and Korean ones. A good all-purpose chile sauce is Sriracha, named for the town in southern Thailand where it was first produced. It is hot but not as hot as SAMBAL OELEK. Sriracha often comes in a handy squirt bottle; store it and other chile sauces in the refrigerator, where they will keep indefinitely.

BAHARAT — This Middle Eastern and North African spice mixture typically includes allspice, cinnamon, clove, cumin, MARAS PEPPER FLAKES, and black pepper, but the versions can be as varied as the merchants who sell them (there are about a hundred of them in Istanbul's spice bazaar). It's used in tagines and couscous, and with grilled or roasted meats and fish.

BORLOTTI BEANS, DRIED — *Borlotti* is the Italian name for cranberry beans, and the beans have been cultivated in the United States since Colonial times. The many varieties range in color from ivory speckled with pale red to tan splashed and streaked with maroon; when cooked, the beans turn an unexciting brown but have a wonderful meaty flavor.

CHAYOTE ("chai-*oh*-teh") — Also called *mirliton* (in Louisiana) and *christophene* (in the Caribbean), chayote is a member of the enormous gourd/squash family. It has crisp, mild flesh like that of a cucumber or very firm squash and is about the size and shape of a pear. Although chayote is usually cooked, it can be eaten raw in salads. It is sometimes peeled, but that is not always necessary.

CHILE GARLIC PASTE — Spicy seasoning pastes are used in many parts of Asia and Indonesia. A brand that we like is Lan Chi Chili Paste with Garlic.

CHILES

Ancho — The dried form of the poblano chile, this is the most commonly used chile in Mexico. Its name means "wide" or "broad," which describes its shoulders. Brick red to dark mahogany in color, it is wrinkled and medium-hot to hot, with a complex, sweet, raisiny flavor. Look for anchos that are pliable and aromatic.

Chipotle — When cherry-red jalapeños are smoke-dried, they are called chipotles ("chi-*pote*-lehs"); the name comes from the Aztec *chilli poctli*, meaning "smoked chile." Their ripeness in their former incarnation helps explain the sweetness underneath the savoriness, and the smokiness partially obscures their heat. They are sold dried as well as canned in a tomato-based adobo sauce, which takes their flavor in a different, more piquant direction. After using part of a can of chipotles in adobo, transfer the remaining portion to a glass jar and store it in the refrigerator; it will keep almost indefinitely.

Chipotle mora — These smoke-dried ripe jalapeños, which are smaller than chipotles, are commonly found on tables in central and northern Veracruz.

Guajillo ("gwa-*hee*-yo") — This shiny, burgundy-colored dried chile has mild to medium heat and a flavor that is rather direct, tart, and just a bit smoky. Elongated and tapering to a point, it is sold in a variety of sizes but is usually 4 to 6 inches long and an inch to an inch and a half across.

Mulato — This large, fleshy dried chile resembles an ancho but is slightly darker and has a full-bodied, moderately hot flavor.

Pasilla ("pah-*see*-yah") — *Pasilla* means "little raisin" in Spanish, a reference to the dark brown color and wrinkled texture of this dried chile. About 5 or 6 inches long and three quarters of an inch to an inch and a half across, it is medium-hot to hot and has a deep, complex flavor.

CHINESE BLACK VINEGAR — Made from grains including wheat, millet, and sorghum, this vinegar is often compared to balsamic vinegar, but its flavor is a bit more rustic. Quality varies widely. Gold Plum brand, produced in the city of Chinkiang, on China's eastern coast, is considered to be the best. It's made from glutinous rice and malt, then aged for several years. The label has a distinctive yellow design, but look closely — many competitors have mimicked it.

CHINESE LONG BEANS — Also known as yard-long beans or snake beans, these are not simply overgrown green beans; they're actually a subspecies of Southern field peas. They are harvested young, while they are pencil-thin, supple, and about a foot and half long. They are denser in texture than green beans, and their flavor is more like that of fresh black-eyed peas.

CHINESE MUSTARD — Made from mustard seeds, one of the world's oldest spices, this condiment is pungent and fiery.

CHINESE RICE WINE — Made from fermented glutinous rice, millet, and yeast, this alcoholic beverage is usually aged for ten years or more and is used for drinking as well as for marinades and sauces. Shaoxing is China's most renowned rice wine; it's been made for more than two thousand years. Chinese rice wine is drier than sake, the Japanese rice wine, which can be substituted in many recipes. Medium-dry sherry and Scotch are other good substitutes.

CHINESE SAUSAGES — These dried sausages (known as *lop chong*) are similar to **CHORIZO** and andouille, which share an intensely porky flavor. Chinese sausages are milder, though, and slightly sweet. Recipes for them vary, so, if possible, taste before you buy.

CHORIZO — *See* **MEXICAN CHORIZO** and **SPANISH CHORIZO**.

CHOY SUM — According to the vegetable authority Elizabeth Schneider, *choy sum* can mean three different things. Most commonly, it refers to a small, white-stemmed, yellow-flowering plant that resembles (but is different from) bok choy. The term can also mean the tender central stalks and small leaves of any plant in the choy family, and it is the southern Chinese (especially Hong Kong) name for *yau choy*, which is a denser, more assertive green that's similar to Chinese broccoli.

CREMA — This tangy cultured cream from Mexico and Central America can be thin or almost as thick as crème fraîche, which is usually a good substitute.

CURRY LEAVES — Spicy and citrusy, these dark green, aromatic fresh leaves (often sold on the stem) from a small deciduous tree are widely used in the cooking of southern India. Sealed in a plastic bag, they will keep for up to 2 weeks in the refrigerator or for about a month in the freezer. The dried leaves can sometimes be found in ethnic markets, but they are nothing like their fresh counterpart.

DASHI, INSTANT — This is the commercial version of the subtle sea stock made with **KOMBU** (dried kelp) and **DRIED BONITO FLAKES** that is used extensively in Japanese cooking.

DENDÊ OIL — This orange oil is made from the nuts of the dendê palm, brought to Bahia, in eastern Brazil, from West Africa by slave traders. Although it's now used throughout Brazil and Africa, *dendê* remains especially popular in Bahia, where it's prized for its silky, nutty richness and brilliant hue. (Like all tropical oils, *dendê* has a

high saturated-fat content, so it's best consumed in moderation.) *Dendê*'s high smoke point makes it perfect for deep-frying fritters and sautéing chicken and vegetables; it's also added to finished dishes as a condiment, much as Italians use olive oil.

DRIED BONITO FLAKES (*katsuobushi*) — Paper-thin shavings of dried bonito (a fish related to mackerel and tuna) have been used as a smoky-salty seasoning in Japan since the fifteenth century. Along with KOMBU, dried bonito is an integral component of *dashi*, the simple sea stock that is the basis of many Japanese dishes. Dried bonito flakes come in cellophane packages. Stored in an airtight container in a cool, dry, dark place, they will keep almost indefinitely.

DULCE DE LECHE ("*dool*-sey deh *leh*-chey") — Argentineans and Uruguayans both claim their countries invented this sweetener, but in all likelihood it originally came from Spain or Italy centuries ago, and similar products exist throughout Latin America. It's made by slowly cooking down sweetened milk into a gooey, caramel-like confection; that long, slow evaporation, because of the amount of liquid involved, is what differentiates dulce de leche from caramel. Sodium bicarbonate is added to commercial versions to prevent coagulation of proteins, and corn syrup is mixed in for sheen and to prevent crystallization.

DULSE FLAKES — These are flakes made from the dramatic reddish purple, ribbonlike fronds of dulse that grow in rocky crannies along the northern coasts of the Atlantic and Pacific Oceans. Considered a red sea vegetable, dulse is popular in Ireland, Iceland, and Atlantic Canada. (One Nova Scotia miniature variety is marketed as Sea Parsley.) Crisp, almost leathery dulse can be eaten raw or cooked.

FARRO — Also known as emmer wheat (*Triticum dicoccum*), this was the staple grain that fueled the Roman Empire. It has a nutty, pleasant chewiness and is rich in protein and vitamins.

FENUGREEK SEEDS — Fenugreek seeds are from a legume native to southeastern Europe and western Asia. The plant's Latin name, *Trigonella foenum-graecum* ("Greek hay"), is a clue that it was livestock fodder in the ancient world, and that is still true today. The hard, angular, tan seeds are herbaceous, and the flavor and aroma are also reminiscent of India. The seeds are used in chutneys and Indian pickles, as well as in various spice blends, dals, and curries. They're also a component of the Ethiopian spice mixture called *berbere*, and in Turkey and the Republic of Georgia, they're used in stews and other dishes.

FERMENTED BLACK BEANS — Not the turtle beans you see in black bean soup or burritos, these are black soybeans, also known as Chinese black beans, that have been steamed and then fermented with salt and spices, especially ginger. They come in plastic packages; after opening them, transfer them to a tightly sealed jar or doubled sealable plastic bags (they are very pungent) and store them in a cool, dark place or the freezer. They'll keep almost indefinitely.

FIDEO — *Fideo* means "noodle" in Spanish. In Spain, *fideos* are short noodles that are used as an alternative to rice; in Mexico, the term refers to vermicelli.

FLEUR DE SEL — The most famous sea salt from France's Brittany region, fleur de sel adds not just flavor but also a spiky crunch to food. As opposed to *sel gris*, which acquires its distinctive color when the salt crystals sink to the gray earth at the bottom of the salt ponds, fleur de sel consists of lightweight white crystals that float to the ponds' surface and are skimmed off. Because of its relative scarcity, fleur de sel is expensive, but a little goes a long way; it's generally reserved for finishing a dish.

GALANGAL — This rhizome, cultivated throughout Southeast Asia, Indonesia, and India, resembles ginger but is thicker and pinkish near the base. Although its flavor is like that of young ("spring") ginger, it is more piquant, with notes of pepper and cardamom, and more fragrant. Galangal is sold fresh or frozen; it's also available dried (in slices), but we don't recommend the dried. Fresh galangal keeps in a sealable plastic bag in the refrigerator for about 2 weeks and can be frozen for up to 3 months.

GARAM MASALA — This classic northern India ground spice blend (*garam* means "warming," *masala* means "spices") varies from household to household, but it always includes spices that "heat" the body according to the ancient tenets of ayurvedic medicine. A typical blend might include cardamom, cloves, black peppercorns, black cumin, cinnamon, nutmeg, and mace.

GREEN WHEAT — The immature (green) hard wheat (*Triticum turgidum* var. *durum*) known as *farīk* in Egypt is harvested just as the leaves begin to turn yellow and the grains are soft and creamy; the grains are then dried and roasted, which gives them a subtle smoky flavor. Green wheat is used in pilafs and added to soups, stews, and meat dishes.

GUANCIALE — Similar to pancetta in flavor, *guanciale* ("gwan-*cha*-leh") is pork jowl that is cured but not smoked. It has a higher proportion of fat than pancetta, enriching whatever it is cooked with.

HALVAH — This term refers to a wide variety of confections in the Middle East, central Asia, and India. It's often made of ground semolina or sesame seeds, and flavorings may include honey, nuts, dates, or coffee.

HARISSA — This searingly hot chile sauce is common to North Africa, especially Tunisia. It is used both in cooking and as a condiment. An opened jar keeps in the refrigerator almost indefinitely. Some harissa comes in cans; after using, transfer the sauce to a small jar and refrigerate it.

HIJIKI — This calcium- and iron-rich sea vegetable, with its black spaghetti-thin fronds, grows along the coasts of Japan, China, and Korea. Dried, it's used in vegetable dishes, soups, and a tealike infusion in Japan and China.

KAFFIR LIME LEAVES — These glossy bright green leaves (sometimes called *bai makroot*) give many Southeast Asian dishes a distinctive citrus tang and floral aroma. Fresh leaves are becoming more readily available, because they are now grown in Florida and California. They keep for about a week refrigerated in a sealable plastic bag and can be frozen for months. The leaves are also available dried, but we don't recommend them; they do not deliver the fragrance and flavor of fresh (or frozen) leaves, and they can't be thinly sliced.

KETJAP MANIS — This dark, sweet, thick soy sauce (also spelled *kecap manis*) flavored with star anise and garlic is used as an ingredient in Malay and Indonesian cooking and as a table condiment.

KIMCHI — This flavoring staple of the Korean kitchen, pickled fermented cabbage seasoned with lots of garlic and red chile, is spicy-hot and pungent.

KOMBU — This salty-sweet dried brown sea vegetable (kelp), harvested mainly around the northern Japanese island of Hokkaido, is renowned as a flavor enhancer, which is why it's long been used as a base for the sea stock called *dashi*. In 1908, Japanese chemist Kikunae Ikeda discovered that kombu has a high concentration of monosodium glutamate (MSG), and he isolated the strange, savory, almost meaty taste sensation he called *umami*, perhaps best translated as "richness" or "deliciousness." (*Umami* is also present in various fermented foods, including soy sauce, wine, and cheese.) All types of kombu are several yards long, so they're sold in different lengths that are easily cut with scissors and folded into cellophane packages. Don't wash off the white salt residue that coats kombu; simply wipe it lightly with a damp cloth or paper towel before using. As with any dried product, humidity is detrimental; keep kombu tightly wrapped in plastic or in an airtight container in a cool, dry, dark place, where it will keep for up to a year.

LEMONGRASS — A dramatic tropical grass with long blade-shaped leaves, lemongrass gives a clean citrus aroma and flavor to the cuisines of Southeast Asia. Only the lower 6 inches or so of the interior stalks are used; before slicing, remove the dry, fibrous outer layers (use them, along with the tops, for making tea or stock). Lemongrass is generally used fresh (sliced paper-thin) or chopped fine and pounded into pastes; avoid dried lemongrass. The herb keeps, wrapped in plastic, in the refrigerator for up to 2 weeks; it can also be frozen for several months.

LILY BUDS, DRIED — Called *jin zhen* ("golden needles") in Chinese, these are actually the long, thin, unopened flowers, not buds, of a type of daylily. They have a slightly fuzzy, velvety texture and earthy sweetness; shredded, they are used in Chinese soups and vegetable dishes.

LIME PICKLE — This popular Indian condiment is made from whole or chopped limes that are pickled in a spicy brine; it can be fiery hot, sour and hot, or sweet and mellow.

MARAS PEPPER FLAKES — These mildly hot, brightly flavored pepper flakes are an essential pantry item for cooks in Turkey and the Middle East. **URFA PEPPER FLAKES** can be substituted, as can dried red pepper flakes or paprika.

MEXICAN CHOCOLATE — Dark coarse-ground Mexican chocolate is whipped with hot milk or water for hot chocolate or ground with spices for a classic *mole* sauce.

MEXICAN CHORIZO — Unlike **SPANISH CHORIZO**, which is a cured sausage, this is a fresh pork sausage, crumbly and rich with chiles, which must be cooked before it is eaten. It is not generally a good substitute for the Spanish version.

MIRIN — This syrupy, golden Japanese cooking wine, made from glutinous rice, adds sweetness and flavor to many dishes. Look for *hon-mirin* (naturally brewed) rather than *aji-mirin*, which contains additives such as corn syrup and salt. Mirin keeps for months in a cool, dry, dark place.

MISO — The fermented soybean pastes called miso are a protein-rich staple of Japanese and Korean kitchens, used in dressings, soups, sauces, marinades, and grilled dishes. Miso comes in various strengths and colors. White miso (*shiro miso*), which is actually pale yellow or golden, is the mellowest; yellow miso (*shinshu miso*), which ranges from pale yellow to yellowish brown, is the most versatile; and the darkest, headiest miso, *hatcho miso*, which looks like chocolate fudge, is pungent and almost meaty in flavor. The lighter-flavored misos are all-purpose. Use stronger-flavored misos only when they are specifically called for. Miso keeps in the refrigerator for several weeks.

MUSTARD SEEDS — There are three common types of mustard seeds: black, brown, and yellow. The colors refer to the hulls; inside, all three are pale yellow. Black seeds are the hottest; yellow, the mildest; and brown are in between. True black seeds are difficult to find; brown seeds, most suitable for high-yield harvesting, are often labeled "black mustard seeds." Mustard seeds should be kept in a cool, dry, dark place or in the freezer. In very traditional Indian recipes, we don't substitute yellow mustard seeds for brown ones, but in more generic recipes, it's fine to substitute one for the other.

NORI — This dried green sea vegetable is used to wrap sushi and is crumbled or shredded for garnish. It comes in cellophane packages of large flat sheets, strips, or broken-up pieces. Nori should always be toasted until crisp before using; otherwise, it is tough and flavorless. Many brands now come already toasted and are labeled as such. Tightly wrapped and stored in a cool, dry, dark place, nori keeps almost indefinitely. In Britain, nori is called laver (Latin for "water plant") and is used in bread and cakes. There, unlike in Japan, where it's dried in sheets, it is sold either wet and fresh from the sea or washed well, pulped, and pureed.

ORGEAT ("*or*-zat") — This sweet, almond-flavored syrup, originally made from barley, is primarily used today for flavoring cocktails such as the mai tai.

PICKLED GINGER — Paper-thin, translucent slices of peeled ginger pickled in salt, sugar, and vinegar are used primarily as a condiment for sushi. The ginger ranges in color from beige to delicate pink. It comes in small glass jars, plastic containers found in the refrigerated case, or vacuum-packed packages on the shelves of Japanese markets. Do not confuse it with the bright red pickled slivered ginger called *kizami shoga*, or *beni shoga*, which is salty and pungent. Kept in the refrigerator, pickled ginger lasts almost indefinitely.

PIMENTÓN (SPANISH SMOKED PAPRIKA) — In the remote Extremadura region of Spain, deep-flavored paprika chiles aren't dried in the sun, as they are in Hungary, but roasted over smoldering oak fires before being ground to a velvety powder. We like La Chinata brand, which comes in three strengths — sweet, bittersweet, and hot.

POMEGRANATE MOLASSES — This thick, dark syrup made from pomegranate juice carries a concentrated boost of tart, fruity flavor. It is used in Middle Eastern and Indian cuisines. It keeps indefinitely in a cool, dry, dark place.

QUESO FRESCO ("*keh*-so *fres*-co") — Mild and salty, this crumbly fresh cow's-milk cheese from Mexico and elsewhere in Latin America is similar to ricotta salata (which can be substituted), not creamy like young goat cheese or briny like feta.

Because it's relatively low in fat, it doesn't melt; it softens into a dish, imparting a gentle richness. The terms *queso fresco* and *queso blanco* are often used interchangeably; almost every country in Latin America has a different name for the cheese, depending on how mature (firm) it is. *Queso fresco* keeps in the refrigerator for about a week.

RAS EL HANOUT — The Arabic name of this sophisticated Moroccan blend of twenty or so spices means "the best the shop has to offer," and the exotic versions you are likely to find in North Africa may include ash berries, chufa nuts, grains of paradise, and dried rosebuds. It's used in lamb, game, and rice dishes as well as in couscous.

SAMBAL OELEK — This Indonesian chile sauce, used as a condiment throughout Southeast Asia, is thin in consistency yet coarse, since it includes the seeds from the chiles. Red to orange and very hot, it comes in a jar and keeps indefinitely in the refrigerator. If you can't find *sambal oelek*, any other nonsweet Asian chile sauce will work.

SICHUAN PEPPERCORNS — Unrelated to black and white peppercorns, this aromatic, tongue-tingling spice, which comes from south-central China, is made from the dried pods of the prickly ash; inferior brands include the seeds too. It is different from the "Szechwan seasoning" or "Szechwan-style pepper blend" (neither of which contains Sichuan peppercorns) sometimes found in supermarket spice racks. Until recently banned from import by the U.S. Department of Agriculture because of the small chance that they may carry a canker destructive to citrus trees, Sichuan peppercorns are becoming increasingly easy to find.

SPANISH CHORIZO — This famous rust-red cured Spanish sausage is made from pork, garlic, and a generous quantity of Spanish smoked paprika. Do not substitute MEXICAN CHORIZO, which is a fresh pork sausage. Spanish chorizo keeps for up to 6 months at room temperature (scrape off any mold that forms) or in the refrigerator.

SUMAC — A Middle Eastern spice, sumac comes from the funky-tart berries of the Sicilian, or elm-leafed, sumac tree. The berries are dried and ground to a purplish red powder. Especially essential to Lebanese cuisine, sumac is used as an acid, to brighten other flavors. A key ingredient in the spice blend called *za'atar*, it's also used in fattoush, seafood, lamb, yogurt, and vegetable dishes.

TAMARIND — Tamarind's complex fruity-sour taste has made it a staple in the cuisines of India, Southeast Asia, the Caribbean, and Latin America, where it is used as an acid, much as we use lemon or lime. The pulp found in the long, reddish brown seedpods comes in several forms; most common are pliable pressed blocks of pulp and a smooth, jellylike concentrate that comes in a jar. Tamarind trees, which can reach a height of nearly eighty feet, are indigenous to eastern Africa but grow in tropical climates all over the world. To use a block of tamarind pulp, break off a chunk, soften it in warm water, and force it through a sieve; discard the fibers and seeds and use the collected brown liquid or puree. Once you have opened tamarind blocks, double-bag them in sealable plastic bags and store in a cool, dry, dark place. Keep the concentrate in the refrigerator.

TASSO — This traditional Cajun seasoning meat (its name comes from a Cajun-French corruption of the Spanish word *tasajo*, meaning "smoked meat") is usually highly spiced, heavily smoked pork, but it may be beef or even turkey. It adds intense flavor to jambalayas, gumbos, and other Cajun dishes.

THAI CURRY PASTE — Pungent, complex Southeast Asian curry pastes are categorized by color as well as heat. The two we use most often are red curry pastes, which are highly versatile, and green curry pastes, which are more herbal in flavor and generally hotter. Store-bought curry pastes come in jars, plastic tubs, or cans. After opening them, keep them in the freezer (transfer them from their jars or cans to plastic containers) or in the refrigerator (adding a thin film of vegetable oil will make them last longer; pour off the oil before you use the paste). Refrigerated or frozen, curry pastes keep almost indefinitely.

THAI SHRIMP PASTE — Pungent blocks of shrimp paste add a savory, not fishy, depth to all sorts of Asian dishes. The Thai shrimp paste called *ga-pi* is essentially interchangeable with the Malaysian one called *blacan* (the word is sometimes spelled *belacan* or *blacang*, but it's always pronounced "*blah*-chan").

TOMATILLOS — These tart fruits, native to Mexico and Guatemala, are sometimes referred to as Mexican green tomatoes, but they are only distantly related to backyard beefsteaks. When fresh, tomatillos are enclosed in papery husks; pull these off before you use the fruit and rinse the tomatillos under warm water. Husked whole tomatillos are also available canned.

URAD DAL — Commonly called black lentils but more closely related to mung beans, these dried beans are also known as *urd* or black gram beans.

You'll see them in the market in three forms: whole (about the size of a BB), with black skins; split, with their skins; and split, without their skins, when they are ivory in color.

URFA PEPPER FLAKES — Like MARAS PEPPER FLAKES, these warm, darkly sweet pepper flakes are essential to many Middle Eastern dishes. One can be substituted for the other, as can dried red pepper flakes or paprika.

WASABI — This pungent green rhizome is often called Japanese horseradish, but it is not related to true horseradish. Most of what's sold in this country is ground dried horseradish with or without ground mustard and sometimes a bit of true wasabi. Wasabi comes in powder or paste form. The powder is mixed with water much as dry mustard is; let it sit for about 10 minutes to allow the flavor to bloom. True wasabi is slowly becoming available here; it is slightly sweeter and more herbal than our "wasabi."

SOURCES

*To contact specific sources,
see the directory on page 936.*

INGREDIENTS

ALEPPO PEPPER — Middle Eastern markets, specialty foods shops, Kalustyan's, and Penzeys Spices

ALMOND OIL — Some supermarkets and Kalustyan's

ALMOND PASTE — Specialty foods shops, many supermarkets, and New York Cake & Baking Distributors

AMARETTI (Italian almond macaroons) — Italian markets and Formaggio Kitchen

AMCHOOR (ground dried mango) — Indian markets and Kalustyan's

ANNATTO (ACHIOTE) SEEDS — Latino markets, some supermarkets, and Penzeys Spices

APRICOTS, DRIED CALIFORNIA — Specialty foods shops, natural foods stores, the Apricot Farm, and Nuts Online

ARAME — Asian markets, natural foods stores, and Eden Foods

AREPA FLOUR — Latino markets, some supermarkets, and Amigo Foods

BACON — Benton's Smoky Mountain Country Hams and Nueske's

BAHARAT — Middle Eastern markets, Formaggio Kitchen, and Kalustyan's

BLACK BEANS, FERMENTED — Asian markets and Uwajimaya

BLACK VINEGAR, CHINESE — Asian markets and Asia Foods

BONITO FLAKES, DRIED (*katsuoboshi*) — Japanese markets, Chefshop, and Uwajimaya

BORLOTTI BEANS — Italian markets, Chefshop, and Rancho Gordo

BUFFALO, TENDERLOIN STEAKS, AND GROUND BUFFALO — Butcher shops and Wild Idea Buffalo Company

CANDIED FRUIT (including pear and citron) — Chefshop and Kalustyan's

CANDIED ORANGE PEEL — Chefshop and Kalustyan's

CAPER BERRIES, BOTTLED — Specialty foods shops, some supermarkets, and Chefshop

CAPERS, SALT-PACKED — Specialty foods shops and Chefshop

CARDAMOM PODS — Indian markets, some supermarkets, Kalustyan's, and Penzeys Spices

CASHEWS, RAW — Natural foods stores and Kalustyan's

CAVIAR ALTERNATIVE — Cavi-Art

CHAYOTE — Latino markets, specialty produce markets, and many supermarkets

CHESTNUTS, BOTTLED — Specialty foods shops and Kalustyan's

CHILE PASTE, ASIAN — Asian markets and specialty foods shops

CHILE POWDER
Indian red — Indian markets, some Asian markets, and Kalustyan's
pure (such as New Mexico) — Many supermarkets, specialty food shops, and Kalustyan's

CHILES
ají dulce — Latino markets and some supermarkets
ancho — Specialty foods shops, many supermarkets, Adriana's Caravan, MexGrocer, and Penzeys Spices
chipotle, ground dried — Mexican markets, many supermarkets, Kalustyan's, and Penzeys Spices
chipotles in adobo, canned — Mexican markets, many supermarkets, Kalustyan's, and MexGrocer
chipotle mora — Mexican markets and Adriana's Caravan
guajillo — Mexican markets, many supermarkets, Adriana's Caravan, Chefshop, MexGrocer, and Penzeys Spices
mulato — Mexican markets, Adriana's Caravan, Kalustyan's, and MexGrocer
New Mexico, dried — Mexican markets, Adriana's Caravan, and Chef Shop
pasilla — Mexican markets, Amigo Foods, and MexGrocer
Thai, fresh (green or red) — Southeast Asian markets, specialty produce markets, and Temple of Thai

CHINESE LONG BEANS — Asian markets and Melissa's/World Variety Produce

CHINESE SAUSAGE, SWEET *(lop cheong)* — Asian markets, Temple of Thai, and Uwajimaya

CHOCOLATE, MEXICAN — Mexican and other Latino markets, many supermarkets, and MexGrocer

CHORIZO
Mexican — Mexican and other Latino markets and some supermarkets
Spanish — Latino markets, specialty foods shops, many supermarkets (look for Palacio or Goya brand), La Tienda, and the Spanish Table

CHOY SUM — Asian markets, specialty produce markets, and farmers markets

CIPOLLINI — Italian markets, specialty produce markets, and farmers markets

CITRON *See* Candied fruit

CORN HUSKS, DRIED — Latino markets and Mexgrocer

CRAB BOIL — Some supermarkets, Cajun Grocer, and Zatarain's

CRAWFISH TAIL MEAT — Seafood shops and Louisiana Crawfish Company

CREMA — Mexican and other Latino markets and La Tienda

CURRY LEAVES — Indian and other Asian markets and Kalustyan's

CURRY PASTE, THAI (green or red) — Asian markets, many supermarkets, specialty foods shops, Temple of Thai, and Uwajimaya

DASHI, INSTANT (*hon dashi*) — Japanese markets, Asia Foods, and Uwajimaya

DENDÊ (PALM) OIL — Brazilian markets, West African markets, and Kalustyan's

DUCK
breasts, Moulard (also called magrets) and Muscovy — Butcher shops, specialty foods shops, and D'Artagnan
legs (confit and fresh) — Butcher shops, specialty foods shops, and D'Artagnan

Pekin (Long Island) — Butcher shops, some supermarkets, and D'Artagnan

DUCK FAT, RENDERED — Specialty foods shops and D'Artagnan

DULCE DE LECHE — Latino markets, many supermarkets, and Amigo Foods

DULSE FLAKES — Asian markets, natural foods stores, and Maine Coast Sea Vegetables

EPAZOTE, DRIED — Latino markets and Penzeys Spices

ESPRESSO POWDER, INSTANT — Supermarkets and the Baker's Catalogue

FARRO — Italian markets, natural foods stores, Anson Mills, and Formaggio Kitchen

FENUGREEK SEEDS — Indian markets, specialty foods shops, Kalustyan's, and Penzeys Spices

FIDEOS — Some supermarkets and La Tienda

FIVE-SPICE POWDER, CHINESE — Asian markets, specialty foods shops, and Penzeys Spices

FLEUR DE SEL — Specialty foods shops, La Cuisine, and SaltWorks

GALANGAL, FRESH OR FROZEN — Southeast Asian markets, specialty produce markets, Temple of Thai, and Uwajimaya

GARAM MASALA — Indian markets, Kalustyan's, and Penzeys Spices

GINGER, PICKLED — Japanese markets, many supermarkets, Sushi Foods Co., and Uwajimaya

GOAT (shoulder, neck, and leg) — Nicky USA, Inc., and halal markets

GORGONZOLA DOLCE — Cheese shops, Artisanal Premium Cheese, and Murray's Cheese Shop

GRAPESEED OIL — Specialty foods shops, many supermarkets, and Chefshop

GREEN WHEAT (*farīk*) — Natural foods shops and Kalustyan's

GRITS, STONE-GROUND — Specialty foods shops, Anson Mills, Bob's Red Mill Natural Foods, and Hoppin' John's

GUANCIALE — Italian markets, Niman Ranch, Salumeria Biellese, and Salumi Artisan Cured Meats

HALVAH — Middle Eastern markets, natural foods stores, some supermarkets, and Kalustyan's

HARISSA — Middle Eastern markets, specialty foods shops, and Kalustyan's

HIBISCUS FLOWERS, DRIED (*flor de Jamaica*) — Latino and Caribbean markets, natural foods stores, Kalustyan's, and MexGrocer

HIJIKI — Natural foods stores, Asian markets, and Eden Foods

HOG CASINGS — Butcher shops and the Sausage Maker, Inc.

HOT SAUCE
habanero — Specialty foods shops, some supermarkets, and Mo Hotta Mo Betta
Scotch bonnet — Specialty foods shops, some supermarkets, and Mo Hotta Mo Betta

JAGGERY SUGAR — Indian markets and Kalustyan's

JUNIPER BERRIES — Specialty foods shops and Kalustyan's

KAFFIR LIME LEAVES — Asian markets, specialty produce markets, and Temple of Thai

KASHA — Some supermarkets (look in the kosher foods section), natural foods stores, and Kalustyan's

KETJAP MANIS (Indonesian sweet soy sauce) — Asian markets and Uwajimaya

KIMCHI — Asian markets, some supermarkets, and Koa Mart

KOMBU — Asian markets, natural foods stores, Eden Foods, and Sushi Foods Co.

LAVASH — Middle Eastern markets, some supermarkets, Damascus Bakeries, and Kalustyan's

LAVENDER FLOWERS, DRIED (untreated) — Specialty foods shops, Adriana's Caravan, and Kalustyan's

LILY BUDS, DRIED (golden needles) — Asian markets, Temple of Thai, and Uwajimaya

LIME PICKLE — Indian markets and Kalustyan's

LINGONBERRY SAUCE — Specialty foods shops and Sweden's Best

LYLE'S GOLDEN SYRUP — Some supermarkets and Kalustyan's

MANGO PUREE — Indian markets, some supermarkets, and Kalustyan's

MANGOES, CANNED ALPHONSO — Indian markets and some supermarkets

MAPLE SUGAR, GRANULATED — Specialty foods shops, some farmers markets, the Baker's Catalogue, and La Cuisine

MAPLE SYRUP, GRADE B — Farmers markets, the Baker's Catalogue, and Dakin Farm

MARAS PEPPER FLAKES — Middle Eastern markets, Formaggio Kitchen, and Kalustyan's

MASA HARINA — Mexican markets, some supermarkets, and MexGrocer

MEYER LEMONS — Many supermarkets and Melissa's/World Variety Produce

MIDDLE EASTERN ROSE WATER — Middle Eastern markets and Kalustyan's

MISO — Asian markets, natural foods stores, and Uwajimaya (phone order only)

MOCHIKO (sweet rice flour) — Asian markets and Uwajimaya

MUNG BEANS, DRIED YELLOW — Asian markets and Kalustyan's

MUSHROOMS
   enoki, fresh — Specialty produce markets and some supermarkets
   Korean pyogo, dried — Korean and other Asian markets
   morels, dried — Specialty foods shops and D'Artagnan
   shiitake, dried — Asian markets, some supermarkets, and Uwajimaya
   tree ear, dried — Asian markets, Temple of Thai, and Uwajimaya
   wood ear, dried — Asian markets and Asia Foods

MUSTARD, SPICY CHINESE — Asian markets and Kalustyan's

MUSTARD SEEDS
black — Indian markets and Kalustyan's
brown — Indian markets, Kalustyan's, and Penzeys Spices

NOODLES
bean thread (cellophane) — Asian markets and Uwajimaya
Chinese egg, fresh — Asian markets and Uwajimaya
rice stick (rice vermicelli) — Asian markets, some supermarkets, and Temple of Thai
soba — Japanese markets, natural foods stores, many supermarkets, and Uwajimaya
sweet potato vermicelli — Korean markets, some Asian markets, and Koa Mart
wide rice (he fun, ho fun, or ho fan) — Asian markets and Uwajimaya

ORANGE-FLOWER WATER — Specialty foods shops and Kalustyan's

ORGEAT SYRUP — Specialty foods shops and Fortunes Coffee Roastery Inc.

PALM SUGAR — Asian markets and Temple of Thai

PANCETTA — Italian markets, specialty foods shops, some supermarkets, Salumeria Biellese, and Salumi Artisan Cured Meats

PASSION-FRUIT PULP, FROZEN — Latino markets and some supermarkets

PASTA, DRIED EGG (Cipriani brand) — Specialty foods shops and Dean & DeLuca

PIMENTÓN (Spanish smoked paprika) — Specialty foods shops, La Tienda, and the Spanish Table

PIQUILLO PEPPERS, BOTTLED — Specialty foods shops, some supermarkets, and Amigo Foods

PISTACHIOS, PERSIAN (Iranian) — Kalustyan's

PLUMS, DRIED ANGELINO — J & D Fine Foods and Nuts Online

POMEGRANATE MOLASSES — Middle Eastern markets, Indian markets, specialty foods shops, Formaggio Kitchen, and Kalustyan's

PORCINI MUSHROOM POWDER — Specialty foods shops and Adriana's Caravan

PORK BELLY — Asian markets, butcher shops, and Niman Ranch

POUSSINS — Butcher shops, specialty foods shops, and D'Artagnan

PRESERVED LEMONS — Specialty foods shops and Kalustyan's

PUFFED RICE, INDIAN — Indian markets and Kalustyan's

PUMPKIN SEEDS, RAW (*pepitas*) — natural foods stores and many supermarkets

QUAIL
semiboneless — Butcher shops, specialty foods shops, some supermarkets, Cavendish Game Birds, and D'Artagnan
whole — Butcher shops, specialty foods shops, Cavendish Game Birds, and D'Artagnan

QUESO FRESCO — Mexican and other Latino markets and some supermarkets

QUINOA — Natural foods stores, many supermarkets, and Kalustyan's

RABBIT — Butcher shops, many supermarkets, and D'Artagnan

RAS EL HANOUT — Middle Eastern markets, specialty foods shops, Formaggio Kitchen, and Kalustyan's

RICE

Bomba — Specialty foods markets and the Spanish Table

Chinese black (forbidden) — Asian markets, specialty foods shops, Kalustyan's, and Lotus Foods

Chinese or Japanese short grain sticky (sweet) — Asian markets and Uwajimaya

sushi — Japanese markets, specialty foods markets, some supermarkets, Sushi Foods Co., and Uwajimaya

Thai sticky, black — Asian markets and Temple of Thai

Thai sticky, long-grain — Asian markets, specialty foods shops, Temple of Thai, and Uwajimaya

RICE PAPER ROUNDS (*bahn trang*) — Asian markets and Asia Foods

RICE WINE, CHINESE — Asian markets, specialty foods shops, some supermarkets, and Asia Foods

ROSE PETALS, DRIED — Kalustyan's

SAFFRON — Some supermarkets, Kalustyan's, and Penzeys Spices

SAMBAL OELEK (Asian chile sauce) — Asian markets, Temple of Thai, and Uwajimaya

SEMOLINA (semolina flour) — Italian markets, specialty foods shops, natural foods stores, D. Coluccio & Sons, Inc., and Kalustyan's

SEV, UNSEASONED (thin crispy chickpea noodle pieces) — Indian markets and Kalustyan's

SHERRY PEPPER SAUCE — Specialty foods shops, Mo Hotta Mo Betta, and Outerbridge's

SHERRY VINEGAR (including "Reserva") — Specialty foods shops, many supermarkets, Formaggio Kitchen, and the Spanish Table

SHRIMP PASTE, THAI (*ga-pi*) — Southeast Asian markets and Temple of Thai

SICHUAN PEPPERCORNS — Asian markets and Penzeys Spices

SOUR CHERRIES — Farmers markets, some specialty produce markets, and Friske Orchards

SOUR ORANGES — Latino markets and some supermarkets

SRIRACHA (Asian chile sauce) — Asian markets, many supermarkets, Koa Mart, and Uwajimaya

STONE CRAB CLAWS, COOKED — Many seafood shops, some supermarkets, Joe's Stone Crab, and Wild Edibles

SUCKLING PIG — Citarella and Esposito Meat Market

SUGAR

Demerara — Specialty foods shops, some supermarkets, and La Cuisine

muscovado — Specialty foods shops, some supermarkets, and Kalustyan's

sanding — Specialty foods shops, the Baker's Catalogue, La Cuisine, and New York Cake & Baking Distributors

yellow rock — Asian markets and Adriana's Caravan

SUMAC, GROUND — Middle Eastern markets, Formaggio Kitchen, and Kalustyan's

TAMALE MASA (tortilla masa) — Mexican markets and MexGrocer

TAMARI — Asian markets, natural foods stores, and Uwajimaya

TAMARIND, BLOCK — Indian and Asian markets and Kalustyan's

TANGERINE PEEL, DRIED — Asian markets

TARAMA (carp roe) — Specialty foods markets, some supermarkets, Greek Internet Market, and Kalustyan's

TASSO — Butcher shops, specialty foods shops, and Cajun Grocer

TEA LEAVES, LAPSANG SOUCHONG — Specialty foods shops, some supermarkets, Nuts Online, and Upton Tea Imports

TRUFFLE BUTTER — Specialty foods shops and D'Artagnan

TRUFFLE OIL, BLACK OR WHITE — Specialty foods shops and Dean & DeLuca

URAD DAL — Indian markets and Kalustyan's

URFA PEPPER FLAKES — Middle Eastern markets, Formaggio Kitchen, and Kalustyan's

VEAL DEMI-GLACE — D'Artagnan and More Than Gourmet

VENISON, LOIN AND TENDERLOIN — Butcher shops, Nicky USA, Inc., and Venison America

VENISON STOCK — Specialty foods shops and More Than Gourmet

VINDALOO PASTE — Indian markets and Kalustyan's

VINEGAR, CHINESE BLACK — Asian markets and Asia Foods

WAKAME — Japanese markets, natural foods stores, and Uwajimaya

WASABI PASTE — Asian markets, specialty foods shops, some supermarkets, and Uwajimaya

WHEAT BERRIES — Natural foods stores, Middle Eastern markets, and Kalustyan's

WHITE PEACH PUREE — Specialty foods shops and the Perfect Purée of Napa Valley

WONTON WRAPPERS — Asian markets and many supermarkets

YUCA
  fresh — Latino markets, specialty produce markets, and Melissa's/World Variety Produce
  frozen — some supermarkets and Latino markets

ZUCCHINI BLOSSOMS — Farmers markets and specialty produce markets

KITCHENWARE

BAKER'S PEEL — Cookware shops, the Baker's Catalogue, and Sur La Table

BAKING (PIZZA) STONE — Cookware shops, the Baker's Catalogue, and Broadway Panhandler

BLOWTORCH, KITCHEN — Cookware shops, the Baker's Catalogue, and Chefs Catalog

FOOD GRINDER — Cookware shops and Williams-Sonoma

GRILL SHEET, PERFORATED — Cookware shops, discount retail stores, and Sur La Table

ICE POP MOLDS AND STICKS (3-ounce) — Cookware shops and Fante's Kitchen Wares Shop

KUGELHOPF PAN — Cookware shops and New York Cake & Baking Distributors

NONSTICK BAKING SHEET LINERS (such as Silpat) — Cookware shops and Broadway Panhandler

OMELET PAN, 9½-INCH CARBON-STEEL FRENCH — Cookware shops and Fante's Kitchen Wares Shop

PAELLA PAN — Cookware shops, La Tienda, and the Spanish Table

PIE SHIELD — Cookware shops, the Baker's Catalogue, and New York Cake & Baking Distributors

PIE WEIGHTS — Cookware shops, the Baker's Catalogue, and New York Cake & Baking Distributors

PUDDING MOLD (6-cup) — Cookware shops and A Cook's Wares

RAMEKINS (including 14-ounce) — Cookware shops and Fante's Kitchen Wares Shop

RING MOLD (8½-by-2¾-inch) — Cookware shops, Fante's Kitchen Wares Shop, and Sur La Table

ROLLING PIN COVER AND PASTRY CLOTH — Cookware shops and Fante's Kitchen Wares Shop

SAUSAGE STUFFER — Cookware shops and Williams-Sonoma

SCALLOP SHELLS (5-inch) — Cookware stores and Bridge Kitchenware

SPATULA, CHINESE — Asian specialty stores and the Wok Shop

SOUP BOWLS, OVENPROOF (deep 16- to 18-ounce bowls, no more than 4½ inches across the top; also called "lion's head") — Cookware shops and Sur La Table

WOK, 14-INCH FLAT-BOTTOMED — Asian specialty stores and the Wok Shop

DIRECTORY OF SOURCES

A COOK'S WARES
800-915-9788
www.cookswares.com

ADRIANA'S CARAVAN
Retail location
120 Coulter Avenue, #15-009
Ardmore, PA 19003
800-316-0820
www.adrianascaravan.com

AMIGO FOODS
800-627-2544
www.amigofoods.com

ANSON MILLS
803-467-4122
www.ansonmills.com

THE APRICOT FARM
800-233-4413
www.apricot-farm.com

ARTISANAL PREMIUM CHEESE
Retail location
2 Park Avenue
New York, NY 10016
877-797-1200
www.artisanalcheese.com

ASIA FOODS
888-274-2380
www.asiafoods.com

THE BAKER'S CATALOGUE
Retail location
135 Route 5 South
Norwich, VT 05055
800-827-6836
www.kingarthurflour.com

BENTON'S SMOKY MOUNTAIN COUNTRY HAMS
Retail location
2603 Highway 411
Madisonville, TN 37354
423-442-5003
www.bentonshams.com

BOB'S RED MILL NATURAL FOODS
800-349-2173
www.bobsredmill.com

BRIDGE KITCHENWARE
Retail location
563C Eagle Rock Avenue
Roseland, NJ 07068
800-274-3435
www.bridgekitchenware.com

BROADWAY PANHANDLER
Retail location
65 East 8th Street
New York, NY 10003
866-266-5927
www.broadwaypanhandler.com

CAJUN GROCER
888-272-9347
www.cajungrocer.com

CAVENDISH GAME BIRDS
800-772-0928
www.vermontquail.com

CAVI-ART
425-967-0149
www.caviart.us

CHEFS CATALOG
800-338-3232
www.chefscatalog.com

CHEFSHOP
800-596-0885
www.chefshop.com

CITARELLA
Retail location
2135 Broadway
New York, NY 10023
631-324-9190
www.citarella.com

D. COLUCCIO & SONS, INC.
Retail location
1214-20 60th Street
Brooklyn, NY 11219
718-436-6700
www.dcoluccioandsons.com

DAKIN FARM
800-993-2546
www.dakinfarm.com

DAMASCUS BAKERIES
800-367-7482
www.damascusbakery.com

D'ARTAGNAN
800-327-8246
www.dartagnan.com

DEAN & DELUCA
Multiple retail locations
800-221-7714
www.deandeluca.com

EDEN FOODS
888-424-3336
www.edenfoods.com

ESPOSITO MEAT MARKET
Retail location
500 9th Avenue
New York, NY 10018
212-279-3298

FANTE'S KITCHEN WARES SHOP
Retail location
1006 South 9th Street
Philadelphia, PA 19147
800-443-2683
www.fantes.com

FORMAGGIO KITCHEN
Retail locations
120 Essex Street
New York, NY 10002
244 Huron Avenue
Cambridge, MA 02138
888-212-3224
www.formaggiokitchen.com

FORTUNES COFFEE ROASTERY INC.
Retail location
2005 Penn Avenue
Pittsburgh, PA 15222
888-327-5282
www.fortunescoffee.com

FRISKE ORCHARDS
Retail location (farm market)
 10743 North U.S. 31
 Ellsworth, MI 49729
 888-968-3554
 www.apples-cherries.com

GREEK INTERNET MARKET
 800-755-8067
 www.greekinternetmarket.com

HOPPIN' JOHN'S
 800-828-4412
 www.hoppinjohns.com

J. B. PRINCE
 800-473-0577
 www.jbprince.com

J & D FINE FOODS
 800-763-1890
 www.jdfinefoods.com

JOE'S STONE CRAB
 800-780-2722
 www.joesstonecrab.com

KALUSTYAN'S
Retail location
 123 Lexington Avenue
 New York, NY 10016
 800-352-3451
 www.kalustyans.com

KOA MART
 www.koamart.com

LA CUISINE
Retail location
 323 Cameron Street
 Alexandria, VA 22314
 800-521-1176
 www.lacuisineus.com

LA TIENDA
Retail location
 3601 La Grange Parkway
 Toano, VA 23168
 800-710-4304
 www.tienda.com

LOBEL'S OF NEW YORK
Retail location
 1096 Madison Avenue
 New York, NY 10028
 800-556-2357
 www.lobels.com

LOTUS FOODS
 866-972-6879
 www.lotusfoods.com

LOUISIANA CRAWFISH COMPANY
 888-522-7292
 www.lacrawfish.com

MAINE COAST SEA VEGETABLES
 207-565-2907
 www.seaveg.com

MELISSA'S/WORLD VARIETY PRODUCE
 800-588-0151
 www.melissas.com

MESA MEXICAN FOODS
 www.mesamexicanfoods.com

MEXGROCER
 877-463-9476
 www.mexgrocer.com

MO HOTTA MO BETTA
 800-462-3220
 www.mohotta.com

MORE THAN GOURMET
 800-860-9385
 www.morethangourmet.com

MURRAY'S CHEESE SHOP
Two locations in New York City
888-692-4339
www.murrayscheese.com

NATIONAL BISON ASSOCIATION
Buyer's guide
8690 Wolff Court, #200
Westminster, CO 80031
www.bisoncentral.com

NEW YORK CAKE & BAKING DISTRIBUTORS
Retail location
56 West 22nd Street
New York, NY 10010
800-942-2539
www.nycake.com

NICKY USA, INC.
800-469-4162
www.nickyusa.com

NIMAN RANCH
866-808-0340
www.nimanranch.com

NUESKE'S
Multiple locations in Wisconsin
800-392-2266
www.nucskes.com

NUTS ONLINE
800-558-6887
www.nutsonline.com

OUTERBRIDGE'S
441-296-4451
www.outerbridge.com

PENZEYS SPICES
Multiple retail locations
800-741-7787
www.penzeys.com

THE PERFECT PURÉE OF NAPA VALLEY
800-556-3707
www.perfectpuree.com

RANCHO GORDO
707-259-1935
www.ranchogordo.com

RUSS & DAUGHTERS
Retail location
179 East Houston Street
New York, NY 10002
800-787-7229
www.russanddaughters.com

SALTWORKS
800-353-7258
www.saltworks.us

SALUMERIA BIELLESE
Retail location
376-378 8th Avenue
New York, NY 10001
212-736-7376
www.salumeriabicllese.com

SALUMI ARTISAN CURED MEATS
Retail location
309 3rd Avenue South
Seattle, WA 98104
877-223-0813
www.salumicuredmeats.com

THE SAUSAGE MAKER, INC.
888-490-8525
www.sausagemaker.com

THE SPANISH TABLE
Multiple retail locations
206-682-2827
www.spanishtable.com

STOLT SEA FARM
916-991-4420
www.sterlingcaviar.com

SUGARCRAFT
Retail location
2715 Dixie Highway
Hamilton, OH 45015
513-896-7089
www.sugarcraft.com

SUNBURST TROUT COMPANY
Retail location
128 Raceway Place
Canton, NC 28716
800-673-3051
www.sunbursttrout.com

SUR LA TABLE
Multiple retail locations
800-243-0852
www.surlatable.com

SUSHI FOODS CO.
888-817-8744
www.sushifoods.com

SWEDEN'S BEST
877-864-8503
www.swedensbest.com

TEMPLE OF THAI
877-811-8773
www.templeofthai.com

UPTON TEA IMPORTS
800-234-8327
www.uptontea.com

UWAJIMAYA
Multiple retail locations in Washington
800-889-1928
www.uwajimaya.com

VENISON AMERICA
Retail location
494-B County Road A
Hudson, WI 54016
800-310-2360
www.venisonamerica.com

WILD EDIBLES
Multiple locations in New York City
212-687-4255
www.wildedibles.com

WILD IDEA BUFFALO COMPANY
866-658-6137
www.wildideabuffalo.com

WILLIAMS-SONOMA
Mail-order catalog
3250 Van Ness Avenue
San Francisco, CA 94109
800-541-1262
www.williams-sonoma.com

THE WOK SHOP
Retail location
718 Grant Avenue
San Francisco, CA 94108
415-989-3797
www.wokshop.com

ZATARAIN'S
888-264-5460
www.zatarains.com

INDEX

C

Fudge
  sauce, hot, 877
  truffle, 706

G

H

M

Nuoc cham (Vietnamese dipping sauce), 72, 80, 94
Nut(s). *See also* Almond(s); Cashew(s); Chestnut(s);
      Hazelnut(s); Peanut(s); Pecan(s); Pine nut(s);
      Pistachio(s); Walnut(s)
  banana bread, 666–67
  and fruit chocolate chunks, 704–6
  mixed, shortbread, 700–701
  toasting, 911–12
  toffee, chocolate-covered, 710

O

OAT(MEAL)(S)
  butter-toasted, with sticky apple topping, 647
  cookies
    chocolate chunk coconut, 681–82
    with dried fruit, 681
  crisps, 813
    plum berry, 827
    red and green grape, 820–21
  fruit and spice granola, 648
  wheat bread, 671–72
Offal, 464–66
  calf's liver with bacon and onions, 464–65
  sweetbreads meunière, 465–66
Oils
  basil, 337
  olive, fennel-infused, 162
OKRA, 610–11
  fried cornmeal-coated, 610
  grilled spiced, 555–56
  preparing and cooking, 611
  roasted potato, and fava bean salad, 181–82
  shrimp and tasso gumbo, 370–71
  and smoked sausage dirty rice, 269–70
  spicy African chicken and peanut soup, 145–46
Old-fashioned (cocktail), 19–20
OLIVE(S), 38–39, 48
  black and purple, 38–39
    clementine, and endive salad, 167–68
    Kalamata, carrot puree with, 586
    oregano relish, 535
    and pine nut salsa, spaghetti with, 206
    poached chicken with tomatoes, green beans
      and, 396–97
  curing methods for, 38
  green, 38
    catfish with, 344–45
    and hazelnut rugelach, 54–55
    lemon relish, 356–57

    marinated, 40
    poached chicken with tomatoes, green beans
      and, 396–97
  varieties of, 38, 39
Olive oil, fennel-infused, 162
Omelet pans, seasoning, 651
Omelets, 648–51
  about, 651
  fluffy egg white, with basil and tomatoes, 650
  parsley-crouton, with Gruyère, 649–50
  rolled, with arugula–goat cheese filling, 648
  summer vegetable frittata, 649
ONION(S), 612–13
  balsamic-roasted, 613
  and barley soup, buttered, 135–36
  braised red cabbage and, 582
  browned, kasha with walnuts and, 279
  browned, kugels, 239
  caramelized
    and mushroom pizza, 303–4
    and roasted butternut squash tart, 306–7
    tartlets, 55
  chicken liver, and sage topping (for crostini), 42
  creamed, 612
  egg noodles with cabbage and, 238
  and fennel bisque, 121
  frizzled, 330
  Israeli couscous salad with grilled shrimp and veg-
    etables, 182–83
  marmalade, beet carpaccio with, 87–88
  molasses-baked, 613
  pearl, in vegetable potpie with cheddar biscuit top-
    ping, 320–21
  and pepper salad, warm, 545–46
  pickled, Mexican, 300
  pierogi with coating of, 247–48
  porcini stuffing, 426
  preparing and cooking, 612
  red
    grilled, with balsamic vinegar and soy, 556
    pickled, 62–63
    tomato salad with herbs and, 171–72
    white bean, and celery salad, 191
  rings, 612
  sweet, and ramp soup, 121–22
  tomato, and goat cheese tart, 305
Opera cake, 753–56
ORANGE(S)
  ambrosia, 818
  candied, and cranberry compote, 788
  caramel sauce, 742–43